1989

"Racial Matters"

"Racial Matters"

The FBI's Secret File on Black America, 1960–1972

Kenneth O'Reilly

THE FREE PRESS
A Division of Macmillan, Inc.
NEW YORK

Collier Macmillan Publishers
LONDON

The Free Press
A Division of Macmillan, Inc.
866 Third Avenue, New York, N.Y. 10022

Collier Macmillan Canada, Inc.

Printed in the United States of America

printing number
1 2 3 4 5 6 7 8 9 10

Library of Congress Cataloging-in-Publication Data

O'Reilly, Kenneth.
   Racial matters: the FBI's secret file on Black America, 1960–1972/
Kenneth O'Reilly.
       p.   cm.
   Bibliography: p.
   Includes index.
   ISBN 0–02–923681–9 :
   1. Afro-Americans—Civil rights.   2. United States.   Federal
Bureau of Investigation—History—20th Century.   3. Civil rights
movements—United States—History—20th century.   4. United States—
Politics and government—1961–1963.   5. United States—Politics and
government—1963–1969.   6. United States—Race relations.
I. Title.
E185.615.O74   1989   89–1554
973'.0496073—dc19   CIP

The author is grateful to Broadside Press for permission
to quote from James A. Emanuel, "Panther Man,"
copyright 1970 by James A. Emanuel.

for
Eamon and Teddy
and Sam

Contents

Civil Rights, Civil Liberties

She was a child of Sunflower County, Mississippi, the youngest of twenty children born to two delta sharecroppers, and she had lived all forty-five of her years in a world of white over black. A large woman with soft eyes and a limp in her walk from a bout with polio, she never dreamed Jim Crow could be knocked down until 1962 when three voter registration workers from the Student Nonviolent Coordinating Committee (SNCC—pronounced "snick") changed her sense of the possible. "When they asked for those to raise their hands who'd go down to the courthouse the next day, I raised mine. Had it up as high as I could get it," she said, describing her decision in the spirit of the Exodus. "Headin' your flock out of the chains and fetters of Egypt—taken' them yourself to register—tomorra—in Indianola." A lifelong fear of the white men who ran Sunflower County disappeared that day. "The only thing they could do to me was kill me," she reasoned, "and it seemed like they'd been trying to do that a little bit at a time ever since I could remember." During the months ahead, they would certainly try.

Her name was Fanny Lou Hamer and her first encounter with J. Edgar Hoover's Federal Bureau of Investigation occurred after she attempted to place her name on the voter rolls at the courthouse. Arrested by county police and evicted from a shack on a cotton plantation that had been her home for eighteen years, she fled the state when gunmen fired shots into the Ruleville house of the friend who had put her up. FBI agents told her they could do nothing about the arrest, the eviction, or the shooting. Gathering the courage that led her to Indianola in the first place, Hamer came home to Mississippi after a few weeks to become one of the most beloved movement leaders in the

1

state. She had a rousing singing voice, and few civil rights workers easily forgot the sight of her swaying, crying, and shouting out the verses of "We Shall Overcome," the movement "anthem." "I'm going to stay in Mississippi," she announced, once and for all, "and if they shoot me down, I'll be buried here."

Fanny Hamer's second encounter with the FBI occurred on the second Sunday in June 1963, after she stepped off a bus in Winona, Mississippi. Hamer and five companions were returning from a voter registration workshop in nearby South Carolina when their bus pulled in for a rest stop. June Johnson and James West went to the lunch counter to sit with Annell Ponder. Euvester Simpson and Rosie Mary Freeman went to the whitesonly restroom. What might have been an uneventful encounter— perhaps ending with a white waitress mumbling about how she "can't take no more" and white customers mumbling about Negroes using the wrong toilets—ended disastrously. Winona Police Chief Thomas Herod ordered the five blacks out and arrested them on the parking lot when Ponder began jotting down the license plate number of his cruiser. "Get that one, too," the chief told Montgomery County Sheriff Earl W. Patridge, after Hamer left the bus to see if she could help.

The officers brutalized four members of the group at the Montgomery County jail. They botched the first beating. June Johnson, a fourteen-year-old girl in a pink dress, bled profusely. So they used blackjacks on the others, interrogating Ponder about her interest in the license plate while batting her head and shoulders. "They wanted to know who we would make a report to. I told him the federal government. They said: 'Who do you mean, Bobby Kennedy?'" They forced two black prisoners to pound Hamer, an assault that permanently damaged a kidney and an eye. A few hours later, Chief Herod and his men locked up a seventh voter registration worker, Lawrence Guyot, who had come to the jail to see about charges and bail. Standing Guyot up against a cell wall, they pummeled him with fists and gun barrels. "They beat him just as bad as they did me," Hamer said. "The only difference was they taken paper and tried to burn his private off," and then turned him over to the private sector for a terror-filled automobile ride and another beating in the hills surrounding the town. Things ended as they had begun, with blood.

Everyone knew the FBI would investigate the Winona incident to determine whether the police had violated the civil rights of

Hamer and her companions. After returning Guyot to the jail, one of the officers flashed a phony federal badge and asked him to "tell me all about what happened." When four or five real FBI agents showed up it appeared to Ponder that "they were cooperating with the chief, in a way. . . . I gave them a statement and they wrote it down," she remembered. "[But] they didn't ask me to sign it." "I just don't *trust* 'em, you know?," Hamer said, after her jailhouse interview with the FBI. "He say, 'Well, we would like to talk to you,' and I said, 'Well, I just can't do it.' You see, I didn't know whether if I said what had happened to me then he could tell the jailer, and I just couldn't do it—I just *couldn't!* But we sho' wanted—if we could have just seen any-body . . . I reckon now God is the only refuge we have because there wasn't nobody there from the Justice Department, nobody there to say *nuthin'*—just the Negro out by theirself."[1]

For Fanny Hamer, the FBI was too intimidating, too friendly with the other side, and above all too late. She found herself alone in her cell, alone with her God, even with the FBI there to interview her and to write a report for the Justice Department. The Bureau's agents had been with Hamer in a more timely man-ner, though, on the day in Sunflower County when she joined SNCC as a field secretary. They were with her a year later in Atlantic City, New Jersey, too, when she served as vice-chair of the Mississippi Freedom Democratic party and told the Winona story before network television cameras and the credentials committee at the Democratic National Convention. And they were with her when she went to Washington, D.C., at the begin-ning of the new decade to speak for a national holiday in honor of Dr. Martin Luther King, Jr. Bureau agents filed information about Hamer under the "Racial Matters" caption and some-times even under the "100" classification, the subversive classi-fication. They followed her not to protect her but to spy on her.[2]

John Lewis, SNCC's chairman in 1963 and later a United States congressman from Georgia (elected in 1986), posed a sim-ple question a few months after the Winona incident: "I want to know—which side is the federal government on?" Lewis's orga-nization had recruited Mrs. Hamer as a nonviolent soldier for a peoples' army engaged in a protracted conflict with the formal racism that ruled in Mississippi and across the South. In fight-ing that larger war, SNCC activists saw an ambivalence in the United States government's apparent refusal to choose sides in a conflict where right and wrong were clearly marked. Good and evil were easy to see with Hamer on one side and Mississippi segregationists on the other, yet it remained unclear whether the only federal representatives sent to the scene sided with the police or their victims. FBI agents had done nothing of consequence in Indianola and Ruleville, when Hamer was arrested, evicted, and shot at, and as far as she could tell they had done nothing but file a perfunctory report with the Justice Department after her assault in Winona. If the FBI, "the most symbolic example of a federal presence," actually stood against black people, as Hamer's experiences led her to believe, where did the federal government stand? Wasn't "the party of Kennedy," Lewis asked, also the party of Senator James Eastland, the man SNCC called "the massa' of Sunflower County himself"?[3]

The FBI investigation of the Winona incident was typical of its civil rights work. Bureau agents investigated thousands of skirmishes between movement troops and the segregationist resistance, and to describe one of these investigations is to convey a sense of them all. Federal agents stood by, to all appearances allied through their own studied neutrality with the enemies of black people rather than with those who risked their lives to demand justice, dignity, and a fair share of the democracy that white America always seemed to be celebrating. Hamer concluded her story in Atlantic City by "askin' the American people, 'Is *this* the land of the free and the home of the brave?'"[4] That such a thing could happen in the United States was bad enough. It was even worse that federal policemen seemed to encourage such brutalities by their refusal to protect people like Hamer in the first place or pursue justice after the fact.

During the first half of the 1960s the struggle for black equality raged around a "states' rights" ideology and a single basic question: who would protect the constitutional rights of black Americans in the Jim Crow South, where segregation was written into county ordinances and state law, and enforced by sheriffs, Ku Klux Klansmen, and white-collar Klansmen from the Citizens Council? A reluctant federal government assumed the burden, with the Justice Department shouldering most civil rights responsibilities and funneling those responsibilities to one of its parts—the Civil Rights Division. Division lawyers, in turn, considered what sort of legal action was appropriate in any given case. The police officer or Klansman or Citizens Council patriot who enforced segregation with a nightstick or a rope or an eviction notice might be prosecuted under an old federal law from the Reconstruction Era. A southern county might be sued under the modest civil rights legislation of the Dwight D. Eisenhower years (the Civil Rights Acts of 1957 and 1960) for refusing to allow Negroes to vote. To make informed choices about who to prosecute or sue, Civil Rights Division lawyers relied on the part of the Justice Department that gathered evidence and performed investigative work for the Department as a whole—the FBI.

FBI Director J. Edgar Hoover had no desire to be at the center of the struggle for racial equality and justice, but at the center is where he and his agents found themselves—in Winona and in every other dusty southern town and cotton county where that struggle raged. Hoover's objections to his involvement in the civil rights movement centered on questions of law and constitutional tradition. He argued, with some justification, that federal statutes provided little authority for the FBI to act in Winona or anywhere else. Intent on separating questions of law and morality in the age of racism, he confronted the southern legal system without reference to the values underlying that system.[5] The irony is that the director adopted such a view only on matters of civil rights enforcement. In all other areas, he bound up law and morality as tightly as any man. Hoover also argued that the FBI had no constitutional right to usurp the responsibilities of state and local police to maintain law and order. The culpability of Mississippi lawmen in denying Fanny Hamer her civil rights was not the issue. The director did not condone white violence. He simply dismissed it as a local problem.

With the government and the people of the United States uncertain about how to respond to the black struggle in June 1963, Hoover had no difficulty in locating broad constituencies for his position. President John F. Kennedy and Attorney General Robert F. Kennedy respected and sometimes deferred to the director's strict interpretation of federalism, while many whites in the South and across middle America shared the director's belief that "the Constitution . . . does not deal in general with the relationships between one private individual and another." Hoover made that point early on, in 1947. Four years later, Walter White of the National Association for the Advancement of Colored People asked him to protest the refusal of the Stork Club in New York to serve Josephine Baker, the singer and actress, on the grounds that "such discrimination . . . anywhere in the

United States plays directly into the hands of communists and other enemies of democracy." Though once a regular patron of that nightclub, Hoover ordered his agents to ignore White's request, scribbling the following comment. "I don't consider this to be any of my business." A states' righter in 1947 and 1951, he remained one in 1963.[6]

Hoover justified his reluctance to investigate the Winona brutality aggressively by reference to the constraints of existing federal statutes, states' rights principles, and the lack of consensus on the question of whether the nation needed a Second Reconstruction. Caught up in a mass movement determined to close the gap between "the theory and the practice of the republic," he fully mobilized his Bureau only when conducting domestic intelligence investigations. Given the absence of specific federal laws on which to base these investigations, Hoover cited no states' rights principles to justify his policy of monitoring the civil rights movement. Speaking only in terms of the cold war necessity of rooting out communists and other subversives who would manipulate the black struggle for their own ends if left alone, he developed a constituency among states' rights southerners for this investigative mission nonetheless. The director preferred the familiar comforts of dossier collecting to the alien business of civil rights law enforcement, and he had a mandate to follow the trail of the Communist party wherever it led. So the FBI spied on anyone interested in the state of race relations in the United States, including Hamer and her Mississippi Freedom Democratic party, from the first sit-ins and voter registration campaigns to the historic march in Selma, Alabama, that led to the Voting Rights Act of 1965; and the FBI spied on blacks as a potentially dangerous class of activists thereafter, a period that spanned the years of urban riots and Vietnam war protests.

More than Hoover's preference and ability to function as a semiautonomous political entity determined the FBI's investigative priorities. Presidents, attorneys general, and other government officials ratified the Bureau mandate. Decent men, for the most part, they tried to use the FBI's investigative resources within the limits of the conventional theories of federalism that governed race relations at the time. In Winona, for example, they pushed for an FBI investigation and a federal civil rights law indictment of the police officers who beat Hamer and her companions.[7] But they accepted the idea that the specter of communist influence in the civil rights movement justified FBI spying. They were reassured that the director's domestic intelligence resources would provide advance warning of civil rights demonstrations and thereby increase the government's chances of heading off anti–civil rights violence.

The ways in which Hoover explained FBI behavior to the public and to the men in the Justice Department and the White House seemed eminently reasonable. Constrained by law, the Constitution, and public opinion, the director lacked the authority to act decisively against Fanny Hamer's tormentors or other enforcers of white supremacy. If the American people and their representatives in the Congress had not decided to rid their land of Jim Crow, why should the FBI be expected to take the lead in doing so? Hoover saw no great question of right and wrong in the Winona jail, only the question of states' rights. How does the federal government go about protecting Hamer's civil rights without disrupting the federal balance? Exactly where do the rights of minorities end? Exactly where does the power of the majority begin? Defending his surveillances, Hoover said he spied on civil rights workers for their own good, keeping track of communist infiltrators and purging them when possible, and using the data gathered on demonstration plans to construct an informal system of protection. If the law and the Constitution and even public opinion prevented him from protecting civil rights workers directly, the director would improvise and use his domestic intelligence resources to do so indirectly.

Hoover's explanations appeared convincing for two reasons. First, he claimed to have no political agenda. He had spent most of his adult life battling against the twentieth century's great movements of social change, and no greater engine of social change roared through the century than the civil rights movement. Though uniquely positioned to obstruct the movement in the 1960s, Hoover apparently spurned the temptation. He simply claimed to be following orders, doing his job under trying circumstances in a manner that pleased neither side entirely. For every Fanny Hamer or John Lewis who criticized the Bureau for standing with the white southern resistance, a segregationist could be found to criticize the Bureau for standing with the integrationists. Second, FBI investigations of specific cases suggest that Hamer and Lewis were wrong. The Winona law enforcement officials ultimately escaped punishment in federal court through no clear fault of the FBI. A case-by-case examination of the FBI record does in fact reveal a bewildering collage, with

Hoover and his men appearing to stand with the movement on one day and with the resistance the next.

To understand the FBI's behavior and the consequences of that behavior, it is less important to look at FBI actions in isolation, or to listen to the apolitical explanations Hoover offered to the public and his ostensible superiors in the government, than to examine the totality of the FBI response to the black struggle for freedom and justice for all. Such an examination raises questions of motivation and agenda that go beyond Hoover's stated reasons for acting as he did, eroding the legal, constitutional, and national security expediencies that purportedly underlay those reasons. An inclusive examination suggests that personal, bureaucratic, political, and ideological choices shaped FBI actions. Regardless of the positive contributions individual FBI agents made to the black struggle, Hoover's perceptions, values, and vision gave rise to a politics which cannot be held legitimate in either a legal or moral sense.

A further examination suggests that the FBI's performance cannot be considered apart from the decisions of responsible federal officials in the White House and the Justice Department. No matter how autonomous it seemed, Hoover's bureaucracy was part of a larger structure, the federal government's executive branch. In the final analysis, then, the story of the FBI and black America is part of the larger history of a government that has been at odds, more often than not over the past two hundred years, with its own nonwhite citizens and its own professed values.

"The shadows disappeared," Don Whitehead wrote, in his authorized, celebratory history, *The FBI Story*. "I found in the FBI story a stirring American adventure," a "struggle to achieve incorruptible enforcement of the law by professionals trained to protect civil rights."[8] Black America's FBI story does not confirm the conclusions of Whitehead's best-seller and the Jimmy Stewart movie inspired by the book. It confirms instead a troubling tale filled with unlikely heroes and villains, and with origins that push back past the days of Kennedys and Kings to the World War I era and the beginnings of Hoover's career as a federal policeman, a time before most of those heroes and villains had even been born.

1

━━━━━◇◇◇◇━━━━━

The Negro Question
Origins of a Private War

For better or for worse, the history of the Federal Bureau of
Investigation and the history of black America have been
linked together almost from the Bureau's beginning in 1908,
when Charles J. Bonaparte, nephew of Napoleon III and President Theodore Roosevelt's attorney general, established a "Bureau of Investigation." (The word "Federal" was added in 1935.)
The Bureau's decision to avoid protecting civil rights and to spy
on blacks were more in reaction to directives from the White
House and the Justice Department than results of its own policy.
In 1910, during the second year of William Howard Taft's presidency and in response to a series of particularly brutal lynchings, the Department claimed "no authority . . . to protect citizens of African descent in the enjoyment of civil rights
generally."[1] In contrast, by 1919, the year J. Edgar Hoover began
his association with the Bureau and the seventh year of Woodrow Wilson's presidency, the Department was citing wartime
security needs to violate the civil liberties of those same citizens.
Expected by the Wilson administration to confine itself to gathering political intelligence on the "Negro Question," the Bureau
paid little attention to day-to-day violations of federal civil
rights laws—let alone to the episodic blood rites committed by
Ku Klux Klansmen and other white supremacists to enforce deference and submission.

By the time John F. Kennedy entered the White House in 1961,
Hoover had located his own grievances against black people in

the four decades since the World War I era, when he first brushed against their demand for justice and equality. The director had learned a great deal about racial matters since 1919, but little about racial justice. He had learned that the Negro's fight for equality threatened his personal racial preferences and his Bureau's institutional interests and political objectives. He had learned that blacks who struggled to make the nation live up to its democratic ideals represented a threat to his America that one day might rival the threat posed by his dreaded communists; and he had learned that nearly every administration from Wilson to Eisenhower condoned his all-embracing definitions of subversion. But he had also learned that there was no American consensus on how to deal with the gathering struggle for black equality. So after a fiery start in 1919, he rarely acted forcefully on his feelings about the Negro Question. He proceeded cautiously, nurturing his grievances and studying the battleground, and, like Machiavelli's prince, preparing for war in times of peace.

It would have been surprising if Hoover had reacted otherwise. The director, born in 1895, and his FBI, born in 1908, both grew up at a time when racism was respectable. Jim Crow came to Hoover's native Washington, D.C., in 1900, and by 1920 segregation had visited all public accommodations save the buses and trolleys, the libraries, and the grandstands at Griffith Stadium. Hoover lived in a white city and an even whiter neighborhood, Seward Square, where restrictive housing covenants insulated his family and the larger community of middle-class civil servants. Other than domestic servants, like the maid who came to help Hoover's mother, Annie, with the cooking and cleaning, no Negroes came to Seward Square. In young Edgar's world, a white family's employment of a colored servant constituted a visible sign of gentility, even if that servant worked for an hourly wage. Hoover's school, Central High, the District's oldest, most prestigious public school, and, of course, all-white, represented another confirmation of status. From Central High, Hoover moved on to a position at the Library of Congress while studying law at George Washington University's night school. In the summer of 1917 he joined the Justice Department, where he kept alive the vision of the white, Christian America he grew up with, until he died on the job, fifty-five years later.[2]

While segregation swept over Hoover's city and other southern towns, the judicial and executive branches of the federal government were dispensing what the historian of Jim Crow, C. Vann Woodward, called "permissions-to-hate." In *Plessy v. Ferguson* (1896), the Supreme Court held separate-but-equal facilities to be good enough for the black man. The Republican party's Reconstruction Era crusade to make all men free had died twenty years before William McKinley's new crusade to project American rule over the eight million people in the Caribbean and the Pacific recently liberated from the Spanish empire. Theodore Roosevelt offered blacks at home no economic or civil reforms, only gestures—most notably inviting Booker T. Washington to dine at the White House. William Howard Taft offered blacks even less. Woodrow Wilson, a Democrat and a native southerner who told "darky" stories to his cabinet, brought the separate-but-equal doctrine of the *Plessy* decision to the federal bureaucracy. What Woodward called "the liberal retreat on the race issue" became a self-imposed rout under the missionary president. Wilson promoted segregation as an enlightened and scientific response to racial divisions, a progressive solution, his postmaster general said, for the good of "the negro and the Service." While the nation prepared to fight a war to make the world safe for democracy, workmen in the capital tacked up "White Only" or "Colored" signs over every federal toilet.[3]

Within the culture at large, respectable racism flourished. The man in the street hummed such popular turn-of-the-century tunes as "If the Man in the Moon Were a Coon," while students at Yale and Columbia listened to their professors lecture on the black man's incorrigible morals. With reputable periodicals pondering the fate of the "varied assortment of inferior races" recently acquired from Spain, the *Atlantic Monthly* posed a rhetorical question. "If the stronger and cleverer race is free to impose its will upon 'new-caught, sullen peoples' on the other side of the globe, why not in South Carolina and Mississippi?" And the *Saturday Evening Post* offered its pages to Thomas Dixon, author of *The Clansman* and other racist tracts, "orgies of hatred" whose "Negro characters, when they were not clowns, all seemed to be either contemplating or swiftly fleeing after the rape of a white woman." In 1915 Dixon's novel inspired D. W. Griffith's *Birth of a Nation*, the first great motion-picture extravaganza and a film that portrayed deceitful, lustful, and dangerous blacks laying seige to a prostrate white South during Reconstruction times. "History written in lightning," President Wilson said, after a private screening of this eulogy to the Ku Klux Klan at the White House.[4]

FBI surveillance activities aimed at black Americans began in this climate of respectable racism two years after Griffith's film appeared and immediately after Congress declared war on Germany. At first, Bureau agents visited black communities to assess attitudes toward the draft and to investigate rumors of subversion. The controversy over the infamous Zimmermann telegram, in which Germany had offered to help Mexico regain territory lost seventy years before in the Mexican-American war, led to a particularly outrageous rumor of German agents organizing an army of Mexicans and black Americans to fight a rearguard action in the Southwest on Kaiser Wilhelm's behalf. In addition to the cultural racism of the time, the FBI's behavior in investigating such rumors reflected the widespread wartime belief that traitors, spies, and saboteurs had provoked the race riots that shook some two dozen cities in 1917 and the "Red summer" of 1919. The epic Red scare of the immediate postwar years included a black scare.[5]

Concluding that second-class citizens would have second-class loyalty, the FBI dismissed every black dissident as subversive, every criticism of American policy as un-American. While Woodrow Wilson defended national self-determination at the Versailles peace conference, his State Department solicited intelligence reports from the Bureau on any black American who complained about riots and lynchings. While the president promised to bring democracy to the world, black activists reminded him that he had not yet brought democracy to blacks in his own country or to the not-very-white peoples who lived in America's overseas possessions. When Monroe Trotter, editor of the *Boston Guardian* and head of the all-black National Equal Rights League, pressed Senator Henry Cabot Lodge (R., Mass.) to read the Thirteenth, Fourteenth, and Fifteenth Amendments of the U.S. Constitution into the Treaty of Versailles, Hoover, already adept at making himself useful to the incumbent administration, called upon the Bureau to monitor "Negro leaders" and their "political stand . . . toward the peace treaty and the league of nations."[6]

By the fall of 1919 the FBI had institutionalized surveillance programs aimed at blacks. Bureau field offices across the country covered "the Negro Question" systematically, recruiting "reliable Negroes" as informants in the "various negro lodges and associations" and having them report on "negro ministers" and anyone else who preached "social equality" and "equal rights." The informants infiltrated every racial advancement and black nationalist group, from the moderate National Association for the Advancement of Colored People to the immoderate African Blood Brotherhood, hoping to detect "ultra radical activities" or even "liberal activities" in the "race riots, etc." The field agents who controlled the informants organized the mass of data collected and forwarded highlights covering "the entire field of so called 'Liberalism'" to the Justice Department's General Intelligence Division (GID), then headed by the twenty-four-year-old Hoover.[7]

From his study of liberalism and radicalism and his previous experience with the Department's Alien Enemy Bureau, Hoover concluded that "the Reds have done a vast amount of evil damage by carrying doctrines of race revolt and the poison of Bolshevism to the Negroes." Black Americans, he suspected, were "seeing Red," snuggling up to "the Bolsheviki" and even the one-big-union doctrines of Bill Haywood and the Industrial Workers of the World. Along with the "contemptible and wicked deeds" of Reds and Wobblies among the subversively inclined colored people, Hoover emphasized Thomas Dixon's theme—namely, the threat oversexed black men posed to white women. The GID chief located the "direct cause" of the riot that visited Washington in "the numerous assaults committed by Negroes upon white women."[8]

The most ambitious of the thousands of FBI/GID investigations of the Negro Question in these early years targeted Marcus Garvey, the Jamaican-born founder of the Universal Negro Improvement Association (UNIA), arguably one of the twentieth century's most important black American leaders. Concluding that Garvey was "the foremost radical among his race," Hoover decided, "once and for all," to "put" him "where he can peruse his past activities behind the four walls of the Atlanta clime"—that is, behind the walls of the federal penitentiary in Atlanta. In his search for an appropriate crime, Hoover hired four black men to work the case, and he assigned one of those men, James W. Jones ("undercover agent '800'"), to infiltrate the UNIA and shadow Garvey in Harlem. Among other strategies, Hoover tried to prove Garvey was an operative of the British and Canadian governments. He even pursued a "white slavery" case—a fa-

vored approach that may have reflected his own sexual anxieties. The White Slave Traffic Act, also known as the Mann Act,
made it a federal crime to transport a woman across a state line
for immoral purposes. Finally, in 1923, Hoover secured an indictment against Garvey on a charge of using the mails to defraud in the course of raising money for his Black Star Steam-
ship Line. A federal court found Garvey guilty, and he served
nearly two years of a five-year prison sentence before President
Calvin Coolidge pardoned him in 1927—and ordered his deportation as an undesirable alien.[9]

Hoover attacked Garvey because of the black leader's all-
around "pro-negroism," and Garvey's "doctrine of the negro for
the negro"—not because Hoover considered him a Wobbly or a
communist or a White Slaver or a British agent or even because
he used the Post Office to cheat "many old Negroes" out of their
hard-earned money, as then FBI Director William J. Burns
claimed. Burns said Garvey was "the most prominent Negro agitator in the world today and we have been 'on' him." A magnetic
black leader who rejected the accommodationist ideas of "the
conservative element" had to be watched closely and brought
down if possible, so Hoover's GID, along with Burns's FBI, destroyed "the Negro Moses."[10]

While pursuing Marcus Garvey, the FBI and the GID launched
a major investigation of "the colored press." Hoover's disapproval here centered on "a well-concerted movement" among
black newspaper and magazine editors to subvert "the established rule of law and order" by promoting "defiantly assertive"
ideas about "the Negro's fitness for self-government," "race consciousness," interest in "sex equality" (miscegenation), and hostility "to the white race." In a few cases, claimed the GID director, the black press even threatened "retaliatory measures in
connection with lynching." The FBI's agents considered the editors of the monthly *Messenger*, the young socialists Chandler
Owen and A. Philip Randolph, especially bothersome; they also
had problems with the editors of the "better-behaved" publications—among others, W. E. B. Du Bois of the NAACP's *Crisis*.
Hoover wanted "something . . . done" to black journalists on the
grounds that their comments had incited "the negro elements of
this country to riot and to the committing of outrages of all
sorts." Under the name of law and order, Hoover proposed the
repression of any black dissident who challenged second-class
citizenship.[11]

By focusing on subversion, broadly defined (race riots, misce-genation, and all black political activity), the FBI barely had time for civil rights investigations. Prior to the 1930s, the only type of civil rights case where the FBI formally recognized federal jurisdiction involved involuntary servitude. Local law enforcement officers and prison officials in many southern states tolerated peonage—the practice of holding persons in servitude or partial slavery to work off a debt. In some instances, state laws permitted employers to pay a prisoner's fine in return for a contract forcing the prisoner to work out a debt. The FBI opened its most spectacular peonage case in 1921 against a Georgia farmer, John S. Williams, who had been buying black prisoners from state and county road gangs and jails for years. Upon learning of the Bureau's interest, a panicked Williams eliminated as many potential prosecution witnesses as possible—killing ten or twelve of his "slaves." Williams's brutality "so aroused [public sentiment] against these practices," *FBI Story* author Don Whitehead concluded, "that peonage became a charge rarely heard in courts of law." Offered as proof that the FBI had destroyed peonage, Whitehead's point of fact actually represented a tacit admission that the FBI had decided to avoid peonage investigations.[12]

Having begun a review of such cases in the summer of 1922, about a year after his appointment as an assistant FBI director, Hoover discovered that the numbers did not add up. The Atlanta office investigated 115 peonage violations under federal law in 1921–1922, an effort that led to a single conviction. (The state of Georgia tried Williams on murder charges.) Hoover did not like to lose cases. Always the good bureaucrat, he wanted his agency to look successful and to use its time as effectively as possible. He concluded that the peonage conviction rate was so low because "the standing of a colored person, as a witness, against a white man, does not amount to a great deal, in this section of the country," as Lewis J. Baley, then head of the Atlanta office, put it. Later, after he became director of the FBI, Hoover wrote what Baley had to say into the field agents' bible, the *Manual of Instruction,* along with a comment that "the type of person usually held a peon" was not "particularly intelligent," making it necessary to secure corroborating testimony from "neighboring farmers, or planters." But he had nothing to say about his colleague's suggestion to pursue all peonage cases anyway on the grounds that even unsuccessful prosecution would deter those persons who violated federal peonage statutes. In contrast to Baley, Hoover mixed legitimate bureaucratic concerns with an illegitimate assumption that the Negro was not worth protecting.[13]

The Ku Klux Klan also attracted the FBI's attention during these years, and as in the peonage investigations, Hoover called attention to a single heroic case to hide a larger pattern of neglect. The FBI began its probe in September 1922, when Louisiana Governor John M. Parker requested federal assistance to break the Klan's stranglehold on state political and legal institutions. President Warren G. Harding ordered the Justice Department to investigate on the condition that the state "handle any prosecutions," a decision that Hoover would point to in the years to come to justify the states' rights attitudes that increasingly dominated his approach to civil rights work. Over the next few weeks undercover FBI agents gathered evidence linking the Louisiana Klan to a series of murders and other crimes, but Klan-dominated grand juries refused to indict. Rather than give up, Hoover turned to the handiest federal law, the Mann Act, and had his agents examine the sexual habits of Klan leaders. Eventually, in Houston, Texas, the Justice Department prosecuted Imperial Kleagle Edward Y. Clark and several other officers on white slavery charges. "The red faces which occurred at that time as a result of those convictions soon ended the Klan in the South," Hoover said, in a wildly exaggerated statement about his accomplishment. Though the Ku Klux Klan continued to function, four decades would pass before the director again sent his agents into battle against Klansmen, and to announce, once more, that his Bureau had destroyed their organization.[14]

While cases involving civil rights issues remained consistently rare throughout the New Era of Warren Harding, Calvin Coolidge, and Herbert Hoover, FBI surveillance responsibilities changed dramatically. With Bureau agents implicated in the Teapot Dome scandals (they had been caught breaking into the offices and tapping the telephones of congressmen investigating the Justice Department's role in the Harding administration corruption), the Coolidge administration targeted the FBI for reform. In March 1924 the president fired Attorney General Harry M. Daugherty, replacing him with Harlan Fiske Stone, former dean of Columbia Law School. Stone then fired William J. Burns as director of the FBI and appointed Hoover acting director, dissolved the Red-hunting GID, and ordered the Bureau to confine its investigations to violations of federal law. Technically, then, Stone had abolished the apparatus for the FBI's original mission—domestic political surveillance.[15]

Hoover began to transform the FBI from an agency riddled with corruption and rocked by scandal into an efficient and respected police agency by imposing strict professional standards on the agent corps. He weeded out the political hacks and ex-convicts scattered in Bureau offices from coast to coast and required new agents to hold a college degree—preferably in law or accounting. Perhaps for reasons of race (there is no evidence of political or personal corruption), the new director also weeded out all but two of the handful of black agents employed by the Bureau.[16] By the early 1930s, however, Hoover may have realized that the days of respectable racism had passed. He reprimanded Clyde Tolson, one of his few real friends, for informing a black applicant that "colored messengers" need not apply. Tolson went on to hire a black man, James E. Crawford, who worked out of his office for a few months as a messenger before becoming his chauffeur. When Hoover's own black chauffeur died, Crawford began to drive the director's bulletproof Pierce Arrow. Hoover had room in his car for a black, but no room in his agent corps. There would never be more than a token number of full-fledged black agents in the FBI until after the director's death.[17]

Hoover had no intention of complying fully with Harlan Stone's restrictions on Bureau activities. With regard to the domestic political surveillance mission, he counseled patience, advising Attorney General Stone on November 5, 1924, less than two months before his permanent appointment as director: "Some of these [Bureau] offices have spent considerable time upon investigation of radical matters and seem to be at a loss now as to how to curtail the same." Though sharply curtailed, Negro Question investigations continued, with the director sending reports on the NAACP and the separatist Moorish Science Temple of America to the Herbert Hoover White House. The most extensive of the reformed FBI's Negro Question investigations focused on nine black Alabama teenagers, the so-called Scottsboro boys, sentenced to death for the alleged rape of two white women. The Communist party was active in the Scottsboro boys' legal defense and the propaganda battle that dragged on throughout the 1930s, and Hoover viewed this involvement as a particularly ominous sign. The party represented the single most dangerous subversive force in the nation, and its proposed alliance with the black cause raised the specter of thirteen million colored people willing to follow communist leadership. Though there were few black communists in the United States, Hoover's upbringing, prejudices, and political assumptions led him to question the loyalty of an entire race.[18]

The director's focus on the communist aspects of the Scottsboro case proved to be a harbinger of things to come. More troubled by Communist party activities than Herbert Hoover, President Franklin D. Roosevelt encouraged the FBI, as part of a broad federal investigation of "subversive activities," to gather intelligence on radical efforts to influence black Americans. In 1934, with Hitler in power and a number of boisterous and explicitly racist American fascists active in the United States, Roosevelt ordered Hoover to investigate the American Nazi movement. The director concentrated on "anti-racial" and "anti-American" activities. With the president's approval, FBI responsibilities expanded two years later to include communist activities, a development that led to a rapid reconstruction of the Negro Question surveillance machine. Though Roosevelt had no knowledge of Hoover's agenda on matters of race, he would raise no objections upon discovering the director's expansive notions of black subversion.[19]

Hoover had his agents collect information under a special "Negroes" category as part of their regular investigations of domestic communist and native fascist infiltration, and he invariably included their wartime reports on "Negro Organizations" with reports on "Communism" and "German, Italian, and Japanese" fifth columnists.[20] By the early 1940s the director's surveillance of blacks and their "subversive tendencies" had led to the filing of weekly reports with government policymakers on such expansive subjects as "Negro trends." He sent additional reports directly to the White House on individuals and groups involved in civil rights activities, from the Southern Conference for Human Welfare to the March on Washington Movement organized in 1941 and again in 1942 and 1943 by A. Philip Randolph. Randolph's threat of "monster mass meetings" prompted FDR to issue the first presidential directive on race since Reconstruction: Executive Order 8802 establishing a Fair Employment Practice Commission (FEPC) and prohibiting discrimination in defense industries. (The president ignored Randolph's third demand to desegregate the armed forces.) Because Roosevelt had acted even though the Bureau had offered the opinion that communists had infiltrated the March on Washington Movement and that Randolph himself was bluffing in his threats, Hoover may have concluded that the president's FEPC directive represented a surrender to "a pressure group" willing to ante the national interest in pursuit of a special interest. All black activists and any white liberal who contributed to the black demand for justice and equality represented a potential subversive threat.[21]

In the summer of 1942 the FBI launched its most systematic Negro Question investigation, a nationwide survey of "foreign inspired agitation" in "colored areas and colored neighborhoods." Hoover wanted to know "why particular Negroes or groups of Negroes . . . have evidenced sentiments for other 'dark races' (mainly Japanese) or by what forces they . . . adopted in certain instances un-American ideologies." To answer these questions, Bureau agents investigated all black-owned newspapers, recruited paid black informants, and tapped the telephones and bugged the offices of racial advancement groups, ranging from the procommunist National Negro Congress to the anticommunist NAACP. Investigative fallout included a mail cover on Rev. Archibald J. Carey, Jr.'s, Woodlawn African Methodist Episcopal Church in Chicago, where the Congress of Racial Equality had an office; a file check on Olympic track and field champion Jesse Owens (an agent compared the date of Owens's marriage with the birthday of his first child); and the transmittal of derogatory information on the NAACP and the National Urban League to prospective financial contributors. The director emphasized that any leak should be handled "cautiously as we don't want [name deleted] to ever say he refused money to any organization upon the recommendation of the FBI." Any such revelation would embarrass the Bureau.[22]

Hoover expanded his mandate in accord with his own private agenda, not the government's, with a search for foreign-inspired agitation among Negroes that led to Franklin Roosevelt's wife. Acting on complaints that the cause of black unrest in Alabama and other southern states could be traced "to the encouragement given Negroes by Mrs. Roosevelt," who had visited Tuskegee Institute in 1941 and "was entertained throughout her visit by Negroes," the director made a number of inquiries. He seemed especially interested in rumors about black domestic servants who supposedly joined "Eleanor Clubs" at the urging of "a strange white man and a large Negro organizer traveling in an automobile." He was also sympathetic to those "white people who found difficulty in retaining their servants as a result of better opportunities offered by various Defense jobs." Hoover ordered his men to find out if female black domestics were really "demanding their own terms for working" and using the slogan, "A White Woman in the Kitchen by Christmas." With black servants of his own, he clearly took a personal interest.[23]

Bureau agents never found the ideas and deeds of subversion that the director thought they would find, not even in their full-scale probe of communist attempts to incite "the feelings of Negroes" during the 1943 riots in Detroit and other cities. The Bureau uncovered "no information," Hoover informed the White House, to substantiate the charge that "foreign elements" inspired the riots. But the director's agents kept looking and kept tracking "a definite change in the attitude of some negroes." "A number of them," as the head of the Richmond, Virginia, field office mused, "appear to have become more disrespectful, more assertive of their rights and more discontented with their station in life." The net result, in this view, paralleled the "Axis aim . . . to cause the negro to wonder whether he should support our war effort whole-heartedly."[24]

Within the Communist party itself, the FBI noted the efforts of such black comrades as Hosea Hudson of Birmingham to "conduct classes in cooperation with the NATIONAL NEGRO CONGRESS for the purpose of teaching negroes how to become qualified voters." The immediate goal of the party's voter registration drive, the FBI agent in Alabama emphasized, was to insure "the re-election of President ROOSEVELT." The Bureau's domestic intelligence sphere remained as broad as it had been on the day in 1919 when Hoover took command of the General Intelligence Division, encompassing "the entire field of so-called 'Liberalism.'"[25]

The FBI's formal civil rights enforcement responsibilities also changed during the Roosevelt years, but progress on this front came in slow and fitful increments. Though sympathetic to the black plight, the president refused to expend any political capital or to antagonize southern Democrats on the race issue. Civil rights reformers remained optimistic nonetheless, particularly during the first New Deal years, when Roosevelt promoted the growth of the FBI as part of his administration's broader effort to extend federal authority over crime control, once considered the exclusive prerogative of state and local government.[26] Civil rights reformers hoped that the New Deal "war on crime" would extend to lynching and other crimes directed most often at black people. Federal concern, however, extended only to such crimes as bank robbery, racketeering, and kidnapping, inspired by the apparent inability of the states to take decisive action against the gangsters of the early 1930s, who exploited the limited jurisdiction of local police by fleeing across city, county, and state lines. The public's fascination with the depression era's flamboyant criminals and the media's romanticization of their exploits also troubled President Roosevelt and Attorney General Homer S. Cummings.[27]

When Roosevelt and Cummings moved decisively to solve both problems in a typical New Deal manner, Hoover proved to be the chief beneficiary. "The strong arm of Government," relying on innovative legislation and working through the alphabet agencies, would solve the nation's problems. In May 1934 Congress approved six anticrime bills without even taking a record vote; in June three more bills passed. The New Deal crime-control package extended the FBI's criminal jurisdiction and budget, granting its agents full arrest power and authority to carry any kind of firearm. To counter public adulation of the John Dillingers and George "Machine Gun" Kellys, Cummings supplemented the new legislation with an ambitious public relations campaign "to publicize and make the G-Men heroes."[28] By the mid-1930s Hoover had developed into a celebrity and his heroic bureaucracy rivaled baseball in popularity. Even H. L. Mencken, the scourge of "the booboisie," sat in the director's cheering section. "In general, I am strongly in favor of Hoover," he told *Liberty* magazine editor Fulton Oursler. "He has done more to improve police work in this great Republic than any other twenty men."[29]

For many Americans, the war on crime, initiated by Roosevelt and Cummings and led by Hoover, looked to be a smashing success; but it disappointed NAACP executive secretary Walter White and others who had an interest in racial crimes. Before sending the FBI and its director off to investigate the new federal crimes, New Deal liberals had jettisoned an antilynching bill from their legislative package. Presidential adviser Louis Howe thought the lynching bill might "create hostility to [the] other crime bills" among southern congressmen.[30] The NAACP's White urged the Justice Department to use the newly amended federal kidnapping statute (the so-called Lindbergh Law) against members of lynch mobs in such cases as the Claude Neal murder. A mob had abducted Neal in October 1934 from the Brewton, Alabama, jail where local police held him on suspicion of murdering a young white woman; he was taken across the state line to Marianna, Florida, and hanged after ten hours of torture. Although the press advertised the lynching and thousands of spectators watched, the Justice Department refused to send the FBI to investigate. The Department took "the position," White charged, "that the amended Lindbergh law covered kidnapping for the purposes of gain [ransom], but not for purposes of murder."[31]

Though Hoover and Roosevelt ignored lynchings for different reasons, the two men found common ground in the aftermath of Neal's death, with the FBI director following the New Deal president's lead. When a reporter asked if he would recommend passage of a pending lynching bill, FDR ducked the question by requesting time "to check up and see what I did last year. I have forgotten." Roy Wilkins, White's talented young assistant, said Franklin Roosevelt suffered from "expedient cowardice." Later, when radio commentator, newspaper columnist and Bureau confidant Walter Winchell sent the director a letter about the Neal lynching that he had received from a private citizen (a letter that did not mention the victim by name), Hoover told Winchell he had no idea what case the letter writer had in mind. More interested in promoting the FBI crusade against kidnappers who held white people for ransom, the director sent Winchell the following item for publication in his gossip column:

> The colored boys in Washington who are prone to play
> hunches in the numbers game are reported to have made a
> killing recently when they combined the numbers in
> connection with the days of the month on which the G Men
> apprehended a number of notorious kidnappers. Alvin
> Karpis was apprehended on May 1st; William Mahan and
> Harry Campbell . . . on May 7th, and Thomas H. Robinson,
> Jr., . . . on May 11th. The colored boys combined the
> numbers 1-7-1 and are said to have cashed in on the hunch.

The nation's chief of police preferred to grin and wink at "colored boys" chasing their numbers rather than confront a black corpse at the end of a rope.[32]

FBI responsibilities to protect the civil rights of black Americans expanded in 1939 when Roosevelt administration priorities began to change. With the coming of World War II, native American fascists and Nazis in Germany were drawing parallels between the Third Reich's policy toward Jews and United States policy toward Negroes. The mobilization for war increased the pressure on the administration to protect black citizens from the effects of a states' rights monopoly on civil rights enforcement. Attorney General Frank Murphy responded to this pressure by establishing a Civil Liberties Unit (renamed the Civil Rights Section two years later) within the Justice Department's Criminal Division. Murphy was a former NAACP board member who considered racial intolerance "the most un-American . . . thing in our life today."[33]

The investigative arm of the Justice Department noticed little change in its work load at first. In 1939 the eight attorneys assigned to the Civil Rights Section asked the FBI to investigate a mere seven of the several thousand complaints submitted by the public alleging civil rights/civil liberties violations. "Only a few" of the complaints submitted actually rested "within the jurisdiction of the Federal Government," reasoned the Section's first chief, Henry A. Schweinhaut, and most of these had to do with the rights of labor, not the rights of black Americans.[34] Section attorneys based their authority to conduct investigations on the National Labor Relations Act (the Wagner Act), the New Deal law that guaranteed employees the right to form unions and bargain collectively, and Sections 241 and 242 of Title 18 of the Federal Criminal Code, remnants of two Reconstruction Era statutes (the Enforcement Act of 1870 and the Civil Rights Act of 1866).[35] The Wagner Act contained no criminal provision, but the Reconstruction statutes were intended to guarantee equality of rights and to control Ku Klux Klan terrorism. Section 241, a felony statute, provided specific criminal sanctions of up to ten years in jail and a $5,000 fine against two or more persons who conspired to deprive "any citizen" of their constitutional rights. Section 242, a misdemeanor statute commonly known as the "color-of-law statute," brought local government officials, including police officers, under the umbrella of federal jurisdiction if they abused the powers of their offices to deny citizens their civil rights.[36]

Because Section 241 required proof of conspiracy and Section 242 required specific intent, the statutes raised hard questions about enforcement strategies and sparked a legal debate that dragged on for decades. As a result, the Justice Department and the White House usually indulged the FBI's reluctance to investigate civil rights cases aggressively. Department attorneys never used Section 241 in the manner that one of Murphy's successors as attorney general, Francis Biddle, recommended—as a "criminal catch-all." Instead, they concluded that "the outbreak of ruffian, vigilante activity, not participated in by public officials, whether directed against reds, nazis, negroes, soap-box speakers, or religious groups," lay outside Section 241. Nevertheless, the government either had to rely on Sections 241 and 242 or withdraw from the protection of civil rights. The Reconstruction Era statutes constituted the only available weapon for the federal government to use in defense of black citizens, and they would provide the basic authority for the FBI's civil rights investigations for the next twenty-five years.[37]

Most of the early cases the FBI investigated under these statutes, whether the civil rights of black people or the civil liberties of labor organizers, involved the politically explosive question of police brutality. The brutality issue made Hoover especially uncomfortable, because Bureau success in solving most federal crimes and piling up conviction statistics depended on the assistance of police officers. It could be awkward for a special agent to ask a policeman for help on a stolen car case in the morning, and then to come back to investigate a brutality complaint against the same officer in the afternoon.

Between 1940 and 1943 Hoover engaged the Justice Department in a struggle to define the proper scope of police brutality investigations. The occasion was a case Civil Rights Section attorneys considered to be a perfect test for Section 242. *United States v. Sutherland* involved an Atlanta policeman who used a hot branding iron to extract a confession from a sixteen-year-old black burglary suspect. On appeal, with the defense attempting to establish the good character of the accused police officer, the Civil Rights Section asked the FBI to determine whether the Atlanta Police Department routinely abused prisoners when questioning them and if the said defendant had a history of such conduct. Given Sutherland's good-character defense, these requests seemed reasonable, and the case itself represented one of the few instances where the Department made a sustained effort to force the FBI to confront civil rights enforcement head on. The FBI balked nonetheless.[38]

"The Atlanta Police Department," Hoover complained to Criminal Division chief O. John Rogge, "is not under investigation in this matter." When Rogge failed to respond, Hoover appealed to Deputy Attorney General Matthew McGuire. The initial investigation, he wrote, had created "considerable ill will" between the Atlanta police and the Bureau. A series of conferences "had resolved this problem," but another confrontation would likely "rupture the friendly relationship which has been established." Siding with Hoover, McGuire offered the following opinion: "It is questionable whether a right not to be beaten is secured by any provision of the Constitution or any Federal Statute. It is secured by State laws. . . . Certainly, it is questionable whether a police officer who hits a prisoner in an effort to make him confess is acting under color of any law, because there is no State law that authorizes him to do so." It would be hard to imagine how any reading of the statute could have been more deferential to the director's desire to keep his bureaucracy focused on crime-busting to the exclusion of any civil rights responsibilities. McGuire had no intention of alienating Hoover, let alone the white southern Democrats who made the Roosevelt coalition whole.[39]

No other responsible Justice Department officials endorsed McGuire's argument, but they did make certain concessions to accommodate the FBI and appease the Democratic party's southern wing. Wendell Berge, Rogge's successor as chief of the Criminal Division, narrowed the scope of police brutality responsibilities by requiring full investigations only in the "quite rare" case where "the victim himself," and not "some friend of the alleged victim," filed charges. Berge also required the Civil Rights Section to take "one added precaution," before calling for a full-field FBI investigation, by first requesting "a preliminary investigation . . . in order to ascertain the criminal record of the victim." Less interested in black rights and questions of law than protecting "law enforcement officers from 'smears'" and speculating about the motives of the people who filed civil rights complaints (and the "shyster[s]" who represented them), Hoover welcomed the new policy because it sanctioned his private agenda. By conceding power of discretion, the directive also sanctioned his bureaucratic agenda because it allowed him to treat police brutality investigations as sideshows. Sutherland, in the meantime, came to trial twice before the U.S. attorney in Atlanta gave up and dropped the case.[40]

While FBI agents continued throughout the war years to do all of the investigative work that was done on police brutality cases and other civil rights matters for the Justice Department, their efforts, as in *Sutherland*, were unenthusiastic and invisible to the world outside the Department.[41] The Bureau's public relations corps rarely bothered to mention civil rights. Crime Records Division agents did help Hoover's principal ghostwriter, former Kansas City newspaperman Courtney Ryley Cooper, with an article on peonage and police use of "third-degree tactics," but the initiative came from Cooper. Released under his name and not the director's, the piece reflected the Bureau's distinctly low-key approach—in contrast to "Gun Crazy" and fifteen other Hoover by-line articles Cooper wrote for *American* magazine celebrating the shoot-em-up gangster wars with Dillinger and cohorts. If the director had been left alone, he would have ignored the problem of police brutality in its entirety.[42]

Hoover and his public relations people could not afford to ignore civil rights during the postwar period. The first indication that the FBI role in the federal enforcement effort would pose larger political and institutional problems for the director came on December 5, 1946—when Harry S. Truman established the President's Committee on Civil Rights "to inquire into and determine whether and in what respect current law-enforcement measures . . . may be strengthened and improved to safeguard the civil rights of the people." Hoover, instinctively recognizing the threat the President's Committee posed to his bureaucracy's power and autonomy, dismissed Truman's decision as a capitulation to communist pressure groups. "Certain elements active in the United States are capitalizing upon every alleged violation of civil rights . . . for the ultimate purpose of launching and perpetuating an organized attack against . . . law enforcement agencies." With their "ulterior and often veiled motives," Hoover reasoned, these "selfish and conniving elements" had geared-up for "a widespread 'smear' campaign."[43]

Expecting to be called before the President's Committee and anticipating that the Committee itself would criticize his bureaucracy's record, Hoover acted to contain any damage. He worked with Committee member Morris L. Ernst, for example, to insure a fair hearing for the FBI position. An American Civil Liberties Union official and longtime adviser to the NAACP, Ernst admired the FBI and generally served Hoover as both an informer on these organizations and a public relations man.[44]

When the summons to testify finally came, the director ordered name checks "setting forth all available information in the Bureau's files" on all sixteen Committee members—with the exception of Ernst. The FBI described Sadie T. Alexander, assistant solicitor for the city of Philadelphia and a board member of the National Urban League, as a "Negress" and "Active Fair Employment"; CIO secretary and International Union of Electrical Workers president James B. Carey as "*Now* Anti-Communist"; Frank P. Graham, president of the University of North Carolina, as "An Innocent"; Rev. Francis J. Haas, former chairman of the Fair Employment Practice Commission, as a "Catholic Bishop. Liberal"; Dorothy Tilly, a lay activist in the Methodist Church, as a "Southern Liberal"; and the moderate Channing H. Tobias of the Phelps-Stokes Fund and the YMCA as a "Negro" and an "ultra liberal." Only Committee chairman Charles E. Wilson received a neutral description: "Pres. General Electric." The others were all dissidents, people who made trouble for the director and his America with their reformist ideas and liberal causes.[45]

Preparation for Hoover's appearance before the President's Committee went beyond name checks and furtive meetings with Morris Ernst. The director constructed the details of the FBI position himself, scribbling out a pile of handwritten notes and outlines. He adopted a direct, if inherently contradictory strategy: take the offensive against the liberal and ultra-liberal members of the President's Committee. He began by calling for enactment of "a clear-cut over-all Civil Rights Statute," but then quickly qualified his support for a tougher law. The federal enforcement effort must operate "against a background of reserved States' rights," he cautioned. Civil rights violations usually involved "private relationships," and such relationships should "remain a matter of interest to the States." The director reportedly expressed the same sentiment, in cruder fashion and in a different context, after attorney Joseph Rauh asked Attorney General Tom Clark to have the Bureau investigate the attempted murder of United Automobile Workers chief Walter Reuther. Rauh remembered Clark's account of Hoover's irrelevant though certainly revealing reply. "Edgar says no. He's not going to send the FBI in every time some nigger woman says she's been raped."[46]

Hoover had no intention of publicly commiting his bureaucracy to either side of a fundamental political debate between states' rights advocates and federal interventionists, and his agenda here was overt and somewhat legitimate. At the same time, he acted to protect his right to determine the FBI's workload, image, and investigative priorities, and his agenda here was covert and illegitimate. While spying on Orson Welles, Frank Sinatra, and other prominent supporters of antilynching legislation, he complained to Attorney General Clark about all the time his agents wasted on "murders, lynchings and assaults, particularly in the Southern states." To make matters worse, these investigations had created a public relations nightmare. Because "the public judges the efficiency of law enforcement . . . upon the basis of prosecutions," and because the "nebulous" Reconstruction Era statutes precluded successful prosecution (1,570 investigations and only 27 convictions in the past twenty years), Hoover felt aggrieved by the widespread "feeling and belief that the Bureau has failed to 'solve' many cases into which it has entered." This "completely ineffective" civil rights enforcement effort, he said, had the unhappy side effect of enabling state authorities to "slide out of these cases as soon as the Department and the Bureau enter them."[47]

To solve the problem, Hoover urged Clark to adopt a rigorous policy to prevent the Justice Department's liberal attorneys from "rushing pell-mell into cases in which there is no apparent violation of a Federal Statute." The attorney general agreed that "a large percentage of the investigations initiated in this field prove in the end to be fruitless," but the Department had no choice. "If we do not investigate we are placed in the position of having received a complaint . . . and of having failed to satisfy ourselves that it is or is not such a violation. I know of no way to avoid at least a preliminary inquiry." Besides, "as a matter of policy," the Civil Rights Section had "requested only limited investigations in almost every case."[48]

Hoover's public strategy for containing the President's Committee on Civil Rights emphasized accommodation and not confrontation. He protested on practical, bureaucratic grounds, not theoretical ones, though privately he saw no harm in the white southern way. Inside the FBI, the director and his men accepted segregation in restaurants in New York, let alone Mississippi, and believed "Negroes go to silly extremes at times to obtain social equality." When they wrote memos back and forth, they usually referred to "alleged" civil rights violations and "alleged" lynchings. One executive, the head of the San Francisco office, even referred to the "alleged persecution of negroes in South Africa." When testifying before the President's Com-

mittee, however, Hoover immediately endorsed its basic premise. Racial violence "in free America," he agreed, occasionally
compared to "the horrors of Nazism and Fascism." The problem
was real enough. It simply was not realistic to expect the FBI to
do much—if anything—to solve it. Too many obstacles and too
many interests worked to frustrate the Bureau. And with the
exception of the director's own agents, nearly everyone was to
blame.[49]

When the President's Committee asked why the training programs at the FBI National Academy in Quantico, Virginia, had
no room for black police officers, Hoover falsely explained that
state and local police departments unilaterally selected all candidates. Organized during the New Deal years to train local police "in the latest crime-fighting techniques," the director
thought of the Academy as "the West Point of law enforcement."
"You'd seek out . . . the best guys possible," one former agent
recalled. "They were going to become key local officials. You
took these people to Washington and Quantico, and you inculcated the hell out of them. . . . You really tried to get corruption-
proof, young, upwardly mobile officers—you got some awfully
good people and then they became your buddies in the field." In
every case, the FBI selected the final (all-white) candidates for
admission.[50]

Hoover also dodged the President's Committee when asked to
explain why he assigned no black FBI agents to civil rights
cases. Emphasizing the "hazards of such an assignment" and the
predictable "reaction of local juries in the South to testimony by
colored Agents," he saw no need to point out that the FBI had
only three black agents—his driver, James Crawford, and office
retainer, W. Samuel Noisette, and the sixty-eight-year-old veteran of the Marcus Garvey case, James E. Amos.[51]

Of the three, only James Amos even remotely carried out the
duties of a regular FBI agent. The son of a Washington policeman who ran a chain gang in Rock Creek Park, Amos's work
experience included seven years with the Burns Detective
Agency and twelve years service as Theodore Roosevelt's valet.
His references on the Bureau employment application in 1921
included Henry Cabot Lodge and Elihu Root, and he received his
shield from Hoover himself at the corner of Vermont Avenue and
K Street. A reputed master of disguise who could "shadow a suspect for days" and decode "cypher messages," Amos rarely functioned in such a manner after the Garvey case closed. Beginning

in the mid-1920s, he contributed to the Bureau by providing common-sense advice. "Whenever F.B.I. agents are stymied on a case and don't know what to do next," wrote Fulton Oursler, then a *Reader's Digest* editor and newspaper columnist, "they have a heart-to-heart talk with the 'Dean.' . . . Jim never fails them because he is an expert in techniques of crime detection." Amos remained with the Bureau's New York office, where he supervised the weapons inventory, until September 1953. He died two months later, on Christmas day.[52]

James Amos received an occasional field assignment. Sam Noisette simply hung up the hats and coats of the people who came in to see the director, and James Crawford did nothing more than wear a chauffeur's uniform, complete with cap, and drive the director around. Crawford received his shield in 1941, after Walter White asked Hoover "about the capacities in which Negroes are employed" and the NAACP launched an investigation of the FBI practice of keeping black college graduates in dead-end jobs while "hiring white girls just out of high school and giving them clerkships." Crawford took his training on the segregated course ("I stayed by myself") at the National Academy, and when he returned from Quantico he went back into his chauffeur's uniform. Noisette also attended the Academy on the segregated course, and upon his return he went back to his desk in the director's outer office. Hoover appointed both men special agents not only in response to NAACP criticisms, but to keep them from being drafted and to exempt them from civil service protections.[53]

Having been placed on the defensive by the NAACP, Hoover proceeded to find fault with the nation's most prominent civil rights group. Earlier, in August 1946, the director had tried to pacify the organization after Walter White complained, once again, about "anti-Negro" FBI agents "messing up" lynching and police brutality cases; Hoover gave him the names and telephone numbers of the special agents in charge of all Bureau field offices. The director hoped such a gesture of implied assistance to the NAACP's mission would "aid us in our relations with the Negro race." In fact, he had been attempting to soften NAACP criticism of the FBI's civil rights enforcement record since the war years, when he wrote a testimonial for White on his twenty-fifth anniversary with the NAACP. But when White kept pestering Hoover to hire more black agents and to investigate civil rights cases more aggressively, the director regretted

the "blunder made in committing me to this outfit." White's colleague, NAACP special counsel Thurgood Marshall, was equally
annoying. When Marshall complained to Attorney General Tom
Clark about the FBI's notably "one-sided" policy of investigating segregationist terror, Hoover drafted a letter for Clark's signature that accused the NAACP of frustrating civil rights progress by refusing to cooperate with the FBI. Marshall saw the
document as confirmation of his original point. "I have no faith
in either Mr. Hoover or his investigators."[54]

After complaining about the NAACP, Hoover singled out the
Justice Department for a share of the blame. When the President's Committee asked why the FBI did not investigate civil
rights cases immediately upon receipt of a complaint, the director suggested that the Committee direct the question to Clark.
Justice Department policy required the Bureau to refer all civil
rights complaints to the Criminal Division of the Department for
an opinion before launching an investigation. In practice, this
meant that complaints received by FBI field offices not only
went to FBI headquarters and then on to the Criminal Division,
but back to the nearest United States attorney's office in the
field for an opinion and then back again, step by step. This usually resulted in delays of two weeks, a long enough period for
evidence to turn stale. The Department initiated that policy,
Hoover said, not the FBI. The director did not advise the President's Committee that he absolutely supported this particular
policy.[55]

The Justice Department, Hoover added, rarely acted on the
information that the FBI did gather. As an example, he cited
the case of the recent Democratic party primary in Georgia. The
Criminal Division originally ordered an investigation to determine if "a conspiracy" existed "to deprive the negroes of their
right to vote." After conducting interviews in ninety Georgia
counties, the FBI concluded that gubernatorial candidate Herman Talmadge and "his various colleagues" had removed the
names of thousands of black citizens from voter registration
roles. But the Department declined to prosecute any of the conspirators.[56]

Besides the reluctant Justice Department and over-eager colored organizations, the director told the President's Committee
that public opinion posed an even greater obstacle to law enforcement in civil rights cases. "White citizens . . . opposed to
the very principle involved in the investigation" invariably

blocked prosecution of civil rights cases in southern states. To document his point, Hoover discussed the July 1946 lynching of Roger Malcolm, his wife, and another black couple by a mob near Monroe, Georgia. One of the agents who worked on the case, Clement L. McGowan, Jr., a Peach State native and Notre Dame graduate, remembered the details forty years later. "The guy was taking them from the county seat, back to the farm where they worked . . . and as they came to this one bridge, they were met by a hooded group." It should have been an open and shut case, but "local white citizens" and "the local sheriff's office failed completely to cooperate," and the state police cooperated only "in a perfunctory fashion." After hearing the testimony of 106 witnesses, the grand jury returned no indictments.[57]

By discussing these problems and by casting blame on virtually everyone from the lowliest NAACP worker to the entire white South, Hoover deflected the criticisms of the President's Committee on Civil Rights. Staff director Robert K. Carr, for one, described Hoover's appearance as "magnificent," telling him that he found it "difficult . . . to restrain my enthusiasm." If Carr's staff privately raked the FBI's "superficial and unintelligent work," their public report avoided such direct language. Noting the lack of specialized training, the Committee maintained that Bureau agents simply lacked the background "to cope with the elusive and difficult aspects of a civil rights case." The Committee itself lacked the political courage to confront the Bureau head-on.[58]

"In view of the public consciousness of the problem and the delicacy of it," Hoover responded immediately to the qualified criticisms of the President's Committee. He ordered additional civil rights training for all new agents, the establishment of "a special training school" for "a selected group" of veteran agents ("so that when one of these cases arises we at least might send in several key men"), and an expansion of the civil rights curriculum for police officers at the National Academy.[59] The only other visible response came from the public relations division. Crime Records helped Fulton Oursler with his articles on Jim Amos and arranged another piece in a black-owned magazine, *Ebony*, on Amos and Sam Noisette.[60] In the meantime, Hoover refused to give the persistent Walter White a straight answer when he again inquired about "Negro FBI operators." Obfuscation still reigned.[61]

A few administrative reforms, publicity releases to the press, and creative answers to tough questions deflected the threat to Hoover posed by the President's Committee on Civil Rights. By placing the burden on Congress "to plot our policy for the protection of civil rights," the Committee actually lessened the "terrific pressure" brought to bear on the Justice Department and the FBI to take decisive action in the absence of new legislation, larger appropriations, and more staff. In a sense, the President's Committee itself had taken Hoover's advice to "the various minority groups"—"get after Congress, not the Department of Justice." By emphasizing the legal and practical barriers to the effective enforcement of civil rights law, the Committee concluded that the nation needed better legislation from Congress, not a more dedicated enforcement effort from the executive. The final report eased pressure on the FBI. With so little incentive, other than public relations, Hoover scarcely followed through on the modest administrative reforms he had implemented. Having survived the challenge, retrenchment, not reform, was in order.[62]

Justice Department officials, in fact, tried to impose one single substantive reform, designed to reduce the investigative delays that accompanied the typical civil rights case. From 1939 to 1947 the FBI had accepted complaints alleging violations of federal civil rights law but had launched formal investigations only at the specific request of the head of the Criminal Division. Department officials generally had reserved such a policy for three or four sensitive categories of investigation (antitrust matters, for example) in which there was special need to manage test cases carefully to create a useful legal precedent. In April 1947, Attorney General Clark changed this policy by authorizing the Bureau "to conduct *preliminary investigations* of any civil rights complaints or incidents upon its own motion [emphasis added]."[63] Hoover saw no threat in Clark's order, although two of his closest aides viewed it as an attempt "to 'unload' responsibility onto the Bureau." In the director's view, "the Attorney General asks us merely to institute 'preliminary investigation' and still leaves us free to then forward the basic allegation to the Department for decision as to . . . whether a full investigation should be instituted." The directive, therefore, was "not to be construed as changing the existing instructions." Hoover, not the attorney general, remained in control.[64]

J. Howard McGrath, Clark's successor, continued on this tack. "I wish to make it clear," he informed Hoover in December 1951, "that the Bureau can in the first instance originate, initiate, and carry through to a conclusion any investigation within its jurisdiction." This meant "blanket authority to conduct full and complete investigations in [civil rights] cases." The director responded by ordering all field offices to proceed only with approval from headquarters in any case considered undesirable, overly broad, controversial, or potentially embarrassing. Less than a year later, in October 1952, he convinced McGrath's successor, James P. McGranery, to rescind the directive entirely.[65]

During the Eisenhower years Hoover made a series of unilateral assaults on what remained of Justice Department policy, all designed to reduce his Bureau's civil rights workload.[66] By mid-1958 he had completely revised existing policy pertaining to every type of civil rights case, from police brutality to peonage, simply by declaring previous departmental instructions "permissive rather than mandatory." Hereafter, the Bureau refused to launch even preliminary investigations unless the attorney general issued a specific directive on a case-by-case basis. Besides being insubordinate, this new policy created certain risks. It would no longer be easy "to shut off criticism by the . . . [NAACP] and other groups," FBI Assistant Director Alex Rosen emphasized. "[We will not be] able to say at the very outset that the matter is being inquired into and the facts will be presented to the Civil Rights Division"—a policy that immediately took "the heat off." The benefits, however, outweighed the risks. A continuation of the old policy would expose the Bureau to heat from the other side. Believing that the growing civil rights movement was too "controversial," politics in the South too "inflamed," and community feelings too "emotional," Hoover intended to keep the FBI on the sidelines.[67]

For the time being, the director's "reforms" accomplished their purpose. Before 1958 the FBI's public reports listed the total number of preliminary civil rights investigations *conducted* in any given year—a total of 1,269 in 1958, for example. Beginning in 1959, the FBI simply listed the number of civil rights violations *reported* during the year. Outright insubordination now joined obfuscation and public relations trickery to govern the Bureau's civil rights policy. To keep the FBI on the sidelines, Hoover proved willing to risk direct confrontation with the Justice Department.[68]

No amount of bureaucratic maneuvering could make the issues raised by the President's Committee on Civil Rights or the political problems facing the FBI fade completely away. On nearly every other issue, with the exception of civil rights, Hoover had been able to build bipartisan constituencies—relatively easy to do when the issue was crime control or anticommunism—but this was a nearly impossible task when the issue was civil rights. Hoover knew that the Negro Question threatened to divide his supporters, and that whatever he chose to do (or not to do) would be controversial. By refusing to launch a crusade against civil rights violators along the model of his earlier campaign against the 1930s' gangsters, or his ongoing campaign against communist subversives, he risked censure from "vociferous minority groups" and their liberal allies. At the same time, even the most unenthusiastic investigations of civil rights abuses alienated his conservative, states' rights constituency.

The most dramatic example of this occurred in 1953 when guards at the Pennhurst School for the Feebleminded in Spring City, Pennsylvania, beat a young black inmate named Robert Byers to death. After Byers's father viewed his son's bruised corpse, he demanded that something be done. The Justice Department ordered the FBI to investigate—on the grounds that the Pennhurst guards may have violated Byers's civil rights by killing him. An important case for the Bureau, it demonstrated that states' rights issues cut across regional lines on the problem of police brutality and other matters covered by Section 242, the color-of-law statute.[69]

FBI interest in Byers's death attracted national media attention during a press conference at the annual Governors' Conference in Seattle in August 1953. John S. Fine of Pennsylvania, Allan Shivers of Texas, John Battle of Virginia, and Thomas E. Dewey of New York, among others, criticized the Bureau "and indirectly the Eisenhower Administration for not curbing its activities." "The publicity," Hoover complained to Attorney General Herbert Brownell, left the "general impression" that the FBI had "engaged in an unrestrained program of invading State's rights." A few of the journalists who publicized the charges, the director added, had deliberately incited "ill will on the part of local, county and state law enforcement agencies against the FBI."[70]

One of the worst offenders, Hearst columnist Westbrook Pegler, had been drawn to the civil rights topic earlier in the year—after another newspaperman broke the story of a Justice Department official's agreement with the New York City Police

Department allowing the police to investigate brutality complaints filed against their own officers. Pegler and states' rights advocates in general saw nothing wrong with that policy—and neither did Hoover, at least in theory. When the attorney general rescinded the agreement, however, Pegler suspected that Hoover had leaked the information that broke the story in the first place. Louis B. Nichols, chief of the Crime Records Division, then met with Pegler in an attempt to straighten him out, telling the Hearst columnist "that for a period of time I frankly wondered whether [Max] Lowenthal had converted [you]." (Lowenthal, a friend of Harry Truman's, had written a scathing book on the FBI.) Conceding that the Bureau had "a duty to do," Pegler said he simply believed policemen should use their night sticks "a little more frequently . . . on 'pimps, fairies and labor racketeers.'"[71]

Pegler's carping, Hoover lamented, had contributed to "a rather bad reaction . . . in various sections of the country." The director tried to limit this damage by going directly to the media, reminding *New York Times* publisher Arthur Hayes Sulzberger that the "FBI is not a policy-making organization. It is a service agency," with a mission to enforce federal law. "It makes little difference whether the Act of Congress was passed in 1866 or 1953 so long as it is the law of the land," he continued, adding that persons opposed to Section 242, the color-of-law statute, should stop criticizing the FBI and seek its repeal. He made this same point again in a press release, quoting a long-dead president. "Theodore Roosevelt, I believe, said that the best way to have a bad law repealed was to enforce it."[72] Nichols, meanwhile, solicited positive press coverage from Raymond Moley of *Newsweek*, Hearst columnists George Sokolsky and Howard Rushmore, and Hearst executive Richard Berlin (who had his own troubles with the incorrigible Pegler). Other prominent Americans, including Joseph P. Kennedy and Morris Ernst, volunteered their services to the Bureau. All of this publicity made the point that FBI agents investigated police brutality because they had to and not because they wanted to or were in any way critical of local police practices.[73]

After the flap over Byers's death and the New York police affair finally quieted, Nichols drafted a directive, for Hoover's signature, requiring all field offices "to be alert for any disgruntled public official who may be misinformed as to the Bureau's position in civil rights."[74] By the time Hoover issued that order the

Byers case had been closed for two months. Nearly as tentative
in the face of criticism from states' righters as the FBI itself,
the Justice Department advised the director one week after the
governors' conference that no further investigation into the circumstances surrounding Robert Byers's death would be necessary.

Because the FBI could withdraw only from particular cases
and not from its general civil rights responsibilities, the political
problems facing Hoover continued to mount. This was especially true among his white constituents in the South after the
Supreme Court unanimously ruled racial segregation in public
schools unconstitutional in *Brown v. Board of Education* (1954).
Congressman Mendel Rivers (D., S.C.) told Nichols "that the Bureau is getting itself in a bad situation when it is forced to do
the work of the NAACP." During the school desegregation crisis
in Little Rock, militant whites appeared to be as upset with Director Hoover for sending in the FBI as they were with President
Eisenhower for sending in the 101st Airborne—though Hoover
sent the FBI in only because Eisenhower told him to do so. Little
Rock segregationists failed to recognize the distinction. They
identified the Bureau's agents as enemies of their race because
(among other reasons) the G-men always stopped by the Sky
Room at the Lafayette Hotel, where the Citizens Council cau-
cused, to obtain specimens from the segregation-forever documents that the resistance had stacked up on tables everywhere.[75]

Civil rights matters posed a threat to the FBI and to Hoover's
own directorship. "A lot of the southern folks never know what
a position the Director has been in," Nichols explained, in February 1957, to Senator James Eastland (D., Miss.). A year later
H. L. Edwards, an aide to Senator Olin Johnson (D., S.C.), told
Gordon A. Nease, Nichols's successor as head of Crime Records,
that "many of the Southern Senators," not understanding why
the FBI "must investigate civil rights matters," had already
taken "definite steps" to remove the director "from his job."
Those senators held a meeting on this subject recently "on the
Hill," though "the matter had gradually calmed down."[76] Edwards recommended that Hoover "pressure" the Eisenhower
administration "to set up an investigative staff for the Civil
Rights Division of the Department," thus enabling the FBI to
"keep away from such matters entirely." Edwards said this
"could be accomplished if sufficient interest was aroused in
Congress," in the process suggesting that the director "speak to

his close friends." Hoover dismissed Edwards's "completely un-
tenable" ideas. "It is amazing how utterly unobjective some individuals get," he complained. "We have a job to do and we will
do it."[77]

That comment indicated no change in attitude toward civil
rights work, only a measure of resignation and more than anything else territorial instinct. An institutional interest in preserving the FBI's function as *the* investigative arm of the Justice
Department counterbalanced Hoover's personal interest in preserving segregation within his own Bureau and political interest
in letting it alone in those areas of the country where it already
existed. No matter how unpleasant the investigation, Hoover refused to establish the precedent of farming out particular tasks.

The struggle to retain bureaucratic autonomy on civil rights
enforcement matters plagued Hoover throughout the cold war
years, in contrast to the parallel investigations of civil rights activists on the domestic intelligence front. Here, the FBI and its
director found the pursuit of bureaucratic autonomy considerably easier. The surveillance mission produced no splits in
Hoover's constituency, only files bulging with rumor, gossip,
and allegation, which the FBI collected but did not always
bother to verify, on a range of people interested in civil rights,
from mainstream politicians to Communist party functionaries
and fellow travelers. The FBI did not harass civil rights activists
and their friends as often during the 1940s and 1950s as they
would do during the 1960s, but neither did they leave the movement alone. They were always tracking the radical and not-so-
radical ideas of the people involved in the struggle for black
equality and following the Red menace in and out of movement
groups.

Much of the collected information represented evidence of
subversion only to the FBI. The Bureau overlooked the membership of Eliot Asinof, a blacklisted television writer, in several
left-wing groups on the attorney general's list of subversive organizations, but not his signature on an old petition urging the
New York Yankees to sign black ball players. In the case of Minneapolis Mayor Hubert H. Humphrey, who advocated civil
rights within the Americans for Democratic Action and led the
civil rights platform fight at the 1948 Democratic convention,
the FBI prepared a "blind" memo citing his appearance at an
NAACP-sponsored meeting and implying that he had once paid a
"political debt to the Communists." Typed "on plain white bond,

unwatermarked paper" to disguise the Bureau's authorship, this blind memo was one of thirty the FBI prepared on Humphrey and other members of the National Conference on Prevention and Control of Juvenile Delinquency for Hearst executive Edmond D. Coblentz, one of Hoover's most powerful media allies—though apparently Coblentz never bothered to pick them up.[78]

There were additional blind memos concerning black communists and fellow travelers, which Louis Nichols delivered to Robert E. Stripling, chief counsel for the House Committee on Un-American Activities. One concerned Benjamin J. Davis, Jr., one of the first-string communist leaders convicted in the 1949 Foley Square Smith Act trial of conspiring to teach or advocate the violent overthrow of the United States government. Nichols gave Stripling another memo (with a copy to Illinois Senator Everett Dirksen) on Paul Robeson, the black singer, actor, and friend of the Communist party. FBI agents tapped Robeson's phone, opened his mail, and tried to find out if he really was having a rumored affair with Lord Louis Mountbatten's wife. A report "that Lady Mountbatten has a huge naked statue of Paul Robeson in her home" attracted Hoover's personal attention.[79]

While leaking information from FBI files to HUAC and the Hearst press, the director methodically continued to forward his conclusions about the subversive aspects of the Negro Question to the White House—a practice that reflected his personal bias and not a legitimate political position. Almost every document sent to Truman administration officials blamed the Communist party for "agitating pressure campaigns" on behalf of racial justice. The director even tried to smear Mary McLeod Bethune, former director of Negro Affairs for the National Youth Administration, as a communist agent. He had Bureau researchers compare the Communist party line on lynching with the views of journals like *The Nation* and the *New Republic*. The implication of these reports seemed to be that only communists supported racial justice in America. This notion allowed Hoover to link a consensus opinion (that communists posed a serious threat to American institutions and values) with a more problematic one (that civil rights advocates posed an equally serious threat to those same institutions and values). Hoover may have been even more concerned with undermining the legitimacy of the civil rights movement than in investigating the Negro Question activities of Communist party functionaries. For the director, the advocacy of racial justice was itself a subversive act, and his reports on communism were simply to support this thesis. By equating civil rights activism with un-American activity, he clearly went beyond his internal security mandate.[80]

A surprisingly high number of documents the FBI sent to Truman and then Eisenhower administration officials concerned the NAACP. The FBI claimed that an NAACP resolution praising former Secretary of Commerce Henry Wallace's public statements about lynching had actually been drawn-up "under the direction of the Communist Party." (FBI agents had been monitoring Wallace's "Contacts with Negro Communist-Controlled Organizations and Individuals" at least since 1945, more than a year before Truman dismissed him from the cabinet for criticizing the hard-line policy toward the Soviet Union.)[81] The Bureau's most notable reports on the NAACP to the Eisenhower White House were a 1956 series of letters and memos on communist interest in plans by the Leadership Conference on Civil Rights, led by the NAACP, to send a delegation to meet with congressmen. The director alerted the administration to the meetings that the Leadership Conference held with the senators from Illinois, the Democrat Paul Douglas and the Republican Everett Dirksen, and also briefed the president's aides on the UAW's support for the Conference.[82]

That same year, President Eisenhower's attorney general, Herbert Brownell, urged Congress to give the Justice Department power to file civil suits in support of voting rights, to create a civil rights commission, and to upgrade the Civil Rights Section to full division status within the Justice Department. Hoover showed his antipathy toward Brownell's efforts by making sure he made no statement in his reports on the NAACP or in his conversations with administration officials that the Department might "seize [upon] . . . to support its position in seeking enactment of civil rights legislation." A year later, after Congress adopted Brownell's proposals, the FBI's New York office sent a 137-page report on the NAACP to the White House and the military intelligence agencies. Based on information supplied by 151 informants, "bag squads" (that is, Bureau burglars), wiretaps, and other confidential sources, the report concerned "communist activity" in NAACP chapters from Miami, Florida, to Fairbanks, Alaska.[83]

Whatever his agenda, however, Hoover remained, as ever, determined to ingratiate himself with whatever president was in the Oval Office. Dwight Eisenhower gave the director an unprecedented opportunity in March 1956 when he asked for an extended presentation on the general subject of "Racial Tension and Civil Rights," and offered Hoover a chance to make his report at a cabinet meeting. Hoover told the cabinet that the Supreme Court decision in *Brown* had set the country on a course toward racial crisis. "Delicate situations are aggravated by some overzealous but ill-advised leaders of the NAACP and by the Communist Party, which seeks to use incidents to further the so-called class struggle. . . . The area of danger lies in friction between extremists on both sides"—"both those who stand for and against segregation"—"ready with violence."[84]

Eisenhower expected Hoover to explain (not defend) the white South's point of view. For the most part that is what the director did, but his briefing paper indicated that he stood with the segregationists. "The specter of racial intermarriages" and "mixed education" that haunted the South also haunted the FBI. Black groups and individuals preaching "racial hatred" had spread across the South, Hoover claimed, in contrast to the "pretty much defunct" Ku Klux Klan. "The leading citizens of the South"—that is, "bankers, lawyers, doctors, state legislators and industrialists"—composed the membership of the white-collar (or "readin' and writin'") Klans, the Citizens Councils. One of the director's aides claimed the Citizens Councils posed less of a problem than the "Negro publications" that ran "inflamatory articles concerning these councils."[85]

Hoover emphasized the communist threat for the Eisenhower cabinet in a way that clearly showed how biased he was. In discussing "the alleged lynching" of a fourteen-year-old Chicago boy, Emmett Till, the director worried more about a "pressure campaign on government officials" than a brutal, racist murder. Till had gone to Money, Mississippi, to visit relatives, and made the mistake, one afternoon, of "whistling at a distaff white." The woman's husband and half brother kidnapped Till, murdered him, and dumped his body in the Tallahatchie River. Till was found seven days later, a .45 caliber bullet hole in his crushed skull and a seventy-four-pound cotton-gin fan tied around his neck. After a state court jury acquitted both suspects of murder charges, a federal grand jury refused to issue indictments. (Technically speaking, the FBI never "investigated" the case; the FBI launched a "preliminary" investigation, not a "full" investigation.) When Illinois communists, along with thousands of other people, demanded that President Eisenhower take action, Chicago Mayor Richard J. Daley wired the White House urging federal intervention. The director concluded his discussion of the case by reminding the cabinet "that Mayor Daley [was] not a Communist," only a dupe: "Pressures engineered by the Communists were brought to bear upon him."[86]

Hoover strayed from the Red menace briefly to discuss Elijah Muhammad's Nation of Islam, a separatist group that accepted the general tenets of Islam. He incorrectly described the Black Muslims as one of the "organizations presently advancing integration" and "figur[ing] in the rising tensions." FBI interest in Muhammad's group resulted from their "violently anti-white rhetoric" and occasional verbal support for the Mau Mau in Africa and the Vietminh in northern Vietnam. The Bureau tried to have the Nation of Islam placed on the attorney general's list of subversive organizations and to jail its leaders for conspiring to violate the Smith Act and the Selective Service Act, but the Justice Department refused. Brownell merely approved a wiretap in 1957 on Muhammad's home telephone in Chicago "or any address to which he may move in the future." Interpreting this directive broadly, the Bureau also tapped and bugged Muhammad's winter residence in Phoenix.[87]

What the cabinet did not learn from the director's report was that Hoover privately shared the convictions of die-hard southern segregationists. But despite Hoover's personal hostility toward the integration movement, he would not commit the Bureau fully to the other side. In the decades following the black scare of 1919 and the dismantling of the old General Intelligence Division in 1924, Hoover presided over a bureaucracy that acted, as often as not, ambivalently toward civil rights activists and their alleged ties to communists and other extremists. Bureaucratic expediencies on matters of race determined outcomes as often as ideological assumptions about civil rights activists who demanded justice and equality for all.

FBI officials continued to disseminate alarmist information on the black freedom struggle. They sent a report to the White House on Eleanor Roosevelt's plans to hold a reception for the Southern Conference Educational Fund, and they briefed Vice-President Richard Nixon and Supreme Court Chief Justice Earl Warren on communist plans to infiltrate the Prayer Pilgrimage for Freedom. This was a demonstration to commemorate the third anniversary of *Brown*, during which Martin Luther King,

Jr., delivered his first major address on the steps of the Lincoln Memorial. The FBI also sent radio commentator and newspaper columnist Fulton Lewis, Jr., information about the civil rights activities of G. Bromley Oxnam, liberal Methodist bishop of Washington and president of the World Council of Churches. Hoover always made sure that the White House and the media were aware of Bureau resources and interests.[88]

When dealing with the southern segregationists, however, FBI officials had to proceed cautiously. Hoover regularly supplied information to the Senate Internal Security Subcommittee and its chairman, James Eastland (D., Miss.), and the House Committee on Un-American Activities and its chairman, Francis Walter (D., Penn.). But as a general rule the Bureau left documenting communist infiltration of the civil rights movement to the congressional committees themselves.[89]

HUAC opened its voluminous files to segregationists to help them discredit the civil rights movement. During House debate on Attorney General Brownell's civil rights bill, E. C. Gathings (D., Ark.) read into the *Congressional Record* HUAC reports detailing the "subversive activities" of eighty-nine people connected with the NAACP. In 1957 HUAC staff director Richard Arens released reports on fourteen board members of the Southern Regional Council, the moderate Atlanta-based interracial group, to Congressman James C. Davis (D., GA.). Arens, who often received information directly from the FBI's supposedly classified files, lost his own job with the Committee in 1960 when the press learned he was a consultant for a foundation that tried to prove Negroes were genetically inferior.[90]

Hoover supported the political position of the Un-American Activities Committee. When Congressman Gathings inserted his dossiers on NAACP activists into the *Congressional Record*, FBI Associate Director Clyde Tolson ordered all eighty-nine names run through the Bureau's files. The FBI and HUAC both helped the state of Kentucky prosecute Carl Braden of the Southern Conference Educational Fund on a sedition charge (for selling a black family a house in a white Louisville neighborhood). The FBI also ran name checks on civil rights activists and others who accused HUAC of "manufacturing the impression that liberalism is tainted with communism," and budgeted some $30,000 a year to the task of checking Committee files. When the Un-American Activities Committee published a cumulative name and organization index in 1955, the FBI ordered thirty copies.[91]

Struggling to form an accurate picture of the Communist party's attempts to take over the civil rights movement, FBI agents had a difficult time collecting specific evidence of significant communist influence. One of their best cases was Carl Braden's real-estate maneuver, which they called "one of the few known instances in which *it appears* a racial situation was created by a communist, *but not* necessarily *by the CP* [emphasis added]." Even the Bureau's best case had two qualifications.[92] The FBI concluded that the Communist party never had much success in its campaign to "sway the Negro" despite an "inordinate" investment of "time, funds, propaganda and personnel," including Comintern subsidies as high as $300,000 and dating from 1922. The Bureau would not even credit the party with attracting a significant minority of black members. In 1928 the CPUSA claimed 50 Negro members, though some of the comrades, according to FBI sources, estimated the total number of black recruits could be counted "on the fingers of one's hand." If the party did better in the 1930s and 1940s, it probably never had more than 4,000 active, disciplined, dues-paying Negro members. By 1956 total black membership dropped to less than 1,400. Ironically, as recent scholarship on the history of the party has shown, the FBI consistently *underestimated* the number of black communists and their accomplishments, such as they were, in black communities.[93]

Hoover's aides identified "the opposition of responsible Negro leaders" as "one of the most influential factors in the failure of the Communist Party." Most prominent blacks, they said, including Willard S. Townsend of the United Transport Service Employees, George Schuyler of the *Pittsburgh Courier*, and the firebrand from the GID era and the World War II March on Washington Movement, A. Philip Randolph, then president of the Brotherhood of Sleeping Car Porters, recognized "the specious nature of [the communist] program."[94] Bureau officials singled out Roy Wilkins ("he has been strongly anti-communist, and has done everything possible to keep the NAACP clear of communist infiltration"), along with his predecessor, Walter White, who died in 1955, for particular praise. Thus, the director wrote his testimonial for White at the very time he approved the wiretap on the office telephone of the NAACP branch in Philadelphia. And he had Louis Nichols and New York special agent in charge Edward Scheidt give White (and Wilkins, too) information "regarding Communist activities directed at the NAACP" even while he ordered an escalation of the Bureau's investigation of their group. The FBI could find no more than 467 past or present communists (or suspected communists) active in the NAACP—out of a total NAACP membership of more than 300,000.[95]

Neither the Communist party's failure to recruit blacks nor Hoover's refusal to commit his resources fully to the segregationists had a discernible impact on FBI surveillance policy. Bureau agents continued to monitor communist efforts to infiltrate groups like the NAACP and the Brotherhood of Sleeping Car Porters, and they continued to report even the most far-fetched rumors—including an informant report of a power struggle between White and Wilkins that had Wilkins representing "the Trotskyite element in the NAACP." And FBI officials continued to worry about what they called communist agitation "among the Negroes on the same old themes . . . 'equal rights' and 'self-determination,'" despite the "obvious" fact (obvious to the Bureau) that "the condition of the American Negro has improved materially during the past generation." If they located few registered black comrades, Hoover's agents remained equally interested in "approximately 18,000 other Negroes who have some contact with the Party and its front groups, and who are, to a certain degree, influenced directly or indirectly by its program, propaganda and agitation."[96]

Surveillance of the civil rights movement would continue for reasons of politics, not internal security. Hoover equated the Negro Question with subversion, but as FBI director he rarely accepted the risks involved in acting on that belief. Consequently, he proved quite tolerant of the contradictory belief of the men around him that the Red menace among blacks should not be taken all that seriously.

By the last of the Eisenhower years, despite the ability of the FBI to intervene in the affairs of black Americans, and despite the existence of a long list of FBI grievances against black people, Hoover remained uncertain about how best to use his power to redress his grievances. The director's racial ideas had not changed much since 1919, but he knew that any attempt to link the civil rights movement to the Red menace would not be persuasive outside the white South, and he knew that explicitly racist policies no longer had national support. His 1931 reprimand of Clyde Tolson for refusing to hire a "colored messenger" indicates an early awareness of the delicacy of the Negro Question. Hoover was sensitive in appearance, though he encouraged the practice, of racism within his own bureaucracy. After *Brown v. Board of Education* he tried to eliminate any overt "bias or prejudice" on the part of his field agents in the South. He had Clement McGowan, then a supervisor on the civil rights desk at headquarters, "personally caution that the Supreme Court justices didn't ask anybody's opinion when they were passing on the case and they didn't need any dissenting opinions or concurring opinions when you're out conducting investigations." "Nothing can hurt you quicker," McGowan said, "than somebody opening his mouth. The biggest enemy most of the agents had was their own little mouths—or big mouths."[97] Hoover was a racist, but he always let his political and bureaucratic instincts control his feelings.

The civil rights movement may have been a faceless thing to much of white America, but Hoover knew that after *Brown* the movement was a gathering social and political force that was already beginning to develop its own political culture, its own leaders, and its own ideas. It was a force strong enough to challenge the director's personal notion of the black man's place in a white man's country, and his preference for an orderly national security state rather than one that lived up to its own democratic creed. Hoover's response to the Negro Question was based on his bureaucrat's instinct to avoid the sticky, divisive issue and his politician's understanding of the politically and morally ambiguous context of the government's response to the black struggle. The result was a position not much different from that of other federal officials (no one stood up for full equality), though Hoover's stance certainly differed in degree. The director went beyond the call of duty when fulfilling what he considered to be a states' rights responsibility to avoid civil rights enforcement and a national security responsibility to monitor communist activity among blacks.

While the civil rights battles were being fought, Hoover positioned his FBI and waited, hoping for a Negro Question policy that might somehow minimize "the terrible pressures coming from both sides," from the integrationists and the segregationists, and as well the more modest pressures that had been coming since 1939 from Civil Rights Section (Division, after 1957) lawyers in the Justice Department. His real hope was that the civil rights movement would disappear on its own, that he personally would not have to expose himself to the risk of openly opposing it.

Hoover kept this hope even as the civil rights movement went from the courtrooms into the streets, with the NAACP-preferred strategy of litigation giving way to a protest-oriented politics of mass direct action. When Mrs. Rosa Parks refused to give up her seat on a Montgomery, Alabama, bus to a white man, "somewhere in the universe," as the Black Panther party's Eldridge Cleaver would later write, "a gear in the machinery had shifted." But no gear shifted in Hoover's FBI during the subsequent bus boycott—or during the sit-ins that swept the South beginning in February 1960, when four black students from North Carolina A & T College ordered coffee at a lunch counter in a Greensboro Woolworth and refused to leave when a waitress denied them service. "If you are Hoover," surmised Nashville newspaperman John Seigenthaler, "you look at Greensboro and you think it's going to be a problem. But it's going to be somebody else's problem."[98] The FBI launched a communist infiltration investigation of the Montgomery Improvement Association only in the second year of the bus boycott, and when investigating the sit-ins found few communists at the lunch counters. If Hoover embellished (the CPUSA considered "these demonstrations . . . the next best thing to 'proletarian revolution'"), his ultimate conclusion reflected his agents' findings and his own caution. "The Communist Party took advantage of the [demonstrations]," he told a House Appropriations Subcommittee. "They did not originate them."[99]

Prudence told Hoover to keep a distance from the risky and unpleasant challenges posed by the Negro Question, to avoid the sort of engagement that might push his Bureau towards an open and inextirpable conflict with black America—or, for that matter, his own states' rights constituents. And that is exactly what he did over the course of the four decades since 1919. But he never stopped spying and he never stopped plotting how to avoid civil rights work. He never stopped sniping at the men and women involved in the black struggle for equality, and he never stopped cataloging grievances against civil rights activists and the everyday people who lived in black communities. He never stopped preparing for that day when his Bureau would no longer be able to dodge the Negro Question.

2

Paper Chains

The Kennedys and the Voting Litigation Campaign

For J. Edgar Hoover and his agents, the modern civil rights movement began in a surprising way. The FBI's inextirpable engagement with the movement began not with Mrs. Rosa Parks in December 1955 or the students at North Carolina A & T in February 1960, but in the last months of the Eisenhower presidency and the first year of the Kennedy presidency with a Justice Department litigation campaign designed to win southern Negroes the right to vote. For all the progress the black struggle had made on the Montgomery buses and among the businesses and public facilities visited by the sit-in activists, blacks across much of the South still lacked the most fundamental right of all. With the franchise, all other rights and privileges would follow, and the franchise had to be won in the courts and not the streets. This strategy was especially appealing to President John F. Kennedy, Attorney General Robert F. Kennedy, and the lawyers who served in the Department's Civil Rights Division. The Kennedys viewed voting litigation—a strategy of moderation, compromise, and confrontation avoidance—as the antithesis of direct action.[1]

John Kennedy's interest in civil rights dated from the early 1950s, and he took calculated risks from time to time on behalf of the black struggle—most notably during the 1960 campaign, telephoning a pregnant Coretta Scott King, while her husband sat in a Georgia jail. But the new president believed a legislative assault on segregation would founder before an unsympathetic Congress and that an executive order would alienate key southern committee chairmen. The voting litigation campaign risked the least political capital. Robert Kennedy had no civil rights program at the time. Though White House aide Kenneth O'Donnell would later say "Bobby was in [civil rights work] up to his eyeballs," that description did not apply in 1961. "I did not lie awake at night worrying about the problems of Negroes," Robert Kennedy said. Sleepless nights would come later. In the interim, a voting litigation campaign would suffice.[2]

John Kennedy's predictions about the risks involved in a more aggressive approach proved to be correct. "We had his whole program bottled up," boasted Senate Judiciary Committee Chairman James Eastland (D., Miss.). In the House, Rules Committee Chairman Howard Smith (D., Va.) handled such chores. Hoover considered both men "members of the [FBI] family." They were contacts of the director and his agents in the Crime Records Division, and FBI Assistant Director for Crime Records Cartha D. DeLoach sometimes had the more conservative members of Smith's Committee out to his house for dinner. Hoover and DeLoach actually gave more aid and comfort to Eastland and Smith than to the Kennedys.[3]

Expected by the Kennedy administration to gather the raw data needed to file and win cases against white southern registrars, FBI officials considered the voting litigation campaign immoderate, arbitrary, and contentious. While binding the FBI more tightly to the Negro Question in ways that the director found particularly unpleasant, however, the campaign also bound the FBI more tightly to the politics of the White House. The Kennedy administration balanced its attempts to force the FBI to act on behalf of the civil rights movement with an entirely understandable desire to protect its own political interests, a strategy that led on occasion to the contradictory position of White House and Justice Department support for the director's barely concealed hostility toward black people and their right to vote.

White House aide Lee C. White once described voter registration programs as "something like motherhood—nobody can be opposed to them."[4] Hoover proved him wrong. He shared the white southern fear that the black vote would destroy a way of life, and so he opposed the voting litigation campaign for reasons of race and politics as well as bureaucratic interest. In the director's world, white southern fears took precedence over the civil rights movement's faith that America would one day guard and protect the black voter, just as the FBI's rights as a bureaucracy took precedence over black people's rights as American citizens. Hoover tried on every front to impede the implementation of the voting litigation campaign, and his behavior represented more than a bureaucratic commitment to avoid civil rights work. Despite the obvious problems caused by Mrs. Parks, the sit-in activists, and other proponents of the new direct-action protest, Hoover's behavior during the course of the voting litigation campaign represented the initial engagement of the struggle that the director and his FBI would wage against black America throughout the 1960s.

By the time Robert Kennedy's Justice Department began its attempt in 1961 to guarantee the right to vote for all in the black-belt South, Hoover and his aides had some inkling of what to expect from such a project. Given their experience with voting rights cases since the 1940s, they foresaw "the potential publicity" involved in "any case of this type."[5] Determined to avoid any act that might alienate their southern white constituents, they investigated voting cases only when they had to and never in an aggressive manner. They were somewhat less restrained when snooping around after the National Committee to Abolish the Poll Tax, a group devoted to ridding the land of one of the oldest and most pervasive forms of disenfranchisement. "There were a few Communists around the poll tax committee," said Virginia Durr, a racial liberal from Montgomery and a friend of Rosa Parks. But "we were surrounded by the FBI."[6] Since the Justice Department rarely prosecuted voting cases during the Roosevelt and Truman eras, few conflicts developed. If the Department pursued its voting rights mission more aggressively during the 1950s, the Eisenhower administration still proceeded "with all deliberate lethargy"—especially after March 14, 1956, when nearly one hundred members of Congress from the South issued a manifesto pledging themselves to resist desegregation by every legal means. The president himself had promised, in a letter to South Carolina Governor James F. Byrnes, "to make haste slowly." For most of the Eisenhower years, then, responsible government officials rarely encouraged the FBI to intervene.[7]

On those occasions when an ostensible superior asked the FBI to do something, Hoover warned the Justice Department of undue pressure on the Civil Rights Division. He said the Division should pay less attention to the demands of people like Martin Luther King of the Southern Christian Leadership Conference and Clarence Mitchell of the NAACP, and more attention to "the feeling of the [white] officials and [white] people in the states targeted for voting drives." At the time, the tentative plans of the SCLC and NAACP to launch a Crusade for Citizenship across the South and a voter registration campaign in Mississippi greatly disturbed the director, as did a grand jury probe of six FBI agents in Louisiana who had investigated (and allegedly harassed) the Webster Parish voter registrar at the Civil Rights Division's request. Even the Bureau's minimal involvement in voting rights work led to bureaucratic and political headaches.[8]

Justice Department attorneys generally followed Hoover's go-slow advice until the last six months of the Eisenhower administration, when Harold R. Tyler, Jr., took over the Civil Rights Division. Tall and angular, the thirty-eight-year-old Tyler had served in World War II and Korea and for seven years as a federal prosecutor in New York. Far more aggressive than his predecessors, the first two assistant attorneys general for civil rights, W. Wilson White and Joseph Ryan, he pressed Hoover to enforce the Civil Rights Acts of 1957 and 1960 and used Division attorneys as investigators whenever the FBI appeared unwilling to perform. Both laws emerged from the post-*Brown* climate and Attorney General Herbert Brownell's advocacy of black civil rights. They provided for injunctive relief against any person, "acting under color of law or otherwise," involved in racial discrimination regarding the registration process or voting itself through threats, intimidation, or any other form of coercion. By July 1960, three months after Eisenhower signed the Civil Rights Act of 1960, which granted the "Attorney General or his representative" authority to inspect and photograph voter registration records, Tyler's attorneys and Hoover's agents had undertaken three voter discrimination suits in Georgia, Alabama, and Louisiana, and two economic intimidation cases in Tennessee.[9]

The most important of these early cases, and the one in which the FBI demonstrated most clearly its reluctance to get involved in civil rights enforcement, concerned the Haywood County (Tenn.) Civic and Welfare League, which had been formed to encourage black voter registration. When the white county elite threatened a number of sharecroppers who joined with eviction by their local landlords, the FBI balked at the Civil Rights Division's request for an investigation—arguing that coercion of local blacks merely resulted from League membership and not League members' attempts to place their names on the Haywood County voter lists. When Division attorneys told the FBI to do its job, the FBI filed reports that simply repeated the allegations of Haywood County blacks while ignoring a blacklist organized by county landlords, merchants, and bankers. Bureau agents in Tennessee, much like the director himself, remained more attuned to "the feeling of the [white] officials" who saw this as a local affair than to the black sharecroppers whose civil rights those officials had violated. It would have been surprising if the FBI had reacted otherwise. Several of the Bureau's domestic intelligence programs were intended to police the various Eisenhower-era blacklists of members of the Communist party and other unpopular groups.

The FBI executive responsible for voting rights cases, General Investigative Division chief Alex Rosen, "was very uncompromising," Tyler remembered. "He was stifling the lawyers in the Division, choking everybody with paper"—including lengthy memos detailing the political affiliations of movement people in Tennessee and elsewhere. On one occasion, when the Knoxville Human Relations Council complained about the Bureau's refusal to investigate civil rights cases in Tennessee, Hoover ordered name checks on the Council's board of directors and forwarded the results to Tyler. Several Council members had radical affiliations dating back to the 1930s and another had "unorthodox attitudes." (He once sent flowers and mash notes to a woman in his church.) "Rosen told me I should read all these FBI reports," Tyler said. "'There are subversives in these civil rights groups.' I said, 'Come on, Al. If these guys are subversives we're all in trouble.'" For Hoover, anyone who caused trouble for the Bureau was a subversive.[10]

By September 1960 the Civil Rights Division had gathered enough hard evidence, despite FBI foot-dragging, to file suit against twenty-nine persons in Haywood County. When Division attorneys went down to take depositions, the victims of the blacklist documented an "economic squeeze . . . much worse than had been reflected in the Bureau reports." Written affidavits from fifty evicted sharecroppers, eviction notices from landlords, and interviews with white citizens opposed to the blacklist led the Division to name thirty-six more defendants, and to prevent a large-scale eviction of black sharecroppers scheduled for January 1, 1961. The Division's evidence underscored the Bureau's deliberate omissions.[11]

Tyler teased Hoover about how one of the Civil Rights Division's attorneys, John Doar, "obtained more evidence in West Tennessee with a $19 camera than the whole Bureau. That shamed the Bureau. Hoover called me and said, 'I'd never dreamed you'd do this on your own.' I said we had no choice." Actually, the Division had not acted alone. Tyler hired investigators like Doar with money from a special appropriation secured with the assistance of Senate majority leader Lyndon B. Johnson. With Johnson's help, Tyler established the precedents on which his own successors, former Exeter schoolmate Burke Marshall and Princeton classmate John Doar, would rely.[12]

With the change in administration in 1961 the Civil Rights Division's workload expanded dramatically. At the end of John Kennedy's second month in office, on March 19, the new assistant attorney general for civil rights, Burke Marshall, and a number of other Division attorneys met with the president's brother, Robert, to discuss their plans for extending the right-to-vote litigation drive. The attorney general wanted Hoover to sit in on the strategy session, but the director declined. He was busy on another matter: expediting Frank Wilkinson's one-year prison sentence for contempt of Congress, the result of an encounter with the House Committee on Un-American Activities in Atlanta where HUAC had gone to look for communists in the integration movement.[13] With the director otherwise engaged, Robert Kennedy settled for FBI Assistant Director Courtney Evans, who was a personal friend. Toward the end of the meeting, John Doar remembered Kennedy telling Evans "to be prepared for a large number of voter investigation requests." Evans forwarded the message to Hoover.[14]

With the Kennedys' support, Marshall and Doar planned "a gigantic enforcement assignment" in Alabama, Georgia, Mississippi, Louisiana, and South Carolina, and within three months a reluctant FBI completed voter registration investigations in thirty-four southern counties. By that time the attorney general's commitment to civil rights had taken hold. "[Bob] thought . . . voting rights was the most natural way to move," John Seigenthaler, then one of his aides, said. "If Negroes were voting in places like Mississippi . . . people like Jim Eastland wouldn't be so fresh." By the time Kennedy resigned the attorney generalship in September 1964, the Justice Department had filed fifty-seven voting suits—thirty of them in Mississippi, including one in Eastland's own Sunflower County.[15]

Doar described this litigation strategy as a war against Jim Crow, and he realized that the Civil Rights Division had drafted the FBI's agents ("unwitting soldiers") to take an exposed point position in a crusade unsupported by public backing or a politically strong administration. "What a situation for the Bureau!" Doar noted, some fifteen years later. "At the time *no one* was with the Division . . . and yet the FBI had been involuntarily enlisted." Given the director's assessment of the bureaucratic and political difficulties inherent in such an assignment, even in the best of times it would have been extremely difficult to enlist the FBI in a war *against* segregation in the South. "Mr. Hoover," Seigenthaler recalled, was a white man with white southern values, and he "was not easy to push."[16]

Robert Kennedy expected the director to resist on partisan and ideological grounds as well. "He's basically very conservative," the attorney general said. Whenever Hoover complained about John Doar "causing us headaches," accusing "the Bureau of unnecessary delays," and requesting "expeditious handling of matters," Kennedy reminded the director that the Republicans had hired Doar. (Doar considered himself "a Kennedy Republican.") Hoover's bureaucracy, moreover, reflected the director's conservatism. A week after the March 19 meeting in Kennedy's office, the FBI ran a file check on one of its most persistent media critics, the liberal *Christian Century*, and uncovered the following "derogatory" item: the magazine's condemnation of "the treatment of Negroes . . . during World War II." If FBI officials offered as evidence of *Christian Century* editors' latent subversive tendencies a mere complaint (twenty years old, at that), one wonders what they thought of the Justice Department lawyers who actually ordered their Bureau to do something about "the treatment of Negroes." Hoover continued to equate the Negro Question with subversion, and he found it especially irritating that the Kennedys expected him to defend racial agitators and oppose people who shared his own white, Christian vision of America.[17]

Hoover responded by launching a campaign of his own—a campaign of bureaucratic resistance that circumscribed his contribution to the voting drive. FBI agents in the field photographed registration records and, when requested to do so, conducted interviews of registrars and persons attempting to register to vote. But they did not analyze those records. "We didn't suspect the romance hidden in the records," Doar explained. "Occupied," as they were, "with other duties," Civil Rights Division attorneys failed to recognize that "the FBI was not being fully utilized in its interrogation assignments, and that its agents were utilized in an almost demeaning fashion in inspecting and photographing voter registration records." By accepting a clerical function and abdicating an investigative responsibility, Hoover outmaneuvered the Civil Rights Division. The Division, in effect, signed a treaty with the FBI, a treaty ratified and put into effect even before Marshall's attorneys fully understood how much detailed investigative work their litigation campaign required.[18]

When Marshall and Doar tried to renegotiate, Hoover resisted. "They thought we should . . . draw the conclusions for them," FBI civil rights section chief Clement McGowan remembered. "Photograph the records, go through all of them, and then present us, 'here, this is the whole story.' The analysis of the evidence is up to the Department. As an investigator," McGowan continued, comparing voting cases with stolen car cases to make his point, "you don't go in and check to see how many Cadillacs were stolen there in Georgia, for example. We're investigating the theft of a Cadillac. I'm not interested in how many other Cadillacs were stolen in that same county right at the outset." This approach, however, could not work on voting cases.[19]

Without access to FBI resources the Civil Rights Division was unable to pursue its litigation on the desired scale. Each case needed analysis of voting rolls, comparison of handwriting samples, interviews with registrars and witnesses, identification of the race of the successful and unsuccessful registrants, surveys of literacy tests and poll taxes, compilation of demographic statistics and background data on historical registration patterns. The tedious work taxed the limited capacity of the Division's fifty-three lawyers and fifty-three clerks, taking a heavy toll. Having "found themselves graduated into the view box rather than into the appellate courtroom," many of the Division's young attorneys, "top graduates of the prestigious law schools," began to look "elsewhere for employment." By placing limits on the uses to which his agents' investigative skills could be put, Hoover also placed limits on the uses to which the Division's legal skills could be put.[20]

With over six thousand agents and eight thousand clerical and technical employees, the FBI had the personnel to do the necessary analysis of voter registration records but not the necessary commitment from the director—or from many of the field agents who worked in the South. So the Bureau did as little as possible. "The FBI snaps the shutter on the camera," Marshall complained. "That is all they do." Even then, the FBI camera man needed a Civil Rights Division lawyer on hand to tell him what to photograph—and in some cases to make sure the agent did not sit in a bar for three hours at lunch break "talking football." One of Marshall's lawyers, Hugh Fleischer, who worked in Mississippi and Louisiana, observed Bureau agents "siding up with the people who were being investigated. I talked to the Bureau's agents all the time and a number of them were racists . . . there was one guy whose name was Robert E. Lee." Racism within the agent corps contributed to the success of Hoover's campaign of bureaucratic resistance.[21]

Racism at the top of the FBI pyramid, however, was far more important. "Not all of their agents in the South were antiblack, anti–civil rights, or anti-Kennedy. The real question," as Robert Kennedy's press secretary, Edwin Guthman, noted, "was what happened when the information got to Washington."[22] When responding to Civil Rights Division requests for assistance, FBI officials emphasized "the variety of circumstances which may attend" voting rights and all other civil rights cases. "The investigations themselves will likewise vary, and therefore, a complete list of investigative suggestions is not possible. Ordinarily the Department in its request will outline the type of information desired. . . . In such circumstances, the Field should confine itself strictly to these suggestions."[23]

The literalist policy dated from the 1940s, when FBI executives in Washington imposed it to force a work slow-down on their own field agents. This effectively limited the investigations and sometimes rendered them useless, even in cases where the agents conducting the investigations supported the right of blacks to vote. "We know," FBI Assistant Director Edward A. Tamm complained to Hoover in 1947, after President Truman's Committee on Civil Rights released its report, that agents investigating civil rights abuses often "ignored logical leads" simply because they "went beyond the investigation requested by the Department." Field agents should be allowed to do their job in a "thorough" and "adequate" manner, he argued. Although the

Bureau's public relations people, Louis Nichols and Gordon Nease, favored Tamm's proposal, Hoover and Clyde Tolson decided for the literalist policy because it required "a minimum of investigation." They preferred to live with the complaints of liberals and movement people rather than risk criticism of their Bureau for violating states' rights by engaging in "extensive [civil rights] inquiries." Back in 1947 Hoover told Truman's Committee that protection of civil rights generally should remain a matter of local concern. A states' righter then, so he remained in 1961.[24]

No longer the heroic bureaucracy that would engage machine-gun toting gangsters or search out every detail needed to make a case against a subversive or a car thief, the FBI became humble and hamstrung. The Civil Rights Division wanted G-men. Hoover sent over clock punchers, nine-to-five men who *apologized* before asking any white person a question in a voting rights or other civil rights case. This so-called "disclaimer policy" took the form of a standing directive to inform the public that the FBI investigated "these things" not "because they wanted to but because they were told to." Hoover considered the disclaimer absolutely necessary—"so there can be no misconception upon the part of anybody that it is being done at the whim of the FBI." Hoping to avoid "unfavorable criticism and publicity," particularly "in districts having a large Negro population," he deliberately rendered his agency ineffectual in the fight for civil rights, depriving black people of a resource that could have been an effective weapon in their struggle.[25]

Nearly as old as the Civil Rights Section that Attorney General Frank Murphy had created in 1939, the disclaimer policy went through a series of arcane revisions over the course of the 1960s. During the first two Kennedy years, FBI agents investigating civil rights matters advised interviewees that Robert Kennedy had requested the investigation. Beginning in December 1962 Hoover designated Burke Marshall as the instigator. After Marshall left the Department to take a job with IBM, the FBI selected John Doar and then Robert Kennedy's successor, Nicholas Katzenbach. FBI officials discontinued the disclaimer itself only in 1974—two years after the director's death—on the grounds that they conducted civil rights inquiries "because of a Federal statute . . . not because of a specific request in each instance by the Department." Beyond the veracity problem, field agents complained about having to "apologize at the outset of

each and every interview." Many felt the same way in 1961, but
in the director's day of authoritarian rule, few agents dared to
complain about official Bureau policy.[26]

In practice, the FBI's jurisdictional humility meant that the
Civil Rights Division, in Doar's words, "got exactly the information we asked for—no more, no less." The Division countered
by issuing incredibly detailed instructions to Bureau agents to
collect the data needed to make a voting rights case, a guaranteed performance technique referred to as "the box memo."
Routine requests for readily accessible information often had to
be typed out on pages that ran into the low three figures. Doar
remembered one memo that "went on in the most minute detail
for 174 pages, explaining, anticipating, cautioning and coaching
the Bureau agents," telling them what to do and what not to do.
("Do not go to the sheriff.") Determined to control the FBI investigators in the field and to by-pass the FBI leadership in Washington, Marshall resorted to a bureaucratic solution (coercion)
to combat a bureaucratic vice (inaction). Hoover viewed the box
memo as an inefficient, ineffective method, and it suited him
fine. The box memo allowed him to tell the integrationists that
the FBI completed each and every task assigned by responsible
government officials, and it allowed him (in the manner of the
disclaimer policy) to tell the segregationists that the FBI scrupulously confined its actions to the specific orders of those same
officials. By paying attention to the letter of the law, Hoover ne-
gated the intention of the law.[27]

While adapting the Civil Rights Division's box memo to meet
its own needs, the FBI resisted Marshall's call for "special
squads" of elite agents "who would travel from state to state
. . . handling voting discrimination matters." Hoover had in fact
ordered the creation of "specially trained squads to handle such
investigations" many years before, in response to criticism from
Truman's Committee on Civil Rights. But he mobilized these
squads only for public relations purposes. The director quickly
abandoned even the pretense of a voting rights strike force, and
he had no intention of creating the real thing when the Kennedy-
era Civil Rights Division asked him to do so. When Marshall
brought up this "old routine" in a meeting with Alex Rosen and
Clement McGowan, the two FBI men hit it "on the head and
knocked it down hard."[28]

Marshall also responded to FBI intransigence, as had Harold
Tyler, by relying on volunteers and Civil Rights Division attor-

neys to do the FBI's work. The Division often sent one of its own lawyers to a southern city or county to check on minor matters rather than work through the FBI. Andrew Young of the Southern Christian Leadership Conference suggested that Hoover had Marshall's men "all scared to death." Actually, the motive was convenience more than fear. "[It was] more expensive, but easier," one roving lawyer explained. "You don't fight the FBI. You work around them." John Doar considered it the natural thing to do. "I was a small-town lawyer and used to doing my own investigating," he said. Because the Civil Rights Division had few illusions about the director's views on voting rights, Marshall even segregated the investigations conducted in the South. FBI agents handled interviews with the white majority because Doar and his fellows had "no rapport" with white southerners. "They [wouldn't] talk to us." Division attorneys handled interviews with blacks. "[The FBI] did not have the resources to interview blacks," Marshall explained. "Their mode of operation was to inform the local police of what they were doing and this exposed blacks to economic and physical intimidation." Whenever the Bureau did interview a black man, one of Marshall's men added, "it was unbelievable." "They would . . . scare him out of his pants," and then write up a report giving no indication of the agent's actions. The Bureau kept its paper "clean," another attorney assigned to the U.S. Civil Rights Commission concluded. That attorney never read an FBI report revealing any bias—let alone "an FBI report saying, 'This guy's a nigger.'" Hoover always hid his personal feelings on race, along with the strain of racism that ran through his Bureau.[29]

Over time, John Doar did a fine job, as Anthony Lewis of the *New York Times* observed, "risking his life to gather the evidence that made his law suits irresistible." In the Macon County, Alabama, voter discrimination case, with Division attorneys scrambling to meet a trial date and lacking the time to spar with the FBI, Doar and another lawyer went into the field themselves. Relying on Tuskegee voting league volunteers to organize photostats of registration records, they came "upon a gold mine" when they began to interview black school teachers, professors, and professionals who had been denied the right to vote. Comparing the literacy tests of these well-educated black citizens with those of barely literate whites who had been allowed to register, Doar and his volunteers gathered the documentation needed to make their case.[30]

But a price had to be paid for writing-off the FBI's investigative resources, and the civil rights movement ended up paying it. The policy spread Civil Rights Division attorneys too thin, preventing the filing of voting suits that should have been filed and the prosecution of southern lawmen who should have been prosecuted under the color-of-law statute for harassing voter registration workers. "We closed investigations which I just knew if we had the time and the resources we might have developed into cases," Marshall affirmed. And the good and brave work that Doar performed in the deep South came at a price of inefficiency. "Administratively," Clement McGowan asserted, "he was probably the worst. Apparently, no one [at the Civil Rights Division] could make a closing decision until John approved it. Often, he was off travelling somewhere. Things really got bogged down over there."[31] That was Hoover's idea in the first place—to slow down the Division and its voting litigation campaign.

Hoover's attitude about what the FBI could do and the Justice Department's deference to that attitude also meant that southern sheriffs and Ku Klux Klansmen could beat voter registration workers right under the FBI's nose. According to the Department's office of legal council, Bureau agents could make an arrest if they observed "a crowd of White citizens . . . pursuing and beating a Negro student."[32] But the no-arrest policy ruled, with Hoover finding allies for his position in Attorney General Kennedy and Assistant Attorney General Marshall. They sided with the director for the very reasons of politics that led to the voting litigation strategy in the first place, reasoning that a more aggressive stance might result in conservative southern congressional Democrats blocking even the administration's modest civil rights initiatives. So the FBI stood, watched, and took notes, and sometimes even snapped photos with "35mm cameras disguised in shaving kit, lunch pail, and necktie clasp concealments," while the resistance beat up voter registration workers and other movement people.[33]

Hoover's own analysis of the "technical and general considerations" underlying the no-arrest policy would have complicated matters even if the Kennedys had been more aggressive. For the director, the relevant laws, Sections 241 and 242, provided no authority for on-the-spot arrests. "Independent action by the FBI would . . . only aggravate the problem," Bureau executives concluded, since agents on the scene would probably be outnumbered and outgunned, and an arrest in such a circumstance would be an adventure. It wasn't quite the same thing as shooting it out with John Dillinger, since civil rights cases were "hurried," "often hazardous," and more than anything else "ambiguous." The director found it disturbing that he might have to protect people challenging the values and laws of the white South.[34]

Though Hoover blamed the voter registration workers for bringing the beatings on themselves, he realized that anti–civil rights violence mocked the authority and dignity of the United States. The FBI had always presented itself as a can-do bureaucracy, compiling an impressive and highly publicized record of the spectacular (combat with the gangsters of the 1930s) and the tedious (the millions of man-hours spent tracking spies and subversives during World War II and the McCarthy era). Led by its celebrity director, the FBI did not simply enforce federal law or cooly gather intelligence. It crusaded against evil. On civil rights, however, Hoover was being asked to go against his own sense of good and evil, so he ordered his agents to stay away. In his view, protecting civil rights was not their job, and technically, of course, he had a case. Under the federal system the maintenance of law and order has principally been the responsibility of state and local police officers, though they were the very people who had abdicated their responsibility in the American South of 1961. Those were extraordinary times and the FBI had built its reputation by doing extraordinary things during extraordinary times, but the director would fill no law-and-order vacuum here. In the end, his stance damaged the image and role of the FBI, just as it impeded the progress of the struggle for black equality.[35]

Although racism in the FBI was a serious problem, the director's noninterventionist policy probably perplexed two or three everyday G-men for every one who applauded it. Many of the agents who stood by and took notes on civil rights abuses fought in World War II and Korea, and as a group they were what Hoover said they were—brave men. "You had agents prepared to do anything they could get away with to help black people," Nicholas Katzenbach believed. Joseph Rauh, general counsel for the Leadership Conference on Civil Rights, described the field agents he encountered as "decent guys doing their job." These decent guys made up "a different level of people, the nonpolitical level," and they worked, or at least they thought they did, for "a different Bureau."[36]

On occasion, FBI agents acted decisively. When white by-standers attacked demonstrators in Bogalusa, Louisiana, John Doar said he would "never forget" Joseph A. Sullivan "moving in, dressing down the local police authorities for their failure to do their duty." Clement McGowan said "a number of your SACs [Special Agents in Charge] or assistants or resident agents were going around to the police departments and told them, 'Chief, you've got to put some men out there to [protect the demonstrators],' and talked to them just like a Dutch uncle. And that, basically, was what Sullivan was doing. Hollering at them to get out there and get on the job."[37]

FBI field agents, however, rarely acted in such a manner. Generally, they followed orders and remained on the sidelines. Calvin Williams, a voter registration volunteer for the Congress of Racial Equality, said "we never saw anybody walk up and say, 'I'm an FBI agent.' . . . Never actually saw one come out and throw his shield out and say, 'I'm protecting you.'" "When a case gets national attention, the FBI seems to be able to do an impressive job," C. T. Vivian of the Southern Christian Leadership Conference observed. "But the day-by-day violations don't make headlines. That's where we get disillusioned." "Our experience with the FBI," Vivian's SCLC colleague, Andrew Young, recalled, "was that no matter what kind of brutality [took place] . . . all the FBI agents did was stand over on the corner and take notes."[38]

Hoover and the bureaucrats around him ignored their own field agents who chafed under the noninterventionist policy as well as the voter registration activists in Mississippi or Civil Rights Division lawyers in Washington. "Most of the damage [the FBI hierarchy] did was a failure to do what they should have been doing," Katzenbach maintained. "There was no [commitment to civil rights work]. Hoover would have preferred to keep black people in their places," and in pursuit of that end he made certain that his own agents remained in their proper place.[39]

FBI policy on the issue of physically protecting civil rights workers encountered little resistance in the White House. "It was very important, as far as we were concerned," Robert Kennedy said, that Hoover "remained happy and that he remain in his position because he was a symbol and the President had won by such a narrow margin and it was a hell of an investigative body and he got a lot of things done and it was much better for what we wanted to do in the South, what we wanted to do in organized crime, and what we wanted to do in a lot of other areas, if we had him on our side." The Kennedys understood the limits of their own power and the formidable base of Hoover's power. They lacked the political strength to take an aggressive stand on the protection issue themselves or to force Hoover to do so. Political reality prevented them from making a total commitment to racial justice. Neither John Kennedy the president nor John Kennedy the candidate for reelection in 1964 would risk alienating the FBI director or southern Democrats in Congress.[40]

Hoover always cited a string of legitimate reasons for not protecting civil rights workers, and he based an additional argument here on a tortured version of civil libertarianism. Attempts to assign FBI agents the task of protecting the voting rights activists would lead to a national police force. "This was one of Hoover's favorite *ex cathedra* assertions repeated so often on social occasions," Victor Navasky wrote in *Kennedy Justice,* that the attorney general himself used this convenient formulation. The director found common ground with the administration once again, with the Kennedys willing to protect themselves from the political risks of an aggressive civil rights program and the voter registration workers from "the specter of a national police force *cum* Gestapo." But the Kennedys would not protect movement activists from segregationist terror.

"These kids were out there," John Seigenthaler remembered, referring to the young people who risked their lives to canvass the rural South. "They couldn't get the FBI to answer them." Rather than pressure the Bureau to do something, "Bob gave them my number. And Burke Marshall's number. 'Any hour of the day or night, you call.' God, they called," Seigenthaler continued. "Burke got the most of it. It's no way to tell how many late nights Burke Marshall would wake up out of a sound sleep—some kid in the county store in McComb, Mississippi, who was looking out the front door, at 10 or 15 young white punks who just wanted [him] to come out." McComb, Mississippi, was a long way from Washington, D.C., where Marshall and Seigenthaler lived. What could they do, beyond lending a sympathetic ear and giving advice? Call the FBI? The FBI would tell them the same thing they told the kids. "We are not a protection agency."[41]

The movement and its supporters could not understand the constraints under which the Kennedy administration operated. For them, according to Marshall, "the constitutional question was merely a technicality," especially since "the federal government had enormous power. The government had an army, a navy, an air force—as well as an FBI." For people "whose lives were on the line all the time," Marshall said, "the idea that the power wouldn't be used was incomprehensible. It was lawyers' piddling talk."[42] Over time, the fundamental difference in spirit between Hoover's investigators and Kennedy's lawyers blurred in the minds of "the kids who were out there." Roy Wilkins's nephew, Roger, then with the Agency for International Development and later director of the Community Relations Service, remembered "a lot of people in the civil rights division at the Justice Department [who] kept telling us how complicated matters were and developed to a high art the practice of splitting the difference between right and wrong. . . . But at least the Kennedy-era pragmatists asked the right questions and pressed in the right directions," at least they had a "moral compass." The men who made the decisions in Hoover's FBI had an entirely different sense of right and wrong.[43]

Burke Marshall complained about the FBI's *"pro forma"* civil rights work, saying it was "worth nothing." But his idea of federalism, with its elaborate systems of deference to state and local authority, resembled the director's own self-serving notions about the FBI's jurisdictional humility. When Marshall took those phone calls from voter registration workers in McComb and elsewhere, he proved, finally, no more comforting than Hoover. Marshall's view—that the government lacked the constitutional authority to protect civil rights workers—may have won him the position of assistant attorney general for civil rights in the first place. The Kennedys, according to former Deputy Attorney General Byron White, wanted "a first-class lawyer who would do the job in a technically proficient way that would be defensible in court—that Southerners would not think of as a vendetta, but as an even-handed application of the law." Robert Kennedy did not want a civil rights activist, noted John Seigenthaler, so "Whizzer White brought [in] Burke Marshall," a Yale Law graduate who came to his post from the prestigious firm of Covington and Burling with a background in corporation law.[44]

Marshall's respect for federalism and the Kennedys' respect for political reality, coupled with what one historian has described as the president's "simplistic . . . view of Reconstruction as a vindictive reign of terror and corruption which the North had visited upon the South," make it easy to see why Hoover could function without serious interference. These things also make it easy to see why the administration sided with voter registration workers only in spirit. Ultimately, white southerners would have to take responsibility for the restoration of southern order. "We ought to live through it," concluded Marshall. Robert Kennedy elaborated: "Now maybe it's going to take a decade; and maybe a lot of people are going to be killed in the meantime; and I think that's unfortunate. But in the long run I think it's for the health of the country and the stability of this system; and it's the best way to proceed." The decision to uphold federalism tormented Kennedy and Marshall—Marshall especially. The FBI director did not seem to be bothered in the least. On the contrary, this view best served his private agenda.[45]

Even if the Kennedy administration had succeeded in mobilizing Hoover's agents, the available manpower was inadequate to do the job. The logistics made no sense, Marshall argued. "The only effective protection would have been to give each [civil rights] worker a guard. And there are no civilians that could do that." A public alliance with the civil rights movement on the protection issue would have led to a false sense of security, a stronger backlash, and the mobilization of the only available "political force . . . the United States Army." Marshall said "it was a matter of prudence." If voter registration workers from the Student Nonviolent Coordinating Committee (SNCC) "thought they could push the Civil Rights Division around, they could force confrontation." One single concession in a hard-line state like Mississippi and there would be "no stopping point . . . [short] of military occupation"—Reconstruction II, in other words. Marshall saw no middle ground.[46]

Hoover understood the politics of the issue from the beginning; the voting rights activists who needed federal protection did not. After meeting with Robert Kennedy and Marshall in June 1961, SNCC workers thought they had struck a deal with the administration. The attorney general wanted the movement's action wing to redirect its energies, to move away from sit-ins and freedom rides and toward the Justice Department's more manageable and less confrontational voting litigation campaign. (Historian Vincent Harding called it an attempt "'to get the niggers off the street.'") Kennedy and Marshall suggested that financial support would be made available through private foundations—a promise that the Southern Regional Council (SRC) helped fulfill by administering the Voter Education Project.[47] But Kennedy and Marshall never promised to protect the students from segregationists who were just as prone to beat up voter registration workers as lunch-counter protestors or freedom riders.

Harold Fleming, former SRC executive director, described the price of political innocence. "Not protecting the kids was a moral shock, more than a cold-blooded, calculated reckoning. It was bruising and deeply emotional. To have the FBI looking out of the courthouse windows while you were being chased down the street by brick throwers deeply offends the sensibilities. So people wept and cursed Robert Kennedy and Burke Marshall more than the FBI, whom they never had any confidence in to begin with. . . . SNCC *et al.* thought Justice's bargain was protection in exchange for a shift from direct action protest to a voter registration drive. Because of the Kennedys' own view of reality they encouraged this belief. . . . Nobody would ever forgive the Kennedys for playing politics because they weren't supposed to on this front."[48] John Kennedy's civil rights adviser, Harris Wofford, a man deeply committed to the black struggle and the first white man to graduate from the Howard University Law School, underscored Fleming's point. "What Kennedy liked best in my role and what I liked least," Wofford confided, "was my function as a buffer between him and the civil rights forces pressing for presidential action. . . . I got tired of him accosting me with a grin and asking, 'Are your constituents happy?'"[49]

With Hoover and the administration, each for their own reasons, unwilling to provide the requested protection, the voter registration workers and the entire civil rights movement were bound to suffer. The FBI's investigation of five instances of violence aimed at SNCC in southwest Mississippi in the late summer and fall of 1961 helped dissipate the naiveté Fleming described. The first episode occurred on August 15, when the Mississippi Highway Patrol arrested Robert Moses, a SNCC worker who left Hamilton College and Harvard and a comfortable teaching job for the poverty and danger of the delta. Billy Caston, a cousin of the Amite County sheriff, beat Moses bloody a week later, after he went to the courthouse in Liberty with three local blacks who were trying to register. Two weeks later, a white mob attacked Travis Britt on the Amite courthouse lawn. On September 7, John Q. Woods, registrar of voters in the Walthall County seat of Tylertown, hit John Hardy in the back of the head with a gun barrel, and on September 25 state legislator

Eugene H. Hurst shot and killed Herbert Lee during a confrontation at a cotton gin.

Not only did the FBI refuse to protect these civil rights workers, it neglected its investigative duties in the aftermath of all five cases. Bureau reports sent to the Civil Rights Division failed to note the nine stitches in Moses's scalp and face, and contained little data on the Lee killing regarding powder burns, the angle of the bullet entering the head, and conflicting witness statements. After Moses sent his own report of events in southwest Mississippi to the Justice Department, John Doar compared it to the FBI report and ordered the Bureau's agents back into the field. One of those agents, the resident agent from Natchez, threatened Moses with bodily harm "for going behind his back, for calling him a liar." Doar also sent two Civil Rights Division attorneys, Bud Sather and Gerald Stein, into the field, and they gathered more documentation in four or five days regarding intimidation of blacks in Walthall and Amite counties than the FBI had in a month. "Whatever the shortcomings of the Justice Department, they certainly made a visible impact on the black population of Mississippi," Moses observed. "People like E. W. Steptoe, down in Amite County. His face lit up when John Doar and the Justice Department came out . . . so different from when a local resident FBI agent came."[50]

Moses charged that police officers murdered a black farmer named Louis Allen because he had trusted one of the FBI's resident agents assigned to investigate the Lee killing. Allen agreed to be a witness against Hurst, but he told county police "what they wanted to hear. . . . The FBI leaked this to the local authorities, and the Sheriff, and the Deputy Sheriff, came out, you know," Moses alleged. "And they had been picking on him ever since—that was in September '61. At one point a deputy sheriff broke his jaw—and then they killed him. With a shotgun." Allen's widow remembered "Louis walking through the house before he was killed, saying he didn't want to die, that he knew people who had been dead, died when he was a boy, that when you're dead you're dead a long time."[51]

"The Bureau performed its normal functions," Nicholas Katzenbach explained, "in a situation which was anything but normal."[52] Reluctance to protect voter registration workers before the fact was one thing; reluctance to investigate after the fact quite another. And this reluctance remained throughout the Kennedy years and beyond. In 1962 FBI agents investigated the shots that night riders fired into a Ruleville, Mississippi, home where Charles McLaurin and other SNCC workers stayed. "They asked the people if we did the shooting," McLaurin recalled. In 1963 segregationists attacked Moses and Randolph T. Blackwell of the Voter Education Project while driving near Greenwood, Mississippi, and shot a passenger, SNCC field secretary Jimmy Travis, in the head and neck. An FBI agent asked the victims, "Are you boys sure you didn't shoot up this car?" "[Like] talking to a member of the Ku Klux Klan," Blackwell said.[53] During James Meredith's 1966 march from Memphis, Tennessee, to Jackson, Mississippi, to encourage voter registration, Hoover refused to assign more than a token number of agents. "Just enough," as former FBI Assistant Director William Sullivan charged, "to avoid criticism." Birmingham police officers saw "only ten F.B.I. agents accompanying the marchers from the time they left Hernando, the place where Meredith was shot on the second day of the march, until the tear gas was dispersed in Canton on Thursday night." When Hoover sent in forty more agents after that, a number of them complained to the Birmingham policemen that John Doar used them as "errant [sic] boys." In the meantime, Hoover told Eastland that "67 Commie organizers" had entered Mississippi during the course of the march. The director always kept his priorities straight.[54]

FBI behavior led the American Civil Liberties Union to conclude that Hoover's bureaucracy lacked "a psychology of commitment" when "enforcing laws which guarantee Negroes equal rights." Movement people demanded "the kind of diligence the FBI shows in solving kidnapping and bank robberies." They settled for a bureaucracy that appeared more apathetic than heroic. Even Robert Kennedy began to wonder whether the FBI was more obstacle than resource in the war against the white southern way of black disenfranchisement.[55]

During the first of the Kennedy years the most serious challenge to the FBI's noninterventionist policy on voting rights and other civil rights enforcement came not from the ACLU, the NAACP, or even Burke Marshall's Civil Rights Division, but from the U.S. Civil Rights Commission. With the Civil Rights Act of 1957 authorizing the Commission to hold hearings on any prima facie denial of civil rights, the FBI concluded that publicity surrounding any such hearings would lead to increased pressure for federal intervention. Assistant Director Louis Nichols discussed this possibility with Senator Eastland even before the

Civil Rights Act became law. "I told Jim that one thing that some of the southern folks should think about is that if they get a President's Commission there is going to be an invasion of the South with all sorts of hearings."[56] In preparation for such hearings, the Commission would likely audit FBI investigations. To counter this move, Hoover denied the Commission access to investigative reports on voting rights matters. Ultimately, this policy forced Robert Kennedy to choose between the FBI's *de facto* authority to keep its secrets and the Civil Rights Commission's *de jure* authority to "investigate allegations . . . that certain citizens of the United States are being deprived of their right to vote."[57]

Initially, the FBI's insistence on keeping its secrets caused few problems. Under Eisenhower, the Civil Rights Commission had been "a cautious and rather technical body, compiling information and proposing modest remedies," and making few formal demands on the FBI for voting rights data—especially after the October 1957 resignation of Attorney General Herbert Brownell, the only civil rights advocate in President Eisenhower's cabinet. With the Commission's methods expected to change under the Kennedys, the FBI tried to delay the inevitable. Harris Wofford told President Kennedy that the Bureau's security check of Berl Bernhard, the administration's nominee for staff director and a holdover from the Eisenhower-era Commission, was "holding up staff reorganization."[58]

The FBI's opposition to Berl Bernhard began a few months before John Kennedy put his name up. "I was on a panel at Catholic University on civil rights and in the course of it I made a comment, which got front-page headlines in the *Washington Post*, that was critical of civil rights enforcement by the Bureau," Bernhard remembered. "I was hauled before the Senate Internal Security Subcommittee by Senators Eastland and [Thomas J.] Dodd," a Democrat from Connecticut and a former FBI agent, "and a director named Jay Sourwine, and received a visit from one of Mr. Hoover's people. It became a major issue when I had a meeting with Bob Kennedy about whether the president was going to nominate me. Mr. Hoover determined I was— there's a phrase for it—'not to be contacted.' Then Mr. Hoover did an evaluation of me. He came up with all kinds of stuff I never heard before." Upon completing its investigation in March 1961, moreover, the FBI turned over its report to the chairman of the Senate Judiciary Committee—James Eastland.

Eventually, Bernhard saw his FBI file. "Bob Kennedy showed it to me and said, 'How can I have my brother nominate you with this kind of material?'" Kennedy made that remark in jest, more or less, "because he was having his own problems with Mr. Hoover."

When the FBI finally cleared Bernhard and the Senate confirmed him, he began an ambitious investigation of FBI policy on voting rights, police brutality, and other civil rights enforcement responsibilities—an effort that led to another confrontation with the director. "I was summoned to Mr. Hoover's office," Bernhard continued, along with the chairman of the Civil Rights Commission and then-president of Michigan State University, John A. Hannah. "I called Senator Hart, Phil Hart, who was on the judiciary Committee, and told him about it—he was a friend of Dr. Hannah's from Michigan. He came with us. It was Hart, Hannah, and me. Mr. Hoover was, to say the least, irate. He didn't know what was wrong with us. He launched into a monologue about the irrationality of the civil rights movement and asserted that we had become dupes of the civil rights movement and the left wing of this and that." Although prepared for this outburst, Hannah, Hart, and Bernhard gave ground. "We said, 'Look, we will take another look at the report to be sure that whatever we say is factually accurate before it's published.'"[59]

The Civil Rights Commission did not tone down its report enough to please Hoover. Released as part of the Commission's annual report for 1961, the FBI section reviewed many of the issues Truman's Committee on Civil Rights originally raised in 1947 and in some ways extended that earlier critique. To document Bureau priorities, Commission staff searched back issues of the *FBI Law Enforcement Bulletin* and found dozens of articles on the apathy of the American people toward the Red menace, but only one item focusing on civil rights. The report's principal author, Arnold Trebach, a lawyer who also held a Princeton Ph.D., went into the field to review particular FBI investigations. He had seen hundreds of Bureau case files in the months preceeding the change of administration, courtesy of Civil Rights Division attorney Arthur B. Caldwell—who had the Bureau send over any file Trebach requested without alerting Hoover or any of his aides. Trebach's audit of these investigations provided the foundation for his conclusion that the FBI had a consistent history of avoiding civil rights work. Its record in 1961 was much the same (lethargic and ineffective) as it had been in 1941 or 1951. A packed press conference accompanied the report's release, and Trebach remembered two *Pravda* correspondents sitting in the second row.[60]

Robert Kennedy and Burke Marshall refused to side with the Civil Rights Commission, even though they agreed with nearly everything the Commission had to say about the FBI. Commission members also criticized the Justice Department voting litigation strategy and urged the Department to support a broader attack on inequality through legislation. One Commission member, Harvard Law School dean Erwin Griswold, considered the Marshall-Kennedy emphasis on litigation "a retail operation." The Civil Rights Commission favored a "wholesale operation," a broad attempt to change "the whole situation" by holding hearings and developing new legislation. In the process, Griswold identified Marshall—unfairly—as a particularly "negative influence," a "conservative" and "cautious" man who "had no broad vision of the whole thing at all."[61]

Ultimately, Marshall advised Bernhard not to pressure the FBI. Hoover needed time to cool off.[62] Robert Kennedy identified the Civil Rights Commission—and not Hoover's FBI—as the principal problem. "I didn't have any great feeling that they were accomplishing anything of a positive nature. . . . It was almost like the old House Un-American Activities Committee investigating Communism. . . . They were not objective investigations. . . . So I had no confidence in them," he said, in an ironic comment, as he had worked for Senator Joseph R. McCarthy's Permanent Subcommittee on Investigations during the 1950s and retained "a fondness for McCarthy." At the same time, the Civil Rights Commission had invaded the Justice Department's domain. "Doing what we were really doing," Kennedy complained. "Voting." Bernhard said he "had never seen anyone so angry at the Commission as Robert Kennedy, not even John Patterson or George Wallace." In his struggle with the Commission, the FBI director would find no more valuable ally than the attorney general.[63]

Hoover received Robert Kennedy's help when the Civil Rights Commission asked the FBI for the firsthand information it needed to do its job. Kennedy stopped Arthur Caldwell from giving any more voting rights and police brutality files to Arnold Trebach and other Commission staff. "We should have had access to FBI reports," Bernhard said. "When we'd get complaints my inclination was to defer to the Department because they could take remedial action. But then we'd want to get the factual basis from the Department and they wouldn't let us see the Bureau reports. . . . Justice would come in and we'd have a big meeting with Seigenthaler, Doar, Bob, Burke and me. There'd be lots of give and take. But in the end, we'd lose out because the Attorney General wasn't willing to take on the Bureau."[64]

Bernhard asked Doar and Marshall why segregationist congressmen received FBI data and not the Civil Rights Commission. "I knew that Mr. Eastland, Mr. Thurmond, and the rest of them did not have the investigating capacity to get the facts that they had. . . . I knew they got them from somewhere, from the Civil Rights Division or the Bureau." It did not do much good to raise this issue either. Doar and Marshall shrugged. "They were very chary," Bernhard thought. "They would say, 'We've got material from the FBI, we can't let you see it.'"[65]

Hoover did not leave the Civil Rights Commission entirely out in the cold. Wofford said the Commission accepted Hoover's offer to assign an FBI liaison officer to work with it daily, but this only led to "the FBI knowing everything about the commission's work, without the commission getting any more information from the FBI." Bernhard said "this fellow was at my office every morning. Full time. After I had been taken off the 'not-to-contact' list, he gave me specific documents. I got one or two direct from Mr. Hoover saying, 'You might be interested to see some of the activities of your friend, Dr. Martin Luther King.' That kind of thing. I got one on Roy Wilkins. I remember *very clearly* looking at it and saying, 'Why am I getting this?' The FBI fellow would say, 'Well, we thought it would be helpful.'"[66] The FBI provided "name checks on witnesses" to prevent "people who were just out-and-out communists from testifying," and security reports on applicants for Commission employment—all "throwbacks to the McCarthy era," said William L. Taylor, Jr., the Commission's liaison with the White House. It worried Bernhard that if he put someone on the payroll that the FBI did not approve of, he knew what the director "might do in terms of turning it over to Mr. Eastland. I could just see the McCarthy-like destruction. I've been there."[67]

None of these services lasted very long. J. Edgar Hoover—not Robert Kennedy—cut them off. FBI officials, as Bernhard suspected, were indeed leaking information to Senator Eastland's Internal Security Subcommittee and as well to the House Committee on Un-American Activities. Kennedy knew it, but he could not stop it.[68] The FBI leaked information that might hurt the voting litigation campaign and the civil rights movement to the Civil Rights Commission and the segregationists alike—while closely guarding information that might help blacks. Having reaffirmed its autonomy (winning the only bureaucratic battle that really mattered), the FBI concerned itself with cosmetic reforms to appease the Civil Rights Commission. Clyde Tolson prepared a what-is-to-be-done memo in December recommending civil rights articles for the *FBI Law Enforcement Bulletin* and additional civil rights material in Hoover's annual testimony before the House Appropriations Subcommittee. Tolson also suggested that Alex Rosen meet regularly with the Commission chairman. The FBI, he said, should make every effort "to indoctrinate Hannah in the manner in which . . . [we] function in Civil Rights matters."[69]

Robert Kennedy knew Hoover had no "great sympathy" for voting rights, but he believed the director gave ground and eventually made a positive contribution. "He . . . recognizes where the power is and what he has to do; and, once he reaches that decision, that is paramount. I think he reached the decision that we were going to do things in civil rights and that that's the way it was going to be. . . . So that either you'd have to do it or you'd have to get out." "When they did things," Kennedy added, "frequently they did them damned well." Burke Marshall's number two man in the Civil Rights Division, St. John Barrett, said the FBI's "investigations were vital. They simply happened to be the bureaucratic instrument that was in place and could do things nobody else could do." Barrett gave a backhanded compliment. The FBI was "not in the forefront of the legal implementation of civil rights by any means, but they nonetheless provided invaluable logistical help."[70]

In 1961, however, the FBI did not actively intervene in voting rights cases or other civil rights matters. Marshall considered the Bureau "absolutely useless." Wofford identified the Bureau as the principal "bottleneck." Katzenbach labeled the Bureau's ultimate contribution "marginal and somewhat grudging." Even Doar, while noting the paucity of "written documentation one way or the other" and recognizing the fallacy of transferring "our impatience with America itself, onto the FBI," considered the Bureau's agents "ill-prepared," their performance "lackluster," and their superiors at the "seat of government," as Hoover referred to FBI headquarters, ignorant "about the realities of life in the South."[71]

FBI executives reciprocated in their opinion of the civil rights people in the Justice Department and the White House. They considered Wofford a "security risk," Doar a "bellyacher," Marshall no "friend of the Bureau." Three years later, when Marshall accused the FBI of leaking derogatory "background information" to the press on the alleged subversive associations of Martin Luther King, he received a telephone call from Rosen, who said: "The Director wants you to know that you are a goddamned liar!" "Hoover wouldn't talk to me, basically," Marshall said. The director never spoke much to Doar either, and in fact Doar remembered (vaguely) only one inconsequential conversation. "I think I rode up with him in the elevator once." After John Kennedy's death, the director only spoke to Robert Kennedy when he had no choice.[72]

The FBI's public posture of studied neutrality was anything but neutral in its impact. If the Bureau did not completely torpedo the Civil Rights Commission's grand plans to change "the whole situation," Hoover's refusal to cooperate did not make the Commission's work any easier. The Bureau's resistance to the active advancement of civil rights law further constrained the voting litigation drive. The failure to protect SNCC and other voter registration workers represented the beginnings of a rupture between the movement's action arm and the government they assumed would support them. The defendants in the civil suit SNCC filed a year later, in 1962, to force the government to protect its citizens, were Kennedy and Hoover. Robert Moses himself believed that the Civil Rights Division never pursued a voting rights case down in Amite County, Mississippi, and the other places where blood flowed, "precisely because there was violence. They didn't want a case moving through the courts that opened up the issue of the federal government protecting voter registration workers and black people attempting to register."[73]

The spectacle of the federal government, usually in the form of an FBI agent, passively watching the brutalization of voter registration workers, helped spur "on the movement's determination to succeed," observed Bayard Rustin of the Southern Christian Leadership Conference. But it also led to "battle fatigue" among SNCC activists and other movement "shock troops." "In many ways these young civil rights workers are in a war and exposed to the stresses of warfare," Harvard psychiatrist Robert Coles wrote. "Clinical signs of depression," including "exhaustion, weariness, despair, frustration, and rage," would be visible by the end of the Kennedy years, leading some movement people to walk away and others to question the turn-the-other-cheek assumptions of nonviolent protest.[74]

Government officials' announcements about the inability of the FBI to protect civil rights workers may have encouraged the more primitive elements of the white southern resistance. "That led to injury and death," Roger Wilkins concluded. "And it deterred a lot of people who might have worked for civil rights. Not everyone who believed in civil rights was brave." Berl Bernhard said the FBI and its director had

> almost made civil rights leaders available to bounty hunters. In saying that, I accept the fact that it was a very difficult period because the people who were in control of the Congress by and large had very strong constituencies in the South. No one wanted to antagonize the McClellans and the Eastlands and the Thurmonds. But the result, for the bounty hunter, was that it was 'OK.' . . . The federal government wasn't there.

"The message coming out of Washington, from Mr. Hoover," SNCC's John Lewis reiterated, "was very clear."[75]

Who was responsible? "There's probably enough blame to spread around," conceded Civil Rights Commission attorney William Taylor. "Ultimately, the policy decisions were made at the very top of the government, by the attorney general and by the president, by the head of the Civil Rights Division. There was an excess of caution. Bobby Kennedy came to understand the nature of the problem that he was dealing with in far more depth than he had in the beginning. And when he understood the nature he was an extraordinarily effective and articulate person in dealing with the whole question of civil rights. But I don't think [he] understood it in the beginning." Years later, after Kennedy had moved on to the United States Senate and turned "to peace and populism," he remembered how mad he had been at Taylor and the other people who worked for the Civil Rights Commission, and how willing he had been to take Hoover's side, and he shook his head, laughing bitterly at himself.[76]

Would things have been much different if Robert Kennedy had understood "in the beginning" the things that William Taylor wanted him to understand? If he had tried to force the FBI to plunge headfirst into voting rights work, to protect "the kids," to cooperate with the Civil Rights Commission, to worry less about Bureau rights and more about black people's rights? The FBI director's refusal to enforce the law represented more than bureaucratic politics and bureaucratic arrogance. It was the first systematic and sustained attempt to impede the people of color who were causing so many problems for the Bureau in the first place. Hoover had not asked the Kennedys to put the FBI in the path of the onrushing civil rights movement. But once there and upon discovering that he could not leave, he developed strategies for countering the movement and exploiting the political constraints that the Kennedy administration faced. The director even found common ground with the administration from time to time, forming alliances that caused ruptures between the movement and the government and among those government agencies committed to the struggle for black equality.

Having engaged the civil rights movement during the voting litigation campaign of 1961 largely on his own terms, Hoover would spend the next two years skirmishing with the movement on every imaginable front and expanding the only Negro Question responsibility that he felt comfortable with—domestic political surveillance of anyone, black or white, who undermined the peace and quiet of his Bureau and the internal security of his America by struggling for racial justice.

3

=====≈≈≈=====

Unbecoming Deeds

From FREEBUS to BAPBOMB and the Albany Movement

J Edgar Hoover stopped speaking to Burke Marshall shortly after the first skirmishes of 1961–1963, about a week after Mother's Day in May 1961 when Ku Klux Klan mobs attacked two groups of Freedom Riders at bus station terminals in the Alabama cities of Birmingham and Montgomery. Marshall had criticized the Bureau for its failure to provide adequate intelligence about the plans of the Freedom Riders or the Klan's plans (with its allies in the Alabama law enforcement community) to greet the riders. "When the bus arrived in Montgomery and the local police . . . were purposely not there to meet it," Marshall said, "I realized for the first time that we didn't have any spy system, we didn't have any information."[1] His words reflected an emerging Kennedy administration consensus on the need to collect intelligence about civil rights protest.

Having rejected a protective role, and negligently fulfilled an investigative role, Hoover's FBI now succeeded in turning a surveillance role to its own purposes. If the civil rights movement was active in a particular southern city or county, the Civil Rights Division came to expect police brutality and Ku Klux Klan violence. Division lawyers wanted to know what would happen ahead of time, and they asked the FBI to provide the answers—even though they knew that the intelligence they would receive from the FBI would reflect the director's personal and political assumptions about the Negro Question and his bureaucratic preference for maintaining a smooth working relationship with southern lawmen. Hoover believed all civil rights activists were troublemakers, that many of them were communists or had communist associations. So the intelligence he provided minimized the collusion between the Klan and local police, and exaggerated the political associations of the people who organized the demonstrations and voter registration drives in the first place. No matter how much they objected to these priorities, Kennedy administration officials accommodated themselves to them. Things had changed a great deal since the days of Woodrow Wilson and the black scare of 1919, but the government still viewed surveillance as something far more convenient and far less controversial than an aggressive, all-out effort to enforce federal civil rights law or to protect civil rights workers. Once again, Hoover's private bias and the administration's political expediency led in the same direction.

Under the pressure of events that began with the Freedom Rides and continued over the next two years, Hoover escalated FBI intelligence gathering activities. Earlier, in the mid-1950s, the Bureau conducted investigations of racial disturbances, particularly demonstrations and clashes arising out of school desegregation, but generally did not file reports with the Civil Rights Division. Instead, the Bureau sent its reports to the Department's Internal Security Division, where the Division bumped them back over to Civil Rights after five or ten days. By organizing information from the FBI "around the requirements of internal security surveillance rather than civil rights protection," this procedure focused the Civil Rights Division's attention on the activities of the Communist party and not disenfranchisement, segregated schools and transportation, and other obstacles to black equality.[2]

By Hoover's reckoning, the FBI had no "investigative jurisdiction over . . . general racial matters." His Bureau had an "intelligence function" based on "U.S. Army regulations [which] place responsibility upon the Army to keep advised of any developments of a civil disturbance nature which may require the . . . intervention of Federal troops." On the eve of the Freedom Rides, then, FBI policy required investigation of all "proposed or actual activities of individuals, officials, committees, legislatures, organizations, etc., in the racial field." Between March 1959 and January 1960 Bureau executives disseminated 892 reports on racial matters to the Justice Department. By that time they sent copies directly to Civil Rights Division attorneys, forwarding additional copies to the military intelligence agencies and state and local police departments whenever they detected a rumor of violence.[3]

Compared to what would follow, FBI surveillance activities were minimal and the spy gap that Burke Marshall had complained about would not close until the Freedom Rides ended in mid-summer 1961. To remind Marshall of this fact, the Bureau began calling him at home, at 3:00 A.M., with reports of racial unrest in a Shreveport, Louisiana, diner and other minutia usually gleaned from the daily press. This petty harassment came in the form of middle-of-the-night phone calls from G-men who read Marshall newspaper stories. If the Civil Rights Division wanted intelligence, the FBI would provide it. The problems Marshall and the Kennedys encountered in Birmingham, Montgomery, and the other cities where the Freedom Riders stopped, however, were less the result of inadequate intelligence than the decisions made by FBI officials about how to respond to what was known. For all of his complaints during the Freedom Rides about not having sufficient notice of impending civil rights demonstrations and anti–civil rights violence, Marshall simply misunderstood the FBI "spy system's" hidden agenda: to damage the struggle for black equality.

The idea that led to the Freedom Ride of 1961 actually dated from 1947, when a group of pacifists and socialists from the Congress of Racial Equality (CORE) and the Fellowship of Reconciliation tested a Supreme Court ruling (*Morgan v. Virginia*) against segregation in interstate transportation. They organized a Journey of Reconciliation and traveled on buses and trains through the upper South, attracting only the passing interest of Hoover's FBI. Thirteen years later, when the Supreme Court extended its earlier prohibition against segregation to include all terminal accommodations (*Boynton v. Virginia*), CORE planned a more adventuresome Freedom Ride. James Farmer, the organization's national director and founder, said the riders would tour the Deep South, hoping to "provoke the southern authorities into arresting us and thereby prod the Justice Department into enforcing the law of the land." Roy Wilkins thought it "a desperately brave, reckless strategy, one that made those touch-football games played by the Kennedys look like macho patty-cake."[4]

Farmer saw himself as an "action man" who had pioneered nonviolent direct action against racial injustice for twenty years, since the day in 1941 when he and a pacifist friend, Jimmy Robinson, participated in what may have been the first sit-in at the Jack Spratt Coffee House in Chicago. When more sit-ins followed during the war years, the FBI opened a communist infiltration investigation of CORE—some four years before the first Freedom Ride and eighteen years before the second.[5] Farmer believed a new Freedom Ride might provoke "a crisis"—"an international crisis." He intended to bring a fundamental contradiction of cold war America to the world's attention: the United States' presentation of itself to Third World peoples as freedom's hope while consigning its own nonwhite peoples to an unequal status.

"We were counting on the bigots in the South to do our work for us," Farmer said, promising that the Freedom Riders would "fill up the jails, as Gandhi did in India," with a jail-no-bail strategy designed to move the struggle onto the high moral ground of global politics. To inform everyone of CORE's plans to commit civil disobedience, Farmer "wrote to the Justice Department, to the FBI, and to the President, and wrote to Greyhound . . . Trailways." But the response was always the same. "We got no reply from Justice. Bobby Kennedy, no reply. We got no reply from the FBI. We got no reply from the White House, from President Kennedy. We got no reply from Greyhound or Trailways. *We got no replies*." The Freedom Riders were on their own.[6]

Afterward, the Justice Department's public information director, Edwin Guthman, explained why things did not filter through: someone routed the CORE press release "to Marshall's desk. Marshall did not bring it to the attention of Bob or Byron White. Then Marshall came down with the mumps . . . " More interested in planning for his June 3 meeting with Khrushchev in Vienna, John Kennedy regarded the timing of the Freedom Ride as particularly inappropriate. With the Soviet Union still exploiting Little Rock and the sit-ins for propaganda purposes in the Third World, the president wanted to avoid another racial incident at all costs. He tried to have the Freedom Ride canceled at the very moment he found out about it, telephoning civil rights advisor Harris Wofford with a direct order: "Tell them to call if off!" "I don't think anybody's going to stop them right now," Wofford responded. In the days to come, the Kennedy administration would make several more attempts to abort the riders' journey south.[7]

The FBI probably knew more about the Freedom Riders' itinerary than either the White House or the Justice Department. Assistant Director Cartha DeLoach reported a telephone call at 12:30 A.M. on May 3, only a few hours before the riders boarded their buses, from Simeon Booker, an *Ebony* reporter who would travel with the riders. DeLoach noted that Booker wanted "to tip us off." The assistant director worked with Booker and his employer, Johnson Publishing Company, from time to time, and one Crime Records Division agent remembered that accord. "*Ebony*, Johnson. Yeah, Johnson Publishing. . . . We had a great, we had a good relationship with *Ebony, Jet*. We used the black publications for stories. . . . We gave material to anybody that came to us," the agent claimed, adding that "Simeon Booker was in with Lou Nichols" and then "Mr. DeLoach."[8] Booker's role, nevertheless, is unclear. Farmer had already sent the FBI a copy of the Freedom Riders' schedule in the form of a press release. Booker may have been trying to manipulate the FBI with his middle-of-the-night phone call on the matter of protecting the riders (and himself) from the violent resistance they expected.

The Freedom Riders left Washington, D.C., on May 4, seven blacks and six whites riding South in two interracial groups on a Greyhound and a Trailways. A southerly flow of FBI teletypes from one field office to the next accompanied them. Bureau interest, nonetheless, was casual and in no way related to the issue of protecting the riders—or the *Ebony* reporter who rode with them. With the notable exceptions of arrests in Charlotte, North Carolina, and Winnsboro, South Carolina, and an assault at the bus station in Rock Hill, South Carolina, few serious incidents occurred during the first part of the trip.[9] The FBI began to pay closer attention to the Freedom Riders only on Mother's Day, May 14, when the Greyhound arrived in Anniston, Alabama, sixty miles from Birmingham.

Local FBI agents expected trouble. Alabama Klansmen planned a baseball-bat greeting for the riders, and the FBI forwarded this information on May 13 to the Anniston police.[10] When the Greyhound parked for its scheduled fifteen-minute rest stop, an angry mob surrounded it and began smashing windows and slashing tires. Police officers diverted the mob and the bus pulled out, but Ku Kluxers pursued in cars, catching up to the bus six miles out of town, when the tires either went flat from the earlier slashing or were shot out. A homemade bomb came through one of the windows. The bus quickly filled with smoke. The passengers tried to flee, but the mob held the door shut. The realization that the bus might explode finally convinced them to back up, and they beat the riders as they left the bus. With flames and smoke gutting the inside of the Greyhound, the beating continued until E. L. Cowling, a representative of Alabama Governor John Patterson and of Public Safety Director Floyd Mann, "drew his pistol" and "backed the crowd away," telling "them that if anybody touched anybody he'd kill them." One man's courage brought the first major incident of the Freedom Ride under control.[11]

The FBI watched as the second bus, the Trailways, pulled into Anniston within an hour. Eight toughs boarded, demanded that the black riders move to the rear, and then beat two of the white riders, Dr. Walter Bergman and James Peck, who had been on the Journey of Reconciliation. The sixty-one-year-old Bergman, a retired Detroit school administrator, suffered permanent brain damage. When the bus arrived at its terminal in Birmingham fifty minutes later, a mob of about forty Klansmen and members of the National States Rights party greeted the Freedom Riders. Most carried baseball bats or chains. A few had lead pipes. One of the Klansmen knocked down the unfortunate Peck once more. "Before you get my brothers, you will have to kill me," Gary Thomas Rowe, an FBI informer who had infiltrated the Klan, heard Peck say before he hit the floor.[12]

While the Freedom Riders not in need of overnight hospitalization gathered at the Birmingham home of Rev. Fred L. Shuttlesworth, the FBI launched a civil rights investigation that included interviews with all of the injured riders but only two or three of the uninjured ones. Though Simeon Booker received a telephone call from Robert Kennedy at Shuttlesworth's house, no Bureau agent contacted him or the photographer he had with him. Thereafter, the FBI claimed to have lost track of the Freedom Ride group, making contact only upon discovering that they were on their way out of town.

In Washington, Hoover demonstrated little sympathy for the Freedom Riders' plight. The riders had tried to move on to their next stop in Montgomery before accepting the advice of both Governor Patterson and the United States Department of Justice to get out of Alabama. They tried to arrange a bus to New Orleans, but could not find a driver. A bomb threat prevented them from boarding a special flight on Eastern Airlines (the FBI and the Birmingham police refused to search the plane), so they tried to make arrangements with another airline. The pilot refused to fly.[13] They finally boarded an Eastern flight to New Orleans, and when they arrived Louisiana segregationists heckled them and organized a rally that evening in the Municipal Auditorium. The crowd listened to speakers warn of NAACP plans "to mongrelize the people," Communist party attempts to aid and abet the ongoing "racial revolution," and CORE sponsorship of a mysterious "training school" in Miami. When Hoover received a report on the rally from the New Orleans field office, he asked: "Do we know anything about this school?" That question revealed a great deal about his priorities in the midst of the Freedom Ride crisis.[14]

Clearly, FBI surveillance had not served to protect the Freedom Riders. Back in Alabama, the director's men opened a case file on the Anniston bus burning, captioned FREEBUS, under Title 18, Section 33, of the U.S. Code ("destruction of aircraft or motor vehicle"). Burke Marshall told Hoover he "appreciated the promptness with which we went into this matter," and Robert Kennedy described the FBI's efforts as "magnificent" following the arrest of four members of the mob. The director's private response—Kennedy "should tell off 'bellyachers' like [John] Doar"—was predictable. Doar constantly complained about the FBI's civil rights performance, and he had just requested a sweeping investigation of the Anniston and Birmingham violence, including an FBI survey "of all assaults and violent activities engaged in by the Klan or Klan members in this general area within the last five years." Hoover had no complaint when Ed Guthman put in a request for name checks on the Freedom Riders themselves. The attorney general's office wanted to know if any of the civil rights activists had a criminal record.[15]

FBI agents in Alabama helped federal prosecutors secure indictments against nine people for their role in the bus burning. (No one was indicted in connection with the Birmingham riot.) After the first trial ended in a hung jury, Doar told FBI Assistant Director Alex Rosen "that some of the jurors wouldn't have voted guilty" unless the indictments had included a tenth name—Bobby Kennedy. According to a Bureau informant, moreover, one of the jurors had attended a Klan meeting and had lied about it during the jury selection process. Hoover's men launched a perjury investigation. Ultimately, six defendants changed their pleas from not guilty to nolo contendere. The court placed five on probation, on the condition that they sever their connections with the Klan. One went to prison.[16]

Led by Kenneth N. Raby, assistant special agent in charge of the Birmingham office, and the Anniston resident agent, Clay Slate, a squad of FBI agents spent over 4,800 man hours on the case by June 6, logging some 14,000 miles in Bureau cars. "It seemed like we interviewed everybody in the state of Alabama at least twice," one FBI man recalled. For such trouble, J. B. Stoner and his National States Rights party hung Slate, two other agents, Farmer, Kennedy, and Hoover in effigy. When Slate came to Washington a year later, Doar pulled him out of an in-service training class and took him over to shake hands with Robert Kennedy.[17]

Clay Slate and the other FBI agents assigned to the FREEBUS case had done a fine job; but the bus burning as well as the Birmingham assault might have been prevented in the first place if FBI officials had chosen to act in a timely and judicious manner on the extraordinary intelligence that they held on the collusion between the Ku Klux Klan and the city's law enforcement community. Aware of the planned violence weeks in advance, the FBI did nothing to stop it and had actually given the Birmingham police details regarding the Freedom Riders' schedule, knowing full well that at least one law enforcement officer relayed everything to the Klan.

Local FBI agents had suspected close ties between the Klan and the Birmingham Police Department since September 1960, when their prize informer in the city Klavern, Gary Rowe, first raised the issue. The FBI knew "that Commissioner [of Public Safety] EUGENE (BULL) CONNOR and the great majority of the officers of the Birmingham Police Department [were] strong segregationists." When three young black men visited the mayor's office and started "yapping around about the lunch counters in the department stores," Connor gave one of the officers suspected of helping the Klan, Sergeant Thomas H. Cook, a typical assignment. "I want you to get all the information you possibly can on these three Negroes, and watch them closely from now on." Thomas Jenkins, the special agent in charge (SAC) of the Birmingham FBI office, was also aware that Cook ("one of CONNOR's boys") took "most of his orders directly from CONNOR and not from Chief [of Police Jamie] MOORE," a graduate of the

FBI National Academy and a considerably less extreme segregationist than the commissioner.[18]

Sergeant Cook exercised little restraint when forwarding material to the Klan. Gary Rowe, the FBI informant who would remain in the Klan for four more years and who would play a central role in the history of the civil rights movement on two other occasions, described his access to police files as complete. Cook once opened two file drawers in his office and told Rowe to help himself, "for the use of the KLAN, in general." Material leaked to Rowe and other Klansmen, Jenkins advised headquarters, included "information concerning potential violence given [Cook] by the Birmingham FBI Office." The Klan, in turn, supplied ad hoc personnel for the police department's surveillance squad. Klansmen covered black churches and movement meetings, jotted down license plate numbers, and sometimes rode around on patrol in squad cars.[19]

The FBI considered Rowe one of its best Klan informants and a number of agents had an interest in his cover and credibility, including Thomas Jenkins. "I think Gary Thomas Rowe made him," John Seigenthaler speculated about Jenkins, who advanced rapidly after he left Birmingham. Thus, to protect Rowe's cover, the Bureau restricted dissemination of certain types of information to the police. Official policy allowed the dissemination of "information relating to racial matters . . . only to reliable law enforcement officials and agencies." But the Bureau made a slight modification here because the most unreliable lawman, Tom Cook, furnished information on Edward R. Fields, the Birmingham chiropractor who headed the local branch of the National States Rights party. The doctor carried a gun and had threatened to shoot any FBI agent he caught snooping around.[20]

FBI officials adjusted their dissemination policy to protect Rowe's informant status and their absolute control over the information Rowe and other Klan informants gathered. They would not change this policy in order to protect the Freedom Riders—even though the Kennedy administration wanted a "spy system" that could be used to head off segregationist terror. Hoover had no sympathy for violent resistance to civil rights protest, and his agents had investigated the Klan intermittently since 1919. But he would not allow his "spy system" to be used on behalf of those who struggled for racial justice. In Birmingham, local FBI agents understood the director's position on groups like the Klan and the National States Rights party. These groups were viewed as minor irritants, at worst, and their violent acts were the concern of local law enforcement and not the FBI. In other words, Klansmen created problems from time to time, but they never created serious problems for the FBI. The FBI always went ahead with its investigations. Not even Sergeant Cook, the gun-toting Dr. Fields, nor Commissioner Connor himself created problems for the FBI in Birmingham. Besides, in the FBI view, the Klan and its friends generally did more talking than anything else.[21]

Such claims to the contrary, the segregationists did cause real problems for the FBI. Rowe's reports on the Klan's plans for the Freedom Riders dated from mid-April, three weeks before their scheduled Mother's Day arrival. The FBI knew all along that Klan leaders would divide into two groups, with half their number stationed in the vicinity of the bus terminal and the other half on call at a nearby hotel. The FBI also knew about the police commissioner's encouragement ("By God, if you are going to do this thing, do it right"), his promise to keep all policemen away "until the Klan had time to act." Connor had guaranteed the mob twenty minutes to beat the riders until "it looked like a bulldog got hold of them." In one way, the FBI "spy system" had worked perfectly.[22]

The "spy system" broke down only when FBI agents on the scene asked the executives in Washington how to use their intelligence about Connor, Cook, and the Klan. After conferring with Alex Rosen, civil rights section chief Clement McGowan phoned Kenneth Raby in Birmingham and said to "go ahead," to "tell Chief of Police JAMIE MOORE ... that apparently several groups are interested in the arrival of the CORE party ... and there could be some violence." McGowan said the information should be furnished in "general terms," mentioning neither the Klan by name nor the bus station where the Klan would gather. He said no "information concerning Commissioner CONNOR" should be furnished, on the grounds that "we have to be careful to protect our informant and be alert to any possible 'trap.'"[23] With these instructions in mind, Birmingham field office agents had warned Jamie Moore on at least five separate occasions "that groups hostile to integration were contemplating violence." In Moore's absence, they passed on information to Tom Cook, including details about CORE's itinerary taken directly from their own files. None of this did the Freedom Riders any good, and when the bus station riot ended someone asked Bull Connor why the police had not been present. He said his men were all home with their mothers.

The FBI made no such flippant response, but Hoover admitted no mistake. When advising Robert Kennedy that his men had notified the police "that the Congress of Racial Equality would arrive in Birmingham on May 14," he refused to tell the attorney general how many agents were on the scene. When Kennedy buzzed Hoover on the intercom with this simple request, a non-committal answer ("we have enough") followed a vintage fillibus-ter—a "torrent of words," one of Kennedy's aides recalled. In Hoover's mind, the FBI had done all it could have done and all it should have done by alerting the Birmingham Police Depart-ment. After things had settled down, a headquarters directive reminded the field of the new facts of life regarding dissemina-tion policy to police departments suspected of having been infil-trated by the Klan. "It is immaterial whether the law enforce-ment agency is trustworthy and also whether it will properly fulfill its responsibility." Hoover adjusted policy under the pres-sure of the Freedom Ride, but in a way that made it even less likely that Bureau resources could be used to prevent anti–civil rights violence.[24]

Aware of the Connor-Cook-Klan connection and the Birming-ham police boycott of the bus station riot, the FBI also knew that Cook was the first officer to arrive on the scene. Hoover informed Kennedy of this fact as well.[25] And Kennedy knew that what happened in Birmingham was only the most dramatic ex-ample of the consequences of FBI policy. The Bureau routinely forwarded intelligence regarding movement strategies to police departments across the Jim Crow South. As often as not, the people who received Bureau information opposed the civil rights movement and were willing to use it to their own advan-tage. They may have passed on information from FBI teletypes to Klan groups in other cities.

The FBI argued that it was up to the Department of Justice to issue special instructions in Birmingham and that the Depart-ment failed to do so.[26] Although the FBI provided the Depart-ment with few details ahead of time regarding Cook's and Con-nor's connections with the Ku Klux Klan and its strategy for discouraging the Freedom Riders, it is clear that Kennedy did not press for details. The attorney general accepted the Bureau's assurances, and the director neglected to tell him about Connor's promise to give the Klan twenty free minutes. If Kennedy learned a lesson in Birmingham, he never did challenge the FBI's dissemination policies to police departments that had been infiltrated by violence-prone segregationists. Kennedy never did tell Hoover what to do.

With the Student Nonviolent Coordinating Committee determined to keep the Freedom Ride moving, Hoover continued to act freely on his own assumptions. Two of the original riders, John Lewis and Henry Thomas, returned from New Orleans to Nashville to help Fisk student Diane Nash's group of ten sit-in veterans begin a journey of their own to Birmingham. Connor arrested all ten just outside the city limits, releasing three almost immediately and driving the other seven to the Tennessee-Alabama line. When they returned to Birmingham by car, additional volunteers joined them at the Greyhound terminal, where a more cautious police commissioner confronted them—thanks to Robert Kennedy's apparent threat to bring Connor up on federal charges. When Greyhound could not locate a driver, moreover, Kennedy phoned a company superintendent to suggest he get in touch "with Mr. Greyhound" and find one. Kennedy also convinced Governor Patterson to intervene, prompting Rev. Shuttlesworth to remark with surprise and delight: "Man, what this state's coming to! An armed escort to take a bunch of niggers to a bus station so they can break these silly old laws." Robert Kennedy, not Hoover, protected these riders.[27]

On May 20 the FBI watched twenty-one well-guarded Freedom Riders board a bus for the two-hour trip to Montgomery. Once the bus left the highway and entered the Montgomery city limits, the police car and helicopter escort promised by Governor Patterson disappeared. "We stepped off the bus" at the station, John Lewis remembered, and "people just started pouring out of the station, out of buildings, from all over the place. White people." John Doar phoned in a report to Washington from across the street. "The passengers are coming off. . . . There are no cops. It's terrible." Lewis was soon lying in a pool of his own blood.[28] John Seigenthaler, who had been sent south, as Alex Rosen noted, "because the Attorney General felt his presence might prevent violence," was pulled from a rented car, dragged, and beaten after he tried to help two white Freedom Riders, Sue Harmann and Susan Wilbur. Seigenthaler lay unconscious and bleeding profusely for twenty-five minutes before an ambulance arrived. Commissioner of Public Safety Lester B. Sullivan, who had been alerted to the scheduled arrival of the bus by the FBI, explained the delay. "Every white ambulance in town reported their vehicles had broken down." While the police and ambulance drivers boycotted and the mob attacked the Freedom Riders, the FBI stood across the street, taking notes, "for the specific purpose of observing and reporting the facts to the Department of Justice in order that the Department will have the benefit of objective observations."[29]

FBI policy prevented the agent across the street from coming to Seigenthaler's aid: "If the agent should become personally involved in the action, he would be deserting his assigned task and would be unable to fulfill his primary responsibility of making objective observations." "They had agents all over the place," Seigenthaler complained, but they never fulfilled any of their responsibilities. "When I got out of the hospital and got back to my office, there was a letterhead memo on my desk, from Hoover to the attorney general, indicating who the assailants were," he said. "It galls me to think that the FBI stood there and watched me get clubbed." Remembering Seigenthaler in the years to come as someone who had embarrassed their Bureau, FBI officials eventually opened a file on him—a file that included allegations about "relations with young girls."[30]

Enraged by the Montgomery riot, Robert Kennedy at first planned to write to the governor of Alabama demanding an explanation. "We took the additional precautionary step," he wrote on May 20, "of having the FBI notify the police department that these students were coming and asked the police to take all necessary steps for their protection. . . . The F.B.I. was informed and in turn notified us that all necessary steps had been taken and that no action on our part was necessary," yet "no police were present," only "an armed mob." To prevent any repetition of these sad events, Kennedy said he would have the FBI "send in an extra team to intensify its investigations." The attorney general retained his hope that Hoover could be persuaded to act.[31]

Robert Kennedy never did send that letter to Governor Patterson; instead, on Sunday, May 21, his brother ordered five hundred U.S. marshals into Montgomery with Byron White in command. Reinforced by Floyd Mann's state troopers and finally the Alabama National Guard, the marshals held off another mob that evening at Ralph Abernathy's First Baptist Church, where Martin Luther King, the Freedom Riders, and some fifteen hundred blacks had gathered for a rally. John Lewis called the battle of the First Baptist Church "a real testing moment . . . without the support of the federal government at that time and a commitment, I think it could have been real bad." But when Doar met Lewis in the backyard of Abernathy's Montgomery home, he told him not "to talk to the FBI" before talking with the Civil Rights Division. "From that in itself," Lewis concluded, "I got the feeling . . . that even people within the Department of Justice had somewhat of a mistrust, distrust of their own FBI agents." The commitment from the federal government that Lewis spoke of had nothing to do with the FBI.[32]

Repeating his familiar refrain ("I can't guarantee the safety of fools") in the aftermath, Governor Patterson ordered Public Safety Director Floyd Mann to terminate his department's "working relationship with the FBI." Montgomery city officials hoped at the same time to convince the FBI to investigate the Freedom Riders on the grounds that they had placed an undue burden on interstate commerce—and life in general. City attorney Calvin M. Whitesell used the same argument when he asked Judge Frank Johnson to impose a permanent injunction banning the Freedom Ride. "They put a burden on our police department. They put a burden on our highway patrol. And they put a burden on the FBI. All because they insist upon a right to ride a bus," Whitesell said. Johnson's reply: the police, the patrol, and the FBI had a duty "to maintain law and order." Hoover disagreed.[33]

Thirty years earlier, during the time of John Dillinger, the director and his bureaucracy had grown in power and influence precisely because state and local police could not cope with the depression era's mobile gangsters. Now, the director was unwilling to fill this new vacuum left by the usual guardians of law and order. He dispatched Alex Rosen to Montgomery, but only because Byron White complained about difficulties in securing timely information. Before Rosen arrived, White had to file a request with the local FBI man, Richard Held, and then wait until the request filtered up to Hoover's aides at the seat of government and then back again. When the Freedom Riders moved on from Alabama and Louisiana to Mississippi, Kennedy, as promised, had the FBI send additional agents to Jackson, Meridian, and Hattiesburg. But these agents concentrated on the gathering of political intelligence about the riders almost to the exclusion of any law-enforcement responsibilities.

Because Robert Kennedy never forcefully challenged this priority, Hoover continued to act in a vacuum. The attorney general first suggested a "cooling-off period," prompting James Farmer to remark: "We had been cooling off for 100 years." He then asked the director to have his "Special Agents drive buses loaded with Freedom Riders through Alabama to Mississippi." Hoover "emphatically refused" this attempt "to use the FBI for improper undertakings." In interviews with *U.S. News and World Report* publisher David Lawrence and *FBI Story* author Don Whitehead, he summarized what he told Kennedy. "I stated that as long as I am Director of this Bureau I do not intend to allow it to be misused by pressure groups." "[If] Mr. Kennedy . . . did not like it," Hoover threatened, he could "get himself another Director." Ironically, Bureau agents had curried favor with prominent Americans since the 1930s and they had chauffered Kennedy's father around on several occasions during his travels outside the Boston area. Unwilling to confront the legal and practical merits of Hoover's argument, let alone the uproar that would follow Hoover's resignation (no matter how unlikely that prospect), the attorney general backed off.[34]

FBI policy remained frozen—as if the violence in Anniston, Birmingham, and Montgomery had not occurred. After CORE's James McCain advised the Bureau of the Freedom Riders' schedule on the Illinois Central Railroad from New Orleans to Jackson, Hoover's men alerted railroad security, the Mississippi Highway Patrol, the Hinds County sheriff, and the Jackson Police Department.[35] With their law-enforcement responsibilities fulfilled, they turned to their intelligence responsibilities. When Martin Luther King demonstrated an interest in the Freedom Riders, the FBI ran his name through the files.[36] As Jackson police locked up the Freedom Riders *en masse*, moreover, the director sent the attorney general a *Reader's Digest* article, "I Was a 'Student' at Moscow State," about Soviet-bloc discrimination against visiting African students. The piece had "tremendous counterpropaganda value," Hoover told Kennedy.[37] At other times, FBI officials went to their constituents in the media and Congress with derogatory information on the Freedom Riders, hoping to bring public and congressional opinion around to their view that civil rights advocacy was un-American.

FBI agents assigned to the Crime Records Division helped radio commentator and newspaper columnist Fulton Lewis, Jr., with a Reds-move-in-on-riders story, and Senator Strom Thurmond of South Carolina with a speech after a wiretap revealed the plans of two reputed communists to form a CORE chapter in San Francisco.[38] It was no coincidence that the FBI selected a segregationist to help publicize Communist party interest in CORE. "Thurmond was probably one of our strongest bulwarks in the Congress on law-enforcement problems," one of De-Loach's Crime Records agents reasoned. "We wanted somebody to know that CORE was being infiltrated. And if you would give it to Joe Blow down the street . . . it wouldn't do any good. But if you give it to Strom Thurmond, a powerful senator . . . [CORE] should have done something about getting those people out of there. . . . You can't have everything. You can't have it both ways."[39] CORE had to act in an acceptable manner or accept the consequences. In this case, however, there is no evidence that the Bureau alerted the organization to the Communist party's interest. Hoover had DeLoach go straight to Thurmond.

The FBI could have it both ways, criticizing "the caliber of the people engaged in the freedom rides" as well as their political associations. The abysmal treatment of the riders in the Jackson city jail and the state penitentiary at Parchman led the Civil Rights Division to order an investigation, but Hoover did not object to "the thumps and whacks" of the jailers. Instead, when a rider complained about being held in solitary confinement in a cell kept completely dark during the day and illuminated by a glaring light at night, Hoover told Robert Kennedy that this fellow had "a private cell" with "a window and a street light shines through the window at night." The director then dismissed a hunger strike in the Jackson jail as a hoax, advising Burke Marshall that the conspirators threatened one of the prisoners who had refused to cooperate. In his reports to the White House and the Civil Rights Division, and in his leaks to his contacts in the media and the Congress, Hoover suggested that the riders brought all their troubles on themselves, that they deserved worse than they got.[40]

While the Freedom Riders made their way home from Mississippi at the end of the summer, a number of them accepted an invitation from a former NAACP leader, Robert F. Williams, to stop in Monroe, North Carolina, a Klan stronghold and the scene of numerous civil rights demonstrations.[41] One of the earliest and most militant advocates of armed self-resistance against segregationist violence, Williams began a week-long picket at the Monroe courthouse that provoked violent reactions. He telephoned the FBI office in Charlotte "each time the Freedom Riders would get ready to go on the picket line . . . The FBI would say, 'We're on the way.' But they would never be there when anything happened." After several days of tension, a mob of at least two thousand whites attacked the line—"a moment of death," thought James Forman, who would soon become SNCC's executive secretary—and the police arrested the Freedom Riders. In the aftermath, with Monroe on the verge of a riot, a car carrying a middle-aged white couple happened to wander into Monroe's black neighborhood. The occupants, Williams claimed, stayed at his home for their own protection.[42]

To the FBI and the state of North Carolina it looked like a kidnapping. Edward Scheidt, commissioner of motor vehicles and public safety, and a former FBI executive who had testified against the civil rights bill of 1957 before the House Judiciary Committee, sent in fifty-two highway patrolmen. Two FBI agents on the scene helped out and Governor Terry Sanford's office kept the White House posted.[43] While the state filed charges against Williams and four others, including one of the Freedom Riders, the FBI ran a name check on Forman that included a quick (and apparently routine) search of the files of the Anti-Defamation League. In Cleveland, the Bureau arrested Mae Mallory, a member of Williams's Crusader Family, who claimed "about 25 members of the F.B.I. came into the house with guns drawn and everything." Williams himself fled the country, imagining "500 FBI men . . . setting up a dragnet." While waiting for the rest of the defendants to stand trial for kidnapping, the FBI focused on the Trotskyite Socialist Workers party's attempt to organize a "Committee to Aid the Monroe Defendants." Hoover tried to smash the group for its work on "integration problems arising in the South."[44]

Ultimately, as in the voting litigation campaign, the FBI record during the crusade to desegregate the buses improved. Despite its failures in Birmingham and Montgomery and interest in the politics and integrity of the Freedom Riders themselves, within two years the Bureau claimed that its investigations played a decisive role in victories over Jim Crow. This was an exaggerated claim, to be sure. By 1963 even the Republican National Committee claimed credit for abolishing segregation "in bus and train interstate travel," a preposterous boast based on the coincidence that the Supreme Court had decided *Boynton* (which prohibited segregation in all terminal accommodations) during the last year of the Eisenhower presidency.[45] The FBI, on the other hand, made a contribution, even though the dissemination of derogatory information on the riders suggests that this may have been the last thing that Hoover wanted to do. While some Bureau agents spied on the Freedom Riders, others, at the insistence of Kennedy's Justice Department, conducted surveys of bus, railroad, ferry boat, and airport terminals, surveys that the Department used in the courts and elsewhere to end segregation on the highways, rails, and inland waterways, and in the skies.[46]

Most of the credit belongs to the Freedom Riders themselves and Robert Kennedy. Kennedy prevented the tragedies of Anniston, Birmingham, and Montgomery from escalating into major catastrophes. He also managed to ram through the historic Interstate Commerce Commission order of June 21, 1961, banning segregation in interstate bus facilities. Though far more willing to protect civil rights workers from segregationist violence than Hoover, Kennedy operated within the confines of his own theory of federalism. Even Seigenthaler understood the attorney general's deference, in practice, to the director's position on the matter of protection. "I thought there were some days—one, for sure—when they should have kept [Hoover] in a cage," he said. "It does make you wonder about the milk of human kindness . . . [but] there were legitimate jurisdictional policies . . . I accepted his official explanation." The protection issue remained complex, and within the government nearly everyone with an interest in civil rights responded ambiguously.[47]

On the surveillance front, no complexities or ambiguities existed. No theory of federalism applied. In the months after the Freedom Rides ended, Burke Marshall complained no more about a spy gap. Instead, he expressed "his deep appreciation" to the FBI "for having kept him so fully informed in connection with the current racial disturbances (walk-ins, sit-ins, etc.). He said this was of inestimable value." Eventually, Marshall began filing "Monday and Wednesday" reports with Robert Kennedy regarding "matters of significance in the Division." These reports, all part of "an advanced warning system," invariably contained intelligence data submitted by the FBI.[48]

No complexities or ambiguities clouded Hoover's view of the FBI's mission. "We are an intelligence agency and as such we are expected to know what is going on," he once said. And he announced hundreds of times that his FBI "was not a protection agency." A case could be made for Hoover's position that the FBI had no authority to protect civil rights activists and full authority to spy on those activists. A case could also be made that "legitimate jurisdictional policies" determined the FBI's reluctance to get involved in civil rights enforcement. In fact, however, the director resisted everything the Kennedys asked him to do on behalf of the black struggle, not just the demand that he act more aggressively to protect civil rights activists.

When the attorney general asked the director to assign agents to drive Freedom Riders into Mississippi, Kennedy understood the irony of Hoover's response. At the time, the FBI employed only a handful of black agents (all of them chauffeurs, according to Washington legend), and the attorney general had his staff recruit blacks for the FBI as part of the administration's broader affirmative action plan for all executive agencies and departments.[49] One of the people Ed Guthman brought in, William Lucas, a Fordham Law School graduate and a Catholic, made it through the FBI National Academy and went on to become sheriff of Wayne County, Michigan. Many years later, in 1986, Lucas ran for governor of the state on the Republican party ticket with an "anti-affirmative action, pro-life, tax-cutting" campaign that won praise from President Ronald Reagan. But during his FBI days not even a conservative black could win the director's favor. The *National Review* quoted *Detroit News* columnist Pete Waldmeir that to impress Hoover "a black dude had better talk better than Harry Belafonte and dance better than Sammy Davis."[50]

FBI officials responded to the Kennedy recruiters with cynicism and flim-flam, and a few agents parodied JFK by warning one another to "work with vigah" or "be replaced with a niggah." Hoover responded to Robert Kennedy's requests for the number of black agents employed by the Bureau with a standard answer: the FBI catalogued no employee by race, creed, or color. A commendable sentiment, the attorney general replied, before repeating his request.[51] Hoover finally told Kennedy that the FBI had five black agents on its 5,500-man roster. He did not indicate that at least one (and possibly three) of these agents were in fact drivers, and two others, Sam Noisette and Worthington Smith, as Guthman observed, "took your hat and coat when you went in." In Washington, James Crawford carried a gun and doubled as a bodyguard and handyman. He kept Hoover's house and garden in good shape for thirty-seven years; looked after the dogs,

Cindy and G-boy; and did the cooking and cleaning when Annie Fields, the director's live-in black servant, had to be away. "James worked fifteen hours a day, seven days a week. Holidays, too," wife Dorothea said. The identities of the other two black agents remain a mystery. They were probably among the handful of black Bureau employees who reportedly received field assignments from time to time—Carl V. Mason in Chicago and Kansas City; Jesse S. Strider, Jr., and his son Robert in Los Angeles; Harold A. Carr and James T. Young in New York; and Leo J. McCairen in Miami.[52]

When "leaning on [Hoover]" to hire black agents, Robert Kennedy used an argument he thought the director would understand. "We saw a problem coming in civil rights," former White House aide Kenneth O'Donnell remembered, "and we saw also the possibility that the Communists might attempt to infiltrate the black movement, and a lot of other people might too, and how do you police Harlem with a white guy who is a spy? They send an FBI guy down in a Brooks Brothers suit and a snap brim hat. He couldn't catch cold in Harlem." That policy, in an area so near Hoover's heart, was simply "ridiculous." The director would have to agree.[53]

Affirmative action was one of the issues that lay at the heart of Hoover's intense dislike of Robert Kennedy. The two men "didn't agree on everything," one Crime Records Division agent recalled, with considerable understatement. "Mainly, they didn't agree on black agents. Kennedy wanted us to lower the standards. Hoover said, 'Bring me all the black agents that meet these standards and I'll take them.' Bobby Kennedy said, 'No, you can't get them at Bureau standards, you've got to come down to here.' And Hoover says, 'Forget it.'"[54] Beyond a college degree (preferably in law or accounting), no one could define the director's "terribly high" standards. Harold P. Leinbaugh, another former Crime Records agent and soldier who landed at Omaha Beach, said Hoover had a "concept of the FBI as an absolutely, totally elite [force]—you know, rangers, commandos . . . paramilitary. His defense in all of this was that he was trying to find qualified men . . . a guy hopefully with a Harvard law degree that was black and had an IQ of 147 and had all the physical and other qualifications . . . which is a pretty good argument . . . Hoover demanded a holier-than-thou attitude. You could always find some excuse for not hiring anybody. . . . They could say, 'Well, you had an uncle who signed a Communist party nominating petition in 1939.'" No excuse satisfied Robert Kennedy however.[55]

Hoover believed blacks were inferior, intellectually and otherwise. He even complained, privately, and as late as 1969, about police departments "lowering the physical qualifications so they could get more Negro officers." He also believed blacks could not be easily integrated into his homogenous agent corps, which hardly represented a broad sampling of the white American male. So the FBI hired few black agents, the attorney general's complaints notwithstanding. By the end of 1962 the Bureau had only ten. Hugh Fleischer, a Civil Rights Division lawyer for six years, said he never saw a black FBI agent. "All we heard [was] that there was a chauffeur or somebody who drove J. Edgar around." When the director died in 1972, blacks made up less than .5 percent of the agent corps, and it would be two more years before headquarters permanently assigned a black agent to the Jackson, Mississippi, field office. What one Bureau executive described as "our posture on blacks" had scarcely improved even twenty years after Kennedy resigned the attorney generalship.[56]

During the Kennedy years affirmative action remained what it had always been for Hoover—a public relations problem to be solved by helping place yet another *Ebony* article. The Bureau had done this most recently in 1958, with a photo of a chauffeur assigned to the Los Angeles field office and his son, Jesse and Robert Strider, peering down the sights of Thompson submachine-guns. The latest article, prepared by Simeon Booker, praised the Bureau's past ("the FBI's history . . . sparkles with seldom told exploits of courageous Negro special agents") and again mentioned Sam Noisette as one of Hoover's most valuable employees. "The relationship between the two men virtually sets the race relations pattern for the huge agency," Booker wrote, with no irony in mind. Rather, he hoped to encourage blacks to join the FBI.[57]

Booker's piece focused on the first two legitimate black agent trainees: James W. Barrow, a Brooklyn College graduate from Amityville, New York, and a former Bureau clerk; and especially Aubrey C. Lewis, a twenty-seven-year-old former Notre Dame football star brought in by a Bureau official active in the Notre Dame Alumni Association. The first black candidates to make it through the FBI academy in Quantico on the unsegregated course, both men went on to serve with distinction—though

Lewis did not remain with the FBI for long. Some civil rights people and even a few of his fellow G-men saw him as a token, an honorary Irishman from Notre Dame among Hoover's heavily Catholic agent corps. Such pressures made the opportunities for other employment tempting.[58]

While Hoover and Kennedy battled over questions of affirmative action during the Freedom Rides and beyond, surveillance remained the FBI's primary function in 1962. "They certainly cooperated fully in passing intelligence, but not in other respects," Nicholas Katzenbach recalled. "The Bureau refused to take any kind of responsibility for the maintenance of law and order"—"and they weren't asked to."[59] Katzenbach referred to the Ole Miss crisis in Oxford, where Governor Ross Barnett blocked the door to prevent James Meredith from attending classes at the University of Mississippi; the resulting riot left two people dead and 375 injured. Eventually, President Kennedy sent in Army troops and federalized the state national guard to support the federal marshals already on the scene. The FBI moved in only after the smoke had cleared, to conduct lab tests on the marshals' pistols. There had been little federal gunfire as it turned out, and not a single casualty could be traced to the marshals.[60]

Expected only to collect intelligence at Ole Miss, FBI agents relied on their many sources in and around Oxford, including Hugh H. Clegg, formerly an assistant director for Hoover, and at that time an assistant to university chancellor John D. Williams. From these sources, however, Hoover often received biased information. A graduate of the George Washington University law school and a Kappa Alpha, like Hoover and Tolson, Clegg was also a Mississippi native. He had been the first Bureau agent assigned to coordinate civil rights training for police officers at the National Academy back in the 1940s. From his new post in Williams's office, he forwarded information to the FBI from the moment Meredith's application for admission arrived. He told the Bureau the university rejected Meredith not because of his race, but because he failed to "name five alumni . . . with whom he was acquainted which is a requirement for admission." Clegg described the Citizens Council ("composed of many of the leading citizens of Mississippi") in words nearly identical to those used by the director six years earlier when briefing the Eisenhower cabinet on racial matters.[61]

The Civil Rights Division called upon FBI surveillance services once again a few months later. Alabama Governor George Wallace had pledged to stand in his schoolhouse door, and Burke Marshall encouraged the Bureau to tape-record the governor's speeches. Fortunately, when Wallace tried to prevent the admission of two black students, Vivian Malone and James A. Hood, to the University of Alabama, events were less chaotic than in Mississippi. Katzenbach handed Wallace a proclamation from the president commanding him to cease and desist his unlawful obstructions of a federal court order; the governor did not budge at first, but withdrew after a second confrontation. The students registered. As the drama unfolded, the FBI remained on the periphery, phoning in developments to the Justice Department, photographing the happenings, and trying to remain inconspicuous.[62]

Hoover intended to spy on the civil rights movement, and Robert Kennedy's Justice Department encouraged him to do exactly that. By the spring of 1963 the Civil Rights Division routinely filed specific requests with the FBI for such services as "photographic coverage" of activities planned for the one hundreth anniversary of the Emancipation Proclamation. More often, the FBI reported directly to Marshall's office. One agent discussed forty-two separate racial incidents during a single telephone call. The reports themselves ranged from the Alabama Highway Patrol's use of electric cattle prods on would-be black voters to a report from Paris that "William Marshall, Negro actor, James Baldwin, Anthony Quinn and Gregory Peck . . . plan to present petitions against racial discrimination to American Embassies throughout Europe." Civil Rights Division staff found it difficult to keep pace with both the sheer number of demonstrations (1,580 in thirty-eight states plus the District of Columbia during the summer of 1963) and the volume of FBI intelligence. Bureau officials supplemented their telephone calls with 8,114 letterhead memos (eight copies each) regarding racial matters for dissemination to the Justice Department, Military Intelligence, and other interested government agencies.[63]

Hoover responded ambivalently to the demand for intelligence, sometimes resisting the requests of Robert Kennedy and Burke Marshall, and sometimes volunteering information. In May, Kennedy wired all U.S. attorneys asking them to make surveys of "segregated business facilities" and to list all places where racial demonstrations could be expected in the next thirty days. The attorney general also "asked" the FBI "to cooperate."

Hoover responded to the second request simply by increasing the volume of his reports to the Department. The other request presented problems. Because of his own racial bias, Hoover wanted to investigate civil rights activists, not white southern businessmen; but he had to respond to Kennedy's directive, so he instructed his agents to advise the U.S. attorneys orally, based on their "personal knowledge and views." The Bureau actually conducted no investigation for the purpose of identifying segregated businesses.[64]

That same month, Robert Kennedy met in New York with Jerome Smith, a CORE field worker and Freedom Rider who had been repeatedly beaten and jailed, and a number of friends of novelist James Baldwin—including playwright Lorraine Hansberry, psychologist Kenneth Clark, singers Harry Belafonte and Lena Horne, and actor Rip Torn. Smith set the tone of the meeting when he said that being in the same room with the attorney general made him feel like throwing up. "Bobby took it personally," Baldwin remembered. "And he turned away from him. That was a mistake because he turned toward us. We were the reasonable, responsible, mature representatives of the black community. Lorraine Hansberry said, 'You've got a great many very, very accomplished people in this room, Mr. Attorney General. But the only man who should be listened to is that man over there.'" The group then criticized the FBI. Kennedy passed this issue to Burke Marshall, who said the Justice Department sent in "special men" from the Civil Rights Division whenever the Bureau refused to do its job. The reply "produced almost hysterical laughter."[65]

After accounts of the meeting appeared in the press, Hoover sent unsolicited dossiers on all those present to Kennedy, who sent them to Marshall with a note. "What nice friends you have." The director had spent the past forty-four years linking protest with disloyalty and impugning the integrity of the protesters. It would have been unusual if he had treated Baldwin's group otherwise. Unfortunately, the Kennedy administration tolerated this behavior and even credited it with some validity. The attorney general read the dossiers, as did the assistant attorney general for civil rights and the Civil Rights Division's "special men." Earlier, when Stokely Carmichael and five other anonymous civil rights activists staged a brief sit-in in the attorney general's office, Kennedy had specifically asked for memos on all six. Marshall's number two man, St. John Barrett, said the director "[was always] telling us between the lines that we were accepting uncritically the assertions of people who really weren't as credible as we thought they were."[66]

Neither Robert Kennedy nor the attorneys in the Civil Rights Division were struck by the contradiction between the FBI's strict-constructionist posture on civil rights enforcement and its anything-goes activities in surveillance. "I took the world as I found it," said Marshall. "We got a lot of what you might call letterhead memos," Doar explained. "To tell you the truth, I didn't react too much one way or the other." "We didn't get into any intellectual debate," Barrett conceded. "You kind of shrug and say, 'What are these guys spending their time on this for?' But you never ask them or raise it with them."[67] Kennedy himself encouraged some of this pervasive name checking. He had learned how the FBI worked and how to use its intelligence gathering resources even before his appointment as attorney general. As chief counsel of the Senate Rackets Committee in the 1950s, he received dozens of blind memos on union organizers and mobsters from FBI agent Courtney Evans. Later, when Kennedy was running the Department, Evans was running the Bureau's Special Investigative Division and serving as Hoover's liaison with the administration.[68]

Evans's Division ran the names of hundreds of individuals and groups through the files at the request of Kennedy administration officials.[69] The subjects of these searches ranged from the National Negro Congress, a communist front that had been dead for fourteen years, to James Baldwin, William Faulkner, and fifty other Nobel Prize laureates whose names graced a White House dinner invitation list—part of John and Jacqueline Kennedy's program to encourage and honor cultural and intellectual achievement. In Faulkner's case, the Bureau noted his statement to the Civil Rights Congress, another communist front and successor to the National Negro Congress, on behalf of Willie McGhee, convicted of raping a white woman in Laurel, Mississippi, in 1945. (McGhee exhausted all possible appeals by March 1951, when the Supreme Court refused to hear his case, and to the day the state executed him the FBI seemed most interested in exploring the "Communistic connections" of one of his noncommunist lawyers, Bella Abzug.)[70] W. Mark Felt, former head of the FBI's Inspection Division, said "Attorney General Kennedy thought of the FBI as a kind of private police department, with Hoover as its desk sergeant."[71] Felt was referring less to the name checks and other surveillance services than to Kennedy's attempts to have the FBI assume more responsibilities in the areas of civil rights and organized crime. The Bureau had been running name checks for the White House since the 1920s.[72]

FBI surveillance activities received implicit if limited approval not only from the Kennedy administration, but from some sections of the civil rights movement itself. Civil rights leaders cooperated with the FBI for two basic reasons. The first had to do with the lingering effects of the domestic communist issue. When HUAC investigator W. Jackson Jones visited the Southern Regional Council (SRC) in 1956, he asked executive director George S. Mitchell about "communist[s] climbing aboard." Mitchell told him the SRC had been "set up by an entirely different stripe of people than those that had established the Southern Conference for Human Welfare"—a group that did indeed have communists among its membership—and gave him a "two-minute lecture on the utter Americanism of the NAACP." Mitchell's willingness to deflect HUAC's criticism onto the nearest available group on the left represented a fairly typical attitude within the established civil rights groups.[73]

This attitude represented a concession to the segregationists who Red-baited the movement well into the 1960s. Long before the cold war settled in, a good many people on the left had been driven into the anticommunist camp by the damage they thought the Stalinists in America were doing. Some civil rights groups, like the NAACP, responded to the pressures of the cold war and the stiffening climate by embracing more conservative politics. Uncomfortable with the mass black activism of the New Deal and World War II years, NAACP leadership retreated to the more familiar and cautious turf of litigation and lobbying. At the same time, the NAACP instituted loyalty oaths and created committees to investigate the political histories of prospective members.[74] "We do not want a witch hunt," Roy Wilkins advised Walter White, "but we do want to clean out our organization." To escape the real McCarthyites, the NAACP purged itself.[75]

By the early 1960s the FBI extended name-check services to several civil rights groups in an informal and usually indirect manner as part of its COMINFIL (communist infiltration) and COINTELPRO (counterintelligence program) efforts to purge Communist party members and others from "legitimate mass organizations." The method began with the compilation of "public source or similar material identifying . . . [the targeted] individual with the communist movement," followed by a discreet effort to "ascertain the most logical officer or prominent person in the organization on whom there is no derogatory information." If this person "could be expected to take . . . action to remove the communist from the organization," he would receive an anonymous letter or phone call or perhaps a blind memo delivered in person by an FBI agent.[76]

In practice, this meant FBI mailings about communists or former communists associated with his group to A. Philip Randolph, then president of the Negro American Labor Council. There were FBI briefings for the NAACP's Thurgood Marshall, and anonymous letters, telephone calls, and blind memos for other "anticommunist officers" at NAACP offices in New York. In the case of the Southern Regional Council, FBI agents questioned the politics of specific activists. "Field men would come in to talk to us," former SRC executive director Leslie Dunbar remembered, and ask, "'What do you know about him?' 'What do you know about her?'" The FBI sent letters to "reliable, intelligent" CORE officials who had "expressed concern over possible 'radical' influences."[77] FBI agents from the Atlanta and Washington field offices may have provided name-check services to the Southern Christian Leadership Conference at Rev. Ralph Abernathy's request.[78]

Leaking information on communist infiltration to "responsible leaders" of civil rights groups was only one aspect of what FBI officials described as a broadly based "liaison program." By identifying people who would move against communist infiltration of particular movement groups, Hoover's agents were able to solicit "a constant flow of intelligence-type information" on "the planned activities of . . . the most active groups . . . staging racial demonstrations." "Our liaison program," Hoover told Robert Kennedy, two years after the attack on the Freedom Riders in Birmingham, "has also enabled us to alert local law enforcement agencies in advance in order that these . . . agencies may take appropriate action to maintain peace and order and to prevent unwarranted situations from developing." FBI surveillance could be used to protect civil rights workers, Hoover seemed to be saying, but actually he remained interested only in rooting out communists from civil rights groups and maintaining friendly relations with segregationist southern lawmen.[79]

Robert Kennedy's aide, John Seigenthaler, said the FBI had

excellent sources "within the civil rights movement." Hoover aide Alex Rosen cited Julius Hobson, who was president of CORE's Washington, D.C., chapter until his dismissal in 1964 for being too militant, as one of the Bureau's more effective contacts. Cartha DeLoach met with Freedom Ride organizer James Farmer in 1963 to discuss "the possibilities of the FBI advising him on a confidential basis whenever members of the Communist Party sought to infiltrate and take advantage of CORE." The FBI also claimed to have an "agreement" requiring Farmer to consult with DeLoach before issuing statements regarding the Bureau's civil rights work. Because Farmer had recently criticized an FBI agent in Birmingham who "had not been very helpful to CORE members," DeLoach believed Farmer was not keeping his word and thus tried to arrange another meeting to straighten him out. He had a hard time contacting him; like so many movement people, "Farmer was either in jail or constantly in travel status." Nearly ten years later, Farmer confirmed the existence of a liaison arrangement by noting one occasion where an FBI agent briefed him on a part-time CORE staff member and alleged "card-carrying member of the Communist party."[80]

The FBI rarely helped the black activists who cooperated. Field agents solicited information from members of state NAACP affiliates about local movement strategies—information that they sometimes passed on to local police officers and sometimes used to exacerbate rivalries between the NAACP and other civil rights groups. On the national level, the FBI favored executive director Roy Wilkins, occasionally sending him derogatory personal and political information on other civil rights leaders—most notably Martin Luther King. Crime Records agent Lawrence Heim described the FBI's relationship with Wilkins as excellent, and the NAACP chief even met with DeLoach once to discuss how the Bureau might brighten its image in the civil rights field.[81] The FBI also established liaison with National Urban League executive director Whitney Young, who tried to turn the liaison program around to meet Urban League needs and not Bureau needs. Young told the special agent in charge of the FBI's New York office that he was interested in this program because it might facilitate the recruitment of black applicants for the position of FBI special agent—"inasmuch as one of the functions of the URBAN LEAGUE is to place Negroes in desirable positions." Young's deftness, in Hoover's view, marked him as "a very expedient person," though the director still rated him "one stripe above [Dr. King]."[82]

Few of the movement people who shared information with the FBI thought it was wrong. If the Bureau identified Farmer, Hobson, and Wilkins, as "sources," those men should not be considered "scabs to the movement."[83] They did not resemble people like Julia Brown, a black woman from Cleveland and a longtime FBI operative who surfaced in the early 1960s to testify before HUAC and the Subversive Activities Control Board.[84] Hobson, for example, met regularly with FBI agent Elmer Lee Todd, reported on civil rights demonstration plans at the 1964 Democratic National Convention in Atlantic City, and received $300 from the Bureau for services rendered at the Convention. But Hobson's widow claimed he joked openly about his relationship with the FBI and actually used his stipend to bring more demonstrators to Atlantic City. The Bureau finally "discontinued" Hobson "as a liaison source . . . when he advised the press of his relationship with us"—an admission that prompted Hoover to complain "that Hobson talks from both sides of his mouth." Shortly thereafter, the Bureau tried to interfere with Hobson's campaign for a seat on the District of Columbia School Board by spreading a rumor that he was an "Uncle Tom."[85]

Even when sharing information with the FBI, most movement people believed they were informing on themselves ("us") and not their enemies ("them"). There were exceptions—notably Farmer's dismissal of that CORE staff worker and the willingness of a surprising number of NAACP activists to discuss the activities of rival civil rights groups with the Bureau. But the FBI's so-called liaison sources did not always "name names." Former agent Arthur Murtagh, who operated a number of formal black informants who monitored the Southern Christian Leadership Conference, claimed nearly all of the information they provided could have been acquired simply by picking up the phone and calling SCLC or asking a representative to stop by the Atlanta field office.[86] Similarly, John Lewis said the FBI often called Julian Bond at the SNCC office in Atlanta "to find out what was going on or should they be notified, that sort of thing." North Carolina attorney Floyd McKissick remembered "FBI agents who needed information coming into CORE offices in New York to get it." Medgar Evers, the NAACP leader in Mississippi, kept the FBI posted on events in Jackson from time to

time. Andrew Young, James Farmer, and A. Philip Randolph occasionally alerted the FBI to their travel itineraries. "I agreed
to keep in touch with DeLoach," Young said, with some exaggeration, "when we were moving anywhere."[87] Farmer kept in touch
with the FBI at the suggestion of DeLoach and John Malone, the
FBI executive who ran the New York office. Malone asked
Farmer to have his "secretary give me a call whenever you're
going south."[88]

The goal of obtaining FBI protection, even more than communist infiltration or factionalism within the civil rights movement, was what made some movement people willing to cooperate. "When you were down South and something happened,
you'd call the FBI," SNCC's H. Rap Brown later wrote. "They
represented the federal government, and you didn't want to face
the fact that the federal government wasn't on your side." "They
were a problem almost from the beginning as they sat around
taking notes while people were getting beat up," Andrew Young
said. "But we always felt their presence was welcome and that
they did serve as a restraint on Southern law enforcement . . .
which would have been far more violent without the FBI. So in
spite of the fact that we knew they were somewhat antagonistic
to our goals, we always cooperated with them—all the way
through. . . . For instance, when we were going into Birmingham
for a demonstration, we would call the FBI, call the Justice Department . . . just to make sure that everybody understood exactly what we were there for." "It's hard to remember back
then," Young concluded, "but when you were anxious about
your life, civil liberties seemed a tertiary consideration."[89]

Movement leaders may have been "compulsive about freedom," maybe even paranoid, in Young's view, but those feelings
did not stop the movement from cooperating, in a limited sense,
in its own surveillance. Dr. King himself told Hoover that "it
was vitally necessary to keep a working relationship with the
FBI." Another SCLC colleague, Bayard Rustin, said "we had to
call upon them." Mary King, who handled communications for
SNCC with Julian Bond, said "we believed that we should lay
the groundwork by providing the agency with a steady flow of
information," and that was a mainstream movement view.[90]

Not everyone shared that view however. SNCC's Jim Forman
also wanted protection, but he concluded that it was an impossible task—because the FBI ran the liaison program to gather derogatory information on civil rights activists that could be used

to divide and otherwise discredit the civil rights movement. The liaison program was never intended to protect those who risked their lives for racial justice. The FBI, "a part of the governmental structure," served as a barrier between power and "the people," Forman wrote. In effect, the FBI was "the enemy of black people. . . . We did not say it that way in 1963, but we did know that the FBI was a farce. It wasn't going to arrest any local racists who violated any and all laws on the statute books. Instead, it would play a game of taking notes and pictures. The files in Washington must have been growing thick even then with documents from the civil rights movement and with photographs of us all—doing everything but screwing, and maybe even that."[91]

On June 12, 1963, three weeks after Hoover told Robert Kennedy that the liaison program's principal purpose was "to prevent unwarranted situations from developing," a gunman shot and killed Medgar Evers, the Jackson-based NAACP field representative in Mississippi. (He was one of the movement leaders who sometimes kept the Bureau posted on demonstration plans in his area.) FBI agents entered the case under civil rights law, on the grounds that the murderer or murderers had conspired to deprive Evers of his civil rights; and in the face of the usual criticism. James Wechsler of the New York Post said Evers "went to a lonely death, as he had feared he would, while the G-men slept."[92] The FBI's after-the-fact investigation, however, was thorough and generally impressive, involving agents from forty-eight field offices.[93] They developed ballistic and fingerprint evidence, and identified a new Golden Hawk telescopic site found in a vacant lot near the thicket where the sniper and his 30.06 had waited for Evers. The scope was traced to a fertilizer salesman from nearby Greenwood who wondered "why the world was in the hands of the Communists." Arrested by the FBI on June 22 and turned over to the Jackson police, he faced two murder trials. Both ended in hung juries.[94]

Not all of the FBI agents on the case looked for Evers's killer, however; other agents covered the funeral in anticipation of a riot.[95] Jackson police officers and troopers from the Mississippi Highway Patrol, also expecting trouble, armed themselves with shotguns, carbines, tear gas, and nightsticks. There was a corps of German shepherds and their handlers nearby. Evers's brother, Charles, said he "came back to Mississippi to kill every white man I saw." Roy Wilkins, who spoke at the funeral, condemned "the Southern political system" for putting that crazed white man "behind the rifle." Rocks, bottles, and chants of "we want the killer" filled the air as the mourners moved toward the business district. Only John Doar's courage prevented a bloody confrontation. Stepping out between the two sides, with the FBI on the edges taking notes and pictures, he turned to the blacks, and said, "You can't win this way. . . . Don't throw bottles, that's what they want you to do." When Doar spoke, the mourners, and the cops with their clubs and dogs, all drifted home.[96]

Evers's death had little impact on the FBI in Jackson. The decision to cover the demonstrations after the shooting and to send the photographers and note takers to the funeral was routine. Bureau agents had been sending memos to the Jackson Police Department on the efforts of movement people to organize boycotts of Capital Street stores from the day the first picket appeared. And they had demonstrated a remarkable tolerance for police brutality for just as long a time, making only a perfunctory investigation of the city policemen who beat John R. Salter, Jr., a half-blooded Micmac/Penobscot Indian and a professor at Tougaloo College just outside Jackson, during a march. Salter gave this account of a follow-up interview with two special agents:

> There was now, they said, considerable doubt that the police who had struck me and who had struck the others could be conclusively identified. I pointed out that every major television network had carried film sequences of my beating, at least, if not the other incidents, and that the faces of the police involved were clearly seen. They shrugged and indicated that there would still be difficulty.

The FBI described Salter as "a chronic complainant," a "determined, belligerent, and confused young man . . . [who] obviously does not like the FBI, having without a doubt been influenced by the writings of LOWENTHAL"—referring to the only critical book on the FBI written during the depths of the domestic cold war.[97]

"The FBI," maverick journalist I. F. Stone charged at the time of Medgar Evers's death, "lives in cordial fraternity with the cops that enforce white supremacy." To a degree, this charge was also true in Birmingham during the mass demonstrations of April and May organized by the Southern Christian Leadership Conference.[98] Hoover's men telephoned reports to the police, including details about the planned march and the distribution of leaflets in the Birmingham schools.[99] Bureau officials in Washington kept the White House posted. As the FBI disseminated intelligence, Commissioner Connor hooked up fire hoses and uncaged police dogs—a brutal repression of the schoolchildren that Dr. King had put on the front line. It proved to be a strategic blunder for Connor however. "There were times," Bayard Rustin remembered, "when we didn't have to be supreme strategists. Bull Connor helped us."[100]

With the September 15 bombing of Birmingham's Sixteenth Street Baptist Church, the FBI had the opportunity to do much more than observe demonstrations and send memos off to the local police or to the White House. This was the twenty-first bombing attack against blacks in Birmingham (Bombingham, as it came to be called) during the previous eight years, and it left four girls—Carole Robertson, Denise McNair, Addie Mae Collins, and Cynthia Wesley, ages eleven to fourteen—dead. The first twenty bombing incidents had gone unsolved, and the FBI admitted (privately) that its record "in bombing cases is not good."[101] The city established a reward fund to help solve the twenty-first crime, but one person sent in a few green stamps and a facsimile of an old $100 confederate bond as a contribution to the fund.[102]

FBI agents immediately opened a full-scale investigation captioned BAPBOMB. "It is one thing to explode dynamite outside a house or in an empty building, with the aim of scaring Negroes and integrationists," as one Bureau executive noted, "but it is quite another thing to take the lives of innocent children."[103] The investigation, nonetheless, included questionable decision making by the director. The Bureau wasted time pursuing a wild and completely unfounded rumor about a liaison between a police detective and a female Klan informant; supposedly this had prevented the police from learning about the bomb in time to clear the church. There was an even wilder rumor "as to the possible involvement of members of the Nation of Islam (NOI) in the bombings." The Bureau looked into "all angles," including what Georgia Senator Richard Russell described in a conversation with Cartha DeLoach as the "possibility . . . that Negroes might have perpetrated this incident . . . to keep emotions at a fever pitch."[104]

Hoover's refusal to disrupt his surveillance network in Alabama or to subject his bureaucracy to any possibility of "embarrassment" also hindred the pursuit of justice in the BAPBOMB case. Some of the informant reports Hoover ignored, for example, involved Gary Rowe, the FBI veteran from the Freedom Ride episode at the Birmingham bus station and still the Bureau's number-one informant in Eastview Klavern 13. Another informant, John Wesley Hall, named Rowe as a member of a three-man Klan security committee that held veto power over all proposed acts of violence; this raised the possibility that Rowe might have been involved in the Baptist Church bombing. In fact, the Birmingham police considered Rowe a prime suspect. But the FBI did not investigate. Hall, who went by the nickname of "Nigger," went on the Bureau payroll two months *after* the explosion despite a polygraph test that convinced FBI agents in Alabama that he had been involved in the crime. Hall also admitted having moved some dynamite for the principal BAPBOMB suspect, Robert E. ("Dynamite Bob") Chambliss, a fifty-nine-year-old truck driver for an auto parts company who had joined the Ku Klux Klan in 1924. Two weeks after the bomb exploded on Sixteenth Street, the Birmingham Recorder's Court sentenced Chambliss, Hall, and another suspect, Charles Arnie Cagle, on a misdemeanor charge—possession of an explosive without a permit.[105]

FBI officials devoted substantial resources to the BAPBOMB investigation. They sent Little Rock SAC Roy K. Moore and other top troubleshooters to Birmingham, and assigned as many as 231 agents to the case at a single time—including two men from the FBI lab who flew down on board a military jet from Andrews Air Force Base, accompanied by Burke Marshall. (When the director found out how his lab men got to the scene so quickly, he penned the following order: "hereafter commercial aircraft should be used if available.") Because no indictments followed, it looked like the Bureau had failed, and John Kennedy and then Lyndon Johnson constantly pressured Hoover to do more.[106] With Johnson still reminding him some seven months after the tragedy to leave no stone unturned, the director told the president that everything that could be done had been done, and every known investigative technique (polygraphs, "constant harassment," and at least seventeen microphone surveillances) had been employed.[107]

Hoover was not as enthusiastic about the case as he seemed when speaking with John Kennedy or Lyndon Johnson. He would not proceed until his agents had built an airtight case, and he would not allow Justice Department access to the potentially embarrassing informant files. On more than one occasion he rebuffed the agents in Birmingham who told him they had a good but not conclusive case. They said the government had to move against the principal suspects anyway, playing off their fears until one of them cracked and talked. Hoover would say no, don't present this or that piece of evidence, don't meet with the lawyers, don't give Justice any "details." "We must not give a 'blow-by-blow' account" to the Civil Rights Division, he reasoned, "because it will appear in the Star or Sat. Evening Post." Ironically, Bureau officials limited their own contacts with the media about BAPBOMB to the argument "that primary jurisdiction" in all bombing cases should remain "at the local level." DeLoach claimed to have arranged stories making this point through his high-level contacts at the Copley and Hearst newspaper chains, and through his "sources on the working level at the Washington Post and . . . the [New York] 'Daily News.'"[108]

Hoover's reading of white Alabaman public opinion shaped his course in Birmingham. Believing the chance of conviction remote, he refused to listen to his own agents who saw a "climate of public opinion favoring prosecution." More interested in assigning blame than taking a tough case to court, the director tried to explain why BAPBOMB had not been cracked even though the FBI knew who was responsible—a small group of ambitious Klansmen and ex-Klansmen who broke away from Birmingham's Eastview 13 Klavern to form a tight cell known as the Cahaba River Group. When the Alabama Highway Patrol arrested three suspects from this group on September 30, including Chambliss and Hall, Hoover told Robert Kennedy that the troopers had acted prematurely. "They have certainly 'flushed' the case and I doubt that they will be able to hold these two men."[109] He was particularly upset with the state police because Robert Shelton and two other Klan leaders had been riding around in a patrol car, helping the troopers finger the renegade "Chambliss crowd" and thus scoop the Bureau. "We had been putting tremendous pressure on," one of the director's aides noted, and "obviously the word got back to Shelton's crowd and they apparently felt they had to jump in." Indeed, immediately after the arrests Governor Wallace announced: "We certainly beat the Kennedy crowd to the punch!"[110]

Nevertheless, Hoover wrote to Robert Kennedy that the "Negro elements" were the real villains. Their constant carping about the cozy relationship between the G-men and segregation-ist law enforcement officers in the South had forced the FBI, "over the last year," to refrain "from close contacts or connec-tion with the local authorities." Now "a gulf" had emerged that prevented the cracking of BAPBOMB and the "Negro elements" were to blame. Courtney Evans delivered the document contain-ing this explanation to Kennedy personally, going over every line and adding one additional comment: "If we sent our Negro Agents to the South, the situation would be even worse." Having battled with Hoover over civil rights matters for two and a half years, Kennedy lacked the stomach for another fight. He lis-tened to every word Evans spoke and "only remarked 'Yeah.'"[111]

The state of Alabama finally indicted Chambliss twelve years later. President Jimmy Carter's Justice Department concluded that the trial jury that convicted the seventy-three-year-old Chambliss for the murder of eleven-year-old Denise McNair "heard less direct evidence than was available to Mr. Hoover in 1964, when the Director ruled against prosecution." State Attor-ney General Bill Baxley considered this assessment too harsh, and his chief investigator, Bob Eddy, agreed—even though the director refused to make the BAPBOMB file available in 1971 when the state first started pushing for an indictment. "I wouldn't say Hoover blocked it," Eddy reasoned. "He did turn down the FBI Birmingham request to pursue the case with an indictment. But he pursued the case. He was looking for more evidence and it turned out they never did get any more."[112] Through it all, Hoover focused on his bureaucratic and political interests, and he appeared more interested in indicting the "Ne-gro elements" than convicting Chambliss and the other white men who killed the four little girls.

By pursuing justice in its own way, whether in the Medgar Evers murder or the Sixteenth Street Baptist Church bombing, the FBI contributed to the growing polarization between civil rights activists and the federal government. The movement con-tinued to perceive the Bureau as indifferent to everyday civil rights violations in the South and strangely incompetent even when investigating the big cases—the kind that "so shock the conscience."[113] No single event turned the movement's young people against their most potentially valuable ally, the federal government. Rather, it was a series of events and consequences shaped in part by FBI actions and value preferences from the first days of the voter registration campaign to the Birmingham horror. But those young activists largely directed their rage toward Hoover's boss. There were people in the civil rights movement, Arthur Schlesinger wrote, "who regarded the Attorney General as the devil incarnate."[114]

Jack Newfield, who had grown up in Bedford-Stuyvesant, helped organize SDS, joined SNCC, and went to Mississippi, where he had been jailed twice in civil rights demonstrations, explained this sentiment. "As civil rights activists in 1963 we liked Kennedy as little as the Southern Governors did. We saw him recommend Harold Cox, James Eastland's college roommate, to be a judge in the Fifth District Court [sic], where he was to call Negro defendants 'chimpanzees' from the bench. . . . We saw Negroes trying to register to vote in Greenwood, Mississippi, urinated upon by a white farmer, while lawyers from the Justice Department calmly took notes destined to be filed and forgotten. We agreed with James Baldwin, who pronounced Kennedy, after their stormy confrontation, 'insensitive and unresponsive to the Negro's torment.'"[115] All of Newfield's examples involved the FBI. The Bureau never made on-the-spot arrests of men like the Greenwood farmer, never investigated the charges of a James Baldwin when Baldwin himself could be more easily investigated, and never paid much attention to the segregationist history of any nominee to the federal bench.[116]

If one single event made things clear to the movement, it was Robert Kennedy's decision, and the FBI's enthusiastic response, to prosecute a group of civil rights activists while continuing to uphold the Bureau's noninterventionist policy with regard to the people terrorizing those activists.[117] That August 9, 1963, action grew out of the so-called Albany Movement. In October 1961 SNCC's Charles Sherrod and Cordell Reagon opened an office in Albany, Georgia, a black-belt city in the southwestern part of the state not far from Plains, and tried, with mixed success, to forge alliances with CORE, SCLC, and the NAACP. They also recruited students from Albany State College and area high schools, including Albany High—where Hamilton Jordan, the future chief of staff of the Carter White House, presided over the student body. In December 1961 SNCC sent eight Freedom Riders from Atlanta (among them future SDS activist Tom Hayden) to test the ICC order that had desegregated train facilities and the waiting room at the terminal. When they moved onto Roosevelt Avenue to demonstrate, the police arrested all eight, plus SNCC worker Charles Jones and two city residents who had come to

greet them. Civil disobedience in Albany then became as common as peanuts. This began the Albany Movement, the first city-
wide campaign of civil disobedience to force enfranchisement
and the integration of all public facilities.

The Albany Movement was unpopular among white city residents for the usual reasons, and it did not become any more popular when SNCC began bringing in "white girls" to help. Marion
Cheek, the FBI's resident agent, remembered a scene in a nearby
town. "Huggin' and kissin' in Americus' court house lobby,
black boys and white girls ... that went over like a lead bal-
loon." This also made the white people of Albany and environs
more tolerant of the city's mass arrest tactics. On December 12,
the police locked up 265 demonstrators. By December 16 they
booked and transported to neighboring city and county jails a
total of 735 people. By October 1962 the police made another
600 arrests, including Albany Movement organizers William G.
Anderson and Slater King and SCLC leaders Martin Luther King
and Ralph Abernathy. The cash and security bond approached
$400,000.[118]

The initial focus of attention in southwest Georgia was not
on the FBI and its director but on Albany Police Chief Laurie
Pritchett, who responded to the nonviolent civil rights movement with a "nonviolent movement by the Albany Police Department"—on the grounds that the city "can't tolerate the
N.A.A.C.P. . . . or any other nigger organization to take over this
town with mass demonstrations." To find out what the Albany
Movement was up to, Pritchett stationed his officers inside the
black churches that served as meeting places and solicited tape
recordings from newsmen who attended the meetings. He had
other sources as well, mostly black adults who passed on what
they had heard from their teenage children. At least two of his
contacts, NAACP member E. D. Hamilton and Albany Movement
secretary Marion Page, also kept in touch with the FBI. With
Albany jails filled beyond capacity, however, Pritchett had to
ship hundreds of demonstrators to neighboring jails where the
police had more faith in night sticks than a "nonviolent movement" of informants and undercover cops.[119]

Not even the most disturbing incidents of brutality unduly
troubled the FBI. Perhaps the worst single incident involved
Slater King's wife, Marion. When she took food and clothing to
a group of demonstrators held in the Mitchell County Jail in
nearby Camilla, the sheriff and his deputy greeted her, seven

months pregnant with a one-year-old in her arms, a three-year-old held by the hand, and her third child looking on, by knocking her to the ground and kicking her. Later, when investigating the officer to determine whether he had violated Mrs. King's civil rights by assaulting her, the FBI said Slater King "abused" the agent assigned to the case "and 'damned' [the] Federal government." A month later, Mrs. King suffered a stillbirth.[120]

There were other incidents—Dougherty County Sheriff Cull Campbell caned Slater King's brother, the attorney C. B. King—but Laurie Pritchett outmaneuvered the Albany Movement activists. "We were naive," SNCC worker Bill Hansen concluded. "[We thought] we could fill up the jails . . . we ran out of people before [the chief] ran out of jails." Unlike Birmingham and Montgomery, there were no roving bands of Klansmen carrying baseball bats, and most of the overt police brutality took place beyond the Albany city limits. President Kennedy saw no need to send marshals or troops to counter the "Nazi-like forces" about which the SNCC people were complaining. Besides, "SNCC has got an investment in violence. They're sons of bitches," the president said. Pritchett, in contrast, had his men under control, and his relationship with the FBI was good. "They cooperated with us one hundred percent." Claude Sitton of the *New York Times,* an Atlanta native and one of the most knowledgeable reporters assigned to the movement beat, said FBI agents needed the cooperation of Pritchett's men to solve stolen car cases and apprehend fugitives, so "they worked hand in glove with the local police and the local police were trying to destroy the civil rights movement."[121]

Albany Movement activists reported the assaults on Marion King and C. B. King to the FBI and the Justice Department. The FBI investigated. Nothing happened. There was simply not enough evidence, the Department said, to prove a federal case. When Vincent Harding, a deeply religious activist, led a group to city hall to pray for Slater King's wife, Pritchett told the group to move on. Harding and his people said they had a right to be there. They kept coming back, until the police arrested them just before midnight and charged them with refusing to obey an officer and blocking the sidewalk. The Albany Movement again reported the details of these arrests, along with dozens of other cases and signed statements by the people who claimed their civil rights had been violated. Again, nothing happened. The complaints always filtered through the Bureau's resident agent, Marion Cheek. The Albany FBI office always described its relationship with the local police as excellent. Responsible Bureau executives always said they were investigating. The Department always said there was not enough evidence to file under the civil rights statutes.

Albany Movement activists never had any confidence in the FBI; but they did have hope that the Justice Department would finally intervene. C. B. King remembered his attempt to convince Burke Marshall to do something. "I had worn his patience a little bit. And he said, 'Mr. King, you talk like these people are communists or affirmed criminals.' . . . I reminded him that it wouldn't make a damn bit of difference to me in terms of the bludgeoning quality of the blow that struck me on my head, whether it was a damn communist or whether it was a damn good sheriff." The meeting itself "was a rather tragic commentary," King thought, reflecting the Albany Movement's gradual erosion of confidence in the Justice Department. Marshall had adopted a "kind of milk-toast position . . . and it was quite distressing." All the federal government had to offer was the FBI, King concluded, an agency most proficient at demonstrating "empathy for . . . the white, hostile community."[122]

FBI agents who worked in Albany in those times had a different perspective, arguing that the broader problem of public opinion among whites in southwest Georgia prevented law enforcement in civil rights cases. "We solved every church burning, every house shooting, every attempt to interfere with voting rights," Marion Cheek claimed. "I didn't work a single criminal case for eighteen months. I worked 7 A.M. to midnight seven days a week . . . I was on the phone to Washington four times a day and I rolled out of bed many a morning to investigate a civil rights case. We brought in stenos, clerks, and everything else— we took over a motel, we handled the whole thing as a special. But we couldn't get a grand jury indictment even with a signed confession. We lost every case over a two and a half year period."[123] There was some truth in what Cheek said, but such efforts remained invisible to the black community, civil rights leaders like Martin Luther King, and newsmen like Claude Sitton. Those who came to Albany with sympathy for the black struggle carried away no memory of the things Cheek spoke of. Instead, they formed a clear image of the close relationship between Hoover's agents and Pritchett's officers.

One of the lost cases Cheek mentioned led directly to the indictment of the Albany Nine. The case, which involved the FBI only briefly, concerned L. Warren ("Gator") Johnson, sheriff of Baker County. Johnson had pistol-whipped the pregnant wife of a black man, Charley Ware, then beat Ware, handcuffed him, and shot him three times in the neck. Miraculously, Ware lived. "Gator walked scot free," Cheek recalled. A powerful man in southwest Georgia, "he was strong enough to keep the state patrol out of his county. . . . They were afraid of him. Johnson was crazy. He'd kill you and get away with it down there." Later, Johnson walked free from a subsequent civil action in federal court. In the aftermath, one of his jurors, Carl Smith, the owner of a foodmarket in the Harlem section of Albany, claimed the Albany Movement picketed his store as punishment for his vote. Smith was "a cool, clever individual who got rich selling to blacks" (Cheek's description), and the movement had put similar pressure on other Albany business owners to force them to change their hiring and promotion practices. No picket sign made reference to Johnson's trial, and the picketing itself lasted about an hour on the morning of April 20, 1963. Pritchett's men arrested several pickets; the line broke up and never reorganized. On April 22 Smith announced that he would close his store permanently. "The last day Carl Smith was in business he took in $9," said Cheek.[124]

Albany Mayor Asa D. Kelley, Jr., a racial moderate by southwest Georgia standards, called for a federal investigation, and J. Edgar Hoover and Robert Kennedy responded. A grand jury convened in Macon and summoned fifty-eight blacks to testify. "Marion Cheek issued everybody in the neighborhood a subpoena," recalled Robert Thomas, who had only passed by the pickets and waved on his way to work at the Harlem Barbershop. At first, almost everyone assumed the FBI had finally gathered enough information to seek the indictments of the officers who beat Marion King and C. B. King and deprived hundreds of others of their constitutional rights. Instead, the grand jury indicted three movement people for conspiring to obstruct justice (that is, for conspiring to injure a juror) and six for perjury, including Robert Thomas, Slater King, and Joni Rabinowitz. A student doing voter registration work in Albany in partial fulfillment of an Antioch College work-study assignment, Rabinowitz denied she was at the store, denied she saw the picketing, denied she knew about the picketing. The result: a three-count perjury indictment. "Marion was the one who got on the stand and lied

about Joni," C. B. King charged. "A vicious guy, really vicious."
Robert Kennedy, however, said the grand jury's proceedings
were "fair and reasonable throughout . . . a completely nonpref-
erential exercise of Federal responsibility."[125]

Not surprisingly, Albany Movement activists, city police, and
Hoover's agents all saw things clearly, each in their own way.
A police officer told one Albany veteran, "Now that the federal
government is going to put the Movement's ass in jail, we will
put your ass in too, if you don't stay off the street." C. B. King
remembered "a rather elderly Negro woman" telling him, "You
know what, lawyer, the Federal government ain't nothing but
a white man." Attorney William M. Kunstler called the Albany
prosecutions "a bone thrown" by the Kennedys "to the segregationists," and the National Committee for the Albany Defendants published an aptly titled pamphlet, *Upside-Down Justice*.
Martin Luther King served as honorary chairman of this Committee and two reputed communist sympathizers, Carl and Anne
Braden, helped write the pamphlet. In response, the FBI dusted
off HUAC's old characterization of the Bradens' group, the
Southern Conference Educational Fund, and dismissed the Albany Movement's concerns out of hand. "Criticism of the F.B.I.
is typical of communist propaganda attacks." Cartha DeLoach
attempted to contact Dr. King in order to tell him "the true
facts," but never could arrange a meeting. So he did the next
best thing. He contacted the publishers of the *Chicago Defender*
and other black-owned newspapers that carried "King's lies,"
and told Hoover he had "set [them] straight."[126]

Movement people in Albany and beyond criticized the FBI's
law enforcement priorities. "At least thirty-eight" FBI agents
worked on the Albany Nine prosecutions, according to U. S. Attorney Floyd Buford's estimate. C. B. King's estimate was considerably higher. "The Justice Department sent eighty-six FBI
agents in here to investigate that case. They were thick as hogs."
When the police knocked down Marion King, in contrast, the
only Bureau agent in sight melted "right in with the total white-
ness of the community." One of the few other arrests the FBI
made was when a white man attacked an agent near the site of
a burned-out church.[127]

The Albany Movement did not know that the FBI intercepted
two telephone calls placed by New York attorney Victor Rabinowitz to C. B. King one week after the grand jury handed down
the indictments. Rabinowitz wanted to discuss strategies for

having the charges against his daughter and the others withdrawn by the Justice Department.[128] Movement activists suspected that the government engaged in electronic snooping, a suspicion seemingly confirmed by their own "informants" within the telephone companies—that is, sympathetic phone company workers. But at the time the charge sounded like so much conspiracy fodder. "I hate this about Robert Kennedy," Slater King said. "We knew our phones were tapped by the Federal government, that he was a pretty vindictive guy and he damn sure meant to get even with us. . . . It also happened that Victor Rabinowitz's daughter [was indicted]. . . . Victor represents Cuba, Algeria. I think that [Victor] had beat [Robert] on several cases. . . . I think that [Kennedy] wanted to tie us all together."[129]

Attorney General Kennedy was probably aware of the wiretap, and he was almost certainly aware of the FBI effort to extend the Albany Nine prosecutions. "They tried to get me too," Charles Sherrod recalled. "Once I was sick in my bed and old Cheek came in there, in the house there, and told me I had to get up because I was impeding justice." Harvard Law student Elizabeth Holtzman, later United States representative from New York and Brooklyn district attorney, was nearly the eleventh person indicted, according to Cheek. "She sat in C. B. King's office and told them what to tell the grand jury," he claimed. "We tried to indict her for subornation of perjury. We weren't allowed to. The Justice Department wouldn't allow it. The reins were pulled in."[130]

Hoover acted in Albany as an enemy of the civil rights movement; Robert Kennedy acted as a lawyer and as a politician—as the attorney general of the United States and as a member of his brother's administration. Robert and John Kennedy did not believe they could ignore political reality as they saw it. Early in Robert's tenure, as biographer Arthur Schlesinger wrote, "he saw civil rights . . . as an issue in the middle distance, morally invincible but filled for the moment with operational difficulty." That operational difficulty never quite faded, even in the summer of 1963, so the attorney general continued to speak the language of federalism whenever it was convenient. The last thing the Kennedy brothers wanted to do was alienate the white South. "The Justice Department," to quote Roger Wilkins, "wasn't trusted in the civil-rights community. It had too often seemed an impartial arbiter between two equally valid compet-

ing views in the South when the basic civil-rights assumption
was that we were right and the Southern bigots were wrong."[131]

Hoover contributed to the Kennedys' mixed record. The
Kennedy brothers stood with the movement. They made substantive contributions to the struggle for black equality, and on
the whole John Kennedy's presidency was an activist one in civil
rights matters. Caution and inaction on protecting activists
must be balanced by the record of executive actions, the introduction of the civil rights bill of 1963, and the voting litigation
suits.[132] But the Kennedys were active on another civil rights
front, spying on the movement through the FBI. They accepted
Hoover's domestic intelligence services as an inevitable part of
the governing process, and they tried to sweep away operational
difficulties in civil rights by turning to the FBI director, by selecting his intelligence services as the best available means of
"protecting" civil rights workers.

Robert Kennedy and the people who worked in his Justice Department, from John Doar to Burke Marshall, agreed with Hoover on one point: namely, the need to limit somehow or direct
the struggle for black equality. They viewed the FBI's domestic
intelligence services as inherently useful, something that might
help with the complex task of managing the civil rights movement. "When you say John and Burke did it for the noblest of
reasons, I don't agree with that," Wilkins added. "They wanted
to know ahead of time so they could do the things the government wanted to do . . . Burke and Bobby and those guys didn't
want the movement to be as aggressive as it was in the early
days. John and those guys, Burke and those guys, they were for
civil rights . . . but they wanted it on their terms, on their timetable, to their end, their agenda." "The Kennedys were tough
people," affirmed former Civil Rights Commission attorney Arnold Trebach. "They wanted to do it their way."[133]

The Kennedy way included tolerance of the FBI's ways. Responsible government officials went along with Hoover's notion
that the Bureau did not have the necessary authority to protect
civil rights workers, while encouraging the director to conduct
widespread surveillance (which he was disposed to do). The New
Frontier reformers who debated the constitutionality of federal
protection never considered the constitutionality of federal surveillance. In retrospect, it seems surprising that movement
people did not forcefully challenge these assumptions and priorities at the time. The idea of civil liberties, to quote Andrew

Young once more, "seemed a tertiary consideration." The movement itself, along with the movement's friends in the White House and the Justice Department, made it easier for FBI officials to operate on their own terms, on their own timetable, to their own end, their own agenda—even before Hoover's bureaucracy moved beyond the skirmishes of the first two Kennedy years to destroy the movement's most charismatic leader, before the movement itself turned left and the government right during the Vietnam peace demonstrations and the riots of the late 1960s.

Black Dream, Red Menace

The Pursuit of Martin Luther King, Jr.

Nineteen days after the grand jury handed down the Albany indictments, on August 28, 1963, J. Edgar Hoover and the Kennedys turned their attention to Martin Luther King, Jr., and the 200,000 Americans, black and white, who had gathered around the Lincoln Memorial on the mall in the nation's capital. The civil rights movement came to participate in the March on Washington, the largest of the civil rights demonstrations of the summer of 1963. They came to demand justice, to hold hands and sing freedom songs, to pressure Congress on the Kennedy administration's civil rights bill, and to listen to Dr. King talk about a dream "deeply rooted in the American dream."

> I have a dream that one day, down in Alabama, with its vicious racists, with its governor having his lips dripping with the words of interposition and nullification, one day, right there in Alabama, little black boys and black girls will be able to join hands with little white boys and white girls as sisters and brothers. . . .
> When we allow freedom to ring, when we let it ring from every village and every hamlet, from every state and every city, we will be able to speed up that day when all of God's children—black men and white men, Jews and Gentiles, Protestants and Catholics—will be able to join hands and sing in the words of the old Negro spiritual, "Free at last, free at last; thank God Almighty, we are free at last."

FBI agents and informants were on hand to observe the great majority of the civil rights movement seize the moment to dream King's dream, but even within the movement there was more than a little ambivalence. The radicals wondered if the Kennedys had co-opted the "Farce on Washington," as Malcolm X called the March. Based on "a body of experience" that "definitely" included encounters with Hoover's FBI during the past two years, SNCC chairman John Lewis wanted to tell the crowd wading among the lily pads in the Washington Monument reflection pool not to "support the Administration's civil rights bill. . . . There's not one thing in the bill that will protect our people from police brutality." But Burke Marshall talked to UAW chief Walter Reuther, and Reuther, among others, including Washington's Archbishop Patrick O'Boyle, and King himself, convinced Lewis to tone it down. "Two Kennedy aides stood ready to pull the plug on the public address system in case anything went amiss," and Lee White said the administration "had troops all over," stationed in "places where they could get here" quickly in the event more serious problems developed. Some of the people on the mall that day would have preferred the original version of Lewis's text. As King delivered his own speech, one black man kept shouting, "Fuck that dream, Martin. Now, goddamit, NOW!" Even at its most optimistic moment the movement still wondered, to use Lewis's unspoken words, "which side is the federal government on?"[1]

The March on Washington convinced Hoover that the civil rights movement would not wither away on its own, that he would have to smash it before it irreparably damaged his America. Before the summer of 1963 ended, the FBI began to transform what had been a holding action against black demands for justice and equality into a frontal assault on Dr. King and the movement he helped lead. By FBI standards, it was a conventional war. "The director fell back on the cry that had never failed him in the past," Arthur Schlesinger wrote: "The ineluctable threat, evidently undiminished despite all his effort, of Communist infiltration into American institutions." After the March on Washington, FBI officials devoted as much time and energy to the communists-in-the-civil-rights-movement issue as they had once devoted to "the cause"—that is, the McCarthy-era purge of communists and other dissidents from the government and the professions.[2] The director had spent his life destroying communists and their causes, and now he would try to destroy King and his cause.

Hoover's decision in August 1963 caught even his closest aides by surprise. The director saw communism as "secularism on the march," but few of his executives could detect this secularist advance, since Martin Luther King and other black Baptist churchmen were among the primary organizers of the civil rights movement. Ever since the sit-ins began in February 1960, the FBI had been predicting a revival of communist activity in the southern black belt.[3] But it never came. When Bull Connor and King faced off in Birmingham, the local FBI office informed the seat of government that no "CP activity" could be found "in connection with these demonstrations and no Communists are known to be participating." Even Hoover's public pronouncements lacked their old ring of conviction: all he could say was that the party merely attempted to infiltrate "the legitimate Negro organizations for the purpose of stepping up racial prejudice and hatred."[4]

The dearth of communists simply encouraged FBI officials to look harder. On the eve of the March on Washington, a headquarters directive advised twenty-seven field offices to "be extremely alert to data indicating interest, plans, or actual involvement of the [Communist] Party in the current Negro movement." And the FBI devoted its entire Current Intelligence Analysis of August 21 "to the communist plans for the Negro March," distributing at least 149 copies to forty-four government agencies.[5] Other agents searched the files for "subversive data" on March leadership and filed reports with the Civil Rights Division. In one case, a wiretap revealed "extensive contact" between black Communist party functionary Ben Davis and Bayard Rustin, the organizing genius behind the March and longtime associate of A. Philip Randolph. The New York office proposed to mark Davis as an informant. Educated at Amherst and Harvard Law School, Davis had worked for the party since the 1930s, when he served as an attorney in the Angelo Herndon case; in the summer of 1963 he was dying of cancer.[6] While headquarters considered Rustin's associations and the New York proposal, other field offices forwarded reports on more obscure March participants. San Francisco reported that Vivian Hallinan, the wife of the Progressive party's presidential candidate in 1952, Vincent Hallinan, planned to bring her six sons to Washington. "All of the

Hallinans," Burke Marshall learned, "have been active in communist party front and civil rights affairs." The FBI opened a new file, captioned Communist Influence Racial Matters (CIRM), for all the inbound information.[7]

While the field filed its reports, Hoover requested a general summary of communist attempts to infiltrate the civil rights movement, assigning the task to the Domestic Intelligence Division (Division Five). On August 23, five days before the March on Washington, the Division submitted a sixty-eight page brief that minimized the Red menace. Communist efforts to infiltrate such groups as the NAACP and SCLC had been "limited," at best, while most "other legitimate . . . organizations in the Negro, civil rights and integration fields," including CORE, SNCC, and the National Urban League, merely provided inviting, "ready-made targets" for communist infiltrators. According to FBI informants in New York, however, many party members did not even try to infiltrate CORE. They did not want "to harm CORE's work." If they stayed away, perhaps the Red-baiters and spies would leave CORE alone. In those few cases where the party had succeeded in its infiltration schemes, Division Five concluded, the civil rights groups generally policed themselves.[8]

The closest thing to a Communist party front in the civil rights field, the Southern Conference Educational Fund (SCEF), was active, by the Division Five estimate, in "raising bail funds for those arrested in connection with integration activities, sending food and other relief shipments to depressed southern Negro areas and holding conferences." Of the eleven SCEF officers, the FBI *suspected* only three "of being CP members." An informant identified Carl and Anne Braden as communists back in 1954, and another "source reported that in the past he has considered James Dombrowski . . . to be a communist, if not actually a CP member, because he followed communist principles." The standard Bureau description of the Bradens' and Dombrowski's group was just as thin. "The source stated SCEF is a progressive, liberal organization which he considers a CP front . . . because it has gone along with the CP on certain issues, particularly the racial issue." Division Five was not even sure about its own best case.[9]

Neither the Communist party's efforts nor its record of failure surprised Hoover's aides in Division Five. "Control of the Negro population in this country" simply represented a logical goal "tied to the dictates of the Soviet Union and not . . . any benevolent or altruistic principles." No matter how troubling in a theoretical sense, in the real world communist ideology guaranteed the party's inability "to appreciably infiltrate, influence or control large numbers of American Negroes." "The CP does not seem to understand," Division Five concluded, "that its failure can be attributed to its adherence to Marxism-Leninism. The Party views the struggle for equal rights as part of the Marxist concept of the never-ending class struggle and not, as most Negroes see it, an attempt to solve a racial issue. Thus, the Party would involve the Negro in a much broader struggle than the already titanic one in which he is now engaged." Perhaps if America's Reds had stopped being Reds, Division Five seemed to be saying, they would have had a better chance.[10]

Although Division Five qualified the report before sending it on to Hoover, its conclusion was unambiguous—given the FBI's unwritten rule that it was far more important not to be wrong than it was to be right. "We are right now in this Nation involved in a form of racial revolution," FBI executive Fred J. Baumgardner advised the assistant director in charge of the Domestic Intelligence Division, William C. Sullivan, "and the time has never been so right for exploitation of the Negroes by communist propagandists. The Communist Party in the next five years may fail dismally with the American Negro as it has in the past. On the other hand, it may make prodigious strides and great successes with the American Negroes, to the serious detriment of our national security. Time alone will tell." In the meantime, the communist menace merited little attention.[11]

When Hoover read the report of August 23 he rejected its premise (that communist influence was "infinitesimal") and lectured Division Five chief William Sullivan. "This memo reminds me vividly of those I received when Castro took over Cuba. You contended then that Castro and his cohorts were not Communists and not influenced by Communists. Time alone proved you wrong." The report, Sullivan remembered, "set me at odds with Hoover. . . . A few months went by before he would speak to me. Everything was conducted by exchange of written communications. It was evident that we had to change our ways or we would all be out on the street." When the director began scribbling sarcastic notes on routine Division Five memos, Sullivan's agents "discussed how to get out of trouble. To be in trouble with Mr. Hoover was a serious matter. These men were trying to buy homes, mortgages on homes, children in school. They lived in fear of getting transferred." The Division had to give Hoover what he wanted, or risk the consequences.[12]

William Sullivan had the most to lose. It had taken him twenty years in the FBI to rise to the rank of assistant director for Domestic Intelligence, an appointment he received in 1961, a mere two years before the March on Washington. An odd creature in Hoover's FBI, Sullivan was certainly the oddest of "the Gandy dancers," as field agents referred to the director's immediate circle of aides in honor of Helen Gandy—"a wraithlike, grim-faced spinster from New Jersey who . . . was Hoover's secretary and administrative assistant from the day of his appointment until the day of his death." A farm boy from New England and a former school teacher whose management style matched the wrinkled suits and spotted ties he wore, Sullivan was always misplacing things, whether a pen or a classified file or his own train of thought, and always losing control of his terrible temper. When not berating his colleagues, he liked to describe himself as "a lifelong Democrat," probably the only FBI executive who voted for John Kennedy and not Richard Nixon. Known inside the Bureau as the house intellectual, Sullivan buried his nose in a book at every opportunity, reading most everything from Marx's *Kapital* to Schlesinger's *Age of Jackson*. He rubbed elbows at cocktail parties with Henry Kissinger, then a Harvard professor, and lectured three years running at the Harvard Graduate School of Business Administration. Whenever he wanted to flatter Hoover, he compared him to German Chancellor Konrad Adenauer or French President Charles de Gaulle.[13]

In no position to challenge the director, Sullivan submitted Division Five's apology on August 30: "The Director is correct. We were completely wrong . . . the Communist Party, USA, does wield substantial influence over Negroes which one day could become decisive." He discussed King's "I Have a Dream" speech, labeling it "demagogic," and marked King "as the most dangerous Negro leader of the future in this Nation from the standpoint of communism, the Negro and national security." To meet the threat, the FBI must concentrate on "the many Negroes who are fellow-travellers, sympathizers or who aid the Party, knowingly or unknowingly, but do not qualify as members." It would "be unrealistic to limit ourselves as we have been doing to legalistic proofs or definitely conclusive evidence that would stand up in court or before Congressional Committees."[14]

A few weeks after the March on Washington, on September

16, Division Five again recommended "increased coverage of communist influence on the Negro," stressing the "urgent need" to use "all possible investigative techniques." Hoover responded with more sarcasm. "No. I can't understand how you can so agilely switch your thinking and evaluation. Just a few weeks ago you contended that the Communist influence in the racial movement was ineffective. . . . Now you want to load the Field down with more coverage." Sullivan thought the director was "egging us on." After returning from a brief vacation, he made another attempt to repair the breach. "As we know, facts by themselves are not too meaningful. . . . It is obvious that we did not put the proper interpretation upon the facts." Division Five had always been "in complete agreement with the Director," particularly with regard to Dr. King, "the most dangerous and effective Negro leader in the country." Sullivan resubmitted his proposal for an escalation of "our coverage of communist influence on the Negro," the CPUSA's "favorite target."[15] Explaining this reversal years later as "a lot of nonsense which we ourselves did not believe in," he said he instructed his aides to "state the facts just as they are and then let the storm break," knowing full well that Hoover believed the civil rights movement was riddled with Reds and thus would be enraged by the Division Five conclusions.[16]

In Hoover's FBI orthodoxy on matters of policy was sacred. If Sullivan understood this simple fact better than most of the men who became special agents, he did not realize, at the time Division Five prepared the August 23 report, that Hoover was reevaluating previous policy, and that the March on Washington itself would convince him to make the change.[17] "The FBI saw the march, in a sense, as far more important than we did," said Bayard Rustin. "The March terrified them. People in the Congress and the White House were beginning to change their attitude toward us."[18] The movement's explosive growth convinced Hoover that he could no longer contain it through a noninterventionist policy on the law-enforcement front or a relatively passive surveillance policy on the intelligence front. The tactic now would be all-out surveillance (that is, counterintelligence) based on the ongoing operations aimed at the Communist party—specifically, the COMINFIL (communist infiltration) and COINTELPRO (counterintelligence) programs designed to "expose, disrupt, or otherwise neutralize" party members.

The original Division Five report and accompanying memo of

August 23 represented a rational attempt to explain the CPUSA's utter irrelevance to the civil rights movement. That position had been FBI policy, more or less, since the Second World War, and the Division had stated it in similar language on numerous occasions during the 1950s and early 1960s, notably in two monographs on "the Communist party and the Negro" and in a counterintelligence program "idea book." The latter, entitled "Current Weaknesses of the Communist Party, USA," included three sections on the party's *incompetence* in the racial field and recommended counterintelligence actions designed to exploit the party's *"self-defeating policies relative to the Negroes* [emphasis added]." If Hoover never agreed with Division Five conclusions on a personal level, he accepted them as policy. He even approved the writing and publication of a pamphlet comparing the positive results achieved by the NAACP with the CPUSA's dismal failures. Sullivan, then an inspector in the central research section, received the assignment—but he gave up after six months, citing a lack of pertinent material.[19]

By the standards of the mid- and late 1960s, FBI surveillance of black political activists prior to the summer of 1963 was limited and cautious because Hoover deemed the political risks of more aggressive involvement to be too great. But beginning in the summer of 1963 there was a fundamental change in Hoover's willingness to assume the risks of more aggressive involvement, a change that can be explained by his belief that blacks had gone too far with their protests and now posed an imminent threat to the established order. Bureau documents immediately before, during, and after the March on Washington are filled with references to an impending "social revolution." Sullivan himself saw it in those terms. "It was a classic confrontation: Hoover vs. Communism, blacks, and social change, and Hoover gave it everything he had, which in his case was considerable."[20] It was no coincidence that President Kennedy and the FBI director concluded at roughly the same time that a strategy of limited intervention in the civil rights movement was neither prudent nor politically feasible. It was a reflection of Hoover's arrogance that he thought he had just as good a chance to influence the nature and direction of the coming revolution as the president of the United States. It was a reflection of Hoover's power that he was probably right.

Hoover based his case for a more aggressive intervention in the civil rights movement on the contention that communists were manipulating Martin Luther King. Neither the director nor any of his aides considered King an actual member of the Communist party, a charge widely circulated in the white South and among right-wing circles in the Southwest and in California. In the FBI view, King was merely a "security risk," to use one of William Sullivan's more restrained descriptions, because of his associations. At least eight persons, according to the FBI's count, who had helped King and SCLC, particularly during early movement days, were Reds of one sort or another—either former communists or the spiritual, never-had-a-card kind. Stanley Levison, Clarence Jones, and Hunter Pitts (Jack) O'Dell headed the list, followed by Harry Wachtel, C. T. Vivian, Randolph Blackwell, Lawrence Reddick, and Bayard Rustin. The charges were soft, products of a utilitarian definition of communism. FBI officials knew they had little to work with. How much mileage could they obtain from King's signature on petitions demanding abolition of the old House Committee on Un-American Activities?[21]

The FBI had explored Dr. King's communist associations prior to the summer of 1963, but Hoover did not act forcefully. Even the case of Stanley Levison, one of King's closest advisers and a man who had been named by prize informants during the early 1950s as a Soviet courier, failed to stir the FBI at first. By the late 1950s Bureau officials knew that Levison had "been closely associated with Reverend Martin Luther King" and at least a few other civil rights leaders, including A. Philip Randolph. But they collected "public source information" only on King's Southern Christian Leadership Conference and did not open a COMINFIL file until October 1962.[22] Sullivan himself was not quite sure what to make of Levison. He contacted Donald E. Roney, the assistant special agent in charge of the New York office, the office of origin in the Levison investigation, and asked (according to Roney's summary of their conversation): "Exactly what is LEVISON's status within the CP?; is he or is he not a member of the Party?; is he subject to Party discipline, or not?; has he actually broken with GUS HALL and other CP leaders?" The FBI moved against King and used his association with Levison as a pretext for doing so, but the decision to destroy King was not made until the March on Washington demonstrated that the civil rights movement had finally muscled its way onto the nation's political agenda.[23]

Bureau surveillance of Levison produced a tremendous

amount of information on the civil rights movement and little information on communist attempts to infiltrate the movement. Some of the information picked up through wiretaps on Levison's telephone was actually supportive of the FBI's work and critical of King. Levison reportedly "commented that King is a poorly read man who probably has not looked at a book in 20 years." On another occasion, after the Bureau arrested thirteen Ku Klux Klansmen in Mississippi, the wireman heard Levison say the director's men had done a "terrific" job. Most of the intelligence gathered through electronic surveillance on Levison and sent on to Burke Marshall and the Kennedys was political, highlighting Levison's contacts with King, Clarence Jones, and Jack O'Dell—his advice on fund-raising and speech-writing, his recommendations that King hire O'Dell as an administrative assistant and support the Negro judge William Henry Hastie in the event the president nominated him for a seat on the Supreme Court.[24]

With Burke Marshall and the Kennedy brothers genuinely troubled by the communists and communist sympathizers who, in Marshall's words, were "always hanging around" the movement, Hoover's steady stream of memos on Levison and O'Dell served to reinforce their fears. By the summer of 1963, with the administration "staking its future on the integrity of the civil rights movement," John Kennedy decided to explain the facts of life to King. The president met him at the White House and took him outside—"I guess Hoover must be bugging him too," King later speculated—for a walk in the Rose Garden. "They're Communists," Kennedy said. "You've got to get rid of them." Public exposure would harm the movement and jeopardize the administration's civil rights bill. "If they shoot *you* down, they'll shoot *us* down too—so we're asking that you be careful." Hoover had already told the president's brother that King would "hurt his own cause" if he did not cut his ties to Levison and O'Dell. "There are more and more communists trying to take advantage of the hate movement," the director advised, in words that he used interchangeably to describe both the civil rights movement and the violence-prone wing of the white resistance. "And bigots down South who are against integration are beginning to charge King is tied in with communists."[25]

The FBI had already compiled an intermittent record of Red baiting. When Hoover, or perhaps one of his aides, mentioned

Bureau interest in Stanley Levison and communist infiltration of the civil rights movement to James Eastland, the Senate Internal Security Subcommittee promptly subpoenaed Levison, who took the Fifth Amendment. The FBI obtained the transcript of Levison's executive session testimony and sent copies to Kennedy and Marshall at the Justice Department and Kenneth O'Donnell at the White House.[26] Other incidents also predated the March on Washington, notably the New York field office's suggestion that an anonymous mailing be sent "to appropriate southern newspapers to expose the communist background of Hunter Pitts O'Dell." After a slight modification at headquarters, Division Five gave a blind memo to Crime Records chief Cartha DeLoach "for his consideration and possible use by his contacts in the news media field." DeLoach alerted the *Augusta* (Georgia) *Chronicle* and a number of other papers "in such southern states as Alabama where King has announced that the next targets for integration of universities are located." FBI officials may have been interested in putting optimum pressure on King to fire O'Dell, but their method represented a direct form of assistance to the segregationists.[27]

In reality, there were few ties between the Communist party and the civil rights movement and only one dusty connection (Stanley Levison) serious enough to give reasonable men pause. Though the cry of communist infiltration remained a false (or at least greatly exaggerated) issue, it was impossible to prove or disprove the validity of the FBI's communist-search justification for spying on civil rights groups. There might not be any hard proof one way or the other. In the case of Bayard Rustin, the FBI conceded the absence of "direct evidence placing him in the Communist party," and then argued that evidentiary voids cut both ways. "While there may not be any direct evidence that [Rustin] is a Communist neither is there any substantial evidence that he is anticommunist."[28] The director's proposition justified a request to Robert Kennedy for a wiretap on Rustin's home telephone. (The attorney general approved the tap.) On an informal level, John Lewis suspected, it also led the FBI to leak derogatory information on Rustin to Whitney Young and Roy Wilkins in an attempt to exacerbate divisions among the so-called Big Six (King, Lewis, Young, Wilkins, Farmer, and Randolph) during the planning stages of the March on Washington. "It was over this whole thing of being too close to . . . subversive elements in the larger society," Lewis said. Wilkins was especially upset about Rustin's prominent role in organizing the march.[29]

For Hoover, the Red menace was a commodity as well as a threat, something to be possessed and used, something to justify the surveillance of any group because "the CPUSA views every noncommunist organization as a target for infiltration."[30] Many years later counsel for a House committee asked former FBI executive Charles D. Brennan, one of the principal authors of the Division Five report of August 23, why the FBI tried to "neutralize" Dr. King if he was the victim of communist infiltration? Why didn't the Bureau spend more time under the counterintelligence and communist infiltration programs targeting the alleged perpetrators, Levison and the Communist party, for "disruption" and "neutralization"?[31] Brennan had no good answer to that question, but it seems clear that Hoover wanted to destroy more than the CPUSA. The director intended to smash the equally serious (and certainly more imminent) threat to the existing social and political order posed by the civil rights movement and its most charismatic leader.

In late September, Hoover finally approved the Division Five request to use "all possible investigative techniques" in its "coverage of communist influence on the Negro."[32] In October, Robert Kennedy approved the director's request to wiretap the phones in King's home in Atlanta and SCLC offices in New York and Atlanta. Two months later, on December 23, representatives from the Atlanta field office and Division Five met at headquarters for nine hours to discuss how best to expose "King for the clerical fraud and Marxist he is." Constrained only by a desire to avoid "embarrassment to the Bureau," Sullivan's group proposed to infiltrate "King's office" with "colored" agents or perhaps "a good looking female plant," and to utilize "specialized investigative techniques [break-ins, in other words] at the SCLC office." Six days after the Division Five gathering, when *Time* magazine named King its "Man of the Year," Hoover responded: "They had to dig deep in the garbage for this one." Nearly a month later, he described King as "a 'tom cat' with obsessive degenerate sexual urges." The director clearly supported the Division Five proposals.[33]

Hoover scribbled this last comment on a document about a microphone that Division Five had installed in King's room at the Shroeder Hotel in Milwaukee. This bug, as well as the other fourteen microphone surveillances the Bureau employed against King (without bothering to obtain Robert Kennedy's authorization for a single one), presented a minor managerial problem. Hoover had to find the money and personnel necessary to transcribe hundreds of reels of tape. Given such a pervasive and intrusive surveillance, SCLC leaders knew they were being tapped and bugged, and they often moved from one lodge to the next in the hope of staying a step ahead of the inevitable FBI wireman. The parking lot of virtually every hotel and motel used by King's group, Andrew Young remembered, had one or two of "these little plain green Plymouths with two-way radios in them," a sure sign the Bureau had already checked in.[34]

By expanding its surveillance of the civil rights movement in the wake of the March on Washington, the FBI moved beyond peripheral operations in civil rights areas where the Communist party was thought to be active. From the fall of 1963 onward, FBI officials used counterintelligence tactics to "expose, disrupt, discredit, or otherwise neutralize" the civil rights movement itself. A few field offices had difficulty finding their targets. Describing the Communist party's southern California district as dormant in "the Negro field," the head of the Los Angeles office said there was nothing to "counter." In Chicago, the special agent in charge advised headquarters that the only current Negro Question counterintelligence operations concerned Claude Lightfoot, a black communist and longtime party functionary. There were "no incidents of misuse of the Negro or the Negro civil rights movement . . . available to us [to exploit]," he continued. Nor were there "any Negro communists," besides Lightfoot, worth targeting. None of the black party members in Chicago, Lightfoot included, were "influential professionally and in the civil rights movement."[35]

Both field offices missed the point; FBI officials wanted their agents in Los Angeles and Chicago and elsewhere to focus on Dr. King and the civil rights movement, not obscure activists like Lightfoot. By targeting King rather than the Communist party, the FBI broadened its assault. King himself, not Levison or some controller in faraway Moscow, was the explicit threat to law and order, and so he was the target of dozens of counterintelligence operations carried out by William Sullivan's Division Five with the cooperation of Cartha DeLoach's Crime Records Division. Crime Records disseminated the embarrassing personal and political information collected through the taps and all those hotel-room bugs not only to the media and King's own wife, but to virtually any individual or organization courted by the movement.[36] The FBI bombarded the White House with data on King, along with select members of Congress—Congressman John Rooney (D., N.Y.), Speaker of the House John McCormack (D., Mass.), and Senator Leverett Saltonstall (R., Mass.), among others. Vice-President Hubert Humphrey, U.S. Information Agency director Edward R. Murrow, Community Relations Service director LeRoy Collins, United Nations representative Adlai Stevenson, and dozens of other government officials, moreover, received oral or written briefings. A leak to the office of the National Science Foundation (NSF) was typical. The Foundation received a Bureau monograph on King as part of a general effort to convince the agency to purge the Southern Christian Leadership Conference from "the NSF program to obtain qualified Negro students from southern schools."[37]

In the private sector, FBI officials tried to discredit Dr. King and the movement through leaks to various university administrators, foundation trustees, and labor leaders. In some cases, the Bureau targeted those persons who promised support for the movement. When King aborted a meeting with Teamster boss Jimmy Hoffa after Crime Records alerted reporters for the *Washington Daily News*, the *Washington Star*, and the *New York Daily News*, the FBI tried to exploit "the white backlash within [Hoffa's] own union ranks." (King had thought the Teamsters might be a possible source of funds.) While King was concluding negotiations for a $3 million grant from the Ford Foundation, DeLoach arranged for an ex-agent and current Ford Motor Company employee, John Bugas, to brief Foundation president McGeorge Bundy. In this case the approach failed. When Bundy asked if the FBI was the source of the allegations, DeLoach told Clyde Tolson it was useless. "Bundy is of the pseudo-intellectual, Ivy League group that has little respect for the FBI." Bundy, however, was the exception. Most of the people who greeted Bureau agents bearing dirt on King were considerably more gracious.[38]

The FBI quickly expanded its intelligence and counterintelligence operations beyond King and SCLC. Many of the COMINFIL reports on such groups as the American Friends Service Committee, for example, bore the Racial Matters caption and were directed at the civil rights movement as well. (The Bureau even ran a name check on George Fox, the founding Quaker who died in 1691.) Bayard Rustin, who went on from the March on Washington to organize the New York City school boycott in 1964, was the target of a press leak that had the FBI salivating over the prospects for dissension within the movement. A long-time pacifist and former member of the Young Communist League, Rustin had gone with a group of fellow pacifists to the headquarters of the Soviet delegation to the United Nations in the hope that they might somehow keep dialogue between the two superpowers open in a nuclear age. FBI agents pointed him out to newspaper photographers, a story appeared the next day in the *New York Daily News* implying that he had a close rela-tionship with Soviet leaders, and a number of "embarrassing" articles followed—including an item in *Time* magazine.[39]

Most COINTELPRO schemes attempted to influence public opinion on the un-American nature of the civil rights movement and its leaders in a similar manner. Cartha DeLoach helped ar-range an interview in the August 19, 1963, issue of *U.S. News and World Report* featuring S. B. Fuller, a wealthy black busi-nessman and publisher from Chicago, who claimed, as quoted by the FBI, "the current civil rights demonstrations (which are being supported by the Communist Party) do not encourage the Negro to work harder or become more self-reliant." With his advocacy of self-help and modest sixth-grade education, Fuller symbolized black mobility and the efficacy of the American dream. Because "his success gives the lie to the communist con-tention that the Negro is downtrodden," Hoover ordered De-Loach to circulate the article widely, "particularly with the Ne-gro press," in the wake of the March on Washington.[40]

The Martin Luther King investigation was the most sustained and adventuresome because King was the most influential civil rights leader; but the FBI counterintelligence campaign against the whole civil rights movement, as Sullivan later explained, was in accord with "Mr. Hoover's policy" and FBI practices dat-ing back to the early cold war years. Since 1946 Bureau officials had pursued counterintelligence actions designed to develop an informed public opinion about "the basically Russian nature of the Communist Party in this country"—an ambitious program that they described as "a campaign of education directed to the proposition that Communism is dangerous." In linking King to the Communist party, they hoped to make a public case about the basically un-American nature of the civil rights movement. They devoted themselves to a campaign of education directed to the proposition that racial justice was dangerous, and their action in so doing was "not an isolated phenomenon." Sullivan said it was "a practice of the Bureau down through the years."[41]

By the summer of 1964 the FBI had focused its attention not only on Dr. King but on all civil rights leaders and all race-related events, including the riots in New York, the Mississippi Summer Project, the national conventions of the Democratic and Republican parties, and, more generally, the emergence of civil rights as "the primary domestic issue on the political front today." With "both sides" in the Senate debate on the civil rights bill bombarding the Bureau with requests for information on "communist penetration with the racial movement," internal security section chief Fred Baumgardner said Division Five had to be in a position to make "a proper presentation of the facts." The Inspection Division concurred, advising Hoover of the "urgency" in the Bureau's attempt to "stay ahead" of civil rights debate and of "complex political situations in an election year where civil rights and social disturbances will play a key role in campaign efforts and possibly election results." Political concerns, not internal security concerns, were in the forefront.[42]

Granted the necessary resources to stay ahead, Division Five executives set up a special desk in the internal security section to coordinate its Communist Influence Racial Matters investigation (a CIRM unit manned by two supervisors) and reminded every agent assigned to a CIRM case to interpret the term "communist" in the "broadest sense." If they directed field agents to "separate . . . the bona fide communist from the mere 'do-gooder'" and to avoid the inclusion of "information concerning legitimate efforts in the racial movement where there is no communist taint," they required the filing of detailed reports on "cummunist infiltration in various organizations, such as the Congress of Racial Equality, Student Non-Violent Coordinating Committee, and the like; . . . subversive individuals active in the racial movements; . . . communist fronts and other miscellaneous organizations; and racial disturbances and other racial matters."[43] The apparent restriction—"if a particular event had no communist involvement, it should, of course, not be included in the report"—was intended to direct general "Racial Matters" intelligence into the proper file and not the CIRM file. When the FBI ran its first name check on King's young and ambitious SCLC colleague, Jesse Jackson, the Chicago field office, having failed to develop an appropriate "subversive characterization," provided "descriptive data" instead. Division Five sent out instructions requiring the field to file "matters which do not fit into any other specific category" under "the character of 'Racial Matters.'"[44]

No matter how sweeping, the FBI's domestic political intelligence activities clearly centered on Dr. King. "King is no good," as Hoover put it back in February 1962.[45] The ferocity of the Bureau's pursuit does suggest a vendetta, an overreaction to a new and potent social force. But King's targeting was quite rational. He was the available man, the most well-known, effective, and charismatic civil right leader. After the March on Washington, King and the movement were inseparable in the public mind. If King could be damaged, the movement could be damaged. King was vulnerable to a subversion charge, FBI officials reasoned, because of his associations with Levison, O'Dell, and others. Beyond that, as the FBI discovered first through the wiretapping of Clarence Jones's telephone, King's personal life made him vulnerable on another front. The ease with which the FBI slid from the communist issue to the morality issue indicates that the director and his aides were looking for something—anything—that might work to discredit King. It also paralleled the typical racist belief in the sexual prowess of the black male and the threat to white society that posed. Hoover's fears were deeply personal.

No matter how promising, the FBI drew a blank on the Levison-Moscow connection—despite "electronic surveillances on Levison dating back to 1954" and forward to the first of the Nixon years, and at least twenty-nine entries (burglaries) into Levison's business office in New York between 1954 and 1964.[46] The Jones tap and then the bugs in King's hotel and motel rooms, however, provided another connection to exploit. If King could not be ruined by publicity charging him with subversion, perhaps he could be ruined with publicity charging him with adultery. "Hoover was a strict Presbyterian–brought up individual," Crime Records Division agent Lawrence Heim said. "If the Ten Commandments said 'Thou Shalt Not Covet Thy Neighbor's Wife,' that meant [exactly that]." Years later, after the tragedy in Memphis, the director initially suspected that King's assassin had been a vengeful husband.[47]

Hoover dreamed of destroying Dr. King and replacing him with "a manageable black leader," another former Crime Records agent, Harold Leinbaugh, said. And a few of the more confident FBI officials, William Sullivan included, tried to find one. In January 1964, when Sullivan proposed to remove King from his pedestal, he suggested that the Bureau replace King with the "right kind" of black leader. John F. Malone, the FBI's man in New York, nominated Roy Wilkins. Division Five agents also favored Wilkins ("a man of character"), but in this instance Sullivan overruled his men—offering instead Samuel R. Pierce, Jr., a talented, conservative attorney who joined the Ronald Reagan cabinet seventeen years later as secretary of housing and urban development. Both men, Wilkins and Pierce, were unaware of the plans of their Bureau cheerleaders.[48]

The FBI campaign to take King off his pedestal went on and on, finally cresting in the late fall and early winter of 1964. Upon learning on October 14 that King would receive the Nobel Peace Prize, Hoover sent a flood of reports to the White House, the Department of Justice, the State Department, the U.S. Information Agency, and American embassies across Europe concerning King's character. Then, during a November 18 meeting with a group of women reporters, the director labeled King "the most notorious liar in the country." DeLoach passed Hoover three notes asking him to retract the statement or at least request the reporters to consider it off-the-record, but the director threw each note in the trash and finally told the assistant director to mind his own business. Needless to say, the notorious-liar quote was the one item that stuck out during Hoover's three-hour oration. "The girls," DeLoach noticed, "could hardly wait to leave to get to the telephone." King learned of the remark while vacationing in Bimini, and he responded in kind, labeling his sixty-nine-year-old adversary senile and expressing his "sympathy for this man who served his country so well."[49]

Hoover's specific reference in calling Dr. King a liar was a year-old statement the civil rights leader had made to the New York Times. A reporter asked King if he agreed with a report on the Albany, Georgia, protests prepared by the historian Howard Zinn for the Southern Regional Council. One of the statements in the report charged FBI agents assigned to civil rights cases in the South with racism, and King said he agreed with Zinn. Too many agents were "white Southerners who have been influenced by the mores of the community." Southern agents were "friendly with the local police and people who are promoting segregation," he added. "Every time I saw FBI men in Albany, they were with the local police force."[50]

This was a serious charge. It could not be answered with a file check on Howard Zinn or explanations about how blacks considered black agents "finks" because they worked in law enforcement. Hoover ignored the racism issue, concentrating instead on the accuracy of King's statement—specifically, the notion that all agents assigned to the Albany office were southerners. Only one was a native southerner. The other four were from New York, Indiana, Minnesota, and Massachusetts.[51] If wrong on the specific question, King was quite correct on the larger issue. Calling him a liar was not "simply a matter of calling a spade a spade," as DeLoach, in an incredible choice of words, told CORE's Val Coleman. Any FBI agent assigned to the Deep South would have to confront his own "psychological needs," Albany movement attorney C. B. King said. "He wants social approbation. He wants his wife to be accepted as the wife of a regular fellow in this community. He wants her to have friends to be invited to dinner. And the only people who are relevant to him are white people." In the end, the agent would likely be a reformed Yankee, just another "local redneck with an FBI tag."[52]

Many of the FBI's agents supported civil rights, Bayard Rustin said, but the executives in Washington did not send in "flaming liberals. By and large they did what they could to send in people who were not going to be helpful." The one native southerner assigned to the Albany FBI office, Marion Cheek, whose family had once owned a large piece of land in DeKalb County, just north of Atlanta, land that Sherman's troopers had once camped on and tore up, found himself at the center of the entire controversy. Arthur Murtagh, the Atlanta agent who sometimes worked out of the Albany office and whose waistline exceeded Hoover's notion of what the proper girth of a G-man should be, said he considered Cheek "a friend, but on the question of race I could not discern much difference between his view and the view of the Ku Klux Klansmen that I would have occasion to interview from time to time." Hoover spoke to Cheek only once in Cheek's twenty-six-year Bureau career, to advise him that Martin Luther King was trying to "get you transferred out of there."[53]

Division Five responded aggressively as Hoover's mostly one-sided feud with King moved into the public realm after the March on Washington. The Division had the FBI lab make a composite tape of the "highlights" of the various microphone surveillances (mostly "dirty jokes and bawdy remarks . . . plus the sounds of people engaging in sex" in King's room at Washington's Willard Hotel), and in November 1964 William Sullivan himself drafted a ghastly note recommending suicide as a way out:

> King, look into your heart. You know you are a complete fraud and a great liability to all of us Negroes. . . . King, like all frauds your end is approaching. You could have been our greatest leader. . . . But you are done. . . . No person can overcome facts. . . . The American public, the church organizations that have been helping—Protestant, Catholic and Jews will know you for what you are . . . So will others who have backed you. You are done . . . there is only one thing left for you to do. You know what this is. You have just 34 days in which to do (this exact number has been selected for a specific reason, it has definite practical significant [sic]). You are done. There is but one way out for you. You better take it before your filthy, abnormal fraudulent self is bared to the nation.

On November 21, thirty-four days before Christmas, Sullivan put the tape and letter in an unmarked package, gave the package to one of his agents, Lish Whitson, and instructed him to fly to Miami. Once in Miami, Whitson called headquarters, and Sullivan (or one of his men) told him to address and mail the package to the SCLC office in Atlanta.[54]

Three days later, on November 24, Hoover again went public with his attack on King, with an indirect reference in a speech at Loyola University in Chicago to "pressure groups" headed by "Communists and moral degenerates." In the meantime, De-Loach offered a copy of a King microphone surveillance transcript to Benjamin Bradlee, *Newsweek* Washington bureau chief. When Burke Marshall and Nicholas Katzenbach learned of this, they asked President Johnson to look into the matter. Johnson did so by warning the FBI about Bradlee. He was unreliable, the president said, and was telling the story all over Washington.[55]

These and other FBI efforts to smear Martin Luther King led to a series of meetings between Bureau officials and various civil rights leaders intent on making peace. Roy Wilkins approached Cartha DeLoach first, shortly after the director's Loyola speech. According to the assistant director, however, Wilkins was on the Bureau's side and willing to assist in the planned removal of "King from the national picture."

> I told [Wilkins] that the Director, of course, did not have in mind the destruction of the civil rights movement as a whole . . . [but] if King wanted war we certainly would give it to him. Wilkins shook his head and stated there was no doubt in his mind as to which side would lose if the FBI really came out with all its ammunition against King. I told him the ammunition was plentiful and that while we were not responsible for the many rumors being initiated against King, we had heard of these rumors and were certainly in a position to substantiate them.

"The monkey was on his back and that of the other Negro leaders," DeLoach reiterated. Wilkins promised to "tell King that he can't win in a battle with the FBI," that "the best thing for him to do is to retire from public life." With that comment, the meeting concluded. Not surprisingly, Wilkins described DeLoach's account of what was said at their meeting as "self-serving and filled with inaccuracies." Hoover passed along that account, nonetheless, to President Johnson.[56]

Wilkins's assessment of what actually transpired in his meeting with DeLoach is no doubt closer to the truth. Indeed, Hoover abruptly (if briefly) cut off Wilkins a few months later. "I don't want anything given to [him] . . . in view of [his] visit to the President demanding my dismissal because of what I had to say re King." Edwin Guthman, who went back to his office and typed up a memo for the files after every one of his meetings with DeLoach, had the opportunity to compare his recollections with the assistant director's several years later. "It was like we were at two different meetings," he said. Even within the Bureau, neither field agents nor his fellow executives completely trusted DeLoach. "Many FBI colleagues observed that [he] seemed to fulfill the role of a son to Hoover," Sanford Ungar wrote. "Others thought it was more like a hatchet man." In either case, Hoover trusted DeLoach absolutely.[57] Born poor in Claxton, Georgia, DeLoach had been with the FBI since 1942, when he dropped out of the Stetson College School of Law in Florida to sign up, and since 1951 he had been under the director's wing at headquarters. In meeting with Wilkins, DeLoach did exactly what Hoover wanted him to do.[58]

Another Big Six civil rights leader who had a close relationship with the FBI, James Farmer, met with DeLoach on December 1, in the back seat of a limousine while driving around Washington. According to DeLoach, the two men discussed "warfare" between Hoover and King. "I told him that if this war continued that we, out of necessity, must defend ourselves. . . . Farmer got the point without any difficulty whatsoever. He immediately assured me that there would be no further criticism from him. He stated he felt certain there would be no further criticism from King." Farmer also disputed DeLoach's recollection. He did not remember DeLoach saying anything about "warfare," and he did not make any commitment to stop sniping at the FBI. Farmer said he knew what DeLoach and Hoover were up to. "They wanted to isolate King."[59]

Later in the day, Martin Luther King himself, accompanied by Ralph Abernathy, Andrew Young, and Walter Fauntroy, met with Hoover and the ever-present DeLoach. The civil rights leaders discovered what everyone who had ever been in the same room with the director already knew—as Robert Kennedy once put it, "You know, he talks a hell of a lot, J. Edgar Hoover." When King did say something, the director maintained, it was generally "laudatory about the Bureau's work." DeLoach described the meeting as "a love feast," and for once the civil rights leaders agreed with him. "You would have thought you were watching a mutual admiration society," Young said, calling it "a completely nonfunctional meeting."[60]

While Hoover and DeLoach met with King and the other civil rights leaders, William Sullivan planned the secret convening of a group of prominent black leaders—Roy Wilkins and two or three other movement leaders (Farmer and Randolph), "top Negro judges" (James B. Parsons and William Henry Hastie), "top reputable ministers" (Robert Johnson of the Washington City Presbytery), and "other selected Negro officials from public life such as the Negro Attorney General from one of the New England states." Division Five intended to enlist these men in the campaign to topple King and to promote "the stature of Roy Wilkins." The group could learn "the facts" about the FBI's many civil rights accomplishments, the truth about King's sexual and political transgressions. While trying to make the necessary arrangements, Division Five blackballed Carl Rowan, director of the U.S. Information Agency, and Ralph Bunche, undersecretary-general of the United Nations, on the grounds that "they might feel a duty to advise the White House of such a contemplated meeting." In this case, the proposal was simply too incredible. The meeting with "reputable Negroes" never happened.[61]

William Sullivan's Division Five and Cartha DeLoach's Crime Records Division remained active on other fronts and they sometimes acted in concert. They wanted to be certain King's rivals in the civil rights movement had the facts, so DeLoach offered the microphone recordings that Sullivan's agents had compiled to various civil rights leaders. C. Sumner Stone, Jr., editor of the *Chicago Defender* and later in the year a special assistant to New York Congressman Adam Clayton Powell, Jr., said a fair number of movement people "claimed to have heard the tapes. Whitney Young heard them. Roy Wilkins heard them." And of course King himself heard them. The Division Five package mailed on November 24 had sat in the SCLC office in Atlanta until January 5, when Coretta King stumbled over it. She listened to a brief portion ("just a lot of mumbo jumbo"), read the accompanying letter, and then called her husband, who had returned from Oslo only the week before. A Nobel laureate to the world, to the FBI, in Sullivan's words, King was "a dissolute, abnormal moral imbecile," "an evil, abnormal beast."[62]

FBI interest in Martin Luther King's private life was not unprecedented. Some of the older movement people had a clear sense of *déjà vu*. What Jesse Jackson called the director's "Peeping Tomism," his "sick interest of the white male in black sexuality," was arguably present in his predecessors as well. (Heavyweight boxing champion Jack Johnson had his troubles with the FBI and "the Mann" in 1912.) In December 1964, only a few days after he met with King, Hoover told *U.S. News and World Report* publisher David Lawrence that the White Slave Traffic Act was "supposed to protect the virtue of womanhood."[63] His interest in interracial sex and the morality of individual black activists was nothing if not consistent.[64] The old General Intelligence Division of 1919 focused on the specter of miscegenation, but so did the Domestic Intelligence Division of 1953. "It is interesting to note that one of [the Communist party's] 'concrete demands' . . . advocated 'the removal of all legal restrictions and social censorship of intermarriage in the Southern States.'"[65] For the director, interracial sex, extramarital sex, premarital sex, homosexuality, bisexuality, and sexual deviancy was all something that could be used to discredit political adversaries. And it was something to which Martin Luther King—and in a broader sense the civil rights movement as a whole during the 1960s—appeared to be particularly vulnerable.[66]

FBI interest in Dr. King as "the 'top alley cat'" accompanied a parallel interest in the sex lives of virtually anyone interested in the subject of racial justice. New York agents tried to find out who the Communist party's top black functionaries were "carrying on" with, while Washington agents worked up a memo on a Civil Rights Division attorney who had gone off on an interracial date. Division Five investigated "the moral character" of Andrew Young and Jesse Jackson and looked into a rumor about Stanley Levison "having a paramour." In the meantime, Hoover discussed the "immoral conditions" within the black family with the ubiquitous David Lawrence, told the House Appropriations Subcommittee that Bayard Rustin (who was in fact homosexual) had once been "convicted for sodomy," and flooded the White House with memos concerning the "personal behavior" of Community Relations Service workers. "He spread garbage about us," Roger Wilkins charged, "and he spread garbage about everybody in the civil rights movement."[67]

Having documented "the depraved nature and moral looseness" of Dr. King and other black activists, FBI officials' attempts to use the information uncovered met with little success. Sumner Stone said "Hoover was a real prude—he misjudged the morality of the average American." When DeLoach offered transcripts based on the King buggings to a variety of newspaper reporters, columnists, and editors, nobody accepted the offer. Jim Bishop of the Hearst chain even claimed to have seen photographs, snapped by the FBI "through a one-way mirror," of King chasing "White women . . . in motel rooms." "The old man," Bishop concluded, "saw the preacher as a buffoon" and "could barely mention the name without bubbling at the lips."[68]

Hoover could not even convince the Catholics to do anything. The Chicago archdiocese published a pamphlet describing King as being "like Jesus," and Marquette University, a Jesuit school, invited him to receive an honorary degree. (Since World War II the FBI recruited heavily at Jesuit schools, and by the 1960s Protestant agents considered themselves a distinct minority, members of a "PU"—a Protestant underground.) In this last case the FBI claimed to have convinced a source at Marquette that King was unworthy, and King did not receive the degree—but the excuse was that he was unable to attend the ceremonies and Marquette had a policy against awarding honorary degrees in absentia. The FBI agent who approached University officials, nonetheless, received a monetary award from his superiors. All this was quite minor compared to King's plans to meet with the Pope. That audience had to be "nipped in the bud," so the director sent New York SAC John Malone off to brief Francis Cardinal Spellman and to have Spellman alert the Vatican. "Hoover always . . . kept a Cardinal in the background," Harold Leinbaugh remembered, and Malone said the King matter had been handled. But it did not do any good. "I am amazed that the Pope gave an audience to such a degenerate," Hoover responded, upon discovering that Malone and Spellman had failed.[69]

Hoover's obsession with the sexual habits of Martin Luther King and other civil rights activists posed an irony. The suspicion that the director himself was homosexual followed him for most of his career. Not even the FBI's own agents were quite sure about Hoover, a result of his "strange relationship" with Clyde Tolson, his second in command, with whom he took all his meals and vacationed over a period of thirty years. "I don't think anybody really knows," Leinbaugh concluded.[70]

Whatever the nature of Hoover's own sexuality, his concern with and condemnation of other people's sexuality was severe, and he was determined to use anything, including sexual inferences, to damage Dr. King and other black activists. "The Negro community" was not much troubled by "a conventional standard of morality," however, and FBI programs designed to discredit movement people by emphasizing "alleged immoral or un-American political inclinations" simply were not working. If anything, the "moral turpitude" label enhanced "the status of these individuals among their peers." Promiscuity, much like "a criminal record or associations with radical groups," was less "a thing of shame to be hidden from public view" than "a badge of honor," sometimes even "a prerequisite to leadership."[71] "Can you imagine anything sillier than somebody starting a rumor that Martin liked women?," asked Charles Evers, the NAACP leader in Mississippi and brother of the slain Medgar Evers. "Now, if he had a hankering for men, that's something else. That's my argument with J. Edgar Hoover. I mean, who's talking about whom? I'd say this to Hoover: You don't have any women anywhere. We might go and check *you* out."[72]

The FBI kept trying to use sexual rumor and innuendo nonetheless, usually in the form of anonymous telephone calls or letters to the spouse of a key activist. Typically, the FBI phone caller—"a Negro agent," if one could be found, or, more likely, "a Negro . . . male clerk"—would "attempt to leave the impression that he is the current lover of the wife." Letter writers concentrated on similar themes, with a Bureau "soul sister" addressing the following to the husband of a white woman active in ACTION: "Look man, I guess your old lady don't get enough at home. . . . Like all she wants to integrate is the bed room and us Black Sisters ain't gonna take no second best from our men. So lay it on her."[73]

Despite the FBI's all-out attempt to destroy Dr. King, whether as a communist dupe or an adulterer (in order to smear and thereby slow down the black struggle which King helped lead), neither the director nor the men who ran Division Five found themselves completely free from constraints. In standing against the civil rights movement, Hoover's Bureau had to distance itself from other groups that opposed the movement. The FBI could not stand with the Ku Klux Klan, or even such nonviolent resistance groups as the American Flag Committee and its preposterous claim that all civil rights law could be traced to a modest Communist party civil rights initiative known as the Lincoln Project. The FBI investigated the obscure Flag Committee, as well as those southern newspapermen who spread its ideas, on the grounds that they were plotting "to defraud the public." Hoover opposed the black struggle by upbringing, temperament, politics, and bureaucratic instinct, but he would not allow extremists to control or even influence the nature and form of his resistance.[74]

Perhaps the best example of the FBI's refusal to join the lunatic fringe involved the charge raised by Mississippi Governor Ross Barnett in July 1963 at Senate hearings on the civil rights bill. Barnett displayed a poster-sized reproduction of a photograph, snapped by an agent of the Georgia Commission on Education, showing Martin Luther King attending a "communist training school." The photo depicted "the 'four horsemen' of racial agitation"—King, former *Daily Worker* writer Abner Berry, Aubrey Williams of the Southern Conference Educational Fund, and their host, Myles Horton—at the twenty-fifth anniversary celebration of the Highlander Folk School just outside of Monteagle, Tennessee. Highlander had provided training for labor organizers and civil rights activists since the Work War II years, and right wingers in the South and elsewhere took the "communist training school" claim seriously; but the FBI did not. The

Georgia Commission distributed over 100,000 copies of the Highlander photo, and it graced hundreds of billboards along the highways in the Deep South. After Governor Barnett displayed his copy, Clyde Tolson recommended a file check and Robert Kennedy requested "a brief squib on" the three men in the photo with King.[75]

FBI officials knew all about Horton's Highlander Folk School and King's appearance there six years earlier. They had gathered and occasionally leaked information on the school since the early 1950s, sending Senator James Eastland and other more respectable segregationists blind memos on Horton. In the 1960s, moreover, someone from Cartha DeLoach's office briefed Congressman Roman C. Pucinski (D., Ill.) on "the background" of the Highlander Folk School. When King explained his appearance there on *Meet the Press*, the Atlanta and Knoxville FBI offices ran name checks on all officers, teachers, and students.[76] After Governor Barnett waved his copy of the Highlander photo and Senators Mike Monroney (D., Ok.) and Warren G. Magnuson (D., Wash.) wrote Hoover to ask about the authenticity of the photo, however, the director simply forwarded the letters to Attorney General Kennedy—along with a memo summarizing the extent of communist influence in the Southern Christian Leadership Conference. John Kennedy responded to Barnett by dismissing the Red menace at a news conference. Robert Kennedy responded to the Monroney and Magnuson letters with a similar disclaimer. "Based on all available evidence from the FBI and other sources, we have no evidence that any of the top leaders of the major civil rights groups are Communists, or Communist controlled."[77]

Rather than risk the uncertainties of involvement in the public debate over the Highlander photo, Hoover pursued his opposition to the civil rights movement on safer ground. He sought the safety of a formal alliance not with Governor Barnett and other extreme segregationists, but with the Kennedys, pressing Robert Kennedy to approve an FBI wiretap on King's home phone and SCLC office phones in New York and Atlanta. The attorney general was considering that request at the time he responded to the Monroney and Magnuson letters. That fall, as noted earlier, he approved another FBI request for electronic surveillance on King and SCLC.

FBI agents installed the wiretaps while President Kennedy considered a response to yet another query from a member of

Congress, Richard Russell, chairman of the Senate Armed Services Committee, whose interest in King's association with Jack
O'Dell presented particular problems. An ardent segregationist
who had worked tirelessly on behalf of Jim Crow America since
the 1940s, Russell was also one of the most powerful men in the
Senate.[78] After Burke Marshall wrote the first draft of the reply,
he sent it to the Bureau. He wanted to know, as FBI executive
Alan Belmont said, "whether it would jeopardize our informant
or otherwise interfere with our investigation." The Bureau had
a number of objections, most of which concerned a reference to
sensitive sources. But when Marshall eliminated this reference,
Tolson complained once more: "[It] still 'clears' King." Marshall
and Kennedy ended up writing three drafts, each of which they
read to John Kennedy over the phone, before the president decided that Marshall and Courtney Evans should deliver "an innocuous letter" to Russell personally. On November 1, Evans
and Nicholas Katzenbach (substituting for Marshall) took the
Bureau's file on O'Dell to Russell's office.[79]

This would not be the last time Senator Russell's interest in
Martin Luther King led to a conference with an FBI agent, dossier in hand. Nearly two years later to the day, Cartha DeLoach,
who served the Johnson White House as Courtney Evans had
served the Kennedy White House, met with Russell and brought
along files on King and someone else. Russell, nevertheless,
proved to be less of a problem than Hoover. During the floor
fight against the administration's civil rights bill, he did not use
the information about King that he had received from the FBI.
Evans said Russell "did not believe Martin Luther King himself
was a communist," only "that obviously the Negro Movement
was ready for exploitation by the Communist Party." Katzenbach remembered the senator as being "a pretty good fellow on
[not] hitting below the belt."[80]

Less restrained than Russell, Hoover sent a "highly explosive"
document on Dr. King, entitled "Communism and the Negro
Movement," to the White House, the attorney general, the secretaries of state and defense, the CIA director, and the military
intelligence agencies. Alan Belmont had pointed out that the
eleven-page document would likely "be regarded as a personal
attack on Martin Luther King" and "may startle the Attorney
General," who "may resent" the decision to circulate such information outside the Justice Department. Beyond that, if one of
the recipients were to leak all or part of the Bureau's analysis,

it would "add fuel to a matter which may already be in the cards as a political issue during the forthcoming Presidential campaign." Hoover made his decision ("we must do our duty") despite the guarded advice of his number-two man.[81]

Alan Belmont's predictions were astute. When Robert Kennedy found out that the Army had received a copy of "Communism and the Negro Movement," he called Courtney Evans to ask "what responsibilities" the Army had "in relation to the communist background of Martin Luther King"? "He was obviously irritated," Evans said. Since the FBI's "explanation seemed to serve no purpose" and he believed the "information would leak out as the military didn't like the Negroes," Kennedy ordered the report recalled. In off-the-record testimony before John Rooney's House Appropriations Subcommittee on January 29, 1964, Hoover said "both of us had feared a leak might get out from the Departments which had copies of the monograph; and if it happened during a sensitive time of negotiations going on with the Negro leaders, it would have caused a ruckus." Actually, only Kennedy had such a fear. The director was merely trying to cover himself before the Democratic members of the Rooney Subcommittee. He had approved the distribution of the report, after all, in the face of Belmont's pointed warning.[82]

Blaming "someone on Rooney's Committee" for betraying the confidence of his off-the-record remarks, Hoover reverted, for a time, to a more cautious policy. This new tack was in evidence when Edwin Willis (D., La.), chairman of the House Committee on Un-American Activities, tried to arrange a meeting between Cartha DeLoach and Howard Smith (D., Va.), chairman of the House Rules Committee and progenitor of the rider to the Alien Registration Act of 1940 that bears his name. At this particular time, Smith was sitting on the administration's civil rights bill. When DeLoach met Smith on March 13, the congressman "asked if he could receive information concerning King," stating "that he would be glad to make a speech on the Floor of the House at any time" and pointing "out that this would offer immunity to him and to newspapers who might desire to quote his remarks." Afterward, DeLoach submitted his recommendation. "Judge Smith is an honorable reputable Congressman. His word carries great weight on the Hill. It may be that after a period of time the Director might desire to have me furnish Judge Smith with information concerning King [deleted] so that he can make a speech. . . . Undoubtedly newspapers all over the Nation would

pick this story up." Given his recent conflict with Robert
Kennedy over the Rooney Subcommittee briefing, Hoover put
the project on hold. "I do *not* want anything on King given to
Smith nor anyone else at this time."[83]

Hoover's reluctance to help Howard Smith represented only a
pause in the campaign to discredit Martin Luther King and the
civil rights movement. The director sent eleven letters about
King to Walter Jenkins at the White House between early February and late April. And he had DeLoach orchestrate a HUAC
hearing a month after he met with Smith for the purpose of having a friendly witness "publicly expose . . . [name deleted] communist background and thus have a neutralizing effect on his
activities and influence in the legitimate Negro freedom movement."[84] When the House Appropriations Subcommittee released the on-the-record portion of the director's testimony that
same month, it became clear that the FBI was the principal
source of allegations about Reds in the civil rights movement.
"Communist influence does exist in the Negro movement," Hoover said, "and it is this influence which is vitally important. It
can be the means through which large masses . . . lose perspective" and "succumb to the party's propaganda lures." Communists, he added, had "magnified and dramatized" every "racial
incident" to date "in an effort to generate racial tensions"—part
of a sinister campaign to "control . . . the Negro population" and
embarrass the United States "in the eyes of the rest of the world,
particularly among the African and Asian peoples."[85]

With his warnings about subversives on the loose in Georgia
or Mississippi, Hoover performed a valuable service for the
white southern resistance. The press widely reported his testimony, with the *New York Times* running the story under the caption "Hoover Says Reds Exploit Negroes," and movement activists regarded his remarks as an attempt to influence debate over
the 1964 civil rights bill. John Lewis said FBI agents should
spend less time worrying about phantom Reds and more time
tracking down "the bombers, midnight assassins, and brutal
racists who daily make a mockery of the United States Constitution." Dr. King was equally direct. He wanted to hit the director
"hard—he made me hot and I wanted to get him"—and his statement read, in part: "Mr. J. Edgar Hoover . . . has allowed himself
to aid and abet the salacious claims of southern racists. . . . It
would be encouraging to us if Mr. Hoover and the FBI would
be as diligent in apprehending those responsible for bombing

churches and killing little children as they are in seeking out alleged communist infiltration in the civil rights movement."[86]

The civil rights movement's strategy had always been to force the FBI to choose sides, to turn toward civil rights law and away from the segregationists and the Red menace. "We were not so stupid as not to understand that other Americans who were opposed to what we were doing were also pressuring them," Bayard Rustin said.[87] The FBI's strategy had usually been to avoid a clear-cut choice, a rather predictable strategy regardless of Hoover's own conservatism and fundamental assumptions about the Negro Question. Since the twilight of Reconstruction nearly every American politician with dreams of forging a national constituency had tried to dodge the race issue. The March on Washington, nonetheless, demonstrated that the movement was finally strong enough to force the FBI, and the rest of the federal government as well, to choose sides.

"It was all taking sides," recalled Harold Leinbaugh, the former agent whose Crime Records Division served as the "carrier" of FBI information to Senator Eastland and other segregationists on the Hill. "If Hoover could be disembalmed, he'd probably say, 'I'm taking the side of America.'"[88] Obviously, Martin Luther King did not see it that way at the time. And when he said the director had chosen to move his bureaucracy alongside the cause of the southern racists, he was right.

5

=====≫≪=====

Mississippi Burning
Freedom Summer 1964

While the Johnson administration's civil rights bill moved through Congress and into the federal statute books during the summer of 1964, the FBI was wrestling with the civil rights movement in Mississippi. The battleground was not the choice of J. Edgar Hoover and his Bureau or Martin Luther King and the Southern Christian Leadership Conference, but of Robert Moses and the Student Nonviolent Coordinating Committee. Earlier, when returning to Mississippi after the March on Washington, SNCC activists mobilized the Council of Federated Organizations (COFO), a nearly dormant umbrella organization of racial-advancement groups established in 1961 to assist the jailed Freedom Riders in Jackson, and organized a Freedom Vote Campaign. Assisted by CORE's David Dennis, Moses served as program director. Aaron Henry, the respected Clarksville druggist and head of the state NAACP, was named president. Volunteers from all the major civil rights groups participated, but COFO was primarily a SNCC operation, and Moses as one civil rights worker noted, was "more or less the Jesus of the whole project."

Hoover's FBI watched events in Mississippi closely as the Freedom Vote Campaign in the fall of 1963 led to Freedom Summer in 1964. In November nearly 80,000 disenfranchised Mississippi blacks participated in a mock election, casting ballots for Aaron Henry for governor and Rev. Edwin King, the white chaplain of Tougaloo College, for lieutenant governor. A week later

in Greenville, forty- five COFO representatives (forty from SNCC
and five from CORE) organized a massive voter registration
drive for the summer months and invited white college students
from the North to participate. Such an effort, Moses and Dennis
reasoned, would incite unprecedented segregationist violence
and thus force the federal government to protect the lives of civil
rights workers and the voting rights of Mississippi's 916,000
blacks.

Allard Lowenstein, a thirty-four-year-old activist in the National Student Association who taught at the University of North
Carolina, had recruited nearly a hundred college students,
mostly from Yale and Stanford, to help with the earlier Freedom
Vote Campaign; and the FBI director had seemed to demonstrate
a token interest in their safety. When a handful of Yale students
had visited the SNCC office in Hattiesburg, Lawrence Guyot recalled, "it was really a problem to count the number of FBI
agents who were there to protect the students. It was just that
gross." It seemed the Bureau might guard northern college students in Mississippi once again during Freedom Summer.
"While these people are here national attention is here," Stokely
Carmichael promised. "The FBI isn't going to let anything happen to them." If Carmichael believed the first part of that prediction, it is doubtful that he or any other civil rights worker in
Mississippi believed the second. "It simply made good copy,"
Robert Moses admitted. Hoover may have understood power,
but everyone understood the director's lack of sympathy for student activists ("young punks") of any color.[1]

No one expected white Mississippi to respond to Freedom
Summer peacefully, and no one expected Hoover's FBI to do
much about it unless forced to. "The question," as Moses remembered, "was this: Were we gonna be able to force the rest
of the country to take a look at Mississippi. The white students
brought the rest of the country down with them for a look and
we knew Mississippi couldn't stand a hard look." "We all understood that whites could be used as a force," Marion Barry,
SNCC's first chairman, said. "Whenever you had blacks who
were killed who cared about that? They die everyday. Blacks
were jailed by the hundreds, who cared? When you've got a Congressman's son or you've got some white professor's son or
you've got some white students who are jailed or killed, then the
whole focus comes. You know, 'Boom.' " A few COFO people even

considered how the death of a student volunteer might benefit the movement.[2]

Hoover actually expected more trouble during the summer of 1964 from Dr. King's Alabama Project. Robert Moses and his co-workers knew better, and they prepared for a violent confrontation with the white resistance. On June 15 the first three hundred Summer Project volunteers gathered in Oxford, Ohio, for a week-long training session. They listened to the administration's representative, John Doar, lecture on civil rights law, and they heard him say the government would do "nothing" to provide protection. "There is no federal police force." They listened to Moses's prediction of guerilla war "not much different from that in Vietnam," and they heard him outline COFO's modest goals: to go, to register black voters, to "come back alive." One of the students, Stephen M. Bingham, remembered being "told that people *would* not return, not that they *might* not return." Moses also told the volunteers about the attempt to arrange a meeting with Lyndon Johnson. "His secretary said that Vietnam was popping up all over his calendar and he hadn't time to talk to us." White House special counsel Lee White found it "nearly incredible that these people who are voluntarily sticking their head [sic] into the lion's mouth would ask for somebody to come down and shoot the lion." In one way, the administration view paralleled the FBI view. The COFO activists were a nuisance, with their unreasonable demands for protection and a federal war on the Klan.[3]

While Hoover and Johnson hesitated, white Mississippi made time for the summer volunteers. Expecting an "invasion" of "mixers" and "outside agitators," the city of Jackson doubled the size of its police force, modified its garbage-truck fleet to double as paddy wagons, and bought what Guyot called "a damn armored truck—satirically referred to as [Mayor] Thompson's tank." The two hundred troopers added to the Highway Patrol helped intercept the SNCC activists who had begun to trickle into Mississippi by late spring, seizing their property and sometimes leaking such things as address books and copies of Communist party historian Herbert Aptheker's study of slave revolts to the press and the FBI. Sam Bowers, Jr., founder and imperial wizard of the White Knights of the Ku Klux Klan, developed the most explicit strategy for dealing with "COFO's nigger-communist invasion." "Catch them outside the law," he advised his fellows, according to an FBI informant report, "then under Mississippi law you have a right to kill them."[4]

According to the FBI's uniform crime reports, however, Mississippi was a picture of tranquillity. The state had the lowest crime rate in the nation. But for blacks it was, as Moses said, "the middle of the iceberg." The state had a seige mentality. Automobile bumper stickers advised motorists to "Drive Carefully: You Are Now In Occupied Mississippi," while the Citizens Council listed the FBI as subversive—along with the Elks, the Red Cross, the YMCA, and even the United States Air Force. In a few counties it was actually a status symbol among segregationists to have been under investigation by the FBI.[5] John Doar said Mississippi "didn't have to intimidate via violence," at least "until December of 1963," when COFO began to organize Freedom Summer, "because the legal structure was impervious. That was the Maginot line." When it "began to crack ... Mississippi turned to violence." And that was the precise time, "as the curve started up," that "Bob Moses and his guys decided the way to confront that curve was to bring a lot of white kids down and get some white kids hurt and the country would be up in arms."[6]

COFO activists from SNCC and CORE called the voter registration drive Freedom Summer, but it was really the summer of the Ku Klux Klan. By the FBI's conservative count, "SNCC and its supporters endured at least 1,000 arrests, 35 shooting incidents, eight beatings, and six murders."[7] With the Bureau continuing to speak the language of federalism, and responsible officials in the Justice Department and the White House continuing to do the same whenever the protection issue forced itself upon them, the Klan rode strong in Mississippi during the summer of 1964. The people on the front line registering black voters wanted to know which side the federal government was on. By the time Freedom Summer ended, the movement had an answer to their question, and a few thought they saw blood on the FBI's hands. The director investigated the Klan and the horrors committed by its members during that summer, but his performance reflected his belief that those who challenged white rule had committed a crime worse than murder.

While the movement and the resistance prepared for Freedom Summer, Robert Kennedy and Burke Marshall pressed the FBI to expand its coverage of Ku Klux Klan violence. They tried to convince the Bureau "to come down and shoot the lion." On one night, April 21, Klansmen burned sixty-one crosses in southwest

Mississippi. Between April 1 and July 1, they firebombed three black homes and a barbershop in Pike County. In Adams County, they chased and shot at two civil rights workers, and killed two local blacks. In Madison County, they bombed the Freedom House and a church. In the rest of Mississippi, they damaged or destroyed at least seven churches and bombed or shot up eight homes. The FBI submitted memos to the Civil Rights Division on every incident, but did not appear to be interested, as Marshall complained, in taking the necessary steps to combat "terrorism in Mississippi."[8]

Kennedy and Marshall hoped to pressure the FBI into launching a counterterrorism program. First, the attorney general dispatched ex-FBI and National Security Agency man Walter Sheridan, along with six or seven members of his "Terrible Twenty" (the "get Hoffa squad"), a crack team of Criminal Division investigators, "to get something on the Klan." "We were sent," Sheridan recalled, "because the Bureau wasn't doing anything. There were twenty FBI guys in the state . . . but they weren't doing anything unless they had to. Talk to John Doar. He would do whatever was done. The Bureau would say it didn't have jurisdiction." Marshall and Kennedy understood Hoover's territorial instincts. When Sheridan's squad arrived in Jackson, the director began sending memos to Marshall about "a man in Mississippi named Walter Sheridan who claims to be doing investigative work for the Department of Justice. This is to inform you that he is not a member of the FBI." The director also dispatched an agent to read the riot act to Doar: "Either the Bureau is going to be *the* investigative agency of the Department or it's not. Either it's going to do all of it or none of it." The irony is that Hoover wanted no other federal investigators in Mississippi, but neither did he want to do the civil rights work that the Department demanded. Caught between his bureaucratic interests and his personal and political preferences, for the time being, as Marshall remembered, the director "sealed off the Bureau from the Civil Rights Division," throwing up a wall of institutional resistance.[9]

Anticipating Hoover's reaction, Kennedy and Marshall next launched a Pennsylvania Avenue end run. Marshall drafted a memo to President Johnson in which he tried "to avoid . . . any appearance of criticism. . . . The problem is not one that can be cured by reprimands to particular agents on particular incidents, even if the Bureau could be persuaded that the agents did

not perform their investigative function well." Hoover had to be
stroked, not criticized. Above all, the director should not be told
how to do things in Mississippi once the commitment had been
made, Marshall wrote. "The problem is rather to describe what
is happening in such a way as to permit the Bureau to develop
its own new procedures for the collection of intelligence." When
investigating "fundamentally lawless activities" in Mississippi
"which have the sanction of local law enforcement agencies, political officials, and a substantial segment of the white population," Kennedy and Marshall offered, as a model, "the information gathering techniques used by the Bureau on Communist or
Communist related organizations." Describing these techniques
as "spectacularly efficient," the attorney general recommended
that President Johnson "take up with the Bureau the possibility
of developing a similar effort to meet this new problem."[10]

Robert Kennedy was in an awkward position. Despised by
Johnson and Hoover, and embroiled in feuds with both men, he
was, in effect, immobilized during the summer of the Klan. President Johnson had long hated the Ku Klux Klan. When he was
thirteen, Klansmen had threatened to kill his father, and young
Lyndon had spent a night in the cellar of the family home with
the women and children while his father and uncles stood watch
on the porch with shotguns.[11] But in 1964 LBJ seemed more worried about RFK than the KKK. He saw in Kennedy a rival who
could challenge his claim to legitimacy and to party and national
leadership; the president used the FBI to investigate "Bobby
Kennedy's boy[s]"—that is, members of the administration who
"had more loyalty to the Attorney General than . . . the President"—while getting "ready to take Bobby on." Hoover probably hated Kennedy even more that he hated Martin Luther
King. His objections ranged from the trivial—the attorney general let Brumus the dog run up and down the halls of the Justice
Department building and let his children run back and forth in
the director's office—to the substantive. Kennedy turned up at
field offices to ask hard questions. He did not want a public relations visit; he wanted to know how the Bureau did things. And
he made Hoover do civil rights work. "Why would he like it?,"
Kennedy asked. "He hadn't made any changes himself in twenty
years."[12]

Hoover refused to launch the kind of operation against the
Mississippi Klan that Marshall and Kennedy wanted, and Johnson saw no reason to pressure him to reconsider his decision.

The attorney general believed the FBI lacked "civilian control," that its director was "rather a psycho," a "senile" and "frightening" head of "a very dangerous organization," who realized "after November 22, 1963, [that] he no longer had to hide his feelings. . . . He no longer had to pay attention to me; and it was in the interest, evidently of . . . President Johnson to have that kind of arrangement and relationship." When a Justice Department attorney summarized the view from Kennedy's office, Cartha DeLoach passed the information on to Hoover: "A number of individuals close to the Attorney General felt that the President's body had not even become cold before you started circumventing the Attorney General and dealing directly with [President Johnson]."[13] LBJ began to pressure the director to act in Mississippi only on June 21, when COFO reported three civil rights workers missing in Neshoba County.

The FBI held files on two of the three, and Michael Schwerner was of particular interest. A native New Yorker, Schwerner had joined New York's downtown CORE the previous summer and went to Mississippi with his wife, Rita, to run the COFO community center in Meridian—a particularly dangerous assignment. In early June 1964 they received a letter from Richard Haley, assistant to CORE's national director, indicating a concern for their safety. "Obviously the tension is gradually rising as your activities probe more deeply into direct action. I am pushing very hard for the national office to set up a high level Justice Department conference to discuss specific protective measures."[14] A few days later, the Schwerners and James Chaney, a twenty-one-year-old black high-school drop out and CORE field worker who had also attracted the FBI's attention, drove up to Oxford to help prepare the summer volunteers. They came back almost immediately, accompanied by one of the volunteers, Andrew Goodman, a student at Queens College in New York, to investigate the beating of three blacks following a meeting at the Mt. Zion Church in Longdale and the burning of the church.

On Sunday morning, June 21, unknown to the FBI or anyone else outside the Mississippi civil rights network, the three young men drove a CORE station wagon from Meridian to Longview. On the return trip Neshoba County Deputy Sheriff Cecil Price arrested them for speeding, jailed them in Philadelphia, and finally released them a little after 10:00 P.M. and told them to leave town. A few miles outside of Philadelphia, the deputy stopped their car again—this time after a wild chase—and turned them over to a group of Neshoba County Klansmen. One of the Ku Kluxers, with one hand on Schwerner's shoulder and a gun in the other, asked, "Are you a nigger lover?" Schwerner, "the Jewboy with the beard" and the bright blue New York Mets baseball cap, was the Klan's principal target during the evening's "missionary work." When he started to say, "Sir, I know how you feel," the night riders shot him dead. The Klan then murdered Goodman and Chaney, set fire to the CORE station wagon in a sweetgum thicket deep in the Bogue Chitto Swamp, and carted the three bodies off for burial at a dam construction project.[15]

The FBI learned almost immediately that Schwerner, Chaney, and Goodman had failed to return to Meridian on time Sunday evening. Hoping to convince someone to investigate, SNCC workers called everybody on their "hot list"—starting with the authorities in every town along the Longview to Meridian route. Using the name of "Margaret Fuller," a "reporter" for the *Atlanta Constitution*, Mary King spoke to Deputy Sheriff Price himself, who denied knowing the whereabouts of the three young men. At 10:00 P.M., only minutes before Price released his prisoners from the Philadelphia jail, Sherwin Kaplan, a law student, spoke to Hunter E. Helgeson, one of the FBI's resident agents in Jackson. Helgeson asked to be kept informed. Thirty minutes later the COFO office in Meridian contacted Frank Schwelb, a Justice Department lawyer who was staying in town. More phone calls followed at 11:00 P.M.. At midnight, Schwelb "stated that the FBI was not a police force." When Robert Weil of the Jackson COFO office phoned Helgeson once more, the FBI agent "took in the information curtly and did not allow a chance for further conversation." Aaron Henry had a similar experience when he called the FBI.[16]

SNCC kept pressure on the FBI and other government agencies throughout the early morning hours and into the next day. At 1:00 A.M. the Atlanta office telephoned John Doar, and following more phone calls at 3:00 A.M. and 6:00 A.M. Doar said the FBI would "look into the matter." At 7:30 A.M. and again at 8:30 A.M. SNCC contacted Helgeson, who said he could do nothing until he heard from the FBI field office in New Orleans. Another phone call to Doar followed at 9:15 A.M. At 11:00 A.M. Helgeson said the Bureau would now "take the necessary action." Because Schwerner, Chaney, and Goodman may have been beaten after their arrest and before their release from the Philadelphia jail, the civil rights statute may have been violated. This "threw new light on the FBI's role in the case." At noon, however, Helgeson said the New Orleans office still had not ordered an investigation. Fifteen minutes later, an agent from the field office told a SNCC volunteer that no instructions had been received from the seat of government. At 1:40 P.M., and again an hour later, SNCC tried to get through to Doar. At 5:20 P.M., Doar called back with news that the FBI resident agent in Meridian, John Proctor, was coordinating a search. Proctor had in fact interviewed Cecil Price—an interview that concluded with the deputy slapping Proctor on the back and saying, "Hell, John, let's have a drink." The two men then imbibed from a cache of contraband liquor in the trunk of Price's cruiser.

Meanwhile, the movement continued to press the FBI and the Justice Department to intervene. The first clear sign of progress, other than Proctor's casual inquiries, occurred around 6:30 P.M., when Robert Kennedy instructed the FBI to treat the disappearance as a kidnapping. But when Bill Light of the SNCC office in Jackson asked the Bureau to confirm the investigation, the agent he spoke to told him to direct "all inquiries . . . to the Justice Department." At 8:45 P.M. SNCC placed a collect call to Doar at his home. He refused to accept charges. Later in the evening the movement finally learned, from the newspaper reporters who had converged on Philadelphia, that the FBI was indeed organizing a search. New Orleans SAC Harry Maynor sent five agents and an inspector to Meridian on June 23. "We're going to see if we can find those guys," Maynor told Proctor. Agents from other field offices, including the Bureau's major case inspector, Joseph A. Sullivan, soon joined the New Orleans squad. On the night of June 24, FBI Assitant Director Alex Rosen arrived on the scene, having flown down from Washington aboard one of President Johnson's jets.[17]

By then, the movement had assumed the worst. "The kids are dead," Robert Moses told the summer volunteers back at their training site in Ohio. "No privileged group in history has ever given up anything without some kind of blood sacrifice." COFO wanted the FBI to mobilize and find Schwerner, Chaney, and Goodman, but there was more to their concern that that: they intended to force the protection issue. Moses urged the parents of the summer volunteers "to use their influence" to pressure President Johnson and Attorney General Kennedy into a commitment to protect workers *before* violence occurs." The chronology of the SNCC/COFO attempt to force an FBI investigation,

Moses added, "shows that it took 24 hours—undoubtedly the critical 24 hours—to get the Federal Government to act." Bureau officials found the chronology especially troubling. They suspected movement people had tape recorded phone conversations with field agents, and they took the time to see if any wiretapping statutes had been violated.[18]

Eventually, COFO had more success in forcing Lyndon Johnson to act than J. Edgar Hoover. Pressure on LBJ built slowly, and in a distinctly political mode. "Congressman Bill Ryan [D., N.Y.] called me," Lee White recalled, "so I go to the president and say, 'Mr. President, Bill Ryan's calling on behalf of the parents . . . they really want to see you.' " "*What for?*," Johnson asked. "Well, they just want the world to know and they want to be reassured that you're doing everything you can to find those kids." "This is June," Johnson told White. "Every goddamn time somebody's going to be missing, I got to meet with all those parents." "He sort of said, 'No,' " White continued. "I said, 'Well, it's not a case of whether we're gonna invite them. I have to go back and tell Ryan no. . . . The *Herald-Tribune* is going to have an article saying the president refuses to see the parents of the missing civil rights workers.' Now he's really getting mad. . . . In any event, the president saw 'em"—Schwerner's and Goodman's parents, anyway—and "while they were all there, Hoover called and said we found the station wagon." Actually, several Choctaw Indians had come across the car by chance.[19]

To Michael Schwerner's wife, a slight, pale woman with black hair, it looked like nobody cared. A secret service agent took her late-night telephone call to the White House, declining to wake the sleeping president. "Mrs. Schwerner sounded quite upset," the agent concluded. "She wished to know how many agents of the FBI were working on the case and where they were working" and "could possibly cause embarrassment."[20] Two days later, on June 25, Rita Schwerner tried to see Mississippi Governor Paul Johnson in Jackson. Accompanied by Edwin King and Bob Zellner, SNCC's first white field secretary, she was kept out of the governor's waiting room by "a fat man" who "zoomed ahead . . . and slammed the door." After a few knocks, the group spoke briefly to one of the governor's assistants and a receptionist—who "started telling Rita what a beautiful state Mississippi was." They caught a glimpse of Governor Johnson later that day at his mansion, escorting Alabama Governor George Wallace and Jackson Mayor Allen Thompson up the steps. When Governor Johnson saw who they were he "started walking," leaving Michael Schwerner's wife facing another closed door. From Governor Johnson to President Johnson, and from Mayor Thompson to FBI Director Hoover, everyone hoped Rita would simply go away.[21]

Mrs. Schwerner and her companions had better luck seeing President Johnson's special emissary, former CIA Director Allen Dulles, over at the Federal Building. Dulles granted the group an audience of two minutes. The government was doing all that it could, he said. When Rita said the government was not doing much of anything, an FBI agent sitting in the room told her the remark "was a poor joke in poor taste." The two minutes were up. When Dulles offered his hand, she refused to shake it. She "didn't want sympathy," she "wanted her husband back." She headed out the door and toward Philadelphia to confront Neshoba County Sheriff Lawrence Rainey. Dulles moved on to his next appointment, receiving Henry, Moses, Dennis, and Guyot. When he told them "we want this mess cleaned up," Henry asked what he meant. "Well," Dulles said, according to Henry's recollection, "these civil rights demonstrations are causing this kind of friction, and we're just not gonna have it, even if we have to bring troops in here." The COFO delegation was incredulous. "You talkin' to the wrong people," Henry told the president's emissary.[22]

On the evening of June 25, the same day that Rita Schwerner saw Paul Johnson and Allen Dulles, television newsman Walter Cronkite described the search for the three civil rights workers as "the focus of the whole country's concern."[23] Lyndon Johnson finally met with Mrs. Schwerner on June 29, and with Chaney's mother in early July, and he had more on his mind than public relations. Burke Marshall described the apparently "silly idea" of sending an aging ex-CIA chief to Mississippi as a "pretty effective" strategy in the long run. "There's three sovereignties involved," Marshall explained. "There's the United States and there's the State of Mississippi and there's J. Edgar Hoover." The president "dealt with them separately, and he used Allen Dulles to do that, and it worked." When Dulles returned to Washington he advised Johnson to send more FBI agents to Mississippi, and further noted that the agents already there were too close to segregationist politicians. Having been "maneuvered" (Marshall's word) by Johnson, Hoover decided to open "a new big office in Jackson"—a bit of presidential persuasion that an amazed Ramsey Clark described as "one of the great positive feats of contemporary American history."

It was also an Oval Office end run around Robert Kennedy. Nobody bothered to tell the attorney general. When Kennedy asked about the new Jackson office after reading about it in the newspapers, Hoover told him to "direct his inquiries to President Johnson." That comment best reflected the director's reasons for succumbing to White House pressure. He would act in Mississippi in exchange for more independence from the Justice Department.[24]

Roy K. Moore, the new special agent in charge, arrived in Jackson on July 5, giving him only five days to have an office ready for opening. Hoover was due to arrive on July 10. The FBI had not had a field office in Jackson since the Second World War. Bureau agents in northern Mississippi operated out of six resident agencies and reported to the Memphis field office. The seven resident agencies in the southern portion of the state reported to New Orleans and Jackson was the largest of the resident agencies, with six agents quartered in a few rooms in the Federal Building. So Moore looked up an old friend from Charlotte, who was then president of a Jackson bank, and talked him into leasing the top three floors of the bank's new office building. More contractor and carpenter than G-man for the next four days, Moore beat his deadline with "a dummy office—a sort of false-front Potemkin village—just opposite the elevators on the top floor."[25]

FBI Assistant Director Cartha DeLoach arrived on July 9 to handle arrangements for Hoover's security. In most ways, as syndicated newspaper columnist Nicholas Von Hoffman commented, the director was the rarest of human beings in Mississippi—"a popular Federal official." Even the July edition of the White Knight's *Klan Ledger* had something good to say about him. Dismissing the Schwerner-Chaney-Goodman "disappearance" as "a communist hoax," the Klan recommended that any person who did not understand the ways of America's subversives "do a little reading in J. Edgar Hoover's primer on communism, MASTERS OF DECEIT." The director had powerful friends in Mississippi, too. He included the names of both United States senators, James Eastland and John Stennis, on his Special Correspondents List. But neither DeLoach nor Hoover took any chances. Among other services, DeLoach screened all phone calls to the Sun 'n' Sand Motel where the director had reservations, including at least one anonymous, threatening call.[26]

When Hoover and his associate director and constant companion Clyde Tolson arrived on the morning of July 10, they were greeted at the airport by Mayor Thompson, State Commissioner of Public Safety T. B. Birdsong, Jackson Police Chief W. D. Rayfield, "and other city and state dignitaries"—the very people the civil rights workers said they needed protection from. After meeting briefly with Moore, Rosen, and Sullivan, and accepting their recommendation that he not visit Philadelphia, Hoover went to the governor's mansion for his first appointment. He promised to help professionalize the Highway Patrol by reserving space in the FBI National Academy for additional Mississippi applicants and by lobbying in Washington for money to upgrade the state police academy. He also gave Governor Johnson and Commissioner Birdsong the names of those highway patrolmen who had joined the Klan. The meeting lasted about an hour. Hoover's group moved on to their second appointment at the capitol building with Mississippi Attorney General Joe T. Patterson, who introduced his entire staff, most of his family, and "a large number of state employees." Hoover found everyone "friendly" and "warm."[27]

The ceremonies opening the new FBI field office began at 1:00 P.M. At the press conference that followed, Hoover made it clear that he had not sent 153 agents into Mississippi to protect civil rights activists. Earlier, he offered COFO workers the opportunity to leave their fingerprints at the nearest FBI field office and that was about as far as he would go. The director went on to describe Governor Johnson, who had called NAACP activists "Niggers, Alligators, Apes, Coons and Possums" during a recent campaign, as "a man I have long admired from a distance." Neil Welch, the assistant special agent in charge of the Jackson office, said Hoover "had declared war, but, unlike the Justice Department, he had carefully avoided making Mississippi the enemy." "The FBI comes in here everyday and we have coffee everyday," the sheriff of nearby Clarksville told reporters after the press conference. "We're good friends." Though SNCC workers had named this particular law man in dozens of affidavits charging brutality, his faith in the FBI was well put. "A few Civil Rights Division attorneys," Welch claimed, "actually manufactured" a good many of the police brutality complaints in Mississippi.[28]

Hoover's last appointment was with Charles Evers of the Mississippi NAACP. "Evers was difficult to reach," Joseph Sullivan remembered. "He appeared to feel he had no need for liaison

with the FBI." But Evers talked to Hoover. When he mentioned
the burden of constantly living under the threat of violent death,
the director "suggested he carry on in the tradition of his late
brother. . . . I told him that while I could understand his feelings,
he must expect some degree of personal danger—particularly in
view of his position of leadership during an era of turbulent social upheaval. I mentioned the numerous threats to my life over
the years, mostly from the lunatic fringe." Before moving on,
Hoover lectured Evers on the criticism leveled by "a number of
[his] followers" in the wake of the FBI's investigation of Medgar's assassination. Evers himself remembered Hoover as "a
racist. . . . He didn't have time, he didn't want to sit down. . . . I
kept pressuring him about why there were no Negroes in the
FBI," but all he wanted to do was look "for a bugger bear behind
every stump."[29]

Having spent twenty-four hours and five minutes in Mississippi, Hoover returned to Washington the next morning, where
he found a grateful Lyndon Johnson. "I find it a great solace
to lean on an old friend, such as you in handling such delicate
assignments," the president wrote. "You left behind you in Mississippi a feeling of good will." With Martin Luther King scheduled to speak in Greenwood ten days later, Johnson asked Hoover for one more favor. He wanted the FBI to protect King, to
station agents "in front and back of him when he goes in; that
at least there ought to be an FBI man in front and behind to
observe and see what happens." The director agreed to do so.[30]

Hoover's largess set no precedent. His FBI provided protection for one civil rights leader during one speech—and only after
a phone call from the president. Johnson placed that phone call
six minutes after Robert Kennedy told Hoover to protect King.
The director said no. "I told the Attorney General that once we
start protecting [one of] them, we are going to have to do it for
all of them. The Attorney General stated he had raised the point
with the President so perhaps I would want to discuss it with
the President. I told the Attorney General that I will do whatever
he thought should be done . . . but I had taken a firm stand on
it. The Attorney General stated he had never asked me to do it."
When refusing Kennedy's request, Hoover created a paper record denying his own insubordination.[31]

Afterward, the FBI received letters from two suspects in the
Philadelphia murders, Sheriff Rainey and a Neshoba County
judge, complaining about the twenty or twenty-four agents who

protected Dr. King "at all times." Both men argued, as Hoover had countless times in the past and would continue to do so once King had left Greenwood, that state and local police should have handled the assignment. The SNCC people also noted the Bureau presence when King arrived in Mississippi, and a few responded with sarcastic comments. When four car loads of FBI agents showed up with King in Jackson, summer volunteer Sally Belfrage said no one knew why they were there—"since they were not, of course, a police force and could not, of course, protect anyone."[32]

Both the civil rights community and the white resistance adopted a skeptical, wait-and-see attitude toward the new FBI presence in Mississippi. During an interview for the Walter Cronkite broadcast on CBS, King referred to the publicity regarding the Jack Gilbert Graham case that had accompanied Roy Moore to Jackson. Graham had detonated a bomb aboard a commercial airplane, and the case was one of the toughest in the FBI's history. Moore broke it nonetheless. King wondered how "a plane can be bombed and its pieces scattered for miles and the crime can be solved, but they can't find out who bombed a church." Dick Gregory, the black comedian and activist, dismissed the Bureau as "a joke . . . a second Ku Klux Klan." "If these Mississippi white Klansmen, who do not know how to plan crimes, who are ignorant, illiterate bastards, can completely baffle our FBI," Gregory asked, "what are those brilliant Communist spies doing to us?" Three days after the murders, a group of SNCC workers "went into the county (Neshoba)," but "didn't see any police cars or FBI and we went over lots of portions of the county. The only thing we saw was a marine helicopter flying above us . . . we didn't see any FBI."[33]

The reason for the skepticism about the FBI presence was obvious. The violence had not abated. By COFO's estimate 450 incidents marked the three months beginning June 15. Segregationists assaulted three voter registration workers in Hattiesburg as Hoover made his speech in Jackson. In Canton, when police officers beat another voter registration worker, McKinley Hamilton, Minnie Lou Chinn described the reaction of two FBI agents. "[They] saw it all just as we did, and them bastards had the nerve to ask what happened." When assistant SAC Neil Welch arrived in early July, he saw fresh blood on the sidewalk outside the bank building that housed the new FBI field office, evidence of the axe-handle beating three black COFO activists had received on Jackson's main street. The victims of this assault, still bleeding, were inside waiting in Welch's office, and they told Welch their story while another FBI agent crawled around on the floor, spreading newspapers to keep the blood from staining the carpet. Even the reporters who helped make 1964 "a banner year for the Mississippi motel and car-rental business" invariably checked in at The Embassy—their name for the Jackson field office. "People coming in from outside, that is, from anywhere except Mississippi," Roy Moore said, "were afraid for their lives. And with good reason . . . we had about ten murders altogether."[34]

COFO workers never received adequate protection from the FBI, but they did notice a few encouraging signs. Moore launched a speech-making campaign to alert the public to the danger posed by terrorism, and the FBI arrested three white men in Itta Bena for threatening two summer volunteers who were canvassing with SNCC staff member Willie McGhee. Over time, Moore and his men accomplished most of their goals. They identified all of the Klan officers in Mississippi, escalated their Klan infiltration investigations of city, county, and state police, and notified "the head of the law enforcement agency involved," along with the governor of the state, if "any member of his organization . . . [had] been sworn into the Ku Klux Klan." This was not done in every southern state—Hoover said his men could not deal with the Alabama Highway Patrol because of Governor George Wallace's "psychoneurotic tendencies." In Mississippi, though, things worked smoothly. Governor Johnson "summarily fired" five troopers identified in this manner, and ordered uniformed members of the Highway Patrol to interrogate every known Klansman "out in the rural." All this was accomplished, Nicholas Katzenbach later advised President Johnson, "at the urging of the FBI."[35]

A few FBI agents resigned rather than go to Mississippi with Roy Moore. For a time, Jackson became a "voluntary office." The hours were too long, community pressures too intense, the danger too imminent. A few young, aggressive agents, however, leapt at the chance to go South and work the tough cases in a tough environment. It was glamorous, or at least exciting, to crawl under a black grocery store or a COFO Freedom House to look for a bomb on your first night on the job. "The breakdown in local law and order" appalled most of the agents who did volunteer, John Doar concluded. "They were ashamed of the Bureau's prior performance," its deference to the rule of white over black and its indifference to the rule of law.[36]

FBI Inspector Joseph Sullivan led the effort in the field to solve the Philadelphia murders. Robert Wick, a Bureau executive who had worked on the Mack Charles Parker lynching in Poplarville, Mississippi, back in 1959, said Sullivan was "absolutely the best there is. If I ever did anything wrong, the last man in the world I'd want after me would be Joe Sullivan." The people who buried Schwerner, Chaney, and Goodman learned that first hand. Sullivan headed a massive investigation, captioned MIBURN (a reference to the burning of the church in Longdale), that involved 258 agents. They interviewed over 1,000 Mississippi residents, including 480 Klansmen—"just to let them know we know who they are," Hoover said; spent $815,000; and "worked in swamps infested with rattlesnakes and water moccasins." The dredging process turned up several black corpses and parts thereof—including a torso clad in a CORE t-shirt. Many agents missed vacation time, and "only a few got home for Christmas." They overlooked nothing, missed no angle. "We also have a long line of individual Negro women with whom the Sheriff has had sexual relations," the director told the president. "We are digging into that more for persuasive evidence on him when we bring him in," so "[we can] put pressure on him."[37]

The pressures on the FBI were enormous. "You got questions everyday," civil rights section chief Clement McGowan recalled. "Have you found the bodies, have you found the bodies, what are we doing? We got just an awful lot of heat from Mr. Hoover. . . . That was a rough one to handle." "You know, they went like a pack," McGowan continued, describing the subjects of the investigation. "Everybody knows everybody else and they could see, say, that Agent A and Agent B were interviewing suspect No. 5 here. . . . As soon as the agents left they moved in on him to see what was going on and what he told him. That made conducting interviews extremely difficult." Joseph Sullivan said nobody would talk "save for a few brave ladies"—Florence Mars, Ellen Spendrup, and a few of their friends. Mrs. Mars and her friends did what they could, but they did not really know very much and no one else in the Philadelphia area would talk. "Fear of the Klan overlay the uncooperative attitude of some," Sullivan noted. "Others perceived that the civil rights workers were outside troublemakers who had received their just dues."[38]

Things were so tough that Hoover nearly brought in the marines to help—after the White House garbled a message about sailors from a nearby naval air station participating in the search for the bodies. When President Johnson told Hoover to "get two hundred marines down there right away," the director delegated the task to William Sullivan, who phoned Secretary of Defense Robert McNamara and Undersecretary of Defense Joseph A. Califano, Jr. After Califano called back with a progress report—the corps supposedly had one helicopter carrying twenty or thirty marines in the air and was lining up the rest at Fort Bragg and Paris Island—Hoover phoned the White House once again. In the interim, with Governor Johnson and Senator Eastland threatening to go to the press ("Marines Invade Mississippi!"), the commander in chief aborted the mission, with the chain of command flowing, as ever, through Sullivan's Division Five desk to the Pentagon. The marines never landed.[39] The whole thing was more unusual than most of the requests for FBI assistance that emanated from President Johnson's Oval Office, but Hoover knew that he had to respond—that it was part of the price he had to pay for the greater independence he gained from the Justice Department. The president concluded that the director's promptness in handling such requests indicated an absolute loyalty. He was mistaken, and he would ultimately pay a price for misreading Hoover.

The FBI forced the first real break in the Neshoba County case by paying an informant $30,000. "We bought the informant," one agent said. "Cheap. We'd have paid a lot more if we'd had to. We'd have paid anything." On August 4 the informant's tip led Joseph Sullivan's men to a dam construction project on the Ollen Burrage farm. Working with a Link-Belt dragline and a Caterpillar bulldozer with a ten-foot blade, the digging went on for nearly six hours in 106-degree heat before the blow-flies began gathering, "numerous vultures or buzzards were observed reconnoitering," and Michael Schwerner's body appeared, face down in the Mississippi clay. The three civil rights workers had not "gone to Cuba," as the Klan kept telling everyone. When the FBI telephoned the White House to say that two "WBs" (white bodies) and one "BB" (black body) had been found, the president interrupted a National Security Council meeting to take the call.[40]

By early September the FBI had sent the Justice Department thousands of pages of investigative reports and other documents on the murders, the beating of the three blacks at Longdale, the burning of the Mt. Zion Church, and dozens of other civil rights complaints against Neshoba County law enforcement officers. By the end of the month, in the wake of a state grand jury's refusal to return a single indictment (and the FBI's understandable refusal to share information with segregationist state prosecutors), Department attorneys began their presentation of evidence to a federal grand jury in Biloxi. Acting Attorney General Katzenbach, nonetheless, cautioned President Johnson not to expect too much. The FBI had not "solved the murder case" and thus its reports contained "no evidence which can form the basis of an indictment for these murders."[41] Instead, the Bureau and the Department pushed for a Section 241 indictment against Rainey, Price, and others, on the grounds that they had conspired to deprive the victims of their constitutional right to do voter registration work in Mississippi. State authorities charged no one with murder or conspiracy to commit murder.

Indictments and convictions on federal civil rights charges were difficult to obtain even after the FBI obtained the confessions that broke the case wide open. On December 1, after Martin Luther King met with the director and told the press immediately thereafter that arrests were imminent, Roy Moore told Hoover that it appeared to white Mississippians "that King was calling the shots." Hoover sent Moore's message to the White House. Three days later, on December 4, the Bureau arrested the sheriff, his deputy, and seventeen other men on the conspiracy charge. Six days later, United States Commissioner Esther Carter dismissed all charges at a preliminary hearing.

The FBI and the Civil Rights Division persisted, however, and in January 1965 secured indictments against all nineteen suspects. When Judge Harold Cox threw out the substantive part of the indictments (that is, the Section 241 counts), the Division appealed to the Supreme Court. In March 1966 the Court overruled Judge Cox, reinstating the original indictments. Nearly a year later, in February 1967, a new federal grand jury convened (defense counsel had argued that the original grand jury pool of potential jurors had not included a sufficient number of blacks, Indians, and women), and handed down indictments against seventeen conspirators. Finally, on October 20, 1967, based in part on the testimony of two paid FBI informants, an all-white jury found seven of the defendants guilty of violating Section 241. They found Rainey not guilty. Klan leader Sam Bowers received the maximum ten-year sentence; the others, including Price, received three to ten years. "They killed one nigger, one Jew, and a white man," Judge Cox explained, years later. "I gave them what I thought they deserved."[42]

At one time, there appeared to be a consensus that the FBI had done a good job. Hugh Fleischer, a Civil Rights Division attorney who worked in Mississippi, said the FBI acted throughout "as if it were a real investigation." Martin Luther King said the FBI's work "renews again my faith in democracy," while Whitney Young praised the FBI's "outstanding effort" and Roy Wilkins noted simply, "the FBI has done its job." After Cartha DeLoach briefed the black-owned *Chicago Defender*, Sumner Stone raved over the G-men in his "Orchid for the Day" column: "To the FBI for its usual relentlessly brilliant and painstaking police work," the same "kind of magnificent detective work that traced the bullet which killed Medgar Evers." Stone urged his readers to write the Bureau to say thanks. Hoover sent a copy of the column to the White House. Later, when Joseph Sullivan left the Bureau, about four hundred agents and two former Civil Rights Division lawyers attended his retirement party. The two lawyers were John Doar and D. Robert Owen, the man who presented the Neshoba County case to the federal jury.[43]

Not everyone was appeased. "It's a shame," John Lewis said, "that national concern is aroused only after two white boys are missing." SNCC placed "the full responsibility for these deaths directly in the hands of the United States Justice Department and the Federal Bureau of Investigation." That statement reflected, more accurately than the words of praise from King, Young, and Wilkins, or the comments of Sumner Stone's "Orchid for the Day," the view of the people who had organized Freedom Summer in the first place.[44] Joseph Sullivan and the other FBI agents in Mississippi had done a good job, but SNCC activists still believed they had enemies within the hierarchies of the FBI and the Justice Department. Other FBI actions during the course of Freedom Summer would show that the SNCC people were right about Hoover and his men, and nearly right about the Department.

In Mississippi and elsewhere, SNCC and the larger civil rights movement were always in a state of flux. The pace of change, however, quickened after the tragedy in Neshoba County. Berl Bernhard, the former staff director of the Civil Rights Commission, said the government's conservatism on the protection issue "broke down a trust on the part of people who were on the front lines of what was nothing less than a battle. . . . It had a detrimental effect on respect for the authority and the dignity of the United States of America," and contributed to "a further severing of the possibility of resolution. . . . The streets became the battleground and violence enveloped the movement." The movement began to split, moderates versus radicals, moderates moving to the left and a few radicals beginning a slide towards nihilism.[45]

There was a break in the movement and some abandoned the longtime commitment to nonviolence. The fracture was there for the FBI to exploit. Hoover ordered Roy Moore to set up a special squad to exacerbate the growing divisions within the movement, and the "civil rights desk" in the Jackson field office handled the counterintelligence responsibilities. One of the agents on the special squad, James O. Ingram, had originally requested a transfer to Mississippi because he wanted to work on civil rights cases. The chief counsel for the Jackson office of the National Lawyers Committee for Civil Rights Under Law, Lawrence Aschenbrenner, remembered him as "a good guy . . . the head of the Klan detail." But Ingram ended up on the Black Nationalist Unit-West of Division Five's Racial Intelligence Section, where he worked under another former Jackson agent, Hunter E. Helgeson, and he was sued, along with Moore and yet another Jackson agent, for violating the civil liberties of a black man. Bureau agents went after the Klan in Mississippi, but they also went after black nationalists and even moderate advocates of racial justice.[46]

FBI priorities did not change much during Freedom Summer. The Philadelphia horror and the pressure of events had combined to get the Bureau moving in Mississippi. But the bureaucratic priorities of Hoover and his men continued to prevail. In one way, Robert Kennedy and Burke Marshall received what they had hoped for on the eve of Freedom Summer. "The problem," to quote Marshall again, was "rather to describe what is happening in such a way as to permit the Bureau to develop its own procedures for the collection of intelligence." Hoover ended up with a brand new field office (and another one in Columbia, South Carolina, the next year), larger budgets, more agents, and control over his bureaucracy's destiny.

A few weeks before his agents arrested Price, Rainey, and the rest, Hoover described himself at a press conference as a "states' righter" who believed civil rights enforcement should remain the responsibility of local police officers. He praised the Mississippi Highway Patrol and "rapped," in an oblique reference to Robert Kennedy's attorney generalship, "the harsh approach toward Mississippi taken by the Justice Department during the past three years." He made a few references to "water moccasins, rattlesnakes, and red-necked sheriffs," then repeated the familiar refrain: "We don't guard anybody. We are fact-finders. The FBI can't wet-nurse everybody who goes down and tries to reform or educate the Negroes in the South." A few weeks later, in an interview with David Lawrence, Hoover again chose those code words for racism to describe himself. "I had spoken of being a states' righter . . . I was a states' righter." President Johnson had forced the director to send a positive signal to the civil rights community by opening a new FBI office in Jackson, and the director was determined to send a signal of his own to his white southern constitutents.[47]

Hoover knew what he was (a states' righter) and what his white constituency in the South demanded (surveillance of civil rights workers). Even during the most desperate days of Freedom Summer, when his agents scrambled to find the bodies, he did not neglect the Red menace. He briefed Burke Marshall on the "subversive activities" of Michael Schwerner's father back in New York, and his agents investigated anyone who had any connection with Freedom Summer whatsoever. In the case of Allard Lowenstein, who had visited South Africa and written on what he saw there, the Bureau noted his opposition to apartheid. The Bureau also clipped a newspaper article about Lowenstein's appearance at a dinner party given by Arkansas Senator J. William Fulbright. Other guests included Robert McNamara, Adlai Stevenson, and Lyndon and Lady Bird Johnson.[48]

Meanwhile, at FBI headquarters, Division Five directed the field to identify the college students who signed on as summer volunteers and to run their names through the files.[49] This type of trolling was not very useful. Few twenty-year-olds possessed old-left pedigrees. Bureau agents carried on nonetheless. They followed the students home through the late summer and early fall, visiting anyone who had criticized their organization's work in Mississippi and characterizing them in the files as "immature, unreliable and obnoxious." And they opened files on every resident of every COFO Freedom House—including one house whose residents included a Catholic nun, a former FBI agent, the son-in-law of a newspaper publisher, the daughter of a Communist party member, a newspaper reporter, and "an oversexed Vassar girl." "Of course there were associations," Roy Moore said. "There were quite a few hard-core communists, but they weren't any more important than any other group." The most extreme example of communist infiltration involved a newlywed couple in southwest Mississippi—"the son and daughter of two of the leading Communist party leaders in Wisconsin and Illinois" who came down "on their honeymoon" to handle "communications out of a COFO house."[50]

The FBI investigated another COFO house resident, Larry Rubin, a summer volunteer from Pennsylvania who had been assaulted in Holly Springs, Mississippi, after receiving a phone call from Senator James Eastland. Because he had been co-chair, along with Joni Rabinowitz, of the Fair Play for Cuba Committee back at Antioch College, the Bureau lumped Rubin with its uncounted group of "individuals with communist backgrounds [who] are known to have assisted in SNCC's 1964 'Mississippi Project.' " Moore may have been low key about the Red menace in the Magnolia state; Hoover was not. Three weeks after the call from Senator Eastland, he briefed New York Governor Nelson Rockefeller on the "communist problem" in connection with "the racial situation in Mississippi."[51] The FBI disseminated information to interested politicians like Rockefeller, "cooperative news media sources, educational officials and other sources in an effort to expose the background and activities of these communists."[52]

FBI officials also pursued their anticommunist goals by cooperating with the law enforcement community in Mississippi, sharing information with the intelligence units of the Jackson Police Department and the Highway Patrol. This last agency claimed to have files on "all known radical agitators in the State." The FBI received additional information from the Mississippi State Sovereignty Commission, one of the more primitive public-sector agencies formed in the wake of Brown v. Board of Education to "resist the usurpation" of states' rights. The Commission channeled tax dollars to the Citizens Council, hired informants, organized mass mailings, and, according to director Erle Johnson, Jr., "turned over information on subversives to the FBI." For a time during the late 1950s and early 1960s, chief investigator Zak Van Landingham—an FBI agent for twenty-seven years—coordinated these activities.[53]

The FBI's relationship with groups like the Sovereignty Commission and far-rightists like Erle Johnson and Zak Van Landingham was ambiguous. Hoover had only contempt for the methods of the Ku Klux Klan, but he recognized his constituency on the radical right. When Senator Karl E. Mundt (R., S.D.), a former member of HUAC and the McCarthy Committee, wanted a speaker for a Sioux Falls television station, he asked Bureau officials what they thought of Fred C. Schwarz of the Christian Anti-Communist Crusade. "The FBI reports Schwarz's material is intelligent, high level, and helpfully informative," Mundt advised the station manager. "They also told me that if you can't get Schwarz you might get an equally high level discussion on the Communist menace by Paul Harvey."[54] FBI officials even tried to manipulate far-right groups that they clearly identified as threats to the peace and stability of their America, sending information on black activists to J. B. Stoner's National States Rights party. They also sent Klan publications or "any other literature that can be obtained from organizations having an extreme hatred for black people" to black activists in Mississippi.[55]

Hoover never ignored the right, but he always focused on the left, and in Mississippi that focus led to the Medical Committee for Human Rights and especially the National Lawyers Guild (NLG), whose members had volunteered their respective medical and legal services. The FBI characterization of the NLG ("the foremost legal bulwark of the Communist Party") had been released under the name of the House Committee on Un-American Activities back in the 1950s, a time when Louis Nichols briefed a variety of groups and individuals on the Guild—from the American Bar Association to Senator Eastland's Senate Internal Security Subcommitee (SISS) and even Walter White and the NAACP. The damage was extensive. The Guild shrank to about 500 attorneys, with only a handful of members at large in the South and only four active chapters.[56]

The FBI had been monitoring the National Lawyers Guild's interest in the civil rights movement since 1959, when two attorneys from New Orleans, Benjamin Smith and Bruce Waltzer, tried to convince the Guild to become more involved in the black struggle. Not much happened until 1962 when two black attorneys from Norfolk, Virginia, Len Holt and E. A. Dawley, made an emotional plea for assistance at the NLG's national convention in Detroit. After extensive debate, the Guild decided to organize a Committee for Legal Assistance in the South (CLAS), selecting as co-chairmen two Detroit attorneys—one black, George Crockett, Jr., and one white, Ernest Goodman—and naming Holt and Smith field secretaries. In the months that followed, NLG members watched events in the South closely, particularly an October 1963 raid on the law offices of Smith and Waltzer, the two attorneys who had originally solicited their assistance.[57]

FBI officials also monitored these events closely. Louisiana police officers, acting on behalf of Jack Rogers, counsel for the Joint Legislative Committee on Un-American Activities, arrested Smith, Waltzer, and Southern Conference Educational Fund (SCEF) board member James A. Dombrowski, charging them with failing to register with the Department of Public Safety as agents of the Communist party. They confiscated all SCEF records—including a copy of Thoreau's *Journal* and a photograph inscribed for Dombrowski by Eleanor Roosevelt.[58] Rogers told the press that he had not coordinated the raid with local FBI agents because "they would have to tell Bobby Kennedy. We cannot trust him and expect he would tell his friend Martin Luther King." When King himself sent a telegram to the Civil Rights Division protesting the raid and requesting federal intervention, Burke Marshall said there was nothing the Department or the Bureau could do. The FBI had more freedom to act on the day after the raid, when SISS Chairman James Eastland sent Jay Sourwine, staff director of the Subcommittee, to New Orleans. Sourwine subpoenaed all 30,000 items seized in the raid and brought them back to Washington, where several FBI agents reviewed them. In March 1964, while the FBI indexed the names listed in the SCEF files, the Guild accepted an invitation from Bob Moses and SNCC to open an office in Jackson.[59]

The SNCC alliance with the National Lawyers Guild troubled nearly everyone. Senator Eastland told Cartha DeLoach that he was conducting "extensive" research "into House and Senate hearing records to build up a case against . . . [NLG] attorneys." He wanted "to show communist influence in the civil rights movement in the South," and planned "to make a talk very soon in the Senate on this matter."[60] Guild involvement even troubled the movement and its friends. SNCC said that Jack Greenberg and the NAACP Legal Defense and Education Fund had threatened to cancel plans to provide legal aid to the Summer Project unless Guild lawyers were purged. "We didn't want a lot of people barreling in here, spending thirty-six hours in Jackson, and then going home and telling people what great civil rights lawyers they were," Greenberg explained.[61] Others, including Carl Rachlin, CORE's chief counsel; Edwin J. Lukas, general counsel for the American Jewish Committee; and Leo Pfeffer, general counsel for the American Jewish Congress, met with De-Loach to discuss the "plans of the National Lawyers Guild . . . to encroach on the role of CORE lawyers." All three groups were "perturbed," Rachlin said. "Many of the younger attorneys in their own organizations had not had any experience in opposing the communists such as Messrs. Pfeffer, Lucas, and he had en-countered during the 1930s."[62]

After giving DeLoach a list containing the names of lawyers who had volunteered to work in Mississippi, the Rachlin delega-tion left to meet with Burke Marshall. Hoover ordered a memo sent to Walter Jenkins at the White House—Marshall having al-ready received a memo characterizing the National Lawyers Guild as a communist front. From there, the FBI ran additional name checks, disseminated follow-up memos on the Guild's civil rights strategies to Jenkins, Kennedy, and Marshall, and placed George Crockett and Ernest Goodman on the counterintelli-gence program target list. In one operation, a John Birch Society official who was "very close to the Bureau" obtained a Birch booklet (*It's Very Simple—The True Story of Civil Rights*) for the FBI, and the FBI sent it, along with an anonymous letter, "to numerous ministers, priests and rabbis in Detroit." The Bureau hoped to discredit Crockett and his work in Mississippi, and eventually tried to sabotage his campaigns for seats on the De-troit City Council and the Recorder's Court by working with an extremist group called Breakthrough. The Detroit FBI office fantasized about taking over Breakthrough and directing its "right-wing conservative" activities. Hoover approved any "jus-tifiable expenditure of funds to further this operation at any ap-propriate time."[63]

Besides Crockett and Goodman, the FBI focused on Guild members Henry Wolf and Martin Popper. Both men happened to represent Andrew Goodman's family, and Popper had been part of the Hollywood Ten defense team back in the late 1940s. (Goodman's parents were in fact part of leftist circles in New York; their dinner parties were attended by Zero Mostel, Alger Hiss, and others.) Popper and Wolf had accompanied Goodman's parents, Schwerner's parents, and Congressman William Fitz Ryan, among others, to the Justice Department, where they met with Nicholas Katzenbach and, briefly, with Robert Kennedy.

Hoover responded, once again, by sending memos to Walter Jenkins—with copies to Kennedy and Marshall and presumably Katzenbach as well. Describing the Lawyers Guild as a communist front, the director noted Popper's own conviction (later reversed) for contempt of Congress following his appearance in 1959 before the House Committee on Un-American Activities.[64] Turning from the Goodman family lawyer to Schwerner's parents, Hoover approved a wiretap (NY 4539-C*) on the home telephone of Michael Schwerner's father. Mostly, the tap uncovered information regarding "contacts of NAT SCHWERNER, in his activities to raise money for COFO."[65]

The FBI had also focused on Popper in early July, when he phoned Katzenbach to complain "that the Goodmans, as parents of one of the victims, have in effect been told nothing about the investigation to locate their son; that the parents want to know more; and are entitled to be told more than that the FBI is doing everything that can be done." "It appears," Courtney Evans wrote, after Katzenbach briefed the FBI, "that the Goodmans have been reading . . . highly speculative . . . newspaper items"—stories inferring "that possibly the local county sheriff at Philadelphia, Mississippi, has been involved." That was "an understatement," Hoover said. The director did not "care what the Goodmans nor Popper say or do. They are not going to intimidate me with their threats and innuendos. We have nothing to say and we will stick to 'no comment.' " If the FBI did tell the family anything, the director added, in a revealing comment, they would simply run "to the press—probably N.Y. Post or Worker."[66]

The FBI's pounding took a toll. By mid-summer, James Forman said "pressure on SNCC" to drop the National Lawyers Guild was coming "from the heartland of the administration itself." "[SNCC] workers are also involved in the COFO plans for the summer," Robert Kennedy told Lyndon Johnson. "They are seeking assistance from [the] National Lawyers' Guild . . . and some of them are more interested in forcing federal action in connection with street demonstrations than anything else."[67] (By relying on FBI reports for his understanding of the situation, Kennedy did not seem to realize that Freedom Summer was largely a Student Nonviolent Coordinating Committee project.) Forman's reference had its roots in a mid-summer meeting with Justice Department officials arranged by Alfred M. Bingham, who had left his Connecticut home for Jackson to see his son,

Stephen M., a summer volunteer from Yale. Bingham "almost had a fit" when he saw "the Lawyers Guild in operation there." Upon returning North, the senior Bingham, Burke Marshall, John Doar, and Arthur Schlesinger, whose own son Stephen planned to go to Mississippi, met with Steve Bingham, Forman, Moses, and Guyot. The ostensible purpose of the gathering, to discuss the situation in "the hill country of McComb and Natchez where the Klan rode strong," seemed secondary. "The Lawyers Guild," Forman said, "seemed to be the main subject on the minds of our hosts."[68]

From Forman's perspective, the civil rights workers might just as well have met with J. Edgar Hoover and his top aides. When they pressed the protection issue, Marshall "pleaded with us to go slow." When they said "all the United States Government had to do . . . was throw one of the racist sheriffs in jail," there was no reply. Only silence. After Marshall finally said something about the threat of "a guerrilla war in Mississippi" if the government locked up even one sheriff, Schlesinger brought up the Guild's tolerance of communists in its ranks. He made a point about the fight against communism in the 1930s and 1940s and then, "out of the blue," told the activists straight out, according to Forman's recollection: "We find it unpardonable that you would work with them." (Schlesinger does not remember using that particular locution.) The group emphasized "freedom of association" and "the unwillingness of the Justice Department and the NAACP Legal Defense and Education Fund to take aggressive action," but it did not do any good. Moses and Marshall "had a hot exchange on this point."[69]

Neither Bingham nor Schlesinger shared Hoover's alarmist assumptions about subversion, but in this particular case they believed communists in the National Lawyers Guild intended to send the sons of well-known people into dangerous areas. They called the meeting "out of a perhaps excessive but not unnatural concern for the lives of [their] sons." Nevertheless, as Forman later wrote in *The Making of Black Revolutionaries*, "the rupture with the government was complete and the issues absolutely clear. The words of Schlesinger echoed in my head, 'We find it unpardonable . . . ' What blindness and arrogance, I thought. He knew nothing of our struggle in the South." Forman and the others had gone into the meeting with the idea that they might finally convince the federal government to act in Mississippi. They walked out convinced that the government was the enemy of black people.[70]

Both Stephen Bingham and Stephen Schlesinger lived through Freedom Summer, and one of them went on to attract the FBI's interest. Schlesinger remained a liberal, eventually writing a book about the CIA overthrow of the Arbenz government in Guatemala and serving as special assistant to New York Governor Mario Cuomo. Bingham slid over to the far left. Grandson of Hiram Bingham (archeologist, governor of Connecticut, United States senator, chairman of the Loyalty Review Board), and great- and great-great grandson of two more famous Hirams (the Hawaiian missionaries), he moved on to law school at Berkeley, the Peace Corps, and Cesar Chavez's farm workers. He ran into trouble with the FBI and the law in California, after allegedly slipping a gun to the Soledad brother, George Jackson, at San Quentin Prison. Three white guards, two white trustees, and three black inmates, including Jackson, died in the violence that followed. (Bingham escaped and went underground for thirteen years before surrendering himself to authorities; in 1986 he won acquittal on two counts of murder and one count of conspiracy to commit murder.)[71]

Had Doar or Marshall told Hoover about the drift of their Freedom Summer conversation with Forman, Moses, Guyot, and Bingham, the FBI director probably would have been pleased. With three of their own buried under thirty feet of Mississippi mud, the movement asked for protection. The listened instead to a lawyer speak the director's language, the language of federalism, and a professor lecture on the director's issue, the communist issue.[72] The movement was told the truth—told to look for shades of gray because "the constitutional issues" were complex. The movement saw right and wrong, black and white, the corpses of summer volunteers and grinning sheriffs and deputy sheriffs with cheeks full of Redman. Jim Forman recognized "a pattern. If government agents take a position that, 'well, we don't care,' or 'it's complex, and so therefore we won't do anything, and so you can continue to beat people, you can continue to lynch people,' and so forth, then people will know that they're encouraged," he said. "I mean, you can encourage the Klan or you can discourage them."[73]

For the FBI, during the third month of Freedom Summer, spying remained the preferred task. This was especially true when

President Johnson asked Hoover to cover the Democratic National Convention in Atlantic City, New Jersey. Two events planned for the convention troubled the president. The first was a tribute to John Kennedy to be delivered by his brother, who had just announced his candidacy for his party's nomination for United States senator from New York.[74] The second was the Mississippi Freedom Democratic party (MFDP) challenge to the seating of the regular, all-white Mississippi delegation. Formed and staffed by native Mississippians from SNCC and other veterans of the Freedom Vote Campaigns and the Summer Project, the MFDP threatened LBJ's dream of convention harmony. White House interest dated from late July when Walter Jenkins submitted the inevitable name-check request to the FBI. John Doar followed this request with another on August 19, submitting the names of forty party leaders, delegates, and alternate delegates—including Fanny Lou Hamer.[75]

At the same time, and at the president's specific request, Hoover sent what Arthur Schlesinger described as a special squad of "snoops and wiretappers" to Atlantic City to spy on Robert Kennedy and the Mississippi activists.[76] Not surprisingly, the director selected Cartha DeLoach to run the operation. (The president called for assistance so often and on so many fronts that he ordered a direct telephone line installed in the assistant director's bedroom.)[77] DeLoach organized a squad of twenty-seven agents, one radio maintenance technician, and two stenographers. He also received an agent from New York who had accompanied Robert and a pregnant Ethel from the Kennedys' Manhattan apartment to LaGuardia Airport and then on to Atlantic City on the family plane. DeLoach's team set up a command post in the Post Office Building, averaged eight hours of overtime a day, and "approached each assignment as a challenge and with enthusiasm." They completed one assignment while Dr. King testified on the MFDP's behalf before the credentials committee—by tapping the telephone in his room at the Claridge House Hotel. They tried to install a bug, too, but "had to get out before they could get mike coverage." From there, they tapped the phone in Bayard Rustin's room, and planted a microphone in the storefront serving as the SNCC–CORE headquarters. CORE was an incidental target. The real targets, DeLoach said, were the "sixty members of the SNCC from Jackson, Mississippi, [who] plan to . . . assist in seating the Mississippi Freedom Democratic Party delegation."[78]

FBI agents monitored every tap and bug from their own room in the Claridge House, and the two-way radios used by the Freedom Democratic party and several of the other civil rights groups from "one of the rooms in the Post Office Building." Whenever they intercepted an interesting bit of conversation on MFDP strategy, they telephoned it to Robert Wick at Crime Records offices in Washington, and Wick dictated the information to stenographers (who typed it up on "plain bond paper") and then rushed the document to the White House by special messenger. President Johnson, as one commentator later put it, "had the convention wired—literally."[79]

To keep track of the Mississippi activists in Atlantic City, the FBI also secured press credentials, with "the cooperation of management of NBC news," for two or three agents who went out onto the convention floor, posing as newsmen. One agent "was so successful," DeLoach bragged, "that [name deleted] was giving him 'off the record information' for background purposes, which he requested our 'reporter' not to print." Another agent, Lloyd Nelson, posed as a news photographer, and yet another, Ben Hale, interviewed "key persons in various groups, using walkie-talkie equipment" and broadcasting not to NBC but to the Bureau control center in the Post Office. Other agents operated an informant who "penetrated" MFDP headquarters in the Gem Motel and the place where the delegation held strategy sessions, the basement of the Union Temple Baptist Church. Most of the remaining agents watched the demonstrations out on the Atlantic City boardwalk. Michael Schwerner's widow, older brother, and mother and father were there, along with about 120 SNCC and CORE activists. DeLoach's squad ended up with "separate files" on the MFDP, King, and SCLC; several far-left and far-right groups; local hoodlums; and what seemed like every single movement group—CORE, SNCC, COFO, ACT, and the NAACP; among others.[80]

The Johnson White House had other sources of information on the Freedom Democratic party besides the FBI. One of Bill Moyer's friends, Robert Spike of the National Council of Churches ("one of these quiet, anonymous, little guys who devotes his life to causes like this"), had "the confidence of the Negro groups working in Mississippi" and relayed what he had learned. Martin Luther King himself kept in contact with Lee White, though he no doubt sought leverage of his own. He told White to expect "demonstrations and riots . . . unless some sort of satisfactory adjustment of the 'Freedom Party' issue is found."[81] Attorney Joseph Rauh, who represented the MFDP, also kept in touch with Johnson administration officials and responded, in the manner of Dr. King, with his own form of pressure. After the president had Walter Reuther and Hubert Humphrey ask him to drop his efforts on the party's behalf, Rauh told Humphrey "if I get out, the National Lawyers Guild fellows are going to take this fight over and they're going to be really wild. You guys just don't know. At least you've got a sensible guy here."[82]

Nearly all of the information gathered by DeLoach's squad on the Mississippi activists and their strategies and allies, much like the information gathered by the administration's other sources, had a political slant. The FBI supplied the type of information President Johnson craved. What would King and Rauh do if the president met with them? What did the movement think about the possible vice-presidential nominees? Would the MFDP accept the compromise engineered by Oregon Congresswoman Edith Green? Was New York Congressman Adam Clayton Powell, Jr., carrying a revolver on the boardwalk? What was the NAACP up to? Why was CORE planning to picket the office of Charles Diggs, the black congressman from Detroit? Although they were not always right, DeLoach and his team always had an answer.[83]

Among other services, DeLoach convinced White House aides Bill Moyers and Walter Jenkins, through "counseling," to support changes in procedures for granting admission to the convention floor. This enabled the FBI to "preclude infiltration of the illegal Mississippi Freedom Democratic Party (MFDP) delegates in large numbers into the space reserved for the regular [all- white] Mississippi delegates." Through other "counterintelligence efforts, Jenkins, et al., were able to advise the President in advance regarding major plans of the MFDP delegates." Because the FBI overheard a number of congressmen, state governors, and other prominent political figures on the various taps and bugs in use during the convention, DeLoach furnished intelligence that ranged far beyond MFDP strategies.[84]

"It was obvious that DeLoach wanted to impress Jenkins and Moyers with the Bureau's ability to develop information which would be of interest to them," special agent Bill D. Williams conceded. On one occasion, during a lengthy telephone conversation with Jenkins, DeLoach "appeared to be discussing the President's 'image.' At the end of the conversation [the assistant director] told us something to the effect, 'that may have sounded a little political to you but this doesn't do the Bureau any harm.' " "[I was merely keeping] Jenkins and Moyers constantly advised by telephone of minute by minute developments," DeLoach explained. "This enabled them to make spot decisions and . . . adjust Convention plans to meet potential problems before serious trouble developed."[85]

When DeLoach returned to the seat of government on August 28, Jenkins called Hoover to let him know the president "thought the job the Bureau had done in Atlantic City was one of the finest [he] had ever seen," that "there were a lot of bad elements up there and because of the work some of the Bureau people did [the administration] knew exactly where they were and what they were doing." Upon hearing this, the director recommended DeLoach for "a meritorious award." A few days later, on September 10, DeLoach thanked Moyers for his "very thoughtful and generous note concerning our operation. . . . It was a pleasure and a privilege. . . . All the boys that were with me felt honored in being selected for the assignment. . . . I'm certainly glad that we were able to come through with vital tidbits from time to time which were of assistance to you and Walter."[86]

The FBI continued to monitor the Mississippi Freedom Democratic party in the aftermath, even as party activists returned home to prepare for the elections and to suffer continuing harassment at the hands of the white resistance. October 21 was a typical day in the town of Marks: "Campaign worker forced off highway, beaten by 4 whites and urinated upon: suffered concussion." Things had not changed much since June 21. The Klan still rode strong. Johnson administration officials, for their part, ignored the defection of most of the Mississippi delegates recognized by the credentials committee in Atlantic City to Barry Goldwater in the November elections. The administration continued to view the MFDP as part of the "leftist elements of the civil rights movement," and the FBI continued to feed that view by sending alarmist reports on the party to the White House. "There was a fear in this country of ordinary people havin' power," Freedom Democractic party chairman Lawrence Guyot said. "And there was no better illustration of that in American history than sharecroppers, and day laborers, and beauticians, and barbers, and preachers, sittin' and sayin' to the president and everybody else in the Democratic party, 'NO.' "[87]

Hoover helped Johnson achieve his goals in Atlantic City, but the president paid a price for his success. Joe Rauh said the civil rights movement never quite trusted LBJ after August 1964. Theodore H. White had once described LBJ as the man who made "the matter of race relations again a subject for discussion and legislation in Washington." And Johnson helped bring the country the Civil Rights Act of 1964 in the middle of Freedom Summer. "Lincoln struck the shackles off the slaves," Virginia Durr contended with a rhetorical flourish that nonetheless contained a kernel of truth. "Lyndon struck the shackles off the South." But Atlantic City was not forgotten. Fifteen years later, Edwin King said the spying was "led by Lyndon Johnson, endorsed by some of the most respectable people like John Doar," and not much different from "the kind of things for which we impeached [sic] Richard Nixon." Roy Wilkins noted the "lasting sense of grievance" that followed Atlantic City, the "terrible damage to relations between white liberals and black organizers in the South."[88]

On the eve of the next Democratic National Convention in 1968, William Connell, an aide to Hubert Humphrey, asked Hoover to assemble another Atlantic City-type team and "do the same thing for the Vice President out in Chicago." The director said it was already in the works. The assistance actually provided was neither so pervasive (in part because Attorney General Ramsey Clark refused to authorize wiretaps in Chicago) nor political (in part because "Hoover was friendly with Nixon and supported his candidacy"). The Jackson field office, however, did send seven informants to cover the Chicago convention—assigning five of them to the Loyal Democrats of Mississippi, a coalition group whose members included MFDP representatives. This time, the Loyal Democrats successfully challenged Mississippi's segregated delegation after a stormy convention floor fight, thus enabling three of the FBI informers to sit in the convention hall and vote as delegates or alternate delegates.[89]

Back in Mississippi during the summer of 1964, the FBI hung a picture of the director in its new Jackson field office. In their own office nearby, SNCC hung a sign that read:

There is a place in Mississippi called Liberty
There is a department in Washington called Justice.

The disillusioned SNCC people hung that sign and wondered whether they should carry guns. After Klansmen firebombed the home of one of the black farmers who worked with SNCC to register voters in Holmes County, the farmer said "I got a automatic shotgun, Remington, twelve gauge, them high-velocity buckshot. So I jumped up and run out and turn it loose a time or two." Julian Bond remembered the farmer, who served as a Freedom party delegate in Atlantic City, and the debate in SNCC about carrying guns. "This old guy, Hartman Turnbow . . . He used to carry an army automatic in a briefcase and it's funny to see a man who looks like a farmer and is dressed like a farmer in coveralls and boots and, let's say, an old hat, with a briefcase. And he opens the briefcase and nothing's in it but an automatic." By the time Freedom Summer was half over, most SNCC field workers were carrying guns of their own.[90]

One week after the FBI found the bodies of Michael Schwerner, James Chaney, and Andrew Goodman, Cartha De-Loach met with Roy Wilkins to discuss SNCC and Forman. According to the Crime Records Division account of that meeting, "Wilkins advised . . . that James Forman, whom other Negroes refer to as 'the Commissar,' was actually the man who was in control of SNCC and that John Lewis was merely a front man. . . . Wilkins also felt that Forman had brought Lewis instructions from the CP."[91] Nearly a year to the day after the Philadelphia murders, on June 15, 1965, Attorney General Katzenbach finally acted on such reports, approving Hoover's request for a wiretap on SNCC—because the FBI had identified the group as "the principal target for Communist Party infiltration among the various civil rights organizations." Eventually, Katzenbach would call for the creation of "a militant but peaceful organization of young [black] people which could successfully compete with SNCC."[92]

While the FBI wiretap request made its way back through channels, Neshoba County Deputy Sheriff Cecil Price arrested a volunteer attorney for the Lawyers Constitutional Defense Committee (LCDC), Dennis Seinfield; a law student, J. V. Henry; and a young black man, Richard Tinsley, who had just been bailed out of the Philadelphia jail. When Price released all three men in the early evening, they telephoned Alvin Bronstein, director of the Jackson LCDC office, who asked the FBI to alert the Highway Patrol and to call the sheriff in Philadelphia. When the agent who took the call refused his request, Bronstein asked, "Do I need three more corpses to prove jurisdiction?," hung up the phone, and called John Doar. "It's a shame that Doar yields to such hysterical calls from obviously biased *sources* in these situations," Hoover wrote, upon learning about the incident and the belated mobilization of his Bureau. "I do not intend that our Agts. waste time and money following out unfounded calls."[93]

That same summer, when responding to Civil Rights Division requests to send more men to Mississippi, the FBI assigned at least a few agents with no civil rights experience but plenty of experience in communist infiltration matters. Hugh Fleischer, who was working on a segregation case in Greenwood at the time, remembered "guys who spent most of their careers watching the Lawyers Guild in Chicago or wherever. That's all they did. This one guy said, 'That's what I do. I watch the Lawyers Guild.' "[94]

Hoover was sending a message to civil rights workers and his own white southern constituents alike: The young people who came to protest the ways of white Mississippi had committed the crime of subversion, a crime worse than the crimes of the Klan on the night when Cecil Price stopped that CORE station wagon. Hoover's message exacerbated the dilemmas created by the Justice Department's own civil rights enforcement strategies. Two months before Schwerner, Chaney, and Goodman died, Burke Marshall noted "the loss of faith in law . . . among Negro and white civil rights workers. The consequences in the future cannot be foreseen."[95] The consequences were easier to see after Freedom Summer. The great majority of SNCC workers never really had that much direct contact with the FBI before Freedom Summer. In the aftermath, they did not remember the job Hoover's agents did in solving the Philadelphia murders or in breaking the back of the Neshoba County Klan. They remembered the Bureau's coldness during those first twenty-four hours after three of their fellows disappeared. They remembered the Bureau as a symbol of the federal government's caution, its interest in splitting the difference between right and wrong.

Seven years after Michael Schwerner, James Chaney, and Andrew Goodman had been buried, Charles Evers asked the FBI field office in Jackson to come to the aid of two Georgetown University students trapped in a barn in Scott County by Klansmen who were throwing a rope over a tree branch. Mayor of Fayette and candidate for governor of Mississippi, Evers telephoned "one of the top brass" and told him "to get some men over there." He stopped talking for a minute before frowning and shouting into the phone: "Listen! I don't give a damn *what* FBI policy is! You can observe and take notes all you want. But if I don't hear about those kids gettin' out safe in ten minutes, I'm goin' down there myself, *with* my bodyguard, *in* my campaign cars! I got forty reporters from all over creation sittin' right out here in the lobby who're gonna go with me. An' they'll tell the whole world how y'all never saved those kids after you were tipped off. Now that'll make one damn fool outa J. Edgar Hoover!" In some ways, white Mississippi changed faster than the director and his FBI.[96]

=====>XXX<=====

Klan Wars

The Ku Klux Klan and the Good Name of White America

On September 2, 1964, one month after the retrieval of the three civil rights workers' bodies in Neshoba County and five days after Cartha DeLoach and his team returned from Atlantic City, the FBI declared war on the Ku Klux Klan. Eventually, the Bureau would fight that war directly on two fronts, an extralegal front of COINTELPRO (counterintelligence program) dirty tricks and a legal front of investigation of Klansmen suspected of violating the old Reconstruction Era statutes; and indirectly on a public relations front of newspaper stories, magazine articles, books, and television specials designed to tell the story of its battles with the Klan on the other two fronts. For the first six months of this war, however, not much happened. It was a time of phony war, and it ended only on March 25, 1965, in Selma, Alabama, a former slave market town on the Alabama River, with a Klan murder of another white civil rights worker, Viola Liuzzo, a red-haired Detroit housewife and mother of five.[1]

For differing reasons, the movement, the FBI, and the Johnson administration expected trouble in Alabama. J. Edgar Hoover told Martin Luther King "that FBI Agents would be in Selma, not for the purpose of protecting anyone, but for the purpose of observing and reporting to the Department of Justice."[2] The director warned President Lyndon Johnson and Vice President Hubert Humphrey that communists and other radicals might provide confrontations.

But when Andrew Young and Ralph Abernathy asked Cartha De-Loach to identify the communists in the civil rights movement and to describe their influence, the assistant director referred the two civil rights leaders to HUAC and the American Legion. "The very racists we've been fighting," in Young's view. Nicholas Katzenbach centered on SNCC participation in the Selma demonstrations and James Forman's alleged threat "to send some of the toughest SNCC members to Washington with a view of demonstrating here." The attorney general was depending on the FBI for "intelligence."[3]

Under Hoover's watchful eye, the movement had been in Alabama since January for the Selma voting drive, and by early February state and local police had arrested Dr. King and three thousand others.[4] On March 9 segregationists beat Rev. James Reeb, a Boston Unitarian, and when he died two days later the movement had its first white martyr in Selma. Reeb's death attracted national attention, in contrast to the earlier killing of a young black man, Jimmy Lee Jackson, by a state trooper. On March 12 Katzenbach told Hoover he was "trying his best to keep troops out of there, and wondered whether an operation like [the FBI] ran in Neshoba County, with a special detail and a fellow like [Joseph] Sullivan [in charge]" might "keep the situation from getting too far out of hand." Hoover said Sullivan and a nine-man squad had already left to join the twenty-six agents on the scene—although he complained to his senior staff about "a situation where almost everyone is having hallucinations." On March 13 President Johnson asked Congress to act on the pending voting rights bill. On March 21 King began the Selma-Montgomery march, after the police had turned back two earlier attempts, including the attempt that led to the Bloody Sunday spectacle of March 7—the single most brutal repression of any civil rights demonstration. Katzenbach spoke to Hoover again on March 23 to thank him "for the help Bureau people have been on the march in Alabama, particularly the way they are getting information to the Army and to Ramsey Clark."[5]

The FBI had seventy agents in and around Selma by March 25, a day Viola Liuzzo spent on Highway 80 shuttling marchers back to the city in her car. On the last trip of the day, near Big Bear Swamp in Lowndes County, twenty-five miles from the Edmund Pettus Bridge, another car carrying four Klansmen drove past and one of the passengers shot Mrs. Liuzzo in the head. The bullet cut her spinal cord in two at the base of the brain, sending blood spurting from her temple, and she died instantly, crashing her car into the ditch. The man who reportedly pulled the trigger, Collie Leroy Wilkins, said to one of his companions as the Klan sped away, "Baby brother, I don't miss. That bitch is dead and in hell." The only passenger in the victim's car, Leroy Moton, a nineteen-year-old black barber and sometime SCLC volunteer, hitchhiked into Selma for help.

President Johnson ordered the FBI to "find the perpetrators of this heinous crime," to "do everything possible around the clock." He telephoned FBI headquarters twice and Hoover himself two or three times in the middle of the night, and again at 6:00 A.M. He followed this last telephone call with a call to Katzenbach at 8:00 A.M. By that time, the president learned, the Bureau had already solved the case. Most of the conversations that followed concerned White House strategies for maximizing press coverage of the forthcoming announcement that FBI agents had arrested four Klansmen. Johnson suggested that Hoover and Katzenbach "come over to the White House; that maybe we could get there before the statements and let television cover us as we come in; that we don't need to have any appointment, to just call [press secretary] George Reedy and tell him I'm coming over to see the President, then tell the Attorney General and just get in the car and come over." The only problem, Hoover reasoned, "is the astronauts get there at eleven o'clock and we can't complete matters by that time." It would be better to wait until "right after" the forty-five minute ceremony for the spacemen.[6]

A few minutes after noon, on live, nationwide television, flanked by his FBI director and attorney general, President Johnson announced the arrests. Hoover understood Johnson's interest in orchestrating this publicity, the use of the occasion to denounce the Klan and to pressure Congress to enact the voting rights bill the administration had submitted on St. Patrick's Day. The publicity helped LBJ and the movement obtain one of the things they wanted—the Voting Rights Act of 1965. "I don't know what they would have done if it hadn't been for Selma," Burke Marshall said. "But President Johnson at that time, at least, was very responsive and pretty smart about public opinion. When the Selma march took place, he saw that as an opportunity."[7]

Hoover understood that Selma could also help him achieve one of his own goals. Unlike the president, the director had no interest in "the colored people" and their right to vote. "Many who have the right to register very seldom do register," he said. But Hoover and Johnson were alike in one way, as a Crime Records Division agent noted. They were both "totally consummate, skilled politician[s]."[8] The FBI's public relations people accelerated their activities in the wake of Liuzzo's murder in order to change the Bureau's image as a silent ally of the white southern resistance and its brutalities. After Selma, as every consummate politician recognized, Jim Crow America was doomed. The new consensus would no longer tolerate the visible, on-the-books discrimination that had ruled in the South for so long, let alone the horrors and idiocy of the Ku Klux Klan.

Hoover made no concession to protect movement activists. He continued to oppose them even in the midst of his Bureau's battles with the Klan. From beginning to end, the Klan wars remained a sideshow to the real war against the black struggle for racial justice. Hoover saw the Ku Klux Klan as another subversive threat to the peace and stability of middle America, but he also saw the Klan as a threat to the good name of the anti-civil rights movement. Klansmen were discrediting all forms of resistance, including the FBI's preferred forms, and for that, the director decided, they had to be stopped.

The Klan wars began with the launching of a formal FBI counterintelligence program against "white hate groups." This was the third COINTELPRO, the first two having been launched in 1956 against the Communist party and in 1961 against the Socialist Workers party; and like its predecessors the Bureau designed the new program "to expose, disrupt, discredit or otherwise neutralize" the targeted group. Individual counterintelligence operations (dirty tricks) often violated federal criminal statutes relating to mail fraud and incited violence, and sometimes involved the sending of obscene material through the mail and extortion. But neither the COINTELPRO against the Klan nor any of the other programs had the solitary goal of invoking sanctions against dissidents. They had an explicitly "educational purpose" of bringing Klansmen or communists or Trotskyites "into disrepute before the American public." While William Sullivan's Division Five supervised the COINTELPROs, Cartha DeLoach's Crime Records Division had counterintelligence responsibilities of its own—including the recruitment of over three hundred newspaper reporters, radio commentators, and television news investigators. These sources could be counted on to publicize the FBI's position on virtually any issue and to discredit the KKK and the CPUSA and even "the liberal press and the bleeding hearts."[9]

The roots of the White Hate Group counterintelligence program lay in Philadelphia, Mississippi. During a White House meeting in June 1964, President Johnson said, "Edgar, I want you to put people after the Klan and study it from one county to the next. I want the FBI to have the best intelligence system possible to check on the activities of these people." The question was not whether a counterintelligence program should be launched, but which FBI division should handle it. Division Five had responsibility for Klan matters, including informant and intelligence functions, until 1958, when Bureau executives transferred those responsibilities to the organized crime section of the General Intelligence Division. "One of the prime factors" in this original transfer was "the almost complete absence of Communist Party activity in the racial area." Since the Bureau did not consider the Klan subversive and the communists were nowhere in sight, the experts in Division Five were not needed. Alex Rosen's General Investigative Division handled the Philadelphia murders, not William Sullivan's Domestic Intelligence Division.[10]

By mid-summer 1964 the FBI found "the KKK and supporting groups" to be "essentially subversive" after all. "They hold principles and recommend courses of action that are [as] inimical to the Constitution as are the viewpoints of the Communist Party." The Bureau used the Red menace to justify the recommended transfer of Klan matters back to the Domestic Intelligence Division. The party's more recent focus on "the racial problem" indicated a "definite need for an intelligence type penetration of these racial and hate groups," and only one FBI unit could handle such a responsibility. Division Five agents had spied on "subversive organizations through informants, anonymous sources, sophisticated microphone and technical surveillances, interview programs of highly specialized nature, etc.," for years, and they "could put this experience to excellent use in penetrating the Klan." If prosecution of individual Klansmen for violating the Reconstruction Era statutes and other federal civil rights law remained "an ultimate objective," the Bureau now deemed "intelligence" and "informant" needs to be more pressing.[11]

Though hardly routine, the transfer was not unusual. FBI officials' notions of exactly what type of word or deed constituted subversion were constantly in flux. They not only debated whether the Klan was subversive, but many other groups as well—including CORE and SNCC and even SDS. As late as June 1965, the Chicago field office advised headquarters flatly and without fear of reprisal: "These are not subversive organizations." This sort of debate, however, had little, if any, impact on surveillance priorities. Katzenbach approved the Bureau request to tap SNCC's office telephone during the same month that the Chicago field office filed its report. The attorney general had approved a tap of the SDS telephone the previous month.[12]

Division Five proposed a counterintelligence program against the Ku Klux Klan at the end of August. Hoover quickly approved a directive targeting seventeen Klan groups and nine far-right hate groups, ranging from the American Nazi party to the National States Rights party. The names of several unaffiliated racists, people who referred to the G-men as "Nigger babysitters," were also included on the target list. Division Five intended "to expose, disrupt and otherwise neutralize the activities of the various Klan and hate organizations," to continue "the policy of aggressively seeking out persons addicted to violence even though they have not violated a Federal law as yet." Sullivan expected the results to rival "our accomplishments in similar-type programs directed against [communist] subversives."[13]

Even though Hoover disliked the Klan for making white supremacy disreputable, he would not have attacked it as he did on his own. Of all the FBI's counterintelligence programs—against the CPUSA and the Socialist Workers and eventually black nationalists, Puerto Rican nationalists, New Left activists, and Chicanos and Mexicans on both sides of the border—only the Klan effort resulted from outside pressure. The pressure came from the press and the White House, from Robert Kennedy and then from Nicholas Katzenbach, and from the civil rights movement itself. The proof can be found in the contrast between the FBI preference for the intelligence investigation and the counterintelligence action over the criminal investigation and courtroom prosecution.

When asked to protect civil rights workers, Hoover's FBI claimed limited jurisdiction, warned about the constitutional dangers of a national police force, and posed as a disinterested, apolitical, fact-gathering investigative agency. Yet, during the counterintelligence period, it swallowed "an intelligence offensive completely outside the forms of the law." The goal in both cases was not so much prosecution as intimidation. Only the means differed. (Hoover once told Martin Luther King "that the FBI had put the 'fear of God' in the Ku Klux Klan.") In the manner of its investigations of civil rights violations and more ambitious investigations of civil rights activists, the Bureau thus entrenched its intelligence and counterintelligence mission as an alternative to its law enforcement mission "in connection with activities unrelated to internal security."[14]

In the process, Hoover largely avoided a public clash with the police in the South, so the FBI's "buddy system" remained intact. By relying on extralegal action, he avoided the headaches of bringing routine cases of Klan harassment before white juries in the South. By pursuing the Klan wars outside the legal system and in a secretive way, he increased his authority to act without interference from the Justice Department's dreaded liberal lawyers. Movement people demanded protection and asked the government to enforce the civil rights conspiracy statutes, Sections 241 and 242. The Johnson administration prescribed a heavier dose of FBI surveillance. The movement sought the rule of law and received a lawless counterintelligence program.

Hoover closely proscribed the Klan wars nonetheless. During the life of the White Hate Group program (1964–1971), the FBI authorized 287 operations, or roughly 40 per year compared to the 100 plus of the Communist party program. Few disruptive actions, moreover, were undertaken against individuals who did not belong to the various Klan organizations. Nothing rivaled the open-ended COMINFIL (communist infiltration) investigations, where the Bureau targeted "legitimate mass organizations in the integration field." There were no KLANINFIL or KLUX-INFIL investigations, no effort to determine whether the Klan had infiltrated "legitimate mass organizations in the segregation field." As a general rule, the Bureau did not bring the Citizens Councils under conventional passive surveillance operations. "We have never had any formal investigation of the Mississippi Council," Burke Marshall complained. "We have also had no results from suggestions that the Bureau should keep itself informed in the same way it does with the Klan."[15]

Once Division Five began to implement COINTELPRO–White Hate Group in the months that followed Viola Liuzzo's murder, Hoover briefed Katzenbach on the FBI's accomplishments. The attorney general thanked the director for the "detailed information," but he kept pressuring him to do more. Hoover said his men were "getting on the Klan—that this was well begun in Alabama but had not been developed as far in Mississippi." He promised to "pass on the order to intensify our efforts," and to seize "every opportunity to disrupt the activities of Klan organizations." Over time, Katzenbach thought the FBI had done its job, investigating, penetrating, and disrupting "activities of the Ku Klux Klan . . . vigorously, actively, overtly and with outstanding success." But he made no effort to find out exactly how the Bureau got on the Klan. How many "black bag jobs" (burglaries) of Klan members' offices and homes did FBI agents carry out? How many taps and bugs did they plant? The attorney general never asked.[16]

The operations against the Klan legitimized the FBI's preferred response to all forms of dissent, since they paralleled the more ambitious operations implemented first against Martin Luther King and later against broad sectors of the black movement. Division Five, the driving force behind the Klan wars (just as it had been in the campaign against King), exerted constant pressure on the field to pursue the new mission. The field reacted ambivalently however. Roy Moore dismissed William Sullivan's plan to "embarrass" the Klan by placing a bogus order for twelve cases of embalming fluid in the name of the Mississippi-based Americans for the Preservation of the White Race. Yet he reportedly authorized a number of operations too extreme even for the COINTELPRO file. Rumors flourished concerning the kidnapping of a Klansman to help solve the fire-bombing of a black family's home. On another occasion, after the Klan had threatened to kill any FBI man seen in Natchez, Paul Cummings "organized a squad of G-men and headed for the Klansmen's favorite bar." The KKKs did not come into the street when called out, so Cummings shot the windows out of the bar. "We were at war and we used some muscle," he said. The macho appealed to Hoover. While a few fist fights broke out between Klansmen and G-men, on the whole, the director bragged, the Kukkers were "yellow," "afraid to 'mix' with our Agents." The FBI could "outshoot and outfight" anybody, from Mafia soldiers to Klan missionaries.[17]

In Charlotte, North Carolina, FBI agents experienced the same ambivalence, sometimes resisting pressure from Division Five and sometimes submitting proposals as controversial as William Sullivan's ideas. After the special agent in charge filed a report about Klansmen donning dresses, padded bras, and wigs,

and strolling through black neighborhoods, Division Five ordered "a critical cartoon" prepared for release to a Crime Records source in the media. The SAC protested because it would
"make 'heroes' of the Klan." A group of white men "willing and
able to take steps to prevent the molestation of white women by
Negroes would be heartily endorsed by most of the white population." The KKKs, hardly "shrinking violets," "homosexuals or
transvestites," "did not indicate a 'desire' to wear female clothing." On the contrary, they were "eager to, and feel capable of,
engaging Negroes in physical combat." On another occasion, the
Charlotte office proposed to arrange for "this country's leading
evangelist," a person whose name (Billy Graham?) was included
on the FBI's Special Correspondents List, to preach a sermon on
the Klan. Division Five liked the idea. Hoover vetoed it.[18]

Most counterintelligence operations involved physical, economic, and emotional harassment. When the Alabama Klan met
for its national Konvocations, the Birmingham field office sent
anonymous letters and placed last-minute phone calls canceling
motel reservations. If a Klansman was a veteran and receiving
benefits of any kind, Hoover sent his name to the Veterans
Administration. Division Five published a joke book, *United
Klowns of America* ("light in presentation," but "a serious
effort at counterintelligence"), and established "a Bureau-
approved vehicle for attacking Klan policies and disputes from
a low-key, common sense, and patriotic position." Named the
National Committee for Domestic Tranquillity, this organization
had "chapters" in eleven states and published a regular bulletin
"under the signature of Harmon Blennerhasset, an obscure figure in American history who gave financial support to Aaron
Burr." The Bureau advised readers of the bulletin to quit the
Klan and support "our boys" in Vietnam.[19]

The FBI pursued the two most notable Ku Klux Klan leaders,
Sam Bowers of Mississippi's White Knights and Robert Shelton
of the Alabama-based United Klans of America, with special
zeal—but with nowhere near the ferocity that characterized the
pursuit of Martin Luther King. Roy Moore called several meetings with his field agents to discuss how they might harass Bowers, and at headquarters Division Five had the IRS send over
his tax returns. In Shelton's case, Division Five asked field
agents in Alabama and Georgia for "a summary of information
concerning [his] close associates, likes and dislikes, drinking
habits, and social habits . . . his relationship with his wife, any

other females or males." Bureau executives already knew Shelton did not like grits. They wanted to know more—facts, rumors, whatever. The information compiled did not have to be "accurate. . . . If [American Nazi party chief George Lincoln] Rockwell printed a report that Shelton had some Negro ancestors, it would [only] be necessary for us to know the names of certain ancestors who could, perhaps, have been an illegitimate child related to Shelton."[20]

Shelton had enough problems with the House Committee on Un-American Activities; a Division Five agent wrote those words about "Negro ancestors" two days after HUAC chairman Edwin Willis (D., La.) asked the House to cite the imperial wizard for contempt of Congress. Shelton had refused to cooperate with the Committee's investigation of the Klan—an investigation supported by the Johnson administration and the FBI and opposed by the civil rights movement on the grounds that HUAC's real interests lay elsewhere. While the Bureau directed the Committee to an ex-agent who Willis hired to head up a fact-gathering team, the movement wondered whether the Klan hearings would be followed by hearings on their own organizations. SNCC's Charles Cobb remembered a visit to Washington and a side trip to the Hill, where he wandered into HUAC's offices. "They had charts right on the wall. I mean, our names and photographs graphed out and where we were in SNCC or CORE or SCLC." After a wiretap revealed Southern Christian Leadership Conference concern, Hoover ordered the Un-American Activities Committee alerted "as a matter of cooperation."[21]

The FBI helped HUAC with its investigation after Willis met with DeLoach in March 1965, the same month Viola Liuzzo died, and admitted his Committee had "no information currently concerning Klans." DeLoach gave Willis a Division Five document, entitled "The Klan Today," and worked out a more ambitious delimitations agreement two months later—principally because the staff investigators HUAC had sent into Alabama and Mississippi were interfering with the Bureau's work. When Willis agreed to keep his people out of the South, the FBI agreed to provide information on Klan members "so that the Committee can intelligently question the individuals when they are on the witness stand." In Hoover's view, the HUAC investigation raised only one substantive problem: "We will be doing all of the digging and staff of House committee will take the bows." Both the Committee and the FBI wanted the credit for destroying the un-

Americanism of the Ku Klux Klan. Neither sought credit for protecting the equally un-American civil rights movement from Klan violence.[22]

While pursuing its counterintelligence assaults against the Ku Klux Klan, the FBI played a role in several civil suits and criminal prosecutions. One of the most important cases, outside of the Philadelphia murders, involved the shooting of Lemuel A. Penn, director of adult and vocational education for Washington's public schools and a lieutenant colonel in the Army Reserve, who died in rural Georgia while driving with two other black officers. Penn was on his way home after a two week tour at Fort Benning when a Klansman noticed the District of Columbia tags. "Must be some of President Johnson's boys," he said. "Out of town niggers." Hoover learned of the incident while returning to Washington himself, having just opened the new FBI office in Jackson. Calling it "cold-blooded murder," he assigned eighty-three agents to the case under Assistant Director Joseph J. Casper's direction. Those agents quickly arrested a small group of Ku Klux Klansmen, and Georgia authorities tried two of them in state court for murder. With defense counsel attacking a "carpet bagging administration of justice" headed up by a horde of FBI agents "infiltrating our land" in search of "white meat," an all-white jury found both Klansmen not guilty.

That decision, Hoover suggested, privately, was in part the FBI's fault. The agents assigned to the Penn case "made it known" that the Bureau would trade cash for information, an offer that "created suspicion upon part of jury against FBI." "I didn't know that FBI had become an arm of the 'poverty campaign,'" the director complained, in a revealing comment, upon learning of his agents' actions in Georgia. He intended to smash the Klan in a way that would not align his Bureau in the mind of the white South with the cause of the civil rights movement— or the larger cause of liberalism. Eventually, in two trials in federal court, two Klansmen were convicted and four other acquitted of violating the Reconstruction Era statute for their actions on the day Lemuel Penn died.[23]

Hoover's men had other successes. In Bogalusa, Louisiana, an area where the FBI had been collecting intelligence on the Ku Klux Klan since the mid-1920s, a federal judge issued an injunction against segregationist violence ("an act of the Nation against a klan") based primarily on the results of a massive FBI investigation.[24] Roy Moore set up a field post in nearby Hattiesburg, Mississippi, to investigate the murder of Vernon Dahmer, a black farmer and leader in the state NAACP who died when terrorists firebombed his home. FBI agents arrested fourteen Klansmen in connection with that murder. They made additional arrests when investigating bombing incidents in Mc-Comb, Mississippi, and New Bern, North Carolina.[25] Because the prospect of convicting a segregationist in any southern court, state or federal, remained problematic, the FBI escalated its intelligence and counterintelligence functions while pursuing indictments against specific Klansmen. The Bureau fully mobilized its law enforcement function only in those cases, such as the Penn and Dahmer murders and especially the Liuzzo murder, that attracted major media coverage.

The media itself represented the third battleground in the Klan wars. A media campaign enabled the FBI to publicize its accomplishments on the other fronts, and for Hoover it was a natural direction to move. Few Americans paid more attention to public opinion. Even fewer had tried to influence national politics over such a long period of time. Back in the 1940s, Senator George Norris (R., Neb.) called Hoover "the greatest publicity hound on the American continent." In the 1960s, John Kennedy described him as one of "the three masters of public relations in the last half century," along with financier Bernard Baruch and CIA Director Allen Dulles.[26] Hoover knew his task would be difficult. In the wake of Selma, the nation would not only take pride in destroying the Ku Klux Klan, but the entire segregationist apparatus. The new consensus had no patience for the Jim Crow sign let alone the Klansman's rope, and yet the FBI director, with his record of lethargic civil rights enforcement, charges of communist influence in the civil rights movement, and feud with Martin Luther King, was firmly allied in the minds of civil rights activists—and many other Americans as well—with the old and now thoroughly discredited order. Hoover would continue his opposition to the black cause, but for the time being his principal task was to improve the FBI's image.

Hoover used all the media skills he had acquired over the years. He had worked tirelessly to promote his Bureau's politics and reputation since his tenure as General Intelligence Division czar. In 1927 Franklin Dodge, a former agent, helped Senator Thomas J. Walsh (D., Mont.) document Hoover's history of granting "writers, who wrote articles that met with the Bureau's approval," "desk space" and access to "the radical files."[27] Hoover moved into radio in the early 1930s with *The Lucky Strike Hour,* a program that recounted Bureau exploits. During the New Deal years, he established the FBI building as one of the principal tourist attractions in the capital. Bureau displays treated the public to such sights as a plastic replica of Dillinger's death mask and the fingerprints of prominent Americans. The director kept everything up to date. When his favored ghostwriter, Courtney Ryley Cooper, committed suicide in 1940, the Bureau pulled his prints from the exhibit room and replaced them with Walt Disney's. The fingerprints were symbolic. Hoover cultivated support from prominent Americans systematically. People as diverse as Bruce Barton, America's first advertising and sales guru, and William Allen White, the Republican editor of the *Emporia* (Ka.) *Gazette,* sat in his "cheering section."[28]

FBI agents assigned to the Crime Records Division, under Louis Nichols and then Cartha DeLoach and Thomas Bishop, supervised these efforts to enhance the FBI's image and to promote the menace of crime and communism. Special agents in charge of the various field offices established ties with the media, and as well business leaders, law enforcement officers, mayors, and other prominent public officials in their respective cities. Following the establishment of the first counterintelligence program against the Communist party in 1956, Crime Records developed its Mass Media Program, a program that Bureau executive James B. Adams described as a modest effort "to get the truth out, to get a proper picture of the FBI's jurisdiction, its activities."[29]

By the early 1960s Crime Records had arranged extensive media coverage of the FBI's accomplishments, such as they were, as an equal-opportunity employer. On occasion, the Division had unexpected allies in publicizing the Bureau's record in the civil rights field. Hoping to manipulate Hoover with praise, Robert Kennedy urged his brother to mention the FBI in his 1962 state of the union address. "It would make a big difference for us," the attorney general said. More often, Crime Records mobilized its own allies. All special agents in charge received ten copies of Hoover's article in the August 1963 edition of *Yale Political* magazine, "The FBI's Role in the Field of Civil Rights," for distribution to "civil rights leaders." DeLoach had already sent copies to all "SAC contacts" and "other special friends of the Bureau." At the same time, said *St. Louis Globe-Democrat* reporter Patrick J. Buchanan, who would go on to serve the Nixon White

House during Watergate and the Reagan White House during the Iran-Contra scandal: "The FBI channeled up constant information on local Communists, radicals, and even national civil-rights leaders." The director never forgot his real enemies.[30]

As the movement criticized the FBI's civil rights record more effectively, Crime Records became more aggressive. Cartha De-Loach had lunch in February 1964 with Drew Pearson and Jack Anderson, the investigative columnists who at one time received preferential treatment but were by then on the Bureau's not-to-contact list. When they asked about civil rights, they heard De-Loach mention Hoover's recent interview with "a cub reporter from the 'Afro-American,'" and then sat and listened to a monologue:

> I told Pearson of the Director's insistence that there be no discrimination in the FBI and of the rapid progress made by a number of Negro Agents in our organization. I told him . . . of my association with Negroes in The American Legion, of the FBI's sponsorship of a boy scout troop at the Juvenile Training Center where 90% of the membership is Negroes, and of the fact that our Civil Rights investigations have always been very clear-cut and incisive.

"Jack Anderson spoke up at this point," according to DeLoach's account of the conversation, and said "he felt the Director would go down in history for the protection of civil rights. Pearson agreed and stated the Director's record in this regard was very clear."[31]

DeLoach also tried to cultivate contact with the black press. The case of C. Sumner Stone, Jr., of the *Chicago Defender* provides an example. Describing Stone in 1963–1964 as a "reliable contact," DeLoach gave him a scoop on the arrest of Medgar Evers's assassin, arranged an exclusive interview with Hoover, and provided other services. Whenever Stone needed something he would telephone DeLoach ("a very likable guy"). After the *Defender* fired him in 1964, for jeopardizing the paper's advertising revenue by criticizing Chicago Mayor Richard Daley, Stone went to work for Congressman Adam Clayton Powell and continued to receive services from the FBI—with DeLoach once running a name check on one of the persons invited to attend the First Black Power Conference. Stone wanted the FBI to check for any "communist connections," and that was the last time he remembered hearing from DeLoach.[32]

In the wake of the Philadelphia and Selma murders, Crime Records again escalated its public relations. Concentrating on conservative white newspapermen and not blacks like Sumner Stone, DeLoach sent Walter Winchell twelve blind memos regarding "the outstanding work the FBI has done under Mr. Hoover's leadership." With Hoover's feud with Dr. King spinning out of control, Winchell reciprocated by sending the director information on the civil rights leader. (Winchell had been doing this sort of thing since the 1940s, when he sent in dirt on Paul Robeson.) From there, Hoover granted David Lawrence an exclusive interview, giving him the FBI version of what he and King had said during their much-publicized meeting. The director hoped to counter a critical story in *Newsweek* magazine with a piece in Lawrence's *U.S. News and World Report*. Lawrence, like Winchell, was one of Hoover's favorites. His syndicated column had run in the *Washington Star* since 1918, and in 1919 he received an advance copy of a lengthy General Intelligence Division memo that questioned the loyalty of Negro newspaper and magazine editors. In the 1960s he received an edited version of Division Five's Current Intelligence Analysis.[33]

Other Crime Records activities included assistance with the preparation and publication of an article, "The FBI's Secret War Against the Ku Klux Klan," for *Reader's Digest*. DeLoach then had Senator Karl Mundt (R., S.D.) insert the piece into the *Congressional Record*. "People are amazed," Hoover told Katzenbach, "when I begin to tell them of the things that have been done."[34] The director contributed an article of his own, "The Resurgent Klan," for the *American Bar Association Journal*. Besides arranging for publicity and distribution of this piece, Crime Records found time to help prepare a children's book— *Kids' Letters to the FBI*—and to help David Sentner, Andrew Tully, and Harry and Bonaro Overstreet with more serious books on the Bureau and its achievements in the civil rights and other fields. Tully concluded a section on "Civil Rights and Civil Wrongs" with a chapter entitled "A Look at the Record." Chapter twenty ("That Bitch Is Dead . . . ") focused on the Liuzzo murder and the Klan wars.[35]

Most Crime Records projects were covert. FBI publicists camouflaged their activities with great care under DeLoach's mentor, Louis Nichols. He was the "master," Lawrence Heim said. "Nobody can track Nichols." Nichols recorded his contacts with newsmen in memos marked FOR ADMINISTRATIVE

PURPOSES TO BE DESTROYED AFTER ACTION IS TAKEN AND NOT SENT TO FILES, and he also tried to control the paper record outside the Bureau. When *Reader's Digest* editor Fulton Oursler died, Nichols asked Oursler's widow to purge her husband's papers, before donating them to a college library, of the "numerous [FBI] memoranda" that had been furnished "over the years." DeLoach, more flamboyant than Nichols, left tracks everywhere. His leaks to journalists include the following greeting to *Chicago Tribune* Washington bureau chief Walter Trohan in a letter about a minister at the St. Luke African Methodist Episcopal Church in East Chicago, Indiana: "Hi Comrade: This is certainly a person who should be exposed."[36]

One of DeLoach's most ambitious projects involved a publicity drive as Hoover's feud with King moved into the public arena. After receiving his orders—"the Director has instructed that we have friendly news sources use an approved blind memorandum which sets forth the FBI's numerous accomplishments in the civil rights field"—DeLoach went to work. He convinced some of the nation's most prestigious conservative newsmen to come to bat for the Bureau—among others, Jeremiah O'Leary of the *Washington Star*, Ed O'Brien of Newhouse Newspapers, Ray McHugh of the Copley chain, Warren Rogers of the *New York Journal-American*, David Lawrence of *U.S. News and World Report*, and Hearst columnist Fulton Lewis, Jr. Lewis's column alone appeared in "approximately 318 newspapers." Clyde Tolson had read an advance copy and was quite pleased. Lewis also used the FBI-prepared material on his national radio program.[37]

For DeLoach, this was routine. He did it again during the summer of 1965 in response to Joseph Rauh's criticisms in a speech before the National Student Association. Rauh said Hoover was the wrong man for the job of enforcing federal civil rights law. When Tolson read the speech, he told DeLoach to do his job. The first reporter contacted, Miriam Ottenberg of the *Washington Star*, had supported the director on a number of previous occasions, most recently in a February 23, 1965, *Look* magazine article, "What's Ahead for the FBI." Crime Records promised to "prevail on her" once again. Tolson wanted an article by the weekend. In the meantime, DeLoach "sent material . . . to a number of columnists including . . . Paul Harvey, Bob Allen of the *Hall Syndicate*, Ray Cromley of Newspaper Enterprise Association, [and] Ed Mow[e]ry of General Features and the Newhouse chain." "That was the system we had," Crime Records agent

Lawrence Heim remembered. "If somebody came out with something erroneous about the Bureau, we were going to correct it. . . . We would put out the correction to as many people as we could.[38]

With or without Cartha DeLoach, Crime Records always corrected people like Joe Rauh. Rauh recalled his review of Max Lowenthal's book on the FBI in the *Washington Post* back in 1950, a review that had noted Hoover's attempt to ingratiate himself with southern congressmen by playing up his own segregationist credentials. "The first thing that happens is Justice [Felix] Frankfurter calls me up and says, 'Honestly, Joe'—that's the way he talked—'Honestly, Joe, that's the best thing that could have happened. Somebody had to say all that. I think you're absolutely great.' I'm feeling top of the world. I go to the football game, the Redskin game, and over the loudspeaker its says, 'This is a great afternoon for the Redskins—J. Edgar Hoover is attending the game.' I went home and told my wife. I said 'We're in. Hoover didn't even think enough to spend the afternoon smearing me.' How wrong I was. At 12:00 the next afternoon, Senator Bourke Hickenlooper [R., Iowa] takes the floor, my whole FBI file is spilled all over it. What I forgot when he was at the game, was that there were fifty assistants doing the work."[39]

The FBI kept coming back to Rauh—in 1965 after the National Student Association speech and again eight years after that. In anticipation of Rauh's testimony at the Senate confirmation hearings on Hoover's proposed successor, L. Patrick Gray III, Bureau executives prepared a seven-page blind memo for another group of friendly reporters because they expected Rauh to raise the civil rights specter once again.[40] By that time DeLoach had been out of the Bureau for three years, and Crime Records had been renamed the External Affairs Division.

The public relations machine ran before DeLoach came to the FBI and it ran after he left; but DeLoach served at a time when the FBI had more things to sell than ever before, and Hoover greatly appreciated his efforts. Promoted in December 1965 to the rank of assistant to the director, DeLoach's responsibilities broadened to include supervision of Division Five. Opinions concerning DeLoach vary, but all agreed that he represented power. Hearst reporter Jim Bishop described him as the "abbot" of the FBI "monastery" and "the coolest man under stress I had ever seen." Edwin Guthman said he never trusted DeLoach. "I was fully warned about him" by "other people in the Bureau, field agents who were friends of mine." Andrew Young said he had "almost a kind of fascist mentality." Joe Rauh said if you were a liberal and you met him (or any of his Crime Records agents), so was he. "These guys, when they saw you, you were really a fine fellow. 'Hail and well met' type of stuff. . . . A lot of people were fooled." When DeLoach received his promotion, Martin Luther King, who was not fooled, sent an ingratiating telegram nonetheless. "It makes me doubly proud," King wrote, in his own hand, "to know that a fellow Georgian has been elevated to such a key position in the federal government."[41]

To counter the adverse publicity regarding civil rights cases in the South, the Crime Records Division commissioned its most notable 1960s' project, the ABC television show *The FBI*. "We finally decided," DeLoach explained, "to clarify for the public what the FBI does. We're simply an investigative agency. We can't protect people—like civil rights workers, for instance. There's some confusion about what we do and I hope this program will show people how we really work." Crime Records routinely rejected scripts on police brutality or any other phase of civil rights responsibilities. David W. Rintels, who went on to chair a Writers Guild committee on censorship, chose a plot based on the bombing of Birmingham's Sixteenth Street Baptist Church when asked to write an episode for the series. After checking with the FBI, the producers told him "they would be delighted to have me write about a church bombing subject only to these stipulations: The church must be in the North, there could be no Negroes involved, and the bombing could have nothing at all to do with civil rights."[42]

Hoover and DeLoach worked out the arrangement for the television series with James Hagerty, ABC's president and Dwight Eisenhower's former press secretary; Jack Warner of Warner Brothers; and Quinn Martin, producer of *The Untouchables*. (The director considered *The Untouchables* "rotten from every view point.") They struck the deal in December 1964, two weeks after Hoover met with King, when Warner Brothers and ABC purchased motion picture and television rights to Hoover's book on the communist menace, *Masters of Deceit*, for $75,000, plus $500 for each television episode during the second and each subsequent year of production. Thanks to the promotional efforts of DeLoach and Nichols, *Masters of Deceit* was a best-seller. Among other efforts, Crime Records worked with the anticommunist

Operation Alert in the early fall of 1961 to distribute 5,500 copies to freshmen entering South Carolina colleges and universities.[43] But neither the book's subject matter nor format lent itself to television or the big screen. No network or motion picture
company every filmed under the *Masters of Deceit* rubric.
Warner and Hagerty, nonetheless, had ingratiated themselves
with Hoover by guaranteeing him a profit. *The FBI* began its
nine-year, Ford Motor Company-sponsored run on ABC television in September 1965, with Crime Records maintaining control over scripts, personnel, and sponsorship.[44]

Another major Crime Records project involved a book on the
Philadelphia murders by Don Whitehead, a writer with a history
of telling the story of Hoover's bureaucracy. Louis Nichols first
brought him in for "a special project" in the mid-1950s, after
investigating his "character, reputation and loyalty." The Crime
Records chief needed someone to write a history of the FBI, and
Whitehead seemed to be the best candidate. He received a
United States Army Medal of Freedom for his combat reporting
in North Africa and Europe during World War II, and his work
as a feature writer after the war won two Pulitzer prizes. In
March 1956, upon winding up his special FBI project, he joined
the *New York Herald Tribune* as its Washington bureau chief.
Whitehead's *FBI Story,* published later in the year by Random
House, remained on the best-seller list for thirty-eight weeks,
and at least 170 newspapers ran excerpts. When Whitehead sold
the books' movie rights to Warner Brothers, Hoover and Nichols
accompanied him to the closing. James Stewart ("Special Agent
Chip Hardesty"—starred in the movie.

Whitehead began his next Crime Records project in 1964, a
series of articles for the Associated Press on the FBI's handling
of civil rights matters. Crime Records set him up with desk
space at the seat of government and asked Hoover to grant an
interview. "Don is anxious to do a good story in order to assist
the Director and the FBI," DeLoach advised. Hoover granted the
interview on December 1, only a few minutes after meeting with
King. The director talked for fifty minutes about his weight and
having to give up chocolate cream pie, his "long and close friendship" with Lyndon Johnson, his "strained" relationship with
Robert Kennedy, his trip to Jackson, Mississippi ("without the
knowledge of Robert Kennedy"), his "thoroughly" enjoyable
statement labeling King "the most notorious liar in the country," and his assessment of the "tricky decisions" of the Warren

Court—"the type that interferes capriciously with efficient law enforcement."[45]

From there, Whitehead, DeLoach, and "officials of 'Reader's Digest'" began planning the book on the Philadelphia murders. *Reader's Digest* intended to publish a condensed version of *Attack on Terror* and have a subsidiary company, Funk and Wagnalls, publish the hardback. Crime Records agents set Whitehead up with desk space once again, pulled files, reviewed chapter drafts and galley proofs. Hoover complained about Joseph Sullivan and the other agents who worked on the case receiving too many accolades ("the Bureau is a 'We' organization not an 'I' organization"); but the book had redeeming features. Whitehead, as Crime Records agent Milton Jones pointed out, "deals briefly with the antics of the Mississippi Freedom Democratic Party at the August, 1964, Democratic National Convention in Atlantic City." The FBI Recreation Association bought 2,000 copies, and Whitehead remained close to the director. Whenever he traveled, an FBI agent from the nearest field office met him at the airport with a car. When he checked into Emory University Hospital in 1972 for surgery, Hoover sent flowers.[46] Years later, after Hoover died, FBI Director Clarence Kelley struck a deal with Quinn Martin for a full-length feature film based on Whitehead's book for the CBS television *Thursday Night at the Movies. Attack on Terror* premiered on February 21–22, 1975, and enraged Michael Schwerner's father, who responded with a one-page article ("Mississippi: Whitewashing the FBI") in a civil liberties magazine with a tiny circulation; and former Neshoba County Sheriff Lawrence Rainey, who filed (and lost) a lawsuit.[47]

DeLoach resigned from the FBI the same year Whitehead's book appeared. He went to work for Richard Nixon's friend, Donald Kendall, at Pepsico, and Paul Harvey said the stock market jumped thirteen points on his first day in the world of free enterprise. Pontificating in his usual style, Harvey was trying to make a point about DeLoach's remarkable skills. In the civil rights field, however, even such Bureau friends as Harvey realized that DeLoach had failed to accomplish his purpose. While Crime Records worked to establish a heroic image, events reinforced the lingering image of FBI agents standing off to the side, notebooks and pencils in hand, while movement people suffered harassments and beatings and much worse. These problems of image emerged from the tragic events of Selma.

Hoover's men had solved the Viola Liuzzo murder so quickly because they had a paid informant among the Klansmen in the murder car. The questions arising from that fact, questions about the Bureau's ability to control its own operatives and possible use of *agents provocateur*, cut across the ideological lines that separated the civil rights movement from its more civilized enemies, and remained to haunt the FBI for the next twenty years. Even such staunch allies as Fulton Lewis, Jr., an active participant in DeLoach's Mass Media Program who had defended the Bureau regularly since the school desegregation crisis at Little Rock Central, wondered why the FBI man in the car had not tried to prevent Liuzzo's murder. Didn't he have a moral obligation to do something, Lewis asked?[48]

The movement's friends in the government expected no such problems. If they had, Lyndon Johnson might not have arranged his dramatic announcement on national television and Ramsey Clark might not have applauded the FBI for doing an "incredible job" in breaking the Liuzzo case. There was even praise from within the movement. "The Agents assigned to Alabama," Dr. King told Hoover, "have done an outstanding job." Although his comments came before the government announced the informant's presence, King had spoken on an earlier occasion about the need to work "within secret groups" to find out "what is going on in conspiratorial racist circles." Similarly, James Wechsler of the *New York Post* called for the FBI to infiltrate the Ku Klux Klan and its fronts. "If only a fraction of the FBI manpower dedicated to the care and feeding of the Communist treasury had been allocated to undercover work in the rightist network," he wrote, "perhaps at least a few of the more deadly Southern explosions might have been forestalled."[49]

John Doar knew better. "You take informants as they come. You and I might have saved Mrs. Liuzzo's life, but you or I could never become FBI informants." That comment was right on the mark. It was difficult to recruit Ku Klux Klan informants in the rural areas where the Klan flourished, and the FBI took them as they came. A Laurel, Mississippi, agent compared the recruiting process to hunting quail. "Once the covey has scattered, you look for the singles." Hoover's men compensated by loosening standards. "The Bureau is willing," Assistant Director Fred J. Baumgardner noted, "to pay an informant to give you negative information, that nothing is going to happen or that nothing is going on." Informants would be dismissed if they drank too much or if they engaged in "sex perversion," and headquarters would not put "a screwball" on the payroll. "Most of them," Crime Records agent Harold Leinbaugh said, "were unguided missiles. You can't tell a criminal informant too much. You hope and pray a lot. He's probably not too bright, he's certainly unreliable, but you've got to . . . hook him somewhere." Baumgardner was more direct: Informants "did not have to be lily white."[50]

Gary Thomas Rowe, the FBI informer who rode with Collie Leroy Wilkins, Eugene Thomas, and William O. Eaton the day they murdered Viola Liuzzo, was not lily white. "He couldn't be an angel and be a good informant," one of the FBI handlers explained. Rowe grew up in Savannah, Georgia, married a nurse at sixteen, and moved to Birmingham where he joined the East-view Klavern of the Alabama Knights and was recruited as an informant by special agent Barrett Kemp. A big man who suffered bouts of macho fantasy, Rowe liked to fight and sit on bar stools. When he began collecting his stipend, a little over $400 per month, plus expenses, an agent told him "the FBI took no position on the question of segregation or integration." The Bureau only wanted intelligence, particularly information regarding violence. It was not "our policy," Division Five agent Fred Woodcock reiterated, "to ask the informant to engage in any forms of violence." On the other hand, the FBI knew that only a tiny "inner group" of Klansmen in any given Klavern engaged in violent acts. If the informant failed to "get selected for the inner group . . . he may never know what is actually going on."[51]

In Rowe's case, that was not a problem. The FBI's principal source of information on the Klan in the Birmingham area from 1960–1965, Rowe attained a position in the Klan's own Bureau of Investigation, and he said the FBI instructed him to be "where the action was." He led a Klan attack squad when the Freedom Riders arrived in Birmingham and accompanied the two Klansmen who smashed radio newsman and "SAC contact" Clancy Lake's car window. The first person to put in a call to the police that Mother's Day, Lake was broadcasting on the car radio when Rowe and the others approached, tore his microphone out of the dashboard, pulled him out of the car, and nearly beaned him with a lead pipe. After things had quieted down around the bus station, Rowe returned in search of black people to beat up, this time receiving all he could handle—including a knife slash on the throat. For the day's work Rowe received a $125 bonus from the FBI, plus medical expenses. The cut took eight stitches.[52]

Rowe went out regularly for missionary work—boarding buses and kicking people, raiding the home of a white family raising a black child, entering integrated restaurants and even an amusement park and beating blacks "severely . . . with black jacks, chains, pistols." There were rumors of Rowe's involvement in the firebombing of the home of a wealthy black Birmingham resident, A. G. Gaston, the detonating of shrapnel bombs in black neighborhoods, and the murder of a black man in 1963 during the spring demonstrations. There was even some speculation that FBI agents in Birmingham helped cover up Rowe's involvment in segregationist terror because he was such a good informant. Rowe reported on all the violence, as well as the regular stuff—the cross-burning rallies, the conversations about "Jews and Dagos" and fluoridated water and movie stars changing their names, and his Klavern's showing of *Birth of a Nation*, D. W. Griffith's eulogy to the Klan. The projector kept breaking down, he said. Rowe also alerted the FBI to a Klan plot to assassinate Fred Shuttlesworth, a tip that may have saved Rev. Shuttlesworth's life. The segregationist who allegedly volunteered to kill Shuttlesworth, John Wesley Hall, later joined Gary Thomas Rowe as an FBI informant.[53]

Within six months of the Liuzzo murder, the FBI operated nearly 2,000 informants, 20 percent of overall Klan and other white hate group membership, including a grand dragon in one southern state. Bureau agents set up and financed one Klavern, with an exclusive, charter membership of informants, to siphon recruits from regular Klan groups. Eventually, the Klavern grew to 250 members. (FBI officials were only slightly less enthusiastic in their quest for a substitute and acceptable Klan leadership as they were in their quest for a substitute and acceptable black leadership.) When Hoover told Katzenbach and White House aide Marvin Watson that his men had been developing two "informants and sources" per day, the attorney general said he hoped it might be possible "at some point . . . to place these achievements on the public record, so that the Bureau can receive its due credit."[54]

Crime Records was taking care of that; but it was a sensitive business because dozens of Klan informants rivaled the controversial Gary Rowe. One informant, when addressing a Klan rally attended by thousands, predicted "peace and order in America" even "if we have to kill every Negro." Another informant, a key witness in the Neshoba County case, Delmar Dennis of Meridian, was a bona fide member of the John Birch Society. When the House Committee on Un-American Activities requested his presence during its Klan investigation, he worked with Roy Moore's men to avoid the subpoena. The FBI thought HUAC might jeopardize the trial of Bowers, Price, and the others, so agents from the Jackson field office reportedly pushed Dennis's empty car down a thirty-five foot slope and into a creek, helped Dennis get back in, and then waited for someone to spot the wreck and call an ambulance. After Dennis wired HUAC from a hospital bed, Committee staff said they would get back to him. They never did.[55]

A number of other informants posed a threat after they broke cover and discovered they could no longer count on the FBI. One bitter ex-informant, who said his reputation as "a 'Nigger Lover'" cost him his home and job in Georgia, asked Robert Kennedy for help in finding "a more democratic environment." He even offered to "take a civilian job in Viet Nam." The man turned to Kennedy because he considered it "useless to ask the F.B.I. to assist," complaining that "they use a person then desert them when they are through regardless of the predicament it leaves you in."[56]

FBI officials did not desert Gary Rowe. Their initial reaction to the murder on Highway 80 had less to do with Rowe, a live informer with a history of involvement in violence against civil rights workers, than whether there was something in the history of Mrs. Liuzzo, a movement martyr, that might be considered derogatory. Upon completing name checks on Viola Liuzzo and her husband, Anthony, Hoover's phone started ringing. Katzenbach called first, a few hours before President Johnson planned to announce the arrests. He wanted to know if there was anything in the files that might prove embarrassing to the president once the television people turned off their klieg lights.

What had the FBI found out? "The man doesn't have too good a background"—he was a Teamster business agent—"and the woman had indications of needle marks in her arms." "[She] was sitting very, very close to the Negro in the car," Hoover added. "It had the appearance of a necking party." The president called a few minutes later and the director elaborated. "I don't say the man has a bad character but he is well known as a Teamster strongarm man." Mrs. Liuzzo may have "been taking dope although we can't say that definitely because she is dead."[57] The autopsy said nothing about needle tracking anywhere on the body, and that fact slowed Hoover. When sending additional information to the White House and the Civil Rights Division, he left out most—but not all—of the voyeuristic speculation that revealed more about himself and his Bureau than the victim and her husband. "They didn't like Mrs. Liuzzo," Lee White remembered. "In their description of her she didn't come off looking like a virtuous woman."[58]

Where Hoover's reports were not absurd, they were soft, and so President Johnson ignored them. Viola Liuzzo had been arrested once, in June 1964, for refusing to send her children to school. She was protesting a Michigan law allowing children to drop out of school at age sixteen. The court's probation department described her as "emotionally disturbed," and she had received psychiatric treatment at one point. Letters found in her car after the shooting also indicated an emotional involvement in the movement.[59] FBI officials' interest in Anthony Liuzzo led to a check with the Detroit Police Department regarding the funeral—because they expected various labor leaders (Hoffa and Reuther) and movement people (King and Wilkins) to attend. Later, when Liuzzo complained about the refusal of Alabama authorities to release the family car, which he had to make payments on, or his wife's wedding ring, Hoover said he "seems more interested in cash . . . than in grief."[60] Nothing in any of the FBI's reports imperiled the dramatic announcement the president had planned. The director kept digging, but even he expected to find nothing. Viola Liuzzo was neither promiscuous nor a drug user. The worst anyone could say was that she left her husband and children behind (temporarily) for duty on the movement's front line in Selma.

The FBI apparently did not leak much on the Liuzzos beyond a few items to Klan informants and one or two newspaper reporters. But on March 31, six days after Mrs. Liuzzo's death, Crime Records did brief Douglas Smith, an aide to Congressman George W. Andrews (D., Ala.), on James Farmer of CORE, John Lewis of SNCC, and Hosea Williams of SCLC. "An urgent request from Governor George Wallace," Smith said, had "precipitated" his visit to the Bureau in search of "information indicat-

ing communist connections on the part of civil rights leaders."
The public-source data supplied by the FBI, he added, "would
not satisfy the Governor."[61]

The segregationists, in contrast to the FBI, remained anxious
to use anything to discredit the civil rights movement. Another
Alabama politician, Sheriff Jim Clark of Dallas County, a man
who often greeted would-be black voters in Selma with electric
cattle prods and organized the brutal police assault on Bloody
Sunday, received more detailed help from his fellow policemen
in Michigan. The FBI collected most of its information on the
Liuzzos from the Detroit police, and one officer, the head of the
criminal intelligence bureau, sent copies of the reports to Marvin G. Lane, police commissioner of suburban Warren and former captain of detectives in the Detroit Police Department. Commissioner Lane sent the reports to Sheriff Clark,who told a UPI
reporter that Liuzzo's murder might have been averted if the
FBI had alerted his office. "They had a carload of Ku Klux
Klansmen under surveillance" and did not tell anybody, he said.
The Bureau issued a rebuttal, but quickly dropped the matter to
avoid a feud with the sheriff. When the Detroit police reports
ended up in Clark's hands, Hoover quietly blackballed all members of Lane's department from the FBI National Academy.[62]

Clark's comment about the carload of Ku Kluxers was revealing; because the FBI's man was in the murder car, even the segregationists suggested the FBI was somehow responsible for Liuzzo's death. For Hoover, this represented the beginning of a
major public relations problem, but he had no idea how to respond—beyond his wild swing at Warren police officers, men
who had nothing to do with Sheriff Clark or Commissioner
Lane's indiscretion. DeLoach and his Crime Records agents
were not necessarily of much use here.

The prosecution of Collie Leroy Wilkins and the other Klansmen who killed Viola Liuzzo also created public relations problems for the FBI. On the matter of legal representation, Gary
Rowe's attorney of record, Matt Murphy, was a Klan attorney,
an "Imperial Klonsel." Once the Bureau and the Justice Department removed the client from that attorney-client relationship,
Murphy sued Rowe to recover fees of $6,000 for professional ser-
vices allegedly rendered. The FBI's Mobile field office responded by proposing a leak to HUAC to publicize "the role of
the subversive lawyer in promulgating the aims of the KKK."[63]
Next, Rowe faced indictment for murder. Eventually, in the fall

of 1978, a Lowndes County grand jury acted against Rowe, contending that he had fired the murder weapon. Finally, the prospects of convicting the three other KKKs in state court were remote. With the prestige of the FBI and the Justice Department at stake, Hoover and Katzenbach "both felt that if we only got disagreement" among the members of the jury "it would be a victory."[64]

FBI agents in Alabama checked jury panels, defense attorneys, and state prosecutors, looking for ties to the Citizens Council or the Klan. Civil Rights Division attorney St. John Barrett put in the request for a check on Arthur Gamble, the Lowndes County circuit solicitor. Barrett wanted "to know what kind of prosecutor Gamble is; whether or not he is or has been affiliated with organizations such as Klan groups; and any information concerning his background which might indicate what kind of a job he will do."[65] The FBI expected Gamble to do a good job, and he did; but the three Klansmen, Wilkins, Thomas, and Eaton, escaped conviction. "Do you know those big black niggers were driven by the woman?" Matt Murphy asked the jurors, in a manner reminiscent of Hoover's necking party innuendo. "One white woman and these niggers. Right there. Riding right through your county." When the first trial ended in a hung jury in May 1965, the FBI tried to identify the two jurors who had voted for acquittal.[66] At the second trial in October, another jury acquitted Wilkins. The FBI encountered embarrassment during this trial in the form of defense attorney Arthur J. Hanes, former mayor of Birmingham and FBI agent who replaced Murphy, who died in a car crash, after the first trial.

"I was hired by these boys," Hanes said, "but as far as I know the Klan had nothing to do with paying me." FBI executives in Washington weren't so sure. Hanes was a pallbearer at Murphy's funeral, as the Crime Record Division painfully noted, and he went on to represent Martin Luther King's assassin, James Earl Ray, for a short time. Hoover said Hanes was "no good," "a very strong supporter" of Bull Connor "in the use of police dogs," "a fellow who has certainly a strong smell of the Klan about him." Hanes never noticed any animosity on the part of local FBI agents. He always found "the Bureau boys" in Alabama "very friendly."[67]

The best hope for a conviction in the Liuzzo case rested in federal court where the charge would be violation of the Reconstruction Era statutes and not murder. There were problems here, too. The FBI had a terrified Rowe hidden in the San Francisco area. He was "torn to pieces" and needed to be "toned down a bit," Hoover concluded. "I thought the Attorneys who are going to try the case should see Rowe and size him up and see if he is going to explode on the witness stand." But Rowe had "no confidence in the attorneys of the Department." The Justice Department's "leverage," Hoover told Katzenbach, could be found in Rowe's "confidence in the FBI." Fearing leaks and Klan vengeance, Bureau officials refused to "furnish information to the Department in writing concerning [Rowe's] status." They briefed John Doar orally. Division Five, nonetheless, screened the cash offers from reporters seeking an interview and more ambitious writers attempting to purchase rights to Rowe's story.[68]

Rowe held up through the trial in Birmingham, and none of the FBI's taps or bugs proved to be an embarrassment. Apparently, the only technical surveillance relevant to the Liuzzo case was a microphone (BH 325-R) planted in Rowe's car, with Rowe's consent.[69] In December 1965 Justice Department prosecutors succeeded where the Lowndes County circuit solicitor had failed. Thomas, Wilkins, and Eaton received the maximum ten-year prison term under Section 241. While free on appeal bond, Eaton dropped dead of a heart attack.[70] The FBI held open its file on Thomas, a suspect in the Sixeenth Street Baptist Church bombing as well. At the end of the month, Hoover informed Katzenbach that the Bureau would "no longer accept responsibility" for the temperamental Rowe, "either financially or security wise."[71]

While the director washed his hands of Gary Rowe, President Johnson's advisers debated the question of how to address the lingering protection issue, with Katzenbach noting the continuing pressure from "civil rights groups . . . for legislation which would greatly expand federal jurisdiction with respect to crimes affecting civil rights workers." The administration recognized the need for "modest legislation," but was not willing to go as far as the civil rights organizations or to trust the House Judiciary Committee. Committee members might give movement people everything they wanted. "Pressures from the left" and the prospect of "a run-away House Committee" would make "the Administration the target of civil right criticism without any compensating political advantage."[72]

Convictions in the Liuzzo case took some of the pressure off the FBI and the White House. Hoover was pleased that things had worked out. "This case [was] being viewed rather as a 'symbol' case," but the convictions marked a "turning point." The "Mississippi thing," he told Katzenbach, referring to the anticipated federal court trial of the suspects in the Schwerner-Chaney-Goodman murders, still needed watching, but "there was a different attitude today and the Governor had helped materially." The attorney general agreed, according to Hoover's account. The corner had been turned in Alabama. "The Bureau did a terrific job not only originally but in the way the testimony went and the way they conducted themselves and it was really a victory for the Bureau." "The Bureau was itself on trial in a sense," Katzenbach said. "The Bureau was held back . . . in the state court trials," but Department prosecutors obtained convictions in federal court because they "relied on the reputation of the Bureau . . . that is what won it."[73]

Three months after this victory, on March 24, 1966, William Sullivan recommended an escalation of intelligence and counterintelligence actions against the Klan. He told an executives' conference that the FBI was "not adequately coping with the problem created by the Ku Klux Klan." Policy required investigation of all "Klan members who are violence prone," but Division Five did not have "sufficient manpower" to do so. Of the 152 Klaverns, Sullivan said, the FBI desperately needed informant coverage of 81. Of the 14,000 Klan members in the United States, Division Five had the resources to investigate a mere "300 violence prone" members, "of whom there are many more," and "only 1,500" officers.[74]

Although Hoover rejected Sullivan's call for "a special squad directed against the Ku Klux Klan," Division Five gradually escalated its counterintelligence program and general intelligence gathering efforts. It was, perhaps, another example of the empire-building that has often been raised to explain Sullivan's actions in particular, and the FBI's accelerated racial matters activities in general. On the other hand, it took the FBI more than a few months to gear up. Division Five implemented most of its COINTELPRO operations against the Klan after the executives' conference met to discuss the new proposals. It also took the FBI time to wear down the Klan. In Mississippi alone from 1964–1970, Roy Moore remembered, "we averaged 250 acts of violence per annum. After 1970, practically nil. It took us that long to put the fire out."[75]

By the late 1960s, FBI surveillance of white hate groups had moved beyond coverage of Klan "rallies and demonstrations" to include the investigation of all segregationists regardless of their "potential for violence." This did not mean a parallel expansion of COINTELPRO—White Hate Group. It increased the number of intelligence targets, as opposed to counterintelligence targets, leading to more "informant coverage of the Klan, White Hate groups, and *white ghetto areas* [emphasis added]." The FBI opened files on "unaffiliated white racial extremists" and "neighborhood groups" in the suburbs ("white ghetto areas of the large cities which border on minority group living areas"), particularly if "these groups are known to sponsor demonstrations against integration and against the bussing of Negro students to white schools." Because "many of these organizations" were founded "on principles of fear rather than hate" and thus could not "be classified as hate groups," all Bureau investigations were "discreet." Whenever a white neighborhood group formed, the FBI sent in informers and "established sources" to gather "background data" and to document "the aims and purposes of the organization."[76]

Hoover brought the FBI to the ghettoes of black America as he reached out to the suburbs—though with a difference in scope and intensity and intent. As a general rule, in the director's view, fear motivated white Americans and hate motivated black Americans. "White citizens are primarily decent, but frightened for their lives," he told a group of newspaper editors in April 1965, less than three weeks after Mrs. Liuzzo died out by Big Bear Swamp. "The colored people are quite ignorant, mostly uneducated."[77]

Hoover's FBI waged war on the Klan, but it was a limited war, a sideshow to the real war. In 1967 the Miami field office helped an NBC television affiliate prepare documentaries on the National States Rights party and the Florida Klan. In 1968 the same office and its "friendly and reliable" media contacts began work on a far more ambitious series of documentaries on the Nation of Islam and other black groups. Hoover's heart was with the frightened people in the "white ghettoes" and their racist nightmares about an American Mau Mau or declining property values or black schoolchildren enrolling in *their* schools. The director may have ordered his agents to spy on the frightened people along with the frightening Klan, but he was on their side. He waged war on the Klan because the Klan had discredited the good name of white America.

Johnson administration officials knew as much as they wanted to know about the FBI's activities. They were neither shocked nor outraged. Instead, they encouraged the FBI to do more, to gather more intelligence on the civil rights movement, to do a better job disrupting the Klan. The surveillance went as far as it did not only because Hoover wanted it that way, but because he was allowed to have his way. His politics and genius, his bureaucratic priorities and maneuverings enabled him to pursue a private agenda. Along with the men around him, men who invariably shared his conservative values, and the deference of the men in the White House and the Justice Department, men who certainly did not share those conservative values, he fought a private war against black people at the very time he was destroying the Ku Klux Klan.

Exactly what did the FBI accomplish during the Klan wars? "In five years we blew them all to hell," a former Division Five agent concluded. "We never got any credit for that." "By the time I left the South in 1966," Joseph Sullivan said, "an entire society had resolved to suppress outlawry in racial matters. This goal was achieved through a team effort by Lyndon Johnson, J. Edgar Hoover, and the prosecutors representing the Justice Department. Hoover did his job well, and much credit must go to the president for providng the sources and support the FBI needed for this task."[78] But to Hoover and the men in Crime Records, it was not the hour of the FBI's greatest triumph. They could not escape the embarrassing details of the Liuzzo case, from the informant's presence in the murder car all the way down to the sight of a former agent helping to carry a Klan attorney's coffin.[79] Charles Morgan, Jr., the Birmingham lawyer who opened the ACLU's first southern office a few months before the Selma march, recognized the irony. "Years before those miserable, ignorant white men killed Mrs. Liuzzo, FBI agents surreptitiously peddled the lies which those killers believed and which lawyer Matt Murphy openly argued"—namely, that "Communists dominate them niggers."[80]

While Nicholas Katzenbach, John Doar, Burke Marshall, and a few other Civil Rights Division lawyers stood by the FBI when the revelations of intelligence and counterintelligence abuses poured out a decade later, they struck a defensive posture. When asked what type of "civil rights work" the FBI did best, Marshall said "the only thing they were good at" was waging war on the Klan. The FBI won the Klan wars by doing what had to be done:

> It was done . . . by bribery, by payments to informers, by whatever eavesdropping was then permitted under the bureau's rules, by the sowing of suspicion among Klan members so that none knew who was an informer and who was not, by infiltration and deception, and in at least one incident by the participation of a bureau informer in the planning and attempted execution of a murder.
>
> It did not appear to those involved at the time, and it does not appear to me now, that the criminal conspiracy of violence that existed in the State of Mississippi then could have been handled by less drastic measures.[81]

The Klan moved outside the law, so the FBI moved outside the law. For every counterintelligence trick, the FBI had a story about Klansmen putting rattlesnakes in an agent's car or leaving a coffin on the porch of an agent's home, ringing the bell, telling the wife that her husband's body was inside. "The Bureau was up against it," one agent said, "up against the wall."

In the end, the FBI pleased only the men in the middle, the men in the Justice Department and the White House. Hoover and his agents pleased neither the Klan (obviously) nor the movement. The Klan has always been resilient. If Klansmen are no longer as prone to leave civil rights people for dead along Alabama highways or buried under thirty feet of Mississippi mud, they are likely nowadays to engage in voter registration drives ("If you are a White American you owe it to your wife and children to register and vote"); campaigns to gain access to cable television channels ("And now, a word from the Klan"); and the filing of at least a few civil suits against the FBI.[82]

The victims of Klan violence have also taken FBI agents to court, with two major suits filed by movement people or their families emerging from the Klan wars. Walter and Frances Bergman, two of the Freedom Riders beaten in Anniston and Birmingham, filed after learning about Gary Rowe's participation and warnings to the FBI to expect a Klan riot.[83] Viola Liuzzo's husband and five children put in the other suit. Mrs. Liuzzo's family did not win their suit; the issues, after all, are complex, especially if one accepts the assumptions of the surveillance consensus. And it is difficult to sue the government in the government's courts. The FBI won, but not convincingly. The FBI had to open its files and provide fodder for newspaper headlines and clips on the evening news and even a *Playboy* article entitled, "Did the FBI Kill Viola Liuzzo?"[84]

That was not the kind of publicity Lyndon Johnson wanted back on March 26, 1965, when he stepped in front of the klieg lights. It certainly was not the kind of publicity Hoover and his Crime Records agents wanted. Even Gary Thomas Rowe, a troubled man in search of a separate peace was telling anybody who would listen that he was just as perplexed as the next fellow. "I inquired several times as to, 'Jesus, why wasn't something done after those acts were carried out'; and I was told that the FBI was not a police body, that the FBI was simply an investigating body and that their function was to gather information. That's all they needed."[85]

CHAPTER
7

===❯❮❯===

White Backlash

LBJ and the Politics of the Urban Riots

Viola Liuzzo's tragic murder presented a public relations dilemma for J. Edgar Hoover and a public relations opportunity for Lyndon Johnson. The riots that began in New York in the summer of 1964 and swept through the urban North in the years thereafter were tragic, too, but they presented opportunities only for the FBI director, not the president. The ghetto eruptions in Watts in 1965 and especially Newark and Detroit in 1967 seemingly confirmed Hoover's lifelong assumptions that subversion and not racism lay at the heart of the Negro Question, that the fires in the cities could be explained by the deeds of communist conspirators and not by the forces of poverty and despair. Yet the new rhetoric of "law and order" and not the archaic rhetoric of the domestic cold war structured the nation's response to the riots. The riots led to a search for communists in the ghetto, but that search was secondary to a national and increasingly partisan debate over the causes of the riots that placed liberalism and not communism at the center of controversy.

Initially, Hoover merely observed while the Johnson administration argued for its war on poverty and other Great Society initiatives as a solution to the great American dilemma, and the president's adversaries in the Republican party and the conservative wing of his own party blamed the permissiveness of liberal reform for causing the chaos and crime of the cities in the first place. For Johnson, the words "law and order" were "code words for racism."[1] For Hoover, law and order meant more money and agents, and therefore a more powerful base from which he could march against the black demand for justice on new fronts in the urban North. By reorienting American politics, the riots eventually provided Hoover the opportunity to abandon his alliance with the segregationists and their doomed cause, and to form new alliances with the administration's adversaries and their efforts to mobilize the "white backlash vote."

On the surface, Hoover's conduct during the course of the riots appears bewildering. The director moved from one riot to the next, sometimes in the same direction as the president, at other times in conflicting directions. His domestic intelligence reports often blamed subversives for instigating the riots, but at other times he provided a voice of reason in a White House increasingly dominated by a president's "incursions of paranoia."[2] Hoover's fundamental beliefs about race, nonetheless, remained unchanged. Black America represented a subversive threat, with or without communists, to the peace and stability of middle America, and the FBI had a responsibility to counter that threat. Hoover formed and pursued his agenda accordingly, building up a surveillance empire capable of intruding into every corner of black America and obtaining authorization for that empire from the Johnson administration—even as he gradually moved the FBI out from under the president's thumb and formed new alliances with the president's law-and-order adversaries.

By the time the riots had run their course, Lyndon Johnson was back on the ranch in Texas, Richard Nixon was president of the United States, and J. Edgar Hoover was in absolute command of an FBI with an ever-expanding "Racial Matters" mandate. Johnson's decision not to seek his party's nomination in 1968 can be best understood by reference to a failing policy in Vietnam and particularly the North Vietnamese army's Tet offensive of January 1968. But his decision was also influenced by the law-and-order politics of the riots, and Hoover's success in influencing those politics against the president's interests and in favor of those who chased the "white backlash vote." Johnson was the thirty-sixth president of the United States; Hoover was merely the sixth director of the FBI. Yet, when they clashed over ways to respond to the civil disorders, the director won, and the

president, surely one of the most adept politicians ever to occupy the Oval Office, lost.

The riots themselves took the Great Society by surprise. Few
people in the White House, the Department of Justice, or the FBI
for that matter expected the "racial problem" to jump the
Mason-Dixon Line. "When we thought of the North we didn't
think of civil rights," Ramsey Clark remembered.[3] Things
changed on July 18, sixteen days after President Johnson signed
the Civil Rights Act of 1964. The riots began in New York after an
off-duty police officer shot a fifteen-year-old Negro boy, James
Powell ("a young colored hoodlum," in the FBI view), and CORE
organized a rally and march on a police station to demand the
officer's ouster. Rioting broke out in Brooklyn the next day, and
yet another riot followed in Rochester upstate five days later. In
August rioting swept through cities in New Jersey, Illinois, and
Pennsylvania.

The riots posed a threat to President Johnson's Great Society
programs, to his administration's attempt to promote consensus
and achieve racial and economic justice.[4] A political threat, it
took the form of Barry Goldwater, the Republican party's presidential candidate in 1964.[5] Aware of (and perhaps encouraged
by) the strong showing of an unabashed racist, Alabama Governor George Wallace, in Democratic presidential primaries in
Wisconsin and Indiana, Goldwater conservatives argued that
liberal reform in general, and LBJ's war on poverty and civil
rights legislation in particular, would encourage civil disobedience and a new permissiveness. Black Americans, who stood
most to gain from the Great Society, would have no incentive to
work. They would simply be granted money, food, jobs, scholarships, affirmative action promises, even their own special law.
The work ethic would die. Disrespect for law, laziness, and criminality would emerge as the new values. The Republican right
pointed to the riots ("Goldwater rallies," as they were sometimes called in Democratic circles) as proof of their predictions
about Great Society permissiveness and the lax law enforcement
policies of elite reformers who saw the roots of crime in poverty.[6]

The conservative critique fed a resentment that first surfaced
among blue-collar whites in the South and quickly spread into
the North, as Wallace's success in the primaries attested. William F. Buckley, Jr.'s, *National Review* published a symposium

on the opportunities for a new political alignment made possible by this embryonic white backlash, with one writer predicting "Suburbia May Explode." On a far cruder level, the Ku Klux Klan issued constant reminders that Great Society reform was for blacks only. While watching FBI agents drag the Pearl River in search of the bodies of Michael Schwerner, Andrew Goodman, and James Chaney, a Neshoba County farmer called out: "Hey, why don't you hold a welfare check over the water. That'll get that nigger to the surface." Another Klansman, a grand dragon in North Carolina, said "the only contact" poor white trash had "with the federal government is the FBI bug."[7]

The Democratic party had worried about a Republican "southern strategy" even before the riots and Goldwater's candidacy. By 1960, Theodore H. White, the chronicler of the campaign trail, pointed out that millions of southerners had begun to recognize Republicans as "natural allies in preserving state sovereignty in race relations." By 1963 Andrew Young and other movement people interpreted federal recalcitrance on civil rights issues by reference to the Kennedys' attempt to undercut the GOP's southern strategy. John and Robert Kennedy, Young said, were trying "to assure the nation that they are still 'white.'" Less than a year later—and two months before the riots began—in an appearance on *Face the Nation*, Martin Luther King said the Republican party might become a "white man's party."[8]

The Goldwater-Republican attempt to capitalize on the breakdown of law and order threatened to cost President Johnson votes in the November 1964 elections. In a meeting with Cartha DeLoach after the summer rioting had run its course, White House aide Walter Jenkins described the political impact of the riots as the administration's "Achilles' heel." Hoover's agenda had little in common with Johnson's. The two men, as Arthur Schlesinger noted, "had been Washington neighbors and friends for many years. They understood each other."[9] Johnson turned to the FBI for assistance in managing the politics of the riots because he thought the FBI could be controlled. He wanted his FBI director, the most respected policeman in the nation, out front, in the public eye, and on his side. If Hoover said Johnson was tough enough, who could criticize the administration for being soft on law and order? The president was "toying with many possibilities," DeLoach told Hoover after his meeting with Jenkins, "which will give him favorable publicity inasmuch as he considers the various riots to have lost him many votes."[10]

The most ambitious plan involved the solicitation of an FBI report intended to counter Goldwater's law-and-order politicking and to recapture those lost votes. Johnson coaxed from the very conservative Hoover an endorsement (of sorts) for the war on poverty, and brought in a prominent if decidedly anti-Goldwater Republican, Thomas E. Dewey, to put all the memos the FBI had submitted on the riots into a final draft.[11] In late September the media received a report surveying nine cities where rioting had occurred. The report had Hoover's name on it, but Dewey, who ran for president in 1944 and 1948 on the Republican party ticket, wrote it. (Johnson held Dewey's authorship in reserve, just in case Hoover's name alone had failed to do the job.)[12] The episode deserves further attention because it demonstrates just how seriously the president took the threat posed by the new politics of race, and the reasons why he assumed that Hoover would stand with the administration during the more serious rioting and law-and-order politicking in the years to come.

Dewey's name first surfaced in the White House in mid-July, when he spoke to Max Kampelman, the lawyer, businessman, sometime diplomat, and former legislative counsel to Senator Hubert H. Humphrey (D., Minn.). Dewey would not "bolt with fanfare," a White House aide concluded, but he was "fed up with the GOP. . . . Should the President call him after the convention Max is certain that Dewey will promise his support and quiet help during the campaign." The idea intrigued Johnson, Nicholas Katzenbach remembered. "The president was always a big fan. . . . He liked Dewey's image, the image he had as the district attorney, as the special prosecutor in New York." With Dewey's offer in mind, Johnson met with Hoover on July 22 to discuss the Goldwater candidacy and how the administration might counter any attempts to exploit the riots. The president wanted the FBI "to get in there and see about the communist groups and the right wingers." Hoover promised to "dig into it at once." When the White House finally contacted Dewey a few weeks later, he agreed to help.[13]

Dewey came to the FBI riot project with ghost-writing experience (having received data from the FBI during the 1948 campaign), and with a desire to find a middle ground between Jo son's welfare state and Goldwater's warfare state.[14] When speculating with Hoover on "the new permissiveness," he asked about the salacious novel *Fanny Hill*. The director sent a memo. When the two men talked about the "timidity of prosecutors and judges," Dewey told Hoover about his recent conversation with the New York district attorney on the subject of Michael Schwerner, who had been arrested back in the summer of 1963 during CORE demonstrations against building trades discrimination in Manhattan. "[Frank] Hogan had said that one of the civil rights workers killed in Mississippi had been convicted in New York and was out on appeal and had the Judge affirmed the appeal [sic], he would have been in jail and it would have saved his life, that this was the fellow with the communist parents."[15]

Johnson expected Dewey to be the more moderate half of the partnership. He expected Dewey to control Hoover, to keep Hoover's crusty anticommunism out of the report. As it turned out, the director was on occasion the more moderate of the two men. When Dewey mentioned the culpability of "the responsible Negro organizations" and the "more violent" actions (as he designated the nonviolent "sit-ins, et cetera") of the past three years, Hoover counseled caution. "All of those actions" have contributed to "a breakdown of law and order and respect for the administration of justice," the director agreed. But "it was a delicate situation," and it might be best to avoid any reference to this in the report "because Roy Wilkins of the NAACP and [Whitney Young of] the Urban League" were "trying to be the restraining influence." When Dewey said "they started it and now want to put out the fire," Hoover pointed out that "they are being called by the younger generation 'Uncle Toms' and are being disregarded and people of more violent disposition are taking over and that is the thing I would hesitate about and think over very carefully about attaching blame to them."[16] In the meantime, the director sent Dewey memos (with copies to the White House) on the involvement of any CORE, NAACP, SCLC, or SNCC member in the riots.[17]

Hoover and Dewey agreed on the big question—whether communists or other radicals sparked the riots. Because the riots "caught" them "by surprise," Communist party members "moved in" only "after the riots started." The violence that followed, the director admitted, was merely "communist encouraged," "not communist inspired." At the same time, neither man intended to ignore the radicals, whether they were card-carrying Reds or not.[18] When Hoover telephoned Nelson Rockefeller at Jackson Hole, Wyoming, on the second day of the riots, the governor complimented the director on the work of the New York State police superintendent, former FBI agent Arthur Cornelius, Jr., and then complained about the "left-wing groups." "[Wasn't] anyone at the Federal level going to say anything about the kind of encouragement this is getting from radical groups," he wanted to know? Hoover told Rockefeller not to worry. "I have been keeping the President advised. . . . I send him a summary each day on the racial situation in Mississippi and Georgia, where there is the same communist problem, and also New York."[19]

Because the riot report, released to the press on September 26, identified poverty and discrimination as the principal causes of unrest, the FBI implied that Johnson administration programs designed to address those problems represented the best possible response. Not surprisingly, many conservatives worried about Hoover's apparent defection from right-wing orthodoxy.[20] The report emphasized social and economic factors, not subversive conspirators, and "cleared the civil rights movement completely," Roy Wilkins wrote. "After the F.B.I. report there was no excuse for race to be drawn into the campaign." When William Buckley objected, the liberal Catholic magazine *Commonweal* conceded a "twinge of sympathy," pointing out that "there is nothing wrong with coming out in favor of the Johnson war on poverty, but it is not for Mr. Hoover to do so in a report on civil rights disturbances."[21]

Johnson achieved a significant success. He had covertly maneuvered a prominent Republican and overtly maneuvered his anticommunist FBI director into issuing a report that endorsed the war on poverty, helped blunt the Goldwater challenge, and played down every sort of conspiracy theory. There was no evidence, the report concluded, that any group or person organized the riots on a national basis or that any of the disturbances were a "direct outgrowth of conventional civil rights protest." And there was little black-white violence—the only interracial clash of note involved blacks and Puerto Ricans in Brooklyn. In the Hoover-Dewey view, the incidents in New York, Illinois, Pennsylvania, and elsewhere were not even "race riots." That was a comforting thought, exactly the sort of message Johnson had hoped to propagate when he first called on his FBI director and a disaffected Republican. Because Hoover had evidently abandoned his traditional focus on communism, it is easy to see why the president concluded that he had the FBI under contol.[22]

Hoover and Dewey raised the radical specter, but in a calm manner. They explained the government's interest in the politics and everyday doings of the people who inhabited America's black ghettoes in the language of federalism *and* of federal surveillance: "Keeping the peace in this country is essentially the responsibility of the state government. Where lawless conditions arise, however, with similar characteristics from coast to coast, the matter is one of national concern even though there is no direct connection between the events and even though no federal law is violated."[23]

Johnson commissioned the report for reasons of politics, not policy. The report's value was therapeutic, its usefulness confined to public relations. Hoover, however, managed to tell the president what he wanted to hear, much to Buckley's chagrin, and to expand his bureaucracy's surveillance mission. He did so, not by promoting the Red menace but by downplaying it. "In certain instances," a headquarters directive of August 20 reminded all Bureau field offices, the evidence "clearly indicated that such [racial] disturbances were sustained and nurtured, if not actually initiated by, subversive elements and/or other organizations." FBI officials could not even define who they wanted to spy on. The "subversive, criminal, or other elements" who interested them were not connected in any way with "so-called civil rights groups." These elements were simply people who "may initiate and fan such smoldering racial resentments into violence solely to serve their own purposes."[24]

In the aftermath, while Dewey returned to the business of his law firm, Johnson asked Hoover to expand the riot control curriculum at the FBI National Academy.[25] The FBI also published a manual on urban violence, "Prevention and Control of Riots," with the assistance of the U.S. Army and the approval of the Civil Rights Division. According to an agent in the Training Division, John Doar reviewed every word of the manual, which included instructions for state and local police officers in baton techniques, among other things. All strokes, including the "smash," should be "short and snappy," the FBI advised.[26] The president's decision to expand FBI riot control responsibilities after the summer's violence cut across the grain of his political instincts. Always the good politician, he hedged his bet. But he did not expect the riots to continue. When they did, he sounded, at times, like former president Herbert Hoover, who implied that blacks had no reason to riot because "our 19 million Negroes probably own more automobiles than all the 220 million Russians and the 200 million African Negroes put together." "How is it possible," LBJ asked, "after all we've accomplished? How could it be? Is the world topsy-turvy?" Johnson had matured politically under the patronage of the New Deal, and in his experience the disadvantaged did not respond to federal largess in such a manner.[27]

Hoover expected the riots to continue; but not a single policeman trained by the FBI's riot control instructors was on hand when the Watts ghetto exploded in August 1965. The chief of the Los Angeles Police Department, William H. Parker, was a fiercely independent man often at odds with Hoover, and as punishment the director denied Parker's officers entry to the FBI National Academy. In any event, Los Angeles police needed no introduction to "the smash." Roger Wilkins, then an assistant director of the Justice Department's Community Relations Service and a member of a federal team sent to Watts, identified police brutality as one of the fundamental causes of the riot. The LAPD "was not fond of Negroes," he concluded. "Its members had killed about thirty looters and many of them called their nightsticks 'nigger sticks.'" With the exception of Ramsey Clark, however, no one listened to Wilkins. The Johnson administration seemed more concerned with subversives than with brutal police officers or Director Hoover's feud with Chief Parker.[28] With the law-and-order issue building all over again, the president—unable to comprehend the visible rage of Watts—turned to the FBI once more. This time, he used the Bureau's agents as the professional countersubversives they were and not as amateur sociologists.

On August 17 Hoover submitted a long memo on the Watts riot to Nicholas Katzenbach, who forwarded it to the president. If there was little "in the way of evidence as to subversive involvement," Katzenbach advised Johnson, the FBI would keep looking and investigate "this aspect" more "directly." But there would be no "general investigation through the FBI of other aspects of the riot." That remained the responsibility of city and state police. After reading the FBI memo and Katzenbach's proposals, the president approved a "limited investigation."[29]

The Johnson administration expected Hoover to help control

the political damage. Earlier, in a June 4 speech at Howard University, the president had called for a White House conference to propose strategies for moving black Americans "beyond opportunity to achievement." Preparations for the conference on civil rights, however, took on a different character after Watts. Berl Bernhard, who was then organizing a planning session for the conference, told Cartha DeLoach that the real purpose of the affair was "to prevent 'rioting' in major metropolitan cities . . . to let the participants freely 'sound off' and to let off steam."[30] The administration then requested name checks on every person the president intended to invite, and briefings for Democratic National Committee (DNC) officials on the alleged plans of certain "elements . . . to disrupt the White House Conference on Civil Rights." Louis Martin, one of the president's black advisers and the DNC deputy chairman for minorities, asked the Bureau to identify "the sources of revenue which enable these bomb throwers to carry out their programs." He found Hoover "very warm and cordial," anxious to cooperate. The director promised to prepare a report "for the chief."[31]

After more summer rioting in 1966, Hoover began preparing semimonthly summaries of possible racial violence in major urban areas. The director anticipated a long, hot summer for 1967, predicting "trouble" in "8 or 9 cities"—an overly optimistic forecast, as it turned out.[32] In all, black neighborhoods in nearly 150 cities experienced disorders—from minor disturbances to widespread looting, arson, and sniping in Newark and Detroit.

Republicans and conservative Democrats blamed the permissiveness of the Great Society once more. In Congress, the Johnson administration's adversaries favored an investigation of the urban disorders, but fortunately for the White House they had no idea "how to handle [it]." There seemed to be a "vacuum of Leadership," as Chalmers Roberts of the *Washington Post* described it to White House aide Douglass Cater. "The Leadership doesn't seem to have any policy." The administration was particularly worried about Senator James Eastland, who wanted to "carry the ball" on the proposed riot investigation, and Senator Everett Dirksen, who had set "out to make hay on the issue." Outside of Washington, the FBI described the riots and the decision to commit paratroopers in Detroit as "a political football between the President and the [Republican] Governor of Michigan," George Romney. In Maryland, another Republican governor, Spiro T. Agnew, claimed the riots had been "thoroughly planned beforehand" by subversive conspirators. Even Dwight Eisenhower discerned "a pattern" to the riots. Implying that Johnson had Hoover on a short leash, the former president called on Congress to pass whatever legislation was necessary to "empower the FBI to move into the situation."[33]

Administration officials controlled the damage as best they could, with Johnson himself asking Hoover to confront Agnew and Eisenhower. In the former case, when two FBI agents buttonholed the governor, he admitted "he had no firsthand information." "He is now backwatering completely," the director said. In the latter case, Johnson told Hoover to contact General Andrew Goodpaster, Eisenhower's aide, and to let him know the FBI had "full authority to spend anything to get the facts." The director summarized LBJ's order:

> Tell Eisenhower we don't want to put it on full page headlines the FBI is going to 'eat you up' and scare everybody and put them on notice what we are doing, but I have the authority and the President is on top of it and called me weeks ago when in Newark and insisted I get anybody, including their wife if she contributed. The President then stated he noticed this Rap (Brown) outfit said he was going to get a gun and shoot Lady Bird.

Before hanging up, Johnson told Hoover once again to "call General Goodpaster and say I have all the approval and authority and money and if I don't he, the President, will go to Texas and get it, and to tell Goodpaster to get Eisenhower fully briefed." Hoover responded, "I told the President I would do this." Goodpaster said "he would talk to General Eisenhower and straighten him out."[34]

Johnson faced a dilemma. While the Republican law-and-order strategy was growing in appeal, the Great Society faced criticism from an unexpected source. Radical black nationalists said the war on poverty and the civil rights reforms confirmed the elitism of liberal politicians. The movement's left wing demanded power, not paternalism, and offered a critique of the Great Society that undermined the president's constituency. From the skewed perspective of the radical left, the movement's principal enemy was not the red-necked southern sheriff or the reactionary senator from Mississippi or the nihilistic rioters or even the reluctant FBI director. Liberal reform was the enemy; LBJ was the enemy. The radicals' exaggerated focus on liberalism as an enemy of black people fractured the movement and put one more crack in Johnson's constituency.

To compound things, many black groups, from the moderate SCLC to the immoderate SNCC, were emerging as critics of the Vietnam war.[35] The radicals thought they had more in common with the world's colonial peoples and former colonial peoples, including the North Vietnamese, than their erstwhile benefactors, the liberal reformers of the Great Society. The United States raised a lower-class and disproportionately black army to fight a white man's war against a nonwhite people, a war to eradicate communism in a far-off country that made it increasingly difficult to eradicate poverty and racial injustice at home. "Johnson did make a brave—and in the end tragic—effort to resolve that visceral contradiction in the imperial way of life," wrote historian William Appleman Williams. "He tried to make major improvements in the quality of life for the poor and disadvantaged of all colors . . . and at the same time secure the frontier in Indochina. That proved to be impossible . . . [he] was trying to swim in the sky. But at least he tried."[36]

So the radicals turned their backs on Johnson and the reformers. They went off to confer with LBJ's enemies (Marxist-Leninists in Cuba, Algiers, China, and North Vietnam), threatened to shoot his wife, and insulted his family. "War," Stokely Carmichael said, was "for the birds, Lynda Bird and Lady Bird." This new black radicalism, in turn, alienated the administration's constituency in the Congress. After "approximately 300 Negroes brought in by CORE" confronted Congressman Lionel Van Deerlin (D., Cal.) and accused him of being a racist during a speech before a youth leadership training program in San Diego, Van Deerlin complained to Office of Economic Opportunity head Sargent Shriver. "Was [it] OEO's function to finance Black Power rioters?"[37]

Desperately trying to hold their voting block together, Johnson and his White House staff tried to discredit their leftist adversaries as followers of Trotsky or Marx or Mao.[38] They did so while trying to contain the growing conservative critique of the administration's lax law-and-order policies. Edwin Willis, the Louisiana Democrat who chaired the House Committee on Un-American Activities, reminded the president of how effective such Republican party tactics might turn out to be. "Just like some years ago the Republicans made a dent in the Democratic column on the false issue that Democrats were 'soft' on Commu-

nism, so I regret to say that in my opinion they will try to portray the Democrats in general, and you in particular, as being
'soft' on law enforcement and respect for law and order."[39] Johnson had even less luck in countering such charges than Harry
Truman had had twenty years earlier; at least Truman won his
election. LBJ claimed the left-wing critics of the Great Society
and the Vietnam war were all radicals or revolutionaries or
plain criminals. Richard Nixon, who had experience with this
sort of thing (Alger Hiss and the New Deal), said the radicals
and revolutionaries and criminals were all children of the Great
Society. The radicals and Nixon had one thing in common: they
were all critics of liberal reform.

Concerned about the continuing implications of the law-and-
order issue in the midst of the Detroit riots, Johnson called upon
Hoover once again on July 25, summoning him to a White House
meeting with Secretary of Defense Robert McNamara, Attorney
General Ramsey Clark, Supreme Court Justice Abe Fortas, Secretary of the Army Stanley R. Resor, and Army Chief of Staff
Harold K. Johnson. Cyrus Vance called in every half hour with
a report from Detroit. Obsessed with "intelligence," according
to Hoover's account of the meeting, the president said "there
was a concerted action and a pattern about all of these riots . . .
[and] that members of the Poverty Corps had been participants."
He told the director to keep his "men busy to find a central character to it, to watch and see and we will find some central
theme."[40]

Hoover said he "would dig into that thoroughly," but advised
Johnson not to expect much. Standing with the advocates of law
and order who traced the causes of the riots to liberal permissiveness and not communist conspiracy, Hoover actually minimized the Red menace. In a notable irony, the liberal president
rambled about subversives while the conservative director
calmly advised him that "outsiders" did not initiate any of the
riots. "Carloads of individuals," including communists, merely
arrived after the riots were "in full force." With regard to the
poverty workers, Hoover did single out Julius Hobson, then an
HEW economist and local chairman of the civil rights group
ACT who was "making militant speeches throughout [the District of Columbia]." (Hobson had filed a suit against the Washington school board that had resulted, the previous month, in a
federal court ruling against de facto segregation in the District's
schools.) Hoover also mentioned Marion Barry, SNCC's first

chairman and then director of the group's Washington office and a $50-a-day consultant for a community relations program that received federal funds. Johnson asked for memos on both men and a general summary of subversive influences in the riots.[41]

Hoover submitted a Division Five report that summarized rioting in twenty-nine cities. The basic conclusion was restrained and accurate. In almost every case "a single incident generally following an arrest of a Negro by local police for some minor infraction" sparked the disturbance. From that modest conclusion, however, Division Five credited "the exhortations of 'Black Power' advocates Stokely Carmichael and H. Rap Brown" with triggering "volatile situations . . . into violent outbreaks" in specific cities; condemned "the involvement of other violent, criminal, subversive and extremist elements" for fanning the flames of "spontaneous outbursts of mob violence"; and suggested that the principal blame for the riots could be traced to the civil rights movement. "Certain individuals who have been prominent in civil rights activities must bear a major burden of the guilt and responsibility for the turmoil created by the riots," Division Five concluded. "Hypocritical individuals" and "false prophets," movement people "who have openly professed abhorrence for violence," had worked "the civil rights field," sowing "seeds of confusion and disorder. . . . The Nation is [now] reaping the harvest of their handiworks."[42]

The Division Five report also included a section on the connection between the antiwar and civil rights movements. Hoover's conclusions here more closely reflected the traditional FBI view that communist subversion lay at the heart of the problem.[43] The director had been delivering reports to the White House about Martin Luther King's position on the Vietnam war since the summer of the Watts riot, when Nicholas Katzenbach ordered the preparation of a memo ("The Position of Martin Luther King, Jr. and the Communist Party, USA, on Vietnam") for Secretary of State Dean Rusk. Katzenbach wanted Hoover to pay particular attention to "any hard Communist Party line tying together Vietnam and the civil rights movement." And that is exactly what the director did, here and especially in the Division Five report prepared in the midst of the Detroit riot, by fusing Vietnam protests and urban rioting with the communist line. The CPUSA's "massive effort to create a united front in opposition to United States military presence in Vietnam" supplemented a parallel effort "to exploit racial issues." The ultimate goal, the Bureau concluded, was to create "the chaos upon which communism flourishes"—an entirely "predictable" Communist party policy. Though Hoover developed little hard information to support such conclusions, he advised the Justice Department on perhaps a dozen occasions that electronic surveillance in the King investigation had produced general intelligence on "the Vietnam situation." The director did not indicate that his ubiquitous wiremen even listened in on one of King's telephone conversations with President Johnson himself.[44]

Hoover had DeLoach brief Speaker of the House John McCormack (D., Mass.) and other members of Congress, including former FBI agent and then Senator Thomas J. Dodd (D., Conn.), on the link between civil rights leaders and antiwar sentiment. When Dodd criticized Dr. King's call for negotiations with the Vietcong, DeLoach told Dodd about King's relationship with Stanley Levison. Dodd had been on the movement's side, more or less, during the early 1960s, commending SCLC for its "excellent work" during the Albany demonstrations. (Nine of the people arrested in southwest Georgia were from his home state.) But King's brief comments on Vietnam ended all that. When Dodd questioned his "competence to speak out about complex matters of foreign policy," King dismissed the senator as a "supporter of the FBI and its invasion of privacy."[45] Meanwhile, King praised Robert Kennedy's position on Vietnam and, more broadly, "contemporary colonial revolutions." SCLC also debated a resolution condemning "the immorality and tragic absurdity of our position" in Vietnam, and a few antiwar activists fantasized about a Kennedy-King ticket in the 1968 presidential elections—a prospect, no matter how unlikely, that alarmed both Johnson and Hoover. "What a pair!," the director wrote.[46]

By breaking with the administration over the war, SNCC's John Lewis said, Dr. King was no longer LBJ's "head nigger when they come to the White House." "It is clear that he is an instrument in the hands of subversive forces seeking to undermine our nation," one of Hoover's agents in Division Five concluded, with far more crudity: "A traitor to his country and his race."[47] Condemning American involvement in Vietnam as an attempt "to perpetuate white colonialism," King called on young black and white men to boycott the war. It appeared, for a time, that the civil rights movement and the antiwar movement might indeed unite under the leadership of a single individual. Hoover responded by increasing the flow of letters and phone calls to the White House, the attorney general's office, and the Civil Rights Division, and most of these communications described King's ideas as identical to "the communist line." Not surprisingly, the White House was receptive. Johnson aide Harry McPherson described King as "the crown prince of the Vietniks."[48]

Hoover and Johnson found common ground on the question of communist influence of the antiwar movement. The modern civil rights movement started out in an uneasy alliance with the liberal reform state, engaging Jim Crow in limited moral skirmishes under conditions that pleased neither the government nor the movement itself. The government never controlled the movement and the movement never convinced the government to intervene on anything but its own terms. The campaign to force the FBI to protect civil rights workers was only the most dramatic element in that larger struggle. By the time the long, hot summer of 1967 began, some civil rights leaders had moved beyond a limited moral struggle to raise questions about power and national policy from Watts to Saigon. It was one thing to challenge Bull Connor and the city of Birmingham or J. Edgar Hoover and the Federal Bureau of Investigation; quite another to challenge Lyndon Johnson and the United States.

With black activists challenging the policies of the reform state at home and abroad, emphasizing the connections between racism, poverty, and militarism, Hoover's assessment of the seriousness of the threat posed by these activists grew exponentially. The antiwar rhetoric of the militants scarcely differed from Dr. King's. Black people, Black Panther Eldridge Cleaver said, "are asked to die for the system in Vietnam. In Watts they are killed by it." Calling for "a radical redistribution of economic and political power," King said "we are not interested in being integrated into *this* value structure." No longer content merely to change the segregated South, many black leaders once considered "responsible" now proposed to remake America. From segregated buses and swimming pools and voting booths, the movement moved on to battle the less visible racism in the North and the far reaches of the Third World where "God's military agent on earth" was doing so much damage.[49]

The call to remake America looked dangerous to Hoover, and the critique of the liberal reform state offered by men like King and the more disjointed critiques offered by men like Carmichael and Cleaver looked dangerous to LBJ. "The war engulfed the poor man," Roger Wilkins remembered, "and then Martin came out against the war. Johnson was distracted and angry, and his cities were burning. His soul hardened against us then . . . and he liked very few of us."[50] Fully committed to discrediting the civil rights movement by the time Detroit exploded in July 1967, the president relied on the FBI to provide the evidence he needed to make his case. Bureau officials flooded the White House with intelligence on the radicals and the moderates, and the sheer volume of information overwhelmed Johnson's staff. When asked to hold the "more or less minor" stuff and send over "the major information" only, Hoover refused. "If they don't want to use it after they get it, it is their responsibility." Even when pursuing an assigned agenda, the director stuck to the myth that his Bureau never evaluated the intelligence gathered.[51]

The White House wanted Hoover to supply "correct information" showing that all the riots and demonstrations were "well-planned" and "in very many cases" organized by "the same people"—the sort of information, secretary to the cabinet Robert Kintner suggested, that could be "authentically prepared" and disseminated in "a speech by someone who cannot be criticized as a McCarthyite." The FBI's reports, however, were short on hard evidence and long on rhetoric. Rather than conclude that they were searching for something that did not exist, administration officials responded by asking Hoover to dig deeper. They also assigned foreign policy adviser Walt W. Rostow the task of collecting "such evidence as there is on external involvement in the violent radical fringe of the Negro community in the U.S." Rostow mobilized the entire intelligence community, but his people realized that "the hard evidence will have to come from inside the U.S. via the FBI." Once again, however, Hoover and his agents could not get the job done. "[They] came up with a blank."[52]

Hoover had no intention of deflecting the law-and-order focus away from liberal permissiveness. In mid-September 1967 the Justice Department received a tip from Walter Sheridan, the former FBI agent and troubleshooter for Robert Kennedy's Justice Department, that his employer, NBC News, had interviewed a number of black citizens who claimed the riots were thoroughly organized. The network planned to use those interviews, along with photographs of several Soviet-made AK-47 assault rifles confiscated in Detroit, during a special television documentary

on urban violence. Attorney General Clark responded by ordering the FBI to "use the maximum available resources, investigative and intelligence, to collect and report all facts bearing upon
the question as to whether there has been or is a scheme or conspiracy by any group of whatever size, effectiveness or affiliation, to plan, promote or aggravate riot activity." The FBI nearly
balked at Clark's order and at Doar's attempts to follow up. "Up
to now," one Division Five executive complained, "we have run
out any logical leads indicating possibility of a conspiracy. . . .
The attached [memo] appears to be an attempt on the part of
John Doar to involve the Bureau in a fishing expedition of the
rankest type."[53]

FBI surveillance responsibilities would expand, and along
with that expansion would come more money and more agents.
But Hoover was never interested in trading autonomy for a
larger taxpayer subsidy. If the FBI was to move into community
surveillance, Hoover would do so on his own terms and not the
terms imposed by the Johnson administration. FBI Inspector Joseph Sullivan, who was assigned to the Cleveland field office at
the time, questioned the desirability of a greatly expanded domestic intelligence mission by asking, "Where do we go from
here?" "The primary troublemakers throughout the riots were
not organized groups in the sense that they represented some
subversive forces in some civil rights or racist collectives. They
were, rather, the street-corner hoodlum gangs," he concluded.
"Do we now program ourselves into coverage, into the development of sources, in these teen-age, street-corner gangs?" The Bureau must define its "interests" before committing major resources to this "whole new field of racial operations" where
questions of law and order would take precedence over questions of subversion. When Sullivan proposed a conference of
field agents to discuss the possibilities, Hoover said no. If the
senior staff at the seat of government hadn't made up their
minds yet and didn't have "the answer," the director wrote, "certainly no field group would be of aid."[54]

In the interim, Hoover advised the field of the facts of life.
"There exists in high Government circles a tremendous interest
in all information regarding the racial situation throughout the
United States."[55] In Chicago, that meant a leak to Mayor Richard
J. Daley regarding Dr. King's (alleged) assessment of the riots.
"They don't plan to burn down the West side. They are planning
to get the loop." In Detroit, where the violence was much worse,

it meant surveillance of a citizens action committee and its plans to hold a "people's tribunal," a mock prosecution of Detroit policemen for the crime of murder. On the national level, it meant the dissemination of a Bureau monograph on SNCC to fifty-one government officials and agencies. The INS received fifty copies and the marines thirty-one. Hoover sent a more modest number of copies (two) to West Point.[56]

This "tremendous interest in . . . the racial situation" also led to an escalation of the FBI's investigation of Office of Economic Opportunity personnel who might have been involved in the riots. Law-and-order advocates and other opponents of liberal reform "were trying to put us out of business," OEO inspector general Edgar May recalled. "They were going to use the riots to do it," by charging subversive infiltration of the poverty corps and poverty worker responsibility for creating a climate ripe for rioting. The White House was interested in damage control, once again, and had more confidence in an FBI probe than in OEO chief Sargent Shriver's in-house investigation. The president himself had mixed feelings on the whole question of poverty worker involvement in the riots. "Johnson was genuine in his concern for the poor and the blacks," OEO general counsel Donald M. Baker said. "He understood as well as anyone how the old fogies over in the Senate can take advantage of bad publicity and do a lot of damage to programs. At the same time, he never quite approved of community action and never really approved the participation of the poor. He talked to Sarge about it. He was never sure we were doing the right thing." So Johnson pushed the FBI investigation.[57]

Officials at the OEO were always bothering Hoover with requests to investigate harassment of poverty workers. Baker recalled one incident where Klansmen shot up a car carrying "do-gooder liberals" from the Child Development Group of Mississippi. "We called the FBI . . . their report came back about three months later and it was sort of typical. Random hunter's shots! That was their opinion! They put it in writing, for God's sake! Just absolutely ridiculous." FBI officials routinely sent reports on organizations that received war-on-poverty funding, in contrast, to OEO through Robert Emond, Edgar May's deputy and a former Bureau agent. One report described a tutorial program for children in Memphis as a fraud, with an emphasis on teaching the "black thing" and not "constructive black history."[58]

Concerned about the potential political impact of poverty worker involvement in the riots, the White House took the FBI's reports seriously. When one of the first reports came in on August 12, 1967, President Johnson met with Marvin Watson to discuss Leander Scott, a black activist and a member of the board of directors of the Kane County (Ill.) Council. The Council received OEO funds and the Bureau linked Scott to the racial disturbances in Elgin, Illinois. More reports followed. In Harlem, the FBI said, OEO funded a "hate school" and antipoverty organization, Haryou (Harlem Youth Opportunities Unlimited)-Act, Inc., whose employees included two members of a gun club formed by the Revolutionary Action Movement. Student Nonviolent Coordinating Committee firebrand Rap Brown, moreover, had used a car leased to the Haryou-Act employment center. These and other FBI reports prompted Sargent Shriver to fire or suspend a number of persons connected to OEO, including a consultant to a Harlem youth group and a Peace Corps trainee who also happened to be an antiwar activist. But no wholesale purge took place. "We never got a marching order from the FBI," Edgar May said.[59]

Instead, the FBI sent "around reports saying this Community Action guy or that Community Action guy was a communist"— a measured charge of communist infiltration of a Great Society program as opposed to the wild charge that communists had instigated the riots. "What did they expect me to do with this stuff?" Donald Baker remembered asking himself. "There were people in the White House from time to time who used to get antsy about some of this crap. Joe Califano once crawled all over us for not [firing] LeRoi Jones [Amiri Baraka]," the poet and playwright then with Haryou. Shriver himself had once complained to Hoover, according to Cartha DeLoach, about "the difficulty encountered in being able to summarily dismiss an individual who had subversive, homosexual or a bad criminal record."[60] There were radicals in OEO, mostly people described by one of Shriver's executives, Hyman Bookbinder, as "ultra left-wing elements in the program who saw this as an opportunity to give hell to both major political parties." There was some corruption, too, in terms of misuse of funds or unaccounted funds.[61] FBI officials showed some interest in this type of corruption, but they showed more interest whenever a countersubversive angle surfaced—like the Rap Brown connection with Haryou-Act. Hoover understood how the white middle class would react to news that the Harlem group received at least some money from OEO, from their war-on-poverty taxes. One way or another, the largess of LBJ's Great Society had provided a rental car for Rap Brown.

Hoover remained less than enthusiastic about President Johnson's OEO probe nonetheless. He would monitor OEO personnel, but not for the purpose of helping the president contain political fallout. After Marvin Watson requested an escalated investigation, the director informed the White House that the FBI had already given the National Commission on Civil Disorders (the Kerner Commission) everything in the files. Armed with a brief prepared by Division Five and "a summary of available information concerning each Commission member," Hoover had just finished detailed testimony on OEO before the Kerner Commission. His briefing papers were divided into seven sections, with the sixth section devoted entirely to the "conduct of anti-poverty workers."[62]

The Kerner Commission itself settled nothing for either the director or the president. Johnson had appointed the Commission on July 28, 1967, to investigate the origins of the riots and to make recommendations "to prevent or contain such disorders in the future," an exercise similar in intent, though certainly not in scope, to the effort to use Hoover and Dewey in 1964.[63] He brought in prominent people, Governor Otto Kerner of Illinois to serve as chairman and New York Mayor John Lindsay as vice-chairman, among others, and ordered the director to cooperate. Hoover supplemented his testimony on OEO before the Commission with a general discussion of the causes of the riots and his bureaucracy's responsibilities, though he qualified his call for stronger antiriot legislation. FBI agents photographed rioters and took notes, he testified, but arrested no sniper or fire bomber because looting and arson were local crimes outside the Bureau's jurisdiction. On the intelligence side, Hoover described for the Commission the "catalytic effect of extremists," focusing on the "vicious rhetoric" of SNCC (Rap Brown and Stokely Carmichael) and SCLC (Martin Luther King), and finding time to mention the Communist party, the pro-Chicom (Chinese communist) Progressive Labor party, Students for a Democratic Society, and various teenage gangs.

On the whole, the Kerner Commission rejected Hoover's conclusions. Its final report, submitted in February 1968, dealt less with the "catalytic effect" of the Browns and Carmichaels than with the social problems facing the United States. America was "moving toward two societies, one black, one white—separate and unequal." To reverse the "deepening racial trend," the Commission called for a massive and sustained "commitment to national action," recommending sweeping reforms in the areas of employment, education, welfare, housing reform, news reporting, and law enforcement. "Discrimination and segregation have long permeated much of American life," the report concluded. "They now threaten the future of every American." Dr. King compared the report to "a physician's warning of approaching death (of American society) with a prescription to life."

The Johnson administration rejected most of the Kerner Commission proposals on budgetary grounds. "That was the problem," LBJ later wrote, "—money." Because the money simply was not there, the Commission, as one of the president's most thoughtful advisers, Harry McPherson, noted in his memoirs, created more problems for the administration than it solved. "It intensified arguments about the war, raised impossible demands, and implicitly diminished the significance of what was already being done."[64] Hoping to break the conservative monopoly of the law-and-order issue at the very least, the administration seized upon one of the Kerner Commission's less costly recommendations—namely, its unintentional embrace of the surveillance mission that Hoover had advocated. A minor recommendation, buried in the appendix, called for the creation of police intelligence units "staffed with full-time personnel," including "undercover police personnel and informants."[65]

Not bothering to wait for publication of the Kerner Commission's findings, the administration encouraged local police departments to establish intelligence units and to funnel any information collected to the Justice Department through the FBI. As a result, the domestic intelligence apparatus became bigger, harder to control, more intrusive—and more incompetent. A Cook County grand jury investigation of the Chicago Police Department's security section concluded that its "inherently inaccurate and distortive" data contaminated federal intelligence. The security section forwarded to the FBI the name of "any person" who attended two "public meetings" of any group under surveillance. The Bureau then passed along the *"fact"* of membership in a subversive organization when conducting background checks on persons seeking federal employment or grants. "Since federal agencies accepted data from the Security

Section without questioning the procedures followed, or methods used to gain information," the grand jury noted, "the federal government cannot escape responsibility for the harm done to untold numbers of innocent persons."[66]

Hoover felt the Kerner Commission paid too much attention to the sociological side of urban violence and not enough to the law-and-order side. When Johnson appointed yet another study group, the National Commission on the Causes and Prevention of Violence, and selected Dwight Eisenhower's brother Milton to chair it, the director told Ramsey Clark that there was too much "emphasis today in the press that society is sick. . . . I said I hoped the new Commission . . . will keep a balanced viewpoint as to that because the other Commission went far astray in regard to white racism. I said there is racism but not as predominantly as the Kerner Commission found it to be."[67] When testifying before the Eisenhower Commission in September 1968, Hoover stressed the "Mau Mau–type tactics" of SNCC and other militant black groups. (The FBI could not decide whether SNCC was a Mau Mau–type New Left group or "a Ku Klux Klan in reverse—a black Klan.") On the issue of police brutality in the ghetto, the director returned to first principles, linking Moscow-directed revolutionaries with "vicious, hate-filled . . . black extremists." The "communist policy to charge and protest 'police brutality' . . . in racial situations" was part of an "immensely successful" and "continuing smear campaign," he said. "The net effect . . . is to provoke and encourage mob action and violence by developing contempt for constituted authority."[68]

An Eisenhower Commission study group headed by Jerome Skolnick saw things differently, placing Hoover, not communists, at the center of the problem. The director's propaganda about subversives "who misdirect otherwise contented people" was particularly effective among police officers. How many radical squads resembled the Nashville Police Department's intelligence division, with its subscriptions "to all known communist publications," its filing system patterned after the Bureau's, its exclusive focus on "subversive organizations," and its "almost daily" contacts with G-men? The FBI, according to Skolnick's group, had helped politicize the police and was at least partly responsible for the "police violence" that so often preceded a riot or accompanied a civil rights demonstration.[69]

The Kerner Commission and the Eisenhower Commission prompted the FBI to take "counterintelligence action" to negate the impact of their findings. One Bureau field office responded to the Kerner Commission's tendency "to absolve the Negro rioters from any large blame" by suggesting that the Crime Records Division publish a public-opinion poll, "either a true poll or a false poll," that would indicate the public's tendency to place all blame on "the Negro rioters."[70] Although Hoover rejected the proposal, he moved quickly to support a law-and-order alternative to the presidential commissions by working with Senator John L. McClellan (D., Ark.), chairman of the Permanent Subcommittee on Investigations (PERM) and a longtime, hard-line foe of the civil rights movement.

McClellan's Subcommittee, the same Subcommittee that Joseph McCarthy had once chaired, was actually the third and last of the old cold war–era investigating committees to probe the origins of the riots. The Senate Internal Security Subcommittee had begun such hearings, but the House Committee on Un-American Activities did not expect much on that front. HUAC Chairman Edwin Willis told Cartha DeLoach "the Senate hearings would amount to only a lot of 'socialistic crap,'" in that the Senate would . . . demand better housing, better jobs, et cetera." Willis wanted to know whether the FBI would provide "guidance" for his Committee's law-and-order hearings. Although the Bureau helped with other hearings, including the SDS investigation, and would continue to help in the coming years with reports on such things as the stockpiling of weapons by radical black groups, HUAC's position on the riots was too extreme. To say "that subversive influences had triggered the riots," DeLoach told Willis, was irresponsible and "bad . . . for the country."[71]

The FBI preferred to work with Senator McClellan. He was far more powerful than any HUAC member, and his PERM staff were far more reliable (and therefore far less likely to compromise their relationship with Bureau agents) than the HUAC people. In their political responses to the riots there was little difference between Willis and McClellan, DeLoach's comment to the contrary notwithstanding. Before the Senate had even voted to fund his inquiry, McClellan said he would emphasize "law enforcement rather than the social causes underlying the disorders." When the authorization came through in August 1967, the McClellan Committee began work on a twenty-five part, three-year investigation into the causes of the urban riots. Sixty-three policemen from local Red squads testified, including a sergeant from the Chicago intelligence unit who assured the Committee that "the Communist threat . . . does exist."[72]

Senator McClellan explained the origins of the riots with the sort of logic favored by the late Senator McCarthy. In September 1967, following a state police raid on the home of two poverty workers in Pike County, Kentucky, Margaret and Alan McSurely, a local prosecutor gave the papers seized in the raid to one of the Committee's investigators. The state charged the McSurelys, organizers for the Southern Conference Educational Fund, with violating a sedition statute. The defendants attracted PERM's interest, McClellan said, because Stokely Carmichael had addressed a SCEF staff meeting and had spoken at Vanderbilt University a few days before the Nashville riots. There was a thread connecting everything back to SCEF, and back through that organization to the Communist party. (McClellan, Hoover, and even a few civil rights leaders believed SCEF to be "communist controlled.") Since the McSurelys were poverty workers, the thread could be traced all the way back to the Great Society. The Pike County prosecutor, however, was not a disinterested Red hunter. He had political ambitions and economic interests. As a candidate for lieutenant governor on the Republican ticket and owner of property leased to coal mine operators, he intended to drive the McSurelys and all other poverty workers out of Kentucky.[73]

These facts slowed the FBI, but not the McClellan Committee. A federal judge ordered the McSurelys' papers sequestered, but a member of McClellan's staff took them to Washington anyway. The senator centered on love letters that newspaper columnist Drew Pearson had sent Margaret McSurely, with whom he had once had a brief affair. A persistent critic of McClellan, Pearson had most recently discussed the senator's activities in a column dated August 10—the day before the Pike County raid. It was indeed a small world. Ultimately, PERM summoned the McSurelys and had them indicted for contempt of Congress. Now facing prosecution on a second front, the McSurelys sued the Committee and the Bluegrass prosecutor. Meanwhile, terrorists (literally) bombed them out of their Kentucky home, and the FBI gave everything it had on the McSurelys and Joseph Mulloy, a worker with an antipoverty group (Appalachian Volunteers) who was also arrested, to the Kentucky State Police. Admittedly, it was not much, and in Mulloy's case there was absolutely nothing in the files. But it was "a matter of police cooperation." Back in

Washington, an FBI agent reviewed the records seized in the raid, and Hoover sent a memo to the White House.[74]

The whole thing was part of what the White House called a "nationwide investigation of the OEO involvement in the riots," an effort that confirmed the president's concern about the vulnerability of the Office of Economic Opportunity and the whole war on poverty.[75] The White House, however, did not realize that the FBI had entered that nationwide investigation on John McClellan's side, not Lyndon Johnson's. If FBI officials kept a reasonable distance from the McSurelys' civil suit and the "political fight" down in Kentucky, they helped with other aspects of the McClellan Committee investigation. In September 1967, when McClellan asked for "the cooperation of the FBI in checking names," Hoover assured him "we would give . . . every assistance we could." The director ordered Crime Records executive Thomas Bishop to handle all requests from the Committee's chief counsel, Donald O'Donnell, "promptly."[76]

A typical PERM request called for the FBI to list all "the militant organizations" in a given area and to provide identifications "of the individual members." Blind memos followed. This was done in about two dozen cities. In Boston, the FBI provided dossiers on such groups as Mothers for Adequate Welfare and such individuals as a Roxbury housewife and sit-in veteran—"a Negress . . . married to . . . a white male" and an antiwar activist to boot, the Bureau said. Other FBI offices kept PERM posted on the activities of their rivals. Whenever something interesting turned up, Hoover issued the appropriate order. "Let our contact on McClellan's Com. know." Since Kerner Commission investigators often focused on police brutality, Hoover countered by sending McClellan data on "bombings" and other "attacks on police."[77]

McClellan was always asking Hoover for help. A week after working out the terms of assistance for the riot hearings, on September 13, 1967, DeLoach met McClellan over lunch to discuss the agenda of another appendage to the Senate Government Operations Committee, the Subcommittee on Criminal Laws and Procedures. Their conversation centered on a provision in "the pending legislation involving the Crime Control Act" that authorized an expansion of the FBI National Academy. McClellan asked DeLoach to write a speech for him on law and order and to provide backup information on the Bureau's desires in the area of police training. Crime Records agents wrote the speech and prepared blind memos, though DeLoach did not believe this latter service was necessary. "Senator McClellan apparently was not aware of the tremendous amount of information we had already furnished his Staff Director, James Calloway."[78]

McClellan also offered the FBI help. He gave DeLoach a copy of his omnibus crime control bill, and "asked that the FBI study this bill very carefully and actually prepare language which could be inserted into the bill for his usage." "This would be done," DeLoach said, "on a confidential basis." When Calloway finished work on a new version of the bill, he handed Bishop a copy of another bill, the law enforcement assistance bill (which would be added to the omnibus bill), and requested, "on an informal basis," the FBI's "views with regard to it. This would include not only the portions dealing with the FBI, but all other portions of the Bill."[79]

A few weeks later, in November 1967, Deputy Attorney General Warren Christopher phoned DeLoach to discuss an amendment to one of the pending crime control bills concerning law enforcement training. "Our conversation," as DeLoach summarized it for Tolson and Hoover, "was not a pleasant one." "[The Deputy Attorney General] and the Attorney General both felt that perhaps the FBI did not want to be saddled with the tremendous responsibilities it was being given." DeLoach told Christopher that was not the case. "To the contrary, we insisted upon such responsibilities . . . we would have no part of recommending legislation which would establish useless substructures or a waste of the taxpayer's funds." Senators McClellan and Eastland, he added, sided with the FBI. While acknowledging the FBI's "powerful allies," Christopher said the attorney general thought "another agency," a national office on law enforcement, should at least "*share* the responsibilities with the FBI." The director favored McClellan's version. "We will not agree to *sharing* any part of this." If Christopher tried to do something about it, "he would meet considerable resistance on the Hill."[80]

The skirmishes here were part of a larger battle between Justice Department attorneys who believed crime would disappear if poverty disappeared and FBI officials who believed crime would disappear if the permissivists in the Department (Ramsey Clark) and on the Supreme Court (Earl Warren) would disappear. Having failed to persuade DeLoach and Hoover to modify the crime control bill, the Department turned to Senator Robert Kennedy for assistance—hoping "to knock out the FBI provision." The Johnson administration experienced some success in attaining a "consensus between hard-line demands for crack-down and constitutional solicitude for civil liberties and due process."[81] When the Omnibus Crime Control and Safe Streets Act became law in 1968, it included a provision creating the in-house bureaucracy Clark and Christopher wanted, the Law En-forcement Assistance Administration, and another provision in-creasing the number of police officers authorized to attend the FBI National Academy from 200 to 2,000. Title I appropriated $5,110,000 to the Bureau in fiscal year 1969 for training pro-grams at the Academy.[82]

While the FBI expanded the National Academy, published pamphlets and instructed local police in the "fundamentals" (DeLoach's word) of riot control, Hoover sought an exemption from the Justice Department policy requiring an automatic pre-liminary investigation upon the receipt of a police brutality complaint. The number of police brutality cases was expanding at an alarming rate by 1968, and movement radicals were pub-lishing pamphlets of their own—for example, a *Black Survival Guide* subtitled *How to Live Through a Police Riot*. But the FBI had no time for investigating police brutality. The FBI had plenty of time for the people who raised the issue, however. The special agent in charge of the Pittsburgh field office tried to "neutralize" a National Urban League grant proposal on the grounds that it called for the creation of a citywide civilian po-lice review board. The Bureau furnished "documentation oppos-ing such civilian review boards" to a "source at the Mellon Foun-dation."[83]

Even the Orangeburg, South Carolina, "riot" of February 8, 1968, was little more than a minor irritant for the FBI. Highway patrolmen fired on 400 students from State College and other young people protesting a segregated bowling alley near the campus, killing three and wounding nearly thirty. Twenty-eight people were shot in the side or back. A few were hit in the soles of their feet. The FBI agent assigned to supervise the subsequent civil rights probe shared a motel room with one of the subjects of the investigation, and two of the agents on the scene at the time of the shooting told the Civil Rights Division that they had not been there. Hugh Fleischer, who worked on the case when it came to trial during the Nixon years, said they "falsified the information to protect the [nine indicted] troopers. . . . I hap-pened to get the call from Dick Kleindienst," then deputy attorney general, "to not crossexamine the Bureau agents because it would be detrimental to the relationship between the Department and the Bureau." Under pressure from Division lawyers who threatened to resign and go to the press, "[we] got the department to back off," Fleischer continued. "Sadly, it didn't help. The jury was out for twenty minutes and acquitted," having concluded that the troopers had not imposed summary punishment "under color of law" by firing into the crowd.[84]

That decision pleased the director. He sympathized with law enforcement officers caught in "an intense demoralizing situation where [black people] cry 'police brutality' on the slightest provocation" and insist on being addressed "in courteous language"—"particularly in the case of Negroes as instead of saying, 'Boy, come here,' they want to be address[ed] as 'Mr.'" Hoover's sympathies, as ever, were with the "officers above" and their nightsticks and guns, not the "Negro on the ground."[85] In South Carolina, the director also stood with state officials. While the civil rights case worked its way through the federal courts, state prosecutors blamed the Orangeburg violence on one of the wounded protestors—SNCC's Cleveland Sellers. "The biggest nigger in the crowd," the governor's representative said. Sellers was locked up "in a tiny cell on death row," where he said he found it hard not to think about Schwerner, Chaney, and Goodman. Seven weeks after the massacre, moreover, he went to trial on a federal charge of violating the Selective Service Act. The court found him guilty, though that action was complicated when the FBI admitted reviewing Sellers's file at his draft board and monitoring his telephone conversations. In the fall of 1970 the state finally convicted him of participating in a riot *two nights before the shootings*. The events in Orangeburg, Tom Wicker of the *New York Times* wrote, suggests "how casual is this country's sense of justice for black people, how careless it is of its own humanity."[86]

Things had changed since the spring of 1964. The FBI had provided "civil rights training" for law enforcement officers, but it was a token effort, in effect a public-relations gimmick. Riot training for these same policemen, in contrast, was a serious business. It may have been public relations, too, but it was a way for the FBI to expand in size, and to spread its ideology about racial matters and subversives and what Ramsey Clark described as its "hostile view of the life of poor blacks in America." The same thing could be said about the FBI's commitment to affirmative action within its ranks. If black agents were still hard to find in Hoover's FBI, the few the director had hired were easy to see. When the Bureau arrested Rap Brown in late July 1967, Hoover immediately called the White House. "I took the occasion," he told Marvin Watson, "to have a Negro Agent participate in the arrest."[87]

FBI riot training for policemen, arrests of people like Rap Brown, and covert assistance to Senator McClellan provided a law-and-order alternative to the social, cultural, and economic prescriptions of the Kerner Commission. It was no coincidence that John McClellan had turned to the FBI for help with the PERM hearings and the Omnibus Crime Control and Safe Streets Act. Hoover knew the Kerner Commission and McClellan's projects symbolized a division in the nation. With the war and the riots, the United States was coming apart. Richard Nixon, with his slogan of "bring us together again," updated version of Goldwater's southern strategy, and politics of resentment, best understood the depth of the division. "The whole secret of politics . . . [is] knowing who hates who," said Kevin Phillips, aide to John Mitchell and the Nixon campaign expert on ethnic voting patterns. "The Republicans have the political freedom to disregard [Negroes]," to "build a winning coalition" by exploiting "Negro-Democratic mutual identification."[88]

Alone in the White House, with his three-screen television console, Lyndon Johnson watched his own tragedy unfold each evening on the network news. He knew what was happening, but did not know what to do about it. He never really made the choice, never really decided on a political strategy, never really gave up his dream of consensus for a more cold-blooded politics of "positive-polarization" (Spiro Agnew's words). Perhaps he was too decent a man, after all. He kept drifting from the world of the Great Society and the Kerner Commission's sociology to the segmented world of Hoover and McClellan and the Nixon campaign.[89] "It is time to rip away the rhetoric and to divide on authentic lines," Vice-President Agnew said without apology after the election. "When the President said 'bring us together' he meant the functioning, contributing portions of the American citizenry." The FBI director agreed. "To Hoover," as one of his biographers noted, protesters of every stripe, whether ghetto rioters or college students marching against the war, "were not part of the real America, 'the hard-working, tax-paying, law-abiding people of this country.'"[90]

President Johnson never gave up completely on the citizens the new vice-president and the old FBI director held in contempt. If he could explain the riots by reference to "a few hoodlums sparked by outside agitators who moved around from city to city making trouble. Spoiling all the progress I've made," in the next breath he could say, "God knows how little we've really moved on this issue despite all the fanfare. As I see it, I've moved the Negro from D+ to C−. He's still nowhere. He knows it. And that's why he's out in the streets. Hell, I'd be there too."[91]

When the riots began, Lyndon Johnson was not sure he could trust Hoover. Ironically, by the time the riots had run their course, he was certain of Hoover's loyalty—and that certainty may have been his grandest delusion. "Dick, you will come to depend on Edgar," LBJ told the new president-elect. "He is a pillar of strength in a city of weak men. You will rely on him time and time again to maintain security. He's the only one you can put your complete trust in."[92] The director, nonetheless, had been working for the McClellans and Nixons all along. In the end, Hoover made things harder for Johnson and the social reformers of the Great Society, and he made things easier for Nixon and Nixon's heirs. He helped make the Republican party the white man's party Martin Luther King had feared it might become, back in the spring of 1964, a few months before the fires started burning.

The FBI director's maneuverings during the riot years suggest that he was no shrill anticommunist ideologue or practitioner of what Richard Hofstadter once called the paranoid style of American politics. Rather, he was a sophisticated politician who understood power and public opinion. He ingratiated himself with the president and with the president's domestic political adversaries while pursuing his own personal, bureaucratic, and political interests. Johnson tried to use Hoover to help him manage the politics of the riots, but he had no more success in controlling the director than had any of his Oval Office predecessors dating back to Franklin D. Roosevelt. He used the FBI to help him manage particular problems and to help him govern, and Hoover damaged Johnson's interests on both fronts. In the end, the director's bureaucracy, the FBI, and the director's mode of operation, federal surveillance, became further entrenched in the governing process.

One of Hoover's aides said "he handled the presidents as well or better than any bureaucrat in the city of Washington ever has."[93] It would be hard to argue with that assessment, and harder still to overstate the consequences for black Americans. Throughout the riot years Hoover's pronouncements on the menace of subversion oscillated wildly, with the director sometimes exaggerating the communist role in the riots and sometimes minimizing it depending on the particular audience to be addressed and the bureaucratic imperatives of the moment. That inconsistency of word, however, should not obscure the fundamental fact about the FBI agenda in those times, whether the director spoke the language of anticommunism or the new language of law and order—or even on occasion the language of social scientists who saw poverty and despair at the center of the riots and not Reds or liberal permissivists. Hoover worked every day to build up a surveillance system that reflected his belief that all of black America, not just Brown and Carmichael and the always troublesome King, posed a subversive threat to the real America—the hard-working, tax-paying, law-abiding white people of this country. He worked every day to spread the white backlash that had infected American politics during the riot years.

CHAPTER
8

=========××××=========

Black Hate
Community Surveillance and Counterintelligence

J Edgar Hoover focused on the black menace and not the Red menace during the last of the Great Society years, and he framed the FBI response to the chaos and crime of the cities accordingly. With black activists sowing seeds of discontent and militant protest in the ghettoes, and with the Johnson administration giving him free reign to march against the new black menace in any way he saw fit, the director constructed a pervasive two-track surveillance system. Hoover mobilized the FBI to smash the vanguard (black political activists of liberal and radical views) and to keep track of the masses (the everyday people who lived in black communities). In August 1967, with the Great Society consensus crumbling amidst burning cities and war in Southeast Asia, the FBI launched a new counterintelligence program, patterned after the Communist party and Ku Klux Klan operations, that targeted civil rights movement leaders and black power advocates alike under a "Black Hate Group" caption. At the same time, the FBI targeted all of black America under a series of community surveillance programs.

Lyndon Johnson might have been ignorant about the details surrounding the "black hate" disruption effort, and it is possible, perhaps likely, that he was not even aware of its existence. Yet Hoover and his principal aides interpreted the president's obsession with militants and nationalists, and as well with those

261

civil rights leaders who opposed the Vietnam war, as an Oval Office grant of authority to do whatever was necessary to neutralize them. On the other hand, community surveillance clearly resulted from White House pressure. Though structured more by the conservative politics and values of internal security bureaucrats than the liberal politics and values of LBJ's social reformers, FBI counterintelligence programs aimed at black leadership and community surveillance programs aimed at blacks as a group were as much a Great Society legacy as the Civil Rights Act of 1964 or the Voting Rights Act of 1965. By giving the FBI carte blanche, the Johnson administration contributed to the emergence of surveillance as the principal element in the federal government's relationship with its black citizens during the president's last two years in office.

The FBI director found the Great Society tolerant of surveillance even before the riots and the antiwar movement led President Johnson to imagine dissent as a gigantic conspiracy led by his enemies.[1] Washington legend credits Johnson for remarking how he would rather have Hoover inside the tent pissing out than outside the tent pissing in. Perhaps the best proof of that LBJism lies in the volume of names submitted to the FBI for clearance during the Great Society years. Even the president's grandson received a check. At his first birthday party, his grandmother joked with the press corps about the White House pass around the toddler's neck. The clearance had included "a letter from J. Edgar Hoover himself, saying that 'nothing derogatory was found in the files of the FBI against Patrick Lyndon Nugent!'"[2] Johnson's people so often sent Hoover's people into the files for more serious work that Mildred Stegall, who served as the designated White House recipient of the FBI's reports, thought the administration abused the service.[3] A low-profile, tight-lipped employee known as "the sphinx," Stegall reportedly went on the FBI payroll for a time. The real name-check person on the staff was Marvin Watson, one of the president's closest aides and a man who had much faith in the integrity of the FBI.[4]

When submitting requests for reports on "matters of extreme secrecy," Waston asked the FBI not to "respond in writing by formal memoranda." "The President actually wanted," as Cartha DeLoach advised Clyde Tolson, "blind-type" memos bearing "no government watermarks or letterhead." Neither DeLoach nor Tolson needed detailed instructions. The Bureau had been preparing blind memos for decades and marking documents

PERSONAL AND CONFIDENTIAL AND NOT FOR FILES since 1920, if not earlier. And the Bureau had been handling "delicate" matters, matters, as Hoover said, "that we don't want any publicity on" because they "would just be terribly embarrassing to the big boss," at least since the Franklin Roosevelt years. The FBI knew how "to put a special on" whenever the chief executive requested assistance, and how to ingratiate itself with the White House when doing so.[5]

Mildred Stegall's "special files" include sixty-two boxes of FBI reports on "individuals other than staff." The FBI even dug up "derogatory information" on Joe Louis and Jesse Owens. "Owens . . . sent greetings to the National Negro Congress on October 15, 16, 1937," the FBI said. On one January 1967 day Stegall submitted the names of thirty black Democrats—elected officeholders and party organizers. The FBI uncovered "no pertinent derogatory information" on Harold Washington, then a member of the Illinois State Senate and later mayor of Chicago, and sixteen others. The FBI did uncover some on two future members of the U.S. House of Representatives, George Crockett (D., Mich.) and Mervyn M. Dymally (D., Cal.), and eleven others.[6] Another nineteen boxes in Stegall's files concern subjects ranging from the Harlem Freedom Forum to South African Affairs and Vice President Humphrey's Files on FBI Investigations. From 1964 to 1968 Stegall received 738 Bureau reports, most of which were not specifically solicited, under a single category, Race Relations and Related Matters.[7]

A broad FBI community surveillance program on Race Relations and Related Matters had begun in 1966, when the Justice Department assigned a handful of law students to a so-called Summer Project and told them to organize newspaper clippings, data from United States attorneys, and "some Bureau material." The Department wanted to find out "what's going on in the black community." A year later, in the wake of the Newark and Detroit riots and President Johnson's "standing instructions," Department attorneys pursued the law students' effort on a more systematic basis. What Joseph Califano described, many years later, as an appalling "lack of intelligence . . . for us in the White House," however, was actually a lack of analysis. The real need was to coordinate the already "heavy flow of FBI reports."[8] Califano believed the White House pressured Justice to produce the wrong type of intelligence. The emphasis should have been on "physical intelligence" (basic urban geography) and "social intelligence" (socioeconomic data) in cities racked by rioting. It was more important to know the location of the hospitals and power stations and schools and the unemployment and high school dropout rates than what the local SNCC contingent or the Revolutionary Action Movement people were up to.[9] But no one even thought of that at the time. The president's men seemed interested only in compiling "advance intelligence about dissident groups."[10]

FBI officials continued to dodge Attorney General Ramsey Clark and Assistant Attorney General for Civil Rights John Doar when they issued directives regarding police brutality or voting rights matters. They were receptive, however, when Clark and Doar spoke of expanding surveillance. At Clark's request, Doar studied the Justice Department's "facilities for keeping abreast" of the racial intelligence the Bureau kept sending over, recommending the establishment of "a single intelligence unit to analyze the FBI information we receive." He also suggested the solicitation of data from the Great Society bureaucracies—"the poverty programs, the Labor Department programs, and the Neighborhood Legal Services." "This is a sensitive area," Doar conceded, but the administration could maintain its "credibility with people in the ghetto" by keeping the unit's existence secret. He recommended no limitation on FBI coverage, arguing that the past surveillance consensus, with its relatively narrow focus on "a limited number of traditional subversive groups" and "individuals" suspected "of a specific statutory violation," was part of the problem. "A broad spectrum approach" was essential—at least until the proposed intelligence "unit became knowledgeable and sophisticated and could make reasonable judgements and . . . [narrow] its spectrum to a more limited target." In the interim, Doar saw no alternative to community surveillance.[11]

Clark created an Interdivisional Intelligence Unit (IDIU) in December 1967, assigning supervisory responsibility to Doar, Assistant Attorneys General Fred Vinson (Criminal) and J. Walter Yeagley (Internal Security), and Community Relations Service Director Roger Wilkins.[12] The IDIU proposed to use FBI reports to compile "a master index," organized on a city-by-city basis, "on individuals, or organizations." Clark based his authorization on executive discretion and criminal statutes regarding rebellion and insurrection that dated from the Civil War era. He also cited the Smith Act, the World War II–era law that made it a crime to conspire to teach or advocate the violent overthrow of the government. Clark thus emerged as one of the founding fathers of community surveillance. Complaining about the limits of "existing intelligence sources," he championed instead a "broad investigation," one that would monitor all possible riot conspirators in "the urban ghetto." He ordered the FBI to "use the maximum available resources, investigative and intelligence, to collect and report all facts" regarding any "scheme or conspiracy by any group." This included the development and expansion of "sources or informants in black nationalist organizations," from SNCC to "other less publicized groups."[13]

Roger Wilkins, then the highest ranking black man in the Justice Department, said "Johnson despised us ... because we wouldn't put Stokely Carmichael in jail." Fred Vinson said the Department averaged "fifty letters a week from Congress" demanding that "people like Carmichael be jailed." In this view, the IDIU and the other community surveillance programs that followed were a product of "the atmosphere of the time." Vinson remembered one congressman saying "to hell with the First Amendment." So the Department kept trying to put Carmichael behind bars; only Clark's men never could figure out which, if any, federal law he had violated. "The only thing you could get Stokely on was speech," Wilkins said. The administration intended to collect advance intelligence about possible disorders in the ghetto and at the same time focus the blame for the riots on subversive conspirators. This last goal came directly from the Oval Office, and Clark and Doar grudgingly acceded to it even as they dismissed the president's obsessions.[14]

"The Department made a judgment that you could [gather intelligence] for a good purpose," Doar said, reflecting on the origins of the IDIU and the decision to rely so heavily on FBI data. "We didn't think it through, I didn't think it through—that if you could do it for a good purpose, there was concern that some people might be able to do it for a bad purpose. . . . If I'd been smarter I'd probably have figured out that's what's going to happen." Doar based his original recommendations on his experiences in the South during the voting litigation campaign of the early 1960s. To change society for the better, he said, "you had to be on the scene, you had to know the territory." But by relying on the FBI to provide information about the black community in the urban North, the IDIU functioned in the manner of a "crazy counterintelligence program"—a "lunatic operation," in White House aide John Roche's words. "Clark was in charge of it," Roche added. Years later, "[he] tried to pretend he never heard of it." Clark said he was only aware of about 10 percent of what the FBI was doing, and while that may have been true overall, he was certainly aware of the IDIU and the birth of community surveillance.[15]

The irony is that the Republican party singled out Clark, along with Supreme Court Chief Justice Earl Warren, as the main target of its law-and-order politicking during the 1968 presidential campaign. Even a few members of Johnson's White House staff referred to Clark as "Ramsey the marshmallow," and Hoover himself labeled him a coddler of crooks and black terrorists and an enemy of the law-and-order values of Richard Nixon's silent majority. The attorney general's record, in his own words, of denying "a good many" FBI requests "to wiretap or bug people that worked in this [civil rights] area," was especially irritating.[16]

Attorney General Clark may have encouraged the FBI director to recruit informants and spy, but Hoover, as ever, did so on his own terms, considering primarily the needs of the FBI, not the needs of the Great Society reformers who ran the IDIU. While reminding field agents to take advantage of opportunities whenever "an entree to develop sources in the Negro community" presented itself, the director had supervisors at headquarters review "the informant situation in all areas for each field division" and submit recommendations for new informant programs that ranged far beyond the typical communist or communist infiltration investigations.[17] Recruitment of black informants to cover the Communist party had always been a priority, in part because the CPUSA's lingering obsession with white chauvinism protected black members from suspicion. White communists who accused Negro comrades of working for the FBI often found themselves accused of racism and drummed out of the party. As a result, the Bureau recruited a disproportionately high number of black informants. In some local communist units during the early 1960s, all of the FBI's informants were black. By the mid- and late 1960s, however, black informant coverage of the CPUSA gave way to new priorities—in the words of FBI Assistant Director W. Mark Felt, "live coverage of (1) black nationalist groups, (2) ghetto areas, and (3) groups expected to capitalize on racial disorder and civil disobedience."[18]

The CPUSA fit the third category, but even here party members were not the focus of attention. The FBI centered on black activists and black people in general, emphasizing a black menace almost to the exclusion of the communist menace. The major FBI operation in the first and last categories mentioned by Felt was the TOPLEV (Top Level) Informant Program, later known by the more appropriate acronym, BLACPRO. By the fall of 1967 each field office assigned at least one (and often as many as four) agents to work exclusively on the development of "quality non-organizational sources . . . for the purpose of expeditiously infiltrating militant black nationalist organizations." A more convoluted BLACPRO objective required the placement of informants in "new groups" that *might* "spring from the mass Black Nationalist movement." These informants reported on "obscure community activists" who *might* "become agitators for violent protest," and they allowed the Bureau "to position" itself "ahead of the growth of these groups and leaders and to record their development and demise." The striking thing about such programs is the dearth of references to communism—the traditional subversive bogey.[19]

Under BLACPRO and various other informant programs, the FBI covered the entire spectrum. Division Five, the Bureau unit responsible for the great majority of the "Racial Matters" investigations, operated informants within the Southern Christian Leadership Conference national office in Atlanta and among Stokely Carmichael's entourage. The FBI man in the SCLC was comptroller James A. Harrison. William Sullivan described the informant assigned to Carmichael, a bodyguard named Peter Cardoza, as a "tough customer" and "a real discipline problem for the bureau."[20] Most informants were not positioned as well as Harrison and Cardoza. They operated out of cities like Minneapolis, where FBI agents asked "criminal informants in the Negro community" to "furnish information on racial matters." As in the parallel Ku Klux Klan informant program, black informants also operated out of remote regions like southwest Texas, where the FBI had seventeen "Negro informants and sources" in El Paso, four in Midland, nine in Odessa, and two in Pecos.[21]

In October 1967 FBI officials launched an even more pervasive informant program—a "Ghetto Listening Post" or a "Ghetto Informant Program." Their definition of a "listening post" embraced "any individual who resides in a ghetto-type area" or "who frequent[s] ghetto areas on a regular basis." Prospective recruits for the Bureau's "grass-roots network" included em-

ployees and owners of taverns and liquor stores, drugstores and
pawnshops, candy stores and barbershops, and other ghetto
businesses; honorably discharged veterans and especially members of veterans organizations; janitors of apartment buildings;
newspaper and food and beverage distributors; taxi drivers;
salesmen; and bill collectors. Bureau agents steered these
sources toward "Afro-American type book stores" and asked
them to identify their "owners, operators and clientele." The informants also reported on persons with criminal records or
teen-age gang members "operating in the ghetto," "changes in
the attitude of the Negro community towards the white community," and "the sentiments and feelings of individuals" who
reside in black neighborhoods. By the summer of 1968 FBI
agents had recruited a 3,248-person army to carry out these
tasks.[22]

Why would a black person in those times knowingly inform to
the FBI? There is no single answer to this question. In the great
majority of cases, fiscal and ideological motives were secondary.
Ghetto informants, as a general rule, only received modest, sporadic payments "on a c.o.d. basis," with local special agents in
charge having the authority to dispense up to $400. Informant
recruiters, moreover, did not look for hostility toward a particular black nationalist group. The recruiters sought persons who
owned property in the ghetto or had an interest in protecting
ghetto property. In fact, age may have been the key factor in
ghetto informant recruiting—with the FBI trying to establish
contacts with the parents and grandparents of the militants.
Amiri Baraka remembered one time, in Newark, when the FBI
came "snooping around," and "my father told the FBI where I
was, not knowing he didn't have to say shit to them." Most of
the informants probably cooperated with the FBI in a similar
manner. The initial decision to talk to the Bureau was an un-
thinking one.[23]

Because Hoover deemed the 1968 number (3,248) inadequate,
Division Five developed "a kind of quota system" that required
all field agents to develop ghetto informants. It was part of their
job. If an agent's territory included no predominantly black
communities, he had to "so specify by memorandum"—"so that
he will not be charged with failure to perform." The special
agents in charge of Bureau field offices never knew how many
informants were enough, only that they had to recruit "a large
number of additional racial informants." FBI Assistant Director

Felt told the men who ran the New York office to be grateful for all the ghettoes in their territory. "Opportunities to engage in racial informant development," he said, were boundless.

A few FBI field offices met their big-number quotas by reclassifying criminal informants as ghetto informants, and a few agents simply invented ghetto informants. A small though perhaps not insignificant percentage of informants existed only on paper. This type of fudging could not satisfy Hoover's concomitant demand to improve the quality of the information provided. To meet the director's goals, the field "converted . . . exceptionally intelligent and knowledgeable" ghetto sources to "regular racial informants" (as opposed to "probationary racial informants"); gave them "specific assignments where appropriate"; and encouraged them to speculate "on the general mood of the Negro community concerning susceptibility to foreign influences"—"whether this be from African nations in the form of Pan-Africanism, from the Soviet or Chinese communist bloc nations, or from other nations." The New York office even assigned informants to report on "Subversive and/or Communist Links Between Harlem and Africa."[24]

FBI officials forwarded much of the information gathered by their ghetto and BLACPRO informants directly to the IDIU, where Justice Department attorneys processed 3,500 incoming intelligence reports a month. By the time Nixon took his oath of office, Department attorneys had reviewed 32,000 FBI documents "concerning individuals and organizations involved primarily in the area of racial agitation." Hoover disseminated a more modest amount of cable traffic regarding "selected racial developments" to the White House.[25] In either case, the FBI reviewed the intelligence collected from over 3,000 ghetto informants and an unknown number of BLACPRO informants, passing on the worst of the black-scare stories and feeding President Johnson's fears. Were "black nationalist organizations, as well as independent Negro extremists," really planning to dynamite the Empire State Building? Were the radicals plotting to assassinate "white political candidates" in retaliation "for the killing of Martin Luther King"? Were a handful of black men in Santa Barbara scheming "to 'get' Governor Ronald Reagan"?[26] FBI headquarters required the field to prove or disprove all these rumors and the countless others that showed up in informant reports.[27]

The Johnson administration provided a context for the FBI to proceed on an intrusive and provocative course. The IDIU itself did not extend community surveillance fast enough or far enough to please either the administration or the FBI. The Unit had been functioning for less than a month when Attorney General Clark, Deputy Attorney General Warren Christopher, presidential assistants Joseph Califano and Matthew Nimetz, Deputy Secretary of Defense Paul Nitze, and Acting Army General Counsel Robert Jordan attended a White House strategy session on the riots expected for the summer of 1968. When briefing the group on the new "secret intelligence unit" and its study of "Black Nationalist groups," Clark complained about "the lack of intelligence these groups have received in the past." He stressed "the difficulty of the intelligence effort," pointing out that the FBI's continuing refusal to hire black agents complicated the government's surveillance mission. At the time, the FBI had some forty black agents.[28]

The purpose of this White House meeting had not been to moan about FBI employment practices. The president's men intended to mobilize the Army's intelligence resouces, thereby requiring better coordination between the Justice Department and the Pentagon, for drawing up "contingency plans for troop movements, landing sites, facilities, etc.," for rating "various cities as to their riot potential." According to former Army Chief of Staff Harold K. Johnson, this was only one of several meetings where the administration urged the military to accept a greater responsibility in the civil disturbance collection effort. Clark asked the Defense Department to "screen'" all "incoming intelligence," and to forward "key items" to the Justice Department and the IDIU. Because FBI officials based their own authority to collect "racial matters intelligence" on "Army regulations," they proved willing to assist a more aggressive military surveillance program and did not exhibit undue concerns about the intrusion of Army agents into their internal security domain.[29]

The FBI also began to solicit "racial matters intelligence" systematically from another intelligence bureaucracy, the Central Intelligence Agency, and one of its mail-opening operations, Project Hunter. CIA agents read the mail of thousands of Americans, black and white, from Richard Nixon to Mrs. Martin Luther King, and FBI agents themselves opened and photographed at least 130,000 first-class letters. The most ambitious of the CIA's domestic intelligence gathering projects, CHAOS, concentrated on foreign links to the peace and black movements and even the Nation of Islam. The Agency tried to prove that the Black Muslims received funding from Libya, and that "U.S. Negro Militants" received training "in guerrilla warfare" from Cuba. A third CIA program, RESISTANCE, concentrated on "the influence of Communists and Revolutionaries on the [black] movement" and the "brown [Mexican-American] movement." Another CIA source, the Weekly Situation Report, covered such topics as the 1968 Democratic National Convention. Of all the groups planning to demonstrate, the Agency said, the black groups were "the most dangerous."[30]

Despite an intense jurisdictional rivalry, intelligence on black militants and antiwar activists flowed freely between the FBI and the CIA. The collection of information bearing upon "foreign influences in the Black Nationalist movement" emerged as a priority for both the Bureau and the Agency in 1967, and FBI officials solicited data from the sophisticated CIA sources in Langley, Virginia, just as they had solicited the opinions of the best and the brightest of the ghetto informants in Watts and Detroit.[31]

Investigation of "foreign influences" was only one of the FBI's priorities. Hoover required "immediate and priority handling" of all racial matters investigations—particularly coverage of "those groups which appeal to the young militant Negro." His agents identified one of these groups, the Congress of Racial Equality, as a formerly "legitimate civil rights organization" that had recently adopted a "black nationalist posture." Because CORE leaders Floyd McKissick and then Roy Innis condoned "violence as a means of obtaining Negro rights," and because communist infiltration remained "negligible," the FBI shifted its CORE file from the COMINFIL category to the Racial Matters category and escalated the entire investigation. This was only one of many adjustments made in the late 1960s, and it reflected Hoover's view that blacks represented a greater threat to white America than did the communists.[32]

By this time FBI interest in communist infiltration was secondary even in the case of Martin Luther King and the Southern Christian Leadership Conference. When King went to Memphis in 1968 to help with the garbage collectors strike, the FBI was already there. The Bureau interjected itself into the politics of a labor dispute between the city and 1,300 garbage workers, nearly all of whom were black, by monitoring at least a few of

the negotiating sessions organized by the city council and Local
1733 of the American Federation of State, County and Municipal
Employees. The Bureau also monitored the principal black
power group in Memphis, the Invaders, describing its members
not as communists per se, but as a "conniving," "criminal-
minded," "monkey-like," "sullen," "loud-mouth" collection of
teen-age "dope-head[s]," "movement pimps," and "Beale Street
bums" who were also "serious reader[s] of Afro-American literature."[33]

At the same time, FBI officials considered how best to respond
to the Poor People's Campaign that King and SCLC planned for
May and June 1968 in Washington, D.C. In the past, according
to a Division Five analysis, the presence of "a large, well-
established, responsible Negro middle class" had combined
with the city's physical geography ("its Negro ghettos are spread
out and interspaced with pleasant neighborhoods") to prevent
the outbreak of large-scale racial disturbances. The Poor
People's Campaign, however, threatened the capital's stability.
"King's spring project could easily get out of control, degenerate
into violence, and thus endanger peace and order." To compound
things, Stokely Carmichael had recently formed a Washington-
based Black United Front. If King's project represented "the immediate threat to Washington," Division Five reasoned, Carmichael represented "the long-range peril."[34]

When Poor People's Campaign participants began arriving
after King's assassination on April 4 and after major rioting in
the District, the FBI ran the names of as many people as possible
through the files—including those who "appeared to be of the
'hippie variety'" and various "black power sympathizers." William Sullivan even donned some old clothes and went for a stroll
through Resurrection City, the plywood and canvas encamp-
ment built near the Lincoln Memorial to house some 3,000 campaign participants, where he tried to strike up a conversation
with Carmichael. The Division Five chief's presence supplemented the work of regular racial informants in Resurrection
City. The informants tracked no Communist party member however. Instead, they gathered "valuable information about the
personality traits, weaknesses, and strengths of these people."
Division Five told the informants "to document such things as
immorality, dishonesty, and hypocrisy."[35]

Hoover sent copies of his reports on the Poor People's Campaign to the Army and the CIA, with sanitized versions going to

newspaper reporters, "responsible Negroes," and congressional leaders. Speaker of the House John McCormack (D., Mass.), Senate Majority Leader Mike Mansfield (D., Montana), and PERM Chairman John McClellan (D., Ark.) all received oral briefings, write-ups, and photographs showing "the militant, aggressive appearance" of the young black men and women who came to Resurrection City.[36] The director sent additional reports on the campaign and its aftermath and related topics to the IDIU and the White House. Dr. King had been dead for only a few weeks when Hoover wrote Mildred Stegall with news that Nelson Rockefeller had contacted Coretta Scott King to ask if SCLC or her family needed money. The FBI picked the information up from the Stanley Levison wiretap. Bureau agents followed Levison himself to King's funeral and later Robert Kennedy's funeral, where he was observed talking with Detroit Congressman John Conyers and Gary, Indiana, Mayor Richard Hatcher. By offering to raise funds for the National Committee of Inquiry, a group formed to evaluate candidates for the presidency and other national offices and how they might "respond to the needs of America's black community," Levison inspired the director to send yet another letter to Mrs. Stegall.[37]

Concerned about their own response to the Poor People's Campaign, Johnson administration officials proceeded cautiously. Matthew Nimetz urged Joseph Califano to read what Arthur Schlesinger had to say about Herbert Hoover and the Bonus Expeditionary Force (BEF) in his book, *The Crisis of the Old Order*. The Johnson White House simply had to "deal with the Poor People's Campaign in a more civilized manner" than the Hoover White House had dealt with the BEF, Nimetz wrote, implying that FBI dossiers were more civilized than Army bayonets.[38] Given the scope of the intelligence programs and the counterintelligence programs to come, the FBI was certainly not part of a measured, civilized response to the dissent of the Poor People's Campaign.

FBI officials continued to downplay the communist menace even as they watched their surveillance empire grow day by day. They defined the problem posed by "the black movement" by reference to "militant racial agitators" who "go about the land inciting riots and preaching and instigating anarchy and revolt." This "new type of . . . agitator," Mark Felt concluded, when reviewing the New York field office's coverage, "evolved from unsettled racial and social conditions" and posed a completely new set of problems "which parallel the dangers presented by the pure communist elements." Thus, Felt attributed "most racial disturbances" to "semi-professional hate-mongers and rabble rousers who spend much of their time" waging war on "the status quo" and "teaching the ghetto's . . . receptive elements doctrines of hate."[39] Labels had changed, with the communist menace now becoming the black menace, but the threat stayed the same. Viewing all black citizens as potential threats to his America, Hoover had his justification for violating their rights.

To meet its responsibilities in New York, the FBI assigned twenty-five special agents to the racial squad (Division Four, Section 43) and supplemented that number with at least twenty-five more agents during the summer months. The squad spent its time supervising and recruiting informants for the Ghetto and BLACPRO programs, locating forty-two "ghetto areas" in the city's five boroughs, opening case files on individuals, and occasionally tailing black militants. Squad members used this last tactic rarely—three physical surveillances on Rap Brown by the fall of 1967, two on Stokely Carmichael, three on Revolutionary Action Movement members, and two on Black Muslims—because "surveillances in Negro areas are not generally practical without Negro agents."

In all, the FBI had between 5,000 and 10,000 active cases on matters of race at any given time nationwide. In 1967 some 1,246 FBI agents received civil rights enforcement or racial intelligence assignments each month. By President Johnson's last year in the White House, that number jumped to 1,678 with the vast majority of those agents undertaking intelligence responsibilities and not civil rights responsibilities.[40]

To keep track of the most prominent "racial agitators," the FBI relied on the so-called Security Index (formerly the Custodial Detention Program)—a listing of dissidents ranked according to their "degree of dangerousness" that dated from 1939 and remained an integral part of "Bureau War Plans" until the Watergate era. Intended to facilitate mass arrests in the event of a national emergency, the Security Index contained the names of 15,000 Americans by the early cold war years and included a special section, a Prominent Individuals Subdivision, listing persons whose "apprehensions might be attended by considerable publicity tending to make martyrs of them and thereby [embarrass] the Bureau." FBI officials rarely included black radicals in this section. Not even Paul Robeson rated a "prominent Negro" listing.[41]

Though the Security Index shrank to less than 10,000 names by the early 1960s, the main listing included the names of Martin Luther King and 1,497 other black Americans. The FBI added the names of an additional 400 blacks during the Kennedy and Johnson years. The largest category listed 673 Black Muslims, followed by 476 communists (or former communists or suspected fellow travelers), 66 SNCC activists, 60 Revolutionary Action Movement members, and 222 persons in a general black nationalists' category. Beginning in the late 1950s and continuing throughout the 1960s, the Security Index facilitated target selection for the COINTELs and the Mass Media programs. For a six-month period beginning in April 1961, the time when the Civil Rights Division made its most serious effort to enlist the Bureau in the voter registration campaign, the FBI leaked blind memos detailing the communist associations of 91 Security Index subjects to the press, and sometimes sent clippings from the resulting newspaper stories to the children of the subjects.[42]

The percentage of communists listed on the Security Index declined steadily throughout the decade—from 83.8 percent in 1961, to 55.9 percent by the time LBJ left the White House. According to the FBI's count as of November 1968, party membership stood at 3,198, and that number included a great many who could hardly be considered part of a Leninist vanguard. Others, perhaps as many as one-third, were informants. An FBI executives' conference considered these facts and unanimously recommended a six-month suspension of "investigations, and particularly report writing, in routine Security Matter–Communist cases throughout the field." "It got to be nothing more than a statistical burden," one Division Five executive said. Communist matters now absorbed too much manpower. The "anarchistic tendencies" of New Left and racial militants needed greater attention.[43]

Hoover himself seemed more concerned about noncommunist racial militants than card-carrying communists. Earlier, when testifying before the Kerner Commission, he discussed the impact of "rabble-rousers who initiate action and then disappear," mentioning King, McKissick, Brown, and Carmichael. "Any law that allowed law enforcement the opportunity to arrest . . . vicious rabble-rousers," he said, "would be healthy to have on the books." One Commission member, New York Mayor John Lindsay, asked "if it would be possible to total up and fully identify the number of militant Negroes and whites who were in the same category as Carmichael and Brown." He wanted to know "just exactly what the hard core in this country amounted to." Hoover responded by ordering Division Five to compile a more refined listing of "vociferous rabble-rousers" than provided by the Security Index.[44]

Hoover hoped the first edition of the new Rabble Rouser Index of "individuals who have demonstrated a potential for fomenting racial discord" would facilitate target selection for the new black nationalist counterintelligence program, launched on August 25, 1967. Initially, FBI officials defined a rabble-rouser "as a person who tries to arouse people to violent action by appealing to their emotions, prejudices, et cetera; a demagogue." They quickly broadened these standards to include persons with a "propensity for fomenting" any type of disorder affecting the nation's "internal security." New Rabble Rouser Index categories included "black nationalists, white supremacists, Puerto Rican nationalists, anti-Vietnam demonstration leaders, and other extremists." Subcategories pertaining to black dissidents included CORE, SNCC, SCLC, Revolutionary Action Movement, Nation of Islam, Black Panther party, and a black nationalist catchall. Everything was computerized.

In March 1968 the Rabble Rouser Index received a new name, the Agitator Index, and headquarters directed the field to submit "visual material relating to violence by black extremists." Division Five wanted "clear, glossy, 8″ by 10″ photographs." Sullivan's men also requested a photograph of each of the one hundred or so persons listed on the Agitator Index. Upon receiving and pasting the photos in the Black Nationalist Photograph Album, Division Five sent copies of this mug book to the field, along with a Racial Calendar highlighting "the dates of . . . racial events." To make sure that his agents could track any "militant black nationalist" who might "turn up" in another country, Hoover approved distribution of the Black Nationalist Photograph Album to the CIA and the Royal Canadian Mounted Police.[45]

The original edition of the Rabble Rouser Index was a disappointment. Bureau field offices had submitted a mere one hundred names.[46] Consequently, the agents assigned to select targets for the new counterintelligence program (COINTELPRO–Black

Hate Group or –Black Nationalist) had little to do. The entire program floundered despite Williams Sullivan's best efforts. Hoover approved the transfer of black nationalist intelligence and counterintelligence responsibilities to Division Five following the summer riots, and Sullivan immediately organized a racial intelligence section to manage the new work. George C. Moore moved over from the nationalities intelligence section to supervise racial intelligence and Theron D. Rushing ran the new COINTELPRO.

Deeming the initial Rabble Rouser/Agitator Index inadequate, Division Five sent another directive to the field in March 1968 requesting an "estimate" of the "propensity for violence" within specific black groups. Interested in "target evaluation," not "record purposes," Division Five told the field to concentrate on "the most violent and radical groups and their leaders"—among others, Martin Luther King of the Southern Christian Leadership Conference, Stokely Carmichael and Rap Brown of the Student Nonviolent Coordinating Committee, Maxwell Stanford of the Revolutionary Action Movement, and Elijah Muhammad of the Nation of Islam.[47]

FBI field agents searched their files and sent their target evaluations back to the seat of government. The new listings, however, were hardly more encouraging than the first edition of the Rabble Rouser Index. The Omaha office reported no "organized Black Nationalist Movement" in Nebraska, and ten other field offices reported no black nationalists beyond the membership of the Nation of Islam (NOI). And nearly every special agent in charge believed Black Muslims merited little attention. In Milwaukee, the FBI man said NOI members were not involved in civil disturbances or civil rights activity of any kind. "A counterintelligence program," he added, "may change the present situation." In Kansas City, two racial informants covered the local mosque, but their reports never indicated any involvement in situations "conducive to tension or violence." Given the Nation of Islam's "present indicated ineffectuality," the SAC wrote, COINTELPRO targeting would not be "suggestible as practicable at this time." This last assessment applied to black nationalist activity in general, he added, advising Division Five not to waste its time with target lists. The FBI man in Kansas City thought it more valuable, when preparing "for future contingencies," to encourage "public and private expressions of favorable Negro leader-figure contacts," to work with "trustworthy liberals," and to "delicately utilize, where practicable, Negro school and church teachers and persons influential with Negro youth."[48]

Division Five subjected Black Muslims to dozens of counterintelligence actions nonetheless. George Moore, the racial intelligence chief, conceded that Muhammad kept his followers "under control, and . . . did not have them on the streets at all during any of the riots." Moore could only emphasize the NOI's "paramilitary . . . potential." The special agent in charge of the Jackson office, Roy Moore, claimed that Muhammad operated a "hit group"—a vague reference, apparently, to the renegade Muslims who had murdered Malcolm X in Harlem's Audubon Ballroom.[49] Thus, Bureau officials had all the justification they needed. They approved the mailing of cartoon leaflets intended to ridicule Muslim life-styles and beliefs to the media in nearly a dozen states, and in Texas they had local agents investigate a mosque in search of a White Slave Traffic Act violation. In Washington, D.C., they attempted to close a Muslim grade school by unleashing the local zoning, tax, and health and safety bureaucracy, and by opening files on the parents of each of the approximately 150 children enrolled in the school.[50]

Every FBI field office experienced difficulty in locating targets for the counterintelligence program beyond the membership of the Nation of Islam. Pittsburgh identified a grand total of two potential targets: the Afro-American Institute, "a study group whose purpose is to promote an interest in black culture," and the Organizers, a teenage group active in issuing "public letters protesting . . . the solicitation of Negro girls in ghetto areas by white males." In Newark, most black groups (SNCC, SCLC, RAM) had "not been factors thus far." The field office merely suggested the targeting of the general membership of the United Afro-American Association and LeRoi Jones (Amiri Baraka). New York identified fewer than one hundred prospective targets, and even that number included members of groups with the sole mission of spreading African culture in Harlem.[51]

The Detroit FBI office identified few potential targets beyond members of the Malcolm X Society, the SNCC contingent (mostly teenagers from city high schools), and the City-Wide Citizens Action Committee. This last group, the SAC noted, continually harassed "the Detroit Police Department, accusing the department of police brutality." Marlin Johnson, head of the Chicago office, listed nine groups, but one of those was inactive and another was "a one man operation." The most likely candidates for the counterintelligence program in Cleveland were New Libya and the Afro American Sect. Members of the first group met at an astrology shop, spending their time "drinking wine, smoking 'pot,' . . . playing cards, and engaging in various forms of criminal activity" and "sexual promiscuity." These "heavy drinking" black nationalists, the local FBI man concluded, possessed a "great potential for violence." The members of the second group spent their time taking "instructions in Karate" and planning "the takeover of Cleveland and the entire country by black revolution." In California, a growing Black Panther party and about forty-five or fifty "hard core" members of Maulana Ron Karenga's US (as opposed to "THEM") attracted some concern, along with various student associations and at least one group whose membership studied "the Swahili language and Karate."[52]

Black nationalists with a propensity for violence were particularly hard to find in the South. In all of South Carolina, the FBI could find only two SNCC representatives and two black student organizations. In Mississippi, Roy Moore located a Political Action Committee at Tougaloo College. Miami described CORE and SCLC as "relatively inactive." The Bogalusa Voters League was the only viable target in Louisiana. The Mobile and Birmingham special agents in charge noted the presence of various SCLC and SNCC representatives, but said they expected no violence in Alabama.[53] The Jacksonville office had seven or eight sources (students, faculty, staff) at Florida A&M University, and "constantly" worked "to increase . . . informant coverage." But to what purpose? In Tennessee, the Bureau ran file checks on faculty at Tennessee A&I University and other predominantly black colleges where students supported SNCC and opposed "the school administration," and sent the names of "black militants . . . enrolled at the various universities [in the state] . . . to trusted and reliable sources at these . . . universities."[54]

On balance, few of these targets posed a danger, and thus required little attention. Still, the FBI ended up harassing, as one COINTELPRO supervisor admitted, "a great number of organizations that you might not today characterize as black nationalist but which were in fact primarily black."[55] The breadth of targeting resembled the pattern under the Communist party counterintelligence program, where the FBI used a loosely defined notion of "communist association" to focus on broad noncommunist sectors. COINTELPRO–Black Nationalist was unique in that the FBI defined "black nationalist" loosely enough to include, in theory, at least, every member of a particular race who happened to be a member of any organization whatsoever.

The target evaluation request sent to the FBI field offices in March 1968 was part of a broad expansion of the black hate group operation. The original directive establishing the program emphasized the immediate goals in a straightforward manner: "to expose, disrupt, misdirect, discredit, or otherwise neutralize the activities of black nationalist, hate-type organizations and groupings, their leadership, spokesmen, membership, and supporters." Long-range goals followed: to prevent militant black groups from forming coalitions, building up their membership, gaining respectability, and developing a charismatic leader. Twenty-three field offices participated, with the various special agents in charge assigning "experienced and imaginative" agents as "counterintelligence coordinators."[56]

The FBI had been engaged in "felonious" harassment of Dr. King and other black activists long before the summer of 1967. All of this harassment, a Justice Department task force later concluded, was "very probably" in violation of the old Reconstruction Era statutes, Sections 241 and 242, that provided for criminal penalties against any person, acting "under color of law" or otherwise, who denied any other person their civil rights.[57] Some of it was carried out informally. Other actions were part of other formal, structured COINTELPROs—against the Communist party, the Socialist Workers party, and, inexplicably, the Ku Klux Klan. One of the Cleveland field office's most ambitious operations, against the Jomo Freedom Kenyatta House, arose from the white hate group program even though no segregationists were involved. FBI activities increased in the first few weeks and months following the launching of COINTELPRO–Black Nationalist, but not dramatically. To cite a rather typical case: the Bureau failed to prove that Herbert Aptheker, the historian and Communist party functionary, provided bail money for Rap Brown, and thus had nothing to leak to its "cooperative and reliable" newspaper sources.[58]

One of the few early efforts deemed successful, an effort that actually began several months before the birth of the black nationalist program, involved Revolutionary Action Movement members in Philadelphia, Pennsylvania. While arguing, as ever,

that police brutality was a false issue, the FBI arranged for Philadelphia police officers to arrest RAM members "on every possible charge until they could no longer make bail." On one occasion, after the police had been sent around for still another
nuisance arrest, a RAM leader lay down in frustration and rage,
and began to beat the floor of his apartment with his fists.[59]

In anticipation of the approach of summer, Division Five proposed an expansion of counterintelligence activity to disrupt
and discredit civil rights activists and black nationalists. In
March 1968 representatives from forty-one field offices met at
the seat of government for a racial conference, and on the second day of that conference they agreed upon the new request for
target evaluation. They also developed the original long-range
goals of COINTELPRO–Black Hate Group in considerable detail. When seeking "to provent the . . . *growth* of militant black
nationalist organizations," the field was told to implement "specific tactics to prevent these groups from converting young
people." This goal was closely related to another basic investigative mission—to prevent violence by "pinpoint[ing] potential
troublemakers and neutraliz[ing] them before they exercise
their potential for violence." "Obviously," one COINTELPRO supervisor reasoned, "you are going to prevent violence or a
greater amount of violence if you have smaller groups." In other
words, "the programs were to prevent violence indirectly, rather
than directly, by preventing possibly violent citizens from joining or continuing to associate with possibly violent groups."[60]

The remaining long-term COINTELPRO goals demonstrate
FBI officials' more explicitly political and elitist assumptions
about their duty to smash any perceived threat to the existing
social order. These counterintelligence goals were also representative of the social and cultural conservatism that permeated
Hoover's FBI, a conservatism that sometimes expressed itself in
a cartoon view of the changes occurring in American society.
Division Five mused over an old truism, "in unity there is
strength," and considered it "no less valid for all its triteness."
Sullivan's men found justification here for a fundamental objective: to "prevent the *coalition* of militant black nationalist
groups." "An effective coalition," Division Five concluded, in a
wild assessment of one highly unlikely outcome, "might be the
first step toward a real 'Mau Mau' in America, the beginning of
a true black revolution." While waiting for the real thing to arrive, the Division placed the fifteen or twenty members of

Charles 37X Kenyatta's Harlem Mau Mau on the COINTELPRO target list. Kenyatta's group armed itself with bayonets and machetes, but nonetheless cooperated with John Lindsay and Nelson Rockefeller to keep peace in the ghetto following King's assassination.

Division Five also worked to "prevent the *rise of a 'messiah'*— someone "who could unify, and electrify, the militant black nationalist movement." Malcolm X had been the most likely candidate, but his assassination removed that threat. Malcolm was simply "the martyr of the movement today." Muhammad was hardly a more viable threat "because of his age." In the final analysis, Division Five said, Carmichael and King were the only serious candidates. They both dreamed of becoming a messiah and had "the necessary charisma." Not even Sullivan considered King to be a militant, but that was beside the point. "King could be a very real contender for this position should he abandon his supposed 'obedience' to 'white, liberal doctrines' (nonviolence) and embrace black nationalism."[61]

This particular counterintelligence goal represented one of the few areas where current FBI policy proved less ambitious than previous policy. Its fears of an American Mau Mau aside, Division Five demonstrated a more rational view of the black movement here than it had in 1963–1964, when it assumed that King was already a messiah, someone who needed to be "taken off his pedestal." At the time, Sullivan believed King would be destroyed, and that the subsequent "confusion . . . among the Negro people" and "the emotional reaction that will set in" would provide opportunities for the FBI. King's collapse would be followed by "ridiculous developments similar to the Old Father Devine and Daddy Grace organizations," leaving "the Negroes . . . without a national leader of sufficiently compelling personality to steer them in the proper direction."[62] The apparent unity of the civil rights movement at the time of the March on Washington had disappeared by 1968, with the new militants deriding King as an "Uncle Tom" and much of white America no longer considering King a wholesome, respectable Negro—given his comments on Vietnam and his increasingly strident call for an economic restructuring of American society. Division Five intended to keep black activists bickering among themselves and to focus white America's attention on the inherently un-American nature of black protest.

While subverting the efforts of black activists to build bridges between their mostly tiny organizations and plotting to quash the rise of a black messiah, Division Five directed the field to prevent those activists and groups "from gaining respectability." Sullivan hoped to discredit black nationalists in the eyes of "three separate segments of the community"—"the responsible Negro community," "the white community," and the black "followers of the movement." Division Five broke down the white community into a responsible element and an irresponsible element, with the latter consisting of "'liberals' who have vestiges of sympathy for militant black nationalist[s] simply because they are Negroes."

Field office response to this last goal was mixed. What was the point, Chicago SAC Marlin Johnson asked? "There remain very few hard core white liberals who continue to attempt to work with and aid the militant black nationalists as opposed to the more legitimate civil rights groups." Other FBI men, particularly those who lived and worked in the South, were more enthusiastic about this part of the counterintelligence program. The special agent in charge of the Charlotte office saw nothing wrong with a campaign "to eliminate the facade of civil rights," a campaign to "show the American public the true revolutionary plans and spirit of the Black Nationalist movement and its leaders." Hoover's man in North Carolina also saw nothing wrong with giving the campaign a boost by "counterfeiting literature damaging to the [movement]."[63]

The FBI effort to discredit black dissidents before "the responsible Negro elements" and "the followers of the movement" was more complex. It required "entirely different tactics," Division Five reasoned, because "publicity about violent tendencies and radical statements merely enhance" the prestige of black nationalist leaders in the eyes of the rank and file. "It adds 'respectability' in a different way." Bureau officials hoped to accomplish their goal here by developing "news media" contacts from coast to coast "that cater to the Negro community." If the special agent in charge of a particular office did not have any "established, reliable, contacts among Negro news media," he was told to develop such contacts—an order that led to some fudging in the field.[64]

Both the New York and San Francisco offices claimed columnist Carl Rowan as "a responsible Negro" media contact, but Rowan's assessment of that claim, in these years, at least, is probably correct. "J. Edgar Hoover hated my guts; nobody from the F.B.I. ever fed me any information." In 1964, as director of the U.S. Information Agency, Rowan did receive a two-page document from the FBI entitled "Martin Luther King, Jr., His Personal Conduct." In the late 1960s, however, the director dismissed Rowan as a "racist columnist." The FBI had only a handful of black media contacts, and no evidence indicates that Rowan was one of them. Mostly, the Bureau relied on anonymous mailings to Rowan and other black newspapermen, with Crime Records sending clippings from mainstream newspapers or the NAACP's *Crisis* that were critical of the new militants.[65]

FBI agents also disseminated "anti-violent statements" issued by such prominent black citizens as former boxing champion Archie Moore, and arranged for another boxer, Olympic gold medalist George Foreman, to receive an award from the Freedoms Foundation. Foreman, as Division Five noted, "gave every American an emotional lift" by beating "a Soviet fighter in the finals," by showing "the world . . . he was proud to be an American by waving a small American flag," and by singing "the national anthem at the award ceremonies." This conspicuous patriotism stood in "sharp contrast with the earlier despicable black power-black gloved demonstration of Tommie Smith and John Carlos on the Olympic victory stand and the anti-Vietnam stand of Cassius Clay." The Freedoms Foundation was a logical choice. Headquartered in Valley Forge, Pennsylvania, and closely connected to the J. Edgar Hoover Foundation, the Freedoms Foundation had at one time or another been associated with a number of right-wing personalities and segregationists, from Billy Hargis to Howard "Bo" Callaway. When Foreman finally received his award in February 1969, Cartha DeLoach arranged appropriate media coverage.[66]

With regard to white-owned newspapers widely read in black neighborhoods, the FBI faced something of a dilemma. To circulate Bureau propaganda, as the Boston office reminded Division Five, it was necessary to work with such relatively liberal newspapers as the *Boston Globe*. If the *Globe* was basically "anti-Bureau in tone," "a much larger percentage of Negroes in the Roxbury area" read it "than any other Boston paper." The *Globe* covered "Negro complaints against discrimination, segregation, and poor housing," and "was a vigorous supporter of the Negro complaint of 'de facto' segregation in the Boston Public School system," the SAC pointed out. FBI officials at the seat of government did not care for the *Boston Globe*'s politics or its implied criticisms of their bureaucracy. They denied the request to work with the paper.[67]

A month after the counterintelligence program expanded in March 1968, Division Five sent the COINTELPRO file to a special room at FBI headquarters. Sullivan controlled access even within the Bureau to the "sensitive" and "highly confidential" paperwork generated by the black hate program.[68] From there, Division Five ordered the field to consider "the entire racial field" for potential counterintelligence action, and to "use every possible technique" in pursuit of the program's immediate and long-range goals. At least one field office positioned itself by breaking into a SNCC office and filming "all the SNCC records." Another field office kept itself up to date by monitoring the credit-card purchases of prospective targets.[69]

The FBI supplemented the black nationalist counterintelligence program with yet another program intended "to expose, disrupt and otherwise neutralize" the antiwar movement—the so-called COINTELPRO–New Left. Hoover sent Bureau data on the antiwar and civil rights linkage to virtually anyone with an interest, from Vice President Humphrey to the commandant of the Marine Corps. And specific COINTELPRO operations included blatantly racist and obscene mailings filled with casual references to niggers, sexual deviancy, and even the diet of black antiwar activists. "Let them eat bananas," one FBI-authored communication read, in a thinly veiled allusion. The FBI also launched a news media campaign to counter coverage of the police riot at the 1968 Democratic National Convention. New Left activists, along with "the liberal press and the bleeding hearts," Division Five complained, "continually and falsely" charged police brutality and "on many occasions viciously and scurrilously attacked the Director and the Bureau in an attempt to hamper our investigation" and "drive us off the college campuses." In one way, not much had changed since the early 1960s. The FBI investigated Chicago's club-swinging policemen at the Civil Rights Division's request, but FBI headquarters assigned the local field office a conclusion: to "develop all possible evidence . . . to refute these false allegations [of police brutality]."[70]

To gather data for the New Left disruption efforts, FBI agents submitted quarterly reports and opened subfiles under RACE RELATIONS and seventeen other headings. In June 1968 the Bureau embarked on a campaign to expose the membership of various "'pacifist' type organizations" as de facto segregationist.

New Left groups, the FBI said, were invariably composed "almost 100 per cent of Caucasians." By the end of the year, Bureau efforts expanded to include "the use of informants to encourage, within the Negro community," the idea that SDS, the principal antiwar group, was "a racist organization." "They are just like the commies and all the other white radical groups that suck up to the blacks," read one of Division Five's anonymous communications. FBI officials pursued this line of attack even though they knew that a sweeping charge of racism was not true. The special agent in charge of the Newark office nominated Tom Hayden for the Rabble Rouser Index precisely because the SDS leader had "worked with and supported the Negro people in their program."[71]

Even though Hoover and his men in Division Five had free rein when implementing both the Black Hate Group and the New Left programs, the COINTELPROs did not develop in a vacuum. Various White House aides and the president himself had encouraged Hoover to do more than simply gather intelligence on black and white antiwar activists since mid-1966, one full year before the Bureau launched COINTELPRO–Black Hate and two years before COINTELPRO–New Left. President Johnson noticed little difference between antiwar demonstrators and ghetto rioters. He saw every dissident as a personal enemy, and he saw all of his enemies united and plotting against him. The civil rights movement and the peace movement never fully embraced each other, but in Johnson's mind they did.

President Johnson's assumptions about the nature of dissent led to some strange alliances. Earlier, when watching televised HUAC hearings in August 1966 on a series of bills to criminalize "assistance to enemies of U.S. in time of undeclared war," the president ordered Marvin Watson to arrange Hoover's appearance "before this group." He wanted his FBI director to name "rioting participants as members of various subversive groups." He told Watson to call DeLoach and have him make the necessary arrangements. Watson told DeLoach not to do anything unless he called back. He never did.[72] Nearly a year later, Johnson summoned DeLoach again and filed a similar request. "[He] asked if the FBI knew anything regarding the activities of King, Carmichael and McKissick. . . . He asked if the FBI could have Chairman Ed Willis of the House Committee on Un-American Activities hold hearings." "[HUAC had] little reputation at the present time," DeLoach responded, adding that "hearings on

McKissick and Carmichael might react to their advantage rather than hurting them. The President then asked how much information could get out."[73]

Turning away from the proposed HUAC alliance, DeLoach fed Johnson's fears without agreeing to any of Johnson's suggested plans of action. He told the president that Carmichael, McKissick, and King "had realized that there was more financial gain and more publicity in being in anti-Vietnam activities than in heading up civil rights drives. . . . The general public is gradually beginning to realize that the civil rights activities of these men have been phoney since the start." Since the president wanted to know "who was behind these people," DeLoach mentioned Stanley Levison, again—falsely identifying him as a "prominent member of the National Committee of the Communist Party." The assistant director dismissed Carmichael and McKissick as "self-styled civil rights leaders who were seeking only to get as much money out of a troubled situation as possible."[74]

If DeLoach thought little of the president's suggestion regarding the Un-American Activities Committee, he found nothing unusual about the general drift of the conversation. The president also announced his intent to mobilize the American Legion in the Vietnam propaganda wars, and he expected the FBI to help on this front as well. A national vice-commander in the Legion, DeLoach's Crime Records Division more or less ran the Americanism Committee. Walter Trohan, Washington bureau chief of the *Chicago Tribune* and a recipient of the American Legion's fourth estate award, described the Legion as "an adjunct of the FBI with FBI men writing speeches for prominent orators, drafting resolutions and sparking the show generally." If Trohan exaggerated (only the Americanism Committee and to some extent the national office were adjuncts of the FBI), his point was well taken. He thought the FBI was doing a wonderful job. Johnson, in contrast, wanted the FBI and the Legion to do more. He did not want Legionnaires running around "placing flowers on black coffins when dead servicemen were returned." He wanted them out "meeting troop ships, having parades, giving presents to returning servicemen and generally stirring up great publicity."[75]

With Hoover's help, the Johnson administration tried to mobilize the old McCarthy-era internal-security machinery. HUAC worked with the Pentagon to run the names of news correspondents in Vietnam through its files, and held hearings on "subversive influences in the riots." Johnson himself helped the Committee get the money it needed to do its job. With civil rights people still complaining about the Justice Department's failure to enforce existing civil rights law, the Department attempted to register the communist-controlled W. E. B. Du Bois Clubs, among other groups, with the Subversive Activities Control Board (SACB). (SNCC activists said the president had a greater interest in registering his Vietnam war critics than in registering Negro voters in the South.) These efforts, nonetheless, frustrated both Hoover and Johnson. The FBI kept sending over files on individuals and organizations (all "good cases," the director declared), but Ramsey Clark kept complaining about tainted evidence. Almost everyone the White House and the FBI wanted to haul before the SACB had been the specific target of electronic surveillance or had been overheard on other taps and bugs.[76]

With the SACB case against the Du Bois Clubs fizzling, Crime Records wrote and disseminated, under the name of the Pennsylvania department of the Catholic War Veterans, some 30,000 copies of a leaflet on the group. DeLoach then worked with the national office of the Junior Chamber of Commerce to discredit the Du Bois Clubs, and arranged for the Catholic War Veterans to publish yet another item. Walter Winchell announced the release of this last document, an FBI-authored pamphlet, in his column.[77]

A few White House aides rivaled DeLoach in his aggresiveness. In April 1967 press secretary George Christian contacted Carl Rowan to discuss Dr. King's antiwar statements—particularly his speech at New York's Riverside Church. Christian told Johnson that Rowan was "exploring the . . . King matter. He said everyone in the Civil Rights movement has known that King has been getting advice from a communist, and he (Rowan) is trying to firm up in his own mind whether King is still doing this. He wants to take out after King, because he thinks he has hurt the Civil Rights movement with his statements."[78]

Another White House aide, John Roche, a political scientist and former head of Americans for Democratic Action, told Johnson that he would try to find out who had written King's Riverside Drive speech. Roche described the speech, in an eyes-only memo for LBJ, as "quite an item," a clear indication "that King—in desperate search of a constituency—has thrown in with the commies" and their "ideological valet service." The civil rights movement was "shot—disorganized and broke," led by an "inordinately ambitious and quite stupid" man who was being "played," along with "his driving wife," "like trout," by "the Communist-oriented 'peace' types." "The president was deeply committed to civil rights," Roche explained, "and upset at the thought that real leaders such as Whitney Young, Roy Wilkins, Clarence Mitchell would be displaced by opportunistic loudmouths using Martin as their front man." Ironically, Roche admired Bayard Rustin—"Martin's original guru on nonviolence and close adviser until he was defenestrated by the 'Abernathys.'"

Roche later advised Watson of his wry plan to neutralize Carmichael: "I have planted a rumor that Stokely is really *white*." In yet another, more serious eyes-only memo, Roche outlined a strategy to discredit the Senate's most persistent dove, J. William Fulbright, the Arkansas Democrat whose segregationist voting record marred his liberal credentials. "I have 'encouraged' my old friend Sidney Hook to take up the franchise," Roche wrote. "He has written a blistering piece for the *Los Angeles Times*. . . . He is also willing to testify before the Senate Foreign Relations Committee 'as an expert witness on Communism and Democracy' to indicate the damage Fulbright's views on civil rights have done to the cause of freedom." "This would be an *event*," Roche told Johnson. "Could it be arranged?"[79]

At the same time Roche was sending his proposals to the Oval Office, the FBI was dreaming up its own ideas—though it is important to note, once more, that the Bureau saw no need to launch a formal counterintelligence program against the New Left until the summer of 1968.[80] Indeed, FBI officials were relatively passive until well after the Tet offensive of January 1968 in Vietnam—that is, until they fully understood the disastrous political implications for the president and his party.[81] Roche's proposals, moreover, were not out of place in the Johnson White House. Other presidential aides also searched for political fodder in the murky world of the subversive.

On one occasion Joseph Califano telephoned Hoover to find out what he thought about King. The director said he was "under active and tight control of the communists," a comment that reflected the habits of rhetoric more than the actual FBI focus at the time, a focus "grounded purely in political-intelligence concerns."[82] From there, Hoover told Califano what he thought about newspaper reaction to General William C. Westmoreland's recent speech on the war. "The Administration came out aces high," he said, adding that Westmoreland should be more active on the speaking circuit. "The man knows what he was talking about as he was just in from Viet Nam." Califano passed on a rumor of his own about the influence Herbert Aptheker, of all people, supposedly had with King and other civil rights leaders who had spoken out on Vietnam. The director knew all about Aptheker, the historian of American Negro slave revolts who had been to Hanoi and the man the Bureau described, quite accurately, as "the principal link between the Communist party and the Nation's campuses." FBI agents kept track of Aptheker by wiretapping his phone and consulting with a source within the Organization of American Historians. At one point Division Five planned to commission a scholarly book-length critique of his work in the field of black history, but Hoover blocked the project. Too expensive. Division Five settled for a pamphlet. All this was routine, and in no way the result of Califano's farfetched rumor of a relationship between Aptheker and King.[83]

Despite the general enthusiasm for counterintelligence action within the White House and within Cartha DeLoach's Crime Records Division and William Sullivan's Domestic Intelligence Division, as often as not the FBI's own field agents remained indifferent to the new COINTELPROs. Bureau executives chastized several offices, including the largest, New York, for not submitting a sufficient quantity of counterintelligence proposals.[84] It is significant that even New York, with its sizeable ghettoes and great numbers of black activists, failed to identify enough targets or to launch an appropriate number of dirty tricks. If the Black Panther party for Self Defense had not emerged in the director's mind by the fall of 1968 as "the greatest threat to the internal security of the Country," the new counterintelligence program might have remained a sideshow—something roughly comparable to the COINTELPRO against the tiny Socialist Workers party. Members of this Trotskyite group, all "home grown tomatoes," the Bureau conceded, had been initially targeted because they supported "such causes as . . . integration problems arising in the South."[85]

The Black Panthers had not even made the initial FBI counterintelligence target lists of August 1967 and March 1968—even though they had received their first major wave of publicity in 1966, when twenty party members, wearing black leather jackets and black berets and toting rifles and shotguns, walked into the California capitol building to protest a bill outlawing the carrying of loaded weapons within incorporated areas. But the FBI's San Francisco field office was not sufficiently impressed, and Division Five somehow neglected to list the Black Panther party. Hoover and Sullivan would not make up for that oversight until Lyndon Johnson's last few months in the White House. Ultimately, Division Five subjected the Panthers to 233 of the total 295 formal counterintelligence actions carried out against black nationalists.

Counterintelligence was far more pervasive than the readily available record indicates. It is impossible to say how many COINTELPRO actions the FBI implemented against the Panthers and other targets simply by counting the incidents listed in the COINTELPRO–Black Hate Group file. The Bureau recorded COINTELPRO-type actions in thousands of other files. Most of the operations to discredit Martin Luther King, for example, were not part of the black nationalist counterintelligence program. The FBI often filed documents recording these actions under King's name or, to a lesser degree, under the name of his organization—and not in the central COINTELPRO file. Still other written records repose in the files of King's associates and advisers, and there are even documents regarding COINTELPRO-type tactics in the files of the newspaper reporters who received derogatory personal or political information leaked by Crime Records. (One FBI executive described the COINTELPRO caption as simply an "administrative device to channel the mail to the Bureau.") To cite another example, the counterintelligence program against the Socialist Workers party consisted of a mere forty-five actions. But, in the more recent past, the FBI implemented a much greater number of informal operations, including some two hundred incidents that occurred after April 1971 when Hoover terminated all the COINTELPROs for security reasons.[86]

The same point could be made about the pervasiveness of the FBI community surveillance programs, from the Ghetto Informant Program to the Rabble Rouser Index and all those other indices. No matter how intrusive and institutionalized these programs may have been, they represented only the tip of the proverbial iceberg. At times, Hoover himself complained about his staff simply throwing money at the problem of black nationalism. Where were the resources needed to run all the new community surveillance and counterintelligence programs going to come from, he wondered?[87] With black activists sowing seeds of discontent and militant protest in the ghettoes, and with the Johnson administration encouraging him to react to the black scare in any way he saw fit, Hoover constructed an unprecedented surveillance system—a system that reflected his belief that any movement for social change was dangerous, and that black demands for social change represented the single most dangerous subversive threat facing the nation.

9

The Only Good Panther

The Pursuit of the Black Panther Party for Self-Defense

By word, and sometimes by deed, the Black Panther party
came to occupy a special place in the history of black radicalism at a time when the outrageous was commonplace, and to
incite FBI actions as outrageous as anything the Panthers did. Of
the thousands of domestic intelligence and counterintelligence
investigations launched against black activists, only the Martin
Luther King case rivaled the Panther case in its ferocity, with
FBI officials pursuing the most prominent proponents of violent
resistance to white racism with the same zeal that had characterized their pursuit of the most prominent proponent of nonviolence. Just as King had been a symbol to so many Americans,
black and white, of all that was good and wholesome about the
struggle for racial justice, the Panthers were a symbol of all that
was bad and frightening about that struggle. While King was in
the mainstream of the civil rights movement, Panther leadership
never moved off the fringes of a quite different black liberation
movement.

Huey Newton, Bobby Seale, and Eldridge Cleaver were all peripheral characters who relied on the rhetoric of revolutionary
prophets and not the rhetoric of Christian prophets. They preferred Fanon's *Wretched of the Earth* and Mao's *Little Red Book*
to the Bible, armed self-defense to passive resistance, power to
morality. The Panthers never built a black army and never at-

293

tained mass support even among the most frustrated and bitter young men and women who lived in the ghettoes. They did learn how to use the media however. With their manifestos and predictions of race war, and their poster of Newton, the supreme commander, sitting in a wicker chair, in black leathers, holding a shotgun in one hand and a spear in the other against a background of African shields and a pelt, the Black Panther party made good copy. "Shoot-outs, revolutions, pictures in *Life* magazine of policemen grabbing Black Panthers like they were Vietcong," journalist Tom Wolfe wrote. While the media and the Panthers engaged in a form of mutual exploitation, other Americans romanticized Newton and his comrades. The Panthers inspired awe among white antiwar activists in SDS, who called them "the vanguard of an anticapitalist revolution involving the whole of American society," and they acquired what Wolfe called "radical chic" among some affluent urban liberals.[1]

The Black Panthers attracted the nation's attention, so J. Edgar Hoover decided that they had to be destroyed. Launched in the last lame-duck months of Lyndon Johnson's presidency, the Panther campaigns had entered their most repressive phase before the Nixon administration began to pressure the FBI to do more. Hoover's pursuit of the Black Panther party was unique only in its total disregard for human rights and life itself. The 1960s had begun with FBI agents standing by while southern lawmen beat black activists, and ended with FBI agents inciting police violence against black activists in the urban North. Just as the Bureau's policies of the earlier period represented official government policy, its interventionist law-and-order policies of the later period also received an implicit authorization.

During the Nixon years the FBI's covert counterintelligence campaign accompanied an overt Justice Department assault against the Panthers, all part of a broader attempt to exploit the new white backlash. While Hoover and his superiors in the Justice Department marched against Black Panthers, the Nixon administration urged Congress to impose a moratorium on court-ordered school busing, and to defeat a fair-housing enforcement program and the extension of the Voting Rights Act of 1965. The president also had the Civil Rights Division plead before the Court for a postponement in the desegregation of public schools in Mississippi. And Vice President Spiro Agnew traveled the country, stoking the racial anxieties of Richard Nixon's silent majority wherever he stopped. "It is clear that for the bulk of our (nominal) countrymen," James Baldwin concluded about those times, "we are all expendable. And Messrs. Nixon, Agnew, Mitchell, and Hoover . . . will not hesitate for an instant to carry out what they insist is the will of the people."[2]

Though the Black Panthers would not make the FBI's initial counterintelligence target lists, Hoover's agents gathered intelligence on the party's gun-carrying cadres from the day in 1965 when they began following police cruisers through the streets of the Oakland ghetto, pledging to intervene whenever they felt "the man" had stepped out of line. Confrontations and arrests occurred almost daily, until October 1967, when a shootout left Newton wounded and Oakland police officer John Frey dead. Following Newton's indictment in November on a charge of involuntary manslaughter, the Panthers began a national recruiting drive. In April 1968 another confrontation resulted in the wounding of two Oakland policemen and the death of the Panther's minister of finance, Bobby Hutton. In September, Newton was convicted on the manslaughter charge, receiving a sentence of two to fifteen years imprisonment. By that time the Panthers had established themselves nationally, building a modest following in the streets and on the campuses, and among print and broadcast newspeople eager to write about Negroes predicting race war, the overthrow of capitalism, and a North American liberation front to help the yellow people of Vietnam. Eldridge Cleaver even went to Hanoi in October 1969, where he made a radio broadcast urging black GIs to desert and otherwise sabotage the American war effort.

With their rhetoric and what Yippie-founder Jerry Rubin called their "far-out guerrilla theater," the Black Panther party invited the sort of FBI repression that typified Lyndon Johnson's last two years in the White House and Richard Nixon's first four.[3] Cleaver's threat to torch the White House ("I'll burn the mother fucker down") and to beat California Governor Ronald Reagan ("the punk") to death with a marshmallow attracted Hoover's attention, as did an off-the-pig Christmas card, a coloring book depicting black children challenging white law and order in the ghetto, and a call for black terrorists to infiltrate the law-enforcement and intelligence communities. "We need Black FBI agents," as one anonymous Panther put it, "to assassinate J. Edgar Hoover, John Mitchell and Richard Nixon, and Black Boss agents in New York City to do the same to Mayor Lindsay and Police Commissioner Murphy. Nigger CIA agents are obliged to kidnap the Rockefellers . . . and the Kennedy's [sic] and hold them for ransom."[4]

Black Panther party rhetoric was anything but crazy to the FBI or the Panthers themselves. For many of the young men and women who joined the party, all social ills could be traced back to the police who patrolled the ghettoes and the larger law enforcement establishment. "Off the Pig!" became the Black Panther slogan, and it suggested to some, Hoover included, that the party had assumed the right to liberate black people from a police army of occupation by murdering anyone who wore a badge. The Panthers saw the image of lawmen who enforced Jim Crow with nightsticks and arrangements with the Ku Klux Klan on the face of every cop and G-man in the ghettoes of the North. When Bobby Seale first heard about Malcolm X's assassination, his mind filled with thoughts of "Bull Connor" and "white-ass cops," along with "the mother fucking white racist president and the FBI." "The FBI killed him," Seale charged, so "let's talk about shooting the God damn FBI." That Malcolm died at the hands of black men was beside the point.[5]

FBI officials also saw connections between the black civil rights workers of the early 1960s and the angry young black men and women of the late 1960s. Whether working to register voters in the Jim Crow South or riding around with the Panthers on community patrol, black activists were challenging the existing social order. It made no difference to the FBI that most of white America supported wholesome civil rights goals like voter registration and opposed the Black Panther party's revolutionary goals. The director's form of resistance might vary in scope, intensity, and intent from case to case, depending on his assessment of the imminence of the threat and his reading of public opinion, but Hoover always stood against leftist demands for social change.

The rhetoric of the ghetto made the Black Panthers an especially safe target. Panther pronouncements on matters of war and revolution allowed FBI officials a degree of credibility when presenting their war with the Panthers as a simple matter of self-defense. Hoover told a House Appropriations Subcommittee that the Communist party might "unite" with the Black Panther party. He told Nixon's attorney general, John Mitchell, that the Panthers intended to stage "an armed black revolution against the Government of the United States." He told the field that the Panthers were "armed and extremely dangerous," and "reportedly attempting . . . to kidnap and kill FBI agents"—a prelude of sorts to their "'Third World' idea which envisions the eventual destruction of the white race." Ironically, given the temper of the times, these outbursts, and especially the grand charge labeling the party as "the greatest threat to the internal security of the country," may have made "J. Edgar Hoover . . . the nation's greatest Panther recruiter."[6]

Hoover and the men around him had an interest in blurring the distinction between verbal violence and frustration and hard-core revolutionary activity. In Andrew Young's view, "their intelligence into the black community was so far fetched they really couldn't understand the information they were getting. They didn't understand minorities." Roger Wilkins elaborated. "A bunch of black guys sitting around drinking in the middle of the night, yelling about how mean white folks are and what they'd like to do to them, is part of the catharsis. But the Bureau was not equipped to deal with black hyperbole. So, if some black guy said, 'I'm going to kill that so-and-so,' the Bureau took it fairly literally." In either case, as Wilkins knew from firsthand experience, the FBI passed the information up to responsible federal officials "who were unsettled themselves and frightened about what was going on in the ghettos. They took the Bureau's information seriously," and "the information . . . provided did not illuminate the stream, it polluted it."[7]

There was more to the Black Panther party than preening ghetto generals spouting off-the-pig rhetoric and sporting black leathers, Cuban shades, and unkempt Afros. Counting the Newton and Hutton incidents, party members engaged police officers in more than a dozen firefights from October 1967 to December 1969, and at least two policemen and as many as ten Panthers died in that two-year period.[8] In 1969 alone law enforcement officers arrested 348 Panthers on murder, armed robbery, rape, bank robbery, drug trafficking, burglary, and dozens of other charges. The shootouts and arrests overshadowed the Panthers' main interests. By the time Nixon moved into the White House, the party was trying to rid itself of criminal elements and to move away from direct confrontations with police officers and toward a program of community control of the police and the schools, tenant strikes, free breakfasts for ghetto children, clothing drives, community day care, and health clinics. The Panthers mixed the rhetoric of revolution with a legitimate social agenda. Every Black Panther who broke the law should have been investigated and called to account in a court of law. But no Panther should have been subjected to any kind of extrajudicial punishment, let alone the illegal and immoral punishments imposed by the FBI, for what they said.

Jerris Leonard, the head of the Nixon-era Civil Rights Division, admitted that he could support many things in the Black Panther party's "serve the people" program. But on the whole the Panthers were "nothing but hoodlums," he said. "We've got to get them." The Justice Department set up a Panther task force in 1969 "to develop a prosecutive theory against the BPP [Black Panther party]," and dispatched five line lawyers to the Bay area to run a special grand jury investigation. "Whatever they say they're doing," the United States attorney in San Francisco charged, "they're out to get the Panthers." Other federal grand juries convened in other cities. In Philadelphia, Pennsylvania, the Department subpoenaed Nathan Schwerner, the father of one of the three young men murdered outside of Philadelphia, Mississippi, and then an official of the International Committee to Defend Eldridge Cleaver. In Seattle, Mayor Wes Uhlman refused a federal request to have city police roust Panther offices by announcing, "We are not going to have any 1932 Gestapo-type raids against anyone."[9]

The FBI responded to the flurry of departmental activity by compiling hundreds of prosecutive summary reports on the Panthers under a "Racial Matters–Smith Act" caption. By June 1969 the Bureau was investigating all forty-two Panther chapters and approximately 1,200 members and sympathizers in order "to obtain evidence of possible violations of Federal and local laws." This effort included the examination of every aspect of Panther affairs, from financial records to the Free Huey posters. The FBI even conducted a survey to determine "how many members are on welfare."[10]

There were limits to this assault nonetheless. In April 1969, when Hoover told Nixon he had "been trying to get the [Justice] Department to move against the Black Panthers," "the President said he would put a word in on this himself" and then asked the director if he "had put it up to the Department." When Hoover said he had and the Department's attorneys were considering it, Nixon "said they should do more than that." Three months later, in July 1969, Hoover discussed the matter again with Mitchell. The attorney general wanted to know if the director thought "their recommendations [for prosecution] are going to be too onerous." He intended to seek the indictment of Panther leaders and wanted "to hang" the "Chicago rioting business" on Bobby Seale, even though Seale had little to do with the demonstrations during the Democratic National Convention in August 1968. At the same time, Mitchell deferred to Hoover. Not wanting to expose sensitive Bureau sources in open court, he asked for the director's clearance and reminded him that "we always have the ultimate action of dropping prosecutions . . . if it too materially affects internal security."[11]

The FBI pressured the Justice Department to get on with the conspiracy prosecutions, and the Department asked the Bureau how far it was willing to go. Neither the Department nor the Bureau were willing to disclose the electronic surveillance records that facilitated the covert war against the Panthers but greatly complicated any overt action in federal court. Thus, the Department dropped a number of prosecutions, including actions against Seale and against Panther functionary David Hilliard, who had threatened Nixon's life in the course of a speech. "The Department," William Sullivan wrote, "needs to be . . . educated to some of the ugly realities of the Black Panthers" and "pushed into getting some prosecutive action underway. People around the country are beginning to wonder why something isn't being done." Hoover and his second-in-command, Clyde Tolson, doubting "the wisdom" of a conspiracy prosecution under the Smith Act, rejected Sullivan's recommendations on the grounds that Supreme Court decisions dating from 1957 had rendered the Smith Act "technically unenforceable." Law enforcement had failed, one counterintelligence supervisor explained. "There were [no] adequate statutes" on which to proceed against any subversive or extremist organization.[12]

Division Five also encountered resistance from the San Francisco field office, the office of origin in the Black Panther party investigation and the office responsible for implementing counterintelligence proposals against national Panther headquarters in Oakland. Most of the resistance came from Charles W. Bates, the special agent in charge who considered William Sullivan ("Crazy Billy") a "kind of wild man" who "had a lot of ideas" but lacked "street sense" and skill as an administrator. Favored by Hoover and popular with the agents who worked under him, Bates was an uncommon Bureau executive. Field agents liked him because he was a "stand-up guy," a man who refused to search for scapegoats among the underlings and resisted unrea-

sonable requests from headquarters. When he thought a directive was foolish, he said so.[13]

With regard to the counterintelligence program, Bates and his
Panther squad, particularly thirty-year veteran agent William
Cohendet, questioned how serious was the Black Panther threat
to the nation's security, and the appropriateness of the Division
Five response. "It did not mean that we didn't feel it had some
merit. We just felt it wasn't the way to go. . . . There were parts
of COINTELPRO we didn't agree with," Bates said. "We can pat
ourselves on the backs when we harass a [Nation of Islam] grade
school and have local police arrest [Revolutionary Action Move-
ment] leaders on every possible charge," Cohendet told Division
Five, "but this is not solving any problems. It is only buying time
and building up greater resentment among persons who already
hate the system. Shall we continue to have all black nationalists
locked up all summer, every summer, or perhaps all year long?"
The FBI was wasting too much "talent, time and money" on
"what amounts to harassment techniques, often euphemistically
called counterintelligence. . . . The likelihood is that it will be
too little too late and we will win a few battles and lose the war.
. . . The Bureau does not have enough Agents, enough concentration of effort, nor enough money to insure foreknowledge of
what is likely to follow in the next few years."[14]

When Division Five first singled out the Panthers for special
attention in the fall of 1968, local San Francisco agents continued to downplay the menace, responding with minimal compliance to the flood of Panther directives pouring out of Division
Five. They did what was required, but no more. They submitted
bimonthly summaries on the Black Panther party, "recommendations as to the best method of creating opposition to the BPP
on the part of the majority of the residents of the ghetto areas,"
and the names of "prominent Negroes" who would receive the
anti-Panther mailings prepared by Division Five. Sullivan's men
drafted dozens of "treatises," including one entitled "The Black
Klan," for "referral to appropriate news media representatives."[15]

By the end of the year the Black Panther party had replaced
the Student Nonviolent Coordinating Committee as the FBI's
principal black threat. With Stokely Carmichael proposing an
alliance with the Panthers, however, SNCC remained a problem.
To keep the two groups apart, Division Five engaged in petty
harassments, having a fictitious SNCC member calling the Pan-

thers "pinheads" and so forth, while singling out Carmichael, whom Newton had "drafted" to serve as the party's East Coast field marshal, for special attention. Attributing the Panthers' growth during the late 1960s to the charismatic Carmichael, the FBI overlooked nothing. His sister's marriage "to a white man of Jewish background" provided fodder for a leak to "a cooperative news media source," and his mother received a telephone call warning of an alleged Panther assassination plot against her son. The Bureau made the whole thing up. No technique, no matter how ruthless, was rejected outright. Division Five even considered labeling Carmichael an informant for a government agency—the so-called "snitch jacket" technique used frequently in counterespionage investigations of Soviet-bloc spies and domestic intelligence investigations of CPUSA functionaries. "This is really nasty treatment from a country that is supposed to be free," complained Carmichael's wife, singer Miriam Makeba, a native of South Africa.[16]

George Moore, the chief of Division Five's racial intelligence squad, defended the use of the snitch jacket. "You have to be able to make decisions"—the decision here was to "tag" Carmichael with a "CIA label"—and "you'd want to make certain that it served a good purpose before you did it. . . . It's a serious thing. . . . As far as I am aware, in the black extremist area, by using that technique, no one was killed. I am sure of that." Was this the result of luck or careful planning? The snitch jacket, after all, had been used against Panther chapters in at least half a dozen cities. In Newark, for example, the FBI falsely implicated a Panther sister for a tip that led to the arrest of a fugitive. Division Five's anonymous letter writers asked the Newark Panthers, "How come the FBI pig fascists knew . . . ?" Another COINTELPRO supervisor admitted that the practice of labeling Panthers as informants may have led to injury or death. "You always have an element of doubt when you are dealing with individuals that I think most people would characterize as having a degree of instability."[17]

Despite this covert assault on the Black Panther party, the frontline FBI office in San Francisco remained reluctant to join the campaign. Things changed dramatically only in May 1969, after Charles Bates advised headquarters that the Panthers were not likely to "overthrow the Government by revolutionary means." That statement, if left unchallenged, would have undermined the entire internal security rationale for the Bureau's domestic intelligence network. "The Panthers right now are not many people and perhaps do not represent many people, as far as most of their actions are concerned," Bates explained. "However, they do represent an idea, or a voice in the ghetto, and are often called upon by Negro residents, to come quell a disturbance in a playground or talk to someone alleging police brutality." Counterintelligence activities, therefore, might "convey the impression that . . . the FBI is working against the aspirations of the Negro people." On this point, Bates of the FBI and Andrew Young of the SCLC were in agreement. The Panthers did not have any support, Young said, "until they became the victims of the persecution campaign of the FBI."[18]

Division Five did not agree. The Panthers' rhetoric alone justified their inclusion on the counterintelligence target list. If they downplayed the talk about guns and offing pigs in favor of social programs intended to overcome their isolation in the ghetto, Division Five reasoned, that would indicate their evolution into a more dangerous form and thus make them a more righteous COINTELPRO target. Sullivan's men lectured the San Francisco office on its responsibilities:

> Your reasoning is not in line with Bureau objectives. . . . You state that the Bureau . . . should not attack programs of community interest such as the BPP "Breakfast for Children." You state that this is because many prominent "humanitarians," both white and black, are interested in the program as well as churches which are actively supporting it. You have obviously missed the point. The BPP is not engaged in the "Breakfast for Children" program for humanitarian reasons, including their efforts to create an image of civility, assume community control of Negroes, and to fill adolescent children with their insidious poison.

Sullivan gave Bates two weeks to assign his best agents to the COINTELPRO desks and get on with the task at hand: "Eradicate [the Panthers'] 'serve the people' programs."[19]

The San Francisco office complied. "There was tremendous fear of Hoover out there," said agent Charles Gain. "It was almost all they could talk about. They were afraid of being sent to some awful post in Montana." So Gain, Cohendet, and the four other agents assigned to the BPP squad supervised the taps and bugs on Panther homes and offices; mailed a William F. Buckley, Jr., column on the Panthers to prominent citizens in the Bay area; tipped off *San Francisco Examiner* reporter Ed Montgomery to Huey Newton's posh Oakland apartment overlooking Lake Merritt; disrupted the breakfast-for-children program "in the notorious Haight-Ashbury District" and elsewhere by spreading a rumor "that various personnel in national headquarters of the BPP are infected with venereal disease"; tried to break up Panther marriages with letters to wives about affairs with teenage girls; and assisted with a plan to harass the Panthers' attorney, Charles Garry, after learning that Garry intended to represent Seale at the Chicago conspiracy trial. They carried out dozens of other counterintelligence operations as well.[20]

The attitude of FBI agents in other field offices balanced Charles Bates's lack of enthusiasm in San Francisco. The Chicago office focused on a proposed alliance between the Black Panther party and the Blackstone Rangers, a confederation of "violence-prone Negro street gangs" under a collective leadership known as the Main 21. The Panthers hoped to politicize the Rangers, to turn the black youths who flocked to the city's gangs away from street crime and toward constructive community action. The Rangers had in fact received some $1 million in Office of Economic Opportunity funding for a "high-risk" job-training program, but OEO terminated the grant in the midst of Senator McClellan's riot hearings. The Chicago Police Department's gang intelligence unit had linked the Rangers to extortion and gun and drug trafficking, and the principal Ranger leader, Jeff Fort, a seasoned felon who had been arrested twice for murder, had used OEO money to further the gang's criminal activities. City police had also linked the Rangers to several ritualistic murders of black teenagers in the course of intermittent warfare with the rival Gangster Disciples. In the FBI view, nonetheless, Ranger criminality was secondary. The "ever present danger," as one Chicago agent later put it, was that "this large Negro youth gang [might] develop black nationalism and align themselves [sic] with the black extremist BPP."[21]

The proposed Black Panther–Blackstone Ranger alliance had enough problems without the meddling of the FBI. On the evening of December 18, 1968, following the shooting of a Panther by a Ranger and the arrest of twelve Panthers and five known members of the Rangers, Jeff Fort met at the gang's headquarters with the two founders of the Panther's Chicago chapter, Fred Hampton, former youth leader of the NAACP branch in suburban Maywood, Illinois, and SNCC activist Bobby Rush.

Fort took the occasion to parade his firepower. According to an FBI informant report:

> Everyone went upstairs into a room which appeared to be a gymnasium, where Fort told Hampton and Rush that he had heard about the Panthers being in Ranger territory during the day, attempting to show their "power" and he wanted the Panthers to recognize the Rangers "power." . . . Fort then gave orders, via walkie-talkie, whereupon two men marched through the door carrying pump shotguns. Another order and two men appeared carrying sawed off carbines then eight more, each carrying a .45 caliber machine gun, clip type, operated from the shoulder or hip, then others came with over and under type weapons. . . . After this procession Fort had all Rangers present, approximately 100, display their side arms and about one half had .45 caliber revolvers. Source advised that all the above weapons appeared to be new.

Fort himself carried a .45 in a shoulder holster and a smaller caliber revolver in his belt. He gave the Panthers one of the machine guns to "try out," but "did not appear over anxious to join forces." A follow-up meeting on December 26, held at a southside bar, broke up when several of the Panthers and Rangers began arguing. Fort telephoned Hampton the next day to tell him the Panthers had twenty-four hours to join the Rangers or else. Hampton told Fort he had the same time to bring his people over to the Panthers and hung up. Later, when Chicago Panthers criticized Ranger leadership's "lack of commitment to black people generally," Fort said he would "'take care' of [the] individuals responsible for the verbal attacks."

Marlin Johnson, the special agent in charge of the FBI's Chicago office, saw in the "enmity and distrust" of these events an opportunity to end the proposed Panther-Ranger alliance once and for all. His office drafted the following letter to Fort and requested authority from Division Five to mail it:

Brother Jeff:

> I've spent some time with some Panther friends on the west side lately and I know what's been going on. The brothers that run the Panthers blame you for blocking their thing and *there's supposed to be a hit out for you.* I'm not a Panther, or a Ranger, just black. From what I see these

Panthers are out for themselves not black people. I think you ought to know what they're up to, I know what I'd do if I was you. You might hear from me again [emphasis added].

(sgd.) *A black brother you don't know.*

Johnson thought the letter would work because the Rangers were "violence prone." "Consideration [had] been given to a similar letter to the BPP alleging a Ranger plot against the BPP leadership," he advised Division Five. "However, it is not felt this would be productive principally because the BPP at present is not believed as violence prone as the Rangers," for whom "violent type activity—shooting and the like—[was] second nature." An explicit suggestion of an assassination plot (a contract "hit"), Johnson continued, might "exact some form of retribution toward the leadership of the BPP." Fort, after all, had already threatened to blow Hampton's head off if he stepped onto Ranger turf. Division Five considered Johnson's proposal, and with Hoover's concurrence authorized the mailing on January 30.

In the months that followed, the Chicago field office used an informant to maintain the division between the Panthers and Rangers, and sent another anonymous letter to Hampton about "Brother Jeff." Yet another anonymous letter, mailed to a rival youth gang, the Mau Mau's, implied that two Panthers were gay. "They're sweethearts" and one of them "worked for the man," the letter writer added. "That's why he's not in Viet Nam." It was all part of a pattern of continually escalating political violence, a pattern that could be traced back to the first voter registration campaigns when FBI agents stood and took notes while the Klan or southern lawmen brutalized civil rights workers. Encouragement of violence through inaction had given way to incitement to violence.[22]

FBI men in southern California were even more calculating in their attempts to egg on a feud between the Black Panther party and US (as opposed to "THEM"), a black group headed by Maulana Karenga that challenged the Panthers' revolutionary political nationalism with its own cultural nationalism. "In the beginning the Panthers and US worked together," Karenga explained. "We used to do community patrol together." Amiri Baraka, who was caught up in the conflict, said Karenga's followers had "a kind of neo-African military quality," with their Karate training, armed security, and olive-drab, homeland garb. For their part,

the Black Panther party ridiculed Karenga's cultural nationalism, claiming US believed power flowed from the sleeve of a
Dashiki and not the barrel of a gun.[23]

FBI agents fueled the US-Panther feud in Los Angeles, San
Diego, and other California cities by mailing anonymous letters
and cartoons to the combatants. The goal was twofold: To inspire an "'US' and BPP vendetta" and to prevent that vendetta
from fizzling out. This was a reckless strategy. "Many of the
younger brothers in Karenga's organization were from eastside
youth gangs," wrote Earl Anthony, a former Black Panther functionary. "The young Panther cadre were from the same, or rival
gangs," and "both sides felt obligated to defend their respective
camps, regardless of whether there were orders to do so. By the
code of the street this was known as gang fighting and they had
been gang fighters long before they were nationalists." The FBI
wanted action, "shootings, beatings, and a high degree of unrest," and attained exactly that with an "imaginative and hard-
hitting" campaign that ran from November 1968 to May 1970.[24]

There is no evidence that the FBI inspired the initial violence
of the Panther-US feud. On November 5, 1968, Los Angeles
agents first noticed the "threats of murder and reprisals" and
informant reports about an US "assassination list" that supposedly included Cleaver's name. Initially, the Bureau saw this
merely as an opportunity to recruit informants and to feed the
Panther suspicion ("fecal material," Karenga said) that US members were cooperating with the CIA and the Los Angeles Police
Department. Things changed in January, at Campbell Hall on
the Westwood campus of the University of California at Los Angeles, where the two groups were competing for the right to advise administrators regarding the selection of a director for a
proposed Afro-American studies program. Four or five US members gunned down two Panthers then attending UCLA, Alpren-
tice ("Bunchy") Carter, on parole from an armed-robbery sentence, and John Huggins. One US member, Larry Stiner, was
wounded in the thirteen-shot, mostly one-sided firefight. Elaine
Brown and three other Panthers testified for the state at the subsequent murder trial, and Stiner, along with his brother, George,
received life sentences. The state sent a third member of Karenga's Simba Wachuka (Young Lions) to a prison for youthful offenders. Two others charged with the killings remained at large.

Baraka saw the roots of the conflict in macho fantasies and
personalities, especially "Cleaver's arrogance and shallow bohe-

mian anarchism which he passes off as Marxism, plus Karenga's Maulana complex." These delusions "sped up the tragic collision that finally saw Bunchy and Huggins dead." "From that point on," Baraka added, "the FBI escalated their 'intervention' into conflict."[25]

That conflict was most visible in San Diego, where the FBI inflamed the existing tensions between the two groups.[26] In early March local agents began mailing cartoons to the homes of Panther activists and the offices of two underground newspapers. These mailings included flyers that had US members gloating over the corpses of Huggins and Carter, and Panthers calling US a collection of "pork chop niggers." Bureau agents and informants tacked up additional copies of the cartoon flyers on walls and telephone poles. Mostly, the crude art work and even cruder captions ridiculed the Black Panther party, and were drawn and phrased to invite the inference of US origin. The Panthers, as expected, suspected Maulana Karenga and not J. Edgar Hoover. While all this was going on, the San Diego office placed anonymous telephone calls to Panther leaders naming other Panthers as police informants. FBI officials had no way of knowing exactly what would happen in the wake of these actions, but they could not have been surprised and were in no way disturbed when violence erupted once again. On March 16, after the Panthers fired into the home of an US member during a retaliatory raid, an US gunman wounded another Panther.[27]

Troubled by the specter of reconciliation in the aftermath (the two groups were actually trying "to talk out their differences"), the San Diego FBI office requested authority to mail a follow-up set of cartoons. The Bureau repeated the whole routine in May when an US activist named Tambuzio shot and killed yet another Panther, John Savage. In June, Division Five learned, US members began drilling with handguns and rifles and purchasing large quantities of ammunition. William Sullivan responded by approving the mailing of yet another inflammatory letter, forged under the signature of a Panther. Blood flowed again in August, when an US gunman shot three Panthers, including Sylvester Bell, who died. The Panthers responded by bombing US offices. In November, after learning that Karenga feared for his life, the San Diego field office mailed a letter asking why he had not retaliated. In January the FBI sent Panther leaders a third set of cartoons attributed to US. One cartoon labeled a Los Angeles Panther a brutalizer of black women and children, another accused the party of instigating a Los Angeles Police Department raid on US headquarters, and a third portrayed Karenga as a strongman who had "the BPP completely at his mercy."

Special agent in charge Robert Evans placed the name of a Panther attorney on the counterintelligence target list that same month—because the attorney had filed suit on behalf of two party members against the San Diego Police Department charging harassment. FBI agents not only encouraged this harassment; they held "racial briefing sessions" for police officers in order to increase their unwitting "contributi[on] to the over-all Counterintelligence Program." They also orchestrated a number of police raids. An especially successful raid, inspired by a Bureau tip about the alleged "sex orgies" occurring at the Panthers' San Diego headquarters, again resulted in violence. Evans considered the raid an outstanding success because, in the aftermath, "the brothers" beat up the woman who opened the front door of the Panther office at the command of the raiding party.

With merit incentives (cash) hanging in the balance for his men, Evans noted the violence "in the ghetto area of southeast San Diego" and tried to take the bows when describing the "tangible results" of his COINTELPRO efforts. "A substantial amount of the unrest is directly attributable to this program," he advised Division Five. "Feuding between representatives of [the Black Panther party and US] has in the past had a tendency to limit the effectiveness of both." Indeed, by March the Panther chapter in San Diego had disintegrated, a development that reduced Evans's men to watching a "former member . . . 'politicking' for the position of local leader if the group is ever reorganized." Division Five, nonetheless, authorized an anonymous mailing, to "selected individuals within the black community," identifying this person as a "police informant."[28]

Other FBI field offices helped out. In Los Angeles, where Karenga had held private meetings with police officials and even Governor Ronald Reagan in an effort to keep the city calm after Martin Luther King's assassination, FBI agents conducted a stringent interview program "in the hope that a state of distruct [sic] might remain among the members and add to the turmoil presently going on within the BPP." The SAC hoped to trigger "internecine struggle" by bringing the two organizations together and thus granting "nature the opportunity to take her course." "They'd shoot at one organization knowing that the other would get blamed, and ... retaliate in kind," Baraka charged, in an exaggerated if understandable participant's assessment of what was going on.[29] Even the faraway Newark office hyped the conflict with a fraudulent letter, allegedly from an SDS activist, to a Panther office in New Jersey. The letter went on about black racists and a "hankerchief head mama" before concluding with a warning ("watch out: Karenga's coming") and a scoreboard (bodycount?):

US - 6
Panthers - 0.[30]

"Our basic policy was to divide and conquer," one former Division Five executive said. "But I can guarantee that nobody was saying, 'Let's get these guys killing each other.'" The surviving combatants had a different perspective, obviously. "These motherfuckers intended to kill everyone of us," Elaine Brown charged.[31] Karenga said the FBI "interjected the violence into it," into the "normal rivalries of two groups struggling for leadership of the black movement. Hoover took his paranoia and imposed that as public policy. It was a violent time. Vietnam. Talk about power from the barrel of a gun. It was a time and context in which the gun was considered a political god, the ultimate arbiter of all conflicts. . . . If somebody tried to do this now, we wouldn't be vulnerable in the same way. We're still recovering and rebuilding from that. We knew it wasn't going to be a tea party, but we didn't anticipate how violent the U.S. government would get. This is obviously an American problem, not an isolated campaign against rantin' and ravin' radicals."[32]

FBI attempts to incite violence ended, more or less, in the spring of 1970. In May the troublesome San Francisco field office asked Division Five if "we are ready to assume responsibility for the death of BPP members we 'set up' as FBI informants"? In fact, William Sullivan had lectured the same field office a few months earlier on this very point, after the SAC offered to drop some "dog eared" FBI paper in a Panther car recently used by Ray ("Masai") Hewitt, the party's Los Angeles–based minister of education. Division Five rejected the proposal on the grounds that "it could result in a Panther murder of one of their leaders."[33] There were two reasons for the Bureau's newfound caution. The first had to do with the torture-murder of New Haven Panther Alex Rackley, a suspected police informant, and the second with the Bureau's involvement in an Illinois State's Attorney's police raid on the Panthers in Chicago. Both had to do with the specter of "embarassment to the Bureau."

The Panther who falsely accused Rackley of working for the FBI went over to the government during the subsequent state court murder trial. That after-the-fact informant, George W. Sams, Jr., a seriously disturbed Panther security enforcer who had spent two years in an institution for the mentally handicapped, had in fact engineered the events that resulted in Rackley's death. Bobby Seale, who was indicted along with Sams and twelve other Panthers, expelled him from the party in the aftermath. Seale had launched a purge of "provocateur agents, kooks, and avaricious fools" seeking to use the party as a base for criminal activities, but Sams had slipped through. Now here he sat as the principal prosecution witness, though he pleaded guilty, along with two other Panthers, to charges of second-degree murder and conspiracy to kidnap. The state dismissed its case against Seale when the jury reported itself hopelessly deadlocked. Sams, meanwhile, was pardoned after serving four years, given a new identity, and placed under the federal witness protection program. He returned to prison many years later, in 1977, following a series of arrests involving violent assaults.

Sams ended up in the witness protection program because he was being groomed for services at a Black Panther party trial in Chicago, a trial that had its roots in the State's Attorney's police raid of December 1969 to seize illegal weapons at the party's Monroe Street "crib," where the twenty-year-old Fred Hampton stayed. The FBI had been involved in the raid during the planning stages, when one of its sixty-seven informants in the Black Panther party, William O'Neal, helped his control agent, Roy Mitchell, sketch out a floor plan of the apartment. A captain of security in the Chicago chapter and for a time one of Hampton's bodyguards, O'Neal worked with the Bureau to label innocent Panthers as informants. He used a bull whip and a homemade electric chair to coerce confessions from accused party members and thereby ease his spy hunting burdens, and pocketed some $30,000 of Bureau money from 1969 to 1972 in salary and perks (a car maintenance allowance). He was worth it, though the Bureau knew he was unreliable. (A wiretap established his involvement in a drug sale.) Neither O'Neal's actions nor his efforts to convince Hampton and the other decision makers to

move the Panthers into the world of bank robbery worried the
FBI. No matter how unstable, no matter how unreliable, O'Neal
was a prize informant, a man adept at "harassing and impelling
the criminal activities of the Black Panther Party locally."[34]

The events leading to the charge that the Panthers kept illegal
weapons at the Monroe Street apartment and the State's Attorney's police raid began in June—a time when Fred Hampton was
in prison, having received a two- to five-year sentence for stealing $71 worth of ice cream bars. An FBI visit to the Panthers'
Chicago office later that month led to eight arrests. Gun battles
with city police followed in July and October. Another shootout
on November 13 resulted in the deaths of two Chicago policemen
and a former Panther, Jake Winters. Although Hampton had not
even been released from prison on appeal bond until August and
was out of town at the time of the November 13 tragedy, he received the blame—principally because he was the main Panther
leader in Cook County, a charismatic and skilled organizer who
formed a shaky alliance with SDS, organized a number of community welfare, medical, and educational programs, and somehow kept the rivalry with the Blackstone Rangers in check. The
FBI placed his name on the Rabble Rouser Index on November
19, and sent William O'Neal's control agent, counterintelligence
man Roy Mitchell, off to the State's Attorney's office with the
sketch of the Panther apartment. Ironically, the Illinois Supreme
Court had ordered Hampton back to prison by the first of the
year, having denied his appeal.

Mitchell's sketch clearly marked the bed where Hampton normally slept with his eight-and-one-half month pregnant girl
friend, Deborah Johnson—thereby making things easier for the
fourteen Chicago policemen detailed to the Special Prosecutions
Unit of the Cook County State's Attorney's Office who raided the
apartment at 4:00 A.M. on December 4. They carried twenty-
seven guns, including five shotguns and a submachine gun, and
Sergeant James "Gloves" Davis, a black cop with a reputation
for brutalizing black citizens, led them into combat. "Davis went
in there with a grease gun," Civil Rights Division chief Jerris
Leonard said, and his crew, poet James A. Emanuel wrote, came
in

> behind guns cursin Black men
> makin gut noises
> wakin up the WORLD

They fired about ninety shots. The occupants of the apartment fired one shot. With a large dose of secobarbital in his system (there are claims that he was drugged), Hampton never woke up, never made it out of bed. He died in a one-way firefight, in his sleep, along with Mark Clark, a member of the Panthers' Peoria chapter.[35]

Shot through the heart at the moment Davis broke open the front door, Clark fired the only Panther round—into the floor, as he fell down dead. Four other Panthers, all teenagers, received serious wounds. Davis's crew directed a pattern of cross-fire, mostly from an M-1 carbine and a Thompson submachine gun, from the front room through the rear bedroom wall, at the location where the floorplan showed the head of Hampton's bed. At least one bullet from the M-1 hit Hampton, though the fatal shots apparently came from a handgun. Circumstantial evidence indicates that one of the officers fired two .45 caliber rounds, perhaps downward at close range, into Hampton's right forehead and right temple. The officer then dragged the body out into the dining room. The two bullets exited below Hampton's left ear and through his left throat, and were never found.

In the aftermath, O'Neal went out to Maywood, to pay his respects to Hampton's mother and father, and to circulate rumors that one of the other Panthers in the apartment that morning was a police informant. A few days later, he picked up a special $300 bonus from the FBI.[36] Over the next two years, he reported to the Bureau on such things as the strategies of the lawyers for the Hampton and Clark families. While O'Neal continued his services, State's Attorney Edward V. Hanrahan said the police "exercised good judgment" and "considerable restraint," a Cook County grand jury indicted the surviving Panthers for murder and attempted murder, and Emanuel wrote these lines about the *Panther Man*, Fred Hampton:

> Wouldn't think
> t look at m
> he was so dam bad
> they had to sneak up on m,
> shoot m in his head
> in his bed
> sleepin
> Afroed up 3 inches
> smilin gunpowder[37]

"Hampton and Clark were not good citizens," Jerris Leonard conceded. "On the other hand, no one had a right to summarily execute them. The Hampton-Clark killing was a perfect example of how a local police department, using bad judgment in dealing with a very serious situation, simply did not execute their attempt to arrest those people properly. The FBI was faced with similar situations, but they had real expertise, and they should have been used in the Hampton-Clark situation."[38] Leonard had it wrong. The FBI had mobilized, and had in fact "used" the State's Attorney's police. Under pressure from the press and public opinion generally, Leonard's Civil Rights Division opened a civil rights case. As always, the FBI did the investigating, and the agent assigned to the case worked under the close supervision of SAC Marlin Johnson. No Division executive recognized the irony in that or said anything when a federal grand jury convened in the winter of 1970 and the FBI withheld information regarding the roles of O'Neal and Mitchell. Leonard, who also served as the prosecutor in charge of the grand jury, said "O'Neal had nothing to do with the investigation we conducted."

In Leonard's view, the FBI conducted an exemplary civil rights investigation. "The Monroe Street apartment was a mess when I arrived there," he remembered. "Frozen pillars of water came down from the ceiling. There was water frozen on the floors and in the bathrooms. The FBI knew that the targets of our investigation were Chicago police officers, who were assigned to the State's Attorney's Office"—including "the chief of police himself. But the Bureau did its job. It did a tremendous mock-up of the apartment showing where every bullet hole had been fired. Bureau agents were on their hands and knees looking for shell casings and bullet fragments. If Clark or Hampton hadn't fired the first shot from inside the apartment, I have no doubt that the Chicago police who were involved, including the higher-ups, would have been indicted."[39]

When the grand jury finished its preliminary report, Leonard told Marlin Johnson there would be "no indictments of police officers."[40] In return, Hanrahan remained silent regarding the FBI role in setting up the raid. Because any sort of prosecution might compromise the Bureau, Hanrahan also agreed to the dismissal of indictments against the surviving Panthers. Not surprisingly, given the total corruption of the investigative process, the details of the Bureau's involvement surfaced only in the mid- and late 1970s. The families of the victims and the survivors of the raid filed a civil suit in 1970, and nearly a decade later a federal court of appeals held that the government had obstructed the judicial process by withholding information. "I thought that our Justice Department team had done a superb job in surfacing what actually happened at the Monroe Street apartment," Leonard said. "I was frankly never able to understand why the Hampton and Clark families filed their suit against us. I thought it was a harassment type case. But the Bureau got into trouble because they didn't cough up the evidence that they had on the informant. And the federal judge out there . . . got very angry about it." The FBI held onto the administrative memo indicating O'Neal's $300 bonus until the end, submitting the document in the very last volume of files surrendered in response to the court's order.[41]

Special agent in charge Johnson had no more luck when he claimed that the FBI had done nothing wrong. The information acquired by O'Neal and disseminated to the police was routine and strictly a matter of local interest, he said. "What they did with the information was none of our concern." The documents, however, were included in the counterintelligence file and bore such captions as "Operations Being Effected and Tangible Results Obtained." They showed that Johnson's office had tried to persuade the Chicago Police Department to conduct the raid before State's Attorney Hanrahan finally agreed to do it. Roy Mitchell, furthermore, had met with Hanrahan's representatives in a series of preraid, off-the-record conferences. And when arguing for the informant's bonus, the Racial Matters squad supervisor, Robert Piper, claimed that O'Neal's information provided "the only source of the raid."

O'Neal's last preraid report stated that there were no illegal weapons on the premises. All the guns were legally purchased and registered. The State's Attorney, nonetheless, had based the probable-cause evidence during the warrant-application process on information supplied by an unidentified informant (O'Neal). The ostensible purpose of the raid was to seize contraband that O'Neal said did not exist. Because Cook County authorities based their request for a warrant on hearsay (O'Neal told Mitchell and Mitchell told the police and the police went to the judge), the warrant itself was invalid. A valid affidavit, under Illinois law, would have required the signature of the informant's contact—the signature of the FBI's counterintelligence man, Roy Mitchell.

The raiding party chief, Sergeant Daniel Groth, helped cover up the FBI's role by claiming that the "probable cause" evidence in his original affidavit for the search warrant came not from O'Neal but from another informant in the Panthers' Chicago chapter. This claim presented a problem for the Bureau on another level, because the weapons referred to in Groth's affidavit, a sawed-off shotgun and a stolen police riot gun, were in violation of federal law. The normal FBI procedure would have been to notify the Alcohol, Firearms and Tobacco Division of the Treasury Department about these weapons. Because Bureau agents failed to do this, and because they avoided any reference to the shotgun or the riot gun in their summaries of the information O'Neal supplied, the survivors of the raid concluded that Groth invented the informant to validate the warrant and conceal the arrangement between the FBI and the Cook County State's Attorney's Office. Perhaps it was just another example of what one police official described to Hoover, a year before Hampton and Clark died, as "the wonderful, wonderful cooperation and rapport that exists between . . . [the] Chicago [FBI] Office, SAC Marlin C. Johnson, and the Chicago Police Department." "I was glad to hear that," the director replied. "We want to work hand in hand with them."[42]

In November 1982, thirteen years after Gloves Davis and the others entered the Monroe Street apartment, the Hampton and Clark families and the survivors agreed to a $1.85 million settlement that their attorney, G. Flint Taylor, Jr., described as "an admission of the conspiracy that existed between the F.B.I. and Hanrahan's men to murder Fred Hampton." Robert Gruenberg, the assistant U.S. attorney who handled the case, said the federal government settled merely to avoid another costly trial. That multimillion dollar cost included $36,000 paid to O'Neal for his services as a witness. Hampton's relatives used their money to endow their family project, the Fred Hampton Scholarship Fund, for "young blacks who want to become lawyers," brother William said.[43]

Initially, the deaths of Fred Hampton and Mark Clark caused few problems for the FBI. First, a number of counterintelligence proposals had to be scrubbed, as one Division Five executive noted, "in view of the fact that Hampton was recently shot and killed." Second, the killings had "triggered an avalanche of publicity favorable to the BPP," a development which inspired an FBI campaign to "portray the BPP in its true light as an aggregate of violence-prone individuals who initiate violence rather than persecuted victims of unprovoked police brutality."[44] By the spring of 1970, however, the Bureau anticipated criticism of its handling of the Panther investigations and its role in the events that led to the Monroe Street tragedy.

FBI officials confined their newfound caution to areas where they could conceivably be held legally responsible for inciting violence or even murder. Counterintelligence, the preferred option before Chicago, remained just that in the aftermath. The entire program continued on a similar if more subdued track. In San Diego, local agents supplemented their efforts to keep the Panther-US conflict simmering with several operations designed to drive the Panther breakfast-for-children program out of the basement of a Catholic church. Division Five ordered the field office to "keep the pressure on the Catholic hierarchy," and eventually it worked. The archdiocese transferred the priest who helped the Panthers, Frank Curran, to "somewhere in the State of New Mexico." "Completely neutralized," the Bureau said. New York agents tried to "deter individuals from joining" the Black Panther party by contacting anyone who showed an interest. They even interviewed the parents of grade-school children who had spoken to Panther organizers.[45]

Counterintelligence assaults occurred in every area of the country. In Detroit, the special agent in charge submitted a proposal involving forged letters to black businessmen demanding financial support for the Panthers or else. Agents assigned to the Jackson, Mississippi, office drafted a letter about "some colored boys" hanging around Senator Eastland's Sunflower County "with hair like Stokely Carmichael" and "jackets with the initials BPP on the back," and apparently sent it to several state and county government officials. They wanted to know why the Panthers had not been "run . . . out of Mississippi." The FBI sent another bogus letter, from an "irate [black] parent," to a Rochester, New York, school board official about a high school history teacher who ordered twenty subscriptions to the Panther newspaper for use in his class. When confronted, the teacher canceled the subscriptions. Sponsors of the breakfast-for-children program also received letters, along with copies of the outrageous Panther coloring book. Party leaders had rejected the coloring book and Bobby Seale ordered it destroyed, but that did not stop the FBI from adding violent captions and sending it around.[46]

One of the FBI's favorite tactics was to accuse the Panthers and other black nationalists of anti-Semitism, a tactic designed to destroy the movement's image "among liberal and naive elements." Bureau interest in anti-Semitism grew during the summer of 1967 at the National Convention for New Politics, when SNCC's James Forman and Rap Brown led a floor fight for a resolution condemning Zionist expansionism. The convention's black caucus introduced the resolution and SNCC emerged as the first black group to take a public stand against Israel in the Mid-East conflict.[47] Brown went on to become well known for his burn-baby-burn and violence-is-as-American-as-cherry-pie quotes, and he was only slightly less well known for another. "If America chooses to play Nazis, black folks ain't going to play Jews." In the FBI view, the black caucus resolution and Brown's rhetoric indicated an anti-Semitic attitude within the black movement as a whole. Division Five responded by directing the field "to compile all evidence of anti-Semitic activity by militant black nationalist extremists and their sympathizers," with a particular emphasis on the Black Panther party.[48]

The issue of anti-Semitism was an old one for FBI officials, so it is surprising that they did not react in a more timely manner. During the 1950s Division Five mailed literature detailing the extent of anti-Semitism in the Soviet Union to Jewish communists in the United States and disseminated a lengthy monograph entitled "Communism Versus the Jewish People" on a more selective basis to a number of prominent Americans, inside the government and out, including former President Herbert Hoover. And Crime Records chief Louis Nichols kept in touch with Hearst columnist George Sokolsky on the fact that so many of the persons exposed by the McCarthy-era committees had "names . . . of Jewish origin." Sokolsky was "a great American. A great Jew, too," Nichols said. The FBI assistant director also kept in touch with Herman Edelsberg, director of the Anti-Defamation League (ADL), who briefed Nichols on the ADL's arrangement with the House Committee on Un-American Activities on "the handling of witnesses." HUAC agreed to check ADL files before subpoenaing leftist Jews—"to insure that such witnesses didn't climb all over the Committee."[49]

When attempting to publicize the "anti-Semitic and unchristian posture" of the Panthers more than a decade later, Hoover's agents employed many of the same tactics that they had used to document the anti-Semitism of the Soviet state. The New York

office enlisted one of its veteran and completely fictitious creations—"a disgruntled Jewish member of the Communist party"
named "Irving." Division Five tried to disrupt the Panthers by
manipulating Rabbi Meir Kahane and the "vigilante-type" Jewish Defense League (JDL), leaking information to college administrators and sources in the Anti-Defamation League, and working with newspaper columnists. The FBI compared Panther
ideology with "the traditional anti-Semitism of organizations
like the American Nazi Party" and the even more traditional
anti-Semitism of the late Adolf Hitler. In the case of the JDL, the
FBI did not limit itself to "the furnishing of factual information" because Kahane's group could not "be motivated to act"
unless "the information . . . concerning anti-Semitism and other
matters were furnished . . . [with] some embellishment."[50]

Another of the FBI's favorite counterintelligence tactics—the
attempt to create dissension and factionalism within the Black
Panther party—also continued unabated. The most dramatic episode involved the split between the West Coast followers of
Huey Newton and the mostly East Coast followers of Eldridge
Cleaver. When the FBI launched this campaign in March 1970,
Newton sat in a California prison and Cleaver sat in Algiers in
self-imposed exile. The Cleaver faction revolved around the so-
called Panther 21—twenty-one Black Panthers indicted in New
York City on April 2, 1969, on conspiracy charges to commit
murder and arson. New York police officers and FBI agents
gathered most of the evidence for the prosecution, presented by
New York County District Attorney Frank Hogan and Assistant
District Attorney Joseph A. Phillips. Complications arose within
the party itself in February 1971, when Newton expelled the Panther 21, a purge that prompted rumors of kidnap plots and frat-
ricide. Finally, on March 13, with the jury deliberating less than
an hour, thirteen of the Panthers on trial won their freedom.
Other Panthers were acquitted in absentia.[51]

The first COINTELPRO operation occurred in April 1970,
when the FBI sent an anonymous letter to Cleaver in Algiers accusing Panther leaders in California of plotting against him.
After Cleaver expelled three of the party's international representatives, Hoover gave "incentive awards" to the agents who
sent the letter.[52] A follow-up letter to David Hilliard, the Panther
chief of staff in Oakland, suggested that Cleaver had "tripped
out." When FBI wiretaps on the Panthers' national office confirmed the effectiveness of this particular letter, the stage was

set for more bogus letters. Following Newton's release from prison on August 13, an FBI informant distributed a "directive" to rank and file Panthers, with a copy to the national office in Oakland, questioning Newton's competence. Thereafter, the FBI mailed "a barrage of anonymous letters" to Newton and Cleaver and their respective followers. A letter of January 1971, drafted to appear as if it had been written by Newton's personal secretary, Connie Matthews, was typical:

> Things around headquarters are dreadfully disorganized with the comrade commander [Newton] not making proper decisions. The newspaper is in a shambles. No one knows who is in charge. The foreign department gets no support. . . . I fear there is a rebellion working just beneath the surface. . . . We must either get rid of the Supreme Commander or get rid of the disloyal members.

Division Five again noted the results of "our counterintelligence projects": Newton was prepared "to respond violently to any question of his actions or policies."[53]

In February, twenty-nine FBI field offices extended the campaign by promoting factionalism between Panther chapters and the national office. Another barrage of anonymous letters followed, including one to Newton's brother, Melvin, warning him that the Cleaver faction planned to assassinate him, and one to Cleaver warning about the possibility of violence directed against his wife, Kathleen. Newton believed an informant had infiltrated Panther headquarters, and his secretary went into hiding. FBI officials tried to take credit for everything, including Cleaver's expulsion from the party. But they were not prepared to rest on their laurels. They sent out more bogus letters, under the signatures of Newton and Hilliard, describing Cleaver as "a murderer and a punk without genitals." This last insult seemed particularly appropriate, since the Panthers sometimes talked about "pussy power" being good for the revolution.

"We absolutely felt Cleaver was a danger," San Francisco Panther squad agent William Cohendet explained. "Matter of fact, the party should be thankful for whatever help they got [from the Bureau]. Getting rid of Cleaver was a big thing; he took all those hoodlums with him. And so Huey didn't have any problems anymore. . . . Read the language in those letters. Would you think that was written by a bunch of white men? When you listen to them everyday for a couple of years you get to know their vocabulary. . . . Don't you think it was a pretty good operation, if you had to give a candid opinion of it?" [54]

The FBI campaign to split the Black Panther party finally stopped at the end of March, a few weeks after a gunman shot Cleaver-faction member Robert Webb while Webb was selling the party newspaper in Harlem. The Bureau concluded that "the differences between Newton and Cleaver . . . [were now] irreconciable." A few days later in Queens, another gunman shot and killed Samuel Lee Napier, the circulation manager of the Newton-faction newspaper. [55]

The Panther compaigns had unintended consequences. They corrupted the criminal justice system in the Hampton-Clark killings and the Cleaver-Newton conflict, and in every case where a black activist faced indictment under a criminal statute. In 1970 the president of Yale University, Kingman Brewster, Jr., questioned "the ability of black revolutionaries to achieve a fair trial anywhere in the United States." The experience of Elmer ("Geronimo") Pratt provides an example of Brewster's point. [56] In 1968 Pratt was a Vietnam war hero, "a sergeant in the 82nd Airborne . . . with a chest full of medals, including two Purple Hearts." Upon returning home, he enrolled at UCLA and joined the Black Panther party. The FBI placed him on the counterintelligence target list in 1969, and a Los Angeles County grand jury indicted him in 1970 on various counts of murder, assault, and robbery. On top of everything else, Huey Newton expelled Pratt after Melvin ("Cotton") Smith called Pratt a police agent. Another ex-Panther and sometime FBI probationary racial informant, Julius Butler, then wrote a letter to the Bureau identifying Pratt as the culprit in the $18 robbery and murder of a twenty-seven year old white woman back in December 1968.

Convicted on the murder and robbery charges, Pratt received a life sentence and claimed Hoover's FBI framed him—a claim based on a number of revelations about the Bureau's conduct that began to surface three years later, including the fact that the FBI sent "COINTELPRO informants" off to infiltrate the defense. Pratt's lawyers raised other points regarding Butler's "extensive contacts with the FBI" and a "lost" wiretap log that might have confirmed their client's presence in North Carolina at the time of the murder. None of it mattered. After Pratt had served eight years in San Quentin, including five years in solitary confinement, the court of appeals rejected his contentions in a majority decision that conceded his main point. "There is

no dispute that FBI informants . . . were in the defense camp."
But the court contended that the informants had "as much effect
on whether or not defendant Pratt was afforded a fair trial conducted in California's superior court as did the furniture in the
areas where the [attorney-client] discussions were conducted."[57]

An equally troubling case in New York involved another
COINTELPRO target, R. Dhoruba Moore. A codefendant in the
Panther 21 case who believed Newton had ordered his assassination, Moore jumped bail, fled the country, and was acquitted in
absentia in March 1971. Police officers arrested him three
months later at an after-hours club in the Bronx, booking him
as a John Doe. The officers also confiscated a .45 caliber machine gun at the club. When they uncovered Moore's identity,
they charged him with the attempted murder of two patrolmen
who had been assigned to guard the Riverside Drive home of
Panther 21 prosecutor Frank Hogan. Moore was indicted, tried,
and convicted, with the court handing down a sentence of
twenty-five years to life. The question that went to the heart of
the criminal justice system had less to do with Dhoruba Moore's
guilt or innocence than whether he had received a fair trial.

After the Black Liberation Army claimed responsibility for the
Riverside Drive shooting, and as well the murder of two other
patrolmen at a Harlem housing project, Richard Nixon ordered
Hoover to conduct a "no punches pulled" investigation. The
president did not want the FBI in "on a case by case basis," only
those police killing cases where the director had "the scent and
smell of a national conspiracy . . . like the Black Panthers." Hoover immediately launched a NEWKILL (New York police killings) investigation, and he had the New York FBI office send "a
Panther expert to brief the police."[58] His aides also used these
crimes to open more domestic intelligence files. "The Newkill
case and other terrorist acts have demonstrated that in many
instances those involved in these acts are individuals who cannot be identified as members of an extremist group," one executive concluded. "They are frequently supporters, community
workers, or people who hang around the headquarters of the
extremist group or associate with members of the group." Division Five ordered the field to round up Cleaver-faction Panthers
and members of other visible black groups, and to list "supporters and affiliates of these groups with your file numbers on
each, if you have a file. If you have no file, open files."[59]

FBI officials did not let up even after the Black Panther party's collapse and Hoover's own death, and even with President Nixon, in the midst of the Watergate muck, barely hanging on to his Oval Office desk. In May 1973, following a firefight on the New Jersey turnpike between three black radicals and state troopers that left one black man and one trooper dead, the Bureau opened its CHESROB file. Named after one of the badly wounded radicals on the turnpike that day, the CHESROB investigation attempted to hook former New York Panther Joanne Chesimard (Assata Shakur) to virtually every bank robbery or other violent crime involving a black woman on the East Coast. This "queen of the Black Liberation Army," as the press liked to call her, was subsequently indicted for robbery (twice) and armed robbery, the kidnapping and murder of a drug dealer, and the attempted murder of a policeman. The courts dismissed three indictments and juries acquitted on two other charges after three separate trials. A seventh indictment led to a mistrial when the court learned of Chesimard's pregnancy—a development that reportedly prompted the FBI "to conduct an investigation to determine how [she] got pregnant." Finally convicted on the seventh indictment at a new trial in March 1977, she received a life sentence for her role in the turnpike incident. Chesimard lives in exile today, having escaped in November 1979 from New Jersey's Clinton Correctional Institute. She surfaced in Cuba eight years later, to promote her autobiography.[60]

The post-Hoover FBI followed Panthers and other black radicals into the prisons with its PRISACTS program. Inspired by the terrorism of the Symbionese Liberation Army and an investigation by HUAC's successor, the House Committee on Internal Security, PRISACTS countered "extremist, revolutionary, terrorist, and subversive activities in penal institutions." Bureau officials launched the program in February 1974 "with the primary goals of promoting liaison and cooperation between the FBI and prison administrators nationwide relative to above elements, and to generally provide for two-way exchange of information."[61]

Most of the black radicals tried and jailed for murder and other violent crimes knew what they were doing. Some of them no doubt believed they were making a statement, spilling a little pig blood, to use the crude words of the day, for the people. Others came to recognize nihilistic terror for what it was. More than anything else, the notion that those black nationalists who went to war with the state and shot police officers in the back are somehow martyrs is a legacy of the FBI's counterintelligence program against the Panthers. To a lesser degree, another legacy of this Bureau program was the continuing harassment of imprisoned Panthers and others under such open-ended investigations as NEWKILL and CHESROB. In San Diego and Los Angeles, the FBI fed the bloody rivalry between the Black Panther party and US, and then helped local police and state prosecutors build murder and conspiracy cases against the survivors. The FBI targeted Geronimo Pratt and Dhoruba Moore under the counterintelligence program, and then helped prosecutors in California and New York put them behind bars. The FBI assisted prosecutors in the New Haven and Panther 21 conspiracy cases against other COINTELPRO targets, and in Chicago two more targets, Fred Hampton and Mark Clark, ended up dead.

A reasonable person could read the files pertaining to two operations (at least), the letter to Blackstone Ranger leader Jeff Fort and the raid on the Panthers' Monroe Street apartment, and conclude that the FBI responded to off-the-pig rhetoric with crazed schemes to off Panthers. The FBI did not plan Fred Hampton's death, but the FBI has had to spend considerable time since the morning of December 4, 1969, explaining that his corpse was not, in bureauspeak, the "tangible result" of a year-long campaign to "otherwise neutralize" one of the Black Panther party's most effective community organizers. The FBI once told Tom Charles Huston, Nixon's man and the principal author of the president's blueprint for a police state, that Hampton was responsible for the deaths of two Chicago police officers. That claim was absurd. Fred Hampton, by most accounts, is a legitimate movement martyr. But were people like Pratt and Moore martyrs or monsters? Cold-blooded killers or victims of Hoover's operatives in Division Five?

Amnesty International, an organization more accustomed to the torture and death squads that roam the jackboot world of military dictators, apartheid governments, and religious and political fanatics, studied the Pratt case and concluded that justice in the United States during those times had neither the appearance nor the reality of fairness. The FBI's counterintelligence program interfered "with the judicial process as selective enforcement of the law. Undoubtedly there is a clear distinction between framing an individual"—Pratt's claim—"and selective enforcement of the law; but both measures stem from an official willingness to abuse the criminal justice system. . . . The effect of COINTELPRO has been to destroy confidence in the *bona fides* of the FBI."[62]

Geronimo Pratt and Dhoruba Moore remain incarcerated, and, perhaps, they deserve to be. A reasonable person might also conclude that their words and deeds deserved whatever FBI response they provoked. The record of FBI conduct, nonetheless, is there for Amnesty International to write reports about and for everyone to see. "The chief investigative branch of the Federal Government, which was charged by law with investigating crimes and preventing criminal conduct, itself engaged in lawless tactics and responded to deep-seated social problems by fomenting violence and unrest."[63] Physical violence, as opposed to violent rhetoric, was never more than a peripheral part of the black struggle for equality. Political violence, in contrast, was a central part of the FBI response to that struggle—something located within the mainstream of government policy toward blacks.

10

Citizens and Radicals
Hoover, Nixon, and the Surveillance State

T he FBI's Panther campaigns were part of a larger strategy of intelligence and counterintelligence that expanded and grew bloodier and finally came to an end during the Richard M. Nixon years. The Watergate president sometimes tried to force the FBI to do things J. Edgar Hoover would not accept, and when the director resisted the president tried to fire him.[1] Eventually, in the midst of the events that drove him out of office, the president's recklessness would contribute, in an ironic and fortuitous way, to the dismantling of the FBI's "Racial Matters" surveillance apparatus. This took place after Hoover's death in 1972, when the Watergate scandal and its repercussions made it clear that the civil liberties of all Americans were at stake. When Nixon took the oath of office in 1969, however, it appeared to the director that the FBI's community surveillance and counter-intelligence programs would flourish under the new administration. For a time, they did so.

Nixon's ties to the FBI dated from late 1947, when he worked closely with FBI Assistant Director Louis Nichols and cracked the Alger Hiss case, as Hoover often said, "almost single-hand-edly."[2] In the 1940s he vacationed with Hoover in Miami, attended an occasional Washington Senators baseball game with him, and met with him in the White House from time to time. In 1960 the director reportedly did a bit of covert campaigning for his friend. Nichols, though retired from the Bureau by then, helped too, and in 1968 he got Nixon his first electronic surveillance expert for the campaign, former FBI agent John J. Ragan. Nixon once compared the FBI favorably to the Central Intelligence Agency with its "muscle-bound bureaucracy which has completely paralyzed its brain," advising White House chief of staff H. R. Haldeman that CIA "personnel, just like the personnel in State, is primarily Ivy League and the Georgetown set rather than the type of people that we get into the services and the FBI." The president and the director assumed they would work well together.[3]

Nixon's policies confirmed that Hoover had more in common with this man than any of the other seven chief executives he had served. Nixon had his White House enemies list, while Hoover had a Not to Contact list of liberals and others. "The Nixon White House got the idea of the Enemies List from us," said William Sullivan. Hoover's list included all representatives of the CBS and NBC television networks and such newspapers as the *Washington Post,* the *New York Times,* the *Baltimore Sun,* and the *Los Angeles Times.* They were all "left-wing and trying to downgrade law enforcement," the director concluded. In the case of the *Los Angeles Times* ("a melting pot of garbage"), national editor Edwin Guthman, Robert Kennedy's former special assistant for public relations and a practicing member of "the Kennedy clique," directed the "smear gathering." The so-called liberal media ("jackals of the press") also made one of Nixon's enemy lists. "No one from AP. on social for 3 mos," Haldeman wrote on a notepad during a White House meeting. "No one Time, Newsweek, Post, Times." "Shaft . . . one by one." "Chop their heads—Screw them."[4]

When it came to biased use of the FBI name-check process, the Nixon White House rivaled the Johnson White House. Hundreds of requests filtered down from then counsel to the president John Ehrlichman and deputy assistant to the president Alexander P. Butterfield, white (Billy Graham, David Lawrence, Mr. and Mrs. Pat Boone) as well as black (Roy Wilkins, Joe Louis, Mr. and Mrs. Lionel Hampton).[5] The administration also solicited Hoover's opinion on a discussion draft of a presidential message on crime (the draft neglected campus and ghetto violence, the director said), and enlisted the FBI indirectly in its crude appeals to the George Wallace constituency. Bureau officials kept such ardent segregationists as Senators James Eastland and Strom Thurmond up-to-date, advising both men of the vague plans of SCLC activist Hosea Williams to organize demonstrations on Eastland's Mississippi plantation and Thurmond's South Carolina farm. Meanwhile, the president offered black America the "delusion" (Bayard Rustin's word) of black capitalism, refused to meet with black leaders, and nominated a segregationist, Clement F. Haynsworth, Jr., of South Carolina, for a seat on the U.S. Supreme Court. When Haynsworth's nomination collapsed, Nixon sent up the name of another segregationist, G. Harrold Carswell of Florida.[6]

Hoover described Haynsworth as "very conservative," "definitely in favor of law and order," a man with "a slight lisp but . . . a brilliant mind." A background check uncovered "no derogatory information" (other than the lisp?). Nor did the background check on Carswell—"a good man," Hoover thought—reveal any hint of a segregationist past. The FBI simply catered to the Nixon administration. Bureau agents routinely collected information regarding the attitudes of southern congressmen, judges, and other politicians toward integration, and Bureau officials routinely kept this information out of the reports they sent to the White House or the attorney general or Senator Eastland's Judiciary Committee. Eastland's own file, in the words of one Crime Records Division agent, "reflects that he is a strong advocate of 'White Supremacy.'"[7]

The FBI had been keeping information regarding segregationist sympathies to itself at least since the Kennedy years. Whenever John Kennedy considered nominating a liberal for a seat on the federal bench, in contrast, Hoover cited the most minute details concerning "subversive" affiliations. While President Kennedy mulled over the possible Supreme Court nomination of William Henry Hastie, a black circuit court of appeals judge, the director sent a memo to Robert Kennedy connecting the judge to ten groups on the attorney general's list of subversive organizations or other lists compiled by such bodies as the House Committee on Un-American Activities. Later, when Lyndon Johnson sent up Thurgood Marshall's name, the FBI extended such services to the press. "When I wrote an editorial telling . . . Eastland to cut the hijinks and get on with the nomination," recalled Patrick Buchanan, then a *St. Louis Globe-Democrat* reporter, publisher Richard H. Amberg "came by to let me know I had made a mistake. . . . A great admirer of J. Edgar Hoover, the publisher was in regular contact with the FBI." The director pursued these policies in the face of opposition from the Kennedys and LBJ, but with the support of Richard Nixon.[8]

"Hoover was more than a source of information" for the administration, John Ehrlichman wrote. "He was a political advisor to whom Nixon listened." The president and the director discussed the black and antiwar movements generally, and the need for more law-and-order judges on the Supreme Court. "[We need] a real man" on the court, Hoover told Nixon.[9] They also discussed the "thing at Cornell," where 250 well-armed black undergraduate and graduate students had occupied the student union building. Cornell President James A. Perkins's capitulation to their demands prompted Nixon to remark, "Basically the faculty does not have any guts." Hoover said "the Presidents [of other schools under siege] don't either," with the exception of S. I. Hayakawa of San Francisco State, who "brought order out of chaos by firing a number of the faculty who had been sparking the demonstrations."[10] Hoping to exploit these types of situations for political advantage, the White House expected the FBI to help make the case. "We simply have got to keep the label of radical sympathizers on the Democrats," Charles Colson noted. "We've got to show that their rhetoric over recent years has encouraged the kind of attitude of permissiveness that has allowed the revolutionaries to hold sway among the moderate students."[11]

National Security Adviser Henry Kissinger, Attorney General John Mitchell, and Vice President Spiro Agnew also used the director as a sounding board. The names of these three men graced the FBI's dissemination list for the weekly "Racial Digest," and as well the INLET (Intelligence Letter) Program, a service launched in late 1969 and intended to channel "items with an unusual twist or concerning prominent personalities." The Bureau scanned all racial matters intelligence, among other items, on a daily basis in search of items suitable for INLET.[12]

Hoover had his agents sweep Kissinger's home and office for taps and bugs, and forwarded information on topics ranging from the late Martin Luther King to Pentagon "employees who are still McNamara people and express a very definite Kennedy philosophy."[13] Hoover rated Mitchell as the best attorney general ever. Patricia Collins, a Justice Department lawyer who worked under fourteen attorneys general, said the director and the new attorney general "were the same kind actually. Hoover was a Republican from beginning to end." The director had his men check Mitchell's telephone for wiretaps and "the locks on the windows and doors" of his apartment at the Watergate.[14] With the campaign to declare Dr. King's birthday a national holiday gathering momentum, Hoover sent Agnew information on the civil rights leader's "highly immoral personal behavior." The vice president wanted "to be thoroughly conversant with all of that because if the crisis comes where we need to throw it, he will." Agnew, as Garry Wills once noted, was Nixon's Nixon—a baiter of blacks and kids. Hoover understood ("the President can't say some of the things the Vice President can"), and he admired Agnew "largely because he spoke out and named names." When Agnew's aide, Kent Crane, told the director "that 'you two' are birds of a feather," Hoover said he "was glad to be in that company."[15]

When Agnew asked for material on the Black Panther party and Ralph Abernathy of the Southern Christian Leadership Conference, the FBI dug into the files. "He wants to be able to let them have it," Hoover surmised. Agnew had expressed an interest in "especially graphic incidents that could be used as examples, which Governor Ronald Reagan has done a beautiful job with."[16] While the director briefed the vice president on the Panthers' financial contributors, especially "the entertainment industry people" and the whole "question of liberal support," the Los Angeles FBI office sent a letter from a fictitious person to Hollywood gossip columnist Army Archerd regarding Jane Fonda and her support for the party. "Jane and one of the Panthers," the letter read, had led the following refrain at a rally: "We will kill Richard Nixon, and any other M . . . F . . . who stands in our way."[17]

In April 1970, the same month that Agnew expressed his interest in "especially graphic incidents," FBI officials approved the mailing of a letter to another gossip columnist suggesting that actress Jean Seberg, star of *Paint Your Wagon* and *Airport* and a Black Panther supporter with a long history of psychiatric problems and suicide attempts, was pregnant by a party member. The Los Angeles office hoped to "cheapen her image," and gossip columnist Joyce Harber did publicize Seberg's pregnancy in the *Los Angeles Times*, without mentioning any names. Haber said "the FBI did not plant me directly because I don't know anyone in the FBI." The FBI claims that the original plan was canceled, an unconvincing denial of responsibility given the sequence of events and the director's close interest in the episode.

On the same day that the Haber column appeared, Hoover sent reports on Seberg to the White House. Even if the FBI's disclaimer is accepted at face value, it is clear that senior FBI officials felt no moral revulsion in any of the episode's outcomes.[18]

Seberg's problems only began with the *Los Angeles Times* piece. On June 8 the *Hollywood Reporter* identified her as the white actress carrying a Black Panther's child, and on August 7, nearly seven months pregnant, Seberg tried to kill herself by swallowing an overdose of sleeping pills. On August 23 she gave birth by Caesarian to a girl weighing less than four pounds. The August 24 edition of *Newsweek* said the father of her unborn child was not a former husband, the French novelist and World War II fighter pilot Romain Gary, but "a black activist she met in California"—presumably Los Angeles Panther Ray ("Masai") Hewitt. Based on information acquired through a wiretap, Hewitt emerged as the FBI's principal designated-father. The FBI also pursued an investigation of Seberg's prior relationship with sometime Panther Hakim Abdullan Jamal (Allen Donaldson), a cousin of Malcolm X. On August 25 Seberg's baby died, prompting a Division Five executive to advise his colleagues "of premature birth and death of child of" this "supporter of extremist Black Panther Party," this "alleged promiscuous and sex perverted white actress."

Four months later, on December 29, the FBI placed Seberg's name on the Security Index. One West Coast agent, in a reference to Seberg and Hewitt fraught with racist and sexual anxieties, reportedly said (according to *Jean Seberg Story* author David Richards), "I wonder how she'd like to gobble my dick while I shove my .38 up that black bastard's ass?" Seberg eventually sued *Newsweek* and two other publications which picked up the story, winning a modest award of $8,333. Gary, the real father of the dead baby, received $2,777. Not surprisingly, the FBI monitored the suit closely, from the day it was filed to the day of the court's final decision.

Jean Seberg's discovery, many years later, that she had been a COINTELPRO target fed her paranoia. She killed herself in Paris, in August 1979, by taking an overdose of barbiturates and alcohol. "Destroyed by the FBI," Romain Gary said, with some exaggeration. Seberg had been having trouble carrying the baby even before the *Newsweek* story broke. Gary committed suicide a year later, in his apartment on the Left Bank. By then, Hakim Jamal had been dead for seven years, murdered in Roxbury,

Massachusetts, by members of a black nationalist group called De Mau Mau, a crime that prompted the Boston FBI office to request approval from headquarters "to delete subject from the Extremist Photograph Album." Ray Hewitt left the Panthers and found work on a construction crew. "What a way to go down in history," he reflected, after the Seberg story spilled out. "The black man who went to bed with a white woman."[19]

On May 18, 1970, a month after the Seberg operation started, Spiro Agnew requested Hoover's assistance in a White House campaign to destroy Ralph Abernathy's credibility. This campaign began when the director and Attorney General Mitchell discussed the tragedy on the campus of predominantly black Jackson State College. A confrontation in front of a women's dormitory ended with city police and Mississippi troopers opening fire with rifles, shotguns, and carbines loaded with military ammunition, and a submachine gun. Some 400 bullets and pieces of buckshot, including armor piercing shells from two 30.06 rifles, struck the dormitory in a twenty-eight second fusillade, killing two black youths, Phillip Gibbs and James Earl Green, and wounding twelve. "[All] nigger gals . . . [and] nigger males," the police said. Hoover said there seemed "to be substantial proof . . . that there was sniper fire on the troops from the dormitory before the troops fired." The only provocations were words, chants ("Pigs! Pigs! Pigs!") and obscenities ("motherfucker!"). Mitchell planned to visit Jackson, and he asked Hoover to find out if there were any plans to picket him. The director advised him not to worry. Roy Moore had a new Cadillac and a chauffeur ready to drive him around, and a squad of agents standing by "in case any disturbance takes place."[20]

Agnew spoke to Hoover that same day, May 18, about Jackson State and Kent State as well. Hoover described the Kent State massacre (four dead white students and nine wounded—including an ROTC cadet) as "six of one and a half dozen of another, as you can't say it was proper to shoot, but we found . . . they were throwing 7 pound rocks at the soldiers and they hit one Guardsmen in the back and knocked him down. There is just so much a human being can stand." The Bureau opened a civil rights investigation (KENFOUR), but Hoover had already formed a conclusion. The students had "severely provoked" the guardsmen.[21]

Focusing on Jackson State, Agnew charged Abernathy with inciting the demonstrations there as well as rioting in Atlanta and

Augusta. Agreeing with this assessment of Abernathy ("I commented that he is one of the worst"), Hoover promised to do everything possible when Agnew asked for "information" for "executive use." The vice president wanted to document "the involvement of those people"—"whether fleeing from looting or what is going on." According to the director's account, Agnew "said he saw a picture about Augusta showing some of the Negroes jumping out of store windows with loot and booty and fleeing and you never hear anything about that." When Hoover again asked what the FBI could do to help, Agnew said he wanted anything "that can ameliorate some of the impact," anything that might assist in "destroying Abernathy's credibility." The director sent over a write-up the next day that included gossip about Abernathy's private life and connections with "suspect organizations."[22] A few months later, when an independent presidential commission condemned the Jackson State shootings as "an unreasonable, unjustified overreaction," Agnew dismissed the report as "pablum for the permissivists." He sided instead with the view of a Hinds County grand jury and a Kennedy judge. Students participating in civil disorders, Harold Cox said, "must expect to be injured or killed."[23]

The FBI continued its assault on Martin Luther King's memory while helping Agnew make his case against Abernathy. In fact, Hoover began this campaign even before Nixon assumed his duties as commander in chief. On Janury 17, 1969, Division Five executive George Moore recommended a memo detailing "the extensive communist influence on King" be sent to Nixon and Mitchell immediately after the inauguration. The director approved the plan, personally delivering additional documentation regarding King's "highly immoral behavior." "'His basic problem was he liked white girls,'" John Ehrlichman recalled the director saying. "Hoover went on at great length. . . . It was pretty obvious. He was trying to rewrite history. . . . In the great marketplace of ideas, Hoover was trying to establish a position on the civil rights issue by impugning the morality and rectitude of Martin Luther King."[24]

From there, Division Five placed the field on alert for "any efforts by city, county, or state governments to pass resolutions commemorating or honoring King." Hoover himself approved a briefing, after House Internal Security Committee member John Ashbrook (R., Ohio) approached the Crime Records Division, on behalf of two members of a subcommittee from the House Judiciary Committee. Crime Records felt the congressmen might be able to keep a bill regarding King's birthday bottled up in Committee if "they realize King was a scoundrel." Cartha DeLoach said it was "a delicate matter—but can be handled very cautiously." A few days later, on April 3, 1969, the Atlanta field office proposed a "counterintelligence action against Coretta Scott King and/or the continuous projection of the public image of Martin Luther King." This plan, like the House subcommittee briefing, was probably aborted. "The Bureau," as Division Five advised the Atlanta office, "does not desire counterintelligence action against Coretta King of the nature you suggest *at this time* [emphasis added]."[25]

Division Five was more receptive when DeLoach alerted "a friendly newspaper contact, on a strictly confidential basis," to the alleged plans of Mrs. King and Rev. Abernathy "to keep King's assassination in the news by pulling the ruse of maintaining that King's murder was definitely a conspiracy."[26] Crime Records also found the time "to choose a friendly, capable author, or the Reader's Digest, and proceed with a book" on the so-called MURKIN case—that is, a book on the FBI's civil rights investigation of King's murder.[27] DeLoach said there was a real need "to have a book . . . on college and high school library shelves so that the future would be protected." When Hoover approved the project, DeLoach tried to reach an agreement with *Reader's Digest* and a writer, Jim Bishop, with whom Crime Records had worked in the past. "Even though Bishop . . . [was] 'somewhat pompous and a little overbearing at times,'" DeLoach conceded, "he nonetheless has both the name and ability to produce a book on the King case which would give proper credit to the outstanding work done by the FBI."[28]

By early 1970 the FBI felt secure enough to back off a bit. When Congressman Peter Rodino, Jr. (D., N.J.), introduced yet another bill, the fifteenth since the assassination, to declare King's birthday a national holiday, Crime Records chief Thomas Bishop said no action was needed. Although passage of "such a bill would be a national calamity," Bishop argued that congressmen like Rodino were simply looking for black votes in their districts. The chances of any bill passing were "virtually nil," principally because Crime Records had already briefed the House leadership. In the Senate, Roman Hruska (R., Neb.), a member of the Judiciary Committee and a Bureau ally, chaired the Subcommittee on Federal Charters, Holidays, and Celebrations. Senator McClellan sat on the Subcommittee while Senator Eastland chaired the full Judiciary Committee. Bishop also said the FBI could count on the Senate minority leader, Hugh Scott (R., Penn.).[29] Hoover and Tolson agreed with Bishop's assessment, and the FBI did not mobilize in response to the Rodino bill. Bureau interest in such matters, nonetheless, remained high. When the Washington Committee for a Martin Luther King Holiday sponsored a program at Howard University, FBI agents and informers showed up to digest the speeches of Fannie Lou Hamer and Congressman John Conyers (D., Mich.). Division Five wrote everything up, and the director sent it on, once again, to the president, the vice president, and the attorney general.[30]

While Hoover worked on the King birthday case and handled special assignments for Nixon, Agnew, and Mitchell, FBI agents in the field and at headquarters tended to the community surveillance programs. At the time Lyndon Johnson left the White House, the Bureau operated some 3,300 "racial ghetto-type informants." That number jumped to nearly 7,500 by the end of Nixon's first term, with individual field offices engaged in crash programs to develop "Negro racial informants and Negro ghetto informants," even if their territory had no "militant black extremist organizations" in existence or "attempting to organize." For all practical purposes, the extent of black nationalism was irrelevant. FBI policy required every field office "to thoroughly saturate every level of activity in the ghetto."[31]

Other specialized FBI informant programs, including BLACPRO, also expanded during the Nixon years. Hoover approved the recruitment of eighteen-year-olds and a general escalation of "the scope and depth of the coverage provided by current racial ... informants." Each field office submitted the names of informants with at least two of the following characteristics: "above average imagination and initiative"; "leadership ability"; "intelligence"; "unique knowledge or ability"; and "a willingness to expand his current affairs." Division Five hoped to create an elite informant squad and to send its members around the country and the world in pursuit of "domestic subversive, black militant, or New Left movements."[32] Information supplied by the informants led to the confiscation of explosives and the indictment of black radicals in Detroit, Richmond, and elsewhere on weapons and conspiracy charges. Most of the information provided, however, was far less dramatic, serving only as fodder for the files. The following report, filed on the

Black United Liberation Front (BULF) in Philadelphia, Pennsylvania, was typical:

> Informant advised . . . that the BULF is not going to buy a type setting machine. They are buying an electric typewriter. . . . Members are fighting and drinking more than ever. . . . There are only four persons staying at the BULF Headquarters now, SCHELL, RONNIE, CURTIS and PHIL. ROBIN stays there from 9 am until closing time but no longer sleeps there. She said SCHELL is 'fed up' and seems to be 'blowing his stack.' He is even talking about getting a job.[33]

Mundane information would not satisfy the Nixon White House. In June 1970, when the Ad Hoc Interagency Committee on Intelligence, the Huston Plan Committee that Hoover chaired, met to discuss the Panthers and the Muslims and especially "black student extremist influence," the director mentioned the events of the past school year: a total of 227 college disturbances and 530 secondary-school disturbances had "racial overtones." Demanding more informant coverage of "militant black student groups," along with more "live" informant coverage of "unaffiliated black militants," the Huston Plan Committee recommended recruitment among "former members of the Armed Forces presently attending college." The administration also needed additional nonhuman sources, including the "maximum use of communications interceptions," to determine the extent of foreign involvement in black student extremist matters.

The foreign angle was particularly important. Here again, the FBI, along with officials from other departments and agencies with internal security responsibilities, lumped everyone together—black students with white students, dissidents with spies and saboteurs, 1960s' militants in the United States with 1930s' popular fronters in Great Britain. Although Tom Charles Huston himself dismissed "old line Communist fronts" as "largely irrelevant to our current problem," the Huston Plan Committee pointed out that "H. A. R. (Kim) Philby, Guy Burgess, and Donald Maclean were all students at Cambridge during the depression period of the 1930's and were in the vanguard of what was then the New Left.[34]

Though Hoover eventually blocked the formal implementation of the Huston Plan Committee's reckless recommendations, he supported the escalation of surveillance aimed at black students. Nixon had been in office for a month when the FBI's four-year-old Columbia field office reported on its success in notifying the draft board of black student militants in 1-A status and developing black informants at South Carolina universities. The Norfolk field office plotted the dismissal of a faculty member at "the predominantly Negro Norfolk State College," while the Pittsburgh office contemplated counterintelligence plans to "neutralize" a person who had "been named coordinator of a drive to recruit black students for scholarships at the University of Pittsburgh." Even the Butte field office mobilized after discovering that a class at the University of Montana required a book entitled *The Student as Nigger*. The University had also hired a black man "to teach Afro-American classes at UM," the Bureau noted, "when the approximately twenty black students" complained they "had no one to relate to."[35] In California, the FBI assisted Governor Reagan's investigation into the use of public funds and facilities to further black extremist activities on the campuses.[36]

The scope of the dissemination and the general interest in black faculty and black student groups was routine. Black student unions (BSUs), quite common by the late 1960s, particularly after 1966 when Amiri Baraka formed one of the first at San Francisco State, were natural targets for the FBI. Investigative criteria—advocacy of "scholarships for black students, more black instructors on the faculty, and introduction of black and African courses in the curriculum"—had been established by the summer of 1968. But Hoover did not drop the minimum age of campus informants from twenty-one to eighteen until September 1970, on the grounds that the FBI needed to counter "violence-oriented youthful groups" and "fanatics . . . at large who are at war with the Government and the American people." Two months later, in November, Hoover approved the automatic investigation of "all BSUs and similar organizations organized to project the demands of black students." At that point, the FBI selected targets "regardless of their past or present involvement in disorders." The Inspection Division estimated a total new case load of 3,500 extending to 750 black student groups on 500 two- and four-year campuses.[37]

A number of black student unions and other student groups attracted the attention of FBI men assigned to the COINTELPRO desks. In Jackson, Mississippi, special agent Thomas Fitzpatrick offered the following rationale for placing a SNCC-affiliated Political Action Committee on the counterintelligence list: "The Tougaloo College PAC activities have, in the recent past, pertained to the sponsoring of on campus out-of-state militant Negro speakers, voter-registration drives, and African cultural seminars and lectures. Additionally, the group has vocally condemned various publicized injustices to the civil rights of Negroes in Mississippi."[38] Neither local FBI agents nor the executives in Washington saw anything wrong with these criteria. Tougaloo was as an "anything goes" campus, "a very liberal school," a "staging area for civil rights and militant Negro activities in Mississippi."[39] So Jackson agents shared informant reports with city and state police officials, and otherwise worked to intimidate the student body.[40] They even proposed to "neutralize" Tougaloo College itself, a suggestion that prompted Division Five to remind them about the Political Action Committee and its chairman, Howard Spencer, "since Tougaloo College, per se, is not a counterintelligence target."[41]

Division Five settled for a letter to the SNCC office in Atlanta implying that one or more Tougaloo PAC members were police informants; and a vague plan to label Jan Hillegas, a Southern Conference Educational Fund field worker who had recruited on the Tougaloo campus for "the Women's Liberation Movement in Mississippi," as an informer for the Mississippi Sovereignty Commission. Another action involved a rumor campaign against Tougaloo student and antipoverty worker Muhammad Kenyatta (then known as Donald Jackson). To drive him out of the state, the Bureau accused Kenyatta of various criminal activities, including the theft of a television set from the campus.[42] The most routine operations in Mississippi involved a series of leaks to *Jackson Daily News* columnist James ("Jackson Jimmy") Ward. The FBI eventually reached beyond the Tougaloo campus to black groups at other campuses, from area high schools to the University of Mississippi, Delta State College, and (of course) Jackson State. Bureau agents sometimes had city police and state troopers arrest "Negro Black Militants" from these schools on minor infractions. Nuisance arrests.[43]

The FBI continued to share the information gathered by its informants in the ghetto and on the campuses with the Central Intelligence Agency, the National Security Agency, state and local police, and various foreign intelligence agencies—though there is no hard evidence that the Bureau went as far as the

House Internal Security Committee. Chairman Richard Ichord (D., Mo.) ran file checks on the African National Congress and the Southwest Africa People's Organization for David Loewe of the South African embassy.[44] At the recommendation of CIA executive Richard Ober, the FBI submitted the names of black militants, Panthers and SNCC members, among others, to the agency for inclusion on its New York mail-opening "watch list." When requesting the assistance of the National Security Agency in "racial extremist matters," Hoover cast a net broad enough to encompass most every group interested in race and class, from the Panthers to the Society of Friends. The FBI submitted the names of "white and black racial extremists" ("natural allies of foreign enemies of the United States," Hoover said) directly to the NSA's so-called MINARET "watch list." The FBI also fed names to a computerized Secret Service list of 5,500 Black Nationalists that included the names of Jackie Robinson and Roy Wilkins.[45]

One of the FBI's own listings, the Agitator Index, included among its 1,191 names that of Jesse Jackson—the subject of a Racial Matters-Black Nationalists investigation. At least thirty-four human and other informants (taps, bugs, trash covers, and so forth) reported on Jackson's activities at any given time, and the FBI eventually opened parallel files on Operation Breadbasket and PUSH.[46] Hoover abolished the Agitator Index in the spring of 1971 and the more pervasive Security Index in the fall, following congressional repeal of the emergency detention provision (Title II) of the Internal Security Act of 1950, and replaced them with an Administrative Index (ADEX). Since FBI officials deemed subversives an "even greater" threat "than before repeal of the Act, since they no doubt [felt] safer . . . to conspire in the destruction of the country," they continued "the essence of the Security Index," and the Agitator Index as well, "under Presidential powers." John Mitchell approved the name change, and the new ADEX included "four categories representing degrees of dangerousness."[47]

Black activists were well represented on the ADEX. Category I listed the names of "national leaders of black extremist separatist organizations," and Category II the names of "secondary leadership," along with "active participants"—that is, people who furthered "the aims and purposes of the revolutionary or black extremist separatist organization with which affiliated." Category III listed "rank-and-file membership," along with the name of any "individual who, although not a member of or participant in activities of revolutionary organizations or considered an activist in affiliated fronts, has exhibited a revolutionary ideology." Category IV listed *"individuals whose activities do not meet criteria of Categories I, II, or III* [emphasis added]." All four categories were purposefully elastic, allowing the inclusion of "the new breed of subversive," the free-lance black radical who had "a seething hatred of the white establishment" and might at any time "assassinate, explode, or otherwise destroy white America." A parallel Reserve Index incorporated into ADEX the names of persons who did not engage in subversive activities ("teachers, writers, lawyers, etc."), but "were nonetheless influential in espousing their respective philosophies."[48]

If skin color attracted a casual interest, a politics of any stripe attracted the more serious interest of the Division Five COINTELPRO agents.[49] The Key Black Extremist (KBE) Program, the most refined Nixon-era list and the last of the targeting mechanisms for the counterintelligence program, had its roots in an October 1970 FBI racial conference. Noting the need for "intensified coverage on a group of black extremists who are either key leaders or activists and are particularly extreme, agitative, anti-Government, and vocal in their calls for terrorism and violence," the racial conference demanded the systematic identification and neutralization of such persons. "Certain elements" were simply "more likely to resort to or order terrorism as a tactic," and these types required "particular attention."[50]

Headquarters solicited nominations from the field, stressed the need for "initiative and imagination," and issued the inevitable guidelines for cataloguing Key Black Extremists and selecting candidates for timely counterintelligence action. Division Five listed the names of all KBEs in the ADEX (Priority I) and pasted their pictures in the Black Nationalist Photograph Album; monitored all bank accounts, safe-deposit boxes, investments, and other financial assets, as well as all travel and "financial arrangements for such travel"; obtained handwriting specimens and tape recordings of inflammatory statements and kept them in "the national security file" at the FBI laboratory; "vigorously investigated" all "possible" violations of federal law; processed individual reports every ninety days; and checked federal income tax records annually. On this last point, when the FBI requested the tax returns of seventy-two Key Black Extremists, the IRS honored every request, without asking any questions.[51]

With regard to the monitoring of financial assets, the FBI overlooked no bank account, even an account in the low two figures. A spot check at a Chester, Pennsylvania, bank revealed a grand total of $44.32 in the name of the National Black Economic Development Conference. The Invaders' bank account in Memphis totaled $33. The FBI obtained this sort of information routinely, through sources at the banks that held the accounts. Such sources were ubiquitous, in banks and other private-sector institutions, and they made things easier for field agents. It made no difference whether the Bureau wanted information from a source in a bank or the help of a source in "the membership section of the National Rifle Association" to purge a black militant member. The FBI mobilized all its resources.[52]

Division Five executives also tried to make things easier for field agents by expanding the Racial Calendar once again in late 1970, and by February 1971 they included "telephone numbers of black, New Left, and other ethnic extremists" in the Computerized Telephone Number File (CTNF)—an investigative tool originally confined to interstate gambling cases. They "entered into the CTNF" the names of all "black extremist groups, black extremist Security Index [ADEX] subjects, and individuals included in the Black Nationalist Photograph Album." The Photo Album alone contained the names of 484 activists.[53]

An even more valuable investigative technique, electronic surveillance, supplemented the "extremely valuable" CTNF. Though FBI wiremen pulled the plug on the Stanley Levison tap during the Nixon years, they installed new taps and bugs in other places. As of March 1971 the Bureau had a microphone hidden in Huey Newton's San Francisco home, and operated at least thirteen telephone surveillances. Six of these were on Black Panther offices (in San Francisco, Oakland, Los Angeles, Chicago, New Haven, and the Bronx), and another was on Newton's phone.[54] Mostly, the information uncovered by the Panther wiretaps had to do with pregnancies, transportation and telephone problems, the lack of heat in offices, calls home to mom. Hoover justified his request to Mitchell for a continuation of the tap on the Panthers' Chicago office on the grounds that it provided valuable information on such topics as Panther attempts "to organize the black workers employed by the Chicago Transit Authority."[55]

This justification contrasts with Hoover's argument when originally requesting authority to tap Panther offices in San

Francisco and Chicago. One Panther leader, the director wrote in April 1969, "has been involved in the direction of racial disturbances, has attempted to obtain dynamite to blow up public buildings, and has stated that if contact could be made with Negroes on the White House staff a plan might be formulated to poison people attending functions there." Party members, the director added, "possess guns" and "use the telephone extensively." That last point was perhaps the one that mattered most. On the whole, the wiretap transcripts "show how far removed the Panther reality was from its bloody guerrilla mystique." "Some of the things we used to hear on the wiretaps were funny," said William Cohendet, the FBI agent assigned to the Panther squad in San Francisco. "It reminded me of *Amos and Andy*. Fundamentally, I think, black people are jovial, happy and fun loving."[56]

The other six FBI wiretaps in place as of March 1971 were on the telephones of two nonwhite "racial extremist groups" (one of which was the Tampa-based Junta of Military Organizations), two "militant black extremist group members" (including a SNCC activist), yet another black extremist group functionary, and a member of a "racial group." Of these unidentified taps, one was on the telephone of the Jewish Defense League in New York, and another was on the telephone of an SDS affiliate in Chicago, the Worker Student Alliance. This modest number of taps and the equally modest number of bugs must be balanced against FBI access to the transcripts based on the hundreds of electronic surveillances installed by state and local police. In New Haven alone the wiring extended beyond the Panthers to include antiwar activists, Yale faculty, journalists, lawyers, housewives, and professional gamblers.[57]

Bureau agents used electronic surveillance less frequently during the Nixon years than they had during the Kennedy years or the early Johnson years. Between 1960 and 1966 they planted 738 "microphone sources" and an unknown number of wiretaps, informing the Justice Department of only 158 of the mikes.[58] "The risk potential," as Mark Felt put it in 1971, in reference to another illegal technique, "specialized mail coverage," was simply too high "in today's world of civil libertarians and 'blabbermouths'" to continue such extensive surveillances.[59] Hoover had first cut electronic surveillances in response to "hearings on bugging" by the Senate Subcommittee on Administrative Practice and Procedure, and the willingness of "hostile Department attorneys" like Ramsey Clark to send the Subcommittee "electronic surveillance memoranda dating back to 1925."[60] The controversy over who authorized the King wiretaps, Robert Kennedy or J. Edgar Hoover, compounded the FBI's problems. After documents produced in the Selective Service Act case against Muhammad Ali revealed that the ex-champ was overheard on one of the King taps, Hoover sent letters defending the FBI's position to Nixon, Agnew, and Mitchell.[61] He also sent letters of thanks to North Carolina television executive and future United States Senator Jesse Helms and anyone else who took the Bureau's side. When Congressman Robert L. Leggett (D., Cal.) asked for a briefing on the controversy, in contrast, the FBI ran his name through the files, noted his vote against HUAC's appropriation back in 1965, and then declined to help him. For Hoover, this was a standard test for distinguishing friends from enemies.[62]

A more restrained use of electronic surveillance and other questionable investigative techniques, including mail openings and break-ins, had no effect on the quantity of intelligence collected. The Nixon administration faced the same problem the Johnson administration faced: the need to organize and evaluate all the racial matters items the FBI kept sending over. Attorney General Mitchell and his deputy, Richard Kleindienst, planned to refine the intelligence apparatus. They wanted more "computer power," more control over the Interdivisional Intelligence Unit (IDIU) and the other Great Society things they had inherited. They ended up with an absolute mishmash of bureaucratic reform.

As a first step, in March and April 1969, Mitchell and Kleindienst, with the help of Secretary of Defense Melvin Laird, developed an Interdepartmental Action Plan for Civil Disturbances. The three men designated the attorney general ("the logical choice") as "the chief civilian officer in charge of coordinating all Federal Government activities relating to civil disturbances," including the accumulation of "raw intelligence data." Three months later, in July 1969, Mitchell created an ad hoc Intelligence Evaluation Committee (IEC), selecting Cartha DeLoach to chair it. Membership included the heads of the Justice Department's Civil Rights, Internal Security, and Criminal Divisions, and the Community Relations Service; and representatives from the IDIU, the Secret Service, and Army Intelligence. In late 1970, in the aftermath of the Huston Plan, Mitchell secretly resconstituted the IEC as a permanent body, expanding its membership to include representatives from the CIA and the National Security Agency. The new Committee held its first meeting on December 3 in John Dean's office, with Division Five executive George Moore representing a skeptical Hoover. The Committee met sporadically until 1974, when it was finally abolished and its functions absorbed by yet another new bureaucracy—the Civil Disturbance Unit, formerly the IDIU.[63]

Intelligence Evaluation Committee staff, together with staff from the old IDIU, processed some 42,000 incoming intelligence reports per annum in the years before the Civil Disturbance Unit organized. The FBI sent over most of the data.[64] Field agents read "all appropriate black extremist publications" in search of names to index, and their annual "subversive" and "extremist" case loads increased during Nixon's first term from 30,000 to 45,000 and from 17,000 to 25,000 respectively. Many of the individual reports forwarded to the IDIU and the IEC, moreover, were quite detailed. A strike organized by "blind black workers" at an Industries of the Blind plant in North Carolina rated sixteen pages. Division Five sent another copy of the report on this strike, based on information supplied by a state police intelligence unit, to the Civil Rights Division.[65]

While forwarding information to John Mitchell's new bureaucracy, Hoover embraced at least one of the attorney general's other priorities—namely, the emphasis on "computer power." To keep track of black and antiwar activists "against whom warrants are not outstanding," in February 1970 the director approved a "Stop Index" program for the computer in the FBI National Crime Information Center. Launched in January 1967, the Crime Information Center provided computerized searches for criminal histories, and was used most often by state and local police officers when making routine stops of motorists who had committed moving-code or vehicular-safety violations. By inserting a "Stop Index" for black and antiwar dissidents, Hoover had politicized the Crime Information Center and its law-enforcement mission.[66]

FBI files provided much of the information for yet another surveillance bureaucracy, the Special Service Staff (SSS) of the Internal Revenue Service. IRS officials set up the SSS in the summer of 1969 after IRS Commissioner Randolph W. Thrower, a former FBI agent, met with Tom Charles Huston and Arthur Burns, Nixon's economic counselor and later chairman of the

Federal Reserve Board. When Paul Wright, the IRS executive selected to run the Special Service Staff, told Hoover that Senator McClellan's PERM had asked for files on twenty-two groups, the director agreed to put the new bureaucracy on his dissemination list. He hoped to "deal a blow to dissident elements." In all, Bureau executives sent over COINTELPRO and other racial matters files (11,818 separate reports), principally because SSS staff did not feel competent to define an "ideological organization." Relying on the FBI for direction, IRS agents processed the reports in the basement of the Internal Revenue Service building under "red seal" security.[67]

The Nixon-era Special Service Staff institutionalized something the IRS and the FBI had dabbled in since the Franklin D. Roosevelt years.[68] Moving beyond Senator McClellan's 22 mostly left-wing groups to 77 organizations by the end of 1969, SSS files exploded thereafter. By August 1973, when IRS Commissioner Donald Alexander abolished the SSS just as it was preparing to put everything on the computer, the listings included 2,873 organizations and 8,585 individuals. The FBI contributed a list of more than 2,300 groups and more than 80 percent of the individual names in five basic categories: "liberal establishment," "New Left," "antiwar," "white right-wing extremist and racist," and "black and ethnic."[69] In all, SSS held files on fifty chapters of the National Urban League; the U.S. Civil Rights Commission; the Head Start program; the Ford Foundation; a black congressman from Detroit, Charles Diggs (and presumably all other black elected officials); and even "persons associated with or 'disassociated' with various racially oriented groups." None of this satisfied the White House however. "Dominated by Democrats," in the Nixon administration view, the IRS was unwilling to go as far as the president intended.[70]

While monitoring black activists with the help of the Special Service Staff and other surveillance appendages, the FBI pursued its other assigned "racial matters" task, the investigation of alleged violations of federal civil rights law, in the usual manner. Civil Rights Division chief Jerris Leonard, who was himself considered by a few of his own attorneys to be in "no way committed to civil rights" ("clearly in the McCarthy mold," "kind of a vile guy"), said the "Division had big problems with the FBI," particularly on police brutality matters, in the beginning. "We had to prod the Bureau at times in order to get them to respond to our requests. It might take three memoranda to them instead of one or two." But the Bureau came around, Leonard continued. "The fact of the matter is, they did the tough interviews in civil rights cases. . . . By the time I left the Civil Rights Division, the earlier problems had generally gone away."[71] Leonard's words could have been spoken by Harold Tyler or Burke Marshall or John Doar, three predecessors who also considered the FBI's performance terrible "in the beginning" but nonetheless believed that the FBI eventually came around. In a sense, the box memo of the Kennedy-era Civil Rights Division had given way to the three-memo cajoling of the Nixon-era Civil Rights Division.

Hoover told Egil Krogh at the White House that 2,301 agents were working in the "civil rights . . . area alone, and it has almost paralyzed us." He did not tell Krogh that most of those agents had racial intelligence responsibilities, not Civil Rights enforcement responsibilities. The Justice Department continued to request numerous "limited or preliminary" investigations of civil rights complaints. "They have been dumping them on us by the hundreds," Hoover said. But as Assistant Director Alex Rosen noted in July 1970, a time when the surveillance programs were flourishing, the FBI did "not have any full investigations in civil rights matters pending at this time."[72]

Eight months after Rosen wrote those words, on the evening of March 1, Hoover and his constant companion for the last forty years, Clyde Tolson, saw a "negro girl . . . in the 9th Street elevator" as they left their offices and headed home. The young woman, a file clerk assigned to the main FBI headquarters building, "had an extremely large hairdo which Mr. Tolson felt was a wig," prompting both the director and the associate director to ask who she was. The FBI executive who received the identification assignment located a likely candidate ("we feel [name deleted] may be empl Mr. Tolson referring to"), noting that "many of our female empls wear wigs of different types in accordance with current fashion and we have not objected to this practice." Upon hearing this, Tolson wrote: "Transfer to Ident Bldg. T." By scribbling a simple "Yes. H." next to his friend's words, Hoover banished the "negro girl" with the Afro wig to the Identification Building. The director acted here as he always did, in opposition to any visible form of protest, whether real or imagined.[73]

All in all, the year 1971 was a trying one for Hoover. He had to terminate the counterintelligence programs, for "security reasons," following the burglary of an FBI resident agency in Media, Pennsylvania, by an antiwar group, the Citizens' Commission to Investigate the FBI, on March 8, the night of the first Ali-Frazier fight. The director also endured a broadside of criticism from House Democratic majority leader Hale Boggs of Louisiana and two Democratic contenders for the presidency, Senators George McGovern of South Dakota and Edmund Muskie of Maine. Then, the surfacing of an FBI memo recording surveillance of Muskie and others attending the nationwide Earth Day environmental rallies further embarrassed the Bureau, despite White House press secretary Ron Ziegler's attempt to dismiss the resultant publicity as "blatantly political." In a sense, Ziegler was right. A Nixon aide had specifically requested an FBI report on Earth Day. All this paled in the face of the Media burglary. The Citizens' Commission liberated approximately 1,000 pieces of Bureau paper, sending a steady stream of samples to the press and members of Congress throughout the months of March and April.

In addition to the counterintelligence programs, the pilfered FBI documents compromised the Ghetto Informant Program and several other community surveillance programs aimed at black America. For Hoover, it was a public relations nightmare. The documents revealed surveillance of black student groups, the names of racial matters informants, the Black Panther party wiretaps, and miscellaneous pieces of surveillance paraphernalia. "Informant loss" was "moderate," Division Five said. "Most of the sources compromised could possibly be replaced within [a] reasonable period of time." The most "potentially . . . damaging item," one of William Sullivan's men concluded, "involved our interest in various Black Student Union groups. . . . Unfriendly critics could seek to portray our investigations as invasion of academic freedom or racially inspired investigations."[74]

Hoover had already given John Mitchell a more alarmist "damage assessment." With regard to one of the black organizations identified in the Media papers, James Forman's National Black Economic Development Conference, the director said the informants named in the Media papers were "in serious personal jeopardy." "Even death is a possibility," he predicted, mentioning the Panthers and Angela Davis's sister, a student at Swarthmore College and best childhood friend of Carole Robertson, one of the victims of Birmingham's Sixteenth Street Baptist

Church bombing, as extremists who might kill someone. Fania Davis was capable of "fatal violence," Hoover told Mitchell. She "intended to foment revolutions after she graduated," and had led a black student sit-in at the Swarthmore admissions office. That sit-in ended, the director added, only when the College president dropped dead of a heart attack.[75]

Attorney General Mitchell wanted the FBI to issue a press release urging the media not to print the purloined documents. He intended to appeal to patriotism, to emphasize the harm to the national security. Hoover would not do it. Instead, he urged the Justice Department, in the words of FBI legal counsel Dwight J. Dalbey, to "sponsor enactment of legislation similar to The Official Secrets Act which is a part of English law." "If we had such an act at this time," Dalbey reasoned, "it could be used against any person or organization, including the new media, which misused the data or failed to return upon demand." In the interim, the FBI looked for the Media burglars. But the director's agents never found them; the MEDBURG case never closed.[76]

Hoover's problems compounded. Under the sponsorship of the Committee for Public Justice (CPJ) and the Woodrow Wilson School of Public and International Affairs, a group of academics, journalists, celebrities, and former Justice Department lawyers met in October 1971 for an investigating-the-FBI conference at Princeton University. Their agenda included the Bureau's civil rights investigations as well as its domestic intelligence investigations. Arthur Schlesinger, Ramsey Clark, John Doar, and Roger Wilkins attended, and Burke Marshall, then deputy dean of the Yale Law School, chaired the conference. D. Robert Owen, the former Civil Rights Division attorney who had presented the grand jury case against the persons indicted in Neshoba County for denying Schwerner, Chaney, and Goodman their civil rights, and Victor Navasky, author of *Kennedy Justice*, were there, too. The FBI described Marshall as "no friend of the Bureau," Doar as "obnoxious," and Navasky "as a Kennedy apologist."[77] Intending to "handle" this "group of anti-FBI bigots," Hoover had his Crime Records agents brief at least fifteen of the FBI's "good friends in the news media" and "on the Hill."[78]

Hoover was still troubled by the Media burglary and the Princeton Conference on May Day 1972. In most every way it was an uneventful day in his life—nine hours at the office, dinner with Tolson, a late evening phone call to retired special agent/chauffeur and then all-around handyman James Crawford. Hoover wanted Crawford to come by the next morning, to help decide where to plant some new rose bushes just delivered by a nursery. After speaking with Crawford, Hoover went to bed. "Another May Day had passed," as his biographer noted, "without the Revolution he had predicted for a May Day in 1920, fifty-two years before. He had been twenty-five years old then; now he was seventy-seven."[79]

Hoover died alone in his room on the morning of May 2, with his three black servants, all in their proper place, waiting for him to come down for breakfast. When he did not come out of his room on time, they crept up the stairs to find out what was wrong. Annie Fields, the live-in housekeeper, wearing her gray maid's outfit, led the way, followed by Crawford and his brother-in-law, special agent Tom Moton, the director's driver for the past three years. They found Hoover's naked body sprawled on the floor. Following a state funeral with full military honors, a hearse carried the thousand-pound casket containing the director's remains to Congressional Cemetery. As the chaplain of the United States Senate, Edward L. R. Elson, sprinkled a handful of dirt across the casket, "black children from the neighborhood hung on nearby gravestones." Elson had barely finished before the kids began "to snatch away the big cottonball mums from the outlying flower baskets," even before the men from the funeral home began to lower the casket into the earth.[80] Afterward, James Crawford went to work as a handyman for Tolson and to wait for his inheritance. He received $2,000 and half of Hoover's clothes. Sam Noisette, the director's black office retainer, received the other half. Annie Fields received $3,000. Hoover left the great bulk of his estate to Tolson.

The Media burglary, the Princeton conference, and even the director's death were only a prelude to the collapse of the FBI domestic intelligence apparatus. "One of the things people forget," as Nicholas Katzenbach said, "is that J. Edgar Hoover was just about as powerful as anyone in the United States of America. Congressmen were scared to death of him. They got very brave after he died." Indeed, a month after Hoover passed away, the Congressional Black Caucus held hearings on government lawlessness, and one of the witnesses, investigative columnist Jack Anderson, brought along dozens of files on black activists provided by a source in the FBI.[81] Though the media largely ignored the Black Caucus's closed-door hearings, with the director gone and the Watergate scandal unraveling, the issue was no longer whether the FBI could avoid a substantive congressional investigation of its domestic intelligence activities but whether the inevitable investigation could be properly managed.

The House Subcommittee on Civil and Constitutional Rights posed the most immediate threat. Chaired by a former FBI agent, Don Edwards (D., Cal.), "the Democratic members of this Subcommittee," in the FBI view, were "extreme liberals." Edwards's proposed hearings "on COINTELPRO could be most troublesome." Bureau officials knew they would fare better by working with the "far friendlier" James Eastland, chairman of the Senate Committee on the Judiciary, and chairman as well of a hastily created appendage to that Committee—the FBI Oversight Subcommittee. Eastland brought in John McClellan and Strom Thurmond to sit on the Oversight Subcommittee, and informed Hugh Clegg, the former Bureau executive and Mississippi native, "that if he received any complaints concerning the FBI he would pitch them into the wastepaper basket and not bother to call together the Committee." He later "indicated his willingness to initiate hearings at any time at [the FBI's] request," agreeing that any report "should not be made public."[82]

In the House, the FBI worked with another sweetheart committee, Richard Ichord's Internal Security Committee. The Committee launched its own investigation of FBI domestic intelligence operations in 1973, part of a more general campaign "to insure that the FBI," in its time of trouble, "is given full Congressional support." Ichord told Clarence Kelley, the Nixon appointee who replaced the hapless L. Patrick Gray III, the acting director who managed to embroil himself and the Bureau in the Watergate cover-up, that the FBI's surveillance responsibilities represented "the backbone of all the Government security programs." Committee staff director Robert M. Horner told Ichord the investigation was timely. "If we don't do it other committees will but probably with a restrictive purpose in mind." With FBI agents helping Horner's staff behind the scenes and senior FBI officials agreeing to testify in public session, HISC finally held its hearings in 1974. But no one paid much attention. The media had no interest in the "'chilling' effect" all the revelations of surveillance abuses had on the FBI. By the end of the year the hearings ended the way they had begun, in obscurity.[83]

Clarence Kelley presided over the FBI during its time of trouble, working with Ichord and other friends in the Congress to defend the Hoover-era record.[84] At best, his success was mixed. When the Edwards Subcommittee finally held its hearings on COINTELPRO, the new director's testimony did not go well. He seemed "to be at his inarticulate worst," as Sanford Ungar observed. When attempting to limit the Bureau's domestic intelligence activities, moreover, Kelley met resistance from the Justice Department. On one occasion, in August 1974, he requested guidance from the Department regarding Bureau responsibilities for gathering and reporting data on civil disturbances. He wanted to limit FBI coverage "to those particular situations which are of such a serious nature that Federal military personnel may be called upon for assistance." Henry E. Petersen, the chief of the Criminal Division, rejected the proposal on the grounds that it was "not practical."[85]

Kelley wanted to extract the FBI from its traditional surveillance role *and* from a looming civil rights quagmire. At the time, the most pressing concern of the Justice Department's Civil Disturbance Unit was the busing issue and attendant violence. In October 1974, the same month that Petersen issued his directive, the Department ordered the Bureau to maintain "a constant oversight monitoring of troubled areas" and "school desegregation disturbances" in South Boston. The White House also monitored FBI activities in South Boston regularly until mid-December 1974, a time when it became clear that the Bureau's surveillance network would collapse.[86]

Newspaper stories about such things as FBI spying on Robert Kennedy and civil rights leaders at the 1964 Democratic National Convention were followed by the death of the Bureau's last hope for a friendly congressional investigation. On January 14, 1975, the House abolished its Committee on Internal Security, the Red-hunting Committee that traced its roots back to Martin Dies. The Senate established a Select Committee to Study Governmental Operations with Respect to Intelligence Activities (the Church Committee) thirteen days later, and the House created it own Select Committee (the Pike Committee) on February 19.[87] Inheriting most of this Watergate fallout, the Gerald Ford administration suspected the FBI would be the least cooperative of all the intelligence community bureaucracies. In that respect, the FBI might prove to be the least troublesome. The administration knew it would have "little control over the intelligence investigation," but proposed to do the best it could. That meant stonewalling.[88]

As the administration suspected, it did not work. Watergate had damaged the national security mystique. Intelligence community files, including the FBI's records, opened to an unprecedented degree. Even Ichord asked to see his file. "Requests for such files are not new," as one White House adviser noted. "What is new is that people—particularly in Congress—no longer give up when they are told no." With the "band wagon" effect of the investigating committees becoming "increasingly partisan" and impossible to control, the White House worried about Congresswoman Bella Abzug (D., N.Y.) and Senator Walter Mondale (D., Minn.), and wondered "how long it will be before we hear from [Ronald] Reagan." Secretary of State Kissinger, among others, thought a series of executive orders restricting "all intelligence agencies except the FBI" would be the best way to contain the committees, to limit the dangers posed to the national security and the Republican party's political prospects.[89]

Amendments to the Freedom of Information Act (FOIA) in 1974 and the sweeping investigations of the intelligence community in 1975–1976 posed no threat to the national security. The Church and Pike Committees and a functioning FOIA threatened only an unrestrained and unaccountable domestic intelligence mission. No one was surprised when the committees zeroed in on the FBI and the racial matters investigations. Bureau surveillance of blacks had never been a well-kept secret, and the earlier revelations, everything from the Martin Luther King wiretaps to the Media papers, gave the investigators a hint of what they would find. There was plenty of fodder for the conspiracy theorists who actually believed that the Bureau "neutralized" Dr. King by killing him. More rational people, like Harris Wofford, John Kennedy's civil rights adviser, merely charged "Hoover and the FBI" with helping to "create the climate that invited King's assassination."[90]

Church Committee members and staff did the most thorough job of all the congressional investigating committees, preparing reports on the FBI campaigns against King and the Black Panther party and questioning many of the principals. They asked Cartha DeLoach about the Atlantic City operation and the activities of the Crime Records Division, while grilling William Sullivan and his former Division Five deputy, George Moore, about the COINTELPROs.[91] "When things blow up," another former Division Five executive said, "they turn their backs on you." The Church Committee brought in Gary Rowe to discuss the Klan wars, and several Great Society reformers, notably former Attorneys General Katzenbach and Clark, to testify regarding the community surveillance programs—and what they knew or did not know about the counterintelligence programs. John Doar, having just completed a yearlong assignment with the House Judiciary Committee as special counsel during the impeachment inquiry, contributed a report on the Bureau and the voting litigation campaign.[92]

The FBI rode it all out. In the House, when the Pike Committee's staff director asked W. Raymond Wannall, one of Kelley's aides and a die-hard Hoover loyalist, a question about the Bureau's political philosophy, he replied: "I don't think the FBI [has] a political philosophy." Another Hoover loyalist, James B. Adams, thought the whole thing much ado about nothing. The civil liberties issue, the racism issue, and the abuse of power issue were all irrelevant. "Is the public afraid of us," Adams asked, "or the fact that they can't walk the streets at night?" The full House never debated that question. But with visions of political pendulums swinging back, the House voted to suppress the Pike Committee's final report following the unauthorized disclosure of information from that report to the *Village Voice*.[93]

In the aftermath, the only reforms were administrative. Congress made no law restricting the use and abuse of the FBI's domestic intelligence resources. The chief executive offered directives and guidelines that could be repealed with the stroke of one future president's pen. The courts called no Bureau official to account for the King or Panther campaigns, but President Jimmy Carter's Justice Department did pursue three top executives for the handling of one other investigation: the Department obtained indictments against L. Patrick Gray, Edward S. Miller, and W. Mark Felt in April 1978, charging them with conspiracy to violate the civil rights of friends and relatives of the Weather Underground—specifically, for authorizing burglaries of their homes in a "hard hitting" and "innovative" search for the antiwar group's fugitive bombers.

There is an irony in those indictments and subsequent convictions of Felt and Miller. (The government dropped its charges against Gray.) All three indictments came under the old Reconstruction Era statute, Section 241 (as revised in the Civil Rights Act of 1968), and the case began in the Civil Rights Division before the attorney general moved it out to the Criminal Division. When Hoover was alive he constantly complained about the inadequacy of the statute, about how "the colored elements" kept bothering him with requests to enforce an unenforceable law. Section 241 was good enough to convict two FBI men, even if President Ronald Reagan pardoned them in March 1981, without even bothering to read the trial transcript, on the basis of their good-faith attempt to safeguard the national security.

Hoover would never have appreciated the irony, though he would have appreciated President Reagan's deference to the FBI's historic mission. The director spent the last fifty-three years of his life protecting the national security, always guarding the republic from the terrible and timeless communists, and in the 1960s guarding the republic against the new enemies of middle America. He opposed the nihilists on the fringes of the black nationalist movement at the end of the decade just as he had opposed the men and women in the mainstream of the civil rights movement at the beginning of the decade. Hoover will always be remembered for standing against the Red menace, for fueling the periodic hysterias of the Red scare. He should also be remembered for standing against justice for blacks, for fueling the fears of a black scare in the time of Kennedy, Johnson, and Nixon.

CONCLUSION

Racial Matters,
Racial Justice

J Edgar Hoover had always been a racist. He once referred to
Martin Luther King as a "burr head," if William Sullivan is
to be believed, and he marked hundreds of FBI documents, only
recently released under the Freedom of Information Act, with a
blue-ink scribble that reveals a racism that was casual when not
primitive. Hoover's FBI, moreover, had always had a racist com-
ponent in its organizational culture. The director and the men
around him had a private preference for segregation within
their own bureaucracy, and an institutional interest in letting it
alone in those areas of the country where separate-but-equal
ruled. The racism that infected the director and his FBI, however, cannot by itself explain the decision to stand against black
America. A final, absolute commitment to bring the weight of
Bureau resources against the black struggle for equality was not
made until the late summer of 1963, in the thirty-ninth year of
Hoover's directorship.

After intermittent conflict and constant preparedness over the
course of four decades (1919–1960), and then three years (1960–
1963) of continuous skirmishing over voting rights responsibilities and Freedom Ride failures, Hoover made his decision to destroy the civil rights movement in the wake of the March on
Washington. Only then did the director reconcile himself to the
fact that the movement would not go away, that the nation was
"in the midst of a social revolution with the racial movement at
its core," that his own bureaucracy was destined to play "an
integral part [in] this revolution." Hoover's decision came at a
time when he had the unqualified support of the segregationists,
who pestered him for documentation that all integrationists

355

were Reds, and the qualified support of the Kennedys, who approved his request to wiretap the telephone of the civil rights movement's most visible leader. In the years after 1963 the gathering white backlash offered Hoover a chance to move away from the segregationists and to form new alliances, and he did so without losing sight of his original enemies. The director developed a political agenda flexible enough to accommodate the destruction of Jim Crow America and even a sideshow war on the Ku Klux Klan, but not the promise and vision of the largest democratic mass movement of the twentieth century.

Responsibility for the FBI record does not stop with Hoover himself or his fellow internal security bureaucrats. In the forefront were elected officials and the men they brought with them to Washington, men who solicited "racial matters" intelligence from the FBI even as they pursued racial justice through the Civil Rights Act of 1964 and the Voting Rights Act of 1965. Bureau officials came to the movement with a contradictory mandate from the chief executive requiring them to protect black rights and to control black people, and they acted freely on that mandate according to their own priorities. No one in the Kennedy or Johnson administrations challenged their autonomy. No one questioned their pervasive intelligence gathering activities. The man who resisted the most, Ramsey Clark, presided over the birth of community surveillance. Bureau officials fought against the struggle for black equality for so long and with so much firepower because responsible government officials allowed them, and encouraged them, to do so.

During the March on Washington, SNCC Chairman John Lewis wanted to know which side the federal government was on. In 1979, fifteen years after Freedom Summer, a group of movement veterans gathered in Jackson, Mississippi, to reconsider those times and to try to answer Lewis's question. When one of them railed against "the subversion" of the movement by "the self-styled 'pragmatism' of those splendid scoundrels residing in the Camelot on the Potomac," he received "a cheering, standing ovation." One of the persons in the audience, *New York Times* columnist Anthony Lewis, said he came expecting a celebration of amazing change but instead found bitterness directed not at "the old segregationists of Mississippi but Northern liberals and, especially, the Kennedy and Johnson Administrations."[1] Neither the attempt of the Jackson radicals to tie the Kennedys "to Jim Eastland" nor Anthony Lewis's observation sufficiently

illuminates the complexities of those times. The conduct of the
FBI from Kennedy to Nixon has much to tell us about the way
we governed ourselves. No better gauge of the moral state of
United States' domestic policy exists than the history of the federal government's relationship with its most disadvantaged citizens; and that history cannot be understood without confronting the government's tolerance of the assaults Hoover's
bureaucracy launched against blacks. The FBI's conduct and the
executive leadership that tolerated it constitutes as much a legacy of the 1960s as the Civil Rights Act of 1964 or the Voting
Rights Act of 1965. "Racial matters" dossiers remain as much a
part of John Kennedy's New Frontier and Lyndon Johnson's
Great Society, let alone Richard Nixon's surveillance state, as
anything else they accomplished. When the FBI stood against
black people, so did the government.

Hoover explained his willingness to spy on blacks by reference to national security responsibilities; and he explained his
avoidance of civil rights enforcement responsibilities by reference to the constraints imposed by public opinion, federal law,
and the United States Constitution. Looked at in isolation, Hoover's defense of FBI behavior to the public and to the men in the
Justice Department and the White House seems reasonable. But
the totality of the FBI response to the black struggle shows that
Hoover viewed it as a threat to his way of life, his bureaucracy,
and his vision of a white, Christian, and harmonious America.
The nation's number-one law enforcement officer violated black
people's civil liberties under the guise of Red hunting, and
avoided civil rights enforcement under the guise of a commitment to the Constitution. Ultimately, his public justifications
collapse under the weight of his unbecoming secret deeds.

While spying on civil rights workers, Hoover refused to make
a commitment to protect them from anti–civil rights violence. A
commitment would have placed his bureaucracy in a vulnerable
position between states' rights advocates and civil rights activists calling for federal intervention. He offered federalism as a
defense against the movement's cultural and political challenges
as he offered federal surveillance to contain those challenges.
Unwilling to establish a national criminal police force to investigate segregationist terror and other violations of civil rights law,
he established a national political police force to investigate the
personal lives of civil rights workers. If Hoover's agents had devoted the same amount of time and energy to civil rights enforce-

ment as they devoted to dossier collecting and petty harassment, the controversy over the protection issue would have been far less pervasive and far less debilitating.

Because of its antagonistic attitudes and positions, the FBI adversely affected the course of black history in the time of Kennedy, Johnson, and Nixon. The FBI fed the internal tensions and rivalries among the myriad of groups that made up the mass-based civil rights movement, making it harder for the movement to present a united front during the years of urban riots and white backlash. By leaking derogatory information on activists to the media, the FBI dissuaded others from joining movement groups, from giving money, from otherwise supporting the black struggle. The FBI also limited the movement's potential by disseminating derogatory information to federal officials in the executive, legislative, and judicial branches of government—a practice that led, perhaps, to a lessened commitment to protect civil rights workers, and contributed, certainly, to John Kennedy's assessment of SNCC ("they're sons of bitches") and Lyndon Johnson's desperate search for subversives. During the last of the Johnson years and the first of the Nixon years, specific COINTELPRO actions against the Black Panther party and many of the lesser-known groups that made up the semisecret, hierarchical, and radical wing of the black movement provoked conflict and violence which might otherwise have been avoided. In some cases, individuals suffered psychological and physical harm.

From the director on down, the executives who ran the FBI constituted a disciplined, resourceful, and highly motivated political elite. Neither racism nor Red-hunting zealotry alone explain FBI officials' actions. The director and his closest aides were idealists who had long-term goals and tried to shape their political and social environment as well as their bureaucratic environment. They had their own dream of what America could and should be, no less than Martin Luther King, and in their America "racial matters" took precedence over racial justice. The FBI developed its own ideas and its own politics about matters of race, and the director worked tirelessly to insure that the Bureau's values would help shape the federal government's relations with its nonwhite citizens. Though Hoover contributed, in his own way, to the destruction of the Ku Klux Klan and its violent methods, he contributed to the rise of a more sophisticated and perhaps more damaging racism as an intractable force in national politics. He helped make the Republican party a white man's party, as Dr. King had feared, acting not so much on behalf of a hopeless cause (the salvation of Jim Crow America), but on behalf of the new law-and-order politics of race.

That Hoover experienced some success in accomplishing what he set out to do is no more important than the fact that he met such feeble resistance from within the White House and the Justice Department. Because so many Kennedy and Johnson administration officials accepted FBI actions, and because the FBI, no matter how autonomous it seemed, was part of a larger structure, the federal government's executive branch, the history of the FBI abroad in black America is nothing less than the history of a government at war with its own citizens. Don Whitehead celebrated the FBI by calling its record "the story of America itself."[2] Black America's FBI story is also America's story, but it evokes a sense of shame, not celebration.

Though Hoover cared very much for posterity, he left only a legacy of misfortune. It was the particular misfortune of those blacks who were tapped, bugged, or harassed that the director stood at the center of the struggle for racial justice, where he could do so much damage. It was the particular misfortune of the Kennedy and Johnson administration officials who accommodated themselves to the director's location that he did so much damage to their efforts to promote consensus and achieve racial and economic justice. It was the particular misfortune of those FBI agents who did brave work on civil rights cases whenever they were given the chance to have been soldiers in an army whose general did so much damage to the democratic promise of the civil rights movement itself. In the end, it was the particular misfortune of the nation that Hoover's obsession with "racial matters" did so much damage to the civil rights and civil liberties of all Americans.

Acknowledgments

===>>>><<<<===

There was something odd about sitting up here in Alaska, especially during the winter months of four-hour sunshine days and ten or whatever below, and writing about Freedom Summer in Philadelphia, Mississippi, or Bloody Sunday in Selma, Alabama. For some reason it was nice to see the *National Geographic* come one day, with a slick picture of Robert Kennedy all bundled up and standing, back in 1967, on top of 13,905-foot Mt. Kennedy in the Yukon, less than ten miles from our state line. The picture went up on the wall of my office, next to the other pictures of Robert Kennedy. There are advantages to living and writing in Alaska, but there are disadvantages as well. It is especially difficult to conduct research from such a faraway place. If it were not for the help offered by a great many people and institutions, it would have been far more difficult. What follows here is a modest and no doubt inadequate attempt to express my gratitude. I have no idea how to thank everyone, and a few people have requested anonymity.

Colleagues and students at the University of Alaska Anchorage, particularly Sean Murphy, Cynthia Weinzetl, Joe Davies, Kathleen Rapp, Stephen Haycox, and Will Jacobs, were a constant source of inspiration. My University offered travel aid and other funding during the early stages of research. The National Endowment for the Humanities, the American Philosophical Society, and the Gerald R. Ford Library provided additional financial assistance. I should also mention Don W. Wilson, then director of the Ford Library and now Archivist of the United States, who answered my questions about the grant-application process forthrightly. Project '87, a joint venture sponsored by the Ameri-

361

can Historical Association and the American Political Science Association, awarded a grant to attend a summer seminar, on "Bureaucracy, Positive Government, and Politicization: The Twentieth Century Challenge to Constitutionalism," chaired by Herman Belz. I tested many of the ideas developed more fully in this book at the seminar, particularly in conversations with Paul Rosen. I also tested my ideas in journal articles. Portions of Chapters 3 and 7 appeared in slightly different form in the *Journal of Southern History* and the *Journal of American History* respectively, and a very small portion of Chapter 1 appeared in *Phylon*. I am grateful to the editors of these journals for permission to draw upon this work. The articles themselves are cited in the bibliography.

Nell Irvin Painter and J. Jeffrey Mayhook read the manuscript, and August Meier read part of it. My gratitude for their respective critiques is immense. At the Free Press, I am in debt to production supervisor Celia Knight and copyeditor Jack Rummel. My editor, Joyce Seltzer, prodded me through each successive draft, and in a sense her talents—and endurance—are largely responsible for whatever merit the reader may find in this final draft.

Among the archivists who always pointed me in the proper directions were: William H. McNitt of the Gerald R. Ford Library; Bob Tissing, Linda Hanson, David Humphrey, and especially Tina Houston of the Lyndon B. Johnson Library; Martin M. Teasley and John E. Wickman of the Dwight D. Eisenhower Library; Joan Howard, Bonnie Baldwin, Cynthia Fox and John W. Roberts of the National Archives; Michael Desmond, Jane E. Ward, and Ronald Whealan of the John F. Kennedy Library; Elinor DesVerney Sinnette of the Moorland-Spingarn Research Center at Howard Univeristy; Menzi Behrnd-Klodt and Joanne Hohler of the State Historical Society of Wisconsin; Dovie T. Patrick of the Robert W. Woodruff Library at the Atlanta University Center; Richard Shrader of the Wilson Library at the University of North Carolina at Chapel Hill; Marvin Y. Whiting and Thomas C. Haslett, Jr., of the Birmingham Public Library; Sheryl B. Vogt of the Richard B. Russell Memorial Library on the campus of the University of Georgia; Eileen Boyle of the San Diego Public Library; Tamara Silver of the Center for National Security Studies; D. Louise Cook of the Martin Luther King, Jr., Center for Nonviolent Social Change; Hank Holmes and William Hanna of the Mississippi Department of Archives and History; Kathleen McIntyre of the State Historical Society of Missouri Manuscripts; and Mary Ann Bamberger of the University of Illinois at Chicago Library.

Helen Near and Susan Rosenfeld Falb of the FBI, along with the FBI Office of Congressional and Public Affairs, solved some of the access problems that inevitably accompany a study of this nature. Others who helped me locate files released under the Freedom of Information Act (FOIA) or otherwise include Tony Freyer, Douglass Cassel, Jr., Michael Krinsky, Ann Mari Buitrago, Jack Novik, Anne Pilsbury, William Goodman, Joan Washington, Ron Kuby, Alan McSurely, Karl Evanzz, James Forman, John R. Salter, Jr., Edwin King, Clyde R. Appleton, Robert F. Williams, and Robert J. Boyle. For their courtesy and prompt replies to my questions about FOIA releases and other matters, I should also mention Katherine Taylor, Richard Smyser, Frances Keller, Ernest Holsendolph, Lennox Hinds, Louis Martin, Walter Naegle, Diane McWhorter, Frank Sikora, Robert Zangrando, Hugh Davis Graham, Nancy J. Weiss, Rick Blake, John Ricks, Pablo Eisenberg, David Burnham, Sanford J. Ungar, Flint Taylor, Juan Williams, Edith Tiger, Richard Gid Powers, Clayborne Carson, Howard Zinn, Arthur M. Schlesinger, Jr., Athan Theoharis, Mary Gail Gerebenics, Dan E. Moldea, David Garrow, and Theodore Kornweibel.

The great majority of the information contained in the pages of this book comes directly from over 150 of the FBI's only recently declassified files. I supplemented archival spelunking by interviewing former FBI executives and field agents, Justice Department and Civil Rights Commission attorneys, White House advisors and staff, newspaper reporters, movement activists, and members of the resistance. A good number of people took the time to talk to me, whether in person or on the telephone, and I thank them for doing so. Most of their names are listed in the bibliography.

While traveling Outside, as we say here in Alaska, a number of people fed me or housed me or did things for me that were quite inconvenient for them. Special thanks are offered to Elizabeth Moore, Robert Zeidel, Alan McSurely and his family, Rachel Rosen-DeGolia and Peter DeGolia, Susan and Michael Cooney (and all the other Cooneys as well), and the Gibbons people at Catholic. My parents allowed me to use their home in

Atlanta as a base of sorts during my research trips, and my sister, Mary Ann, loaned me her car. Finally, there is the matter of Maureen O'Reilly and our children, who put up with all those trips Outside and always took me back. For that, the great number of plenary indulgences to come will be well earned.

Notes

===========◇◇◇===========

INTRODUCTION

1. Guyot, Johnson interviews; DeMuth, "'Tired,'" 548–51; Watters and Cleghorn, *Climbing*, 136–37, 146 n20, 363–75; Cagin and Dray, *We Are Not Afraid*, 23–24, 86–88; Zinn, *SNCC*, 93–96; Hamer Oral History; Hamer, *Praise*, 11–12; Misseduc Foundation, *Mississippi*, 19–24.
2. One of the last references to Hamer in the FBI's files, dated Jan. 12, 1970, no. 3697, FBI–King File (100-106670), concerns the D.C. Committee for the Martin Luther King Holiday. When Hamer died of cancer seven years later, Andrew Young delivered the eulogy at the funeral service in Ruleville. In 1963 it was Young who finally obtained the release of Hamer and the others from the Winona jail, on the same day a sniper shot and killed Mississippi NAACP leader Medgar Evers.
3. Grant, ed., *Black Protest*, 376; Lewis interview.
4. Evans, *Personal Politics*, 91.
5. In the timeless and contentious debate among jurists, Hoover unknowingly sided with "legal positivists."
6. "Civil Rights and Domestic Violence," March 15, 1947, Civil Rights and Domestic Violence Folder, FBI–Hoover O&C Files: Walter White to J. Edgar Hoover, Oct. 20, 1951, no. 601, FBI–NAACP File (61-3176).
7. "They were gonna' prosecute," Lawrence Guyot said. "The Bureau was interested." The Justice Department filed misdemeanor brutality charges in Oxford, but a jury acquitted the defendants after a brief trial.
8. Whitehead, *FBI Story*, vii, 396, 403.

CHAPTER 1.
The Negro Question

1. Memo, re Authority of the United States to Protect Negroes . . . , March 31, 1910, no. OG 3057, Bureau of Investigation (BI) Files.
2. Powers, *Secrecy and Power*, 9–10, 27, 36–41, 324.
3. Kluger, *Simple Justice*, 111; Woodward, *Strange Career*, 69, 81.
4. Kluger, *Simple Justice*, 104–5; Woodward, *Strange Career*, 93–96, 102–5.
5. Kornweibel, "FBI and Black America," 6.
6. Dept. of Justice, *Investigation Activities*, 162, 187. See also *Federal Surveil-*

lance of Afro-Americans, reels 17–18 (microfilm). A few Bureau agents submitted reports listing "NEGROES" and "IRISH MOVEMENT" under the same "Racial Activities" heading.

7. Henry G. Sebastian to A. B. Coxe, Aug. 9, 1919, Box 14, Glasser File, Dept. of Justice Files; William J. Neale to all SACs, Oct. 2, 1920, FBI–SAC File; James P. Rooney to William J. Burns, Sept. 20, 1921, no. BS 202600-1778-66, BI Files; Henry H. Stroud to Rooney, Sept. 19, 1921, no. BS 202600-1778-66, ibid.

8. John Edgar Hoover, Memo upon the work of the Radical Division, Oct. 18, 1919, no. OG 374217, BI Files; Dept. of Justice, *Investigation Activities*, 13, 162–67.

9. Hoover to Ridgely, Oct. 11, 1919, in *Marcus Garvey . . . Papers*, ed. Hill, vol. 2, p. 72; Hoover to George F. Ruch, June 8, 1920, ibid., vol. 2, p. 345; Hoover to Anthony Caminetti, Feb. 24, 1921, ibid., vol. 3, p. 235; Hoover to John B. Cunningham, Aug. 10, 1922, ibid., vol. 4, p. 841; Stein, *World*, 189–90.

10. Kornweibel, "F.B.I. and White American Hegemony," 7–26; Dept. of Justice, *Investigation Activities*, 163–64, 166; Stein, *World*, 186–208; Hill, "Foremost," 229.

11. Dept. of Justice, *Investigation Activities*, 162–63, 187; Kornweibel, "FBI and Black America," 17.

12. Whitehead, *FBI Story*, 73.

13. Lewis J. Baley to Director, July 18, 1922, no. 50-0-5, BI Files; Section 17, *FBI Manual of Instruction* (1936 ed.). Daniel, *Shadow*, touches briefly on the FBI role.

14. Whitehead, *FBI Story*, 69–73; Hoover, "Off-the-Record Remarks."

15. Mason, *Stone*, 151; Powers, *Secrecy and Power*, 520 n8.

16. Hoover failed to undertake a parallel purge of hard-core racists. He disciplined one such agent, but only because the agent accused him of trying to "whitewash" the patronage case against Perry Howard, the black Republican National Committeeman from Mississippi. The director, in fact, called the Howard case "bigger than Teapot Dome." See case file 70-40-1, Dept. of Justice Files; McMillen, "Howard," 212.

17. Director to Clyde Tolson, July 15, 1931, no. 142, FBI–Tolson Personnel File (67-9524); Demaris, *Director*, 33–34.

18. Hoover to Attorney General, Nov. 5, 1924, FBI–SAC File; Hoover to all SACs, Nov. 5, 1924, ibid.; Hoover to Charles P. Sisson, April 19, 1930, Colored Question, Pres. Papers, Herbert Hoover Papers; Hoover to Attorney General, Sept. 12, 1931, Moorhead, He., PSF, ibid.; Rhea Whitley to Director, Sept. 12, 1931, no. 1, FBI–Moorish Science File (62-25889).

19. Senate Select Committee to Study . . . Intelligence Activities (hereafter Church Committee), *Book II*, 25.

20. The Justice Department filed sedition charges in 1942 against eighty blacks, including Elijah Muhammad of the Nation of Islam, chiefly on the grounds that they had a "pan-colored" identification with the Japanese.

21. Hoover to Marvin McIntyre, May 7, 1942, OF 4952, Roosevelt Papers; Hoover to Edwin P. Watson, June 19, 1941, no. 835, June 26, 1942, no. 2194, OF 10-B, ibid.; Hoover to Harry Hopkins, Sept. 4, 1942, no. 2248-B, Feb. 1, 1943, no. 2304-A, July 3, 1943, no. 2355-C, July 6, 1943, no. 2356-A and -B, July 8, 1943, no. 2357-A, Sept. 15, 1943, no. 2346-A, OF 10-B, ibid.; Edward A. Tamm to P. E. Foxworth, June 24, 1941, no. 18X1, FBI–NAACP File (61-3176); D. Milton Ladd to Director, April 25, 1944, no. 9, FBI–CORE File (100-225892).

22. E. G. Fitch to Ladd, March 11, 1942, no. 220, FBI–National Negro Congress

File (61-6728); Klehr, *Heyday*, 460 n54; Hoover to SAC Philadelphia, n.d. [ca. Dec. 18, 1943], no. 178, FBI–NAACP File; Hoover to Tolson, Tamm, and Ladd, Sept. 30, 1942, no. 56, ibid.; Chicago Field Office Rept., Nov. 6, 1943, no. 2, FBI–CORE File; "Survey of Racial Conditions in the United States," n.d. [ca. Sept. 1943], in CF, Justice Dept. (5–6), Truman Papers.

23. Ladd to Director, Sept. 11, 1942, FBI File 62-116758; Ladd to Tamm, Oct. 21, 1942, ibid.; Richmond Field Office Rept., Jan. 26, 1943, no. 9, FBI–Moorish Science File; Hoover to SAC Louisville, Aug. 5, 1943, no. 12, FBI–Civil Rights Policy File (66-6200-44).

24. Richmond Field Office Rept., Jan. 26, 1943, no. 9, FBI–Moorish Science File; Ladd to Director, Sept. 30, 1943, no. 156, FBI–Detroit Riot File (44-802); Robert C. Hendon to Tolson, June 24, 1943, no. 55, ibid.; Hoover to McIntyre, June 23, 1943, no. 8, ibid.; Hoover to Attorney General, June 25, 1943, no. 14, ibid.

25. William Neale to all SACs, Oct. 2, 1920, FBI–SAC File; Birmingham Field Office Rept., Jan. 11, 1945, no. 20, FBI–Hudson File (100-24548).

26. Millspaugh, *Crime Control*.

27. Rosenman, ed., *Public Papers*, vol. 3, pp. 12–13, 242–45.

28. The White House press secretary's description. Stephen Early to the President, July 12, 1940, PPF 2993, Roosevelt Papers; Early to Lowell Mellett, July 30, 1940, OF 880, ibid.

29. H. L. Mencken to Fulton Oursler, May 15, 1939, no. 51, FBI–Oursler File (94-4-692).

30. Rable, "South," 201–20. Howe is quoted in Manchester, *Glory*, 107.

31. White, "U.S. Department of (White) Justice," 310.

32. Hoover to Walter Winchell, May 19, 1936, no. 42, July 6, 1938, no. 99, FBI–Winchell File; [name deleted] to Winchell, June 16, 1938, no. 99, ibid. FDR is quoted in Weiss, *Farewell*, 109; Wilkins in *Standing*, 132.

33. Fine, *Frank Murphy*, vol. 3, pp. 79, 82.

34. Schweinhaut's comments are paraphrased in W. Cleon Skousen to [File], Feb. 22, 1940, no. 2, FBI–Civil Rights File.

35. Sections 51 and 52, during the Roosevelt years; Congress recodified both provisions in 1948 and they are referred to throughout the text as Sections 241 and 242.

36. Section 242 penalties were of course less severe—a maximum fine of $1,000 and a maximum prison sentence of one year.

37. Dept. of Justice Circular no. 3356, April 4, 1942, no. illegible, FBI–Civil Rights File. See also Carr, *Federal Protection*.

38. Elliff, "Aspects," 609–18.

39. Ibid., 610–13.

40. Ibid., 617–18; Marcus B. Calhoun to Hoover, June 12, 1944, no. 17, FBI–Civil Rights File; SAC Dallas to Director, Aug. 31, 1949, no. 98, ibid.; Leland V. Boardman to Alex Rosen, Jan. 23, 1957, no. 487, ibid.; Hoover, "Protecting Our Freedom," n.d. [ca. March 1947], in Civil Rights and Domestic Violence Folder, FBI–Hoover O&C Files. The Supreme Court read a specific-intent requirement into the color-of-law statute in 1945, in *Screws v. United States* (325 U.S. 91).

41. There were exceptions. Capeci, "Lynching," 859–87.

42. Louis B. Nichols to Tolson, Oct. 13, 1939, no. 525, FBI–Cooper File (94-3-4-20); Courtney Ryley Cooper to Nichols, Oct. 21, 1939, no. 526X, ibid.; Hoover to Cooper, Nov. 3, 1939, no. 527X1, ibid.

43. SAC Letter, Feb. 19, 1946, FBI–SAC File; J. C. Strickland to Ladd, July 15,

1946, no. illegible, FBI–Civil Rights File; Hoover to Tolson, Tamm, and Ladd, July 17, 1946, no. illegible, ibid.; Ladd to Director, Aug. 29, 1946, no. illegible, ibid.

44. Ladd to Director, March 10, 1947, no. 10, Civil Rights and Domestic Violence Folder, FBI–Hoover O&C Files; Ladd to Director, Dec. 13, 1946, no. 40X, FBI–Civil Rights File. See also the Ernst Folder, FBI–Nichols O&C Files.

45. Ladd to Director, March 10, 1947, no. 10, Civil Rights and Domestic Violence Folder, FBI–Hoover O&C Files.

46. Rauh interview. Hoover's position on states' rights is set out in "Civil Rights and Domestic Violence," March 15, 1947, Civil Rights and Domestic Violence Folder, FBI–Hoover O&C Files; "Protecting Our Freedom," n.d. [ca. March 15, 1947], no. 6, ibid.

47. Director to Attorney General, Sept. 12, 1946, no. illegible, Sept. 17, 1947, no. illegible, FBI–Civil Rights File. For Sinatra and Welles, see Guy Hottel to Director, Sept. 18, 1946, no. 569, FBI–National Negro Congress File.

48. Attorney General to Director, Sept. 24, 1946, no. 35, FBI–Civil Rights File; Director to Attorney General, Sept. 12, 1946, no. illegible, Sept. 17, 1947, no. illegible, ibid.

49. "Civil Rights and Domestic Violence," March 15, 1947, Civil Rights and Domestic Violence Folder, FBI–Hoover O&C Files; Tamm to Director, Dec. 12, 1941, Dies Folder, ibid.; SAC San Francisco to Director, Dec. 3, 1946, no. 49, FBI–Robeson File (100-12304); [deleted] to Nichols, July 20, 1942, no. 65, FBI–NAACP File.

50. Leinbaugh interview; Whitehead, *FBI Story*, 15–16.

51. Hoover to Tolson, Tamm, Hugh H. Clegg, and Ladd, March 22, 1947, Civil Rights and Domestic Violence Folder, FBI–Hoover O&C Files.

52. "FBI Agents," 9–13; Nichols to Tolson, June 29, 1949, no. 148, FBI–Oursler File; Hoover to Oursler, Jan. 12, 1951, no. 176, ibid.; clipping, Jan. 7, 1951, no. 176, ibid.; Director to E. J. Brennan, Jan. 18, 1922, FBI–Amos File; Hoover to James E. Amos, Oct. 30, 1935, ibid; Amos to Hoover, Sept. 21, 1953, ibid.; Amos, *Theodore Roosevelt.*

53. Sullivan, *Bureau*, 123–24; Demaris, *Director*, 38–39; Walter White to Hoover, June 17, 1941, FBI, Group II, Series A, Box 268, NAACP Papers; Hoover to White, July 14, 1941, ibid.; C. Herbert Marshall to White, Dec. 13, 1941, ibid.; White to Marshall, Dec. 17, 1941, ibid.

54. Thurgood Marshall to White, Jan. 23, 1947, FBI, Group II, Series A, Box 268, NAACP Papers; White to Robert Carter, Aug. 21 and 27, 1946, ibid.; Carter to White, Aug. 26, 1946, ibid.; Marshall to Tom Clark, Dec. 27, 1946, exhibit 26, Civil Rights and Domestic Violence Folder, FBI–Hoover O&C Files; Clark to Marshall, Jan. 13, 1947, ibid.; Hoover to White, Jan. 13, 1947, no. 367, FBI–NAACP File; note, Hoover, n.d. [ca. April 10, 1947], no. 308, ibid.; Arthur B. Spingarn to Hoover, Sept. 15, 1943, no. 150, ibid.; T. J. Starke to Nichols, Sept. 23, 1943, no. X1, FBI–White File (100-382824); SAC Letter, Aug. 26, 1946, FBI–SAC File.

55. "Civil Rights and Domestic Violence," March 15, 1947, Civil Rights and Domestic Violence Folder, FBI–Hoover O&C Files; "General Problems," n.d. [ca. March 15, 1947], no. 5, ibid.

56. See the documents cited in the previous note.

57. President's Committee, *To Secure These Rights*, 124; McGowan interview; and the documents cited in note 55.

58. President's Committee, *To Secure These Rights*, 123; Robert K. Carr to

Hoover, March 21, 1947, in Civil Rights and Domestic Violence Folder, FBI–Hoover O&C Files.

59. Hoover to Tolson, Tamm, Clegg, and Ladd, March 22, 1947, Civil Rights and Domestic Violence Folder, FBI–Hoover O&C Files.

60. "FBI Agents," 9–13. See also the documents from Oursler's FBI File cited in note 52.

61. White and other NAACP leaders exerted constant pressure on the FBI to change its "'lily white' hiring policy." Leslie S. Perry to White, Sept. 17, 1947, FBI, Group II, Series A, Box 268, NAACP Papers; Perry to White, Sept. 18, 1947, ibid.; White to Hoover, Aug. 21, 1946, no. 349, FBI–NAACP File; W. R. Glavin to Director, Aug. [14?], 1947, no. 395, ibid.

62. Elliff, "Aspects," 628–29.

63. Attorney General to Director, April 22, 1947, no. 49, FBI–Civil Rights File; Director to Attorney General, April 16, 1947, no. 48, ibid.

64. Executives' Conference to Director, May 2, 1947, no. illegible, ibid.; Bureau Bulletin no. 26, May 14, 1947, FBI–Bureau Bulletin File.

65. Attorney General to Director, Oct. 10, 1952, no. illegible, FBI–Civil Rights File; Attorney General to Director, Dec. 19 and 21, 1951, no. not recorded, ibid.; Executives' Conference to Director, Jan. 2, 1952, no. not recorded, ibid.; SAC Letter, Jan. 5, 1952, FBI–SAC File.

66. Bureau officials proceeded with great care. Because the Department "has given us blanket authority to conduct preliminary inquiries in Civil Rights cases," Alex Rosen cautioned, it would not be "advisable to abrogate or abridge that rule by any communication over the Director's signature." Rosen to Boardman, Jan. 27, 1956, no. 395, FBI–Civil Rights File.

67. Rosen to Boardman, April 16, 1958, no. illegible, May 26, 1958, no. illegible, ibid.; Rosen to Alan H. Belmont, Dec. 5, 1961, no. 902, ibid.; Director to SACs Albany et al., April 16, 1958, no. 552, ibid.; SAC Letters, June 24 and July 22, 1958, FBI–SAC File.

68. Commission on Civil Rights, *Report-Book, 5,* 218 n138.

69. Between January 1, 1948, and June 30, 1955, the FBI investigated 9,340 police officers, an effort that led to 189 indictments under Section 242 and 35 convictions.

70. Director to Attorney General, Aug. 5, 1953, no. 216, Aug. 25, 1953, no. illegible, FBI–Civil Rights File; "Certain Governors' Comments," Nov. 20, 1953, no. 286, ibid.

71. Director to Attorney General, Aug. 25, 1953, no. illegible, ibid.; Nichols to Tolson, July 10, 1953, no. 180, Oct. 22, 1953, no. 203, Nov. 20, 1953, no. 207, FBI–Pegler File (62-36434); Rosen to Ladd, Aug. 26, 1953, no. 195, ibid. For the New York police, see House Committee on the Judiciary, *Hearings . . . Department of Justice;* Nichols to Tolson, Feb. 11, 1953, James M. McInerney Folder, FBI–Nichols O&C Files. McInerney, a former Bureau agent who went on to head the Department's Criminal Division, established the policy on his own initiative.

72. Quoted in SAC Los Angeles to Director, Aug. 27, 1953, no. illegible, FBI–Civil Rights File. See also Hoover to Arthur Hayes Sulzberger, Aug. 13, 1953, no. illegible, ibid.

73. Director to Attorney General, Sept. 1, 1953, no. illegible, ibid.; Nichols to Tolson, Sept. 11, 1953, no. 202, FBI–Pegler File; Hoover to Raymond Moley, Sept. 17, 1953, no. not recorded, ibid.; Hoover to Tolson and Nichols, Sept. 22, 1953, no. 200, ibid.; Milton A. Jones to Nichols, Aug. 28, 1953, no. 40X3,

FBI–Rushmore File (100-13058); memo, re FBI's Jurisdiction, Aug. 28, 1953, no. 40X3, ibid.; Belmont to Ladd, Oct. 16, 1953, no. 39, Folder 14, FBI–Hoover O&C Files

74. SAC Letter, Oct. 13, 1953, FBI–SAC File.

75. "Integration in Public Schools," n.d. [ca. Sept. 15, 1958], no. 2673, FBI–Little Rock File (44-12284); Nichols to Tolson, Jan. 10, 1956, no. 1153, FBI–NAACP File.

76. Gordon A. Nease to Tolson, Jan. 22, 1958, no. 6, Directorship Folder, FBI–Hoover O&C Files; Nichols to Tolson, Feb. 26, 1957, no. 19, FBI–Eastland File (94-4-5130).

77. Nease to Tolson, Jan. 22, 1958, no. 6, Directorship Folder, FBI–Hoover O&C Files. The director scribbled his comments on this memo.

78. Jones to Nichols, Oct. 29, 1947, no. not recorded, FBI–Humphrey File (62-26225); memo, re Hubert H. Humphrey, n.d. [ca. Oct. 29, 1947], no. 906, ibid.

79. Tamm to Director, May 10, 1947, no. 71, FBI–Robeson File; note, Hoover, n.d. [ca. May 7, 1947], no. 79, ibid.; memo, re Paul Robeson, May 7, 1947, no. 79, ibid.; Belmont to Boardman, April 18, 1957, no. not recorded, ibid. For Davis, see Nichols to Tolson, Feb. 18, 1948, no. 1495, FBI–HUAC File (61-7582).

80. Kimball, "History," 410; memo, re Mary McLeod Bethune, Dec. 20, 1946, PSF, FBI–B, Truman Papers.

81. Hoover to George Allen, Sept. 25, 1946, PSF, FBI–Communist Data, Truman Papers; Hoover to Harry Vaughan, June 3, 1947, PSF, FBI–W, ibid.; Des Moines Register, Sept. 4, 1983.

82. Church Committee, Book II, 51, 180, 250–51 n151a, Book III, 450; Hoover to Dillon Anderson, Jan. 16 and 24, March 2, 6, and 7, 1956, FBI Series, FBI L–N, Office of the Special Assistant for National Security Affairs, Eisenhower Papers; memo, re Communist Infiltration of the NAACP, Jan. 16, 1956, ibid.; memo, re Communist Party–USA, Negro Matters, Jan. 23, 1956, ibid.

83. Church Committee, Book III, 450; F. L. Price to Rosen, Dec. 27, 1956, no. not recorded, FBI–Civil Rights File.

84. Memo, re Racial Tensions and Civil Rights, March 1, 1956, Whitman File, Cabinet Series, Eisenhower Papers. In the months after the cabinet briefing the director began to send reports to the White House on the Citizens Councils.

85. Belmont to Boardman, Oct. 27, 1955, no. not recorded, FBI–NAACP File; memo, re Racial Tensions, Eisenhower Papers.

86. Memo, re Racial Tensions, Eisenhower Papers. See also Director to Attorney General, Jan, 3, 1956, no. not recorded, FBI–NAACP File; Hoover to Anderson, Jan. 3, 1956, no. not recorded, ibid.

87. Church Committee, Book III, 452–54, Hearings—FBI, 37–39; Hoover to Attorney General, Dec. 31, 1956, no. 61, King Folder, FBI–Hoover O&C Files; Fred J. Baumgardner to William C. Sullivan, Sept. 8, 1961, no. 62, ibid.; New York Field Office Rept., Jan. 28, 1955, no. deleted, FBI–Malcolm X File (file no. also deleted); Lincoln, Black Muslims, 99; FBI monograph, "Nation of Islam," 1960, passim.

88. Jones to Cartha D. DeLoach, Feb. 1, 1960, no. 424, FBI–Lewis File (94-4-2189); Hoover to Fulton Lewis, Jr., Feb. 2, 1960, no. 423, ibid. For Mrs. Roosevelt, see Church Committee, Book II, 51–52. For the pilgrimage, see memo, Feb. 28, 1958, no. 2, FBI–Wilkins File (62-78270). Oxnam requested and received a report of his own from the FBI in 1951 on a black minister

in the Bronx, Edward D. McGowan—because he found McGowan's performance disappointing: "He has not been particularly effective as a Negro." G. Bromley Oxnam to Nichols, Jan. 9, 1951, Louis B. Nichols Folder, Oxnam Papers; letter, Nichols to Oxnam, Jan. 25, 1951, ibid.

89. Senator Eastland held the most ambitious congressional investigation in 1954 in New Orleans—a "Great Southern Commie Hunt"—and the FBI supplied blind memos on several "unfriendly witnesses." Among others, the Eastland Committee subpoenaed Aubrey Williams, former chief of the National Youth Administration, and Virginia Durr, the veteran of the fight against the poll tax and wife of another New Dealer, onetime FCC chief Clifford Durr. For Virginia Durr on Eastland ("a vicious little fat toad of a man"), see Barnard, ed., *Outside,* 171–72, 258, 261, 266.

90. May, "Genetics," 420–22; Richard Arens to James C. Davis, May 3, 1957, Criticisms: HUAC (75-1-21-3), Southern Regional Council Archives. The Stamler Papers contains a lengthy compilation of *Cong. Record* excerpts based on Committee files.

91. Executives' Conference to Tolson, Aug, 4, 1954, no. 2473, FBI–HUAC File; SAC Washington to Director, Oct. 12, 1955, no. 2835, ibid.; Nichols to Tolson, Oct. 12, 1955, no. 2836, ibid.; G. H. Scatterday to Belmont, April 14, 1959, no. 4121, ibid. For the sedition trial, see Braden, *Wall Between.* For Tolson's directive, see memo, Feb. 28, 1958, no. 2, FBI–Wilkins File.

92. See "Integration in Public Schools," n.d. [ca. Sept. 15, 1958], no. 2673, FBI–Little Rock File.

93. FBI monographs, "Communist Party and the Negro," 1953, pp. i, iii, iv, 79–83, and 1956, pp. ii, v, 53. For the Comintern subsidy, see Hoover, *Masters,* 233.

94. Jones to DeLoach, Jan. 27, 1960, no. 5, FBI–Wilkins File; "Communist Party and the Negro," 1953, p. 83.

95. The document cited in note 92 lists these numbers. For Wilkins and White, see Jones to DeLoach, Jan. 27, 1960, no. 5, FBI–Wilkins File; Nichols to Tolson, Dec. 11, 1950, no. 5095, FBI–White File (100-3-81); Nichols to Tolson, June 21, 1951, no. 596, FBI–NAACP File.

96. "Current Weaknesses of the Communist Party," Oct. 1956, no. 47, FBI–COINTEL (CPUSA) File (100-3-104); "Communist Party and the Negro," 1956, pp. 19–25; Jones to DeLoach, March 16, 1965, no. not recorded, FBI–Wilkins File.

97. McGowan interview.

98. Thompson, ed., *Kennedy,* 122–23. For the Montgomery bus boycott, see Garrow, *Bearing,* 11–82.

99. House Committee on Appropriations, *Hearings* (1961), 423. See also C. B. Stanberry to SAC Birmingham, Oct. 31, 1960, no. 137-00-165, FBI–Bergman Freedom Rider Files; "Communist Party, USA—Negro Question," Aug. 23, 1963, no. 253X, FBI–CIRM File (100-3-116).

CHAPTER 2.
Paper Chains

1. A major theme of Navasky, *Kennedy Justice.*

2. For JFK's sensitivity to civil rights, see his correspondence in Subject Files 1953–60 (Civil Rights), Box 9, Sorensen Papers. See also Louis B. Nichols to Clyde Tolson, Jan. 16, 1952, no. not recorded, FBI–Civil Rights File (44-00); Milton A. Jones to Cartha D. DeLoach, July 13, 1960, no. 16,

Kennedy Folder, FBI–Hoover O&C Files. O'Donnell is quoted in Demaris, *Director*, 186; RFK in Navasky, *Kennedy Justice*, 97.

3. DeLoach to John P. Mohr, Feb. 5, 1962, no. not recorded, FBI–Wilson File (94-42524); Eastland Oral History, 22.

4. Lee C. White to Jack Valenti, Dec. 4, 1964, WHCF, Ex HU2, Johnson Papers.

5. R. O. Kittelsen to Alex Rosen, April 27, 1945, no. illegible, FBI–Civil Rights File.

6. Barnard, ed., *Outside*, 188.

7. Dwight D. Eisenhower to James F. Byrnes, July 23, 1957, Whitman File, Diary Series, Box 14, Eisenhower Papers; Schlesinger, *Robert Kennedy*, 299.

8. Director to Attorney General, March 19, 1958, no. not recorded, FBI–SCLC File (100-438794).

9. John Doar and Dorothy Landsberg, "The Performance of the FBI in Investigating Violations of Federal Laws Protecting the Right to Vote, 1960–1967," in Senate Select Committee to Study . . . Intelligence Activities (hereafter Church Committee), *Hearings—FBI*, 892–94.

10. Ibid., 160, 474–75, 912–21; Doar, Tyler interviews.

11. Doar, "Performance," 912–21.

12. Doar, Tyler interviews. "I got along with Hoover," Tyler said, "partly because he was taken, in a Platonic sense, with my mother-in-law, and partly, I like to believe, because he liked and trusted me." Tyler remembered one time, at a party, where his mother-in-law and the FBI chief talked for several hours. Hoover had left his Cadillac outside with the motor running, and his driver, James Crawford, had to come inside to use the phone, having run out of gas.

13. The FBI opened what ultimately matured into a 132,000-page dossier on Wilkinson in 1942, when the city of Los Angeles hired him to manage the first integrated housing project in Watts. Bureau agents routinely checked voting records in California to see if Wilkinson had registered as a communist, and in 1961 they followed his case "closely at the Supreme Court." See serials 106-9, FBI–Wilkinson File (100-112434).

14. Doar, "Performance," 894; Evans interview.

15. Seigenthaler Oral History, 14; McMillen, "Black Enfranchisement," 351–72.

16. Thompson, ed., *Kennedy*, 110; Doar, "Performance," 948.

17. J. Edgar Hoover to [deleted], March 27, 1961, no. 4938, FBI–HUAC File (61-7582); memo, re John Doar, n.d. [ca. Nov. 19, 1971], no. not recorded, FBI–CPJ File (62-113909).

18. Doar, "Performance," 893, 904.

19. McGowan interview.

20. Doar, "Performance," 901, 905–06.

21. Ibid., 975; Fleischer interview.

22. Guthman interview.

23. In June 1944 Bureau executives wrote this language into the *Manual of Instruction*.

24. Edward A. Tamm to Director, Oct. 16, 1947, no. 60, FBI–Civil Rights File; Executives' Conference to Director, Oct. 27, 1947, no. 61, ibid.; J. Patrick Coyne to D. Milton Ladd, Oct. 29, 1947, no. 65, ibid.; Bureau Bulletin No. 66, Nov. 5, 1947, FBI–Bureau Bulletin File.

25. House Select Committee on Assassinations, *Hearings—King,* vol. 6, 93; J. F. Buckley to Ladd, Aug. 19, 1944, no. 19, FBI–Civil Rights File; Rosen to Ladd, Aug. 21, 1953, no. illegible, Sept. 4, 1953, no. not recorded, ibid.; SAC Letter, Aug. 27, 1953, FBI–SAC File.

26. Clement L. McGowan, Jr., to Gebhardt, May 30, 1974, no. 1072, FBI–Civil Rights File. See also serials 761, 927, 951, 982–3, ibid.

27. Doar, "Performance," 895, 903; Barrett interview.

28. Hoover to Tolson, Tamm, Hugh H. Clegg, and Ladd, March 22, 1947, Civil Rights and Domestic Violence Folder, FBI–Hoover O&C Files; Rosen to Ladd, Aug. 19, 1949, no. illegible, FBI–Civil Rights File; Rosen to Belmont, Dec. 22, 1961, no. illegible, ibid.

29. Ungar, *FBI,* 419; Howell, "Interview," 16; Schlesinger, *Robert Kennedy,* 313; Elliff, "Aspects," 652; Navasky, *Kennedy Justice,* 103; Marshall, Trebach, Doar interviews. Until December 1962 the FBI issued a warning to the *victims* in civil rights cases that anything they said could be used against them in a court of law. If a complainant agreed to an interview and insisted on having an attorney present, moreover, the FBI's agents had to request special authority before proceeding. SAC Letters, Sept. 2 and 16, 1965, FBI–SAC File.

30. Doar, "Performance," 897–900; *New York Times,* Nov. 5, 1979.

31. McGowan interview; Navasky, *Kennedy Justice,* 115–16.

32. Norbert A. Schlei to White, Sept. 30, 1964, WHCF, FG135-6, Box 188, Johnson Papers; White to Nicholas deB. Katzenbach, Aug. 4, 1964, ibid. Criminal Division chief Warren Olney III ordered the FBI to make on-the-spot arrests during the Little Rock crisis, but when Hoover complained Herbert Brownell rescinded the order. F. L. Price to Rosen, Oct. 4, 1957, no. 531, FBI–Civil Rights File.

33. D. W. Griffith to Ivan Conrad, March 29, 1963, no. 16, FBI–Forman File (44-21661); Director to SAC Memphis, March 29, 1963, no. 12 and no. 48, ibid.; McGowan to Rosen, March 29, 1963, no. 41, ibid.

34. Quinn Tamm to Tolson, Sept. 25, 1957, no. 529, FBI–Civil Rights File; Joseph J. Casper to Mohr, June 6, 1966, no. illegible, ibid.

35. U.S. marshals dressed in jackets and ties or lightweight riot gear provided whatever protection the federal government offered movement people.

36. Katzenbach, Rauh interviews.

37. McGowan interview; Doar, "Performance," 942–45.

38. Schardt, "Civil Rights," 172, 178; Calvin Williams interview.

39. Katzenbach interview.

40. Robert F. Kennedy Oral History, 637; Evans interview.

41. Seigenthaler Oral History, 17; Navasky, *Kennedy Justice,* 126.

42. Marshall interview; Marshall Oral History, 6–10, Bunche Collection.

43. Wilkins, "Chester Bowles," 813.

44. Seigenthaler Oral History, 9; Navasky, *Kennedy Justice,* 162. Marshall's book, *Federalism and Civil Rights,* contains no reference to the FBI.

45. Kennedy Oral History, 578–80; Belknap, *Federal Law,* 73–74; Brauer, *John F. Kennedy,* 317.

46. Marshall interview; Marshall Oral History, 6–10, Bunche Collection.

47. In the end, SNCC received only a pittance—the result, Fleming said, of the tax-exemption policies of a skeptical Internal Revenue Service and the high-risk policies of SNCC itself.

48. Navasky, *Kennedy Justice*, 118–19.
49. Garrow, *Bearing the Cross*, 170.
50. Doar, "Performance," 921–27; Moses interview.
51. Moses interview; Warren, *Who Speaks*, 93; Misseduc Foundation, *Mississippi*, 30–37.
52. Church Committee, *Hearings—FBI*, 209.
53. Watters and Cleghorn, *Climbing*, 159; Misseduc Foundation, *Mississippi*, 8–9; Burns, "Federal Government," 251. The Ruleville gunmen fired into two houses, missing Fanny Lou Hamer but hitting two voter registration workers from Jackson State College.
54. *Jackson Daily News*, Aug. 4, 1966; Sullivan, *Bureau*, 72, 125–26; Maurice House and C. B. McDavid to Jamie Moore, June 29, 1966, Box 4.4, Hamilton Papers.
55. Schardt, "Civil Rights," 172–73; Warren, *Who Speaks*, 93n.
56. Nichols to Tolson, Feb. 26, 1957, no. 19, FBI–Eastland File (94-4-5130).
57. 71 Stat. 104 (1957).
58. Harris Wofford to the President, Feb. 27, 1961, Office Files—Civil Rights General, Box 97, John F. Kennedy Papers; Schlesinger, *Robert Kennedy*, 326.
59. Bernhard interview. Eastland insisted on seeing the full FBI report on Commission nominees, not just the summary sheet usually provided.
60. Civil Rights Commission, *Report—Justice*, 61–62, 200 n47, 213–16 n134, 217–18 n138, 219 n147, 221–22; Trebach, Bernhard interviews.
61. Griswold interview, Rafferty Papers.
62. Bernhard Oral History, 19; Dulles, *Civil Rights Commission*, 150.
63. Schlesinger, *Robert Kennedy*, 327; Wofford, *Kennedys and Kings*, 161; Bernhard interview.
64. Navasky, *Kennedy Justice*, 110; Bernhard interview.
65. Bernhard interview.
66. Ibid.; Trebach interview.
67. Wofford, *Kennedys and Kings*, 161–62; Bernhard interview, Oral History, 17–19; William Taylor interview.
68. DeLoach to Hoover, Jan. 15, 1964, no. 10, Johnson Folder, FBI–Hoover O&C Files.
69. Tolson to Director, Dec. 5, 1961, no. not recorded, FBI–Civil Rights File.
70. Schlesinger, *Robert Kennedy*, 305; Barrett interview.
71. Doar, "Performance," 890, 949–50; Marshall Oral History, 24, Johnson Library; Schlesinger, *Robert Kennedy*, 303; Church Committee, *Hearings—FBI*, 208.
72. Doar, Marshall interviews; Wofford, *Kennedys and Kings*, 220; DeLoach to Hoover, Feb. 18, 1964, no. 315, FBI–King File (100-106670); Rosen to Belmont, Feb. 25, 1964, no. 317, Feb. 26, 1964, no. 319, ibid.; memo, re Burke Marshall, Nov. 19, 1971, no. not recorded, FBI–CPJ File; Marshall to Attorney General, Feb. 20, 1964, Special Correspondence, Attorney General, Box 8, Marshall Papers.
73. Moses interview.
74. Coles, "Social Struggle," 305, 307–08; Rustin interview.
75. Wilkins, Lewis, Bernhard interviews.
76. William Taylor interview; Wofford, *Kennedys and Kings*, 420.

CHAPTER 3.
Unbecoming Deeds

1. Navasky, *Kennedy Justice*, 23.
2. Elliff, "Aspects," 648.
3. [Deleted] to Alex Rosen, Feb. 26, 1960, no. 25, FBI–Racial Matters Policy File (157-00); Senate Select Committee to Study . . . Intelligence Activities (hereafter Church Committee), *Book III*, 456.
4. Wilkins, *Standing*, 283; Meier and Rudwick, "First Freedom Ride," 213–22.
5. Chicago Field Office Rept., Aug. 10, 1943, no. 1, FBI–CORE File (100-225892).
6. Raines, *My Soul*, 109–10.
7. Wofford, *Kennedys and Kings*, 153; Guthman, *Band*, 167.
8. Cartha D. DeLoach to John P. Mohr, May 4, 1961, no. illegible, FBI–Alabama Freedom Rider Files; Director to SACs Atlanta et al., April 24, 1961, no. 178, FBI–CORE File.
9. Meier and Rudwick, *CORE*, 137-38.
10. Director to Attorney General, May 15, 1961, no. 144-1-554, FBI–Bergman Freedom Rider Files.
11. Raines, *My Soul*, 114.
12. For Peck's account, see *Freedom Ride*. For Rowe, see Barrett G. Kemp to SAC Birmingham, May 17, 1961, no. 149-16-62, FBI–Bergman Files.
13. Meier and Rudwick, *CORE*, 138.
14. Rosen to Parsons, May 17, 1961, no. 321, FBI–CORE File.
15. Clement L. McGowan, Jr., to Rosen, May 18, 1961, no. 268, FBI–CORE File; John Doar to SAC Montgomery, May 22, 1961, no. illegible, FBI–Bergman Files. For Hoover, see his handwritten comments on DeLoach to Mohr, May 22, 1961, no. 149-1684-41, FBI–Alabama Files; UPI ticker, May 14, 1961, no. not recorded, ibid.; Rosen to Parsons, May 15, 1961, no. 215, FBI–CORE File.
16. Rosen to Alan H. Belmont, n.d. [ca. Nov. 13, 1961], no. 149-1684-236, Nov. 16, 1961, no. 149-1684-246, FBI–Alabama Files.
17. McGowan to Rosen, Sept. 5, 1961, no. 149-1684-153X, ibid.; Director to Attorney General, Sept. 6, 1961, no. 149-1684-145, ibid.; SAC Birmingham to Director, June 6, 1961, no. 149-1684-70, ibid.
18. Eugene "Bull" Connor to Thomas H. Cook, Aug. 9, 1960, Box 5.24, Connor Papers; SAC Birmingham to Director, Sept. 30, 1960, no. 157-198-17, FBI–Bergman Files; SAC Birmingham to Director, April 19, 1961, no. 157-198-35, April 26, 1961, no. 157-198-33, ibid.
19. SAC Birmingham to Director, May 5, 1961, no. deleted, FBI–CORE File; SAC Birmingham to Director, April 19, 1961, no. 157-198-35, April 24, 1961, no. 157-198-27, April 26, 1961, no. 157-198-33, FBI–Bergman Files; informant rept., April 25, 1961, no. 170-9-SF-42, ibid.; Kemp to SAC Birmingham, May 18, 1961, no. 149-16-69, ibid.
20. SAC Birmingham to Director, April 19, 1961, no. 157-198-35, FBI–Bergman Files; Director to SAC Birmingham, May 3, 1961, no. 157-198-31, ibid.; Director to SAC Atlanta et al., May 4, 1961, no. 157-198-34, ibid.; SAC Birmingham to Director, May 5, 1961, no. deleted, ibid.; Director to Attorney General, May 9, 1961, no. 144-1-554, ibid.; Seigenthaler interview.
21. Confidential interviews with former FBI officials.

22. Letterhead memo, May 12, 1961, no. 144-1-554, FBI–Alabama Files.
23. Raby interview; McGowan to Rosen, May 12 and 13, 1961, no. illegible, FBI–Alabama Files; Kenneth N. Raby to SAC Birmingham, May 13, 1961, no. 157-48-29, FBI–Bergman Files.
24. Director to SACs Albany et al., July 11, 1961, no. 157-198-39, FBI–Bergman Files; Director to Attorney General, May 15, 1961, no. 144-1-554, ibid.; Navasky, *Kennedy Justice*, 14.
25. Director to Attorney General, May 15, 1961, no. 144-1-554, FBI–Bergman Files.
26. Confidential interviews with former Birmingham FBI agents.
27. Wofford, *Kennedys and Kings*, 153–54; Lewis interview.
28. Schlesinger, *Robert Kennedy*, 309; Lewis interview and Oral History, 83.
29. Seigenthaler interview and Oral History, 41; Navasky, *Kennedy Justice*, 22; Rosen to Parsons, May 17, 1961, no. 321, FBI–CORE File.
30. Seigenthaler interview and Oral History, 41; Navasky, *Kennedy Justice*, 22; Civil Rights Commission, *Law Enforcement*, 166n; *New York Times*, May 8 and 19, 1976, Aug. 25, 1977. Seigenthaler learned about the FBI's file from his desk at the *Nashville Tennessean*, after he fired a copy editor, Jacqe Srouji, who also happened to be an FBI informant and a minor figure in the Karen Silkwood case. Ungar, "Piranhas," 19–27.
31. Robert Kennedy to Governor of Albama, n.d. [ca. May 20, 1961], General Correspondence, Civil Rights/Alabama, Attorney General's Files, Box 10, Robert Kennedy Papers.
32. Schlesinger, *Robert Kennedy*, 309–11; Lewis interview.
33. Yarbrough, *Judge Frank Johnson*, 83; Director to Attorney General, June 8, 1961, no. 157-387-306, June 10, 1961, no. 157-387-180, FBI–Bergman Files.
34. Milton A. Jones to DeLoach, Dec. 2, 1964, no. 126, FBI–Whitehead File (77-68662); J. Edgar Hoover to Clyde Tolson, Mohr, and DeLoach, Dec. 8, 1964, no. 127, FBI–Lawrence File (94-4-3169); Director to Attorney General, May 24, 1961, no. 144-1-554, FBI–Bergman Files.
35. New Orleans Field Office Rept., July 26, 1961, no. 157-387-793, FBI–Bergman Files.
36. George H. Scatterday to Rosen, May 22, 1961, in Dept. of Justice, *King Task Force*, 162–64; Garrow, *FBI and Martin Luther King*, 22, 24, 84.
37. Director to Attorney General, July 18, 1961, no. not recorded, FBI–COINTEL (CPUSA) File (100-3-104); Fred J. Baumgardner to William C. Sullivan, July 12, 1961, no. 2962, ibid.
38. Director to SAC San Francisco, Sept. 19, 1961, no. 2904, ibid.; SAC San Francisco to Director, Sept. 12, 1961, no. 2904, Sept. 22, 1961, no. 2903, ibid.; Baumgardner to Sullivan, Sept. 18, 1961, no. 2905, Oct. 3, 1961, no. 2964, ibid.; press release, Sept. 22, 1961, no. 2964, ibid.; *Cong. Record*, 87 Cong., 1 sess., Sept. 26, 1961, p. 21,329.
39. Confidential interview with former FBI agent.
40. Director to Attorney General, June 1, 1961, no. 157-387-57, June 6, 1961, no. 144-1-554, FBI–Bergman Files; Director to Marshall, June 16, 1961, no. 157-387-249, ibid.; Meier and Rudwick, *CORE*, 140–42.
41. For Williams's story, see *Negroes With Guns*.
42. Forman, *Making*, 158–63.
43. Memo, Susan Stankrauff, Aug. 28, 1961, General Correspondence, Civil Rights, Attorney General's Files, Box 9, Robert Kennedy Papers.

44. Blackstock, *COINTELPRO*, 67–89, 93–104, 152, 163–66; Forman, *Making*, 206; SAC Chicago to Director, Oct. 30, 1961, no. X3, FBI–Forman File (100-443566); Director to SACs New York et al., Oct. 12, 1961, in Church Committee, *Hearings—FBI*, 377. Williams served a self-imposed exile in Cuba, China, North Vietnam, and Tanzania until 1969, when he returned to the United States, clad in a Mao uniform. The FBI men he dreamed about met his plane, followed his "day-to-day activities," and compiled a thirty-two volume file. In March 1970 he testified before the Senate Internal Security Subcommittee and there were charges that he had made a deal with the CIA. FBI agents followed Mallory around, too, and she claimed "[they] got me kicked out of nursing school." Mallory Oral History, 18, 23; Williams Oral History, n.p.

45. Research Division Rept., Republican National Committee, Aug. 1963, in Cong. Papers, Civil Rights (B Series), Ford Papers.

46. Navasky, *Kennedy Justice*, 23.

47. Seigenthaler interview; Thompson, *Kennedy*, 124.

48. Rosen to Belmont, Dec. 22, 1961, no. illegible, FBI–Civil Rights Policy File (44-00); Marshall to Director, Dec. 29, 1961, no. illegible, ibid.; Marshall interview; Marshall to Attorney General, May 14, 1962, Civil Rights Div.—Mon. & Wed. Repts., Box 16, Marshall Papers.

49. Guthman interview. Kennedy's lawyer corps was just as white as Hoover's agent corps.

50. "Michigan's Cool Hand Luke," 32.

51. Schlesinger, *Robert Kennedy*, 304–5; Ollestad, *Inside*, 129.

52. Sullivan, *Bureau*, 125; Guthman, Seigenthaler interviews; Demaris, *Director*, 35, 37; Turner, *Hoover's F.B.I.*, 93; Brauer, *John F. Kennedy*, 83; Schlesinger, *Robert Kennedy*, 304–5; Church Committee, *Hearings—FBI*, 33.

53. Demaris, *Director*, 192.

54. Heim interview.

55. Leinbaugh interview.

56. Hoover to Tolson, DeLoach, James H. Gale, Rosen, and Thomas E. Bishop, April 14, 1969, no. not recorded, FBI–Tolson Memo File (67-9524); House Select Committee on Intelligence, *Hearings*, pt. 3, p. 1070; Fleischer interview; Ungar, *FBI*, 419–20; S. R. Burns to Walsh, Dec. 10, 1975, no. 62, FBI File 157-6160. In 1975 the FBI employed 103 black agents, 113 Hispanics, 14 Native Americans, 21 Asian-Americans, and 37 women—and over 8,300 white male agents.

57. *Ebony*, Oct. 1947, pp. 9–13, July 1958, pp. 46–47, Sept. 1962, pp. 29–34.

58. Heim interview.

59. Katzenbach Oral History, vol. 1, p. 12; Katzenbach interview.

60. FBI agents also investigated Major General Edwin A. Walker, the retired Army officer who commanded the paratroopers sent into Little Rock five years earlier. In Oxford, Walker stood on the other side, and the Bureau's reports provided the basis for a Justice Department attempt to have him committed for mental observation.

61. Director to Attorney General, Jan. 30, 1963, Mississippi File, Box 19, Marshall Papers; FBI letterhead memos, Feb. 13, 1961, Sept. 29 and 30, 1962, ibid.; Lord, *Past*, 199. Clegg was a veteran of the raid in 1934 on the Little Bohemia Lodge in Wisconsin, where John Dillinger and Baby Face Nelson escaped in a shootout that left one FBI agent dead.

62. Memo, re University of Alabama, n.d. [ca. June 11, 1963], General Corre-

spondence, Civil Rights (Univ. of Alabama), Attorney General's Files, Box
10, Robert Kennedy Papers; Director to Assistant Attorney General, Dec.
5, 1962, Alabama File, FBI Repts., Box 18, Marshall Papers; Church Committee, *Book II*, 82.

63. Employee suggestion of March 9, 1964, no. 67, FBI–Racial Matters File;
    Church Committee, *Book II*, 82; Edwin Guthman to Attorney General,
    Oct. 2, 1963, Demonstrations, Chronology, Box 32, Marshall Papers;
    David Marlin to Marshall, Aug. 22, 1963, July—Aug. 1963 Demonstra-
    tions, Box 32, ibid.

64. Director to SACs Atlanta et al., May 27, 1963, no. not recorded, FBI–
    Racial Matters File; Church Committee, *Book II*, 83.

65. *New York Post*, May 28, 1963; Navasky, *Kennedy Justice*, 112–15; Schlesin-
    ger, *Robert Kennedy*, 344–48; Wofford, *Kennedys and Kings*, 224.

66. Barrett interview; Navasky, *Kennedy Justice*, 16, 115.

67. Marshall, Barrett, Doar interviews.

68. Schlesinger, *Thousand Days*, 697, *Robert Kennedy*, 110. See also the docu-
    ments on UAW organizers, officers, members, and attorneys in Box
    701(3), Mundt Papers.

69. John and Robert Kennedy knew Hoover had accumulated information
    on the president's adventures with a string of girlfriends—from a World
    War II–era encounter with Inga Arvad, a one-time Miss Denmark and
    suspected Nazi agent, to a White House fling with Judith Campbell, a
    friend of mobsters Sam Giancana and John Rosselli, who had been intro-
    duced to JFK by Frank Sinatra. The FBI bugged Arvad's room in the Fort
    Sumter Hotel in Charleston, and Hoover had the tapes of her bed-top
    conversations with young Jack. Hoover also had an item on file regarding
    a party in New York attended by Kennedy, Sinatra, and "two mulatto
    prostitutes." The FBI even went to Robert once to alert him to a rumor
    being spread by gangster Meyer Lansky about an affair with a woman in
    El Paso, Texas. The attorney general said he had never been to El Paso.
    Courtney A. Evans to Belmont, Aug. 20, 1962, Folder 9, FBI–Hoover O&C
    Files; Theoharis and Cox, *Boss*, 334–35, 336.

70. James F. Bland to Sullivan, April 10, 1962, no. 94, Kennedy Folder, FBI–
    Hoover O&C Files; Hoover to P. Kenneth O'Donnell, Feb. 3, 1961, no. 720,
    FBI–National Negro Congress File (61-6782); Mitgang, "Annals," 55–56;
    Horne, *Communist*, 82.

71. Felt, *FBI Pyramid*, 62.

72. O'Reilly, "Herbert Hoover," 50–51.

73. George S. Mitchell to Files, Aug. 2, 1956, Criticisms: HUAC, 75-1-21-3,
    Southern Regional Council Archives.

74. Government Red-hunters accommodated blacks with a double-standard.
    Only rarely requiring black witnesses to name names, HUAC usually set-
    tled for a denunciation of Paul Robeson. Navasky, *Naming Names*, 192–
    94.

75. Wilkins to White, July 21, 1950, Communism 1950, Box 22, Wilkins Pa-
    pers.

76. Director to SAC New York et al., March 31, 1960, no. 1577, FBI–COINTEL
    (CPUSA) File; Baumgardner to Sullivan, Oct. 27, 1965, no. illegible, ibid.

77. SAC St. Louis to Director, Oct. 11, 1963, no. 42–43, ibid.; Director to SAC
    St. Louis, Oct. 24, 1963, no. 42–43, ibid. For Randolph, see Baumgardner
    to Belmont, Nov. 30, 1960, no. 2109, Dec. 27, 1960, no. 2170, ibid.; Director
    to SAC Pittsburgh, Dec, 7, 1962, no. 39–32, ibid. For the NAACP, see

memo, Feb. 28, 1958, no. 2, FBI–Wilkins File (62-78270); Director to SAC New York, Dec. 4, 1959, no. illegible, FBI–COINTEL (CPUSA) File; Baumgardner to Belmont, June 7, 1960, no. 1727, ibid.; Baumgardner to Sullivan, Feb. 15, 1965, no. 31-312, March 5, 1965, no. 31-319, ibid.; Director to SAC Detroit, Feb. 19, 1965, no. 15-153, ibid.; Director to SAC New York, March 5, 1965, no. 31-320, March 17, 1965, no. 15-illegible, ibid.; Director to SAC Newark, May 6, 1965, no. 331, ibid. For the SRC, see Dunbar interview.

78. When asked at a press conference about methods SCLC used to screen people, Abernathy made a startling claim. "If we have a person coming to our staff . . . we will check with FBI men. . . . We don't want anything that is pink much less anything that is 'red.'" Hoover responded: "If I find anyone furnishing information to SCLC he will be dismissed." De-Loach to Mohr, July 1, 1965, no. 391, FBI–SCLC File (100-438794); Baumgardner to Sullivan, July 1, 1965, no. 392, July 1, 1965, no. 408, July 6, 1985, no. 521, ibid.

79. Rosen to Belmont, May 22, 1963, no. illegible, FBI–Civil Rights File; Director to Attorney General, May 23, 1963, no. 54, FBI–Racial Matters File.

80. Seigenthaler Oral History, 41; Farmer Oral History, 30; Farmer, *Lay Bare*, 270–71; DeLoach to Mohr, Nov. 20, 1963, no. 3882, Nov. 27, 1963, no. 3882, FBI–COINTEL (CPUSA) File.

81. Heim interview; Jones to DeLoach, March 16, 1965, no. not recorded, FBI–Wilkins File (62-78270).

82. SAC New York to Director, July 19, 1963, no. 51, FBI–National Urban League File (100-23219); DeLoach to Tolson, Oct. 11, 1967, no. not recorded, FBI–Young File (161-3130).

83. *Atlanta Daily World*, June 20, 1978.

84. Brown testified again years later, against a bill to declare King's birthday a national holiday. Senate Committee on the Judiciary and House Committee on Post Office, *Joint Hearings*, 43.

85. George C. Moore to Sullivan, April 18, 1969, no. 13, FBI–Hobson File (157-3707); Baumgardner to Sullivan, Aug. 24, 1964, no. X1, ibid.; Hobson interview; SAC Washington to Director, Sept. 24, 1969, no. 132, Oct. 1, 1969, no. illegible, FBI–COINTEL (Black Nationalist) File (100-448006).

86. House Select Committee on Assassinations, *Hearings—King*, vol. 6, p. 98.

87. McKissick interview; Director to Attorney General, June 6, 1961, no. 144-1-554, FBI–Bergman Files; Lewis Oral History, 172; Young Oral History, 25; A. Philip Randolph to Hoover, Aug. 7, 1964, J. Edgar Hoover Folder, Box 14, Brotherhood of Sleeping Car Porters Records. Even Malcolm X demanded an FBI investigation after police rousted a mosque in Buffalo. And Elijah Muhammad sent Hoover a threatening letter he had received from J. B. Stoner.

88. Farmer, *Lay Bare*, 285. On occasion, the FBI responded when movement activists needed protection. Following Farmer's near lynching in Plaquemines Parish, Louisiana, DeLoach dropped by the CORE office in New York and listened to Val Coleman explain that Farmer had been smuggled out of a church in a hearse to escape a mob and was planning to go back into the Parish the next day. "You guys have got to protect him," Coleman said. When Farmer showed up at the Plaquemines courthouse the following morning, five or six FBI agents were waiting for him on the steps.

89. Howell, "Interview," 14–16, 19–20; Young Oral History, 23; House Select Committee on Assassinations, *Hearings—King*, vol. 6, p. 4; Raines, *My Soul*, 430; Brown, *Die*, 61.

90. King, *Freedom Song*, 229; Rustin interview; DeLoach to Mohr, Dec. 2, 1964, no. 634, FBI–King File (100-106670); Howell, "Interview," 14–16, 19–20; Young Oral History, 23; House Select Committee on Asssassinations, *Hearings—King*, vol. 6, p. 4; Raines, *My Soul*, 430.

91. Forman, *Making*, 353; Forman interview.

92. Overstreet, *FBI in Our Open Society*, 167–68.

93. Even Jim Forman admitted that the FBI agents who worked the case did a good job, but he said "a lot of this is 'the horse is running wild and we caught the horse after the horse is out of the gate.' I mean, who opened the gate?"

94. Frank E. Smith to Robert Kennedy, June 26, 1963, General Correspondence, Civil Rights, Attorney General's Files, Box 9, Robert Kennedy Papers. A former agent claimed that the FBI arranged for one "Julio," a Mafia-connected fellow who was facing prosecution, to kidnap a segregationist who knew the identity of the person who pulled the trigger. Taken to a "safe house" in the Louisiana bayou, the man provided enough information, after "Julio" put a .38 in his mouth, to enable the FBI to reach out for Byron De La Beckwith. Villano, *Brick Agent*, 90–94.

95. SAC New Orleans to Director, June 19, 1963, no. 168, FBI–Desegregation . . . Jackson File (157-896); letterhead memo, re [deleted], June 19, 1963, no. 168, ibid.

96. Evers Oral History, 14; Schlesinger, *Robert Kennedy*, 358; Lewis, *Portrait*, 227–29.

97. After Salter left Mississippi to work in North Carolina for the Southern Conference Educational Fund, the FBI briefed Congressman L. H. Fountain (D., N.C.) on Salter's background.

98. Overstreet, *FBI in Our Open Society*, 167–68 (quotation). The Birmingham Police Department's surveillance apparatus rivaled the Jackson Police Department's. Birmingham wiremen recorded King's telephone call home from the city jail, and squads of detectives followed civil rights activists from one Baptist church to the next throughout the 1960s. They listened to preaching about "the movement" and "how good God has been," and filed uncomprehending reports on "the singing and praying . . . all going on at the same time. Seems as if anyone wanted to sing a different song from everyone else he just goes ahead. There are four different songs being sung at one time plus one Negro man praying." A. J. Cornelius and E. T. Coleman to Jamie Moore, March 13, 1967, Box 3.28, Hamilton Papers.

99. M. H. House to Moore, April 30, 1963, Box 13.4, Connor Papers.

100. Rustin interview.

101. Belmont to Tolson (addendum by DeLoach), Sept. 17, 1963, no. 211, FBI–BAPBOMB File (157-1025).

102. Birmingham police officers assigned to the Baptist Church bombing worked hard to solve the case. But the officers assigned to the "subversive squad" were scarcely more sympathetic than the person who sent in the green stamps. During the burial service for one of the girls at Grace Hill Cemetery, the police ran license-plate checks on the cars of those "few White people standing among the Negroes." Detective M. A. Jones then followed one of the cars, driven by a white man and carrying four girls, two white and two black, back into town, where he forced the driver to stop. When Jones tried to take pictures, "the White girls put their heads down between their knees. The Negro girls just giggled."

Jones kept trying to snap his shots until "a Cadillac loaded with Negroes [pulled up]. " Personal notes, M. A. Jones, Sept. 23, 1963, Box 3.40, Hamilton Papers.

103. Belmont to Tolson, Sept. 17, 1963, no. 211, FBI–BAPBOMB File. In the normal bombing case the FBI's principal goal was to prevent local police officers and politicians from shifting "the burden of their responsibility to us." Rosen to Belmont, April 11, 1964, no. not recorded, FBI–Civil Rights File.

104. DeLoach to Mohr, Sept. 20, 1963, no. 144, FBI–BAPBOMB File; Rosen to Belmont, Sept. 27, 1963, no. 308, ibid.

105. See serials 144, 308, 334, 335, 392, 463, ibid.; Raines, "Birmingham Bombing," 12ff; *New York Times,* Feb. 17 and 18, 1980.

106. Rosen to Belmont, Sept. 16, 1963, no. 28, FBI–BAPBOMB File; Hoover to the President, April 10, 1964, WHCF–CF, HU2/St1, Box 56, Johnson Papers; Lyndon B. Johnson to Edgar [Hoover], April 8, 1964, ibid.

107. Rosen to Belmont, Oct. 14, 1963, no. 485, FBI–BAPBOMB File; SAC Birmingham to Director, Dec. 13, 1966, no. 769, FBI–Liuzzo File (44-28601); Gale to DeLoach, May 27, 1966, no. 2, Microphone Surveillances Folder, FBI–Hoover O&C Files. The Bureau informed Kennedy of only one of its mike sources.

108. DeLoach to Mohr, Sept. 20, 1963, no. 63, FBI–BAPBOMB File; Evans to Belmont, Sept. 16, 1963, no. 67, ibid.; and the articles cited in note 105.

109. Hoover to Attorney General, Sept. 30, 1963, no. 333, FBI–BAPBOMB File.

110. Rosen to Belmont, Sept. 30, 1963, no. 283 and 284, ibid.

111. Hoover to Attorney General, Sept. 30, 1963, no. 333, ibid.; Evans to Belmont, Sept. 30, 1964, no. 337, ibid.

112. *New York Times,* Feb. 18, 1980; Eddy interview. Chambliss, sentenced to life imprisonment, died in the fall of 1985.

113. Rosen to Belmont, April 11, 1964, no. not recorded, FBI–Civil Rights File.

114. Schlesinger, *Robert Kennedy,* 345.

115. Newfield, *Robert Kennedy,* 23.

116. The FBI cannot be blamed for the Kennedy administration's early tendency to appoint segregationists to the federal bench.

117. Newfield, *Robert Kennedy,* 23. Newfield gradually changed his mind, believing Kennedy had been transformed into an "existential hero." Hoover himself described Kennedy as "a kind of Messiah for the generation gap."

118. Cheek interview; Laurie Pritchett to Asa Kelley, Oct. 19, 1962, City Manager's Office, Albany Movement Records.

119. Pritchett to S. A. Roos, Oct. 30 and Nov. 10, 1962, Police Dept., Mayor's Office, Albany Movement Records; memos, re statements from Chief Pritchett et al., July 23 and 24, 1962, ibid.; Pritchett interview; C. B. King Oral History, 1; *New York Times,* Dec. 14, 1961.

120. Rosen to Belmont, July 24, 1962, no. not recorded, FBI–King File.

121. Pritchett, Sitton interviews. Hansen is quoted in Carson, *In Struggle,* 61, 84. In the South as a whole, Sitton added, the conduct of the FBI "depended on the individual agents—some were very good, some were terrible ... extremely cooperative with the local police. Albany especially."

122. C. B. King Oral History, 18, 21.

123. Cheek interview.

124. Ibid.
125. Ibid.; C. B. King, Thomas interviews; Robert Kennedy to Martin Luther King, Jr., Dec. 4, 1963, King Papers. Jack Miller's Criminal Division brought the action, not Burke Marshall's Civil Rights Division.
126. DeLoach to Mohr, Jan. 15, 1963, no. not recorded, FBI–King File; R. W. Smith to Sullivan, Oct. 15, 1964, no. not recorded, FBI–SCLC File; C. B. King Oral History, 18; Barkan, *Protestors*, 69; Zinn, *Southern*, 212.
127. Zinn, *Southern*, 211, *Albany*, 31; Navasky, *Kennedy Justice*, 121–22; C. B. King interview.
128. This surveillance was on Rabinowitz's law office, not C. B. King's.
129. Slater King Oral History, 26.
130. Cheek, C. B. King, Sherrod interviews. Holtzman had criticized the FBI performance in Albany. *Harvard Law Record*, Oct. 3, Nov. 14, and Dec. 5, 1963.
131. Schlesinger, *Robert Kennedy*, 298; Wilkins, *Man's Life*, 173–74.
132. Brauer, *John F. Kennedy*, 319.
133. Wilkins, Trebach interviews.

CHAPTER 4.
Black Dream, Red Menace

1. Schlesinger, *Robert Kennedy*, 365–66; White, Forman, Lewis interviews; Garrow, *Bearing*, 282–83.
2. Schlesinger, *Robert Kennedy*, 366–67; Louis B. Nichols to Clyde Tolson, July 23, 1953, Misc. A–Z Folder, FBI–Nichols O&C Files.
3. In preparation for the expected southern influx of Soviet-directed agents, FBI officials advised field agents to recruit informants by waving "the flag" and using their own "sons and daughters" at the high schools and colleges. C. B. Stanbery to SAC Birmingham, Oct. 31, 1960, no. 137-00-165, FBI–Bergman Freedom Rider Files.
4. House Committee on Appropriations, *Hearings* (1962), 343–44; SAC Birmingham to Director, April 12, 1963, no. 199, FBI–Levison File (100-392452).
5. William C. Sullivan to Alan H. Belmont, Aug. 30, 1963, in Dept. of Justice, *King Task Force*, 166; Director to SACs Atlanta et al., July 18, 1963, no. not recorded, FBI–CIRM File (100-3-116).
6. Milton A. Jones to Cartha D. DeLoach, March 16, 1965, no. not recorded, FBI–Wilkins File (62-78270); Director to SAC New York, Aug. 13, 1964, no. 856, FBI–COINTEL (CPUSA) File (100-3-104); SAC New York to Director, Aug. 24, 1964, no. 867, ibid.
7. David Marlin to Burke Marshall, Aug. 22, 1963, Aug. 1963 Demonstrations, Box 32, Marshall Papers; "Communist Party, USA—Negro Question," Aug. 23, 1963, no. 253X, FBI–CIRM File.
8. "Communist Party, USA—Negro Question."
9. Ibid.
10. Ibid. See also the cover memo, Fred J. Baumgardner to Sullivan, Aug. 23, 1963.
11. Baumgardner to Sullivan, Aug. 23, 1963, no. 253X, FBI–CIRM File.
12. Baumgardner to Sullivan, Aug. 23, 1963, no. 253X, Aug. 28, 1963, no. 230 and no. not recorded, ibid.; Senate Select Committee to Study . . . Intelligence Activities (hereafter Church Committee), *Book III*, 107.

13. Ungar, *FBI*, 295–314; Theoharis and Cox, *Boss*, 105.

14. Sullivan to Belmont, Aug. 30, 1963, no. 253X, Sept. 16, 1963, no. 367, Sept. 25, 1963, no. illegible, FBI–CIRM File; J. Edgar Hoover to all SACs, Sept. 24, 1963, no. not recorded, Oct. 1, 1963, no. illegible, ibid.; Tolson to Director, Sept. 18, 1963, no. 253X, ibid.; Dept. of Justice, *King Task Force*, 165–74.

15. Church Committee, *Book III*, 107–11. The Church Committee concluded that "preconceptions" and "bureaucratic squabbles" led to the intensification of surveillance after the March on Washington—and not "genuine concerns based on hard evidence that communists might be influencing the civil rights movement." The FBI position is that the initial decision to investigate King was fully justified and the excesses that followed resulted from Sullivan's recklessness. Sullivan himself testified before the Church Committee, but he was hardly an objective witness, having left the Bureau in 1971 under fire.

16. Ibid., 106, 108.

17. Internal debates over surveillance policies were common—as Hoover's comments about Castro suggest. The same type of debate occurred on the question of organized crime and would occur again during the height of the anti–Vietnam war demonstrations, when Division Five argued that "knowledgeable sources and confidential informants have failed to substantiate claims by the CP of substantial influence within the new Left movement." R. L. Shackelford to Charles D. Brennan, Dec. 31, 1970, no. 68, FBI–Kirk File (134-14771).

18. Rustin interview.

19. Sullivan to Belmont, Oct. 9, 1956, no. 47, FBI–COINTEL (CPUSA) File; "Weaknesses of the Communist Party, USA," Oct. 1956, no. 47, ibid.; FBI Monographs, "Communist Party and the Negro," 1953 and 1956. See also Hoover, *Masters*, 236.

20. Church Committee, *Book III*, 139; Sullivan, *Bureau*, 137–38.

21. Memo, re Martin Luther King, n.d. [ca. June 1963], King Folder, FBI–Hoover O&C Files.

22. Director to SAC New York, April 22, 1959, no. not recorded, FBI–Levison File; Baumgardner to Belmont, April 22, 1959, no. not recorded, ibid.; Garrow, *FBI and Martin Luther King*, 21–77; Director to SAC Atlanta, Sept. 20, 1957, no. X1, FBI–SCLC File (100-438794); Director to SACs New York et al., Dec. 1, 1964, no. 2108, FBI–COINTEL (CPUSA) File.

23. D. E. Roney to SAC New York, March 9, 1964, no. 1391, FBI–Levison File (New York Field Office File) (100-111180); Dept. of Justice, *King Task Force*, 141; note, April 30, 1962, no. not recorded, FBI–King File (100-106670).

24. Memo, re Stanley David Levison, June 3, 1963, no. 128, FBI–King File; SAC New York to Director, March 30, 1966, no. 2425, ibid.; note, March 30, 1966, no. 2425, ibid.; memo, re CIRM and Stanley Levison, Dec. 9, 1963, no. not recorded, ibid.

25. Schlesinger, *Robert Kennedy*, 372; Hoover to Tolson, Belmont, DeLoach, Alex Rosen, and Sullivan, June 17, 1963, no. 150, FBI–King File.

26. Garrow, *FBI and Martin Luther King*, 47–48. Division Five objected to the SISS subpoena.

27. Baumgardner to Sullivan, Oct. 8, 1962, no. 34-306, FBI–COINTEL (CPUSA) File; SAC New York to Director, Sept. 28, 1962, no. 34-295, ibid.; *Augusta Chronicle*, Oct. 25, 1962; *Birmingham News*, Oct. 26, 1962.

28. Director to SAC New York, April 24, 1964, in Church Committee, *Hearings—FBI*, 695–96; idem, *Book III*, 139.

29. Lewis interview.
30. Quoted in the SNCC monograph, Aug. 1967, no. 1386, FBI–SNCC File (100-439190).
31. House Select Committee on Assassinations, *Hearings—King*, 351.
32. Hoover to all SACs, Oct. 1, 1963, in Church Committee, *Book III*, 110–11.
33. Sullivan to Belmont, Dec. 24, 1963, no. not recorded, FBI–King File; memo, re Questions to be Explored, Dec. 23, 1963, no. 684, FBI–CIRM File; Church Committee, *Book III*, 133, 135; Sullivan to Belmont, Jan. 27, 1964, no. 15, King Folder, FBI–Hoover O&C Files.
34. Raines, *My Soul*, 430.
35. SAC Chicago to Director, Aug. 25, 1965, no. 9-531, FBI–COINTEL (CPUSA) File; SAC Los Angeles to Director, Oct. 28, 1963, no. 26-103, ibid. The most aggressive action launched against Lightfoot occurred in 1966, after he inherited a row house from his mother, when the FBI arranged publicity portraying him as a "slum lord." Division Five timed this action to coincide with an SCLC slum clearance campaign, hoping to divert attention from King's work in Chicago. Berlet, "Journalists."
36. The FBI campaign to destroy King has been meticulously chronicled in Garrow, *FBI and Martin Luther King* and *Bearing*.
37. Church Committee, *Book III*, 145.
38. DeLoach to Tolson, Oct. 25, 1966, no. 2756, Oct. 26, 1966, no. 2754, FBI–King File; Baumgardner to Sullivan, Nov. 3, 1966, no. 2782, ibid.
39. *Time*, Feb. 14, 1964; SAC New York to Director, Feb. 11, 1964, no. 34-565, Feb. 14, 1964, no. 34-582, FBI–COINTEL (CPUSA) File; Senate Select Committee On Intelligence, *Hearings on National Intelligence Reorganization*, 484–86.
40. Baumgardner to Sullivan, Sept. 17, 1963, no. 9-214, FBI–COINTEL (CPUSA) File.
41. Church Committee, *Book II*, 66, *Book III*, 430, 438–39.
42. Church Committee, *Book III*, 135, 139, 479; Baumgardner to Sullivan, Oct. 1, 1964, idem, *Hearings—FBI*, 609–11.
43. Church Committee, *Book III*, 139, 481–83.
44. Director to SACs Atlanta et al., July 14, 1964, no. illegible, FBI–Civil Rights Policy File (44-00); SAC Chicago to Director, May 26, 1966, no. 1442, FBI–SCLC File.
45. James F. Bland to Sullivan, Feb. 3, 1962, no. 135, FBI–Levison File.
46. Director to Assistant Attorney General, Dec. 18, 1975, no. X65, FBI File 62-117166; Director to Attorney General, Oct. 1, 1969, no. 353, FBI–Levison File.
47. Heim interview; Bishop, *Days of Martin Luther King*, 83.
48. SAC New York to Director, Oct. 14, 1963, no. 34-502, FBI–COINTEL (CPUSA) File; Navasky, "FBI's Wildest Dream," 716–18; Leinbaugh interview.
49. Statement, re J. Edgar Hoover, Nov. 19, 1964, Box 27.41, SCLC Papers; Church Committee, *Hearings—FBI*, 173; Garrow, *FBI and Martin Luther King*, 122–23; "FBI and Civil Rights," 56–58.
50. Garrow, *FBI and Martin Luther King*, 54–55; Zinn, *Albany*. King had been on record as a critic since February 4, 1961.
51. Hoover had monitored the percentage of southern-born agents assigned to civil rights cases since the mid-1950s.

52. DeLoach to John P. Mohr, Nov. 19, 1964, no. not recorded, FBI–King File; Navasky, *Kennedy Justice*, 122.

53. Cheek interview; House Select Committee on Intelligence, *Hearings*, pt. 3, p. 1047; House Select Committee on Assassinations, *Hearings—King*, vol. 6, pp. 92–96; Rustin interview.

54. Garrow, *FBI and Martin Luther King*, 125–26, 133–34, *Bearing*, 373–74.

55. Church Committee, *Book III*, 162; Garrow, *FBI and Martin Luther King*, 127.

56. DeLoach to Mohr, No. 27, 1964, no. 16, FBI–Wilkins File; Hoover to the President, Nov. 30, 1964, no. 15, ibid.; Church Committee, *Book III*, 162–63, *Hearings—FBI*, 172; Garrow, *Bearing*, 687–88n, *FBI and Martin Luther King*, 271 n41.

57. Guthman interview; Ungar, *FBI*, 281; Baumgardner to Sullivan, Feb. 15, 1965, no. 312, and March 5, 1965, no. 319, FBI–COINTEL (CPUSA) File.

58. Ungar, *FBI*, 279–95; Theoharis and Cox, *Boss*, 105n.

59. Church Committee, *Book III*, 168–71; Farmer, *Lay Bare*, 269–70.

60. Howell, "Interview," 16; Kennedy Oral History, 636; Hoover to Tolson, Belmont, Mohr, DeLoach, and Rosen, Dec. 1, 1964, no. 563, FBI–King File; DeLoach to Hoover, Dec. 2, 1964, no. 634, ibid.

61. Joseph A. Sizzo to Sullivan, Dec. 1, 1964, no. 3, King Folder, FBI–Hoover O&C Files. Rowan and Bunche, nonetheless, received derogatory information on King from time to time.

62. Stone interview; Garrow, *FBI and Martin Luther King*, 125–26, 133–34, *Bearing*, 373–74. The King flap continued to occupy a good deal of the FBI's time. On March 30, after Edwin C. Berry of the Urban League in Chicago criticized the director, SAC Marlin Johnson gave him a ninety-minute going over in the chambers of federal judge James B. Parsons, a Bureau ally. Another Chicago resident, Rev. Archibald Carey, met with DeLoach in May in a futile attempt to end the King-Hoover feud. Afterward, Hoover gave DeLoach the ultimate accolade ("Well handled. H."), though in this case it was a bit gratuitous. Carey had once named the director, along with the entire "Jewish community," as one of the ten living whites who had done the most to help black America. D. C. Morrell to DeLoach, March 31, 1965, no. not recorded, FBI–National Urban League File (100-23219); Archibald J. Carey, Jr., to [deleted], March 3, 1964, no. 27, FBI–Carey File (161-2040); DeLoach to Mohr, May 19, 1965, no. 30, ibid.

63. Hoover to Tolson, Mohr, and DeLoach, Dec. 8, 1964, no. 127, FBI–Lawrence File (94-4-3169); Roberts, *Papa Jack*, 144–84; *Chicago Defender*, Aug. 11 and 15, 1970.

64. Hoover's prurient interests extended beyond blacks. His old General Intelligence Division held a file on birth-control crusader Margaret Sanger; in the late 1930s his agents investigated several condom manufacturers on the grounds that their products were "often found in the possession of high school students"; and throughout his forty-eight year tenure his senior staff remained on alert for "sex deviates" among the faculty and staff of his alma mater, George Washington University.

65. "Communist Party and the Negro," 1953, p. 10.

66. Sexism within the movement should not be exaggerated, but it did exist—as evidenced by Stokely Carmichael's casual remark: "The only position for women in SNCC is prone."

67. Director to SAC New York, May 11, 1960, no. 1649, FBI–COINTEL (CPUSA) File; Director to SAC Atlanta, Aug. 19, 1964, no. not recorded, ibid.; Na-

vasky, *Kennedy Justice*, 16; Hoover to Tolson, Mohr, and DeLoach, Dec. 8, 1964, no. 127, FBI–Lawrence File; Director to SAC New York, Aug. 25, 1966, no. not recorded, FBI–Levison File; Director to SAC New York, Sept. 14, 1966, no. 1964, ibid. (New York Field Office File); House Committee on Appropriations, *Hearings* (1966), 296; Wilkins interview; SAC Chicago to Director, April 16, 1968, no. 2116, FBI–SCLC File; Dept. of Justice, *King Task Force*, 136.

68. Stone interview; Bishop, *Confessions*, 432.

69. Leinbaugh interview; Baumgardner to Sullivan, March 4, 1964, no. 312, Aug. 31, 1964, no. 450, Sept. 17, 1964, no. 479, FBI–King File; UPI ticker, Nov. 9, 1963, no. 264, ibid.; Hoover to Tolson, June 2, 1967, no. not recorded, FBI–Tolson Memo File (67-9524); Garrow, *FBI and Martin Luther King*, 121.

70. Leinbaugh interview.

71. Serials 59, 66, FBI–COINTEL (Black Nationalist) File (100-448006).

72. Evers, *Evers*, 112.

73. Church Committee, *Book III*, 52–53; SAC St. Louis to Director, Oct. 11, 1968, no. illegible, FBI–COINTEL (Black) File.

74. Director to SAC Philadelphia, June 17, 1965, no. 37-6, FBI—COINTEL (White Hate) File (157-9).

75. Press release, July 13, 1963, in Box 27.25, SCLC Papers; Courtney A. Evans to Belmont, July 16, 1963, no. 166, FBI–King File; Jones to DeLoach, July 16, 1963, no. 164, ibid.

76. Belmont to D. Milton Ladd, Aug. 25, 1953, no. not recorded, FBI–Highlander File (61-7511); Nichols to Tolson, Aug. 30, 1957, no. 198, ibid.; Director to SAC Savannah, April 29, 1959, no. not recorded, ibid.; Baumgardner to Sullivan, July 26, 1963, no. 286, ibid.; Director to SAC Knoxville, July 29, 1963, not recorded, ibid.; Jones to DeLoach, July 27, 1964, no. 299, ibid.; Director to SACs Atlanta and Knoxville, April 6, 1965, no. 1154, FBI–King File.

77. Church Committee, *Book III*, 98–100.

78. Russell was the man who laundered "the CIA budget in the Defense budget," said Secretary of State Dean Rusk. Rusk himself "never saw a budget for the CIA." Rusk Oral History, n.p.

79. Robert Kennedy to Russell, Nov. 1, 1963, Civil Rights Series, Civil Rights General, Special Correspondence, Box 4, Russell Papers; Kennedy Oral History, 683; Belmont to Tolson, Nov. 1, 1963, no. not recorded, FBI–King File; Evans to Belmont, Nov. 1, 1963, no. not recorded, ibid.

80. WHJ to File, Oct. 23, 1965, Intra Office Communications Series, Box 15, Russell Papers; Schlesinger, *Robert Kennedy*, 379.

81. Belmont to Tolson, Oct. 17, 1963, in Dept. of Justice, *King Task Force*, 176.

82. Hoover to Tolson, Belmont, Rosen, Sullivan, DeLoach, and Evans, Feb. 5, 1964, no. 297, FBI–King File; Hoover to Tolson, Belmont, Mohr, DeLoach, Rosen, and Sullivan, Oct. 25, 1963, no. 10, King Folder, FBI–Hoover O&C Files; Director to Attorney General, Oct. 25, 1963, no. 11, ibid.; "Communism and the Negro Movement—A Current Analysis," Oct. 16, 1963, no. 416, FBI–CIRM File; Evans to Belmont, Oct. 25, 1963, no. not recorded, FBI–Robert Kennedy File (77-51387).

83. Hoover to Tolson, Belmont, Rosen, Sullivan, DeLoach, and Evans, Feb. 5, 1964, no. 297, FBI–King File; DeLoach to Mohr, March 16, 1964, no. 320, ibid.

84. Baumgardner to Sullivan, April 17, 1964, no. 34-713, FBI–COINTEL (CPUSA) File.

85. House Committee on Appropriations, *Hearings* (1964), 308–09.

86. Church Committee, *Book III*, 155; Garrow, *Bearing*, 322; *New York Times*, April 22, 1964. Lewis is quoted in Carson, *In Struggle*, 107.

87. Rustin interview.

88. Leinbaugh interview.

CHAPTER 5.
Mississippi Burning

1. Belfrage, *Freedom Summer*, 55; Raines, *My Soul*, 287; Guyot, Moses interviews; J. Edgar Hoover to Clyde Tolson, Alan H. Belmont, Cartha D. De-Loach, and William C. Sullivan, Jan. 28, 1965, no. not recorded, FBI–Tolson Memo File. Senator Paul Douglas (D., Ill.) once asked the FBI, when compiling arrest records, to indicate if arrests had been made during nonviolent racial demonstrations. "Innocent" college students, he felt, should not be burdened by the stigma of a police record. Hoover refused the request—and not only because of the expected clerical burden. In 1960, when San Francisco municipal judge Albert Axelrod warned sixty-three students and others who had been arrested at a demonstration against HUAC about matters "which would be on their record for the rest of their lives," Hoover dismissed Axelrod as "another 'bleeding heart.'" SAC San Francisco to Director, May 28, 1960, no. 4508, FBI–HUAC File (61-7582); Navasky, *Kennedy Justice*, 10–11.

2. Barry Oral History, n.p.; Moses interview.

3. Belknap, *Federal Law*, 141; Aaron Henry, Robert Moses, and David Dennis to President Johnson, May 25, 1964, White House Aides' Files—Lee C. White, Miss. Summer Project, Box 6, Johnson Papers; Miller, ed., "Mississippi," 290.

4. Atlanta Field Office Rept., Sept. 28, 1964, no. illegible, FBI–SNCC File; Guyot interview; Whitehead, *Attack*, 4, 9.

5. During the Bureau's probe of the Mack Charles Parker lynching in 1959, a candidate for sheriff of Pearl River County invariably reminded his audiences that the FBI "talked to me like I was a nigger, or a dog." Tully, *F.B.I.'s Most Famous Cases*, 217.

6. Navasky, *Kennedy Justice*, 125.

7. See the SNCC monograph, Aug. 1967, no. 1386, FBI–SNCC File (100-439190).

8. John Doar and Dorothy Landsberg, "The Performance of the FBI in Investigating Violations of Federal Laws Protecting the Right to Vote, 1960–1967," in Senate Select Committee to Study . . . Intelligence Activities (hereafter Church Committee), *Hearings—FBI*, 929–30; Burke Marshall to Attorney General, June 5, 1964, Alphabetical File, Box 3, Marshall Papers.

9. Marshall interview; Doar, "Performance," 931–32, 936; Navasky, *Kennedy Justice*, 105–06, 437–38; DeLoach to Tolson, Jan. 9, 1967, no. 1911, FBI–Robert Kennedy File (77-51387).

10. Robert F. Kennedy to the President, June 5, 1964, WHCF, Ex HU2/St24, Box 26, Johnson Papers; Marshall to Attorney General, June 5, 1964, Alphabetical File, Box 3, Marshall Papers.

11. Brown, *Strain*, 294–95.

12. Kennedy Oral History, 639, 655–56, 666; DeLoach to Hoover, Jan. 15, 1964, no. 10, March 6, 1964, no. 31, March 9, 1964, no. 26, Johnson Folder, FBI–Hoover O&C Files; DeLoach to Tolson, June 17, 1965, no. 34, ibid.; Hoover to Marvin Watson, June 29, 1965, no. 36, ibid.

13. DeLoach to Hoover, March 6, 1964, no. 31, Johnson Folder, FBI–Hoover O&C Files; Kennedy Oral History, 639, 655–56, 666.

14. Meier and Rudwick, *Core*, 276.

15. "Prosecutive Summary," Dec. 19, 1964, no. 1613, FBI–MIBURN File (44-25706); Cagin and Dray, *We Are Not Afraid;* Whitehead, *Attack.*

16. Henry Oral History, n.p; King, *Freedom Song,* 378–85; "Chronology of Contacts," June 21–22, 1964, in WATS/Neshoba, SNCC Papers.

17. Lee C. White to File, June 23, 1964, White House Aides' Files—Lee C. White, Miss. Summer Project Voter Registration, Box 6, Johnson Papers; Cagin and Dray, *We Are Not Afraid,* 324–25.

18. Moses to Parents of all Mississippi Summer Volunteers, n.d. [ca. June 22, 1964], White House Aides' Files—Lee C. White, Miss. Summer Project Voter Registration, Box 6, Johnson Papers; Alex Rosen to Alan H. Belmont, July 8, 1964, no. not recorded, FBI–Racial Matters Policy File (157-00).

19. White interview; White to File, June 23, 1964, White House Aides' Files—Lee C. White, Miss. Summer Project Voter Registration, Box 6, Johnson Papers.

20. Memo, re telephone call, Rita Schwerner to the White House, June 23, 1964, White House Aides' Files—Lee C. White, Miss. Summer Project Voter Registration, Box 6, Johnson Papers.

21. Memo, re telephone call, Rita Schwerner to Mary King, June 25, 1964, WATS Repts., Box 37, SNCC Papers; Misseduc Foundation, *Mississippi,* 62–63.

22. Memo, re telephone call, Rita Schwerner to Mary King, June 25, 1964, WATS Repts., Box 37, SNCC Papers; Raines, *My Soul,* 289.

23. Transcript, CBS News, June 25, 1964.

24. Clark Oral History, 30; Marshall Oral History, 24, 30, Johnson Library; House Select Committee on Assassinations, *Hearings—King,* vol. 7, p. 142; Milton A. Jones to DeLoach, Dec. 2, 1964, no. 126, FBI–Whitehead File (77-68662).

25. Ungar, *FBI,* 413–14. For Moore's career, see Tully, *F.B.I.'s Most Famous Cases,* 191–201; Subject File—Roy K. Moore, Mississippi Dept. of Archives and History, Jackson.

26. Jones to Thomas E. Bishop, Aug. 14, 1970, no. 18, FBI–Whitehead File (94-64866); Von Hoffman, *Mississippi,* 38; Sutherland, ed., *Letters,* 118.

27. Hoover to Walter Jenkins, July 13, 1964, WHCF, Ex HU2/St24, Box 26, Johnson Papers; Jones to Bishop, Aug. 14, 1970, no. 18, FBI–Whitehead File (94-64866).

28. Welch, *Inside,* 102, 106–7; Navasky, *Kennedy Justice,* 107; letterhead memo, July 1, 1964, WHCF, FG135-6, Box 188, Johnson Papers. In addition to the fingerprint service, SNCC's Lawrence Guyot remembered an FBI agent who "said, 'Look, Guyot, we want to . . . identify any scars on your body. . . . If anything happens to you we want to know how to be able to identify you.'" "They were as much a part of the fear apparatus as anything else," Guyot concluded.

29. Evers interview; and Hoover's letter to Jenkins, cited in note 27.

30. Johnson to Edgar [Hoover], July 13, 1964, WHCF, FG135-6, Box 188, John-

son Papers; Hoover to the President, July 16, 1964, WHCF, Ex HU2/St24, Box 26, ibid.; Hoover to Tolson, Belmont, Rosen, William C. Sullivan, and DeLoach, July 21, 1964, no. not recorded, FBI–King File (100-106670).

31. Hoover to Tolson, Belmont, Rosen, Sullivan, and DeLoach, July 21, 1964, no. not recorded, FBI–King File.

32. D. C. Morrell to DeLoach, Aug. 4, 1964, no. 422, ibid.; Lawrence A. Rainey to Hoover, July 28, 1964, no. 425, ibid.; Belfrage, *Freedom Summer*, 155, 164.

33. Memo, re telephone call, Freddy Lee Watson to Mary King, June 24, 1964, WATS Repts., Box 37, SNCC Papers; Clement L. McGowan, Jr., to Rosen, July 22, 1964, no. 405, FBI–King; "Mississippi Eyewitness," 38–39.

34. Moore interview; Welch, *Inside*, 100; *Jackson Daily News*, July 12, 1964; Warren, *Who Speaks*, 125n; Ungar, *FBI*, 415; Von Hoffman, *Mississippi*, 39, 54; Doar, "Performance," 941; Moody, *Coming*, 338.

35. Nicholas deB. Katzenbach to the President, Sept. 28, 1964, WHCF, Ex HU2/St24, Box 27, Johnson Papers; Director to Attorney General, Dec. 19, 1967, in Church Committee, *Hearings—FBI*, 526. For Hoover on Wallace, see DeLoach to Mohr, Dec. 2, 1964, no. 634, FBI–King File.

36. Doar, "Performance," 936-37; Ungar, *FBI*, 414–15.

37. As relayed by the director to his senior staff. He offered no evidence. Hoover to Tolson, Belmont, Rosen, Sullivan, and DeLoach, July 16, 1964, no. not recorded, FBI–Penn File (44-25873). For the statistics and the other quotes, see House Committee on Appropriations, *Hearings* (1965), 285; Doar, "Performance," 937; Demaris, *Director*, 207.

38. McGowan, Sullivan interviews; Mars, *Witness*.

39. Sullivan, *Bureau*, 74–77.

40. DeLoach to Mohr, Aug. 5, 1964, no. not recorded, FBI–Penn File; Prosecutive Summary, Dec. 19, 1964, no. 1613, and the Supplemental Summary, March 5, 1965, no. 1822, FBI–MIBURN File.

41. Katzenbach to the President, Sept. 4, 1964, White House Aides' Files—Lee C. White, Law Enforcement (Riots), Box 5, Johnson Papers. See also the prosecutive summaries cited in the previous note.

42. Cagin and Dray, *We Are Not Afraid*, 435, 452.

43. McGowan, Doar, Fleischer interviews; Hoover to Jenkins, Aug. 11, 1964, WHCF, FG135-6, Johnson Papers. King, Young, and Wilkins are quoted in *Whose FBI?*, ed. Wright, 381; Sullivan in Whitehead, *Attack*, 142.

44. Suggested statement re Katzenbach, Jan. 2, [1967?], Dept. of Justice, Box 58, SNCC Papers; Carson, *In Struggle*, 115.

45. Bernhard interview.

46. Aschenbrenner interview; deposition of James O. Ingram, Oct. 10, 1978, p. 7, *Muhammad Kenyatta v. Roy Moore et al.*, no. J77-0298(R) (N.D., Miss., 1985). Kenyatta's suit failed.

47. Hoover to Tolson, Mohr, and DeLoach, Dec. 8, 1964, no. 127, FBI–Lawrence File (94-4-3169); *Jackson Daily News*, Nov. 22, 1964. After a gentle nudge from Lawrence, Hoover qualified this characterization. "I thought it more appropriate to say state obligations than rights."

48. SAC Charlotte to Director, April 24, 1964, no. deleted, FBI–Lowenstein File (file no. also deleted).

49. Director to SACs Albany et al., June 12, 1964, no. 73, FBI–Racial Matters File. By this time the FBI had begun to experiment with "counterintelligence education" on the campuses of the schools that sent students into

the South. "Certainly," the head of the Milwaukee office wrote, in a clear statement of this ambitious campaign, "we should educate our students in Democracy" by supplying "information" to "reliable, dedicated, loyal college faculty," by developing "an outstanding student leader on each campus," and by disseminating data to "established sources of all college newspapers." SAC Milwaukee to Director, May 31, 1963, no. 34-47, FBI–COINTEL (CPUSA) File (100-3-104).

50. Moore interview; Ungar, *FBI*, 415–16; Harris, *Dreams*, 87.

51. DeLoach to Mohr, July 2, 1964, no. 44-25790-5, FBI–NLG Files; Hoover to Tolson, Belmont, Rosen, Sullivan, and DeLoach, July 21, 1964, no. not recorded, FBI–King File.

52. SAC Seattle to Director, Dec. 4, 1964, no. 50-157, FBI–COINTEL (CPUSA) File; Director to SAC Seattle, Nov. 30, 1964, no. 50-156, ibid.; Church Committee, *Book III*, 56.

53. SAC Jackson to Director, Sept. 16, 1969, no. 54-14, FBI–COINTEL (New Left) File (100-449698); Smead, *Blood*, 147–48. See also Subject File—State Sovereignty Commission, Mississippi Archives.

54. Karl E. Mundt to Joe Floyd, Feb. 23, 1962, Box 165(3), Mundt Papers. A few weeks after discussing Schwarz with Mundt, DeLoach recommended that Dwight Eisenhower not allow his name to be "used to lend prestige to such individuals." DeLoach to Mohr, June 27, 1962, Eisenhower Folder, FBI–Nichols O&C Files.

55. Director to SAC Atlanta, July 2, 1970, no. 2-16, FBI–COINTEL (New Left) File; SAC New Orleans to Director, July 31, 1970, no. illegible, FBI–COINTEL (Black Nationalist) File (100-448006).

56. Louis B. Nichols to Tolson, Feb. 26, 1954, no. not recorded, FBI–NAACP File (61-3176); "Plaintiff's Principal Factual Papers . . . ," Sept. 26, 1984, pp. 220–22, in NLG Papers; *National Lawyers Guild v. Attorney General et al.*, 77 Civ. 999 (S.D.N.Y.); Belmont to Leland V. Boardman, April 4, 1958, no. not recorded, May 15, 1958, no. not recorded, FBI–COINTEL (CPUSA) File; Director to SACs Baltimore et al., April 11, 1958, no. not recorded, ibid.

57. Goodman, "NLG," 1–7; Holt, *Summer*, 88–94.

58. The FBI described Dombrowski as "a preacher at heart who has gone 'nuts' on the brotherhood of man."

59. Baumgardner to Sullivan, Oct. 9, 1963, no. illegible, Feb. 26, 1964, no. 1065, FBI–McSurely Files (100-10355); Rosen to Belmont, Oct. 8, 1963, no. 1040, Feb. 20, 1964, no. 1066, ibid.; DeLoach to Mohr, March 4, 1964, no. 1067, ibid.; SAC Washington to Director, March 19, 1964, no. 1068, ibid.; McGowan to Rosen, Oct. 17, 1963, no. not recorded, ibid.; Marshall to Martin Luther King, Jr., Oct. 16, 1963, King Papers.

60. DeLoach to Mohr, July 2, 1964, no. 44-25790-5, FBI–NLG Files; *Cong. Record*, 88 Cong., 2 sess., July 22, 1964, pp. 16593-97.

61. Barkan, *Protestors*, 41–46; Greenberg interview. From the Inc. Fund's perspective, the problem was with SNCC. "Initially, we represented them very readily," Greenberg said. "As time went on they probably didn't want us."

62. Conversations recorded in DeLoach to Mohr, June 10, 1964, no. 100-7321-not recorded, FBI–NLG Files.

63. "Plantiff's Principal Factual Papers," 320–24; Church Committee, *Book III*, 59; *Atlanta Constitution*, Dec. 28, 1979. Crockett won election to the Recorder's Court and eventually won a seat in the U.S. House of Represen-

tatives. Hundreds of FBI informants reported on NLG members over the years, and a few of them sat on the executive boards of the major chapters. As late as September 1979 the FBI forwarded some four hundred pages of documents on the Guild to Senator Strom Thurmond in connection with a nomination for a federal judgeship. Thurmond specifically requested data on the executive board of the Detroit chapter for the years 1960–1965. "Plantiff's Principal Factual Papers," 390–92.

64. James F. Bland to Sullivan, June 24, 1964, no. 105-1913-362, FBI–NLG Files; UPI ticker, June 23, 1964, no. 105-1913-362, ibid.; Director to Attorney General, June 25, 1964, no. 105-1913-360, ibid.; memo, re Martin Popper, June 24, 1964, no. 105-1913-360, ibid.; Hoover to Jenkins, June 25, 1964, no. 105-1913-361, ibid.

65. SAC New York to Director, Aug. 10, 1964, no. not recorded, FBI–CIRM File (100-3-116).

66. Courtney A. Evans to Belmont, July 3, 1964, no. 44-25706-473, FBI–NLG Files. Hoover scribbled his comments on this memo.

67. Kennedy to Johnson, May 21, 1964, WHCF, Ex HU2, Box 2, Johnson Papers.

68. Forman, *Making*, 381–82.

69. Ibid.

70. Ibid.; Arthur M. Schlesinger, Jr., to author, June 11, 1986.

71. For the Bingham family, see Miller, *Fathers and Sons*.

72. The FBI, nonetheless, considered Schlesinger a parlor revolutionary. Belmont to Boardman, April 4, 1958, no. 1060, FBI–Winchell File (62-31615).

73. Forman interview.

74. Clifford Oral History, 39–41; Hoover to Tolson et al., Sept. 2, 1965, no. 1792X, FBI–Robert Kennedy File. Hoover began collecting information on Kennedy's campaign team as early as August 25, but there is no evidence that he interfered with Kennedy's Senate bid.

75. H. N. Bassett to Nicholas P. Callahan, Jan. 29, 1975, in Church Committee, *Hearings—FBI*, 503.

76. Schlesinger, *Robert Kennedy*, 692.

77. Evans to Belmont, Aug. 25, 1964, no. 1648, FBI–Robert Kennedy File. For DeLoach, see Ungar, *FBI*, 279–80, 287–89, 291–92; the documents in WHCF, Name File (Cartha DeLoach), Johnson Papers; Roche, McPherson interviews.

78. E. T. Turner to W. A. Branigan, Aug. 23, 1964, no. 440, FBI–King File; DeLoach to Mohr, Aug. 29, 1964, in Church Committee, *Hearings—FBI*, 495–502; DeLoach to Jenkins, Aug. 25, 1964, ibid., 715–16. See also ibid., 20–21, 175–78; idem, *Book III*, 335, *Book II*, 117 n575; Wise, *American Police State*, 288–91.

79. Wise, *American Police State*, 288.

80. See the sources cited in note 78.

81. Lee C. White to the President, Aug. 13, 1964, WHCF, PL1/St24, Box 81, Johnson Papers; Moyers to the President, Aug. 19, 1964, WHCF, Ex HU2/St24, Box 27, Johnson Papers.

82. Rauh Oral History, 15; Rauh interview.

83. White to the President, Aug. 19, 1964, WHCF, PL1/St24, Box 81, Johnson Papers; DeLoach to Jenkins, Aug. 25, 1964, in Church Committee, *Hearings—FBI*, 717; DeLoach to Mohr, Aug. 29, 1964, ibid., 498–99; Bassett to

Callahan, Jan. 29, 1975, ibid., 505–6; idem, *Book II*, 118–19, *Book III*, 347–49.

84. DeLoach to Jenkins, Aug. 25, 1964, in Church Committee, *Hearings—FBI*, 714–16; DeLoach to Mohr, Aug. 29, 1964, ibid., 495.

85. Bassett to Callahan, Jan. 29, 1975, ibid., 503–7; DeLoach to Mohr, Aug. 29, 1964, ibid., 496–97. See also ibid., 175, 178.

86. Bassett to Callahan, Jan. 29, 1975, ibid., 508–9 (for Jenkins's phone call); DeLoach to Mohr, Aug. 29, 1964, ibid., 502 (for Hoover's comment); DeLoach to Moyers, Sept. 10, 1964, WHCF, Name File (Cartha DeLoach), Box 117, Johnson Papers.

87. Katzenbach to the President, Feb. 14, 1966, WHCF, Ex HU2/St24, Box 27, Johnson Papers; MFDP Fact Sheet, n.d., [ca. Oct. 30, 1964], in WHCF, Name File (Miss. F-K), ibid.; Guyot interview. Forman, Lewis, Hamer, and seven other SNCC staffers traveled to Africa before returning to Mississippi.

88. Wilkins, *Standing*, 306; "Mississippi Freedom Democratic Party," 46 (for Edwin King); Rauh Oral History, 11; White, *Making of the President 1960*, 133.

89. SAC Jackson to Director and SAC Chicago, Sept. 5, 1968, no. 54-5, FBI–COINTEL (New Left) File; Hoover to Tolson, DeLoach, Bishop, and Sullivan, Aug. 16, 1968, no. not recorded, FBI–Humphrey File (62-77485); Church Committee, *Hearings–FBI*, 732–37, 756–59; Sullivan, *Bureau*, 159. Only one delegate, Kenneth Dean, then director of the Mississippi Council on Human Relations, has admitted to having a relationship with the FBI. He reported on convention activities under the code name "Mr. Magnolia," but denies that he was an informant.

90. Raines, *My Soul*, 265, 267.

91. Jones to DeLoach, March 22, 1965, no. X16, FBI–Forman File (100-443566); Jones to DeLoach, March 16, 1965, no. not recorded, FBI–Wilkins File (62-78270).

92. Church Committee, *Book III*, 334; Katzenbach to Harry C. McPherson, Jr., Sept. 17, 1966, Civil Rights(2), Box 22, White House Aides' Files—Harry McPherson, Johnson Papers.

93. Rosen to Belmont, June 7, 1965, no. deleted, June 17, 1965, no. deleted, FBI–Bronstein File (File no. also deleted); John de J. Pemberton, Jr., to Katzenbach, June 10, 1965, no. deleted, ibid.; Director to Attorney General, June 18, 1965, no. deleted, ibid.

94. Fleischer interview.

95. Marshall, *Federalism and Civil Rights*, 81.

96. Berry, *Amazing Grace*, 322–23.

CHAPTER 6.
Klan Wars

1. "The emphasis on all the intelligence investigations is to hit the left hard," former FBI agent Arthur Murtagh charged. "The only time they investigated the Klan was when there was actual murder." House Select Committee on Intelligence, *Hearings*, pt. 3, p. 1,067.

2. Cartha D. DeLoach to John P. Mohr, Dec. 2, 1964, no. 634, FBI–King File (100-106670); Hoover, "Off-the-Record Remarks."

3. James H. Gale to Alan H. Belmont, March 17, 1965, no. X14, FBI–Forman File (100-443566) (for Katzenbach); Young Oral History, 26.

4. Garrow, *Protest at Selma.*

5. The director's conversations with the attorney general are summarized in J. Edgar Hoover to Clyde Tolson, Belmont, DeLoach, and Alex Rosen, March 23, 1965, no. not recorded, FBI–Tolson Memo File (67-9524); Hoover to Tolson, Belmont, DeLoach, Gale, Rosen, and William C. Sullivan, March 12, 1965, no. not recorded, ibid.; Hoover to Tolson, Belmont, Rosen, Sullivan, and DeLoach, Feb. 19, 1965, no. not recorded, ibid.

6. Hoover to Tolson, Belmont, DeLoach, and Rosen, March 26, 1965, no. 15 and 16, FBI–Liuzzo File (44-2860) (for the director's conversations with the attorney general and the president); Belmont to Director, March 26, 1965, no. 33, ibid.

7. Marshall Oral History, 35–37, Bunche Collection.

8. Leinbaugh interview; Hoover, "Off-the-Record Remarks."

9. For the COINTELPROs, see Senate Select Committee to Study . . . Intelligence Activities (hereafter Church Committee), *Book III,* 3–77.

10. Gale to Tolson, July 30, 1964, no. 3, FBI–COINTEL (White) File; Whitehead, *Attack,* 91; Sullivan, *Bureau,* 127.

11. Gale to Tolson, July 30, 1964, no. 3, FBI–COINTEL (White).

12. SAC Chicago to Director, June 4, 1965, no. 5756, FBI–HUAC File (61-7582); Church Committee, *Book III,* 334.

13. Fred J. Baumgardner to Sullivan, Aug. 27, 1964, no. 2, Dec. 16, 1965, no. 21, FBI–COINTEL (White) File; Director to SACs Atlanta et al., Sept. 2, 1964, no. 1, ibid.; Gale to Tolson, July 30, 1964, no. 3, ibid.; Director to SACs Los Angeles et al., Dec. 17, 1965, no. 20, ibid.; Sullivan, *Bureau,* 127–28.

14. Donner, *Age,* 207; DeLoach to Mohr, Dec. 2, 1964, no. 634, FBI–King File.

15. Burke Marshall to Attorney General, Nov. 13, 1963, Special Correspondence, Attorney General, Box 3, Marshall Papers.

16. Katzenbach interview; Church Committee, *Hearings—FBI,* 213; Director to Attorney General, Sept. 2, 1965, Dec. 19, 1967, ibid., 513–14, 519; Nicholas deB. Katzenbach to Hoover, Sept. 3, 1965, ibid., 515; Hoover to Tolson, Belmont, DeLoach, Gale, Rosen and Sullivan, March 12, 1965, no. not recorded, FBI–Tolson Memo File.

17. DeLoach to Mohr, Dec. 2, 1964, no. 634, FBI–King File; Welch, *Inside,* 105; Ungar, *FBI,* 415; Director to SAC Jackson, Sept. 6, 1966, no. 54-38, FBI–COINTEL (White) File.

18. Charles D. Brennan to Sullivan, March 31, 1967, no. 8-83, FBI–COINTEL (White) File; SAC Charlotte to Director, Oct. 14, 1966, no. 8-61, Nov. 1, 1966, no. 8-66, ibid.; Director to SAC Charlotte, Oct. 19, 1966, no. 8-61, ibid.

19. Baumgardner to Sullivan, March 10, 1966, no. 24, April 20, 1966, no. 31, Aug. 9, 1966, no. 10-15, ibid.; Director to SACs Dallas et al., May 12, 1966, no. 28, ibid.; George C. Moore to Sullivan, Sept. 24, 1968, no. illegible, ibid.; Director to SAC Birmingham, Aug. 26, 1970, no. 4-162, ibid.; Hoover to Office of Management and Evaluation, Nov. 9, 1964, no. 2-11X, ibid.

20. Director to SAC Birmingham, Feb. 4, 1966, no. 4-40, ibid.; SAC Jackson to Director, April 14, 1965, no. 54-4, April 21, 1966, no. 54-25, Jan. 28, 1965, no. 6, Oct. 20, 1965, no. 54-14, ibid.; Baumgardner to Sullivan, May 19, 1965, no. illegible, ibid.

21. Baumgardner to Sullivan, April 23, 1965, no. 318, FBI–SCLC File (100-438794); Cobb interview.

22. DeLoach to Mohr, March 12, 1965, no. 5656, March 22, 1965, no. 5649, June

17, 1965, no. 5762, FBI–HUAC File; Baumgardner to Sullivan, March 12, 1965, no. 5657, June 25, 1965, no. 5763 ("digging" quote), June 25, 1965, no. 5657, ibid.; "The Klan Today," March 12, 1965, no. 5657, ibid.; Director to SAC Atlanta, July 14, 1965, no. 5784, ibid.

23. Rosen to Belmont, March 5, 1965, no. 378, FBI–Penn File (44-25873); Tully, *FBI's Most Famous Cases*, 205–11. See also Shipp, *Murder*.

24. The FBI also opened a file on the Deacons for Defense and Justice, one of the first black self-defense groups that had been formed in Bogalusa and environs in February 1965, and sent reports on this "gun-carrying black vigilante group" to "appropriate . . . authorities in the state of Louisiana." See serials 5, 12, 23, 111, FBI–Deacons for Defense and Justice File (157-2466).

25. Director to Attorney General, Dec. 19, 1967, and the accompanying memo, re Ku Klux Klan Investigations, Dec. 19, 1967, in Church Committee, *Hearings—FBI*, 516–27.

26. Schlesinger, *Robert Kennedy*, 266.

27. Franklin L. Dodge to Thomas J. Walsh, Feb. 2, 1927, Investigations, Dept. of Justice (1), Box 278, Walsh Papers; Edward J. Brennan to Dodge, Nov. 22, 1920, ibid; memo, re Facts Furnished, Jan. 21, 1927, ibid. See also Joseph E. Bayliss to Carl Mapes, March 26, 1929, Cabinet Offices, Justice, FBI (1929), Pres. Papers, Herbert Hoover Papers.

28. Louis B. Nichols to Tolson, Oct. 4, 1940, no. 676, FBI–Cooper File (94-3-4-20); William Allen White to Hoover, Dec. 11, 1940, Correspondence, J. Edgar Hoover, Series C, Box 343, White Papers; and the voluminous, if mostly perfunctory, correspondence in Box 29, Barton Papers.

29. Church Committee, *Hearings—FBI*, 88.

30. Buchanan, *Right*, 283; SAC Letter, July 16, 1963, FBI–SAC File; Attorney General to the President, Jan. 9, 1962, President's Office Files, Depts. and Agencies–Justice, Box 80, John Kennedy Papers. The president mentioned the FBI, but only in connection with "organized crime, racketeering, and youth delinquency."

31. DeLoach to Mohr, Feb. 4, 1964, no. 94-8-350-129, FBI–McSurely Files.

32. Stone interview.

33. DeLoach to Mohr, Dec. 8, 1964, no. 126, FBI–Lawrence File (94-4-3169); Hoover to Tolson, Mohr, and DeLoach, Dec. 8, 1964, no. 127, ibid.; Thomas E. Bishop to DeLoach, Sept. 6, 1967, no. 136, ibid.; Milton A. Jones to DeLoach, June 2, 1964, no. 1194, FBI–Winchell File (62-31613); John [Hoover] to Walter Winchell, Oct. 15, 1964, no. 1222, ibid.

34. Hoover to Tolson, Belmont, Rosen, and DeLoach, Nov. 24, 1965, no. 635, FBI–Liuzzo File; Belmont to Tolson, Aug. 31, 1965, no. not recorded, FBI–COINTEL (White) File; Hoover to Karl E. Mundt, Jan. 17, 1966, Box 167(6), Mundt Papers; Barron, "FBI's Secret War," 87–92.

35. Tully, *FBI's Most Famous Cases*, 205–30; Hoover, "Resurgent Klan," 617–20; Overstreet, *FBI in Our Open Society*; Sentner, *How the FBI Gets Its Man*; Adler, *Kids' Letters*.

36. DeLoach to Walter Trohan, June 9, 1961, Correspondence, Cartha DeLoach, Trohan Papers; Nichols to Mrs. Fulton Oursler, Aug. 3, 1955, no. 227, FBI–Oursler File (94-4-692); Grace Oursler to Nichols, Aug. 5, 1955, no. 228, ibid.; Heim interview.

37. DeLoach to Mohr, Nov. 3, 1964, no. not recorded, FBI–Lewis File (94-4-2189).

38. Heim interview; Sullivan, *Bureau*, 93; Jones to DeLoach, Feb. 9, 1965, no. not recorded, FBI–King File.

39. Rauh interview; *Washington Post*, Nov. 26, 1950; *Cong. Record*, 81 Cong., 2 sess., Nov. 30, 1950, pp. A7,342–50.

40. Thomas J. Jenkins to Richard Baker, March 5, 1973, no. not recorded, FBI–Civil Rights Policy File (44-00).

41. Martin Luther King, Jr., to DeLoach, Dec. 6, 1965, King Papers; Bishop, *Confessions*, 402; Guthman, Rauh interviews; Young Oral History, 26.

42. Sherrill, "Selling," 18–19.

43. Jones to DeLoach, Sept. 8, 1961, no. 37, FBI–Wilson File (94-42524); Executive Vice President, Warner Brothers, to DeLoach, Dec. 11, 1964, no. 1, FBI Television Series Agreement Folder, FBI–Hoover O&C Files.

44. The star, Efrem Zimbalist, Jr. ("Inspector Erskine"), presented the image of a "housebroken G-man." ABC wanted "a more adult approach," including "bigger and longer action sequences in which Inspector Erskine does not always get his man with one shot." Quinn Martin also asked the FBI to liberalize its name-check activities. The "derogatory information" the Bureau uncovered on "actors, actresses, writers, and directors" had led to a mini-blacklist of "a number of name personalities who could help the show." Assistant Director in Charge Los Angeles to Acting Director, Feb. 1, 1973, no. 4, FBI Television Series Agreement Folder, FBI–Hoover O&C Files; Brownfield to Jenkins, Feb. 6, 1973, no. 4, ibid.

45. DeLoach and Hoover are quoted in Jones to DeLoach, Nov. 19, 1964, no. 124, Dec. 1, 1964, no. 125, Dec. 2, 1964, no. 126, FBI–Whitehead File (77-68662).

46. Jones to Bishop, April 23, 1968, no. X, Aug. 26, 1969, no. not recorded, Sept. 17, 1969, no. 3, April 14, 1970, no. 8, May 21, 1970, no. 9, June 25, 1970, no. 11, July 20, 1970, no. 94, Aug. 25, 1970, no. 20, Jan. 31, 1972, no. 23, ibid. (94-64866); SAC Letter, Sept. 1, 1970, no. not recorded, ibid. (94-64866).

47. *New York Times*, Feb. 20 and 22, 1975; J. H. Campbell to George C. Moore, Sept. 12, 1975, no. not recorded, FBI–Whitehead File (94-64866); Schwerner, "Mississippi," 15.

48. Radio broadcast of April 7, noted in Jones to DeLoach, April 7, 1965, no. 518, FBI–Lewis File.

49. Wechsler, "FBI's Failure," 20–23; Clark Oral History, 29. For King's comments, see DeLoach to Mohr, March 28, 1965, no. not recorded, FBI–Liuzzo File; Schlesinger, *Robert Kennedy*, 669.

50. Doar interview, in Rafferty Papers; Leinbaugh interview; C. B. Stanberry to SAC Birmingham, Oct. 31, 1960, no. 137-00-165, FBI–Bergman Freedom Rider Files (for Baumgardner). The Laurel agent is quoted in Whitehead, *Attack*, 23.

51. Paraphrased in Stanberry to SAC Birmingham, Oct. 31, 1960, no. 137-00-165, FBI–Bergman Files. For Rowe's account of his life and times, see *My Undercover Years*; his deposition of Oct. 17, 1975, before the Church Committee; Church Committee, *Hearings—FBI*, 115–31.

52. SAC Birmingham to Director, Nov. 5, 1960, no. 170-9-64, FBI–Alabama Freedom Rider Files; SAC Birmingham to Director and SAC Mobile, May 14, 1961, no. 149-1684-2, ibid.; Barrett G. Kemp to SAC Birmingham, May 17, 1961, no. 149-16-62, FBI–Bergman Files; Rowe deposition, 10.

53. *New York Times*, Feb. 17 and 18, 1980; Church Committee, *Book II*, 13. See also the informant reports in FBI–Alabama Files.

54. Katzenbach to Hoover, Sept. 3, 1965, no. 16, FBI–COINTEL (White) File; Director to Attorney General, Sept. 2, 1965, no. 15, ibid.; Hoover to Marvin Watson, Sept. 2, 1965, no. not recorded, ibid.; Church Committee, *Hearings—FBI*, 18; *New York Times*, July 9, 11, and 14, 1978.

55. Church Committee, *Book III*, 252; McIlhany, *Klandestine*, 60–61.

56. L. E. Rogers to Robert F. Kennedy, Dec. 14, 1966, Legislative Series, Un-American (1965), Box U1, Russell Papers.

57. Hoover to Tolson, Belmont, DeLoach, and Rosen, March 26, 1965, no. 15, and 16, FBI–Liuzzo File.

58. White interview.

59. Director to Attorney General, March 26, 1965, no. 1, FBI–Liuzzo File; Rosen to Belmont, April 5, 1965, no. 162, ibid.; Detroit Field Office Rept., April 1, 1965, no. not recorded, ibid.; Mobile Field Office Rept., April 1, 1965, no. not recorded, ibid.

60. Letterhead memos, March 29, 1965, no. 48, Jan. 17, 1966, no. 684, ibid.; Rosen to Belmont, June 28, 1965, no. 407, ibid.

61. Quoted in Jones to DeLoach, April 1, 1965, no. not recorded, FBI–King File.

62. SAC Detroit to Director, May 12, 1965, no. 354, May 17, 1965, no. 351, FBI–Liuzzo File; DeLoach to Mohr, March 28, 1965, no. not recorded, ibid.

63. SAC Mobile to Director, May 4, 1965, no. 277, ibid.; Director to Attorney General, April 2, 1965, no. 110, ibid.

64. The director's assessment, as recorded in Hoover to Tolson, Belmont, De-Loach, Rosen, and Sullivan, May 7, 1965, no. 302, ibid.

65. Clement L. McGowan, Jr., to Rosen, March 27, 1965, no. 23, ibid.; SAC Mobile to Director and SAC Birmingham, March 27, 1965, no. 108, ibid.

66. McGowan to Rosen, May 8, 1965, no. illegible, ibid.; Morgan, *One Man*, 37.

67. Hanes interview; Hoover to Tolson, DeLoach, Rosen, Bishop, and Sullivan, June 20, 1968, no. 44-38861-4660, in House Select Committee on Assassinations, *Hearings—King*, vol. 7, p. 88; Rosen to Belmont, Oct. 13, 1965, no. 497, FBI–Liuzzo File; note, CDC, no. 444, ibid.; Jones to DeLoach, Aug. 24, 1965, no. 441, ibid.

68. Hoover to Tolson, Belmont, DeLoach, and Rosen, March 26, 1965, no. 16, Nov. 24, 1965, no. 635, FBI–Liuzzo File; Rosen to Belmont, March 30, 1965, no. 158, ibid.; Hoover to Tolson, Belmont, DeLoach, Rosen, and Robert E. Wick, Dec. 3, 1965, no. 617, ibid.

69. SAC Birmingham to Director, Dec. 13, 1966, no. 769, ibid.; Rosen to De-Loach, Dec. 22, 1966, no. 774, ibid.; DeLoach to John Doar, Dec. 23, 1966, no. 774, ibid.

70. The court of appeals upheld the conviction of the surviving defendants on April 27, 1967.

71. Director to Attorney General, Dec. 27, 1965, no. 676, FBI–Liuzzo File.

72. Katzenbach to Joseph A. Califano, Jr., Dec. 13, 1965, Civil Rights 1965 (1), White House Aides' Files—Harry McPherson, Johnson Papers.

73. Conversations summarized in Hoover to Tolson, Belmont, DeLoach, Rosen, and Wick, Dec. 3, 1965, no. 617, Nov. 24, 1965, no. 635, FBI–Liuzzo File.

74. Church Committee, *Book III*, 474.

75. Moore interview; Hoover to Tolson et al., March 25, 1966, no. not recorded, FBI–Tolson Memo File.

76. SAC Letters, April 30, 1968, Nov. 10, 1969, FBI–SAC File. See also Church Committee, *Hearings—FBI*, 679–80, *Book III*, 474–75.

77. Hoover, "Off-the-Record Remarks."

78. Sullivan interview.

79. A number of other embarrassing, tragic incidents followed. The most notable occurred in 1968, when the FBI and police officers in Meridian, Mississippi, paid $36,500 to two Klansmen as part of a plot to entice two other Klansmen to bomb the home of a Jewish businessman. One of the suspects showed up, unexpectedly accompanied by a woman—Kathy Ainsworth. A shoot-out followed, leaving the man wounded and Ainsworth dead. Hoover responded, in part, by gathering intelligence on Jack Nelson and other reporters who criticized the Bureau's judgment.

80. Morgan, *One Man*, 37–38.

81. *Conspiracy*, ed. Raines, 157–58; Marshall interview.

82. This is not to minimize more recent racist violence. In 1985 alone the FBI devoted "52 agent-years of attention" to the Aryan Nation investigation. Ungar, "F.B.I. On the Defensive," 78.

83. One FBI agent said the victims of Klan violence should have sued the city of Birmingham and its police department and not the FBI.

84. Greene, "Did the FBI Kill Viola Liuzzo?," 100ff.

85. Rowe deposition, 8.

CHAPTER 7.
White Backlash

1. McPherson, *Political Education*, 377.

2. Goodwin, "War Within," 42, *Remembering America*, 392–416.

3. Clark Oral History, 22; Milton A. Jones to Cartha D. DeLoach, March 16, 1965, no. not recorded, FBI–Wilkins File. In May 1964, Princeton historian Eric F. Goldman, one of the White House advisers who did think of civil rights in the North, pondered "the breakaway from the established organizations of the more irresponsible Negroes"—warning LBJ of the need for the administration to "re-establish control and keep the movement going in its legitimate direction." Otherwise, cities in the North would burn, a development which would "present a weapon to the Republicans in the election." Eric F. Goldman to the President, May 4, 1964, WHCF, Ex LE/HU2, Box 65, Johnson Papers.

4. The riots also had foreign policy implications. Dean Rusk to All Diplomatic and Consular Posts, July 18, 1964, Civil Rights (vol. 1), National Security File—Subject File, Johnson Papers.

5. "'Violence in our streets,'" political commentator Richard Rovere wrote, was Goldwater's "number-two issue. It came hard on the heels of 'the wall of shame in Berlin, [and] the sands of shame at the Bay of Pigs, [and] the slow death of freedom in Laos.'" *Goldwater Caper*, 85.

6. Wills, *Reagan's America*, 290; Greenfield, "Senator Goldwater," 27; "'Backlash' Issue," 24; *New York Times*, July 17, 18, 21, and 25, 1964; White, *Making of the President 1964*, 332–33n.

7. Task Force, *Prevention of Violence*, 224–25; Horowitz, "Alienation," 173–200; de Toledano, "Negro Minority," 814–15; Croce, "Backlash in New York?," 816–17; Wheeler, "Backlash in California?," 817; Wills, "Who Will Overcome?," 818–20.

8. King is quoted in Fred J. Baumgardner to William C. Sullivan, May 11, 1964, no. not recorded, FBI–King File (100-106670); White in *Making of the President 1960*, 203; Young in Andrew Young to Martin Luther King, Jr., Oct. 21, 1963, Box. 35:15, King Papers.

9. Schlesinger, *Robert Kennedy*, 657; DeLoach to J. Edgar Hoover, Sept. 9, 1964, no. 42, Riots Summer 1964 Folder, FBI–Hoover O&C Files.

10. DeLoach to Hoover, Sept. 9, 1964, no. 42, Riots Summer 1964 Folder, FBI–Hoover O&C Files.

11. The Bureau also sent over intelligence on two "white kids" riots that occurred over the Labor Day weekend in Seaside, Oregon, and Hampton, New Hampshire. "The President felt free to move in strongly," Dewey reasoned, according to Hoover's account, "because he had a couple of white riots to deal with." Hoover to Clyde Tolson, Alan H. Belmont, Alex Rosen, Sullivan, and DeLoach, Sept. 10, 1964, no. 54, Riots Summer 1964 Folder, FBI–Hoover O&C Files.

12. Goldwater had enough problems with disaffected Republicans operating in the sunshine. Goldwater, *With No Apologies*, 179.

13. Hoover to Tolson, Belmont, Rosen, Sullivan, and DeLoach, July 22, 1964, no. not recorded, FBI–King File; Hoover to Tolson, Belmont, Rosen, Sullivan, and DeLoach, Sept. 16, 1964, no. 52, Riots Summer 1964 Folder, FBI–Hoover O&C Files; Dick Nelson to Walter Jenkins, July 13, 1964, WHCF, Name File (Thomas E. Dewey), Box 161, Johnson Papers; Katzenbach interview.

14. Hoover to Tolson and Louis B. Nichols, April 27, 1948, no. 1 and 2, FBI–Nichols O&C Files; Sullivan, *Bureau*, 41, 44.

15. Conversations summarized in Hoover to Tolson, Belmont, Rosen, Sullivan, and DeLoach, Sept. 10, 1964, no. 22, Sept. 15, 1964, no. 54, Riots Summer 1964 Folder, FBI–Hoover O&C Files. See also Hoover to Thomas E. Dewey, Sept. 10, 1964, no. 9, and the accompanying blind memo, ibid.

16. Hoover to Tolson, Belmont, Rosen, Sullivan, and DeLoach, Sept. 15, 1964, no. 54, ibid.

17. In Philadelphia, Pennsylvania, for instance, city police arrested two SNCC workers and one CORE worker who had been at the boardwalk demonstrations in Atlantic City and were then on their way to Mississippi. The FBI ran name checks and consulted records at the University of Chicago (where one of the movement people was a student), the New York, Philadelphia, and Jackson police departments, and the House Committee on Un-American Activities. Philadelphia Field Office Rept., Sept. 9, 1964, no. 6, ibid.

18. Memo, re Communist Involvement in Racial Disturbances, Sept. 14, 1964, no. not recorded, ibid.; James F. Bland to Sullivan, Sept. 10, 1964, no. 4, ibid.; Hoover to Tolson, Mohr, and DeLoach, Dec. 8, 1964, no. 127, FBI–Lawrence File (94-9-3169).

19. Hoover to Tolson, Belmont, Rosen, Sullivan, and DeLoach, July 21, 1964, no. not recorded, FBI–King File.

20. White House staff and the president himself had only a few "nit-picking" objections to the report. "They took exception particularly to page four," Hoover advised his aides, "wherein the word 'Negro' is used three times and they felt that was overdoing it." Ironically, the FBI had once tried to discredit the Communist party by publicizing its frequent use of the word "Negro" as opposed to "Afro-American." SAC New York to Director,

March 24, 1961, no. 2439, FBI–COINTEL (CPUSA) File (100-3-104); Director to SAC New York, April 4, 1961, no. 2439, ibid.

21. "F.B.I. Report," 119; Wilkins, *Standing*, 304; *New York Times*, Sept 27, 1964 (for the report itself); *National Review*, Oct. 13, 1964, p. 1.

22. *New York Times*, Sept. 27, 1964; Senate Select Committee to Study . . . Intelligence Activities (hereafter Church Committee), *Book III*, 475. Johnson sought Hoover's endorsement from the beginning, asking him to comment on the proposed war-on-poverty speech. DeLoach to Mohr, March 10, 1964, no. 29, Johnson Folder, FBI–Hoover O&C Files.

23. *New York Times*, Sept. 27, 1964; Church Committee, *Book III*, 475.

24. Church Committee, *Book III*, 475–76; Director to SACs Albany et al., Aug. 20, 1964, no. 76, Sept. 8, 1964, no. 77, FBI–Racial Matters Policy File (157-00).

25. In March 1965 Johnson administration recruiters proposed another mission for Dewey. "How about asking him to come see you now," Bill Moyers suggested, "to discuss the crime problem. It might [also] help what with Nixon running around the way he is to have Dewey briefed on foreign policy." This time, Dewey declined. Dewey to the President, May 20, 1965, WHCF, Name File (Thomas E. Dewey), Box 161, Johnson Papers; William D. Moyers to the President, March 5, 1965, ibid.

26. Hoover to Jenkins, Oct. 1, 1964, WHCF, FG135-6, Box 188, Johnson Papers; "Prevention and Control of Riots," 70–76.

27. Hoover, "From Herbert Hoover," 144; Kearns, *Lyndon Johnson*, 305.

28. Wilkins, *Man's Life*, 166; Jacobs, *Prelude*, 13–60.

29. Katzenbach to the President, Aug. 17, 1965, WHCF, FG135-6, Box 188, Johnson Papers; Church Committee, *Book II*, 83, *Book III*, 490.

30. Conversations recorded in DeLoach to Mohr, Nov. 10, 1965, no. not recorded, FBI–King File.

31. Louis Martin to Marvin Watson, May 20, 1966, Civil Rights, Negroes (2), Box 18, White House Aides' Files—Marvin Watson, Johnson Papers; Baumgardner to Sullivan, Nov. 8, 1965, no. not recorded, FBI–SCLC File.

32. Hoover to Tolson, DeLoach, Sullivan, and Robert E. Wick, April 27, 1967, no. not recorded, FBI–King File.

33. Douglass Cater to the President, July 26, 1967, WHCF, Ex HU2, Box 5, Johnson Papers; Joseph J. Casper to Mohr, Sept. 7, 1967, no. 15-2145, FBI–Detroit Riot File (157-6); Hoover to Tolson, DeLoach, Sullivan, and Wick, July 27, 1967, no. 961, ibid.; Director to Attorney General, July 28, 1967, no. 967, ibid.; Hoover to Mildred Stegall, July 28, 1967, no. 988, ibid.

34. Hoover to Tolson, DeLoach, Sullivan, and Wick, July 26, 1967, no. 971, FBI–Detroit Riot File.

35. A January 1966 SNCC statement, signed by John Lewis and calling upon all young American men "to seek work in the civil rights movement as a 'valid alternative to the draft,'" threw the White House into a panic. Lewis suspected that the FBI responded by instigating a change in his own draft classification as a conscientious objector. When Burke Marshall intervened, Lewis received a 4-F deferment. "They said I was morally unfit," he recalled, because of a long civil rights arrest record. Another SNCC veteran, Robert Moses, who withdrew from an active role in the organization in 1965, also received a 1-A classification. Like Lewis, he suspected the FBI had visited his draft board.

36. Williams, *Empire*, 201.
37. An OEO official briefed the FBI on the episode. D. J. Brennan, Jr., to Sullivan, March 30, 1967, no. 180, FBI–McSurely Files (62-109683).
38. The secretary to the cabinet conceded that the administration's methods were similar to the methods of the late Senator Joseph R. McCarthy. Robert E. Kintner to the President, May 18, 1967, WHCF—CF, HU4, Box 57, Johnson Papers.
39. Lovin, "Lyndon B. Johnson," 567.
40. Hoover to Tolson, DeLoach, and Sullivan, July 25, 1967, No. 958 and 959, FBI–Detroit Riot File.
41. Ibid.; Hoover to Stegall, July 26, 1967, no. 2X, FBI–Hobson File (157-3707).
42. Director to Attorney General, July 26, 1967, no. 965, and the attached report, FBI–Detroit Riot File.
43. When Johnson pushed the FBI to find communist conspirators at the roots of the urban riots, Hoover resisted—largely because he agreed with the law-and-order advocates that liberal permissivists were the real culprits. On the issue of communist infiltration of the antiwar movement, Hoover needed no pushing.
44. Baumgardner to Sullivan, July 7, 1965, no. 1555, Aug. 16, 1965, no. 1768, Sept. 15, 1965, no. 1858, FBI–King File; letterhead memos, Sept. 15, 1965, no. 1866, Sept. 16, 1965, no. 1858, ibid.; Hoover to Rusk, July 7, 1965, no. 1538, ibid.; Hoover to Tolson, Belmont, Sullivan, and DeLoach, July 6, 1965, no. 1551, ibid. King even attracted the benign attention of Henry Kissinger, who invited him to participate in the international seminar at Harvard. King declined. Henry Kissinger to King, June 3, 1965, Henry Kissinger Folder, Box 14.5, King Papers; King to Kissinger, June 16, 1965, ibid.
45. DeLoach to Mohr, Aug. 14, 1965, no. 1782, FBI–King File; Bland to Sullivan, Sept. 20, 1965, no. 257, FBI–Levison File (100-392452); Thomas J. Dodd to Robert F. Kennedy, n.d. [ca. Aug. 29, 1962], Albany Movement Aug. 1962, Box 1:27, King Papers; Dodd to King, Aug. 31, 1962, ibid.
46. See the notation on UPI ticker, Dec. 7, 1966, no. 2796, FBI–King File.
47. George C. Moore to Sullivan, Oct. 18, 1967, no. 3129, ibid.; Garrow, *Bearing*, 555; Lewis Oral History, 157.
48. Hoover to Stegall, June 18, 1968, no. 2198, FBI–SCLC File; Hoover to Stegall, April 19, 1967, no. 2893, FBI–King File; Marvin [Watson] to the President, May 16, 1967, WHCF—CF, HU4, Box 57, Johnson Papers; Fairclough, "Martin Luther King," 19; Lawson, *In Pursuit of Power*, 8.
49. Cone, "Martin Luther King," 462; Garrow, *Bearing*, 564, 581.
50. Wilkins, *Man's Life*, 230–31.
51. Hoover to Tolson and Sullivan, Aug. 2, 1967, no. 985, FBI–Detroit Riot File.
52. Richard Helms to Walt W. Rostow, Aug. 9, 1967, National Security File—Subject File, Civil Rights and Antiwar Personalities, Johnson Papers; Rostow to the President, July 27, 1967, ibid.; W. G. Bowdler to Rostow, Aug. 3, 1967, ibid.; Kintner to the President, May 18, 1967, WHCF—CF, HU4, Box 57, Johnson Papers; Kintner to Attorney General, May 19, 1967, ibid.
53. Note, TJS, Sept. 16, 1967, no. 15-2159, FBI–Detroit Riot File; Ramsey Clark to Director, Sept. 14, 1967, in Church Committee, *Hearings—FBI*, 528–30.
54. Joseph A. Sullivan to Director, Aug. 2, 1966, no. not recorded, FBI–Racial Matters File. Hoover scribbled his comment on this document.
55. SAC Letter, Aug. 15, 1967, FBI–SAC File.

56. Director to SAC Detroit, Sept. 6, 1967, no. not recorded, FBI–Detroit Riot File (157-6); Moore to Sullivan, July 25, 1967, no. 1937, FBI–SCLC File; R. W. Smith to Sullivan, Aug. 8, 1967, no. 1386, FBI–SNCC File (100-439190).

57. Baker, May interviews.

58. Ibid.; McKnight, "Harvest," 11.

59. May interview; Hoover to Tolson and Sullivan, Aug. 2, 1968, no. 985, FBI–Detroit Riot File; DeLoach to Tolson, Aug. 3, 1967, no. 15, ibid.; Hoover to Stegall, Aug. 17, 1967, no. 115, FBI–McSurely Files (62-109683); Bland to Sullivan, Aug. 17, 1967, no. 115, ibid.; Marvin [Watson] to the President, Aug. 12, 1967, WHCF, FG135-6, Box 188, Johnson Papers; Larry Levinson to Joseph Califano, April 11, 1968, WHCF, FG135-6, Box 188, ibid.; Sargent Shriver to the President, Aug. 14, 1967, WHCF—CF, HU4, ibid.

60. DeLoach to Tolson, Oct. 11, 1967, no. not recorded, FBI–Young File (161-3190); Baker interview.

61. Bookbinder interview. The FBI, the Manhattan district attorney's office, and OEO itself investigated Haryou for fiscal mismanagement.

62. See the outline of Hoover's testimony, Aug. 1, 1967, in Witness Outline Digest, Box 1, National Advisory Commission on Civil Disorders Records; and the brief Division Five prepared for his use, "Racial Disturbances," Aug. 1, 1967, no. 988, FBI–Detroit Riot File. See also Hoover to File, July 31, 1967, no. not recorded, FBI–Tolson Memo File.

63. It was all part of the way LBJ governed. "[He] appointed 28 presidential commissions and, by rough count, 134 secret task forces in a tour de force of presidential advisement." Graham, "Ambiguous Legacy," 20.

64. McPherson, *Political Education*, 376; Johnson, *Vantage Point*, 173.

65. Donner, *Age*, 283; National Advisory Commission on Civil Disorders, *Report*, 1, 201–2, 487.

66. Cook County Grand Jury, *Improper Police Intelligence Activities*, July 10, 1975; Church Committee, *Book II*, 77.

67. Hoover to Tolson, DeLoach, Rosen, Bishop, and Sullivan, June 20, 1968, no. 4660, FBI–King Assassination File (44-38861). The Kerner Commission itself fed "white racism," according to Harry McPherson, by provoking "the deepest resentment among white workers whose unions had helped to pass the laws of the Great Society. The charge against white racism was true—but so was the bitterness of white families . . . when they were told that they were responsible for the sacking of the cities. . . . The commission had weakened the liberal bloc by charging part of it with crimes against the other." *Political Education*, 376.

68. "Statement of J. Edgar Hoover . . . Before National Commission on the Causes and Prevention of Violence," Sept. 18, 1968, in Church Committee, *Hearings—FBI*, 870–82.

69. Task Force on Violent Aspects of Protest and Confrontation, *Politics of Protest*, 263, 280, 288; Navasky, *Kennedy Justice*, 36. For the Nashville operation, see David Orange to Melvin Bailey, Aug. 22, 1967, Box 30.26, Boutwell Papers.

70. SAC Houston to Director, March 15, 1968, no. 26, FBI–COINTEL (Black Nationalist) File (100-448006).

71. Conversations recorded in DeLoach to Tolson, July 27, 1967, no. 5926, FBI–HUAC File (61-7582); Bishop to DeLoach, Aug. 3, 1967, no. 5928, ibid.

72. Senate Permanent Subcommittee on Investigations, *Hearings on Riots . . .* , pts. 1–25.

73. The FBI filed a report on the prosecutor and someone at OEO leaked the information to the press. Joseph A. Sizoo to Sullivan, Sept. 1, 1967, no. illegible, FBI–McSurely Files (105-164714); D. J. Brennan, Jr., to Sullivan, Sept. 6, 1967, no. 28, ibid.

74. Hoover to Mildred Stegall, Aug. 17, 1967, no. 115, ibid. (62-109683); SAC Louisville to Director, Aug. 14, 1967, no. 14, ibid. (105-164714); Bland to Sullivan, Aug. 28, 1967, no. 16, ibid. (105-164714). For the McSurelys' ordeal, see Harris, *Freedom Spent*, 125–311.

75. James Gaither to Califano, Oct. 17, 1967, White House Aides' File—James Gaither, Pres. Task Forces—Subject File, Riot Control, Poor People's March(1), Box 36, Johnson Papers.

76. Hoover to Tolson, DeLoach, Bishop, and Sullivan, Sept. 19, 1967, no. 1112, FBI–McSurely Files (62-18810).

77. Richard D. Cotter to Sullivan, June 30, 1970, no. 1186, ibid.; Donald F. O'Donnell to Bishop, Nov. 8, 1967, no. 1123, and the attached blind memos, ibid.; SAC Milwaukee to Director, Oct. 3, 1967, no. 1118, ibid.

78. DeLoach to Tolson, Sept. 13, 1967, no. not recorded, ibid.

79. DeLoach to Tolson, Nov. 7, 1967, no. not recorded, ibid.; Bishop to DeLoach, Oct. 12, 1967, no. not recorded, ibid.

80. DeLoach to Tolson, Nov. 7, 1967, no. not recorded, ibid.

81. Graham, "Ambiguous Legacy," 20–21; Bishop to DeLoach, Nov. 22, 1967, no. not recorded, FBI–Robert Kennedy File (77-51387).

82. The FBI had an interest in a number of other sections of the Omnibus Act, especially Section 2511, which pertained to electronic surveillance.

83. SAC Pittsburgh to Director, Dec. 18, 1968, no. 540, FBI–COINTEL (Black) File. The FBI source at the Mellon Foundation furnished "information on a confidential basis relating to . . . requests for financial grants made by various civil rights and racial–type organizations." SAC Pittsburgh to Director, Sept. 24, 1968, no. 2, Oct. 9, 1968, no. 3, FBI–Young File (157-10774).

84. Fleischer interview. When Jack Bass and Jack Nelson were researching a book on the incident, the FBI opened files on both men—and as well those Civil Rights Division attorneys who granted them interviews. Memo, re David Robert Owen, n.d. [ca. Nov. 19, 1970], no. not recorded, FBI–CPJ File (62-113909).

85. Hoover to Tolson, DeLoach, and Wick, July 6, 1966, no. not recorded, FBI–Tolson Memo File (67-9524).

86. Sellers, *River*, 223, 226; Carson, *In Struggle*, 250; *New York Times*, Sept. 29, 1970.

87. Hoover to Tolson, DeLoach, Sullivan, and Wick, July 26, 1967, no. not recorded, FBI–Tolson Memo File; Clark interview. Ultimately, the courts found Brown guilty on a charge of carrying a rifle from New Orleans to New York while under indictment. Another charge had to do with "this ol' negro FBI agent" who "testified against me in court," Brown wrote. "I said to him, 'I hope your children don't grow up to be a Tom like you' . . . The judge charged me with threatening an FBI agent and set $50,000." *Die*, 133.

88. Phillips, *Emerging*, 468, 472; Wills, *Nixon*, 247.

89. See McPherson, *Political Education*, 377: "I was concerned that Johnson, having earned recognition as the country's preeminent civil libertarian, might be forced to become its chief of police."

90. Powers, *Secrecy and Power*, 434; Schell, *Time of Illusion*, 62.

91. Kearns, *Lyndon Johnson,* 305.

92. Nixon, *RN,* 238.

93. Leinbaugh interview.

CHAPTER 8.
Black Hate

1. Goodwin, "War Within," 42.

2. Johnson, *White House Diary,* 687.

3. "I realize that emergencies arise," Stegall complained, on the FBI's behalf, "but . . . you can't make me believe there isn't some way we could get our hands on the lists sooner." DeLoach had just called to tell her the FBI "had to keep over fifty people *all night* to check [a] list of around 400 names." Mildred Stegall to Marvin Watson, Oct. 1, 1965, WHCF, PE6, Johnson Papers.

4. "His sophistication in rating the importance of a person's having attended a John Reed Society meeting back in 1938," Harry McPherson remembered, "left a hell of a lot to be desired."

5. Transcript of telephone conversation, J. Edgar Hoover and Vincent Astor, July 5, 1941, Roosevelt Folder, FBI–Nichols O&C Files. For the desires and policies of the Johnson White House, see Cartha D. DeLoach to Clyde Tolson, March 1, 1966, Johnson Folder, FBI–Hoover O&C Files; William Moyers to White House Personnel, Dec. 3, 1964, WHCF, Ex PE6, Johnson Papers; Walter Jenkins to White House Staff, Oct. 7, 1964, ibid.; DeLoach to Tolson, July 10, 1967, no. not recorded, FBI–King File (100-106670). For the early Do Not File files, see Edward J. Brennan to Franklin L. Dodge, Jr., Nov. 22, 1920, Investigations, Dept. of Justice (1), Walsh Papers.

6. Hoover to Watson, Jan. 20, 1967, no. 53, FBI–NLG Files (100-367743); Hoover to [deleted], March 14, 1968, no. 27, FBI–Owens File (77-72778). The name checks did not focus exclusively on blacks. The FBI ran Vince Lombardi's name through the files at White House request, too.

7. According to an inventory prepared by Johnson Library staff.

8. Senate Select Committee to Study . . . Intelligence Activities (hereafter Church Committee), *Book II,* 79 n338, 83, *Book III,* 495, 498.

9. The Office of Economic Opportunity collected the sort of physical and social intelligence that Califano referred to, but the White House considered the community action centers to be part of the problem. OEO's inspector general, Edgar May, "had an extraordinary staff," Sargent Shriver said. "Very independent, very quick, very street oriented. . . . FBI didn't have any people in those poverty-stricken areas—to begin with, at all. . . . The OEO people were in there where the poor people lived—in there where the 'revolutionaries' were . . . almost as if we had 2,000 or 3,000 'spies' in there. They weren't spies at all, but I'm trying to say that those poverty-stricken areas were where our OEO people lived."

10. Church Committee, *Book II,* 79 n337.

11. Ibid., 79, 84, *Book III,* 495–97.

12. Fred M. Vinson, Jr., to Ramsey Clark, Sept. 15, and Oct. 20, 1967, White House Aides' Files—James Gaither, Pres. Task Forces, Subject File, Riots 1967, Box 36, Johnson Papers; Church Committee, *Book II,* 79–84; *Book III,* 495–97.

13. Clark to FBI Director, Sept. 14, 1967, in Church Committee, *Hearings—*

FBI, 528–30. "The Ramsey Clark of 1967," as one FBI executive put it in 1974, "not only directed the Bureau to be certain that every attempt was made to get all information but to 'take every step' to determine the plans for racial violence." T. J. Smith to W. Raymond Wannall, March 18, 1974, no. not recorded, FBI–COINTEL (White Hate) File (157-9).

14. Wilkins, *Man's Life*, 230–31; Church Committee, *Book II*, 280; J. Walter Yeagley to Richard Russell, Aug. 10, 1967, Legislative Series, Un-American (1967), Box U1, Russell Papers. The FBI added to its files on Carmichael in the years that followed—trying to find something from his high school days in the Bronx, when he "read Karl Marx" and palled around with Eugene Dennis, Jr., to his black power days, when he embarked on a SNCC purge of "Caucasians" and was diagnosed, the FBI said, by Selective Service psychologists as a schizophrenic with psychopathic, pseudoneurotic, and paranoid tendencies.

15. Doar, Roche interviews; Theoharis and Cox, *Boss*, 87.

16. Roche interview; DeLoach to Tolson, May 7, 1968, no. not recorded, FBI–McSurely Files (62-98810); Clark Oral History, 21.

17. [Deleted] to William C. Sullivan, June 28, 1967, no. not recorded, FBI–Racial Matters Policy File (157-00). See also the references to an Aug. 7, 1967, directive in New York Field Office Inspection Rept., Oct. 27, 1967, FBI–Moore Files.

18. See Felt's comments in the inspection report cited in the previous note. In an attempt to "increase the quantity and quality of coverage of racial matters," the FBI also considered mobilizing thousands of American Legion Contact Program and Plant Informant Program sources. SAC Letter, Feb. 23, 1965, in Church Committee, *Hearings—FBI*, 678.

19. SAC Letter, March 12, 1968, FBI–SAC File; New York Field Office Inspection Rept., n.d. [ca. May 1968], FBI–Moore Files. See also the inspection report of Oct. 27, 1967, ibid.; SAC Letter, March 12, 1968, FBI–SAC File; Church Committee, *Book III*, pp. 493–94.

20. Sullivan, *Bureau*, 133; Garrow, *FBI and Martin Luther King*, 173–203.

21. SAC El Paso to Director, April 17, 1968, no. 16-4, FBI–COINTEL (New Left) File (100-449698); SAC Minneapolis to Director, April 3, 1968, no. 59, FBI–COINTEL (Black Nationalist) File (100-448006).

22. SAC Letter, Oct. 17, 1967, FBI–SAC File; Church Committee, *Book II*, 75–76, *Book III*, 253, 494, *Hearings—FBI*, 17.

23. Baraka, *Autobiography*, 269; SAC Letters, March 12 and April 30, 1968, FBI–SAC File.

24. SAC Philadelphia to all Field Office Agents, Feb. 26, March 29, and Aug. 12, 1968, in "Complete Collection," 52–54; New York Field Office Inspection Rept., Oct. 27, 1968, FBI–Moore Files; George C. Moore to Sullivan, Sept. 3, 1968, no. not recorded, FBI–Racial Matters File; Church Committee, *Book II*, 75–76, *Book III*, 253, 494, *Hearings—FBI*, 17.

25. Clark to Kevin T. Maroney, Thomas J. McTiernan, Hugh Nugent, and James P. Turner, Nov. 9, 1967, in Church Committee, *Hearings—FBI*, 531–32; Attorney General to John Doar, Vinson, Roger Wilkins, and J. Walter Yeagley, Dec. 18, 1967, ibid., 533–34; idem, *Book II*, 79–80, 83–84, *Book III*, 493, 497–98, 500.

26. SAC Letters, March 26, May 7, and June 4, 1968, FBI–SAC File; Moore to Sullivan, May 1, 1968, no. 153, FBI–Racial Matters File; Church Committee, *Book III*, 517–18.

27. Church Committee, *Book III*, 517–18.

28. Joseph A. Califano, Jr., to the President, Jan. 18, 1968, WHCF, Ex HU2, Box 7, Johnson Papers; Church Committee, *Book II*, 84–85, 260; Roche interview.

29. Church Committee, *Book II*, 84–85, 260; Roche interview.

30. M. E. Triplett to W. A. Branigan, Aug. 24, 1966, in Church Committee, *Hearings—Mail Opening*, 245–48; Senate Select Committee on Intelligence, *Hearings on National Intelligence Reorganization*, 503; Howard J. Osborn to Deputy Director for Support, Dec. 11, 1967, CIA–Brown File; memo, re Information [deleted] on Cuban Comments on Contacts with U.S. Negro Militants, April 25, 1968, ibid.; memo, re West Coast Subversive Organizations and their Interaction and Proposed Goals, March 20, 1968, CIA RESISTANCE/Black Student Unions File; Guiterrez, "Chicanos," 29–58.

31. Church Committee, *Book III*, 520–21.

32. SAC Letter, March 12, 1968, in Church Committee, *Hearings—FBI*, 681.

33. McKnight, "Memphis Sanitation Strike," 138–56, "Harvest," 8.

34. R. W. Smith to Sullivan, March 6, 1968, no. 53-1284, FBI–Levison File (157-6); memo, re Outlook for Racial Violence in Washington, D.C., n.d. [ca. March 6, 1968], no. 53-1284, ibid.

35. Milton A. Jones to Thomas E. Bishop, Jan. 17, 1968, no. 3193, FBI–King File; Director to SACs Washington, Atlanta, Boston, and Philadelphia, June 18, 1968, no. not recorded, FBI–SCLC File (100-438794); DeLoach to Tolson, May 3, 1968, no. 2130, ibid.; Sullivan, *Bureau*, 133.

36. For the FBI's general interest in disrupting the Poor People's Campaign, see serials 63, 82, 131, and 203, FBI–COINTEL (Black) File.

37. Hoover to Stegall, April 23, 1968, no. not recorded, FBI–SCLC File; Hoover to Stegall, Aug. 12, 1968, no. 315, Aug. 19, 1968, no. 316, FBI–Levison File (100-392452); SAC New York to Director, June 5, 1968, no. 306, ibid.; letterhead memo, June 19, 1968, no. 306, ibid.; letterhead memo, Aug. 16, 1968, no. 4, ibid.—Detroit Subfile (100-35176).

38. Matthew Nimetz to Califano, May 16, 1968, White House Aides' Files—James Gaither, Pres. Task Forces, Subject File, Riot Control—Poor People's March (1), Box 36, Johnson Papers.

39. See the comments of Felt and other FBI supervisors and agents in New York Field Office Inspection Division Rept., Oct. 27, 1967, FBI–Moore Files.

40. Ibid. See also the other inspection reports in these files.

41. Director to SAC New Haven, April 9, 1951, no. 227, FBI–Robeson File (100-12304); Church Committee, *Book III*, 417–22, 436–42, 542–48.

42. [Deleted] to [deleted], March 19, 1969, no. 3919, June 26, 1961, no. 2930, Feb. 11, 1969, no. not recorded, FBI–Security Index File (100-358086); James F. Bland to Sullivan, June 6, 1961, no. illegible, ibid.; memo, re Subversive Control Section Programs and Accomplishments, Oct. 20, 1961, no. 2980, ibid.; [deleted] to Director, Jan. 10, 1952, no. deleted, ibid.; D. Milton Ladd to Director, Feb. 12, 1951, no. 56, FBI–Responsibilities Program File (62-93875); Louis B. Nichols to Tolson, Feb. 12, 1951, no. 4, ibid.

43. Church Committee, *Book II*, 92; Charles D. Brennan to Sullivan, Nov. 22, 1968, no. 4046, FBI–COINTEL (CPUSA) File; Executives' Conference to [deleted], Feb. 27, 1969, no. not recorded, FBI–Security Index File.

44. Church Committee, *Book III*, 491–92.

45. Director to SACs Albany et al., Jan. 17, 1969, no. 181, FBI–Black National-

ist Photograph Album File (157-8415); SAC Letters, Aug. 4, 1967, Jan. 16, 1968, FBI–SAC File; Moore to Sullivan, March 20, 1968, no. 229, FBI–Rabble Rouser Index File (157-7782); Director to SACs Albany et al., Dec. 6, 1968, no. 473, FBI–COINTEL (Black) File; Church Committee, *Book II*, 89–90, *Book III*, 510–12, 517–18.

46. P. L. Cox to Sullivan, Sept. 5, 1967, no. 67, FBI–Rabble Rouser File.

47. Director to SACs Albany et al., March 4, 1968, no. 19, FBI–COINTEL (Black) File.

48. SAC Kansas City to Director, March 18, 1968, no. 30 and 31, ibid. See also serials 44–45, 58, 62, 64–65, 75, 80, and 91, ibid.

49. *Jackson Capital Reporter*, June 22, 1978; Church Committee, *Book III*, 20–21 n90.

50. SAC Washington to Director, Oct. 27, 1967, no. 4, Dec. 18, 1967, no. 7, FBI–COINTEL (Black) File; Director to SAC Washington, Nov. 14, 1967, no. 4, ibid.

51. SAC Newark to Director, April 2, 1968, no. 61, ibid.; SAC Pittsburgh to Director, March 28, 1968, no. 42, ibid.; SAC New York to Director, April 4, 1968, no. 69, ibid.

52. SAC San Francisco to Director, April 3, 1968, no. 95, ibid.; SAC San Diego to Director, April 3, 1968, no. 78, ibid.; SAC Los Angeles to Director, April 2, 1968, no. 76, ibid. For the other field offices, see serials 52, 87, 102, ibid.

53. SAC Birmingham to Director, April 3, 1968, no. 51, ibid.; SAC Mobile to Director, March 27, 1968, no. 33, ibid. See also serials 38, 56, 70, and 73, ibid.

54. SAC Memphis to Director, May 22, 1968, no. illegible, Aug. 30, 1968, no. not recorded, ibid.; SAC Memphis to Director, April 19, 1967, no. 28-19, FBI–McSurely Files (100-439190); SAC Jacksonville to Director, July 2, 1968, no. 53-5, FBI–COINTEL (New Left) File.

55. Church Committee, *Book III*, 4.

56. Director to SACs Albany et al., Aug. 25, 1967, no. 1, FBI–COINTEL (Black) File.

57. Dept. of Justice, *King Task Force*, 141.

58. SAC New York to Director, Sept. 25, 1967, no. not recorded, FBI–COINTEL (Black) File; Fred J. Baumgardner to Sullivan, April 22, 1966, no. 11-5, FBI–COINTEL (White) File.

59. Director to SACs Albany et al., March 4, 1968, no. 19, FBI–COINTEL (Black) File.

60. Moore to Sullivan, Feb. 29, 1968, no. 19, ibid.; Church Committee, *Book III*, 6.

61. Director to SACs Albany et al., March 4, 1968, no. 19, FBI–COINTEL (Black) File.

62. Navasky, "FBI's Wildest Dream," 716–18.

63. SAC Charlotte to Director, April 4, 1968, no. 77, FBI–COINTEL (Black) File; SAC Chicago to Director, April 22, 1968, no. illegible, ibid.

64. Director to SACs Chicago et al., May 3, 1968, no. illegible, ibid.

65. Director to SACs Albany et al., Jan. 7, 1969, no. 580, ibid.; SAC San Francisco to Director, Aug. 7, 1968, no. 230, ibid.; *New York Times*, Oct. 19, 1980; Bishop to DeLoach, June 25, 1969, no. 155, King Folder, FBI–Hoover O&C Files; Hoover to Gerald Ford, Oct. 29, 1969, FBI, Cong. Papers, Box B140-19, Ford Papers; Moore to Sullivan, June 27, 1969, no. 3660, FBI–King File.

66. Moore to Sullivan, Nov. 1, 1968, no. illegible, FBI–COINTEL (Black) File; SAC San Diego to Director, May 31, 1968, no. illegible, ibid. The FBI gathered background data on Smith and Carlos; placed the principal organizer of a black athlete boycott/protest at the Olympic games, Harry Edwards, on the Rabble Rouser Index; and recruited a student in Edwards's sociology class at San Jose State as an informant. Edwards, *Struggle*, 181, 185, 193.

67. SAC Boston to Director, Feb. 1, 1968, no. 9, FBI–COINTEL (Black) File; Director to SAC Boston, Feb. 8, 1968, no. 9, ibid.

68. Moore to Sullivan, April 17, 1968, no. 96, ibid.

69. Director to SAC New York, July 10, 1968, no. 100-161140-illegible, FBI–Moore Files; Director to SAC Washington, April 2, 1968, no. 43, FBI–COINTEL (Black) File; SAC Houston to Director, March 14, 1968, no. 27, ibid.; SAC Charlotte to Director, July 9, 1968, no. illegible, ibid.

70. Church Committee, *Book III*, 25; Brennan to Sullivan, May 9, 1968, idem, *Hearings—FBI*, 393–94; Director to SACs Albany et al., July 7, 1968, ibid., 395–97.

71. Hayden, *Reunion*, 150; SAC Chicago to Director, Dec. 31, 1968, no. 9-29, FBI–COINTEL (New Left) File; Director to SAC Chicago, Dec. 23, 1968, no. 9-28, ibid.; SAC Baltimore to Director, June 7, 1968, no. 3-1, ibid.; Church Committee, *Book III*, 42.

72. DeLoach to Tolson, Aug. 22, 1966, no. 5888, FBI–HUAC File (61-7582).

73. Bishop to DeLoach, Aug. 3, 1967, no. 5928, ibid; DeLoach to Tolson, July 10, 1967, no. not recorded, FBI–King File. In addition to the suggested HUAC campaign, Johnson urged the Bureau to work with Drew Pearson. DeLoach "doubted Pearson would print derogatory information concerning these characters."

74. DeLoach to Tolson, July 10, 1967, no. not recorded, FBI–King File.

75. Ibid.; Walter Trohan to Comrade [DeLoach], Sept, 24, 1964, Correspondence, J. Edgar Hoover, Trohan Papers.

76. Larry Temple to the President, May 28 and June 19, 1968, White House Aides' Files—Larry Temple, SACB, Johnson Papers; Temple to the President, Jan. 19, 1968, WHCF—CF, FG285, ibid.; note, LBJ, Aug. 27, 1967, WHCF, Ex FG285, ibid.; Barefoot Sanders to the President, Feb. 29, 1968, WHCF, Ex FG411/U-Z, ibid.; Hoover to Tolson, DeLoach, and Sullivan, July 25, 1967, no. 959, FBI–Detroit Riot File (157-6); Lovin, "Lyndon B. Johnson," 94–112; Francis J. McNamara to Richard H. Ichord, June 1, 1966, Accredited Newsmen Covering War in Vietnam, Box 184, Ichord Papers; press release, re Du Bois Clubs, n.d. [ca. Oct. 1967], U.S. Dept. of Justice, Box 58, SNCC Papers. The Du Bois Clubs formed after Dr. Du Bois joined the Communist party in 1961, at the age of ninety-three. The FBI responded by leaking derogatory information through the U.S. Information Agency "in view of the esteem in which Du Bois is held in African nations." Bland to Sullivan, Nov. 21, 1961, no. 193, FBI–Du Bois File (100-99729).

77. Director to SACs New York et al., June 7, 1965, no. 3931, FBI–COINTEL (CPUSA) File; Baumgardner to Sullivan, Oct. 27, 1965, no. illegible, Nov. 16, 1965, no. not recorded, ibid.; Brennan to Sullivan, Oct. 13, 1967, no. not recorded, FBI–COINTEL (Black) File.

78. George Christian to the President, April 8, 1967, WHCF—Name File (Martin Luther King, Jr.), Box 144, Johnson Papers.

79. John P. Roche to the President, Sept. 1, 1967, WHCF—CF, Name File (Hon), Box 4, ibid.; Roche to the President, April 5, 1967, WHCF—CF, HU2, Box

56, ibid.; Roche to Watson, Dec. 22, 1967, WHCF—CF, PU1-2, ibid. The Carmichael rumor, Roche explained, "was a joke which grew out of a photo in the *Post* (I think) of Julian Bond, Andrew Young, and Stokely C. with a bunch of African nationalists at some conference (Lagos?). They looked like whites. My Irish irony always got me into jams, but I loved to work over Marvin who was a solemn Fundamentalist."

80. The Catholic War Veterans operations (see note 77) were carried out under the Communist party and black nationalist COINTELPROs.

81. The President lost his enthusiasm for counterintelligence action against his antiwar critics after Tet. Lovin, "Lyndon B. Johnson," 564.

82. Garrow, *FBI and Martin Luther King*, 207.

83. Aptheker interview; SAC Cincinnati to Director, March 28, 1966, no. not recorded, FBI–COINTEL (CPUSA) File; Hoover to Tolson, DeLoach, Sullivan, and Robert E. Wick, April 27, 1967, no. not recorded, FBI–King File.

84. Director to SAC New York, July 10, 1968, no. illegible, FBI–Moore Files.

85. Director to SACs New York et al., Oct. 12, 1961, in Church Committee, *Hearings—FBI*, 377; idem, *Book III*, 18.

86. Idem, *Book III*, 12–13 n54–55.

87. Hoover to Tolson, DeLoach, John P. Mohr, James H. Gale, Alex Rosen, and Sullivan, March 11, 1968, no. not recorded, FBI–Tolson Memo File (67-9524).

CHAPTER 9.
The Only Good Panther

1. Wolfe, *Radical Chic*, 8.

2. Davis, et al., *If They Come*, 21.

3. Rubin, *Do It!*, 142.

4. For Panther rhetoric, see the party newspaper, the *Black Panther*.

5. Seale, *Lonely Rage*, 134–36.

6. Sheehy, *Panthermania*, 6; John Ehrlichman to J. Edgar Hoover, Dec. 22, 1969, Black Panther Party, WHSF—John Ehrlichman, Box 15, Nixon Papers; Director to SACs Albany et al., Sept. 3, 1968, no. illegible, FBI–Hampton Files.

7. Watters and Gillers, eds., *Investigating*, 196, 214, 216.

8. The casualty counts in Black Panther mythology and police department lore are considerably higher. Epstein, "Panthers," 45–77.

9. Elliff, *Crime*, 130, 140; Leonard interview; Pinkney, *Red, Black*, 110; Harris, *Justice*, 236.

10. Director to SAC San Francisco et al., June 25, 1969, no. illegible, FBI–Hampton Files; Director to SACs Chicago et al., June 25, 1969, no. illegible, ibid.; Director to SAC New York, June 6, 1969, no. 999, FBI–COINTEL (Black Nationalist) File (100-448006).

11. Conversations recorded in Hoover to Clyde Tolson, Cartha D. DeLoach, James H. Gale, Alex Rosen, and William C. Sullivan, April 23, 1969, no. not recorded, FBI–Tolson Memo File (67-9524); Hoover to Tolson, DeLoach, Sullivan, and Thomas E. Bishop, July 14, 1969, no. not recorded, ibid.

12. Senate Committee to Study . . . Intelligence Activities (hereafter Church Committee), *Book III*, 10–11, 528–29. A federal grand jury indicted Seale and seven others under the antiriot provision of the 1968 Civil Rights Act, the so-called Rap Brown Law which made it a federal crime to cross a

state line with intent to incite riot. Verbal clashes between Seale and Judge Julius J. Hoffman marked the early stages of the trial, and the judge finally ordered the Panther publicist gagged and chained to his chair in the courtroom. When Seale persisted, Hoffman found him in contempt, sentenced him to four years in prison, severed his case from that of the others, declared an individual mistrial, and set a new trial date.

13. Bates interview; Ungar, *FBI*, 208.

14. Bates interview; SAC San Francisco to Director, April 3, 1968, no. illegible, April 3, 1968, no. illegible and 95, FBI–COINTEL (Black) File. A liberal cadre had not infiltrated this FBI office. San Francisco had more operatives (eighty-nine) assigned to domestic intelligence than any other field office, and their reports on the New Left were filled with musings about attacks on "the Establishment"—that is, "the organized, lawful society which the Bureau represents." SAC San Francisco to Director, Jan. 27, 1969, no. 47-44, FBI–COINTEL (New Left) (100-449698).

15. George C. Moore to Sullivan, Dec. 17, 1968, no. illegible, FBI–COINTEL (White Hate) File (157-9); Moore to Sullivan, Sept. 27, 1968, no. 306, Oct. 28, 1968, no. illegible, Oct. 10, 1968, no. illegible, FBI–COINTEL (Black) File; Director to SAC San Francisco et al., Sept. 30, 1968, no. 306, ibid.

16. Makeba, *Makeba*, 162; Church Committee, *Book III*, 9, 47, 199 n60; Director to SAC Washington, July 1, 1968, no. 113, FBI–COINTEL (Black) File; Moore to Sullivan, Nov. 8, 1968, no. 465, April 15, 1970, no. 1751, ibid. The FBI also placed anonymous calls to SNCC's James Forman, informing him that the Panthers intended to "get him," and sent threatening letters to the twenty-one person board of directors of the Black United Front. One of the recipients, Sumner Stone, remembered sitting "up half the night" with his wife. "I thought I was going to be assassinated."

17. Church Committee, *Book III*, 9, 40, 46–48.

18. SAC San Francisco to Director, May 14, 1969, no. 961, FBI–COINTEL (Black) File; Watters and Gillers, eds., *Investigating*, 196.

19. Director to SAC San Francisco, May 27, 1969, no. 964, FBI–COINTEL (Black) File. The reluctance of a particular field office to go along with Division Five was not unusual. When Detroit SAC Neil Welch balked at a directive to intensify surveillance of the League of Revolutionary Black Workers, a small group of UAW dissidents, suggesting that the matter be referred to the attorney general, Division Five told him that the attorney general's "authority is not necessary for our intelligence operations." Welch, *Inside*, 172-73.

20. See the San Francisco subfile, FBI–COINTEL (Black) File. Gain is quoted in Bergman and Weir, "Revolution," 47.

21. The discussion of the Ranger-Panther conflict in this and the next three paragraphs is based on serials 534, 591, 599, 606, 608, FBI–COINTEL (Black) File; Church Committee, *Book III*, 195–99.

22. See the sources cited in the previous note. The Rangers later changed their name to the Black P. Stone Nation. In the more recent past they have called themselves the El Rukn tribe of the Moorish Science Temple of America, and finally El Rukn, Sunni Muslims under their religious leader, Malik (Jeff Fort). In late 1987 a federal jury convicted Fort and four other members of conspiring to commit terrorist acts against the United States on behalf of Libya. El Rukn bought an antitank rocket from an undercover FBI agent, and the FBI implicated Fort as the mastermind of the entire terrorism-for-hire plot—even though he was incarcerated in Texas at the

time, serving a thirteen-year sentence. He received eighty years on the conspiracy charges.

23. Baraka, *Autobiography*, 254; Karenga interview; Karenga, *Roots of the US/Panther Conflict*.

24. Anthony, *Picking Up the Gun*, 75–76. The US-Panther vendetta can be traced in serials 466, 482, 541, 795-6, 813, 833, 1234, 1283, 1435, 1600, 1777, FBI–COINTEL (Black) File; Church Committee, *Book III*, 41, 43, 47–48, 189-95, 199, 213, 221–22.

25. Baraka, *Autobiography*, 279.

26. San Diego agents also launched a campaign against New Leftists that included the incitement of the paramilitary Secret Army Organization to acts of violence against Vietnam war protestors.

27. See the sources cited in note 24; and the following issues of the *San Diego Union* (all 1976), Jan. 4 and 15, March 11, May 6, 7, 19, and 20, June 11, 18, and 25.

28. Ibid. In 1972 Evans and another agent who helped egg on the feud received a nonpunitive transfer to Butte, Montana. The agent who headed up the counterintelligence program in San Diego, Robert L. Baker, left the Bureau in 1975 at the mandatory retirement age of fifty-five.

29. Baraka, *Autobiography*, 279; Church Committee, *Book III*, 194, 199; Karenga interview.

30. Director to SAC Newark, Sept. 16, 1969, no. illegible, FBI–COINTEL (New Left) File; SAC Newark to Director, Aug. 25, 1969, no. illegible, ibid.

31. Bergman and Weir, "Revolution," 49.

32. Karenga interview; Karenga, *Roots of the US/Panther Conflict*, 7. A year later, in June 1971, Karenga was sentenced to a year in prison for allegedly torturing two young black women.

33. SAC San Francisco to Director, May 11, 1970, no. 211, June 17, 1970, no. 221, FBI–COINTEL (Special Operations) File (105-174254); Director to SAC San Francisco, June 26, 1970, no. 221, ibid.; Church Committee, *Book III*, 208; SAC San Francisco to Director, Dec. 29, 1969, no. 1569, FBI–COINTEL (Black) File.

34. The discussion of the Hampton case is based on Flint Taylor interviews; Donner, *Age*, 226–30; the voluminous documents in FBI–Hampton Files; *Iberia Hampton et al. v. Edward V. Hanrahan et al.*, 600 F.2d 600 (1979); Commission of Inquiry, *Search and Destroy*.

35. Leonard interview; James A. Emanuel, "Panther Man" (c. 1970).

36. Director to SAC Chicago, Dec. 17, 1969, no. illegible, FBI–Hampton Files; SAC Chicago to Director, Feb. 11, 1970, no. illegible, ibid.

37. Emanuel, "Panther Man." Hanrahan is quoted in Commission of Inquiry, *Search and Destroy*, ix.

38. Leonard interview.

39. Ibid.

40. SAC Chicago to Director, April 8, 1970, no. illegible, FBI–Hampton Files.

41. Flint Taylor, Leonard interviews.

42. Flint Taylor interviews; Hoover to Tolson, DeLoach, Bishop, Rosen, and Sullivan, Sept. 19, 1968, no. not recorded, FBI–Tolson Memo File.

43. *New York Times*, Nov. 14, 1982.

44. Berlet, "Journalists," 22; Director to SAC Chicago, Dec. 10, 1969, no. 1448, FBI–COINTEL (Black) File.

45. This program began in late 1968 and by the spring of the following year the FBI had conducted over 500 interviews. Director to SAC New York, Nov. 14, 1968, no. 100-161993-illegible, FBI–Moore Files; SAC New York to Director, April 8, 1969, no. 100-161993-illegible, ibid. For the "Catholic hierarchy" quote, see Director to SAC San Diego, Sept. 11, 1969, no. 1269, FBI–COINTEL (Black) File.

46. Church Committee, *Book III*, 208–12. The FBI proposed hundreds of fraudulent letters; it is not always clear which ones were mailed out and which ones were not. For the examples cited here, see serials 743, 1233, 1771, 1826, 1861, FBI–COINTEL (Black) File.

47. Carson, "Blacks and Jews," 126–27.

48. Director to SACs Albany et al., May 6, 1968, no. 32, FBI–Moore Files (157-601).

49. Herman Edelsberg to Louis B. Nichols, July 7, 1953, no. not recorded, FBI–HUAC File (61-7582); Hoover to Herbert Hoover, Feb. 20, 1957, J. Edgar Hoover Folder, Post–Pres. Individual, Herbert Hoover Papers; Nichols to Tolson, March 9, 1955, no. not recorded, FBI–Sokolsky File (62-89885).

50. Moore to Sullivan, Jan. 8, 1969, no. 586, Sept. 22, 1969, no. 1306, Nov. 21, 1969, no. 1444, FBI–COINTEL (Black) File; SAC New York to Director, Sept. 10, 1969, no. 1306, ibid.; Director to SAC New York, April 10, 1969, no. illegible, ibid.; SAC Boston to Director, Aug. 13, 1970, no. illegible, ibid.; SAC San Francisco to Director, May 28, 1970, no. illegible, ibid.; Director to SAC Baltimore, Feb. 25, 1969, no. illegible, ibid.; Moore to Charles D. Brennan, Aug. 20, 1970, no. not recorded, ibid.; Director to SAC Boston, July 29, 1970, no. illegible, ibid.

51. The indictments included 150 counts involving plans to dynamite five midtown department stores, the Morrisania (Bronx) police station, and Penn Central Railroad tracks above 148th Street.

52. Moore to Sullivan, May 14, 1970, no. 1820, FBI–COINTEL (Black) File. Division Five listed this as one of five COINTELPRO highlights, alongside syndicated columns on the Panthers by Robert S. Allen and John A. Goldsmith; the collapse of a Panther chapter in Cleveland, Mississippi, in the wake of a leak to James Ward of the *Jackson Daily News;* the eviction of US from its San Diego headquarters; and a Miami television documentary on the Nation of Islam.

53. Church Committee, *Book III*, 200–07.

54. Bergman and Weir, "Revolution," 47, 48.

55. Church Committee, *Book III*, 200–07.

56. *New York Times*, April 25, 1970.

57. Amnesty International, *Proposal*, 15–33; *Sixty Minutes* (CBS Television network), Nov. 29, 1987, pp. 6–10.

58. Director to SAC Newark, Aug. 13, 1971, no. 9X10, FBI–Moore Files (152-22627); Hoover to Tolson, Sullivan, Brennan, Gale, Rosen, and Casper, May 26, 1971, no. not recorded, May 27, 1971, no. not recorded, FBI–Tolson Memo File. Hoover had no intention of having the FBI "assume the responsibility for taking over the killing of all police officers." Nixon agreed, because, among other reasons, Senator Harrison A. Williams, Jr. (D., N.J.), had charged "the President of not backing up law and order, et cetera"— specifically, by "blocking his attempt to let the FBI go into these police killings." Raising the specter of "a national police force," once again, Hoover said "Williams wants to make a Lindbergh case where there is a pre-

sumption of Federal jurisdiction at the end of 24 hours and we would be
in every case in the country," adding that "Williams is the last man who
should be doing any talking as his background is so bad it ought to be
looked into." Years later, the FBI targeted Williams under its ABSCAM
sting operation. Hoover to Tolson, Sullivan, Bishop, Brennan, Joseph J.
Casper, Gale, and Rosen, May 28, 1971, Folder 128, FBI–Hoover O&C Files.

59. Director to SAC Newark, Aug. 13, 1971, no. 9X10, FBI–Moore Files (152-
22627); Hoover to Tolson, Sullivan, Brennan, Gale, Rosen, and Casper, May
26, 1971, no. not recorded, May 27, 1971, no. not recorded, FBI–Tolson
Memo File.

60. Shakur, *Assata*, 123; National Conference of Black Lawyers, et al., *Human
Rights*, 1–83 (Appendix VII).

61. SAC Letter, Feb. 19, 1974, FBI–SAC File; A. B. Fulton to W. Raymond Wannall, Feb. 7, 1974, no. 6162, FBI–HUAC File; Director to Attorney General,
Feb. 8, 1974, no. 6162, ibid.; memo, re PRISACTS, July 15, 1975, no. 57,
FBI–Moore Files (157-12065); House Committee on Internal Security, *Revolutionary Target*. See also the more recent report, Dept. of Justice, *Prison
Gangs*. By 1975, if not earlier, the FBI had extended the PRISACTS dissemination program to include Ku Klux Klan literature entering the nation's
prisons and Klan activity in general among inmates.

62. Amnesty International, *Proposal*, 32–33. Bureau counterintelligence actions also served as the foundation for a petition on human rights violations submitted in December 1978 to a United Nations commission by the
National Conference of Black Lawyers and other groups. Hinds, *Illusions*.

63. Church Committee, *Book III*, 189.

CHAPTER 10.
Citizens and Radicals

1. When Hugh Sidey mentioned Nixon's plan in his *Life* magazine column,
the FBI ran its mandatory file check. Milton A. Jones to Thomas E. Bishop,
Oct. 18, 1971, no. not recorded, FBI–CPJ File (62-113909).

2. See the director's introduction of the vice president at the FBI National
Academy graduation exercises, June 11, 1954, in Folder 8, FBI–Hoover O&C
Files.

3. Richard Nixon to H. R. Haldeman, May 18, 1972, Pres. Memos, WHSF—
H. R. Haldeman, Box 230, Nixon Papers.

4. Haldeman notes, May 31, 1970, WHSF—Haldeman, Box 41, ibid.; Cartha
D. DeLoach to Clyde Tolson, Feb. 27, 1970, no. 5, Press Media Campaign
Against Director Folder, FBI–Hoover O&C Files; newspaper clippings,
May 18, 1971, no. 2049, May 27, 1971, no. 2051, FBI–Robert Kennedy File
(77-51387); J. Edgar Hoover to Tolson, DeLoach, John P. Mohr, Bishop, Jo-
seph J. Casper, and William C. Sullivan, May 1, 1970, no. not recorded,
FBI–Tolson Memo File (67-9524); Tolson to Director, Aug. 26, 1971, in Sen-
ate Select Committee to Study . . . Intelligence Activities (hereafter Church
Committee), *Hearings—FBI*, 443. Sullivan is quoted in Demaris, *Director*,
84.

5. Charles Colson to John Dean, April 28, 1972, Misc. Intelligence, WHSF—
John Dean, Box 89, Nixon Papers; John Ehrlichman to Hoover, Dec. 17,
1971, Charles Evers, WHSF—John Ehrlichman, Box 18, ibid.; Hoover to
Alexander P. Butterfield, March 16, 1970, no. not recorded, FBI–Lawrence
File (95-54-3169); Hoover to Ehrlichman, July 2, 1969, no. 42, FBI–Wilkins
File (62-78270).

6. Rustin, *Down the Line*, 260; notes, June 12, 1969, no. not recorded, June 14, 1964, no. not recorded, June 16, 1969, not recorded, FBI–SCLC File (100-438794); letterhead memo, July 18, 1969, no. not recorded, ibid.; George C. Moore to Sullivan, Jan. 22, 1969, no. not recorded, FBI–Eastland File (94-4-5130); Jones to DeLoach, July 14, 1965, no. 47, ibid.; Jones to Bishop, March 5, 1969, no. 2, Folder 131, FBI–Hoover O&C Files; Director to Deputy Attorney General, March 5, 1969, ibid.

7. Jones to Louis B. Nichols, Sept. 3, 1954, no. 12, FBI–Eastland File; Hoover to Tolson, DeLoach, and James H. Gale, July 1, 1969, no. 23, Mitchell Folder, FBI–Hoover O&C Files; Director to Attorney General, July 1, 1969, no. 24, ibid.; Hoover to Tolson, DeLoach, Gale, and Bishop, Jan. 19, 1970, no. not recorded, FBI–Tolson Memo File; Turner, *Hoover's F.B.I.*, 91–92.

8. Buchanan, *Right*, 282–83; Director to Attorney General, April 2, 1962, no. not recorded, FBI–Levison File (100-392452).

9. Hoover to Tolson, DeLoach, Gale, Alex Rosen, Sullivan, and Bishop, April 23, 1969, no. not recorded, FBI–Tolson Memo File; Powers, *Secrecy and Power*, 440.

10. Hoover to Tolson, DeLoach, Gale, Rosen, Sullivan, and Bishop, April 23, 1969, no. not recorded, FBI–Tolson Memo File.

11. Colson to Jim Keogh, Sept. 22, 1970, Campus Unrest, WHSF—Charles Colson, Box 44, Nixon Papers.

12. Director to SACs Albany et al., Nov. 26, 1969, in Church Committee, *Hearings—FBI*, 368–69; Richard D. Cotter to Charles D. Brennan, Nov. 3, 1970, no. 1X3, FBI–Racial Digest File (157-19573).

13. Hoover to Tolson, DeLoach, Sullivan, and Bishop, May 9, 1969, in House Committee on the Judiciary, *Statement of Information—Book VII*, pt. 1, p. 143; Hoover to Tolson, Sullivan, Mohr, Bishop, and Ivan W. Conrad, Feb. 4, 1971, no. not recorded, FBI–Tolson Memo File.

14. Hoover to Tolson, DeLoach, Nicholas P. Callahan, Rosen, and Bishop, March 19, 1969, no. not recorded, FBI–Tolson Memo File; Conrad to Mohr, March 14, 1969, no. 6, March 18, 1969, no. 1, March 27, 1969, no. 4 and 5, June 17, 1969, no. 17, June 18, 1969, no. 19, Mitchell Folder, FBI–Hoover O&C Files; Director to Attorney General, March 20, 1969, no. 8, March 28, 1969, no. 10, ibid.; Demaris, *Director*, 140.

15. Moore to Sullivan, June 18, 1969, no. 3602, FBI–King File (100-106670); Hoover to Spiro Agnew, June 19, 1969, no. 3602, ibid.; Hoover to Tolson, DeLoach, Rosen, Sullivan, and Bishop, May 14, 1970, no. not recorded, May 18, 1970, no. not recorded, FBI–Tolson Memo File; Hoover to Tolson, DeLoach, Sullivan, and Bishop, April 21, 1970, no. not recorded, ibid.; Hoover to Tolson, Sullivan, Bishop, and Brennan, Jan. 7, 1971, no. not recorded, ibid.

16. Egil Krogh, Jr., to Hoover, June 27, 1969, Black Panther Party, WHSF—Ehrlichman, Box 15, Nixon Papers; Krogh to Attorney General, Jan. 28, 1970, ibid.; Krogh to Haldeman, March 12, 1970, ibid.; Krogh to Brad Patterson, Jan. 14, 1970, ibid.; Ehrlichman to the President, May 8, 1970, OA #103, WHSF—Egil Krogh, Box 58, Nixon Papers; Hoover to Tolson, DeLoach, Sullivan, and Bishop, April 21, 1970, no. not recorded, FBI–Tolson Memo File; Hoover to Tolson, DeLoach, Rosen, Sullivan, and Bishop, May 14, 1970, no. not recorded, ibid.; Hoover to Tolson, Sullivan, Bishop, and Brennan, Jan. 7, 1971, no. not recorded, ibid.

17. House Committee on Appropriations, *Hearings* (1971), 743; Director to SAC Los Angeles, June 25, 1970, no. 1868, FBI–COINTEL (Black Nationalist)

File (100-448006); SAC Los Angeles to Director, June 17, 1970, no. 1868, ibid.; SAC New York to Director, March 6, 1969, no. 2085, FBI–Moore Files (100-161993).

18. The discussion of the Seberg case is based on Richards, *Played Out*, 220, 237–41, 245, 247, 253, 277, 325, 374, 378; Moore to Sullivan, April 14, 1970, no. 28, FBI–Seberg File (157-13876); Hoover to Ehrlichman, May 19, 1970, no. 30, ibid.; Hoover to Attorney General, May 19, 1970, no. 30, ibid.; Moore to Brennan, Aug. 28, 1970, no. 32, ibid.; Director to SACs Los Angeles et al., Sept. 11, 1970, no. 33, ibid.; Director to SAC Los Angeles, May 6, 1970, no. 1766, FBI–COINTEL (Black) File; SAC Los Angeles to Director, April 27, 1970, no. 1766, June 3, 1970, no. 1831 (Haber's column is filed under this serial), June 10, 1970, no. 1837, ibid.; SAC San Francisco to Director, April 23, 1970, no. 26-1137, FBI–Black Panther Party File (105-165706); SAC Boston to Director, May 4, 1973, no. 125, FBI–Jamal File (100-44622).

19. See the sources cited in the previous note.

20. Hoover to Tolson, DeLoach, Rosen, Sullivan, and Bishop, May 18, 1970, no. not recorded, FBI–Tolson Memo File; President's Commission, *Campus Unrest*, 436, 438–39. Moore disagreed with Hoover on Jackson State, saying "the trouble began with 'the street corner boys,' youngsters who dropped out of school" and "were on campus looking for trouble, spreading rumors—'Did you know Charlie Evers was shot?'" Moore interview.

21. Memo, Hoover to Tolson, DeLoach, Rosen, Sullivan, and Bishop, May 18, 1970, no. not recorded, FBI–Tolson Memo File. Field agents, in contrast, were critical of the guardsmen in Kent and the policemen in Jackson. When the *Washington Post* ran a story "to the effect that the FBI has said that the (National) Guards are to blame in the Kent State matter," Nixon called Hoover to complain. "The President said that from what he had seen . . . it looks like the Guard had a lot of provocation. I said I thought they definitely had. The President said he told his people he was going to have [the FBI report] 'shot down' as he was not going to have this student business erupting as, basically, what do you expect the Guards to do." Hoover to Tolson, Sullivan, Bishop, and Rosen, July 24, 1970, no. not recorded, ibid.; Hoover to Tolson, Sullivan, Bishop, Brennan, Gale, and Rosen, July 24, 1970, no. not recorded, ibid.; Leonard interview.

22. Director to SACs Atlanta and Philadelphia, May 19, 1970, no. 2932, FBI–SCLC File; Director to SAC Atlanta, May 19, 1970, no. 2929, ibid.; Moore to Sullivan, May 18, 1970, in Church Committee, *Hearings—FBI*, 493; Hoover to Agnew, May 19, 1970, ibid., 494; Hoover to Tolson, DeLoach, Rosen, Sullivan, and Bishop, May 18, 1970, no. not recorded, FBI–Tolson Memo File.

23. Graham, "On Riots," 22; President's Commission, *Campus Unrest*, 436, 450, 458–59.

24. Ehrlichman interview; Moore to Sullivan, Jan. 22, 1969, no. 3562, FBI–King File; Hoover to the President, Jan. 23, 1969, no. 3560, ibid.; Director to Deputy Attorney General, March 3, 1969, no. 3571, ibid.; Moore to Sullivan, Jan. 17, 1969, no. 127, King Folder, FBI–Hoover O&C Files.

25. Church Committee, *Book III*, 183; Director to SAC Atlanta, April 14, 1969, no. not recorded, FBI–SCLC File; Director to SACs Baltimore et al., March 27, 1969, no. 3581, FBI–King File; Jones to Bishop, March 18, 1969, no. 3586, ibid.

26. DeLoach to Tolson, March 11, 1969, no. 5654, FBI–King Assassination File (44-38861); Moore to Sullivan, March 5, 1969, no. 772, FBI–COINTEL (Black) File; Director to SAC Atlanta, March 13, 1969, no. 772, ibid.

27. When the FBI finally made an arrest in June, the director told the attorney

general that "the supporters of Dr. King will do everything in their power to kill [James Earl Ray]." Hoover to Tolson, DeLoach, Rosen, Bishop, and Sullivan, June 20, 1968, no. 4660, FBI–King Assassination File.

28. DeLoach to Tolson, March 11, 1969, no. 5654, FBI–King Assassination File; Jones to Bishop, March 20, 1969, no. 5655, ibid.; Rosen to DeLoach, Jan. 16, 1970, no. 5854, ibid. Bishop wrote his book, but it was not the type of book DeLoach wanted and it is not clear whether Crime Records provided much assistance.

29. Moore to Sullivan, Feb. 28, 1970 (addendum by Bishop), no. 3728, FBI–King File; Jones to Bishop, May 22, 1968, no. 149, King Folder, FBI–Hoover O&C Files.

30. Moore to Sullivan, Jan. 13, 1970, no. 3699, FBI–King File; SAC Washington to Director, Jan. 12, 1970, no. 3697, ibid; letterhead memos, Jan. 5, 1971, no. 3871, Dec. 31, 1970, no. 3867, ibid.; SAC Washington to Director, Jan. 11, 1971, no. 3689, ibid.

31. SAC Letter, May 27, 1969, in Church Committee, *Book III*, 518. See also ibid., 228, 252–55, *Book II*, 75, *Hearings—FBI*, 17; SAC Richmond to Director, May 14, 1969, no. 918, FBI–COINTEL (Black) File.

32. Director to SACs Baltimore et al., July 16, 1970, no. 230, FBI–COINTEL (Special Operations) File.

33. Richard E. Logan to SAC Philadelphia, Jan. 27, 1971, in "Complete Collection," 50; Church Committee, *Book III*, 246–50.

34. House Committee on the Judiciary, *Statement of Information—Book VII*, pt. 1, pp. 398–402; Tom Charles Huston to Haldeman, Aug. 25, 1970, HRH Security/FBI, WHSF—Haldeman, Box, 147, Nixon Papers.

35. SAC Columbia to Director, Feb. 28, 1969, no. illegible, May 28, 1970, no. illegible, FBI–COINTEL (Black) File; SAC Pittsburgh to Director, Sept. 4, 1969, no. 1257, ibid.; SAC Norfolk to Director, April 6, 1970, no. 932, FBI–COINTEL (New Left) File; SAC Butte to Director, Sept. 12, 1968, no. 7-6, March 12, 1969, no. 7-14, ibid.

36. SAC Sacramento to Director, April 1, 1970, no. 931, FBI–COINTEL (New Left) File; SAC Los Angeles to Director, July 31, 1968, no. 26-7, Sept. 30, 1968, no. 26-13, ibid.; Director to SAC San Diego, Sept. 18, 1969, no. 1284, FBI–COINTEL (Black) File; Director to SAC San Francisco, Feb. 27, 1969, no. illegible, ibid.; SAC San Diego to Director, Oct. 6, 1969, no. 1338, Nov. 10, 1969, no. illegible, Feb. 18, 1970, no illegible, ibid.

37. Note, re Domestic Intelligence Division Inspection, Jan. 12, 1971, in Church Committee, *Hearings—FBI*, 709; Director to SACs Albany et al., Nov. 4, 1970, ibid., 698-99; Executives' Conference to Tolson, Oct. 29, 1970, ibid., 701; SAC Letter, Sept. 15, 1970, FBI–SAC File. See also Director to SACs Albany et al., Jan. 31, 1969, no. 2, FBI–Black Student Groups on College Campuses File (157-12176).

38. SAC Jackson to Director, April 4, 1968, no. 73, Feb. 11, 1969, no. illegible, FBI–COINTEL (Black) File; deposition of Thomas Fitzpatrick, April 27, 1978, pp. 87–88, 208, *Muhammad Kenyatta v. Roy Moore, et al.*, no. J77-0298(R) (S.D. Miss., 1985).

39. SAC Jackson to Director, Feb. 26, 1969, no. illegible, March 7, 1970, no. illegible, FBI–COINTEL (Black) File.

40. Church Committee, *Book II*, 46; SAC Jackson to Director, March 7, 1970, no. illegible, FBI–COINTEL (Black) File.

41. SAC Jackson to Director, Feb. 26, 1969, no. illegible, FBI–COINTEL (Black) File; Director to SAC Jackson, March 3, 1969, no. illegible, ibid.

42. Aschenbrenner interview; SAC Jackson to Director, Sept. 16, 1969, no. 54-

14, Oct. 13, 1969, no. 54-15, FBI–COINTEL (New Left) File; Director to SAC Jackson, Oct. 1, 1969, no. 54-14, ibid. Bureau agents insist that Kenyatta did in fact steal the television in question.

43. *Jackson Capital Reporter,* June 22, 1978; SAC Jackson to Director, Oct. 13, 1969, no. 1348, FBI–COINTEL (Black) File; Director to SAC Jackson, Aug. 17, 1970, no. illegible, Feb. 8, 1971, no. 2195, ibid.; SAC Jackson to Director, July 21, 1970, no. 1893, Aug. 5, 1970, no. 1910, Aug. 4, 1970, no. 1914, Aug. 3, 1970, no. 1911, Feb. 1, 1971, no. 2195, ibid.; Moore to Brennan, Aug. 7, 1970, no. not recorded, ibid. Moore's agents also helped Ward write about the Republic of New Africa.

44. Richard H. Ichord to William H. Stapleton, July 2, 1974, Misc. Memoranda 1973-74, Box 175, Ichord Papers.

45. Bamford, *Puzzle Palace,* 322; Church Committee, *Book III,* 573, 624, 631, 751, *Book II,* 107; National Conference of Black Lawyers, et al., *Human Rights,* Appendix VI.

46. Letterhead memo, Jan. 29, 1971, no. 27, FBI–Jackson File (157-6760); Moore to Brennan, Aug. 14, 1970, no. 22, Aug. 17, 1970, no. 23, ibid.; Moore to Brennan, Aug. 18, 1970, no. 3834, FBI–King File; Director to SAC Chicago, Aug. 21, 1970, no. illegible, FBI–COINTEL (Black) File; Moore to Brennan, Aug. 18, 1970, no. 2981, FBI–SCLC File.

47. Cotter to Miller, Sept. 17, 1971, no. illegible, FBI–Security Index File (100-358086); Thomas J. Smith to Miller, Nov. 11, 1971, no. 4116, ibid.; Moore to Brennan, April 21, 1971, no. 294, FBI–Agitator Index File (157-7782).

48. Church Committee, *Book II,* 125–26, *Book III,* 546–47.

49. This also applied to people with red skin, with Division Five preparing a directive to the field requiring the counting of Indians! All reservation and nonreservation natives were to be tallied up and spied upon. "We are *outraged* by the conduct of these Indians," L. Patrick Gray III agreed, but Division Five "rhetoric" needed to be toned down. Gray aborted the directive in favor of a more moderate one requiring the surveillance of all American Indian Movement chapters. Moore to Edward S. Miller, Nov. 27, 1972, no. 73, FBI–AIM File (100-462483); Acting Director to SACs Albany et al., Nov. 28, 1972, no. 73, Dec. 29, 1972, no. 108, ibid.; note, F [Felt], n.d. [ca. Nov. 27, 1972], no. 73, ibid.; note, G [Gray], Nov. 29, 1972, no. 73, ibid.

50. Moore to Brennan, Oct. 29, 1970, no. 2053, Nov. 2, 1970, no. 2113, FBI–COINTEL (Black) File; Director to SACs Albany et al., Dec. 23, 1970, no. not recorded, ibid.; Church Committee, *Book II,* 91, *Book III,* 530–31.

51. See the sources cited in the previous note.

52. SAC Washington to Director, Feb. 17, 1969, no. 680, FBI–COINTEL (Black) File; [deleted] to SAC Philadelphia, June 18, 1970, in "Complete Collection," 49–50.

53. Church Committee, *Book III,* 534; Director to SACs Albany et al., Feb. 26, 1971, no. 227, FBI–Computerized Telephone Number File (62-3491). A year later, Division Five renamed the Black Nationalist Photograph Album the Extremist Album and added the names of about twenty-five or thirty Ku Klux Klansmen.

54. For a day in the life of a wiretap (PH 1209-R), see Ronald Butler to SAC Philadelphia, Feb. 4, 1971, no. illegible, in "Complete Collection," 26–28.

55. John Mitchell to Hoover, July 14, 1969, no. illegible, FBI–Hampton Files; Hoover to Attorney General, April 29, 1969, no. illegible, Oct. 19, 1970, no. illegible, ibid.

56. Koning, *Nineteen Sixty-Eight,* 52; Bergman and Weir, "Revolution," 46;

Hoover to Attorney General, April 29, 1969, no. illegible, Oct. 19, 1970, no. illegible, FBI–Hampton Files.

57. Houlding, "Wiring," 685. For the Levison tap, see SAC New York to Director, Sept. 24, 1969, no. 353, FBI–Levison File; Hoover to Attorney General, Oct. 1, 1969, no. 353, ibid. For the breakdown of electronic surveillances, see W. Raymond Wannall to Brennan, March 29, 1971, no. 3, Intelligence Coverage, Domestic and Foreign Folder, FBI–Hoover O&C Files.

58. Gale to DeLoach, May 27, 1966, no. 2, Microphone Surveillances Folder, FBI–Hoover O&C Files.

59. Felt to Tolson, July 7, 1971, no. 2, Folder 142, ibid.

60. Director to Attorney General, Sept. 14, 1965, no. 14, Microphone Surveillances Folder, ibid.; Ramsey Clark to the President, Vice President, Members of the Cabinet, and Robert E. Kintner, Jan. 6, 1967, WHCF—CF, FG100/RS, Box 102, Johnson Papers.

61. FBI surveillance of Muhammad Ali sucked in everyone around him, from Howard Cosell to Angelo Dundee and even Johnny Carson. Whenever Ali appeared on the *Tonight Show*, an agent stayed up to watch and record the telecast.

62. Moore to Sullivan, July 2, 1969, no. 3643, FBI–King File; Hoover to Jesse Helms, July 7, 1969, no. not recorded, ibid.; Hoover to Attorney General, June 10, 1969, no. 92, King Folder, FBI–Hoover O&C Files; Hoover to the President, June 16, 1969, no. 95, July 1, 1969, no. 156, ibid.; Hoover to Agnew, June 16, 1969, no. 97, ibid.

63. Leonard interview; Church Committee, *Book II*, 80–81, *Book III*, 500–04, 536; memo, for the President, April 1, 1969, Civil Rights, Busing(1), Box 3, Domestic Council—Geoffrey Shepard Files, Ford Papers.

64. The FBI compiled "estimates" on such topics as "The Interrelationships of Black Power Organizations in the Western Hemisphere."

65. Church Committee, *Book II*, 256–57, *Hearings—FBI*, 349–50; Director to SACs Albany et al., Nov. 6, 1969, no. 6049, FBI–Moore Files (100-161993).

66. Executives' Conference to Tolson, Feb. 12, 1970, no. 1, FBI–Stop Index/National Crime Information Center File (62-115784); W. G. Campbell to Thomas J. Jenkins, Feb. 22, 1974, no. 71, ibid.

67. D. J. Brennan, Jr., to Sullivan, Aug. 15, 1969, no. 1000, FBI–McSurely Files (62-17909); Senate Committee on the Judiciary, *Political Intelligence in the IRS*, 17; Joint Committee on Internal Revenue Taxation, *Investigation of the Special Service Staff*, 23-27; John L. McClellan to Henry Fowler, Sept. 19, 1968, IRS-McSurely Files; D. O. Virdin to File, March 14 and May 28, 1969, ibid.

68. FDR's secretary of the treasury, Henry Morgenthau, Jr., had a Bureau of Internal Revenue intelligence unit compile a report, complete with thirty-seven exhibits, on Paul Robeson. At the time, the IRS rarely shared data with the FBI. Tolson and Edward A. Tamm to Director, Dec. 12, 1941, Dies Folder, FBI–Hoover O&C Files; Elmer Irey to the Secretary, Aug. 7, 1941, Confidential Repts. About People 1941, Morgenthau Papers; Internal Revenue Intelligence Unit Rept., July 31, 1941, ibid.

69. Joint Committee, *Investigation of the SSS*, 7–8, 13–14, 37, 101–10; Senate Committee on the Judiciary, *Political Intelligence in the IRS*, 39–40, 43–47; Church Committee, *Book II*, 95, *Book III*, 842. The IRS also had an informal name-check arrangement with the FBI. Memo, Sept. 19, 1966, no. 14X1, FBI–Forman File (100-443566).

70. Joint Committee, *Investigation of the SSS*, 7–8, 11, 37; Committee on the

Judiciary, *Political Intelligence in the IRS*, 39–40, 43–47; Church Committee, *Book II*, 95, *Book III*, 842.

71. Leonard, Fleischer interviews; Greenberg, "Revolt," 32–40.

72. Rosen to DeLoach, July 9, 1970, no. 1015, FBI–Civil Rights Policy File (44-00); Hoover to Tolson et al., Sept. 11, 1970, no. not recorded, Oct. 12, 1970, no. not recorded, FBI–Tolson Memo File.

73. W. S. Tavel to Mohr, March 2, 1971, Folder 83, FBI–Hoover O&C Files; Tavel to Mohr, March 2, 1971, ibid.

74. Brennan to Sullivan, March 15, 1971, no. 215, FBI–MEDBURG File (52-94527).

75. Director to Attorney General, March 5, 1971, no. 91, ibid. In 1969, when Forman presented his "Black Manifesto" calling for reparations from white churches, the Bureau opened a racketeering/extortion investigation of the Black Economic Development Conference.

76. Rosen to Sullivan, March 24, 1971, no. 264, ibid.; Dwight J. Dalbey to Tolson, March 24, 1971, no. 425, ibid.

77. For the conference, see Watters and Gillers, eds., *Investigating*. For the blind memos and other documents on conference participants, see FBI–CPJ File.

78. Director to Attorney General, April 30, 1971, no. 4, FBI–CPJ File; Rosen to Sullivan, Sept. 24, 1971, no. 10, ibid.; C. Bolz to Charles W. Bates, Oct. 13, 1971, no. 14, Oct. 19, 1971, no. 18, ibid.; Jones to Bishop, Oct. 1, 1971, no. 8, Oct. 27, 1971, no. 25, ibid.; *Cong. Rec.*, 92d Cong., 1st sess., 1971, Oct. 19, pp. 36,883–84, Oct. 28, pp. 38,091–92, Nov. 2, pp, 38,792–94, Nov. 9, pp. 40,073–79, Nov. 19, p. 42,222.

79. Powers, *Secrecy and Power*, 479–80.

80. Ibid., 478–85; *Washington Evening Star*, May 5, 1972, in U.S. Congress, *Memorial Tributes*, 229.

81. National Conference of Black Lawyers et al., *Human Rights*, Appendix V; Katzenbach interview.

82. R. R. Frank to Jenkins, March 21, 1974, no. not recorded, FBI–HUAC File (61-7582); Jenkins to Callahan, Nov. 15, 1973, no. not recorded, FBI–Eastland File.

83. Robert M. Horner to Ichord, Sept. 19, 1973, FBI (Oversight Hearings), Box 179, Ichord Papers; Ichord to Clarence M. Kelley, June 25, 1973, Justice Dept., Box 175, ibid.

84. A former FBI agent who headed the Birmingham office from 1957 to 1960, Kelley came to the directorship with the reputation of being an innovative law enforcement man. A single blemish marred his record as police chief of Kansas City—the charge that he was insensitive to minorities. Ungar, *FBI*, 582, 587–88.

85. Henry E. Petersen to Director, Oct. 22, 1974, in Church Committee, *Hearings—FBI*, 703–5; idem, *Book III*, 555–56.

86. Laurence H. Silberman to Donald Rumsfeld, Dec. 12, 1974, Civil Rights, Busing-Boston, Domestic Council—Geoffrey Shepard Files, Box 3, Ford Papers.

87. Chaired in the Senate by Frank Church (D., Ida.), and in the House by Lucien N. Nedzi (D., Mich.) and then Otis Pike (D., N.Y.).

88. Mike Duval to Jack Marsh, Oct. 23, 1975, Draft Plans for IGC, Box 11, Raoul-Duval Papers.

89. Henry A. Kissinger et al. to the President, Sept. 18, 1975, WHCF, ND6,

Ford Papers; Dudley Chapman to Buchen et al., Nov. 5, 1974, Counsel to the President, Exec. Priv., Gen. (1), Box 13, Edward C. Schmults Files, ibid.; Duval to Marsh, Oct. 23, 1974, Draft Plan for IGC, Raoul-Duval Papers; Ichord to Kelley, Oct. 23, 1975, Departmental: Justice–FBI, Box 139, Ichord Papers; Kelley to Ichord, Oct. 30, 1975, ibid.

90. Wofford, *Kennedys and Kings*, 206.
91. Sullivan died in a deer hunting accident in November 1977.
92. Katzenbach submitted Doar's report, originally prepared for the Princeton conference. *Hearings—FBI*, 888–991.
93. House Select Committee on Intelligence, *Hearings*, pt. 3, pp. 1,035, 1,042; Stone, "Schorr Case," 6–11; Freeman, "Investigating," 103–18.

CONCLUSION

1. *New York Times*, Nov. 5, 1979; Salter, "Reflections," 23–24.
2. Whitehead, *FBI Story*, 396.

Selected Bibliography

Books and Pamphlets

ADLER, BILL. *Kid's Letters to the F.B.I.* Englewood Cliffs, N.J.: Prentice Hall, 1966.

Amnesty International. *Proposal for a Commission of Inquiry into the Effect of Domestic Intelligence Activities on Criminal Trials in the United States of America.* London: Amnesty International, 1981.

AMOS, JAMES E. *Theodore Roosevelt: Hero to His Valet.* New York: John Day, 1927.

ANTHONY, EARL. *Picking Up the Gun.* New York: Dial, 1970.

BAKER, WILLIAM J. *Jesse Owens: An American Life.* New York: Free Press, 1986.

BAMFORD, JAMES. *The Puzzle Palace.* New York: Penguin ed., 1983.

BARAKA, AMIRI. *The Autobiography of LeRoi Jones.* New York: Freundlich Books, 1984.

BARKAN, STEVEN E. *Protestors on Trial.* New Brunswick, N.J.: Rutgers University Press, 1985.

BARNARD, HOLLINGER F., ed. *Outside the Magic Circle: The Autobiography of Virginia Foster Durr.* University: University of Alabama Press, 1985.

BARNES, CATHERINE A. *Journey from Jim Crow.* New York: Columbia University Press, 1983.

BELFRAGE, SALLY. *Freedom Summer.* New York: Viking, 1965.

BELKNAP, MICHAL R. *Federal Law and Southern Order: Racial Violence and Constitutional Conflict in the Post-Brown South.* Athens: University of Georgia Press, 1987.

BELL, DERRICK A., JR. *Race, Racism and American Law.* Boston: Little, Brown, 1973.

BERMAN, WILLIAM C. *The Politics of Civil Rights in the Truman Administration.* Columbia: Ohio State University Press, 1970.

BERRY, JASON. *Amazing Grace: With Charles Evers in Mississippi.* New York: Saturday Review Press, 1973.

BISHOP, JIM. *A Bishop's Confessions.* Boston: Little, Brown, 1981.

———. *The Days of Martin Luther King, Jr.* New York: G. P. Putnam's Sons, 1971.

BLACKSTOCK, NELSON. *COINTELPRO: The FBI's Secret War on Political Freedom*. New York: Vintage, 1975.

BRADEN, ANNE. *The Wall Between*. New York: Monthly Review Press, 1958.

BRANCH, TAYLOR. *Parting the Waters: America in the King Years, 1954–1963*. New York: Simon and Schuster, 1988.

BRAUER, CARL M. *John F. Kennedy and the Second Reconstruction*. New York: Columbia University Press, 1977.

BROWN, H. RAP. *Die, Nigger, Die*. New York: Dial Press, 1969.

BROWN, JULIA. *I Testify: My Years as an F.B.I. Undercover Agent*. Belmont, Mass.: Western Islands, 1966.

BROWN, RICHARD M. *Strain of Violence*. New York: Oxford University Press, 1975.

BUCHANAN, PATRICK J. *Right From the Beginning*. Boston: Little, Brown, 1988.

BURK, ROBERT F. *The Eisenhower Administration and Black Civil Rights*. Knoxville: University of Tennessee Press, 1984.

CAGIN, SETH, and PHILIP DRAY. *We Are Not Afraid: The Story of Goodman, Schwerner, and Chaney and the Civil Rights Campaign in Mississippi*. New York: Macmillan, 1988.

CAMPBELL, CLARICE T., and OSCAR ALLAN ROGERS, JR. *Mississippi: The View from Tougaloo*. Jackson: University Press of Mississippi, 1979.

CARLSON, JODY. *George C. Wallace and the Politics of Powerlessness*. New Brunswick, N.J.: Transaction Books, 1981.

CARMICHAEL, STOKELY, and CHARLES V. HAMILTON. *Black Power: The Politics of Liberation in America*. New York: Random House, 1967.

CARR, ROBERT K. *Federal Protection of Civil Rights: Quest for a Sword*. Ithaca, N.Y.: Cornell University Press, 1947.

CARSON, CLAYBORNE. *In Struggle: SNCC and the Black Awakening of the 1960s*. Cambridge, Mass.: Harvard University Press, 1981.

CARTER, DAN T. *Scottsboro: A Tragedy of the American South*. Baton Rouge: Louisiana State University Press, 1969.

Chicago Commission on Race Relations. *The Negro in Chicago: A Study of Race Relations and a Race Riot*. Chicago: University of Chicago Press, 1922.

CLARK, RAMSEY. *Crime in America*. New York: Simon and Schuster, 1970.

CLEAVER, ELDRIDGE. *Soul On Ice*. New York: Random House, 1968.

COLBURN, DAVID R. *Racial Change and Community Crisis: St. Augustine, Florida, 1877–1980*. New York: Columbia University Press, 1985.

Commission of Inquiry Into the Black Panthers and the Police. *Search and Destroy*. New York: Metropolitan Applied Research Center, 1973.

CUMMINGS, RICHARD. *The Pied Piper: Allard K. Lowenstein and the American Dream*. New York: Grove, 1985.

DANIEL, PETE. *The Shadow of Slavery: Peonage in the South, 1901–1969*. Urbana: University of Illinois Press, 1972.

DAVIS, ANGELA. *Angela Davis: An Autobiography*. New York: Random House, 1974.

———, ET AL. *If They Come in the Morning*. New York: Signet, 1971.

DEMARIS, OVID. *The Director: An Oral Biography of J. Edgar Hoover*. New York: Harper's Magazine Press, 1975.

DE TOLEDANO, RALPH. *J. Edgar Hoover: The Man in His Time*. New Rochelle, N.Y.: Arlington House, 1973.

DONNER, FRANK J. *The Age of Surveillance.* New York: Knopf, 1980.

DULLES, FOSTER RHEA. *The Civil Rights Commission, 1957–1965.* East Lansing: Michigan State University Press, 1968.

EDWARDS, HARRY. *The Struggle That Must Be.* New York: Macmillan, 1980.

EHRLICHMAN, JOHN. *Witness to Power.* New York: Simon and Schuster, 1982.

ELLIFF, JOHN T. *Crime, Dissent, and the Attorney General.* Beverly Hills, Calif.: Sage Publications, 1971.

EVANS, SARA. *Personal Politics: The Roots of Women's Liberation in the Civil Rights Movement and the New Left.* New York: Knopf, 1979.

EVERS, CHARLES. *Evers.* New York: World, 1971.

FAIRCLOUGH, ADAM. *To Redeem the Soul of America: The Southern Christian Leadership Conference and Martin Luther King, Jr.* Athens: University of Georgia Press, 1987.

FARMER, JAMES. *Lay Bare the Heart.* New York: Arbor House, 1985.

FELT, W. MARK. *The FBI Pyramid from the Inside.* New York: G. P. Putnam's Sons, 1979.

FINE, SIDNEY. *Frank Murphy.* 3 vols. Ann Arbor: University of Michigan Press, 1975–1984.

FORMAN, JAMES. *The Making of Black Revolutionaries.* New York: Macmillan, 1972.

FRADY, MARSHALL. *Wallace.* New York: World, 1968.

FREYER, TONY. *The Little Rock Crisis.* Westport, Conn.: Greenwood, 1984.

FRIEDMAN, LEON, ed. *Southern Justice.* New York: Random House, 1965.

GARROW, DAVID J. *Bearing the Cross: Martin Luther King, Jr., and the Southern Christian Leadership Conference.* New York: Morrow, 1986.

———. *The FBI and Martin Luther King, Jr.: From "SOLO" to Memphis.* New York: Norton, 1981.

———. *Protest at Selma: Martin Luther King, Jr., and the Voting Rights Act of 1965.* New Haven, Conn.: Yale University Press, 1978.

GITLIN, TODD. *The Sixties: Years of Hope, Days of Rage.* New York: Bantam, 1987.

GOLDWATER, BARRY M. *With No Apologies.* New York: Morrow, 1979.

GOODWIN, RICHARD N. *Remembering America.* Boston: Little, Brown, 1988.

Governor's Commission on the Los Angeles Riots. *Violence in the City—An End or a Beginning.* Los Angeles: College Book Store, 1965.

GRANT, JOANNE, ed. *Black Protest.* Greenwich, Conn.: Fawcett, 1968.

GUTHMAN, EDWIN. *We Band of Brothers.* New York: Harper and Row, 1971.

HAMER, FANNIE LOU, ET AL. *To Praise Our Bridges.* Jackson, Miss.: KIPCO, 1967.

HARRIS, DAVID. *Dreams Die Hard.* New York: St. Martin's/Marek, 1982.

HARRIS, RICHARD. *Freedom Spent.* Boston: Little, Brown, 1976.

———. *Justice.* New York: Avon Books ed., 1970.

HAYDEN, TOM. *Reunion: A Memoir.* New York: Random House, 1988.

HILL, ROBERT A., ed. *The Marcus Garvey and Universal Negro Improvement Association Papers.* Los Angeles and Berkeley: University of California Press, 1983–.

HINDS, LENNOX S. *Illusions of Justice.* Iowa City: School of Social Work, University of Iowa, 1979.

HOLT, LEN. *The Summer That Didn't End.* New York: Morrow, 1965.

HOOVER, HERBERT. *Memoirs*. 3 vols. New York: Macmillan, 1951–1952.

HOOVER, J. EDGAR. *Masters of Deceit*. New York: Pocket Books ed., 1959.

HORNE, GERALD. *Black & Red: W. E. B. Du Bois and the Afro-American Response to the Cold War, 1944–1963*. Albany: State University of New York Press, 1986.

——. *Communist Front? The Civil Rights Congress, 1946–1956*. Rutherford, N.J.: Fairleigh Dickinson University Press, 1988.

JACOBS, PAUL. *Prelude to Riot*. New York: Vintage ed., 1967.

JOHNSON, LADY BIRD. *A White House Diary*. New York: Holt, Rinehart & Winston, 1970.

JOHNSON, LOCH K. *A Season of Inquiry: The Senate Intelligence Investigation*. Lexington: University of Kentucky Press, 1985.

JOHNSON, LYNDON B. *The Vantage Point*. New York: Holt, Rinehart & Winston, 1971.

KARENGA, M. *The Roots of the US/Panther Conflict*. San Diego: Kawaida Publications, 1976.

KEARNS, DORIS. *Lyndon Johnson and the American Dream*. New York: Harper and Row, 1976.

KELLEY, CLARENCE. *Kelley: The Story of An FBI Director*. Kansas City, Mo.: Andrews, McMeel and Parker, 1987.

KING, MARTIN LUTHER, JR. *Why We Can't Wait*. New York: New American Library, 1964.

KING, MARTIN LUTHER, SR., with CLAYTON RILEY. *Daddy King: An Autobiography*. New York: Morrow, 1980.

KING, MARY. *Freedom Song*. New York: Morrow, 1987.

KINOY, ARTHUR. *Rights on Trial*. Cambridge, Mass.: Harvard University Press, 1983.

KIRBY, JOHN B. *Black Americans in the Roosevelt Era*. Knoxville: University of Tennessee Press, 1980.

KLEHR, HARVEY. *The Heyday of American Communism*. New York: Basic Books, 1984.

KLUGER, RICHARD. *Simple Justice*. New York: Knopf, 1975.

KONING, HANS. *Nineteen Sixty-Eight*. New York: Norton, 1987.

KORNWEIBEL, THEODORE, JR. *No Crystal Stair: Black Life and the* Messenger, *1917–1928*. Westport, Conn.: Greenwood, 1975.

KRUEGER, THOMAS A. *And Promises to Keep: The Southern Conference for Human Welfare, 1938–1948*. Nashville: Vanderbilt University Press, 1967.

LAWSON, STEVEN F. *Black Ballots: Voting Rights in the South, 1944–1969*. New York: Columbia University Press, 1976.

——. *In Pursuit of Power: Southern Blacks and Electoral Politics, 1965–1982*. New York: Columbia University Press, 1985.

LEWIS, ANTHONY. *Portrait of a Decade*. New York: Random House, 1964.

LEWIS, DAVID L. *King: A Critical Biography*. New York: Praeger, 1970.

LINCOLN, C. ERIC. *The Black Muslims in America*. Rev. ed. Boston: Beacon, 1973.

LORD, WALTER. *The Past That Would Not Die*. New York: Harper and Row, 1965.

LOWENTHAL, MAX. *The Federal Bureau of Investigation*. New York: William Sloane, 1950.

MCADAM, DOUG. *Freedom Summer*. New York: Oxford University Press, 1988.

McCoy, Donald R., and Richard T. Reutten. *Quest and Response: Minority Rights and the Truman Administration*. Lawrence: University Press of Kansas, 1973.

McGovern, James R. *Anatomy of a Lynching: The Killing of Claude Neal*. Baton Rouge: Louisiana State University Press, 1982.

McIlhany, William H., II. *Klandestine: The Untold Story of Delmar Dennis and His Role in the FBI's War Against the Ku Klux Klan*. New Rochelle, N.Y.: Arlington House, 1975.

McMillen, Neil R. *The Citizens' Council: Organized Resistance to the Second Reconstruction, 1954–1964*. Urbana: University of Illinois Press, 1971.

McPherson, Harry C., Jr. *A Political Education*. Boston: Little, Brown, 1972.

Makeba, Miriam, with James Hall. *Makeba: My Story*. New York: New American Library, 1988.

Malcolm X. *The Autobiography of Malcolm X*. New York: Grove, 1965.

Manchester, William. *The Glory and the Dream*. New York: Bantam ed., 1975.

Marable, Manning. *Race, Reform and Rebellion: The Second Reconstruction in Black America, 1945–1982*. Jackson: University Press of Mississippi, 1984.

Mars, Florence. *Witness in Philadelphia*. Baton Rouge: Louisiana State University Press, 1977.

Marshall, Burke. *Federalism and Civil Rights*. Foreword by Robert F. Kennedy. New York: Columbia University Press, 1964.

Mason, Alpheus Thomas. *Harlan Fiske Stone: Pillar of the Law*. New York: Viking, 1954.

Matusow, Allen J. *The Unraveling of America*. New York: Harper and Row, 1984.

Mazón, Mauricio. *The Zoot-Suit Riots*. Austin: University of Texas Press, 1984.

Meier, August, and Elliott Rudwick. *Along the Color Line*. Urbana: University of Illinois Press, 1976.

———. *CORE: A Study in the Civil Rights Movement, 1942–1968*. New York: Oxford University Press, 1973.

Mendelsohn, Jack. *The Martyrs*. New York: Harper and Row, 1966.

Meredith, James. *Three Years in Mississippi*. Bloomington: Indiana University Press, 1966.

Miller, Char. *Fathers and Sons: The Bingham Family and the American Mission*. Philadelphia: Temple University Press, 1982.

Millspaugh, Arthur C. *Crime Control by the National Government*. Washington, D.C.: Brookings Institution, 1937.

Misseduc Foundation. *Mississippi Black Paper*. New York: Random House, 1965.

Mitgang, Herbert. *Dangerous Dossiers: Exposing the Secret War Against America's Greatest Authors*. New York: Donald I. Fine, 1988.

Moody, Anne. *Coming of Age in Mississippi*. New York: Dial Press, 1968.

Moore, Jesse T., Jr. *A Search for Equality: The National Urban League, 1910–1961*. University Park: Pennsylvania State University Press, 1981.

Morgan, Charles, Jr. *One Man, One Voice*. New York: Holt, Rinehart and Winston, 1979.

Morris, Aldon D. *The Origins of the Civil Rights Movement*. New York: Free Press, 1984.

MYRDAL, GUNNAR. *An American Dilemma*. New York: Harper and Row, 1944.

NAISON, MARK. *Communists in Harlem during the Depression*. Urbana: University of Illinois Press, 1983.

National Conference of Black Lawyers et al. *Human Rights Violations in the United States*. Petition to the United Nations Commission on Human Rights. December 1978.

NAVASKY, VICTOR. *Kennedy Justice*. New York: Atheneum, 1971.

———. *Naming Names*. New York: Viking, 1980.

NELSON, JACK, and JACK BASS. *The Orangeburg Massacre*. New York and Cleveland: World, 1970.

NEWFIELD, JACK. *Robert Kennedy: A Memoir*. New York: Dutton, 1969.

NIXON, RICHARD M. *RN: The Memoirs of Richard Nixon*. New York: Grosset and Dunlap, 1978.

NORRELL, ROBERT J. *Reaping the Whirlwind: The Civil Rights Movement in Tuskegee*. New York: Knopf, 1985.

OATES, STEPHEN B. *Let the Trumpet Sound*. New York: Harper and Row, 1982.

OLLESTAD, NORMAN. *Inside the F.B.I.* New York: Lyle Stuart, 1967.

O'REILLY, KENNETH. *Hoover and the Un-Americans*. Philadelphia: Temple University Press, 1983.

OVERSTREET, HARRY and BONARO. *The FBI in Our Open Society*. New York: Norton, 1969.

PAINTER, NELL IRVIN. *The Narrative of Hosea Hudson*. Cambridge, Mass.: Harvard University Press, 1979.

PECK, JAMES. *Freedom Ride*. New York: Simon and Schuster, 1962.

PHILLIPS, KEVIN P. *The Emerging Republican Majority*. New Rochelle, N.Y.: Arlington House, 1969.

PINKNEY, ALPHONSO. *Red, Black, and Green: Black Nationalism in the United States*. New York: Cambridge University Press, 1976.

POFFORD, TIM S. *Lynch Street: The May 1970 Slayings at Jackson State College*. Kent, Ohio: Kent State University Press, 1988.

POWELL, ADAM CLAYTON, JR. *Adam by Adam*. New York: Dial, 1971.

POWERS, RICHARD GID. *G-Men: Hoover's FBI in American Popular Culture*. Carbondale: Southern Illinois University Press, 1983.

———. *Secrecy and Power: The Life of J. Edgar Hoover*. New York: Free Press, 1987.

RAINES, HOWELL. *My Soul Is Rested: Movement Days in the Deep South Remembered*. New York: G. P. Putnam's Sons, 1977.

RAINES, JOHN C., ed. *Conspiracy*. New York: Harper and Row, 1975.

RECORD, WILSON, *The Negro and the Communist Party*. Chapel Hill: University of North Carolina Press, 1951.

———. *Race and Radicalism: The NAACP and the Communist Party in Conflict*. Ithaca, N.Y.: Cornell University Press, 1964.

RICHARDS, DAVID. *Played Out: The Jean Seberg Story*. New York: Random House, 1981.

ROBERTS, RANDY. *Papa Jack: Jack Johnson and the Era of White Hopes*. New York: Free Press, 1983.

ROBESON, PAUL. *Here I Stand*. New York: International Publishers, 1960.

ROSENMAN, SAMUEL, ed. *The Public Papers and Addresses of Franklin D. Roosevelt*. 13 vols. New York: Random House, 1938–1950.

ROTHSCHILD, MARY A. *A Case of Black and White: Northern Volunteers and the Southern Freedom Summers, 1964–1965*. Westport, Conn.: Greenwood, 1982.

ROVERE, RICHARD. *The Goldwater Caper*. New York: Harcourt, Brace and World, 1965.

ROWE, GARY THOMAS, JR. *My Undercover Years with the Ku Klux Klan*. New York: Bantam, 1976.

RUBIN, JERRY. *Do It!* New York: Simon and Schuster, 1970.

RUSTIN, BAYARD. *Down the Line*. Chicago: Quadrangle, 1971.

SALTER, JOHN R., JR. *Jackson, Mississippi*. Hicksville, N.Y.: Exposition Press, 1979.

SCHELL, JONATHAN. *The Time of Illusion*. New York: Knopf, 1976.

SCHLESINGER, ARTHUR M., JR. *Robert Kennedy and His Times*. Boston: Houghton Mifflin/Book Club ed., 1978.

———. *A Thousand Days*. Boston: Houghton Mifflin, 1965.

SEALE, BOBBY. *A Lonely Rage*. New York: Times Books, 1978.

SELLERS, CLEVELAND, with ROBERT TERRELL. *The River of No Return: The Autobiography of a Black Militant and the Life and Death of SNCC*. New York: Morrow, 1973.

SENTNER, DAVID. *How The FBI Gets Its Man*. New York: Avon Books, 1965.

SHAKUR, ASSATA. *Assata: An Autobiography*. Westport, Conn.: Lawrence Hill, 1987.

SHAPIRO, HERBERT. *White Violence and Black Response: From Reconstruction to Montgomery*. Amherst: University of Massachusetts Press, 1988.

SHEEHY, GAIL. *Panthermania*. New York: Harper and Row, 1971.

SHIPP, BILL. *Murder at Broad River Bridge*. Atlanta: Peachtree Publishers, 1981.

SILVER, JAMES W. *Mississippi: The Closed Society*. New York: Harcourt, Bracc and World, 1963.

SIMS, PATSY. *The Klan*. New York: Stein and Day, 1978.

SITKOFF, HARVARD. *A New Deal for Blacks*. New York: Oxford University Press, 1978.

SMEAD, HOWARD. *Blood Justice: The Lynching of Mack Charles Parker*. New York: Oxford University Press, 1986.

STEIN, JUDITH. *The World of Marcus Garvey*. Baton Rouge: Louisiana State University Press, 1986.

SULLIVAN, WILLIAM C., with BILL BROWN. *The Bureau: My Thirty Years in Hoover's FBI*. New York: Norton, 1979.

SUTHERLAND, ELIZABETH, ed. *Letters from Mississippi*. New York: McGraw-Hill, 1965.

THEOHARIS, ATHAN. *The Boss: J. Edgar Hoover and the Great American Inquisition*. Philadelphia: Temple University Press, 1988.

———. *Spying on Americans*. Philadelphia: Temple University Press, 1978.

THOMPSON, KENNETH W., ed. *The Kennedy Presidency*. Lanham, Md.: University Press of America, 1985.

TULLY, ANDREW. *The FBI's Most Famous Cases*. New York: Morrow, 1965.

TURNER, WILLIAM W. *Hoover's F.B.I.* New York: Dell ed., 1971.

UNGAR, SANFORD J. *FBI*. Boston: Little, Brown, 1975.

VILLANO, ANTHONY, with GERALD ASTOR. *Brick Agent*. New York: Quadrangle/New York Times Book Co., 1977.

VON HOFFMAN, NICHOLAS. *Mississippi Notebook*. New York: David White, 1964.

WADE, WYN CRAIG. *The Fiery Cross*. New York: Simon and Schuster, 1987.

WARREN, ROBERT PENN. *Who Speaks for the Negro?* New York: Random House, 1965.

WASHBURN, PATRICK S. *A Question of Sedition: The Federal Government's Investigation of the Black Press during World War II*. New York: Oxford University Press, 1986.

WASHINGTON, JOSEPH R., JR., ed. *Jews in Black Perspectives*. Rutherford, N.J.: Fairleigh Dickinson University Press, 1984.

WASKOW, ARTHUR I. *From Race Riot to Sit-In: 1919 and the 1960s*. Garden City, N.Y: Doubleday, 1966.

WATTERS, PAT, and REESE CLEGHORN. *Climbing Jacob's Ladder*. New York: Harcourt, Brace and World, 1967.

———, and STEPHEN GILLERS, eds. *Investigating the FBI*. Garden City, N.Y.: Doubleday, 1973.

WEISS, NANCY. *Farewell to the Party of Lincoln: Black Politics in the Age of FDR*. Princeton: Princeton University Press, 1983.

———. *The National Urban League, 1910–1940*. New York: Oxford University Press, 1974.

WELCH, NEIL J., and DAVID W. MARSTON. *Inside Hoover's FBI*. Garden City, N.Y.: Doubleday, 1984.

WHEATON, ELIZABETH. *Codename GREENKILL: The 1979 Greensboro Killings*. Athens: University of Georgia Press, 1987.

WHITE, THEODORE H. *The Making of the President 1960*. New York: Atheneum, 1962.

———. *The Making of the President 1964*. New York: Atheneum, 1965.

WHITEHEAD, DON. *Attack on Terror*. New York: Funk and Wagnalls, 1970.

———. *The FBI Story*. New York: Pocket Books ed., 1958.

WHITFIELD, STEPHEN J. *A Death in the Delta: The Story of Emmett Till*. New York: Free Press, 1988.

WILKINS, ROGER. *A Man's Life*. New York: Simon and Schuster, 1982.

WILKINS, ROY, with TOM MATHEWS. *Standing Fast*. New York: Penguin Books ed., 1984.

WILLIAMS, ROBERT F. *Negroes With Guns*. Chicago: Third World Press ed., 1973.

WILLIAMS, WILLIAM APPLEMAN. *Empire as a Way of Life*. New York: Oxford University Press, 1982.

WILLS, GARRY. *The Kennedy Imprisonment*. Boston: Little, Brown, 1981.

———. *Nixon Agonistes*. New York: New American Library, 1971.

———. *Reagan's America: Innocents at Home*. Garden City, N.Y.: Doubleday, 1987.

WILSON, JAMES Q. *The Investigators*. New York: Basic Books, 1978.

WISE, DAVID. *The American Police State*. New York: Random House, 1976.

WOFFORD, HARRIS. *Of Kennedys and Kings*. New York: Farrar, Straus and Giroux, 1980.

WOLFE, TOM. *Radical Chic and Mau-mauing the Flak Catchers*. New York: Farrar, Straus and Giroux, 1970.

WOODWARD, C. VANN. *The Strange Career of Jim Crow*. 2d rev. ed. New York: Oxford University Press, 1966.

WRIGHT, RICHARD O., ed. *Whose FBI?* LaSalle, Ill.: Open Court, 1974.

YARBROUGH, TINSLEY E. *Judge Frank Johnson and Human Rights in Alabama.* University: University of Alabama Press, 1981.

ZANGRANDO, ROBERT L. *The NAACP Crusade Against Lynching, 1909–1950.* Philadelphia: Temple University Press, 1980.

ZAROULIS, NANCY, and GERALD SULLIVAN. *Who Spoke Up? American Protest Against the War in Vietnam, 1963–1975.* Garden City, N.Y.: Doubleday, 1984.

ZINN, HOWARD. *Albany.* Atlanta: Southern Regional Council, 1962.

———. *SNCC: The New Abolitionists.* Boston: Beacon, 1964.

———. *The Southern Mystique.* New York: Knopf, 1964.

Articles, Papers, Essays

BARRON, JOHN. "The FBI's Secret War Against the Ku Klux Klan." *Reader's Digest,* Jan. 1966, 87–92.

BELKNAP, MICHAL R. "The Vindication of Burke Marshall: The Southern Legal System and the Anti-Civil Rights Violence of the 1960s." *Emory Law Journal* 33(Winter 1984): 93–133.

BERGMAN, LOWELL, and DAVID WEIR. "Revolution on Ice: How the Black Panthers Lost the FBI's War of Dirty Tricks." *Rolling Stone,* Sept. 9, 1976, 41–49.

BERLET, CHIP. "Journalists and G-Men." *Chicago Reader,* June 12, 1978, 1, 8ff.

BILLINGTON, MONROE. "Lyndon B. Johnson and Blacks: The Early Years." *Journal of Negro History* 62(Jan. 1977): 26–42.

BOOKER, SIMEON. "J. Edgar Hoover—The Negro in the FBI." *Ebony,* Sept. 1962, 29–34.

BURNS, HAYWOOD. "The Federal Government and Civil Rights." In *Southern Justice,* ed. Leon Friedman, 228–54. New York: Random House, 1965.

CAPECI, DOMINIC J., JR. "The Lynching of Cleo Wright: Federal Protection of Constitutional Rights during World War II." *Journal of American History* 72(March 1986): 859–87.

CARSON, CLAYBORNE, JR. "Blacks and Jews in the Civil Rights Movement." In *Jews in Black Perspectives,* ed. Joseph R. Washington, Jr., 113–31. Rutherford, N.J.: Fairleigh Dickinson University Press, 1984. ·

COLES, ROBERT. "Social Struggle and Weariness." *Psychiatry,* 27(1964): 305–15.

COMMAGER, HENRY STEELE. "'To Form a Much Less Perfect Union.'" *New York Times Magazine,* July 14, 1963, 5ff.

CONE, JAMES H. "Martin Luther King, Jr., and the Third World." *Journal of American History* 74(Sept. 1987): 455–67.

CREWDSON, JOHN. "Seeing RED: An FBI 'Commie Hunter' Rebels at Illegal Tactics." *Chicago Tribune Magazine,* March 2, 1985, 8ff.

CROCE, ARLENE. "Backlash in New York?" *National Review,* Sept. 22, 1964, 816–17.

DEMUTH, JERRY. "'Tired of Being Sick and Tired' . . ." *The Nation,* June 1, 1964, 548–51.

DE TOLEDANO, RALPH. "A Negro Minority vs. a White Majority." *National Review,* Sept. 22, 1964, 814–15.

ELLIFF, JOHN T. "Aspects of Federal Civil Rights Enforcement: The Justice Department and the FBI, 1939–1964." *Perspectives in American History* 5(1971): 605–73.

EPSTEIN, EDWARD JAY. "The Panthers and the Police." *New Yorker*, Feb. 13, 1971, 45–77.

FAIRCLOUGH, ADAM. "Martin Luther King, Jr. and the War in Vietnam." *Phylon* 45(Spring 1984): 19–39.

FLEMING, HAROLD C. "The Federal Executive and Civil Rights: 1961–1965." *Daedalus* 94(Fall 1965): 921–48.

FREEMAN, J. LEIPER. "Investigating the Executive Intelligence." *Capitol Studies* 5 (Fall 1977): 103–18.

GLEN, JOHN M. "The Making of a Southern Radical: Myles Horton and the Highlander Folk School." *Southern Historian* 7(Spring 1986): 5–22.

GOODMAN, ERNEST. "The NLG, the FBI, and the Civil Rights Movement: 1964— A Year of Decision." *Guild Practitioner* 38(Winter 1981): 1–17.

GOODWIN, RICHARD N. "President Lyndon Johnson: The War Within." *New York Times Magazine*, Aug. 21, 1988, 35ff.

GRAHAM, HUGH DAVIS. "The Ambiguous Legacy of American Presidential Commissions." *Public Historian* 7(Spring 1985): 5–25.

———. "On Riots and Riot Commissions: Civil Disorders in the 1960s." *Public Historian* 2(Summer 1980): 7–27.

GREENBERG, GARY J. "Revolt at Justice." *Washington Monthly*, Dec. 1969, 32–40.

GREENE, JOHNNY. "Did the FBI Kill Viola Liuzzo?" *Playboy*, Oct. 1980, 100ff.

GREENFIELD, MEG. "Senator Goldwater and the Negro." *Reporter*, Oct. 8, 1964, 27–28.

GUTIÉRREZ, JOSE ANGEL. "Chicanos and Mexicans Under Surveillance: 1940–1980." *Renato Rosaldo Lecture Series Monograph* 2(Spring 1986): 29–58.

HACKER, ANDREW. "The States' Righters Still Wage War." *New York Times Magazine*, Oct. 21, 1962, 31ff.

HALISI, IMAMU CLYDE. "Maulana Ron Karenga: Black Leader in Captivity." *Black Scholar*, May 1972, 27–31.

HARRIS, LOUIS. "The 'Backlash' Issue." *Newsweek*, July 13, 1964, 24–27.

HART, JOHN. "Kennedy, Congress and Civil Rights." *Journal of American Studies* 13(Aug. 1979): 165–78.

HILL, ROBERT A. "'The Foremost Radical Among His Race': Marcus Garvey and the Black Scare, 1918–1921." *Prologue* 16(Winter 1984): 215–31.

HOOVER, HERBERT. "From Herbert Hoover on His 90th Birthday." *Reader's Digest*, Sept. 1964, 144.

HOOVER, J. EDGAR. "Off-the-Record Remarks." Informal Reception for Editors of Georgia and Michigan Newspapers, April 15, 1965, Washington, D.C.

———. "The Resurgent Klan." *American Bar Association Journal* 52 (July 1966): 617–20.

HOROWITZ, DAVID ALAN. "White Southerners' Alienation and Civil Rights: The Response to Corporate Liberalism." *Journal of Southern History* 54(May 1988): 173–200.

HOULDING, ANDREW. "The Wiring of New Haven." *The Nation*, June 7, 1980, 685–88.

HOWELL, LEON. "An Interview with Andrew Young." *Christianity and Crisis*, Feb. 16, 1976, 14–20.

KARENGA, M. "A Response to Muhammad Ahmad." *Black Scholar*, July–Aug. 1978, 55–57.

KIMBALL, PENN. "The History of *The Nation* According to the FBI." *The Nation,* March 22, 1986, 399–426.

KLIBANER, IRWIN. "The Travail of Southern Radicals: The Southern Conference Educational Fund, 1946–1976." *Journal of Southern History* 49(May 1983): 179–202.

KORNWEIBEL, THEODORE, JR. "Black on Black: The FBI's First Negro Agents and Informants and the Investigation of Black Radicalism during the Red Scare." Annual Meeting of the American Historical Association, Dec. 30, 1986, Chicago.

———. "The F.B.I. and White American Hegemony: The Campaign Against Marcus Garvey during the Red Scare." American Studies Convention, Nov. 2, 1985, San Diego.

———. "The FBI and Black America, 1917–1922." Annual Meeting of the Organization of American Historians, March 13, 1984, Los Angeles.

LICHTMAN, ALAN. "The Federal Assault Against Voting Discrimination." *Journal of Negro History* 54(Oct. 1969): 346–67.

LOVIN, HUGH T. "Lyndon B. Johnson, the Subversive Activities Control Board, and the Politics of Anti-Communism." *North Dakota Quarterly* 27(Winter 1986): 94–112.

———. "The Lyndon Johnson Administration and the Federal War on Subversion in the 1960s." *Presidential Studies Quarterly* 17(Summer 1987): 559–71.

McKNIGHT, GERALD D. "A Harvest of Hate: The FBI's War Against Black Youth—Domestic Intelligence in Memphis, Tennessee." *South Atlantic Quarterly* 86(Winter 1987): 1–21.

———. "The 1968 Memphis Sanitation Strike and the FBI: A Case Study in Urban Surveillance." *South Atlantic Quarterly* 83(Spring 1984): 138–56.

McMILLEN, NEIL R. "Black Enfranchisement in Mississippi: Federal Enforcement and Black Protest in the 1960s." *Journal of Southern History* 43(Aug. 1977): 351–72.

———. "Perry W. Howard, Boss of Black-and-Tan Republicanism in Mississippi, 1924–1960." *Journal of Southern History* 48(May 1982): 207–24.

MAY, RONALD R. "Genetics and Subversion." *The Nation,* May 16, 1960, 420–22.

MEIER, AUGUST, and ELLIOTT RUDWICK. "The First Freedom Ride." *Phylon* 30(Fall 1969): 213–22.

MILLER, CHAR, ed. "The Mississippi Summer Project Remembered: The Stephen Mitchell Bingham Letter." *Journal of Mississippi History* 47(Nov. 1985): 284–307.

MITGANG, HERBERT. "Annals of Government: Policing America's Writers." *New Yorker,* Oct. 5, 1987, 47ff.

NAVASKY, VICTOR. "The FBI's Wildest Dream." *The Nation,* June 17, 1978, 716–18.

O'REILLY, KENNETH. "The FBI and the Civil Rights Movement During the Kennedy Years: From the Freedom Rides to Albany." *Journal of Southern History* 54(May 1988): 201–32.

———. "The FBI and the Politics of the 1960s' Riots." *Journal of American History* 75(June 1988): 91–114.

———. "Herbert Hoover and the FBI." *Annals of Iowa* 47(Summer 1983): 46–63.

———. "A New Deal for the FBI: The Roosevelt Administration, Crime Control, and National Security." *Journal of American History* 69(Dec. 1982): 638–58.

————. "The Roosevelt Administration and Black America: Federal Surveillance Policy and Civil Rights During the New Deal and World War II Years." *Phylon* 48(March 1987): 12–25.

RABLE, GEORGE C. "The South and the Politics of Antilynching Legislation, 1920–1940." *Journal of Southern History* 51(May 1985): 201–20.

RAINES, HOWELL. "The Birmingham Bombing Twenty Years Later: The Case that Won't Close." *New York Times Magazine*, July 24, 1983, 12ff.

RICKS, JOHN A., III. "'De Lawd' Descends and Is Crucified: Martin Luther King, Jr., in Albany, Georgia." *Journal of Southwest Georgia History* 2(Fall 1984): 3–14.

ROWAN, CARL T. "Martin Luther King's Tragic Decision." *Reader's Digest*, Sept. 1967, 37–42.

SALISBURY, HARRISON E. "The Strange Correspondence of Morris Ernst and John Edgar Hoover, 1939–1964." *The Nation*, Dec. 1, 1984, 575–89.

SALTER, JOHN R., JR. "Reflections on Ralph Chaplin, the Wobblies, and Organizing in the Save the World Business—Then and Now." Unpublished paper. Dec. 1984.

SCHWERNER, NAT. "Mississippi: Whitewashing the FBI." *Rights*, April–May 1975, 15.

SHERRILL, ROBERT. "The Selling of the FBI." In *Investigating the FBI*, ed. Pat Watters and Stephen Gillers, 3–32. Garden City, N.Y.: Doubleday, 1973.

STONE, I. F. "The Schorr Case." *New York Review of Books*, April 1, 1976, 6–11.

TOLBERT, EMORY J. "Federal Surveillance of Marcus Garvey and the U.N.I.A." *Journal of Ethnic Studies* 14(Winter 1987): 25–47.

UNGAR, SANFORD J. "Among the Piranhas: A Journalist and the FBI." *Columbia Journalism Review*, Sept.–Oct. 1976, 19–27.

————. "The F.B.I. On the Defensive Again." *New York Times Magazine*, May 15, 1988, 46 ff.

WALL, ROBERT A. "Special Agent for the FBI." *New York Review of Books*, Jan. 27, 1972, 12–18.

WECHSLER, JAMES. "The FBI's Failure in the South." *Progressive*, Dec. 1963, 20–23.

WHEELER, RICHARD S. "Blacklash in California?" *National Review*, Sept. 22, 1964, 817.

WHITE, WALTER. "U.S. Department of (White) Justice." *Crisis*, Oct. 1935, 309–10.

WICKER, TOM. "What Have They Done Since They Shot Dillinger?" *New York Times Magazine*, Dec. 28, 1969, 4ff.

WILKINS, ROGER. "Chester Bowles." *The Nation*, June 14, 1986, 813.

WILLIAMS, DAVID. "The Bureau of Investigation and Its Critics, 1919–1921: The Origins of Federal Political Surveillance." *Journal of American History* 68(Dec. 1981): 560–79.

WILLS, GARRY. "Who Will Overcome?" *National Review*, Sept. 22, 1964, 818–20.

"The 'Backlash' Issue." *Newsweek*, July 13, 1964, 24.

"The Complete Collection of Political Documents Ripped-Off From the F.B.I. Office in Media, Pa." *WIN*, March 1972 (entire issue).

"Father and Son FBI Team." *Ebony*, July 1958, 46–47.

"FBI Agents in Action." *Ebony*, Oct. 1947, 9–13.

"The FBI and Civil Rights—J. Edgar Hoover Speaks Out." *U.S. News and World Report*, Nov. 30, 1964, 56–58.

"F.B.I. Report." *Commonweal*, Oct. 23, 1964, 119.

"Michigan's Cool Hand Luke." *National Review*, Nov. 7, 1986, 32.

"Mississippi Eyewitness." *Ramparts*, Summer 1964 (special issue).

"Mississippi Freedom Democratic Party and the Atlantic City Convention." Freedom Summer Reviewed Conference, Millsaps College, Nov. 2, 1979, Jackson.

"Opinion: 'Leave It to Experts.' " *Time*, Aug. 17, 1962, 18–19.

Government Documents

U.S. Commission on Civil Rights. *Law Enforcement: A Report on Equal Protection in the South*. Washington, D.C.: Government Printing Office, 1965.

———. *Report—Book 5, Justice*. Washington, D.C.: Government Printing Office, 1961.

U.S. Congress. Joint Committee on Internal Revenue Taxation. *Investigation of the Special Service Staff of the Internal Revenue Service*. 94th Cong., 1st sess., 1975.

U.S. Congress. Senate Committee on the Judiciary and House Committee on Post Office and Civil Service. *Joint Hearings on Martin Luther King, Jr., National Holiday, S.25*. 96th Cong., 1st sess., 1979.

U.S. Congress. House. Committee on Appropriations. Subcommittee on Departments of State and Justice, the Judiciary, and Related Agencies. *Hearings*. 87th Cong., 1st sess.-92d Cong., 1st sess., 1961–1971.

U.S. Congress. House. Committee on Internal Security. *Hearings on Domestic Intelligence Operations for Internal Security Purposes*. 93d Cong., 2d sess., 1974.

———. *Revolutionary Target: American Penal System*. H.Rept. 738. 93d Cong., 1st sess., 1973.

U.S. Congress. House. Committee on the Judiciary. *Hearings Before the Special Subcommittee to Investigate the Department of Justice*. 83d Cong., 1st sess., 1953.

———. *Statement of Information—Book VII, White House Surveillance and Campaign Activities*. 93d Cong., 2d sess., 1974.

U.S. Congress. House. Committee on Un-American Activities. *Communist Infiltration and Activities in Newark, N.J.* 85th Cong., 2d sess., 1958.

———. *Hearings on Bills to Make Punishable Assistance to Enemies of U.S. in Time of Undeclared War*. Pts. 1–2. 89th Cong., 2d sess., 1966.

U.S Congress. House. Select Committee on Assassinations. *Hearings on Investigation of the Assassination of Martin Luther King, Jr.* Vols. 1, 6–7. 95th Cong., 2d sess., 1978.

U.S. Congress. House. Select Committee on Intelligence. *Hearings on Domestic Intelligence Programs*. Pt. 3. 94th Cong., 1st sess., 1975.

U.S. Congress. Senate. *Memorial Tributes to J. Edgar Hoover in the Congress of the United States and Various Articles and Editorials Relating to His Life and Work*. 94th Cong., 2d sess., 1974.

U.S. Congress. Senate. Committee on Government Operations. Permanent Subcommittee on Investigations. *Hearings on Riots, Civil and Criminal Disorders*. Pts. 1–25. 90th Cong. 1st sess.-91st Cong., 2d sess, 1967–1970.

U.S. Congress. Senate. Committee on the Judiciary. Subcommittee on Constitutional Rights. *Hearings on FBI Counterintelligence Programs.* 93d Cong., 2d sess., 1974.

———. *Political Intelligence in the Internal Revenue Service.* 93d Cong., 2d sess., 1974.

U.S. Congress. Senate. Select Committee on Intelligence. *Hearings on National Intelligence Reorganization and Reform Act of 1978.* 95th Cong., 2d sess., 1978.

U.S. Congress. Senate. Select Committee to Study Governmental Operations with Respect to Intelligence Activities. *Final Report—Book II, Intelligence Activities and the Rights of Americans.* 94th Cong., 2d sess., 1976.

———. *Final Report—Book III, Supplementary Detailed Staff Reports on Intelligence Activities and the Rights of Americans.* 94th Cong., 2d sess., 1976.

———. *Hearings—Federal Bureau of Investigation.* Vol. 6. 94th Cong., 1st sess., 1975.

———. *Hearings—Mail Opening.* Vol. 4. 94th Cong., 1st sess., 1975.

U.S. Department of Justice. Investigation Activities of the Department of Justice. S. Doc. 153, 66th Cong., 1st sess., 1919.

———. *Prison Gangs: Their Extent, Nature, and Impact on Prisons.* Washington, D.C.: Government Printing Office, 1986.

———. *Report of the Department of Justice Task Force to Review the FBI Martin Luther King, Jr., Security and Assassination Investigations.* Washington, D.C.: Government Printing Office, 1977.

U.S. National Advisory Commission on Civil Disorders. *Report of the National Advisory Commission on Civil Disorders.* New York: Bantam ed., 1968.

U.S. National Advisory Commission on Selective Service. *In Pursuit of Equity.* Washington, D.C.: Government Printing Office, 1967.

U.S. National Commission on the Causes and Prevention of Violence. Task Force on Historical and Comparative Perspectives. *Violence in America.* Ed. Hugh Davis Graham and Ted Robert Gurr. New York: Signet ed., 1969.

———. Task Force on Violent Aspects of Protest and Confrontation. *The Politics of Protest.* Under the direction of Jerome H. Skolnick. New York: Simon and Schuster ed., 1969.

U.S. President's Commission on Campus Unrest. *The Report of the President's Commission on Campus Unrest.* Washington, D.C.: Government Printing Office, 1970.

U.S. President's Committee on Civil Rights. *To Secure These Rights.* New York: Simon and Schuster ed., 1947.

Other Government Documents and Records

Bureau of Investigation Files, 1908–1922. Record Group 65. National Archives. Washington, D.C.
    Bureau Section Files.
    Mexican Files.
    Miscellaneous Files.
    Old German Files.
Central Intelligence Agency Files.
    H. Rap Brown File.
    HTLINGUAL Files.
    RESISTANCE/Black Student Unions File.

Department of Justice Files. Record Group 60. National Archives. Washington, D.C.
　　Numerical Files.
　　Abraham Glasser File.
　　Perry Howard File.
Department of State Files. Record Group 59. National Archives.
Federal Bureau of Investigation Files and Records (Freedom of Information Act and other releases; including partial releases).
　　Agent's Handbook.
　　Agitator Index Files.
　　Alabama Freedom Rider Files.
　　American Civil Liberties Union (ACLU) File.
　　American Indian Movement (AIM) File.
　　James E. Amos Personnel File.
　　Walter and Frances Bergman Freedom Rider Files.
　　Birmingham Sixteenth Street Baptist Church Bombing (BAPBOMB) File.
　　Black Nationalist Photograph Album File.
　　Black Panther Party File.
　　Black Student Groups on College Campuses File.
　　Alvin J. Bronstein File.
　　Bureau Bulletin File.
　　Archibald J. Carey, Jr., File.
　　Civil Rights Policy File.
　　Clergy and Laity Concerned About Vietnam File.
　　Committee for Public Justice (CPJ) File.
　　Communist Influence Racial Matters (CIRM) File.
　　Communist Party of the United States of America—Negro Question File.
　　Computerized Telephone Number File.
　　Congress of Racial Equality (CORE) File.
　　Courtney Ryley Cooper File.
　　Counterintelligence Program (COINTEL) File.
　　　　Black Nationalist Subfile.
　　　　Communist Party, United States, Subfile.
　　　　New Left Subfile.
　　　　Puerto Rican Nationalists Subfile.
　　　　Special Operations Subfile.
　　　　White Hate Group Subfile.
　　Deacons for Defense and Justice File.
　　Desegregation of Jackson Business Establishments and Public Facilities File.
　　Detroit Race Riot Files (1943 and 1967).
　　Dissemination of Information Policy File.
　　W. E. B. Du Bois File.
　　James O. Eastland File.
　　Wallace D. Fard File.
　　Filing and Records Procedures (microfilm; Scholarly Resources).
　　Five Percenters File.
　　James Forman File.
　　Fred Hampton Files.
　　Highlander Folk School File.
　　Julius Hobson File.
　　J. Edgar Hoover Official and Confidential Files.
　　　　Inga Arvad Folder.
　　　　Civil Rights and Domestic Violence Folder.
　　　　Martin Dies Folder.

FBI Directorship Folder.
FBI Television Series Agreement Folder.
Intelligence Coverage, Domestic and Foreign Folder.
Lyndon B. Johnson Folder.
John F. Kennedy Folder.
Martin Luther King, Jr., Folder.
George McGovern Folder.
Microphone Surveillances Folder.
John Mitchell Folder.
Press Media Campaign Against Director Folder.
Riots Summer 1964 Folder.
Adlai Stevenson Folder.
Other folders: 8, 9, 14, 76, 83, 96, 128, 131, 136, 142, 151, 161, and 163.
J. Edgar Hoover Personnel File.
House Committee on Un-American Activities (HUAC) File.
Hosea Hudson File.
Hubert H. Humphrey File.
Jesse Jackson File.
Hakim Abdullan Jamal File.
June Mail File.
Robert F. Kennedy File.
Kent State File.
Muhammad Kenyatta File.
Martin Luther King, Jr., File.
Martin Luther King, Jr., Assassination File.
Gerald Kirk File.
Law Enforcement Assistance Administration (LEAA) File.
David Lawrence File.
Stanley Levison File.
Fulton Lewis, Jr., File.
Little Rock, Arkansas, School Desegregation File.
Viola Liuzzo File.
Huey Long File.
Allard K. Lowenstein File.
Alan McSurely Files.
Malcolm X File.
Manual of Instruction (1927, 1936, 1941, and 1978 editions, microfilm;
    Scholarly Resources).
Media Burglary (MEDBURG) File.
Medical Committee for Human Rights File.
Mississippi Burning (MIBURN) File.
Montgomery Improvement Association (MIA) File.
R. Dhoruba Moore Files.
Moorish Science Temple of America File.
Elijah Muhammad File.
National Association for the Advancement of Colored People (NAACP) File.
National Black Economic Development Conference File.
National Lawyers Guild (NLG) Files.
National Negro Congress File.
National Urban League File.
Louis B. Nichols Official and Confidential Files.
    American Youth Congress Folder.
    Hugh H. Clegg Folder.
    Thomas E. Dewey Folder.
    Dwight D. Eisenhower Folder.

    Morris L. Ernst Folder.
    James M. McInerney Folder.
    Misc. A-Z Folder.
    Kermit Roosevelt Folder.
  Operation Breadbasket File.
  Fulton Oursler File.
  Jesse Owens File.
  Westbrook Pegler File.
  Lemuel Penn File.
  PUSH File.
  Rabble Rouser Index File.
  Racial Digest File.
  Racial Matters Policy File.
  Responsibilities Program File.
  Revolutionary Union File.
  Paul Robeson File.
  Howard Rushmore File.
  John R. Salter, Jr., File.
  Jean Seberg File.
  Security Index File.
  Senate Internal Security Subcommittee (SISS) File.
  Clarence 13X Smith File.
  George Sokolsky File.
  Southern Christian Leadership Conference (SCLC) File.
  Southern Conference Educational Fund (SCEF) File.
  Special Agent in Charge (SAC) Letter File.
  Stop Index/National Crime Information Center File.
  Student Nonviolent Coordinating Committee (SNCC) File.
  Clyde Tolson Memo File.
  Clyde Tolson Personnel File.
  Walter White File.
  Don Whitehead File.
  Roy Wilkins File.
  Frank Wilkinson File.
  Lyle Wilson File.
  Walter Winchell File.
  Whitney Young File.
  Misc. Files.
    62-116758.
    62-117166.
    157-6160.
Federal Bureau of Investigation Monographs and Reports.
  "Certain Governors' Comments on Civil Rights Investigations" (1953).
  "Civil Rights and Domestic Violence: A Summary" (1947).
  "Communism and the Negro Movement—A Current Analysis" (1963).
  "The Communist Party and the Negro" (1953 and 1956).
  "Communist Party, USA—Negro Question" (1963).
  "Integration in Public Schools, Little Rock" (1958).
  "The Nation of Islam" (1960 and 1965).
  "Prevention and Control of Riots" (1965).
  "Racial Disturbances" (1967).
  "Student Nonviolent Coordinating Committee" (1967).
  "Survey of Racial Conditions in the United States" (1943).
  "Weaknesses of the Communist Party, USA" (1956).
Federal Surveillance of Afro-Americans (1917–1925): The First World War, the

Red Scare, and the Garvey Movement (microfilm; University Publications of America).
Internal Revenue Service Files (Freedom of Information Act and other releases).
   Alan McSurely Files.
   Special Service Staff Files.
Military Intelligence Division Files. Record Group 165 (War Department). National Archives.

Manuscripts

Albany Movement Records. Martin Luther King, Jr., Center for Nonviolent Social Change. Atlanta.
Americans for Democratic Action Papers. State Historical Society of Wisconsin. Madison.
Bruce Barton Papers. State Historical Society of Wisconsin.
Randolph Battle Papers. King Center.
Berl Bernhard Papers. John Fitzgerald Kennedy Library. Boston.
Francis Biddle Papers. Franklin D. Roosevelt Library. Hyde Park, New York.
Albert Boutwell Papers. Birmingham Public Library. Alabama.
Carl and Anne Braden Papers. State Historical Society of Wisconsin.
Brotherhood of Sleeping Car Porters Records. Library of Congress. Washington, D.C.
Tom Clark Papers. Harry S. Truman Library. Independence, Missouri.
Congress of Racial Equality Papers. King Center.
Congress of Racial Equality Papers. State Historical Society of Wisconsin.
Eugene "Bull" Connor Papers. Birmingham Public Library.
Council of Federated Organizations Papers. State Historical Society of Wisconsin.
Dwight D. Eisenhower Papers. Dwight D. Eisenhower Library. Abilene, Kansas.
   Office of the Special Assistant for National Security Affairs.
   Ann Whitman File.
Gerald R. Ford Papers. Gerald R. Ford Library. Ann Arbor, Michigan.
   Congressional Papers.
   Office of Domestic Council.
      Geoffrey Shepard Files.
      Edward C. Schmults Files.
   White House Central File.
William C. Hamilton Papers. Birmingham Public Library.
Arthur J. Hanes Papers. Birmingham Public Library.
Herbert Hoover Papers. Herbert Hoover Presidential Library. West Branch, Iowa.
   Post-Presidential Papers.
   Presidential Papers.
   President's Secretary's File.
Hosea Hudson–Nell Irvin Painter Papers. Southern Oral History Collection. Southern Historical Collection. University of North Carolina, Chapel Hill.
Richard H. Ichord Papers. Western Historical Manuscripts Collection/State Historical Society of Missouri Manuscripts. Columbia.
Lyndon B. Johnson Papers. Lyndon Johnson Library. Austin, Texas.
   Administrative Histories.

Department of Justice.
Federal Bureau of Investigation.
National Security File.
White House Aides Files.
James Gaither.
Harry McPherson.
Mike Manatos.
William Moyers.
Larry Temple.
Marvin Watson.
Lee C. White.
White House Central File.
John F. Kennedy Papers. Kennedy Library.
Office Files.
White House Central File.
Robert F. Kennedy Papers. Kennedy Library.
C. B. King Papers. King Center.
Edwin King Papers. Tougaloo College. Tougaloo, Mississippi.
Martin Luther King, Jr., Papers. King Center.
Slater King Papers. King Center.
Burke Marshall Papers. Kennedy Library.
Mississippi Freedom Democratic Party Papers. King Center.
Henry Morgenthau, Jr., Papers. Roosevelt Library.
Karl E. Mundt Papers. Dakota State College. Madison, South Dakota.
National Advisory Commission on Civil Disorders Records. Johnson Library.
National Association for the Advancement of Colored People Papers. Library
of Congress.
National Lawyers Guild Papers. New York.
Richard M. Nixon Papers. Nixon Presidential Materials Project. National Ar-
chives. Washington, D.C.
White House Special Files.
Charles W. Colson.
John Dean.
John D. Ehrlichman.
H. R. Haldeman.
Egil Krogh.
White House Central File.
G. Bromley Oxnam Papers. Library of Congress.
Scott J. Rafferty Papers. Kennedy Library.
Michael Raoul-Duval Papers. Ford Library.
Franklin D. Roosevelt Papers. Roosevelt Library.
Official File.
President's Personal File.
Richard B. Russell Papers. Richard B. Russell Memorial Library. University
of Georgia. Athens.
John R. Salter, Jr., Papers. Mississippi Department of Archives and History.
Jackson.
Theodore Sorensen Papers. Kennedy Library.
Southern Christian Leadership Conference Papers. King Center.

Southern Regional Council Archives. Atlanta University Center.

Jeremiah Stamler Papers. State Historical Society of Wisconsin.

Student Nonviolent Coordinating Committee Papers. King Center.

Walter Trohan Papers. Hoover Library.

Harry S. Truman Papers. Truman Library.
    Confidential File.
    President's Secretary's File.

Thomas J. Walsh Papers. Library of Congress.

William Allen White Papers. Library of Congress.

Alexander Wiley Papers. State Historical Society of Wisconsin.

Roy Wilkins Papers. Library of Congress.

Interviews and Oral Histories

Aptheker, Herbert. Feb. 5, 1987 (phone), San Jose, Calif.

Aschenbrenner, Lawrence. Sept. 9, 1987, Anchorage.

Baker, Donald M. July 21, 1986, Washington, D.C.

Barrett, St. John. July 21, 1986, Washington, D.C.

Barry, Marion. By Katherine Shannon, Oct. 3, 1967. Marion Barry Oral History. Ralph J. Bunche Oral History Collection. Moorland-Spingarn Research Center. Howard University. Washington, D.C.

Bates, Charles W. Aug. 14, 1986 (phone).

Bernhard, Berl. July 23, 1986, Washington, D.C.

――――. By John Stewart, June 17, 1968. Berl Bernhard Oral History. John F. Kennedy Library. Boston.

Bookbinder, Hyman. July 9, 1986, Washington, D.C.

Braden, Anne. Feb. 5, 1987 (phone), Louisville, Ky.

Branton, Wiley. July 20, 1987 (phone), Washington, D.C.

Cheek, Marion E. July 2, 1986 (phone).

Clark, Kenneth B. April 8, 1987 (phone), Hastings-on-Hudson, N.Y.

Clark, Ramsey. Oct. 26, 1987 (phone), New York.

――――. By T. H. Baker, Oct. 30, 1968, Feb. 11, March 21, April 16, and June 3, 1969. Ramsey Clark Oral History. Lyndon B. Johnson Library. Austin, Tex.

Clifford, Clark. By Larry J. Hackman, Feb. 4, 1975. Clark Clifford Oral History. Kennedy Library.

Cobb, Charles. July 20, 1987, Washington, D.C.

Dean, Kenneth. Sept. 14, 1987 (phone).

Derian, Patt. July 14, 1987, Washington, D.C.

Doar, John. Jan. 14, 1987 (phone), New York.

――――. By Scott J. Rafferty, Jan. 26, 1976. Scott J. Rafferty Papers. Kennedy Library.

Dunbar, Leslie. Sept. 2, 1986 (phone), Pelham, New York.

Durr, Virginia. Feb. 12, 1987 (phone), Montgomery, Ala.

Eastland, James O. By Joe B. Frantz, Feb. 19, 1971. James O. Eastland Oral History. Johnson Library.

Eddy, Bob. Jan. 26, 1987 (phone), Mobile, Ala.

Ehrlichman, John. Feb. 16, 1987 (phone), Santa Fe, N.M.

Evans, Courtney A. July 25, 1986 (phone), Washington, D.C.

Evers, Charles. Sept. 18, 1987 (phone), Fayette, Miss.

———. By John Jones, Feb. 10, 1981. Charles Evers Oral History. Mississippi Department of Archives and History. Jackson.

Farmer, James. By Paige Mulhollan, July 20, 1971. James Farmer Oral History. Johnson Library.

Fleischer, Hugh. Jan. 16, 1987, Anchorage.

Fleming, Harold. July 15, 1987, Washington, D.C.

Forman, James. July 24, 1986, Washington, D.C.

Greenberg, Jack. Sept. 10, 1987 (phone), New York.

Griswold, Erwin. July 9, 1987, Washington, D.C.

———. By Scott J. Rafferty, Oct. 29, 1975. Rafferty Papers.

Guthman, Edwin O. Jan. 14, 1987 (phone), Philadelphia, Penn.

Guyot, Lawrence. July 10, 1987, Washington, D.C.

Hamer, Fannie Lou. By Robert Wright, Aug. 9, 1968. Fanny Hamer Oral History. Bunche Collection.

Hanes, Arthur J. Feb. 4, 1987 (phone), Birmingham, Ala.

Heim, Lawrence J. July 23, 1986.

Henry, Aaron. By John Dittmer and John Jones, April 22, 1981. Aaron Henry Oral History. Mississippi Archives.

Hobson, Tina C. July 13, 1988, Washington, D.C.

Holtzman, Elizabeth. Aug. 19, 1988 (phone), Brooklyn.

Johnson, June. July 15, 1987, Washington, D.C.

Karenga, Maulana. Jan. 13, 1987 (phone), Los Angeles.

Katzenbach, Nicholas deB. Aug. 13, 1986 (phone), Morristown, N.J.

———. By Paige Mulhollan, Nov. 11 and 12, and Dec. 11, 1968. Nicholas deB. Katzenbach Oral History. Johnson Library.

Kennedy, Robert F., and Burke Marshall. By Anthony Lewis, Dec. 4, 6, and 22, 1964. Robert F. Kennedy and Burke Marshall Oral Histories. Kennedy Library.

King, C. B. Jan. 14, 1987 (phone), Albany, Ga.

———. By Stanley Smith, Aug. 1968. C. B. King Oral History. Bunche Collection.

King, Edwin. April 20, 1986 (phone), Jackson, Miss.

King, Slater. By Stanley Smith, Aug. 1968. Slater King Oral History. Bunche Collection.

Leinbaugh, Harold P. July 24, 1986.

Leonard, Jerris. July 10, 1986, Washington, D.C.

———. By Robert Wright, Feb. 11, 1970. Jerris Leonard Oral History. Bunche Collection.

Lewis, John. July 21, 1987, Washington, D.C.

———. By Katherine Shannon, Aug. 22, 1967. John Lewis Oral History. Bunche Collection.

McGowan, Clement L., Jr. July 9, 1986.

McKissick, Floyd. Sept. 22, 1987 (phone), Oxford, N.C.

McPherson, Harry C., Jr. July 21, 1987, Washington, D.C.

McSurely, Alan. July 23, 1984, Amherst, Mass.

Mallory, Mae. By Malaika Lumumba, Feb. 27, 1970. Mae Mallory Oral History. Bunche Collection.

Marshall, Burke. June 18, 1986 (phone), New Haven, Conn.

———. By T. H. Baker, Oct. 28, 1968. Burke Marshall Oral History. Johnson Library.

———. By Robert Wright, Feb. 27, 1970. Burke Marshall Oral History. Bunche Collection.

May, Edgar. Sept. 12, 1987 (phone), Springfield, Vt.

Moore, Roy K. Aug. 13, 1986 (phone).

Moses, Robert. Sept. 11, 1987 (phone), Boston.

Pritchett, Laurie. July 2, 1986 (phone), Southmont, N.C.

Raby, Kenneth N. July 3, 1986 (phone).

Rauh, Joseph L., Jr. July 10, 1986, Washington, D.C.

———. By Paige Mulhollan, July 30, and Aug. 1 and 8, 1969. Joseph L. Rauh, Jr., Oral History. Johnson Library.

Reedy, George. April 20, 1982, Milwaukee.

Roche, John P. Sept. 16, 1986 (phone), Boston.

Rusk, Dean. By Hugh Gordon Cates, Feb. 22, 1977. Dean Rusk Oral History. Richard B. Russell Memorial Library. University of Georgia. Athens.

Rustin, Bayard. Jan. 22, 1987 (phone), New York.

———. By T. H. Baker, June 17 and 30, 1969. Bayard Rustin Oral History. Johnson Library.

Sanders, Harold Barefoot. Oct. 27, 1987 (phone), Dallas.

Schwerner, Nathan. Sept. 2, 1986 (phone), Pelham, N.Y.

Seigenthaler, John. Jan. 16, 1987 (phone), Washington, D.C.

———. By Robert Campbell, July 10, 1968. John Seigenthaler Oral History. Bunche Collection.

Sherrod, Charles. Feb. 2, 1987 (phone), Albany, Ga.

Shriver, Sargent. July 25, 1986, Washington, D.C.

Sitton, Claude. Sept. 18, 1987 (phone), Raleigh, N.C.

Stone, C. Sumner, Jr. Aug. 29, 1986 (phone), Philadelphia, Pa.

Sullivan, Joseph A. Aug. 18, 1986 (phone).

Taylor, G. Flint. Sept. 16, and Oct. 16, 1987 (phone), Chicago.

Taylor, William L. July 18, 1986, Washington, D.C.

Thomas, Robert. Jan. 15, 1987 (phone), Albany, Ga.

Trebach, Arnold. July 12, 1988, Washington, D.C.

Tyler, Harold R., Jr. April 1, 1987 (phone), New York.

Watson, Marvin. Sept. 16, 1987 (phone), Dallas.

White, Lee C. July 9, 1987, Washington, D.C.

Wilkins, Roger. Aug. 8, 1986 (phone), Washington, D.C.

Wilkins, Roy. By T. H. Baker. April 1, 1969. Roy Wilkins Oral History. Johnson Library.

Wilkinson, Frank. Oct. 17, 1986, Anchorage.

Williams, Calvin. Feb. 7, 1987, Anchorage.

Williams, Robert F. By James Mosby, July 22, 1970. Robert F. Williams Oral History. Bunche Collection.

Wofford, Harris. By Larry J. Hackman, Feb. 3, 1969. Harris Wofford Oral History. Kennedy Library.

Young, Andrew. By T. H. Baker, June 18, 1970. Andrew Young Oral History. Johnson Library.

Index

THE
ENCYCLOPEDIA OF
CENSORSHIP

THE ENCYCLOPEDIA OF CENSORSHIP

Jonathon Green

Facts On File

New York

The Encyclopedia of Censorship

Copyright © 1990 by Jonathon Green

Facts On File, Inc.
460 Park Avenue South
New York, NY 10016
USA

Library of Congress Cataloging-in-Publication Data

Green, Jonathon.
    The encyclopedia of censorship / Jonathon Green.
      p. cm.
    Bibliography: p.
    ISBN 0-8160-1594-5
    1. Censorship—Dictionaries. I. Title.
Z657.G73   1989
098'.13'0321—dc19   89-1210
                                   CIP

British CIP data available on request.

Jacket design by Robert Santora
Composition by Facts On File, Inc.
Manufactured by Maple-Vail Manufacturing Group
Printed in the United States of America

10 9 8 7 6 5 4 3

This book is printed on acid-free paper.

CONTENTS

INTRODUCTION

There is no such thing as a moral or an immoral book. Books are well written or badly written. That is all.

—Oscar Wilde, Preface to *The Picture of Dorian Gray* (1891)

The "what should be" never did exist, but people keep trying to live up to it. There is no "what should be," there is only what is.

—Lenny Bruce (ca. 1963)

It is hardly possible that a society for the suppression of vice can ever be kept within the bounds of good sense and moderation … Beginning with the best intentions in the world, such societies must, in all probability, degenerate into a receptacle for every species of tittle-tattle, impertinence and malice. Men whose trade is rat-catching love to catch rats; the bug destroyer seizes upon the bug with delight; and the vice suppressor is gratified by finding his vice.

—Sydney Smith, quoted in *Anthony Comstock: Roundsman for the Lord* by Heywood Broun and Margaret Leech (1927)

And always keep a-hold of nurse, for fear of finding something worse.

—Hilaire Belloc (1908)

The word "censor," both as verb and noun, as well as in its various derivatives—censorship, censorious, censure—comes from the Latin *censere* (itself based in the Sanskrit word for "recite" or "announce"), which meant to "declare formally," to "describe officially," to "evaluate" or to "assess." The Roman Censor's original task was to declare the census; quite simply, to count the city's population. From this responsibility there developed a further charge: the administration of the *regimen morum,* the moral conduct of the Roman people. The word, the office, and the prime concern of both have lived on, evolving as required by time and geography, but essentially immutable and pervasive.

Censorship represents the downside of power: proscriptive, rather than prescriptive; the embodiment of the status quo, the world of "don't rock the boat," of "what you don't know can't hurt you," of *pas devant les enfants*; the "nanny state" incarnate, whether administered by the Renaissance Church, the "vice societies" of 19th-century Europe and America, or the security sections of the contemporary Third World. The dates may differ, the ideologies may quite confound each other, but the world's censors form an international congregation, worshipping in unison at the same altar and taking as their eternal text Jehovah's "Thou shalt not." Censorship takes the least flattering view of humanity. Underpinning its rules and regulations is the assumption that people are stupid, gullible, weak and corrupt. They need, so the

censor intones, protection from themselves. Censorship thrives in the land of euphemism and doublethink, taking color from its own operations, lying keenly the better to tell "the truth." It is not, of course, a monolith, but just as one can talk, however broadly, of communication, so too can one consider its symbiotic rival, censorship.

Communication has always been subjected to control. The two phenomena are linked in mutual adversity and as communication has proliferated, so has censorship. Today's institutionalized systems, aimed primarily at the mass media, are rooted in the laws that emerged to challenge and limit the spread of the first of such media. All across Europe the invention of movable-type printing was paralleled by the elaboration of the means of its suppression—first by the church, militant against heresy and new faiths; then by governments, fearing sedition within and treason without; and, in their wake, by the successive campaigns of self-appointed moralists, dedicated to an imposed purity. As new media developed they too were subjected to restrictions. The history of communication is also a history of the censor's toll on the free exchange of ideas and information, on unrestricted entertainment and on the individual's right to choose.

All censorship, whether governmental or cultural, can be seen to spring from a single origin—fear. The belief that if the speech, book, play, film, state secret or whatever is permitted free exposure, then the authorities will find themselves threatened to an extent that they cannot tolerate. Throughout history governments have sought to, and succeeded, in banning material that they consider injurious. Initially there was no thought of obscenity or pornography; the first censorship was purely political. Treason, the betrayal of the state and its secrets, has always been rewarded with harsh punishments; sedition, which might be termed internal treason, has been suppressed with equal rigor, even if the sedition of one regime might later become the orthodoxy of the next. The status quo, whatever its current basis, must be fiercely maintained. State censorship continues to thrive today. The old monoliths persist, and the fledgling governments of newly independent nations follow suit.

The first cultural censor was the Roman Catholic Church, which dominated all Europe until the Reformation, although its determination to suppress heresy derived as much from a desire to maintain its political power as to propagate true belief. The early Indexes of Prohibited Books dealt in ideology, not obscenity, but the very nature of the church as the arbiter of public morality meant that these lists soon expanded to encompass the sins of the flesh as well as those of the cerebrum. Like the censorship of the state courts that later usurped its powers, clerical censorship was capricious, variable and sensitive to the power struggles among numerous warring interest groups. Fortunately, it was no more capable of completely suppressing what it disliked than any other apparatus of suppression, however dedicated.

As clerical power waned, the secular authorities took over censorship as they did a multitude of other powers. Church courts gave way to civil justice, even if the earliest prosecutions for obscenity seemed to tax the legal imagination. Faced with offenses of this sort, 17th-century English civil courts simply had no powers with which to punish offenders, and such powers evolved relatively slowly. Obscene libel, the original charge under which prosecutions were brought, was based less on the pornographic content of such works as by Aretino or James Reade, than on the idea that this material would provoke a breach of the peace. As the original indictment under English law pointed out, the "divers wicked lewd impure scandalous and obscene libels" contained in such works were in "violation of common decency, morality, and good order, and against the peace of our said Lord the King ..." When, in 1663, the rakehell Sir Charles Sedley "excrementiz'd" from a Covent Garden balcony and harangued the crowds below, thus initiating the interference of the state courts in obscenity offenses, the essence of the charge was concerned not with his language, foul though it may have been, but with the fact that the bespattered onlookers might riot.

The wider moral censorship that was to come as a product of the 18th and 19th centuries abandoned any connection with a breach of the peace but instead saw its purpose as simply to maintain control of "dirty books" (and, later, films, television and other media)—ushering in the modern concept of "obscene publications." It was also to a great extent—if one excludes the increasingly isolated role of the Catholic Church, which continued to issue its Indexes to the world's faithful until 1966—a phenomenon restricted to the English-speakers of Britain and America. Here one finds the private moralists, each setting him or herself up as a regulator of mass behavior, both by pressuring the government and by running a personal and often vociferously supported campaign. This new style of censorship, designed to protect not the power of those at the top, but the alleged weakness of those at the bottom, was the creation of a rapidly changing society, a response by the emergent (and still insecure) middle class to the new, mass literacy of the era. It has continued ever since. Philanthropy might ordain that the masses should be educated; self-interest still dictates the curriculum.

Hitherto the idea of one man or woman volunteering for the task of imposing his or her own standards on their fellow citizens had been generally unknown. Now there arose legions of the decent, maintaining their own moral status quo by emasculating plays, poetry and prose that until scant years before had been considered the flower of English literature. Their influence ran unabated, touching even on the Bible itself, for at least a century, and, while much diminished, has yet to vanish completely. Today's generally illiberal social drift, in both America and Britain, confers more rather than less power on groups that might, 20 years ago, have been dismissed as cranks. Their style, of course, spread throughout the world, an inevitable adjunct of cultural colonialism, but if such censorship seems to have been originally an Anglo-Saxon phenomenon, the apparatchiks of the Soviet Union have shown themselves equally assiduous in spreading, through suppression, their own cultural norms. Presumably they would feel some kinship with the Western mainstream: Anthony Comstock, the vice societies of the 1880s, today's citizen censors, all are self-appointed moralists, asserting their own beliefs in order to control those of others, and challenging wider public mores with their own narrow ideology. The Puritan sensibility, whatever its doctrinal basis, dies hard.

Today's censor works essentially from one of two premises, which stem from a common, fearful root. The first premise can be loosely classified as security and the second as the castration (a word blithely employed, without the slightest irony, by the censors of the 18th and 19th centuries) of the culture. In practice security, a concept popular among most governments, says, in effect, "what you (the public) don't know won't hurt you." This is ratified on the documents concerned as "need-to-know" or "eyes only" and varies in its severity as to the actual democracy of the given government. While even the most dedicated libertarian reluctantly accepts a degree of governmental secrecy, the problem, even in the most liberal of democracies, lies in the gulf between theory and practice. Despite the evolution of Freedom of Information Acts, painfully extracted from unwilling governments (and never, it seems, to be permitted by the Mother of Parliaments, in London), the bureaucracies hang as tight as they can, their filing cabinets and computer data bases bulging with obsessively restricted trivia.

The second premise, castration, stems from the belief, held both in government departments and as commonly among self-appointed arbiters of standards, that certain individuals have the right to dictate the reading, viewing or listening matter of the rest. To many people it is this encroachment on culture and morals that represents what they see as censorship, but in the end cultural control is inextricable from the political variety. The same fear of a "breach of the peace" that informed the earliest obscenity prosecutions underlies the modern system. If one is to accept the theories of the clean-up campaigners, reading or viewing pornography undermines the family and since the family supports the state, in the subversion of one lies the destruction of the other. Governments, as self-interested as any other power-holders, duly take the point in framing their obscenity laws.

Censorship is international, continuous and pervasive, but it is not a seamless monolith. Concerns that seem paramount to one nation are meaningless to another. But political and moral/cultural censorship can be seen as falling into a recognizable, even predictable geographical pattern. The sort of cultural censorship that pervades America, Britain and to a lesser extent Europe and other Western nations such as Australia, is often irrelevant elsewhere. For the poorest nations the whole concept is meaningless: The population are unlikely to call for the dubious delights of X-rated videocassettes. Here the obscenity is child starvation, not kiddie porn. The basis of Third World censorship is political, rooted in the desire of a ruling party to preserve its privileged status. The censorship trials that reach the headlines concern the rebellious, not the rude. Closed societies—whether religious, such as those of Libya or Iran, or secular, as in the Soviet Union or China—undoubtedly proscribe pornography, but only as part of a wider imposition of political and cultural norms. Once again, the censors, and those who defy them, are playing a rougher game than those who can indulge the niceties of "secular humanism" or "fighting words."

Conversely in some of those countries loosely allied as "The West," political controls are less stringent; the governments, backed by their voluntary cohorts, have a greater inclination to indulge in the prosecution of allegedly titillating material. For governments who persist in believing that cultural license runs hand-in-glove with social license—and as such subverts the state—this form of censorship is not trivial, however petty it seems in the face of the battles fought out in more repressive countries. But the ability of certain countries, notably France and Holland, and the Scandinavians to abandon all such legislation, other than where they affect the young, calls into question the necessity for such controls.

Censorship is an enormous, wide-ranging topic, far more complex than simply cutting the "naughty bits" out of the movies, shutting down adult bookshops, or muzzling civil service whistleblowers. It affects the quality of every life—aesthetically, emotionally, socially and politically. The petty freedoms of the four letter word are allied (as much in governmental as in moral eyes) to the greater freedoms, of speech, of the press, of opinion—indeed, of freedom itself. Those who burn books today will burn people tomorrow, remarked a witness of the bonfires on which the Nazis burned Jewish, communist and other ideologically impure publications. This is the essentially libertarian view, and one that has traditionally informed the great mass of anti-censorship, pro-freedom-of-speech campaigning. It is, broadly, the view that underlies the compilation of this book. Yet to intensify the complexity there have emerged new strands of opinion, ostensibly unallied to those of the moral censor, but stemming from the complaints of feminists, blacks, male and female homosexuals, the aged and similar activist groups. Their fight against "isms"—sexism, racism, ageism—has led to calls for a new version of ideological censorship. It claims, admirably, to target only negative stereotyping, but seeks, inevitably, to secure its own position by denying that of its opponents. Thus it is possible to applaud these groups' aims but to deplore their actions.

I have tried to tabulate as comprehensively as possible in this encyclopedia the history, development and present-day state of the censor's art. I have taken as a model the essential catholicity of the Oxford Companions to English and to American Literature. I have concentrated, inevitably, on America and Britain, followed closely by other Western nations (including South Africa), Europe and the communist bloc, China and the Third World. As far as the latter is concerned, there is relatively little historical material. I am further constrained by the inescapable fact that countries in which censorship is most successful offer the fewest details on their system, other than those available from its victims. I have not included every single instance of censorship, even in those areas with which I have dealt under many entries. While, in the West at least, the large-scale censorship of books is sufficiently rare as to deserve individual consideration, that of films is so continual, if only by cuts that run to a few frames, that there simply is insufficient space to catalog them all. I have, however, included some general lists of books or films that have suffered censorship, a number of which I have treated individually, to help give some perspective on the vast breadth of worldwide censorship as well as illustrating the way in which one country's high school textbook is another's seditious tract.

I have generally ignored wartime military censorship. The fine points of national security under fire defeat simple analysis. Prior to the 19th century the concept was irrelevant and the level of communications that might worry the generals was nonexistent. Since then the military who fight the war and the media who cover it have fought a parallel battle all their own. The increasing independence of those media, and the evolving sophistication of its techniques and technology (rivalling those of the battlefield weaponry itself), have intensified the argument. The nature of military strategy must involve secrecy; the nature of the media requires quite a contrary concept. According to the current military posture, as far as the press is concerned, less is definitely more. One point might be noted: If the war is popular, e.g. World War II, the media, and the public whom they serve, are far more willing to accept whatever strictures are established.

The topic of censorship, of course, remains perennially fascinating. As communications's doppelganger it will not go away, only bend, perhaps, in the prevailing political and social winds. No one has so far managed to write about censorship without inferring at least some slight, personal opinion. The archivist, even (or perhaps especially) of so contentious a subject, must strive for the disinterested stance. However, as must be clear from this introduction as well as from what follows, I am no supporter of censorship. Indeed, with very few exceptions, I have found in my researches very little material published by those who are—although their complaints remain well-publicized. I also note that for all the superficial confidence of their public pronouncements, there is an undeniable strain of defensiveness underlying every statement. I do not pretend that this book, therefore, can be so disinterested as to ignore my own position. On the other hand, I hope to have avoided sacrificing accuracy for mere polemic.

Aside from any other failings endemic to an undertaking such as this, and for which I take full blame, the simple march of historical events stands in the way of achieving absolute accuracy in the encyclopedia's every entry. The world is in continual flux, and the chronicler of any aspect of international events can but do his or her best to keep up. Immediately before the massacre in Tiananmen Square, it might have seemed that a substantial new section would have to be added to what I had already written about China. The events of June 4, 1989, rendered that unnecessary. China's censors go on as ever. Today, I can survey a world as much in turmoil as ever. For instance, what appears at the moment as the imminent collapse of the postwar Soviet empire renders events there particularly unpredictable, although *glasnost* will presumably give observers a better view of what is happening than was made available during the Cold War.

Thus, here and elsewhere the simple necessities of publication schedules will guarantee, unfortunately, that some entries will still stop short of immediacy. The Solidarity-led government in Poland may be assumed to have relaxed controls there, while Hungary is already a quasi-Western state. What will happen in the Baltic states, in Armenia and Azerbaijan, even in Soviet Russia itself remains to be seen. In these and other parts of the world, events defy prediction. I trust that the reader will make allowance for my inadequacy as a seer.

If a number of figures, particularly today's self-appointed censors, appear to have been treated with greater respect than some others may feel they deserve, suffice it to say that it is due to the impartiality that a reference work demands.

JONATHON GREEN

THE
ENCYCLOPEDIA OF
CENSORSHIP

A

ABC Trial, The   The ABC Trial was the name given by the British media to the trial in September 1978 of two journalists, Crispin Aubrey and Duncan Campbell, and one former soldier, John Berry, whose names on the Old Bailey trial lists conveniently fell into alphabetical order. The background to the trial lay in the campaign by the British government to deport two Americans—ex-CIA agent Philip Agee and journalist Mark Hosenball—both of whom had been served in 1978 with Deportation Orders under the Immigration Act (1971) (see *Haig* v. *Agee*). It was alleged that the continued presence of both men on British soil would be prejudicial to national security, although the British security services refused to reveal any details. It was known only that Agee's memoirs had fallen afoul of his former bosses, and Hosenball had written a piece on GCHQ (General Communications Headquarters) in Cheltenham, the center of Britain's electronic signals monitoring.

John Berry was a former lance-corporal in a British Army signals unit in Cyprus who had left the Army in 1970 and since then worked as a truck driver and a social worker. Since 1970 his politics had shifted to the left and so enraged was he by the Agee-Hosenball deportations that he wrote to their defense committee offering to tell them about his own military experiences. It is assumed that his letter was opened and that the committee's phones were tapped.

On February 18, 1977, Aubrey, the community affairs correspondent for the London listings and features magazine, *Time Out*, accompanied by Campbell, whose knowledge of electronics had been used previously by the magazine in a piece on the government monitoring center (Government Communications Headquarters [GCHQ]) entitled "The Eavesdroppers" (which he had coauthored with Mark Hosenball), went to meet Berry at his north London flat. When they had finished their two-hour meeting, which Aubrey taped, all three were arrested by waiting police and charged under section 2 of the OFFICIAL SECRETS ACT. The Home Secretary, Merlyn Rees, already suffering criticism over the Agee-Hosenball deportations, remarked, according to author James Michael (op cit), "My God, what are they trying to do to me now?" A large van was required to carry away Campbell's personal library.

The onus of prosecution lay in the hands of Sam Silkin, the attorney-general. Although the initial charge was under only section two of the Act, he chose to add a further charge, against Campbell alone, under section one—which had never previously been used against a journalist. The case began to face legal problems from the outset. The charges against the two journalists were on the grounds of "mere receipt" of Berry's confessions. In 1976 the government had made it clear that "mere recept" was due to be dropped from the Act at such time as it came round to achieving its proposed revisions. Although the original law still lay on the statute books, the attorney-general had the option of whether or not to use it. In the event, he did. The next problem emerged at the committal proceedings at Tottenham Magistrates Court. Here a witness declined to give his name, and was identified in court simply as "Colonel B." Checking a publicly available service journal, *The Wire*, made it easy to identify him as Colonel H.A. Johnstone, until 1977 the head of Army Signals in the U.K.

The first attempt at an Old Bailey trial began on September 5, 1978, and lasted just 10 days before it was abandoned when it was discovered (and revealed on a television talk show) that the jury had been vetted by the security services, which had informed the prosecution of their findings, but not the defense. When the new trial began, on October 5, the judge, Mr. Justice Mars-Jones, made it clear he was unimpressed with the section one charge and noted that the attorney-general could as easily drop it as he had imposed it. Silkin, who must have realized that a meaningful result was slipping fast away, did just that. His decision was helped by the fact that the material Campbell was supposed to have obtained clandestinely was all available from published sources. Mars-Jones then told the court, although the media were prohibited from saying so, that he had no intention of imposing custodial sentences.

Campbell clashed with the security services again in early 1987 when as a *New Statesman* reporter, he assembled a proposed series of films for the BBC on Britain's defenses, "The Secret Society." Among his revelations was the Zircon Project, a long-running scheme to put a British spy satellite into space. Spurred on by an increasingly intemperate Conservative government, the police raided Campbell's home, as well as the offices of the *New Statesman* and those of the BBC in Glasgow, where the programs had been made. The government obtained an injunction against the showing of the film in question, although administrative bungling failed to suppress a piece by Campbell in his journal in which he mentioned the project, and the government did not stop a number of MPs from arranging, with the security of parliamentary privilege, private showings. The consensus of opinion outside the government, which claimed Zircon to be of paramount security importance, was that the furor had arisen because Campbell's film revealed a piece of notable government mis-spending, hitherto sedulously hidden from report. As for the satellite itself, keeping it a secret during development seemed irrelevant: As soon as it actually went into operation, its targets, presumably in the Soviet Union, would be able to spot it for themselves. Campbell's series, "Secret Society," was finally screened in April 1987, although the BBC's new director-general, Michael Checkland, chose to excise the contentious segment.

Abelard, Peter Peter Abelard (1059-1142) was born in Brittany and moved to Paris where he proved himself a brilliant disputant and lecturer in the schools of St. Genevieve and Notre Dame. His book *Sic et Non* is generally seen as the basic text of scholastic theology, a discipline that attempted to reconcile Aristotle and the Bible and reason with faith. The practitioners of scholasticism were known as the Schoolmen and their numbers included Peter Lombard (1100-60), William of Ockham (?1300-49), Duns Scotus (1270-1308) and Thomas Aquinas (?1225-74), whose *Summa Theologica* is considered the greatest work of a movement that flourished between 1100 and 1500 and still persists in French Thomism, named for Aquinas. Abelard's works, notably *Introductio ad Theologiam*, like those of many of his peers, were anathematized by the church as contrary to orthodoxy, although the teachings in time became orthodox themselves. Abelard's writings were burnt on various occasions after 1120, and his entire theological work was declared heretical in 1142 at the Council of Sens. His works were cited in the ROMAN INDEXES OF 1559 and 1564. The U.S. Customs' ban on his writings was not lifted until 1930. Abelard is best known to non-philosophers and theologians as the lover of Heloise, his pupil. Their affair ended tragically, but when she died in 1163 she was buried in his tomb.

Ableman, Paul SEE *The Mouth*.

Abrams v. *United States* (1919) Under the ESPIONAGE ACT (1917), it was forbidden for U.S. citizens to engage in any activity prejudicial to their country's involvement in World War I. The jingoistic atmosphere of the time, which had intensified even though the war had been won, militated against even the milder forms of agitation. A number of Jewish radicals, headed by Jacob Abrams, ignored the act and distributed a number of anti-war leaflets, condemning America's declaration of war and urging munitions workers, and especially those who had emigrated from Russia, to register their protest in a general strike. Among their leaflets were those entitled "The Hypocrisy of the United States and Her Allies" and "Workers Wake Up" (this latter written in Yiddish). The leaflets were couched in bombastic revolutionary tones, attacking the "hypocrisy of the plutocratic gang in Washington and vicinity" and urging workers to "spit in the face of the false, hypocritic, military propaganda." In a majority opinion written by Justice Clarke, the Supreme Court affirmed the men's conviction by a lower court and their sentences of 20 years imprisonment each, stating that the leaflets were "obviously intended to provoke and encourage resistance to the United States in a war ..." In their dissenting opinion, Justices Holmes and Brandeis supported the defendants' plea that their freedom to publish was backed up by the First Amendment to the U.S. Constitution (see United States 7. Constitution), saying that they had the right to publish and that they had been "deprived of their rights."
SEE ALSO: *Adler* v. *Board of Education* (1952); Debs, Eugene; *Frohwerk* v. *United States* (1919); *Gitlow* v. *New York* (1925); *Lamont* v. *Postmaster-General* (1965); *Pierce* v. *United States* (1920); *Schaeffer* v. *United States* (1920); *Schenck* v. *United States* (1919); *Sweezy* v. *New Hampshire* (1957); *Whitney* v. *California* (1927); *Yates* v. *United States* (1957).

Academie des Dames, L' This dialogue, by NICOLAS CHORIER, represents the most advanced form of pornography circulating in late-17th-century Europe and was widely and consistently seized and destroyed. Originally written in Latin as a supposed translation by the Dutch scholar Meursius of a Spanish work by one Luisa Sigea of Toledo, and titled *Satyra Sotadica*, it appeared in 1659 or 1660. By 1680 it appeared in a French translation as *L'Academie des Dames* and the English translation of 1688, now titled *A dialogue between a married lady and a maid* (subsequently retitled *The School of Love* [1707] and *Aretinus Redivivus* [1745]), is the earliest surviving piece of prose pornography in England. This substitution of prose for verse, the usual and acceptable format for such writing, immediately placed the work beyond the literary pale; Chorier emphatically denied his authorship, claiming that a literary thief had stolen those pieces attributed to his pen, and the printer went bankrupt. Despite such disapproval, this novel hastened the decline of erotic verse and stimulated an increasing flood of erotic prose, initally in the dialogue form but leading by the 19th century to the full-blown erotic novel. The dialogues are those between the sophisticated Tullia and her 15-year-old cousin Ottavia and deal with the sexual initiation of the latter by the former. They are divided into four volumes, the first of which has four dialogues (*L'Escarmouce* [The Skirmish], *Tribadicon*, *Anatomie* and *Le Duel*) and the other three, one each (*Voluptes*, *Facons et Figures*, *Historiettes*). The author has left the most lurid episodes in Latin, but a glossary is provided. Unlike earlier dialogues of the era, e.g. L'ESCHOLLE DES FILLES, the speakers become actors too, engaging in a variety of heterosexual and female homosexual acts. The book also stresses the sadistic and perverse side of sex, with several scenes of defloration, incest, flagellation and sodomy. Most of the themes that inform subsequent pornography, up to the present day, can be found, all based on the premise that sexual pleasure, of whatever sort, justifies its own indulgence. Editions of the English translation, or similar books adapted from it, appeared regularly. The first, titled *The Duell*, appeared ca. 1676 and has survived as the earliest example of English pornography. *The Duell* was also the first piece of printed pornography to be prosecuted in England: One William Cademan was convicted in 1684 for "exposing, selling, uttering and publishing the pernicious, wicked scandalous, vicious and illicit book entitled A Dialogue between a Married Lady, and a Maid ..." Subsequent editions were published until at least 1894, when one was advertised in a catalog issued by the pornographer, CHARLES CARRINGTON.

Achilles Statue, The In 1822 a statue of Achilles, subscribed for by the women of England, and celebrating the invincibility of the Duke of Wellington, victor of Waterloo (1815), was unveiled in Hyde Park, London. The crowd attending the ceremony was duly appalled to see that the statue represented the hero fully naked, including the genitals. The ensuing outcry, magnified through the legions of female subscribers, ensured that within a few days the offended parts had been masked, as they still are on the extant statue, by a fig-leaf.

Acta Pauli This unauthenticated life of St. Paul was the first item to suffer the censorship of the church. Banned by an edict at the council of Ephesus in 150, the book was an historical romance written around the middle of the 2nd century and aimed to glorify the life and labors of SAINT PAUL. The Council, made up of a synod of bishops who met at Ephesus (or, according to some authorities, at Smyrna), condemned the book on the grounds that, while written by an orthodox, if anonymous, Christian, it did not conform to the orthodox presentation of Paul's life. Nonetheless it continued to circulate and was cited by such later authors as Eusebius and Photius, as well as by Tertullian. The ban set in motion a process that accelerated greatly after the invention of printing in the 15th century, reached its peak in the censorship of the various Inquisitions and has not wholly died out today.
SEE ALSO Christian Church 1. early censorship (150-814); Spanish Inquisition.

Acts and Monuments of these latter perillous dayes, touching matters of the Church SEE *Foxe's Book of Martyrs.*

Adler v. Board of Education **(1952)** SEE New York 1. Civil Service Law (1952).

Adult Film Association of America The AFAA was formed in 1969 at a time when attitudes to what was euphemistically known as "adult" entertainment had emerged from the restrictions of the Fifties and were preparing for the promotion of even greater license in the Seventies. The association is based in Los Angeles and is made up of the producers, distributors and exhibitors of X-rated and erotic films. The aim of the AFAA is to combat the censorship of such films; this is becoming increasingly hard to sustain on a local level, in the face of the current resurgence of conservatism in America. They have filed a number of amicus curiae briefs, offering their expert aid to defendants in censorship cases.

advocacy Advocacy has been condemned as an illegal act by the U.S. Supreme Court. In the case of GITLOW V. NEW YORK (1925) the court stated that those who incite the overthrow of government by violent means, even if they take no action to carry out their threat, "involve danger to the public peace and to the security of the State." Using the metaphor of a smoldering fire, kindled by a "single revolutionary spark," the court claimed that the State was not "acting arbitrarily or unreasonably" when it sought to extinguish that spark, in the interest of public safety, "without waiting until it has enkindled the flame or blazed into the conflagration." As such, those who promote revolution might legitimately be suppressed, irrespective of their supposed freedom of speech under the First Amendment of the U.S. Constitution. This opinion was reversed in 1957 when, in the case of *Yates* v. *United States*, the court accepted that simple advocacy, even when it taught "prohibited activities ... with an evil intent" came under the category of protected speech, so long as that advocacy dealt only in words and not deeds. Thus it was possible both to preach extreme left- and extreme right-wing philosophies, so long as it did not extend to action. A typical recent case was that of *Brandenburg* v. *Ohio* (1969), in which a Ku Klux Klan leader was acquitted (on appeal) of "advocating the duty, necessity, or propriety of crime, sabotage, violence, or unlawful methods of terrorism" and of "criminal syndicalism" after a speech in which he used highly racist language, attacking Jews and blacks. Since his speech was not promoting "imminent lawless action," he could not be made to serve his sentence of 1-10 years, nor pay a $1,000 fine.
SEE ALSO incitement.

Age D'Or, L' This film by surrealists Luis Bunuel and Salvador Dali opened at Studio 28 in Paris in 1931. Allegedly the greatest-ever cinematic repository of shocking material, it played to packed houses for six nights, but the mounting pressure of right-wing pressure groups threatened its run. Agitation from conservative groups such as Les Camelots du Roi and Les Jeunesses Patriotiques as well as from the right-wing press attacked both the filmmakers and their patron, Charles de Noailles, who was expelled from the aristocratic Jockey Club and very nearly excommunicated by the Pope. At the end of the first week's showings, patriotic enthusiasts attacked the cinema, breaking up exhibits in the foyer and smashing the seats in the auditorium. This gave the police the excuse they required and *L'Age D'Or* was officially closed down a week later. Other than in film clubs it was not screened publicly until 1980 in New York and in 1981 in Paris.

Age of Reason, The *The Age of Reason* was written by the expatriate English radical THOMAS PAINE during his stay in Revolutionary France between 1792 and 1795. The first part appeared in 1793 at the height of the Terror, but no copies have survived. The whole work, completed while Paine was imprisoned for his opposition to the execution of Louis XIV,

appeared in 1795. It is a wholesale attack on the Bible and on Christianity, written in a deliberately flippant, and thus shocking, style. It takes the Deist point of view, epitomized by Paine's statement "I believe in one God, and no more." Belief in a deity as justified by one's reason was acceptable; the tenets of organized religion were not. More specifically, Paine condemned the Old Testament as being filled with "obscene stories and voluptuous debaucheries"; the New Testament was inconsistent and the Virgin Birth merely "hearsay upon hearsay." The book concludes with a plea for religious tolerance. It was generally condemned as blasphemous and joined Paine's other works both as a target for the censor and a textbook for the freethinker and radical.
SEE ALSO *Rights of Man, The*.

Agee, Philip   SEE *Haig* v. *Agee*.

Agrippa, Henry Cornelius   Agrippa, born in Cologne, was a scholar and writer (1486-1535) who specialized in the occult sciences. He is probably the origin of the astrologer "Her Trippa" of RABELAIS' *Third Book of Gargantua and Pantagruel* (1546). Both of Agrippa's major works—*De Occulta Philosophia libri tres* (1529) and *De Incertitudine et vanitate Scientiarum et Artium* (1530)—were seen as heretical by the church and duly banned. Even before he had written them, in 1509, Agrippa was charged with heresy for his lectures at the University of Dole in France, and he chose to suppress his early treatise, *On the Excellence of Wisdom*, for fear of offending the Scholastics. To escape a trial he fled to the Netherlands, where he took refuge with the Emperor Maximilian. He fought in Italy under Maximilian, whose private secretary he was and who knighted him for his efforts. When *De Incertitudine*—a sarcastic attack on the pretensions of the supposedly learned and on the state of existing sciences—appeared in 1530 Agrippa was imprisoned in Brussels and his book was burnt as heretical. He complained in his *Epistles* that he wrote only "for the purpose of exciting sluggish minds" but instead "there is no impiety, no heresy, no disgrace with which they do not charge me … with clapping fingers, with hands outstretched and then suddenly withdrawn, with gnashing of teeth, with raging, by spitting, by scratching their heads, by gnawing their nails, by stamping with their feet, they rage like madmen." In 1533 charges of magic and conjury were brought against him, after the Inquisition had examined *De Occulta Philosophia* and heard a number of stories in which the scholar was credited with exercising the black arts himself. His support for witches, against whose persecution he argued, did not endear him to the church and his works were included on the TRIDENTINE INDEX.

Alexander, William   SEE *The Bible*.

Alfred A. Knopf Inc. v. Colby (1975)   SEE *United States* v. *Marchetti* (1972).

Aliens Registration Act, 1940 (U.S.)   This act, the first peacetime anti-sedition act passed by the U.S. Congress since the Alien and Sedition Acts of 1798, was generally known as the Smith Act, after Rep. Howard W. Smith (Virginia) who introduced it. The act made it a crime to advocate forcible or violent overthrow of the government, or to publish or distribute material that advocated such a violent overthrow. In the 20 years in which the act was enforced, some 100 persons, usually from the left wing, were prosecuted, suffering fines and/or imprisonment. The act has not been used since 1957, when in *Yale* v. *United States* the conviction of 14 communists under its provisions was overturned in the Supreme Court, but it remains on the U.S. statute book.
SEE ALSO advocacy; Espionage Act (1917) and Sedition Act (1918).

Amann, Max   SEE Germany 4. Nazi press controls (1933-45).

Amants, Les   *Les Amants* (*The Lovers*) was made in France by Louis Malle in 1958. Based on the 19th-century novel *Point de Lendemain* by Dominique Vivant, it starred Jeanne Moreau as a bored provincial housewife, seeking solace first in the dubious pleasures of an affair with a Parisian sophisticate, followed by her more satisfying dalliance with a young intellectual. She rejects both the provincial bourgeoisie and the metropolitan chic. On arrival in America *Les Amants* was banned in major theaters in Ohio, Illinois, Massachusetts, Rhode Island, Oregon, Tennessee, and throughout the states of New York, Virginia and Maryland. A number of cases arose from this, most notably JACOBELLIS V. OHIO (1964), in which Nico Jacobellis, a cinema manager who was convicted under his state's anti-obscenity laws for showing the film, took his case to the U.S. Supreme Court and enabled that body to deliver an important decision, using the ROTH STANDARD of 1957 to overturn the state court ruling and declare Jacobellis innocent.

The film also bothered the English censor, notably as regarded a scene clearly implying the practice of cunnilingus. This problem was solved when the censor, JOHN TREVELYAN, persuaded Louis Malle to shoot extra material to cover the mandatory excisions. The film was then passed for exhibition.

Amatory Experiences of a Surgeon, The   SEE Campbell, James.

America the Beautiful   This picture by G. Ray Kerciu, assistant professor of art at the University of Mississippi, was painted in April 1963. Inspired by the desegregation riots on the campus at Oxford, Mississippi, in September 1962, the picture featured a large Confederate flag—"the Stars and Bars"—daubed with a variety of slogans, all used during the riots. The graffiti included "Impeach JFK!," "Would You Want Your Sister To Marry One?" and "———[expletive deleted on artwork] the NAACP." On April 6 Kerciu opened a one-man show of 56 canvases at the University Fine Arts Center. Local members of the White Citizens' Council and the Daughters of the Confederacy complained at this "desecration of the Confederate flag" by "obscene and indecent words and phrases." University Principal Charles Noyes acknowledged their campaign and ordered that *America the Beautiful* and four other offending pictures be removed from the exhibition.

American Civil Liberties Union (ACLU) The ACLU was founded in 1925 and has approximately 250,000 members today. Like its British counterpart, the National Council for Civil Liberties (NCCL), it takes an active role in fighting censorship and advocating freedom of speech, expression and inquiry. It promotes a number of test cases to point up what it sees as repressive legislation and regularly files amicus curiae briefs to assert its involvement in censorship cases.
SEE ALSO Committee on International Freedom to Publish; Committee to Defend the First Amendment; First Amendment Congress; Freedom to Read Foundation; National Coalition Against Censorship; National Committee for Sexual Civil Liberties; Reporters Committee for Freedom of the Press; Scholars and Citizens for Freedom of Information.

American Convention on Human Rights This convention was created in 1950 to cover all the states of the Americas, North, South and Central. Although it is modeled on the American declaration of the rights and duties of man it has been ratified neither by the U.S. nor Canada. Its signatories are 19 countries from Central and South America. Under Artical 13:

1. Everyone shall have the right to freedom of thought and expression. This right includes the freedom to seek, receive and impart information and ideas of all kinds, regardless of frontiers, whether orally, in writing or in print, in the form of art, or through any other medium of one's choice. 2. The exercise of the right provided for in the foregoing paragraph shall not be subject to prior censorship but shall be subject to subsequent imposition of liability, which shall be expressly established by law and be necessary in order to ensure: (a) respect for the rights and reputations of others; or (b) the protection of national security, public order or public health or morals. 3. The right of expression may not be restricted by indirect methods or means, such as the abuse of government or private controls over newsprint, radio broadcasting frequencies, or implements or equipment used in the dissemination of information, or by any other means tending to impede the communication and circulation of ideas and opinions. 4. ... public entertainment may be subject by law to prior censorship, for the sole purpose of ... the moral protection of childhood and adolescence. 5. Any propaganda for war and any advocacy of national, racial or religious hatred that constitutes incitements to lawless violence or any other similar illegal action against any person or group of persons on any grounds including those of race, color, religion, language or national origin shall be considered as offenses punishable by law.

SEE ALSO European Convention on Human Rights; International Covenant on Civil and Political Rights.

American Legion SEE blacklisting.

Andrea de Nerciat, Andre-Robert Andrea de Nerciat (1739-1800) has been recognized as one of the foremost writers of erotic novels in the 18th century. His work was frequently seized as obscene. He was born at Dijon, the son of a lawyer who worked in local government. As a young man he traveled, exploiting a facility for learning foreign languages, and spent a period as a soldier in Denmark prior to returning to France and joining the royal household as one of the *corps des gendarmes de la garde*. After his regiment was disbanded in 1775 he began traveling again, visiting Switzerland, Belgium and Germany, during which time he was possibly working for the French secret service. He was employed in Prussia, first as an adviser and sub-librarian to the landgrave of Hessen-Kassel, and then as director of building works to the duke of Hessen-Rothenburg. After this he resumed his travels and espionage work, visiting Holland and Austria in 1787, and was awarded a French honor, presumably for these efforts, in 1788. Subsequent assignments in Italy, working for Queen Marie-Caroline of Naples, led to his imprisonment by French troops in Rome. After his release his health was broken; he died in January 1800, in poverty and ill-health.

Andrea de Nerciat began writing around 1770 and produced, as well as some generally unexceptional straight work, five erotic novels and many compilations of shorter pieces, indecent verses, erotic dialogues and similar material, typical of the era. For many of these works he adopted the pseudonym of "Le Docteur Cazzone—membre extraordinaire de la joyeuse Faculte Phallo-coiro-pyro-glottonomique." His first erotic novel was *Felicia* (written ca. 1770, first edition 1775). It has been reprinted many times, although the first edition was full of mistakes and only the subsequent edition of 1778, probably corrected by the author, provides a definitive text. His most famous works appeared later: *Le Diable au corps* (1785) and *Les Aphrodites, ou Fragments thali-priapiques pour servir a l'histoire du plaisir* (1793). The first half of *Le Diable* appeared originally in Germany, titled *Les Ecarts du temperament, ou le Catechisme de Figaro*, and a geniune, three-volume edition was not published until 1803. It is a novel in dialogue form, and, like a play, includes stage directions. It details the sexual adventures of an anonymous marquise and her infinitely aroused companion, the Comtesse de Motte-en-feu, both members of a libertine club, presumably the Societe des Aphrodites, also the topic of the eponymous novel of 1793. In the pornographic tradition, the two heroines encounter a number of sexual experiences, growing gradually more bizarre and involved, until the book ends with a massive orgy, with all the participants in fancy dress. *Les Aphrodites* concerns the members of an expensive sexual club, quite probably based on an actual establishment that flourished before the Revolution wiped out such aristocratic amusements—although *Les Aphrodites* proclaims the equality of all members, high and low. As well as the continuing descriptions of the sexual antics of its members, the author lists in some detail the rules that govern the club, offering debates on the eligibility of pederasts and similar species of "other business." Like all of Andrea de Nerciat's best writing, these two books, peopled with grotesques, both of character and experience, and composed with wit, style and a feel for the real world in which his characters moved, transcend the repetitious couplings of much erotic composition. Other erotic novels, generally less well reviewed, by Andrea de Nerciat include *Mon Noviciat, ou les Joies de Lolotte* (1792), which appeared in London as *How to Make Love* (1823); *Monrose, ou le Libertin par fatalite* (1792), a sequel to *Felicia*; and *Le Doctorat impromptu* (1788), a "galante" rather than an overtly erotic work.

Aphrodites, ou Fragments thali-priapiques pour servir a l'histoire du plaisir, les (1793) SEE Andrea de Nerciat, Andre-Robert.

Apollinaire, Guillaume

Apollinaire (1880-1918), whose poetry earned him a place among the pioneers of futurism and cubism, was also the author of a number of erotic writings, both in his own right and on commission for George and Robert Briffault. For these publishers, who specialized in issuing reprints of 18th-century "galante" novels, from 1909 Apollinaire contributed introductions and bibliographies; and, when dealing with their series "Maitres de l'Amour" and "Coffret du Bibliophile," he chose, on occasion, to make his own bowdlerizations. He wrote these both under his own name and under that of "Germain Amplecas."

The first of his own efforts appeared in 1900, called *Mirely, ou le petit trou pas cher*, a novel commissioned by a specialist bookshop in Paris. In 1907 he wrote two more books: *Les Memoires d'un jeune Don Juan* (latterly titled "Les Exploits . . .") and his best known erotic piece, *Les Onze mille verges*. While *Don Juan* is mild enough, for all that it includes episodes of sodomy and incest in its tale of a young man's sexual development, *Les Onze mille verges* takes a more Sadeian direction, indulging a full range of bizarre sexual fantasies as the hero, a Rumanian prince named Mony Vibescu, makes his way through the Russo-Japanese war of 1904. Such extremes have been attributed to Apollinaire's desire to create a surrealist parody of de SADE (and Picasso declared it the finest book he had ever read), but the book is none the less hard-core for that. As an exemplar of what British censors and readers termed "French novels," it was regularly seized in raids on London's pornographic bookshops. Among its subsequent translators was Alexander Troc-

chi, author of CAIN'S BOOK. Apollinaire's subsequent erotica was published after his death in 1918. It was all verse and included the collector's *Le Verger des amours* (1927) (although this may have been written by PIERRE LOUYS), *Le Cortege priapique* (1925), *Julie, ou la rose* (1927) and *Poemes secretes a Madeleine* (1949), in which the erotic aspects are coincidental to their real subject, the poet's letters written from the World War I front to Madeleine Pages in 1916.

Apollinaire was also the coauthor, with publishers LOUIS PERCEAU and Fernand Fleuret, of a bibliography of those erotic works held in the Paris Bibliotheque Nationale—*L'Enfer de la Bibliotheque National: icono-bio-bibliographie . . .* , which appeared in 1913.

Archer, John SEE book burning in England 4. Puritans.

Areopagitica, The SEE Puritan Censorship: the Commonwealth.

Aretino, Pietro

Aretino (1492-1556), whose name comes from his Italian birthplace, Arezzo, and who was known as "Flagello de principi" (The Scourge of Princes) for his biting wit, was author of five comedies and a tragedy and a wide variety of satires and other works condemned as scandalous or licentious. "One of the wittiest knaves God ever made" said Thomas Nashe, but Aretino, who liked to see himself as "censor of a proud world," was unloved by the authorities in Rome. In 1527 Pope Clement VII condemned and had suppressed every edition of his *Sonetti Lussuriosi* (otherwise known as *La Corona di Cazzi*), published in 1524. The illustrations, by Giulio Romano, depicted a number of "Posizioni," the positions of sexual intercourse. Such lubricity affronted the authorities and Romano and Aretino were forced to flee Rome to avoid prosecution. The artwork survived, engraved by Marcantonio Raimondi—the greatest engraver of the era—who was also exiled for his efforts. As Aretino's *Postures*, the bound sets, with or without their accompanying commentary, survived for centuries as one of the indispensable titles in any collection of sophisticated erotica. The *Postures* appear regularly in English literature, mentioned by Jonson in *The Alchemist* (1612), Wycherley in *The Country Wife* (1678), in Rochester's SODOM (1684) and so on. Subsequent rumors claimed that Oscar Wilde essayed a translation but no copy exists. For all their notoriety, Wayland Young, writing in *Eros Denied*, dismissed them as "coy, guilty, timid and periphrastic . . ."

The first of Aretino's works to appear in England was *The Crafty Whore* (1658), subtitled "The Mistery and Iniquity of Bawdy Houses laid open . . . ," but in fact a free translation of part three of his "Ragionamenti," a series of dialogues on sexual life conducted between an older and a younger woman, first published in Italy between 1534 and 1536 and in England (in Italian) in 1584. In 1889 a six-volume translation of the "Ragionamenti" into English appeared, published in Paris. In

1674 fellows of All Souls, Oxford, printed the complete "Sonnets" and their accompanying "Postures" on the university's press in the Sheldonian Theatre. As the sheets were appearing, Dr. John Fell (of "I do not love you, Dr. Fell" fame) appeared. As head of the press, he was enraged and destroyed all the material, threatening the errant dons with expulsion.

Paradoxically, when the nudes in Michelangelo's Sistine Chapel *Last Judgment* caused such a furor in 1541, Aretino wrote to the artist, attacking the "licentiousness and impurity" he found in the painting, claiming that such pictures made him, "as a baptized Christian," blush. He died apparently after falling off a chair in a fit of laughter—when hearing about his sister's sexual escapades—and breaking his neck.

Argentina   Under the Argentine Constitution, dating from 1853, the state guarantees freedom of the press (Article 31) and the right to publish one's opinions without censorship (Article 14). While the vagaries of Argentine government since 1930 have led to the suspension of such rights, notably under the military junta which ruled from 1976 to 1983 and whose death squads actually assassinated 100 opposition journalists, the administration of President Raoul Alfonsin (December 1983-July 1989) has returned to more liberal principles. Nonetheless the persistent efforts of the ousted military leaders to regain control has led to a degree of censorship, although no actual regulations have been passed. The censorship operates equally against the left and right. In 1984 Congress passed a "right of reply" law, giving to those who feel they have been attacked unfairly in the press the opportunity to air their own views. The new president, Peronist Carlos Menem, appears to be concentrating on his country's economic problems.

The right wing, while out of office, remains active. Thus, while the government has outlawed the publication or import of anti-Semitic material, a good deal still circulates. Likewise the right still dominates television's news and current affairs programming, although Argentine radio has been reborn as a vocal forum of popular debate. The Catholic Church has attempted to influence both publishing and the cinema, campaigning against less restrictive attitudes to sex and blasphemy in both media. A number of films have been withdrawn at its insistence.

Ars Amatoria   SEE Ovid.

art censorship   SEE art: religious prohibitions; Germany 3. Nazi art censorship; China 5. art censorship; USSR 1. art censorship.

art porn   SEE *Deep Throat*; *The Devil in Miss Jones*.

art: religious prohibitions
1. Jewish   The proscription of graven images (second commandment as laid down in Exodus 20:4) precluded Jewish sculptors from attempting busts or statues of human beings until the 17th-18th centuries. Such a ban was extended in Deuteronomy 4:17-18, which forbade the likeness of "any beast that is on the earth ... any winged fowl that flies in the heaven ... any thing that creepeth upon the ground ... any fish that is in the water." Not until Maimonides, rabbi of Cairo in the 12th century, were these prohibitions modified.

2. Zoroastrianism   No representations of the godhead, other than symbolic ones, were permitted.

3. Buddhism   No representation of Buddha is permitted; the deity must always be shown symbolically, as a pair of footprints or as an empty throne.

4. Christian   Still influenced by the Old Testament ban, early Christian painters generally avoided depicting Christ. Origen, a teacher and writer of Alexandria ca. 240, and one of the Greek Fathers of the Church, advocated that Christians should follow the Jewish prohibitions on representation. In "Contra Celsum" he praised as their contribution to "pure religion" their rejection of all "Painters and makers of images ... an art which attracts the attention of foolish men, and which drags down the eyes of the soul from God to earth." By the Edict of Milan in 313 Christianity took on its institutional and doctrinal form, delineating, among other things, the precise style permissible in religious paintings, all on the basis of "sacred dogma." The arrangement, form, and symbolism of form and color of all such work was made "fixed and absolute." The *Confessions* of St. Augustine of Hippo (ca. 400) underlined the growing Christian belief in visual art as standing contrary to all prescribed standards of piety.

5. Islam   On the basis of a belief that a painted or sculpted image is not separate but exists in some way as the double of its subject, Islam has always prohibited painting. While the Koran makes only a passing, condemnatory reference to statues as an abomination, traditions of the Prophet claimed that "those who will be most severely punished ... on the Day of Judgement will be the painters." The later-codified *Hadith*—a collection of the Prophet's sayings—explained that the artists' fault was their inability to breathe life into their creations. The response of Islamic artists to this ban was the development of artistic calligraphy.

Article 19   Article 19 was established in 1986 as an international human rights organization dedicated to the promotion of the rights of freedom of opinion and expression and the right to receive and impart information and ideas through any form of media, regardless of national frontiers. It takes its name from Article 19 of the UNIVERSAL DECLARATION OF HUMAN RIGHTS. The organization is based in London, where it has set up an international research and information center on censorship.

Asgill, John   The pamphlet, "An Argument proving that According to the Covenant of Eternal Life, revealed in the Scriptures, Man may be Translated from Hence into that Eternal Life without Passing Through Death, although the

Human Nature of Christ Himself could not be thus Translated till He had Passed Through Death," appeared in 1700. Its author was John Asgill, a barrister known after his theories as "Translated Asgill," who claimed that death, which had originated with Adam, had been deprived of its legal power by Christ. Asgill was elected to two seats in the Commons—of Enniscorthy in Ireland in 1703 and of Bramber in Sussex in 1707—but his inability to resist promoting his theory ensured that he was deprived of both within a matter of days. Both Parliaments had his book burned, even though among its crazy paragraphs were such aphorisms as "It is much easier to make a creed than to believe it after it is made" and "Custom itself, without a reason for it, is an argument only for fools." Asgill died in the Fleet prison, after contracting a mass of unpayable debts.

Ashbee, Henry Spencer   Henry Ashbee (1834-1900), ostensibly a model Victorian bourgeois businessman and traveler, was simultaneously the leading bibliographer of the erotic and pornographic literature of his own and previous eras. He combined his life as a member of the Royal Geographical Society, the Royal Historical Society, the Society of Arts, and Master of the Worshipful Company of Curriers, with the investigation of every aspect of published erotology and with the society of hacks and pornographers. Ashbee was born in Southwark in 1834. He worked first as a traveling salesman for a firm of Manchester warehousemen, then joined a firm of Hamburg silk merchants, founding their branches in London and Paris and marrying his employer's daughter in 1862. He lived with his family in Bedford Square, returning from his City counting house to entertain enthusiastically, playing host to writers, businessmen, explorers and a series of exotic foreigners. He collected books and paintings, always of the most conservative type. He was a particular devotee of Cervantes, having the best library of that author's work outside Spain. He was also a devoted traveler, touring the world in 1880—and making several other trips. His writing on these journeys was popular.

Ashbee's collecting of rare books led him toward some of the most esoteric: the erotic and pornographic publications that were officially ignored by the Victorian world but were produced for an enthusiastic market. Like many successful Victorians, he wished to add a degree of scholarship to his business pursuits. In his case the scholarship embraced the world of forbidden literature. He took the pseudonym "Pisanus Fraxi," a piece of cod-Latin easily accessible to those who cared to unravel it. *Fraxinus* was Latin for "ash" and the remaining four letters were an anagram for *apis*, a bee. The smutty wit of "Pis Anus" may have added charm to this sobriquet. While Ashbee pretended ignorance of his alter ego, even going so far as to plant pieces of disinformation in the journal *Notes and Queries*, there were few in literary London who did not know of his double identity. Apart from any more subtle inferences, Ashbee had written since 1875 a

number of pieces in *Notes and Queries*, signed "Fraxinus" and usually dealing with erotic literature.

Using his pseudonym, Ahsbee wrote and published his great erotic bibliography. *The Notes Bio-Biblio-Icono-graphical and Critical, on Curious & Uncommon Books* appeared in three volumes: "Index Librorum prohibitorum" (its title indulging his obsessive anti-Catholicism) in 1877, "Centuria librorum absconditorum" in 1879, "Catena librorum tacendorum" in 1885. Each edition was limited to 250 copies. Despite a number of successors, all of whom have drawn to some extent on his efforts, Ashbee's *Notes ...* remains the examplar of such bibliographies. The work is by no means flawless. Ashbee was a pedantic scholar, no great fault in a bibliographer, but he delighted in exhibiting his scholarship, never quoting in English where a foreign source could be found, and letting his various passions take over his critical commentary, to the extent that a single line of text would be adorned with almost a page of footnotes. And, as one critic suggested, it sometimes appears that he took up his work as a penance, so unrelievedly negative is he about the material he considers.

Ashbee died in 1900, a comparatively rich man, his image as a staid Victorian success in no way diminished by his closet compilations. He left 15,229 books to the British Museum, including his collection of pornography, which formed the basis of today's PRIVATE CASE and which was allegedly accepted only because without it the museum would not have gained possession of the Cervantes material. His wife and family, from whom he had been separated since 1893, were disinherited. For himself he asked for "no demonstration of grief, no mourning, no monument."
SEE ALSO Gay, Jules; Perceau, Louis; Reade, Rolf S.

Attorney General's Commission on Pornography, The (1986)   The Attorney-General's Commission on Pornography was established in February 1985 by then-U.S. attorney-general, William French Smith. It was delivered in July 1986 to his successor, Edwin Meese III, by its chairman, Henry E. Hudson, the United States Attorney for the Eastern District of Virginia. The findings of the 1,960-page, two-volume report were based on public hearings in six cities, a review of published articles relating to pornography, the work of staff investigators and the views expressed in more than 3,000 letters from the public. Budgeted at only $500,000 it was prevented from commissioning independent research.

The 11-member panel acknowledged that its conclusions were diametrically opposed to those of the 1970 PRESIDENT'S COMMISSION ON OBSCENITY AND PORNOGRAPHY that said erotic material was not a significant cause of crime, deliquency, sexual deviancy or emotional disturbances. The new panel claimed that times had changed, the problem of pornography had grown much worse and the conclusions of the earlier report were "starkly obsolete."

The panel concluded that "there is a connection between the pornography industry and organized crime." The panel also concluded that there was a "causal relationship" between certain kinds of pornography and acts of sexual violence. On this, and on other important points, the panel was not unanimous, and two of its members issued a dissenting statement, pointing out that the printed and video materials presented to the commission as evidence "were skewed to the very violent and extremely degrading." They also stressed that efforts to "tease" the current social science data into "proof of a causal link" between pornography and sexual crimes "simply cannot be accepted" and claimed that there had not been enough time for "full and fair discussions of many of the more restrictive and controversial proposals."

The commission rejected proposals to broaden the legal definition of obscenity, which embraces some but not all pornographic material, and said that current laws were basically adequate but woefully underenforced by federal, state and local prosecutors. They cited the Supreme Court's judgment in MILLER V. CALIFORNIA (1973), in which it was stated that "obscene material is unprotected by the First Amendment," and that judges can apply "contemporary community standards" to determine what is obscene. Many laws at various levels regulate or prohibit obscene material. The panel called for much more vigorous enforcement of laws against obscene materials.

It also said that sexually explicit material portraying the violent abuse of women by men led to "antisocial acts of sexual violence," sometimes including sex crimes. "With somewhat less confidence," the commission concluded that material showing the nonviolent humiliation or degradation of women might lead to "attitudinal changes" producing similar results: "sexual violence, sexual coercion or unwanted sexual aggression." Intensified enforcement should focus on child pornography and material showing sexual violence, the panel said. It also recommended that the "knowing possession of child pornography" should be made a felony under state law. It further recommended that a second or subsequent violation of obscenity laws should be a felony punishable by at least one year in prison. The panel said "extraordinary caution" must be exercised in prosecuting purveyors of materials composed entirely of printed words, with no photographs, pictures or drawings. "The written word," it said, "has had and continues to have a special place in this and any other civilization," adding that "Books consisting entirely of the printed word text only" seem to be among the "least harmful" types of pornography. Not all pornography, which the commission defined as any material that was "sexually explicit and intended primarily for the purpose of sexual arousal," might actually be actionable in court under current laws. The committee recommended that citizens "use grass-roots efforts to express opposition to pornographic materials." Such efforts may include "picketing and store boycotts," as well as the filing of protests with sponsors of radio and television programs deemed "offensive."

The commission recommended that Congress should authorize the forfeiture and recovery of any money gained through violation of federal obscenity statutes. It should also amend the obscenity laws to eliminate the need to prove transporation in interstate commerce. In addition, any form of indecent act by or among "adults only" pornographic outlet patrons should be unlawful.

Meese supervised the establishment of a special team of prosecutors to handle pornography cases as part of an "all-out campaign against the distribution of obscene material." He also promised to recommend changes in the federal law to limit sexually explicit material provided on cable television and through pornographic telephone services. Federal officials resisted the ballyhoo, stressing that the team would be small and that campaigns against espionage and illegal drugs took far greater priority. The main use of the prosecutors would be to train up expert witnesses who could be dispatched across the United States to help any local anti-pornography prosecution.

Attwood, William SEE book burning in England 7. United Kingdom (1688-1775).

Austin v. *Kentucky* SEE *Redrup* v. *New York* (1967).

Australia

1. film censorship All film censorship in Australia is controlled by the Commonwealth Film Censorship Board, established in 1917. The various states have delegated their responsibilities in this area to the board under a series of acts passed between 1947 and 1949. The basis of all Australian censorship is the right of adults to enjoy such entertainment as they desire. Under the principle of protecting the young the following classification system has been established:

G: for general exhibition. "Family entertainment" films suitable for all ages, which specifically contain no scenes that could perturb the youngest viewer or his or her parents.

NRC: not recommended for children under 12. Films in which the content is slightly harder than those classified G. There may be some above-the-neck sex scenes, some violence and some strong language, although the overriding message will still be moral

M: mature audiences, 15 years and over (advisory only). Films that deal with essentially adult concepts but are slightly more restrained than those falling into the R classification. There may be open sexuality, unrestrained language and a good deal of violence but all such content is still relatively inexplicit.

R: restricted. This classification, the only one governed by law, prohibits the exhibition of such films to anyone between the ages of 2 and 18. These films deal with adult themes in an overt and explicit way. R-rated films may be considered harmful to minors and may cause offense to some sections of the community. They number some 21 percent of all films exhibited in Australia.

Films may be refused a license on grounds that:

(1) they are indecent, obscene or blasphemous;
(2) they are injurious to morality, condone or incite to crime;
(3) they are offensive to an ally or to the people of a part of the queen's dominions;
(4) they are undesirable in the public interest.

Some 2.5 percent of films examined are banned absolutely, usually on the grounds of pornographic or obscenely violent content. Films that glorify drug abuse are similarly rejected. The censor may also vet the advertising prepared for a given film.

While the states generally accept the board as final arbiter, conservative Queensland has established certain extra regulations. A five-member Films Review Board, established under the Films Review Act (1974), reexamines any film against which a complaint has been made. It bans any "objectionable" films, working on the basis that such a film is either of an indecent nature or suggests indecency or portrays, describes or suggests acts or situations of a violent, horrifying, criminal or immoral nature. The effect of this double-check is to bar many films that have satisfied the Commonwealth Board; a large proportion, therefore, of R-rated films are never distributed in Queensland.

2. Freedom of Information Act (1982)   Australia enacted its Freedom of Information Act in December 1982; its aim was to create a public right of access to documents, to amend or update incorrect government records and to appeal against administrative decisions that attempted to curtail such freedom of access, and to ensure that it was no longer necessary to establish any special interest before being given access to documents. Progress toward the act began in January 1973, when the attorney-general began assessing the U.S. Freedom of Information Act. A committee was established to modify the American model for Australian use. The main provisos suggested by the committee were the maintenance of cabinet and ministerial confidentiality and of the authority of ministers for their own governmental departments. A second committee, set up in 1976, then assessed other freedom of information legislation that existed around the world, notably the Scandinavian systems, as well as those in Canada and Holland. The Freedom of Information Bill was proposed in 1978, put through a senate standing committee for further fine-tuning and finally passed into law in February 1982.

Under the act all Australian citizens and persons entitled to permanent resident status are entitled to information held in government offices in Australia, although not to government offices overseas. Government departments and authorities are required to publish information about their powers and their operations as well as make available manuals and other documents used in making decisions or recommendations that affect that public. The authorities must provide access to all documents unless they fall into an exempted category (see below). If a document to which the individual has gained access is found to be inaccurate or incomplete, that individual has the right to alter it. No one need establish any special interest before gaining access to such documents that are available. The act covers most government departments but wholly exempts Parliament and its departments.

A number of areas are exempted from access, rendering the act far less sweeping than it might otherwise be. These include documents affecting national security and defense, dealing with international relations and relations between the government and individual Australian states; cabinet and executive council documents; internal working documents; documents dealing with law enforcement and the maintenance of public safety; documents covered by any form of security legislation; documents covering Commonwealth financial or property interests; documents covering the operations of certain agencies (notably those dealing with security, the economy, industrial relations, farming as regards its competitive commercial activities, banking, health and national pension funds); documents covering personal privacy; legal proceedings and documents subject to legal privilege; documents relating to business affairs; documents relating to the national economy; documents containing material disclosed in confidence; documents that if disclosed would breach parliamentary privilege; documents arising from companies and securities legislation.

In addition to these broad zones of exclusion, the act, on the basis that time, money and staffing would preclude earlier investigations, does not apply to any material that existed prior to December 1, 1982. Agencies are not obliged to make available material that is not already in documentary form, although they must produce printouts of electronically stored computer records or transcripts of sound recordings. Those seeking access are not allowed to make fishing expeditions through the files but must make a reasonable identification of the document in question. The government has no obligation to help the searcher in any way. The government is obliged to inform applicants as to whether they may see a document within 60 days after the application is received. If only a part of a document is considered exempt, that is sufficient to exempt the whole document, although an excised copy may be provided.

If an agency or minister refuses to reveal a document the reason for this refusal must be produced in writing. Individuals who wish to appeal may approach either the ombudsman or the Administrative Appeals Tribunal (AAT). This latter deals with refusals made by a minister of the principal officer of an agency. The AAT may refer an applicant to the Document Review Tribunal (DRT) in the case of documents that have been exempted on the grounds of national security, defense, international relations or relations with states, cabinet and executive council documents, and internal working documents. The minister retains the final decision, even though the DRT may recommend access.

Third parties, about whose personal, business or other activities there is information in a document that has been requested, must be consulted about the proposed access and may apply to the AAT, when access has otherwise been granted, to reverse that decision.

SEE ALSO Canada 1. Access to Information Act (1982); Denmark 2. Law on Publicity in Administration (1970); Finland 2. Freedom of the Press Act (1919); France 6. freedom of information; Netherlands 3. freedom of information; Sweden 3. Freedom of the Press Act.

3. obscenity laws Responsibility for the control of obscene material is divided between the Commonwealth and state governments; the former deals with the importation of material while the latter variously control the publication, advertising and display of all printed material within their borders.

Commonwealth: Under regulation 4(A) of the Customs (Prohibited Imports) Regulations no goods that are either blasphemous, indecent or obscene or that unduly emphasize matters of sex, horror, violence or crime may be imported. Administration of the regulations is shared between the attorney-general and the Bureau of Customs. The former deals with general policy and the examination of seized material; the latter undertakes the practical work of inspection and detention, seizure and destruction of obscene material. The basis of the national censorship is the prohibiting of "verbal or pictorial publications devoted overwhelmingly to the explicit depiction of sexual activities in gross detail, with neither acceptable supporting purpose or theme, nor redeeming features of literary or artistic merit."

New South Wales: The state laws cover various offenses dealing with "indecent articles" ("indecent" is not defined). Items prosecuted for indecency may offer a defense of artistic or literary merit and call on expert witnesses to prove this. Under the premise agreed by both major political parties in the state, no adult should be denied the right to see and read whatever form of literature he or she desires; concurrently no one need have anything he or she considers distasteful thrust upon them and young people must be protected. Under the Indecent Articles and Classified Publications Act (1975) the minister may classify all publications into four categories: unrestricted; restricted; direct sale; child pornography. Restricted and direct sale publications are limited to over-18 purchasers and must be marked clearly with the relevant notice "R" or "Direct Sale" and plastic-wrapped unless sold in a shop, usually a sex shop, or part of a shop dedicated to such sales and advertising itself and clearly designating itself as such. Child pornography is wholly illegal. There is no theatrical censorship, although the option, very rarely exercised, exists to regulate the stage on the grounds of decorum or good manners.

Queensland: The test for obscenity remains that established in 1868 under the HICKLIN RULE, and the overall attitude to printed obscenity is conservative. Obscenity is defined, other than in Hicklin, as emphasizing matters of sex or crime and calculated to encourage depravity. Under the Objectionable Literature Acts (1954-67), a literature board of review was established. This acts as a state censor, reviewing all literature and banning the distribution of anything it classifies as objectionable. Such items have included a variety of men's magazines, the *Kama Sutra*, *The Perfumed Garden*, *Health and Efficiency*, and INSIDE LINDA LOVELACE. Medical and legal works are exempt, as are works claiming geniune artistic or literary merit, as do the recognized stories of myth, legend, the Bible and of history. A first offense is fined $500 (Australian); subsequent offenses up to $1,000.

Tasmania: All obscene material is dealt with by the Restricted Publications Acts (1974 and 1977). These prohibit completely all child pornography and bestiality, and deal with less extreme material under the Restricted Publications Board. This five-member panel shares the New South Wales attitude that adults must have freedom to read but that the young must be protected and no one coerced into experiencing what he or she dislikes. Thus the board reviews questionable material. Classifying it, when necessary, as restricted and either prohibiting its distribution absolutely or subjecting it to various restrictions as to advertisement, display etc.

Victoria: The state laws deal with obscene material under the Police Offences Act (1958) and the Police Offences (Child Pornography) Act (1977). The legal test for obscenity governs material that is both a variation of Hicklin ("to deprave and corrupt persons whose minds are open to immoral influences") and that unduly emphasizes sex, horror, violence, gross cruelty or crime. Legitimate defenses for articles prosecuted under the acts are their artistic, literary, scientific or technical merit or, if the charge refers to the manufacture of an obscene article, that it was made for personal use only. There exists a five-member State Advisory Board for Publications. This reports on any material against which complaints have been made and judges whether such material is unsuitable, through its references to "sex, drug addiction, crimes of violence, gross cruelty or horror, or … disgusting or indecent language or illustration" for those under 18. The minister, on the basis of this advice, can mark certain items as restricted for sale to adults only; such a restriction also indemnifies the retailer against any future charges of selling obscene material.

Western Australia: The state laws deal with obscene material under the Indecent Publications and Articles Acts (1902-74). The legal test depends on whether an article is "indecent or obscene," but this fails to define either term other than making automatically obscene all material relating to any illegal operation or medical treatment. A defense of artistic, literary or scientific merit is allowed, but the onus is on the defense to prove such merit. Under the current act a State Advisory Committee on Publications has been set up. The seven-person committee, of which one member must be a woman, one a recognized literary, artistic or scientific expert and one a solicitor, meets three times a month to report on any pertinent publication to the minister. On the basis of their recommendation the minister may restrict a publication to those over 18. If the committee recommends prosecution, which it will when dealing with child pornography, bestiality, sadistic or incestuous material and any explicit illustrations, this decision is not intended in any way to prejudice the outcome of the subsequent trial.

Austria: Federal Ministries Act (amendment, 1973)
Under the amendment to the Federal Ministries Act, passed in 1973, the Austrian government made uncumbent upon its constituent ministries a duty to inform the public of such administrative documents that they generate. Although this in theory supports the principles of open government propounded at the Council of Europe colloquy held in September 1976, critics argue that the amendment has created more of an unfulfilled promise to the people than a realistic threat to the authorities. Civil servants retain their overriding duty of keeping government affairs secret when such secrecy is considered "in the interests of the administrative authority." All inquiries must cite a specific document and no information will be released until the ministry concerned has assessed its importance. As in the Dutch system (q.v.), even when it agrees to disclosure, the government is not bound to show a document, merely to detail its contents. If a search among the files is seen as too time-consuming or labor-intensive, the request may be rejected. Frustrated inquirers may appeal to the administrative courts.

Austria passed in 1978 a Data Protection Act that is in the vanguard of parallel European legislation. It covers individuals and companies, extends to government and private data banks and deals with both manually compiled and computer-generated files (although the emphasis is on the latter). Everyone included in a data bank has the right to see his or her own file on request. The legislation is monitored by a Data Protection Council.

average person   For the purpose of the American legal definitions of obscenity contained in the cases of ROTH V. UNITED STATES (1957), MILLER V. CALIFORNIA (1973) and *Memoirs* v. *Massachusetts* (see MEMOIRS OF A WOMAN OF PLEASURE), and those cases derived from them, an "average person" is an average adult person who is applying contemporary community standards in his or her consideration of the alleged "obscenity" in question. Unlike the HICKLIN RULE (1868), this legal "person" does not embrace those of an especially sensitive or susceptible nature, but this definition can include specific groups, such as minors or homosexuals, assuming that they represent the target group at which the material is deliberately aimed.

aversion   The concept that pornography may not only titillate but also repel and disgust is the basis of the "aversion defense," which has sometimes been offered in trials of allegedly obscene books or films. Defendants have attempted to show that the material in question is so vile and disgusting that rather than excite the AVERAGE PERSON, whose tastes are at the heart of most tests for obscenity, it is far more likely to repel him or her from such material. Some individuals may still be titillated, but these cannot be considered "average" and thus fall outside the test. The aversion defense concentrates on the context and purpose of the publication. It stresses the opposite point of view from that of the traditional prosecutor of obscene material, who generally suggests that any exposure to such material would ensnare the reader or viewer in the same corrupt pleasures. If a book or film points out that while such practices do exist, they are by no means wholly pleasurable, and in fact may be quite the opposite, the defense will stress the aversive side of the book or film. Among the trials in which the aversion defense was used were those of LAST EXIT TO BROOKLYN, and OZ.

Avery, Edward   Edward Avery was one of the main publishers and sellers of pornography in late-Victorian London; he managed from 1879 for 25 years to combine a relatively legitimate trade as a remainder publisher (reissuing, under his own imprint, books that had failed for other publishers) with a substantial business in pornography, both domestic and imported from France and Belgium. Avery ran both businesses from the same address in Greek Street, Soho, London, using the remainders as a convenient front for the erotica. In October 1900, after a plainclothes policeman, acting as a customer, bought a volume of "a grossly obscene nature" from the shop, Avery's twin businesses were raided. Vast stocks of pornography, text, drawings and photographs were unearthed and confiscated. Avery was able to hire in his defense Horace Avory, who had prosecuted Oscar Wilde and defended HAVELOCK ELLIS; and thanks to his advocacy, which was based on the fact that in 25 years of illicit business, this was the only time his client had been caught, the bookseller was sentenced to a mere six months in jail. After his release Avery vanished forever.

While Avery's stock had contained both printed books and unbound sheets, as well as the visual material, only one volume has been firmly attributed to him as a publisher rather than as a vendor. This is a collection of material devoted to flagellation, entitled *The Whippingham Papers*, which appeared in 1887. It was priced at two and a half guineas (£2.62) and limited to 250 copies. Its author was allegedly one St. George H. Stock, who had previously concocted *The Romance of Chastisement*. The fame of *The Whippingham Papers* rests on its inclusion of a poem in unashamed celebration of the whipping of schoolboys, written by the poet A.C. Swinburne (1837-1909) and first published in the pornographic periodical, *The Pearl*. It is possible that Avery also published a series called "The Rochester Reprints," which specialized in such 18th-century works as CLELAND's *Memoirs of a Coxcomb* and other "galante" rather than overtly pornographic material.
SEE ALSO Carrington, Charles; Dugdale, William; Hotten, John Camden.

B

Babeuf, Francois Noel Babeuf (1760-1797), known popularly as "Gracchus," the Roman tribune of the people after whom he named his own newspaper *Le Tribun du Peuple*, was the father of modern revolutionary socialism. A precursor of Proudhon, Babeuf challenged first Robespierre and his fellow Terrorists and then the Directory in his paper, originally called *Journal de la Liberte* and from 1794, *Le Tribun*. In 1795 Babeuf began attacking the government of the Directory, which had emerged after the fall of Robespierre and, in its Constitution of the Directory, published in late 1795, sanctified the rule of the new elite, "les nouveaux riches." Babeuf was a member of the Society of the Pantheon, a body composed of many former Jacobins, still dedicated to the ideal of genuine equality. The *Tribun* served as the movement's public voice. Issue 33 was burnt in the Theatre des Bergeres by the anti-Jacobins in 1795. In February 1796 the Society seemed sufficiently threatening to the authorities for them to send General Napoleon Buonaparte to shut down its meeting place and dissolve the membership. Babeuf and fellow extremist Sylvain Marechal countered by forming the six-man Secret Directory and planning a full-scale insurrection based on the slogan "Nature has given to every man the right to the enjoyment of an equal share in all property"—a concept he coined in issue 40 of the *Tribun*. Babeuf's intent was the revival of the Jacobin Constitution of 1793 and the proclamation of a Republic of Equals. The Secret Directory sent agents to infiltrate the army, police and bureaucracy; meanwhile, preparations were put under way for the new revolution. However, the Babeuf Plot came to nothing. The army and police remained loyal; the revolt's leaders were arrested before they could launch their plans and the mob failed to rise. Babeuf was tried in 1797 in a three-month spectacle that served as a platform for his attack on the regime. Such pure socialism was too much even for the French Revolution and Babeuf was condemned to the guillotine. He attempted to stab himself to death but was saved for a judicial demise. His colleague Phillippe Buonarroti, who escaped prosecution, immortalized Babeuf in his book *Conspiration pour l'egalite dite de Babeuf* and consecrated Babeuf as one of the great republican martyrs of the 19th century, inspiring a number of European socialist revolutionaries.

Baby Doll Playwright Tennessee Williams adapted this film from two of his plays, *27 Wagons Full of Cotton* and *An Unsatisfying Supper*; it was filmed for Warner Brothers by Elia Kazan in 1956 and starred Carroll Baker, Karl Malden and Eli Wallach. The plot deals with the frustrations of one Archie Lee, a bigoted, impoverished specimen of "poor white trash," whose life is tortured both by his inability to outwit various business rivals and by a promise that he once made to Baby Doll's father whereby he would not touch his 19-year-old bride, who is fully developed physically but still sleeps in a crib and sucks her thumb, until she was "ready." The film received a certificate from the MOTION PICTURE ASSOCIATION OF AMERICA but was given a C (condemned) rating by the LEGION OF DECENCY, which in 1951 had forced cuts in Kazan's adaptation of Williams' A STREETCAR NAMED DESIRE.

The Legion's attack on *Baby Doll* cited its plot as "morally repellent both in theme and treatment" and claimed that the action concentrated "almost without variation or relief upon carnal suggestiveness in action, dialogue, and costuming. As such it is grievously offensive to Christian and traditional standards of morality and decency." Kazan, who had the right of final cut, fought back, rejecting the Legion's claims and stating that he "wasn't trying to be moral or immoral, only truthful." He suggested that the Legion should restrain its interference and allow Americans to judge this and any other picture for themselves. His defense was not helped by the critics: The *New York Times* shrank from the film's "foreignness," while *Time* called it "the dirtiest American-made motion picture that has ever been legally exhibited." Former ambassador and political patriarch Joseph Kennedy banned it from his chain of New England cinemas, and Cardinal Spellman, while studiously avoiding seeing the film himself, sermonized in St. Patrick's Cathedral for the first time in eight years to condemn a film that was "an indictment of those who defy God's law, and contribute to corruption in America." This smear on Kazan's patriotism was duly noted by many cinemagoers. Of the leading clergy only Bishop James A. Pike was willing to defend the film, condemning Spellman's outburst as the "efforts of a minority group to impose its wishes on the city."

Outside New York the film gained only mixed reviews, although all this publicity ensured reasonable business, even though 16,000 of America's 20,000 theaters refused to screen it. It met legal censorship only in Aurora, Illinois, where the city was persuaded by a mass meeting of its citizens to bring out an injunction against the film, because of a scene they saw as "scandalous, indecent, immoral, lewd and obscene." The lower court duly granted the injunction and this ruling was sustained on appeal, although the court also accepted that the film was still entitled to constitutional protection since it was not wholly obscene in the constitutional sense.

Bacon, Roger Bacon (ca. 1214-ca. 1292), otherwise known as "Doctor Mirabilis" was the author of three philosophical works, the *Opus Maius*, *Opus Minus* and *Opus Tertium*, all written between 1265 and 1268 at the request of his friend Pope Clement IV and generally accepted as the foundation of English philosophy. Bacon, who studied at Oxford and Paris, was a Franciscan, but his philosophy, as well as his treatises on grammar, logic, mathematics and physics, brought him into conflict with his order and in 1257 his Oxford lectures were placed under the interdict (anyone attending them faced excommunication), and he was sent to Paris to undergo surveillance. Here he was imprisoned for ten years, accused of propounding heresy and forbidden to write for publication.

Despite this ban he managed to write his three major works during this period. In 1278, after Clement, his protector, had died, Bacon fell prey to ecclesiastical persecution again. This immensely learned man, who invented spectacles and worked out a design for a telescope, was an essentially conservative theologian, but his interest in science, and his belief that religious error could best be cured by knowledge rather than blind belief, brought him into conflict with the church. Accused of practicing the black arts, and characterized by the ignorant as a necromancer, he saw his books condemned by Jerome de Ascoli, general of the Franciscans (subsequently Pope Nicholas IV), and Bacon himself was imprisoned for a further 14 years. He died in jail and was supposedly buried in Oxford.

Bastwick, John   Dr. John Bastwick (1593-1654) whose honorific was, according to one of his judges, "unknown to either University or the College of Physicians"—was one of the most consistent scourges of the established church in the era leading to the English Civil War. His first trial followed the seizure of his books *Elenchus Papisticae Relionis* (1627) and *Flagellum Pontificis* (1635) by the Court of High Commission in 1635. His outspoken condemnation of episcopal venality infuriated Archbishop Laud and his fellow senior clerics. Both books were burnt and Bastwick was fined £1,000, excommunicated and ordered to be imprisoned in the Gatehouse until he recanted, which event would not be, as Bastwick declared, "till Doomsday, in the afternoon." While thus imprisoned he wrote "The Letany" and the "Apologeticus ad Praesules Anglicanos"; the first attacked the High Commission and the second the bishops, the Prayer Book and the doctrine of the Real Presence. Bastwick's attacks were splendidly coarse and almost ridiculous, and he attacked the bishops as "the very polecats, stoats, weasels and minivers in the warren of Church and State" and as "Anti-Christ's little toes." On a more serious note he attacked the excessive privileges and powers accorded to all senior clergy. He was condemned, along with WILLIAM PRYNNE and Henry Burton in 1637, to mutilation, the pillory, a fine and imprisonment for life. He was not freed until the advent of the Long Parliament in 1640.

Bauhaus, The   The Bauhaus, founded by Walter Gropius and generally recognized as the most influential design school of modern times was provisionally shut down by the Nazis as a "breeding place of cultural Bolshevism" after a raid by the Gestapo on April 11, 1933. A number of students were arrested, but the leading architects who had worked at the school had already fled. The exiles, part of the cultural exodus that paralleled the Nazis' increasing domination of Germany, included Gropius, Ludwig Mies van der Rohe, Herbert Bayer, Laszlo Moholy-Nagy, Paul Klee, Marcel Breuer and Lyonel Feininger. The school had already been forced to quit its home in Dessau in October 1932, when the authorities closed it down. In August 1933 the Bauhaus was officially closed for good. The Nazis loathed its architectural style, pronouncing that its architecture was fit only for factory buildings, and that flat roofs (one of the hallmarks of Bauhaus design) were oriental, and oriental was a synonym for Jewish. Purges of architects continued on a wider scale throughout Germany and only those who adhered to the grandiose neo-classical styles epitomized in the designs of Albert Speer were permitted to practice or to teach.

SEE ALSO Germany 3. Nazi art censorship

bawdy courts   These courts were established in England shortly after the Norman Conquest and lasted until the 17th century. Administered by the church they were responsible for the regulation of heresy and similar deviations from true religion up to and including misbehavior during divine service, as well as for a variety of fleshly excesses, including fornication, bastardy, adultery, incest, homosexuality, brothel-keeping and, on occasion, white slavery. The bawdy courts dealt largely in lower-class vices; the peccadilloes of the powerful were presumed to be inviolate. They were similarly limited by commercial desires (the development of the legalized brothels or stews was tolerated on the church's own land in Southwark) and by social realities (the pregnant bride, while technically guilty of fornication, was an accepted figure in contemporary society). Despite these restrictions, the courts were sufficiently powerful to control a good deal of venial sin. All defendants were forced to pay costs and their court appearances were made in a white sheet, the symbol of contrition. They could be sentenced to humiliating public penances. Operated under the ex officio oath, defendants were made to testify against themselves; to refuse would be to lay oneself open to charges of perjury. The courts lasted until the Puritan Revolution when they were abolished and moral authority was turned over to the secular courts. They were reinstated by Charles II, but the ex officio oath was abandoned. They declined quickly thereafter and a new style of moral arbiter, typified by the self-appointed moral vigilantes of the SOCIETIES FOR THE REFORMATION OF MANNERS, fulfilled much the same function.

BBC

1. balance The BBC, while avowedly opposed to any form of censorship, has always stressed in its news and current affairs coverage the concept of balance. While both left- and right-wing critics of the corporation claim that this means no more than a formula for ensuring that no opinion, however, valid, can be broadcast without an automatic right of reply being built into the program, spokesmen for the BBC see it differently. The best definition of the concept was provided in a lecture given in 1968 by Sir Huw Wheldon, whose idea of program control was equated with that of the editing of a large newspaper—not censorship per se but editorial decision that took into account the nature both of the paper and of its readers:

> The BBC cannot accept dismissal by artists and writers and men and women of sensibility as a purveyor of pap … A middle ground is inhabited. The concept of the "middle ground" leads on to the concept of "balance," which is central to the Corporation's control of its subject matter. The word "balance" in connection with the BBC … [is] an idea deeply embedded in the practices of the Corporation; it has to do with truth and coverage … It has to do with an effort, in all kinds of programs, to go further than two sides, an intelligent effort to make sense of all the facts, however difficult and not just some of them. "Balance" does not preclude attacks and passion and lampoons and deep conviction in given programs. But it precludes a "BBC line" as a whole … The BBC cannot be in a position where it could be described consistently and widely in terms of a particular "line." "Balance" also precludes pornography and propaganda in any programme … "Balance," or truth, also assumes and must assume that the state of public opinion is not at one or unchanging.

SEE ALSO BBC 2. broadcasting censorship.

2. broadcasting censorship Immediate control of BBC programming is in the hands of the producers who are responsible to the director-general and thus to the governors, but the director-general takes very few programming decisions compared to the men and women on the spot. Producers are guided by a number of codes, such as "Guidance Note on the Portrayal of Violence" (1979), "Tastes and Standards in the BBC" (1973), "Principles and Practices in News and Current Affairs Programs," and "Principles and Practices in Documentary Programs." In light entertainment and allied areas there are lists of taboo topics, notably the royal family and the church. All such codes are subject to widely-varying interpretation, but they have embraced on the one hand the banning from "Women's Hour" of an astrology feature, and on the other of major plays by Dennis Potter and Ian Mac-Ewan, even though such plays had been commissioned by the BBC itself. It is not unknown for controversial lines to be rewritten, without their author's knowledge.

Radio and television were specifically excluded from the OBSCENE PUBLICATIONS ACT (1959), although attempts are now underway to amend this situation and the government White Paper on television (published November 1988) promised to extend the act to TV. Broadcasters are still liable for criminal prosecution on charges of CONSPIRACY TO CORRUPT PUBLIC MORALS or CONSPIRACY TO OUTRAGE PUBLIC DECENCY. Unlike the IBA, the BBC charter contains no statutory requirements as to taste, but ever since Lord Reith, whose own moral standards ensured that he eschewed the employment of divorcees, let alone the discussion on air of divorce, the BBC has been acutely aware of its role as the purveyor of the national culture. In 1964 the then-chairman stated that "the Board [of Governors] accept that, so far as possible, the programs for which they are responsible should not offend against good taste or decency, or by likely to encourage crime or disorder, or be offensive to public feeling." He added that while programs should stimulate thought, they should not give general offense. If in doubt the BBC rule is always "reference up": the passing of controversial decisions up through the corporation's multi-layered hierarchy until a sufficiently senior figure gives or withholds a final imprimatur.

Under the royal charter by which the British Broadcasting Corporation is incorporated, the home secretary has the ultimate power of licensing the BBC. Given this power the minister can call for the publication of various programs, and under section 13(4) of the charter may force the BBC to refrain from broadcasting any material that the Home Office sees fit to proscribe. In turn the BBC may, if it wishes, tell the public that it has been censored by a section 13 order. Section 19 of the charter, promoted during the general strike of 1926 by Winston Churchill, who wished to use the corporation as a propaganda outlet, allows the home secretary to send in the troops "to take possession of the BBC in the name and on behalf of Her Majesty." Its programs must not offend against good taste or public decency, nor should they encourage crime or public disorder or be offensive to public feeling. If the BBC deliberately ignores a ministerial diktat, the home secretary has the power to revoke its license and even to abolish, with parliamentary approval, the royal charter.

Under its concept of balance it accepts an obligation to treat all topics impartially. The BBC may not broadcast its own opinion on current affairs and public policy, nor may it broadcast matters of political, industrial or religious controversy. Such a restriction obviously carries with it a good deal of built-in difficulty and allows for a variety of interpretations of what may or may not be seen as controversy. As any observer of BBC-Government relations will be aware, the two bodies are rarely in complete agreement.

It is in the area of parliamentary and political affairs that the censorship bites most obviously. A succession of directors-general have agreed to remove from the schedules topics that were seen as too sensitive for broadcasting. These have included the views of such extremist organizations as the IRA, the portrayal of the police in an unfavorable light, attacks on the government itself, and, against the background of the government's campaign against ex-MI5 officer Peter

Wright's memoirs, *Spycatcher*, any material deemed dangerous to national security. The BBC's refusal during the Falklands War of 1982 to restrict its broadcasting to government-approved coverage particularly enraged Tory backbenchers, and their media committee called in Director-General Alistair Milne for a lengthy and hostile dressing-down.

SEE ALSO Broadcasting Complaints Commission; Broadcasting Standards Council; IBA: broadcasting censorship.

3. The Green Book   Prior to the so-called swinging Sixties, the BBC, created by its first director-general Lord Reith as Britain's austere guardian of the national culture, was particularly careful of preserving the standards of the light entertainment content of television programming. To this end there was issued to all writers, producers and directors of the corporation's comedy, variety and other light entertainment shows, the "Variety Program and Policy Guide for Writers and Producers." Packaged in green covers it was known as the Green Book and was not withdrawn until 1963, when a very different style of humor arrived at the BBC. The Green Book read, in part, "Programs must at all cost be kept free of crudities. There can be no compromise with doubtful material. It must be cut. There is an absolute ban upon the following: jokes about lavatories, effeminacy in men, immorality of any kind, suggestive references to honeymooning couples, chambermaids, fig leaves, ladies' underwear (e.g., 'winter draws on'), animal habits (e.g., rabbits), lodgers, commercial travellers. When in doubt—cut it out." There were also to be no mention whatsoever of drink or religion, the royal family was sacrosanct and while comedians might "take a crack at the government," this must only be "without undue acidity." The term working class was not to be used as a pejorative and there was to be no personal abuse of politicians.

Beardsley, Aubrey   There was in the 1960s a brief but widespread revival of interest in the works of Beardsley (1872-98), a black-and-white illustrator of the 1890s, who had died young, beseeching his hearers to destroy his "obscene" works. On January 30, 1967, the firm of Jepson's Stores Ltd. was charged in an Edinburgh court with selling and keeping indecent prints in a shop: to wit, the exhibiting for sale of a number of Beardsley prints in their shop The Bodkin, at North Bridge, Edinburgh, during the previous August. Eschewing the OBSCENE PUBLICATIONS ACT (1959), the prosecutuion brought charges under an Edinburgh Corporation bylaw of 1961, which prohibited the display for sale of indecent or obscene books or pictures. Although the prints in question were on display in London's Victoria & Albert Museum, and the catalog, in which one of the offending prints was pictured, was on sale widely throughout England and Scotland, including over the counter of Her Majesty's Stationery Office, the magistrate, Mrs. Margaret Ross, stated that she had "no doubt at all" that the Beardsley works were indecent; she fined Jepson's £20 and confiscated the prints.

On May 5, 1967, an appeal against this conviction failed to impress the Judiciary Appeal Court in Edinburgh and the verdict was upheld.

Beaumarchais, Piere-Augustin Caron de   Beaumarchais (1732-99) was the author of two comedies of manners, *The Barber of Seville* (1775) and *The Marriage of Figaro* (1784). The tone of both was sufficiently mischievous to antagonize the authorities. Beaumarchais' *Memoirs* had already been burnt in France in 1774 for its criticisms of the state government, containing "scandalous charges against the magistracy and the members of the Parliament"; now *The Barber of Seville* was banned from the stage, between 1775 and 1777, and in 1781 *The Marriage of Figaro* was suppressed by Louis XVI both at Court and on the public stage on the grounds of profound immorality. Beaumarchais was imprisoned at St. Lazaire in 1781, then charged with treason the same year and had all his works suppressed. By the 19th century, after the two plays had inspired works by Mozart (1786) and Rossini (1816), Beaumarchais' reputation had been reprieved.

Becker, Regnier   A French journeyman carpenter of Meru (Oise), Becker augmented his craftsman's income by selling a variety of obscene prints, engravings and lithographs. Between 1839 and 1842 Becker's wares were seized and destroyed by the authorities and on August 9, 1842, he was imprisoned for six months and fined 200 francs for outraging public morals and decency. Among the engravings, albums and drawings available from Becker and judged obscene were *Album heretique*, *Les Apprets du Bel*, *Le Don du Mouchoir*, *Le Coup de vent*, *La Rosee*, *Les Moeurs de Paris* and many more.

Behind the Green Door   *Behind the Green Door*, made by Art and James Mitchell in 1973, was one of the first efforts to capitalize on the success of DEEP THROAT and keep rolling the lucrative bandwagon of what was known as the art porn boom. It was allegedly adapted from an anonymously penned pornographic story, featuring a beautiful young woman who is kidnapped and turned into the bemused but increasingly enthusiastic star performer of a private sex club. The film featured Marilyn Chambers, whose almost innocent beauty belied her on-screen sexual voracity and was, in effect, the record of a protracted and inventive orgy. When the film was exhibited at a new cinema in Suffolk County, New York, the authorities charged the owner with violation of section 1141 of the state's penal laws, which prohibited the exhibition of any film that "appeals to prurient interest in sex, goes substantially beyond the customary limits of candor, and has utterly no redeeming social value." The film was also prosecuted in New York City, where the city's district attorney and corporation counsel sought to have it banned from exhibition in certain theaters.

Both attempts at censorship were successful. The Suffolk County judge resisted the offer to see the film in the owner's "modern non-sleazy theater," which had recently exhibited *The Sound of Music*; he also rejected the testimony of a string of expert witnesses, all of whom testified to the film's excellence. The theater owner was duly found guilty and the film banned. The New York City prosecution, which included another allegedly obscene film, *The Newcomers*, was similarly effected and *Beyond the Green Door*, which was described as involving "multiple and variegated ultimate acts of sexual perversion [which] would have been regarded as obscene by the community standards of Sodom and Gomorrah," was banned. The film has also been banned in Texas, Colorado, Georgia and California.

Belgium

1. film censorship Reverse censorship operates in Belgium under a law of September 1, 1920, whereby no one under the age of 16 is permitted to enter a cinema. This prohibition is modified by the pronouncements of a Royal Commission, which can authorize certain films as being suitable for families and children. This five-member commission is appointed by the minister of justice and has nominees from the film industry and from the Tribunal of Youth. An Appeals Commission exists to hear appeals against the Royal Commission's decisions. Films can be cut or even prohibited on the grounds of violence and cruelty or, even if not actually pornographic, when they are considered likely to stimulate in children those senses that it is felt should still remain dormant. Individual scenes will also be cut if they trouble children's imagination or endanger their equilibrium or moral health. Since 1951 the Ministry of Justice has recommended that films (or scenes in them) that are derisive of family life or the social status quo, uphold free love or adultery and attack marriage and family life should be banned from general audiences.

2. obscenity laws While the Belgian constitution guarantees freedom of expression and prohibits state censorship, certain laws pertaining to morality, and as such included in those designed to preserve public order, do exist. Legislation governing obscene material is conditioned by a variety of undefined phrases: "contraire aux bonnes moeurs" (immoral), "qui blessent la pudeur" (which offend modesty) and "de nature a troubler leur imaginations" (as regards to children: of a nature that causes them to worry). There is no specific definition of any of these, and thus the administration of the law varies with the state of current opinion. The main offense, prohibiting the writing, advertising, importing, distributing etc. of "immoral publications," is covered by Article 383 of the Penal Code. If the offense is by the press, then the author of the piece or, failing him or her, the publisher, then printer, then distributor become liable. If the offense is not journalistic, then anyone dealing in the material becomes liable. Article 385 creates the offense of publicly outraging morality by immodest actions. Children are specifically protected, with higher penalties for those who sell obscene material to a child or who commit a public outrage to morality

in the child's presence. Material dealing with violence is not restricted, unless it incites the reader or viewer to crime. There is no exemption in law on the grounds of literary, artistic or scientific merit, but such exemptions are tacitly assumed by the legislature. Penalties exist on various scales, with the heaviest punishments, up to and including the closing down of a shop that sells obscene materials to minors, reserved for those who involve the young. A list of publications, which may not be imported or which have been banned internally, is issued annually. Prohibited material, unless it is in small quantities imported by foreigners for personal use, is seized by the Customs; a detailed report is sent to the crown prosecutor. Further action depends on his or her advice.

Bellamy, John   SEE *The Bible*.

Benbow, William   Benbow, an artist and illustrator, had the dubious honor of being the object of attack by two of England's earliest anti-obscenity groups, the CONSTITUTIONAL ASSOCIATION and the SOCIETY FOR THE SUPPRESSION OF VICE. In 1820 the association's case against two Benbow cartoons—"The Brightest Star in the State, or, a Peep Out of a Royal Window" and "The Royal Cock and Chickens, or, the Father of His People"—both of which were deemed unacceptable attacks on George IV, was thrown out when the jury refused to convict on the pressure group's evidence. In June 1822 a prosecution for obscene libel was brought by the society, which claimed that Benbow had published two obscene pictures—"Mars, Venus and Vulcan" and "Leda"—which had been used as frontispieces in the January and February issues of *The Rambler's Magazine*, a popular publication of soft-core pornography. Again, Benbow was acquitted.

Bentley, Elizabeth   SEE House Committee on Un-American Activities (HUAC).

Besant, Annie   SEE *Fruits of Philosophy, The*

Best, Paul   SEE book burning in England 1. Puritans.

The Bible   Subsequent to the publication of the King James authorized version of the Bible in 1611, there have been a number of attempts to bowdlerize the scriptures. In 1782 Mrs. Sarah Kirby Trimmer published the first edition of her *Sacred History*. Aimed at children between seven and 14 it appeared in six full-length volumes. The history derived from a bundle of manuscripts created to introduce her own 12 children to the more innocent parts of the Bible. Around half of the original text had been cut and the rest rearranged to give a generally rosier view of Biblical events than the actual Scriptures do. All references to sex are absent. The Bible's language is sometimes replaced by the editor's own expositions, aimed directly at the young. Certain chapters are simply dropped and replaced by Mrs. Trimmer's own paraphrases.

A brief commentary for 8- to 10-year-olds is inserted after each portion of scripture.

When the *Sacred History* proved popular with adults Mrs. Trimmer began revising it upwards to meet their needs. The expurgations were replaced, with suitable cuts made where necessary. Although some readers resented her work, Mrs. Trimmer defeated most critics by maintaining that her efforts were not a real Bible, even if her contemporaries had no illusions. The post-Reformation tradition of updating and altering sacred tests for comtemporary applications similarly helped her position. In 1796 Bishop Beilby Porteous, the bishop of London (and a leading member of the SOCIETY FOR THE REFORMATION OF MANNERS), brought out the first Bible to use a PORTEUSIAN INDEX. This method of ensuring that one could read the Bible safely involved four discrete levels of marking, placed at the head of each chapter. His indexes proved popular and sold widely, but they provided only a guide, not the full-scale purge required by purists.

Such a purge was attempted by four editors between 1818 and 1824. The *Holy Bible, Newly Translated by John Bellamy* appeared in 1818. Bellamy, a Swedenborgian, based his bible on the assumption that no major biblical figure, e.g., Lot or Jacob, could possibly have performed the unacceptable actions with which he is credited. Since the Bible itself was sacrosanct, the translation from the Hebrew must be at fault. He went through the Bible, carefully working out new meanings for previously indecent passages. Bellamy was helped by the fact that Hebrew has no vowels and thus consonant clusters can be reinterpreted as desired. His scheme began well, attracting subscriptions from the Prince Regent and ten other royals, but established Bible scholars savaged the new translation despite Bellamy's elaborate explanations. His royal patrons quickly abandoned the scheme, but Bellamy persisted in his plans until the money ran out. His efforts to obtain a grant from public funds were rejected and his enterprise collapsed for good in 1832.

The New Family Bible and Improved Version by Dr. Benjamin Boothroyd appeared in 1824. Boothroyd was a Congregationalist who wanted to bring the language of the Bible up to date and also to find a way of circumventing the "many offensive and indelicate expressions" in it. This undertaking proved difficult and Boothroyd was often reduced to deprecatory footnotes, condemning the moral tone of his subject matter. Unlike Bellamy, he was a real scholar, and was awarded an honorary D.D. from Glasgow University for his translation from the Hebrew. He also corrected a number of errors in the authorized version. A second edition appeared in 1835-37 and a third (posthumous) edition in 1853, 15 years after his death.

Also in 1824 appeared *The Holy Bible Arranged and Adapted for Family Reading* by John Watson, a layman of the Church of England. Watson's main change was to drop the numbering of traditional chapters and verses, replacing them by sections of his own making. Thus it was harder to see immediately just what had been cut. As an expurgation it stands between *The Sacred History* and *The Family Bible*. Watson's efforts, which were never widely circulated, also suffered from the editor's absolute belief that Moses wrote every word of the Pentateuch personally and thus any alterations were sacrilege.

In 1828 William Alexander, a Quaker, published *The Holy Bible, Principally Designed to Facilitate the Audible or Social Reading of the Sacred Scriptures*. Alexander was a printer, and his effort reflects his profession. Based on Porteusian principles, its typography defeats every effort to read it usefully. Every page offers a mixture of faces: Gothic, italic, three or four sizes of Roman. Like Porteus he cited three levels of scripture: the devotional, the general and the private perusal series. Good and bad parts of the Bible were to be kept separate, yet each chapter and verse were to be kept in their normal order. The devotional and general series were also intended to form independently coherent and readable books. There were also substantial footnotes. The private series was unnumbered and printed in italics at the bottom of each page. Unlike the other series, it intentionally makes no sense if read as a continual book. Alexander made it clear that this series would not have been included at all had the Bible not put it in the original. To embellish the visual and textual chaos, he carefully changed any word or passage "not congenial to the views and genius of the present age of refinement." His efforts were not successful and printing was discontinued after only six of the proposed 20 parts had been published.

The first and last deliberate expurgation of the Bible in America was published in 1833 by the lexicographer Noah Webster (1758-1843). He had started "the most important enterprise of my life" in 1821. A specimen section was offered to the Andover Theological Seminary in 1822 but the experts thought he had gone too far. For the next decade he devoted himself to his great dictionary and to the expurgation of the entire canon of English poetry. In 1830 he returned to the Bible and in 1833 his version appeared. He retained every incident but changed words ad lib, offering thousands of alterations, every one dedicated to euphemism and absolute decency. He also changed much Biblical poetry into prose. Although Webster's Bible had its brief success—it was adopted by the state of Connecticut in 1835 and endorsed by Yale University—his sheer pedantry and his refusal to leave unaltered even the "decent" parts of the Bible alienated many readers. After second and third editions appeared in 1839 and 1841 Webster's version vanished.

SEE ALSO the Bowdler Family.

Bibliographie des ouvrages relatifs de l'amour, aux Femmes, au Mariage et des Facetieux, Pantagrueliques, Scatalogiques, Satyriques, etc.   This bibliography, the third edition of which remains generally accepted as the best source of information on French literary erotica published prior to 1870, was compiled by the publisher JULES GAY, writing as "M. Le C. d'I***." It is heavily annotated with scholarly references, as was Gay's habit in all his publications. The first editions, appearing in 1861 and 1864, list books by their subjects; the third lists them by title. A fourth edition, with extra material contributed by J. Lemonnyer, appeared between 1894 and 1900. Comprising four large volumes, this has often been cited by bibliophiles as the optimum edition, but in it Gay's notes have either been excised wholesale or seriously abridged. The *Bibliographie* is useful for French and Italian books but has little of value concerning the English output. As ASHBEE noted, the only trustworthy material regarding English erotica is that contributed by his own associate JAMES CAMPBELL, whose efforts are acknowledged in the third edition. Subsequent critics have found it unreliable, in many details, and relying too often on secondary sources, such as catalogs, rather than on detailed studies of the books themselves.

SEE ALSO *Bibliographie du roman erotique au XIXe siecle*; Perceau, Louis; Reade, Rolf S.

Bibliographie du roman erotique au XIXe siecle T h i s bibliography of clandestine French erotic literature was compiled by LOUIS PERCEAU and published in 1930. Unlike the efforts of his predecessors ASHBEE and GAY, Perceau chose to concentrate on a single country and a relatively short period: French prose works between 1800 and 1929. There are 388 articles. The bibliography is arranged in chronological order, with each successive first edition being listed under the relevant year. Reprints are listed under the year of their appearance. There are two appendices, one covering works that have been announced but have not yet appeared and one covering unpublished manuscripts; there are 10 indices, running to 200 pages.

SEE ALSO *Bibliographie des ouvrages relatifs de l'amour …*; Reade, Rolf S.

Bibliotheca Arcana … The *Bibliotheca Arcana seu Catalogus Librorum Penetralium, being brief notices of books that have been secretly printed, prohibited by law, seized, anathematised, burnt or bowdlerized*, was published in 1885. Its compiler and author, "Speculator Morum," has been cited variously as HENRY S. ASHBEE and CHARLES CARRINGTON, but the most reliable authorities attribute "Speculator" to two men: Rev. John McLellan, who wrote the preface, and Sir William Laird Clowes, sometime author of *Confessions of an English Haschish Eater*, who actually compiled the entries. Compared with Ashbee's INDEX LIBRORUM PROHIBITORUM, this is a thin, second-rate collection of just 630 items, none of which offer any useful commentary. It lacks Ashbee's critical notes, although it does list certain volumes that he overlooked, but it suffers most from its lack of bibliographic rigor and the simple fact that the volumes are not listed in alphabetical order.

SEE ALSO Reade, Rolf S.

Bibliotheca Germanorum Erotica This book, the standard reference work on German erotic writing, was originally published in Leipzig in 1875, compiled by Hugo Hayn. A second edition, keeping pace with the output of literary erotica, appeared in 1885. The third edition (1912-14) enlisted the aid of Alfred N. Gotendorf and was expanded to eight large volumes. The most recent edition appeared in 1929 and included an "Erganzungsband" or supplementary volume, running to a further 668 pages and compiled by Paul Englisch, himself the compiler of the *Gesichte der erotischen Literatur* (1927, cited as the best ever history of erotic writing) and the *Irrgarten der Erotik* (1931, a bibliography of erotic bibliographies). The *Bibliotheca* lists as many books as possible and describes them in the traditional bibliographical style; only occasionally does an editor add his own critical comment.

Hayn remains German's leading bibliographer of the erotic. As well as the *Bibliotheca Germanorum* he compiled several other major bibliographies. These include: the *Bibliotheca Germanorum Gynaecologica et Cosmetica* (1886), a compendium of erotic as well as medical and cosmetic items, some of them exceedingly rare; the *Bibliotheca erotica et curiosa monacensis* (1889), based on the library in Munich; the *Bibliotheca Germanorum Nuptialis* (1890), concentrating on marriage; *Vier neue Curiositaten-Bibliographieen* (1905), on several hundred volumes of erotica in the library in Dresden; *Floh-Literature* (1913), a listing of all those erotic works that center on the adventures of a flea, such as *The Autobiography of a Flea* and *L'Origine des Puces* by Villart de Grecourt.

SEE ALSO *Bilderlexikon der Erotik*.

Bidle Bidle (1620-62), a tailor's son, followed a brilliant school career in Gloucester with the study of philosophy at Magdalen College, where he was found to be "determined more by Reason than Authority." He returned to Gloucester to become master of the town's Free School, where he began evolving his theory that the doctrine of the Trinity "was not well grounded in Revelation, much less Reason." This statement brought him before the Gloucester magistrates on a charge of heresy in 1644. He was jailed briefly, the first of a succession of sentences that ensured that for the rest of his life "he seldom knew what liberty was." In 1647 his "Twelve Arguments drawn out of Scripture wherein the Commonly Received Opinion touching the Deity of the Holy Spirit is Clearly and Fully refuted" was burnt by the hangman on the orders of the House of Commons but still proved so popular as to be reprinted that same year.

In 1648 it was declared a capital offense to deny the Trinity. Despite this Bidle published the "Confession of Faith touching the Holy Trinity, according to Scripture" and "Testimonies of Different Fathers," both of which proclaimed his refusal to accept government doctrine. The Assembly of Divines demanded that Parliament should pass the sentence of death on Bidle, but it refused, choosing rather to release him. In 1654 Bidle attacked again, with *The Twofold Catechism*; this time he was jailed in the Westminster

Gatehouse, deprived of all writing materials and his books were all burned. Cromwell released him soon afterward, but exiled him to the Scilly Isles. He was jailed again in 1662 and died in prison. Bidle was also allegedly the translator of the "Racovian Catechism," an anti-Trinitarian tract originally composed in Poland in 1605 and published in England in 1652. Another supposed translator, who was questioned by the House of Commons, was Milton.

SEE ALSO Puritan censorship: the Commonwealth.

Big Character Poster   SEE dazibao.

Bijoux indiscrets, les   This relatively little-known work, a mixture of literary criticism, satire and the erotic, gains its reputation from that of its unlikely author, the French philosopher and encyclopedist DENIS DIDEROT (1713-84). Diderot apparently wrote the book to prove to his mistress Madame de Puisieux that he could manage popular as well as intellectual work. It took a mere fortnight to compose, and it appeared in January 1748; the proceeds, some 50 louis, were turned over to his mistress. The novel satirizes, in a Turkish harem setting, Louis XV, Madame de Pompadour and members of their court. Interwoven with the satire are Diderot's opinions on French literature and drama, and a number of contemporary authors are parodied. The erotic aspects of the book are derived from the sultan's (Louis') sexual ennui and his attempts, aided by an aged hypochondriac djinn who gives him a magic ring, to alleviate this by probing the intimate secrets of the ladies of his court, which device allowed Diderot to catalog a variety of sexual adventures. An English edition appeared in 1749. The most recent version, corruptly translated and heavily embroidered with extra obscenity to suit the modern marketplace, appeared in 1968, published in California by Collectors Publications (an imprint owned by Marvin Miller, the well-known publisher of such material) and entitled *The Talking Pussy*. A French film, called *Pussy Talk*, was made in the 1970s.

Bilderlexikon der Erotik   This bibliography of erotica, published in Vienna between 1928 and 1931, was edited by one Leo Schidrowitz. It is in four volumes, of which only volume two and part of volume four deal exclusively with its alleged subject matter. The other volumes cover a wide range of eroticism, but move beyond the world of books. The full title of volume two is *Ein bibliographisches und biographisches Nachschlagewerk, eine Kunst-und Literaturegeschichte für die Gebiete der erotischen Belletristik, der galenten, skandalosen und sotadischen Literaturen, der facetien, folkloristischen und skatalogischen Curiosa von der Antik bis zur Gengenwart: ein Sammelwerk der sexuell bettonten Produktion aller Volker und Zeiten, auf den Gebieten der bildenden Kunst.*

The book is illustrated throughout and consists of a number of essays by a variety of authors. Many of its illustrations came from the files of the Institut für Sexualwissenschaft, whose library was burned by the Nazis. While some experts feel that it ranks with ASHBEE and other bibliographers of the erotic, critics have pointed out its many inadequacies and cite its arbitrary and capricious manner. It lacks the scholarly depth that other volumes of this type have achieved, and such failings cannot simply be attributed to the elusive nature of the material.

SEE ALSO *Bibliotheca Germanorum Erotica.*

Birth Control   The campaign to make available both the physical means of contraception and, equally important, the knowledge of its use and implementation, was spearheaded by a number of notable women, most particularly Marie Stopes in Britain and Margaret Sanger in America. The authorities, still immured in slowly shifting Victorian attitudes, were less than supportive. In 1912, aged 29, Sanger wrote a number of frank pieces about the dangers of venereal disease in the magazine *The Call*. The Post Office, citing the COMSTOCK ACT, claimed that material of this nature was obscene, and banned *The Call* from the mails. Sanger retaliated with a headline in the next issue, declaring: "What Every Girl Should Know: NOTHING! By Order of the Post Office Department." In 1915 she opened a birth control clinic in Brooklyn. Appealing directly to the poor immigrants of New York, the center printed its circulars in Italian and Yiddish, as well as in English. Despite this, Sanger, like Stopes, was an elitist, whose slogan was "More children from the fit, less children from the unfit—that is the chief issue of birth control." The police department sent an undercover policewoman to investigate. Sanger was arrested and served 30 days in jail.

Sanger hit back with her film *Birth Control*. This was in effect a documentary, largely autobiographical, charting the career of a nurse (Sanger) who wishes to advise poor women on contraceptive methods but is restrained through a draconian state law. She is unable to hold back and opens a clinic. Tipped off by private detectives, the police move in and arrest her. The film ends with Sanger in jail and a final title proclaiming "No matter what happens, the work shall go on." The New York City license commissioner refused to permit the film to be shown. Sanger appealed and his decision was reversed, only to be reinstated by a higher court. In his opinion *Birth Control* was "not a proper film to be exhibited … [because it] sought to teach immorality and was entirely opposed to the public welfare." The film also tended to bring law enforcement officials into disrepute. The commissioner charged that the film had a tendency to arouse class hatred, showing as he felt, that the rich were able to use contraceptive methods denied, through their ignorance, to the poor. Finally the commissioner claimed that *Birth Control* would lead to the corruption of society, encouraging "many unmarried people to indulge in liberties from which they would otherwise refrain on account of the danger of being placed in a position of shame."

Judge Nathan Bijur refused to accept any of this, stating that the commissioner had no right to revoke the license of any theater exhibiting the film. In his eyes, films, like the print media, were entitled to FIRST AMENDMENT protection. The Appellate Division of the New York State Supreme Court reversed this decision, however, stating that as determined by the case of MUTUAL FILM CORPORATION V. INDUSTRIAL COMMISSION OF OHIO (1915) film was not a medium but simply a business and as such exempt from special consideration. Not until the case of *Griswold* v. *Connecticut* (1965), when the U.S. Supreme Court decided that any state laws censoring contraceptive advice were unconstitutional, was it possible to circulate such material without fear of prosecution.

The Hand That Rocks the Cradle, a similar attempt to use the medium to pioneer the knowledge of birth control and sexual hygiene, was similarly prosecuted in 1917. Once again the New York censor refused to give his license, claiming that there had been widespread complaints "from persons of high standing" against it. Citing the example of the "Birth Control" decision, and pointing out that "a confessed violator of the law is represented as a martyr and held up to the admiration and applause of promiscuous authorities because of her violation of the law," the courts duly upheld the banning.

Sanger's written work was also widely suppressed. Her book "Family Limitation" (1915) was prosecuted by the SOCIETY FOR THE SUPPRESSION OF VICE and found to be "contrary not only to the law of the state but also to the law of God"; Mrs. Sanger was jailed, as was her husband William, for distributing her pamphlets on birth control. In 1923 the book was suppressed in England. In 1929 the New York City police, acting in response to a complaint from the right-wing Daughters of the American Revolution (DAR), raided the Sanger clinic, arrested three nurses and two doctors and seized vast quantities of records. Sanger was completely acquitted and the authorities were warned off similar raids. Her work was subsequently banned in Ireland, Yugoslavia and fascist Italy.

SEE ALSO *The Birth of a Baby*; *Love without Fear*; *Married Love*; *The Sex Side of Life*.

Birth of a Baby, The   This 1938 health education film quite simply portrays the subject of its title, dealing with the progress of a couple's life through pregnancy and climaxes with actual childbirth. Produced by the American Committee on Maternal Welfare it was scrupulously dignified and if anything tended to be excessively earnest. Such care notwithstanding, the local censors of New York, Lynchburg (Virginia), Cincinnati and Omaha all found the film in contravention of their statutes against indecent or immoral movies. In New York, where the film was branded as tending to corrupt morals, the censor offered to give it a special dispensation for showing strictly as an educational film, but refused to permit its exhibition in places of amusement. Despite the dissenting opinion of two judges, the New York Court of Appeals refused to overturn this ban. The state

censors in Virginia, after an initial attempt to ban the film, were persuaded to relent, but in the town of Lynchburg, the city manager claimed that its exhibition violated local ordinances and it must not be seen. This attempt to place municipal scruples above state licensing was not upheld in the courts and the town's attempt to obtain an injunction against the film was denied.

The film provided the illustrations for a major feature in *Life*'s issue of April 11, 1938. The publisher, Ralph Larsen, wrote to subscribers, suggesting that since the feature had been put in the center-spread it could be removed by those readers who so desired, but in many cases the magazine arrived before the letter. When a number of squeamish readers complained, Larsen was arrested and charged with selling an obscene magazine. The charges were quashed and the judge stated that "the picture story ... does not fall within the forbidden class. The picture story was directly based on a film produced under the auspices of a responsible medical group. There was no nudity or unnecessary disclosure. The subject has been treated with delicacy."

When the film was submitted to the British Board of Film Censors (BBFC) in 1939 it was rejected outright. Despite this ban the London County Council allowed its exhibition to those over 18. Accepting the film were a number of other local authorities, including those in Manchester, where it was shown separately to audiences of men and women. Resubmission to the BBFC in 1947 was similarly unsuccessful, but this time the LCC passed it with an A certificate. The board did not assess the film again, although in 1957 it passed a similar documentary—*Birth Without Fear*—with a X certificate.

SEE ALSO *Birth Control*; *Love without Fear*; *Married Love*; *The Sex Side of Life*.

Birth of a Nation, The   D.W. Griffith's film *The Birth of a Nation* was first shown on February 8, 1915, at Clune's Auditorium in Los Angeles. It was released as *The Clansman*, which was the name of the novel by Thomas Dixon Jr. on which much of its plot was based. The story fell into two parts: The first is a conventional enough narrative of the Civil War; the second is a view of postwar Reconstruction as seen very much from a native Southerner's point of view. The story forsook narrative for controversy when it portrayed every black as animalistic, moronic and lusting after white women, while the overtly racist Ku Klux Klan appeared as the saviors of not merely the South, but the North as well. Griffith, whose father had fought for the Confederacy, presented a film with a definite message: the South was to be made safe for whites.

After it had been viewed by members of the influential NATIONAL BOARD OF REVIEW OF MOTION PICTURES it appeared to Dixon, the author, that its nature might result in a ban, and he appealed for help to his old friend, President Woodrow Wilson. Wilson saw it and told Dixon, "It is like writing history in lightning." He did not particularly like the film, but he had not attacked it, and Dixon moved on to canvass the support of the Supreme Court, where the chief justice, Edward Douglass White, was himself a former Klansman.

Despite this support, *The Birth of a Nation* has faced continual controversy. It became the most banned film in American history. By 1980 it had amassed a total of 100 challenges, in some 60 of which the film was banned outright or partially censored. Griffith himself claimed in a pamphlet called "The Rise and Fall of Free Speech in America" (1916) that "the moving picture is simply the pictorial press. The pictorial press claims the same constitutional freedom as the printed press …" The law, as promulgated by the Supreme Court in MUTUAL FILM CORPORATION V. INDUSTRIAL COMMISSION OF OHIO (1915), stated otherwise, designating the whole film industry as a commercial enterprise pure and simple and as such excluded from FIRST AMENDMENT rights, a situation that persisted until 1952. The film was variously banned in Boston, where it caused race riots, in the states of Colorado and Ohio, and in Pittsburgh, St. Louis and many other cities. The NAACP has continued to campaign against it.

Black, Sir Cyril   SEE *Last Exit to Brooklyn*; Public Morality Council.

blacklisting   The main result of the informer system, both official and amateur and encouraged in America by the activities of the HOUSE COMMITTEE ON UN-AMERICAN ACTIVITIES (HUAC) and Senator JOSEPH McCARTHY, was the creation, particularly in the film and entertainment industry, of a blacklist of individuals who were deemed unacceptable for employment. The blacklist was never acknowledged, indeed it was strenuously denied. A number of freelance blacklisters worked closely with the employers whose tacit acceptance of the lists legitimized the system. Most powerful of these citizen censors was the American Legion. At its National Convention in October 1951 its officers were directed to undertake a program of public information designed to disseminate data on the communist associations of individuals in the entertainment, and especially the film, business. The Legion then started picketing theaters showing films made by unfriendly HUAC witnesses, and backed this up by lobbying, letter-writing campaigns and phonecalls, all aimed at stopping the studios from employing these supposed communists. In December the *American Legion Magazine* ran an article, "Did the Movies Really Clean House?" by a former Committee informer, J.B. Matthews. In his piece, Matthews named 66 communists still involved in the movies. The studios, as desired, took note and throughout the blacklist era sought actively to placate the Legion. Other freelance blacklisters included the American Business Consulants (ABC), three ex-FBI agents who published the booklet *Red Channels: the Report of Communist Influence on Radio and Television*, known facetiously as "The Bible of Madison Avenue," and Aware Inc., which published the newsletter,

Counterattack. Counterattack also investigated the teaching profession, the United Nations, trade unions, clergymen, scientists, lawyers, and many other establishment figures. Its particular hatred was reserved for *Time* magazine and the *New York Times.* Hollywood's hard right—John Wayne, Adolphe Menjou, Ward Bond—led the Motion Picture Alliance for the Preservation of American Ideals (MPAPAI). The Catholic Church and the Catholic War Veterans had their own proscriptions. HUAC itself distributed annual lists of names and namers, which, unlike the freelance material, at last had the virtue of accuracy, if only in nomenclature. The committee also leaked many stories to syndicated gossip columnists like Walter Winchell and Hedda Hopper and the sleazier magazines like *Confidential.*

The corollary of the blacklist was the concept of clearance. If one could sin, then one could recant and be received back amongst the blessed. The paradox of clearance was that outcasts were seeking to escape a blacklist that officially did not exist. The tragedy was that by undergoing the clearance ritual they were giving legitimacy to the blacklist system. All the freelance organizations were as keen to help one off the list as they were to include one on it. Aware Inc. published a pamphlet, "The Road Back (Self-Clearance): A Provisional Statement of View on the Problem of the Communist and Communist-Helper in Entertainment Communications Who Seeks to Clear Himself."

Once again the employers, while never acknowledging that the blacklist actually existed, cooperated as willingly with the listers as they did with HUAC. Companies such as ABC were hired "for expert assistance in detecting Communist propaganda," a euphemism for accepting cash to remove certain names. Studios set up departments to screen employees. Errant employees could write letters, which often had to be rewritten until the correct level of abject humiliation was achieved, which could then be submitted by a studio to a given blacklister in the hope of achieving the required absolution. The American Legion formulated five tests under which one might achieve clearance: the suspect must denounce and repudiate all past communist sympaties; he must appear before HUAC and make full public disclosure, most importantly by naming names; he must join organizations that are actively anti-communist; he must condemn Soviet imperialism publicly; and promise not to do it again. It was also vital to proclaim oneself an innocent who had been duped. Blacklisting lasted throughout the 1950s and sometimes beyond. The stigma of guilt by association was hard to remove. The pusillanimity of employers vanished very slowly. Careers were wrecked, families destroyed and friendships smashed. Above all, some have suggested that the emasculation of U.S. creativity accomplished by the blacklist is in part responsible for the weakness of mass popular culture ever since.

blasphemous libel   SEE blasphemy.

blasphemy A statement is blasphemous under English common law, if it denies the truth of Christianity, or of the Bible, or the Book of Common Prayer or the existence of God. Blasphemy was not a matter for the church courts when they existed, but was actionable under criminal law. As stated by Justice Bayley in 1823, when sentencing one Susannah Wright for blasphemous libel: "Christianity is parcel of the English law, and we cannot permit that point to be argued now." The common law of blasphemous libel has gradually developed since the courts first entered in this area in Attwood's case in 1618. A series of cases followed, starting with that brought against John Taylor in 1676 and progressing to that against J.S. Gott in 1922. Such works as THOMAS PAINE's THE AGE OF REASON and Shelley's "Queen Mab" were indicted.

While the majority of ancient statutes referring to blasphemy have been repealed, the prevailing definition dates from Lord Coleridge (1883): The mere denial of the truth of Christianity is not in itself blasphemous, but "indecent and offensive attacks" on Christianity "calculated to outrage the feelings of the general body of the community" do constitute an offense. This definition was most recently reiterated in 1977 in the trial of GAY NEWS. Under British law no other religion is afforded similar protection from attack. A series of statutes, such as the Blasphemy Act (1698), have maintained the legal as well as spiritual integrity of the Church. Since *Bowman* v. *the Secular Society* (1916), the basic definition has been amplified: Blasphemous words or representations are only punishable "for their manner, their violence, or ribaldry, or, more fully stated, for their tendency to endanger the peace then and there, to deprave public morality generally, to shake the fabric of society and to be a cause of civil strife." Blasphemy, thus codified, existed only if it led to a breach of the peace. This refinement was not backed by statute, but stands as obiter dicta, a verbal guideline for legal convenience.

So wide-ranging is the concept of blasphemy, and so dependent is its existence on assessing the degree of offense that certain words or representations will cause to a given witness (accepting the widely varying religiosity of individuals), that it defies simple application in the courts. In 1922 the Court of Criminal Appeal offered as justification for upholding a judicial direction the concept that, were a deeply religious individual to have read a particular anti-Christian pamphlet, then he might have become so enraged as to attack its seller. Thus the pamphlet's blasphemy was proved as far as leading to a breach of the peace was concerned. In the same judgment, the Court also affirmed blasphemy if the pamphlet had been "calculated to outrage the feelings of the general body of the community."

The first man to be tried for blasphemy was one John Taylor, who claimed in 1676 to be Christ's younger brother, at the same time as denouncing the Savior as a whoremaster and orthodox religion as a cheat. After a period in Bedlam on bread and water failed to alter his views, he faced trial, the result of which was Taylor's being placed in the pillory, wearing a placard that said, "For blasphemous words and tending to the subversion of all Government." A number of cases followed this, notably those against Thomas Woolaston (1728), Peter Annet (1763), Thomas Williams (1797), WILLIAM HONE (1817), Richard and Jane Carlile (1819), Robert Taylor (1827), Henry Hetherington (for an attack on the violence and obscenity of the Old Testament, in 1841), GEORGE HOLYOAKE (1842), Matilda Roalfe (1843), Henry Seymour (1882) and CHARLES BRADLAUGH (1883).

A number of these cases provided the basis of future movements toward legal reform, but, since that against Gott, there have been few successful prosecutions for blasphemy in the 20th century. A National Asssociation for the Repeal of the Blasphemy Laws was formed in 1883 and dissolved, assuming its task complete, in 1959. More recently Lord Scarman has suggested that if blasphemy were to remain a crime, then its provisions must be extended to non-Christian beliefs. As stated by Baron Alderson in 1838, blasphemy protected only the "established religion of the country" and "Judaism, Mahometanism, or even any sect of the Christian religion" may be attacked freely.

In 1981 The Law Commission proposed that the crime should be abolished completely, saying that the current law had too wide an ambit, that there was no way of legislating for the sincerity of the publisher and that "the criminal law is not an appropriate vehicle for upholding sectional religious tenets." The most recent prosecutions were both brought privately and without any substantial Anglican support. They were those of Lady Birdwood against the play *Council of Love* (1971), which failed, and that by Mrs. MARY WHITEHOUSE of the magazine *Gay News*, when it published James Kirkup's poem "The Love That Dares to Speak Its Name" in 1976. This latter, tried in 1978 as *R.* v. *Lemon and Gay News*, stressed the modern interpretation of blasphemy—not as an attack on Christianity, but as a probable cause, through the outrage such an attack might cause among believers, of a breach of the peace. On the basis of this case, in which the magazine was found guilty, as lawyer Geoffrey Robertson has pointed out (*Obscenity*, 1979), "it appears that the law of blasphemy no longer relates to attacks on, or criticisms of Christian doctrine, but is concerned solely with indecent or offensive treatment of subjects sacred to Christian sympathisers."

In addition to the specific law of blasphemy, religion in Britain is protected by clauses in a number of acts, including the OBSCENE PUBLICATIONS ACT (1959), The Post Office Act (1953), the Public Order Act (1936), the Metropolitan Police Act and the Town Police Clauses Act, and the Ecclesiastical Courts Jurisdiction Act. The Customs are also empowered to ban the importation of any indecent articles that might deal with the sexuality of Christ or any other religious figure. Outside the law, religion is protected by both the BBC and IBA, who tend generally to shy away from real religious controversy. The BBC has only recently permitted the expression of rationalist views, which are consistently assailed by orthodox complainants. Religious themes are usually kept out of non-religious programs as well as advertisements. But channels reserve some 70 minutes every Sunday—the "God slot"—for religious programming.

SEE ALSO *Satanic Verses, The.*

Blue Movie/Fuck *Blue Movie*, alternative title *Fuck*, was made by Andy Warhol and Paul Morrissey in 1969 and starred one of the Warhol superstars, Viva (Waldon), and her husband Louis. The film watches as the couple spend an afternoon in bed in their Manhattan apartment. They chatter about current affairs, including the Vietnam War, watch the TV, enjoy sexual foreplay and intercourse. After a shower and more sex, Viva acknowledges the camera to ask "Is it on?" New York City police officers who had already seen a part of the film obtained warrants to seize the film and to arrest the theater manager, the ticket taker and the projectionist, although charges against the latter pair were dropped. The New York Court found the manager, one Heller, guilty of promoting obscene material. This conviction was upheld in the Appellate Court and, two years after the original seizure, by the New York Court of Appeals. The courts also stated that the issuing of warrants for the seizure of the film prior to its having been judged obscene in an adversary proceeding was constitutionally sound.

By the time the case reached the U.S. Supreme Court, as *Heller* v. *New York* (1973), the legal definition of obscenity as accepted in such cases had been redefined by the Court's opinion in MILLER v. CALIFORNIA (1973) and set down as the MILLER STANDARD. As far as the aesthetic aspect of the appeal was concerned, the Supreme Court preferred to return the film to the New York courts, which could thus use the new standard to reassess it. As far as the seizure was concerned, Chief Justic Burger, in a majority opinion, accepted that the police had acted within their rights. When the case returned to the New York courts, *Blue Movie* was again found obscene and duly banned.

Blyton, Enid Enid Blyton (1897-1968) was, and remains, Britain's best-selling author of children's books. After three years at a Froebel Institute, she became involved in the theoretical side of education, editing a variety of journals. In 1923 she published a small collection of verses for children but her real fame began in 1933 when she began editing and single-handedly writing the weekly magazine, *Sunny Stories*. For the next 35 years she dominated the children's market, writing at peak a book a month, producing in all some 400 titles, translated into 30 languages and selling five million copies a year. Her creations—Noddy, Big Ears, the Famous Five and Secret Seven—form part of a myriad childhoods.

Despite this, Blyton has long been a target of censorship, notably in British and Commonwealth public libraries. The problem with Blyton was obviously not that she corrupted the young, but that her lookalike, readalike volumes of anodyne pap, low on vocabulary and imagination, high on minimal reading ability, appalled educators and librarians who looked for quality in children's literature. Characters and plots were at best two-dimensional and demanded nothing of the children who consumed them. While her supporters claimed that Blyton's own wish "to take a child by the hand when he is three and walk with him all his childhood days" helped promote early reading, her detractors pointed out that her undemanding, unstimulating texts might becalm those same readers in a sea of mediocrity, beyond which they might never move.

For a number of librarians the response was simple: Blyton's books were either removed from the shelves or from the lists of titles to be ordered. When copies wore out, they were not replaced. Blyton was dropped from libraries in Australia, New Zealand and the U.K. With them went Richman Crompton's "William" books (although these were seen as dated rather than simply illiterate) and W.D. Johns' "Biggles" series (arraigned for their outmoded Kipling approach to the "natives"). Perhaps the most notable ban was that instituted by the St. Pancras libraries in London. This caused a brief furor in 1963 and gave the nation's agonized letter-writers an opportunity to parade their loyalties. The press duly played it all up. In 1964 the Nottingham Public Libraries followed suit, and similar sensationalism followed. In 1966 it was the turn of Sittingbourne in Kent. By 1968, the year of Blyton's death, they had been removed from every library in Hertfordshire and by 1971 from those in Wiltshire. Despite the bans the books remain all-pervasive and this minor censorship issue will undoubtedly continue to rankle.

Board of Education v. Pico (1982) This case is central to the current rash of local- or state-level attempts to censor works that would otherwise escape federal obscenity laws in America. *Board of Education* v. *Pico* is the result of the attempt by the Board of Education of the Island Trees Union Free School District No. 26, in New York State, to brand a number of books as "anti-American, anti-Christian, anti-Semitic and just plain filthy" and remove them from both junior and senior high school libraries. The board appointed a committee composed of parents and teachers and empowered them to review the books in question and make their own decision as to whether they should be returned to circulation. When the committee proved itself less susceptible to literary threats than it might have hoped, the board simply ignored its recommendations and stated unequivicoally that certain books would not return to the shelves.

The books thus criticized were *The Best Short Stories by Negro Writers* (ed. Langston Hughes), which had reasonably explicit references to sex; *Black Boy* (by Richard Wright) and *The Fixer* (by Bernard Malamud), both of which were cited for anti-Semitism; *Go Ask Alice* (anonymous) and *Slaughterhouse Five* (by Kurt Vonnegut), which were anti-Christian; and *A Hero Ain't Nothing But a Sandwich* (by Alice Childress) and *Laughing Boy* (by Oliver LaFarge), which were "plain filthy." British pop socio-biologist Desmond Morris' best-selling *The Naked Ape* was also attacked, presumably for its passing references to masturbation and homosexuality; former black radical Eldridge Cleaver's *Soul on Ice* was included for its references to miscegenation.

Faced by this local censorship, a number of students brought a suit against the board, claiming that, on no better grounds than the supposed insult to their social, political and above all moral tastes, the authorities had arbitrarily taken the law into their own hands and as such had violated the students' rights under the FIRST AMENDMENT. The federal district court ruled in favor of the board; an appeals court, backed by the U.S. Supreme Court, remanded the case for a trial on the students' allegations. The Supreme Court was in fact severely divided, but ruled that the district court did not have the right to give a summary decision against the students. Justice Brennan stated that while local school boards did indeed have "broad discretion in the management of school affairs, this discretion must be exercised in a manner that comports with the transcendent imperatives of the First Amendment." In other words, a board could not simply excise books from a library because they happened to conflict with the views of individual members. The more conservative justices, led by Chief Justice Burger, refused to set the Court up as a super-censor, and assured parents, teachers and local school boards that it was up to them, and not to the judiciary, to establish standards of "moralty and vulgarity ... in the classroom." The case remains undecided at this writing.

SEE ALSO Eagle Forum; Gabler, Mel and Norma; Moral Majority; Texas State Textbook Committee.

Boccaccio, Giovanni *Decameron, The.*

Bodkin, Sir Archibald The British director of public prosecutions (DPP) from 1920 to 1930, Bodkin worked alongside Home Secretary WILLIAM JOYNSON-HICKS in a campaign against what they both considered obscene and immoral literature. He described a work by Freud as filth and threatened its publishers, Allen and Unwin, with prosecution unless they restricted its circulation to doctors, lawyers and university dons, all of whom had to give their names and addresses when purchasing the book. ULYSSES was condemned as "indescribable filth" and Bodkin sent policemen to interrogate the critic F.R. Leavis, then a young Cambridge lecturer, who had requested the publishers in Paris to send him a copy for teaching purposes. The police duly infiltrated Leavis' lectures, with special orders to count the number of women present. In 1923 Bodkin attended, as British delegate, a League of Nations conference considering the international trade in pornography. At the conference Bodkin refused to permit the making of any definition of what material was and what was not to be classified as pornography; he listed his own efforts in convicting even those who swapped such material between themselves. His most notorious prosecution was that in 1928 of Radclyffe Hall's WELL OF LONELINESS.

Bonfire of the Vanities SEE Savonarola, Girolamo.

book burning in England

1. Tudor period These were among the most important works, mainly condemned as heretical, that were burned by the English authorities during the reigns of Henry VIII (1509-47), Edward VI (1547-53), Mary (1553-58) and Elizabeth I (1558-1601):

MARTIN LUTHER: various works burned in 1521 after the Vatican had condemned Luther's Protestant doctrines. The bishop of Rochester, Fisher, preached a sermon as they were piled on a bonfire in St. Paul's churchyard.

WILLIAM TYNDALE: *New Testament*, burned in 1525—the first book written by an Englishman to be burned in England. Various heretical works: burned in 1546; the list comprises books by Frith (10), Tundale (9), WYCLIF, Joye (7), Basil (13), Bale (28), Barnes (3), Coverdale (12), Turner (6) and Tracy.

WILLIAM THOMAS: *The Historie of Italie*, burned by the common hangman in 1549, the first book so to suffer.

Hendrick Niclas: *Joyful Message of the Kingdom, Peace on Earth, The Prophecy of the Spirit of Love*, burned 1579; Niclas, of Leyden, was the founder of a sect, the Family of Love or House of Charity, which preached that Christ's teachings were more important than the church rituals that had come to surround them. Highly popular among the peasantry, the family preached obedience to no law other than that of God, and imputed all their sins to their desire to show, by sinning, how wonderful God's mercy was in that He chose immediately to pardon them. This doctrine seemed dangerously seditious and Elizabeth ordered Niclas' works destroyed, although the sect survived this setback.

SIR JOHN STUBBS: *Discoverie of a Gaping Gulf whereinto England is like to be swallowed by another French marriage, if the Lord forbid not the banes by letting her Majestie see the sin and punishment thereof*, burned in 1579.

MARTIN MARPRELATE tracts: some of these were burned in 1589.

Parsons, Allen et al.: *The Conference about the Succession to the Crown of England*, burned 1594. The intent of this book, which was attributed to one Doleman, but more likely the creation of the leading Jesuit intriguer, Robert Parsons, of Cardinal Allen and similar pro-Catholics, was to discredit the claims of James VI of Scotland on the English throne and to prove that either the earl of Essex or the infanta of Spain were Elizabeth's true heirs. On the basis of these claims, the book suggested that it would be lawful to depose the queen herself. It was widely burned, and the printer hanged, drawn and quartered. Its arguments, paradoxically, were used by Bradshaw, an arch-Puritan, to argue the validity of executing Charles I in 1649. It was burned again in 1683, when Oxford University attempted to prove its loyalty by destroying quantities of "unsound" books.

Peter Wentworth: *A Pithy Exhortation to Her Majesty for Establishing her Successor to the Crown*, burned 1594. This was an answer to *The Conference* (above) and written in the knowledge that "the anger of a Prince is as the roaring of a Lyon, and even the messenger of Death." In it Wentworth humbly advocated the claims of James VI. The queen was no more impressed than she had been by *The Conference*; she required no amateur advice. She may have also wondered how sincere its author's humility may have been: He had already spent two periods in prison for his speeches advocating the House of Commons' Right of Free Speech, in 1575 and 1587. Wentworth was sent to the Tower, where he died; his book was burned.

Christopher Marlowe (1564-93), *Elegies of Ovid*; Sir John Davies (1569-1626), *Epigrammes*; John Marston (1575?-1634), *Metamorphosis of Pygmalion's Image*; Joseph Hall (1574-1656), *Satires*; Cutwode, *Caltha Poetarum; or, the Bumble Bee*. All these books of poetry and satirical verse were burned by order of Archbishop Whitgift, 1599.

Samuel Rowlands (1570?-1640?): *The Letting of Humour's Blood in the Headvein* and *A Merry Meeting; or, 'Tis Merry When Knaves Meet*. These satires were burned in public and in the kitchen of Stationers' Hall in 1600.

2. James I (1603-25)   These were among the most important works, mainly condemned as heretical or anti-monarchical, that were burned by the English authorities during the reign of James I:

REGINALD SCOT (1538?-99): *The Discoverie of Witchcraft*.

Cowell: *The Interpreter*, burned 1607; this tract on monarchy was considered to be dealing, for all its high monarchical attitude, with matters that were outside the domain of public opinion.

Sir Walter Raleigh (1554?-1618): *History of the World*. In 1614, Volume One was called in by the king "especially for being too saucy in censuring princes."

David Paraeus: *Commentaries* on the Old and New Testaments; the works of Paraeus, Protestant professor of divinity at Heidelberg, were condemned when it was found that in one gloss, to Romans 13, he had advocated the violent overthrow by the people of a tyrannical ruler. All his books were declared dangerous and seditious and burned on July 1, 1622.

Richard Mocket: *Doctrina et Politia Ecclesiae Anglicanae*; these translations into Latin of The English Prayer Book, Jewell's Apology and Newell's Catechism by the warden of All Souls, Richard Mocket, were designed to spread the doctrines of the Anglican Church outside England. James I felt that Mocket's work was overly Calvinistic and ordered the book to be burned in 1622. This destruction left Mocket "so much defeated in his expectations to find punishment where he looked for preferment, as if his life were bound up by sympathy in his book, he ended his days soon after." He died, aged only 40.

Suarez: *Defensio Catholicae Fidei contra Anglicanae Sectae Errores*. This massive tome (778 pages) was written at the express order of Pope Paul V after James I had responded to his order of 1606, forbidding Catholics to attend Protestant churches or take Protestant oaths, with his own *Apology for the Oath of Allegiance* (1607), which James had followed

with the *Premonition to all most Mighty Monarchs*, a warning to secular rulers of the designs of the Papacy. James forbade any Englishman to read Suarez' volume, ordering it to be burned at London, Oxford and Cambridge.

Conrad Vorst: *Tractatus Theologicus de Deo*. Vorst was the professor of theology at Leyden University and his book was condemned by the king as thoroughly heretical. Claiming that "such a Disquisition deserved the punishment of the Inquisition" and forbidding any English student to attend Leyden so long as Vorst held tenure, James demanded that the university should expel its author—a demand that was satisfied, after some delay in 1619—and had the book burned publicly at London, Oxford and Cambridge in 1611.

3. Charles I (1625-49)   These were among the most important works, mainly condemned as anti-monarchical, that were burned by the English authorities during the reign of Charles I:

ROGER MANWARING: *Religion and Allegiance*, burned by order of the king, but only after the intercession of Parliament, in 1628.

RICHARD MONTAGU: *Appello Caesarem*, burned in January 1628.

ALEXANDER LEIGHTON: *Syon's Plea against the Prelacy*, burned 1628.

WILLIAM PRYNNE: *Historio-matrix; or, the Player's Scourge*, burned 1633.

JOHN BASTWICK: *Elenchus Papisticae Relionis* (1627), *Flagellum Pontificis* (1635), *The Letany* (1637), *Apologeticus ad Praesules Anglicanos*—all burned soon after publication.

Henry Burton: *For God and King*. This "masterpiece of mischief" was condemned along with the works of Prynne and Bastwick and burned in 1637 and its author pilloried, during which experience he felt himself "in heaven, and in a state of glory and triumph if any such state can possibly be on earth."

St. Francis de Sales: *Praxis Spiritualis; or, The Introduction to a Devout Life*. This book was licensed by Archbishop Laud but was found to have been altered during the printing process to emphasize various points of Roman Catholic dogma. Laud had it called in and as many copies as could be found were burned at Smithfield in 1637.

4. Puritans   The following books and pamphlets were among the most important of those burned during the English Revolution, from 1640 to 1660:

JOHN POCKLINGTON: *Sunday no Sabbath* (1635), *Altare Christianum* (1637)—burned 1641.

Sir Edward Dering: *Speeches*. Dering was a moderate who managed to antagonize both Archbishop Laud and the new Puritan authorities. In May 1641 he attempted to curb Laud's powers by moving the first reading of the Root and Branch Bill, designed to abolish the episcopacy. When the Puritans replaced the monarchy, Dering alienated them by his refusal to embrace their beliefs without question. His book of speeches on religion was therefore burned and Dering confined to the Tower of London for the week of February 2, 1642.

The Kentish Petition: drawn up by the gentry, clergymen and common people of Kent, and delivered to Parliament on April 17, 1642. This petition sought the preservation of episcopal government and the settlement of all religious schisms by a synod of the clergy. This petition was written in uncompromising language and for that reason, if for no other, so incensed Parliament that it was burned by the common hangman.

A True Relation of the Proceedings of the Scots and English Forces in the North of Ireland: burned on June 8, 1642, as being overcritical of the Scots.

King James: his Judgement of a King and a Tyrant: burned on September 12, 1642.

A Speedy Post from Heaven to the King of England: burned on October 5, 1642.

Letter from Lord Falkland: to the earl of Cumberland, dealing with the battle of Worcester—burned on October 8, 1642.

David Buchanan: *Truth's Manifest*, an account of the participation of the Scots in the Civil War—burned April 13, 1646.

George Wither: pamphlets, including "Mercurius Elenichus," "Mercurius Pragmaticus" and "Justicarius Justificatus" were all burned ca. 1646.

Various royalist squibs, including "The Parliament's Ten Commandments," "The Parliament's Pater Noster, and Articles of the Faith" and several others were burned in 1648, "in the three most public places in London."

James Okeford: *Doctrine of the Fourth Commandment, deformed by Popery, reformed and restored to its primitive purity*; all copies burned on March 18, 1650.

JOHN FRY: "The Accuser Shamed" (1648), "Clergy in their True Colours" (1650)—both tracts burned on February 21, 1651.

John Archer: "Comfort for Believers about their Sinnes and Troubles." This pamphlet suggested that God was not only responsible for all sins but also condoned them as part of His plan for mankind; it was the first theological work to be suppressed by the Revolution and was burned in July 1645.

Paul Best (d. 1657): "Mysteries Discovered, or a Mercurial Picture pointing out the way from babylon to the Holy City, For the Good of all such as during that Night of General Error and Apostasy, II Thess. ii.3, Rev. iii. 10, have been so long misled by Rome's Hobgoblin, by me, Paul Best, prisoner in the Gatehouse, Westminster." Best, who had been condemned to be hanged for his heretical opinions on the Trinity, was pardoned by Cromwell and freed in 1647, but this pamphlet was burned in three different places on three different days in July 1647.

BIDLE: *Twelve Arguments drawn out of Scripture wherein the Commonly Received Opinion touching the Deity of the Holy Spirit is Clearly and Fully refuted* (1647); *Confession of faith touching the Holy Trinity, according to Scripture* (1648); *Testimonies of Different Fathers* (1648); *The Racovian catechism* (translator). All these were burned soon after their publication.

Abiezer Coppe (1619-72): *The Fiery Flying Roll; or, Word from the Lord to all the Great Ones of the Earth whom this may concern, being the Last Warning Peace at the Dreadful Day of Judgement*. Coppe was a Ranter, preacher, mystic and pamphleteer, who preached naked in the streets of London, denouncing the sins of the rich, and produced his *Fiery Roll* in 1649. All discoverable copies were condemned to be burned on February 1, 1650, but Coppe, whose prose style was quite unique to its period, was released from jail on recanting his opinions. Parliament responded to his work by issuing on August 9, 1650, an ordinance for the punishment of "atheistical, blasphemous and execrable opinions."

Laurence Clarkson (1615-67): *A Single Eye All Light, No Darkness* (1650). Clarkson was successively an Anabaptist, Seeker, Ranter and Muggletonian (see MUGGLETON). He believed that sin was part of God's plan and declared, inter alia, that "What act soever is done by thee in light and love, is light and lovely, though it be that act called adultery." His book was burned in September 1650 and he was first jailed and then banished under the threat of death were he to return to England.

LODOWICKE MUGGLETON: *A Looking Glass for George Fox, the Quaker, and other Quakers, wherein they may See Themselves to be Right Devils*; written during the Commonwealth but burned in 1676.

5. Oxford University (1683) In the aftermath of the Rye House Plot of 1683, in which a number of conspirators attempted to assassinate King Charles II and his brother, the Duke of York, the Convocation of the University of Oxford issued its "Judgement and Decree … passed [on] July 21, 1683, against certain pernicious books, and damnable doctrines, destructive to the sacred persons of princes, their State and Government, and of all Human Society." The decree explained at length how Oxford had reflected upon "the barbarous assassination lately enterprised … with utmost detestation and abhorrence on that execrable villainy, hateful to God and man." And although suitably grateful to Divine Providence for the king's delivery from "the pit which was prepared for him," "we find it to be a necessary duty at this time to search into and lay open those impious doctrines, which having been of late studiously disseminated, gave rise and growth to these nefarious attempts, and pass upon them our solemn public censure and decree of condemnation."

The practical result of the document was the burning of the works of eight authors:

Samuel Rutherford: *Lex Rex*
George Buchanan: *De Jure Regni apud Scotos*
Bellarmine: *De Potestate Papae*; *De Conciliis et Ecclesia Militante*
John Milton: *Eikonklastes*; *Defensio Populi Anglicani*
John Goodwin: *The Obstructours of Justice*
Richard Baxter: *The Holy Commonwealth*

Dolman: *Succession*
Thomas Hobbes: *De Cive*; *Leviathan*

6. The Restoration

John Goodwin: *Obstructours of Justice* (1949); this book was written by Goodwin, a Puritan minister and prolific author, as a justification for the execution of Charles I. At his trial, in absentia, Goodwin was alleged to have been the leader of the fanatical Fifth Monarchists, but his real sin was to have justified the act most repugnant to the restored monarchy. His book was burned in June 1660.

John Milton: *Eikonoklastes* (1649), *Defensio Populi Anglicani* (1650). Both these books, attacks on Charles I, were called in by royal proclamation on June 16, 1660, and burned at the next assize, two months later.

Samuel Rutherford: *Lex Rex; or, the Law of the Prince* (1644). Rutherford's book, which stated flatly that "The king is subordinate to Parliament, not co-ordinate … What are kings but vassals to the State who, if they turn tyrants, fall from their right?" was burned in both Scotland and England in October 1660 and its author summoned on a charge of high treason before Parliament in Edinburgh. He was immediately deprived of all his academic and ecclesiastical offices and only his death in 1661, before the trial had ended, saved him from execution.

A variety of acts passed by the Commonwealth: all ordered to be burned on May 17, 1661. These included the creation of a High Court to try Charles I, the annulling of the title of Charles Stuart (Charles II), the securing of the position of lord protector.

JOHN LOCKE (1632-1704): "Letter from a Person of Quality to his Friend in the Country."

Delaune: *Plea for the Nonconformists* (1683), *The Image of the Beast*. Delaune, a teacher, was foolish enough to take literally a suggestion by Dr. Calamy, a royal chaplain, that there should be a friendly discussion of doctrine between Anglicans and Dissenters, of whom he was one. On publishing his *Plea* Delaune was arrested and imprisoned in Newgate, and was charged with intending to disturb the peace of the kingdom, with bringing the king into the greatest hatred and contempt, and with printing and publishing, by force of arms, a scandalous libel against the king and the Prayer-Book. Dr. Calamy refused all his requests for help and Delaune was fined heavily and imprisoned with his family in Newgate. He died there in 1685, preceded by his wife and two small children. His book was reprinted several times after the Act of Toleration (1689), with a preface by DEFOE.

7. United Kingdom (1688-1775)

These are among the most important books burnt in England between the Glorious Revolution of 1688 and 1775, when the last book to be so treated was consigned to the flames by the authorities:

William Molyneux: *The Case for Ireland being bound by Acts of Parliament in England* (1698). This argument for the constitutional rights of the Irish to absolute legislative independence from England, which concluded by warning the government of dire consequences if the Irish were not freed of English laws, infuriated the Parliament in London. Whether the book was actually burned is debatable—it is possible that its dedication to King William saved it—but Molyneux was certainly interrogated by the Commons and both he, and his book, were severely censured.

Arthur Bury: "The Naked Gospel" (1690); Bury, the rector of Exeter College, Oxford, had proved his loyalty to the church and the monarchy when in 1648 he was expelled from the college and exiled from Oxford on pain of death because he refused to deny Anglican doctrine. He wrote "The Naked Gospel" anonymously, signing it only "a true son of the Church." The pamphlet was in support of the king's plans to alter the litany in an attempt to reconcile various differences between the English and European Protestant communities. Instead of praise, Bury's work infuriated those members of the clergy to whom he showed it and he was tried as a heretic, deprived of his rectorship and his book was burned by the university.

JOHN ASGILL: *An Argument Proving that According to the Covenant of Eternal Life, revealed in the Scriptures, Man may be Translated from Hence into that Eternal Life without Passing Through Death, although the Human Nature of Christ Himself could not be thus Translated till He had Passed Through Death* (1700); burned in Ireland in 1703 and in England in 1707.

Dr. Coward: *Second Thoughts concerning the Human Soul* (1702), *Grand Essay: a Vindication of Reason and Religion against the Impostures of Philosophy* (1704). Coward, a fellow of Merton College, Oxford, usually wrote poetry and books on medicine. His ventures into metaphysics and philosophy, by all accounts dry and unexciting works, managed to antagonize the House of Commons. He was called to its bar and his books were condemned to be burned in Palace Yard on March 18, 1704. The main result of this attack was that they achieved an otherwise unlikely popularity and clandestine editions appeared within the year.

JOHN TOLAND (1670-1722): *Christianity not Mysterious* (1696); this book, which launched Deism and the concept of a natural rather than a received religion, was burned in Dublin in 1696.

DANIEL DEFOE (1660-1731): "The Shortest way with Dissenters"; this pamphlet, an ironical reply to Dr. SACHEVERELL's attack on Dissenters (among whom Defoe had been educated), was burned in 1702; Defoe was fined, pilloried and jailed from May to November 1703.

John Humphrey: "A Draught for a National Church accomodation, whereby the subjects of North and South Britain, however different in their judgements concerning Episcopacy and Presbytery, may yet be united." This pamphlet, authored by an aged Nonconformist minister, was burned in 1709.

Dr. Drake: "Memorial of the Church of England"; Drake published his pamphlet anonymously in 1705 as a complaint against the rejection by Parliament of the Bill against Occasional Conformity, a measure that would have outlawed

Dissenters from holding office. His high Tory complaint clashed with the government's desire to promote a united church and a royal proclamation censured Drake, albeit as an anonymous author, and condemned the pamphlet to be burned by the common hangman. It was similarly destroyed in Dublin. This was not the first of his books to suffer: his *Historia Anglo-Scotia* was burned in Edinburgh as insulting to the Scots in 1703.

DR. HENRY SACHEVERELL: two sermons—"The Communication of Sin" and "Perils among False Brethren"—preached in August and November 1709; burned after Sacheverell's trial before the House of Lords.

Matthew Tindal (1657-1733): *The Rights of the Christian Church, asserted against the Romish and all other Priests who claim an independent power over it* (1706). Written by Tindal, a fellow of All Souls' and a leading Deist, this book concentrated on attacking the attempts of the church to set itself above the state. Tindall attacked the independent powers of the clergy as having "done more mischief to human societies than all the gross superstitions of the heathen, who were nowhere ever so stupid as to entertain such a monstrous contradiction as two independent powers in the same society ..." As he noted, while writing the book, it "would drive the clergy mad." Despite Tindal having been given £500 by Queen Anne, and an assurance that popery was eternally banished from England, his book was still burned, at the same time as Dr. Sacheverell's sermons, a gesture designed as as a sop to the High Church party who were outraged by the verdict against their champion.

Boyse: sermon on "The Office of a Scriptural Bishop"; burned on the orders of the Irish House of Lords in November 1711.

William Fleetwood: four sermons on various matters pertaining to the royal sucession preached in 1712. All these were burnt on June 10, 1712, as "malicious and factious, highly reflecting on the present administration of public affairs under Her Majesty and tending to create disorder and sedition among her subjects." The upshot of the burning was that Addison's *Spectator* reprinted the material and sold 4,000 copies of its no. 384.

Joseph Hall: *A Sober Reply to Mr. Higgs' Merry Arguments from the Light of Nature for the Tritheistic Doctrine of the Trinity with a Postscript relating to the Rev. Dr. Waterland*; burned in February 1721 on the orders of the House of Lords because it "in a daring, impious manner, ridiculed the doctrine of the Trinity and all revealed religion."

George King: "His Majesty's most Gracious Speech to both Houses of Parliament on Thursday, December 2nd, 1756"; King, a bookseller, created this "audacious forgery and high contempt of His Majesty, his crown and dignity." It was condemned by the House of Lords to be burned on December 8, 1756, and King was fined £50 and jailed in Newgate for six months.

Timothy Brecknock: *Droit le Roy: or, a Digest of the Rights and Prerogatives of the Imperial Crown of Great Britain*; this work, written by a hack writer in February 1764, was an attack on popular rights, claiming that such rights represented "a false, malicious, and traitorous libel, inconsistent with the principles of the Revolution to which we owe the present happy establishment, and an audacious insult upon His Majesty ..." The Commons and the Lords ordered the book to be burned in Palace Yard and at the Royal Exchange on February 25 and 27, 1764. Brecknock himself was hanged soon afterwards, after being convicted of murder in Ireland.

"The Present Crisis with regard to America Considered": this anonymously produced pamphlet was the last book to have been burned by parliamentary order in England. It was disposed of on February 24, 1775.

William Attwood: *Superiority and Direct Dominion of the Imperial Crown of England over the Crown and Kingdom of Scotland, the true Foundation of a Compleat Union reasserted.* This book, written by a Whig writer and barrister who was briefly chief justice of New York but died in penury, was burned in Scotland as being "scurrilous and full of falsehoods." Another of Attwood's works, *The Scotch Patriot Unmasked*, was similarly destroyed in 1715.

book burning and the Jews Many books written by Jews have been burned, but there are a number that have been burned by Jews, usually orthodox zealots, desperate to destroy new and potentially revolutionary ideas. Such bookburners both aped the Christian authorities, notably the Dominicans of the Inquisition and the hard-line Protestant Calvinists, and attempted to curry favor with them by using such techniques. Few rulers, either clerical or secular, required much encouragement to purge what they were informed was seditious literature.

Probably the first Jewish author to have his works burned by his coreligionists was Maimonides (1135-1204), the supreme theologian of medieval Jewry, whose writings, notably *The Guide of the Perplexed* (1200), were condemned by his orthodox opponents as heresy. Copies of *The Guide ...* were burned when discovered, it was barred from Jewish homes, and anyone reading it was excommunicated; the work was still facing bans in the 19th century. The rabbis were appalled by suggestions that it was foolish to take the Bible as a literal text.

The prejudice that consigned Maimonides to the flames—that any form of rationalism was incompatible with religious orthodoxy—similarly informed the attacks on other books. Any attempt to reconcile spiritual and secular topics was outlawed and the *Sefer Milhamot Adonai* (*Book of the Wars of the Lord*), written in the 13th century by Rabbi Levi ben Gershon, was ordered to be burned. So abhorrent was the book that this burning might even be carried out on a sabbath, a day on which the orthodox would not usually light a fire; this suspension of normal theology was extended even to such sabbaths as coincided with the even holier Day of Atonement. The appearance in Italy in 1713 of the false messiah Sabbati Tsvi led to the burning of any works supporting his claims, as well as to the destruction by his allies of many books that attacked him.

Similar bonfires, both pro and con, dealt in 1780 with the works of the Hassidim (who are today still campaigning against the excesses of 20th-century permissiveness), notably the *Toldot Ya'kov Josef*, written by a follower of the Hassid Baal Shem Tov. Individual copies suffered, as did whole editions that were bought up in bulk by rabbis who promptly consigned them to the flames. A translation of the Pentateuch in German by Moses Mendelssohn, who appended a commentary, was proscribed: German Jews condemned it and its potential readers; the Eastern community burned it wholesale, despite an introduction in which the author pleaded for tolerance. Any attempts at religious reform, of which there were a number during the 18th century, were burned by conservatives, as were the publications of nascent Zionists who had the audacity to talk of a Jewish homeland in the absence of the ever-awaited messiah.

book burning in Nazi Germany   Four and a half months after Hitler became chancellor, on the evening of May 10th, 1933, a torchlight procession of students marched into a square on Unter den Linden opposite the University of Berlin. Here they used their torches to ignite a bonfire of books that had been piled up in preparation. As the flames consumed these volumes, more were added to the bonfire; an estimated 20,000 books were burned on this single pyre and similar book burnings were carried out in other German cities on this and further nights. Prompted by Dr. Josef Goebbels, Reich propaganda minister in charge of the Nazification of German culture, the students added to the flames any book that was considered to "act subversively on our future or strike at the root of German thought, the German home and the driving forces of our people." Authors who fell into this category included, among German writers—an estimated 2,500 of whom had prudently fled the country subsequent to the mid-February purge of the Prussian Academy of Poetry—Bertolt Brecht, Thomas and Heinrich Mann, Lion Feuchtwanger, Jakob Wassermann, Arnold and Stefan Zweig, Erich Maria Remarque, Walther Rathenau, Albert Einstein, Alfred Kerr and Hugo Preuss (who had drafted the Weimar Constitution). Foreign victims included Jack London, UPTON SINCLAIR, Helen Keller, Margaret Sanger, H.G. Wells, HAVELOCK ELLIS, ARTHUR SCHNITZLER, Sigmund Freud, Andre Gide, EMILE ZOLA and Marcel Proust.

For those who had valued German culture, the bonfires epitomized the tragedy of Hitler; for Goebbels "these flames not only illuminate the final end of an old era; they also light up the new." In place of the discredited "degenerates and racial undesirables," such unknowns as Werner Beumelberg, Hans-Friedrich Blunck, and Hans Grimm were elevated to *volkisch* glory. The book-burning was backed up by stringent censorship of new publications and the proscription of many volumes hitherto on public library shelves. Such literature as did appear suffered no pre-censorship, but publishers and authors knew what ideological purity demanded. The bestseller of the era, unsurprisingly, was the Führer's *Mein Kampf* which had sold six million copies by 1940.

SEE ALSO Germany 4. Nazi press controls (1933-45).

Boothroyd, Dr. Benjamin   SEE *The Bible.*

Borri, Joseph Francis   Borri (1627-1685) was both a famous chemist and a well-known charlatan, born in Milan and educated by the Jesuits in Rome. After a wild youth he ws forced to retire into a seminary, at which point he professed a deep religious faith and wrote a book—*La Chiave del gabinetto del cavagliere G. F. Borri* (*The Key to the Cabinet of Borri*)—in which he put forward a number of highly idiosyncratic opinions as regards the Trinity and the role of the Virgin. Despite the immediate condemnation of this heresy by the ROMAN INQUISITION, Borri gained a number of enthusiastic followers, although the chemist prudently fled Rome and moved first to Milan and then to Amsterdam and finally to Hamburg. In his absence the Inquisition examined his book and declared that its author should be punished as a heretic. He was excommunicated and his effigy was handed over to the cardinal legate who duly burned it on January 3, 1661, along with his writings. His goods were all confiscated. Borri remarked, in Hamburg, that he had never felt so cold than on that day. He then moved to Denmark, seeking asylum with King Frederick III. Borri lived in Denmark until Frederick died. Moving on to Vienna, he was arrested and turned over to the papal authorities, who brought him back to Rome. He was condemned to perpetual imprisonment and died in 1685, in the Castle of St. Angelo, to which heretics were traditionally sent.

Bowdler family, The   Three generations of the Bowdler family, of English country gentry stock, were concerned in the business of literary expurgation. The most famous, Thomas Bowdler, M.D., gave his surname to the language, in the form of *bowdlerize*. Thomas Bowdler's parents, Thomas Bowdler Sr. (1720?-1800) and his wife, were both adept at expurgation. The squire restricted his efforts to ruthless excisions in his nightly reading to his children, especially in his cutting of Shakespeare's more dramatic scenes. Mrs. Bowdler, an intellectual woman and Bible scholar, published in 1775 *A Commentary on the Song of Solomon Paraphrased* in which she considered an earlier expurgated version of the *Song* edited by Bishop Percy in 1764. His version had already cut many passages, but she demanded that the cutter himself be further cut.

These elder Bowdlers had four children. Jane, the eldest, was a clever but miserable spinster. She died in 1786, aged 40. Jane expurgated nothing but believed firmly in the practice and urged that "continued watchfulness must restrain the freedom of conversation." A posthumous and anonymous book, *Poems and Essays by a Lady Lately Deceased*, proved a popular seller. John, their second child, was a country squire like his father. Obsessed with purity, he composed a form letter despatched to friends' daughters on the eve of their wedding, advising them on the means of being a good wife; it concentrated on avoiding "everything which has the least tendency to indelicacy or indecorum." After his younger brother's FAMILY SHAKESPEARE proved so successful, he released in 1821 his own anthology of censored verse, *Poems Divine and Moral*. John had several children, including three sons. The eldest, another Thomas Bowdler, helped his uncle with the expurgated *Family Gibbon* of 1826. Charles, the youngest, resisted the family fascination, but the middle son, John more earnest than any other Bowdler, devoted himself to expurgation. He demanded, without success, that his law school should expurgate the classical texts it used. Had he not died young, in 1815, he was destined to take over revisions of the *Family Shakespeare*.

The two most important Bowdlers were Squire Thomas' youngest children: Thomas Bowdler M.D. and Henrietta Maria (Harriet). They were both consciously high-minded intellectuals. She was a bluestocking of deepest dye who could not bear the indelicacy of dancers at the opera. Her anonymous book, *Sermons on the Doctrines and Duties of Christianity*, ran into 50 printings in 52 years. Thomas Bowdler (1754-1825) qualified as a doctor but abandoned his practice in 1785; he had, it appeared, a physical aversion to the sick. He spent the next 15 years working on prison reform in London, a task he combined with being a leading member of various straitlaced intellectual circles. He became a great friend of Mrs. Elizabeth Montagu (1720-1800), "Queen of the Blues" and cofounder of the Blue Stocking Circle of learned contemporary ladies. Particularly impressed by her 1769 "Essay on the Writings and Genius of Shakespeare," he dedicated the *Family Shakespeare* to her. In 1800 Bowdler left London, disgusted by the failure of his prison reforms. He took an estate on the Isle of Wight, then in 1806 married Mrs. Trevennen, the widow of a naval officer. The marriage lasted only a few years; there were no children.

In 1807 there appeared the *Family Shakespeare*. No name appeared in the first edition but in the second of 1818, Bowdler announced himself, thus confirming rumors that had persisted since 1809. What he refused to admit was that he was neither the sole nor even truly a coeditor of the 1807 edition—that responsibility devolved upon his sister Harriet. While Bowdler refused ever to amend this piece of misinformation, the true authorship of the original work was attributed both in the family and among many recipients of the book to the correct, if anonymous, individual. While Harriet's pioneering efforts had received only marginal interest, Thomas' new edition, after a slow start, became the best-selling edition of Shakespeare in England. Bowdler, as its editor, gained great celebrity. He turned next to Edward Gibbon's *Decline and Fall of the Roman Empire* (1776-88), in which the author's dealings with early Christianity had always worried those of a more devout bent. Assisted by his nephew, the Rev. Thomas Bowdler, he prepared a suitably expurgated edition but did not live to see it in print. *The Family Gibbon* appeared in 1826; its creator died in 1825, leaving only his surname as an eponym and his adulterated Shakespeare as a multi-editioned memorial.

Boyse. SEE book burning in England 7. United Kingdom (1688-1775).

Bradlaugh, Charles SEE *Fruits of Philosophy, The*.

Brancart, Auguste Brancart, about whom little biographical information is available, was one of the major publishers of erotic literature in the late 19th century, working first from Brussels and subsequently from Amsterdam between approximately 1880 and 1896. He is seen today as a link between the 19th and 20th centuries, falling between the scholarly elegance of such as GAY and POULET-MALASSIS and their less scrupulous modern successors. Among his many publications were two of the most famous erotic autobiographies: *The Amorous Prowess of a Jolly Fellow*, an 1892 reprint of EDWARD SELLON's *The Ups and Downs of Life*, and, on the best authority, the first edition of the anonymous MY SECRET LIFE, sometime between 1885 and 1895. He reprinted a number of erotic classics and produced many English translations, aimed both at visiting tourists and at such London booksellers as EDWARD AVERY. Like Gay, who founded a spurious book club through which to publish his productions, Brancart founded the Societe des bibliophiles cosmopolites and in a series called the "Musee secret du bibliophile anglais" published a number of translations of English flagellation novels, including *Le Colonel Spanker, Conference experimentale*. He also capitalized on the output of Edmund Dumoulin, a prolific author who wrote 14 novels, a collection of poetry and a volume of plays between 1887 and 1894. Dumoulin, who signed his books "E.D." was in fact a wine merchant from Bordeaux. Another hihgly productive writer employed by Brancart was Alphonse Momas, a civil servant attached to the police, whose later life was devoted to spiritualism, but who first, under the name "Le Nismois" among many other pseudonyms, wrote some 76 novels between his first *Un Caprice* (1891) and his last *Un Lupanar d'hommes*, written before the First World War but published in 1924. Momas, whose work is typified by its slovenly, third-rate style, covered every aspect of sexuality in 30 years of hackwork.

Brazil

1. censorship Under Law No. 5.250 of February 9, 1967, "Law on the freedom of expression of thought and information," there exist the following provisions. Chapter 1 states that "Speech is free, and also the procuring and dissemination of information and ideas by whatever means, and without the submission to censorship, as long as the terms of the law are obeyed." However, these "terms" are broad. Public entertainments and shows may be censored, "propaganda in favor of war, of subversion of a political and social nature, and of race or class prejudice will not be tolerated." Publishing and broadcasting are free "unless clandestine or offending against morality and public decency"; the establishment of radio or television stations must be licensed by the state. No foreigner or even naturalized Brazilian may own a general information source—newspaper, radio or TV station—although they are permitted involvement in specialist publications.

Chapter 3 details "Abuses against free speech," all of which carry a penalty of up to four years imprisonment, penalties designed to reinforce internal as well as external security. The abuses include: propaganda for war, for political and social subversion and for race or class prejudice; publication of state secrets or information relating to national security; publication of false or distorted information, referring to public disturbances or which undermines confidence in the national institutions, notably government bodies and the banking system; offenses against morality and public decency; attempts to restrict publication or communication of information by bribery; incitement to lawbreaking or a defense of such incitement; libel (the truth of the libel is a defense unless it is against the president, senior officials or foreign heads of state).

A variety of possibly contentious subjects are permitted, unless they are performed "in bad faith" (a concept that is not further defined and proves hard to refute): criticisms of artistic, scientific, literary and sporting matters; references to the proceedings of the legislature or of the courts; criticism of laws and other matters of public interest; the discussion of ideas. Anyone thus criticized, other than in literary, sporting or artistic criticisms, has the right of absolutely equal reply to state their own position. Texts of radio and television programs must be kept for 60 days after transmission. Any publication may be imported so long as it satisfies the internal laws. Publications offending public decency or threatening public order may be seized summarily by the Ministry of Justice and Internal Affairs without any legal preamble. If the author of a piece or of a broadcast cannot be found, then the editor or producer is held responsible. If a journalist is detained he or she must be held apart from common criminals; no journalist need reveal the source of a story. Many topics are taboo, including political subversion and any news considered to present a negative image of Brazil.

Law 5.250 has been modified subsequently. Act Number Five, published on December 13, 1968, was essentially a modification of the constitution. It gave the president (under article five) the right to suspend the political rights of any citizen, dismiss anyone from his job and to fix restrictions or prohibitions related to any other public or private rights. Under article ten it provided for the suspension of habeas corpus in the case of political crimes against national security, the economic and social order and the popular economy. This provided for the detention of any writer or broadcaster who transgressed section 16 of Law 5.250, which prohibits anti-social propaganda, the undermining of the government or

economic system and the dissemination of false or distorted information.

The National Security Law (1969), termed by the International Commission of Jurists "a formidable weapon of repression," extended the control of Brazilian activities to citizens living outside the national borders. The intention to commit the relevant crimes was declared as culpable as the fact of performing that crime. It was forbidden to distribute any propaganda of foreign origin or in any way to attack the constitution; to form, join or maintain any organization, in any way associated to foreign states or ideas, that might be seen as anti-Brazilian; to incite through mass comunication—either through lies, half-truths or distortions—any anti-authority feelings. Subversive propaganda and attacks on the honor or dignity of senior officials are forbidden. This rule can be used to suppress any complaints against corruption, incompetence or torture. Draconian powers enable the minister of justice to maintain absolute control of the media, confiscating and suppressing material and closing down papers and broadcasting stations. The crime of incitement—which is not defined in the act—can be met by imprisonment and even capital punishment.

Decree-Law no. 1077, of January 26, 1970, banned the transmission of any live broadcasts, other than the news, which had not been submitted to pre-censorship. Print media were similarly checked: books to be submitted 20 days before publication, magazines, 48 hours. All foreign material must be similarly assessed by censors acting for the Ministry of Justice and any attempts to communicate otherwise prohibited material to foreign media are suppressed wherever possible. Letters may be opened and phones tapped. Under National Security Law no. 477, of February 26, 1969, education is strictly controlled. Potentially subversive teachers and students are excluded from higher education; student unions are banned; many classes are checked for ideological purity by a police agent who also reports on any suspicious students. Social science courses were replaced on the curriculum by one in morals and civics, a text book for which was written by a leading Brazilian fascist. Modern languages are seen as a threat, offering the opportunity to obtain information from external sources.

On June 8, 1978, censorship was officially ended in Brazil. The authorities stated that this implied the end of dictatorship; cynics referred to a cosmetic operation. Certainly a period of liberalization did ensue and for the first time it was impossible to impose censorship without the formal suspension of constitutional guarantees. However, as an emergency measure (a "Safeguard of the State"), a number of special powers remain.

Under the National Security Law of January 1, 1979, a number of articles give a legal basis to these powers. Art. 11 prohibits the dissemination of any internal or externally inspired propaganda designed to attack the state and its constitution; Art. 14 forbids the dissemination of "false or tendentious information ... in such as way as to incite ... the people against the constitutional authorities"; Art. 19 protects foreign heads of state from public criticism; Art. 25 makes it a crime to use the media "for the execution of a crime against national security"; Art. 42 bans all forms of subversive propaganda, whether by using the communications media, by psychological or revolutionary or subversive warfare, by indoctrinating people at work in the universities, by holding rallies and marches, by staging unofficial strikes, by slandering the political or business authorities or by expressing solidarity with any such action; Art. 44 deals with incitement to any of the crimes covered under this law; Art. 49 provides for the suspension, differing as to the gravity of the offense, of any medium for up to 60 days; Art. 50 empowers the minister of justice to seize any form of printed, filmed or recorded medium that is considered to have broken the law and to "take other steps necessary to avoid the perpetration of these crimes ..." In addition to these legal punishments, certain magazines, notably those considered to be irresponsible, face a variety of extralegal threats, including arbitrary seizure, anonymous bomb attacks, prosecutions and similar problems.

2. film censorship The first law to censor films in Brazil was passed in 1932. In 1939 all censorship passed into the control of the powerful Department of Press and Propaganda, which maintained a strict rule over all media. The DPP laid down many of today's standards, including the compulsory reservation of some exhibition time for home-produced films. Radio, TV and film broadcasts or exhibitions are now controlled by the regulations of the Public Entertainments Censorship Service, as set down by Art. 41 of decree No. 20.493 (January 24, 1946). These specify that authorization for transmission, presentation or exhibition will not be given to any material that: (a) contains anything offensive to public decorum; (b) contains scenes of violence or is capable of encouraging crinimal acts; (c) gives rise to, or induces evil habits; (d) is capable of provoking incitement against the existing regime, public order, the authorities or their agents; (e) might prejudice cordial relations with other countries; (f) is offensive to any community or religion; (g) in any way prejudices national dignity or interests; (h) brings the armed forces into disrepute.

The Public Entertainment Censorship Service is responsible to the Ministry of Justice. It looks at all films (the majority on exhibition are the usual Hollywood blockbusters) and can cut, suppress completely and allot certificates restricting the age of those who see the films. To back up these regulations, the government can use direct censorship, economic pressures to influence the distribution and exhibition of a given film, and force cinemas to show a variety of state-sponsored films and newsreels. Such native filmmaking as exists was savaged by repressive regimes between 1964 and 1978 and the nascent "film novo" effectively wiped out. TV and radio censorship is aimed directly at news broadcasting and many items are banned, dealing with all major political and social issues.

Brecknock, Timothy SEE book burning in England 7. United Kingdom (1688-1775)

Breen, Joseph I. Breen (1890-1965) first involved himself in the campaign for the reform of the movies in 1925 when, as a reporter in Philadelphia, he was working as director of public relations for the 1925 Catholic Eucharistic Congress. Noting that a Universal Pictures script for *Seed*, based on the eponymous novel by Charles Norris, was "hardly more than subtle propaganda for birth control," Breen nagged the company until it agreed to rewrite the script, excising the unacceptable material. When the MOTION PICTURE PRODUCTION CODE was in its early stages, Breen allied himself with its framers, Martin Quigley and Daniel Lord, in their campaign for on-screen purity, and when the LEGION OF DECENCY was established, Breen was placed at the head of the Production Code Administration (PCA).

Breen proved an extremely conservative censor, attacking the slightest suggestion of sex, left-wing politics or anti-Americanism. He was an absolute and self-satisfied autocrat who boasted, "There are two Codes: one written, the other one mine" and "I don't interpret the Code, I make it." An individual of staggeringly narrow mind, he made WILL HAYS, who at least liked the movies, seem liberal in comparison. Among the many films he attacked were ECSTASY (Hedy Lamar's nude bathing), *Gone With the Wind* (Clark Gable's "damn"), *It Can't Happen Here* (too anti-fascist) and *The Outlaw* (Jane Russell's breasts, "which are quite large and prominent.")

Breen met his match in 1953 when he attempted to cut Otto Preminger's innocuous comedy *The Moon Is Blue*, finding the words "virgin," "seduce" and "pregnant" and the line "You are shallow, cynical, selfish and immoral, and I like you" beyond the pale. Preminger, backed by critics who called the film "as pure as Goldilocks," refused to back down and despite all Breen's efforts, and those of the entire pro-censorship lobby and the Catholic Church, the film went on to gross $6 million, proving that a film could contrary to carefully fostered belief, still go out without a seal of approval and make money. Breen's response after losing this round was to quit the game. He resigned from the PCA and was replaced by New York City Family Court Judge Steven Jackson. On his retirement Breen received the industry's special Golden Academy Award for his work.

Brennan, William SEE *Board of Education* v. *Pico* (1982); *Carnal Knowledge*; *Don Juan*; *Magic Mirror*; *Mishkin* v. *New York* (1966); *New York Times Company* v. *Sullivan* (1964); New York Times Rule; *Roth* v. *United States* (1957); Roth, Samuel; *Stanley* v. *Georgia* (1969); *Titicut Follies*; unprotected speech.

British Board of Film Censors

1. history This is the industry-created body, established in its current form in 1921, under which the British film business submits itself voluntarily to censorship. It is not, as Lord Denning stated in 1976, "a legal entity. It has no existence known to law. It is but a name given to the activities of a few persons." The existence of the board ensures that there is no statutory film censorship in the U.K. although local authorities, since 1909, have possessed and will still sometimes use their own regulatory powers. The legislative basis that provides for the existence of all subsequent film censorship in Britain is the CINEMATOGRAPH ACT (1909). This act was described by the then under secretary of state at the Home Office, Herbert Samuel, as intended "to safeguard the public from the danger which arises from fires at cinematograph entertainments" (stemming possibly from the inflammable nitrate film stock). It was "a small departmental Bill of a somewhat urgent nature," and though critics derided such fears as "the acme of absurdity," the act duly became law. It coordinated the various measures introduced by many local authorities to ensure that the burgeoning occupation of cinema-going, and the picture palaces in which it was indulged, was subject to the same type of safety regulations as were such places of mass entertainment as theaters and music halls. Under the act, starting in January 1910, local authorities were empowered to license all premises used for exhibiting films "on such terms and conditions and under such restrictions as the council may determine."

The Cinematograph Act was not ostensibly designed for censorship, but the very existence of the cinema meant that its content would come under scrutiny. In March 1908 a letter in the *Daily Telegraph* deplored a film biography of the notorious criminal, Charles Peace, and the commissioner of the Metropolitan Police expressed his worries over any film that might glorify crime. In July 1910 there were complaints concerning a film of the World Championship fight in which Jack Johnson knocked out Jim Jeffries, presumably because the new champion was black (see WILLARD-JOHNSON BOXING MATCH). The home secretary was asked to ban the film but had no authority to do so; the London County Council (LCC), using the restrictions embodied in the Cinematograph Act, issued its own ban. The same film elicited from the councils of Walsall and Birkenhead the demand that such pictures, which in the former town "tended to demoralize and brutalize the minds of young persons," should be interdicted. More generally important was the decision in 1910 by the LCC whereby it prohibited the showing of films on Sundays, Good Friday and Christmas Day. This ban was challenged in the courts a month later, when the Bermondsey Bioscope defied its ruling. The lower court dismissed the council's case, but on appeal the lord chief justice confirmed that the 1909 act did indeed "confer on the county council a discretion as to the conditions which they will impose, so long as those conditions are not unreasonable." It was on this pronouncement, delivered in 1911, that the future provisions of film censorship would be based.

In 1912 the film industry suggested to the home secretary that its members should take the initiative in setting up their own self-regulating censorship. They were both keen to preempt further efforts at local council censorship and wished to counteract a growing trend of films that belied their claim to offer only wholesome family pictures. The home secretary, whom they suggested should appoint an overall appellate censor, backed the plan in principle, but refused to give his practical support, pleading that the local authorities had the legal powers of censorship and that the industry must deal with them. The British Board of Film Censors, the result of the industry's deliberations, was established in 1912 under its president, Mr. G.A. Redford, formerly an EXAMINER OF PLAYS for the LORD CHAMBERLAIN, and its first secretary, Mr. J.B. Wilkinson. They began their work as censors in January 1913. The BBFC was to be "a purely independent and impartial body, whose duty it will be to induce confidence in the minds of licensing authorities and of those who have in their charge the moral welfare of the community generally." The president's decision on a film would be "in all cases ... final." All the major distributors promised to submit their product to the board, which would assess it and then issue one of two certificates, either permitting universal exhibition or indicating that the material was unsuitable for children, even though this was simply advice and the young would not be excluded automatically.

Although the BBFC was intended to work with the local authorities, and take from them the burden of film censorship, the immediate effect of its creation was that many councils became even more enthusiastic over imposing their own standards. As these sometimes differed notably from those offered by the BBFC, it became obvious to all concerned that the system must be refined. In response to this the home secretary suggested in April 1916 that a government-appointed but non-statutory censorship board should be established. The local councils gave their support. A circular accompanying this proposal made it clear that government censorship would impose the severest possible restrictions on the film content. The industry did not approve. The home secretary persisted, and announced the establishment of official censorship as of January 1917. A new home secretary, the death of Mr. Radford, and his replacement by the far more imposing figure of T.P. O'Connor, MP, all combined to defeat official censorship. The new government was less inclined toward such measures and O'Connor asked for the BBFC to be given official recognition. This was refused and until 1921 censorship was operated in parallel by the board and by the local councils.

Gradually the BBFC gained precedence. A report published in 1917 by the National Council of Public Morals backed its efforts; the industry itself made its support ever clearer and, most important, the public's acceptance and use of the two certificates made their existence increasingly valid. In 1920 the Middlesex County Council made the granting of a BBFC certificate a prerequisite of issuing their own licenses and in 1921 the LCC followed suit. The "Sankey condition," based on the decision of Mr. Justice Sankey who had adjudicated in the Middlesex C.C. action above, became standard for all authorities. It was issued by the Home Office in June 1923, following the case of *Mills* v. *London County*, and stated: "No film—other than photographs of current events—which has not been passed for 'universal' or 'public' exhibition by the British Board of Film Censors shall be exhibited without the express consent of the Council." Henceforth there were no attempts to impose official censorship on the film industry, but the parallel powers of the local authorities still exist.

The board remains under the aegis of the Incorporated Association of Kinematograph Manufacturers. In law it has no official statutory existence, but is a private body set up by the film industry that derives its authority finally from the fact that local authorities choose almost invariably to accept as valid the standards and classifications that it lays down. It is not profitmaking and its income derives entirely from fees, assessed on the length of the film, charged to distributors who submit their films. The annual subscriptions paid by local authorities in return for the board's monthly reports augment this income. The president of the BBFC controls all matters as regards public decision-making. Other than a variety of minor alterations in the precise categorization of certificates issued—from the basic two-tier system, to the introduction of H (for Horror) and then X, to today's system, which has included the American PG (parental guidance) category— film censorship by the BBFC has been operated in much the same way since 1921. The Cinematograph Act of 1952 extended the 1909 act in certain areas of safety, health and welfare, particularly in stressing the resonsibility of councils for the protection of children. It also extended the powers of licensing to non-inflammable films and widened exemptions allowed to cinema clubs. Since 1977 the cinema has been within the scope of the OBSCENE PUBLICATIONS ACT OF 1959. The Local Government Act of 1972 made district councils the only licensing authority, other than in London, where the Greater London Council was the licensing body, up to its abolition in 1986. Since 1985 the board has been renamed the British Board of Film Classification.

SEE ALSO British Board of Film Classification.

2. mandatory cuts (pre-1945) Unlike America, the British film industry has never composed a voluntarily accepted production code, but the records of the BBFC, issued regularly between World Wars I and II, make it clear that a wide variety of topics were taboo. The following list, which quotes verbatim from the published lists of excisions for the years 1926 and 1931, typifies the standards that governed the permitted exhibition of films, whether made in England, America or elsewhere, at the time. Each entry denotes the reason for a cut; many such cuts were repeated in a number of films.

Religious: the materialized figure of Christ; irreverent quotations; travesties of familar biblical quotations and well-known hymns; titles to which objection would be taken by religious organisations; travesty and mockery of religious services; holy vessels amidst incongruous surroundings; comic treatment of incidents connected with death; painful insistence of realism in death-bed scenes; circumcision; themes portraying the Hereafter and the Spirit World; the Salvation Army shown in an unfavourable light.

Political: lampoons of the institution of Monarchy; propaganda against Monarchy, and attacks on Royal Dynasties; references to Royal persons at home and abroad; references to the Prince of Wales; unauthorized use of Royal and University arms; themes which are likely to wound the just suceptibilities of our allies; British possessions represented as lawless sinks of iniquity; white men in a state of degradation amidst native surroundings; American law officers making arrests in Britain; inflammatory sub-titles and Bolshevist propaganda; equivocal situations between white girls and men of other races.

Military: officers in British regiments shown in a disgraceful light; horrors in warfare and realistic scenes of massacre; reflection on wife of responsible British official stationed in the East.

Social: the improper use of the names of well-known British institutions; incidents which reflect a mistaken conception of the Police … sub-titles in the nature of swearing, and expressions regarded as objectionable in this country; painful hospital scenes; scenes in lunatic asylums and particularly in padded cells; workhouse officials shown in an offensive light; girls and women in a state of intoxication; "orgy" scenes; subjects which are suitable only for scientific or professional audiences; suggestive, indecorous and semi-nude dancing; nude and semi-nude figures … girls' clothes pulled off, leaving them in scanty undergarments; men leering at exposure of women's undergarments; abortion; criminal assault on girls; scenes in, and connected with, houses of ill repute; bargain cast for a human life which is to be terminated by murder; marital infidelity and collusive divorce; children following the example of a drunken and dissolute father; dangerous mischief, easily imitated by children; venereal disease; reflections on the medical profession; marriages within the prohibitative degree; son falling in love with his father's mistress; employee selling his wife to cover defalcations; harem scenes; psychology of marriage as depicted by its physical aspects; liaison between coloured men and white women; intimate biological studies; immodest scenes of girls undressing.

Questions of sex: the use of the phrase "sex appeal" in sub-titles; themes indicative of habitual immorality; women in alluring or provocative attitudes; procuration; degrading exhibitions of animal passion; passionate and unrestrained embraces; incidents intended to show clearly that an outrage has been perpetrated; lecherous old men; indecorous bathroom scenes; extenuation of woman sacrificing her honour for money on the plea of some laudable object; female vamps; indecent wall decorations; men and women in bed together.

Crime: hanging, realistic or comic; executions … objectionable prison scenes; methods of crime open to imitation; stories in which the criminal element is predominant; crime committed and condoned for an ostensibly good reason; "crook" films in which sympathy is enlisted for the criminals; "Third Degree" scenes; opium dens; scenes of, traffic in and distribution of illegal drugs; the drugging and ruining of young girls; attempted suicide by asphyxiation; breaking bottles on men's heads; criminals shown in affluence and apparently successful in life without retribution; severed human heads.

Cruelty: cruel treatment of children; cruelty to animals; brutal fights carried to excess ... knuckly fights; girls and women fighting; realistic scenes of torture.

SEE ALSO Motion Picture Production Code 2. and 3. (texts).

3. films banned (1913–50) While the British Board of Film Censors has never had a list of specific prohibitions, such as the MOTION PICTURE PRODUCTION CODE, which for many years dominated mainstrean U.S. filmmaking, there were a number of taboo areas that films might or might not be permitted to explore. Many films were cut; in addition to these, the following were banned wholesale. Although no copies survive of many of the earlier films, their titles alone, redolent of sexual misadventure, underline the censor's abiding interests. This list excludes films that were passed at a later date:

1913: *The Crimson Cross; Frou Frou; Funnicus the Minister; The Good Preceptress; The Great Physician; His Only Son; La Culotte de Rigadier; The Lost Bag; The Love Adventures of the Faubles; Love Is Blind; Mephisto; The Night Before; The Priest and Peter; Religion and Superstition in Baluchistan; A Salvage; A Shop Girl's Peril; A Snake's Meal; Spanish Bull Fight; The Story of Sister Ruth; Why Men Leave Home.*

1914: *The Blue Room; Coralie and Co.; Dealers in Human Lives; The Diva in Straits; The Hand that Rules the World; The Last Supper; Little White Slaves; Miraculous Waters; My Wife and I; The Sins of Your Youth; Three Men and a Maid; The Word that Kills.*

1915: *Cupid Arthur and Co.; Hearts in Exile; Human Wrecks; Hypocrites; The Inherited Burden; Innocent; The Lure; Nobody Would Believe; Vera; A Woman; The Yoke.*

1916: *The Double Room Mystery; The Dragon; The Eel; The Fire; A Fool There Was; Greed, No. 14; Glittering Broadway; A Hero of Gallipoli; Inspiration; The Kiss of Kate; Little Monte Carlo; A Man without a Soul; A Mother's Confession; Nabbed; A Night Out; A Parisian Romance; The Rack; Tanks; Those Who Toil; Toil and Tyranny; The Unpainted Portrait.*

1917: *The Battle of Life; The Black Terror; Conscience; Fear; The Four Feathers; The Fourth Estate; The Girl from Chicago; It May Be Your Daughter; Just As He Thought; The Land of Their Forefathers; The Libertine;The Marionettes; The Scarlet Mask; Sealed Lips; Skirts; A Splendid Waster; Strafing the Kaiser; Trapped for Her Dough; Under the Bed; The Wager; What Happened at 22; The Whelp; The Whispered Name.*

1918: *Blindfolded; The Crimson Stain; God's Law; Honor's Cross.*

1919: *At the Mercy of Men; The Case of a Doped Actress; Damaged Goods; The Divided Law; Free and Equal; Her White God; Mother, I Need You; The One Woman; Riders of the Night; The Spreading Evil; Woman, Woman.*

1920: *A Friend of the People; The Great Shadow.*

1921: *Beyond the Barricade; Greater than Love; Leaves from the Book of Satan; Love; The Price of Youth; The Women House of Brescia.*

1922: *A Bachelor Apartment; Bolshevism on Trial; Cocaine; Dracula* ("Nosferatu"); *Handcuffs and Kisses; The Kitchener Film; The New Moon.*

1923: *Animals Like Humans; The Batchelor Girl; Boston Blackie; Children of Destiny; Fit to Marry; I Also Accuse; Nobody; A Royal Bull Fight; A Scream in the Night; Shootin' for Love.*

1924: *The Downfall; Getting Strong; Human Wreckage; The Last Man on Earth; Love and Sacrifice; Open All Night; Through the Dark; A Truthful Liar; A Woman's Fate.*

1925: *Battling Bunyon; The End of the Road; Grit; Lawful Cheaters; North of Fifty-Fifty; Our Little Bell.*

1926: *The City of Sin; Flying Wheels; Irish Destiny;* (Battleship) *Potemkin; The Red Kimona; Rose of the Tenements.*

1927: *The Ace of Cards; Birds of Prey; Life's Shadows; Outside the Law; Plusch and Plumowski; Salvation Jane; Two-time Mama; The Weavers; The White Slave Traffic.*

1928: *Cabaret Nights; The Compassionate Marriage; Dawn; The Girl from Everywhere; The Haunted Ship; Mother; Night Life; Two's Company; You Can't Beat the Law.*

1929: *Below the Deadline; Casanova's Son; Love at First Sight; Marriage; The Mysteries of Birth; The Seashell and the Clergyman.*

1930: *Born Reckless; Gypsy Code; Her Unborn Child; Hot Dog; Ingagi; Liliom; The Parlour Pests; The Party Girl; Possession; The Stronger Sex; Who Killed Rover.*

1931: *An American Tragedy; Are These Our Children; The Blue Express; Captain Lash; Civilisation; Devil's Cabaret; Easy to Get; Enemies of the Law; The Fainting Lover; The Ghost that Never Returns; The Gigolo Racket; Girls About Town; Hidden Evidence; Just a Gigolo; Laugh It Off; Leftover Ladies; The Miracle Woman; The Naggers; Night Shadows; The Road to Reno; Ships of Hate; Siamese Twins; Song of the Market Place; Take 'em and Shake 'em!; Too Many Husbands; Town Scandal; The Victim; The Virtuous Husband; Women Go On for Ever.*

1932: *La Chienne; Divorce a la Mode; False Faces; The Flirty Sleepwalker; Freaks; Good Sport; Her Mad Night; Here Prince; Lady Please; The Last Mile; Life Begins; The Line's Busy; Minnie the Moocher; The Monster Walks; Night Beat; Night Life in Reno; L'Opera de Quat' Sous* (French version of Brecht's "Threepenny Opera"); *The Sultan's Cat; Tango.*

1933: *Alimony Madness; Bondage; Caliente Love; The Deserter; Fanny's Wedding Day; Gold Diggers of Paris; Hello Sister; Her Resale Value; India Speaks; Kiss of Araby; Malay Nights; Picture Brides; Poil de Carotte; Private Wives; Terror Abroad; Thirteen Steps; What Price Decency?; What Price Tomorrow?.*

1934: *Animal Life in the Chaparral; Black Moon; Casanova; Elysia; The Expectant Father; Fluchtlinge; Le Grand Jeu; La Guerre des Valses; Hell's Fire; Hitler's Reign of Terror;*

Honeymoon Hotel; Leningrad; March of the Years No. 5; Medbury in India; Men in Black; Nifty Nurses; Old Kentucky Hounds; A Penny a Peep; Red Hot Mama; Struggle for Existence; Sultan Pepper; The Wandering Jew; World in Revolt.

1935: *Arlette et les Papas; The Crime of Dr. Crespi; Death Day; The Fighting Lady; Free Thalmann; Good Morning Eve; Harlem Harmony; Oh, What a Night; The Prodigal; Puppets; Show Them No Mercy; Storm; Suicide Club; Yiddish Father.*

1936: *Club des femmes; Hunter's Paradise; Jenny; One Big Happy Family; Red Republic; Spring Night.*

1937: *Cloistered; Lucrezia; Skeleton Frolics; Sport's Greatest Thrill; Sunday Go to Meetin' Time; That Man Samson; Wrestling.*

1938: *Avec le Sourire; Wedding Yells.*

1939: *Entente Cordiale*

1940: *Buried Alive*

1944: *The Mystic Circle Murder*

1948: *Behind Locked Doors*

1949: *Body Hold; Dedee d'Anvers;* THE MIRACLE; *Sins of the Fathers; Street Corner.*

1950: *Devil's Weed; The Story of Birth* (BIRTH OF A BABY)

SEE ALSO British Board of Film Censors 2. mandatory cuts (pre-1945); Production Code Administration.

British Board of Film Classification   As operated in contemporary Britain, the exercise of film censorship by local authorities is regularly delegated to the Watch Committee, which is often similarly responsible for police affairs, and which in turn bases its assessments, other than in exceptional cases, on the model conditions laid down by the BBFC. These three conditions are essentially that:

No film shall be shown nor poster or other advertisement be exhibited that would offend against public taste or decency or would be likely to encourage or incite to crime or lead to public disorder or be offensive to public feeling. If the licensing body feels that a film or its advertisements offend on any of these grounds, they are entitled to ban it. No film that has not been passed by the board itself shall be allowed exhibition unless the licensing body expressly permits it.

Second, films shall be classified as U, PG, 12, 15 and 18, a group of categories that are worked out with the Cinema Consultative Committee, which body includes delegates from all sections of the industry and from the local authorities.

Third, a local licensing authority, if it so desires, can reject the board's classification and either alter the classification itself or simply refuse to allow the film to be shown; alternatively, as was relatively common under the Greater London Council, the authority may choose to permit a film that the board prefers to ban. Local authorities may, if they wish, abandon all censorship of films for adults, although children must at all times be protected.

BBFC examiners are selected from individuals with no professional interest in the film industry; they are appointed by the president of the BBFC, an official who himself is appointed by the Council of the Incorporated Association of Kinematograph Manufacturers, a body drawn from the film industry. The association consults on its choice with the current home secretary and representatives of the local authorities. The council's secretary, who is also the secretary to the BBFC, is the most important figure, and the only British censor of any sort who is generally known to the mass public. As in any censorship system, practical contemporary considerations have a substantial influence on the letter of the law; and fluctuations in current moral standards, as well (most vitally) as the personal attitude of the current censor himself, have inevitably influenced the application of these statutes. Dedicatedly conservative censors, such as Colonel J.C. Hanna and Miss N. Shortt in the 1930s, or liberal ones, such as John Trevelyan in the 1960s, have not merely categorized and classified cinematic product, they have profoundly influenced the viewing attitudes and, by extension, the overall climate of the society in which they worked.

The influence wielded by the secretary is further boosted by the fact that, unlike the comparable American body, the BBFC neither publishes a list of does and don'ts, often a subject of sophisticated ridicule, nor is it subjected to the kind of continuous, vociferous pressure of groups ranging from the right-wing LEGION OF DECENCY or MORAL MAJORITY to militant feminists, such as WOMEN AGAINST VIOLENCE AGAINST WOMEN and similar organizations. In Britain the activities of the anti-pornography and feminist lobbies do impinge on film, but they tend to concentrate on television.

SEE ALSO British Board of Film Censors 1. history.

British Broadcasting Corporation (BBC)   SEE ABC Trial; BBC 1. balance; BBC 2. broadcasting censorship; Broadcasting Complaints Commission (U.K.); Clean Up Television (U.K.); D Notices; National Viewers and Listeners Association; USSR 2. broadcasting censorship; Whitehouse, Mary.

British Library   The British Library collection of "suppressed books," bearing the pressmark S.S. has the same bearing on politically or legally unsound books as does the P.C. pressmark of the PRIVATE CASE on erotica and pornography. The section was set up in the 19th century to remove from public access a wide selection of books considered unsuitable. It covers books printed abroad that reflected badly on U.K. governments, books declared libelous in court, books in which an infringement of copyright has been proved, books suppressed by the courts for alleged obscenity, publications that contain official or police secrets or that detail criminal techniques and expertise, and books critical of the administration of the British Museum.

The ban on such material is absolute, although the list of suppressed material is occasionally revised. As stated in the handbook, "Information for Those Superintending in the Reading Room" (1966):

Suppressed Books: The so-called suppressed books comprise mainly those which have been withdrawn by publishers or authors, those which have been the subject of a successful action for libel, and those which are confidential and are deposited on condition that they are not issued for a certain period … none of the books in these classes is available to readers in any circumstances …

Broadcasting Complaints Commission (U.K.)   T h o s e who consider themselves to have been unfairly treated by a broadcast on British radio or television may appeal to the Broadcasting Complaints Commission. This body was established by the Broadcasting Act (1981) after a committee under Lord Annan recommended in 1977 that a new complaints procedure should be created to replace the separate bodies that had hitherto been used, respectively, by the BBC and IBA. The five part-time members of the BCC, appointed by the home secretary, were initially all unconnected with the broadcasting industry. Worries about such a commission—composed completely of individuals sitting in judgement over a profession of which they knew nothing—were slightly alleviated when the Home Office agreed to include "one or more persons … with substantial experience in Broadcasting."

All complaints must be made in writing and must deal with programs that have already been broadcast; the commission does not deal with prior restraint of material, however potentially controversial. Complaints deal with such topics as unjust treatment, invasion of privacy (although the common law does not recognize a right to privacy) or the way in which material used in the program was obtained by its makers. The individual making the complaint may authorize a third party actually to write the pertinent letter. Frivolous complaints are not considered; nor are those made too long a time after transmission or those that deal with an individual who died more than five years before the broadcast. No complaint that is already the subject of court proceedings or that could be dealt with were court proceedings initiated will be considered. The commission has the right to demand a recording—aural or video—of the program in question and will make its adjudication at a private hearing at which the complainant, the program maker and a representative of the broadcasting company may be present. The commission will publish its ruling, and a regular summary of all rulings is made available.

SEE ALSO Broadcasting Standards Council (U.K.)

Broadcasting Standards Council (U.K.)   The establishment of a Broadcasting Standards Council was announced to the British public by Home Secretary Douglas Hurd in spring 1988. Headed by Lord Rees-Mogg, a former editor of the *Times* and leading member of the British establishment, it is designed to reduce levels of sex and violence on television. The BSC, which is to become a statutory body according to the government white paper on broadcasting (published fall 1988), has aroused predictable responses. The broadcasters

see it as unnecessary state interference in the media, especially as regards Rees-Mogg's demands for hitherto unknown pre-censorship of programs that have been "bought in" from abroad. Those in favor of more rigorous controls are delighted, especially long-time campaigner Mrs. MARY WHITEHOUSE, who has been advocating such a body for 25 years. Rees-Mogg himself stresses his desire to maintain the standards of British TV, especially in the face of the coming influx of satellite-transmitted programs, on schedule for the 1990s and certain to destroy the traditional duopoly of the BBC and the commercial network. As regards pre-transmission censorship, he hopes that an amicable agreement will be reached between the BSC and the broadcasting authorities. These latter have so far refused such an accommodation, but Rees-Mogg has made it clear that if the companies will not cooperate, they will be forced to comply.

SEE ALSO Broadcasting Complaints Commission(U.K.).

Bruce, Lenny   In 1963 Lenny Bruce was America's hottest comic. The media snickered over his "sick humor" and the conservative columnist Walter Winchell labeled him "America's No. 1 Vomic," but for the sophisticated, the hip, and particularly for the young who would make the Sixties their own decade, Bruce was the tops. In a series of inspired free-form fantasies, mini-dramas that he called his "bits," he gutted the safe prejudices and assumptions of contemporary American, and thus Western, life. An acidulous satirist, whose efforts influenced a whole generation of imitators, he revolutionized America's still cozy, folksy sense of humor, destroying preconceptions, stereotypes and, eventually, through his manic drug use and driven lifestyle, himself. Unsurprisingly Bruce, who spared no one in his diatribes, came up against America's censors. From his point of view, any restriction of free speech was ludicrous: "A knowledge of syphilis," as he put it, "is not an instruction to contract it." The courts thought differently. He was arrested continually, seven times in Chicago alone, and faced three obscenity trials. He was tried in Philadelphia, in Beverly Hills and, in 1963, in Chicago. In 1964, attempting to appear at London's Establishment Club, he was promptly deported.

In the Chicago case, *People* v. *Bruce*, he was charged under the state's obscenity laws with giving an obscene performance. By now Bruce's career was becoming inextricably involved with his lawsuits. He was becoming increasingly obsessed by the authorities' attempts to suppress his freedom of speech and believed, foolishly, that he could conduct his own defenses better than could his lawyers. This failed to impress the Chicago court where Judge Michael Ryan made it clear that he saw little that was amusing in the comedian's humor. Chicago held many devout citizens and the prosecution harped deliberately on Bruce's mockery of the church. Bruce's act, for which he faced prosecution, was also rendered less than funny when reduced to the court's dry description:

The performance … consisted of a 55-minute monologue upon numerous socially controversial subjects interspersed with such unrelated topics as the meeting of a psychotic rapist and a nymphomaniac who have both escaped from their respective institutions, defendant's intimacies with three married women, and a supposed conversation with a gas station attendant in a restroom which concludes with the suggestion that the defendant and the attendant both put on contraceptives and take a picture. The testimony was that defendant also made motions indicating masturbation and accompanied these with vulgar comments …

Bruce was duly convicted, in absentia since he was constrained to stay in Los Angeles, awaiting another trial (this time for narcotics possession). Ryan, of whom one expert opined, "If capital punishment were available for this crime, [he] would have given it," sentenced Bruce to the state's maximum penalty: a fine of $1,000 and one year in jail. Bruce appealed to the Illinois Supreme Court, which overturned the conviction in 1964. The court rejected his lawyers' submission of the ROTH STANDARD as justification for his use of "terms which ordinary adult individuals find thoroughly disgusting and revolting as well as patently offensive." However, it acknowledged reluctantly that under JACOBELLIS v. OHIO the U.S. Supreme Court had accepted that if any social importance could be found in the material under review, then it was no longer obscene. While the court made it clear that "we would not have thought that constitutional guarantees necessitate the subjection of society to the gradual deterioration of its moral fabric, which this type of presentation promotes," it conceded with undisguised distaste that "some of its topics commented on by the defendant are of social importance … the entire performance is thereby immunized …" This victory was Bruce's only one. In 1965 he was convicted again, this time in New York. He planned to appeal his conviction up to the U.S. Supreme Court, but he died of a drug overdose in 1966, before he could make what he envisaged as his greatest appearance.

Bruno, Giordano   Bruno (1550-1597) was born at Nole in Italy, 14 years before GALILEO GALILEI. Educated in a Dominican convent he abandoned theology for philosophy and science. His first book, *De Umbris idearum*, appeared in 1582. This was followed in 1584 by *Spaccio della bestia triomphante* ("The expulsion of the triumphing beast"), which was published in London. In this allegory Bruno both attacked superstition and satirized the errors of Roman Catholicism. He scoffed at the worship of God, declared that the Scriptures were no more than fantasy, claimed that Moses was a magician and Christ no messiah. As long as he avoided Italy, this gross heresy remained unpunished, and Bruno lectured only in Wittenberg, Frankfurt and Prague, taking as his text the idea that God is the substance of life in all things and that the universe is a huge animal, of which God represents the soul. When in 1595 he dared to return to Italy, to lecture in Padua and Venice, he was arrested by the ROMAN INQUISITION. He was imprisoned for two years and then in 1597, burned alive. He told his judges, "You pronounce sentence upon me with a greater fear than I receive it."

Buchanan, David   SEE book burning in England 4. Puritans.

Buckley, Jim   SEE *Screw*.

Bulgaria   The press in Bulgaria is strictly controlled on a number of levels, including pre-publication censorship, the proscription of many topics and the denial of access on a variety of important subjects on the domestic and international fronts. Government statements are kept minimal; officials generally eschew interviews by the mass media and brand many otherwise anodyne documents as state secrets. Hard news remains at a premium, and newspapers thus print reams of copy that in a less restricted country would be relegated to official publications. Almost one quarter of Bulgarian newspaper space is filled with protocol information—lists of dignitaries, their honors and their current status. Even if a portion of the required information can be elicited from a source and then written up as a news story, the Bulgarian journalist has no control over the subsequent editing of the material. However, journalists, as members of the Bulgarian Journalists' Union (BJU), are members of the state's elite, enjoying unusual privileges and luxury. They live well, travel widely (if mainly in communist and Third World countries) and receive good pay. Their morale, nonetheless, is reportedly low.

Burger, Warren   SEE *Blue Movie/Fuck*; *Board of Education* v. *Pico* (1982); *Carnal Knowledge*; *Magic Mirror*; Miller Standard; *Miller* v. *California* (1973); *Myron*; *Ratchford … v. Gay Lib* (1978); *Schad* v. *Board of Mt. Ephraim* (1981).

Burstyn* v. *Wilson   SEE *The Miracle*.

Burton, Henry   SEE book burning in England 3. Charles I (1625-49).

Burton, Sir Richard   Burton was a British explorer, anthropologist and linguist (1821-90), who combined his academic and traveling pursuits to create a persona that made him one of the most flamboyant characters of his time. His travels covered most of the world, both as an explorer in Arabia and Africa, as a soldier in the Indian Army and a diplomat in Europe, South and North America. He wrote extensively about his journeys, compiling some 40 volumes, including translations and volumes of poetry. He is best known today for his interest in erotica, and the translations he made of two Indian erotic classics: THE KAMA SUTRA and THE PERFUMED GARDEN. Burton's translation of *The Arabian Nights* ran to 16 volumes and featured the explorer's own annotations on clitoral surgery, homosexuality and bestiality. The unfinished "Perfumed Garden Men's Hearts to Gladden" was to be "a marvellous repository of Eastern wisdom: how eunuchs are made and married ... female circumcision ... the fellahs copulating with crocodiles." Burton was also part responsible, with LEONARD SMITHERS, for the erotic publications of the Kama Shastra Society and the EROTIKA BIBLION SOCIETY.

His wife, Lady Isobel, was less entranced by such material and on his death in 1890 appointed WILLIAM COOTE, the secretary of the NATIONAL VIGILANCE ASSOCIATION, as her husband's literary executor. Coote's interpretation of his role, in which he was encouraged by Lady Isobel, was to burn a quantity of Burton's papers, including Burton's translation of *The Perfumed Garden* from the original Arabic, on which he had been working for 14 years.

SEE ALSO Hankey, Frederick; Nichols, H. Sidney.

Bury, Arthur   SEE book burning in England 7. United Kingdom (1688-1775).

***Butler* v. *Michigan* (1957)**   SEE Michigan—protection of minors.

By-road News   SEE Hsiao tao hsiao hsi.

C

Cabell, James Branch Cabell (1897-1958), "a lingering survivor of the ancien regime, a scarlet dragonfly imbedded in opaque amber," was the sole writer spared from the disdain of H.L. Mencken in his condemnation of the American South as "The Sahara of the Bozart." Cabell worked as a journalist and genealogist, and from 1904 began publishing a variety of novels, poetry and essays to increasing acclaim. The high point of his success came with *Jurgen* (1919), set in the imaginary nation of Poictesme. But Cabell's style was somewhat too rarified for mass appeal and even his devotees moved elsewhere. By 1930 his fame, respected by Mencken in 1924, was no more. *Jurgen*, as well as bringing him his transitory success, also outraged the censorious. It was prosecuted in 1920 by the SOCIETY FOR THE SUPPRESSION OF VICE (U.S.); the publicity this case created may well have done as much as anything to promote the book. By 1922 it was cited only as a work of art although the refusal of many public libraries to carry the book did give the censors somewhat of a victory by default, and in Ireland the novel remained off-limits into the 1950s.

Cagliostro, Alessandro Cagliostro, the pseudonym of Guiseppe Balsamo (1743-1795), was one of the most notorious necromancers of the 18th century. In 1789 he was imprisoned on the orders of the ROMAN INQUISITION after he had been denounced by his wife as a heretic. In April 1791, after a session at which the Pope presided, it was decided that Cagliostro had transgressed against the penalties provided by both canon law and municipal law that dealt with heresy, heresiarchs, astrologers, magicians and freemasons. The mandatory sentence of death was commuted to one of life imprisonment, on condition that he abjured all heresy. His collection of books, including his *Memoires* (1786) and a manuscript, "Maconnerie Egyptienne" (1789), as well as certain instruments were burnt in public. A further manuscript, also destroyed, claimed that the Inquisition itself had made Christianity godless, superstitious and degrading. His books were placed on both the Roman and Spanish Indexes.
SEE ALSO Roman Indexes (1670-1800) and Spanish Inquisition 2.

Cain's Book This novel by Alexander Trocchi appeared in 1960, published in New York by Grove Press. Trocchi, who had worked both as an editor and pseudonymous author for MAURICE GIRODIAS, had already written his acknowledged autobiography, *Young Adam*, in 1955. *Cain's Book* appeared with a demurring preface, stating that the narrator's heroin use and allied adventures were not those of the author.

Trocchi's junkie hero lives on a garbage scow in New York, musing on the necessity to defy utterly any prohibitions either on hard drugs or on the arts.

When the book was issued by JOHN CALDER in 1963, at the then high and thus safe price of £1.25, Trocci was feted as a new star. Aware of the crackdown that followed the conviction of MEMOIRS OF A WOMAN OF PLEASURE in 1964, the publisher limited distribution to legitimate bookshops. Nonetheless some copies still appeared in the seedier stores and in February 1964 *Cain's Book* was seized, along with 48 other novels and 906 magazines, in a series of police raids in Sheffield. At a preliminary hearing the police stated that the book "seems to advocate the use of drugs in schools so that children should have a clearer conception of art. That, in our submission, is corrupting."

The trial began on April 15. The defense put forward the book's literary merit. The prosecution challenged this and after a 45-minute retirement, the jury found against the publishers. Trocchi arranged a public burning of his novel as his personal response. An appeal was unsuccessful. Lord Chief Justice Parker made it clear that such a book "highlighting as it were, the favourable effects of drug taking," must never be allowed to fall into innocent hands. While there was no actual obscenity, the hero's addiction to heroin was sufficient reason for censorship.

Calder, John John Calder was to British publishing in the 1960s what BARNEY ROSSET was contemporaneously in America and MAURICE GIRODIAS had been in France a decade before. Calder, with his partner Marion Boyars, was the supreme promoter of modern literature in the decade. His intention was to disseminate the works of a number of discrete groups: "the New British School" (consisting of Ann Quin, R.C. Kennedy, Aidan Higgins and Alan Burns); "the American Scene" (Henry Miller, William Burroughs, Robert Creeley and various Beat writers); "the Nouveau Roman" (French writers Alain Robbe-Grillet, Nathalie Sarraute, Marguerite Duras); "the Avant-Garde Theater" (Eugene Ionesco, Peter Weiss, David Mercer, Fernando Arrabal and Samuel Beckett). He also published various former victims of JOSEPH MCCARTHY, such as Albert Maltz and Alvah Bessie. In 1962 and 1963 he organized the Edinburgh Writers' Conference, which attracted many of his favored authors. Many of his titles had previously appeared in Girodias' OLYMPIA PRESS and were currently published in the U.S. by Rosset's Grove Press.

Unlike his peers in America and France Calder suffered relatively rarely from censorship, although he was willing, as in the case of Trocchi's CAIN'S BOOK or Hubert Selby's LAST

EXIT TO BROOKLYN, to fight when necessary for his author's rights. He was also a founder of the Defence of Literature and the Arts Society, formed in 1968 in the wake of the *Last Exit* ... trial to help coordinate a variety of anti-censorship campaigns. In general he preferred caution to confrontation, ensuring as far as possible that Calder books eluded the authorities, rather than challenged them. He priced his books high, above the prevailing hardback prices. Finally, he avoided any descent into pornography, eschewing Girodias' pseudonymous creations or Rosset's disinterred Victoriana.

Caldwell, Erskine   SEE *God's Little Acre.*

California

1. Criminal Syndicalism Act   Under this act, sections 11400 and 114001 of the California Penal Code, "criminal syndicalism" is defined as:

> any doctrine or precept advocating, teaching or aiding and abetting the commission of crime, sabotage (which word is hereby defined as meaning wilful and malicious physical damage or injury to physical property), or unlawful acts of force and violence or unlawful methods of terrorism as a means of accomplishing a change in industrial ownership or control, or effecting any political change ... Any person who: 1. By spoken or written words or personal conduct advocates, teaches or aids and abets criminal syndicalism or the duty, necessity or propriety of committing crime, sabotage, violence or any unlawful method of terrorism as a means of accomplishing a change in industrial ownership or control, or effecting any political change; or 2. Willfully and deliberately by spoken or written words justifies or attempts to justify criminal syndicalism ... or 3. Prints, publishes, edits, issues or circulates or publicly displays any books, paper, pamphlet, document, poster or written or printed matter in any form ... teaching ... criminal syndicalism; or 4. Organizes or assists in organizing ... any organization ... assembled to advocate ... criminal syndicalism ... is guilty of a felony and punishable by imprisonment in the state prison not less than one nor more than fourteen years.

2. obscenity statute   Under section 311 of the California Penal Code it is stated that "Every person who wilfully and lewdly, either ... writes, composes, stereotypes, prints, publishes, sells, distributes, keeps for sale, or exhibits any obscene or indecent writing, paper, or book; or designs, copies, draws, engraves, paints or otherwise makes any obscene or indecent figure; or writes, composes or publishes any notice or advertisement of such writing, paper, book, picture, print or figure ... is guilty of a misdemeanor." Within the statute "obscene matter" is defined as "matter, taken as a whole, the predominant appeal of which to the AVERAGE PERSON, applying contemporary community standards, is to prurient interest, i.e., a shameful or morbid interest in nudity, sex or excretion; and is matter which taken as a whole goes substantially beyond customary limits of candor in description or representation of such matters; and is matter which

taken as a whole is utterly without redeeming social importance."

3. offensive language   Under section 415 of the California Penal Code, "Every person who maliciously and wilfully disturbs the peace and quiet of any neighborhood or person, by loud and unusual noise, or by tumultuous or offensive conduct ... or use(s) any vulgar, profane, or indecent language within the presence or hearing of women or children, in a loud and boisterous manner, is guilty of a misdemeanor." SEE ALSO *Cohen* v. *California* (1971).

Caligula   Gaius Caligula (31-60) was the fourth Roman emperor to be profiled in Suetonius' book, *The Twelve Caesars*, which he wrote sometime during the early part of the second century A.D. Caligula earned his nickname, translated as "bootikin," from the diminutive army boots that he wore as a child. He was a monstrous figure even by the bloody-minded standards of such peers as the Emperors Tiberius and Nero; a penchant for arbitrary, sadistic violence was matched by unbridled sexual self-indulgence. In 1980 Caligula's life was portrayed on film via a screenplay by the novelist Gore Vidal. The film starred Malcolm McDowell, Peter O'Toole and Sir John Gielgud. As shot, under the auspices of *Penthouse* magazine's owner, Bob Guccione, the film was a profane hymn to the glories of sex and violence. Nothing was apparently missing, neither as to cruelty or perversion, and the screen seemed constantly awash with naked bodies, writhing either in pleasure or in pain. So excessive did it appear even to its participants that Vidal, O'Toole, McDowell and Gielgud all stated that they wished to be officially disassociated from it. Vidal's name was removed from the credits, but the actors remained on screen.

Unsurprisingly the film met a number of local objections on its release in America. The most notable of these were in Boston, and in Atlanta. In neither case were the prosecutors able to have *Caligula* declared obscene. In Boston the judge, prompted by the testimony of social scientist Andrew Hacker, was forced to accept that while the film was indeed highly prurient, it could not be denied that throughout the script ran a political truth—absolute power corrupts absolutely—that as such satisfied the standard laid down in MILLER v. CALIFORNIA. The judge in Atlanta echoed his Massachusetts colleague, accepting that the film did have sufficient serious political value to offset the charge of obscenity. In March 1984 the Supreme Court backed both judges and added not only that the film had political and artistic value but also that, far from stimulating the viewer's prurient interests, it tended rather to sicken and to disgust. The film went on to become one of America's most successful independently produced X-films.

Calvin, John   The French theologian and Protestant reformer (1509-1564) took up and accentuated the essential puritan condemnation of art that had been developing in the works of St. Augustine, SAVONAROLA and other divines. Art in general was dismissed as popish and idolatrous, with painting and sculpture, depicting the Roman saints, standing particularly condemned. In his *Institution de la religion chretienne* ("Institutes of the Christian Religion," first published in Latin in 1536), Calvin preached Bible-based fundamentalism as the authority for all belief, quoting Jeremiah and Habakuk to castigate both "art that is against Christ" (the images found in Catholic churches) and "art for art's sake" (any form of art created simply for pleasure) as "a doctrine of vanities" and a "teacher of lies." Art was sensual, immoral and, most repellent to the puritan mind, a waste of time that could be put to far better, productive use.

Cameroons   The Press Law of July 1980, itself a modification of previous press laws of December 1966, November 1969 and December 1973, makes the following provisions for the national press in an attempt to suppress the dissemination of material that might be considered prejudicial to the security and unity of the state: No publication may be established without official authorization; the government may censor or ban any imported news materials if they are seen to popularize anti-government criticisms; punishments are authorized for those who publish any material previously prohibited; once banned, an article or document must await a revised government decision before it may (if ever) appear; propagating false news and "causing grievous injury to the public" are grounds for banning; fines and imprisonment (maximum one year) may be levied on those who break the law.

Further restrictions were placed on the press after Presidential Decree 81/244 of June 22, 1981, defining "the conditions of authorisation or prohibition of a newspaper, periodical or magazine." Given the vulnerable state of the press, the decree was seen as another means of restricting non-governmental publications in the Cameroons. Specifically,

1. Any physically normal person wishing to begin publication must produce a dossier containing a stamped application detailing the name, intent and frequency of the publication; the names of all officials and executives involved; the addresses of the directors; the name and address of the printers; comprehensive details of the financial position of the company, both past, present and planned; proof of the lodging with the authorities of a 500,000 fr. security; proof that those involved have no criminal record.

2. This dossier must also be compiled by any state- or political party-owned institution wishing to establish a publication.

3. This dossier must be checked by the Ministry of Territorial Administration prior to giving or withholding permission to publish. While the ministry may take up to 60 days to return a positive decision, a silence of more than 90 days implies that the application has been rejected.

4. The minister, "without prejudice to the criminal sanctions stipulated by the law," may either on his own decision, or on the advice of a local official, "temporarily or permanently stop the publication of a newspaper, periodical or magazine

that has previously been authorized to exist, on the grounds of serious disturbance of public peace or morals." A further clause states that a publication that has been censored and confiscated three times may forfeit its authorization to exist. All those concerned had to comply with the decree within 90 days of its appearing.

The assumption of power by President Paul Biya in November 1982, replacing the regime of President Ahmadou Ahidjo, appears to have improved the situation of the press, but substantial censorship, still using the 1981 Press Law, remains. Publications that attempted to use the new freedom to criticize the regime have been condemned as purveyors of half-truths and forced to reform or close. A number of papers have already shut down and all publications are subject to checks by the military. All foreign publications are checked for stories on the Cameroons prior to being imported.

Campbell, James   James Campbell Reddie (d. 1878), who consistently styled himself "James Campbell," was an expert in pornography who collected, wrote and annotated much erotic material. An autodidact who read in Latin, French and Italian, Campbell was dedicated to his studies, and his friend and fellow erotophile HENRY ASHBEE noted that "hardly an obscene book in any language has escaped his attention." In Ashbee's opinion he "viewed erotic literature from a philosophic point of view—as illustrating more clearly than any other human nature and its attendant foibles." But his own novel, *The Amatory Experiences of a Surgeon* (1881), reveals an interest more devoted to sex than sociology. With its "nostalgie de la boue ... fantasy and a disguised sadism" (Pearsall, op. cit.), it was one of many popular pornographic works regularly seized and destroyed by the police and the vice societies.

Campbell's most important contribution to erotic scholarship was his life's major work, the three-volume *Bibliographical Notes on Books* (pre-1878), a bibliography of some 1,000 works of erotica that was part of Ashbee's bequest to the British Museum—and a vital aid to Ashbee in compiling his own NOTES ON CURIOUS AND UNCOMMON BOOKS. He also supplied the pornographer WILLIAM DUGDALE with a number of original works for reprinting in new editions and contributed translations of European erotica to Dugdale's magazine, *The Exquisite*. In 1877 his declining health and failing sight took him out of London, first to Bath and then to Crieff in Scotland where he died.

Canada

1. Access to Information Act, 1982   The Canadian Parliament passed an equivalent to the U.S. Freedom of Information Act, the Access to Information and Protection of Personal Information Act, on July 7, 1982. While the act, the bill for which was introduced in 1980, had been modified and, some would say, weakened by the exemption of cabinet documents and discussions from its provisions, it provides the public with access to a great deal of hitherto restricted material. As under the American act, individuals may use the law to request any files on themselves and to correct erroneous information contained within them. With the exception of cabinet material, over which the courts have no jurisdiction, the onus in disputed applications for access is on the government to prove why specific material may not be released and it is up to the judiciary to decide whether the information should be made available. Assuming the information is made available, the government must produce required materials within 20 working days and a fee of $10.00 must be paid on receipt of the information. An information commissioner, appointed by the government and directly responsible to Parliament, has been appointed to deal with complaints and denial of information. His decision may be countermanded by the minister of communications, but the complainant may make a further appeal to the federal and then the Supreme Court of Canada.

2. censorship As a Western democracy Canada is relatively free of overt censorship, and freedom of thought, belief, expression and of the press and other media is guaranteed in Canada's Charter of Rights and Freedoms. Nonetheless nationalists would claim that the country's cultural identity is overwhelmed by the U.S. entertainment industry, and French speakers (other than in Quebec) feel that despite constitutional guarantees as to the equal legitimacy of French as an official language, it is in effect swamped by the English-speaking majority.

Common law, based on the British model, protects individuals from defamation (as both libel and slander); those thus defamed will gain monetary compensation. Allegations of defamation can be opposed by four defenses: the absolute privilege of Parliament or the courts; the qualified privilege of those who report the defamatory statement; the concept of fair comment, whereby everyone may comment fairly and honestly on matters of public importance; justification, whereby the material under consideration is true, even if published with malice. Discrimination on grounds of race, color, religion, gender, age and physical disability is uniformly forbidden, by federal, provincial and territorial governments. The federal Human Rights Act outlaws all "hate messages" and the criminal code cites four offenses germane to such material.

Canadian obscenity laws are governed by Section 159 of the Federal Criminal Code, which makes it an offense to publish, distribute, sell or expose to view any obscene written, visual or recorded article or any other obscene thing. This section also covers crime comics. Further sections (163, 164) deal with theater and cinema and with the mails. These laws remained based on the "deprave and corrupt" test established in 1868 by Hicklin until 1959, when an effort to provide an objective test for obscenity was made. The new legal test defined an obscene publication as one in which a "dominant characteristic … is the undue exploitation of sex, or of sex and any one or more of the following subjects, namely crime, horror, cruelty and violence." The original intention was for

the two definitions to coexist, but some legal argument has ensued as to which is to take precedence. There is no defense of artistic or literary merit; the concept of public good is permissible, but there exists no definition of this term as regards an allegedly obscene article. Those who are convicted under these sections face penalties of up to two yers imprisonment and/or a fine of up to $500.

SEE ALSO the Hicklin Rule.

caricature In 1729 the book *State Law; or, the Doctrine of Libels Discussed and Examined* laid down the legal liability in England of those who used caricature or allegorical painting to attack a victim; "and paints him in any shameful posture, or ignominious manner, 'tho no name be to it; yet if the Piece be such, that the Person abused is known by it, the painter is guilty of a Libel … They that give Birth to a Slander are justly punished for it." This restriction was amplified in 1769 when the verdict in the case of *Villers* v. *Mousley* established that "to publish anything of a man that renders him ridiculous is a libel." However, in the case of *Sir John Carr, Kt.* v. *Hood and Another* (1808) it was accepted that ridicule, at least, might be a fit weapon of criticism and that truth, used as a defense in a libel case, might prove suffficient for an acquittal.

SEE ALSO *Presentation, The.*

Caricature, La *La Caricature*, a weekly satirical sheet published in Paris by CHARLES PHILIPON, first appeared on November 4, 1830, and for four years spearheaded the opposition to the government of Louis Philippe, established after the Revolution of July 1830. The struggle between the government and its critics was intense, fought over a battleground defined by William Thackeray, visiting France in 1834 to observe the political situation, as "half a dozen poor artists on one side, and His Majesty Louis Philippe, his august family, and the numberless placement and supporters of the monarchy on the other." That those "poor artists" included Daumier, Raffet, Grandville, Monnier, Pigalle and several other leading painters and printmakers helped the opposition cause. The government, nonetheless, held the real power. As Philipon battled with pictures and prose to show how the brave promises of 1830 had declined into empty mouthings, the authorities fought to silence his efforts, seizing 27 separate issues of the paper. A typical seizure was that of May 5, 1831, when a cartoon—*Soap Bubbles*—showed governmental promises of reform as bursting bubbles. Of all the paper's efforts, the most telling was Philipon's coinage in November 1831 of a nickname for the king: La Poire, a name derived both from the French equivalent of "fathead" and the shape of the royal face.

Most notorious of the paper's caricatures was Daumier's *Gargantua*, drawn for an issue of December 1831 but never published, since the authorities seized the plates as they were being prepared. The picture was frankly scatological and quite defamatory of Louis Philippe, who was pictured on a throne-cum-lavatory. As tiny figures, each bowed beneath baskets of produce, labor up a ramp ending at the royal mouth, ranks of aristocrats, traders and placemen queue beneath the royal buttocks, carrying off the excreta, transmuted by Louis Philippe into favors, monopolies, commissions and similar financial gains. Daumier, who had already been cautioned for a "rash lithograph," was sentenced to six months in jail and a 500 franc fine.

The paper's demise in 1834 followed another Daumier print, this time of the massacre of 12 workers in the Rue Transnonien, when soldiers ran amok after one of their officers had been killed during the uprising of the Lyons silkworkers. Queues of spectators attempted to see the original work, but the authorities seized the stone and all available prints. *La Caricature* closed down, leaving Philipon only his daily paper, LE CHARIVARI.

Carlile, Richard SEE Society for the Suppression of Vice (U.K.).

Carnal Knowledge *Carnal Knowledge* was made for AVCO Embassy Pictures by Mike Nichols in 1971; it starred Jack Nicholson, Art Garfunkel, Candice Bergen and Ann-Margaret. The plot concerns the sexual development of two college students, one of whom looks for bodies, the other for minds. The film falls into two sections, their college years and their middle age, when we see what has become of them. Touting traditional morals, the film ends with the seeker after intellect happily married to a beautiful woman, while the sensualist is still wretchedly pursuing some unattainable dream of feminine perfection. The film was well and widely reviewed, earning an Oscar nomination for Ann-Margaret. It was screened in nearly 5,000 theaters and was seen by about 20 million people.

In 1972 police in the town of Albany, Georgia, acting on a search warrant, seized the film and arrested the manager of the theater where it was being shown on charges of distributing obscene material. The state courts upheld the charges and fined the manager $750, but when the case—*Jenkins* v. *Georgia* (1974)—reached the U.S. Supreme Court the conviction was reversed. The court refused to accept that under the MILLER STANDARD *Carnal Knowledge* could be defined as hard-core pornography; it was not obscene, even if the subject of the film was certainly sex. There were no overt portrayals of sexual activity, even when it was plain that such activity was taking place, and although there was nudity, this was not in itself sufficient grounds to uphold a conviction. None of the justices felt the film was remotely obscene (Justice Marshall stating off the record that "the only thing obscene about this movie is that it is obscenely boring"), but the liberal justices wanted Chief Justice Burger to accept that had he not forced the Miller Standard on the country, such cases would not even have to be heard. This Burger would not do, preferring to make sure that the country still appreciated that there must be some limits on obscenity; Justice

Brennan, representing the court's liberals—Brennan, Douglas, Marshall and Stewart—wrote a concurring opinion in which he made this point.

Carranza, Bartolomeo Carranza was archbishop of Toledo, a conspicuously rich and powerful figure, who as a favorite of Philip II of Spain accompanied that monarch to England in 1551 and presided over the burnings of a number of Protestant heretics. In 1558 he wrote his *Commentaries on the Catechism*, which was published in Antwerp. It was condemned as Lutheranism and Carranza was arrested by Ramirez, the inquisitor-general of Toledo, and imprisoned in Valladolid. In 1566 he was summoned to Rome by Pope Pius V and imprisoned there for a further six years. He was finally tried by Pius' successor, Gregory XIII, who pronounced him guilty of false doctrine. His catechism was condemned, he was forced to abjure 16 propositions and, beside a number of other penances, he was imprisoned in a monastery for five years. Although he had been paying some 1,000 gold pieces each month to have his life spared, Carranza proved too weak to suffer further punishment and died 16 days after receiving Gregory's sentence. The citizens of Toledo, who were unimpressed by the Inquisition's theology, treated his funeral as a major event, shutting all shops and honoring him as a saint and martyr.

SEE ALSO Martin Luther.

Carrington, Charles (aka Paul Fernandino) Carrington (1857-1922) was the best known and most proficient of those British publishers of pornography whose actual offices were based abroad. The continuing harassment of pornographers in the late 19th century drove many abroad; as well as Carrington, H.S. Nichol (the former partner of LEONARD SMITHERS), H. Ashford and others preferred the relative safety of Brussels or Paris. Carrington, who came from a Portuguese family, worked as an errand-boy, van-boy and lavatory attendant before, aged 16, he set up a bookstall in the Farringdon market. Here he met Leonard Smithers and through Smithers such fashionable figures as BEARDSLEY, Dowson and Wilde. After Wilde's trial Carrington published the full transcript, including material that was unprintable in the daily press; when Wilde died in 1901, Carrington bought the copyright to *The Picture of Dorian Gray*.

In 1893 Carrington immigrated to France and established a shop at 13, Faubourg Montmartre in Paris. Here he began a business in pornography, salted with a number of genuine scientific works, that lasted almost until his death. His books were well printed and designed and often claimed to have originated from "The Imperial Press." They appeared simultaneously on both sides of the Channel, and Carrington was generally recognized as a considerable annoyance to the British police. Foremost on the list of banned books issued by the British Customs was "any" book published by Carrington. The French police obtained expulsion orders against him in 1901 and 1907, but he managed to ignore both. To the irritation of their British peers, the French allowed him to continue his lucrative export trade, since by sending his packets of pornography in sealed wrappers he offended no French law.

Carrington's list, a good deal of which was taken up after his death by another expatriate publisher, JACK KAHANE, included MY SECRET LIFE, *Colonel Spanker's Experimental Lecture* (1879), the DON LEON poems, *The Lives of Fair and Gallant Ladies* by the Abbe Brantome, *The Memoirs of Dolly Morton* (1889), Rosenbaum's *The Plague of Lust, Flossie, a Venus of Fifteen* (1897), and the genuinely scholarly *Manual of Classical Erotology* ("De Figuris Veneris"), with a Latin text and its English translation by Friedrich Karl Forberg (1899). He also published the first unexpurgated English translation of *The Satyricon* by Petronius. Carrington also compiled two works of bibliography: *Forbidden Books: notes and gossip on tabooed literature, by an old bibliophile* (1902) and *Biblioteca Carringtonensis* (ca. 1906), a composite volume that combined the publisher's sale catalogs and advertising pamphlets.

Carrington's last years were wretched. Virtually blind from the effects of syphilis, he was unable to stop the depredations of his mistress and her five children who robbed him of money, possessions and his own collection of erotica. So extensive were the thefts that a shop was hired to dispose of the booty. In 1917 they had him confined in a lunatic asylum, where he died in 1922. His magnificent funeral, with full Roman Catholic rites, was paid for, no doubt, out of the profits from the deceased's former treasures.

Casanova, Giovanni Jacopo de Seingault   Casanova was an Italian adventurer (1725-98) who wrote a number of historical works in Italian but whose real reputation rests on his sexual exploits, an impressive number of which are cataloged in the 12 volumes of his *Memoirs*, which were published posthumously between 1826 and 1838. The original manuscript was held in the safe of his German publisher, Brockhaus, in Leipzig and could not be published as written until the 20th century. An expurgated version did appear but even this scandalized the authorities. The memoirs were first placed on the Roman Index in 1834 and were never removed. The French banned them in 1863, and the book only became available in general circulation in America after 1929, a situation that did not prevent its seizure by the Detroit police in 1934. IRELAND, where the control of reading persisted well into this century, banned it in 1934 and Mussolini's Fascists outlawed the work in 1935.

SEE ALSO Roman Indexes.

Catena librorum tacendorum SEE   *Index Librorum Prohibitorum* (of Henry Spencer Ashbee).

Cato   "Cato" was the pseudonym of two London journalists, John Trenchard and William Gordon, who began in 1720 to issue the "Cato Papers," in which they argued pseudo-

nymously against the prevailing law of SEDITIOUS LIBEL, asserting that a defendant should have the right to prove the truth of such a libel—since the people had the right to know the facts about those who governed them—and that the truth, once proved, should be a sufficient defense. Instead of prosecuting libels, the best means of dealing with them was to "laugh at them, and despise them." Despite Cato's splendid rhetoric, and the lasting influence of the Letters on a century of libertarian campaigning, the law did not change until 1843.

The Papers became immensely popular both in England and in its American colonies, where the growing opposition to British rule found itself increasingly frustrated by the constraints of seditious libel, which affectively precluded criticism of the government. The four volumes of the Papers, initially published in the London press, were collected as *Cato's Letters: Or, Essays on Liberty, Civil and Religious* and went through six editions between 1733 and 1755. In Colonial America, wrote historian Clinton Rossiter in *Seedtime of the Republic* (1953), the Letters "rather than Locke's *Civil Government* was the most popular, quotable, esteemed source of political ideas."

> To Cato: Without Freedom of Thought, there can be no such Thing as Wisdom; and no such Thing as publick Liberty, without Freedom of Speech; Which is the Right of every man, as far as by it he does not hurt and countroul the Right of another; and this is the only Check which it ought to suffer, the only Bounds which it ought to know. This sacred Privilege is so essential to free Government, that the Security of Property; and the Freedom of Speech, always go together; and in those wretched Countries where a Man cannot call his Tongue his own, he can scarce call any Thing his own. Whoever would overthrow the Liberty of a Nation, must begin by subduing the Freedom of Speech …
>
> That Men ought to speak well of their Governors, is true, while their Governors deserve to be well spoken of … The Administration of Government is nothing else, but the Attendance of the Trustees of the People upon the Interest and Affairs of the People … Only wicked Governors of Men dread what is said of them … All Ministers, therefore, who were Oppressors, or intended to be Oppressors, have been loud in their complaints against Freedom of Speech, and the Licence of the Press; and always restrained, or endeavoured to restrain both. In consequence of this, they have browbeaten Writers, punished them violently, and against law, and burnt their Works. By all of which they shewed how much Truth alarmed them … Freedom of Speech, therefore, being of such infinite Importance to the Preservation of Liberty, everyone who loves Liberty ought to encourage Freedom of Speech.

SEE ALSO Father of Candor; Zenger, John Peter.

Cato the Censor   Marcus Porcius Cato (234-149 B.C.) was an exemplary ROMAN CENSOR with personal responsibility for the moral standards of the Roman state. The nature of his position did not extend his authority to a modern censorship of the arts, but in his drive to regiment the *regimen morum*, or the discipline of moral practices, he stamped his authority on his contemporaries. He attempted through legislation to implement wide-ranging reforms, outlawing ostentatious public display, the building of new public works, and similar tendencies toward conspicuous consumption by individuals and the state. Despite his own loathing of commemorative statuary, an effigy was raised in his honor. The inscription read: "In honor of Cato, the censor, who, when the Roman Commonwealth was degenerating into licentiousness, by good discipline and wise institutions, restored it."

Censor, The Roman The office of censor was established in Rome under the Lex Canuela of 443 B.C. Two censors were appointed, both patricians, although the office was thrown open to plebeians following the Licinian laws of 367 B.C. and 351 B.C. The initial task of the censors was to hold the census, the register of Roman citizens and their property ("censes," or wealth), that was in theory taken every five years, although these intervals varied considerably. Although the censors lacked certain of the highest degrees of Roman authority, the office was regarded as one of the most powerful in the state. This respect stemmed less from their duties in assessing the size of the population, than in their subsequently developed, but infinitely more important role as regarded the *regimen morum*: the discipline of moral practices.

Essentially, this meant determining to what extent each individual male citizen (women were not citizens and therefore not responsible to the censors) fulfilled his duty to the state. The censors were thus in control of both public and private morality and were empowered to call before them any citizens who were seen as transgressing the performance of the *mos maiorum*, a hypothetical collection of standards and characteristics that were presumed to have been those of an earlier and more admirable brand of citizen. A citizen thus summoned would face the *nota*, the official accusation, after which, if one failed to provide an adequate defense, one would lose a variety of privileges. These could be reinstated by later censors and the citizen was not disqualified from serving the state in war or peace. There was no appeal.

Breaches under which the *nota* was served included such offenses in private life as: the irregular dissolution of marriage or betrothal, neglect of the obligation of marrying, ill-treatment of one's wife or children, neglect or carelessness in cultivation of one's land, cruelty to slaves, trading malpractice, general venality, legacy-hunting. Offenses in public life included corruption, perjury, military misconduct as well as a variety of offenses simply considered to be injurious to the public morality. Censors also administered state finance, especially as regarded setting and collecting property and other taxes. They superintended the construction and maintenance of public buildings and had responsibility for all aspects of worshiping the Roman gods. The office lapsed in 22 B.C., after which the emperor took on all of its duties, under the title of *Morum Praefecti*.

SEE ALSO Cato the Censor.

Centuria librorum absconditorum SEE *Index Librorum Prohibitorum* (of Henry Spencer Ashbee).

Chambers, Whittaker SEE House Committee on Un-American Activities (HUAC).

Chant d'Amour, Un This film is the only one made by the French writer JEAN GENET. Like some of his prose works, it reflects his own experiences in a Paris prison and deals particularly with overt homosexuality. Made in the style of a silent film of the 1920s, *Un Chant d'Amour* has no soundtrack or titles, is shot in harsh artificial light and lasts 26 minutes. Its actors, all male professionals, portray a guard and four prisoners, and the plot focuses on the affair going on between two of the latter. When in 1966 distributor Sol Landau attempted to exhibit the film in Berkeley, California, he was informed by a member of the local police special investigations department that were he to continue screening it, the film "would be confiscated and the person responsible arrested." Landau responded by instituting the case of *Landau v. Fording* (1966) in which he sought to show Genet's work without police harassment. The Alameda County Superior Court watched the film twice and declared that it "explicitly and vividly revealed acts of masturbation, oral copulation, the infamous crime against nature [a euphemism for sodomy], voyeurism, nudity, sadism, masochism and sex …" The court rejected Landau's suit, further condemning the film as "cheap pornography calculated to promote homosexuality, perversion and morbid sex practices." He was similarly rebuffed in the District Court of Appeal of California, which accepted that Genet was a major writer but cited this as a lesser work of an early period and declared that in the end it was "nothing more than hard-core pornography and should be banned." When the case reached the U.S. Supreme Court, the decision was confirmed once more, in a 5-4 per curiam decision in which the justices simply stated that *Un Chant d'Amour* was obscene and offered no further explanation.

Chanting Cherubs, The The first marble statue ever commissioned by one American from another was ordered by the writer James Fenimore Cooper from the sculptor Horatio Greenough in 1831. Greenough's *Chanting Cherubs* was copied from the putti in the painting *Madonna del Trono* by Raphael. When the sculpture was put on exhibition in New York the public was scandalized and the resulting outcry forced the artist to place little aprons on the marble infants "for the sake of modesty." The great moral indignation caused by the cherubs was compounded by the fact that many were equally infuriated that the carved stone failed, despite its title, to sing. Enraged puritans conspicuously mutilated the three-foot-high statue. In 1832, inspired by the attacks of an anonymous critic, "Modistus," the painter Charles Cromwell Ingham successfully persuaded the U.S. National Academy of Design to replace the obvious mutilations with plaster fig leaves.

Chaplinsky v. *New Hampshire* **(1942)** This case was the basis of the Supreme Court's landmark decision regarding the doctrine of FIGHTING WORDS, those words that, like libel, slander and obscenity, are not protected by the First Amendment of the U.S. Constitution. The initial prosecution was brought against the defendant Chaplinsky who was charged under New Hampshire's Offensive Conduct Law (chap. 378, para. 2 of the N.H. Public Laws), whereby it is prohibited for anyone to addresss "any offensive, derisive or annoying word to any other person who is lawfully in any street or other public place ... or to call him by any offensive or derisive name." Chaplinsky had called certain individuals in the town of Rochester "goddamned racketeers" and "facists," and had stated that "the whole government of Rochester are fascists or agents of fascists." When the case reached the Supreme Court it was declared that Chaplinsky's abuse did fall into the category of "fighting words" and as such was not protected by the laws regarding freedom of speech. The court stated that "resort to epithets or personal abuse is not in any proper sense a communication of information or opinion safeguarded by the Constitution" and defined the word "offensive" in this context not "in terms of what a particular addressee thinks ... [but] ... what men of common intelligence would understand would be words likely to cause an average addressee to fight."

SEE ALSO *Cohen* v. *California*; United States 7. Constitution.

Charivari, Le Published by CHARLES PHILIPON, *Le Charivari* appeared daily in Paris from its launch in 1832; defying a number of prosecutions and a six-month period when government censors banned so many illustrations that the paper was composed of virtually blank pages, each one carrying only a declaration against censorship in a plain black frame. One successful government prosecution was of Charles Vernier for his engraving *Actualities* in 1851; and the work of Daumier was subject to continual censorship. Satire did defeat the censors in December 1835 when the editor appeared on a charge of lese-majeste concerning an illustration. When it was proved that the same picture had already been published to illustrated a book by Thiers, one of the king's favorites, the government case was promptly abandoned.

SEE ALSO *La Caricature*.

Charter 77 In January 1977 a number of Czechoslovak intellectuals issued Charter 77 (Charta 77), a gloss on the progress of the Final Act of the Helsinki Conference (1975) (see Helsinki Final Act) regarding their own country. Charter 77 is not an organization and has no formal rules of membership; it is a "loose, informal and open association of people of different shades of opinion, faiths and professions united by the will to strive individually and collectively for the respecting of civic and human rights." Its aim is not to organize political activity, but to create a dialogue between the population and its government. The original spokesmen saw it as "an attempt to rehabilitate the individual as a unique and irreplaceable human being and to take the individual back to where he belongs, namely, at the center of social activity, as the measure of politics, the law and the system ..." It also aims to document violations of civil rights, to suggest the amelioration of such violations and to act as an intermediary in situations of conflict. A variety of sub-groups combine to create a number of programs, notably VONS (the Committee for the Defense of the Unjustly Persecuted), which continues to publish details of the abuses of law in Czechoslovakia, and *Information on Charter 77*, a monthly bulletin that details all Charter 77 statements and other documents.

Although the authorities declared continually that Czechoslovakia was "consistently fulfilling all the requirements" of Helsinki (itself based on the International Covenants on Civil and Political Rights and on Economic, Social and Cultural Rights), the Charter 77 signatories, most notably Dr. Jan Patocka, Dr. Vaclav Havel and Professor Dr. Jiri Hajek, condemned this claim as illusory. The charter specifies the extent to which in Czechoslovakia, "basic human rights ... exist, regrettably, on paper alone."

The original signatories of the charter numbered 242; they increased swiftly to 631. The authorities responded almost immediately by arresting and interrogating a number of those involved; although they were not imprisoned permanently, a number lost their jobs as a result of their stance.

chastity of records SEE *Commonwealth* v. *Sharpless*.

Chesser, Dr. Eustace SEE *Love Without Fear*.

Chicago film censorship In 1908, under an ordinance passed in November 1907 providing for the licensing of any films shown in the city, the Chicago chief of police banned two films—THE JAMES BOYS IN MISSOURI and *Night Riders*—thus making himself the first public official to ban a film in America. This local censorship has persisted ever since. Under section 155 of the Chicago Municipal Code: "It shall be unlawful for any person to show or exhibit in a public place [any motion picture] without first having secured a permit therefore from the commissioner of police ..." This permit is only granted once the film in question has been submitted to the commissioner and has been viewed by him, after which he has three days to either grant or withhold his permission. A picture may be banned if it is "immoral or obscene, or portrays depravity, criminality or lack of virtue of a class of citizens of any race, color, creed, or religion and exposes them to contempt, derision or obloquy, or tends to produce a breach of the peace or riots, or purports to represent any hanging, lynching or burning of a human being ..." The code has been challenged on many occasions, but while the fine print regarding definitions, rights of appeal and similar points may have been revised, the necessity for a police-authorized permit remains.

Children and Young Persons (Harmful Publications) Act (1955, U.K.) Horror comics, invariably imported into Britain from America and featuring what for Britain were hitherto unprecedented depictions of gruesome, bloody and violent carnage, were the video nasties of the 1950s. Such material was seen as potentially injurious to the morals and manners of the young, and backbench parliamentarians and the tabloid press joined forces in the creation of what disinterested observers criticized as a somewhat hysterical response. However, the furor was sufficient to persuade the authorities, and in 1955 this act was passed, designed specifically to outlaw such publications. The solicitor-general was determined to prevent "the state of mind that might be induced in certain types of children by provoking a kind of morbid brooding or ghoulishness, or mental ill-health." The act defines a child as a person under 17 years.

The law bans those comics that portray "the commission of crimes ... or acts of violence or cruelty ... or incidents of a repulsive or horrible nature," with the additional prohibition of any work that "as a whole would tend to corrupt a child or young person into whose hands it might fall." The act has never been tested in the crown courts (as has the OBSCENE PUBLICATIONS ACT [1959]), but has generally succeeded simply by frightening the distributors of such material into inactivity, although the maximum penalty is only four months in jail or a fine of £100.00. Of the 40 cases involving horror comics referred to the director of public prosecutions up to 1978, six had resulted in further action, all of which led to convictions. Trial is always held in a magistrates court.

Chile

1. censorship Although the domination of General Augusto Pinochet Ugarte was technically rejected by the people in the plebiscite of October 1988, his 15 years of authoritarian rule (from 1973) have stamped a definite, repressive image upon Chile's media and book publishing. After the immediate onslaught on all areas of media and the arts that followed his assumption of power, many of the new controls were codified in the constitution of 1980. While article 19, clause 12 guarantees freedom of expression and private opinion in the press and media, bars the state from establishing a monopoly over the media, and allows prior censorship only to uphold general norms in the arts, further clauses effectively refute these freedoms. Article 24 gives Pinochet the right to restrict freedom of assembly and freedom of information; such restrictions cannot be questioned by any court. Article 41 allows for the curtailing of freedom of information and opinion during a state of emergency. This can be proclaimed by the president at any time and allows for complete censorship if necessary.

As well as laws governing libel, slander and privacy (it is illegal to publish material concerning an individual's private life that damages or could damage the individual), a major plank in Pinochet's control of free expression is the Law for Internal Security. This law forbids any subversion of public order either by calling for anti-government demonstrations or by publishing such material.

2. literary censorship In the immediate aftermath of the military coup that overthrew the left-wing President Salvador Allende in 1973, the new government set out to take absolute control of Chilean culture. A wholesale attack was launched on the arts, including the destruction of much literature, all condemned as subversive of the new regime. This censorship was further organized under the Direccion de Inteligencia Nacional (DINA) and the Direccion Nacional de Comunicacion Social (DINACOS), which latter organization, as part of the Ministry of the Interior, ran a censorship board. Under two military decrees of 1977 and 1978 all publications (both Chilean and imported) were to be checked by this board. All books were also subject to a value-added tax of 20 percent of their cover price.

The new constitution of 1980, enforced after March 1981, elaborated further rules regulating books. Although freedom of expression is guaranteed, article 24 provides that all new publications must undergo censorship, with the threat of substantial fines for noncompliance. Few books were actually banned, but since the government had an unlimited period of time to decide whether a publication was to be allowed distribution, a publication could simply vanish, unpublished, into the bureaucracy, a victim of administrative silence. To defend writers and readers, the Chilean Society of Authors set up the Permanent Committee for the Defense of Freedom of Expression, lobbying for greater freedoms, challenging censorship and generally defending books. So successful were their efforts that in June 1983 all provisions of prior government censorship were abandoned, thus improving the position of literature. Some argue, however, that self-censorship has become so ingrained that Chilean writers remain largely muted. In addition, the soaring prices of books tends to keep readership small, restricting any real impact.

3. media censorship The immediate consequence for the Chilean press of the fall of President Allende in 1973 was the purging of its ranks: Several hundred journalists were interned in concentration camps, shot dead, or secretly detained without trial; at least 150 escaped into exile. Newspapers that had supported Allende were shut down and a system of pre-censorship was established, for all publications. This system lasted only three months, but was replaced by widespread implicit censorship whereby the press is controlled tightly, but more subtly, relying largely on journalistic self-censorship. Individual journalists were also threatened by vigilantes who break up union meetings, assault "corrupt" journalists and generally add their unofficial weight to more established restrictions. The broadcast media suffered similar purging: All pro-Allende radio and television stations were placed under state control, with senior members of the military assuming controlling positions. Many former employees were blacklisted.

Many censorship regulations were created to control the media, including a lengthy list of taboo topics banned from coverage. Under the ongoing emergency, a magazine or newspaper may be suspended for up to six issues and a broadcasting station for up to six days. Economic pressures, notably the channeling of lucrative government-controlled or private enterprise advertising to the pro-regime press, are used to control the media further. In general, the intensity of control varies directly as to the assumed impact of the medium under consideration: Thus television is the most restricted. The consolidation of President Pinochet's power has led to a certain relaxation in control in the last few years, but the assassination attempt in summer 1986 led immediately to the restoration of a state of siege, with the harsher censorship that this implies. Nonetheless, as seen in the build-up to the plebiscite of 1988, the opposition press, aided by the country's church-backed human rights movement, refused to collapse and, paradoxically, has flourished in the face of repression.

As of mid-1987 the government was again considering proposals, based on the freedoms of communication written into the constitution of 1980 and with an eye to the proposed free elections scheduled for 1989, for legislation regarding the media. A committee under Don Sergio Fernandez, the former minister of the interior, was appointed to make suggestions for a new law. The current project is based on article 12 of clause 19 of the constitution, referring specifically to "Constitutional Rights and Obligations," which guarantees to all citizens "Freedom to express opinions and to disseminate information without prior censorship in any form and by any means, without prejudice to assuming the responsibility for any crimes or abuses committed in the exercise of such liberties, in conformance with the law which is to be approved by a qualified quorum. In no case may the law establish a state monopoly over the mass comunication media."

As well as granting to various institutions and individuals the right to publish, and the proposed establishment of autonomous bodies for the censorship of television, radio, films and other artistic activities, the committee opted for a right of reply to printed or broadcast material: "Every individual or juridical person offended or unjustly alluded to in some mass communication medium has the right to have his declaration or rectification gratuitously disseminated ... by the mass communication medium which issued such information."

The National Board of Radio and Television (responsible for control of the communications media) is designed as a collegiate organization; it is composed of five high-ranking advisers, one appointed by the state president, one by the Senate, one by the Supreme Court, one by the defense staff and one by the Chilean Institute. Although the council is intended to replace direct governmental control it will retain sweeping powers, among which is the provision that "no sanctioning of a radio broadcast or TV channel can be carried out without a favorable vote of at least three of the Council." Despite this the proposed legislation promises "the fullest programming freedom in all fields of cultural, scientific and social affairs." All state- and university-run stations are to devote one hour per day to political programming, when allowed to do so within the relevant legal rules. In theory all parties are allowed equal access to such broadcasts.

This bill was the responsibility of General Pinochet and subject to his revisions and approval. It may be abandoned given the new, post-plebiscite situation. Alternatively, since Pinochet is still officially in power, he may consider it further and, if he finds it satisfactory, it will presumably be forwarded to the government and made into a law. The extent to which the letter of the proposed law will accord with its actual implementation may, on the basis of the Chilean status quo, be limited.

China

1. censorship   Under the 1982 constitution the People's Republic of China guarantees full freedom of expression, but the constitution also contains certain articles that act to restrict such freedom. As well as laws governing libel and insult and false charge, citizens are forbidden to exercise their rights and freedoms if they "infringe upon the interests of the state, of society, and of the collective, or upon the lawful freedoms and rights of other citizens." They must not commit acts detrimental to the motherland and must keep "state secrets, protect public property, observe labor discipline and public order and respect social order." Above all these stand the Four Basic Priciples of the Party: "upholding party leadership, Marxist-Leninism-Mao Zedong thought, the people's democratic dictatorship, and socialism."

Against this background contemporary China has continued the fluctuating policies on cultural and media controls that have typified the whole revolutionary era since 1949. After the apparent liberalization of the early 1980s, the "Anti-Bourgeois Liberalization" policy was launched in 1987. A number of scientists, journalists and writers were expelled from the party, and various books and films have been banned. A number of vociferously critical publications were shut down, although purged journalists were no longer sent to labor camps or subjected to "reeducation" as they were under the Cultural Revolution. Predictably, the nationwide crackdown that followed the student-inspired democracy movement of May/June 1989 has only intensified governmental determination to suppress every vestige of free speech. The students themselves face intense pressures, from propaganda, reeducation and the judicial system. An unknown number of leaders have already been executed. Foreign reporting, surprisingly unfettered even as the troops moved in, is now strictly controlled.

The party owns and dominates the nation's press, radio and TV; as the unashamed propagandizing that has followed the massacre in Tiananmen Square has proved, the party has no scruples in rewriting history as and when required. Senior staff are invariably party cadres and concentrate on their main function: supporting and sustaining the revolution. The ideal proletarian journalist (a Maoist conception) exists for no other purpose. China's national press is geared to serving specific markets. *The People's Daily* (*Renmin Ribao*) and *Red Flag* (*Hong Qi*) are aimed at cadres and filled with theoretical discussion. Other papers are produced for the military, the National Workers Union, intellectuals, writers and artists, the young and so on. This system is replicated on a provincial and local level.

China has two news agencies, which serve internal and foreign media. Incoming news, obtained from foreign agencies, is strictly censored. A number of semi-secret publications based on such material are circulated to various levels of party members. They include *Reference News* (*Can Cao Xiao Si*), *Reference Materials* (*Can Cao Zilino*), and the top secret *Internal Reference* (*Neibu Cankao*), which reaches only the elite.

With party cadres in control of the press and other media, day to day censorship does not require much external supervision. Self-censorship in the promotion of the revolutionary line is automatic and party committees work on various levels to help dictate the line. Only important stories are submitted to senior authorities, as high as the party leadership in some cases, when it is important to disseminate an absolute version of the news.

2. film censorship The Chinese film industry established from its earliest days an influential role both in entertaining the people and conveying to a broad spectrum of audiences a variety of messages, either supportive or subversive of the status quo. Relatively uncensored, it had gained great sophistication by the 1930s and 1940s; among its actors was the future wife of Chairman Mao, Jiang Qing. Like all the Chinese arts, post-Revolutionary films were dominated by the precepts established in Mao's speeches to the Yenan Forum in Literature and Art in 1942. While the industry, with its main centers in Peking, Shanghai and Changchun, continued to flourish, it was gradually suborned to the party line.

A Film Bureau and department of propaganda, both under the Ministry of Culture, were created in 1949 and laid down the obligations of film in China: "A film industry must be created that fully serves the interests of all the people and which speaks out clearly and truthfully on the burning questions of the day." The repertoire included home-produced films, reprints of Soviet originals, documentaries and a number of specially commissioned works, produced in Hong Kong. The first film to be banned, in 1950, was *The Life of a Peking Policeman*. More relevant to the struggles within the party, and a pointer to the repression of the arts that would dominate the Cultural Revolution, was the controversy over, and subsequent banning of, *The Inside Story of the Qing Court*, an allegedly counter-revolutionary film; the attack was inspired by Jiang Qing, now a senior functionary in the Film Bureau.

Conforming to the general development of the arts in China, the film industry suffered the policy fluctuations of the 1950s, when it was rigorously molded into a propaganda agency for the state; of the HUNDRED FLOWERS MOVEMENT,

when it enjoyed temporary liberalization; and of the antirightist movement that followed, when repression was reintroduced. The Great Leap Forward intensified this control, with a new emphasis on high production norms. Like literature and the theater, the film business was viciously attacked during the Cultural Revolution. With Jiang Qing in absolute control of the arts, the "poisonous weeds campaign" of 1964, heralding the Cultural Revolution, proscribed some 400 Chinese films. The industry was suspended: No feature films were produced between 1964 and 1971, and afterwards only film versions of the model operas, followed in 1973 by some productions that had marginally different plots but the same general style.

The death of Mao and the subsequent fall of the Gang of Four (including Jiang Qing) in 1976 instigated a period of liberalization in the arts. Surviving industry personnel, in disgrace since 1964, were rehabilitated, and formerly banned films joined newly created material as the cinema regained its strength. A climate of intellectual freedom prospered until 1978, when attempts to curb it were renewed. In the early 1980s, control, rather than unfettered creativity, seemed to have the upper hand, but by 1986 the pendulum had reversed once more and a liberal tone, by Chinese standards, was more in evidence.

3. music censorship As part of its attempt to remodel the whole edifice of Chinese culture the Revolution of 1949 imposed immediate controls on musical composition, based on the ideology and needs of the new political system, and censoring on both moral and political grounds. While the party's methods of censorship were new, they were the direct development of the tendency of all Chinese rulers to use music for didactic purposes and to place its regulation among the functions of a government. This role was further complicated by the 20th-century incursion of western music into traditional forms, although such experimentation was confined mainly to the sophisticated cities of the Chinese coast. The attempt, as early as the 1930s, by party intellectuals, who appreciated Western composers, to fuse these two incompatible styles developed into a compromise called "walking on two legs," whereby traditional Chinese forms were gradually to be reworked on a Western model. All music, as explained in Mao Zedong's "Talk to the Music Workers" in 1956, was naturally to be suborned to ideological needs. The isolation of China for most of the Maoist period meant that official interference in music was less a matter of suppression than of direction. Decadent Western music was simply unavailable. The most revolutionary changes came in the imposition by the Cultural Revolution of Jiang Qing's "model revolutionary operas," the performance of which dominated Chinese cultural life during that upheaval.

The liberalization that followed Mao's death in 1976 naturally extended to music, with the reemergence of Western influences and the forging of new links with the outside world. While the authorities today tolerate classical works, the gradual incursion of decadent forms, notably rock 'n' roll, even as represented by the more anodyne teen idols, is more threatening, creating as it has a class of alienated young people keen to ape the mores of Western youth and heavily influenced by Hong Kong style. To counter this trend, the People's Music Press of Beijing has issued a guide, "How to Distinguish Decadent Songs," which explains and warns against jazz, rock and disco. On a tougher level, the authorities in March 1982 issued a "Resolution Strictly Prohibiting the Import, Reproduction, Sale and Transmission of Reactionary Yellow Obscene Recordings and Video Recordings," aimed particularly at blue films and teenage music, both of which are prohibited from import and which may be seized from those who have managed to procure them. Party members are encouraged to track down the owners of such recordings and to discipline them. The campaign has also been extended to eradicating the music that developed during the Cultural Revolution. While there is yet no clear line between decadent songs and simple pop music that satisfies the needs of art workers and the popular masses for foreign works, the control of such imports may well be tightened, depending on the fluctuations of Chinese cultural policy.

4. official publishing   Publishing in prerevolutionary China had developed into a large-scale industry, with firms ranging from the massive Commercial Press (with its stock of 8,000 titles) to a variety of much smaller houses. After the Revolution the Maoist government imposed itself upon this network, winnowing out products that were no longer ideologically acceptable. The first National Conference on Publishing, in 1950, established the Publications Administration Bureau, a branch of the Ministry of Culture, which was to be responsible for every aspect of the business: paper supplies, printing and distribution. To empower the PAB, the conference passed the Provisional Regulations Concerning the Control of Book and Periodical Publication and the Provisional Measures Governing the Registration of Periodicals. The latter noted the name and address of every publisher and printing office and extracted from the publisher and printer a pledge to obey the Provisional Regulations.

The regulations laid down that no publisher should "violate the Common Program of the Chinese People's Political Consultative Conference or the decrees of the government." Publishers that satisfied the local branch of the PAB would be given an authorization number, which was to be printed on all issues. The publication might then be distributed through the Post Office. Copies of every publication had to go both to libraries—state and local—and to the local organs in charge of publication administration. This offered some opportunity for post-production censorship, but few publishers, with their large print runs, would have risked their work at this stage, and a system of self-censorship was quickly established. The backlog of pre-1949 titles was checked and cut. Of the Commercial Press' 8,000 titles, 1,234 were permitted distribution; the remainder were sold as waste paper.

Many smaller publishers survived, still publishing until the Cultural Revolution.

"Responsible" publishing was also helped by the general decline of literature in the face of a massive demand, never fully satisfied, for scientific and technological works. Publishing in China is on the whole confined to the major cities. During the Great Leap Forward of 1958 the director of the largest publisher, the People's Press in Peking, was dismissed for advocating an end to state supervision and the development of free buying, selling and criticism of books. This led to an attempt to decentralize publishing into the various regions of the country, but this failed. Among other problems, too many books of similar value on similar topics were thus published, when a single, centralized edition would have been quite sufficient.

Publishing, like the rest of Chinese society, was heavily controlled during the Cultural Revolution (1966-72). For content editors wanted only stories and articles "that present revolutionary content in a healthy way." Such material had to "exalt the great Chairman Mao with deep and warm proletarian feelings" and similarly exalt the party and the revolutionary line, follow the example of Jiang Qing's model revolutionary operas and "zealously strive to create peasant and worker heroes," and reflect the history of the Revolution and its victorious progress. On a stylistic level they required texts with a "mass, revolutionary and militant character"; all should reflect the Maoist-Marxist-Leninist line and extol socialism while intensifying denunciation of "revisionists and swindlers." During the Cultural Revolution the number of works published dropped substantially. All academic journals vanished for at least six years. Many publishers were closed and what did appear was utterly pure.

After the fall of the Gang of Four in 1976, the publishing industry began to regain strength, the number of publishing houses increased and a number of old ones reemerged. Regional publishers also benefited and launched many young, aspirant writers. The main change is the reprinting of work by individuals who were formerly banned and the return of many foreign classics. There also exists a tolerated level of unofficial publishing, appearing in parallel with sanctioned material, which advocates human rights, non-party-line literature etc. Such journals include *Peking Spring*, *Today*, *April 5th Tribune* and others. The publishing output is tabulated, at least in part, in the monthly "National List of New Publications" (*Quan guo xin shu mu*). This bibliography, which appeared throughout the cultural Revolution, is issued by the PAB and is compiled by New China Bookshop (*Xin hua shu dian*) using the facilities of the National Library of Peking. Certain lacunae are evident in the list, because some books appear only in short, trial editions (see below) rather than in the usual monster runs, and because the size of China simply defeats a comprehensive listing.

The distribution of publications, especially as regards their availability to foreigners, falls into five categories. These include: (1) national distribution (*guo nei fa xing*): many of these works are exported as well as being produced for home; (2) overseas distribution (*guo wai ja xing*): specifically for overseas distribution and translated into various foreign languages. These may not be available for foreigners inside China but can be bought elsewhere. Two categories are not distributed to foreigners: (3) restricted to internal distribution (*xian quo nei fa xing*); and (4) internal publication (*ne bu fa xing*). There is also (5) not for distribution (*bu fa xing*).

Much of the material is restricted not on ideological grounds but because it has been pirated, often for university and factory use, from original foreign editions or has been translated unofficially; such works, though well produced and very cheap, are thus embarrassing. Such books are available in special shops for which a pass enabling their purchase must be obtained. A further variety of restricted books are those that appear only in a short, trial edition and are distributed solely to those whose opinions may be useful. Such small runs help the authorities to control the availability of important works.

5. art censorship July 22, 1960: Third Congress of Artistic and Literary Workers established the principles that governed art in China and displayed "the terrifying spectacle of the demoralization of the spirit and the degredation of morals" found in the artistic freedoms of the West. The congress also laid down the criteria upon which works of art and literature were to be purged and banned as contrary to Chinese Socialist ideology. In essence, art in Communist China is the nerve center of the class struggle and as such it must serve "the workers, peasants and soldiers … in the victory of Marxist-Leninist principles."

6. Cultural Revolution, the The Cultural Revolution in China was inspired by the desire of Jiang Qing (Madame Mao) to reform the national arts on the basis of the cultural doctrines set down by Mao at the Yenan Forum on Literature and the Arts in 1942. These doctrines, which established the primacy of political considerations over artistic ones, and that of proletarian standards over bourgeois ones, had dominated cultural life since 1949, but Jiang Qing claimed that they had never been fully implemented. The movement was launched on November 10, 1965, with the publication in the *People's Daily* of a piece by Yao Wenyuan (of the later "Gang of Four") attacking a new historical play, *Hai Rui dismissed from office*. This triggered a massive attack on the play and with it the wholesale disruption of Chinese society termed the Cultural Revolution.

Guided by Jiang Qing the Revolution launched a two-pronged attack on the artistic status quo. Intellectuals were to be repressed, accused wholesale of being pro-bourgeois and labelled "stinking intellectuals." To replace their corrupt works, new aesthetic standards, all strictly proletarian, were to be imposed on the arts and a number of model revolutionary literary and artistic works were to be created. Chinese culture was purged. Nothing created before 1966 was to be tolerated. Those who created such works were persecuted severely. Depending on the enthusiasms of the Red Guards concerned, a writer, artist or intellectual might be beaten to death or tortured savagely (both in public), driven to suicide or madness, or, less fatally, face a round of critical "struggle meetings" led by Red Guard "criticism teams" and spend some years working in a labor camp. Many were exiled permanently to the countryside, judged too politically unsound for the cities. Their families were similarly disgraced and assaulted. The first targets of reform were individuals who held senior positions in a variety of cultural organizations, notably a variety of writer and artist unions on a national and regional level. The attacks soon spread far wider and most of China's leading intellectuals suffered. Only those who chose massively degrading public self-criticism escaped the more savage effects of the Cultural Revolution.

In place of the purged art came the various "models." Jiang Qing, an actress, had been attempting to reform the opera since 1964; she was now able to impose just eight model revolutionary operas as the nation's entire operatic repertoire until her downfall. Literature was dominated by the theory of the three contrasts: among all characters bring out the positive ones, among the positive characters bring out positive heroes, among the positive heroes bring out the principal hero. There was little resistance to the Revolution. The vicissitudes of the previous 20 years had taught intellectuals the value of silence. Fear of the Red Guards ensured that few if any dared come out in open opposition. Only a few younger writers, who have come to prominence since 1976 but were unknown then, dared challenge the movement with clandestinely published works.

SEE ALSO Hundred Flowers Movement.

chopping Chopping is U.S. military jargon for the way in which even unclassified information on military matters and material can be diluted and filtered before it is rendered safe for media and thus public consumption. When a journalist asks for information on any military-related topic, an automatic process of internal censorship takes over: A number of experts, senior officers and other figures must assess both the request and the information that is to be issued. The number of assessments, or "chops," that accompany a question vary as to the importance of the topic, but some chopping is inevitable and the process is always lengthy and often obstructive.

Chorier, Nicolas Chorier (b. 1609?), one of the earliest pioneers of modern pornography, was born in Vienne, Dauphine, in France. He was educated by Jesuit priests, after which he took a law degree in 1639 and practiced successfully as a lawyer until 1658 in the town of his birth, working at the Cour des aides, a court dealing with tax cases. When the Cour des aides was abolished in 1658, Chorier moved to Grenoble, where he published a history of the Dauphine, which earned him a cash endowment from the Provincial States and the rank of count palatine of the church. At this time he also published his most famous work, the often seized L'ACADEMIE DES

DAMES, initially issued as *Aloisiae Sigeae Toletanae Satyra Sotadica de arcanis Amoris et Veneris*, a volume originally printed in Latin and alleged to have been taken by the Dutch philologist and historian Jan de Meurs (1579-1639) from a work written by a Spanish woman, Luisa Sigea (ca. 1530-60), known by her contemporaries as the Minerva of her era. Chorier, hardly the most upright of men, published a number of second-rate histories and on one occasion stole three valuable registers of monastic records from the bishop of Grenoble before selling them back for a good price.

Christian Church

1. early censorship (150-814) The following dates incorporate a list of the decrees and prohibitions aimed by the Early Church at the control of allegedly heretical literature between A.D. 150 and 814:

150: The ACTA PAULI banned by the Council of Ephesus.

325: The First Council of Nicaea banned the *Thalia* by Arrius.

325: Emperor Constantine issued an edict directing the destruction of the works of Arrius and Porphyry. All those who failed to produce their copy would be sentenced to death.

398: Emperor Arcadius issued an edict for the destruction of the books of the Eunomians; failure to comply is punished by death. In 399 Arcadius further forbade the possession of any books on magic. Both these edicts were designed to strengthen the still parlous position of the church.

399: The Council of Alexandria, despite the determined opposition of the Egyptian monks, banned the owning or reading of the works of Origen.

431: The Council of Ephesus banned the writings and the heresy of the Nestorians. This prohibition was further extended by an edict of the Emperor Theodosius in 435: All such books were to be burned, as were those of the Manicheans, banned by Theodosius in 436.

446: Recapitulating virtually all the edicts that have preceded him, Pope Leo I issued his own ban on the works of Porphyry, Origen, the Eunomians, Montanists, Eutychians, Manicheans and any other heretical sects whose teachings contradicted those of the synods of Nicaea and Ephesus.

496: The DECRETUM GELASIUM.

536: After they had first been condemned by the Synod of Constantinople, the works of Severus were proscribed by an edict of the Emperor Justinian.

649: A decree of Pope Martin outlawed certain specified heretical works.

681: The Council of Constantinople condemned certain heretical works and ordered them burned; this was the first time the church ordered the destruction of a work itself— hitherto it had selected the books in question, but left their disposal to the secular authorities.

692: The Council of Trulla ordered the burning of certain histories of the martyrs, because they had been produced in verse form.

768: A Benedictine monk, Ambrosius Autpert, obtained permission from Pope Stephen III prior to writing a treatise. This is the first occasion that such permission had been requested; Aupert claimed that he wished to ensure that his own work conformed with the teachings of the church fathers.

787: The Second Council of Nicaea ordered the destruction of "certain falsified utterances of the martyrs" that had allegedly been prepared by "enemies of the Church."

814: Patriarch Nicephorus ordered the destruction, in Constantinople, of falsified acts of the martyrs.

SEE ALSO *Index Librorum Prohibitorum*.

2. censorship in the Middle Ages (849-1480) This list represents some of the more important attempts by the church to censor heretical material during the period preceding the creation of the Inquisitions of Rome (see Roman Inquisition), Spain and elsewhere. Like all early censorship, these attempts were not cohesive and appear on a somewhat ad hoc basis:

849: Gottschalk, a German monk, was excommunicated and imprisoned for life after he wrote a treatise refuting certain of the doctrines of St. Augustine. This action was taken on the instigation of Hincmar, archbishop of Rheims. Gottschalk died, still imprisoned, in about 869. His book, paradoxically, was never included in an Index.

1050: The Synod of Vercelli condemned the treatise of Berengar of Tours on the Lord's Supper; also that of Ratramnus of Corbu (actually written 200 years earlier) entitled *De Corpore et Sanguine de Christi*. In 1059 Berengar was forced to burn a further work—a thesis he had composed in defense of his earlier book.

1120: PETER ABELARD was forced to burn his *Introductio in Theologiam*; in 1140 Pope Innocent III ordered that all Abelard's works be burned, along with those of Arnold of Brescia. Both authors were confined in monasteries. In 1141 Abelard's entire theological works were declared heretical by the Council of Sens.

1148: Four chapters of a commentary on the works of Boethius by Gilbert de la Porree were condemned by a synod at Rheims. Gilbert had requested that the Pope make any expurgation that he desired—the first recorded occasion on which such expurgation was requested—but the Pope refused to do so, preferring simply to ban the entire book.

1209: The *Physion* of Amalric or Amaury of Chartres (who had died in 1204) was condemned by a synod at Paris. The book was burned and Amalric's remains were disinterred, officially excommunicated and dumped on unconsecrated ground. The book expounded its author's theory that what Aristotle called "primary matter" was the same thing as Divine Nature. A number of the followers of this heresy were burned themselves in December 1210.

1209: The works of David Dinant (de Nantes) were condemned by the Synod of Paris. His book *De Metaphysica* was ordered expurgated and anyone reading the original text was to be excommunicated. Some of those who refused to abjure the teaching of the "misbelieving David Dinanto" were burned at the stake.

1231: Pope Gregory IX forbade the reading of the works of Aristotle until such time as they had been purged of heresy.

1276: Instructed by Pope John XXI, Bishop Stephen Tempier published a condemnation of some 219 propositions that were currently accepted for discussion in the schools. According to Tempier these propositions were undoubtedly philosophically sound, but they clashed with theological orthodoxy. As well as the proposition, a large number of books on magic and necromancy were ordered to be turned in to the authorities within seven days, to await burning.

1311: The writings of Gherardo Segarelli, founder of the heretical Apostolic Brothers and a victim of the stake in 1300, were condemned by the Council of Vienna; this was subsequently confirmed by Pope John XXII. In the first instance of such a decision being reversed, Segarelli's work was officially pardoned by another pope, Sixtus IV, in 1471.

1316: The Inquisition of Tarragona condemned 14 treatises of the physician Arnold of Villanova (who had died in 1310); all copies were to be delivered to the authorities on pain of excommunication.

1321: Seventeen propositions from the works of Meister Eckhardt (Johannes Eckhardt, 1260?-1327), a Dominican friar who was the founder of German Mysticism, were condemned by Pope John XXII as heretical; the remainder as dangerous and suspicious. Eckhardt's works were further condemned by the University of Heidelberg in 1330.

1325-1328: Pope John XXII condemned a variety of works, including those of Marsilius of Padua and John of Jandun (1327), Petrus Johannes Oliva (whose bones were disinterred to be burned alongside his books, although Sixtus IV pardoned him in 1471), Michael of Cesena, William of Ockham, and Bonagratia of Bergamo, as well as all writings on conjuring and exorcism.

1348: The theological propositions of the Parisian Nicholas d'Autrecourt (de Ultricuria) were condemned by Pope Clement VI. The author was forced to destroy his own work.

1378: On the advice of the Inquisitor Nicholas Eymeric, Pope Gregory XI condemned 200 propositions taken from 20 treatises of Raymond Lully (ca. 1235-1315), a Spanish monk, philosopher and missionary to the Arabs. The ban was more a matter of church politics—Lully was a Franciscan, Eymeric a Dominican—than of the genuine heresy of the works involved.

1387: Richard II banned the writings of WYCLIF from England. These were further proscribed in 1408 by the Convocation of Canterbury, which requested the Universities of Oxford and Cambridge to expurgate them for future publication, and in 1415 by the Council of Constance, which simply outlawed all of Wyclif's works, as it did those of John Huss.

3. censorship of Hebrew texts (1239-1775) Even prior to the institution of the various Indexes (see Index of Indexes), the traditional texts of the Jews, notably the Talmud, source of much Jewish doctrine, were prohibited and censored by the church:

1239: All copies of the Talmud, combining the Mishnah (the precepts laid down by the Jewish elders) and the Gemara (the subsequent glosses and annotations on these) were burned on the orders of Pope Gregory IX. Acting on the allegations of heresy brought by Nicholas de Rupella, a converted Jew, letters were sent to France, England, Spain and Portugal to ensure that on a single given day all copies of the work were to be delivered to Dominicans and Minorites. These orders would check the Talmud for heresy and duly destroy that which they found. The order was carried out fully only in France.

1244: Pope Innocent IV ordered Louis IX of France to burn all copies of the Talmud. This order, which met great opposition from the Jewish community, was repeated in 1248 and 1254.

1415: Pope Benedict XIII ordered all copies of the Talmud to be delivered to the bishops of the Italian dioceses and held by them, subject to further instructions. These collections were amassed as part of the general contemporary interest in Cabbalistic studies. The Jews themselves were forbidden to possess any material that was antagonistic to Christianity.

1555: On the instructions of the Inquisition of Rome the houses of the Jewish community were searched and all copies of the Talmud seized; these were burned on the first day of Rosh Hashana, the Jewish New Year's Day. Pope Julius III ordered that no Christian might own or read the Talmud, nor might they print such material, on pain of excommunication.

1559: After the publication of the ROMAN INDEX OF 1559, which prohibited the Talmud and all other works of Jewish doctrine, some 12,000 volumes of Hebrew texts were burned after the Inquisitor Sixtus of Siena destroyed the library of the Hebrew school at Cremona.

1564: Under the TRIDENTINE INDEX all works of Jewish doctrine were banned again, other than those that were purged of possible heresies and printed under a title other than that of "Talmud." This expurgated Talmud was permitted by the Pope only after the Jewish community offered a substantial financial "gift."

1565: All Cabbalistic works were banned by the Inquisition of Rome.

1592: Pope Clement VIII forbade both Christians and Jews from owning, reading, buying or circulating Talmudic or Cabbalistic books or other "godless writings," either written or printed, in Hebrew or in other languages, which contained heresies or attacks on the church, its persons or practices. Any such work, ostensibly expurgated or not, was to be destroyed. In 1596 this ruling was modified when the *Machsor*, the basic Hebrew prayer book, was permitted to be published, but only in Hebrew.

1775: The prohibitions of Jewish doctrinal material as set out in 1559, 1564 and 1592 were all repeated by Pope Clement XIV. No Hebrew books were to be bought or sold until they had been submitted to the magister palatii (the papal chaplain charged with administering the censorship system).

4. censorship of books (1550-1661) As established by the bull COENAE DOMINI, the Papacy controlled the reading of the faithful. This authority was constantly challenged and during the late 16th century successive popes found it necessary to issue a variety of rules in an attempt to strengthen their position. Among the more notable were:

1550: Julius III revoked all previous dispensations still in use for the reading of heretical books. Similar bulls were issued by Paul IV (1558), Pius IV (1564), Paul V (1612), Gregory XV (1623) and Urban VIII (1627). Julius followed his bull by granting permission in 1551 for those cardinals named as presidents of the Council of Trent to read heretical works and, by making personal contact with them, to investigate the growing ranks of Protestants. Pius IV gave his cardinals a similar dispensation in 1564.

1568: Pius V sent a cardinal and two bishops to Germany to encourage Catholic scholars there to begin writing theses counter to those of the German Protestants.

1572: Gregory XIII issued instructions for the production of an INDEX EXPURGATORIUS; this did not actually appear until 1590.

1590: The Index Prohibitorius and Expurgatorius of Sixtus V; this was the first Index, itself a revision of the TRIDENTINE INDEX, to be carried out by the CONGREGATION OF THE INDEX.

1596: INDEX (Expurgatorius) OF CLEMENT VIII.

1607: INDEX EXPURGATORIUS OF BRASICHELLI.

5. early controls on printing (1475-1520)   Johan Gutenberg (ca. 1400-ca. 1468) invented movable type and thus founded the art of typographic printing in the mid-15th century. The church responded, unsurprisingly, with a new effort to establish control of the printing and the distribution of the increased volume of books:

1475: An anti-Semitic tract printed at Esslingen carried the notation that it had been submitted to the bishop of Regensburg for corrections and approval.

1479: Pope Sixtus IV empowered the authorities of the University of Cologne to impose ecclesiastical penalties on those printing, selling or reading heretical works. This was confirmed in 1501, although the city's printers, faced by a severe decline in business, attempted in vain to have the order rescinded.

1486: The archbishop of Mainz ordered that no book was to be printed either in the vernacular or as a translation from the classics until it had been approved by the heads of all four faculties at the Universities of Erfurt and of Mainz.

1487: Pope Innocent VIII issued a bull regulating printing, directed to the authorities of the University of Cologne. Regarded as the first general edict on censorship to come from the Papacy, it aimed to suppress theism, otherwise defined as "scientific liberty," both political and religious anarchism and nihilism, and what were described as "romances," which were considered to be immoral to the point of pornography. Punishments included fines, excommunication and the burning of offending volumes.

1491: Niccolo Franco, bishop of Treviso and papal legate to Venice, issued a "Constitution," considered as the first printed censorship regulation issued by the church and as the first prohibition of printed books, whereby no printed material was henceforth to be issued without the permission of the bishop or vicar-general of the diocese. Miscreants would face excommunication. The edict also banned two titles: the 900 theses of the humanist philosopher Pico della Mirandola (1463-94), who attempted the synthesis of Christianity, Jewish Cabbalism, Plato and Aristotle, and *De Monarchia sive de potestate imperatoris et papae* (*Concerning Monarchy without the Power of the Emperor or the Pope*), both published 1487.

1501: Pope Alexander VI issued the bull INTER MULTIPLICES, dealing with the need to control printing.

1512: The Inquisition of the Netherlands burned Magistrate Hermann of Ryswick as a heretic, together with his books.

1515: Pope Leo X issued the bull INTER SOLICITUDINES, which regulated printing and its products.

1520: The "Directorium Inquisitorium," a list of books classified as heretical, was published by the Inquisitor Nicholas Eymeric. This list was used subsequently as the basis of the catalog of Bernard Lutzenberg, the *Catalogus Haereticorum*, first issued in 1522, which was itself incorporated in the ROMAN INDEX OF 1559, established by Pope Paul IV.

SEE ALSO Index of Indexes [for individual titles]; Roman Inquisition; Spanish Inquisition.

Christian Crusade, The   The Crusade was founded in 1948 and currently claims a membership of 250,000 families, mainly of the white, Southern working class. Headed by fundamentalist preacher Billy James Hargis, the Crusade declares its aims as "to safeguard and preserve the Conservative Christian ideals upon which America was founded; to protect our cherished freedoms, the heritage of Americans; to oppose persons or organizations who endorse socialist or Communist philosophies, and to expose publicly the infiltration of such influences into American life; and to defend the Gospel of Jesus Christ; to oppose U.S. participation in the United Nations, federal interference in schools, housing and other matters constitutionally belonging to the states, and government competition with private business." The Crusade extends its condemnation to "indecent" literature and to rock and roll; its members were among those Americans who burned Beatles albums after John Lennon's comments in 1967 that the Beatles were more popular than Christ.

SEE ALSO Eagle Forum; Mel and Norma Gabler, Moral Majority.

Chronicle of Current Events, A   *A Chronicle of Current Events* was founded in Moscow on April 30, 1968, partly in response to contemporary events in Czechoslovakia, but mainly as a central source of information that brought together the many disparate strands of the dissident movement. Published in SAMIZDAT, the *Chronicle* remains the journal of the dissident movement, covering major political trials, giving news of dissidents throughout the country, collating information on those imprisoned in camps, prisons or psychiatric hospitals, describing the latest developments in extra-legal persecutions and maintaining a running index of the latest samizdat publications. It covers the entire U.S.S.R., providing news from clandestine correspondents in all provinces. Information is collected verbally: The *Chronicle* has suggested that those with something to say should simply tell the person from whom they received the magazine, who will then pass it to the person from whom they received it and so on—the chain supposedly ending at the editor in Moscow. As opposed to some similar publications, the *Chronicle*, the doyen of Soviet underground publishing, has managed to give equal prominence to every aspect of dissidence—religious, national and political. Since 1987 the *Chronicle* has been renamed *Express Chronicle* and continues to appear in samizdat. It is edited by Alexander Podrabinek, a leading dissident, author of *Punitive Medicine* (1980, a study of the use of politically motivated psychiatry), and founder in 1977 of the Working Commission to Investigate the Use of Psychiatry for Political Purposes.

CIA

1. publishing agreements   Anyone employed by the U.S. Central Intelligence Agency (CIA) is required to sign an agreement promising not to "publish ... any information or material relating to the Agency, its activities or intelligence activities generally, either during or after the term of ... employment ... without specific prior approval by the agency." This agreement, designed to preserve U.S. intelligence secrets, was challenged unsuccessfully in 1980 by Frank Snepp, a former employee who wrote his memoir of the last days of American involvement in South Vietnam.
SEE ALSO *Snepp* v. *United States.*

2. secrecy agreements   All CIA employees are bound by two signed secrecy agreements, one on beginning employment and one on leaving the Agency. They run as follows. On joining the CIA:

I, ——, understand that by virtue of my duties in the CIA, I may be or have been the recipient of information and intelligence which concerns the present and future security of the United States ... I do solemnly swear that I will never divulge, publish or reveal either by word, conduct, or by any other means, any classified information, intelligence or knowledge, except in the performance of my official duties and in accordance with the laws of the United States, unless specifically authorized in writing, in each case, by the Director of Central Intelligence or his authorized representatives.

On leaving:

I, —— , solemnly swear, without mental reservation or purpose of evasion, and in the absence of duress, as follows: I will never divulge, publish or reveal by writing, word, conduct, or otherwise, any information relating to the national defense and security and particularly information of this nature relating to intelligence sources, methods and operations, and specifically Central Intelligence Agency operations, sources, methods, personnel, fiscal data, or security measures to anyone, including, but not limited to, any future

governmental or private employer, private citizen, or any other Government employee or official without the express written consent of the Director of Central Intelligence or his authorized representative.

SEE ALSO *United States* v. *Marchetti.*

***Cincinnati* v. *Karlan* (1973)**   In this decision the Supreme Court defined the difference between FIGHTING WORDS, which are not protected by constitutional amendments dealing with freedom of speech, and mere "rude words," which, however offensive they may seem to the individual at whom they are directed, are so protected. The words in question were "fucking, prick-ass cops," and had been uttered by the defendant Karlan when approached by a police officer who had noticed him tampering with a parked car. The policeman had warned Karlan three times, and each time received unequivocal abuse. However, since at no time did the officer lose his temper, although his face did become flushed, and the officer could not honestly say that the words aroused any desire to fight in him, the court acquitted Karlan of having caused public disorder by the use of "fighting wrods."
SEE ALSO *Chaplinsky* v. *New Hampshire* (1942); *Cohen* v. *California* (1971).

Cinematograph Act (1909)   SEE British Board of Film Censors 1. history.

Citizens for Decency Through Law   SEE Citizens for Decent Literature.

Citizens for Decent Literature   The CDL was founded in Cincinnati in 1957 by Charles H. Keating, Jr., a former fighter pilot turned successful executive. Keating, a father of six children, disliked the increasingly accessible displays of what he saw as smut and with the support of various businessmen, local government officials and concerned clergymen, set up his group to battle pornography. The main aim of the CDL was to pressure local politicians and policemen to shut down outlets for what it called pornography, including bookshops, TV programs, cinemas, even racks of allegedly objectionable books in otherwise "clean" stores. It organized letter writing campaigns, economic boycotts and similar tactics both locally and then on a national scale.

Similar in many ways to the Catholic LEGION OF DECENCY, the CDL was initially dismissed as old-fashioned, but by the late 1960s it boasted a membership of 350,000, with 32 chapters in 20 states. Catholic clergymen were particularly enthusiastic, but there were also 11 senators, four governors and 100 members of the House of Representatives among the honorary members. It produced a monthly periodical, the *National Decency Newsletter*, which offered a mixture of personality profiles of successful anti-smut crusaders and lawmen, labelled "Prosecutor of the Month," and gloating reports of victorious raids on "the merchants of smut." The magazine was edited by a formerly obscure Los Angeles accountant, Raymond Gauer, who like Keating had established himself as a one-man anti-vice crusader. In 1968 Gauer worked in Washington as the CDL's official lobbyist. Among his successes was the campaign against the Supreme Court nomination of Justice Abe Fortas.

In 1968 two honorary CDL members, Senator Karl Mundt (South Dakota) and Representative Dominick Daniels (New Jersey), infuriated by the liberal Supreme Court decision on the case of REDRUP v. NEW YORK, introduced legislation that led directly to the creation of the PRESIDENT'S COMMISSION ON OBSCENITY AND PORNOGRAPHY. The CDL gained its greatest success when, on the resignation of one of the commission's members in 1969, President Nixon appointed Keating to fill the gap. When the commission issued its final report in 1970, offering generally liberal recommendations regarding pornography, CDL lobbyists, spearheaded by Keating, ensured that the administration totally rejected its own commission's efforts. The successful prosecution in October 1971 of publisher WILLIAM HAMLING for his illustrated edition of the report was also watched closely by the CDL.

Nixon's appointment to the Supreme Court of four conservative justices—Burger, Blackmun, Powell and Rehnquist (whose names, along with that of Father Hill, a leading anti-pornographer in New York, were substituted in 1974 for those of the private parts in Gore Vidal's MYRON)—ensured a severe and long-term rebuff for liberal forces. Subsequent to 1973 the CDL was renamed the Citizens for Decency Through Law and its newsletter now appears as *The National Decency Reporter*. The CDTL aims "to assist law enforcement agencies and legislatures to enact and enforce Constitutional statutes, ordinances and regulations controlling obscenity and pornography and materials harmful to juveniles. [It] works to create an awareness in the American public of the extent and harms associated with the distribution of pornography through newstands, bookstores, theaters, and television." It provides free legal assistance in the form of research, model legislation, expert witnesses and the filing of amicus curiae briefs in appellate cases. The CDTL also holds seminars instructing police and prosecutors on search and seizure, trial tactics, evidence and proof and appeals.

Clark, Samuel   Clark (1675-1729) was a metaphysician, a moralist and a supporter of rational theology. He was involved with a number of contemporary scientists, including Isaac Newton, and in 1704 and 1705 delivered the Boyle Lectures, which were published in 1705-6. They were entitled *A Demonstration of the being and Attributes of God* and *A Discourse concerning the Unchangeable Obligation of Natural Religion*. A former chaplain to the bishop of Norwich, Clark became chaplain to Queen Anne and rector of St. James'. He was well-known throughout Europe for his theology, and engaged in intellectual controversies with such as Spinosa, Hobbes, Leibnitz and others. In 1712 he published *The Scriptural Doctrine of the Trinity*; this was declared to be opposed to the true Christian faith and possibly tainted with Arianism, a heresy first condemned at the Council of Nicaea in 325. The book was attacked in Parliament and Clarke was deprived of his offices. Despite this he continued as an academic and made substantial contributions to classical scholarship.

Clarkson, Lawrence   SEE book burning in England 4. Puritans.

Classification and Ratings Administration (CARA)   SEE United States 10. film censorship.

classification at birth   In the classification of certain U.S. government documents as secret: the concept that any ideas developed within overall classified areas—nuclear weapons, espionage etc.—are automatically secret from the moment of their creation and require no specific registration on a secrets file.

classification levels   An ascending ladder of secrecy used by the U.S. government and military to classify data: confidential, secret, top secret and special intelligence. A further, widely used category covers material that is not actually secret but is labelled "For Official Use Only." Special intelligence covers a range of super-secret classifications hidden from most government and elected officials, let alone from the general public. There are some 25 of these, including the ultra-secret "SIOP-ESI," which deals with the nation's Single Integrated Operational Plan (SIOP), the nuclear order of battle. The official use category is used to exempt as broad a range of information as possible from the information available to researchers under the Freedom of Information Act (1966).

Clean Up Television Campaign (U.K.)   CUTV was launched in Birmingham, U.K., in January 1964 by two local women—MARY WHITEHOUSE, a schoolteacher and sex educator, and Norah Buckland, a clergyman's wife—as an attempt to challenge the moral laxity that they felt stemmed directly from the increasingly liberal standards of U.K. television in general and the BBC in particular. First, a manifesto exhorted the "Women of Britain" to "revive the militant Christian spirit" of the nation, then a packed public meeting in Birmingham Town Hall proved that the traditional viewpoint still had a large constituency, for all the contemporary touting of the Swinging Sixties. By August 1964 CUTV could claim 235,000 signatures on its manifesto.

CUTV had a simple aim: to rechristianize society. Although some critics claimed otherwise, the movement was not simply an arm of Moral Rearmament, although Mrs. Buckland and many early members belonged to both groups; but MRA's pro-Christian and anti-communist tenets certainly provided much of the campaign's intellectual framework. For CUTV, a distinctly socialist devil was abroad and the BBC, under its unashamedly liberal Director-General Hugh Carlton Greene, was deliberately promoting his works. "Men and women and children," wrote Whitehouse in January 1964, "listen and view at the risk of serious damage to their morals, their patriotism, their discipline and their family life."

As a statutory body, the BBC was under the control of Parliament, yet this institution seemed unwilling to check BBC subversion. CUTV members determined to take the responsibility on themselves. After monitoring 167 programs, CUTV branded a large proportion as objectionable. Such programs were those that included "sexy innuendoes, suggestive clothing and behaviour; cruelty, sadism and unnecessary violence; no regret for wrong-doing; blasphemy and presentation of religion in a poor light; excessive drinking and foul language; undermining respect for law and order; unduly harrowing and depressing themes." Programs otherwise acceptable were ruled objectionable if they included any mention of homosexuality, abortion and kindred topics. The royal family and armed services were sacrosanct.

Many critics of CUTV, while by no means progressive, condemned the campaign for negativism: Its members opposed, but never proposed. By 1965 CUTV moved to change its role. After an initial meeting in February, the NATIONAL VIEWERS AND LISTENERS ASSOCIATION (NVALA) was inaugurated in March 1965. CUTV was incorporated wholesale into the new pressure group, which acted not only to protest against the objectionable but also to represent and lobby for the views of Britain's silent majority.

Clean Up Television Campaign (U.S.)   CUTV was founded in America in 1978 and embraces essentially the same objectives as does its earlier, British counterpart. It describes itself as composed of "religious groups, civic groups and churches; other interested parties." Its aims are "to insist that television programs be revised so that they are no longer an insult to decency and a negative influence on young people. [It] has initiated [a] campaign to boycott products advertised on programs which depict scenes of adultery, sexual perversion or incest or which treat immorality in a joking or otherwise unfavorable light." The campaign emphasizes, as do so many similar organizations, that such demands are "clearly not censorship, but simply responsible action, since companies remain free to sponsor any programs they choose." Such a disclaimer is in practice quite specious, since no company, in the present conservative atmosphere, will risk offending America's influential anti-pornography lobby, whose purse, if not its mind, is profitably suggestible. CUTV has had a number of successes, notably the curtailing of the "anti-soap opera" *Soap*, which won a large liberal audience in the late Seventies but was driven off the screen through the pusillanimity of its sponsors and its network in the face of CUTV's orchestrated campaign.

clear and present danger   "Clear and present danger" is one of the criteria used to determine the validity of laws that restrict or punish the freedom of speech and of the press in America. It is also an expression that points out the way in which a free society must always ensure that the demands of free speech are balanced by those of other democratic freedoms, which may run contrary to absolutely unfettered freedom of speech. In the case of SCHENCK V. UNITED STATES (1919), Justice Holmes defined the concept as concerning "The question … whether the words are used in such circumstances and are of such a nature as to create a clear and present danger that they will bring about the substantive evils that Congress has the right to prevent." From 1919 to 1969 the danger in question needed only to be "probable." Subsequent to 1969, after a Supreme Court judgment in WHITNEY V. CALIFORNIA, the danger needed to be "imminent." The court ruled that: "No danger flowing from speech can be deemed clear and imminent, unless the incidence of the evil apprehended is so imminent that it may befall before there is opportunity for full discussion. If there be time to expose through discussion the falsehood and fallacies, to avert the evil by the processes of education, the remedy to be applied is more speech, not enforced silence."

Cleland, John   Cleland (1709-89) was the son of a Scottish army officer, latterly a civil servant, and an Englishwoman of Dutch and Jewish descent. He attended Westminster School for just two years of formal schooling, leaving aged 12. From 1728 to 1740 he served the East India Company in a successful career first as a soldier, then as an administrator in Bombay. During this period he wrote a preliminary version of MEMOIRS OF A WOMAN OF PLEASURE, better known as *Fanny Hill*. He returned to London on his father's death in 1741. During the 1740s Cleland's fortunes declined. He failed to find backers for the establishing of a Portuguese East India Company and ran up substantial debts. He was imprisoned for debt between 1748 and 1749, during which time he both completed and had published *Memoirs* … The publishers Fenton and Ralph Griffiths bought the copyright for 20 guineas (£21.00). The first edition ran to 750 copies. Subsequent to the government's ban on the book there were many clandestine editions and the Griffiths are supposed to have made some £10,000 profit. In 1749 Cleland and Ralph Griffiths were arrested, but soon discharged, for having published an obscene work. The book itself was declared obscene and banned. Cleland then expurgated his novel, cutting some 30 per cent, all of it sexual. This too was placed under interdict. Griffiths continued to profit both from this edition and from reissues of the unmutilated book.

Between 1749 and 1769 Cleland pursued a diversified and often anonymous career as a journalist, playwright and general author. He wrote three plays; two more novels (*The Surprises of Love*, 1765, and *The Woman of Honour*, 1768), neither of which approached *The Memoirs* … in either sexuality or success; many book reviews; two medical treatises; three philological studies; several translations and much more. None of this prolific output brought him fortune or fame. He was the author of *Fanny Hill* and thus in public eyes he remained. As he aged he grew increasingly depressed, embittered by his experiences and offensive to his once wide and successful circle of friends, including David Garrick, Laurence Sterne, and James Boswell. He lived alone, with one servant and a chaotic book-filled household, a figure on the fringes of smart society. Rumors as to his possible homosexuality abounded. He died in 1789, solitary and wretched, abandoned by his friends and utterly disappointed in his life.

Coalition for Better Television   This organization, one of several that exist in America for the censorship of television, was founded in 1981 by the Rev. Donald Wildman of Tupelo, Mississippi. CBT claims to represent five million families in a fight against "excessive and gratuitous violence, vulgarity, sex and profanity on commercial television." The coalition has yet to influence American federal or state law, but such pressure groups certainly worry commercial sponsors and TV networks, traditionally susceptible to any allegations that may diminish their advertising income.

"Coenae Domini"   The bull "Coenae Domini" ("of the Lord's Supper"), a collection of the various excommunications ordered against a variety of doctrinal miscreants, dates from 1364, when it was first issued by Pope Urban V. It was traditionally read aloud in every church each Maundy Thursday. The form in which it was used during the Reformation and beyond was created by Julius II in 1511 and modified to encompass the growing threat of Protestantism, epitomized in such sects as those of WYCLIF and Huss. Minor alterations were made by later popes. Under the regulations of the bull it was necessary for a book to satisfy five tests before it and those who read it could be declared heretical: (1) the book must be the production of an actual heretic, and not by someone who has never been baptized or by a Catholic who has uttered heresy simply through ignorance; (2) it must contain a specific heresy or have to do with religious matters; (3) the reader must be aware that the author and the content of the book are heretical; (4) the reading must have been done without permission of the Apostolic Chair, i.e., the Pope or those he authorizes; (5) sufficient of the book must have been read to constitute a mortal sin—this amount was variously defined, from a minimum of merely two lines to a single page. Those who had been named as heretics then suffered the *excommunicatio major*: They were barred from receiving the sacraments, from the holding of office, from public worship and from burial in consecrated ground. They lost all legal rights. The excommunication was carried out *latae sententiae* (immediately) rather than *ferendae sententiae* (not until the case had been assessed and a judgment given).

These regulations were modified in the mid-19th century by Pius IX. Journals, newspapers and magazines that contained the occasional writings of those defined as heretics were declared heretical in their entirety, irrespective of the other subject matter they contained; books produced by writers outside the church were to be held as less pernicious than those produced by lapsed Catholics who have become Free-Thinkers, Rationalists or Spiritualists.

The bull was not wholly popular, even in the 16th century. In 1536 a commentary on it by a French jurist was confiscated in Paris; Charles V banned its publication in Spain in 1551 and Philip II confirmed this in 1568, asking the Pope to recall it. During the century the bull was forbidden, variously, in Naples (1570), Venice (1568), Portugal (1580), France (1580), Moravia, Silesia and Bohemia (1586). The Papacy, in the meantime, continued to amend it. In 1524 the name of MARTIN LUTHER and all who read, listened to, distributed, or possessed his writings, or defended the teachings, was added to its provisions. A number of sects, followers of "the godless and abominable heresies of Martin Luther," were cited in 1536. In 1583 "Hussites, Wyclifites, Lutherans, Zwinglians, Calvinists, Anabaptists, anti-Trinitarians" were included.

In 1770 Clement XIV had the annual readings of the bull discontinued, but it remained in force until October 1869 when Pius IX recalled or modified most of its provisions.

Cohen v. *California* (**1971**)   Cohen was convicted of a breach of section 415 of the California Penal Code after he appeared in the corridor of a Los Angeles courthouse wearing a jacket inscribed with the words "Fuck The Draft." He was sentenced to 30 days in jail for this misdemeanor. The Supreme Court reversed the decision, explaining that section 415 dealt with offensive language but not with obscenity and that the crux of the case was not the content and message of Cohen's jacket, but simply whether the word "fuck" thus displayed was in fact offensive. Fuck in other contexts might arouse prurient, erotic instincts, but this was not one of them. The fact that the word was a vulgar and "scurrilous epithet" was unfortunate but insufficient grounds for a conviction. "Whilst the particular four-letter word being litigated here is perhaps more distasteful than most others of its genre, it is nevertheless often true that one man's vulgarity is another's lyric." The court added that the excision of all such words, so as to render all language acceptable to "the most squeamish," might be seen as the first step in the blanket censorship of all unpopular views.

SEE ALSO California 3. offensive language; *Chaplinsky* v. *New Hampshire* (1942); *Cincinnati* v. *Karlan* (1973).

Colman, George, the Younger   Colman, the son (1762-1836) of the successful dramatist George Colman, the Elder (1732-94), was appointed EXAMINER OF PLAYS, effectively the arbiter of permissible taste in the English theater, in 1824. He succeeded John Larpent, who had held the post since 1778. Colman was a dramatist himself, with such successes as *The Iron Chest* (1796), *The Heir-at-law* (1797) and *John Bull* (1803), and in 1797 had himself a "licentious" play banned by his predecessor. From 1819 he had managed, albeit with financial difficulty, the Haymarket Theater. Colman was appointed, as were most examiners, through influence, in his case that of the duke of York and the prince regent, but his previous career made him an exception among censors, who usually lacked any pratical theatrical experience. It was assumed that he would be a liberal censor, but once turned gamekeeper the former poacher went to excesses of prudery. To those who expressed shock, he announced: "I was a careless immoral author. I am now examiner of plays. I did my business as an author at that time and I do my business as an examiner now."

Suiting himself to the increasing morality of his era, Colman savaged the theater. Proclaiming that "nothing on stage is to be uttered without license," he proceeded to eviscerate play after play. Anything remotely suggestive was removed, as well all oaths, including "Lud!" and "Providence!" No religious references, personal allusions or political statements were permitted. The stage was ruthlessly adapted to "the taste of the most conservative, most frightened and most bigoted of English minorities" (Findlater, op. cit.). Colman was an arrogant figure who told the Lytton Committee, investigating the stage in 1832, that his allegiance was to the Crown and not to his nominal superior, the LORD CHAMBERLAIN. He claimed that he could not be removed from office, although the lord chamberlain may well have been about to do just that if the examiner had not died first. The inclusion of this right of dismissal in the Theatre Regulation Act (1832) was certainly due to Colman's obstinacy.

Whether Colman was, in the words of one biographer, "one of the most narrow, humourless and puritanical censors," is debatable. He was idiosyncratic and opinionated, but his puritanism seems to have ended at his office door, from where he would proceed to the witty company of his drinking cronies. He was venal, demanding fees to license plays, but he never pursued his excisions into the theaters, having no desire, as he put it, to become a spy as well as a censor. Colman died on October 26, 1836. The theater did not mourn his passing, but notices were mixed. A "superannuated buffoon," said one critic, but the actor Macready was kinder and probably more accurate: "A man of some talent, much humour, and little principle."

Colombia   As a signatory to the International Covenant on Civil and Political Rights and the American Convention on Human Rights, both of which are included in the nation's domestic laws, Colombia guarantees its people freedom of expression. This ideal situation is mitigated by daily reality: Colombia has suffered non-stop political and social upheavals for the last 30 years, and a variety of freedoms have been suspended or attacked, either by direct government action or by the threats posed by a variety of extreme groups, all of whom prey on the media. Such problems are accentuated by the domination of the country by a small elite of five families who control the main political parties as well as the press and media, whose broadcasts and publications are thus geared to furthering family and political interests. In

parallel to this elite stand the military, who make their own incursions into freedom of expression. Both the military and the rebel guerillas continue to attack and murder journalists whose views annoy them. These attacks, although not yet fatal, extend to the foreign press, some of whom have been hounded from the country. Although President Belisario Betancur attempted to launch a "Peace Process" in the early 1980s, establishing a ceasefire between government and the rebel forces and opening the press to pro-rebel writers, this failed to take root. Both sides flooded the press with disinformation and today there are few reports from the guerilla position.

Under the Press Law (1975) all journalists must hold a valid press card, which acts as a license to work and which can be issued or withheld at the discretion of the Ministry of Education. A National Council of Journalism exists to help the media and the government liaise. A variety of recent laws also appear to be threatening press freedoms. Under the Narcotics Law (1986), created in an attempt to combat Colombia's pervasive cocaine industry, it is forbidden to circulate information about the drug trade. This is a dangerous enough pursuit: Some 27 journalists have been murdered while investigating drugs. Political advertising is now severly restricted; access to newsprint is curtailed by a high import tax, which hits smaller, oppositional newspapers.

Committee on International Freedom to Publish   The committee was founded in 1975 and is dedicated to supporting the efforts of publishers and authors throughout the world in the face of repression, censorship and allied persecution. The organization monitors the position of authors and publishers in countries all round the world and attempts to persuade repressive governments to modify the provisions of their censorship. The committee is linked to a number of similar organizations working from America and other countries.

SEE ALSO International P.E.N.

Committee on Public Information   This committee was established in 1917 once America joined World War I; its task was to check the content and distribution of all printed material and of motion pictures. Any objectionable material that was discovered was to be rooted out. The main committee was paralleled by special bureaus in the Post Office, Justice Department, War Department and State Department. President Woodrow Wilson assured his fellow Americans that "legitimate criticism" of his administration's war policies would not be censored, but in practice no such criticism was permitted. Instead, the country was reduced to hysterical jingoism, epitomized in its vilification of the large German population and backed officially by the ESPIONAGE ACT OF 1917 AND SEDITION ACT OF 1918. The tide of conformity, which would extend beyond the war into the PALMER raids and the red scare of the early 1920s, provided the ideal opportunity for the government to attempt a wholesale purge of dissenters.

Wilson had no illusions as to the value of the cinema and while one hand sought to censor its product, the other clapped its producers firmly on the back and set out, via the CPI, to use Hollywood to "sell the war to America." Films would be used to purvey the official line and give the public a degree of sanitized newsreels. The committee's chairman, George Creel, called upon the business to "carry the gospel of Americanism to every corner of the globe" and saw the medium not as simple entertainment but as "international theological weapons." Simultaneously, the CPI's "voluntary" censorship ensured that no film advocating pacifism, let alone actively attacking the war effort, was ever distributed. Local censors clamped down on the slightest example of such material. America was to be portrayed as an earthly paradise, and nothing that might taint that image, or give aid and comfort to the enemy, might be permitted. The CPI backed its voluntary system with blackmail: If producers didn't play ball, then the only alternative would be direct government censorship. Few filmmakers wanted that, and few dared reject the committee's line. Those that did faced at best the suppression of their work, and at worst prosecution under the Espionage Act.

Committee to Defend the First Amendment   The committee was founded in 1979 as a collection of professionals taken from the media, the law, and various religions, united in their desire to maintain and protect the freedoms guaranteed in the FIRST AMENDMENT to the U.S. Constitution. It raises and provides funds to be used in the securing of "adequate legal services and assistance to individuals whose First Amendment rights are jeopardized by federal, state and local courts." The committee also provides informational material for organizations, government agencies and private individuals concerning the First Amendment and its current position in American life.

SEE ALSO First Amendment Congress.

Commonwealth v. Blanding (1825)   This case, one of the earliest trials for libel in America, established the precept that the truth of a libel is not a defense for committing it. Blanding was the editor of the *Providence Gazette* and published in his newspaper a "scandalous and libellous" attack on an innkeeper, one Enoch Fowler. Fowler protested his good character but Blanding offered to give the court proof that his allegations were true. The judge, Justice Wilde of Massachusetts, rejected this testimony, declaring that, "the provision in the Constitution securing the liberty of the press was intended to prevent any previous restraints upon publications, and not to affect prosections for the abuse of such liberty. The general rule is, that upon indictment the truth of a libel is not admissible in evidence ... [and] publishing a correct account ... but with comments and insinuations [tending] to asperse a man's character, is libellous."

Commonwealth v. Sharpless   The first obscenity trial held in the U.S. came before the Pennsylvania Supreme Court in March 1815. The defendants, the "yeoman" Jesse Sharpless, with five associates, were charged that "in a certain house ... [they] ... did exhibit, and show for money ... a certain lewd, wicked, scandalous, infamous and obscene painting, representing a man in an obscene, impudent and indecent posture with a woman." Although the defense attempted to deny the jurisdiction of the court in such a case, which would under English law still have been tried by an ecclesiastical court, the court was adamant. In order, as the judges declared, to keep the dignity of the community, they condemned Sharpless and company for "filthy conduct" and laid down a ruling that would influence all future obscenity prosecutions and that emphasized the role of the civil courts in dealing with the whole spectrum of public morals: "Any offense which in its nature, and by its example, tends to corruption of morals, as the exhibition of an obscene picture, is indictable at common Law." This trial was also responsible for the concept of "chastity of records," which was adopted by U.S. courts in similar situations. Neither was the relevant picture exhibited in court nor were its details officially recorded. The judge claimed that this omission paid "some respect to the chastity of the records." British courts rejected such niceness as fanciful and imaginary, but it persisted for some time in the U.S.

Commonwealth v. Tarbox (1848)   In this early American obscenity trial Tarbox was indicted for "he did print, publish and distribute a certain printed paper, containing obscene language and descriptions manifestly tending to the corruption of the morals of youth, which printed paper was distributed and left at the doors ... of one hundred of the citizens of Boston." Tarbox was tried and convicted but complained that the charge had been too general: The court had cited only "an obscene paper," it had made no effort to define what exactly was obscene about his publication. The court rejected Tarbox's complaint, stating that it would only compound the obscenity and debase the court's own records if it included the detailed material in its charge and in the trial transcript. It was disgusting and that was all that need be said.

Comstock Act, The   On March 3, 1873, America's foremost anti-vice crusader, ANTHONY COMSTOCK, with the backing of such individuals as Samuel Colgate and J.B. Rockefeller (himself a collector of erotica), and through his own tireless lobbying of Congress, achieved his greatest triumph: a federal bill (U.S. Code: Section 1461, Title 18) that banned from the mails "every obscene, lewd, lascivious or filthy book, pamphlet, picture, paper, letter writing, print or other publication of an indecent character." Comstock himself was appointed a special agent of the U.S. Post Office, and as such allowed to carry a gun and attack pornographers throughout the country. Officially named the Federal Anti-Obscenity Act, it was more generally known by the name of its foremost advocate, as the Comstock Act. This act, which under its originator's dedicated operation stood as the sole federal obscenity law of the U.S., replaced the act of 1865 (q.v.). It threatened more severe punishments and widened the list of actionable obscene materials to include contraceptives and information about where they might be obtained.

Comstock remained the chief prosecutor of his act, arresting in his career, at his own estimation, more than 3,500 individuals (although no more than 10 percent were found guilty) and having destroyed "160 tons of obscene literature," marriage aids, contraceptives, and the like. The Comstock style remained constant: the choosing of a target; the entrapment of that target, either by posing as a legitimate buyer or writing spurious letters of interest; the raid, in which the crusader himself took an enthusiastic part; and the subsequent trial. Despite the increasing hostility toward the act, and its creator, it was not truly abrogated until well after his death in 1915.

Comstock, Anthony The 19th century's foremost crusader (1844-1915) against vice in America was born in New Canaan, Connecticut. An upbringing of fundamentalist puritanism, compounded by his mother's death in 1854, created a supremely priggish youth, obsessed with the extirpation first of his own sins, and then those of others; a man, as his biographer Heywood Broun put it, "terrible in his earnestness." His initial career as a dry goods clerk, interrupted by service from 1863 to 1865 in the Civil War, in no way restrained such enthusiasms.

Comstock's first act as a self-styled "weeder in God's garden" came in 1862, in Winnupauk, Connecticut, when he first shot the rabid dog and then smashed up the store of a local liquor dealer. The self-ordained interference, the personal dealing out of physical violence and the pious satisfaction in performing the Lord's work would typify Comstock's career henceforth. In 1868, still a clerk and now working in New York, he made his first attacks on pornography, supposedly to revenge a personal friend who had, by some lurid volume, been "led astray and corrupted and diseased." Comstock had as yet no authority, but he purchased various books, and with them as evidence, forced the police to act. His entrapment worked, and three major distributors fell before his assault. Allying himself in 1872 with the nascent YMCA, Comstock founded, under their auspices, the Committee for the Suppression of Vice and started in earnest his struggle against "the hydra-headed monster."

Comstock's emergence into real public recognition came in his attacks on two free-thinking sisters—Victoria Woodhull and Tennessee Claflin, joint editors of *Woodhull and Claflin's Weekly*, a journal devoted to women's rights and attacks on puritanism and its supposedly attendant hypocrisy. His attempt to destroy the ladies failed, but his fame spread widely. In 1873 he was appointed by his committee to campaign for the creation of strict laws—both federal and state—to control the sending of potentially obscene material through the mails.

With the backing of such individuals as Samuel Colgate and J.B. Rockefeller (himself a collector of erotica), and through his own tireless lobbying of Congress, Comstock achieved his greatest triumph in 1873: a federal bill that banned from the mails "every obscene, lewd, lascivious or filthy book, pamphlet, picture, paper, letter writing, print or other publication of an indecent character." Comstock himself was appointed a special agent of the U.S. Post Office, as such allowed to carry a gun and attack pornographers throughout the country.

A slight flaw in this success was Comstock's falling out with the YMCA, but he replaced the committee with the Society for the Suppression of Vice. It was under its banner (a diptych representing the arrest of a pornographer and the burning of his stock) that he worked henceforth.

Over the next 40 years Comstock prosecuted at his own estimation more than 3,500 individuals (although no more than 10 percent were found guilty) and had destroyed 160 tons of obscene literature, plus a variety of marriage aids, contraceptives etc. The Comstock style remained constant: the choosing of a target; the entrapment of that target either by posing as a legitimate buyer, or writing spurious letters of interest; the raid, in which the crusader himself took an enthusiastic part; and the subsequent trial.

In his pursuit of evil, Comstock was callously singleminded. When in 1874 an aging, and possibly reformed, specialist in contraception and abortion—one Ann Lohmann, known as Madame Restell—cut her throat rather than face the court, he acknowledged proudly that she was the 15th individual who had chosen such a course after falling beneath his scourge. It surprised only the pious crusader, whose terrible sincerity was never in doubt, that by the 1880s, when his efforts had largely rooted out pornography in the U.S., he was massively hated and seen by many who were far from being smut-dealers not as a figure of reverence and respect but as one who inspired only horror and fear. Unjust, fanatical, bigoted, cruel and relentless, he seemed the image of the modern Inquisitor.

With his primary target largely defeated, Comstock ranged further afield. Turning, as Broun put it, from "real giants to mere windmills," he achieved some success against lotteries, con-men and quack doctors, but less in the face of abortionists. Seeing sex in everything, obsessed by "the fight for the young," he turned to freethinkers, socialists and liberals of every hue, attacking at random "long-haired men and short-haired women."

Despite his increasing unpopularity, no major commentators set themselves against him. An attack on Comstock might be seen as offering support to his bugbears, and no newspaper would risk the smear. Those who did attack—such as D.M. Bennett, an elderly, free-thinking liberal who published a weekly magazine, *The Truth Seeker*—were hounded without mercy. Comstock saw Bennett jailed for 13 months' hard labor, from which he emerged severely broken down.

What H.L. Mencken called his "rugged Berserker quality" drove Comstock to greater and greater excesses. Gradually, as the new mores of the 20th century eroded his position, he became increasingly absurd. Attacks on art students and galleries, proclaiming "Art is not above morals. Morals stand first ... ," merely rendered him ridiculous. His attempt in 1912 to have banned Paul Chabas' *September Morning* (featuring a naked female figure) merely boosted sales of the print. An attack on George Bernard Shaw's *Mrs. Warren's Profession* in 1905 ensured that the queues ran around the block. Shaw turned the crusader into an eponym, telling the *New York Times*: "Comstockery is the world's standing joke, at the expense of the United States."

There were still supporters, especially for his castigation of HAVELOCK ELLIS, MARGARET SANGER and Suffragism, but as his wrath magnified, so did his targets shrink. He died in 1915, still raging, the official U.S. delegate to the International Purity Congress at the San Francisco Exposition. A funeral oration praised the "soldier of righteousness," but his day was over. In 1870, when his crusade began, the puritan ethos was still that of the nation: 40 years later it was a laughing stock. As Mencken put it in 1927, "like all the rest of us, in our several ways, he was simply a damned fool." But he added an ironic tribute, one that Comstock would hardly have appreciated: "More than any other man he liberated American letters from the blight of Puritanism."

comstockery   SEE Comstock, Anthony.

"Confessional Unmasked, The"   SEE *Regina* v. *Hicklin*.

Confucius   Confucius (551-479 B.C.), the Latinized form of K'ung fu-tze (Master K'ung), was born in the state of Lu, present-day Shantung. Until the collapse of the empire in 1911 he was considered to be China's greatest sage and Confucianism overrode Buddhism and Taoism as dominant state ideology. It dominated the educational system and molded morals and political conduct. Confucius believed that the best way of uniting the warring states of China lay in the preservation of the culture of the Chou dynasty (1030-256 B.C.). He failed to gain a place in any of the Chinese courts, and concentrated on teaching his philosophies to the young men who would become the next generation of statesmen. His best known work was the *Analects*, a collection of his sayings and of the history of his native state of Lu from 722 to 481 B.C. Although Confucius was generally revered, his works were not immune from attack. Around 250 B.C. the first ruler of the new dynasty of Ts'in wished to abolish the feudal system. Confucius' work was seen as a central prop for that system and comprehensively searched out and destroyed. Many hundreds of the master's disciples were burned alive at the same time. Fifty years later, the Emperor TSIN CHI WANG-TI, in a massive purge of all forms of knowledge, ordered the burning of the *Analects*, along with all other works, other than those on medicine, divination and husbandry.

Congo   The Congo declared itself a Marxist-Leninst people's republic in 1972. Under article 29 of its constitution opposition parties are uniformly banned—although some operate from exile in France—and under article 18 the use of religion for political purposes is similarly forbidden. Freedom of expression and of the press is guaranteed under article 16, and the Congolese government has ratified the INTERNATIONAL COVENANT ON CIVIL AND POLITICAL RIGHTS, and the African Charter of Human and People's Rights. Despite this a National Censorship Committee was established in 1972, staffed by party cadres, and all forms of print media, as well as literature and the theater, are effectively controlled by this committee. The committee is also responsible for censoring the lyrics of Congolese singers. It meets every three months and publishes regular lists of prohibited material. All daily newspapers, and some periodicals, are owned by the party. All media employees are officially civil servants and as such expected to act as unofficial watchdogs for the party, checking their own media for signs of sedition. Some mild criticism is permitted publication, but those who complain regularly can expect to suffer reprisals. The committee also vets all foreign publications for unacceptable material, and restricts foreign reporters by forbidding their sending home any articles or broadcasts prior to the issuing of an official communique. Congolese radio, dominated by the single, party-run station, is a vital means of communication; it is subject to the censorship of the Ministry of Information.

Congregation of the Index   The Congregation of the Index was established in 1571 by Pope Pius V as an organization that would have responsibility for the running of the church's censorship apparatus. It was composed of a number of cardinals selected by the Pontiff and was charged with the work of updating and issuing editions of the Index (see Index of Indexes) and of developing the regulations that made up the censorship laws. The organization was completed under Gregory XIII in 1572 and by 1588, under Sixtus V, there were 15 such congregations of cardinals, all directed at a given administrative object. The seventh of these was the Congregation of the Index.

As explained in the bull of Gregory XIII:

> In order to put a stop to the circulation of pernicious opinions, and as far as practicable to bring certainty and protection to the faithful, it is our desire to bring the Index of Prohibited Books into a condition of completeness, so that Christians may be able to know what books it is safe for them to read and what they must avoid, and that there may be in this no occasion for doubt or question ... Therefore we give to you or to the majority of your body, full authority and powers to take action in regard to the examination and classification of books and to secure for aid in such work the service of learned men, ecclesiastics or laymen, who have knowledge of theology ... and to permit or to prohibit the use of books so examined, all authority given by my predecessors to their bodies or individuals for the carrying on of the work.

It shall also be the duty of your body to elucidate or eliminate all difficulties or incongruities in the existing Indexes; to arrange for the correction or expurgation of all texts containing instructions of value, the service of which is marred by erroneous and pernicious material; to add to the Index the titles of all works found to be unworthy; and to prohibit the production and the use of all books so condemned; and to give permission for the reading of books approved and of books corrected and freed from error; and for the purpose of facilitating your task, you shall enjoin upon all bishops … doctors, masters, printers, booksellers, magistrates, and others to cooperate … in carrying out the regulations …

Connection, The   *The Connection* was adapted in 1962 by writer Jack Gelber from his eponymous play. It deals with heroin addiction and in its effort to appear naturalistic used a variety of drug-related slang: "connection," for instance, meaning heroin dealer. The use of such slang, in an otherwise unremarkable film, antagonized the New York State censors, who objected specifically to the use of the word "shit," as meaning, not excrement but, in this context, heroin. The Appellate Court annulled this decision and their ruling was upheld by the New York Court of Appeals. The court made a deliberate distinction between the normal use of the word, when as slang for excrement it could be condemned as obscene, and its use here, as part of the jargon of drug addicts whereby it might be vulgar, like much slang, but could not be judged as obscene.

SEE ALSO filthy words.

Connell, Vivian   SEE *September in Quinze.*

conspiracy to corrupt public morals   This charge, while not embodied in any previous statute, is the descendant of the law of conspiracy developed by the 17th-century Star Chamber, which in 1611 defined conspiracy as the agreement between two or more parties to make a false accusation, even if the accusation was laughed out of court. This was further extended in 1616 when Star Chamber cited as conspiracy any agreement to commit any crime. Defendants could be condemned on the grounds of guilt by association and there were no limits to punishment. Responsibility for conspiracy trials was given to the court of King's Bench, which extended its powers during the 17th century to dealing with the morals of all the king's subjects. The law was particularly useful for the punishment of those who, traditionally, might have hoped for the less severe justice of the ecclesiastical courts.

The modern charge was created in 1961 with the express purpose of prosecuting one Shaw, who had issued a guide to London prostitutes: THE LADIES' DIRECTORY. The House of Lords, citing the precedents above, and approving and defining the new law, justified its extralegal action by stating that the peers, as the present-day equivalent of the King's Bench, had a "residual power, where no statute has yet intervened to supersede the common law, to superintend those offences which are prejudicial to public welfare." The charge, after its initial, successful test-run against Shaw, was used against the underground magazines OZ and IT in 1971, as well as against some 120 individuals, often the makers and distributors of blue movies or the sellers of sex aids and erotic toys, whose activities could not be prosecuted under the OBSCENE PUBLICATIONS ACT (1959).

The charge was bitterly attacked, as much within the law as outside it, on the grounds of its implicit vagueness and the opportunity it presented to the authorities to prosecute as a conspiracy any conduct that was considered by them to be immoral and might as such be seen as conduct injurious to the public in that it led them astray morally. For many lawyers the concept directly rejected the legal principle of *nullum crimen sine lege* (no crime without a law)—i.e., one might not prosecute when there was no specific offense to provide the grounds for that prosecution. In the face of this criticism, the Law Lords narrowed after 1971 the area in which the act might operate, limiting its scope in various ways. These included the need for the defendant to have intended to corrupt public morals; the "corruption" thus alleged to be clearly defined as potentially serious enough to disrupt the fabric of society; the rejection of the charge if it covered material for which there might be brought a "public good" defense as allowed under the Obscene Publications Act (1959). Homosexual contact advertising, the basis of the *IT* and *OZ* charges, was not, of itself, to be considered automatically corrupt.

SEE ALSO conspiracy to outrage public decency.

conspiracy to outrage public decency   This charge dated from 1727 when the crime of committing an OBSCENE LIBEL was created for dealing with literary morality. It dealt only with such offenses as exhibitionism, public sexual intercourse, nude bathing, encouragements to women to take up prostitution and such non-sexual activities as exhibiting a deformed child, selling a wife and disinterring a corpse. After the offense of obscene libel was abolished by the OBSCENE PUBLICATIONS ACT (1959) there was no longer any simple way to prosecute publishers whose material might offend but was not technically obscene. The old charge was revived to help fill the gap.

The offense was held by the House of Lords, when judging in 1970 the prosecution of the underground magazine IT, to exist and to be capable of being used against publications that are judged to be "lewd, disgusting and offensive." There is no precise test as to what exactly constitutes such an outrage, and the charge, like that of CONSPIRACY TO CORRUPT PUBLIC MORALS, together with which it has usually been brought, was on the whole an ad hoc proceeding, used in the moral climate of the era to prosecute material that was not simply obscene, but also considered to be politically threatening. The offense was specifically preserved in statutory law—the Criminal Law Act of 1977—but has not been used since then.

SEE ALSO Vagrancy Act (1824).

Constitutional Association, The   A prototype anti-obscenity pressure group, the association was set up in Britain in 1820 under the auspices of the Duke of Wellington and with the approval and backing of William Wordsworth. It was headed by one Dr. John Stoddart, editor of the *New Times*, a London broadsheet, who was known to his many enemies as "Doctor Slop." The intention of the association, setting the course for its many successors, was to work quietly and clandestinely on behalf of the government in bringing private prosecutions, allegedly without taint of official interference, against such satires, parodies, cartoons and similar publications that the authorities disliked but were unwilling to prosecute openly for fear of the political backlash. Among the association's first actions was the prosecution in 1820 for seditious libel of artist WILLIAM BENBOW, whose two cartoons—*The Brightest Star in the State, or, a Peep Out of a Royal Window* and *The Royal Cock and Chickens, or, the Father of His People*—were deemed unacceptable attacks on George IV. The case was dropped, since the jury declared itself unwilling to convict on the evidence of the association, which had, they stated, "a bad reputation." Such rejection undermined the association, and shortly afterwards it was closed down.

SEE ALSO National Vigilance Association; Proclamation Society; Societies for the Reformation of Manners; Society for the Suppression of Vice.

contemporary community standards   Along with that of the AVERAGE PERSON, the concept, under both American and British law, of contemporary community standards is central to the assessment of whether or not material is obscene. In America the concept is as set down in the standards that arose from the cases of ROTH V. UNITED STATES, *Memoirs* v. *Massachusetts* and MILLER V. CALIFORNIA. In all these cases the judgment established a standard of obscenity whereby material was judged on the basis of whether an average person, applying contemporary community standards, would find that the work, when taken as a whole, appeals to the prurient interest. This gives the definition of obscenity to local or state communities, rather than to a national consensus. In Britain the role of "contemporary standards" is embodied in the current statute governing obscenity, the OBSCENE PUBLICATIONS ACT (1959). As amplified in the case of *R.* v. *Calder and Boyars* (1969), the jury "must set the standards of what is acceptable, and what is for the public good in the age in which we live." Given the national basis of the act, the British system is intended to stress the supposed basic common sense of "the man on the Clapham omnibus"; it is less likely than its American equivalent to indulge local prejudice.

Coote, William A.   William Coote (1842-?), for 34 years the secretary of the NATIONAL VIGILANCE ASSOCIATION, was England's equivalent of America's devoted anti-smut campaigner, ANTHONY COMSTOCK. A classic example of the working-class radical puritan, Coote survived an impoverished childhood, brought up by a mother widowed when he was only three, and gained his education through the Working Men's League. Deprived of the chance of a university education he became a printer. At the age of 16 he was handed a religious tract and apparently experienced a profound and lifelong conversion. His innate prudishness made the emergent purity movements of the 1870s inevitably alluring. In 1885, the *annus mirabilis* of the early movement, the campaigning journalist W.T. Stead, whose pamphlet "The Maiden Tribute" had (albeit somewhat salaciously) illuminated the problems of the white slave trade in young prostitutes, launched a vehicle for purity: the National Vigilance Association. As secretary for the association he chose Coote, then working as a compositor on *The Standard* and as a minor official of the Working Men's League, and who had been a marshal at the great purity rally in Hyde Park in August 1885. Stead initially paid Coote's wages and later in the year embarked on a nationwide tour, drumming up support for the fledgling NVA.

Coote's lowly origins worried some of the longer-established puritans at first, but he grew increasingly powerful, a peer of the era's other great moralist, Bishop Winnington-Ingram of the PUBLIC MORALITY COUNCIL. Bernard Shaw, whose excoriation of Coote's American cousin had produced the eponym "comstockery," declared in 1895: "Mr. Coote is a person of real importance, backed by an association strong enough to enable him to bring his convictions to bear efficiently over our licensing authority ... [but he is] in artistic matters an intensely stupid man and on sexual questions something of a monomaniac." Coote overrode such liberal plaints, but was more concerned by the early, faltering years of the NVA, which lacked real funds and efficient administration. His own abilities, backed by a number of rich well-wishers, managed to secure the association's, and his own, future. By 1900, riding the wave of late-Victorian puritanism, Coote stood foursquare in the face of each and every manifestation of obscenity and impurity. His own obsession was with commercial sex: Whether as prostitution and public indecency in London, white slavery in Buenos Aires or pornography in Belgium and France (from where it was imported into England), he was against it. He toured three continents pursuing his aims, and was decorated by the grateful governments of Germany, France and Spain.

As its importance waned in the 1920s, the association turned over its obscenity campaign to the Public Morality Council. But as the direct successor to the SOCIETY FOR THE SUPPRESSION OF VICE (U.K.), the NVA, and Coote, had backed a variety of censorship bodies, including the Pure Literature Society, the National Home Reading Union and the like. His personal contacts with the great circulating libraries—Mudie's and Smith's—ensured that they would ban such works as he requested. Assigned by Lady Isabel Burton as literary executor for Sir Richard's, her husband's papers,

Coote personally purged the late explorer's unrivalled library of many priceless erotic artifacts.

Coote's heyday preceded World War I and he retired in 1919. The Victorian values he had promoted were substantially eroded, but the purity campaigners had laid down the groundwork for an English cultural style that has yet fully to vanish. The self-censorship of a variety of media, notably the still emergent film industry, was largely due to a fear of NVA pressure: It was simpler to accede to puritan demands and still enjoy the profits.

Coppe, Abiezer   SEE book burning in England 4. Puritans.

Council of Trent, The   The 25th and final session of the Council of Trent, the chief center for the pronouncements of the Counter-Reformation, issued on December 4, 1563, a series of decrees that established doctrinal purity as regarded religious art. The iconography that was laid down has essentially dominated devotional imagery ever since, and the restrictions suggested, most notably the denunciation of nudity, survived until the present century. For the church, the Council's edicts, which were put into practice by the Inquisition, were a satisfactory means of curbing the imagination, and thus the potential heresy of the artist and those who looked at his work. For critics, both contemporary and subsequent, December 1563 remains the birthday of prudery.

Counterattack   SEE blacklisting.

Coward, Dr.   SEE book burning in England 7. United Kingdom (1688-1775).

Cowell, Dr.   SEE book burning in England 2. James I (1603-25).

Criminal Law Act (1977)   The following amendments were added to the U.K. OBSCENE PUBLICATIONS ACT (1959) in order to include the exhibition and content of films:

(2) Prohibition of Publication of Obscene Matter:
(3A) Proceedings for an offence under this section shall not be instituted except by or with the consent of the Director of Public Prosecutions in any case where the article in question is a moving picture film of a width not less than sixteen millimeters and the relevant publication or the only other publication which followed or could reasonably have been expected to follow from the relevant publication took place or (as the case may be) was to take place in the course of a cinematographic exhibition; and in this section "the relevant publication" means
(a) in the case of any proceedigns under this section for publishing an obscene article, the publication in respect of which the defendant would be charged if the proceedings were brought; and
(b) in the case of any proceedings under this section for having an obscene article for publication for gain, the publication which, if the proceedings were brought, the defendant would

be alleged to have had in contemplation.
(4A) Without prejudice to subsection (4) ("public good" defence) above, a person shall not be proceeded against for an offence at common law—
(a) in respect of a cinematograph exhibition or anything said or done in the course of a cinematographic exhibition, where it is the essence of the common law offence that the exhibition or, as the case may be, what was said or done was obscene, indecent, offensive, disgusting or injurious to morality; or
(b) in respect of an agreement to give a cinematograph exhibition or to cause anything to be said or done in the course of such an exhibition where the common law offence consists of conspiring to corrupt public morals or to do anything contrary to public morals or decency.

criminal syndicalism   A number of American states have enacted "criminal syndicalism" laws that are aimed at the suppression of criminal anarchism, the incitement to revolution, rebellion and the violent overthrow of the government. The censorship relevance of these statutes, which emerged during the red scare era of the early 1920s, is that in attempting to suppress such incitement, the courts may be violating the rights to freedom of speech guaranteed to all Americans by the FIRST AMENDMENT. The most important decision in this area was that given by the Supreme Court in the case of *Gitlow* v. *New York* in 1925. This upheld the state's criminal anarchy statute, declaring that although the defendant had only spoken on anarchy, and had not put his exhortations into practice, his words were enough of a revolutionary spark to kindle a greater and more destructive conflagration. A more recent decision, *Brandenburg* v. *Ohio* (1969), in which a Ku Klux Klan leader was acquitted of criminal syndicalism despite the overt racism of the remarks that had brought about his prosecution, reversed the court's earlier opinion, saying that criminal anarchy statutes that aimed to suppress ADVOCACY but could cite no imminent danger, were contrary to the Constitution.

Crossman Diaries   Richard Crossman (1907-74) was a cabinet minister in the Labour governments in Britain between 1964 and 1970. A former Oxford don, Crossman was an acute observer of his own experiences and a compulsive communicator of these observations. His main interest was the way government worked in Britain and his tape-recorded diaries, with their wealth of detailed information, revealed as never before the precise and complex manner in which policies were developed and implemented, individuals struggled for primacy, and all the competing interests involved in running a country functioned.

In common with many legally sanctified practices in Britain, where there is no written constitution, but instead a vast body of slowly evolving statutory and judge-made laws, while the writing of such diaries is unrestricted, there exists an unwritten but supposedly generally understood precept governing their publication. Governments and their ministers assumed and accepted, until 1975, that when any such publications dealt with events occurring within the last 30 years, they must be submitted to the pre-publication censorship of the Cabinet Office. Crossman, a devoted advocate of open government (although he had once dismissed a low-ranking DHSS official who had published an unauthorized account of dole frauds), had arranged only weeks before his death in April 1974 for the firms of Jonathan Cape and Hamish Hamilton to publish his diary and its blow-by-blow account of his years in power.

When on April 28, 1974, the London *Sunday Times* announced that it would run excerpts from the forthcoming *Diaries*, the Cabinet Secretary Sir John Hunt wrote to Dr. Janet Morgan, Crossman's editorial assistant, asking her to submit the manuscript for his review prior to permitting any form of publication. Crossman's literary executors duly submitted the ms. on June 10 and on June 21 were informed bluntly that none of it could possibly appear for 30 years. Cape's lawyer, Lord Goodman, persuaded Hunt to accept a strictly censored, abridged version, but he accepted that any publication would give Hunt 14 days notice, enough time for him to get an injunction. On July 1 Harold Evans, editor of the *Sunday Times*, was involved as owner of the *Diaries'* serial rights. He was appalled by cuts in which all details of government meetings, advice by civil servants and policy discussion "fell within forbidden parameters"—epitomized in a conversation in which Goodman asked "What can we say? Can we say that Crossman sat at [the] Cabinet table and looked out at St. James' Park?" And Hunt replied "Yes, provided you don't indicate who else was sitting with him." The theory was that ministers would not talk with necessary frankness without assuming a guaranteed confidentiality.

The newspaper was determined to publish, even though lawyers for all concerned made it clear that challenging the government might well end in a prosecution under the OFFI-CIAL SECRETS ACT. After a series of meetings Evans managed on January 23, 1975, to obtain from Hunt a demand that the *Sunday Times* should give its own undertaking to accept prior censorship; this had to be accepted by January 27. Evans seized this window of opportunity and published the first 10,000-word, uncensored extract on January 26. Instead of meeting an instant injunction, Evans received a call from Hunt, who proposed a compromise. For the next nine weeks the *Sunday Times* and the Cabinet Office watched as nearly 100,000 words of the *Diaries*, some anodyne, some potentially explosive, appeared. The paper accepted some cuts, rejected others, then submitted further material, usually far more than Hunt could handle efficiently.

The government's patience ran out on June 26 when the whole book was to be published. The attorney-general issued an injunction banning the publication and the *Sunday Times* responded to this demand—that the Cabinet had absolute powers of censorship over any discussion, past or present, that involved the formation or execution of policy—by running more unsubmitted material. The paper was duly included in the trial that followed. Cape, Hamish Hamilton and the *Sun-*

day Times were charged with breaching not the feared Official Secrets Act, but an arcane law of confidence, a judge-made precept that had formerly been restricted to commercial secrets but since 1967 had been extended to private rights. The prosecution argued for censorship, the defense against the increasing and unjustifiable secrecy that had accompanied the endless expansion of the civil service. The judge, Lord Widgery, delivered his opinion in October 1975: He agreed with the attorney-general's legal reasoning, accepted that a government must be bound by confidentiality but refused to ban the *Crossman Diaries*. He stated that, "I can find no ground for saying that either the Crown or the individual civil servant has an enforceable right to have the advice which he gives treated as confidential for all time." And added, "I cannot believe that the publication at this interval of anything in Volume 1 would inhibit free discussion in the Cabinet of today even though the individuals involved are the same and the national problems have a distressing similarity with those of a decade ago."

The case had made no law, but it had revealed previously secret government information, including the supposed guidelines for the writing of ministerial memoirs, guidelines that had only been committed to writing when this affair began. The attorney-general chose not to appeal, but he extracted from Widgery a confirmation that his ruling extended only to this case; the courts still retained their powers of restraint in government matters. The government established a committee under Lord Radcliffe. His report suggested that since no useful legal opinion had emerged, judges would in future best be kept out of this sort of controversy and that infinitely preferable was what "rightly or wrongly have come to be known as gentlemen's agreements," in which "everyone knows what is expected of him." In future any memoirs would be vetted for 15 years after the event, or in the case of civil servants until their retirement. During that period no minister past or present is to reveal the opinions or attitudes of government colleagues as to the business on which they have been engaged. He must not comment on the advice given to him by civil servants nor on the competence of those civil servants. On taking up office he must sign a declaration whereby he promises to abide by these conditions. Ex-ministers must submit all proposed memoirs, scripts for TV or radio inverviews and even letters to newspapers to the cabinet secretary in advance. If these are found unacceptable the minister may appeal to the prime minister, whose decision is final. These rules do not specify posthumous memoirs, but it is assumed that an ex-minister will place a codicil to his or her will to ensure that any such material is duly submitted before publication. A dissatisfied author may appeal to the prime minister, whose decision is final. A determined ex-minister may reject the guidelines, which have no legal force. In such a case, only if his or her work contravenes to Official Secrets Act (which Crossman's did not), can a prosecution take place.

SEE ALSO United Kingdom 3. Law of Confidence.

Crusade for Decency The crusade was founded in 1969 as one of the first organizations to challenge the generally permissive consensus of the era and campaign against pornography, abortion and sex education. Its finest hour was the presentation to Congress of a quarter-million-signature Petition for Decency, which focused upon the evils of its particular bugbears. Despite the increasingly conservative tone of American society, and the burgeoning of many comparable groups, the crusade, at best a loose confederation of the like-minded, has been out of operation for some years. Its members, it may be presumed, are still campaigning, albeit under new banners.

Curll, Edmund Curll was a bookseller and pamphleteer (1683-1747) who specialized in the fringes of literary production, issuing near-libellous biographies, seditious tracts, pirated works and pornography. He mixed pamphlets on venereal disease with such curiosities as *Eunuchism Display'd* (1718) and the first English edition of Petronius' *Satyricon*. He also pioneered the sexshop industry, vending a variety of dubious patent medicines, allegedly curative of venereal disease. He was a generally unpopular figure in the literary world and in 1715 incurred the wrath of Alexander Pope when he published, without authorization, some of Pope's poetry. Both parties used satires and squibs as their weapons, although Pope once placed an emetic in a supposedly concilliatory glass of wine. Curll's first brush with authority came when he issued a cheap edition of the proceedings of the House of Lords against the earl of Winton, who had been implicated in the Jacobean rebellion of 1715. The Lords punished Curll for this breach of privilege by having him imprisoned for three weeks and then making him kneel before the lord chancellor for verbal admonition.

In 1717 he was denounced by Daniel Defoe, who coined the word "Curlicism" to denote the publisher's iniquities and demanded that Curll's "abominable catalogue" should be suppressed. Curll was undaunted, publishing *Curlicism Displayed*, an answer to Defoe in which he touted, among other publications, his best-selling series "Cases of Impotency and Divorce." Far from facing the ire of the authorities, as Defoe had wished, Curll joined their ranks, starting work as a political spy for Sir Robert Walpole in 1725. In 1724 Curll published a translation of *De Usu Flagorum in re Medica et Venerea* by John Henry Meibomius (Meybaum), M.D.; he also issued a new edition of VENUS DANS LE CLOITRE, OU LA RELIGIEUSE EN CHEMISE (*Venus in the Cloister, or the Nun in her Smock*). The former was a somewhat anodyne tome, of medical rather than erotic interest, which belied the lurid promise of its title; the latter, allegedly written by the Abbe Barrin in 1683 as a Protestant tract, had developed into one of the staples of contemporary pornography, albeit a mild one. Although at his trial Curll claimed that his *Venus ...* was merely a reprint of an edition that had been circulating for 50 years, it was in fact an entirely new translation, generally thought to have been made by Robert Samber whose more

savory reputation lies in his translation of Charles Perrault's *Contes du temps passe*, as *Mother Goose's Tales*. Hearing that complaints against *Venus ...* had been made to the authorities, Curll tried to forestall any prosecution by printing "The Humble Representation of Edmund Curll, Bookseller and Stationer of London ..." This plea, though timely, failed to influence the secretary of state to whom it was addressed. In March 1725 Curll was arrested, held in prison until July and tried in November on charges of committing an OBSCENE LIBEL.

At this trial, before the King's Bench, arguments centered not on Curll's actions, which were generally accepted to be criminal, but on whether the common or ecclesiastical law—which latter had formerly been responsible for offenses against morals—should hear the case. The lord chief justice argued that since the offense concerned writings, it was in the province of the common law. Curll maintained that there was no libel anyway, but what offense there was fell into the province of the church. The prosecution, citing the case of SEDLEY, claimed that Curll had corrupted the morals of the king's subjects and thus broken the peace and thus the common law. The case was adjourned for fuller discussion. Curll was declared guilty, but, since there was as yet no provision for his punishment, he was bailed to await sentence.

Initially he forswore any more publishing, but was unable to resist two last books. One dealt with alleged monkish degeneracy in Paris, the other, the seditious *Memoirs of John Ker* (a notorious government spy), gave sufficient reason for a new raid on his premises. Curll was arrested again and nine books removed. He remained in prison, still publishing sedition and complaints, until July 1726.

On February 13, 1729, Curll was finally sentenced under common law. He was fined a total of 55 marks—once for the moral offenses and once for the political one—and condemned to stand in the pillory for one hour. Prior to this usually painful appearance he had distributed to the enthusiastic mob a pamphlet in which he maintained that "the Gentleman who stands before you" had been convicted of nothing more than excessive affection for the late Queen Anne, a far more popular monarch than the current George I. Curll survived absolutely unscathed. Curll continued working until his death in 1747; his fortunes, which had declined, improving after Pope singled him out for a scathing attack in *The Dunciad*. He continued as a pornographer, still offering such works as *The Secrets of Coition* in 1745. His case had a greater importance than his life, since for the first time it firmly placed obscene libel within the misdemeanors covered by common law.

Curly *Curly*, made in 1947 by Hal Roach Studios, concerns the escapades of an ostensibly lovable gang of youngsters and their adventures in and out of school. Set in small-town America it mixes blacks and whites without comment. This cinematic miscegenation was unacceptable to the South, and in 1949 the film was banned by the Tennessee state censor, who wrote to United Artists, the film's distributor, to explain that "I am sorry to have to inform you that [the board] is unable to approve ... your picture with the little negroes as the South does not permit negroes in white schools nor recognize social equality between the races even in children." Hal Roach Studios brought suit in the circuit court, claiming that this censorship, brought "solely on the grounds that members of the colored race appear" was "capricious and arbitrary" and as such violated the rights of freedom of speech guaranteed by the FIRST and Fourteenth Amendments. This suit was rejected by the judge, who refused even to view the film and carefully sidestepped the real issue of racism, and its use as a justification for censorship. It was accepted that such a criterion was not acceptable, but ruled that such matters were irrelevant to this case. His opinion stated that there was no ground for controversy since the letter had been "advisory only," and that, since the local censorship laws related only to local exhibitors, a national distributor, who neither showed pictures in the city nor had legally contracted to do so, had no right to sue.

Czechoslovakia The Communist Party, which took control of Czechoslovakia in 1948, inherited a system of censorship legislation that essentially dated from the December Constitution of 1876, in which pre-censorship had been banned and which had lasted, with the exception of the 1938-45 period, ever since. Between 1948 and 1953 there was party censorship, but this was random, operating without a proper institutional framework, and officials tended to delegate the responsibility to individual editors, who were given their positions by the party. Their job was simply to ensure that everything printed concurred with the current ideological line. The situation changed in 1953, following the resolution of five years of internal party struggles. The winning group declared their own infallibility, blaming their opponents for any failings in society. At the same time the mass media began to proliferate, bringing with them a complex of publishing and broadcasting that could no longer be controlled by a few party-appointed editors.

The need for a proper censorship office was accepted and the unpublished government decree no. 17 of April 22, 1953, set up the Office of State Press Supervision as a non-public government body, incorporated in 1954 into the Ministry of Interior. The office was given side powers, controlling the mass media and all cultural and artistic activities. Everything from newspapers and books to matchbox labels had to be checked, and the office assessed any imported publications. Wholesale confiscations and bannings were begun, and a special library of such works, to which very few readers were admitted, was established. Under the office the whole of Czech culture and media were submitted to the needs of the party by both prescriptive and proscriptive measures. As well as constant, all-embracing censorship, under which the party interfered continually in the operation of the mass media, Czech journalists, writers, broadcasters and artists accepted a high degree of self-censorship, encouraged by the concept of party duty whereby they were expected on their own initiative to "take note of all socially significant journalistic ventures and their orientation in order to ensure that their effect was in harmony with the party's overall policy." This situation was largely restored after the brief liberalization of 1968 and is very much the current status quo.

Censorship was slightly relaxed in the period of de-Stalinization that followed the 20th Party Congress of 1956 and some criticisms of society, carefully controlled, were permitted. Such liberality ended with the Hungarian uprising and the party made its dominance clear. In 1966 a new press law was adopted, replacing the law of 1950, which had been mainly concerned with the abolition of private enterprise publishing and the creation of a licensing system. The new law was far more complex. It defined the task of the mass media as "unfolding the socialist consciousness of the citizenry in the spirit of the Constitution and of the ideas of the Communist Party ... as the leading force." Its most innovative provision was the admission in public for the first time that censorship, long established but never acknowledged, actually existed, setting up a Central Publications Office to administer it. It replaced the licensing system with an ostensibly more liberal form of registration, but the party still held absolute control of the qualifications for such registration, as well as of the means—financial, material and technical—to achieve publication.

In the area of disseminating information, the law instructed a variety of state-run cultural, scientific, economic and similar bodies to give to "editors and all other journalists information within the scope of their responsibilities essential for the truthful, prompt and thorough information of the public." But this apparent openness was tempered by permitting the restrain of any information that was a state, official or economic secret or that, if published, might threaten the interests of the state or Czech society. Such vaguely defined areas ensured a wide range of censorable material. Furthermore the party itself has no obligation to provide information, although it maintains the right to interfere extensively in all media.

During the 1960s, despite these controls, a reform movement did begin to find a voice in the Czech media, although this was in the journals and periodicals and on an increasing number of TV documentaries and audience participation shows, rather than in the daily press, still absolutely subject to the party's wishes. The continuing dissatisfaction with Czech society could not be suppressed and undoubtedly spurred the advent of the Prague Spring of 1968. Under the Dubcek reforms, the press law of 1966 was abrogated, but a framework of legislation was maintained, with the vital modification that the party bosses no longer claimed the right to control the flow and content of information. Subsequent analysis suggests that had Dubcek survived, there would have been an increasing liberalization of the mass media.

In the aftermath of the Soviet invasion censorship was quickly restored. The authorities established an Office for Press and Information, *Urad Pro Tisk a Informace* in Czech and nicknamed *Utisk*, the Czech word for "repression." Initially this office had two departments, one Czech, one Slovak. These were amalgamated in December 1980 into the Federal Office for Press and Information. This office has six duties: to propose and implement government policy on the press and information; to register the periodical press; to ensure the protection of important state interests; to oversee the importation of foreign material and check the distribution of publications printed in Czechoslovakia by foreign publishers or distributed by foreign press agencies; to decide on authorization permits for editors-in-chief who are not Czech nationals; to authorize organizations that are entitled to receive or distribute periodicals. No actual censorship is mentioned, but the "protection of state interests" gives the office wide powers to restrict the flow of information.

D

D Notices The British army had campaigned for press censorship since Bismarck noted the extent to which Germany's war planning had benefited from the uncensored French press of 1870. In 1912 the British government set up the Admiralty, War Office and Press Committee, a group that included members from both the press and the armed forces. The purpose of this committee, which came into its own during the First World War, was to advise the press, in the persons of newspaper editors, that it would please the government if certain topics, although otherwise newsworthy, were omitted from their columns. The advice was given in the form of D (for Defense) Notices. Such notices also made it clear to editors just what material fell under the OFFICIAL SECRETS ACT.

The committee did not meet from 1923 to 1946. During the Second World War the D Notices were issued by the Press Censorship Department of the Ministry of Defence. After the war the committee was revived and renamed the Services, Press and Broadcasting Committee. It consists of four government officials, all permanent civil servants, plus 11 delegates from the press and broadcasting, representing variously the Newspaper Publishers' Association, the Newspaper Society, Scottish Daily Newspaper Society, Periodical Proprietors Association, news agencies, one publisher, the BBC and the IBA. The committee, which has no legal basis whatsoever, is responsible for D Notices and P & C Letters, reminders to editors that old D Notices encompass a ban on certain new topics that refer back to the originally censored material.

The D Notice system is ostensibly voluntary, depending on the sense of fair play that supposedly permeates the British establishment. Whether one interprets this gentlemen's agreement as self-censorship or responsible journalism depends on one's position in that Establishment. There is no overt censorship, and editors are only requested to "make no reference to the following" material. As the introduction to a D Notice explains, "Its success depends on good will and in effect on very little else." If an editor chooses to ignore the notice, feeling perhaps that it simply provides a convenient mask for government ineptitude rather than genuine national security, there is no automatic penalty, although in certain cases the material involved may fall under the Official Secrets Act. Like other aspects of security, the wording of a D Notice is deliberately vague, covering as wide as possible an area of information. The normal issuing procedure involves the preparation by the secretary of a draft, geared to satisfying the approval of the press. All members of the committee are circularized, although they only meet as such when there is disagreement or when some new principle of restriction is to

be discussed. Once all are satisfied, the notice is issued. The line between genuine security and convenient cover-up of embarrassing material or governmental error remains fine. On the whole editors tend to give the authorities the benefit of the doubt. Certain D Notices remain in force indefinitely. There are currently nine permanent D Notices, covering references to defense plans, operational readiness and state of readiness; classified weapons and equipment; construction of naval warships and equipment; aircraft and aero engines; nuclear warfare and a variety of defense oriented subjects, including intelligence services and their codes and communications.

The D Notice committee is also responsible for the unofficial but pervasive censorship apparatus, which deals with any books or allied publications that deal with the services. There exists for the guidance of its members a list of prohibited topics; although this is never publicized it is known to include any books on prisoner-of-war escapes, among other service-related areas. The exercise of this form of censorship demonstrates how in the interest of supposed national security a citizen may have his or her livelihood—in this case writing a book—severely curtailed through the operation of a shadowy body dispensing undisclosed regulations. There is no legal means whereby the committee may operate this censorship, other than that the government assumes that all material it sees as relevant will be submitted for assessment. The Official Secrets Act remains in the background as a form of blanket threat and many employees of civil service departments and scientific and research establishments as well as current and former servicemen, have to sign declarations whereby they promise not to disclose any classified material.

The committee lost something of its respect during the 1960s when it appeared to be straying into areas other than those of defense. In 1963 it attempted to ban the publication of the whereabouts of the nation's regional seats of government (RSGs), the proposed underground headquarters for the government during a nuclear war. These sites were published by a group of nuclear disarmers in a book, *Spies for Peace*. In this instance the D Notice was ignored by the press. In 1967 the committee's secretary, Col. Sammy Lohan, was consulted by veteran defense journalist Chapman Pincher who wished to publish a story alleging that the secret service monitored all cables leaving the U.K., whether diplomatic or commercial. He had obtained this information from a telegraphist at Commercial Cables and Western Union. When the piece was published in the *Daily Express* on February 21, the prime minister, Harold Wilson, told Parliament that Pincher's story was unfounded and contravened two D Notices. Pincher denied this, claiming that Lohan had given him a go-ahead to publish, saying that while two notices did exist one, of 1956, did not apply to cables, and the other, of 1961, was of marginal relevance. Lohan contradicted this and said that he had warned Pincher against publication. After an investigation by Lord Radcliffe both the *Express* and Lohan were exonerated, although Lohan was forced to resign his post. The main injury was to the system itself, and hamfisted attempts the same year to cover up stories on the "Third Man," Cambridge spy Kim Philby, with two notices that were ignored by the *Sunday Times*, made things even worse.

Dada On April 20, 1920, the first Dada Event in Cologne was organized by the artists Max Ernst and Hans Arp. It caused such a scandal that it was immediately closed down by the police, ordered to take this action by a magistrate who was Ernst's uncle. It was alleged that "Dadaists were worse than Communists" and the police assumed that they were no more than a gang of gays. The Event could only be entered through the lavatory of the Winter Bierhaus, a local beer-hall. Innocent drinkers found themselves attracted through a gap in the wall to the "Dada-Fair," crammed with bizarre objects, collages and photomontages. After the police had looked closely at the exhibition, and found the most morally reprehensible object to be one created by Albrecht Dürer, they permitted it to continue unhindered. The First International Dada Fair was held in April 1921 in Berlin. The five promoters of the fair were charged with insulting the Reichswehr—the newly reorganized German army—after a caricature put a pig's face on a dummy, which had been dressed in field-gray and which was hanging from the ceiling. The authorities also objected to GEORGE GROSZ's *Gott Mit Uns*, a volume of satirical drawings that were described in court as "gross insults to officers and soldiers" and to the mutilated figure of a woman, a knife stuck in her breast and an iron cross on her back. While the defense claimed that the whole exhibition was a joke, and the anti-militarism was directed at the old German army, not the new, the jury was unimpressed. Two of the promoters were found guilty, and Grosz was fined 300 marks. The verdicts, it was felt, had saved the honor of the German army.

Daily Mirror The London *Daily Mirror* was nearly suppressed under Regulation 2D of the English Defence (General) Regulations after it published on March 6, 1942, a cartoon by Philip Zec in which a torpedoed sailor clung to a life raft, above a caption that read: "The price of petrol has been incrased by one penny—Official." The caption, which the *Mirror* claimed was merely a warning against wasting fuel and a tribute to the herosim of the merchant navy, but which the government read as an attack on the petrol companies and their profits, had been written by the paper's acerbic columnist, "Cassandra" (William Connor). Home Secretary Herbert Morrison, himself a former *Mirror* columnist, summoned C.E. Thomas, the offending editor, and threatened that any

further cheek would have the paper banned. The rest of Fleet Street, excepting the *Daily Telegraph*, *Daily Sketch* and *Sunday Times* united in the paper's defense. The *Daily Mirror* was not banned, but it continued to stay only marginally inside the regulations for the war's duration.

Daily Worker On January 20, 1941, the London *Daily Worker* published a cartoon, *Their Gallant Allies*, which attacked Britain's current allies; the Free French; the hard-right-wing Dr. Antonio Salazar of Portugal; and General Wladyslaw Sikorski, described as fascist, of Poland. All were holding a banner proclaiming "War On USSR, Peace With Italy." The paper had been in conflict with the authorities through its open policy of "revolutionary defeatism" since the outbreak of war and this cartoon was considered justification for a raid by Scotland Yard's Special Branch. The Home Office announced on January 21 that publication of the paper had been suspended indefinitely under Regulation 2D of the English Defence (General) Regulations. The paper was not allowed to recommence publication until August 1942, some 14 months after Hitler's invasion of Russia, since when the U.S.S.R. too had joined the allies.

Daniel, Yuli (aka Nikolai Arzhak) SEE Sinyavsky & Daniel trial (1966).

Dante Alighieri Dante (1265-1321) was born in Florence of a Guelf family. His early years are obscure, other than that, in 1277, he was betrothed to his future wife Gemma Donati and in 1289, he fought for Florence against Pisa and Arezzo. At some stage he fell in love with "Beatrice," the girl he immortalized in the *Vita Nuova* (ca. 1290) and the *Divine Comedy* (ca. 1307), and who is generally assumed to have been Bice Portinari, wife of Simone de' Bardi. After she died in 1290 Dante buried his grief in his study of philosophy. From 1295 he involved himself in the political life of Florence, supporting the White faction there, but during an absence in Rome in 1301 the rival Black faction took control and Dante never returned, spending the rest of his life in a peripatetic existence.

As well as alienating the politicians of Florence, Dante also fell foul of the church in Rome. His treatise on relations between the emperor and the Pope, *De Monarchia* (written sometime between 1309 and 1312), was publicly burned in France in 1318 and a number of his books were included in SAVONAROLA's "bonfire of the vanities" in 1497. *De Monarchia* was placed on the INDEX OF PAUL IV in 1559 and on the TRIDENTINE INDEX in 1564; in both cases the Papacy refused to accept Dante's contention that the authority of kings derived not from the Pope, but from God himself. In 1581 the authorities in Lisbon called in all copies of the *Divine Comedy* for expurgation.

data protection SEE Austria: Federal Ministries Act (amendment, 1973); Denmark 3. Law on Publicity in Administration (1970); Norway 3. Freedom of the Press Act (1971); Sweden 3. Freedom of the Press Act; United States 18. Privacy Act.

David Michelangelo's *David* has frequently worried those who cannot tolerate the marble genitals and pubic hair with which it is unmistakably adorned. The 18-foot-high statue has come to symbolize Renaissance sculpture, but its anatomical perfection has always disturbed some critics. Even on its unveiling in Florence in 1501, onlookers stoned Michelangelo's masterpiece, breaking off an arm. Four centuries later, in 1939, when the cemetery at Forest Lawn Memorial Park, in Cypress, California, erected a copy of the statue, the offending area was masked with a figleaf. Not until July 1969 was the 22-foot-high reproduction revealed as the artist created it. Local residents did complain, but the cemetery chose to leave David naked. In nearby Glendale and West Covina, however, cemeteries chose not to display their own versions of the statue. In November 1969 a *David* poster displayed in a bookshop in Sydney, Australia, then acknowledged as the most censored country in the free world, was seized by members of the vice squad. An impending prosecution of the shop's manager for obscenity was headed off only when the curator of the New South Wales Art Museum pooh-poohed the raid and pointed out that *David* had been displayed undraped in Florence—"A Roman Catholic city"—for nearly 500 years. This reverse failed to prevent a further raid, two months later, when four men involved in running another Sydney bookshop were arrested for selling obscene publications: a print of the statue plus a number of drawings by AUBREY BEARDSLEY.

dazibao The publication of "big character posters" (dazibao), a rash of which appeared in China subsequent to the fall of the Gang of Four in October 1976, represents the liberal side of a tradition of calculated information management under communist rule. Such wall posters had often been used in revolutionary China as an established means of working out the ideologically correct line and were very popular, for instance, during the Cultural Revolution. Their premise was based on Mao's belief that if a variety of erroneous views are made, within reason, public, then the masses, swayed by the leadership and its greater knowledge, will be able to use the "correct" line to refute them and as such embrace ideological purity actively rather than accept it passively. Such subtlety rejects the simple bludgeon of outright repression, although "unmistakable counter-revolutionaries and saboteurs" are simply deprived of any freedom of speech. No posters may be put up within Peking, although unsanctioned ones did appear in April 1976 before they were removed.

Two styles of poster exist: the officially inspired and the privately issued. The former style provides a convenient way for opposition groups within the leadership to air their views, which cannot otherwise appear in the mass media, all of which carry only the official version of the news and the policies and events that comprise it. Such posters may be issued by the individuals concerned, or they may be issued by a support group, often students or factory workers, who have been suitably briefed. Personal posters often concentrate on a single issue: one's detestation of a factory boss or even a neighbor. They are a convenient way for an individual to vent his or her anger; but these posters must not be trivial. A cogent argument is mandatory and writing a poster is an intellectual exercise. Posters must fall within acceptable bounds; those that do not can earn the writer serious punishment, including imprisonment in a labor camp.

In December 1979, in response to Western interest in the posters, a number of regulations were issued governing their content and display: (1) all dazibao were to be displayed on officially authorized sites; (2) all dazibao writers were to register their names and addresses, but the content of their poster would not be checked; (3) those who display the posters are held responsible for the political content and such content must not contain state secrets, libel or false information; (4) it is illegal to create a disturbance at the poster display sites.

De Dominis, Antonio De Dominis was archbishop of Spalatro, a historian and scientist (1566-?) who was the first to discover the cause of a rainbow. He had been educated by the Jesuits, who helped him become professor of mathematics at Padua and of logic and rhetoric at Brescia. After finding himself on the wrong side in a controversy between Venice and the Pope, and subsequently forced to pay an annual pension of 500 crowns to Rome, he applied to the British ambassador to Venice, asking to be received in the Church of England since he found himself unable any longer to tolerate the abuses and corruption of Catholicism. King James I welcomed De Dominis and the English episcopate volunteered to pay for his maintenance. He gained a reputation for his wit and his weight, as well as for his irascibility and learning. Above all, he was outstandingly avaricious and was ridiculed as such in Middleton's play, *The Game of Chess*. While in England he wrote and published his major work, *De Republica Ecclesiastica*, in which he argued, on the basis of the scriptures, that the authority claimed by the Church of Rome was utterly specious; he went on to support the heresies of Huss, and to dismiss the papacy as a fiction invented by men.

De Dominis was further rewarded by James I, but foolishly insulted Count Gondomar, the Spanish ambassador. Gondamar was determined to be revenged and persuaded the Pope, Gregory XV, to help him. Gregory played on De Dominis' greed, offering him vast sums to reject Anglicanism and return to Rome. Despite the efforts of the king and a number of bishops, De Dominis was adamant. The authorities turned against him and he was ordered to leave England within 20 days. A cache of money was removed from his luggage and he fled to Brussels. He stayed there, writing his apologia, *Consilium Reditus*, and waiting for the papal favors that had been promised. When these did not come he began complaining again, citing *De Republica Ecclesiastica* and threatening to change faiths yet again. This time he was arrested by the ROMAN INQUISITION. He was imprisoned and died soon after, allegedly of poison. His body and books were burned by the public executioner and their ashes scattered on the River Tiber. The Catholic Dr. Fitzgerald, rector of the English College in Rome, summed up De Dominis: "He was a malcontent knave when he fled from us, a railing knave when he lived with you, and a motley particoloured knave known he is come again."

De Sales, St. Francis SEE book burning in England 3. Charles I (1625-1649).

Debs, Eugene In 1918 Debs was America's leading socialist and while outside the mainstream of two-party politics still attracted a respectable following in a country then devoted to laissez-faire capitalism. He was by no means an extremist, but still attracted the attention of the authorities. Among the byproducts of America's belated entry into World War I was a flood of sedition prosecutions, brought under the ESPIONAGE ACT of 1917. Speaking in Canton, Ohio, Debs denounced such specious prosecutions, which used the European war as an excuse for the persecution of domestic left-wingers. Debs was promptly arrested under the same act. At the trial, held in Cleveland, Ohio, Debs defended himself, telling the jury: "I admit being opposed to the present form of government; I admit being opposed to the present social system. I am doing what little I can to do away with the rule of the great body of people by a relatively small class ..." Such beliefs did not impress a conservative jury; Debs was found guilty and sentenced to 10 years in prison. An appeal to the Supreme Court was rejected on the grounds that his advocacy of draft-resistance as the best way of stating one's opposition to the war put him within the power of the act. Debs was freed in 1921 after President Harding granted him a pardon, although he had forfeited his citizenship. Until his death he edited the journal of the combined Socialist and La Follette (Progressive Party) parties, the *American Appeal.* His collected speeches were published in 1929.

Decameron, The This collection of tales by Giovanni Boccaccio (1313-75) appeared between 1349 and 1351. A company of seven young ladies and three young men, confined through an outbreak of the plague in Florence in 1348, spend 10 days entertaining each other with stories, each narrator telling one story per day, making a total of 100 tales in all. Many of the stories predate this publication, but Boccaccio set them down in their definitive version. The first English edition appeared in 1620. With its open enjoyment of the more salacious aspects of life and its poking of fun at respectable mores, especially in its imputation of a variety of excesses, mainly sexual, to nuns and priests, the *Decameron* soon gained its critics. SAVONAROLA included it in his "bonfire of

the vanities" in 1498. Pope Paul IV placed it on the ROMAN INDEX OF 1559, but his complaints were not against the courtly licentiousness. When the authorized version was issued by the Vatican, the "gallantry" remained but the immoral clergy had been excised, and their places taken by conjurors and aristocrats.

Secular authorities were less tolerant. France banned the book well into the 19th century. Until the Tariff Act of 1930, the *Decameron* was among those books automatically confiscated from returning travellers by U.S. Customs, and it was occasionally banned from internal circulation. In 1927 Customs mutilated a copy sent from England by the antiquarian booksellers Maggs Bros. and returned the covers to London, minus the text. Even after Customs began permitting its importation in 1931, the book featured in prosecutions, such as that in Detroit in 1934, Boston in 1935 and so on. It is still featured on the black list of the U.S. NATIONAL ORGANIZATION FOR DECENT LITERATURE.

Prosecutions of the book continued in England until the 1950s. The NATIONAL VIGILANCE ASSOCIATION only narrowly failed to have copies burnt in 1886. Between 1951 and 1954 there were eight separate orders for the book's destruction. The one that caused the greatest uproar, and was the last attempt to ban Boccaccio, occurred in 1954 in Swindon. Local Justices of the Peace ordered the book burned, adamant in their demand until they were informed that an identical copy, an unexpurgated edition translated by J.M. Rigg, was held by the local reference library.

SEE ALSO United States 21. Tariff Act (1930).

Decretum Gelasianum In 494 Pope Gelasius issued a catalog of works prohibited for private reading. This is sometimes cited as the first Papal Index, but the better claimant to this title is the Decretum Gelasium, a decree published at the Council of Rome in 496 and confirmed by the Emperor Gratian, which specified those writings composed by the fathers of the church that may be read by the faithful. To this was appended a list of 60 apocryphal and heretical writings and writers that may not be read. This list condemned heretical works, forged acts of martyrs, spurious penitentials, and "superstitious writings." Even this list is not a real Index however, since rather than specify a general prohibition of the reading of works, it simply calls for their rejection and condemnation.

SEE ALSO Christian Church 1. early censorship (150-814).

Deep Throat First exhibited in the U.S. by its director Gerard Damiano in 1972, this film was the first example of hard-core cinematic pornography that transcended the usual audience for such exhibitions. Millions of men, their wives and girlfriends all saw the film, starring actress Linda Lovelace (real name Linda Marchiano). To have seen the film, for many Americans, became a badge of one's sexual liberality. The "art porn" boom that it was thought would follow *Deep Throat,* which defied nationwide attempts to ban it, although it never gained international acceptance outside the traditional porno markets, did not materialize. The film was actually judged obscene in the case of *Sanders* v. *Georgia* (1975), and a year later the Supreme Court affirmed that judgement. Nonetheless the film continued to be exhibited in the U.S., although attempts to show it in British cinemas were swiftly quashed and only a few smuggled copies were imported. Other efforts, notably *The Devil in Miss Jones*, were touted but failed to maintain the trend. The title remains best known as the pseudonym given by reporters Bernstein and Woodward to their most damning official source in the Watergate scandal of 1973-74.

SEE ALSO *Behind the Green Door.*

defamation (U.K.)   The legal concept of defamation is, like libel, slander, FIGHTING WORDS and similar actionable offenses, an area that falls outside those categories protected by laws covering freedom of speech. Defamation may occur when either a printed (libel) or a spoken (slander) statement injures the reputation of a given individual, exposing him or her to public hatred, contempt, ridicule, or financial injury, or impeaches their character, honesty, integrity or morality. Merely making someone into a laughingstock is not enough; his or her reputation or character must be impugned as well. Defamation may also vary as to contemporary circumstances: What is damaging to an individual under one social or political climate, say in wartime, when it might be defamatory to ally someone with the enemy, may be quite acceptable when the climate has changed and the former enemy is now a valued ally. Defamation is a contentious enough concept when it does not affect issues and individuals within the public interest, but when it does, the courts are forced to adjudicate between the desire for the full disclosure of the relevant facts and the need to protect an individual's reputation from unrestrained attacks, only some of which may be accurate but others may not. The best defense in English law against a charge of defamation is that the allegation is substantially true. Prior to the Defamation Act (1952) every fact had to proved, but since then "a defence of justification shall not fail by reason only that the truth of every charge is not proved if the words not proved to be true do not materially injure the plaintiff's reputation having regard to the truth of the remaining charges." Even if the defendant was inspired by malice, or did not even believe the allegations to be true when he made them, if in fact they are true, there is no defamation.

Under parliamentary privilege, even the truth is not vital: An MP may make certain allegations within the House of Commons that would be defamatory if repeated outside. Such allegations may similarly be reported verbatim by the media, who are likewise protected by such privilege for the purpose of their reporting. Whether of parliamentary statements or otherwise, all fair and accurate reporting, even if it is of the inaccurate and even malicious statements of third parties, is protected. Outside Parliament otherwise defamatory statements may claim qualified privilege if they can be proved to have been made without malice, e.g., in the case of a company director alleging, in the interests of his fellow directors and of the company as a whole, that their cashier is falsifying accounts. Fair comment on matters of public interest, e.g., comments on the activities of public figures or reviews of books, plays and the like, is exempt from prosecution.

defamation (U.S.)   As in Britain (above) the offense of defamation embraces any printing or writing (libel) or spoken word (slander) that tends to injure an individual's reputation, and thus expose that person to public hatred, contempt, ridicule, financial injury, or that impeaches someone's character, honesty, integrity or morality. However, unlike the U.S., whcre stringent libel laws severely curtail the public right to know and are heavily biased in favor of the plaintiff, the FIRST AMENDMENT ensures that, possible defamation notwithstanding, there must be full disclosure and debate on matters of public interest. Simultaneously, personal reputations must be protected from defamatory attacks.

In order to resolve this conflict the Supreme Court has given First Amendment protection to certain types of defamation. The rulings are epitomized in the NEW YORK TIMES RULE, whereby a PUBLIC OFFICIAL or PUBLIC FIGURE who sues for defamation must prove malice on behalf of the defendant. Otherwise the material in question is protected by constitutional guarantees of a free press and of freedom of speech.

Defence of Literature and the Arts Society (U.K.)   T h e DLAS was formed as part of the response by publishers JOHN CALDER and Marion Boyars to the prosecution in 1967 of Hubert Selby's LAST EXIT TO BROOKLYN. A distinguished panel of defense witnesses—academics, sociologists, writers, poets, critics and assorted literary and media figures—had been assembled to defend the novel. When their efforts failed to convince the jury that the book was a masterpiece, the publishers faced costs of £10,000-15,000. A Free Art Legal Fund was set up to meet this bill and the DLAS formed, both to administer the funds sent by a sympathetic public and to keep the anti-censorship momentum going. Once established, the DLAS joined with the National Council for Civil Liberties (NCCL) in promoting its beliefs and helping in the defense of various obscenity cases.

The first chairman, until mid-1969, was Stuart Hood, former controller of programs for BBC-TV; he was succeeded by William Hamling, MP. Calder and Boyars were joint secretaries. The first help offered by the DLAS was to Bill Butler of the Unicorn Bookshop in Brighton who was facing charges under the OBSCENE PUBLICATION ACT (1959), following a police raid in January 1968 and the seizure of many avant-garde and underground publications. When Butler was fined £250 plus 180 guineas (£189.00) costs by Brighton magistrates the DLAS helped him pay but was unable to have his case appealed in the High Court. The DLAS involved itself in the defense of a number of similar cases, but they refused to back the defense of MY SECRET LIFE in February 1969, and ensured that while DLAS funds were allotted to *The Mouth*, the society rigidly disassociated itself from the advertising leaflet promoting the book. They also organized a public meeting to support OZ and contributed to the defense of the LITTLE RED SCHOOLBOOK.

The premise of all DLAS efforts, despite the dubious artistic value of some items that it did choose to support, was that in the end the principle of cultural freedom is more important than its practice. In March 1969, Hamling introduced in Parliament the strictly optimistic Obscene Publications (Amendment) Bill, which, in common with many efforts to reform the bill (from both liberals and censors), was rejected. Throughout this period, when there were a number of important cases involving concepts of literary freedom, the DLAS maintained its important role as a front-line defender of the written arts.

SEE ALSO *The Mouth and Oral Sex*.

Defoe, Daniel Defoe was born Daniel Foe (1660-1731), the son of James Foe, a butcher. He changed his name around 1695. Educated as a dissenter he abandoned thoughts of the ministry after he married in 1683-84 and began traveling in Europe as a merchant of hosiery. After joining Monmouth's rebellion and fighting with the forces of William III in 1688 he began writing, publishing his first serious work, *An Essay Upon Projects*, in 1697. In 1701 appeared *A true-born Englishman*, a satirical attack on those whose xenophobia turned them against King William and his Dutch friends. In 1702 Defoe published *The Shortest Way with Dissenters*, in reply to a sermon preached in June 1702 at Oxford by DR. HENRY SACHEVERELL. The sermon, entitled "The political Union," attacked the Dissenters, and suggested that all proper Anglicans "ought to hang out the bloody flag and banner of defiance." Defoe's reply parodied Anglican extremism to perfection, demanding rigorous repression of all dissent and delighting the devout until the pamphlet's true authorship was discovered. He paid dearly for his ironies, being fined, imprisoned from May to November of 1703 and placed for three days in the pillory. During this latter confinement he composed the "Hymn to the Pillory," which was sold widely on the London streets. It read, in part, "Hail, Hieroglyphick State machine,/Contrived to punish fancy in;/Men that are men in thee can feel no pain,/And all they insignificancts disdain/ ... Thou are no shame to Truth and Honesty/Nor is the character of such defaced by thee,/ ... And they who for no crime shall on thy brows appear./Bear less reproach than they who placed them there." Defoe survived this punishment to work for the Tory government as a secret agent between 1703 and 1714, before embarking on a career that produced some 560 books, pamphlets and journals, including *Robinson Crusoe* (1719), *Moll Flanders* (1722), *A Journal of the Plague Year* (1722), *Roxana* (1724), *Colonel Jack* (1724) and a great deal more. Various of these works suffered bans, on the grounds either of Defoe's anti-Catholicism or the "obscenity" of his writing. *Robinson Crusoe* was placed on

the Spanish Index in 1720, the *Political History of the Devil* on the Roman Index in 1743 and *Moll Flanders* and *Roxana* were only permitted into the U.S. after the Tariff Act of 1930. SEE ALSO Roman Indexes; United States 12. Tariff Act (1930).

Dejeuner sur l'herbe Edouard Manet painted *Le Bain* (*The Bathing Party*) in 1863. Hanging in the Palais d'Industrie amongst 4,000 works that formed the Salon des Refuses—those works that had been rejected for exhibition by the jury of the Paris Salon—the painting caused an instant scandal. The picture, with its two fully dressed, dandified young men lolling beside a naked girl, her clothes spread out around her, while a second girl paddles in a pool in the background, shocked the upright. The painting, rechristened by its many viewers *Dejeuner sur l'herbe* (*Picnic* or *Luncheon on the Grass*), was condemned as immoral and shameless. For the conservative art connoisseur, its exhibition justified the blanket condemnation of the Impressionist movement, of which Manet was a leader. Napoleon III, patron of the Refuses, joined the attack, while the empress affected not to see it as they toured the exhibition. The whole scene appeared to most critics as thoroughly degenerate, with the crux of their disapproval being not that the young lady, "a commonplace woman of the demi-monde," was "as naked as can be" but that the two young men were clothed. It was, in the words of critic Louis Etienne, "a young man's practical joke, a shameful open sore not worth exhibiting."

SEE ALSO *Olympia*.

Delaune SEE book burning in England 6. the Restoration.

Delaware's obscenity statute Under volume 43, chapter 239, Laws of Delaware, "Whoever ... exhibits ... or has in his possession with intent to ... exhibit ... or knowingly advertises ... any obscene, lewd, lascivious, filthy, indecent drawing, photograph, film, figure or image ... is guilty of a misdemeanor." This law was used in the case of *State of Delaware* v. *Scope* (1951), brought against a cinema owner, John Scope, who screened the film, *Hollywood Peep Show*. The film was essentially a strip-tease show, with the obligatory third-rate comedians interspersed among the dancers. Scope was charged under the statute and condemned, largely on the evidence of an expert psychiatric witness, Dr. Tarumianz, who claimed that the film's bumps and grinds would corrupt the young and create "a various deviation of thinking and emotional instability in regard to sex problems." After watching *Hollywood Peep Show*, Tarumianz assured the court, "A happily married individual who is considered a mature adult individual, seeing such films, becomes seriously concerned with whether he is obtaining the necessary gratification of his sex desires from his normal and normally endowed and inclined wife. It may deviate him in accepting that there is something which arouses him to become interested in an abnormal type of sex satisfaction which he had perhaps from this picture." The judge agreed and Scope was convicted and fined.

Denmark

1. censorship The Danish Constitution (1953) states at article 77 that "any person shall be entitled to publish their thoughts in printing, in writing, and in speech, provided that they may be held answerable in a court of justice. Censorship and other preventive measures shall never again be reintroduced." While this clause guarantees freedom from prior restraint but still appears to allow for subsequent criminal proceedings, it is generally accepted that the constitution does protect individuals from such action if the matter is considered to be in the public interest. There is thus no censorship of the press or of publications, but section 267 of the Penal Code makes defamation an offense, unless the defendant can prove "justified protection of obvious public interest." Article 265b of the code makes it a criminal offense to attack a person on the grounds of their race.

There is no censorship of the Danish press, all of which is owned privately and has been free of restriction since the Constitution of 1849. The sole restriction states that all material must be credited to a named author. Under article 172 of the Court Procedure Act journalists have the right to protect their sources. This can only be overruled if the case deals with an offense that might lead to the defendant's imprisonment, or if it deals with leaks by civil servants who are legally obliged to maintain confidentiality.

In June 1967 the Danish Parliament by an overwhelming vote abolished all laws relating to printed obscenity in Denmark. In July 1969 those laws relating to visual material, including films and photographs, were similarly abandoned. The immediate result of this was a recorded drop of some 50 percent in the circulation of pornography. It also created the image, cultivated sedulously in less liberal countries, of Denmark as a freewheeling pornocracy. In fact porno shops may not sell to anyone under 17, and all forms of display of their wares—in windows and on stalls—are tightly regulated. The image is hardly accurate.

Radio and television are controlled by Danmarks Radio, established in 1925, an independent public institution that is responsible for all broadcasting. This situation was confirmed in the Radio and Television Service Act, 1975. The organization is controlled by the Radio Council, a 27-member body responsible to the minister for cultural affairs and elected by Parliament. It operates no specific censorship system, but ensures that all programs conform to the provisions of Danish law. The composition of the council is as follows: the chairman and vice chairman are nominated by the minister for cultural affairs, one member is nominated by the Ministry of Public Works, 12 by the Parliament as representatives of public viewers and listeners, 10 by the political parties who hold seats on the parliamentary finance committee, and two by Danmarks Radio. The council meets twice a month; as

well as discussing overall broadcasting affairs, it makes some post-transmission criticism of given programs.

2. film censorship Censorship of films is governed by the Censorship Board, established by statute in 1969. Its function is to decide whether or not a film is suitable for exhibition to children under the age of 16, and it is empowered to ban the exhibition of films to children under the ages of either 12 of 16 if its two members feel such films would be harmful to that age group. The censors have no responsibility for films shown to adults, nor for those shown on television. Both board members are appointed by the minister for cultural affairs and must be teachers or psychologists or have had some professional experience dealing with children. They hold office for four years and act independently, although a Board of Appeal, rarely used and in every case taking a more liberal position, can reassess their decisions. The board checks some 30 percent of the 300 films exhibited on average per year. If the film is not to be seen by 12- or 16-year-olds, it is marked either TO12 or TO16, meaning that only those older than the ages specified may see the film. These restrictions operate only when a film includes explicit shots of the genitals, sexual violence or the degradation of women. A violent film is defined as one in which the ability to feel pity toward another person is lowered. Any frightening film is marked TO12. Public opinion in Denmark has even suggested the complete abandonment of film censorship for all ages, but this does not seem likely, although a new system might be developed.

3. Law on Publicity in Administration (1970) The Danish law on public freedom of access to government material resembles the Norwegian Freedom of the Press Act (see Norway 3) but, possibly as a result of the Danish system of government, which resembles the British parliamentary one, is less far-reaching and more protective of government autonomy. The current constitution, dating from 1953, has no provision for open government. Government commissions on the topic in 1957 and 1963 consistently rejected legislation, but the Law on Party Access in Administration, allowing the parties to administrative cases to see the relevant documents, was passed in 1964. It is similar to the U.S. and Norwegian administrative procedure acts.

On the basis of this law, the Law on Publicity in Administration was passed in 1970. It has proved the least user-friendly of all such legislation. Those requesting documents must identify them in detail but there is no system of listing or indexing available. Exemptions from disclosure are drawn as widely as possible and documents may be retained by the government merely if so required by "the special character of the circumstances." The law is enforced by the ombudsman, an office established in 1953, who is also responsible for upholding standards in advertising. Given the range of exemptions and the structure of Danish law, a complainant is very rarely able to overturn the government's refusal to release a document. Plans to revise the law are pending, but these would retain ministerial control of what was and was not secret; the main change would be to establish an indexing system of available documents. In the meantime the law is relatively underused.

Danish measures for data protection are embodied in two laws, passed in 1979: The Public Authorities Register Act covers government data banks and the Private Register Act deals with commercial ones. Both are supervised by the Data Surveillance Authority and deal only with computer-based lists. Government data banks are regulated only as far as they contain material on individuals; the commercial ones must submit information on institutions as well as on individuals to the law. There is no general right of subject access: the fact that a file exists on a person does not automatically permit him or her to inspect it.

Two laws passed in October 1987 deal with the professional secrecy of employees in the public sector. The Law on Public Administration states that all citizens have the right to demand to be informed of documents received or produced by an administrative authority. The Law on Government Services deals with working documents produced for internal use within the civil service. Access to such documents can be limited in order to protect the state, foreign policy, the investigation of crime, public order or the protection of private and public economic interests.

SEE ALSO Netherlands 3. Freedom of Information; United States 11. Freedom of Information Act.

4. obscenity laws The obscenity laws, or the relative lack of them, in Denmark have made that country a byword—either for sensible liberty or unfettered license, depending on one's attitude toward the topic. Prior to the 1960s it was forbidden to publish or circulate obscene publications, pictures or objects, but in 1964 the minister of justice asked the Permanent Criminal Law Committee to consider a scheme for altering such laws. Following the publication of its report in 1966, in which a three to one majority opted for the complete decensorship of prose and a new set of restrictions for illustrations, a process of liberalization began. The basis for these moves was that, in the first place, there was no proven link between such material and any harmful effects (although there was equally little proof that harmful effects might not occur) and, anyway, so liberal was the interpretation of the existing law that very few books, and certainly none that might claim literary merit, ever suffered prosecution.

The new law went into effect in August 1968. The main offenses it covered were those of selling or giving to minors obscene pictures or objects and publishing, circulating or importing such materials. Further modified by a law of July 1, 1969, there now exist five offenses regarding obscenity: (1) selling obscene pictures or objects to anyone under 16 (section 234 of the Criminal Code); (2) obscene behavior, violating public decency or giving public offense (section 232 of the Criminal Code); (3) exhibiting or distributing offensive pictures in public places (police by-laws); (4) the unsolicited delivery of such publications or objects to any involuntary recipient (police by-laws); (5) mailing any obscene or in-

decent matter (written or visual) to a country where the laws prohibit the import of such material (Postal Act). Danes of any age can import any material they wish. Child pornography and live sex shows, both of which flourished in the immediate aftermath of liberalization, are now banned.

Dennett, Mary W. SEE "The Sex Side of Life."

Dering, Sir Edward SEE book burning in England 4. Puritans.

derivative classification As defined in the U.S. Department of the Army Standard Operating Procedures (July 1, 1971, modified November 11, 1972): "derivative classification ... devolves upon the person who uses, extracts, reproduces, incorporates, or responds to information which has already been validly classified." Amplified by Assistant Secretary of Defense David O. Cooke: "Derivative classification is involved when any person authorized to receive and disseminate classified information in any form treats that information in the same way as the originator with respect to classification of content and markings. In this case the derivative classification merely applies the original classification already made by the original classifier." In other words, once one incorporates in a non-classified project any material that has already been classified, the entire project is rendered classified. An obvious example of this system was the collection of war-planning documents entitled the PENTAGON PAPERS. The Papers were not originally classified, but the incorporation in them of classified information duly conferred secrecy upon all the material involved and led, in 1971, to the clash between the government and the press, which ultimately led to the Papers' publication.

Descartes, Rene Descartes, a French philosopher and mathematician (1596-1650), is generally seen as the founder of modern philosophy. Although his mathematical theories were exploded by Newton, his philosophical works, including *Discours de la methode* (1637), *Meditations philosophiques* (1641), *Principia philosophia* (1644) and *Traite des passions de l'ame* (1649), have all been highly influential on human thought, and his statement defining the self in consciousness—I think, therefore I am (*Cogito ergo sum*)—is still known by many more people than understand quite what he meant. Descartes was a devout Catholic, and on hearing that GALILEO's pro-Copernican theories had been suppressed by the church, he abandoned his own treatise on the same subject. Despite this piety, Descartes still earned the suspicion of the church and his works first appeared on an Index in 1633 and were forbidden until expurgated. The *Meditations* was again placed on the Index in 1665; the authorities claimed that Descartes' work was directly contrary to that of Aristotle and demanded that it be suitably emended. It was further banned in 1772 by the church and in 1926 by the communist government of the U.S.S.R. Descartes remained on the Index until as late as 1948, despite his vital influence on all of European thought.

SEE ALSO Index of Indexes.

Devil in Miss Jones, The   *The Devil in Miss Jones*, like BE-HIND THE GREEN DOOR, was one of those films that aimed to capitalize on the art porn boom that was anticipated in America after the success of DEEP THROAT in 1972. Made by Gerard Damiano (also responsible for *Deep Throat*) in 1973 it concerned the sexual escapades of Miss Jones, a lonely, frustrated virgin who commits suicide and finds herself in hell. Determined to make her damnation worthwhile, she petitions the Devil for a reprieve and back on Earth runs the gamut of sexual experience, before returning to hell and an infinity of frustration. The film met widespread censorship, and was banned in California, Florida, Georgia, Kansas, Massachusetts, Michigan, Missouri, New York, South Dakota, Texas and Virginia. The Michigan court, in condemning a package of porn movies, which included *Miss Jones, Deep Throat, Little Sisters* and *It Happened in Hollywood*, categorized them all as examples of the "trash that a few sick, demented minds are spewing out across our country in search of the easy dollar."

Diable au Corps, Le   SEE Andrea de Nerciat, Andre-Robert.

Diderot, Denis   Diderot (1713-84), the son of a prosperous French artisan, was one of the foremost figures of the 18th-century Enlightenment, whose most important contribution to European culture was as editor, for the 12 years from 1746, of the *Encyclopedie*. The whole work ran to 35 volumes and appeared between 1751 and 1776. Every leading intellectual of the period contributed, including VOLTAIRE, Montesquieu, ROUSSEAU and others. The *Encyclopedie ou Dictionnaire raisonee des Sciences, des Arts et des Metiers, par la Societe des Gens de Lettres* set out to provide a rational explanation for all terrestrial phenomena. The work of all three of the major contributors had already been condemned by the church, and the political and religious outspokenness of the *Encyclopedie* inevitably brought Diderot, and his great work, into conflict with the authorities. The first two volumes were suppressed in France in 1752, although Louis XV issued a personal privilege for the continuation of the work in 1754. In 1759, after only seven volumes had appeared, the Papacy placed the work on the ROMAN INDEX and continued to add each successive volume to its proscription. Political pressure led Louis to withdraw his privilege in the same year, but the work continued to appear, even though the publisher, Le Buffon, took it on himself to censor Diderot's final text without admitting to his alterations. The *Encyclopedie* was first cited in the Index of 1804 and remained prohibited into the 20th century.

SEE ALSO *Les Bijoux Indiscrets*.

Dies, Martin   SEE House Special Committee on Un-American Activities.

Dine, Jim   On September 13, 1966, The Robert Fraser Gallery in London opened an exhibition of 21 paintings and drawings by the American artist Jim Dine. A week later, backed by a warrant issued under the OBSCENE PUBLICATIONS ACT (1959), police from Scotland Yard's "Dirty Squad" raided the gallery, removing 12 paintings and all the catalogs for the show. A number of the pictures, some of which were collaborations between Dine and British sculptor Eduardo Paolozzi, had been sold for prices up to 300 guineas (£315.00), including one bought by the Leicestershire Education Committee. Gallery owner Robert Fraser claimed that "these drawings [are] about as pornographic as Cezanne," adding that while they might have some scatalogical content, "they are not erotic nor are they intended to be so." As itemized by the police, the offending articles, which were in part visible from the street, were "twelve compositions on one wall [depicting] the male genital organ and three on the opposite wall [showing] the female genital organ." The artist denied that his "phallic and vaginal forms" were obscene, saying that they reflected his feelings about London.

As the exhibitor of the pictures Fraser was tried at Malborough Street Magistrates Court on November 28, under the VAGRANCY ACT of 1838. This act works, inter alia, against "any person exposing his person, or exposing in any public place any obscene print or picture or any obscene object." Because the Vagrancy Acts have no provisions for the calling of expert witnesses and deal with the word "indecent" (a concept less susceptible to legal wrangling than is the more notorious "obscene"), the magistrate, John Fletcher, accepted the prosecution plea that, while the pictures might not be obscene under the 1959 act, they were nevertheless indecent under that of 1838, even if that indecency was only on the grounds of "arrangement." Fraser was found guilty and fined £20.00, with 50 guineas (£52.50) costs. The paintings themselves were held in police custody for a fortnight, pending the consideration of an appeal.

dominant effect   The main difference between the British OBSCENE PUBLICATIONS ACTS of 1857 and 1959 is the way that, while the former act made it possible to convict material as obscene on the basis of any single part of the overall work (e.g., a single purple passage) the latter demand that the work be assessed as a whole, weighing off the alleged obscenities against the mass of the complete book. Thus a jury must consider the context in which the alleged obscenity appears, and judge the dominant effect of the book or film in question. This concept works for whole books or films, but is less potent when applied to magazines, which by their very nature are composed of small, separate pieces. The idea of assessing context is underlined by the need for juries to consider the intention of the publisher or filmmaker in creating the material on trial. While obscenity, if proved, cannot be mitigated by a defense that stresses the educative aspect of the work, the publisher can claim that the material is in the public interest and base a defense on that.

Don Juan   The story of Don Juan is one of the most popular in literature, music and the allied arts. The exploits of this eponymous "great lover," the epitome of the cold-blooded seducer, all stem from the play *El burlador de Sevilla* (*The Deceiver of Seville*), written in 1630 by the Spanish playwright Gabriel Tellez (1583-1648). Since then versions of the tale have been essayed by Shadwell, Goldoni, Moliere, Byron, Mozart, Pushkin, de Montherlant, Browning and Shaw. In 1956 the Austrian director H.W. Kolm-Veltee adapted Mozart's opera *Don Giovanni* into a film he called *Don Juan*. It was distributed in America by the Times Film Corporation.

In a new twist on the film industry's ongoing war with the strictures of local and state censorship, Times Film chose to apply to the Chicago Board of Censors for a permit, and to pay the fee required, but refused to submit the film for the viewing that was obligatory under Chicago's statute on film censorship (see Chicago film censorship). The distributor was then refused a permit until he submitted the film to the board. After failing to persuade the mayor of his alleged rights, the distributor then went to court in an attempt to obtain an order that would force the authorities to let *Don Juan* be exhibited. There was no controversy over whether or not the film was obscene, the usual basis of such clashes, but, more centrally, Times Film Corporation was challenging the whole rationale of local pre-censorship of films. Both the district and the appeals courts dismissed the complaint and upheld the board's system.

When the case of *Times Film Corporation* v. *City of Chicago* (1961) reached the U.S. Supreme Court, its members were split 5-4 in favor of upholding prior censorship as constitutionally valid. A seven-page opinion written for the majority by Justice Clark stated that while films are indeed included in the same free speech and free press guarantees as are the print media, there did not exist an absolute right to exhibit each and every film at least once. Film was a specific medium, and like other means of expression, "tends to present its own particular problems." Clark also claimed that films probably possessed a greater power for evil influence than any other medium. A state must retain the right to protect its citizens from the possibility of actionable obscenity by checking the films proposed for exhibition. Assessing whether or not they were obscene fell into an entirely different category, and one that was not under debate in this case. The censor's basic authority must be upheld.

The minority decision was written by Chief Justice Warren, representing the more liberal members of the court, Justices Black, Brennan and Douglas. For him "the decision presents a real danger of eventual censorship of every form of communication ... The Court purports to leave these questions for another day, but I am aware of no constitutional principle which permits us to hold that the communication of ideas through one medium may be censored while other media are immune. Of course each medium presents its own peculiar problems, but they are not of the kind that would authorize the censorship of one form of communication and not others. I submit that ... the Court ... in exalting the censor of motion pictures, has endangered the First and Fourteenth Amendment rights of all others engaged in the dissemination of ideas ..." He rejected the argument that films had an exceptional popular impact and as such should be distinguished from other media. "This is the traditional argument made in the censor's behalf; this is the argument advanced against newspapers at the time of the invention of the printing press. The argument was ultimately rejected in England, and has consistently been held to be contrary to our Constitution. No compelling reason has been predicated for accepting the contention now."

Despite Warren's fears, the decision did not encourage the creation of more local censors, nor did the lower courts appear any more willing to rubber-stamp the decisions of those that did exist. In the 11 lower court decisions taken before the next Supreme Court film censorship case in 1965, the censors were not upheld once. In the same period there was a substantial reduction in the number of state and especially municipal censorship boards. Three lower courts, those of Pennsylvania, Georgia and Oregon, actually ruled that state censorship was unconstitutional, a step that the Supreme Court had resisted.

Don Leon   This poem of 1,455 lines, an extensive defense of sodomy, both homosexual and heterosexual, was published by WILLIAM DUGDALE in 1864 and falsely attributed to Lord Byron. It was assumed to provide the reason—i.e., Byron's alleged sodomizing of his pregnant wife—for the collapse of his marriage. With it were the "Notes to Don Leon," which dealt in gossipy but erudite detail with the scandals of the era, and "Leon to Annabella," of approximately 500 lines, which is a less obscene version of *Don Leon*, although concentrateing on the same subject matter.

Dugdale, London's leading pornographer at the time, received the two manuscripts in 1864 and believed them to be genuine. He initially intended to use them for the extortion of money from the current Lady Byron. But, advised by JAMES CAMPBELL, one of his writers, that such a course would only lead to a prosecution for blackmail and that in any case the poems were forgeries, citing incidents that occurred after Byron's death, Dugdale dropped the extortion but proceeded with the publication. The first edition was advertised as "A Poem by the late Lord Byron" and was supposedly a survivor of his *Memoirs*, which had been burnt in 1824 by his biographer, Thomas Moore (1779-1852).

The two poems, bound together, appeared as Byron's legitimate works, and they soon became staples of the pornographer's stock. A second edition appeared in 1875, luridly titled "The Great Secret Revealed! Suppressed Poem by Lord Byron, never before published ... An Epistle explaining the Real cause of Eternal Separation, And Justifying the Practice which led to it." Dugdale's successor, CHARLES CARRINGTON, published his own edition, advertising it as a work "which far outdistances *Don Juan* both in audacity of conception and licence of language." Copies of the poems were regularly seized and prosecuted. The most recent instance was that of the FORTUNE PRESS edition in 1934. Opinions vied as to the real author. One school believed they came from GEORGE COLMAN THE YOUNGER, a one-time rake and later examiner of plays. G. Wilson Knight (1897-), in his scholarly *Lord Byron's Marriage*, used the poem, for all its spurious character, as the basis for an exposition of the poet's marriage.

Dondero, George A. Congressman George A. Dondero (R, Michigan) spearheaded the U.S. attacks on "Communist art" in a series of speeches as chairman of the House Committee on Public Works between March and October 1949. Basing his campaign on the premise that modern art is synonymous with communism (ignoring the fact that in communist Russia such art was labeled bourgeois) and like it degenerate, Dondero set out to discredit the institutions, museums and a variety of reputable art associations or organizations. Although his attempts to extend McCarthyism into the visual arts met with strong opposition, a number of museums and gallery owners returned to their artists works that Dondero had branded as subversive. In the way of such campaigners, Dondero professed a simple vision: "Modern art is communistic because it is distorted and ugly, because it does not glorify our beautiful country, our cheerful and smiling people, our great material progress. Art which does not portray our beautiful country in plain, simple terms that everyone can understand breeds dissatisfaction. It is therefore opposed to our government, and those who create and promote it are our enemies."

SEE ALSO Joseph McCarthy.

Douglas, James James Douglas worked as book reviewer for the *London Sunday Express* during the 1920s. Through his weekly column he campaigned for the censorship of a number of works that he saw as obscene. A man of splenetically intemperate, conservative views, he spearheaded every attack on what he categorized as immoral or indecent books, often bringing them to the notice of the authorities, and simultaneously excited gullible public opinion as to the alleged obscenity of some hitherto undistinguished work. Douglas' most notorious attack was on Radclyffe Hall's THE WELL OF LONELINESS, in which he declared "I would rather put a phial of prussic acid in the hands of a healthy boy or girl than the book in question ..." Douglas declined George Bernard Shaw's offer to produce a child, a phial and the book in question, the reviewer to carry out his promise to administer the prussic acid as stated. Joyce's ULYSSES he found equally frightening: "I say deliberately that it is the most infamously obscene book in ancient or modern literature. The obscenity

of Rabelais is innocent compared with its leprous and scabrous horrors. All the secret sewers of vice are canalised in its flood of unimaginable thoughts, images and pornographic words ... its unclean lunacies are larded with appalling and revolting blasphemies ... hitherto associated with the most degraded orgies of Satanism and the Black Mass."

Drake, Dr. SEE book burning in England 7. United Kingdom (1688-1775).

Dreiser, Theodore Dreiser (1871-1945) was born into a German immigrant family, with devout Catholic parents. He left his home in Indiana aged only 15 and after working at a number of jobs in Chicago wrote in 1900 his first novel, *Sister Carrie*. This study of a working girl's social climb through ruthlessly self-interested relationships so appalled Dreiser's East Coast publishers that they decided not to distribute the published work. It was withdrawn and toned down. Dreiser worked as a hack journalist until *Jennie Gerhardt*, his next novel, with a similar plot, appeared in 1911. This was followed by a trilogy based on the rise of an unscrupulous businessman, parts of which appeared in 1912, 1914 and posthumously in 1947. His substantially autobiographical study of artistic life, *The Genius* (1915), was suppressed in New York by the SOCIETY FOR THE SUPPRESSION OF VICE, although it was republished in 1923, with a blurb that attempted to play on the vice society's condemnation.

In 1930 Dreiser's best-known work, *An American Tragedy* (1925), in which, inter alia, the hero drowns his pregnant girlfriend, was condemned by Boston's Superior Court; the publisher was fined $300. Ironically, just across the Charles River the book was a required text for Harvard English literature majors. The book remained banned in Boston until 1935. In Nazi Germany both *The Genius* and *An American Tragedy* were proscribed in 1933, because "they deal with low love affairs." A lesser novel, *Dawn* (1931), was banned in Ireland beginning in 1932.

Dugdale, William Dugdale (1800-68) was born in Stockport in Cheshire, implicated in 1819 in the Cato Street Conspiracy to assassinate the prime minister, and pirate publisher in 1822 of Byron's *Don Juan*—and, was, in the words of HENRY ASHBEE, "one of the most prolific publishers of filthy books" in Victorian England. At his shops in HOLYWELL STREET, Russell Court and Wych Street, trading under his own name and his aliases (Henry Smith, James Turner, Henry Young and Charles Brown), Dugdale capitalized for 40 years on the lucrative trade in pornography. His first essay into erotic publishing was *Memoirs of a Man of Pleasure* (1827), a reprint of a little-known novel, *The History of the Human Heart* (1769). In 1832 he published an edition of THE MEMOIRS OF A WOMAN OF PLEASURE. After thus establishing himself, he lowered his standards and devoted the rest of his career to a wide range of pornographic pulp.

His catalogs, written alluringly in the most lavish of prose, included classic and contemporary works, such as *The Battles of Venus, The Bed-Fellows or the Young Misses Manuel, The Confessions of a Young Lady*, DON LEON, *Eveline, The History of the Human Heart, The Ladies' Telltale, Lascivious Gems*, THE LUSTFUL TURK, *Scenes in the Seraglio, The Ups and Downs of Life* and *The Victim of Lust*. The style of all of these was graphically embraced in Dugdale's plug for *Nunnery Tales* (1865): "every stretch of voluptuous imagination is here fully depicted, rogering, ramming, one unbounded scene of lust, lechery and licentiousness." He also produced *The Boudoir* and *The Exquisite*, leading examples of the growing selections of pornographic magazines, as well as blood-and-thunder serials such as *Gentleman Jack* (1850s).

Dugdale was regularly prosecuted for his publications, amassing some nine sentences by 1857. Large amounts of his stock were seized and destroyed. The seizures, fines and imprisonment proved only minor irritations. Selling at three guineas (£3.15), approximately three times the average price of a "straight" three-volume novel, his books made him a rich man. Very occasionally he even defeated the courts, on one occasion suing a member of the SOCIETY FOR THE SUPPRESSION OF VICE who had broken into his shop and removed various books, and on another establishing the precedent that merely possessing obscene material was not actionable unless it could be proved that one intended to sell it. His most important trial was that which, in 1857, inspired the judge, Lord Chief Justice Campbell, to propose and carry through the OBSCENE PUBLICATIONS ACT (1857). Dugdale died in 1868. He was serving a sentence in the House of Correction at the time.

SEE ALSO Avery, Edward; Carrington, Charles; Hotten, John Camden; Sellon, Edward; Smithers, Leonard.

Dworkin-McKinnon bills The Dworkin-McKinnon Bill is the basis of two anti-pornography laws created for the American cities of Minneapolis and Indianapolis in 1983. The Pennsylvania senator Arlen Specter has also introduced a bill based on this model into the U.S. Congress. They were drawn up by author Andrea Dworkin and attorney Catharine McKinnon and are based on the premise that pornography is a form of discrimination against women. The bill's authors thus see it not as censorship, as their critics in and out of the feminism movement allege, but simply as positive and progressive support of women's rights.

The law developed initially in Minneapolis when legislators were unable to put through a zoning ordinance designed to shut down the city's porno bookstores. Working on ways of revising zoning restrictions the Neighborhood Pornography Task Force of South and South-Central Minneapolis asked Dworkin and McKinnon, who were teaching a course on pornography at the University of Minnesota, to testify. Dworkin and McKinnon proposed a new law that would not merely regulate pornography, but also eliminate it altogether by redefining pornography as a form of sex discrimination and outlawing it that way. The bill was passed, but vetoed by the city's mayor.

Anti-pornography groups in Indianapolis heard of these moves and made positive efforts to ally themselves to the proposals. The Republican mayor (and Presbyterian minister) William Hudnut III persuaded the conservative anti-Equal Rights Amendment activist Beulah Coughenour to sponsor a similar bill in the city. She hired McKinnon as a consultant and they both worked closely with the city prosecutor, a well known anti-vice campaigner. The bill, enthusiastically supported by such groups as Citizens for Decency and Coalition for a Clean Community, was passed into law by 25 (Republican) votes to 5 (Democratic). A group of publishers and booksellers challenged the law in the federal district court, and duly had it suspended pending further judgment. A number of other cities are known to be awaiting that outcome, hoping to promulgate parallel legislation.

As defined in the Minneapolis ordinance pornography is "the sexually explicit subordination of women, graphically depicted whether in pictures or in words." The material in question must also satisfy one of the following criteria: "(1) women are presented as dehumanized sexual objects, things or commodities; or (2) women are presented as sexual objects who enjoy pain and humiliation; or (3) women are presented as sexual objects who experience sexual pleasure in being raped; or (4) women are presented as sexual objects tied up or cut up or mutilated or bruised or physically hurt; or (5) women are presented in postures of sexual submission; or (6) women's body parts—including but not limited to vaginas, breasts, and buttocks—are exhibited, such that women are reduced to those parts; or (7) women are presented as whores by nature; or (8) women are presented as being penetrated by objects or animals; or (9) women are presented in scenarios of degradation, injury, abasement, torture, shown as filthy or inferior, bleeding, bruised, or hurt in a context that makes these conditions sexual."

Assuming that material fell within the required categories, its owner could be charged with a variety of offenses: the production, sale, exhibition or trafficking (distribution) in pornography; coercion into pornographic performance; forcing pornography onto a person; assault or physical attack following one's assailant's reading or viewing of pornography. Any "woman acting as a woman against the subordination of women" could file a complaint (as could a man if he could prove to have suffered similar injury). The plaintiff might then file a complaint either in court or with the local equal opportunities commission. Assuming the law had indeed been broken, the court would then levy suitable punishment if guilt was proved.

SEE ALSO Women Against Pornography; Women Against Violence Against Women; Women Against Violence in Pornography and Media.

E

Eagle Forum   The Eagle Forum was founded in 1975 by Phyllis Schlafly. The Forum opposes anything anti-family, anti-God, anti-religion, anti-children, anti-life (i.e., abortion) and anti-American defense. A special subcommittee, named Stop Textbook Censorship, aims to influence the contents of the nation's schoolbooks. The Forum publishes the monthly *Phyllis Schlafly Report*.

SEE ALSO Christian Crusade; Citizens for Decency Through Law; Citizens for Decent Literature; Clean Up TV Campaign (U.S.); Coalition for Better Television; Committee on Public Information; Crusade for Decency; Foundation to Improve Television; Moral Majority; Morality in Media; National Federation for Decency; National Organization for Decent Literature; People for the American Way; secular humanism.

Ecstasy   The film *Ecstasy* was made in Czechoslovakia in 1933 and first scheduled for exhibition in America in 1935. In this story of a young woman who replaces an old, impotent husband with a young, potent lover, the important scene is that in which its star Hedy Lamarr first makes love to the young man. While the camera never ventures below her neck, the look of ecstasy on her face was considered by many to be sensationally erotic. To U.S. Customs, which was empowered under the Tariff Act (1930) to seize any imported material and hold it, pending a court test of its possible obscenity, Lamarr's bliss seemed pornographic. The film was tried in the federal district court—*U.S.* v. *Two Tin Boxes* (1935)—and pronounced immoral and obscene. The federal marshal then burnt the print, although an appeal was still pending. This destruction was cited as sufficient grounds to deny an appeal, since there was no longer a physical object to consider.

The film was then revised, recasting the scenes between Lamarr and her lover as a flashback, thus rendering what had been adultery as acceptable marital love. This version was passed by the Customs, but in 1937 the New York censor refused to license it. Despite an appeal—*Eureka Productions* v. *Byrne* (1937)—this ban was confirmed, lasting until 1940 when a third, doctored version of the film was permitted exhibition in the state.

SEE ALSO United States 21. Tariff Act (1930).

Ecuador   Ecuador's current constitution, promulgated in 1979 when the current civilian government replaced the country's military rulers, guarantees freedom of opinion and expression (article 19.4), freedom of conscience and religious belief (article 19.6) and freedom of association (article 19.13). Only in a state of emergency can prior censorship be imposed. The Penal Code further outlaws the obstruction of

such freedoms and in articles 178 and 179 lays out the penalties for any authority who attempts by artibrary and violent means to impede freedom of expression or obstructs the free circulation of any publication, other than those published anonymously. Despite such promises, the current President Leon Febres Cordero, who took office in 1984, has consistently flouted the law in a variety of ways. He has refused to publish legislation passed by Congress in the official gazette, substituting for it his own, contrary proposals; he has rejected national and local amnesties offered a variety of individuals, notably Air Force General Frank Vargas, who in 1986 rebelled against what he claimed was government corruption. Such amnesties are banned from publication in the gazette and thus, says the president, do not exist. Even when Congress has appealed to the Constitutional Guarantees Tribunal and had Cordero overruled, the president simply accuses the tribunal of political bias, and still refuses to obey the law.

Given this attitude, the president and his government have no hesitation in attacking opposition when voiced through the media. Although there is no official consorship, the authorities crack down as and when they choose. Critical television and radio stations as well as newspapers face bans, albeit temporary, at crucial moments, such as during the Vargas rebellion and the general strike of March 1987. Individual journalists are harassed and lucrative government advertising is allotted with an eye to media loyalty. The government also attempts to restrict the free flow of information concerning Ecuador's guerilla organizations, although the guerillas in their turn are liable to put their own pressures on journalists to promote their rebel policies.

Educational Research Analysts   SEE Mel and Norma Gabler.

Egypt   The Egyptian Constitution (article 47) guarantees freedom of opinion "within the limits of the law. Self-criticism and constructive criticism is the guarantee for the safety of the national structure." It also, at article 48, bans censorship of the press. Despite this, certain laws exist to limit absolute freedom of expression, and the State of Emergency, which has lasted since President Mubarak took office in 1981, further curtails the constitutional guarantees.

The main vehicle of control is the Law of Shame (Qanun al-'eib)—The Law on Protecting Values from Shameful Conduct—which was passed on April 29, 1980, under President Sadat and which has been extended by President Mubarak. It makes a variety of antisocial behavior an indictable crime and introduces harsh punishments at the discretion of the socialist public prosecutor (a post created in 1971 by President Sadat), who has absolute authority to investigate and indict under the law. Article 1 states that it is the duty of each citizen to uphold the basic social values and that any departure therefrom represents shameful conduct, justifying a prosecution.

Under the law the following acts are prosecuted: (1) advocating any doctrine that denies the truth of Sunni Muslim teachings; (2) attacking the state, its economic, political or social systems and calling for the domination of any one class over another or the elimination of any class; (3) corrupting youth by repudiating popular religious, moral or national values or by setting a bad example in public; (4) broadcasting or publishing anything prejudicial to national unity and social peace; (5) broadcasting or publishing gross or scurrilous material that might offend the state or its constitution; (6) forming any unauthorized organization dedicated to undermining the state; (7) broadcasting or publishing information abroad that might undermine the state's political or economic system. Those who break the law face one of a number of sanctions: deprivation of the right to stand for local public office; exclusion from candidacy for any form of governing body, in business, trade unions, clubs, federations and any other organization; prohibition from founding a political party or administering such a party. They may also be barred from holding public office, refused a passport, excluded from setting up residence in certain areas of the country or deprived of transacting in or administering real property. All these penalties last a maximum of five years.

In pursuit of those suspected of breaking this law the authorities may tap telephones, search premises, intercept and monitor all communications and mails between the suspect and outside world. Warrants for such activities are issued by the Court of Values. To ensure that no one who has been banned still seeks election, all lists of candidates for election (both political and in other organizations) must be submitted to the socialist public prosecutor, who is empowered to have any candidate's name removed without appeal. In April 1986 President Mubarak extended the emergency laws, put into operation after the assassination of his predecessor Anwar Sadat, until 1988. Under these laws the authorities may inspect the mails, subject all publications to pre-censorship, and close down any publishing or printing facilities considered in breach of the regulations. The Press Law (1980) adds further restrictions: it is an offense to challenge the orthodox religion (another attack on fundamentalist Shi'ites), to advocate the destruction of state institutions and to publish abroad any "false or misleading" information that might be detrimental to Egypt. Under the Emergency there have been many arrests for "sectarian sedition" or the dissemination of "tendentious rumors."

All Egyptian periodicals must be licensed and those who obtain licenses have to show substantial wealth. Unlicensed publications flourished despite the law and in early 1987 the authorities purged many of these. Print shops were forbidden to print any but licensed periodicals. Imports from abroad are often censored, even if the unacceptable opinions they express on Egyptian politics and society may in fact be found regularly in home-based publications.

The newspaper press is controlled less by overt censorship than by the government's appointment of the editors-in-chief to the three main dailies—al-Ahram, al-Akhbar and al-Gomhouriya—as well as to a number of other important publications. These editors have absolute authority and they reflect government policies without demur. It is illegal to dismiss a journalist for writing other than the official line, but the work involved will simply remain unpublished.

Books, films and theater are all censored on political, sexual and theological grounds. The Ministry of Information is responsible for books, the Ministry of Culture for film and theater. Officials both check the text of each play and attend its rehearsals. Completed films are viewed before public screening by a three-person panel. Any appeals against their cuts can be made to the ministry.

El Salvador El Salvador, under its President Jose Napoleon Duarte, remains one of Central America's most volatile countries. Unsurprisingly the constitution's guarantees of freedom of expression and allied civil liberties are at best tenuous and often abrogated for years on end. Under the state of siege, which had lasted effectively from 1980, the constitution was suspended and its provisions only restored in January 1987. The Ministry of Culture and Communications, which disseminates government propaganda, has made some attempts to manipulate access to information, warning off over-critical media, and financially vital government advertising may be withdrawn at any time.

There is thus no official censorship, but all journalists accept the need for self-censorship. The government makes it clear that such self-regulation is vital—otherwise it will have to clamp down. Even though a degree of liberalization has been noted recently, with the media daring to cover topics hitherto off-limits, fears of government pressure, and the physical harassment of reporters, have ensured that such investigations are still relatively restrained. Television has attempted to broaden its coverage, as have the important national radio stations, but the government has the right to shut down a radio or TV outlet at any time.

The press remains relatively conservative, despite a gradual loosening of restrictions on its stories; when covering such contentious topics as the activities of left-wing guerillas, it often prefers to reprint government communiques. It is accepted that foreign journalists, who must obtain official permission to cover the ongoing civil war, may have a better chance of writing "the truth," although they too have been vulnerable to attack. Between 1980 and 1984 11 Salvadoreans and 10 foreign journalists were murdered. Harassment, albeit not fatal, continues and a number of reporters have been detained, then asked to leave El Salvador.

Ellis, Henry Havelock SEE *Sexual Inversion*.

Ellsberg, Daniel   SEE Pentagon Papers, The.

'Enfer, L   Literally, *The Hell*: the collection of obscene, suppressed and otherwise forbidden books held by the Bibliotheque Nationale of France in Paris; the equivalent to the British Museum's PRIVATE CASE. L'Enfer was established in 1791 and modelled on a similar library in the Vatican.

Enfer de la Bibliotheque Nationale: icono-bio-bibliographie ...   This bibliography of those erotic works held in the Paris Bibliotheque Nationale was compiled by the poet and occasional pornographer GUILLAUME APOLLINAIRE and two coauthors, the publishers of erotica LOUIS PERCEAU and Fernand Fleuret. Appearing in 1913, the bibliography ran to 930 articles, specializing naturally in French works, and contained much valuable information and, unlike many such catalogs, accurate commentary. A supplement, listing works added up until March 1934, was prepared by the English bibliographer ALFRED ROSE (Rolf S. Reade), but this was never published, although typescripts were deposited in the British Museum and the Bodleian Library in Oxford.

Epperson v. *Arkansas* **(1968)**   According to the Arkansas Anti-Evolution Statute of 1928, "it is unlawful for any teacher ... to teach the theory or doctrine that mankind ascended or descended from a lower order of animals, and also it shall be unlawful for any teacher, textbook commission or other authority ... to adopt or use in any such institution a textbook that teaches the doctrine or theory that mankind descended or ascended from a lower order of animals." Those who contravened the statute lost their job and were fined $500. In 1968 Epperson, an Arkansas public school teacher, challenged the constitutionality of the law. The Arkansas Supreme Court took only two sentences to reject his claims. At the U.S. Supreme Court, Epperson received a more respectful hearing. The court declared the statute to be in contravention of the FIRST AMENDMENT, denying free speech and establishing censorship. It also ran contrary to the obligation of all American institutions to permit a plurality of religious belief. The court pointed out that while a state had the right to determine the form that education took in its schools, it could not arrange the content on the dictates of a single interest group, in this case the highly conservative fundamentalist Christians. As Justice Stewart put it, "A state is entirely free, for example, to decide that the only foreign language to be taught in its public school system shall be Spanish. But would a state be constitutionally free to punish a teacher for letting his students know that other languages are also spoken in the world?"

SEE ALSO *Scopes* v. *State* (1927).

Erasmus, Desiderius   Erasmus (ca. 1467-1536) was born at Rotterdam and was pressured by his guardians into becoming an Augustinian monk. He was allowed to travel extensively and communicated with all the major scholars of his era, lecturing at Cambridge between 1511 and 1514 and receiving a benefice from the archbishop of Canterbury. His main works were a translation of the Greek New Testament (1516); the *Encomium Moriae* (1511, *In Praise of Folly*), which was a satire on theologians and church dignitaries; the *Enchiridion Militis Christiani* (1503), a manual of piety taken from Christ's own teachings; *Institutio Christiani Principis* (*Education of a Christian Prince*); *Adagia*, a collection of aphorisms; and *Colloquia* (1518), his autobiographical writings on contemporary life. His work was among the most popular in Europe and its circulation was rivalled only by that of LUTHER. Erasmus is the founder of humanism and, in his telling criticisms of the inadequacies of the contemporary church, a major proponent of the Protestant Reformation, although he resisted the ideological stance of many fellow reformists. As such he was both continually subject to the censorship of the church and decried as a fence-sitter by militant Protestants.

The Papacy was generally friendly toward Erasmus during his lifetime. In 1516 Leo X praised his "sound morality, his rare scholarship and his distinguished services" and accepted the scholar's dedication to him of his Greek New Testament, writing him a fulsome letter in 1518. Adrian VI was similarly congratulatory as was Paul III, who in 1535 made him provost of Deventer, as a tribute to his learning and his services to the church, not least of which were his struggles with apostasy. If the scholar had any major enemies, they came from the Protestants, frustrated at his refusal to commit himself to their campaign. Enjoying the protection of Emperor Charles V his books were excluded from the INDEX OF LOUVAIN in 1546. Only in France, between 1525 and 1530, in Spain in 1550, and in Scotland, by Mary, Queen of Scots in 1555, were his works initially condemned.

The intensification of the Counter-Reformation with the publication of the INDEX OF PAUL IV in 1559 changed the picture. Erasmus was condemned, as harshly as were Luther and CALVIN, as a major influence on the Reformation. His name was placed in the Index's Class I, those authors who were banned absolutely, and "all of his Commentaries, Remarks, Notes, Dialogues, Letters, Criticisms, Translations, Books and writings, including even those which contain nothing concerning Religion" were prohibited. This blanket condemnation was slightly modified by the TRIDENTINE INDEX of 1564, although the expurgations that rendered his work acceptable simultaneously ensured that it was unreadable. Subsequent Indexes, both in Rome and Spain, maintained the attacks on Erasmus. His works were banned by the INDEX OF QUIROGA (1583), where a list of them takes up 55 quarto pages; this list had been increased to 50 double-columned folio pages by 1640. By this time he had been consigned to the elite ranks of the incorrigible heretics, and the words *auctoris damnati* (of a condemned author) were inserted after his name on all title pages.

Erotika Biblion Society   This so-called society was founded in the late 1880s by the publishers LEONARD SMITHERS and H.S. NICHOLS. They used it to distribute a variety of erotic and pornographic material to their circle of discerning customers; its early publications included *Priapeia* by Sir Richard Burton (a collection of sportive epigrams taken from the more risque Latin authors) and *Crissie, a Music Hall Sketch of Today*, the last original piece of English erotica published in 19th-century London. While both its founders ceased operations in the 1890s, the society's name was continued by various imitators. The "Erotica Biblion Society of London and New York," and actually based in France, published a number of works around 1899. The publisher was probably CHARLES CARRINGTON, who had escaped England to set up his business in pornography in Paris. Among the society's publications was *Pauline the Prima Donna, or, Memoirs of an Opera Singer* (1898). This translation of *Aus den Memoiren einer Sangerin*, purportedly the sexual reminiscences of the singer Wilhelmine Schroder-Devrient (1804-60) and probably the first example of German erotica to appear in English or French, was one of a number of erotic books prosecuted in Paris in 1914. It appeared in an expurgated French version in 1913, translated by the French poet APOLLINAIRE. Carrington also produced, in 1899, *The Memoirs of Dolly Morton*, written by "Hugues Rebell" (Georges Grassal [1867-1905]) and ostensibly the reminiscences of a girl caught up in the U.S. Civil War.

espionage   For material dealing with espionage, counterintelligence and allied topics, readers should consult the following headings:

Abrams v. *United States* (1919)

classification at birth

Committee on Public Information

Debs, Eugene

Espionage Act (U.S., 1917) and Sedition Act (U.S., 1918)

Frohwerk v. *United States* (1919)

Masses, The

Official Secrets Acts (1889, 1911, 1920, 1939)

Pierce v. *United States* (1920)

Schaeffer v. *United States* (1920)

Schenck v. *United States* (1919)

Schepp v. *United States* (1980)

Spirit of '76, The

Sweden 4. The Secrecy Act (1981)

United States 13. library censorship (1876-1939)

United States 20. Supreme Court cases and legislation index.

Espionage Act (U.S., 1917) and Sedition Act (U.S., 1918)
Under these acts, it is illegal "wilfully to utter, print, write or publish any disloyal, profane, scurrilous or abusive language about the form of government of the United States or the Constitution ... or to bring the form of government or the Constitution into contempt." The law also states that "Whoever, when the United States is at war, shall wilfully make or convey false reports or false statements with intent to interfere with the operation or success of the military or naval forces of the United States or to promote the success of its enemies and whoever, when the United States is at war, shall wilfully cause or attempt to cause insubordination, disloyalty, mutiny or refusal of duty in the military or naval forces of the United States, or shall wilfully obstruct the recruiting or enlistment service of the United States ... shall be punished by a fine of not more than $10,000 or imprisonment for not more than 20 years, or both." These acts were used against alleged traitors, especially supposed communists, and justified the anti-communist Palmer raids, named for the then-current U.S. attorney-general, under which 1,500 people were arrested, of whom only a tiny fraction were actually charged.

SEE ALSO Debs, Eugene; Sedition Act (U.S., 1798).

Essay on Woman   The *Essay on Woman* by "Pego Borewell, with Notes by Rogerus Cunaeus, Vigerus Mutoniatus, etc.," an indecent parody of Pope's philosophical *Essay on Man* (1732-4), appeared in 1763. It comprised a 94-line poem, the "Essay" itself, dedicated to the demi-mondaine Fanny Murray; an obscene parody of the hymn "Veni Creator," attributed to Bishop Warburton (1698-1779), a notably contentious clergyman; and two further parodies on Pope: "The Universal Prayer" (mocking Pope's poem of the same name) and "The Dying Lover to his Prick" (based on Pope's treatment of the Emperor Adrian's last words, "A Dying Christian to his Soul"). Although the "Essay" was reasonably bawdy, it was on the grounds of its BLASPHEMY rather than its obscenity that it attracted adverse attention.

Although subsequent scholarship attributes the "Essay" to Thomas Potter, MP, a member of the libertine Hellfire Club, contemporary opinion gave the authorship firmly to John Wilkes, MP (1727-97), a lifelong womanizer and the member for Aylesbury, whose flagrant opposition to the government of Lord Bute, as broadcast through his magazine THE NORTH BRITON, had already brought him before the courts. The edition was only of 12 copies, strictly for private circulation amongst Wilkes' fellow-members of the Hellfire Club, but one copy went missing. Whether this was deliberately stolen or, as one account claims, some sheets were erroneously used as wrapping for a printer's lunch, the poems fell into the hands of John Kidgell, a corrupt clergyman and sometime novelist, whose patron, the earl of March, urged on himself by Bute, persuaded Kidgell to turn the sheets over to the authorities. The entire work was recited to the House of Lords, where it was condemned as "a most scandalous, obscene and impious libel." Kidgell received £233.6.8d for his efforts.

Under interrogation, Michael Curry (1722-78), the printer of the "Essay," who bore a personal grudge against Wilkes, admitted that it had been printed at Wilkes' express instruction; the MP's own papers bore this out. Curry appeared in court as the government's chief witness, although even he was unable to prove that Wilkes had actually penned the verses. The authorities remained vengeful and the alleged obscenity of the "Essay" was used to punish its author for the sedition of the magazine. In 1768 Wilkes was found guilty of publishing an OBSCENE LIBEL, fined £500 and jailed for a year. Curry, an unpopular man, was blacklisted throughout the London printing trade. A number of pamphlets appeared, all underlining the popularity of Wilkes among the public and, entitled variously "The Plain Truth" and "The Priest in Rhyme," attacked the authorities in general and Kidgell in particular. To spice the entire proceedings it was generally known that Potter, who was even then suspected of having helped Wilkes in the parodies, was cuckolding Bishop Warburton, whose name "The Essay" had taken in vain.

European Convention on Human Rights   This convention has been accepted by all 21 member states of the Council of Europe since September 1953. Created in the aftermath of World War II its intention was to create some form of legal structure that might help suppress any future resurgence of fascism. Under article 10(1) it guarantees freedom of expression to all citizens of member states, including the freedom to "hold opinions and to receive and import information and ideas without interference by public authorities, regardless of frontiers." The convention accepts national rights, stating in article 10(2) that "the exercise of these freedoms" is subject to such formalities, conditions, restrictions or penalties as "are prescribed by law and are necessary in democratic society in the interests of national security, territorial integrity or public safety, for the prevention of disorder or crime, for the protection of health or morals ... of the rights and reputations of others, for preventing the disclosure of information received in confidence, or for maintaining the authority and impartiality of the judiciary."

Further provisions relevant to censorship are article 6, governing fair and public hearings for the determination of civil rights and obligations and criminal charges; article 8, governing respect for correspondence; and article 1 of protocol 1, the right to the peaceful enjoyment of possessions.

The inevitable drawback to so all-embracing a guarantee is the different standards by which each nation judges what is moral or immoral. At best this limits the authority of the convention and at worst exposes it as an empty threat. As the European Court of Human Rights put it in 1976, "It is not possible to find in the domestic law of the various Contracting States a uniform European conception of morals." And it accepted that the various governments concerned were better equipped to assess such problems in the light of their individual domestic situations. To satisfy this, each state is allowed a margin of appreciation, which extends both to the individual legislative bodies and to the various interpretations and applications of domestic laws. Thus the conviction in England of the LITTLE RED SCHOOLBOOK, which was contested in 1971 by its publisher Richard Handyside, was deemed not to have infringed the convention, since the OBSCENE PUBLICATIONS ACT (1959) under which it was

prosecuted was held to be a law "necessary in democratic society ... for the protection of morals." Nonetheless, the convention, for all that it accepts the right of states to regulate national communications (e.g., with licenses), does work in favor of the media and their freedoms, even if the states concerned may choose on occasion to act less scrupulously.

evolution   SEE *Epperson* v. *Arkansas* (1968); Mel & Norma Gabler; *Scopes* v. *State* (1927); Texas State Textbook Committee.

examiner of plays (U.K.)   While the LORD CHAMBERLAIN was ostensibly the censor of the English stage until 1968, from the 18th century on the official who actually performed the task was the examiner of plays, a post created by Lord Grafton, lord chamberlain in the 1720s. Lords chamberlain might change on average every five years, examiners lasted much longer. Men like John Larpent (examiner from 1778 to 1824), GEORGE COLMAN THE YOUNGER (1824-1836) and William Bodham Donne (1857-1874) dictated the style and content of the stage for decades. It was a job with extensive power: the lord chamberlain had many other preoccupations; he read few if any plays, unless he was expressly asked to do so. Otherwise he simply signed approvals or excisions as his deputy indicated. The chamberlain's powers were not diminished, it was merely that the examiner actually wielded them.

A sensible examiner did not ignore his lord chamberlain, and made sure that he indulged his superior's foibles— whether they centered on morals, politics or the safety of the auditoriums. He was similarly able to indulge his own obsessions, which tended inevitably to conservatism. By the early 20th century, with the emergence of such dramatists as Shaw, Ibsen and other modernists, all of whom fell foul of the examiner, his was the least popular employment in the theater. That his opinion, highly conservative as it often was, was indicative of many of his compatriots did not mollify the writers. Very occasionally the lord chamberlain might contradict his examiner, usually when a third party complained and it did seem that the deputy had gone too far. Largely unsupervised, an early examiner could and did maximize the financial benefits of his office by charging for readings, accepting bribes and similar stratagems. Colman, among others, mulcted his position unashamedly. Larpent assumed that the manuscripts he read became his property and amassed a superb collection in 46 years of examining.

After the THEATRE REGULATION ACT (1843) the job of examiner became more demanding. For the first time the role was give some statutory recognition, but his essentially secondary status was made clear: "The Examiner is nothing but an assistant—a clerk in his office—who does the drudgery for [the Lord Chamberlain] and should advise him." There would be no more Colmans. The financial perks were similarly regulated: Fees were established and there were few opportunities for graft. After 1832 the examiner read plays for the whole country and, between 1857 and 1878, took responsibility for the structural soundness and fire-proofing of theatres, before that task was ceded to the Metropolitan Board of Works. The examiner, in later years assisted by several official readers, lasted as long as did his employer. Under the THEATRE ACT (1968) both offices were officially terminated.

F

Family Shakespeare, The The appearance in 1807 of *The Family Shakespeare*, a small format, four-volume edition published in Bath and bearing no editor's name on the title page, set in motion one of literature's growth industries of the 19th century: bowdlerization, or the expurgation of classical texts. It was, as it transpired, the first book that can be technically described as bowdlerized. In 1809 it was revealed in a letter to the *Christian Observer* that the editor was in fact Thomas Bowdler (see Bowdler Family), a former physician, now country gentleman resident on the Isle of Wight. In fact, as the writer of the letter, signing himself "Philalethes" (Lover of Obscure Things, but in fact Bowdler's nephew, John), pointed out: The editor of this pioneering expurgation was not his uncle but his aunt, Henrietta Maria (Harriet) Bowdler. Why this noted bluestocking had chosen anonymity, and why her brother for the rest of their lives refused to acknowledge her work, remains a mystery. It may be assumed that it was simply out of the question for a lady, even an intellectual such as Harriet Bowdler, to admit to the degree of understanding of Shakespeare that was required to excise his indecencies.

The Family Shakespeare took as its premise the need to cut "everything that can raise a blush on the cheek of modesty," in effect about 10 per cent of Shakespeare's text. Miss Bowdler dealt with 20 of the 36 plays. Most were expurgated, some, like *Hamlet*, lost substantial portions of the text; *Romeo and Juliet* was not even included. When the latter play appeared in the 1818 edition, the Nurse, too earthy for 19th-century scruples, was barely evident. That Miss Bowdler had no conscious desire to destroy Shakespeare's work was underlined in her preface, but nothing could "afford an excuse for profaneness or obscenity; and if these could be obliterated, the transcendant genius of the poet would undoubtedly shine with more unclouded lustre." To this end she excised even a suspicion of profanity: "God!" invariably became "Heaven!" "Jesu!" was simply dropped. The religious preferences were distinctly evangelical; Catholic susceptibilities were not soothed and oaths such as "Marry!" (Mary) and "'Sblood!" (God's blood) were left intact. What mattered most was irreverence: No vestige of humor at God's expense was spared.

The 1807 *Family Shakespeare* received little notice. There were three reviews: one in favor, citing the desirability of such a "castrated" version; one against, feeling such excisions to be unnecessary; and a third, in which the reviewer opined that the only proper edition of Shakespeare would be a folio of blank pages. The most tangible result was the attribution of the work to Thomas Bowdler, who in 1818 produced a revised, more substantial edition. Thomas dealt with all 36 plays, adding his own work on 16 to his sister's original 20. He put his name on the title page and ignored her completely. In many ways Thomas was kinder to his subject, restoring passages Harriet had condemned as boring, as well as reinstating some material that she had removed as improper. But he also cut hundreds of lines that she had left alone, and discovered new improper sections even in passages she had already scrutinized. Like his sister he dealt easily with profanity, but found great problems with his attempts to excise the general flow of indecency that runs through many of the plays without destroying the sense completely. He cut heavily into *Romeo and Juliet*, *King Lear* and *Henry IV, Part 2*. *Measure for Measure* defeated him and had to be printed with a warning, so hard was it to cut, as was *Othello*, which he stated was "unfortunately little suited to family reading" and suggested that it be transferred "from the parlour to the cabinet."

While Harriet's edition virtually vanished, Thomas Bowdler's suddenly took off. In tune with an increasing refinement in public attitudes, and the growing influence of puritan evangelism, it soon became the best-selling edition of Shakespeare in Britain. It was also boosted by the current rivalry between the era's major critical journals: *Blackwoods Magazine* and the *Edinburgh Review*. When in 1821 *Blackwoods* attacked *The Family Shakespeare*, the *Review* automatically extolled this "very meritorious publication." Bowdler's book went into three editions before his death in 1825 and many more followed. Bowdlerization caught on. By 1850 there were seven rival expurgated Shakespeares; by 1900 there were nearly 50. In 1894 Swinburne said of Bowdler, "No man ever did better service to Shakespeare," and his 1818 work remained preeminent among its peers. Not until 1916, when he was finally debunked in the *English Review*, did Bowdler's version of Shakespeare lose its authority.

Fanny Hill SEE *Memoirs of a Woman of Pleasure*.

Father of Candor In 1764, following the prosecution of JOHN WILKES for issue number 45 of the NORTH BRITON, there appeared a tract under the name "Candor"—identified only as "a Gray's Inn Lawyer"—and entitled "A Letter from Candor to the Public Advertiser." This conservative pamphlet backed the status quo regarding freedom of speech, accepting that such freedom extended only to the prohibition of pre-publication censorship, not to subsequent prosecution when the law was seen to be flouted. "Candor" backed any government, asking "In God's name, what business have private men to write or to speak about public matters?" adding that "such kind of liberty leads to all sorts of license and obloquy" and warning the "scribbling race from meddling with political questions, at least from ever drawing their pens a second time upon such subjects."

In reply to "Candor" there was published a small book entitled *An Enquiry into the Doctrine, Lately Propagated, concerning Libels, Warrants, and the Seizure of Papers* ... Authored by the otherwise anonymous "Father of Candor" it went into seven editions between 1764 and 1771. "Father of Candor" was never identified, but he appeared to be an eminent public man with some legal background; he was, more importantly, the first Englishman to attack the prevailing doctrine of SEDITIOUS LIBEL. He laid responsibility for "the whole doctrine of libels and the criminal mode of prosecuting them" on "that accursed court of the star-chamber." What the government called libel was vital to public freedom, without it there would have been no Glorious Revolution in 1688, no Protestant religion nor "one jot of civil liberty." In future, he suggested, juries, drawn from the public, rather than judges, appointed by the crown, should judge the criminality of an alleged libel, and truth, rather than merely compounding the offense as was the current law, should be an absolute defense against further prosecution. He added that, despite prevailing theories, libel was not in fact a breach of the peace, which belief was the basis of all current law. Like all contemporary critics of that law, "Father of Candor" was unable to influence the authorities and the situation remained unchanged until 1843.
SEE ALSO Cato; John Peter Zenger.

Federal Anti-Obscenity Act (1873)   SEE Comstock Act, The.

Federal Communications Act (1934)   As well as permitting rival political candidates equal time, the FCC maintains a rigorous "fairness doctrine," whereby both or all sides involved in any issue of public importance must be permitted to use the media in their own interest. The radio or TV station must in its turn give both or all sides equal coverage. The regulations covering fairness are as follows:

(a) When, during the presentation of views on a controversial issue of public importance, an attack is made on the honesty, character, integrity or like personal qualities of an indentified person or group, the licensee shall, within a reasonable time and in no later than one week after the attack, transmit to the person or group attacked (1) notification of the date, time and identification of the broadcast; (2) a script or tape (or an accurate summary if a script or tape is not available) of the attack; and (3) an offer of a reasonable opportunity to respond over the licensee's facilities.
(b) The provisions of paragraph (a) ... shall not be applicable (1) to attacks on foreign groups or foreign public figures; (2) to personal attacks which are made by legally qualified candidates, their authorized spokesmen, or those associated with them in the campaign, or other such candidates, their authorized spokesmen, or those associated with them in the

campaign; and (3) to bona fide newscasts ... interviews ... and on-the-spot news coverage of a bona fide news event. Section (b) also covers commentary and analysis but not the licensee's editorials, which must offer the right of reply as in section (b).

SEE ALSO BBC 1. balance.

Federal Communications Commission Regulations on Indecency and Censorship   Title 18 USC, section 1464: "Indecency: Whoever utters any obscene, indecent or profane language by means of radio communication shall be fined not more than $10,000 or imprisoned not more than two years, or both."

Title 47 USC, section 326: "Censorship: Nothing in this [Federal Communication] Act [1934] shall be understood or construed to give the Commission the power of censorship over the radio communications or signals transmitted by any radio station, and no regulation or condition shall be promulgated or fixed by the commission which shall interfere with the right of free speech by means of radio communication."

Federal Communications Commission v. *Pacifica Foundation* (1978)   SEE filthy words.

Festival of Light   This evangelical crusade to clean up Britain was founded in 1971 by a Baptist missionary, Peter Hill, to combat "moral pollution." Hill had been in India working for Operation Mobilization, "a militant inter-denominational youth group," before returning to London. To assist him in this program were the Rev. Eddie Stride of Christ Church, Spitalfields, who had been involved with the Dowager Lady Birdwood (the London organizer of NVALA) in the recent campaign against *Council of Love* (Oscar Panizza's stage play that mixed anti-clericalism and syphilis); Eric Hutchings, a radio evangelist; Malcolm Muggeridge (the former radical journalist, now born again, who suggested the name); Lord Longford; Peter Thompson; MARY WHITEHOUSE; Sir CYRIL BLACK; pop singer Cliff Richard; David Kossoff; and the otherwise radical Bishop of Stepney. Lady Birdwood herself was not invited, her views were considered too right-wing.

The Festival of Light was suitably apocalyptic, declaring in 1971 that were the country not purged according to its dictates, the world would end in five years. It claimed, in putting forward its "Savonarola-like programme of social purification" (Sutherland, op. cit.), that it represented the views of ordinary people. The movement, launched as the "Nationwide Festival of Light," attracted much media coverage, and reportedly some 215,000 people gathered in various meetings to support the cause. (The London assembly was marred only by some blaspheming "nuns" who turned out to be members of Gay and Women's Liberation.) The Festival of Light called, together with NVALA, for a Nationwide Petition for Public Decency. This was to entail: (1) the reform of the OBSCENE PUBLICATIONS ACT (1959) "to make it an effective instrument for the maintenance of public decency"; (2) the extension of the act to cover sound and visual broadcasting; (3) the introduction of new legislation aimed directly at protecting children. The petition also called for state-directed film censorship and a boycott of shops selling indecent material.

After enjoying its initial burst of publicity in 1972, the Festival of Light became blurred with the NVALA and has played second fiddle to that leading anti-pornography pressure group. The two organizations act in concert to lobby for their cause and can, when required, produce a large and vocal constituency of supporters.

SEE ALSO: Longford Report; National Viewers and Listeners Association.

Fifteen Plagues of a Maidenhead   SEE obscene libel.

fighting words   The concept of "fighting words" covers certain areas in American law where the speaker may be seen to have sacrificed his or her right to freedom of speech rights as otherwise guaranteed by the U.S. Constitution. As defined by the Supreme Court, specifically in the case of CHAPLINSKY V. NEW HAMPSHIRE, fighting words are "those personally abusive epithets that, when addressed to the ordinary citizen, are, as a matter of common knowledge, inherently likely to inflict injury or tend to incite an immediate breach of the peace."

SEE ALSO *Cincinnati* v. *Karlan* (1973); *Cohen* v. *California* (1971); defamation (U.S.).

"Filthy Words"   In October 1973 the American comedian George Carlin recorded a 12-minute long monologue entitled "Filthy Words" in front of a live audience in a California theater. In it he talked about "the words you couldn't say on the public, uh, airwaves, um, the ones you definitely wouldn't say, ever." He then listed the words in question: fuck, shit, piss, cunt, tits, cocksucker, motherfucker, fart, turd, cock, twat and ass, then repeated them in a variety of colloquialisms. Around two o'clock on the afternoon of October 30, 1973, a New York radio station broadcast the monologue. A man who had been driving with his young son complained to the Federal Communications Commission (FCC). The FCC referred to its own regulations regarding INDECENCY and obscenity and stated that while the monologue was not obscene, it was certainly indecent and "patently offensive." It stated that it would make a note of the broadcast on the station's license file and would decide in due course whether to take further action. The station appealed against this ruling; in its decision, given in 1978, the Supreme Court examined the context of the broadcast and stated that it was not obscene, but that it was indecent and that the FCC, under its own statutory regulations, had the right to make the relevant note in the licensee's file.

Finland

1. censorship   In 1766, when Finland was still part of the kingdom of Sweden, King Gustaf III approved the Act on the Freedom of the Press, advocated by Antti Chydenius, a Finnish member of the Diet. This act was in force only until 1772, but it was the first such legislation in the world. Today there is no overt censorship in Finland, but all the media exercise a degree of self-censorship dictated both by the attitudes of politicians, who have gone so far as to outlaw satire, and by the country's geographical position, on the border of the U.S.S.R.

The proximity of Finland to Russia has meant that the country has suffered periods of harsh censorship; notably during its inclusion in the Czarist Empire from 1809 to 1917; during the Civil War that followed the Russian Revolution; as part of the conservative reaction to the left-wing movements of the 1930s; and during the Second World War. The Russians completely controlled the Finnish media from the end of Swedish rule until 1861, at which point there was established a Supreme Censorship Board. Briefly, in 1864, pre-publication censorship was abolished, but almost immediately reestablished. After the General Strike of 1905, a further attempt to abolish censorship went as far as a new bill, but the Czar refused to give it his assent. In 1917 Finland was declared independent; In 1919 the Freedom of the Press Act, which controls the Finnish press, banned all prior censorship. This act remains in force.

Since the liberation of 1944, when all Nazi propaganda was purged from the country, there has been no official censorship, but a pragmatic approach has ensured that the Finnish media has usually opted for discretion over controversy. This self-censorship has helped successive governments, which, stating that they are promoting self-discipline, have attempted to control excessive criticism of the Soviets. This campaign extends to interfering in, although not actual censorship of, the work of foreign correspondents who may have revealed hitherto secretive relations between Finland and Russia. Such stories are not in the "national interest." The demands of the various political interest groups are most conspicuously influential in radio and television, controlled by the Finnish Broadcasting Company (YLE). The government plays a large role in news selection and programming. All broadcasting organizations must specify a program editor who is responsible for any broadcasts that are criminal in content and whose word on such material is final. All schedules must be published a month in advance; all programs must be taped and held for 90 days. Soviet influence is substantial and a weekly radio program is devoted to praising the Russian system. The Soviet embassy has also managed to outlaw a number of Western productions critical of its policies and revelatory of its military strategy.

Film censorship concentrates on unacceptable pornography, but material that might offend either superpower tends to be excised. The frequency of such bannings tends to fluctuate as to the current state of international tension.

2. Freedom of the Press Act (1919) This act governs press freedom in Finland. Its basic premise, in article 1, states: "Every Finnish citizen shall have the right to publish printed writings, without the public authorities being allowed to set any obstacles to this in advance, as long as the provisions of this Act are observed." Among these provisions are certain restrictions.

article 10: "Every printed work published ... must bear the printer's name and the name of his firm as well as the name of the place where the item has been printed and the year in which it was printed ... Offenses against this regulation shall be punished by fines."

article 12: "Immediately after a printed piece of writing ... has been published in print, the printer should supply the Ministry of Justice with one copy of it ... neglecting to supply this copy shall be punishable by a fine."

section 4, article 19, dealing with newspapers and magazines: The authorities must be notified of the printer, his firm, the place where the publication will appear; "the notification must also state the name of the printed work ... how often the work is intended to appear ... state the person who will, as chief editor, have to supervise the publication of the printed work and supervise its contents."

section 5, article 26: "Without proper permission, nobody may publish in print memoranda or documents belonging to the highest administrative authorities, the publication of which has been forbidden under regulations issued, or information relating to negotiations going on between the Government and a foreign power, which are to be kept secret, nor any documents relating to a matter to be dealt with by the State Treasury Office, the Bank of Finland or any other public authority, insofar as they are to be kept secret under general regulations, before 25 years from the date of issue of the memoranda or the holding of the negotiations have elapsed." In special cases this period can be extended by a further 50 years. Those who contravene this section shall be fined up to 2,000 marks or imprisoned for up to two years.

As modified in 1951 in the Act on Publicity of Official Documents, material classified as secret includes the areas listed in article 26 above, and the interests of national defense, the prevention of crimes or the bringing of charges, certain areas of national or local government, the management of private businesses, court cases in progress, and matters dealing with the church or prisons. Material stemming from any of these can be summarily declared secret. Higher officials can instruct their assistants of such a declaration; juniors without the power to do so themselves can request a classification from their superiors.

article 28, providing for individual privacy: This includes "documents issued by the clergy ... that concern spiritual care or ecclesiastical discipline" and "notes and doctor's certificates written in a prison or hospital." All such material remains secret for 20 years unless otherwise permitted by those concerned or an act of parliament.

Section 6 deals with crimes committed through a printed publication: These crimes include the omission of the printer's and/or chief editor's or author's name from printed matter or a periodical publication, or certain crimes specified in the Finnish Penal Code. The publication in question can be seized and subsequent editions banned. Those reponsible for these omissions are fined or jailed for up to one year. If anyone attempts to sell copies of a banned work, he or she faces a fine or a maximum of six months jail.

Seizures and bans are the responsibility of the Ministry of Justice, which will examine the material in question and decide whether or not to authorize the seizure. Individual chiefs of police may act without a specific order, but must inform the ministry within 24 hours and obtain an order; if the seizure is not backed by the minister, the material must be freed. The material must be submitted to a court for initial examination within three days (eight if the seizure takes place at a distance from the court) and the court must either confirm or cancel the seizure within four days of notification. If the court fails to act or the prosecutor fails to gain a writ within 14 days from the court's upholding of a seizure, the action is nullified. Plays and theatrical performances are similarly regulated. Prosecutions will still be carried out and items banned even if those legally responsible are dead.

First Amendment The First Amendment to the U.S. Constitution was added to the original document of 1787 in 1791, as part of the Bill of Rights. It provides the fundamental guarantee to U.S. citizens of freedoms of speech and expression and stands as the basis of all subsequent legislation in these areas. It reads: "Congress shall make no law respecting an establishment of religion, or prohibiting the free exercise thereof, or abridging the freedom of speech, or of the press; or the right of the people peacefully to assemble, and to petition the government for a redress of grievances."

First Amendment Congress The First Amendment Congress is an association of some 50,000 members, all employed in journalism and other media, whose purpose is to maintain public awareness of the freedom of speech and press guaranteed in the First Amendment to the U.S. Constitution. Further objectives are to "convey the belief that a free press is not a special prerogative of print and broadcast journalists, but a basic right that assures a responsive government; to establish a dialogue between the press and the people across the country; to encourage better education in schools about the rights and responsibilities of citizenship; and to obtain broader support from the public against all attempts by the government to restrict the citizen's right to information." The FAC operates on national, state and local levels to work with the public in its efforts to resolve the problems of media credibility, fairness, objectivity and accuracy.

SEE ALSO United States 7. Constitution.

Fiske v. *State of Kansas* (1927)   The Criminal Syndicalism Act of the state of Kansas states:

> Section 1. Criminal Syndicalism is hereby defined to be the doctrine which advocates crime, physical violence, arson, destruction of property, sabotage or other unlawful acts or methods, as a means of accomplishing or effecting industrial or political revolution, or for profit ... Section 3. Any person who, by word of mouth, or writing, advocates, affirmatively suggests, or teaches the duty, necessity, propriety, or expediency of crime, criminal syndicalism, or sabotage ... is guilty of a felony.

In the case of *Fiske* v. *State of Kansas* (1927), Fiske, a labor organizer, was convicted under this act when he attempted to recruit members into the Workers' Industrial Union, a branch of the Industrial Workers of the World (IWW). The state declared that this organization was a criminal syndicate and duly prosecuted Fiske. The U.S. Supreme Court overturned his conviction, saying that "the Syndicalism Act has been applied in this case to sustain the conviction of the defendant, without any charge or evidence that the organization in which he secured members advocated any crime, violence or other unlawful acts or methods as a means of effecting industrial or political changes or revolution. Thus applied the Act is an arbitrary and unreasonable exercise of the police power of the State, unwarrantably infringing the liberty of the defendant ..."

Flaubert, Gustave   The son of a well known Rouen physician, Flaubert (1821-80) was one of the 19th century's greatest novelists and, as evinced in the painstaking analyses of the creative process incorporated in his correspondence, a supreme artist. Despite this present-day status, his first published novel, *Madame Bovary* (1857), which charts the adulteries and eventual suicide of the wife of a provincial doctor, was considered to be an "*outrage aux bonnes moeurs*" and led to Flaubert's being taken to court, as were his publisher and printer. Because French obscenity law was not bound by the HICKLIN RULE, the author was acquitted, since although the prosecution could cite ·individual passages that it found disgusting, it was unable to prove that the book, when viewed as a whole, was consistently unacceptable. This acquittal failed to impress the Catholic Church and both *Madame Bovary* and Flaubert's second novel, *Salammbo* (1862), a minutely researched recreation of classical Carthage, were placed on the Roman Index (see Roman Indexes) in 1864.

Flaubert was no more popular in America. JOHN S. SUMNER of the SOCIETY FOR THE SUPPRESSION OF VICE attempted without success in 1927 to have banned *The Temptation of St. Anthony*, written in 1874. U.S. Customs seized *November*, a piece of Flaubert's juvenilia, in 1934, but decided on reflection not to submit it to a federal court for assessment. The society joined the attack in 1935, but its case failed, and the magistrate pointed out that "the criterion of decency is fixed by time, place and geography and all the elements of a changing world. A practice regarded as decent in one period may be indecent in another." As late as the 1950s *Madame Bovary* was still on the blacklist of the NATIONAL ORGANIZATION FOR DECENT LITERATURE.

Fleetwood, William   SEE book burning in England 7. United Kingdom (1688-1775).

Fleischmann, Stanley   SEE *Luros* v. *United States* (1968); *Smith* v. *California* (1959).

Flesh   Andy Warhol's film *Flesh* was made in 1969, not by the artist himself but by his assistant Paul Morrissey. It told the story of a young man, played by Joe D'Alessandro, who chose to support his wife and child by working as a homosexual prostitute. The film featured a great deal of nudity, both male and female, and was unrestrained in its use of taboo language. It arrived in England in 1969, where the censor, JOHN TREVELYAN, suggested to its distributor that he should not even bother submitting it to the British Board of Film Censors, who would never be able to pass it. Instead the distributor passed *Flesh* on to the Open Space Theatre, which ran a cinema club, where it was duly exhibited to critical acclaim—the *New York Times* had already chosen *Flesh* as one of the year's 10 best films—and was seen by large audiences.

In Britain the authorities found Warhol's work distasteful. On February 3, 1970, a force of 32 policemen, led by a chief inspector, raided the Open Space during the evening showing. They stopped the screening, seized the film and parts of the projector, took the names and addresses of the entire audience and confiscated the records of the Open Space club membership as well as a number of other papers. The raid immediately began a controversy. Questions were asked in the House of Commons, and Trevelyan himself told the press that he backed the Open Space, approved fully of the film being shown in a club context and deplored the police action.

The authorities initially threatened a prosecution under the OBSCENE PUBLICATIONS ACT (1959) but quickly modified this, sending all the relevant papers on to the Greater London Council, "for consideration as regards the question of proceedings for any offence under the CINEMATOGRAPH ACT of 1909." On March 20 the council summoned the Open Space's directors, Thelma Holt and Charles Marowitz, for failing to observe certain regulations as regarded clubs.

The two directors appeared in Hampstead Magistrates Court in late May. They pleaded guilty as charged and Trevelyan appeared as a character witness. They were fined and made to pay court costs. Warhol himself paid both fines and costs. In 1970 the BBFC gave *Flesh* an X certificate.

Florida: sale of obscene material   Under the Florida Penal Code it is a misdemeanor to have in one's possession "custody or control with intent to sell ... any obscene, lewd, lascivious, filthy, indecent [or] immoral ... figure [or] image." The Florida test of obscenity states: "Whether to the average person, applying contemporary community standards, the dominant theme of the material taken as a whole appeals to prurient interest."

Forever Amber In 1946 the state of Massachusetts attempted to ban the sale of *Forever Amber*, a romantic historical novel by Kathleen Winsor. This was the first book to be prosecuted under the state's new obscenity law, promulgated in 1945, which, while it did not actually alter the definition of obscenity, set up a new procedure whereby in the case of books sold to adults the action was to be instigated by a district attorney or the attorney-general and would be aimed at the book and not at its distributor. Charging the author with obscenity, Attorney General George Rowell cited as due cause for banning the book some 70 references to sexual intercourse; 39 to illegitimate pregnancies; 7, abortions; 10, descriptions of women undressing, dressing or bathing in the presence of men; five references to incest; 13 references ridiculing marriage; and 49 "miscellaneous objectionable passages." Rowell lost his case, and Judge Donahue of the Massachusetts Supreme Court defined the book as "a soporific rather than an aphrodisiac ... while the novel was conducive to sleep, it was not conducive to a desire to sleep with a member of the opposite sex."

Fortune Press, The The Fortune Press, a London publisher that combined the work of unknown new authors with that of older ones, often in translation, was raided by the police in 1933. A number of books were seized, all of which were condemned by the magistrate at the Westminster Police Court, Mr. A. Ronald Powell. They included four contemporary novels, a sex guide and a book in which two poems were included that had mistakenly been attributed to Lord Byron. There were translations of four French novels, including *La-Bas* by J.-K. Huysmans, and a number of historical works. The only book that might be recognized as conventionally pornographic was *The Perfumed Garden*, but this was a bowdlerized edition.

Foundation to Improve Television Founded in 1969 with headquarters in Boston, Massachusetts, FIT aims to promote the "proper utilization of television," especially as regards juvenile viewers. Members of the group carry out research on the psychological effects of TV on all viewers, particularly on children. It also campaigns through the courts and by bringing pressure on the networks to outlaw many of the medium's more violent programs, and especially advocates a legal ban on the transmission of violent material before 10 P.M.

Foxe's Book of Martyrs *Acts and Monuments of these latter perillous dayes, touching matters of the Church*, generally known as *Foxe's Book of Martyrs*, was first published in Latin at Strasbourg in 1559 and in English in 1563. A massive tome, twice the size of Gibbon's *Decline and Fall of the Roman Empire*, it was compiled by the printer and clergyman John Foxe (1516-87). Three further editions appeared in 1570, 1576 and 1583, as well as one posthumous one in 1641, edited by his son. The *Acts and Monuments* was a history of the Christian Church, with special reference to its martyrs, especially those Protestants who had recently been executed in England by Queen Mary. The whole weight of the book is an attack on "the persecutors of God's truth, commonly called papists." The book was not banned itself, but its first edition served as a guide to Roman Catholic censorship, including a list of a number of "Condemned Books," by Protestant authors whose works had been banned by the church. It runs:

> Miles Coverdale, the whole Bible; George Joy; Theodore Baselle, alias Thomas Beacon; William Tindall [WILLIAM TYNDALE]; John Frith ... William Turner, translated by Fysh; Robert Barnes; Richard Tracey; John Bale, alias Haryson; John Goughe; Roderick Mors; Henry Stalbridg, otherwyse Bale ... Urb. Regius; Apologia Melanchthonis; Romerani; Luther ...

France
1. book censorship (1521-51) Literary censorship in 16th- and early-17th-century France was controlled jointly by the crown and by the church. The former would decide what should be controlled, the latter, in the form of the theological faculty of the Sorbonne or the bishops, held responsibility for framing the regulations and putting them into practice. Occasionally a third power, the secular Parlement of Paris, published censorship regulations, but this activity had essentially ended by 1700.

In 1521, at the instigation of the University of Paris, Francois I prohibited the printing of any new works with any relevance to religion, either in Latin or in French, until they had been examined and approved by the theological faculty. The king further instructed the Councils of Bourges and of Sens, both in 1528, to issue decrees forbidding the possession of copies of the writings of LUTHER and his followers. No one might read or circulate any religious book that had not been approved by the bishop. In 1530 the king appointed inquisitors of literature, two of whom were clergymen from the Sorbonne and two of whom were magistrates from the Parlement of Paris. The former were to determine heresy, the latter to authorize its destruction. Their immediate task was to suppress heretical literature, as authorized by the Parlement and the crown and specified by the archbishop of Paris. Lists of prohibited and permitted material were published.

In 1542 the Parlement of Paris forbade the printing of any book without the approval of the authorities of the University of Paris; two members of each faculty had to approve every item and for Bibles there were required the signatures of four doctors of divinity. All bales of books arriving in Paris were to be opened in the presence of four certified bookdealers and examined by divines appointed by the university. A list of permitted literature was to be circulated and severe penalties threatened against anyone who sold heretical material. Between 1542 and 1547 the Sorbonne compiled a number of catalogs of prohibited books, the last of which totaled around 120 titles. A similar catalog was published by the Inquisitor of Toulouse in 1548; it contained 92 titles, often misspelled and confused. The forbidden authors included Luther, Zwingli, Erasmus and others. Anyone guilty of reading, owning, selling, binding or printing such material was to be excommunicated.

In 1551 Henri II prohibited the importation of any books printed in Geneva or any other towns known as Protestant strongholds. No books listed as prohibited by the Sorbonne could be printed or sold, and only those with direct authorization to inspect them for heresy might possess copies. The name of all printers were to be recorded and they were to conduct their businesses only from specified places. All imported books were to be inspected on arrival by a panel of censors, and this same panel was to check the bookstores twice every year. In Lyons, a center of contraband literature, this check took place three times a year. Every bookshop was to display a copy of the Sorbonne's prohibited list. Among those authors condemned were ERASMUS, Faber, Peter Martyr, WYCLIF, Huss, Corvinus and others. These lists ran to five divisions: works in Latin by known authors; anonymous works in Latin; signed works in French; anonymous works in French; French translations of the Scriptures.

The Parlement maintained the compilation of lists of prohibited books throughout the period, issuing them in 1551 (based on the Sorbonne list of 1544) and 1557. A further revision, in 1562, was begun but left unfinished. Instead, the crown issued an ordinance that bypassed the Parlement, simply making any prohibitions listed by the Sorbonne incumbent on all citizens. In 1577 Henri III slightly modified the regulations, allowing the purchase of Protestant works that had been approved by special commissioners.

2. censorship under the Ancien Regime As in other European countries, where printing had begun in the 15th century, the earliest form of censorship in France, as instituted in 1521 by Francis I, was pre-publication control by the church. As in England, the impetus for control lay with the crown, while the framing of the actual regulations and their execution was left to the clergy. This system was replaced in 1629 by an ordinance of Louis XIII, which moved the onus of control to secular authorities, establishing a system of censors operating under the chancellor. This system became decreasingly effective as the 18th century progressed.

The censorship of the Ancien Regime worked on two levels: pre-publication, whereby the Crown authorized certain printers and booksellers, and post-publication, whereby anything that escaped the primary censorship was controlled by the police. The absolutist state had no doubt as to the importance of the printed word and was determined to control it. But it also understood that the control of books reflected not simply on ideological needs, but also on the national economy. As more titles appeared, it became necessary to strengthen the monopolistic Paris publishers. It was necessary to temper control with the need to derive an income. Thus a degree of liberality was necessary, since otherwise the same material would simply appear via clandestine methods and thus rob the state of valuable funds.

The major development of Old Regime censorship was from 1660 to 1680, under Jean-Baptiste Colbert and Nicolas Reynie. Prior to this time things were still relatively fluid; after it the system that lasted until the Revolution was set up. Increasingly close supervision of printed matter was backed by prosecution of illicit, counterfeit or controversial publications, foreign material and "immoral" pictures. This system was firmly established with the appointment in 1699 of Abbé Jean-Paul Bignon as director of the book trade. Under his direction the censors of the Office of the Book Trade (after 1750 the Direction of the Book Trade) subjected all material to pre-publication assessment. After examination the relevant publisher received either "privileges" (exclusive rights of publication and sale) or "tacit permissions" (in the case of books that the state did not wish openly to sanction, nor to condemn). If a book received neither status, some reason had to be given.

Bignon increased the number of censors from 60 to 130 (they numbered 160 by 1789). They were drawn from academics (often clergymen, and as such subject also to church discipline), lawyers, doctors and some noblemen. Often specialists in a given area—e.g., science or religion—they worked closely with the authors, who appreciated the niceties of the state's policy of qualified tolerance and attempted to strike compromises wherever possible. Given a state that required filtration rather than blanket suppression, the system ran smoothly, although Bignon's guidelines made it clear that they worked from assumptions fundamentally opposed to freedom of thought. Prohibition was designed to control anything that attacked religion, the established authorities (notably the king) or the accepted morality. In 1757 a royal declaration condemned to death anyone involved in the publication or sale of "writings that tend to attack religion, excite spirits, injure royal authority, and trouble the order and tranquility of the state." It was unenforceable, but compromise was not always possible and VOLTAIRE, DIDEROT and ROUSSEAU were among the suppressed authors.

The state censors were backed by a number of other regulatory bodies. From about 1700 the "book police," an equally efficient and pervasive body, checked booksellers and publishers, establishing a wide post-publication censorship over what they termed "bad books." The book trade itself established *chambres syndicales*, local organizations where representatives of the trade met with those of the state to iron out their difficulties. Working with these *chambres* were inspectors of the book trade, who would check every consignment of books arriving in the provinces from the Paris publishers. Foreign material suffered similar checks.

Breaking the rules led to serious punishment. Booksellers and publishers faced at best a fine, at worst whipping, the stocks, banishment, prison or the galleys. But many took the risk: Suppression, as ever, made a work even more alluring, and clandestine editions could be priced even higher. There was a substantial trade in illicit books, known in the trade as *livres philosophiques*, or "philosophical works."

3. censorship after the French Revolution The Revolution of 1789, which abrogated the concept of the divine right of kings, ended the old censorship. Article II of the Declaration of the Rights of Man stated, "Free communication of thought and opinion is one of man's most precious rights: Therefore every citizen may speak, write and print freely." But some controls persisted, and throughout the 19th century French governments either tightened or relaxed controls as their politics and inclinations moved them. Whereas pre-publication censorship had been abandoned in 1695 by the English (SEE Licensing Act [1662]), the French authorities retained it, and their fluctuating systems became the model for most European nations.

As early as 1792, the revolutionary National Convention banned all royalist publications; anyone guilty of publishing such material faced the guillotine, although preliminary censorship was abolished. It returned under Napoleon I, who also forced booksellers and printers to take a loyalty oath. Louis XVIII promised an end to all censorship when the Bourbons were restored under the Charter of 1814 but immediately imposed it, although Napoleon's "100 days" made him reverse his position. The press was ostensibly free in 1819 when a new law made it an offense for anyone to publish works that provoked a felony or misdemeanor, and the owners of all political newspapers had to put up a cash bond against their breaking of the law. This was set at a rate aimed deliberately to cripple small, radical papers. All newspapers and magazines were similarly to register a responsible editor, thus providing an automatic defendant against whom the government, if need be, might institute proceedings.

Between 1820 and 1821, while the charter was suspended, preliminary censorship reappeared. When, along with the charter, freedom was restored in 1822, it was further constrained by an extended definition of libel, which included the blanket offense of inciting contempt against the government. Non-jury courts were empowered to suspend, temporarily or permanently, any publication that had been warned repeatedly but still persisted in attacking the status quo. Charles X restored censorship in 1827, ordering that newspapers must apply every three months for the renewal of a license to print, but the press proved sufficiently undaunted to spearhead the campaign that drove him from the throne in 1830. Under Louis Philippe the press was freed, but constrained by strict laws of seditious libel under which there were many prosecutions. In 1835 these laws were extended further and some were upgraded to treasonable offenses; it was forbidden to mention the king in political papers, and all publications were obliged to print government statements. The government's propaganda office, the Bureau de l'esprit publique, issued such statements and actively involved itself in promoting right-wing publications. The press agency Havas (founded in 1835) was similarly employed for the distribution of pro-government material.

The success of the Revolution of 1848, which proved how futile had been the press controls of the July monarchy, and which placed two editors in the 11-man provisional government, did not preclude the continuation of press control. The Second Republic began by abandoning all censorship but a rash of street disorders led to the closing down of many vociferous sheets and the National Assembly moved to reestablish much of the traditional censorship. After his coup of 1852 Louis Napoleon substantially increased the range of seditious libels and temporarily suspended the many opposition papers and created a system of official warnings, followed by proceedings in non-jury courts along the lines of the 1822 system. This system was dropped in 1865. From 1870, under the Third Republic, censorship was again set aside, but when the vast majority of the French press came out for the opposition, the authorities clamped down once more. Finally, in 1881, under Gambetta, "modern" freedom of the press, which has remained largely unchanged other than during wartime and the Occupation, was established.

SEE ALSO France 1. book censorship (1521-51); France 4. freedom of the press.

4. film censorship State censorship of films is the direct responsibility of the minister of culture, who acts according to advice given by a board of film censors, which is made up of three groups of eight members each, divided equally among government officials, members of the film industry and a collection of other interested parties, such as parents' groups, local authorities, teachers and psychologists, all of whom operate under a part-time chairman. Films are viewed by a subcommittee composed of a quarter of the board; members of a larger panel, drawn from the whole spectrum of French society, may be called in, for a small fee, to offer extra advice. Films are placed in four categories: (1) unrestricted and available to children; (2) forbidden to those under 13; (3) forbidden to those under 18; (4) X-films (introduced in 1975), forbidden to those under 18 on the grounds of pornographic sex or incitement to violence. About 20 to 25 films are banned each year, usually on the grounds of sexual violence, although the X certificate, referring to incitement to violence, is only rarely applied. Publicity material designed for films is also subject to censorship.

In 1975 the French government advanced proposals for the complete decensorship of films, maintaining a ban only on those that were offensive to human dignity and maintaining the classification system as regards minors. Appalled by the flood of pornography that this released, the public demanded some form of control. Although a poll showed that 59 percent wanted a return to the old controls, the government created a system that contained rather than suppressed pornography and introduced it in December 1975. Pornography is now confined to specialist cinemas, thus kept away from those likely to be otherwise offended by its existence. When a film has been classified as pornographic it becomes liable to extra taxes both on its production and on the entrance charges for viewing it; it may not be advertised other than in general newspaper listings and its makers forfeit their chance of obtaining government subsidies.

5. freedom of the press   The press and publishing in France are both free, as stated in the Law of July 29, 1881. Certain restrictions under this law forbid the reporting of certain legal cases, to protect the rights of individuals at law, but there is no provision for precensorship. It is possible, however, for a publication that makes attacks on the head of state or on foreign heads of state or incites its readers to political crimes or, if soldiers, to mutiny or collaborate with the enemy, to face punishment after the material has appeared. In this case, the publisher, rather than the author, is held responsible, and it is notable that books, rather than newspapers, are seen as more liable to prosecution for supposed sedition. When the authorities wish to restrain such publishers, who are seen as undermining national security, either the minister of the interior or the minister of defense may seize the offending items; there is no appeal against such an action. An additional statute, passed in the wake of the vast sums made from his autobiography by Jacques Mesrine, a celebrated villain, confiscates any profits made by a criminal who attempts thus to exploit his crimes. Thus once popular instant confession books are outlawed. A new law, that of August 1, 1986, "Act on Reforming the Legal System Governing the Press," updated the act of 1881 and that of November 1945, which reestablished the post-Occupation French press. Dealing mainly with the financial direction of the press, it did not modify the basic freedoms and safeguards.

6. freedom of communication   French broadcasters and citizens were guaranteed freedom of communication by the Act of July 29, 1982, which stipulated the "legal existence of a pluralistic radio network." This placed radio and television within the sphere of the 1881 Act on Press Freedom, gave the public a right of reply and subjected members of the broadcasting media to a variety of legal penalties for offenses either in the 1881 act or the Penal Code. The theory behind the act, however, was constrained by the fact that all major radio and television networks in France were controlled by the government. Attempts by the government to alter this paradoxical situation led to the privatization of Television Francaise-1 (TF-1) and of certain formerly state-run radio channels, as well as a number of allied measures, and an acknowledgment of the effects of the proliferating new telecommunications technology and the chances it offered to autonomous operators. In addition, a new, ostensibly independent, supervisory body was created to take over the powers previously held by the minister for the post office and Telecommunications as regarding the regulation and control of broadcasting.

The legal support for these changes is based in the Act of Freedom of Communication, of September 30, 1986, in which the French government has laid down, in article 1, that:

Telecommunications installations are freely established and used; telecommunications services are freely operated and used. Such freedoms may be restricted on the basis of observance of the principle of equality of treatment, only to the extent required by national defense needs and public-service imperatives, and to safeguard law and order, the freedom and property of others and the pluralist expression of opinion trends. The secrecy of a person's selection of telecommunication services and of programs from among those offered them cannot be lifted without that person's agreement.

In order to maintain the premise of article 1 the act set up, in article 3, the National Commission for Communication and the Freedoms. This body is intended, according to the government, to be "a powerful and independent institution capable both of defining generally accepted rules of play and enforcing them." Designed to "safeguard the exercise of freedom of communication," it has replaced the previous regulatory body, the High Authority, established under the act of 1982 and which was found to be insufficiently independent of government influence to make disinterested judgments of public-sector telecommunications.

The National Commission is composed of three members nominated by the president of France, the president of the Senate and the president of the National Assembly; three drawn from the supreme administrative court (Conseil d'Etat), the supreme court of appeal (Court de Cassation) and the audit court (Cour des Comptes). These six will then co-opt a further four members: a member of the Academie Francaise; a person "with appropriate expertise in the sector of audio-visual creation," one with "appropriate expertise in the telecommunications sector" and a member of the written press. All members will serve nine years and the commission will elect its own chairman. No member may have any professional interest in any medium but will be paid according to French civil service grades.

The immediate task of the commission is to authorize independent telecommunications installations and to supervise the running of those stations. Its reponsibilities fall into three areas: first, ensuring that the new stations operate as the law requires. This includes considering public complaints against the way in which these stations are operated, protecting minors, supporting pluralist views and as well as supervising "by all appropriate means ... the purpose, contents and programming methods of advertisements ..." as well as of electoral broadcasts. Secondly, it is responsible for the various privatization measures now underway within the French broadcasting media. Thirdly, the commission will guarantee the exercise of freedom of communication within private-sector broadcasting, carrying out this duty to ensure that such freedom is exercised "in a legal framework that avoids any kind of disorderly situation." It is responsible for the issuing of permits to broadcast and the allocation of relevant wavebands. The commission also maintains broadcasting pluralism both in the content of the programs and by suppressing attempts to create media monopolies. The commission is now facing increased complaints from the public, who feel it is overly influenced by the government.

7. freedom of information Subsequent to the deliberations of the Council of Europe at Graz in Austria in September 1976, which debated ideas for open government on the basis of article 10 of the EUROPEAN CONVENTION ON HUMAN RIGHTS, which guarantees freedom of expression, France initiated moves toward its own freedom of information law. A committee to research the topic was established in 1977 and it reported in 1978. Four laws were then passed that dealt with this topic:

The Law of January 6, 1978 (on Information and Freedom) deals primarily with access to computer data bases. This law on data protection was the result of the Tricot Commission that had been looking into the topic since 1975. Under this legislation all files, both manually compiled and computer-generated are covered, and both the public and private sectors included, although only individuals and not companies or institutions are given protection. Article 1 of the law states that "computer science has to be at the service of each citizen ... it should not damage human identity, nor human rights, private life or individual and public liberties." The independent and powerful Commission Nationale de l'Informatique et des Libertes (CNIL) is entrusted with monitoring and enforcing the law. No data base may be set up without its permission and regular checks are made.

The Law of July 17, 1978 (on access to administrative documents) was passed subsequent to its recommendations and the decree promulgating it was announced in December 1978. Under the law individuals gained the right of public access to government documents. Ten broad exceptions to disclosure were listed and a commission (CADA) set up to monitor the law and adjudicate on complaints made by those who were unable to see the material they requested. Ironically the law was passed almost without comment until an article in *Le Monde* in 1979 noted its existence. In theory the law should guarantee freedom of information, but in practice there remain problems, notably the delay between application for and delivery of information and the fact that CADA has no legal powers to force an authority to hand over material.

The Law of January 13, 1979, ensures the right of access to documents in French public archives; the Law of July 11, 1979, forces the administration to give reasons if it chooses to reject an individual's request for information.

8. obscenity laws The essential belief of French governments is that adults should be free to read what they please. The publication of items that transcend the test of being *contraire aux bonnes moeurs* ("immoral") is vetoed, and ministers hold certain administrative powers of control, but on the whole French obscenity laws concentrate on protecting minors and permitting adults to read without restriction. Article 283 of the French Penal Code forbids *l'outrage aux bonnes moeurs* ("the outraging of public moral standards"). It governs immoral material, making it an offense to manufacture, distribute, import, export, transport, sell or offer for sale,

hire or offer for hire, display publicly or offer directly or indirectly, even if privately and without payment, any printed matter, writing, drawing, painting, photograph, film, gramophone record or other object or representation that is judged *contraire aux bonnes moeurs*. Violent material is only banned if it advocates violence. It is further illegal to "publicize debauchery." The desire to protect minors works both through a Special Commission set up by the Ministry of Justice, which pre-censors all material aimed at the youth market, and through the law of 1949 under which the minister of the interior can restrict material as to sale, display and advertising.

Following the *Decret-Loi* of July 29, 1939, articles 119-128, a decree promulgated to protect "the family, parenthood and the race," it is an offense to make, possess, transport, distribute, sell, import or export for commercial purposes any writing or pictures *contraires aux bonnes moeurs* or to advertise any such articles. Literary or other merit is no defense but it may be taken into consideration in imposing the penalty. Any obscene articles that are the subject of a prosecution may be seized by the Customs, and the postal authorities may refuse to accept them for transmission. There exist three safeguards: (1) prosecutions must be instituted within three years of commission of the offense; (2) instead of ordering destruction, a court may present obscene items to a state museum; (3) by a decree of January 25, 1940, no book can be prosecuted as obscene until it has been assessed as such by a special commission, the Commission Consultative de la Famille et de la Natalite Francaise.

The French have not established a specific test for obscenity, stating only that is an *outrage aux bonnes moeurs*. In practice this means that mercenary and gross pornography may be outlawed, but works of art and literature are usually exempt, even if they are considered unsuitable for minors. A special commission exists purely to judge what is suitable for the consumption of the young. Pornography has been defined by the Tribunal Correctionel de Paris as any material that "by depriving the rights of love of any emotional context and by describing simply the physiological mechanisms, tends to deprave public decency if, in so describing, deviations are sought for with obvious relish." Under the law of September 25, 1946, any book that has been condemned as obscene can be reassessed after 20 years have passed. The process of review can be initiated by the author, publisher, any of their relations or the Societe des Lettres de France. Under the law of July 16, 1949, designed to protect the young under 18, and modified as recently as March 1987, the minister of the interior has massive powers to forbid the sale, exposure or advertising of any material deemed to be "licentious or pornographic." The breadth of ideas and images covered by the act is enormous and would, it has been noted, remove most children's classic and fairy tales from their intended readers, banning as it does references to, inter alia, bandits, running away from home, lying, stealing, idleness, and a variety of other behavior that qualifies as "deliquent" and that may "demoralize children or young people." In effect the law is not applied to such material, but when it is found useful, may be used in an attempt to suppress a variety of adult publications that are seen as dangerously subversive or pornographic.

In October 1986 the Paris Council set up a working party whose task was to establish a monthly booklist on which librarians must base their choice of new children's books. This was widely decried as censorship and in 1987 librarians, authors and publishers united in a group called Reject Censorship (Renvoyons la Censure).

SEE ALSO Maurice Girodias; Olympia Press.

France, Anatole Born Jacques Anatole Thibault (1844-1924), the son of a Parisian bookseller, France published his first successful novel, *Le Crime de Sylvestre Bonnard*, in 1881. As a journalist and editor he built himself a major reputation and from 1890 was counted among the most influential figures in French literary life. In 1893 there appeared two companion volumes—*La Rotisserie de la reine Pedauque* and *Les Opinions de M. Jerome Coignard*—which together attempted to recreate the mind and sensibility of 18th-century France. Four novels, appearing between 1897 and 1901, comprise the "Histoire contemporaine"; focussing on M. Bergeret, a disenchanted but observant provincial professor, they offer a satirical fantasy on the evolution of human society and institutions. His most popular work is held by many to be *Les Dieux ont Soif* (1912), a study of the excesses of the French Revolution. He was awarded the Nobel Prize for Literature in 1921. Although France had been among the foremost enemies of the freethinking EMILE ZOLA, suggesting that a world without him would have been a better place, he suffered some censorship himself. His entire works were banned by the Roman Index (see Roman Indexes) in 1922 and in 1953 Ireland banned his novel, *The Mummer's Tale*.

Freedman v. Maryland (1965) SEE *Revenge at Daybreak*.

Frohwerk v. United States (1919) Frohwerk was responsible, with others, for the editing and publishing of the *Missouri Staats Zeitung*, a German-language newspaper whose readers were drawn mainly from the German immigrant population. Like many of their fellow-countrymen they were appalled by the jingoistic excesses occasioned by America's entry into World War I. The paper attacked American policy in a number of articles; unlike a more celebrated German, H.L. Mencken, who also railed against American xenophobia, the paper was accused by the government of fomenting disloyalty, mutiny and refusal of duty in the U.S. armed forces. Frohwerk was tried under the Espionage Act (1917) and convicted. The Supreme Court affirmed the conviction, while recognizing a variety of potentially extenuating circumstances, not least of which was the insignificance of the newspaper, but the court still stated that it was "unable to

say that the articles could not furnish a basis for a conviction" and Frohwerk was jailed as required by the act.

SEE ALSO *Abrams* v. *United States* (1919); *Adler* v. *Board of Education* (1952); Debs, Eugene; Espionage Act (U.S., 1917) and Sedition Act (U.S., 1918); *Gitlow* v. *New York* (1925); *Lamont* v. *Postmaster-General* (1965); *Pierce* v. *United States* (1920); *Schaeffer* v. *United States* (1920); *Schenk* v. *United States* (1919); *Sweezy* v. *New Hampshire* (1957); *Whitney* v. *California* (1927); *Yates* v. *United States* (1957).

Fruits of Philosophy, The In 1876 a bookseller in Bristol, England, was convicted under the obscenity laws for selling an edition of Charles Knowlton's *The Fruits of Philosophy: an Essay on the Population Question*, in which there appeared a number of less than academic illustrations. Knowlton was a reputable American doctor, and his pamphlet, a basic sex manual with some advice on contraception, had been on sale without hindrance in England for 40 years, although its author had been prosecuted in two Massachusetts towns when the book was published in 1832. The complaint against the book was twofold: It advocated contraception rather than chastity for the control of pregnancies and, at only 6d. (2.5p) a copy, the poor could afford to buy it. The plates of the pamphlet were owned by Charles Watts, an associate of Charles Bradlaugh (1833-91), the freethinker and reformer. On Bradlaugh's suggestion, Watts appeared in Bristol, declared himself the publisher of Knowlton's work and was committed for trial at the Old Bailey.

The trial was scheduled for January 1877, but before this Watts changed his "Not Guilty" plea to one of "Guilty." He was bailed in the sum of £500 and in court it was contended that it was unlawful to publish the physiological details of sex. Bradlaugh ended his relations with Watts but decided to fight this ruling himself. Allied with fellow freethinker and birth control enthusiast Mrs. Annie Besant (1847-1933), he republished the pamphlet under the imprint of the Free Thought Publishing Company, maintaining the descriptions but dropping the illustrations. The pair were both arrested and committed for trial, first at the Old Bailey and then, after a plea of certiorari by Bradlaugh, to the Queen's Bench.

At this second trial, on June 18, 1877, the jury declared, "We are unanimously of opinion that the book in question is calculated to deprave public morals, but at the same time we entirely exonerate the defendants from any corrupt motives in publishing it." Despite this proviso the judge, Sir Alexander Cockburn (of *Regina* v. *Hicklin*), who had previously shown himself generally favorable to the defense interpreted the jury's remarks as a "guilty" verdict. He was nonetheless ready to discharge the defendants without further penalty until informed by the prosecution that Mrs. Besant had declared her intention of republishing the book, a move that she claimed Cockburn himself supported. The defendants were then sentenced to six months' imprisonment and a fine of £200 each and were to pay recognizances of £500 each for two years. They were then released on bail to await an appeal.

The convictions were duly quashed in February 1878 but so scandalous had Mrs. Besant's involvement been judged that her husband refused to let her see her daughter for the next 10 years. *The Fruits of Knowledge*, which had previously sold only hundreds, went on to sell 120,000 copies.

Fry, John   John Fry, MP, had sat in the High Court for the trial of Charles I and was a generally orthodox Parliamentarian. In 1648 he wrote a tract, "The Accuser Shamed," a rebuttal of charges made against him by a fellow MP, Colonel Downes, who had accused him of BLASPHEMY during a private conversation. This accusation had led to Fry being temporarily suspended from the House of Commons. Dr. Cheynel, president of St. John's College, Oxford, wrote a rejoinder to Fry's pamphlet, after which Fry in turn wrote *The Clergy in their True Colours* (1650), a straightforward attack on the clergy, although he expressed "a hearty desire for their reformation, and a great zeal to my countrymen that they may no longer be deceived by such as call themselves ministers of the Gospel, but are not." Observing the postures that some clergymen adopted to pray, he wondered "Whether the fools and knaves in stage plays took their pattern from these men, or these from them, I cannot determine; but sure one is the brat of the other, they are so well alike." And found, "few men under heaven more irrational in their religious exercises than our clergy." The House of Commons debated the contents of Fry's tracts and declared them highly scandalous and profane. On February 21, 1651, Fry was deprived of his seat in the Commons and both pamphlets were burnt by the common hangman.

SEE ALSO Puritan Censorship: The Commonwealth.

G

Gabler, Mel and Norma Mel and Norma Gabler are the most prominent of America's self-appointed citizen censors, a husband and wife team who have taken it upon themselves to orchestrate a nationwide campaign against what they see as improper books. Based in the industrial town of Longview, in East Texas, where Mel, 66, worked for 39 years as a clerk for the Exxon Corporation, the Gablers and their staff of seven use a 12,000-name mailing list to alert their supporters to what they see as harmful material. They produce the regular *Mel Gabler's Newsletter* as well as the blacklist, "Textbooks on Trial," culled from their library of 7,000 current textbooks, all of which they have checked for improprieties.

The Gablers, who work under the name Educational Research Analysts, are at the center of a growing network of parent groups who are demanding the alteration or removal of curriculums and individual books that they contend are in large part to blame for the high teenage pregnancy rate, venereal disease, declining test scores and other problems of today's youth. They embrace goals similar to those of such national organizations as the MORAL MAJORITY, the EAGLE FORUM, and the Christian Broadcasting Network. All try to provide grassroots parents' groups with the lobbying techniques and literature to wage attacks on individual books or school practices.

Mr. and Mrs. Gabler state that "We feel safe with older books" and concentrate their attacks on certain themes: that textbooks today undermine patriotism, the free enterprise system, religion and parental authority; that the books are negative in their discussions of death, divorce and suicide; that the books erode absolute values by asking questions to which they offer no firm answers. In addition to examining individual books for their improprieties, the Gablers serve as a clearinghouse for other issues and put interested parents in touch with other groups advocating, for example, the abolition of sex education in the schools and the compulsory teaching of creationism alongside the theory of evolution. Like most of their peers, the Gablers advocate the purging from schools of what they see as atheistic SECULAR HUMANISM.

Galilei, Galileo Galileo (1564-1642) began his studies as a medical student but he abandoned these in favor of mathematics, in which he proved himself exceptionally able, first as a student in his native town of Pisa, and subsequently as a teacher in a number of Italian universities. His particular contribution to contemporary science was to support the belief that, in contravention of the 2,000-year-old theory of Ptolemy, the Earth, rather than being at the center of the universe, was simply one more planet revolving around the sun. This concept had already been suggested by his predecessor, Nicholas Copernicus (1473-1543), but since Copernicus had lacked a telescope with which to prove his theory, the church, while condemning all such writings, dismissed him as a harmless crank, and took no punitive measures against him. Similar theories, elucidated by Johannes Kepler (1571-1630), were banned by the Pope in 1619. According to the papal bull that accompanied these bans, "to teach or even to read the works denounced or the passages condemned was to risk persecution in this world and damnation in the next."

Galileo, however, did have the recently invented telescope, and in 1632, despite warnings from the Vatican, which had in 1620 cited all the emendations that would be necessary before any of Copernicus' work might be permitted, he published his monograph, *Dialogo sopra i due massimi sistemi del mondo Tolemaicho e Copernicano (Dialogue Concerning the Two Chief World Systems of Ptolemy and Copernicus)*. In this work, set out as an argument between hypothetical proponents of the two systems, he simply proved Copernicus correct. Galileo attempted to satisfy the authorities by publishing his book with a preface by Ricciardi, the current MAGISTER SACRI PALATII, in which the Copernican theory was described as no more than an interesting intellectual exercise, but the new Pope Urban VII was implacable. He considered that the *Dialogo* brought him into ridicule and duly moved against the scientist. In June 1633 the ROMAN INQUISITION ordered Galileo to abjure his work as error and heresy. Galileo was arrested, twice threatened with torture and made to recant. He was forced to kneel in public and state, "I, Galileo, being in my seventieth year, being a prisoner and on my knees, and before your Eminences, having before my eyes the Holy Gospel, which I touch with my hands, abjure, curse and detest the error and the heresy of the movement of the earth." It was popularly alleged that he then murmured "Eppur si muove" ("And yet it does move"). The Papal theologians further declared that "the first proposition, that the sun is the center and does not revolve around the Earth, is foolish, absurd, and false in theology, and heretical, because expressly contrary to Holy Scripture ... the second proposition, that the Earth is not the center but revolves about the sun, is absurd, false in philosophy, and from a theological point of view, at least, opposed to the true faith." Galileo lived out his life under house arrest at his home near Florence.

The *Dialogo* was formally banned in 1634 along with all of Galileo's works, although the Vatican was still urging its theologians to write copiously in refutation of the new theory. Before he died Galileo managed to complete a new work, a *Dialogue Concerning Two New Sciences*, which was smuggled out of Italy and published by Protestants in the Netherlands in 1638, four years before his death. After Galileo's death his widow presented his work on the telescope and the pendulum to her confessor, who destroyed it has heretical. Not until 1824, when Canon Settele, professor of astronomy at Rome, wished to to publish a work that conformed to modern, Copernican theories, did the church finally accept "the general opinion of modern astronomers" and remove Galileo's and similar works from the Index.

Gamiani, ou une nuit d'exces This novel, among the most important items of French erotica to appear in the 19th century, is generally accepted as being written by the poet Alfred de Musset (1810-57), and was first published in 1833. Like many such works, it was regularly seized and destroyed by the authorities both in France and Britain. The heroine, the Comtesse de Gamiani, who indulges in the book "all extremes of sensuality" has similarly been identified with the writer George Sand (Amadine Aurore Dupin, Baronne Dudevant, 1804-76). The book takes in a wide variety of sexual exploits, including lesbianism, orgies and rape (in a monastery), bestiality and the like. The work climaxes with Gamiani utterly sated and committing suicide by poison, an experience that she combines, for one final fling, with the tricking of another woman into taking the same draught. The slim volume, running to less than 30 pages, combines this short piece of fiction—which takes the form of a supposed dialogue between two lesbians who recount their various sexual exploits—with a number of erotic illustrations and its dimensions are more suitable for an art book than a prose one. It has been reprinted many times, often as a vehicle for fine printing and lavish illustrations.

Gautier, Theophile SEE *Madamoiselle de Maupin.*

Gay News Gay News, founded in Britain in 1972 as the newspaper of the newly emergent gay liberation movement, published in its issue 96, of June 3-16, 1976, a poem by James Kirkup, entitled "The Love That Dares to Speak Its Name." The poem, in which a Roman soldier and Christ indulge in homosexual relations, intends to state that with the growth of gay liberation the traditional Victorian euphemism, used most notably by Lord Alfred Douglas in a sonnet about homosexual guilt, can be abandoned, since homosexuals need no longer feel any shame in declaring their sexual preference. It was illustrated by Tony Reeves with a picture of Christ being taken from the cross. Although the scene is conventional enough, this Christ has unmistakably larger-than-average genitals.

Critics were not particularly impressed with the poem, which takes the form of a dramatic monologue interlarded with slang, but they did not find it especially offensive. Mrs. MARY WHITEHOUSE was less sanguine. In November 1976 she initiated a private prosecution for BLASPHEMOUS LIBEL against *Gay News*, its editor Denis Lemon and its distributor (although charges against the last were eventually dropped). When the trial commenced at the Old Bailey in July 1977 the defense was in disarray. Blasphemy was so intrinsic a part of modern life that no useful defense suggested itself. Mrs. Whitehouse, although lacking the support of the director of public prosecutions, cleverly capitalized on the general resentment of outspoken gays and centered her attack not on Kirkup himself, a respected academic and Fellow of the Royal Society of Literature, but instead on the newspaper and its editor as less respected and thus easier targets.

In a blasphemy case no experts were permitted, merely two character witnesses who defended Lemon. The prosecution case was simply that such a filthy poem was self-evidently blasphemous. The defense mocked the anachronistic charge and claimed that poems could not be treated like lavatorial limericks. In his summing up Judge King-Hamilton asked the jury to ask themselves the following questions: "Do you think that God would like to be recognised in the context of this poem? Did it shock you when you first read it? Would you be proud or ashamed to have written it? Could you read it to an audience of fellow-Christians without blushing?" The jury found against the defendants.

Lemon was fined £500 and jailed for nine months, the imprisonment to be suspended for 18 months. His newspaper was fined £1,000 and faced costs of £20,000. The verdict was upheld in the Appeal Court by a vote of 5-3.

Gay, Jules Gay was one of the two major European publishers of erotica in the mid-19th century. He began publishing in Paris, whence he was hounded by the authorities, and moved first to Brussels and later to Geneva, Turin, Nice and San Remo, finally settling back in Brussels in the mid-1870s. He teamed up with a variety of printers, notably Mertens of Brussels. Like many of his peers Gay was occasionally prosecuted, losing his stock and paying fines to the courts. When in 1863, in Paris, he sufferd such a forfeiture, he celebrated the entire episode in an exquisitely produced volume entitled *Proces des raretes bibliographiques* (1875). This was limited to 100 copies, some 50 of which were subsequently seized and burnt by the Italian police. While in Turin he founded the euphemistically named "Societe des bibliophiles cosmopilites," whose only members were Gay and his son Jean, and which provided a front for the publication of a number of erotic works, notably a series called "La Bibliotheque libre," which was composed of reprints of obscene pamphlets originating in the French Revolution.

Gay published many erotic works, often reprinting the erotic classics of earlier centuries and personally embellishing them with scholarly, if anonymous or pseudonymous, introductions. Among his publications were *Caquire* by "M. de Vessaire," a scatalogical satire on Voltaire's *Zaire*, originally published ca. 1780 and *Nocrion*, an obscene pastiche of a traditional French tale originally published in the 18th century. Gay was the compiler of one of the first bibliographies of erotic literature, the *Bibliographie des Ouvrages* *relatifs a l' Amour, aux Femmes, au Mariage et des Facetieux, Pantagrueliques, Scatalogiques, Satyriques, etc. par M. Le C. d' I****. Preceding ASHBEE by some years, Gay attempted to collect and comment on the titles and content of as many of such works as possible, in French, English and other languages, both ancient and modern. The original edition of some 150 pages, appeared in 1860. It ran, eventually, to some three revised editions, the last of which, comprising four quarto volumes, took the entries up to 1900. Jean Gay, Jules' son, worked with him for some time, then set up his own, parallel enterprise, which mixed in with the inevitable reprints a number of new works, including in 1876 *Marthe, histoire du' une fille* by Joris-Karl Huysmans (1848-1907), a novel that centered on the life of a prostitute working in a licensed brothel; while not actually pornographic, it proved too lurid for France and had to be published in Brussels.

SEE ALSO *Bibliographie des ouvrages relatifs a l' amour*; Poulet-Massis, Auguste.

Gelling v. Texas (1952)   SEE *Pinky*.

Genet, Jean
Genet (1910-1986) was born the illegitimate son of a prostitute and brought up by the state. He entered his first reformatory at the age of 10 and had an extensive career in the prisons of Europe. He wrote his first and still probably most successful book, *Our Lady of the Flowers*, while serving a sentence in Fresnes prison in France, using sheets of brown paper for his manuscript. The novel is a paean to homosexuality, crime and betrayal and as such was deemed too strong for English publication until 1964. Further novels included *Miracle of the Rose* (1965). Genet wrote four plays, *Les Bonnes* (1947, *The Maids*), *Le Balcon* (1958, *The Balcony*), *Les Negres* (1960, *The Blacks*) and *Les Paravents* (1963, *The Screens*). He directed one film, UN CHANT D'AMOUR (1950, *A Song of Love*). All of these works suffered censorship problems. In his essay, "Saint-Genet, actor and martyr" (1953), Sartre claimed that the writer was an existentialist rebel who, having failed to achieve absolute evil in his life, managed it in art. The success of his works reflected the increased tolerance that Genet, predicating his art on society's revulsion, deplored.

Gent v. Arkansas   SEE *Redrup* v. *New York*.

Georgia
1. obscenity statute   Under sections 26-2101, 2105, and 2011 of the Georgia Penal Code:

> A person commits the offense of distributing obscene materials when he ... exhibits or otherwise disseminates to any person any obscene material of any description, knowing the obscene nature thereof ... Material is obscene if considered as a whole, applying community standards, its predominant appeal is to prurient interest, that is, a shameful or morbid interest in nudity, sex or excretion, and utterly without redeeming social value and if, in addition, it goes

substantially beyond customary limits of candor in describing or representing such matters. It is a crime to exhibit a motion picture portraying acts which would constitute public indecency if performed in a public place.

Public indecency is defined as, "(a) an act of sexual intercourse, (b) a lewd exposure of the sexual organs, (c) a lewd appearance in a state of partial or complete nudity, (d) a lewd caress or indecent fondling of another person." Any such indecency is a misdemeanor.

2. possession of obscene material   Under section 26-6301 of the Georgia Penal Code, "Any person who shall knowingly bring or cause to be brought into this State for sale or exhibition, or who shall knowingly sell or offer to sell, or who shall knowingly lend or give away or offer to lend or give away, or who shall knowingly have possession of ... any obscene matter shall be guilty of a felony, and, upon conviction thereof, shall be punished by confinement ... for not less than one year and not more than five years."

SEE ALSO *Stanley* v. *Georgia*.

German Democratic Republic
1. literary censorship   The history of literary creation in the GDR since 1945 has run in parallel to that of state policy as a whole. However, while this state policy initially ran parallel to the situation in the Soviet Union, the emergence of liberal GLASNOST policies in Moscow has not been echoed in East Germany. In censorship, as in all other areas of society, the government persists in its traditional methods, irrespective of promptings from both its own population and the new Soviet ideology.

At the First Writers' Congress in October 1947 the Soviet concept of SOCIALIST REALISM was introduced as the basis of all future artistic efforts. The importance of the relationship of East Germany to the Soviet Union was stressed. There was little resistance among German artists and writers to this imported version of ZHDANOVISM.

At the Second Writers' Congress (November 1950) the committment to the Soviet parent was further emphasized. The minister for people's education stated, "We don't want to impose compulsion on artistic work, nor to prohibit or anything like that ... But it will, and I would like to stress this as strongly as possible, be quite noticeable for some people in the near future that, instead of the former feudal and capitalist commissioners, new commissioners have stepped in." It was also claimed that since traditional German prose had been "short of works describing society," the guidelines for creating such material must be imported from the U.S.S.R. Writers in the GDR suffered a variety of forms of censorship. The Central Committee secretariats and the State Commission for Censorship exercised the official forms including simply the refusal of permission to publish, but in addition to these were public denunciation, pressure on individual writers to accept the party line, and particularly the authorities "persuading" errant writers to rewrite their books on the correct lines. In 1951 the State Commission for Art Affairs was established, with the task of assessing and criticizing various artists and writers. Simultaneously the First Cultural Struggle was instituted, at this stage devoted to censuring various artists accused of "formalism."

At the Third Writers' Congress (March 1952) the power of the Soviet line was stressed once more. East German writers were suitably impressed and if anything held closer to the party line than their Soviet cousins. The authorities were in fact less coercive—the still-open border with the West meant that it was important not to alienate too many creative people—but the writers, still enthusiastic revolutionaries, seemed to prefer state directives to artistic autonomy. This acquiescence was epitomized by the response, or lack of it, to the workers' uprising of June 1953. Even when the Academy of Arts did pass a motion supporting the aims of the uprising, the call was only for the "moderation of administrative interference" and only then because half the membership, led by Bertolt Brecht, had threatened to resign. The result of the motion was that the State Commission was upgraded to a Ministry of Culture. The arts as a whole concentrated on the concept of reconstruction: the celebration of the immediate post-war period, with little reference to more recent history.

The Fourth Writers' Congress (January 1956) reflected the changes in the U.S.S.R. that followed the accession to power of N.S. Khrushchev. A period of liberalism followed the de-Stalinization of the 20th Party Congress in Moscow, but the GDR party resented this, fighting the trend, imprisoning the outspoken and reducing native writers to relative silence. A series of conferences, known as the Second Cultural Struggle, climaxing in that of Bitterfeld (April 1959), attempted to reproduce in East Germany the Chinese Cultural Revolution (SEE China 6). True art was declared to depend on workers writing and writers living among and as workers. The immediate effect of this was the greatest-ever exodus of literary talent from the GDR.

The completion of the Berlin Wall in 1961 encouraged writers to feel that this added security would allow the state to grant them greater latitude. This hope lasted only briefly; Bitterfeld-style standards were reaffirmed at the Writers' Congress of January 1963, self-criticism was demanded of many artists and some lost their posts within the artistic establishment. To minimize this confrontation the polit-bureau established a Cultural Commission. In 1965 Stefan Heym, a leading author, published abroad a manifesto, "The Boredom of Minsk," which propsed four principles: (1) the party has no monopoly on the truth; (2) there is an imminent conflict between writers and authorities brewing; (3) taboos must be disregarded; (4) hardship must be accepted in pursuit of points 1 to 3. Such outspokenness was impermissible. The state response was to launch the Third Cultural Struggle, but now the series of conferences had no effect on the writers who largely ignored the debates and who tended to vanish into introspection, writing only historical plays, poetry and autobiography. Revolutionary enthusiasm vanished and more

leading authors left the country; those who remained have become victims either of suppression or self-censorship.

2. censorship The state constitution (article 27.1) guarantees freedom of expression, of the press, radio and television. This freedom is modified under the official commentary on the constitution (1969), which confers on each citizen the "Constitutional duty to oppose … the spreading of anti-socialist ideology which is practiced in the name of 'freedom' or 'democracy' or 'humanity.'" Six articles in the Criminal Code of the GDR help implement the controls of real freedom of expression. Three deal with crimes against the GDR, and three with crimes against the state and social order. Those who collect and send information to foreign organizations detrimental to the GDR face imprisonment; so too will those who discredit the GDR and its alliances or who citicize the socialist way of life; anyone who seeks help from a foreign organizaiton in leaving the country may be jailed. The general proscription of contacts with foreigners is intensifed by declaring large numbers of the population "carriers of state secrets." Such individuals—the military, the police, government workers and those employed in cultural and scientific areas—are forbidden to contact any foreigner.

Germany

1. book censorship (1521-1555) The bans and edicts of the Roman Catholic Church concerning the printing and distribution of books, aimed mainly at Protestant and allied heresies, were felt throughout Europe, including Germany. The first major ruling of the 16th century came at the Diet of Worms on May 8, 1521, when an edict of Emperor Charles V comprehensively banned the writings of "that stubborn heretic MARTIN LUTHER" as well as institutionalizing the church's current prohibitions on heresy of all varieties. In 1523 the Imperial Diet of Nuremberg ordered that no new writings were to be printed or distributed until they had been examined and approved by trustworthy men. This edict also forbade the selling and printing of libelous books (*libelli famosi*), thus bringing books devoid of religious content into the censorship system. In 1530 the Diet of Augsburg was ordered by the Pope to take stringent measures to enforce the Edict of Worms, since Lutheran heretics were persisting in publishing their theories. The Pope demanded imperial regulations that would ensure the destruction of all such material and the punishment of anyone who refused to give up their copies, as well as the promise of rewards for informers against alleged herctics. The Diet rejected such extremes however, merely renewing the regulations for the examination of books and for the licensing of those that were approved.

In 1550 a provincial Synod at Cologne issued an edict for the protection of "simple and unlearned pastors who are not competent to distinguish pernicious literature from sound teaching." In effect this meant the banning under penalty of the anathaema (excommunication and thus damnation) of the works of Luther, Bucer, Calvin, Oecolampadius, Bullinger, Lambert, Melanchthon, Corvinus, Sarcerius, Brentius and a dozen more heretical authors. The edict further promised the publication of a list of all banned publications, but this failed to materialize. However, this first brief list of 1550 is generally seen as the earliest Index to be compiled in Germany, its successor appearing in Munich in 1582. In 1555 the Augsburger Pact provided that the penalties specified by papal regulations were only to be enforced in those territories classified as Catholic and in 1570 the Diet of Speyer stated that printing offices were to be licensed only to the imperial cities, court cities and university towns and that each printer must be placed under oath to uphold the imperial regulations.

2. Carlsbad Decrees (1819) These repressive decrees, which ushered in an era of suspicion, secret police and military repression in Germany and Austria, were created by the Austrian Chancellor Metternich in 1816. They represented a central part of his system, whereby, in common with many other European authorities, he attempted in the wake of the Napoleonic Wars to suppress all forms of unrest and reestablish order in Europe. The decrees also showed that the authorities in the Austrian Empire had no intention of tolerating the emergent aspirations of German nationalism.

The formation in 1815 of Burschenschaften (students' unions) in the universities of Germany, was a response to national and constitutional feelings created by the Wars of Liberation. The aim of these unions was to create one nationwide organization, as opposed to the existing multiplicity of unions, which divided students according to the state from which they came. In 1817, to celebrate both the 300th anniversary of the Protestant Reformation and the battle of Leipzig, fought against Napoleon in 1813, a festival of the new unions was held at the Wartburg. The festival unified student opinion and proclaimed the depth and intensity of German nationalism and the desire for a unifying constitution. The result of the festival, at which a number of articles symbolizing militarism, as well as some reactionary books, were burnt, was to alert the authorities to the student unrest. In 1819 an activist student, Carl Sand, assassinated the author Kotzebue on account of his reactionary position. In August 1819 10 regional governments met at Carlsbad and issued three decrees, which were accepted by the Diet as law in September 1820. They dealt with the universities, the establishment of a central commission of investigation and with the press.

The main articles of the Press Law, which called for censorship to be carried out in concert by the authorities in all German states, specified, among other things, that: (1) no daily paper or pamphlet of less than 20 sheets shall be issued from the press without the previous consent of the public authority. (2) Each government of the confederation is accountable for the writings published under its jurisdiction; and when these writings offend against the dignity or safety of another state of the confederation, or make attacks upon its constitution or administration, the government that tolerates them is responsible not only to the state that suffers directly therefrom, but also to the whole confederation. (3) All the members of the confederation must enter into a solemn engagement to devote their most serious attention to the superintendence prescribed by the decree and exercise it in such a manner as to prevent as much as possible all reciprocal complaints and discussions. (4) The Diet will proceed also, without a previous denunciation, and of its own authority, against every publication, in whatever state of Germany it may be published, which, in the opinion of a commission appointed to consider thereof, may have compromised the dignity of the Germanic Confederation, the safety of any of its members, or the internal peace of Germany—with no recourse being afforded against the judgment given in such a case, the judgment to be executed by the government that is responsible for the condemned publication. (5) The editor of a publication that may be suppressed by command of the Diet shall not be allowed, during the space of five years, to conduct any similar publication in any state of the confederation.

3. Nazi art censorship Total control of the arts was maintained through the Reich Chamber of Culture, under the direction of Josef Goebbels' Ministry of Propaganda and Popular Enlightenment. Any artist who wished to work under the regime was forced to join the Art Chamber, separate divisions of which were established to deal with every aspect of creative and commercial activity, and which maintained a strict ban on "racially inferior" or "politically unsound" artists, i.e., Jews and Communists. Banned artists were prohibited from working, either for profit or for personal pleasure. The bans were upheld by Gestapo searches, when officials would check that an individual's brushes were dry and paints unused. Goebbels made clear his own stance: "Art for art's sake" was anathema, and "only that art which draws its inspiration from the body of the people can be good art in the last analysis and mean something to the people for whom it has been created. There must be no art in the absolute sense, such as liberal democracy acknowledges." The Nazi director of the Folkwang Museum in Essen delineated the perfect artifact of the totalitarian state: "The most perfect object created in the course of the last epochs did not originate in the studios of our artists. It is the steel helmet."

Degenerate, "cosmopolitan" (Jewish) or Bolshevik art was removed from the galleries and museums, ostensibly to destruction, but often merely into the burgeoning private collections of the Nazi leaders. Among those artists banned were Fritz Winter, Ewald Matare, Arnold Zadikow, Hans Uhlmann, Ernst Barlach, GEORGE GROSZ, Paul Klee and Emil Nolde. In a speech at Nuremburg in 1935 the Führer himself excoriated modern artists: "One will no longer discuss or deal with these corrupters of art. They are fools, liars or criminals who belong in insane asylums or prisons." On November 27, 1936, Goebbels announced the official prohibition of all art criticism in Germany. Henceforth all comments must be purely descriptive and governed by party doctrine. On March 15, 1937, criticism was permitted again, on a simple basis: What fits Nazi doctrine would be acceptable, anything else would not. Critics had to be at least 30 years old and it was stated baldly that aesthetic judgment was irrelevant since "the press policy of the National Socialist State is merely an extension of its political policy into the realm of public opinion." On July 7, 1937, Hitler opened the Haus der Deutschen Kunst (House of German Art) with an exhibiton of 850 pure works. Most of the subjects were rigorously banal, focusing on Nazi themes of race heroes, simple peasants, family scenes, tedious landscapes and female nudes, echoing Hitler's declaration that "Germany forbids any work of art which does not render an object faithfully." Many were the work of Dr. Adolf Ziegler, president of the Reich Chamber of Art, nicknamed by his many critics as "The Master of Pubic Hair," so detailed were his studies of the Aryan nude. On July 18, as a deliberate counterpoint to the "pure" exhibition, there opened the exhibition of Entartete Kunst (degenerate art). This was based on some 16,000 works of art by nearly 1,400 artists, which had been assembled under special decree by Ziegler and was intended to reveal the true horrors of "Kultur-Bolschevismus" and "Jewish-Democratic" art to the German people. This show of degenerate and decadent (*Verfallszeit*) art offered a superb display of modern European art, including works by Dix, Gauguin, Van Gogh, Kandinsky, Klee, Kokoschka, Nolde, Braque, Chagall, Munch, Picasso and Grosz. Although Hitler condemned all these "products of morbid and perverted minds," viewers of the degenerate outnumbered those of the ideologically pure by three to one.

In August 1937 the German museums were purged of their remaining modern pictures, and thousands more paintings were taken from their walls. In June 1938 the confiscation, without compensation, of all "degenerate art … accessible to the public and owned by German citizens" was ordered by the Führer. As Germany's Jews were deported to the concentration camps, their empty homes were pillaged by Gestapo officials, claiming to those few citizens who commented that they were "preserving works of art for the Reich." Special pawnshops were set up at which rich Jews might sell, at grotesquely low prices, their heirlooms, art objects and similar possessions. Similar tactics were expanded as Nazism moved out from Germany into Austria, Czechoslovakia and beyond. In June 1939, 125 confiscated artworks were put up for auction in Lucerne, Switzerland. Despite the quality of the paintings they achieved only half of their estimated value, a total of 600,000 francs ($135,150). The remaining thousands were burnt by the Berlin Fire Brigade in July.

4. Nazi press controls (1933-45) The German press in 1933, at the advent of the Third Reich, was prolific, diversified and culturally broadminded. It embraced the extremes of political thought, from the right-wing Nazi sheets to the left-wing organs of the SPD and KPD (the German Socialist and Communist Parties). It sustained many Catholic publications and a large group of *Generalanzeiger* (non-partisan, independent papers). Despite statements to the contrary, it

was not a particularly Jewish phenomenon, although Ullstein, the largest publisher in Germany, was a Jewish firm.

To the Nazis the press represented just one more aspect of the nation that was due for reorganization and reorientation. The press, as Hitler pointed out in *Mein Kampf*, had a great effect on mass opinion and as such was to be strictly controlled. Such concepts as press freedom were "corrosive" of the state, which "therefore must proceed with ruthless determination and take control of this instrument of popular education and put it in the service of the state and nation."

The initial treatment of the press was part of the overall *Gleichschaltung* (coordination), the "national reconstruction" that took the form of the coordination and centralization under the Nazi banner of all German organizations and institutions. This was generally effected by purging the leadership of such organizations of their former personnel and replacing them with the Nazi faithful. The reaction of the Verein Deutscher Zeitungsverleger (VDZV, the Society of German Newspaper Publishers) was to compromise. Hitler appeared initially to welcome such an approach. While the communist (KPD) and socialist (SPD) press were to be eradicated, the independent *burgerliche* (middle-class) papers would be safe, although they, in common with every cultural institution, must demonstrate their loyalty to the regime. Thus, when the Marxist/Socialist press, some 150 papers, was summarily shut down, the VDZV made no comment, offering only a statement deploring the "atrocious propaganda" appearing in the foreign press, and stressing their own solidarity with the party. Goebbels, the Reich minister of propaganda, who had formerly denounced the "downright mistaken orientation of the German press," praised this contribution to "national discipline."

The VDZV capitulated further in June 1933 when seven of its directors, the least popular with the regime, voluntarily resigned and were replaced by Nazi appointees. Max Amann, Reich press leader and business manager of both the NSDAP and the party newspaper, the *Volkischer Beobachter*, was made chairman and infiltrated his puppet, Rolf Reinhardt, as the chairman's personal representative, a position with disproportionate powers of control and access. The professional associations of journalists and editors were similarly co-opted, with Otto Dietrich, a hard-line opponent of all non-party publications, as head of the Reichsverband der Deutschen Presse (Reich Association of the German Press). Like so many German organizations, remodelled on Nazi lines, the RVDP remained ostensibly autonomous, but in reality became a party cypher, administering rules imposed from above, such as the automatic exclusion from the profession of all Jews and Marxists (1,300 of whom were purged by 1935) and the screening of all journalists for racial and political reliability. Under the direct control of the Ministry of Propaganda, which appointed its president and could veto the enrollment (and thus employment) of any journalist, the RVDP helped ensure that the press, as Hitler desired, was rendered no more than a state mouthpiece.

On October 4, 1933, Goebbels had enacted the *Schrift-leitergesetz* (editor's law), one of a number of laws designed to establish the power and status of the Propaganda Ministry, which was accruing to itself the total control of all German media and culture. The law was aimed mainly at working journalists—the *Schriftleiter*—but also involved owners and publishers. It was a mixture of the proposed but rejected "Journalists' Law" of 1924—which had emphasized the publishers' right to publish what they wanted and the editors' obligation to work in the public interest—and the compulsory organization of newspaper personnel pioneered by Mussolini in Fascist Italy. The Ministry of Propaganda had the absolute right to arbitrate over those who might work as journalists and could set down the educational, racial and professional qualifications necessary for acceptance. A code of professional duties and ethics was established and the journalists' legal status itemized. Overriding every consideration was the demand that journalists "regulate their work in accordance with National Socialism as a philosophy of life and as a conception of government." The chief editor on a paper was responsible for the content of that paper, and any attempt by its publisher to influence that content was a crime, punishable by a fine, imprisonment or loss of the license to publish. An editor was defined as a public educator, who thus owed allegiance only to Adolf Hitler and the Nazi Party. The role of an owner or publisher was extensively diminished, reflecting both the pragmatic needs of the party and its political promises to downgrade the nation's "corrupt capitalists."

The press was further disciplined by the operations of the Reichspressekammer (RPK, Reich Press Chamber), itself subordinate to the Reichkulturkammer (RKK, Reich Chamber of Culture), which was established in September 1933 with responsibility for literature, radio, film, theater, music, fine arts and the press, all under the aegis of the Ministry of Propaganda, which operated as ever by taking over existing organizations and suborning them to the needs of the Nazi party. Max Amann was president of the RPK, with Otto Dietrich as vice president. While the RPK itself was small, working essentially as an administrative body, it controlled both the management and employees of the press in their respective organizations, the VDZV and RVDP, as well as the *Fachverbande*, a number of trade and professional groups that dealt with the production, sale and distribution of printed materials.

Under its implementing ordinances, the president of the RPK had various dictatorial powers, including enforcing compulsory membership on anyone involved in the press (paragraph 4); excluding anyone judged to be unfit for the profession (paragraph 10); establishing regulations governing the opening and closing down of any press-related enterprise (paragraph 25); prohibiting those thus closed down from claiming for damages on grounds of expropriation. The VDZV was renamed the Reichverband der Deutscher Zeitungsverleger (RVDZV) in 1934 and dedicated to purging the press of all undesirable elements—both by screening individuals and checking the editorial content of every paper regarding certain key issues—and establishing uniformity and centralized direction. Everything was to work according to party ideology. By 1936 the purges were complete, with the disqualification of some 1,473 publishers and certificates of reliability issued to the rest.

While its ideological purity was in no doubt, the Nazi press was a vast and unwieldy mix of small papers, mainly controlled by the local Gauleiter, and was in 1933 a generally uneconomic proposition. By a decree of January 31, 1934, this "trumpet press," as Hitler called it, was centralized under the control of Amann and its administration brought under the Standarte GmbH, a subsidiary of the Eher Verlag, the long-established party press. The party press was revitalized with new training plans, increased advertising (often by threatening companies who persisted in placing their advertisements in papers that also accepted the promotions of Jewish firms) and similar encouragement. Many Gauleiters made a subscription to their local paper compulsory. Only the content of the papers, which in common with all the Nazified press became increasingly stultified, failed to improve, and readership, for all the national and local campaigns designed to boost it, continued to fall.

The culminating example of control over the German press came in the passing in April 1935 of the Amann Ordinances, three measures that completed the muzzling and redirection of the nation's press. Using as his justification the implementing decrees of the Reichpressekammer and a lengthy memorandum prepared by Reinhardt, replete with complex legal and economic justifications, Amann achieved behind a masquerade of legitimacy the same destruction of the bourgeois press as had, with open force, been rendered against the left-wing newspapers. The ordinances were as follows: (1) withdrawal of publishing rights from any publisher who by sensationalism, by offenses against public taste or morals, brought the publishing industry and the honor of the press into disrepute; (2) the power to close down any paper in an area where, due to an excess of competitors, it was rendered economically unsound; the RVDZ would indicate such areas and the Cura (the party's department of management specialists) would decide on which papers should go; (3) all papers were to make full disclosure of their ownership since 1800, all of which had to show true Aryan descent; any private enterprise capital investment or subsidies had to be revealed and would in future require the approval of the RPK, a move intended to suppress private involvement in the press. As Amann put it, "Moneybags shouldn't be allowed to make public opinion." And (4) the exclusion of "confessional, vocational or special interest groups." This was aimed at the large Catholic press and such Jewish publications as were still defying the anti-Semitic regulations.

Using the ordinances Amann succeeded in the desired "cleansing and reform" of the German press and achieved his four basic aims: (1) the exclusion from publishing of all non-Aryans and other minority interest groups, whether based on economics, class or religion, as well as all servants and employees of such groups; (2) the elimination of private enterprise that might work contrary to Nazi wishes; (3) the promotion of the educational role of the press on ideologically pure lines; and (4) the enforcement of the principle of a publisher's responsibility (in the face of severe penalties) for the content of his paper. The owners were stunned by the scope and the harshness of the ordinances, but they capitulated and by September 1936 the Nazi *Verlagspolitik* (press policy) was absolutely in place and Amann could state, "We have freed the newspapers from all ties and personalities that hindered or might hinder the accomplishment of their National-Socialist tasks."

Around 600 papers had been closed down, merged or taken over by the Eher Verlag. The sectarian, provincial and independent press had vanished in what constituted the largest single confiscation of private property under the Third Reich. The survivors, those papers considered officially pure, were dull and uniform and were often rejected by their former readers. Few writers of quality chose to become journalists and circulations declined. Not only was criticism of the regime within the press taboo, but under Goebbels' instructions, so too was any criticism of the press itself. As the German armies expanded Nazi rule throughout Europe, so did the Amann Ordinances dictate the status of the conquered newspapers. At the peak of German successes, the Europa Verlag, the company responsible for publishing in the occupied territories, ran some 30 titles, circulating one million copies a day. As fortunes declined, these papers were discarded and gradually, as paper shortages hit Germany, the homegrown press was similarly trimmed and the papers ceased to provide even censored information, churning out only the desperate propaganda of a dying regime.

Germany—Federal Republic

1. broadcasting controls   Radio and television in Germany is in the hands of broadcasting corporations—nine regional stations, controlled by the individual states, two federal stations and one controlled mutually by the federal government and by the regions or "Lander"—which are governed by public law. Despite their responsibility to the law, all these stations are independent from the federal and regional government. They are funded and administered separately from the state governments. The relationship is purely legal and never aesthetic. The state or federal government has no right of censorship, other than to carry out the various broadcasting laws.

All stations are managed and supervised by various bodies. The Broadcasting Board represents members of the general public. Depending on the board in question, the members are chosen by the elected parliaments of the various regions or by a number of public organizations—employers, writers' associations, churches, other media etc. The board controls a station's budget and must approve each year's proposed expenditure in advance. The board is usually

responsible for the appointment of two of the other public bodies: the Board of Administration and the director-general. It ensures that the station complies with the relevant broadcasting law.

The Board of Administration comprises from seven to nine members, all or most of whom are chosen by the Broadcasting Board. This board is designed to oversee the purely business administration of a broadcasting corporation. All major contracts (e.g., in excess of 30,000DM) must be approved by this board. The Program Commission is a 20-member body exclusive to WDR (West-Deutsche Rundfunk of Cologne), Germany's largest broadcasting corporation. Drawn from a variety of socially relevant institutions, its task is to advise the director-general on all matters relating to programming. The director-general is appointed to be the individual personally responsible for the running of the corporation within the structure laid down by the Broadcasting Board of Administration. He represents the corporation in public and, if necessary, in court. His term of office is usually five years.

Like the German press, German broadcasting is based in the legal justification of freedom of communication laid down in article 5 of the basic law (the federal constitution of 1949), which states: "(1) Everyone has the right freely to express and propagate his or her opinions in words, writing or images and to inform himself or herself without hindrance from generally accessible sources. Press freedom and freedom of reporting by means of broadcasting and films are guaranteed. Censorship shall not take place. (2) These rights are limited only by the regulations of general law, legal regulations on the protection of juveniles and the rights of personal honor." The various corporations all have their own constitutional basis, the majority of which acts have been amended within the last decade. The corporations promise to bind themselves to democracy, a sense of cultural responsibility, humanity and objectivity and to adhere to the basic right and commitments of the federal constitution. Any "programs causing prejudices against groups of persons or individuals because of their race, ethnic origin, religion or ideology ... as well as such programs which injure religions or moral feelings shall be forbidden in particular."

2. film censorship   All films are subject to a board of censorship, the Freiwillige Selbstkontrolle (voluntary self-regulation) der Filmwirtschaft (FSK), which was established by the German film industry. In addition to the FSK is the Juristenkommission (JK), which exists to provide technical legal advice about films or scenes within them. Filmmakers have the choice of either of the two bodies when submitting their work for full censorship or simply legal approval. Once the FSK or JK has issued a certificate, the film is exempt from any prosecution. No film exhibited in Germany may: (1) offend moral or religious feelings or human dignity, nor may it disseminate moral depravity or undermine the position, guaranteed under the constitution, to the lawful family, nor may it depict violence or pornography; (2) undermine the concepts of liberal democracy and advocate racist or totalitarian doctrines; (3) encourage breaches of the peace, jeopardize Germany's relations with other nations or advocate militarism, imperialism or glorify war. Government grants to filmmakers may be withheld when material offends religious beliefs, undermines morality or the law and constitution. Films exploiting sex and/or violence will not be given state aid.

3. obscenity laws   Under the federal constitution the republic guarantees freedom of expression and prohibits state censorship. The concept of pornography is not defined under German law, and since 1973 previous laws covering obscene material have been drastically liberalized. The current test for pornography, as set down by the Select Committee of the Federal Assembly on Criminal Law Reform, covers depictions that either expressly demonstrate that they are exclusively or predominantly aimed at the arousal of sexual excitement in the reader or that clearly go beyond society's generally accepted standards of the boundaries of sexual decency. Like most countries that offer to adults the responsibility of reading what they like, the FDR seeks to protect children and those who do not wish to have obscene material thrust upon them. No sadistic material, child pornography or bestiality is allowed. Those who break such prohibitions face a year's imprisonment or a fine. Pictures that glorify violence are similarly prohibited. No other forms of pornography are banned to adults, but restrictions, administered by the Office for the Control of Publications Harmful to Youth, keep such material from those under 18 and also prohibit the unsolicited mailing of possibly offensive publications and pictures. The courts permit no defense of literary or artistic merit. Given the narrow definitions of what must constitute actionable pornography, this does not matter—nothing with such merits would ever appear in court.

4. press control   In 1945 the occupying Allied forces established a new order of German media, replacing the discredited organs of the Nazi era. Some 150 titles were licensed and from the early 1950s the pre-war publishers rejoined the marketplace, and soon some 570 titles—national and local, general and specialized, magazines and newspapers—were available. The main control over the German press is article 5 of the Basic Law (the Federal Constitution of 1949), which states:

> (1) Everyone has the right freely to express and propagate his or her opinions in words, writing or images and to inform himself or herself without hindrance from generally accessible sources. Press freedom and freedom of reporting by means of broadcasting and films are guaranteed. Censorship shall not take place. (2) These rights are limited only by the regulations of general law, legal regulations on the protection of juveniles and the rights of personal honor.

The Basic Law is administered by the Federal Constitutional Court, which guarantees the freedom of the press and ensures its "institutional independence ... from the procurement of information to the dissemination of news and com-

ment." The court also attempts, by regulating mergers and closures, even if it succeeds only partially, in using the Cartels Act to prevent the development of the media monopolies common to most Western countries.

Press freedom is further guaranteed in the regional laws of the eleven *Lander* into which the country is divided. The current *Land* laws all developed in the 1960s and extend beyond basic freedoms to regulating the way in which newspapers and magazines actually function. Such regional laws have only minor variations as to area and deal in such areas as the compulsory masthead, specifying those legally responsible for the publication, the right of reply, a journalist's right to protect his or her sources, the distribution of free copies, the listing of those with financial interests in the paper and so on.

The press is also subject to the criminal law. Under the political criminal law this covers the suppression of treasonable material, incitement to a war of aggression and the betrayal of state secrets to another country. Under paragraph 131, anyone who disseminates literature that recounts violence against persons in a lurid or other inhuman manner, thus expressing glorification or minimization of such acts of violence or incites to racial hatred, is liable to prosecution. Journalists are forbidden to publish "malicious defamation"; they are not obliged to back up every statement that appears, but in the case of a complaint must do so. The belief that the defamatory material was true is no defense. Libellous insult or straightforward libel are punished more severely and malicious defamation and libel against those in political life more so again. Those who feel they have been maligned are also entitled to the statutory right of reply.

As of 1973, the German Press ostensibly adheres to a 16-point press code, known as the "Publicistic Principles" and administered by the German Press Council, whose 20 members are drawn from organizations of publishers, journalists and print workers and which was founded, on a British model, in 1956. The Press Council issued a number of further guidelines in September 1981. This comprehensive list, running in all to 37 points, deals with the journalistic commitment to thoroughness, the duty to rectify, the legitimacy of research, readers' letters, invitations and presents offered to journalists, employment contracts, embargoes, the publication of stories on minors and the release of prisoners etc. However, this code had the unintended effect of turning the council into a complaints department in which its various interest groups constantly bickered and deadlocked over every issue, and attempts are currently underway to restructure the council on more positive lines.

Ghana   Ghana's information media, as well as its film industry, have been essentially well kept under state control since national independence in 1957. Today, the bureaucracy of such censorship is centered on the Secretariat of Information. This body appoints and dismisses the editors of government newspapers—in effect, every large-circulation paper other than a few devoted to sport—and all other senior media figures; it holds regular meetings with all media heads and supervises the training of journalists and filmmakers. The current military government, established in 1981, has made no special laws to govern the media, but in 1982 it abolished the Press Commission, a body established by the relatively liberal government of Dr. Hilla Limann (1979-81) and designed to place some limits on government influence on the media. The Castle Information Bureau, an unofficial but potent body, ostensibly the press unit of the Office of the Head of State, has recently been added to the machinery of press control, issuing regular instructions as to what may or may not be published.

As elsewhere in Africa, censorship can be exerted by regulating the supply of newsprint, by restricting advertising and by forcing newspaper proprietors to pay heavily for the registration of their paper. In addition the government controls the supply of all newspaper equipment, including typewriters—a further means of regulating their content. Since January 1982 it has been forbidden to report any activity by a political opposition, including the views of such (quite legal) bodies as the Ghana Bar Association or the Trades Union Congress. Such stringency means that the government line may be promoted without apparent argument. Laws covering sedition make it an offense to report anything that brings the government into disrepute or contempt or causes dissaffection. In addition the Ghanaian media exercise their own self-censorship. Arrests and detentions are never mentioned, neither are anti-government demonstrations, and while no formal censorship laws exist, such careful screening of anything that might get its writer in trouble ensures a safe press. Investigative journalism hardly exists, and those reporters who are determined to move outside the official communiques must do so at their own expense. Journalists, many of whom have chosen to resign, are also liable to detention without trial under the government's Law 4, dealing with preventive custody.

Gillray, James   SEE *The Presentation.*

Ginsberg v. *New York* (1968)   This case concerned Sam Ginsberg, operator of a stationery store and luncheonette in New York, who sold to a 16-year-old boy a soft-core pin-up magazine and was duly charged, tried and convicted for violation of section 484-h of the New York Penal Code, which covers the exposure of minors to harmful materials. (In New York a minor was defined as a person under the age of 17.) The Supreme Court upheld the conviction, stating that, while the magazine was not obscene and could be sold without fear of prosecution to adults, the supposed inability of a minor to make a mature judgment as to the nature of such a magazine meant that the restrictions on its purchase by a minor were that much more stringent. They used the term "variable obscenity" to illustrate that what might be acceptable for an adult was obscene for a minor. The court stated

that New York's statute did not infringe constitutional freedoms of expression since that freedom presupposed a "full capacity of individual choice" which a minor was presumed not to possess. The court pointed out that it was on this concept of full capacity or its lack, that other laws prohibited minors from voting, buying liquor and so on. In his dissenting opinion, Judge Fortas agreed that minors should not be permitted to buy such magazines, but felt that the idea of variable obscenity was too vague to provide justification for a conviction.

Ginzburg v. *United States*   Ralph Ginzburg was publisher of the magazine, *Eros*, a biweekly newsletter, *Liaison*, and a book titled *The Housewife's Handbook on Selective Promiscuity*, which claimed to be the sexual autobiography of Mrs. Lillian Maxine Serett. In late 1962 there was published in the magazine's fourth issue, which had been mailed out to its usual subscribers, a photoset entitled "Black and White in Color." The 16 pictures were of a black man and a white woman. None showed the genitals, but from the positions assumed, it was obvious that they were meant to be lovers. The blurb alongside them called the pictures "a photographic poem" and extolled interracial sex. Attorney-General Robert Kennedy, who had wished to prosecute *Eros* already, claimed that such pictures would exacerbate racial problems in the South. Ginzburg was charged under Title 18, USC, section 1461, with sending obscenity through the mail.

The trial was arranged for June 1963 in the ultra-conservative city of Philadelphia, where a local journal remarked, "Ralph Ginzburg has about the same chance of finding justice ... as a Jew ... in Nazi Germany." The magazine, stated the judge, "has not the slightest redeeming social, artistic or literary importance or value." *Liaison*, with such features as "Semen in the Diet" and "Sing a Song of Sex Life," was described as "entirely without literary merit" and the *Handbook* as "a patent offense to the most liberal morality ... a gross shock to the mind ... pruriency and disgust coalesce here creating a perfect example of hardcore pornography." More pertinent to the charge was Ginzburg's palpable misuse of the mails. After post offices in the towns of Intercourse and Blue Ball, Pennsylvania, had refused to handle his mailout, Ginzburg had persuaded authorities in Middlesex, New Jersey, to distribute under their postmark millions of circulars, sent to a completely indiscriminate list of prospective customers. It was from recipients of these circulars that witnesses against *Eros* were found. Ginzburg was found guilty, sentenced to five years in jail and fined $42,000.

In his appeal before the Supreme Court in December 1965 Ginzburg claimed again that his magazine was not offensive and did have some social value. The court took five months to consider, and in February 1966 declared that the matter of possible obscenity was irrelevant; what counted was the misuse of the mails—not to mention full-page advertisements in which Ginzburg claimed that *Eros* was the result of decisions by the Court itself. Ginzburg was deliberately pandering to the customer's erotic sensibilities, and the sentence and the fine were upheld. Several justices filed dissenting opinions, one objecting to the condemnation of a magazine on the basis of "sexy advertisements," given that sex was used for promotion in "our best magazines"; another compared the concept of being utterly without redeeming social value to "the unknown substance of the Milky Way." Although legal maneuvering kept him out of jail for some years, and his sentence was reduced, Ginzburg eventually served three years in Lewisburg Penitentiary, Pennsylvania. SEE ALSO *Goldwater* v. *Ginzburg* (1964).

Girodias, Maurice   Girodias was born in 1919, the son of publisher JACK KAHANE. During the Second World War he took his Catholic mother's maiden name to avoid the roundups of Jews under the occupying Germans. When his father died in 1939 Girodias inherited his OBELISK PRESS, where such once risqué luminaries as JOYCE, HENRY MILLER and Lawrence Durrell had first been published. The press naturally went into eclipse during the Occupation, but Girodias revived it after liberation, capitalizing on the wide-open market provided by the U.S. and British forces, all of whom were delighted to purchase books that their own censors prohibited.

In 1953 Girodias sold the Obelisk Press and its subsidiary, Editions du Chene, and set up its successor, the OLYMPIA PRESS. Here he continued his father's tradition of backing the new and the experimental, however much such work might shock the authorities. Girodias made possible the publication of Nabokov's *Lolita*, Donleavy's *The Ginger Man*, Burroughs' THE NAKED LUNCH, the pseudonymous Pauline Reage's *Story of O* and many other titles. Alongside these came what he called unashamedly the "DBs," dirty books: including *White Thighs*, *With Open Mouth*, and *Whips Incorporated*, many of which were written by otherwise reputable, if young authors, under a variety of pseudonyms.

The Girodias mixture of the avant-garde and the gaily pornographic worked well through the early 1950s. His green-jacketed "Travellers' Library" sent Olympia Press titles around the world. The French authorities remained quiescent—as long as Girodias published only in English and left the French language undefiled. As he told an interviewer: "It was great fun. The Anglo-Saxon world was being attacked, invaded, infiltrated, outflanked and conquered by this erotic armada." This liberal atmosphere ended when Girodias published the memoirs of a resistance leader who alleged that various members of the current government had collaborated with the Germans. On December 10, 1956, the press was raided by police. Twenty-five titles were instantly banned. Only when it transpired that the raid had been instigated by complaints from the British Home Office about the sending of "highly obscene books" through the mail did Girodias find some sympathy. Under a compromise his books could not in the future be exhibited nor advertised, but they could be ordered by post or obtained on demand from the Olympia offices.

With the return to power in 1958 of General de Gaulle, Girodias fell victim to what he called the forces of "priggish virtues." In 1958 he was charged with outraging public morals through his books. The punishment was exemplary, even if much of it was commuted or reduced later: an 80-year ban on all publishing, four to six years in prison and £29,000 in fines. By 1960 Girodias had seen 41 titles banned and had faced 25 separate indictments for obscenity. While he had intended to "beat censorship out of existence," the authorities had defeated him. In 1965 he declared "the secular feast" over, quit France and turned to the U.S., taking advantage of the liberal climate that had followed the ROTH V. UNITED STATES decision, and to the U.K. Neither venture really worked. In America the Grove Press had already cornered the art porn market and in Britain Girodias' refusal to mask his products in hypocrisy ruined their charm for many potential customers. His fortunes were further diminished when in 1968 he published in New York an obscene burlesque of the British anti-pornography campaigner, Sir Cyril Black. Black was awarded $100,000 damages and a public apology. By the early 1970s Girodias' career, and the style that engendered it, were over.

***Gitlow* v. *New York* (1925)**   Benjamin Gitlow was a member of the Communist Party who in 1925 published a "Left Wing Manifesto." This rambling, rhetorical document expounded reasonably traditional Marxist views on the necessity of establishing the dictatorship of the proletariat through the implementation of a communist revolution sustained by the historical class struggle. The manifesto was filled with the stock phrases of Marxist jargon and informed its readers that: "Revolutionary Socialism is alone capable of mobilizing the proletariat for Socialism, for the conquest of the power of the state, by means of revolutionary mass action and proletarian dictatorship ... The old order is in decay. Civilization is in collapse. The proletarian revolution and the Communist reconstruction of society—the struggle for these—is now indispensable ... The Communist International calls the proletariat of the world to its final struggle." Nonetheless Gitlow was charged and convicted under the New York statute against criminal anarchy, whereby it was illegal to preach revolution or publish material pertaining to such preaching.

The U.S. Supreme Court refused to overturn the conviction. Justice Sanford wrote of a "single revolutionary spark that may kindle a fire that, smoldering for a time, may burst into a sweeping and destructive conflagration. It cannot be said that the state is acting arbitrarily or unreasonably when in the exercise of its judgment as to the measures necessary to protect the public peace and safety, it seeks to extinguish the spark without waiting until it has enkindled the flame or glazed into the conflagration." Justice Holmes and Brandeis dissented, claiming that Gitlow's rhetoric failed to qualify as threatening a CLEAR AND PRESENT DANGER. They also pointed out that if the concept of free speech was to have any meaning, such opinions as Gitlow's, whether inflammatory or otherwise, must be heard.

SEE ALSO *Abrams* v. *United States* (1919); *Adler* v. *Board of Education* (1952); *Debs, Eugene*; *Frohwerk* v. *United States* (1919); *Lamont* v. *Postmaster-General* (1965); *Pierce* v. *United States* (1920); *Schaeffer* v. *United States* (1920); *Schenck* v. *United States* (1919); *Sweezy* v. *New Hampshire* (1957); *Whitney* v. *California* (1927); *Yates* v. *United States* (1957).

Glavlit   SEE U.S.S.R. 3. censorship of publications (Glavlit).

God's Little Acre   Erskine Caldwell (1903-1987), born in Georgia, the son of a Presbyterian minister, wrote a number of books, the most famous of which were *Tobacco Road* (1932) and *God's Little Acre* (1933). The plot of the latter concerns the family of Ty Ty Walden, a dirt-poor Georgia farmer, his sons, daughters and in-laws. Walden is barely literate and convinced that somewhere beneath his barren acres lies gold. He and his sons dig feverishly for the gold, while their cotton crop is tended by two black sharecroppers. Ty Ty is a religious man and dedicates a single acre of his land to God, promising that whatever is found under that acre will go to the church. In the event no gold appears; instead the Walden sons, daughters and daughters-in-law, enmeshed in a merry-go-round of sexual infidelities, divert attention from gold-digging. As the book ends one brother kills another and may be assumed to be planning his own suicide. Ty Ty is left, digging vainly on.

Both of Caldwell's major novels were attacked for their alleged obscenity in the way Caldwell told his stories of lust, religion and family entanglements among the poor whites of his native state. The *Tobacco Road* prosecution failed, as did the first attempt to ban *God's Little Acre*, which was instituted in 1933 by JOHN S. SUMNER of the SOCIETY FOR THE SUPPRESSION OF VICE. This prosecution, listed as *People* v. *Viking Press* (1933), was balanced between a range of expert witnesses, all testifying to the book's inherent worth, and Sumner's dismissal of such opinions with the words, "The question arises as to whether a criminal prosecution is to be determined by interested parties having access to the newspapers and no interest in public welfare or by the Courts existing for that purpose and representing the whole people and not only the literati." He suggested that "literati" was another way of saying "abnormal people" and added, "Conditions would be deplorable if abnormal people were permitted to regulate such matters." The court was unimpressed by Sumner, coming down on the side of the experts and deciding that "this group of people ... has a better capacity to judge the value of a literary production than one who is more apt to search for obscene passages in a book than to regard the book as a whole." The magistrate added that he believed

Caldwell to have written what he saw as the truth and that "truth should always be accepted as a justification for literature."

God's Little Acre faced prosecution again in 1950 in Massachusetts. In the case of *Attorney-General* v. *A Book Named God's Little Acre* (1950) the court found that Caldwell's book was indeed "obscene, indecent and impure"; it might indeed have some literary merit, but that failed to justify the author's excesses. Despite this successful piece of censorship, *God's Little Acre* sold in the millions and remains a popular book, undoubtedly helped by the frisson that such attacks have lent it. It remains on the black list of the NATIONAL ORGANIZATION FOR DECENT LITERATURE. *Tobacco Road*, which was adapted into a play, was one of Broadway's longest-running hits, amassing 3,182 performances from its first night in 1932, although it too was banned to audiences in a number of American cities. Both books were made into successful films. Both books were banned in Ireland.

Goldstein, Al (1937-   )   SEE *Screw*.

Goldwater v. Ginzburg   In the 1964 American presidential campaign the Republicans nominated Barry Goldwater, a right-wing senator from Arizona, as their candidate. Immediately prior to the election there appeared in *Fact*, a magazine published by Ralph Ginzburg, a piece entitled "The Unconscious of a Conservative: A Special Issue on the Mind of Barry Goldwater." The piece, similar to that published by the British *Sun* newspaper in an attempt to smear the reputation of the left-wing member of Parliament Tony Benn in 1984, claimed to offer a psychiatric profile of the candidate. It was, inevitably, highly unflattering. Ginzburg had concocted a questionnaire in which he entered certain hearsay assessments of Goldwater's mental state, notably that he had allegedly suffered a nervous breakdown, and circulated this to a number of psychiatrists, asking them for their opinion. When such questionnaires as were filled in were returned to *Fact*, Ginzburg then edited them highly selectively, producing the overtly anti-Goldwater piece that he published. Goldwater sued Ginzburg for DEFAMATION, claiming that the statements in the piece "were published and circulated by the defendants with actual malice, or with reckless disregard of whether such statements were false or not, and with the deliberate, wilful and malicious purpose and intent to injure plaintiff and to deprive plaintiff of his good name and reputation as a person, a public official and a candidate for office, and to bring plaintiff into disrepute and subject him to public scorn, contempt, obloquy and ridicule." The federal district court ruled in favor of the candidate, as did the appeals court; the Supreme Court refused to consider Ginzburg's case. The defamation was proved. Ginzburg had employed malice; whether or not the piece was true was therefore irrelevant.

SEE ALSO *Ginzburg* v. *United States* (1966).

Goodwin, John SEE book burning in England 6. The Restoration.

grand blasphemy   Art criticism based on the standards of absolute Catholic dogma defines grand blasphemy as any variety of modern art that exhibits "private pleasures in shapeless and distorted forms." The charge of blasphemy stems from the fact that nature is not represented in such pictures as a hymn to the glory of God but "as a diabolical creation reproducing man's own depravity."

Greece

1. banned books (1967-74)   During the seven years of their military dictatorship, the Greek Colonels banned a number of works. This list gives a representative selection, divided into Greek and foreign writers:

Greek writers: Most of these are Marxist or at least left-wingers; some—Delmouzous, Glinos, Trikoupis—were dead.

E. Antonopoulos, *Hellenism and Democracy*
Markos Avgeris, *Introduction to Greek Poetry*
Delmouzos, *Education and the Demotic*
D. Glinos, *Nation and Language*
S. Gourgouliatos, *The Tale of Constantine*
Gerasimos Grigoris, *Focus of Resistance*
Sofia Kana (editor), *The Prague Spring*
Nikos Katiforis, *While Darkness Lasts*
Konstantine Koresis, *The Life of George Papandreou*
George Koumandos, *High Education*
D. Liatsos, *Capodistria and Greek Rights*
S. Linardatos, *A Little Political Encyclopedia*
D. Maronitis, *The Fear of Freedom*
V. Rafaildis, *Lessons in Cinematography*
G. Rallis, *The Truth about Greek Politicians*
G. Skliros, *Critical Work*
C. Trikoupis, *Who Is to Blame?*
Tasos Vournas (editor), *Memoirs of Kolokotronis*
Tasos Vournas, *The Years of Fire*
E. Yannopoulos, *Patriotic Upbringing*

Foreign writers:
Anonymous, *Classical Texts from German Literature*
Louis Aragon, *Cards on the Table*
Juan Bosch, *Pentagonism: the Successor to Imperialism*
Bertolt Brecht, *Life of Galileo*
Bertolt Brecht, *Terror and Misery of the Third Reich*
Norman Brigarete, *An Exile in Siberia*
Anton Chekhov, *The Lady with the Little Dog*
Isaac Deutscher, *The Unfinished Revolution*
Roger Garaudy, *For a Boundless Realism: Kafka-Picasso*
Roger Garaudy, *The Turning-point of Socialism*
Jean Jaures, *Texts*
George Lukacs, *Problems of Ontology and Politics*
Herbert Marcuse, *Eros and Civilisation*
Jean-Francois Revel, *Without Marx or Jesus*
Jean-Paul Sartre, *What Is Literature?*

Leon Trotsky, *History of the Russian Revolution*
Peter Weiss, *The Investigation*

2. censorship (1967-74)   From 1967 to 1974, when it was replaced by the moderate-conservative government of Constantine Karamanlis, Greece was ruled by a military dictatorship. The Colonels, as the dictatorship was known, maintained rigid censorship of the press through the Press Control Service, which was established under Colonel Elias Papadopoulos of the Department of Military Justice and which was directly responsible to the Prime Minister. All newspapers were to provide page proofs of all editions prior to publication and the censors checked the first printed copies again before permitting the paper to be distributed. It was forbidden to leave blank spaces indicating where copy had been excised; all such spaces must be filled in with acceptable material. The details of the censorship were laid down in a decree of April 27, 1967, which cited not only those topics forbidden to the press, but also those with which it was mandatory to deal. The lists were as follows:

Forbidden Topics:

1. Any article, commentary or news item that was disrespectful, directly or indirectly or in any manner whatsoever, to the person or the king, the queen, the members of the royal family and of the royal court in general; similarly forbidden was the reproduction of such matter from a foreign newspaper or periodical.

2. Any article, commentary or news item and reproduction from any source whether from within the country or abroad that criticized, directly or indirectly or by any means, the premier and members of the Government or their actions in the carrying out of their duties or that injured their honor.

3. Criticism or abuse of foreign heads of state in any manner whatsoever.

4. Historical accounts that by reference to the past could reawaken passions and sow discord.

5. Translations of historical accounts or news items referring to changes of regime, rebellions or revolutions and tending in any manner whatsoever to defame or denigrate other regimes or heads of state.

6. Reproduction of broadcasts by foreign radio stations of the left, including communiques, news items or commentaries from the radio of the Greek Communist Party (KKE).

7. Communiques from any organization of the Left.

8. Caricature or photographs that insulted in any manner whatsoever the sovereign and the members of the royal family or of the court, the government, the armed forces, the functioning of the machinery of government in general.

9. Chronicles, humorous articles, titles of theatrical works, films or books that insulted the above-mentioned persons.

10. Any publication that in the opinion of the Press Control Service, was harmful to the work of the government.

Mandatory Topics:

1. The speeches of the king and court communiques.

2. The speeches, declarations or communiques of the premier and members of the government; similarly, news concerning

the work of the government and the activity of the ministers, without omitting anything.

3. The communiques of the Information Service of the Sub-Ministry of the Press, without omitting anything.

4. Telegrams transmitted by the Athens Agency from abroad, which refer to the situation in Greece, without omitting anything.

5. Photographs issued by the Press Control Service (or by photographers with the approval of the service) referring to the work of the government, on the first or last page.

6. At least one commentary per day referring to the government and its work.

These general regulations were further augmented by daily rulings, often transmitted to the individual editors by phone, to ensure that the media's position on any given topic was dictated by the government. These dealt both with political topics and with areas of morals and of taste. Many stories dealing with foreign reactions to the regime were either distorted or completely fabricated as were those referring to the internal situation, both political and economic. The Colonels, whose accession to power was boosted by CIA intervention, religiously curried favor with their allies. The Soviet Union was never to be presented in anything but a negative light, while America, especially as regarded its incursion in Vietnam, ws always the subject of praise.

3. media censorship (PASOK) After seven years of military dictatorship (1967-74), followed by a further seven years of conservative rule, the 1981 elections brought to power the socialist PASOK (Pan-Hellenic Socialist Movement) government under Prime Minister Adreas Papandreou. In regard to the media, the new government immediately purged the major positions in the Secretariat-General for Press and Information, the state broadcasting networks and the Athens News Agency (a semi-official organization), and placed their own supporters in these strategic jobs. The resulting pro-PASOK bias is cheerfully acknowledged: The Party feels that the sooner the public is reeducated along socialist lines the better. Broadcasting is not wholly devoted to pro-government propaganda: Opposition statements are included, though these are followed by a condemnatory gloss from a government spokesman, and the socialist commitment to "polyphony"—letting as many media voices as possible be heard—means that there is little overt repression. Conversely, PASOK's desire to introduce a wide-ranging program of economic and social reform is not helped by the variety of critics "polyphony" tolerates. To an extent the economic crisis that the press has begun to suffer has helped weed out some newspapers. Hard-right-wing papers have lost circulation; others have found themselves unable to operate in the face of militant print unions, whose wage demands have exceeded management's capacity to pay. To compound the situation, much advertising revenue has been lost to television. While the government, in the tradition of its predecessors, has given the press a number of loans on generous terms, it has stated that once these have been used

up, any future borrowing will be at the normal commercial rate. To compensate for these financial problems, it has been alleged, some left-wing papers have turned to Moscow for aid, although these publications in turn have denied such fund-raising.

Promises to introduce a new press law have yet to be fulfilled. Such laws as do exist are fragmented and date back to the 1930s. Only two major press laws have ever been passed, and, as the product of dictatorial regimes, they have been repealed. The journalists' union has always fought any restrictions, arguing that only an industry-developed code of professional conduct would be acceptable to them. Only in the standing legislation regarding obscene publications has there been any recent change. When one publisher was jailed for 60 days after publishing works by the Marquis de SADE, 47 others immediately put the same books on sale and were duly charged. The minister of culture speedily had the law amended, excluding from prosecution such works as were "generally recognized" as being of artistic or scientific merit. De Sade was thus recognized and all charges were dropped.

PASOK has also promised reforms in the Penal Code, dealing with such articles that insult the public authorities and the dissemination of information liable to disquiet the public. These have not been carried out, but unsurprisingly the papers that now suffer such prosecutions are of the right rather than of the left. Laws that had made the possession of military plans, maps and allied material by civilians an offense were repealed. All previous press offenses against the code were given an amnesty. The government's power, used during the rule of the Colonels, to deprive a paper of duty-free newsprint, is also under review as possibly contravening the Treaty of Rome to which Greece, as a member of the European Economic Community, is subject. Measures to limit newspaper monopolies have been shelved for similar reasons. In radio and television, other than removing the military influences, the new government has generally reversed the old patterns, giving prominence to its own news values, both on national and international topics, although opposition statements (sometimes postponed till after the relevant event and usually balanced by a government reply) are transmitted. When dealing with vital questions of foreign affairs, news editors voluntarily check with the government for the approved line.

Green Sheet, The   The Green Sheet is a monthly consensus of the ratings of films currently circulating in America and as such is the oldest rating system other than that operated by the LEGION OF DECENCY/NATIONAL CATHOLIC OFFICE FOR MOTION PICTURES. The sheet first appeared in 1933, published by the 10-member Film Board of National Organizations. The members of the board are the American Jewish Committee, the American Library Association, the Daughters of the American Revolution, the Federation of Motion Picture Councils, the General Federation of Women's Clubs, the National Congress of Parents and Teachers, the National

Council of Women of the USA, the National Federation of Music Clubs, the Protestant Motion Picture Council, and the Schools Motion Picture Committee. While the board is ostensibly independent, its expenses are underwritten by the MOTION PICTURE ASSOCIATION OF AMERICA (MPAA) and it has an office in the MPAA headquarters in New York. Green Sheet reviews initially dealt only with films granted the MPAA Seal of Approval, although this practice was dropped in 1963.

The Green Sheet rates on the basis of suitability for given age groups. Ratings divide into: A (adult, those of above high school age); MY (mature young people—high school); Y (young people—junior high school); GA (general audience); C (children, under 12 and unaccompanied by adults). A single film may have a rating that embraces several categories, e.g. *A Man for All Seasons*, which was rated A-MY-Y. Films are rated after three or four representatives of each member organization have viewed the material. Each individual writes his or her own report; this is condensed into a single review with a proposed rating attached. These reviews are then sent to the board's main office where an overall editor produces a final, amalgamated version. The editor's decision is final, although dissenting reviews may be and have, on very rare occasions, been filed. Given the organizations involved, the ratings tend to the conservative, although the board claims that using more than one reviewer per group ensures a cross section, and that no one organization can dominate the views of others.

The Green Sheet, described by its MPAA sponsor as "a strong affirmation of the family's right to govern what their children will see," has a relatively limited distribution. Very few individuals receive the sheet, and it tends to be circulated, as a press release, mainly to the mass media: schools, libraries, churches, film exhibitors and of course to the members or the organizations involved. Certain of these organizations produce their own ratings and reviews, listed in their regular magazines.

***Greer* v. *Spock* (1976)**   Dr. Benjamin Spock, the author of the best-selling *Commonsense Book of Baby and Child Care* (1946), emerged in the late 1960s as one of the best-known protestors against American involvement in the Vietnam War. Spock's involvement in the protest movement extended beyond the American withdrawal from Southeast Asia. In 1976, he was the presidential candidate of the Progressive Party; accompanied by Julius Hobson, his vice-presidential candidate, and supported by two members of the Socialist Workers Party, he attempted to distribute campaign literature and hold a political meeting at the U.S. Army's Fort Dix, a military establishment devoted to the basic training of new recruits. Although certain areas of the fort were free to civilian access, post regulations, dictated by the Army, governed the entire area, restricted or otherwise. Under these restrictions any form of political speech or demonstration was strictly banned. Thus, when they attempted to distribute their literature and hold a meeting, Spock and his companions were evicted from the base.

Spock claimed that this ejection violated his FIRST AMENDMENT rights and he sued Greer, the commanding officer of Fort Dix. The Supreme Court upheld the Army's regulations, stating that the prime purpose of the fort was to train soldiers, not to act as a forum for political or any other kind of debate. If certain areas were opened to civilians, that did not exempt them from military rules. As far as the campaign literature was concerned, the commanding officer had the right to exclude anything he felt was prejudicial to the loyalty, discipline or morale of his troops. It might be that some officers would use this power arbitrarily and irrationally, but that did not invalidate its legality.

***Grimm* v. *United States* (1895)**   Grimm was one of the victims of the COMSTOCK ACT of 1873, which banned obscene materials from the U.S. mail. The case hinged, as did so many of Comstock's much-trumpeted successes, on the entrapment of the defendant. Comstock knew that Grimm was a wholesaler of obscene photographs and arranged for a postal inspector, posing as a traveling salesman, to write from Richmond, Indiana, to Grimm in St. Louis. Dated July 21, 1890, the letter read: "Dear Sir, A friend of mine has just showed me some fancy photographs and advised me that they could be obtained from you. I am on the road all the time, and I am sure many of them could be sold in the territory over which I travel. How many different kinds can you furnish? Send me a price list showing your rates by the hundred and dozen. Address me at once … and I will send you a trial order. Herman Huntress." Commercial greed outweighed any caution and Grimm replied the next day, stating his rates as requested and offering "about 200 negatives of actresses."

The authorities duly swooped in, and Grimm was charged with breaking the Federal Anti-Obscenity Act, specifically, for mailing "obscene, lewd or lascivious" materials and for offering information on how to obtain such materials. After his conviction Grimm appealed to the Supreme Court where the conviction was upheld. In its decision the court laid down three important rulings: (1) merely possessing obscene materials does not constitute an offense: Grimm's stock was not an offense, mailing it was; (2) an indictment need not go into the details of what exactly are the "obscene materials": The description "fancy photographs" was sufficient; (3) although Comstock's opponents deplored the use of entrapment, as far as the law was concerned there was no entrapment of Grimm: "When a government detective, suspecting that a person is engaged in a business offensive to good morals, seeks information under an assumed name, directly from him, and that person responding thereto, violates a law of the United States by using the mails to convey such information, he cannot, when indicted for that offense, claim that he would not have violated the law, if the inquiry had not been made by the government official."

SEE ALSO *Stanley* v. *Georgia*.

Grosz, George Grosz (1893-1959) was born in Berlin, where his father, who died when Grosz was only six, was a publican. His mother worked in the officer's mess of a provincial garrison town and he grew up in the narrow world of the petite bourgeoisie. Expelled from military school he turned to art, joining the Academy at Dresden at the age of 16. He returned to Berlin in 1912, and by the end of World War I he had evolved his unmistakable style, concentrating on the seamy, violent side of life, portraying the universe as a gallery of sideshow freaks who had escaped from the circus and taken over the real world.

In 1920 Grosz was arrested and tried for attacking the Reichswehr in his collection of anti-militarist drawings, featuring soldiers, whores and capalists, entitled "Gott Mit Uns," a title parodying the "God On Our Side" slogan of the German army. Grosz was fined 5,000 marks and claimed that what had most infuriated the army was that he had purposely misdrawn the details of the soldiers' uniforms. The appearance of "Gott Mit Uns" at the First International DADA Fair in 1921 earned Grosz a further arrest, and a fine of 300 marks. In 1923 he was tried for his book *Ecce Homo (Behold the Man)* on charges of defaming public morals and "corrupting the inborn sense of shame and virtue innate in the German people." The book is a collection of savage drawings, satirizing—and, to many, epitomizing—life in Weimar Berlin. Grosz's cast of rich and poor, men and women, the ostensibly pure and the unashamedly corrupt are all set against a backdrop of crime, sex and excess. The key emotion is always hypocrisy. Such damning images overwhelmed the jury. Grosz was fined 6,000 marks and some 24 plates were removed from all the remaining unsold copies of the portfolio.

On December 10, 1928, Grosz was tried in Berlin on charges of sacrilege brought by the church authorities because of two satirical drawings in the portfolio "Hintergrund" ("Background"), made up of stage sets for the writer Jaroslav Hasek's play based on his novel, *The Good Soldier Schweik.* One drawing showed a crucified Christ wearing a gas mask, the other a pastor balancing a cross on his nose. The court found Grosz and his publisher Wieland Herzfeld (brother of the satirical collagist John Heartfield) guilty, fining them 2,000 marks each. In 1929 the State Court of Berlin reversed the conviction, explaining that Grosz was "the spokesman of millions who disavow the war" and that a truly Christian Church should not support such a conflict.

Grosz's reputation caused him some trouble abroad when John Sloan, president of the Art Students' League of New York City, offered him a post as a temporary teacher in summer 1932. When the league's board of control first approved, then cancelled the invitation, Sloan resigned. After accepting this resignation, the board then reissued the invitation and Grosz did eventually teach in New York that summer. Earlier, in July 1929, when London police raided a gallery to confiscate works by D.H. LAWRENCE, they also seized a volume of Grosz's drawings.

Grosz returned from New York in October 1932 and, wary of the growing power of the Nazis, left Germany again in January 1933. He did not return for 26 years. Under Josef Goebbels' Ministry of Propaganda and Popular Enlightenment Grosz was branded "Cultural Bolshevik No. 1"; his works were burned, his German citizenship revoked. In July 1937 Grosz featured in the Nazi exhibition "Entartete Kunst" ("Degenerate Art"), which was organized to demonstrate "Jewish-Democratic" and "Kulturbolshevistic" influences in the type of art to which Nazi doctrines were opposed.

Grosz lived in America for virtually the remainder of his life. His style mellowed gradually, but in the atmosphere of McCarthyite America, he could not escape some censure. In March 1955 the Public Affairs Luncheon Club, a 400-member-strong patriotic women's group of Dallas, Texas, issued a press release attacking the alleged concentration of the curators of the Dallas Museum on "futuristic, modernistic and non-objective painting … much of which was produced by Communists, at the expense of various orthodox, patriotic and Texan artists." Among those artists they wished proscribed was Grosz, as well as Diego Rivera, Pablo Picasso and several more. In 1962 four Grosz drawings—*Society, Girl in a Nightdress, Easy Girl* and *The Psychoanalyst*—that were on display at L'Obelisco Gallery in Rome were ordered destroyed by Roman magistrates. The gallery's director, Dr. Gaspare del Corso, was imprisoned for two months and fined $54,000 for publishing a catalog that included the Grosz drawings. All 1,500 copies of the offending catalog were destroyed and the magazine *Mondo Nuovo* was sequestered for reproducing the same four pictures. In March 1969 Grosz's works were among those seized by police in Los Angeles when they raided Erotic Art '69, an adults only art show at the David Stuart Gallery. Gallery owner Stuart contested some 16 misdemeanor counts and was eventually acquitted of them all. In November 1970 a drawing by Grosz was one of 10 "admittedly spicy" works imported into the U.S. as part of a 200-work exhibition of erotic art, which had already been displayed without comment in Scandinavia. U.S. Customs, acting under the Tariff Act (1930), had seized the art on its arrival in Baltimore and the U.S. Justice Department had condemned the 10 works as obscene and was attempting to have them destroyed. Sexologists Phyllis and Eberhard Kronhausen, who had arranged the exhibition, took their case to the Federal Court in Baltimore, where such customs seizures had by law to be assessed. There Judge Frank A. Kaufman rejected the government's suit, stating that the "explicit erotic" works did have "redeeming social value" and permitting the exhibition to take place. Grosz returned to Germany in May 1959. He died in Berlin in July 6 of that year.

SEE ALSO United States 21. Tariff Act (1930).

H

Hagar Revelly   SEE *United States* v. *Kennerley* (1913).

Haig v. *Agee* (1981)   Philip Agee was a former member of the CIA, serving mainly in Latin America, who became disenchanted with his work, which was often centered on the destablization of governments considered to be threatening to the U.S. In 1975 Agee decided to launch a personal campaign "to expose CIA officers and agents and to take the measures necessary to drive them out of the countries where they are operating." Agee then implemented his campaign with a number of activities, notably the publication of an autobiographical book, *Inside the Company: CIA Diary* (1975), which did indeed name CIA agents and officers. His former masters were furious and attempted to link his revelations with the murder of a CIA officer in Greece in 1975. These activities all took place while Agee, an American citizen, was living in London, where he had used the British Museum's preeminent collection of Latin American newspapers to research his book.

American pressure on the British government led to Agee's deportation, under the Immigration Act (1971) in May 1977. He had been promised immunity from prosecution as far as the death in Greece was concerned, but other, civil actions were still feasible. Agee and another American, the journalist Mark Hosenball, who had also been served with a deportation order in November 1976, fought their ejection before a committee of "three wise men" chosen by the Home Office: solicitor and ex-intelligence man Sir Derek Hulton, retired civil servant Sir Clifford Jarrett, and former trade union official Sir Richard Hayward. Their precise reasons for recommending deportation were never stated, but Agee was told that his presence was "not conducive to the public good" and Hosenball was accused of being "involved in disseminating information." The "information" in question was presumably "The Eavesdroppers," an article on governmental communications monitoring that he had coauthored with Duncan Campbell; it had appeared in the listings magazine, *Time Out.* An Agee-Hosenball Defence Committee was formed, but despite Agee's appeal to the European Commission of Human Rights, he failed to stay in Britain. Hosenball, who had worked through British courts, was informed by Lord Denning that in cases of national security "even the rules of natural justice had to take second place" and he too was expelled.

Back in America Agee faced a move by the secretary of state, Alexander Haig, to revoke his passport. Haig claimed that he was entitled to do this under the Passport Act (1926), which provided for such measures when an American citizen's activities abroad "are causing or are likely to cause serious damage to the national security or the foreign policy of the United States." Agee sued Haig, claiming, inter alia, that the revocation of his passport violated his FIRST AMENDMENT rights to criticize U.S. government policy. The Supreme Court rejected his suit, on the grounds that Haig's action had been in punishment of Agee's actions, not his speech. The court explained its judgment by ruling that: (1) a different protection is accorded to beliefs, taken in isolation, than is offered to conduct; Agee's beliefs were his own affair but his conduct seriously jeopardized American security; (2) the Constitution does not protect those who breach national security and Agee's passport had been revoked at least in part as a result of such breaches; (3) the revocation of the passport would restrict only Agee's freedom of movement, it would not affect his freedom of speech. Under the Constitution, the revocation is the only means available to the government to restrict Agee's activities—which would not genuinely conflict with his freedom of speech.
SEE ALSO *McGehee* v. *Casey* (1983); *Snepp* v. *United States* (1980).

Hair   *Hair*, subtitled a "Tribal Love-Rock Musical," graduated with great speed from its status as a hippie cause celebre to fodder for the world's suburbanites. One of the first examples of what came to be known as "Das Hip Kapital" or hippie capitalism, *Hair* traded on all the hippie artifacts of the late 1960s: long hair, beads, bells, peace, protest, love and something called "The Age of Aquarius." It also threw in a fair number of more or less naked bodies and a reasonable selection of dirty words and taboo deeds. Trading on the *faux-naivete* that marked the more earnest hippies, these taboos were delivered with an aura of innocence.

Although in time the suburban matinee addicts would flock to *Hair* with the same enthusiasm as they showed for revivals of *The Sound of Music*, the sexual revolution touted by such lyrics did manage to generate the occasional shock. The most notable of these came in 1972, some years after *Hair* companies had been touring throughout the world, when the show was scheduled to be staged in Chattanooga, Tennessee. The city's municipal board refused to allow an exhibition permit for the performance in one of the city's auditoria, claiming that the show would not be "in the best interest of the community." The board then added that *Hair* was obscene and contained conduct—its naked dancing—that was not protected by the FIRST AMENDMENT.

Southeastern Productions Ltd., who were backing the show, sued the board. The district court rejected their plea, describing *Hair* in the least flattering terms and stressing its language, its nudity and "simulated acts of anal intercourse, frontal intercourse, heterosexual intercourse, homosexual intercourse, and group intercourse." However, the Supreme Court backed the production company, but Justice White, in a minority opinion, suggested that *Hair* should be comprehensively banned from all stages, since such a performance falls outside First Amendment rights. The court's majority opinion stated that the board's actions had been based on a system of PRIOR RESTRAINT, and thus did violate the First Amendment.

Hall, Joseph   SEE book burning in England 7. United Kingdom (1688-1775).

Hall, Radclyffe (1883-1943)   SEE *Well of Loneliness, The.*

Hamling v. United States   William Hamling (1921-) was a publisher whose firm in San Diego, California, had for 10 years been publishing a variety of books, magazines, radical political statements, science fiction novels, a selection of non-fiction material and such notorious best-sellers as HENRY MILLER's *The Rosy Crucifixion*, Terry Southern and Mason Hoffenberg's *Candy*, and works by the MARQUIS DE SADE and LENNY BRUCE. A former altar boy who had considered the priesthood, Hamling had lost his Catholic faith while serving in World War II, disillusioned by the pragmatic flexibility of the wartime church. After the war he had worked for the naturist-cum-pinup magazines published by George von Rosen and had graduated in 1955 to producing his own effort, a monochrome *Playboy* lookalike, *Rogue*, which sold 300,000 copies a month but which was classified as obscene by the U.S. Post Office and lost its vital second-class mailing status. After a court case that cost him $13,000 Hamling had this ruling reversed, a triumph that reinstated his business, but launched him on a conspicuously litigious career.

By 1970 Hamling was possibly the leading publisher of pulp pornographic novels, the staple of every U.S. adult bookstore and newsstand. His Nightstand Books, taking advantage of the increasing liberalism of the 1960s, sold in their millions. The Redrup decision of 1967 (see *Redrup* v. *New York*), based on two Nightstand titles, apparently set aside all limits on the texts he distributed. But this was not strictly true. The backlash against Redrup led in 1968 to the establishment of the PRESIDENT'S COMMISSION ON OBSCENITY AND PORNOGRAPHY. The liberal report produced by this commission was vilified by conservative opinion and repudiated by the authorities who had set it up. Flaunting his own position, Hamling proposed a special edition of the document, embellished with lurid illustrations, all purporting to make more intelligible the context of its recommendations. It was immediately clear that Hamling had overplayed his hand. A supposed ally, HUGH HEFNER, refused to publicize the illustrated report. Conservative opinion, spearheaded by the Nixon White House, was outraged. Hamling and three members of his staff were charged by federal indictments, in San Diego and Dallas, with circulating and selling an unauthorized edition of a government document and with adding obscene pictures to the original report. Hamling fought back with newspaper advertisements decrying the administration and its waste of taxpayers' money.

The trial lasted from October to December 1971. At its conclusion the jury, while worried about convicting for obscenity a document that relied for its text solely on government-sanctioned material, used Hamling's distribution of 55,000 promotional brochures to condemn him. These brochures were sent unsolicited through the mails, offering reprints of the hard-core material included in the report, and were illustrated with equally hard-core pictures; the brochures then moved away from official material to attack President Nixon. In February 1972 Hamling was sentenced to four years in prison and fines totalling $87,000. In June 1973 the Court of Appeals confirmed these decisions. On June 24, 1974, the Supreme Court, in a 5-4 decision, rejected Hamling's appeal. His lawyer, the veteran campaigner against obscenity prosecutions, Stanley Fleishman, managed only to have his sentence reduced to less than a year. The fines stood, as did a five-year probationary period during which Hamling was prohibited from having anything to do with his former business, up to and including writing or speaking about the laws in general and his own situation in particular.

Hamling, William   SEE *Hamling* v. *United States.*

Hankey, Frederick   Hankey (1830?-1882) was born in Corfu, the son of Sir Frederick Hankey, then governor of the Ionian Islands, and his Greek wife. After a career as a captain in the Guards Hankey moved to Paris where he lived his whole life, a move that enabled him both to gain access to the best contemporary erotica and to avoid the success of his elder brother Thomson in the Bank of England. Hankey enjoyed Parisian life and in 1862 met the de Goncourt brothers who duly recorded his existence in their Diaries. "If ever there was a bibliomaniac in the fullest sense of the word it was Frederick Hankey," wrote the bibliographer of erotica, HENRY ASHBEE. He spent freely on his collection, buying both pornographic books and a variety of erotic objects. It was not a scholarly obsession, but an absolute fascination with the sexual. Hankey allegedly resembled his favorite author, de SADE, and Ashbee characterized him as "a second de Sade without the intellect." Hankey once told Ashbee that he had recovered from a serious illness by obtaining a long sought-after edition of de Sade's JUSTINE. His great pleasure was the smuggling—with a variety of couriers, ranging from the embassy's diplomatic bag to a cousin's valet or the manager of the Covent Garden Theatre—of pornography and erotic objets d'art into England. His clients included the HOLYWELL STREET pornographers and such individuals as the explorer SIR RICHARD BURTON. He died in 1882.

Harris, Frank   Harris (1856-1931) was born in Galway, Ireland, moved to America at age 14 and embarked, if he is to be believed, on a life of lurid adventure (much of it sexual) before returning to London sometime around 1880 and devoting himself to journalism. Harris became editor, successively, of the *Evening News* (1882-86), the *Fortnightly Review* (1886-94) and the *Saturday Review* (1894-96), in which last organ he published, among others, Shaw, Beerbohm and H.G. Wells. He was a talented editor but his arrogant manner, defiance of Victorian proprieties and espousal of the German cause during World War I endeared him to few. Harris is best remembered for the four-volume MY LIFE AND LOVES (1922-26); a fifth volume was "edited"—in fact, created by ALEX TROCCHI—for the OLYMPIA PRESS in 1958. These are supposedly Harris' memoirs, a catalog of sexual excess, name-dropping and self-promotion. The book was regularly banned from its initial clandestine publication in Germany onward; it did not appear in an American or English edition until 1963. The book, while hugely entertaining and filled with the celebrities whom Harris undoubtedly knew, is generally accepted as highly unreliable. His best work is a biography of Oscar Wilde (1920) but his books on Shakespeare (he claimed to be the era's greatest Shakespearian scholar) and Bernard Shaw were also well read if poorly reviewed.

"Harris's List of Covent Garden Ladies"   This early version of today's contact magazines was one of a number of similar publications available in the 1780s and 1790s to those who frequented the prostitutes of Covent Garden. It was a simple, descriptive list, offering names, addresses, prices, physical attributes and "specialities." It was freely available, placed, as one observer recalled, between the Racing Calendar and the Book of Common Prayer, "all three being bound in red and lettered in gold." The first prosecution of the List came in 1794, possibly brought by the PROCLAMATION SOCIETY, when one James Roach was convicted, sentenced to 12 months in prison and ordered to put up sureties against his future good behavior. In a further case that year James Aitken was fined for selling the same directory. After this it ceased to be compiled or sold.

SEE ALSO *Ladies Directory, The*.

Hatch Act   This act, Title 5 U.S. Code, section 7324ff., lays out those political activities that are permitted to U.S. civil servants employed by the federal government. The initial justification for the act was to establish protection for the employees from any attempt by the government to exercise undue pressure or intimidation. Its provisions include the following: No federal employee may take part in partisan political activities other than to cast his or her vote in an election; they may not be candidates for an elected office on a national, state or any public level; they may not involved themselves in another person's partisan political campaign nor serve as an officer in any political party, committee or club. The restrictions further cover fund-raising, working at the polls, making political speeches or public endorsements of a candidate both in print and through broadcasts, helping ferry voters to an election, and any similar involvement. In recent years some employees have seen the act as possibly breaching the rights guaranteed under the FIRST AMENDMENT, but to date the Supreme Court has been consistent in upholding its provisions. Individual states have similar laws regulating the political activities of their civil servants.

Hays Office   SEE Hays, Will H.; Motion Picture Association of America.

Hays, Will H.   In 1922, reeling under the appalling publicity engendered by the Fatty Arbuckle scandal, Hollywood's studio bosses decided to find themselves an overseer, who would act both as a dignified figurehead and as an agent of reforming moral fervor. Baseball had rescued itself from the fixing of the 1919 World Series by appointing Justice Kenesaw Mountain Landis as commissioner; Hollywood chose Will H. Hays (1879-1954).

Hays was currently postmaster general in the cabinet of President Warren G. Harding. As a member of a Republican National Committee whose deliberations had led to the coining of the phrase "smoke-filled room," Hays had substantially influenced the success of Harding's candidature. The Hollywood czars fell happily for this Presbyterian elder and member of the Masons, Knights of Pythias, Kiwanians, Rotarians, Moose and Elks—whose public image centered on his campaigns against "smut"—and offered him the job as their new "Mr. Clean": president of the MOTION PICTURE PRODUCERS AND DISTRIBUTORS ASSOCIATION. He accepted a salary of $100,000 per annum and left Washington for Hollywood in March 1922.

Surrounded by a group that included Adolph Zukor, Samuel Goldwyn, William Fox, Carl Laemmle, Marcus Loew and Lewis and Myron Selznick, Hays revealed his new regime. Touting himself as an "unreconstructed Middle Westerner from the sticks," he promised that "this industry must have towards that sacred thing, the mind of a child, towards that clean virgin thing, the unmarked slate, the same responsibility, the same care about the impressions made upon it, that the best clergymen or the most inspired teacher of youth would have." The duty of film, he believed, was "to reflect aspiration, achievement, optimism and kindly humor in its entertainment."

In the event Hays went straight for Hollywood's sex-life—on and off the screen. Passionate clinches were out, as were suggestive situations and anything that smacked of "immorality" or "carnality." His agents set about compiling a Doom Book, a list of 117 Hollywood names now considered unsafe on moral grounds. Hays told the world, "Soon there will be a model Hollywood." Author Elinor Glyn, whose own relatively painless *Three Weeks* had been skilfully touted as salacious by press agent Harry Reichenbach, remarked that "Whatever will bring in the most money will happen."

The immediate effect of the Hays edict was the lowering of overall creative standards. As a critic pointed out,

"Photoplays which deal honestly with life are now banned from the screen while claptrap receives a benediction provided it has a blatantly moral ending and serves up its sex appeal with hypocritical disapproval."

Hypocrisy was by no means restricted to screenplays. In 1928, facing a Senatorial committee enquiring into the Teapot Dome scandal that destroyed the reputation of the Harding administration, Hays was revealed to have received a "gift" of $75,000 and a "loan" of $185,000 as a reward for his efforts at the convention. He narrowly escaped punishment. In 1930 it appeared that the impartial moral experts who were engaged to check the suitability of new films had their expenses and certain "honoraria" paid by Hays. Once again he escaped censure.

In 1930 Hollywood accepted a further extreme of self-censorship: the MOTION PICTURE PRODUCTION CODE—inspired by the Roman Catholic LEGION OF DECENCY—better known as the Hays Office, after the name of its author and administrator. The code, which controlled movie standards for 30 years, imposed sexual and, more important, social censorship on the content of film. While a subtle script could still amuse a sophisticated audience, the attack on "false, aesthetic and immoral doctrines" meant that any criticism of the American way—especially if it suggested a tinge of communism—was strictly off-limits. When Hays retired as the president of the MPPDA in 1945 the industry was further assailed by the purges of the House Un-American Activities Committee and of the blacklist (see blacklisting). These things passed, but Hays' influence, only marginally eroded, lasted for 20 more years.

Hefner, Hugh M.   Failed cartoonist, unenthusiastic magazine promotion man, Hugh Hefner (1926-) produced in December 1953 from his kitchen table in a Chicago apartment, the first issue of the world's best-known and best-selling men's magazine. *Playboy*, as he called it after rejecting such raunchy working titles as *Stag Party*, was loosely modeled on Hefner's favorite magazine and one-time employer, *Esquire*, in whose pages in 1953 Petty girls still rubbed scantily-clad shoulders with literary superstars. Featuring the famous Marilyn Monroe calendar shots, issue one was an enormous success. Looking to 30,000 in sales to break even, the magazine sold almost 54,000, setting the pattern for a phenomenal success. Over the next few years Hefner went on to found what for a while was an unrivalled and apparently boundless sex empire. *Playboy* paraded the fantasies of America's contemporary male yuppies, with its key clubs, its bunny girls, its hip bachelor lifestyle and, above all, the magazine itself, touting unashamed consumerism—of food, drink, technology, pleasure and, of course, pneumatic girls. By 1956 it was outselling *Esquire* itself and by 1972 had peaked at over seven million copies.

Hefner celebrated his good fortune by taking over a 48-room mansion, former property of a Chicago millionaire, and fitting it up as a hedonistic pleasure palace, the epitome of his own "Playboy Philosophy," dutifully published in the magazine, and comprising the thoughts of a man who lived in pajamas on a circular bed, chain-quaffed Pepsi-Cola and videotaped his own copulations. He filled it to the brim with visiting celebrities and complaisant, resident bunnies. Above the door, in dog-Latin, was the message "Si Non Oscillas, Non Tintinnare," loosely translated for the star-studded guests as "If you don't swing, don't ring." A second mansion, in Los Angeles, was set up in 1971. Playboy Mansion West duplicated and gradually came to replace the Chicago pleasure-dome.

Hefner, his magazine, his philosophy and all the ancillary impedimenta, peaked in the late 1960s. A variety of factors conspired to undermine *Playboy*'s success: the careless sexuality of the "permissive era," the anti-consumerism of the young, the emergence of competing publications, either hardercore, such as Larry Flynt's *Hustler*, or more sophisticated, such as Bob Guccione's *Penthouse*. In addition *Playboy* was under attack from the gathering forces, first of feminism and then of the New Right. On top of it all, quite simply, was bad management. Sealed off from real life, cossetted into late middle-age in a fantasy that entranced fewer and fewer people, Hefner gradually lost control of his empire. A chapter of accidents assailed his old success. A variety of employees were mixed up with unsavory drug-related crimes; one committed suicide. Dorothy Stratton, Playmate of the Year for 1980 and considered the first centerfold to have real Hollywood potential, was murdered by a jealous husband-cum-manager. Perhaps the most important was *Playboy*'s failure to satisfy Britain's strict gaming laws, when its London casino was shut down in 1981. This diversification into the potentially lucrative world of gambling was intended to revivify Hefner's increasingly unimpressive balance sheets. Instead it merely underlined the magazine's poor image.

By early 1982 *Playboy* was shedding many assets in an attempt to reach financial solvency. In April 1982 Hefner's daughter Christie took over as president of Playboy Enterprises, Inc. While she has certainly managed to reverse the speed of *Playboy*'s downward trend, the whole idea of *Playboy* remains to many anachronistic and slightly absurd. Hefner, the company's grand old man, retains only the right of selecting the monthly pin-up girls; he still lives reclusively, if self-indulgently, in Playboy Mansion West.

That *Playboy* maintains some ability to shock was proved in 1986 when, in the wake of the ATTORNEY GENERAL'S COMMISSION ON PORNOGRAPHY the 7-11 chain of convenience stores decided to ban the magazine and various similar publications from their shelves.

Heine, Heinrich   Heine (1797-1856) was born to Jewish parents in Dusseldorf, although he converted to Christianity in 1825. The self-styled "last Romantic" left Germany for Paris in 1830, after the disappointment of his hopes for the establishment of a liberal regime to replace the deposed Napoleon; he lived in Paris for the rest of his life. His exile was further spurred by a law passed by the German Bund forbidding the publication of work by any member of the Young German group, of which Heine was one. Beside his poetry, much of which was set to music by German composers, Heine's satirical works, often ostensibly travel pieces, brought him into conflict with both civil and ecclesiastical authorities, who wished to suppress his critical irreverence. His books *Reisebilder* (1826-31, *Travel Pictures*), *De la France* (1835) and *De l'Allemagne* (1836) were placed on the Roman Index (see Roman Indexes) in 1836; they were banned by the church for the duration of the Index. Another work, *Neue Gedichte*, was added to the Index in 1844. As a born Jew and despite his later conversion, Heine's work was included by the Nazis in their destruction of Jewish literature. There was one exception to this rule: So beloved by all Germans was his poem "Die Lorelei" (1827) that, despite his well-known authorship, it was listed in the Nazi catalog as "Anonymous" and thus spared from the flames.

Hellenic Sun Under the Tariff Act (1930), the U.S. Customs has the right to impound any allegedly obscene material that is being imported into the United States. A federal district court is then obliged to decide whether or not the material actually is obscene and should either be released or be held and destroyed. *Hellenic Sun* was a magazine produced in Europe and illustrated extensively with homosexual pinups. A consignment of the magazines was seized on arrival in the U.S. in 1967. Both a district and an appeals court, in the case of *United States* v. *Magazine entitled "Hellenic Sun,"* agreed that the magazine was patently offensive, lacked redeeming social value and appealed exclusively to a defined deviant group, to wit, male homosexuals. Thus it fulfilled the necessary tests and was clearly obscene under the Tariff Act. The magazine was destroyed.

SEE ALSO United States 21. Tariff Act.

Helsinki Final Act The Final Act of the Conference on Security and Co-operation in Europe (CSCE) was signed in Helsinki in August 1975 by leaders of 33 European countries, both East and West, and of the U.S. and Canada. The CSCE had been organized to improve East-West relations on a variety of fronts. The Final Act runs to 40,000 words, divided into three sections, generally known as "baskets." The document, which is not a treaty and not legally binding, set in motion a new appraisal of the international human rights issue, placing it in a central position as regards East-West relations.

The document commences with 10 introductory principles that guide relations between the participants. Following these are the three baskets. Basket One deals with the improving of military security; Basket Two with the improving of trade and economic and scientific cooperation; Basket Three with humanitarian issues, the reunification in a single format of issues that had become overly fragmented, interpersonal contacts and the flow of information between East and West. The

CSCE was controlled by consensus, and each nation could veto any proposition. Given that the accords taken were accepted voluntarily and their implementation depended purely on the good faith of the signatories, the Final Act concluded with an agreement to meet again in Belgrade in 1977 to assess the progress of the decisions taken.

Of the document's 62 pages, only three and a half deal specifically with information, but it is these that have led to the most bitter debate. There are three main fields involved, and on none of them do the two sides find themselves able to agree to the same interpretation: (1) Improvement of the circulation of, access to, and exchange of information. The improvement of the dissemination of newspapers and other publications from one state amongst the others; the increase in the number of places where publications may be bought or in which they can be read or from which they can be borrowed; an improvement in the dissemination of information through the broadcast media. (2) Cooperation in the field of information. The betterment of relations among the various media and their professional organizations. (3) Improvement of working conditions for journalists. Facilitating the granting of visas, accreditation and temporary residence permits; to remove when possible the restrictions on travel in the country in which a journalist is based; to improve the communication of information to journalists by government officials; to permit foreign correspondents absolute freedom to file whatever material they wish with their newspaper at home; the affirmation by participating states that journalists will not be expelled or otherwise penalized for their activities while in the legitimate pursuit of their job and, if a journalist is expelled, for him or her to receive a proper reason for the expulsion and to be allowed an appeal.

The Belgrade meeting, which commenced on June 15, 1977, was heated and acrimonious. The Eastern bloc, demanding "a positive and forward-looking" discussion, attempted to sidestep any assessment of the extent to which the participants had actually put the decisions, especially those involved in Basket Three, into practice. The Western states, plus the neutral and non-aligned members (known as the N+N group) joined forces to persuade the Eastern bloc to consent to a follow-up meeting to focus on the questions of implementation. This meeting, which was held in Belgrade from October 1977 to March 1978, was characterized by bitter arguments, conducted in closed session. At its end a formal statement, reaffirmed "the resolve ... to implement fully, unilaterally, bilaterally and multilaterally all the provisions of the Final Act." Further meetings were arranged for 1980 in Madrid and 1986 in Vienna, at which the accords have been reviewed and the Final Act maintained.

The most contentious points of the Final Act have been points VI and VII of the introductory principles. Point VI prohibits "any direct or indirect, individual or collective" interference by any member in the internal affairs of any other member. Point VII reaffirms "respect for human rights and fundamental freedoms, including the freedom of thought, conscience, religion and belief." The opposing interpretations of these clauses by East and West have yet to be resolved; coupled with the continuing disputes about the dissemination, or lack of it, of information, this has led inevitably to a deadlock between the ideological rivals. Thirty-six further attempts to implement Basket Three were vetoed by the Soviet bloc at Belgrade. One state's propaganda and psychological warfare is another's ideological competition and the arguments remain unresolved.

SEE ALSO Charter 77.

Hemingway, Ernest   In common with a number of other Nobel Prize winners, literary respectability failed to protect Hemingway (1898-1961) from censorship. The Italian government found his novel, *A Farewell to Arms* (1929), which is set against the Italian retreat at Caporetto during World War I, too painful and banned it from Italy; Italian pressure similarly forced certain cuts in the U.S. film version. In 1930 Boston authorities banned Hemingway's first novel, *The Sun Also Rises* (1926), and in 1938 *To Have and Have Not* was variously banned in Detroit, in Wayne County and in the borough of Queens, New York. Hemingway was also banned in Ireland and burnt in Nazi Germany.

Herbert Committee, The   The committee was set up in Britain in November 1954 by the Society of Authors with the intention of assessing the current laws regarding OBSCENE LIBEL and recommending future reforms. Initially under the presidency of Sir Alan Herbert and later of Sir Gerald Barry, the committee was drawn from authors, publishers, printers, critics, lawyers and one member of Parliament. In February 1955 the committee announced its proposals in public, after submitting them, in the form of a bill, to Home Secretary Gwilym Lloyd George.

The main proposed change to the then-current law, the OBSCENE PUBLICATIONS ACT (1857), was to replace the concept of a "tendency" to "deprave and corrupt" with an "intention" to do so. The bill contained no specific definition of obscenity, but urged juries to give maximum attention to any artistic value claimed for or found in a work. Expert witnesses were to be permitted in all prosecutions for obscenity. All previous statutes in this area were to be repealed, but the new act would incude certain parts of the 1857 legislation, with modifications: Proceedings under the Act were to be speeded up and authors, publishers and printers were to be given a "locus standi" in court, a recognized right of appearance that allowed them to call and give evidence on their own behalf. The Customs would no longer be able to destroy seized material without the permission of a magistrate, and all proceedings under the act would have to bear the imprimatur of the attorney-general.

The bill was well-received by the press and public and in March 1955 Roy Jenkins, MP, introduced it as a private member's bill under the 10-minute rule. The bill received an unopposed first reading, but in the end the pressure of other business posponed reform until the committee's efforts, further modified, were embodied in the OBSCENE PUBLICATIONS ACT (1959).

"Here Lies John Penis"   SEE Potocki de Montalk, Count Wladislas.

Hernani   SEE Hugo, Victor.

Hicklin Rule, The   In the case of REGINA V. HICKLIN, in 1868, Britain's Lord Chief Justice Cockburn stated: "The test of obscenity is this, whether the tendency of the matter charged as obscenity is to deprave and corrupt those whose minds are open to such immoral influences and into whose hands a publication of this sort may fall." The Hicklin Rule, which permitted juries to convict if even a single passage in an otherwise "clean" publication was judged obscene, stayed in force in England until the OBSCENE PUBLICATIONS ACT (1959) and in America until UNITED STATES V. ONE BOOK ENTITLED ULYSSES (1934). Both countries revised their tests in the light of judging the entire book for its overall obscenity. In overturning Lord Cockburn's definition, U.S. Judge Curtis Blok commented, "Strictly applied, this rule renders any book unsafe, since a moron could pervert to some sexual fantasy to which his mind is open the listings of a seed catalog."

Hollywood Peep Show   SEE Delaware's obscenity statute.

Holyoake, George Jacob   Holyoake (1817-1892), the eldest son of a Birmingham foundery worker, second of 13 children, was one of the 19th century's leading freethinkers and subject of the last trial for atheism held in England. At the age of 15 he became a Chartist and toured the country, teaching mathematics at poor people's institutes and promoting Chartist opinions. While in Sheffield he joined the "Defiant Syndicate of Four," a highly atheistic group, although Holyoake was himself more of a deist. The group's leader, Charles Southwell, was arrested in November 1841 for his intemperate attack on the Bible—"The Jew Book"—in his magazine, *The Oracle of Reason*. While Southwell faced trial for blasphemous libel, Holyoake took over the magazine.

In May 1842, journeying to visit Southwell in Bristol jail, Holyoake stopped in Cheltenham to give a lecture on socialism to the local Mechanic's Institute. At the end of the lecture he was asked by a local preacher where God fitted into socialism. Holyoake declared, "I do not believe that there is such a thing as a God ... I flee the Bible like a viper, and revolt at the touch of a Christian." His sentiments were received quietly and he left, to walk on to Bristol. Complaints began only after the *Cheltenham Chronicle* wrote, under the headline "Atheism & Blasphemy," an attack on socialism in general, "or as it has been more appropriately termed, devilism," and on Holyoake's lecture in particular, calling for official action. A further piece, headlined "Holyoake the Blasphemous Socialist Orator," talked of "this monster."

Local magistrates announced that his talk was blasphemous and threatened Holyoake with arrest.

While this threat was probably meant merely as a warning against Holyoake's returning to Cheltenham, he took it as a challenge. He walked back to the town, was smuggled into a Chartist meeting and spoke in his own defense. Twelve police were present and he was arrested after the meeting and charged with blasphemy. When he claimed accurately that there had been no warrant nor had information been laid against him, the chairman of the bench, Robert Capper, replied, "We refuse to hold an argument with a man professing the abominable principle of denying the existence of a Supreme Being." He was then charged with a breach of the peace, although both meetings had been orderly. After 16 days in Gloucester jail, where he was treated very poorly, and the transfer of his case to the assizes, Holyoake appeared, now charged with a felony, cited as a "labourer" and "a wicked, malicious and evilly disposed person" who denied God. Despite starting with the sympathy of the court and the relatively unsophisticated rural jury, Holyoake's determination to establish himself as a martyr and to detail, at tedious length, his beliefs and his grievances, both before and after his incarceration, gradually eroded his position. He was duly convicted as charged and jailed for six months.

Once imprisoned he refused to abandon his defiant stance, distancing himself from his peers and maintaining a thoroughly self-righteous posture. He was freed in February 1843 and received a martyr's welcome from his fellow freethinkers. After returning to the lecture circuit, and in 1850 writing *The History of the Last Trial by Jury for Atheism* (in which with hindsight he modified his self-satisfaction), he established in 1855 the London Secular Society, which embodied his own version of freethinking, essentially the bringing of atheistic beliefs to the working classes in such a modified form that it would not alienate them. His philosophy, secularism, existed to promote morality, science, reason and free discussion; he was willing to tolerate open-minded Christians and did not seek to attack the bases of their faith. Holyoake died in 1892, after publishing his memoirs, *Sixty Years an Agitator*. He remained a freethinker to the end, but although revered in such circles, his relatively moderate beliefs had long been superseded by harder-line theorists, such as CHARLES BRADLAUGH, determined to destroy the very roots of Christianity. Ironically when in 1960 the playwright John Osborne wrote his play, *A Subject of Scandal and Concern*, a study of Holyoake, it was banned by the British independent television network. The BBC broadcast it instead.

Holywell Street Holywell Street, off the Strand, was the center of the London pornography trade in the mid-19th century. At the height of its influence, between 1840 and 1860, some 20 shops, owned by such notable pornographers as WILLIAM DUGDALE and George Cannon, flourished in this one street. Lord Campbell's OBSCENE PUBLICATIONS ACT (1857) and the activities of the various Victorian vice societies were aimed directly at Holywell Street, and by the late 19th century the pornographers' citadel had indeed been extirpated. The trade simply moved north, via Charing Cross and Leicester Square to Soho, where its depleted descendants rest today. Holywell Street was torn down around 1900 to make way for the Aldwych development. Its site is currently occupied by the Australian High Commission.

Honduras Freedom of expression and the absence of state censorship are guaranteed under article 72 of the Honduran Constitution. Article 73 further states that the means of communication may not be seized, confiscated or otherwise interrupted for any offense relating to the spread of thoughts or ideas. Under article 74 it is forbidden for the government or other authority to use any form of pressure to exert indirect censorship. Only in the protection of the ethical and cultural values of society (article 75) and especially of the young, may the government exert prior censorship.

All journalists must be licensed by a professional guild; newspapers employing unlicensed writers will be fined and the editor may lose his or her accreditation. A degree of self-censorship is generally exercised, compounded by the control of a paper's coverage by the political stance of its proprietor, who is almost invariably linked to the power structure and thus unlikely to tolerate real criticism of the government. The authorities themselves monitor the press, moving to have over-inquisitive reporters dismissed and, given their support for the Nicaraguan Contras, brand any outspoken reporters—both Honduran and foreign—as "Sandinista spies." The weakness of individual journalists is compounded by their near-subsistence salaries, laying them open to bribery and corruption. The simple fear of losing one's job accentuates the desire to toe the line.

Journalists are further cowed by the physical violence of a number of extralegal kidnap teams and death squads, although the activities of the latter, which accounted for at least 147 disappearances between 1979 and 1984, appear to have largely diminished, despite some resurgence in 1987. Nonetheless reporters are still subjected to intense interrogations, raids and confiscations. The staff of the resolutely independent newspaper *El Tiempo* have been especially targeted.

Hone, William William Hone (1780-1842) was an author and bookseller best known for his frequent publication of parodies, pamphlets and political satires. Born the son of a Bath solicitor's clerk, who espoused a dissident nonconformist sect, Hone gravitated naturally toward radicalism. He established bookshops, first at Lambeth Walk and subsequently at Old Bailey, and began writing and reporting on a variety of social welfare causes and in favor of parliamentary reform. Subsequent to Thistlewood's attempt to seize power in 1816 (the Spa Fields Plot), Hone started his own political broadsheet, *The Reformists' Register*, and was identified by the Tory government as a leading radical.

In 1817 Hone was charged with "impious and seditious libels" after the publication of three political squibs, all parodies on religious texts: "The Late John Wilkes's Catechism of a Ministerial Member," "The Political Litany" and "The Sinecurist's Creed or Belief." The charges in all three cases referred to attacks on the Athanasian Creed, the Book of Common Prayer, and other Christian texts, but the true injured party was the Tory government. In three trials, in which he defended himself superbly, Hone condemned his accusers by their own words and deeds. Among the many books he produced in his defense were copies of two works by JAMES GILLRAY—*The Impious Feast of Balshazzar* and the *Apotheosis of Hoche*. Claiming that each of these was far crueller a parody than any of his efforts, he noted that for the first Gillray had been given a government pension, and that the second had been recognized as a consciously pro government statement. Despite three consecutive trials, Hone was acquitted of all charges.

Hone became a national hero and a subscription raised £3,000 to pay costs and allied losses during his trials. Acquitted, he took no further risks in his pamphleteering, although his radicalism was unabated. *The Political House That Jack Built*, illustrated by the young Cruikshank and scrupulously avoiding religious references, sold 100,000 copies at one shilling (five pence) each. Hone remained a famous but impoverished bookseller until his death. An attack of cerebral spill caused him temporary paralysis and dysphasia from which he never recovered. Dickens, London's latest celebrity, visited him on his deathbed and attended his funeral.

Hosenball, Mark   SEE ABC trial; *Haig* v. *Agee*.

Hotten, John Camden   According to 20th-century slang lexicographer Eric Partridge, Hotten (1832-73) was a "near-scholar" who combined at his shop at 151b Piccadilly the callings of a general publisher, a slang lexicographer and a purveyor of pornography. He was born in Clerkenwell in 1832 and developed a precocious interest in books. In 1848 he visited America and on his return established himself as an expert in modern American literature. His first publishing ventures were in editions of such contemporary Americans as Bret Harte, Oliver Wendell Holmes, James Russell Lowell and Artemus Ward. He also wrote biographies of Dickens and Thackeray. But his fame rests on his exploitation of what Partridge called "the by-ways" of Victorian life. His *Dictionary of Modern Slang, Cant and Vulgar Words* appeared in 1859. It remained the authoritative work for nearly 40 years and still holds an important place in slang lexicography. The other by-way he traveled keenly was pornography.

Compared with less savory publishers Hotten was relatively honest and ASHBEE praised him as "industrious, clever but not always reliable." Hotten had a special affection for this side of the business, calling it his flower garden, in which bloomed such titles as *The History of the Rod*, Thomas Rowlandson's *Pretty Little Games* (a series of 10 erotic plates) and *The Romance of Chastisement*. He also published Swinburne's *Poems and Ballads* (1866), which, while hardly obscene, had been turned down by more timid publishers. Swinburne, who appreciated flagellant pornography himself, helped Hotten with *The Romance of the Rod*. Hotten died in 1873, either of "brain fever" or, as some claimed, of a surfeit of pork chops. His final works were *The Golden Treasury of Thought* and a comprehensive list of those who immigrated to America in the 17th century.

House Committee on Un-American Activities   The pursuit of alleged communists in American society by the House Committee on Un-American Activities was continued after the resignation of MARTIN DIES by two arch-conservatives, Representatives John S. Wood of Florida and John Rankin of Mississippi. The Wood-Rankin Committee maintained the Dies style, combining innuendo, guilt by association and extravagant allegations to attack a variety of victims. As well as having some leaders of the Communist Party of the USA (CPUSA) jailed for contempt of Congress, HUAC turned for the first time on Hollywood, cited as "the greatest hotbed of subversive activities in the United States." "We're on the trail of the tarantula" claimed Wood and Rankin, but their threats proved empty. Only their investigator Ernie Adamson's requisition and condemnation as un-American of a number of radio scripts, which resulted in the panicky networks' dismissal of two of the commentators involved, gave a foretaste of more intensive attacks on the entertainment industry. Wood introduced a bill to have all such commentators register details of their background, politics etc., when applying for a job, on the premise that "the time has come to determine how far you can go with free speech." This bill was defeated, but when The Citizens to Abolish the Wood-Rankin Committee inserted an advertisement in the *New York Times*, the signatories, the newspaper and the advertising agency concerned were all investigated.

The Wood-Rankin administration of HUAC ended in 1946. As a parting gesture it called for veterans' associations to check for "pink teachers." And Adamson, acting in his own initiative, issued a directive alleging serious communist infiltration of the government, demanding curbs on aliens and the creation of a new, independent Washington agency with the power to check out the loyalty of government employees. The imposition of loyalty checks, by taking an oath, was duly implemented by President Truman in 1947. While he lacked enthusiasm for witch-hunting, Truman needed to extract from the conservative Congress funds to contain communism abroad, which necessitated pandering to the committee's demands at home. The attorney general compiled a list of subversive organizations, and Truman issued an executive order demanding an investigation into the loyalty of 2,116,000 federal employees. Dismissable offenses included membership or affiliation or "sympathetic association" with a listed subversive group. Few members or affiliates were discovered, but simply liking Russian music or reading about the U.S.S.R. was enough to make one "sympathetic." One-hundred-and-thirty-nine people were fired, although no one was proved guilty of actual subversion; 600 others resigned, some refusing to take the test on principle, others simply aware that they would fail it.

In 1947 HUAC gained two important members: its new chairman J. Parnell Thomas and the freshman representative from California, Richard M. Nixon, whose career to date had benefited from his well-publicized attacks on the "Red Menace." The Thomas Committee started up on predictable lines, attacking the CPUSA, the remaining New Dealers, unions, leftist groups etc. It also used FBI director J. Edgar Hoover's condemnation of the "pro-Communist" film *Mission to Moscow*, made while America and Russia were allies, to begin a new attack on Hollywood. For the first time HUAC began seriously to influence the film industry. In June 1947, backed by the testimony of 14 friendly witnesses, including Adolphe Menjou and Jack L. Warner, Thomas issued an indictment claiming that the National Labor Relations Board (a New Deal agency) was actively advancing a communist takeover in Hollywood. He promised that hearings would be held. The ensuing investigation failed utterly to find the alleged conspiracy but did engender massive publicity. The movie establishment sided with HUAC, while a number of stars, such as Katharine Hepburn, Humphrey Bogart and Judy Garland formed the Committee for the First Amendment, taking out advertisements and flying en masse to the hearings in Washington. Thirty-five people were finally cited as communists, of whom 12 were called upon to testify. Two of these capitulated, but the remaining 10, nine scriptwriters and a director, refused to answer questions. This Hollywood Ten or Unfriendly Ten were all found in contempt of Congress, fined $1,000 and jailed for terms of six or 12 months. Despite their appeals, all served time in prison. All were blacklisted on their release, and few could work (other than pseudonymously) for many years. The Hollywood hearings were not universally popular, and Thomas abandoned them a week early in the light of adverse press comment. They were, on the other hand, successful, and while HUAC's "methods were gross and its intentions despicable" (Goodman, op. cit.), it successfully terrorized Hollywood, its establishment in Los Angeles and its financiers in New York. The blacklist, albeit clandestine, was instituted and with it came a climate of pervasive fear.

In the buildup to the 1948 elections Republican Committee members Richard Nixon and Karl Mundt concentrated on discrediting the national security measures of Democrats Roosevelt and Truman. Their bill, aimed at outlawing all hard-left groups, was rejected in the Senate, but they successfully undermined confidence in the scientific community, particularly the Atomic Energy Commission with its many European refugee members, and smeared its civilian chairman Dr. Edward Condon as "one of the weakest links in our atomic security." The general escalation of anti-communist investigations—as well as HUAC, a Federal Grand Jury was probing the Communist Party in New York and the Senate had established its own investigating committee—reflected the growing conservatism of the era. Two names stand out as contemporary informers: Elizabeth Bentley and Whittaker Chambers. Bentley, ex-lover of a prominent party member, named two top Roosevelt aides—Lauchlin Currie and Harry Dexter White—among the 11 government figures among whom existed an alleged Soviet spy network for which she claimed to have been a courier. Bentley was by no means a coherent witness, but, as in so many similar "confessions," the publicity created by her testimony far outweighed its factual basis. Currie successfully fended off the smear, but White, who died shortly afterward, never fully cleared his name. Chambers, a former activist, had recanted and named eight government "Communists," two of whom were also on Bentley's list. Chambers is best remembered for the help he gave Richard Nixon in his pursuit of Alger Hiss and for his best-selling book *Witness* (1952), in which he attempted to justify his actions in the name of patriotism.

The committee's image suffered somewhat in 1948 when J. Parnell Thomas was indicted on charges of embezzling government funds and was imprisoned in the same jail as two of the Hollywood Ten. Attempting to accelerate its progress and frustrated by witnesses using the Fifth Amendment to resist testifying, HUAC then persuaded the House of Representatives to approve contempt citations against 56 formerly recalcitrant witnesses. By 1955 every single one had managed to have his or her case thrown out of court.

The effect of the witchhunters' allegations on the American consciousness was devastating. Private censors perhaps surpassed even the national committees. Blacklists proliferated, such as the pamphlet RED CHANNELS and the weekly newsletter COUNTERATTACK (produced, respectively, by American Business Consultants and Aware Incorporated), plus similar documents compiled by a variety of groups, including the Catholic Church and the American Legion.

In 1951 HUAC returned to Hollywood, and took aim at specific individuals. The climate was ideal for such investigations. The Hollywood establishment closed ranks against the left: The association of motion picture producers (the MPAA) threatened to sack anyone not cooperating with the committee; neither the Screen Actors Guild nor Actors Equity would defend "unfriendly" members; and the craft unions, represented by the Motion Picture Industry Council, followed suit. John Wayne headed the Motion Picture Alliance for the Preservation of American Ideals (MPAPAI), and Walter Wagner created the Los Angeles Crusade for Freedom. Both were active HUAC supporters. To refuse cooperation was to be blacklisted; to cooperate was to turn informer. Hollywood as an industry gave in.

After investigating the New York entertainment business, the committee then turned on two still vociferous organizations; the Council of the Writers, Sciences and Professions and the National Lawyers Guild, both of which had represented lawyers who had defended uncooperative witnesses.

Under attack, the legal profession proved itself no more stalwart than Hollywood or Broadway.

After the Republican victory in the 1952 elections, the new President, Eisenhower, had to implement his promises to scour the government of communists. Loyalty oaths, lie detector tests, security checks on federal, state and local government appointees were all employed on a large scale; millions were processed. A new chairman, ex-FBI agent Harold N. Velde, was appointed to HUAC. Working in parallel with William E. Jenner, who ran the Senate Internal Security Subcommittee, Velde continued the investigations. His main innovation was to introduce a number of HUAC subcommittees that toured the country, interviewing witnesses as they went. Velde also attacked the colleges and the Roman Catholic Church. A number of colleges did purge their ranks, but his treatment of such clergymen as Bishop G. Bromley Oxnam, only weakened Velde's position. He lost all credibility when, in trying to resurrect the case of Harry Dexter White, he attempted to subpoena former President Truman, former Attorney General Tom Clark and former Secretary of State James T. Byrne. All three rejected the papers, and even Velde's supporters distanced themselves from his efforts. In 1954, with HUAC in increasing disarray, Velde resigned.

His successor as chairman, Francis Walter, had the reputation of a civilized and sensible person and civil rights activists greeted his appointment with relief. Although Walter briefly showed signs of an increasing appetite for McCarthyism (see Joseph McCarthy), he gradually wound down HUAC's hearings, and the committee's reduced status was evidenced by the fact that courts, although presented with HUAC citations for contempt, such as those issued to Arthur Miller and Paul Robeson, invariably rejected the citations on technical grounds. The committee's decline was accelerated after the defection of most of the CPUSA after the Hungarian uprising of 1956. And in 1959 Truman called HUAC "the most un-American thing in the country today." Walter's attack in 112 California teachers backfired when the press savaged HUAC for basing its investigation purely on smear and hearsay. In May 1960 HUAC hearings in San Francisco were greeted by 5,000 demonstrators.

Throughout the 1960s HUAC's targets were the emergent civil rights and peace groups, as well as the New Left, whose members blithely admitted their socialism and harassed the investigators while leftist supporters packed the public seats. HUAC's final hearings were into the 1966 urban riots and the fracas at the Chicago Democratic Convention of 1968. In February 1969 HUAC was finally disbanded and replaced by the more pacific House Internal Security Committee.

House Special Committee on Un-American Activities
American worries about the threat of communism developed in the face of homegrown radicalism and became entrenched in the light of the success of the Russian Revolution. In 1917 the magazine THE MASSES was suppressed for its anti-war

sentiments; in 1919 Senator Lee Overman launched an abortive investigation into the extent of Bolshevik influence in the U.S.; in 1920 Attorney General A. MITCHELL PALMER, touting his red scare, arrested more than 4,000 people, often without warrants; 240 were deported. The increasing popularity of left-wing causes during the 1930s, whether fighting fascism or campaigning for civil rights, was paralleled by President Franklin Roosevelt's socially experimental New Deal, which enraged conservatives.

Attempts to quell this "leftward" drift continued in 1930 when conservative Congressman Hamilton Fish suggested that, were communism expelled from America, the Depression would vanish with it. He set up a committee to investigate the communists, but had little success. More impressive were the efforts of Rep. Samuel Dickstein of New York, who in 1934 persuaded Congress to establish the first House Committee to Investigate Un-American Activities. Its proceedings, chaired by John J. McCormack, were civilized and offered few revelations. Its mandate expired in 1937 and Congress refused to extend it, despite Dickstein's urging. In 1938 the New Deal was foundering and popular opinion was increasingly conservative, viewing askance the Communist Party-inspired Popular Front under which banner most left-wing groups, of whatever hue, were now amalgamated. In 1938 the veteran anti-communist Rep. Martin Dies (D., Texas), allied himself to Dickstein. He persuaded Congress to reestablish the committee in 1938, then promptly refused Dickstein a seat.

The main impetus of the House Special Committee on Un-American Activities (generally known as the Dies Committee) was the promoting of its chairman's loathing of the New Deal in general and various supposedly left-wing federal "alphabet agencies," notably the FWP (Federal Writers Project) and the FT (Federal Theater). Dies promised to keep the committee on "a dignified plane ... to adopt and maintain throughout the course of the hearings a judicial attitude." He also promised that it would "not permit any character assassination or any smearing of innocent people ... the chair is more concerned with facts than with opinions, and with specific proof than with generalities."

The committee's critics disagreed, suggesting instead that the Dies Committee, with no constitutional justification, used smear tactics, guilt by association, unreliable "friendly" witnesses, circumstantial evidence, and a variety of extralegal methods to set about the systematic destruction of the New Deal and the Left in America. Those called before the committee were often insulted by its members; they were not permitted to testify on their own behalf and many were not allowed counsel; if counsel were present they could not consult with their client during testimony. With the exception of the left-wing papers, the press was generally sympathetic to the committee. Although Dies failed to have convicted a single witness who appeared before the committee, his campaign succeeded, with the help of the anti-Roosevelt Congressional Appropriations Committee under Rep. Clifton

Woodrum (D., Virginia). After the committee the New Deal was forced into a more conservative posture, and the chance of social experiments and reforms was lost.

In 1939 the Dies Committee focused on the CPUSA itself, as well as the ACLU, which, like an increasing number of leftist organizations, swiftly and voluntarily purged itself. In 1940 the committee began investigating Hollywood after one John J. Leech, claiming to be a former member of a Hollywood Communist Party cell, alleged that 42 major Hollywood figures were secret communists. Many of the stars testified, including Humphrey Bogart, James Cagney and Franchot Tone, and all were exonerated.

In 1944 Dies resigned from the committee. He had made possible the rise of his successor: Sen. JOSEPH McCARTHY.

SEE ALSO House Committee on Un-American Activities.

Hsiao tao hsiao hsi   Translated as "byroad news" (literally, "little road news"), this unofficial means of communication in China complements the officially sanctioned, but ostensibly spontaneous "DAZIBAO" or big character posters. The term refers to the dissemination of information in what appears to be (but is not) a genuinely underground manner, relying on handwritten sheets and/or oral communications. Like the posters, the byroad news also stems ultimately from party leaders and is used in parallel to bolster the "correct" line the citizens are encouraged to espouse voluntarily, rather than accept without understanding or appreciation. Particularly common in times of political crisis or during leadership struggles, these rumors, leaks and similar fragments of information are carefully fed downwards from the party to the more responsible and politically aware members of the public. Although such news has been manipulated, it is accepted as an improvement on the monolithic pronouncements of the official mass media. If the process is correctly managed, the required line, which will be implicit in all such information, will be absorbed as desired by the people. And so byroad news provides an essential adjunct to communications in China.

Hugo, Victor   Poet, novelist and dramatist, Hugo (1802-85) was one of the central figures of the 19th-century French Romantic movement. Between 1848 and 1851, he was a member of the General Assembly; after Louis Napoleon's coup d'etat, he went into exile on the island of Guernsey. On his return in 1870 he reentered politics, being elected first as a deputy and then as a senator. Earlier, he had been elected to the French Academy aged only 38. Hugo managed to antagonize the authorities on a number of occasions. His play, *Marion Delorme*, was banned by the official censors in 1829 because in it Louis XIII was portrayed as a "weak, superstitious and cruel prince." This image was seen as conducive to public malevolence and disparagement of the current king, Charles X. When Hugo appealed directly to the king the ban was confirmed, but Charles offered to raise the writer's annual pension from 2,000 to 6,000 francs, in recognition of

his poetry rather than his plays. After Charles had been deposed in the Revolution of 1830 the play was permitted to be performed.

In 1830 the first two performances of *Hernani*, a play that marked a turning point in the style of French drama, scandalized theatergoers, who turned both nights into an uproar. Hugo's supporters, the Romanticists, and his opponents, the Classicists, fought in the auditorium and on the street. The Classicists hired bands of thugs who would deliberately drown out the performance; Theophile Gautier, backing Hugo, organized a group of volunteers, "resolved to take their stand upon the rugged mount of Romanticism." One unfortunate even died in a duel over the rival styles. In 1832 *Le Roi S'Amuse* was banned after a single performance; Prime Minister Quinze had found it derogatory to Louis-Phillipe. It was produced 50 years later, under the supervision of Hugo himself. In 1834 Hugo's novel *Notre Dame de Paris* (1831) was placed on the Roman Index (see Roman Indexes) for its alleged anticlericalism and, in 1864, *Les Miserables* (1836). In 1850 his complete works were banned by Czar Nicholas I of Russia, who saw them as potentially subversive, although after the Revolution of 1917 Hugo became a very popular author in that country. Hugo's final clash with the French government came in 1853 when copies of the satirical *Napoleon le Petit*, which Hugo had written during his exile from France, were seized by the police.

Humphrey, John   SEE book burning in England 7. United Kingdom (1688-1775).

Hundred Flowers Movement   Between the Revolution of 1949 and the mid-1950s, Chinese cultural standards were based on Mao Zedong's lectures to the Yanan Forum on Literature and Art in May 1942, in which he called for a "cultural army" to support the military one and pointed out that after the Revolution had succeeded writers and artists must suppress any instincts of criticism or satire. The effect of this demand was to silence many such individuals, who were further frightened by a series of attacks launched against those seen as counterrevolutionaries.

By 1956 the Revolution seemed secure and in a speech in January Zhou Enlai made it clear that intellectuals were to be given greater freedom, as much for the exploitation of their talents in revolutionary causes as for the encouragement of their art. Writers responded cautiously at first, but were further encouraged by a speech in June by Lu Dingyi, which expounded Mao's slogan, "Let a hundred flowers bloom, let a hundred schools of thought contend." The main source of the newly critical writing was the journal *People's Literature*, whose deputy chief editor, Quin Zhaoyang, stressed the need for a realistic approach to counter the anodyne popular writing that idealized the struggles of workers/peasants/soldiers for the socialist way. He noted that no writer could be faithful both to truth and to propaganda and that, while art for art's sake was impermissible, a socialist message imposed from above would always ring false. Writers, he demanded, should break "the bonds of [their] own dogmatism."

Mao's speech of February 27, 1957, pushed the writers even further. He acknowledged that within society were a number of traditions, the diversity of which in no way threatened the Revolution. He also called for a "rectification campaign" under which, although senior officials deplored it, the party was to be criticized from the outside as well as from within. This speech finally convinced the writers and until June 1957 many critical pieces were published, as well as speeches and wall poster campaigns from many individuals and groups, mainly students and pre-revolutionary authorities who regretted their lost status. The Hundred Flowers wilted by June 1957. The press began to suggest that criticism should be curbed and on June 8 Mao's February speech was published as "On the Correct Handling of Contradictions Among the People." It had been amended in the interim and its liberal promises replaced by new directions for repression. The pejorative term "rightist" appeared, and in the rectification campaign that followed, a preface to the Great Leap Forward of 1958, the short-lived critics were humiliated and denounced. Hundreds of thousands were branded as rightists: students were expelled, workers dismissed, and many writers and artists simply vanished, driven into internal exile and deported to the farthest provinces. Many were not rehabilitated even after Mao's death.

Hungary In comparison to such heavily controlled Soviet bloc countries as Czechoslovakia, there is relatively little overt censorship in Hungary. Under the media's well-functioning and long-established system of self-censorship, the authorities can claim that "editors do not need any kind of special resolution to be able to decide whether something should be published or not." At the same time it is assumed that those "responsible" individuals who occupy senior positions in the media naturally have "their moral and material responsibility." As a senior politician has stressed, those who run the media must know how to strike the right balance between "creative freedom" and "the correct use of the right to decide." Thus censorship is replaced by rejection slips explaining that a piece fails to fit a given profile or endangers the successful publication of a more important piece on the same topic. The government also makes full use of a tactic available to any state-run publishing system: the issuing of works in absurdly small quantities that prohibit adequate distribution. Nonetheless the Hungarian media, unlike their Soviet bloc peers, are able to deal with issues that would be taboo in, say, Poland. As long as one does not offend the

Soviet authorities in Moscow, anything goes. The complaint of many Hungarian intellectuals, most of whom publish their most outspoken pieces in the underground press, yet manage to place less controversial work in state-sponsored organs, is that such repressive tolerance is all too seductive a means of suppressing real dissent.

In 1986, the Hungarian National Assembly passed a new press law, Act II of that year. Enacted on September 1, 1986, the law allegedly conforms to the latest United Nations resolution on civil and political rights. As stated in the preamble to the act: "everybody has the right to publish their opinions and works by way of the press, if these do not contravene the constitutional order of the Hungarian People's Republic." Under section 2, "The duty of the press," it states that everyone has the right to information, and "it is the task of the press to provide … true, precise and timely information." In the pursuit of this information the press shall not infringe state constitutional laws, or the country's "international interests, or the rights and legitimate interest of the citizens and legal entities, or public morals." The act adds that "information shall not offend against human rights, or serve as justification of crimes against humanity, such as war-mongering, arousal of hatred toward other peoples, chauvinism, minority, racial or denominational discrimination, or bias on account of sex."

As provided in section 685 of the Civil Code, the economic and social organizations and associations of the state are "obliged to promote true and timely information by their own initiatives." Information may be withheld only when it is prohibited by the code or "if it interferes with state, official, factory [business] or private secrets and the authentic organ or person has given no exemption from the obligation of official and secrecy." Those who provide information in the public interest are entitled to protection under the law. The press is entitled "even without the consent of those concerned" to examine the open proceedings of state, economic or social organizations or associations and those bodies are duty bound to answer any proposals made by the press. The media are in turn bound to publish these answers as written.

A senior manager must take legal responsibility for what is published and a journalist has the right to remove his byline from any piece that has been so heavily edited that its content no longer represents what he wrote. All publications must contain a statement containing their address and that of the printer. Under the Civil Code, those publications that break the civil law as interpreted by the authorities may be suspended from publication, sequestered or shut down pending legal adjudication.

I

I Am Curious (Yellow) *I Am Curious (Yellow)* is one of the most notorious of relatively recent X-rated films. Its release in 1967 created a furor that far outweighed the alleged obscenity of its content, and that guaranteed far more people would see it than would otherwise have bothered. The film, directed by a protege of Ingmar Bergman, Vilgot Sjoman (whose *491* had already been banned from America in 1964, under the Tariff Act of 1930), centers on the social, moral, political and sexual questioning of a young actress, Lena Nyman, Sjoman's lover, who is making a film within the film about the various problems of the contemporary world. As well as demonstrating against the war in Vietnam, fantasizing a discussion with Martin Luther King, and interviewing men and women in the streets of Stockholm, she is conducting an up-and-down affair with Borje, a married car salesman. Her fantasies of their fights and their love-making are what worried censors across America.

The Maryland attorney general, describing the film to the Supreme Court, cited 16 episodes of obscenity. These included both action—cunnilingus, intercourse in a variety of usual and unusual settings, nudity, fantasized castration—and allegedly obscene dialogue.

Under the Tariff Act (1930) the first copies of the film imported into the United States, in 1968, were seized by U.S. Customs and held, pending the obligatory decision by a federal court as to whether or not they were obscene. The lower court affirmed that they were, but on appeal this decision was reversed, and the film was permitted exhibition on the grounds that it was not "utterly without redeeming social value." The film was shown without problems at 125 theaters, but was found obscene by local authorities in the states of Alabama, California, Colorado, Georgia, Michigan, Missouri, New Mexico and Ohio and in the cities of Phoenix, Kansas City, Baltimore and Boston. One of these local cases, *Grove Press* v. *Maryland State Board of Censors*, reached the Supreme Court in 1971. The distributors' appeal, *Wagonheim* v. *Maryland*, was rejected by the court and the film was declared obscene, but continued to be shown despite this. Sjoman also edited a new version, called *I Am Curious (Blue)*, from which a good deal of the erotic material was removed.

In Great Britain, where the film arrived in 1968, it also faced cuts from the British Board of Film Censors. These included scenes of rear-entry copulation on the floor, male and female frontal nudity and various instances of obvious copulation. The film was then released with an X certificate and duly became a commercial success.

SEE ALSO United States 21. Tariff Act (1930); British Board of Film Censors 1. History.

IBA: broadcasting censorship Independent television, relying on advertising rather than on a nationally levied license fee, was founded in Britain in 1954. By no means initially popular—the BBC's Lord Reith compared it to "smallpox, bubonic plague and the Black Death" and cited its arrival as "a betrayal and a surrender"—it grew to rival and often surpass the success of the BBC, purveying programs that often lacked cultural cachet, but that brought in the viewers and thus money to the advertisers.

The Independent Broadcasting Authority, which oversees commercial radio and television broadcasting in Britain and replaced the original Independent Television Authority (ITA), operates under the INDEPENDENT BROADCASTING AUTHORITY ACT OF 1973, as amended by the Broadcasting Act of 1981. The IBA makes no programs itself but acts as an umbrella for a number of franchised companies who share the lucrative regional broadcasting contracts, both in radio and television. As opposed to the BBC, with its committment to public service broadcasting, the winners of IBA franchises need make no more than token recognizance of such concepts, although some companies have a notable record in investigative, current affairs programming.

The control of all IBA programming is governed by the 1973 act. Section 2 imposes a general duty on the network to ensure that all programs maintain a high general standard as regards their content and quality and offer both a wide range of topics and a balanced, impartial approach. Under section 4(1)(a) no program should include anything that offends against good taste or decency or is likely to encourage or to incite to crime, lead to disorder or offend standards of public feeling. Section 4(1)(b) further calls for a "due impartiality ... as respects matters of political or industrial controversy, or relating to current public policy." Under the act the 18 government-appointed members of the IBA are duty-bound to vet all programs. The Annan Committee of 1977, which was established to investigate independent broadcasting, deplored this pre-broadcasting censorship, but the situation has not changed.

The essential conservatism of IBA standards was underlined in the case of *Attorney-General ex rel McWhirter* v. *IBA* (1973). McWhirter, a member of the FESTIVAL OF LIGHT, had been carried away by lurid prepublicity and attempted to have banned a documentary on the life of artist Andy Warhol, citing the good taste provision of 4(1)(a). In a judgment highlighting the differences between broadcasting and literature, Lord Denning stressed that programs were not to be judged as a whole, but must be considered piece by piece so that nothing must be included in them which might offend. The court did accept that individual "pieces" might be considered in the light of the purpose and character of the whole program.

Like the BBC, the IBA has its own code to cover the presentation of on-screen violence (written in 1971); this is especially related to such material as may be transmitted when children are watching. The code makes no attempt to provide absolute, universal rules, preferring to state that "the program maker must carry responsibility for his own decisions." In so sensitive an area risks require special justification and doubtful material is often cut. Given that most IBA stations are ultimately controlled by conservative big business, the commercial network makes less fuss about such cutting than does the BBC. In addition to the code, the IBA provides a constant flow of directives, all aimed at helping programmers keep within acceptable bounds. Like the BBC, independent companies will be subject to the strictures of the new television censorship body, the BROADCASTING STAND-ARDS COUNCIL.

Under section 5 (2) of the 1973 act, the IBA is allowed to impose extra requirements on certain programs over and above those demanded by the code. All contractors must submit their schedules to the IBA and unscheduled programs may not be broadcast other than under special circumstances. Certain programs—notably the weekday "News at Ten"—are "mandated" and must be shown throughout the network. IBA companies are bound by the Official Secrets Act and, like the BBC, are also subject to the censorship powers of the Home Office. While no government admits to overt political censorship, critics claim that it can be masked beneath the supposed grounds of good taste, balance or impartiality. Unlike the BBC, which may lose its license to broadcast through non-compliance with Home Office directives, the IBA companies are merely bound by a duty to obey. Were a company ever to refuse such a directive, the Home Secretary could presumably have the courts enforce his or her will.

Peculiar to the IBA is the control of the advertising material that it transmits and that provides its contractors with their income. The IBA has drawn up a comprehensive code to deal with these advertisements, their quality, quantity and positioning within the program schedule. Aided by an advisory committee drawn from members of the public and of the advertising industry, the IBA supervises the commercials it broadcasts. The IBA remains the final adjudicator on advertising; there is no court or tribunal above it in this area. It is especially sensitive to "potentially offensive sexual overtones," epitomized in the furor over the advertising of condoms. The IBA is also restricted as to the value of the prizes it may offer in game shows.

SEE ALSO BBC 2. broadcasting censorship; Broadcasting Complaints Commission; Broadcasting Standards Council; Clean-Up Television Campaign (U.K.); D Notices; National Viewers and Listeners Association (NVALA); Official Secrets Acts; Whitehouse, Mary.

If I Die *If I Die* is the autobiography of Andre Gide (1869-1951), a French writer whose personal and professional life were influenced by the continuing conflict he experienced between his orthodox religious upbringing and the inescapable and powerful streak of unorthodoxy that permeated his existence. He produced many noteworthy books, in all of which he attempted to resolve his own literary, sexual, religious, moral and political conflicts. An acknowledged homosexual, Gide's books were regularly attacked as immoral, but he made little attempt to modify his themes. *Les Nourritures terrestres* (1897) was an open exultation of hedonism; *L'Immoraliste* (1902) is devoted to sensuality; both *Corydon* (1919) and *Les Faux-Monnayeurs* (1950) defend and celebrate homosexuality.

The American publication of his biography, a typically opinionated and irreverent piece of writing, angered the New York SOCIETY FOR THE SUPPRESSION OF VICE, whose secretary, JOHN S. SUMNER, brought suit in 1936 against the Gotham Book Mart of New York City. Sumner alleged that the book was obscene as defined under New York's Obscenity Statute and as tested by the Hicklin Rule. Under this rule Sumner was required only to prove that a portion of the book was actionable, and therefore concentrated on some 76 pages, about 20 percent of the whole. Hicklin, however, had already been discredited in American courts, after Justice Woolsey's decision to allow the uncensored sale of Joyce's ULYSSES in 1934. This stated, in essence, that henceforth a book would have to be judged wholly and not merely occasionally obscene. On these grounds Sumner's suit was dismissed by the New York City magistrate Nathan D. Perlman, who also noted that if a writer of Gide's stature was good enough for the world's literary critics, then he was certainly good enough for New York's readers.

SEE ALSO New York 5. Obscenity Statute.

Illinois's obscenity statute Under section 223 of the Illinois Criminal Code: "Whoever ... shall have in his possession, with or without intent to sell or give away, any obscene and indecent ... drawing ... or shall draw and expose any such article, shall be confined in the county jail not more than six months, or be fined no less than $100 nor more than $1,000."

Illustrated Report, The SEE *Hamling* v. *United States* (1974).

incitement Under U.S. law the government has the right to punish anyone who incites or induces another person to commit a criminal act. This can extend to inflammatory speeches, and thus comes up against FIRST AMENDMENT guarantees of free speech. Whereas ADVOCACY of criminal acts need not presume that the acts themselves will occur, incitement must be shown to have represented an immediate, imminent and clear and present inducement to commit the acts in question. This definition is best seen in the case of

YATES V. UNITED STATES (1957), in which a number of individuals were charged under the SMITH ACT for an alleged conspiracy to overthrow the U.S. government and establish a communist dictatorship. The Supreme Court reversed the convictions of lower courts, on the grounds that the defendants had advocated, but not incited these revolutionary activities.

Incitement to Disaffection Act (1934, U.K.) This act, more popularly known as the Sedition Bill, was designed to protect members of the British armed forces from receiving materials that might lead them to become disaffected with the orders it was their duty to carry out. Under section 1 it is an offense "if any person maliciously and advisedly endeavours to seduce any member of Her Majesty's forces from his duty or allegiance to Her Majesty"; under section 2(1) it is an offense "if any person, with intent to commit or to aid, abet, counsel or procure the commission of an offense under section 1 of this Act, has in his possession or under his control any document of such a nature that the dissemination of copies thereof among members of Her Majesty's forces would constitute such an offence." Those convicted under the act face a fine of £200 maximum and up to two years' imprisonment.

The act, condemned by a leading contemporary lawyer, Sir William Holdsworth, as "the most daring encroachment upon the liberty of the subject which the Executive Government has yet attempted at a time which is not a time of emergency," met stern opposition from the then newly formed Council for Civil Liberties. Many groups joined a broad campaign against the bill, including writers, intellectuals and particularly pacifists, who most wished to challenge the military assumptions and would be most threatened by the legislation. Despite these efforts, which included mass demonstrations, the bill became law. It was used occasionally before World War II, and more recently in Northern Ireland, where Republican sympathizers have circulated documents questioning the role of the British Army.

The most celebrated prosecution under the law was that in 1974 of veteran peace campaigner Pat Arrowsmith, who had been charged under the act after distributing to British troops a leaflet explaining how best to leave the army. Arrowsmith jumped bail, fled to Ireland and remained there until February 1974 when the Labour Party won the General Election in England. On her return she was arrested and held without bail until her trial at the Old Bailey in London in May 1974, at which she was found guilty and sentenced to 18 months imprisonment. The Court of Appeal upheld the conviction but reduced her sentence to a length that permitted her immediate discharge. In May 1977 the European Commission on Human Rights upheld her complaint that the conviction had been in violation of the EUROPEAN CONVENTION ON HUMAN RIGHTS.

indecency Under English law there exists in addition to the concept of obscenity the lesser offense of indecency. This has been defined in the case of *R.* v. *Stanley* (1965) as "something that offends the ordinary modesty of the average man ... offending against recognised standards of propriety at the lower end of the scale." In the trial of the underground magazine IT (*Knuller* v. *DPP* [1973]), Lord Reid added that, "Indecency is not confined to sexual indecency; indeed it is difficult to find any limit short of saying that it includes anything which an ordinary decent man or woman would find to be shocking, disgusting, or revolting." As in cases of obscenity, it is accepted that CONTEMPORARY COMMUNITY STANDARDS, varying gradually as they do, must also be taken into account in indecency trials. The concept of DOMINANT EFFECT must also be assessed: material cannot be judged indecent on the basis of certain isolated passages or scenes, on film or television. Indecency offenses are covered by the Post Office Act (1953), the Unsolicited Goods and Services Act (1971), and the Indecent Displays (Control) Act (1981).

Indecent Displays Bill (1979, U.K.) The original Cinematic and Indecent Displays Bill was prepared during 1973 by Home Secretary Robert Carr for Britain's Conservative government, and when that government fell unexpectedly in February 1974 the bill was abandoned. The topic of obscenity was similarly shelved, although the new Labour home secretary deputed the WILLIAMS COMMITTEE to produce a report on the topic. By the time this report appeared, the Conservatives had returned to power and its liberal recommendations were swiftly rejected. In place of the report, there was adopted a private member's bill, proposed by Timothy Sainsbury, MP, that in effect resuscitated Carr's old proposals. On October 27, 1981, the bill became law. In essence it governed the window displays of shops that sold indecent material. Aimed specifically at the Soho sex shops, it aggravated many shopkeepers who sold items, e.g., guns, which might be considered indecent by a passer-by and which might thus face prosecution under the act. The adult bookstores, in compliance with the law, now placed in their windows nothing but a notice advising the public of the nature of their business—thus perhaps adding to their mystique and making the shops even more conspicuous.

Independent Broadcasting Authority Act (1973) The following sections of the act deal with the content of programs and with the code dealing with the treatment of violence on the screen:

4. (1) It shall be the duty of the Authority to satisfy themselves that, so far as possible, the programs broadcast by the Authority comply with the following requirements, that is to say:
(a) that nothing is included in the programs which offends against good taste or decency or is likely to encourage or incite to crime or lead to disorder or to be offensive to public feeling;
(b) that a sufficient amount of time in the programs is given

to news and news features and that all news given in the programs (in whatever form) is presented with due accuracy and impartiality;

(f) that due impartiality is preserved on behalf of the persons providing the programs as respects matters of political or industrial controversy or relating to current public policy.

5. (1) The Authority:

(a) shall draw up, and from time to time review, a codegiving guidance:

(i) as to the rules to be observed in regard to the showing of violence, and in regard to the inclusion in local sound broadcasts of sounds suggestive of violence, particularly when large numbers of children and young persons may be expected to be watching and listening to the programs, and

(ii) as to such other matters concerning standards and practice for programs (other than advertisements) broadcast by the Authority as the Authority may consider suitable for inclusion in the code,

and in considering what other matters ought to be included in the code in pursuance of sub-paragraph (ii) shall have special regard to programs broadcast when large numbers of children and young persons may be expected to be watching or listening; and

(b) shall secure that the provisions of the code are observed in relation to all programs (other than advertisements) broadcast by the Authority.

SEE ALSO IBA: broadcasting censorship.

Index Expurgatorius A list, sanctioned and devised by church authority, specifying passages that had to be removed or altered in books that were otherwise permitted reading for Roman Catholics. The first Index was created in 494 by Pope Gelasius I, proscribing a number of books that should not be read by the faithful. This developed into the INDEX LIBRORUM PROHIBITORUM. The *Index Expurgatorius* was originated in the 16th century as an addendum to the *Index Librorum Prohibitorum*; it was abrogated in 1966. The *Index Expurgatorius* was cited by Thomas James, whose treatise on such Indexes was published in Oxford in 1627, as an invaluable reference work to be used by the curators of the Bodleian library when listing those works particularly worthy of collecting. Writing at much the same time, Bishop Barlow described the Indexes as "invaluable as records of the literature of the doctrines and opinions obnoxious to Rome … we are directed to the book, chapter and line where anything is spoken against any superstition or error of Rome; so that he who has the Indexes cannot want testimonies against Rome."

SEE ALSO Indexes, index of.

Index Expurgatorius of Brasichelli The Dominican monk Guanzelli, who called himself Fr. Joseph Maria Brasichelli and was the current MAGISTER SACRI PALATII, was the author of this *Index Expurgatorius*, issued in 1607 and the second compiled in Rome. The complaints that met Brasichelli's Index convinced the Vatican that the issuance of such expurgatory Indexes was bad policy, especially when, as in this case, the Index appeared under no authority other than that of the individual who published it, and might be seen in its prohibitions and listings as an expression of his own prejudices, even if they did reflect the teachings of the church as a whole. It was decided that this particular Index would bring no credit to the church, and it was quietly suppressed. Only one volume appeared, and when Brasichelli died in 1619 the proposed second one had not been published.

SEE ALSO Indexes, index of.

Index Generalis of Thomas James **(1627)** James was Bodley's librarian in Oxford in 1627 when he published an *Index Generalis*, based on those copies that the library held of the Catholic Church's Indexes. His intention in producing this volume was to point out to the university on the basis of the Indexes just what books the library ought to be specializing in collecting. The "James Index," as it came to be known, developed into a working guide to bookbuyers in England and exercised an important effect on the circulation of the titles it mentioned. Like the works from which it takes its material, it classes authors in three groups: those who have been banned completely; authors whose works have been expurgated; and works of doubtful authorship, which have still to be prohibited. James' preface makes his contempt for the Papacy clear, both because it extended so pervasive a censorship system and, perhaps more so, because the system was so poorly, ignorantly and unprofessionally implemented. The Bodleian Library itself continued using the Index when purchasing certain titles up to the 20th century.

Index Librorum Prohibitorum

1. history A list of books banned to Roman Catholics under the imprimatur of the church in Rome. Guided by the pronouncements of such authorities as ST. PAUL, St. Isidore and St. Augustine, all of whom had recommended the censorship of "bad books," the Catholic Church instituted the banning of books at the First Council of Nicaea (325) when the heresies of Arrius were condemned and his works proscribed. In 431 the Council of Ephesus similarly proscribed the works of Nestorius and in 496 Pope Gelasius issued a list of some 60 works that were not to be read by the faithful. In 1121 the works of ABELARD were banned, as were those of WYCLIF and Huss at the Council of Constance in 1814. The Hebrew Talmud was banned by a succession of Popes beginning, in 1239, with Gregory IX, and continuing until 1329. In 1520 Pope Leo X's bull, "Exsurge Domine," prohibited those books MARTIN LUTHER had already written as well as those he might write in the future.

The first governmental list of banned books was issued in 1526 by the English King Henry VIII, but this was short and dealt only with volumes relevant to England (see United Kingdom: Tudor censorship). At the same time the Emperor Charles V published in the Netherlands a "plakaat," which named certain authors whose works were to be burnt in that country. In Spain, where the Inquisition (see Spanish Inquisition) was growing increasingly influential in the censorship of books, the church issued in 1540 a catalog of forbidden works, although it went only to the Inquisitor of Barcelona and urged him to redouble his efforts against such material. In 1546 a full-scale catalog was prepared at the University of Louvain, submitted in 1547 to the Suprema, and subsequently circulated throughout the inquisitorial tribunals operating in Spain. It was enlarged and recirculated, under the authority of Charles V, in 1551. The first comprehensive attempt to list all such banned material, on a scale applicable to the whole of Europe, was published in 1559 by Pope Paul IV. This index, the *Index Auctorum et Librorum Prohibitorum*, was the first of a series of Papal Indexes that by 1899 totalled 42. The Vatican did not have a monopoly on the banning of heresy, and a variety of local Indexes continued to appear, often at odds with the Roman one, although the lists compiled for one area were often used in another, and vice versa. From 1571, as established by Pope Pius V, the CONGREGATION OF THE INDEX, a panel of cardinals and priests, began supervising the operation and enforcement of the censorship and updating the list of banned writings. The congregation was an outgrowth of a body instituted by Pope Alexander IV, who in 1256 had empanelled four cardinals to examine and subsequently prohibit a highly critical assessment of church affairs by the Parisian, William of St. Amour.

In 1564, at the Council of Trent, the first official *Index Librorum Prohibitorum* was issued. It became known as the TRIDENTINE INDEX. While the Spanish and the Tridentine Indexes overlapped, they operated independently, as the Inquisitors of Spain and of Rome pursued separate courses. The council also compiled 10 rules governing the printing, publishing and reading of books. No heretical or obscene works were to be published and even permissible works had to be vetted by a bishop. These rules lasted until the pontificate of Benedict XIV in 1740, and their institution helped underline the central authority of Rome. In 1753 Pope Pius V, in the bull "Sollicita ac Provida," ordered the Congregation of the Index to begin work on a major revision of the censorship system. The result of their deliberations was the INDEX OF BENEDICT XIV of 1758, the first major redirection of ecclesiastical censorship for two centuries and the church's first acknowledgment that it could not and should not attempt to control the entire volume of worldwide printing. Further reforms modified the form of the Index in 1848, 1897, 1900 and 1917, but these were essentially cosmetic rather than fundamental.

The traditional Indexes, prior to the essentially liberal realignments of Benedict's version, were triumphs of dogmatic hope over practical reality. They were bibliographically inaccurate, compiled in many caess by men whose theological enthusiasm far exceeded their intellectual ability, and based on the fluctuations of papal doctrine and politics rather than on the actual content of the works under discussion. The tenor of an Index might be dictated by which particular faction or religious order happened to be dominant when it was being prepared. Books were condemned as much on the name of their author, their printer or of the city of their origin as on what they actually said. The censors erred toward excess, preferring occasionally to punish the innocent rather than to let slip even one of the allegedly guilty. Even on the basis of the compilers' brief, no Index was ever truly comprehensive or absolutely correct.

As it existed in its final 20th-century form, the Index was divided into three parts: the Congregation of the Index; that part of the Canon law in which the rules and regulations governing its operation were found; and the list of prohibited books itself. Among the most important of the rules laid down was that no Roman Catholic priest or layman might publish any book without prior ecclesiastical approval if it dealt with scripture, theology, canon law etc. (canon 1385). Only the Holy See and the bishops held the right to prohibit books. A papal prohibition applied to the whole church, an episcopal prohibition to the bishop's diocese only (canons 1395, 1396). Certain books and classes of books were automatically prohibited, including heretical and schismatic books, books supporting divorce, duelling, and suicide, or books evoking spirits, advocating magic. Books that dealt with impure and obscene subjects were forbidden. Once a book had been prohibited it could be neither published, read, owned, sold, translated nor in any way be communicated to others of the faith. Cardinals and bishops remained above the prohibitions and, in special cases, they might grant permission to a specific individual to read a specific book. Were a Catholic to defy these rules, he or she faced a variety of penalties. A special excommunication reserved to the Holy See was incurred by those who published heretical, apostate or schismatic books that advocated heresy, apostasy or schism; those who defended, read or simply owned such books were similarly punished. Authors or publishers who published unauthorized commentaries on the scriptures faced a simple excommunication. There was no penalty laid down for reading a book classified as obscene.

The Index went through 300 editions until it was abrogated in 1966 when Cardinal Ottaviani was authorized by the Pope to announce that the Index had forfeited its authority as a document of censorship and existed merely as "an historic document." The sheer volume of publications produced, plus "the increasing maturity and sophistication of Catholic laymen" had rendered the Index obsolete. Throughout its existence the Index dealt with specific books, rather than authors, thus leading to some confusion in the public mind, since it was possible to read one volume by a given author but perhaps not another. The last new edition of the Index was published in 1948 by the Typis Polyglottis Vaticanus. Among the titles listed that year were the complete works of Balzac, D'Annunzio, Anatole France, Hume, VOLTAIRE, ZOLA and Stendhal; CASANOVA's *Memoirs*, Richardson's *Pamela*, John Stuart Mill's *Principles of Political Economy*, J.-J. ROUSSEAU's *Social Contract* and VICTOR HUGO's *Les Miserables*. Despite the end of the list, certain volumes, notably any communist publication, are still automatically banned from Catholic homes and institutions. The periodical issued by the Sacred Congregation of the Faith occasionally publishes lists of those works that, while not actually forbidden, are certainly "not recommended."

2. material that was condemned The Roman and Spanish Indexes (see Roman Indexes) ran for several hundred years, with their most effective or certainly most enthusiastic activities taking place in the 16th and 17th centuries and affecting a large proportion of the known world. During that time many hundreds of books were condemned as heretical or otherwise unsuitable for the faithful. It would be impossible, and unnecessary, to list every title, especially given the bibliographical inaccuracy and ideological inconsistency of the Index compilers, but it is possible to offer a brief overview of the categories of material falling under the bans and a few of the titles concerned. The major works, such as those of LUTHER, ERASMUS, GALILEO and similar prominent heretics, appear under their own heading.

Although a number of polemic works against the Papacy undoubtedly appeared in the 17th century, few of them appeared on an Index. By the 1800s, the controversy over Papal infallibility ensured a wider mention of such material. The Index did take note of historical works on the church, both by Protestants and Catholics, as well as studies of the Index itself, on papal finances and similar topics. Examples of these works include the monographs of Gregorio Leti (1630-1701), which were banned in their entirety in 1686, and Limborch's *History of the Inquisition* (1693), banned in 1694. Writings on the Eastern or Greek Orthodox Church, such as those of Lukaris, Nektarius, Philippus Cyprius and Sylvester Syropoli, were also banned, although the earlier Indexes tended to ignore the Greek theologians. More important were the works of the church fathers such as Chrysostom and Cyprian. These were not of themselves heretical, but tended to have been edited by those who had subsequently been so condemned, and were thus by association condemned themselves. Editions of the pagan classics—OVID, Lucretius, Caesar and others—were all banned.

Apart from the consistent bannings of the TALMUD, certain rabbinical texts were also banned. These were not chosen specifically, but rather plucked from the whole corpus of Jewish writing, based on the large lists compiled in the *Bibliotheca Rabbinica* by Bartolucci and Imbonati, published between 1675 and 1694. This specialized "Index" was augmented in 1775-76, giving the Papacy further titles from which to choose. Conversely, more overtly anti-Semitic tracts, such as that of the monk Vincenti, appearing in 1776, were also condemned. All Indexes prohibited the theological writings of any Protestant, and works from all over Europe were cited during the period. Similarly, works by unorthodox Catholics, especially of certain 19th-century Germans, were forbidden.

A major area of controversy was that of historical writing, and Italian, English and French authors, both Protestant and Catholic, were all banned. Victims include Dupin's *History of the World*, the works of Francis Osborne (banned 1757) and of Pietro della Valle (1629). The writings of Dutch and German Protestant jurists were banned wholesale, and those of Italian Protestants, such as Vicenzo Paravicino, suffered similarly. Given the prerogatives claimed by the church, the whole area of philosophy, natural science and medicine fell under continual suspicion. Most of the work of DESCARTES (1596-1650) was banned in 1663 and again in 1722. Nicholas Malebranche (1638- 1715) was banned, although his peers Gassendi, Mersenne and Maignan were spared. Spinoza (1632-77) was banned, as were Montaigne (1533-92), Bacon (1561-1626), Hobbes (1588-1679), Fludd (1574-1637) and other important 17th-century Protestant philosophers.

VOLTAIRE (1694-1778), ROUSSEAU (1712-78) and Hume (1711-76) were all prohibited absolutely. Gibbon's *Decline and Fall of the Roman Empire* (1776-81) was banned in 1783. The work of such scientists and philosophers as Jeremy Bentham (1748-1832), Richard Whately (1787-1863), John Stuart Mill (1806-73), Erasmus Darwin (1731-1802), Auguste Comte (1798-1857), Hippolyte Taine (1828-93), Leopold von Ranke (1795-1886), Oliver Goldsmith (1730?-74) and many others were all listed in due course. In the field of general literature the Indexes listed, for example, the works of Lamartine, Eugene Sue, Balzac, both Dumas, Feydeau, Sand, Stendhal, FLAUBERT, HUGO, Lessing and Heine.

Books on magic, astrology and similar topics were banned, as were those on the techniques of exorcism and on secret societies, such as the freemasons and the followers of CAGLIOSTRO. A number of poems, satirical squibs, textbooks, periodicals and cyclopedias were listed; in this group come Swift's *Tale of a Tub* (1704), Richardson's *Pamela* (1740) and DEFOE's *Robinson Crusoe* (1719). La Fontaine was banned completely, although Cervantes was merely expurgated.

Corrupt or fraudulent indulgences, the sale of which had inspired Luther's polemic against the church, were prohibited from 1603, by the Inquisition, the CONGREGATION OF THE INDEX and the Congregation of Indulgences. The INDEX OF BENEDICT XIV makes four specifications against such material. Works concerning the saints had to be authorized by the church, and pictures of saints were subject to certain strict rules. Any suggestion that the Blessed Virgin Mary had indulged in any earthly sin was absolutely proscribed; a large number of works on Mariology were forbidden on grounds of exaggeration and bad taste, as well as doctrinal error. Stories of divine revelations afforded to nuns were occasionally suppressed. Quietism, a form of mysticism originated ca. 1675 by Molinos, was generally forbidden, as were the works of Francois Fenelon (1651-1715), a leading Quietist. Controversies arising over the doctrine of probability (a casuistic doctrine, frowned upon by orthodox Catholics, wereby an individual is not always obliged to take the more probable side in a dispute, but may take the less probable, however unlikely that may be) and the role of usury during the papacy of Benedict XIV created a number of rival treatises, many of which were banned.

The French Revolution created a large body of material, all of which was censored, although mainly by the Spanish rather than the Roman authorities. The Revolutions of 1848 were similarly productive of seditious material, which in turn was banned. Communism and socialism fell into a similar category of unacceptability, with the works of Proudhon among the first to be prohibited. Less important were theories of magnetism and spiritualism, both popular in the 19th century, but they too were suppressed. The Catholic population of America increased throughout the 19th century, and the Index took due note. The first work by an American author to be banned was a monograph by a Philadelphia priest, W. Hogan, whose work was banned in 1822. Canadian Catholics were also subject to censorship, but the most extensive effects of the Index were seen in South America, where the church had a far more dominant role than in the North.

SEE ALSO Christian Church 1. early censorship; Indexes, index of.

Index Librorum Prohibitorum (of Henry Spencer Ashbee)

Published in 1877, the Index formed the first part of HENRY SPENCER ASHBEE's monumental three-volume bibliography of erotic and pornographic works, issued under the overall title of *Notes Bio-Biblio-Icono-graphical and Critical, on Curious & Uncommon Books*. Following the *Index librorum prohibitorum* (its title indlulging his obsessive anti-Catholicism) were the *Centuria librorum absconditorum* (1879) and the *Catena librorum tacendorum* (1885). In all, Ashbee listed several hundred erotic and pornographic works, from the classics to the more obscure, giving each one as far as possible a full bibliographical listing and adding a plot summary and/or his own comments where appropriate. Throughout the work he aims for scrupulous scholarly disinterest. He does not comment on the morals either of writing such books, or of the characters within them. He uses obscene language only where no other can be substituted—and never bowdlerizes when he quotes, although he does not translate when a work is not in English. He was keen not to have his excerpts used as mini-pornography, and gave only as much of a book "as is necessary to form a correct estimate of the style of the writer."

No one setting out to compile such a book could pretend to have no interest in its subject matter, but Ashbee is determined to inspire not pleasure but "a hearty disgust" in what he itemizes. Certainly his overall tone is at least ostensibly condemnatory. To ensure that his efforts were appreciated only by the cognoscenti Ashbee limited each edition to 250 copies, many of them bought by members of the exclusive bibliographical clubs to which he belonged. Although there had been some similar efforts, notably that of JULES GAY and the *Pornodidascaliana* compiled by Joseph Octava Delpierre (1802-79), Ashbee's work laid down new standards for the bibliography of erotic literature. Despite a number of succes-

sors, all of whom have drawn to some extent on his efforts, Ashbee's *Notes...* remains the exemplar of such bibliographies.

SEE ALSO *Bibliographie des ouvrages relatifs de l'amour, aux Femmes...*; *Bibliographie du roman erotique au XIXe siecle*; *Bibliotheca Arcana*; *Bibliotheca Germanorum Erotica*; *Bilderlexikon der Erotik*; *Register Librorum Eroticorum*.

Index of Alexander VII (1664)

This Index, the first Roman Index to appear since 1596, was produced by the Pope to bring up to date the ROMAN INQUISITION's censorship system, which had not issued a cumulative and comprehensive list of prohibited material since that of Clement VIII (see *Index of Clement VIII*). This Index offered an alphabetical list of all the works that had been prohibited in the TRIDENTINE and Clementine Indexes, as well as those works that had appeared since then and had been banned on an ad hoc basis. The old division of three classes was abandoned, because the Pope had no wish to promote the illusion that those in classes II and III were any less pernicious than those in class I. The new Index also listed every prohibitory edict that had appeared since the Council of Trent's publication. The Alexandrine Index was reprinted in 1665 and 1667. The most important aspect of the Index of 1664 was that it contained, as well as its more predictable prohibitions, the formal condemnation of the astronomical theories and discoveries of Copernicus and GALILEO.

SEE ALSO Indexes, index of.

index of banned books

This inevitably partial list is a summary of those books that have most often been censored. In many cases they appear separately under their own heading, or that of their author.

Ableman, Paul, THE MOUTH AND ORAL SEX (1971)

Adams, W.E., *Tyrannicide: Is It Justifiable?* (1858)

Albertus Magnus, *De Secretis Mulierum* (1475; translated in 1725 as *The Mysteries of Human Generation Fully Revealed*)

Aldiss, Brian, *The Hand-Reared Boy* (1970)

Algren, Nelson, *The Man with the Golden Arm* (1949)

Alembert, Jean d' & DIDEROT, Denis, *L'Encyclopedie, ou Dictionnaire raisonne des sciences, des arts et des metiers* (1751-67)

Amalrik, Andrei, *Involuntary Journey to Siberia* (1970); *Will the Soviet Union Survive until 1984* (1970)

Anderson, Sherwood, *Dark Laughter* (1925)

Anonymous, A CHRONICLE OF CURRENT EVENTS (1968-   )

Anonymous, *Arabian Nights' Entertainment* (in oral tradition, from the ninth century; published in Arabic in 1839-42, in English 1885-8)

Anonymous, MY SECRET LIFE (ca. 1888)

APOLLINAIRE, Guillaume, *Memoires d'un Jeune (Don) Juan* (1914)

Sterne, Laurence, *The Life and Opinions of Tristram Shandy, Gentleman* (1760-7)

STOPES, Marie, *Contraception: Its Theory, History and Practice* (1923); *Married Love* (1918); *Vestia* (1926); *Wise Parenthood* (1918)

Sue, Eugene, *Mysteres du peuple* (1857)

Suetonius, *The Twelve Caesars* (ca. 100 A.D.)

Swift, Jonathan, *A Tale of a Tub* (1704)

Swinburne, A.C., *Laus Veneris, and other Poems and Ballads* (1865)

Tarsis, Valeriy, *Ward 7* (1965)

Taylor, Robert, *The Devil's Pulpit* (1831)

Tenin, Vlas, *Moscow Nights* (1971)

Toft, Mogens, *Sexual Techniques* (1969)

Tolstoy, Lev, *The Kreutzer Sonata* (1889)

TROCCHI, Alexander, CAIN'S BOOK (1960); *Helen and Desire* (1954); *White Thighs* (1955)

Trotsky, Leon, *The History of the Russian Revolution* (1931-3)

Twain, Mark, *Some Remarks on the Science of Onanism* (1879)

Van Rensburg, Patrick, *Guilty Land* (1962)

Vanbrugh, Sir John, *The Provok'd Wife* (1697)

Vatsyayana, *The Kama Sutra* (originally, fourth century; translated 1883)

Verlaine, Paul, *Femmes* (1890); *Hombres* (1904); as "Pablo de Herlangnez," *Les Amis, scene d'amour sapphique* (1867)

Vian, Boris, *J'irai cracher su vos tombes* (1946)

Vicarion, Count Palmiro (Christopher Logue), books for OLYMPIA PRESS

Vidal, Gore, *Myra Breckinridge* (1968)

Volney, Constantin-Francois de, *Les Ruines, ou meditation sur les revolutions des empires* (1791)

VOLTAIRE, *Candide* (1759); *Dictionnaire philosophique* (1764); *Traite de la Tolerance* (1763)

Wales, Hubert, *The Yoke* (1908)

Wells, H.G., *The World of William Clissold* (1926); *Ann Veronica* (1909)

Whitman, Walt, *Leaves of Grass* (1855)

Wilde, Oscar, *Salome* (1893)

WILKES, John, *The North Briton* (1762-3, 1768-71, journal); *An Essay on Woman* (1763, attributed)

Williams, Tennessee, *Cat on a Hot Tin Roof* (1955); *A Streetcar Named Desire* (1947)

WILSON, Edmund, MEMOIRS OF HECATE COUNTY (1946)

Winsor, Kathleen, FOREVER AMBER (1946)

Wooler, T.J., *The Black Dwarf* (1817-24, journal)

Woolston, Thomas, *Six Discourses on the Miracles of our Saviour* (1727-9)

Wright, Richard, *Native Son* (1940)

Wycherley, William, *The Country Wife* (1675)

ZOLA, Emile, *Nana* (1880); *Pot-Bouille* (1882); *La Terre* (1887)

index of banned films   This inevitably partial list is a summary of those films that have most often been censored, although few of them have been comprehensively banned. In many cases they appear separately under their own heading (and are marked for cross-reference). The listing comprises the title, the year of production, the director (where known), and the country of origin.

AGE D'OR, L' (1930, Luis Bunuel, Fr./Sp.)

Avventura, L' (1949, Michelangelo Antonioni, Italy/Fr.)

Bel Ami (1954, Louis Daquin, Fr./Austria)

Beyond the Valley of the Dolls (1970, Russ Meyer, U.S.)

Bezhin Meadow (1935, Sergei Eisenstein, U.S.S.R.)

Bike Boy (1967, Andy Warhol, U.S.)

BIRTH OF A NATION, THE (1915, D.W. Griffith, U.S.)

Blackmailed (1950, Marc Allegret, U.K.)

Bloody Mama (1969, Roger Corman, U.S.)

BLUE MOVIE/FUCK (1968, Andy Warhol, U.S.)

BODY, THE (1970, Roy Battersby, U.K.)

Bofors Gun, The (1968, Jack Gold, U.K.)

Bread of Love, The (1953, Arne Matteson, Sweden)

Breathless (1959, Jean-Luc Godard, France)

Brig, The (1964, Jonas and Adolfas Mekas, U.S.)

British Sounds (1969, Jean-Luc Godard, U.K.)

Burn (1968, Gillo Pontecorvo, Italy)

CHANT D'AMOUR, UN (1950, Jean Genet, Fr.)

Chelsea Girls (1966, Andy Warhol, U.S.)

Chien Andalou, Un (1928, Luis Bunuel, Fr.)

Christine Keeler Story, The (1963, Robert Spafford, Denmark)

Clockwork Orange, A (1971, Stanley Kubrick, U.K.)

Couch (1965, Andy Warhol, U.S.)

Cranes Are Flying, The (1957, Mikhail Kalatozov, U.S.S.R.)

Cuba Si! (1961, Chris Marker, Cuba/Fr.)

Cuba Va! (1970, Felix Greene, Cuba)

Danish Blue (1968, Gabriel Axel, 1968)

Dawn (1928, Herbert Wilcox, U.K.)

Devils, The (1971, Ken Russell, U.K.)

Dolce Vita, La (1959, Federico Fellini, It.)

East Wind (1970, Jean-Luc Godard, It.)

Eclipse, The (1970, Michelangelo Antonioni, It.)

Encore (1951, Pat Jackson et al., U.K.)

Father Sergius (1917, Yakov Protozanov, U.S.S.R.)

Femme est une Femme, Une (1960, Jean-Luc Godard, Fr.)

Femme Mariee, Une (1964, Jean-Luc Godard, Fr.)

Flaming Creatures (1963, Jack Smith, U.S.)

FLESH (1968, Paul Morrissey, U.S.)

Fortune and Men's Eyes (1971, Harvey Hart, U.S.)

Fuck Off! (*Images of Poland*) (1971, Jorn Donner, Finland)

Futz (1969, Tom O'Horgan, U.S.)

Grande Illusion, La (1937, Jean Renoir, Fr.)

Grissom Gang, The (1971, Robert Aldrich, U.S.)

Growing Up (1969, Martin Cole, U.K.)

Guns of the Trees (1961, Jonas Mekas, U.S.)

Holiday on Sylt (1958, Annelie and Andrew Thorndike, E. Ger.)

How to Stuff a Wild Bikini (1965, William Asher, U.S.)
Human Condition, The (1960, Masaki Kobayashi, Japan)
I AM CURIOUS—YELLOW (1967, Vilgot Sjoman, Swe.)
Ilyich's Gate (1963, Marlen Khutsiev, U.S.S.R.)
Inside North Vietnam (1967, Felix Greene, U.S.)
Jules et Jim (1961, Francois Truffaut, Fr.)
Klute (1971, Alan J. Pakula, U.S.)
Knife in the Water (1961, Roman Polanski, Poland)
L-Shaped Room, The (1962, Bryan Forbes, U.K.)
Language of Love (1969, Torgny Wickman, Swe.)
Lenin in October (1937, Mikhail Romm, U.S.S.R.)
Let There Be Light (1946, John Huston, U.S.)
Lonesome Cowboys (1968, Andy Warhol, U.S.)
Love that Whirls, The (1949, Kenneth Anger, U.K.)
Macbeth (1971, Roman Polanski, U.K.)
Male and Female (1919, Cecil B. De Mille, U.S.)
Mr. Freedom (1968, William Klein, Fr.)
Mondo Cane (1961, Bualtiero Jacopetti, It.)
Mondo Cane 2 (1963, Bualtiero Jacopetti, It.)
Music Lovers, The (1970, Ken Russell, U.K.)
My Hustler (1965, Andy Warhol, U.S.)
My Little Chickadee (1940, Edward Cline, U.S.)
Myra Breckinridge (1970, Michael Sarne, U.S.)
Nazarin (1958, Luis Bunuel, Mexico)
Nine Days of One Year (1961, Mikhail Romm, U.S.S.R.)
Nine Hours to Rama (1962, Mark Robson, U.K.)
No Orchids for Miss Blandish (1948, St. John Clowes, U.K.)
Notte, La (Michelangelo Antonioni, It.)
October (1928, Serge Eisenstein, U.S.S.R.)
One, Two, Three (1961, Billy Wilder, U.S.)
Operation Teutonic Sword (1958, Annelie and Andrew Thorndike, E. Ger.)
Paths of Glory (1957, Stanley Kubrick, U.S.)
PROFESSOR MAMLOCK (1938, Adolf Minkin, U.S.S.R.)
Psycho (1960, Alfred Hitchcock, U.S.)
Quartet (1948, Ken Annakin et al., U.K.)
Room at the Top (1958, Jack Clayton, U.K.)
Saturday Night and Sunday Morning (1960, Karel Reisz, U.K.)
Scorpio Rising (1963, Kenneth Anger, U.S.)
Servant, The (1963, Joseph Losey, U.K.)
Seventeen (1965, Annelise Meineche, Den.)
17th May (1969, Amnja Breien, Norway)
Silence, The (1962, Ingmar Bergman, Swe.)
Singer Not the Song, The (1960, Roy Baker, U.K.)
Soldier Blue (1970, Ralph Nelson, U.S.)
Straw Dogs (1972, Sam Peckinpah, U.K.)
Suzanne Simonin (1965, Jacques Rivette, Fr.)
Sympathy for the Devil/One Plus One (1968, Jean-Luc Godard, U.K.)
Trans-Europe Express (1966, Alain Robbe-Grillet, Fr.)
Trash (1970, Paul Morrissey, U.S.)
Trio (1950, Ken Annakin et al, U.K.)
Triumph of the Will (1936, Leni Riefenstahl, Ger.)
Tropic of Cancer (1969, Joseph Strick, U.S.)

US (1967, Peter Brook, U.K.)
ULYSSES (1967, Joseph Strick, U.K.)
Victim (1961, Basil Dearden, U.K.)
Virgin Spring, The (1959, Ingmar Bergman, Swe.)
Viridiana (1961, Luis Bunuel, Mex.)
Vivre sa Vie (1962, Jean-Luc Godard, Fr.)
WR—Mysteries of the Organism (1971, Dusan Makavejev, Yugo./W. Ger.)
War Game, The (1965, Peter Watkins, U.K.)
Weekend (1967, Jean-Luc Godard, Fr.)
Who's Afraid of Virginia Woolf? (1966, Mike Nichols, U.S.)
Wild Angels, The (1966, Roger Corman, U.S.)
Wild Bunch, The (1968, Sam Peckinpah, U.S.)
Wild One, The (1953, Laslo Benedek, U.S.)
Women in Love (1969, Ken Russell, U.K.)
Woodstock (1969, Michael Wadleigh, U.S.)
Zabriskie Point (1968, Michelangelo Antonioni, U.S.)
SEE ALSO United States 1. banned films.

Index of Benedict XIV (**1758**)   This index, the result of deliberations by the CONGREGATION OF THE INDEX begun in 1753, marked a new direction in church censorship. It states that all previous Indexes are in various ways incorrect and substitutes this new compilation to correct their errors. Its main innovation was the establishment of the "Decreta de libris prohibitis nec in Indice expressis," termed in later editions the "Decreta Generalia." The preface to these "general decrees" explained that there were now so many books being published that it was no longer possible to list every title that deserved condemnation. Instead there would be laid down a variety of general classifications, accompanied by general rules designed to guide the faithful as to what they should or should not read. The "Decreta" listed 11 species of "prohibited books which have been written or published by heretics or which have to do with heresies or the creeds of unbelievers." These included the prayers and offices of the heretics; apologia defending heresy; editions of the scriptures prepared or annotated by heretics; any portions of the scriptures put into verse by heretics; heretical editions of calendars, martyrologies and necrologies; any poems, narrations, addresses, pictures or compositions that contained heresy; catechisms, ABC primers, commentaries on the Ten Commandments or the Apostles' Creed and instructions in doctrine; colloquies, conferences, disputations and similar arguments that concern heresy or are edited by heretics; articles of faith, confessions or creeds of heretics; dictionaries, glossaries and thesauri compiled or printed by heretics and not yet expurgated; works dealing with Islam. In addition to this religious group were "Prohibited Books on Special Subjects," which included such topics as writings on duelling.

This Index, in which the church finally accepted the impossibility of controlling every item of printed material, represents the begining of the modern system of Catholic censorship. It concentrates very much on Catholic writers whose works were primarily aimed at the faithful and as such could be constrained into doctrinal accuracy. Otherwise the world had simply become too large. Even on this basis, Benedict's Index was relatively tolerant, in that it consistently gave the benefit of the doubt to the author rather than to the doctrine. Its premises were still in use as late as 1900, in the INDEX OF LEO XIII.

SEE ALSO Indexes, index of.

Index of Brussels (1735)   A number of Indexes, based initially on those published in Rome, were published for Belgian consumption during the 18th century. The first, the *Elenchus propositionum et librorum prohibitorum*, appeared in 1709; the second, the *Index ou Catalogue des principaux livres condamnes et defendus par l'Eglise*, in 1714. This latter, concentrating on suppressing the works of the Jansenists, was compiled by Jean-Baptiste Hannot, a devoted Jesuit. Neither of these Indexes was issued on ecclesiastical or political authority, although Hannot's work was subsequently approved by the bishop of Namur. The *Index of Brussels*, the work of another Jesuit, Father Wouters Hoynck van Papendrecht, appeared in 1735. A further attack on Jansenism, it is notable for its inclusion of a separate list, related to the list of titles by a numerical code, that explains just why each title included has been banned. The Index also provides regulations for the control of printing and of bookshops. This Index was never put into effect, and served more as a weapon in the long-running Jesuit-Jansenist battles than as a real tool of censorship.

SEE ALSO Indexes, index of.

Index of Casa (1549)   This Index, prepared on the orders of Pope Paul III, was the first to appear in Venice, a city with a thriving publishing industry. Although already nearing the end of its imperial moment, Venice was antagonistically independent of Rome. The Index, named for John della Casa, archbishop of Benvenuto and papal legate at Venice, was the first to be issued under direct papal authority. It condemned and prohibited "all works produced by the heretics and heresiarchs whose names follow, which have to do with theology or kindred subjects." As well as 142 named titles, there is a general ban on "Bibles and New Testaments containing notes or comments opposed to the faith, and of all works which within the preceding twenty-four years have been printed without the name of the author and the address of the printer." The Index was an unimpressive production, full of errors and comparing most unfavorably with those produced at Louvain (see Index of Louvain) and the Sorbonne. Errors and inadequacies notwithstanding, the *Index of Casa* was largely reproduced unedited in the Venetian Index of 1554 and as part of the TRIDENTINE INDEX of 1564. The first list of heresiarchs was also published in Venice in 1549 and also authorized by della Casa.

SEE ALSO Indexes, index of.

Index of Clement VIII (1596)   After the withdrawal of the INDEX PROHIBITORIUS ET EXPURGATORIUS of Sixtus V, when the Pope died in 1590, the new Pope, Clement VIII, instructed the CONGREGATION OF THE INDEX to continue with its preparation of a replacement for the TRIDENTINE INDEX of 1564. A first draft appeared in 1593 and, after substantial revision, the final Index was published in 1596. It was unique in that it concentrated as devotedly on the works of Catholic authors as on those of Protestant heretics. As such it reached a larger audience than any previous Index, other than that of 1564. Regional editions were prepared in all the major Catholic European cities by 1598. In Venice, where the book trade flourished and Roman censorship was less than popular, the Index was duly modified to satisfy local pressure, but it was still accepted.

Its first edition, of 1593, was especially severe in its prohibitions and a number of senior churchmen and scholars worried whether the Index would provoke a backlash even among the loyal faithful. To prevent such a reaction, the Index was revised on more liberal lines. Among the new features was the inclusion in the list of prohibitions of many vernacular titles hitherto listed only in regional Indexes. In turn, the regional authorities were no longer allowed to publish their own lists when they differed from those of Rome. The 22 new rules created for Sixtus V were abandoned and the Ten Rules of 1564 replaced them, although 18 new paragraphs—the "Instructio"—dealt in detail with prohibition, expurgation and printing. The most notable new direction was an instruction ordering the papal authorities to check books that were already in print, as well as the new books that they would automatically examine, for any necessary expurgations or emendations. Realizing that the congregation could not purge every volume, the Index authorized individual readers to expurgate their own copies of certain works; to do this they could check their own copy against that issued, with the official alterations, by the authorities. There was, however, no provision for enforcement. On the other hand, the guidelines under which such expurgations were to be carried out were notably severe. The authorities were to excise heretical, erroneous, schismatic, seditious and blasphemous passages. Further proscribed were ambiguous phrases that might lead a soul to evil opinions; praise of heretics, passages dealing with superstition, prophecy or divination; passages in which Fate or Fortune limited free will; anything paganistic; anything prejudicial to the reputation of a neighbor, clergyman or prince; propositions challenging the liberty, immunity and jurisdiction of the church; squibs that injured another's good name; lascivious passages and obscene pictures.

Further paragraphs tightened up the original Tridentine rules. All printed volumes were to carry the approval ("testamur") of the examining authority; printers were to deposit a mint copy of every new book with the Holy Office; members of the bookmen's guild were to swear an oath before the bishop and inquisitor that they would obey the Index and that they would admit to the guild only those who would also smear the oath. Under a document peculiar to this Index, known as the "Observatio," bishops and inquisitors were deprived of the right to license certain individuals to read or own any Bibles or scriptural works written in the vulgar tongue; the previous partial toleration of Hebrew texts was revoked.

Following 1596 there appeared several supplements to this Index, often when a specific 16th-century volume, possibly in print without comment for several decades, was declared unacceptable by the new authorities. The Index, with these supplementary lists, was reprinted in 1624, 1630 and 1640.

SEE ALSO Indexes, index of.

Index of Information Not to Be Published in the Open Press, The

This 300-page, small-print manual, known colloquially as "The Talmud," is used by the Soviet censors at GLAVLIT to determine what material may not be published in the Soviet press. It falls into several sections, covering General Information, Military Information, Industry and Construction, Agriculture, Transport, Economics and Finance.

Under General Information the following material is impermissible: (1) Information concerning natural disasters on U.S.S.R. territory; (2) information about other disasters, caused by human, mechanical or technological error on U.S.S.R. territory; (3) details of the earnings of government and party workers; (4) comparisons between the budget of Soviet citizens and the price of goods; (5) information about any form of price increase, including seasonal or local ones; (6) reports of increasing standards of living outside the Soviet bloc; (7) reports of internal food shortages; (8) any kind of large-scale statistics not taken from central Statistical Bureau reports; (9) the name of any KGB operative other than the committee chairman; (10) names of workers for the former Committee for Cultural Relations with Foreign Countries, other than that of its chairman; (11) aerial photographs of Soviet cities or the coordinates of any populated point in the U.S.S.R.; (12) mention of the Glavlit organs themselves, or of the jamming of foreign radio broadcasts; (13) the names of certain political figures whose actual roles have been excised from official history.

The "Talmud" has developed over the years, changing as required by the current Soviet political situation. Thus, with the advent of glasnost it has presumably been modified in many areas. Such changes are typified in the fact that since late 1988 the name of Leon Trotsky, for decades an absolute "unperson," now appears in the press, and reports on such internal disasters as Chernobyl and the Armenian earthquake are freely circulated inside and outside the U.S.S.R.

Index of Leo XIII (1881-1900)

1. history The *Index of Leo XIII*, published in 1881, with supplements in 1884, 1896, and 1900, was the last major Roman Index to appear before the censorship system was finally abandoned in 1966. The first version contains 6,800 entries, comprising nearly 4,000 individual books. This 1881 edition cited a number of previous Indexes and rules, notably those of Pius IV, Clement VIII, Alexander VII and Benedict XIV. The 1900 edition is centered on the "Decreta Generalia," first promulgated by Benedict XIV and designed, as the preface of this Index put it, to "prohibit the greatest possible number, indeed almost all, of noxious and tainted books, the reading of which is strongly forbidden by the natural law itself ..." The Index was further intended "not only to temper the severity of the old rules but also, on behalf of the maternal kindness of the Church, to accommodate the whole spirit of the Index to the times." The Pope, in his "Constitution Concerning the Prohibition and Censorship of Books," did not, however, abjure his responsibility to maintain Roman Catholic censorship, in the face of the "great evil" of heresy. Nonetheless, Leo's Index is notably urbane by earlier standards.

The number of books prohibited was reduced: All books hitherto banned but published prior to 1600 were expunged from the Index, "although they are to be considered as much condemned today as they ever were." The works of Class I (absolutely banned) authors were now permitted if they had no relevance to religious topics. The definition of "all works" would now mean only "all religious works." A number of works that were generally accepted by the church as intellectually unassailable, whether heretical or otherwise, were dropped from the lists. Works pertaining to long-dead religious controversies were no longer banned, as were those dealing with defunct questions of liturgy. Many minor works were freed from the ban, as were supposedly dangerous works of which few or possibly no copies still existed. Many periodicals and pamphlets were declared acceptable. The Index as a whole was the most bibliographically accurate of its type, exhibiting a degree of care that had never been exhibited by any previous compilers.

There were issued 10 decrees "on the prohibition and censorship of books." These: (1) reversed the bans on pre-1600 writings; (2) permitted editions of the Bible edited by non-Catholics, so long as they did not impugn the dogma of the church; (3) maintained the ban on all vernacular versions of the Bible, even by Catholics, since "it has clearly been shown by experience that ... more harm than utility is thereby caused, owing to human temerity"; (4) banned obscene books, but permitted those of classical authors, because of "the elegance and beauty of their diction," although only expurgated versions of these were to be permitted to the young; (5) banned any attacks on Catholicism, books of magic and allied superstitions, of prophecies, visions and divinations and that advocate duelling, divorce, suicide and other profane matters; (6) banned false indulgences and any religious pictures that had not previously been authorized; (7) restricted any liturgical and prayer books to those that had been authorized by the church; (8) prohibited newspapers and periodicals, "which designedly attack religion or morality," and forbade Catholics to contribute to such publications; (9)

forbade the possession of any prohibited material unless permission had been specially granted and a license given by the appropriate authority; (10) laid down the rules whereby a Catholic might denounce a bad book, notably requesting not only that a book's title and author should be cited, but also more detailed reasons for its censure.

In addition to these rules, the decrees laid down the ranks of those permitted to administer the censorship, the duties of those censors in the preliminary examination of books, and the categories of books that required a mandatory examination, notably those dealing in Holy Scripture, Sacred Theology, Ecclesiastical History, Canon Law, Natural Theology, Ethics and "other religious or moral subjects of this character." Rules governing printers, publishers and booksellers were laid down, and the punishments, both excommunication and, if required, other canonical penalties conditional upon rejecting the decrees, were set out. There followed the actual Index (q.v.), listing those works banned by the Catholic Church in 1900.

SEE ALSO *Index of Alexander VII*; *Index of Benedict XIV*; *Index of Clement VIII*; Indexes, index of.

2. banned material   This Index, the last major revision of the Roman Index, included the following works amongst those that might still, as late as 1900, not be read by devout Catholics. This is by no means a full listing of authors and titles included, but gives a general view of what was still considered, and in many cases had been considered for some long time, unacceptable to the faithful. The date, not of publication but of banning for the first time, follows each entry.

Acton, Lord, *History of the Vatican Councils* (1871)

Addison, Joseph, *Remarks on Italy* (1729)

Albertus Magnus, *De Secretis Mulierum* (1604)

Arnauld, Antoine, 17 Jansenist works (1656-59)

Balzac, complete works (1841 et seq.)

Bayle, Pierre, complete works (1698 et seq.)

Bentham, Jeremy, four works (1819 et seq.)

Beranger, *Chansons* (1834)

Blackwell, George, *Letter to Clement VIII* (1614)

Boileau, Jacobus, *Historia Flagellantium* (1668)

Bossuet, Evesque, *Response a M. de Tencin* (1745)

Browne, Thomas, *Religio Medici* (1642)

Bruno, Giordano, complete works (1600)

Bunen, C.J.J., *Hippolytus and his Age* (1853)

Burnet, Gilbert, two works (1714, 1731)

Collins, Anthony, *On Free Thinking* (1715)

Combe, George, *Manual of Phrenology* (1837)

Comte, August, *Cours de philosophie positive* (1864)

Condorcet, *Tableau Historique du progres l'esprit humain* (1827)

Darwin, Erasmus, *Zoonomia* (1817)

DESCARTES, Rene, *Meditationes* (1663)

DIDEROT, Denis, *Encyclopedie raisonee des sciences* (1804)

Draper, J.W., *History of the Conflicts between Science and religion* (1876)

Dumas, Alexandre (pere), complete works

Dumas, Alexandre (fils), complete works

Earle, John C., two spiritualist works (1878)

Fenelon, Francois, *Explication des maximes des saintes* (1665)

Ferri, Enrico, *Sociologica criminale* (1895-6)

Feydeau, Ernest, complete works (1864)

Fontenelle, Bernard, *La Republique des Philosophes* (1779)

Fourier, Charles, *Le Nouveau Monde industrial et societaire* (1835)

Frederick II of Prussia, *Oeuvres du philosophe de Sans-Souci* (1760)

Gandolphy, Peter, *A defence of the Ancient Faith* (1818)

Gibbon, Edward, *Decline and Fall of the Roman Empire* (1783)

Goldsmith, Oliver, *Abridged History of England* (1823)

Grotius, Hugo, complete religious works (1757)

Hallam, H., two historical works (1833)

Herbert de Cherbury, *de Veritate* (1633)

Jobbes, Thomas, complete works (1703)

HUGO, Victor, *Notre Dame de Paris* (1834); *Les Miserables* (1864)

James I, *Basilikon Doron* (1606)

Jansen, Cornelius, *Augustinus* (1641 et seq.)

KANT, Immanuel, *Critique of Pure Reason* (1827)

Lamartine, Alphonse, *Souvenirs* (1836)

Lang, Andrew, *Myth, Ritual and Religion* (1896)

Leigh, Edward, *Annotations upon the New Testament* (1735)

Lessing, Gotthold, *Religion of Saint-Simon* (1835)

Limborch, P., *History of the Inquisition* (1694)

Lipsius, Justus, *Orationes* (1613)

LOCKE, John, *Essay on Human Understanding* (1734); *The Reasonableness of Christianity* (1737)

Malebranche, Nicholas, *Treatise on Nature and Grace* (1689)

Mandeville, Bernard de, *The Fables of the Bees* (1744); *Thoughts on Religion* (1732)

Marvell, Andrew, *The Growth of Popery* (1730)

Maurice, F.D., *Theological Essays* (1854)

Michelet, Jules, *Bible de l'humanite* (1852)

Mill, John Stuart, *Principles of Human Economy* (1856)

Milton, John, *Literae pseudo-senatus anglicani* (1694)

Molinos, M. de, complete works (1687)

Montaigne, Michel, *Essays* (1676)

Montesquieu, Charles-Louis de, *Esprit des lois* (1751)

Morgan, Lady S., *Journal of Residence in Italy* (1822)

Murger, H., complete works (1864)

Pascal, Blaise, *Thoughts* (1789)

Puffendorf, S. von, *De jure naturae et gentium* (1711)

Quesnel, Pasquier, complete wroks (1708 et seq.)

Ranke, Leopold von, *The Roman Popes* (1841)

Renan, Ernest, 20 works (1859 et seq.)

Richardson, Samuel, *Pamela* (1744)

ROUSSEAU, J.-J., *The Social Contract* (1766)

Saint-Simon, Claude-Henri, *Science de l'homme* (1859)
Sand, George, complete works (1840 et seq.)
Sarpi, Paolo, *Historia sopra gli beneficii ecclesiastici* (1676)
Scaliger, J., letters (1633)
Spinoza, Baruch, posthumous works (1690)
Stendhal, complete works (1864)
Sterne, Lawrence, *A Sentimental Journey* (1819)
Stroud, William, *The Physical Causes of the Death of Christ* (1878)
Sue, Eugene, complete works (1852)
Swedenborg, Emmanuel, *Principalia verum naturam* (1738)
Taine, Hippolyte, *History of English Literature* (1866)
Thomas a Kempis, *De Imitatione Christi* (1723)
Tillotson, John, *Sermons* (1725)
Volney, Constantin, *Ruins of Empire* (1821)
VOLTAIRE, complete works (1752)
Whatley, Richard, *Elements of Logic* (1851)
White, Thomas, complete works (1665 et seq.)
Wilkins, J., *Discovery of a New World* (1701)
ZOLA, Emile, complete works (1894 et seq.)
Zwicher, G., *Monks and Their Doctrine* (1898)

SEE ALSO Indexes, index of.

Index of Louvain   The *Index of Louvain* was compiled in 1546 by the University of Louvain in the Netherlands, well-known as a bastion of doctrinal orthodoxy, under the instructions of the Emperor Charles V and authorized by the bull, "COENAE DOMINI." It was the first major catalog of prohibited material and, while authorized by the church, it predated Rome's own first Index by 13 years. It was used mainly by the more enthusiastic and more powerful SPANISH INQUISITION, which used a second edition prepared in 1550 and published in 1551. The Index cites various regulations of 1540 and 1544 designed to control the press and complains of the continuing publication of heretical material. Booksellers are subjected, under pain of death, to regulations prohibiting them from selling any book containing heresy, unless, like approved and innocent volumes, it has been inspected and marked as acceptable by the authorities. There is appended a list of banned titles: (1) Bibles and New Testaments in Latin, low German and French; (2) Protestant works written in Latin; (3) heretical works in German and French; (4) those books already condemned in the *ordonnance* of 1540.

The university theological faculty, which prepared the Index, is given the right and duty to examine all material for heresy, and to destroy such material. Libraries and shops were to be purged not simply of heretical material, but also of any writing considered to be "dangerous for the unlearned." As well as specifying pure heresy, the Index created a category of material that should not be made accessible to the young or the general public. With some subtlety the university added that it had chosen to ignore certain obscure but potentially heretical works, assuming that if they received no publicity,

no one would be bothered to search them out. Finally, the index listed its recommendations for school use.

A further Index was published at Louvain in 1558, itself a revised edition of the Index of 1550. It was issued because, according to its preface, "It is well known to all that since 1550, avowed heretics and others whose catholicity is not to be trusted, have brought secretly into the land pernicious and dangerous books, through the influence of which the heretics are confirmed in their errors and the faithful are led astray ..." The Index then reprinted the lists of 1550, supplementing them by another 100 titles.

SEE ALSO Indexes, index of.

Index of Lucca (1545)   The *Index of Lucca* is the first catalog of heretical books to be issued in Italy. It orders that any copies of the books specified are to be delivered to the authorities for burning within 14 days of their publication. It was not authorized by the bishop or by the Luccan authorities but may be assumed to have been inspired by the Inquisition in Rome. A supplementary edition was printed in 1549, naming some 28 major heretical writers, including WYCLIF, Huss, Zwingli and Melanchthon and 100 lesser figures. This local index lasted until 1605 when Pope Paul V repealed it, claiming the prerogative of the church and ordering the establishment of an Inquisitional tribunal in the city.

SEE ALSO Indexes, index of.

Index of Paul IV (1558)   This index, named for the reigning Pope—the former, implacably anti-heretical Cardinal Caraffa, who had succeeded Julius III in 1555—was drawn in part on the 1558 version of the INDEX OF LOUVAIN and was in turn used as part of the TRIDENTINE INDEX of 1564. A Roman commission had begun work on the Index in 1556 but its completion was hindered by the Pope's war against Spain, until December 1558. It took its schedule of punishments from those specified in the bull, "COENAE DOMINI," and divided into three groups its list of prohibited titles, covering the complete works of some 550 authors (583 are listed, but there are duplications and pseudonyms): (1) authors whose output, past or future, is wholly forbidden; (2) books, classified by authors; (3) anonymous works. The list approximately doubled the number of works on the Venetian Index of 1554, including both new authors and extra works by authors already cited.

All permits to read heretical works and exceptions to previous listing were revoked. Anyone who held such material was to deliver it for destruction. Anyone who was aware of the existence of banned material was duty-bound to inform against its owner. All books and tracts that had been written by heretics, irrespective of their content, were forbidden. Any book that had appeared during the previous 40 years without including the name of both its author and printer was forbidden. Any book dealing with aeromancy, cheiromancy, physiognomy, geomancy, hydromancy, oneiromancy, pyromancy, or necromancy, or other divination, magic or astrology (except for certain treatises designed to aid navigators, farmers or doctors), was banned. All previous papal or secular bans were reaffirmed. Sixty-one printers were listed as heretics, and nothing they either had produced or would produce was to be read.

The Pauline Index, the first to be issued in Rome by the Pope in his capacity as the head of the Christian Church, and the first to be called an "Index" rather than a "Catalog," was novel not merely in its size. It was the first such compilation to make unequivocally clear the moral conservatism endemic to the Counter-Reformation. For the first works were included not for their doctrinal error, but because of their tendency to be anticlerical, immoral, lascivious or obscene. Authors such as ARETINO, MACHIAVELLI, RABELAIS and BOCCACCIO appeared for the first time. By banning some 60 different editions of the Bible, Paul added another type of prohibition, hitherto excluded from Roman Indexes.

The publication of the Index, at a time when the Roman Inquisition was at its most powerful, led to near wholesale panic. Hundreds of books were disposed of by their owners, thus helping Paul in his alleged desire to "expunge from human memory the names of heretics." Booksellers were not even permitted to sell off their prohibited stock as scrap paper. Contemporary witnesses estimated that every reader lost some books, and those who specialized in humanism, the law and medicine suffered worst. From the cardinals of the Inquisition itself downward, those who were subjected to the Index complained, albeit quietly. Only the fact that even this Pope, armed with this Index, was unable absolutely to stamp out heresy, mitigates its potentially all-encompassing effect on European culture.

Paul's death in August 1559 relaxed the Inquisition's efforts to enforce the Index as fully as he might have desired, and a number of states, notably Venice, Naples and Milan and cities such as Frankfurt, Basel and Zurich simply refused to allow the measure to be published. Printers in Tuscany were torn between the Papal demands and those of their duke, who threatened with a fine of 100,000 ducats anyone who accepted the Index. Outside Italy the Index was barely acknowledged, except that it infuriated scholars, whose contempt was further aroused by the fact that those authorized to ban books often did not understand them. Even Valdes, the inquisitor general of Spain, a notably zealous censor, refused to accept this Index, possibly because he had produced his own INDEX OF VALLADOLID in the same year.

SEE ALSO Indexes, index of.

Index of Prague   Two indexes, those of 1726 and 1729, were printed in Prague for use by Bohemian (Czech) Catholics, but neither of these was anything more than a reprint of the Roman Index of 1704, with its supplement of 1716. More important was the *Clavis haeresium claudens et aperiens*, a supplement to the 1729 Index that listed those books, in Latin, German and Czech, that were of particular interest to Bohemian readers. This *Clavis* appeared in an enlarged edition in 1749, and in 1767 appeared the *Index of Prague*, which dealt solely with Bohemian books. This listed works in Latin, in Czech and in German, and included a section entitled "Index librorum Veneria vel obscoena tractantium," which covered obscene literature. The original edition of the *Clavis* was compiled by a Jesuit, Anton Konaisch, whose papers, left after his death in 1760, provided the basis for this section edition, printed by Przichovsky, archbishop of Prague. In the first *Clavis* it was ordered that a sermon should be read on the topic of heretical books three weeks after its publication and that from that moment, all owners and readers of such books would automatically be excommunicated.

SEE ALSO Indexes, index of.

Index of Quiroga (1583)   This Index was prepared in 1583 by Quiroga, inquisitor general of the SPANISH INQUISITION. It was designed, its preface stated, to remedy the lack of comprehensive listings of heretical works, since so many new ones had appeared since the last such Index. It was largely based on the TRIDENTINE INDEX both as to the books it prohibited and the 14 rules under which it operated. It lists works in Latin and a variety of European languages, the reading of any of which was penalized by immediate excommunication. Like most Indexes, it drew both on its predecessors and itself to provide the basis for those that followed, notably that of Sixtus V in Rome. The Index was notable for its inclusion of the work of several otherwise devout Catholic authors; this was explained as the result both of their names being used by heretical writers to fool the masses, and by the fact that their complex works were aimed only at the scholarly and thus should be prohibited from appearing in the vulgar tongue.

A second *Index of Quiroga* appeared in 1584, compiled by the Jesuit, Juan de Mariana. It advocated the continuing task of purging literature of heresy and decreed that, if heretical authors managed to create a work of genuine scholarship, it should be expurgated for general use. The list of heresiarchs runs to 67 names, a notably lengthy one, including WYCLIF, LUTHER, Huss, Melanchthon, Zwingli, CALVIN and many others.

SEE ALSO Indexes, index of.

Index of Sandoval   This prohibitory and expurgatory Index was prepared for the SPANISH INQUISITION by its current inquisitor general, Cardinal and Archbishop Sandoval of Toledo, and published in Madrid in 1612. It was reprinted in 1614, 1619 and 1628, with slight variations. The Index cancelled all previous measures and repealed any licenses that may have been given for the reading of heretical works, other than those that might be given by Sandoval himself in the future. The Index includes 14 rules, based on the 10 rules of the TRIDENTINE INDEX of 1564. Books are divided into three classes: the first deals with books by the major heretics, all of which are banned absolutely; the second and third deal with translations of the scriptures and other works into any of the European languages; these latter classes may be expurgated rather than simply banned. The expurgatory listings follow those of the Clementine Index of 1596 and that of Quiroga in 1583. Sandoval also drew in part on the suppressed work of Brasichelli.

SEE ALSO Indexes, index of; *Index Expuratorius of Brasichelli*; *Index of Clement VIII*; *Index of Quiroga*.

Index of Sotomayor (1640)

This Index was published in Madrid in 1640 by Antonio de Sotomayor (1549-1648), the inquisitor general of the SPANISH INQUISITION. It was reprinted in 1662 and 1667. Sotomayor's preface rails at length against all those heretics who have attempted to use the names of the devout to foist their opinions on the innocent and have impugned the orthodoxy of certain doctrinal writings. All heretical books, the titles of which are listed, are to be turned over to the authorities within 10 days, otherwise the owner will face excommunication. This excommunication will be immediate if the book in question is heretical; if the book is merely prohibited, the excommunication will depend on a subsequent judgment in court. Culprits could also be fined. The Index lists 16 rules, which modify the 10 rules of 1564. Those works that quote from the heresiarchs purely for the purpose of analyzing and condemning their errors are not (as they were in 1564) themselves prohibited. Sotomayor also legislated against certain descriptions when applied to those writers who were in class I (absolutely banned). Any description that implied that the subject was abusing one of God's gifts (describing someone with a value judgment such as "pious") rather than simply making a factual statement ("a distinguished mathematician") was forbidden.

SEE ALSO Indexes, index of.

Index of Valladolid

The first *Index of Valladolid* was published for the use of the SPANISH INQUISITION in 1551 and compiled under the authority of Fernando Valdes, archbishop of Seville and inquisitor general of Spain, who had been urged to action by Emperor Charles V. It is modeled on the second edition of the INDEX OF LOUVAIN, published in 1550. As well as listing heretical authors, as cited by Louvain, the Index prohibits Bibles in Spanish or any vernacular version; any representations of the Virgin or saints (two- or three-dimensional) that might be brought into ridicule; any book tainted with heresy; any writing on necromancy; books of any content that had been published anonymously in the preceding quarter-century; books written against the proceedings of the Diet of Ratisbon (1541), which had condemned works by Calvin. The Koran appears for the first time on an Index, although this first inclusion stemmed less from Islamic heresies than from the impiety of its publisher, Theodor Bibliander of Basel.

Valdes produced a second Index named for Valladolid in 1554. It concentrated exclusively on heretical versions of the Bible, and specifies some 103 editions. The Bibles, many of which had been outlawed wholesale in the Indexes of Louvain, are put forward for suitable expurgation, after which they may be approved. This index is thus the first "index expurgatorius," allowing textual modifications in a way never permitted by the Indexes prepared in Rome. All such volumes were to be submitted to the authorities within 60 days, after which the corrections were to be undertaken before the books could be returned. Anyone still retaining tainted works would be excommunicated and fined and the books burnt.

Valdes' greatest achievement was the preparation and publication in 1559 of the third *Index of Valladolid*. This differed from its predecessors in that the lists of works prohibited were compiled by Spanish editors rather than being yet one more recycling of those created in Louvain or elsewhere. The Index, the first real indicator of the extent to which the Spanish Inquisition functioned very much as an entity of its own ruling, deliberately distanced from Rome, was a wide-reaching, comprehensive document, far more thorough than any Papal product. Works were divided by language, and anything that fell into one of these following categories was banned: books by heresiarchs; all religious works written by those condemned by the Inquisition; all books on Jews and Moors biased against Catholicism; all vernacular translations of the Bible, even by Catholics; all devotional works in the vernacular; all works of controversy between Catholics and heretics; all books on magic; all verses using the scriptures profanely; any book printed since 1515 without the name of its author and publisher; all anti-Catholic works; all irreligious illustrations. Any such book, manuscript or picture discovered in the extensive searches of libraries (both private and public), monasteries, bookshops and universities, was forfeit and liable to assessment and then destruction. Apart from these rules, which were largely a development of the 1551 Index, the 1559 Index substantially extended the number of prohibited titles, adding some 253 new books (particularly vernacular works of mysticism) and a number of translations of the Bible. One particular target was ERASMUS, the humanist scholar, despite the fact that his translation of the Greek Testament had, in 1516, earned the personal congratulations of Pope Leo X.

SEE ALSO Indexes, index of.

Index of Zapata (1632)

This prohibitory and expurgatory index was published at Seville in 1632 by Antonio Zapata, the current inquisitor general of the SPANISH INQUISITION. It takes its authority from the desire of Pope Urban VIII to have the Index brought up to date and reorganized, and it notes some 2,500 works of ancient authors and a number of as yet unpurged contemporary authors that have been overlooked by any previous compilation. Zapata's Index was the largest yet to appear, running to some 1,000 pages. It improved upon its predecessors by including an alphabetical index of all titles.

SEE ALSO Indexes, index of.

Index Prohibitorius et Expurgatorius   Published in 1590 by Sixtus V, this was the first Index, itself a revision of the TRIDENTINE INDEX, to be carried out by the CONGREGATION OF THE INDEX. In the intervening period since 1564, during which time the flood of heretical literature had been by no means checked, some of the more notorious new titles had been dealt with on an ad hoc basis, but there had been no general revision of the regulations or of the catalog of prohibitions. The new Index appeared in spring 1590, prefaced, among other things, by a declaration that henceforth no other Index might be prepared other than those issued by the Congregation in Rome or directly authorized by the Pope. There followed some 22 new rules, designed to replace the 10 rules of 1564. The Index extended the book lists substantially, even including a number of Catholic works, otherwise acceptable, that failed sufficiently to stress the importance of the Papacy. Before the new Index could be fully distributed the Pope died, and in accordance with custom, the distribution was suspended. Few copies survived. The Index was replaced by that of Clement VIII, in 1592.

SEE ALSO Indexes, index of.

Index Ultimo (1790)   This Index, issued in 1790 in Madrid by the Inquisitor General Cevallos, brought up to date the censorship provisions and prohibitory and expurgatory listing of the SPANISH INQUISITION. As its name suggests, it was the last index: other listings of banned material were published in the 19th century, but as far as Spain was concerned, there were no further alterations in the censorship system itself. It listed every available title in alphabetical order, and as such is seen primarily as an index to its most recent predecessors. It was the first Index to accept that vulgate translations of the scriptures might be read without danger of heretical corruption. It permitted individuals to expurgate their own books, so long as they submitted the revised copy to the authorities within two months. The *Index Ultimo* had already produced a supplementary list in 1790 (concentrating on the writings of the French Revolution), followed by further additions in 1805. In 1844 there appeared yet another listing, putting into alphabetical order the lists of 1790, 1805 and the new Roman Index of 1843. This was further updated and re-cataloged in 1848 and 1863.

SEE ALSO Indexes, index of.

Indexes, index of   The following versions of the INDEX LIBRORUM PROHIBITORUM are to be found under their individual headings:

Index Expurgatorius of Brasichelli
Index of Alexander VII (1664)
Index of Benedict XIV (1758)
Index of Brussels (1735)
Index of Casa (1549)
Index of Clement VIII (1596)
Index of Leo XIII (1881-1900) 1. history; 2. banned material
Index of Louvain (1546)
Index of Lucca (1545)
Index of Paul IV (1559)
Index of Prague (1767)
Index of Quiroga (1583)
Index of Sandoval (1612)
Index of Sotomayor (1640)
Index of Valladolid (1551/54/59)
Index of Zapata (1632)
Index Prohibitorius et Expurgatorius (1590)
Index Ultimo (1790)
Roman Indexes
Tridentine Index

India

1. censorship   Other than during the 1975 state of emergency (see India 2), independent India has never been subjected to institutionalized censorship of the media. Under the Constitution of 1950 freedom of speech and expression are guaranteed. A further statute does permit "reasonable restriction … in the interests of the security of the State, friendly relations with foreign states, public order, decency or morality or in relation to contempt of court, defamation or incitement to an offense." But judicial restraint has ensured that such restrictions have not usually reduced freedom of expression. Some state legislatures have passed their own laws to prevent journalists breaching individual parliamentary privilege. Obscene publications are covered by the national Penal Code, which prohibits material that may "deprave and corrupt"; the Indecent Representation of Women (Prohibition) Act forbids any material derogatory to women. It is illlegal to publish anything that inflames communal or religious passions, thus leading to a breakdown of public order. The Official Secrets Act (1962) forbids the dissemination of material that might help an enemy, but officials are not barred from communicating with the press.

Despite their freedoms, Indian journalists do exercise a degree of self-censorship. This is accentuated by the domination of the media by powerful business institutions and by the importance of advertising, both commercial and government-backed, the allocation of which is restricted according to the newspaper's acquiescence. The government also controls the allocation of newsprint. Laws on sedition, passed initially to combat violence and terrorism in various areas of India, have also been used to control journalists. Reports on civil rights violations and interviews with dissidents have been suppressed by this means. Prime Minister Rajiv Gandhi has become increasingly exasperated with the media and has accused the press of trying to "stage a coup against the elected representatives of the country." He has also attacked "scurrilous writing."

Given its 64 percent national illiteracy, India's radio and television are far more important than its press. Acknowledging this disparity, the state controls both All India Radio and Doordanshan India, the TV network. A broadcasting study group recommended in 1978 that the electronic media should be made autonomous but this was rejected by the government, which claimed that its controls were vital for the sake of national interest. State censors have absolute control of the extensive Indian film industry, ensuring that nothing immoral, e.g., a screen kiss, is permitted. Cinemas are also bound to preface each program with an official newsreel.

2. press censorship during the 1975 State of Emergency
During the State of Emergency proclaimed by the late Mrs. Indira Gandhi on June 26, 1975, press censorship of an unprecedented severity was levied over India's 12,000-strong newspaper industry. The legal basis for this censorship was the Censorship Order issued under the Defence of India Rules (1971), which themselves stemmed from the Defence of India Act (1971), legislation imposed under the previous State of Emergency and never repealed, although that emergency had officially ended. Although this censorship apparatus existed, it had never previously been used and, although the India press was not absolutely free, neither did it suffer any form of state interference.

Initially, under the new rules, editors were able to ridicule the government by leaving white spaces where unacceptable material had been excised, but a system of precensorship quickly eliminated these jibes. Under the minister of information and broadcasting, government censors were placed in the offices of all major city newspapers and in those of the two national news agencies. Other publications had to submit all material to the Press and Information Bureau before distribution. No news that might embarrass the government was to be printed. It was also forbidden to quote "mischevously" the speeches of previous Indian leaders—Nehru, Gandhi and even Mrs. Gandhi herself—to point up the inconsistencics of the emergency.

Nine topics were made taboo: (1) any attempt to subvert the functioning of democratic institutions; (2) any attempt to compel members of parliament to resign; (3) anything related to agitations and violence; (4) any attempt to incite the armed forces and the police; (5) any attempt to stir up anti-government feelings among the population; (6) reports containing false allegations against leaders; (7) any attempt to denigrate the institution of prime minister; (8) any subversion of law and order; (9) any attempts to threaten internal stability, production and prospects of economic improvement. Foreign correspondents were similarly precensored, although less rigorously than the native press. Restrictions on the foreign press were altered when precensorship was dropped, and a system of restrictive guidelines was introduced.

On the whole the Indian press accepted the censorship, with the exception of L.R. Malkani and Kuldip Nayar, editors respectively of *Motherland* and *The Indian Express*, both of whom were arrested for their anti-government stance. By August 1974 the government was able to end domestic precensorship: the generally acquiescent press had volunteered its own self-censorship for the duration, often inspired by the newspaper owners' backing of Mrs. Gandhi. The prime minister herself justified censorship, which she ostensibly deplored, on the premise that many newspapers had "shed all objectivity and independence, and allied themselves with the Opposition Front and did everything to spread doom and defeatism."

Indonesia The press in Indonesia, a country under military rule since October 1965, is strictly controlled and much depleted since martial law was established. Any artistic or creative work that fails to reflect Islamic aesthetic standards is rigorously proscribed. The duty of journalists is to select information that creates "national unity and stability."

Under the Basic Law on the Press of November 1966 (amended 1982) there was nominal acknowledgment of press freedom, but an absolute ban on all Communist, Marxist and Leninist publications was enforced. Foreign publications deemed injurious to the state could also be banned. A series of crackdowns have eroded press power throughout the era. All of them claim to be suppressing press attempts to foment national disorder and to attack the authorities. The act also set up a Press Council and defines the functions and duties of the press. These duties include the need to "fan the spirit of dedication to the nation's struggle" and similar exhortations. Those who violate the act are subject to various sanctions, including jail.

The means of controlling the press are as follows: All publications must be licensed. This licence requires two permits: a Publishing Licence, issued by the Ministry of Information as demanded by the 1966 law; a Printing Licence, issued by KOPKAMTIB (Operational Command for the Restoration of Security and Order), the state security agency, established in October 1965. Licensing the press gives the government extensive powers of coercion, which it uses without hesitation.

KOPKAMTIB also holds press briefings to control the news to be reported. These briefings have no legal force but editors who choose to ignore them may suffer accordingly. Journalists and editors are regularly arrested for "provocative reporting." The intimidation of all levels of journalist is routine, particularly in regional areas where reporters may be arrested by the military and detained, if not actually beaten up. A number of prominent journalists have been imprisoned for their stance and KOPKAMTIB also holds a blacklist of journalists who worked for banned papers. As in many countries, the press is further reined in by economic pressures. Government advertising, which provides some papers with a substantial income, can be withheld as a punishment. Government office subscriptions, highly important to the small, local press, can be similarly withdrawn.

Journalists are further bound by "the telephone tradition," a system whereby officials simply ring up editors and remind them that certain contentious issues are best left well alone. This system can be expanded to a full-scale blackout of a given topic: journalists are summoned to the Ministry of Information and ordered either to drop a story outright, or print only the official line. Reporters have also been beaten up, jailed or simply threatened.

The state controls Indonesia's single TV station, and has established its aims as the stimulation of "the process of national character building" as well as helping educate the country and promote development programs. Radio is also dominated by the government, although there are a number of independent stations. They are closely monitored and may not produce their own news programs, but must broadcast the official 15-minute news bulletins six times each day. Radio stations may be closed down if they fail to follow government guidelines.

Book censorship is the norm, operated by the attorney general. This censorship is carried out post-publication, when books may be banned. All theater performances must be cleared before they go on in public. This extends to short story readings and other non-theatrical performances. Films and, to a lesser extent, video cassettes, are subject to the Film Censorship Board.

Inside Linda Lovelace Linda Lovelace (the pseudonym of Linda Marchiano) was an American porno starlet who gained international fame as the heroine of the 1972 film DEEP THROAT, in which she played a woman whose clitoris is sited in her throat. In 1973 U.S. publisher Pinnacle Books issued her ostensible autobiography, *Inside Linda Lovelace*. The book was imported into England in 1974 by Johannes Hanau, a Soho distributor. Relatively soft-core, it sold only moderately. In 1976, however, it was rumored that the makers of *Deep Throat*, which had already earned $50,000,000 against a $25,000 budget, were hoping to exhibit the film in England. It was assumed by the authorities that, were its star's autobiography declared obscene, exhibiting the film would be rendered impossible.

The leading defender of such causes, John Mortimer, QC, and a panel of experts managed to convince a jury of the "joy and pleasure" of Ms. Lovelace's many and varied sexual exploits, and their value as instruction to individuals more inhibited but nonetheless interested in widening their sexual vocabulary. The main import was not simply that the book was acquitted. The verdict proved that the OBSCENE PUBLICATIONS ACT (1959) simply did not work. Irrespective of its original purpose—to permit literature while still outlawing pornography—trials brought under the act tended merely to boost sales of the material in question. Prior to the trial sales totaled around 38,000; within three weeks of the acquittal they topped 600,000. Since this case there have been no further trials in Britain that have attempted to prove the obscenity of a purely written text.

The acquittal of *Inside Linda Lovelace* enraged conservative opinion. The news that Peter Cook, "The Cambridge Rapist," had been a devotee of pornography, intensified such feelings. A variety of prosecutions followed, all resulting in guilty verdicts. The home secretary, Roy Jenkins, countered this backlash by announcing a government enquiry into the problem: the WILLIAMS COMMITTEE.

"Inter Multiplices" In his bull "Inter Multiplices," of 1501, Pope Alexander VI stated: "The art of printing can be of great service in so far as it furthers the circulation of useful and tested books; but it can bring about serious evils if it is permitted to widen the influence of pernicious works. It will, therefore, be necessary to maintain full control over the printers so that they may be prevented from bringing into print writings which are antagonistic to the Catholic faith, or which are likely to cause trouble to believers." The Pope went on to authorize bishops and inquisitors to execute censorship decrees and enforce them wherever necessary, against both individuals and institutions, and to keep one half of all fines collected. Were offenses to continue, they could threaten even more severe penalties. The bull, like most medieval decrees, offered guidelines rather than banning specific titles.

"Inter Solicitudines" On his accession in March 1513 Pope Leo X was petitioned by a number of his subordinates as regarded the need for press censorship. The church officials simultaneously condemned the low educational level of the clergy and advised that the flow of books should be restricted as much as possible. The clergy should be limited to a selection of sacred studies in their original texts and there should be established an official board of censors to check any other material. In response the Pope issued in 1515 the bull "Inter Solicitudines," which dealt with printing and its products. This bull, which served as the model for many successors, stated that no printed material might appear prior to approval by either the MAGISTER SACRI PALATII (a papal chaplain appointed to oversee the censorship system) in Rome, or the appropriate local equivalent. These officials were themselves ordered under pain of excommunication to assess works submitted speedily and to pass them for publication unless proper grounds existed for their censorship. Printers who attempted to avoid the system would be fined 100 ducats, payable to the building fund of St. Peter's, and their printing office would be shut for one year. If they still refused to acknowledge the censor, they would be excommunicated "and shall be further so chastened that others may take warning from the example."

International Agreement for the Suppression of Obscene Publications This agreement was signed in 1910 and ratified by the U.K. in 1911. Under a Protocol of 1949, the agreement became an instrument of the United Nations, as administered by the secretary general. The aim of the agreement was to promote and coordinate international attempts to control obscene material by researching its existence and then taking measures for its suppression. Each government designates an authority to coordinate information within his or her own country and to communicate it where relevant to fellow authorities. The agreement, given the varying national attitudes toward obscenity and the variety of laws (or lack of them), has never been seen as a useful practical measure.

SEE ALSO International Convention for the Suppression of the Circulation of and Traffic in Obscene Publications.

International Convention for the Suppression of the Circulation of and Traffic in Obscene Publications   This convention was signed in Geneva in 1923 and by the Protocol of 1949 became an instrument of the United Nations, administered by the secretary general. Article 1 of the convention binds its signatories to taking all measures to discover, prosecute and punish any person distributing obscene articles by way of trade. Article 5 provides for the search, seizure and destruction of obscene material. The effective existence of the convention can generally be seen in the various laws governing obscene publications that exist in the various signatory countries. Certain nations, such as the U.S.A., have never signed, and others, whose policy on such material has changed radically since 1923, such as Denmark and the Federal Republic of Germany, have since renounced their part in the Convention.

International Covenant on Civil and Political Rights
This treaty came into force in 1967 and by the end of 1967 had been ratified by 86 countries. All signatories undertake to report regularly to a Human Rights Committee on the human rights situation in their own country. Countries may also permit their own citizens to complain to the committee about abuses within their country. The covenant guarantees freedom of conscience, religion and belief (article 18); of opinion and expression (article 19) and of the duty to ban propaganda for war or for racial incitement (article 20). Article 19 reads in full:

(1) Everyone shall have the right to hold opinions without interference. (2) Everyone shall have the right to freedom of expression; this right shall include freedom to seek, receive and impart information and ideas of all kinds, regardless of frontiers, either orally, in writing or in print, in the form of art, or through any other media of his choice. (3) The exercise of the rights provided for in paragraph 2 of this Article carries with it special duties and responsibilities. It may therefore be subject to certain restrictions, but these shall only be such as are provided by law and are necessary (a) for respect of the rights and reputations of others; (b) for the protection of national security or of public order or of public health or morals.

Inevitably the interpretation of the convenant differs as to the signatory.

SEE ALSO American Convention on Human Rights; Article 19; European Convention on Human Rights; Universal Declaration of Human Rights.

International P.E.N.   The concept and initial organization of P.E.N. was created in the autumn of 1921 by the British novelist and poet Mrs. C.A. Dawson Scott. Her idea was to bring together, strictly in the interests of the freedom of creative expression and with no overt political stance, the international community of writers. The organization's name stands for the members of that community: poets, playwrights, essayists, editors and novelists, who were to be offered a forum in which they could communicate and act irrespective of individual ideologies, colors and creeds. By the 1970s P.E.N. had 82 centers in 60 countries, but not in the U.S.S.R. and the People's Republic of China.

Developed from a number of resolutions passed at early P.E.N. congresses, there has evolved a P.E.N. charter of four clauses, to which all members of centers must subscribe. These are:

(1) Literature, national though it be in origin, knows no frontiers, and should remain common currency between nations in spite of international or political upheavals. (2) In all circumstances, and particularly in time of war, works of art, the patrimony of humanity at large, should be left untouched by national or political passion. (3) Members of P.E.N. should at all times use what influence they have in favour of good understanding and mutual respect between nations; they pledge themselves to do their utmost to dispel race, class and national hatreds, and to champion the ideal of one humanity living in peace in one world. (4) P.E.N. stands for the principle of unhampered transmission of thought within each nation and between all nations, and members pledge themselves to oppose any forms of suppression of freedom of expression in the country and community to which they belong. P.E.N. declares for a free press and opposes arbitrary censorship in time of peace. It believes that the necessary advance of the world towards a more highly organized political and economic order renders a free criticism of governments, administrations and institutions imperative. And since freedom implies voluntary restraint, members pledge themselves to oppose such evils of a free press as mendacious publication, deliberate falsehood and distortion of facts for political and personal ends.

This charter remains at best the expression of ideals that each center can pursue only in a form best suited to the country in which it operates. The less ostensibly democratic the host country, the harder this is to do.

P.E.N. is run by its Annual Congress, which takes place each year in a different national center. The congress ratifies the work of the executive committee, which is composed of two delegates from each autonomous center officially appointed to serve that year. At the congress everyone can express his or her opinions, except those that are blatantly political. P.E.N. has always paid particular attention to the effects on writers of dictatorships and political upheavals, and lobbies for those who have been imprisoned or otherwise persecuted. Subsequent to a resolution tabled in 1960 by the Centre for Writers in Exile, P.E.N. has sponsored the Committee for Writers in Prison, a section that, as one-time member Arthur Miller pointed out, "is rarely out of business."

Work of this committee, which operates with a minimum of publicity and which by general consensus does not publish detailed reports of its activities, is seen as International P.E.N.'s most important activity.

International Style, The

The "International" style of architecture, pioneered by Mies van der Rohe and Walter Gropius in the 1920s was unpopular with totalitarian governments of the 1930s. So virulently did the Nazis hate the flat roofs and clean lines that typified the style that they forced owners of such buildings to embellish them with gabled roofs, to produce traditional German styles. Such structures that could not be modified were simply destroyed, including van der Rohe's memorial at the Berlin-Lichtenberg Cemetery to the assassinated communists Karl Liebknecht and Rosa Luxemburg. Official cultural policy in Russia also condemned the style, ordering architects to abandon it and seek inspiration instead in classical or Imperial Russian designs.

SEE ALSO Bauhaus.

Iran

1. censorship under the shahs

Censorship of Iranian culture dates from the seventh-century Arab invasion and the subsequent imposition of the religious precepts of Islam. The Moslem prohibition of any representation of the human form put an end to all painting and sculpture, and the general dissaproval of dancing and music severely limited those arts. Successive Persian sovereigns also suppressed opposition to their absolute rule and made the censorship apparatus a part of the government. This had a dual effect on Iranian culture: on the one hand there developed a tradition of panegyrics, the lavish praise of the shah and his works by a coterie of court flatterers; on the other appeared an oral tradition, far more reliable as a cultural indicator, which depended on fables and tales, allegory and metaphor to express its opinions without incurring official displeasure.

The printing press was imported to Iran in 1836 and the first newspaper published that year. By 1840 a number of satirical sheets had appeared, attacking the policies of both the shah and of the Russian and British interests that struggled to dominate the country. In 1847 the first newspaper of note, *Vaghaye-e-Etefaghiyeh* (edited by an Englishman, E. Burgess), espousing a very cautious and moderate tone, was published. Based on translations Burgess made from the European and Turkish press, the paper sometimes displeased the authorities, and became the first Iranian newspaper to be censored, although like most of the press, until the 1940s, it was generally congratulatory of the government.

Censorship remained strict throughout the 19th century. Under Shah Nasser-el-Din penalties for flouting censorship rules included imprisonment, banishment, corporal and even capital punishment. Under this shah censorship became part of the machinery of state, when in 1880 the Imperial Printing Office was established and empowered to seize, ban and burn offending books. The growing opposition to this situation was reflected in the proliferation of newspapers published abroad by a variety of expatriate Iranians. At home, there developed the *shabnameh* ("night letters"): revolutionary pamphlets that were printed secretly and slid anonymously beneath doors. When this opposition crystallized in the Persian Revolution of 1906 and the subsequent adoption of a state constitution (based on that of Belgium in 1831), censorship was abolished.

The resulting flood of journalistic efforts that followed testified to the vigor of the new democracy. When interference from Russian interests replaced the incumbent Shah Mozaffar-al-Din with his son Mohammad-Ali, censorship returned. Only a civil war and the reintroduction of constitutional, democratic rule in 1909 by Ahmed Shah restored freedom to the nation's culture and press. In 1921 the British, taking advantage of their victory in 1918 and the Russians' post-Revolutionary distractions, and determined to maintain control over Iran's oil revenues, replaced Ahmed and the Kadjar dynasty with that established by their puppet, Reza Pahlavi. Reza Shah swiftly restored repression and censorship. Of a once thriving press only 50 publications survived, of which the majority were government mouthpieces.

In 1941, when Reza became too obvious in his pro-Nazi sympathies, the British forced him to abdicate. He was replaced by his son, the last shah of Iran, Mohammad Reza. For a decade Iran enjoyed an unprecedented level of press freedom as the shah restored parliamentary rule, political parties, trade unions and other democratic institutions. There were 464 publications, of every political and cultural shade, despite Iran's 90 percent illiteracy rate. By 1951 the progressive Iranian parties, infuriated by the activities of the British-dominated Anglo-Iranian Oil Company (AIOC), which regularly drained massive funds from Iran, united in the National Front and elected the ultra-progressive Mossadegh as prime minister. Under Mossadegh, who among other things nationalized the oil fields and expelled the British managers and technicians, the country was plunged into unfettered political ferment, with no-holds-barred public debate. In response Britain, calling on American aid, launched an international boycott of Iranian oil. This savaged the Iranian economy, but Mossadegh was undaunted. In August 1953 the Shah, with the support of the U.S. and U.K., ordered that Mossadegh stand down as prime minister and cede his position to General Zahedi, a formerly pro-German military comander. When Mossadegh refused to do, the shah fled to Rome. Zahedi, backed by CIA aid, then ejected the prime minister himself and the shah returned to Teheran.

The shah's return signalled the institution of a police state that lasted until his overthrow. Press opposition was banned, all forms of democratic debate rigorously suppressed. Those criticis of the shah who failed to escape were arrested, tortured and often executed. Victims were estimated at around 5,000 people. The U.S. became the dominant external force and the shah began converting Iranian society into what his critics saw as a debased clone of his major ally, although he carefully excluded any taint of the cultural diversification found in the actual West. His own survival now depended on the long-term suppression of all opposition, using military and police control. SAVAK, a secret police force of great efficiency and viciousness, aided and armed by the CIA, was created to spearhead his policy.

SAVAK censorship of the press operated under a number of guidelines: (1) any news concerning the Iranian royal family could come only from official sources; (2) no plans announced by the shah and the empress were to be caricatured; (3) responsible and high-ranking citizens and anyone appointed by the shah were immune from criticism; (4) official policies as laid down by the shah might never be criticized, but must be mentioned "with great reverence"; (5) news regarding military dispositions and plans, terrorist and anti-terrorist activity, the industrial and economic situation, and anything regarding the nation's physical health (e.g., epidemics) might all come only from official sources; (6) major corruption was never to be mentioned; (7) critics were not to be given space for publication and the press was not to publish news of strikes or anything else that might foment discontent; (8) foreign comment on Iran was to be published only when favorable, and hostile nations were never to be mentioned.

The 500-plus publications of 1952 quickly shrank to 100, most of them dedicated to pro-government propaganda. Only among the exiled opposition did a free press flourish. By the 1970s, when Iran was cited by Amnesty International as having the world's worst record on human rights, absolute conformity was the norm. SAVAK's press section enforced the censorship and recruited its own journalists, who were placed on newspapers to pen the government line. The Iranian press concentrated on reproducing pro-capitalist, pro-Western material, alongside all the attributes of American popular culture. Undoubtedly this attempt to destroy ethnic Iranian culture was one of the main contributory causes of the shah's downfall.

2. censorship under the ayatollahs The censorship that underlies the imposition of an Islamic theocracy has always been part of the revolution in Iran. Even as opposition factions were debating the overthrow of the shah in 1978, the fundamentalist Hezbollahis ("the party of God") were making themselves felt, breaking up meetings, chanting slogans, condemning all but their supporters. With the revolution achieved, the Hezbollahis took up Khomeini's call for unity, attacking anyone who denied the primacy of Islam. These still inchoate gangs developed into the *komitehs*, the Revolutionary Guards, the Foundation of Martyrs and other militantly Islamic groups, urging the absolutes of faith and the dictates of the Ayatollah.

The Islamicization of Iranian culture was set down in a speech by Ayatollah Khomeini on July 29, 1979, in which he set aside the history and developments of the previous 800 years, during which time the people had only been "wandering," and promised a return to "eternal [values] that were temporarily forgotten."

In the autumn of 1979 a seminar was established to work out this Islamic cultural strategy, in which Islamic theologians and secular intellectuals debated the future direction of Iranian culture. Although the arguments of the secular side won the day and as such reflected the view of most Iranians, whose genuine religiosity did include the excesses of the spiritual authorities, the religious leaders were unmoved. Reports of the debates, which had initially been heavily edited to favor Islam, were soon banned completely, and the authorities henceforth refused any public discussion of Islamic culture. The seminar and its suppression preceded a major campaign against all aspects of culture. Thinkers, writers, poets, journalists, teachers and intellectuals in general suffered purges, attacks and an overall pressure to conform to the new Islamic culture. Khomeini exhorted his followers to "Break their pens!" Many were imprisoned or executed after summary trials, or went into hiding or exile. Others have simply censored themselves and begun a life of exclusion.

The attack on culture is widespread. Some five million books, formerly in university and other libraries, have been destroyed; approximately 3,000 publications have been shut down; many Iranian monuments have been smashed, condemned as relics of "The Age of Idolatry"; it has been estimated that museums and private collections have been stripped of some 90 percent of their holdings. The treasures have either been destroyed by zealots or smuggled abroad by opportunists for sale elsewhere. Traditional music, dancing, theater, sculpture and painting have been banned wholesale as *taghuti*—pro-Shah, anti-Islamic activities. The language and history of Iran are similarly under attack, with attempts to destroy all vestiges of Persian antecedents, both written and verbal. Nationalism is condemned as "an invention of the Jews" and the Persian language, cited as "a fortification against Islam," is being replaced by Arabic forms. Only the nine-year Iran-Iraq war, recruitment for which required a degree of nationalist propaganda over and above religious inspiration, restrained the attacks on the nation's past.

To replace the vilified Persian traditions, Islamic culture offers dedication to the Quran and to Islamic history. Writers are encourged to take their themes from these sources, but few of merit have bothered, preferring silence. In the press, this insistence on Islamic polemic, and its general unpopularity, has meant the removal of most byline-published pieces. The visual media have been enlisted, and few people choose to watch what is offered: propaganda films or television programs devoted to religious readings. All television archives were destroyed. Paradoxically, publishing is flourishing, although prior to publication every book must be sanctioned by the authorities; the Hazbollahis burnt many thousands of books, as well as bookshops and libraries. Yet publishing is relatively free, as long as the volume is neither overtly anti-Islamic or by a Jewish author. Banned books are often given new titles, attributed to pseudonymous authors and distributed on the black market. Some Soviet-style

SAMIZDAT is available, mainly from emigre sources, but the circulation of this material is much hindered by the closures of the universities, usually the prime sites of its distribution. All publishing benefits from the essential instability of the regime, which, for all its efforts, cannot maintain absolute control of all media.

3. censorship in education The immediate task of the theological revolution concerning education was to destroy the reforms of the Constituional Revolution of 1906, which had largely eroded the power of the clergy over secular matters and instituted full academic freedom. While such freedoms had been severely curtailed by the Pahlavi shahs, the universities maintained the basic ethos of question and debate and in 1979, after playing a major role in the downfall of the shah, they remained potent centers of radical opinion and encouraged the breadth of intellectual concerns that had always been at the heart of traditional Islamic teaching.

In dealing with education, the fundamentalist faction of the provisional government laid down three vital tenets: (1) the country was to be Islamicized as fast and as comprehensively as possible; (2) so-called "academic freedom" was merely a corrupting ploy, devised by colonial powers who wished to weaken Islam; (3) no teacher might continue working unless qualified under Islamic standards. Given the relative weakness of the Shi'ite clergy in 1979, when warring factions were still competing for ultimate control of Iran, they were forced to commence their purification of the educational system at the bottom, in the primary schools. A number of regulations appeared: All textbooks were rewritten as dictated by the Islamic theocracy; no teacher or pupil might read or research any material not sanctioned by the school's Islamic Association; the sexes were to be segregated in school and girls and female teachers were to wear orthodox Islamic dress; indoctrination in Islam, based on a massive increase in the time allotted to lessons in religion, was to be the priority of all education and those senior theological students responsible for such lessons were to double as informers against backsliders and apostates; all private schools were to be closed.

In November 1979, when the provisional government was replaced by Ayatollah Khomeini's Islamic Revolutionary Council, the full assault on higher education was able to begin. The tone of the attack was epitomized in Khomeini's dictum: "Universities have done more damage than cluster bombs." Although hard-left students resisted fundamentalist militants, the government smashed all opposition, both with physical force and through its edicts. All universities, other than theological institutes, such as the Ayatollah's own foundation at Qom, have remained shut, pending the completion of Islamicization. Further to this suspension, their have been wholesale purges of the teaching staff. All those who held ministerial positions under the shah and all those known to have collaborated with the secret police (SAVAK) were denounced at once. Subsequently a wide variety of charges were laid against the allegedly guilty, ranging from the specific (membership in certain prerevolutionary organizations) to the general ("being known as a corrupt or infidel person" or holding anti-clerical beliefs). The educational reforms have also made academic qualifications, other than theological ones, virtually useless in the job market. Students, once again, other than those sent abroad to propagate Islam, are not allowed to travel in pursuit of research.

Iraq Under the Provisional Constitution of 1968 Iraqis are guaranteed freedom of opinion and publication as well as the ability to form political parties. The practicalities of life are less simple, and circumstances stress constitutional provisos restricting such freedoms to "the limits of law." Since 1963, when the ruling Ba'ath Party took over absolute control of the country, Iraq has been a one-party state, with a press to match. Kurdish and communist parties and papers were permitted a brief revival in the 1970s, but these were banned once more in 1978. This purge had been preceded by the party's eighth regional conference in 1974, when it was made clear that the media were to be completely suborned to the party line. It was further reported that this transformation had yet to be fully achieved since "most organs of culture and information lack competent and revolutionary executives ... many reactionary elements lurk in these organs ..."

By 1981, when reform of the media was embodied in the new Ministry of Culture and Information Act, all such inefficient and insufficiently zealous officials had been removed. The new act summed up Iraq's policy on the media: Its sole function was to be the promotion of the Ba'athist ideology and the revolution. To this end, "the Ministry has the mission to supervise all media functions and activities and to exercise cultural supervision over all public and private libraries, and to inspect and license the recording on tapes and discs of all music and vocal production used for commercial purposes."

Under the Press Code of 1968 the Iraqi press may be widely censored. Even though the state controls both print and broadcast media, which generate a constant diet of praise for President Saddam Hussein and his policies coupled with vilification of the national enemy, Iran, the authorities make sure that no errant journalist diverges from the party line. Among forbidden topics are criticism of Saddam, of the Revolutionary Command Council (the inner cabinet), or of any part of the state or its apparatus. News that may affect the national economy adversely is banned. The censor will also check prior to publication any quotations from the president or his senior officials, from any treaties entered into by Iraq, any reports of criminal cases regarding financial malfeasance. Foreign correspondents, whose publications were banned outright from 1970 to 1981, are strictly controlled. Communications home are strictly monitored and no journalist can use a telex by him or herself. Stories may only be covered in the company of a government official, and all tape recorders, typewriters and copiers must be registered and licensed.

The Penal Code contains heavy penalties for overly free expression and critical journalism. Insulting the president, his officials or the government or Ba'ath Party carries the threat of the death penalty, life imprisonment or confiscation of property. All cultural and literary organizations were dissolved in 1980 and replaced with the General Federation of the Literate and Writers. All writers must join the federation and work by its rules; rebels are jailed, harassed and even killed. All artists must belong to the artists' union; those who prefer retirement or simply refuse to join must pay back to the state the cost of their education, unless they have already worked for 15 years. A number of intellectuals have been tortured and interrogated in an attempt to force them into line; some 400 have left for exile.

Radio and television are state-controlled. The State Organization for Broadcasting and Television, a department of the Ministry of Culture, carries out censorship. Censorship of film is operated by the Ministry's Information and Media Censorship Branch, which controls a censorship committee drawn from the ministries of Defense, Culture and Information, and the Interior, operating under Law number 64 (1973) on Censorship of Classified Material and Cinema. As well as censoring anything alien to party dogma, virtually all imported films are banned.

Ireland Censorship in the Republic of Ireland was established as part of Home Rule, and aimed to replace the old Anglo-Irish standards with a new, nationalist morality. The intention was to preserve the Irish native genius, impose moral strictures dating back to the Old Testament and let Irish culture develop irrespective of the changing modern world.

1. film censorship The Censorship of Films Act (1923) forbids the public exhibition of any films without a certificate granted by the government-appointed censor, appeal against whose decision may be made to a nine-person Appeal Board, which must arrive at a majority verdict. The censor must give some level of certificate for every film "unless he is of the opinion that such a picture or some part of it is unfit for general exhibition in public by reason of it being indecent, obscene or blasphemous, or because the exhibition thereof in public would tend to inculcate principles contrary to public morality or would be otherwise subversive of public morality." Initially film posters were not subject to the act; this loophole was shut in an amendment of 1925, which made it a criminal offense to display film posters without pre-submission to the censor. The act was further amended in 1930 to cover films with sound. In October 1987 a Video Recordings Bill sought to include videos (notably "video nasties") under the same legislation as are cinema films.

2. literary censorship In 1926 the Dail (the Irish Parliament) set up a committee to investigate the nature and extent of the trade in "evil literature" and to report on whether it would be sensible and necessary to establish state censorship over books. The committee unanimously recommended that preventive censorship should take the place of the existing criminal law governing "obscene libel," which had dealt with such cases as emerged. It advised that a Board of Censors be established to ban "books written with a corrupt intent or aiming at circulation by reason of their appeals to sensual or corrupt instincts or passions." It was intended that works "having a purely literary aim in view, but which as part of their reflection of the world admit representation of the vices or the passions that exist" should be excluded from provisions governing straight pornography. The report also stressed that the censorship should consider adult standards, and not base itself on a desire to reduce all acceptable literature to "work intended only for the youth and the maiden." It added that all material in favor of birth control should automatically be illegal.

The Censorship Act of 1929, modified by that of 1946, established Irish literary censorship on the basis of the committee's recommendations. A five-person board of censors was set up, to serve for five years. This board could ban a book if at least three members agreed and only one dissented. The board itself can select the material it considers, but in practice most of the books it assesses are referred by the government or members of the public. The act established no theological censorship, although Ireland, as a Catholic country, naturally followed the INDEX. Articles contrary to Catholic doctrine were automatically banned only if they advocated birth control. Indecency and obscenity are defined as "suggestive of, or inciting to, sexual immorality or unnatural vice or likely in any other similar way to deprave or corrupt." When considering books, the board must give credence to possible literary merit, and publishers and authors are allowed to make statements in their own interest. The Customs can seize banned material from the luggage of arriving travelers, but those travelers cannot be charged with any offense. Periodicals considered obscene or known to advocate birth control can also be banned. The board must maintain a list, available for public inspection, of currently banned material. Those who publish, sell or distribute listed books may be either fined or imprisoned.

Since 1946 a five-member Appeal Board, under the chairmanship of a senior lawyer, has existed before which a book's author, editor or publisher, or any five members of Parliament may challenge a ban. At least three members of the Board must agree on a verdict.

The Health (Family Planning) Act of November 1, 1980, made several major modifications to the state of censorship in Ireland, as set down in the acts of 1929 and 1946. The amendments, under section 12, paragraphs 1-4, all removed from censorship the sale, distribution or advertisement of any publication advocating or describing "the unnatural prevention of conception," and substituted clauses that cited instead "the procurement of abortion or miscarriage" or methods used for such purposes. Advertising such services or methods is banned, as is advertising that refers to "any disease arising from or relating to the regenerative organs of either sex," sexually transmitted diseases, cures for menstrual problems; and any drugs, appliances, treatment or methods dealing with such topics. Books may be seized and banned if they are indecent or obscene or advocate the procurement of abortion or miscarriage. Periodicals fall under the same restrictions, with the added proviso that the amalgamated effect of their back issues is to be considered, and that they may be censored if they tend to give "an unduly large proportion of space to the publication of matter relating to crime."

Under the Censorship Acts of 1929 and 1946, the Irish Board of censors has banned thousands of books and hundreds of periodicals. Although the original target of the board, and its sponsors in the Catholic Church, was apparently the "unclean" British Sunday newspapers, the censors soon went far beyond that modest target. Despite the board's supposed acceptance of the concept of literary merit four Irish winners of the Nobel Prize for literature and virtually every native-born writer of distinction—e.g., St. John Gogarty, Liam O'Flaherty, Sean O'Faolain—have been included. Joyce's ULYSSES, paradoxically, has always been permitted. Among the many authors to suffer censorship are:

Marcel Proust, *Remembrance of Things Past*

Andre Gide, IF I DIE

Charles Morgan, *The Fountain*

Somerset Maugham, *The Painted Veil*

Aldous Huxley, *Point Counter Point*

George Orwell, *1984*

ERSKINE CALDWELL, GOD'S LITTLE ACRE

Theodore Dreiser, *Reprieve*

Daphne du Maurier, *I'll Never Be Young Again*

ERNEST HEMINGWAY, *Across the River and into the Trees*

Christopher Isherwood, *Goodbye to Berlin*

Arthur Koestler, *Arrow in the Blue*

SINCLAIR LEWIS, *Cass Timberlane*

Angus Wilson, *Hemlock and After*

William Faulkner, *Sanctuary*

C.S. Forester, *The African Queen*

Joyce Cary, *Prisoner of Grace*

H.G. Wells

Hugh Walpole

Alberto Moravia

Since the 1970s the board has fallen into increasing disfavor, but it remains implacably opposed to birth control publications, popular attitudes notwithstanding. As recently as 1987 Alex Comfort's bestselling *Joy of Sex* was banned as was an art book, *The Erotic Art of India*. The board, normally secretive, explained its rationale: "What we have in mind is this. You put this book on an ordinary bookshelf. Imagine the effect it would have on a 13 year-old ..."

3. library censorship Irish librarians are bound not only by the official literary censorship but, in addition, by secondary, unofficial bans. Thus, in given public libraries, apart from the listed, banned books, such works as those of Smollett, Tolstoy, Balzac, Dumas, Arnold Bennett, Hardy and many more have been excluded.

Israel There is no official Israeli Constitution, and thus no guarantees of freedom of speech, although Israel, as a vociferously democratic state, has always maintained the necessity for freedom of expression. In the event, the state does censor, varying the severity of this control as to whether it is dealing with the native Israeli, the Israeli Arab and the East Jerusalem or West Bank Arab populations. All Israeli censorship, whether of Hebrew language, Israeli-produced newspapers and magazines, or of licensed Arabic-language publications, produced in Israel or East Jerusalem but read in the West Bank, occupied since the Six Day War of June 1967, originates in a number of regulations enacted by the British Mandatory Government in Palestine in 1945. The rules dealt with the safeguarding of public security, the defense of the country, the maintaining of public order and the suppression of rebellions, uprisings and disturbances. These regulations have been absorbed into Israeli law and were extended to the West Bank under Military Order No. 5 (1967).

The legal justification of censorship is found in Article 88 of the regulations.

(1) The censor may by order prohibit the importation or exportation or the printing or publishing of any publication (which prohibition shall be deemed to extend to any copy or portion of such publication or of issue or number thereof), the importation, exportation, printing or publishing of which in his opinion, would be or be likely to become, prejudicial for the defense of [Israel] or to the public safety or to public order. (2) Any person who contravenes any order under this regulation and the proprietor and editor of the publication, in relation which the contravention occurs, any person (unless in the opinion of the court he ought fairly to be excused) who has in his possession or his control or in premises of which he is the occupier, any publication prohibited under this regulation, or who posts, delivers or receives any such publication, shall be guilty of an offense against these regulations.

The censor, who does not require a court order, may use these articles to shut down publications (either for limited or indefinite periods) and to confiscate their printing equipment. Articles 94–100 cover the publication of newspapers and apply to the Hebrew, Arabic and English-language press. All publications must have a permit to publish (art. #94) and all must submit copy to pre-censorship (art. #97) by the chief censor or one of his deputies, all of whom are members of the army's 50-strong censorship unit, itself a subsection of military intelligence. Two copies must be submitted to a censor the day before publication and may be picked up, suitably amended, by midnight that same day. Israeli and Arab journalists are united in their opposition to the permit system, but the government remains adamant and shrouds the granting and withholding of the permits in secrecy. The censor can define a given topic as harmful as and when he wishes, often laying temporary bans on particular areas of news. Stories on Israel's attempts to contain the Palestinian *intifadeh* are particularly closely monitored, although the press is increasingly unwilling to take the censor's writ without argument.

Prepublication censorship operates for all, but with different criteria for Israelis and Arabs. The Israeli press, under an agreement worked out between the censors and its own editors, need submit only articles touching on military security. These are adjudicated by an Editors' Committee drawn from senior members of the press and of the Israeli Broadcasting Authority (IBA). It may comment freely on everything else, including affairs on the West Bank. The Arab-language press must submit all material and is heavily censored, with very little material referring to West Bank topics permitted. While the Israeli papers may appeal, often successfully, against the chief censor, Arabic papers manage only rarely to have the decisions reversed, and they are far more likely than are their Hebrew-language peers to be suppressed, under article 100 of the regulations, for breaching the censorship law. Since 1967 the censorship of the West Bank is controlled by the military commander, acting personally or through a proxy as an inspector of the regulations. The Palestinian press is controlled on three levels: the licensing system, without which a publication may not exist; strict control of distribution; and censorship itself. Censorship here has been extended to cover all publications and while ostensibly aimed at the preservation of public order, effectively militates against expressions of Palestinian nationalism. No printed matter may be brought to the West Bank, either for mass distribution or for personal use without the relevant permit. Given the pro-PLO stance of these papers, the Israelis claim they have no alternative: "When you have a press that represents your adversary or your enemy," said an army spokesman, "you discriminate against it."

Books receive the same scrutiny as do newspapers, and a list of 1,600 forbidden titles has been compiled. This list does proscribe many overtly anti-Semitic titles, but its main thrust is against writings that promote Palestinian nationalism. It is not made available to the public and the usual means of identifying a banned book is for its owner to find him or herself arrested for possessing it. Like newspapers, a term that embraces every publication, books require a permit. Printing is similarly controlled, under a variety of Military Orders (101 in 1967, 718 in 1977 and 938 in 1981). The basic order states that "it is forbidden to print or publish in the area any publication, any advertisement, proclamation, picture, or any other document which contains any article with political signification except after obtaining beforehand a license ..." A preamble, defining the key words "printing," "publishing" etc., shows that in all cases these words are given the widest possible interpretation to facilitate legal action. Publishing, for instance, has been extended to the making available of a given title by a librarian in his library. At its broadest, "political signification" may simply mean prejudicial to public order.

Over and above the censorship orders, any Israeli soldier serving in the West Bank has the powers of search and seizure without warrant, as justified in Military Orders 101 and 378 (1970). The first of these gives him the authority to implement all censorship procedures; the second to search for suspected publications and their publishers and distributors. Such searches may be extended to private libraries and may include on-the-spot destruction, without a prior court case. Those individuals who are arrested may be held for 96 hours before an arrest warrant must be issued. Nothing of "political significance" may be published without a license from the local Israeli commander; conversely, every military announcement must be printed as written.

Despite the censorship, some illicit publications do appear in the West Bank and the population may receive the broadcasts of Syrian, Jordanian and Egyptian television, which are also censored at source. Given the relatively free movement of individuals between Israel and the West Bank, many publications circulate with them: Material banned in the West Bank may often be obtained freely in Israel.

Foreign journalists are obliged to submit material to the Israeli censor. If otherwise censorable material is published abroad, it may then appear freely in Israel. Thus Israeli journalists often leak material to the foreign press, which publishes abroad and may be reprinted at home. West Bank journalists practice the same tactic as regards the Hebrew press.

There is one television channel in Israel, broadcasting in Hebrew and Arabic; a second one is under consideration. TV is notably independent, although the authorities and the producers have worked out a system of military no-go areas, as have the print media. As in the press, Arab programs are more tightly controlled than are Hebrew ones. Film and theater are controlled by the Board for Film and Theater Review, generally known as the censorship board. Censorship of the theater was supposed to have been repealed in 1972, but the law has never been put into action.

It All Comes Out in the End   SEE *Magic Mirror*.

Italy's obscenity laws   Under Article 528 of the Penal Code it is an offense to manufacture, distribute or import obscene articles of any kind for the purpose of selling, distributing or displaying them publicly. There is no legal definition of "obscene." It is also an offense to give obscene public theatrical or film shows and any such offenses carry three years imprisonment. Those who offer for sale or display publicly articles that offend public decency are fined. The law of February 8, 1948, specifies the provisions of article 528 as regard the protection of children. No material designed for minors may be written in a way that might disturb them, promote violence or anti-social behavior. No real or imaginary events may be depicted in such a manner that they concentrate too heavily on horrific detail or upset common morality or family order or provoke suicide or crime. The law of July 17, 1975, exonerates the retailers working from newspaper and magazine kiosks from any offense that might accrue to the material they sell. Only if their displays are "obviously obscene" or if they sell to persons under 16 do they forfeit this special treatment. Specialist pornography dealers are not exempt.

***IT* trial** *IT* (originally *The International Times*) was England's first underground newspaper, launched in late 1966 to reflect, inspire and generally report on the prevailing youth counterculture of the day. Given that such papers eked out minimal distribution incomes with such advertising as was offered, *IT* made its personal columns as widely open as possible, and as such offered a marketplace to many whose demands could not be satisfied elsewhere. Given the lack of a mass-circulation homosexual press, in which such advertisements would be carried later, *IT* gave space to a variety of gay contact advertising, which was listed as the "Gentleman's Directory" in a column headed "Males."

In January 1970 three directors of *IT* and Knuller Publishing (who published the magazine; *knuller* means "fuck" in Swedish) were charged on two counts: conspiring to corrupt public decency (see conspiracy to outrage public decency) and CONSPIRACY TO CORRUPT PUBLIC MORALS (the latter charge was created to ban the LADIES' DIRECTORY in 1961). The gay contact material was alleged to "debauch and corrupt the morals as well of youth as of diverse other liege subjects of the Lady the Queen." The defendants' counsel argued that since homosexual acts were no longer illegal (subsequent to the Sexual Offenses Act of 1967) gay advertisements should not be either. In November 1970, after a six-day trial, the defendants were found guilty, the court stating that a conspiracy to corrupt public morals had still taken place if a jury believed that the defendants' actions had indeed undermined the nation's morals. Each director was fined £100 and sentenced to 12 months in jail on the first charge and 18 months on the second. The company was fined £1,500 on both charges, with £500 costs.

Despite the verdict, *IT* survived and had its appeal heard in May 1972. Concerning the defense claim that the "conspiracy to corrupt morals" was not a statutory offense, the court admitted that the *Ladies' Directory* case might have been "an unfortunate mistake." They still upheld the morals conviction, but reversed that on the decency charge, accepting that a small ad buried within a paper could hardly corrupt a decent person unless they were determined to find offense. This compromise satisfied no one. The pro-*IT Times* columnist Bernard Levin and the attorney general swapped opinions through that newspaper. Levin claimed that "justice in this country has not been covered in glory," while Sir Peter Rawlinson inferred that *IT*, in effect, was pimping for its gay advertisers. The home secretary then annouced that the "morals" charge was being considered by the Law Commissioners. It has only been used once since, in the prosecution of the Paedophile Information Society's contact magazine aimed at pederasts.

J

***Jacobellis* v. *Ohio* (1964)** In October 1959 Nico Jacobellis, manager of the Heights Arts Theater in Cleveland, Ohio, was arrested on charges of obscenity, emerging from his exhibiting an art film—LES AMANTS—which concerned itself with the infidelities of a bored housewife.

David Frankel, the distributor, and Louis Sher, the cinema's owner, chose to fight and ended up paying $70,000 in legal fees, notably to Ephraim London, the country's top First Amendment attorney. Jacobellis had always kept the theater low-key, showing a series of art films to adults only and minimizing any potential sensationalism. The local police had previously done no more than preview, with Jacobellis' cooperation, the occasional title. Jacobellis' arrest, his fingerprinting and booking on charges of possessing and exhibiting an obscene motion picture, was splashed across the local paper. The police claimed that they had received several complaints, and Jacobellis, who was subjected to constant personal harassment throughout the period, believed that these were orchestrated by the Catholic CITIZENS FOR DECENT LITERATURE. On June 9, 1960, he was convicted by three judges in the local court, fined a total of $2,500 and held for six days pending the preparation of a probation report.

The case reached the U.S. Supreme Court in June 1964, and the lower court's decision was reversed, the court declaring that under the ROTH STANDARD, while the subject matter of the film might in part have been obscene, it was not "utterly without social importance" and thus must transcend an opinion based purely on differing attitudes concerning morality. The Jacobellis verdict was subsequently used on many occasions in an attempt to justify otherwise actionable material. Its most immediate effect was to cause a federal court in Illinois to reverse its own ruling on charges against the comedian LENNY BRUCE: while the language of his performance might be considered obscene, the content undoubtedly had a degree of social importance.

James Boys in Missouri, The This film, a 1,000-foot silent short made by the Essanay Company in 1908, concerned the criminal adventures of the James Gang, headed by the notorious Jesse James, an outlaw who had pursued his villainies within living memory. The film's banning in 1908 is the first recorded example of local film censorship in the United States. Under an ordinance of 1907 it was unlawful to show any moving pictures in a public place unless they were previously licensed by the city's chief of police. When *The James Boys* and another western, *Night Riders*, were banned from exhibition, one of the exhibitors, Jake Block, who had been showing it up until then, took the city to court, claiming

that he had been deprived of his constitutional rights. Block argued that the films in question were based on highly moral stage plays and that the ban "discriminates against the exhibitors of moving pictures, delegates descretionary and judicial powers to the chief of police, takes the property of complainants without due process of law and is unreasonable and oppressive." The lower court upheld the ban, as did the Illinois State Supreme Court. In his opinion, Chief Justice Cartwright claimed that enforcing morals, in the films as elsewhere, was police business and that the low admission prices charged by contemporary cinemas—nickels and dimes—meant that many minors could and would be watching. It was right to delegate authority to the police and while it was "doubtless true" that individual definitions of "immoral" and "obscene" might differ, "the average person of healthy and wholesome mind knows well enough what [the terms] mean and can intelligently apply the test to any picture …" The court "presumed" that the police chief would possess such faculties and would perform his task "with reasonable intelligence."

Jansenism In 1640, two years after the death of Cornelius Jansen (1585-1638), bishop of Ypres, his religious treatise was published: *Augustinus seu doctrina S. Augustini de humanae naturae sanitate, aegritudine et medicina, adversus Pelagianas et Massilienses*. The book was divided into three parts: the first dealt with the Pelagian and Massilian heresies; the second with St. Augustine's doctrine of the fall, maintaining that human beings were naturally perverse and could attain the love of God only by conversion, the presence or absence of which was only determined by God; the third dealt in 10 books with the grace of Christ. Jansen's implication, in an epilogue, that the Massilian heresies were currently paralled by Jesuit orthodoxy caused an immediate controversy. The book was condemned by the ROMAN INQUISITION in 1641, but no specific opinion was pronounced on its doctrine and the treatises written in refutation by the Jesuits were also condemned. Those espousing what became known as Jansenism based themselves at Port-Royal, a former Cistercian monastery, where the doctrine flourished until it was shut down by Louis XIV in 1710. The doctrine was also particularly popular in the Netherlands.

Jansen's book was condemned by successive Popes after 1642, and in 1651 85 French bishops demanded a specific condemnation of the five propositions that made up the heart of Jansenist doctrine and that emphasized man's natural inability to achieve goodness, other than granted by God at his discretion through the agency of the Catholic Church.

In 1653, under the bull "Cum occasione impressionis libri," Innocent X stated that Jansen's propositions were heretical; it was added that to suggest, as they did, that Christ died only for an elect (as Calvin would have proposed) was impious and blasphemous. The Jansenists accepted the bull, but claimed that the specific propositions condemned in it were not essential to their faith. All Catholics must obey the Vatican, but the Vatican could be wrong. The Pope responded by condemning all Jansenist writings in April 1654, and this condemnation was upheld throughout the 17th century. In 1856, Alexander VII, asserting his own infallibility, rejected the idea that the propositions were not essentially Jansenist. He demanded that all the clergy should accept this judgment and swear an oath to that effect. By the end of the century some 100 Jansenist works, mainly by French authors, had been placed on the Index. The works of Jansen's main supporter, Antoine Arnauld, were particularly condemned, although this did not restrict their great popularity. Among other contentious works were the *Letters* of Blaise Pascal (1623-62), first condemned in 1657, a year after their publication. The *Commentary on the New Testament*, written in 1671 by PASQUIER QUESNEL (1634-1719), provoked in 1713 the bull "UNIGENITUS," urged on Pope Clement XI by Louis XIV and designed to suppress Jansenism.

Jenkins v. *Georgia* (1974)   SEE *Carnal Knowledge.*

Joint Select Committee on Censorship (1909)   As agitation against stage censorship in Britain increased in the early 20th century, Parliament responded in 1909 with the establishment of a Joint Select Committee on Censorship, under the chairmanship of Herbert (later Viscount) Samuel. The creation of the committee had been particularly stimulated by a letter signed by 71 members of the theatrical establishment following the banning in 1907 by the LORD CHAMBERLAIN (Britain's theatrical censor) of Edward Garnett's *The Breaking Point* and Harley Granville-Barker's *Waste*, which condemned "an office autocratic in procedure, opposed to the spirit of the Constitution, contrary to justice and common sense." The committee heard some 49 witnesses during the summer of 1909. The lord chamberlain himself declined to appear, but his assistants were called and were unable to set out what his office saw as its precise role. Such luminaries as Shaw, Barrie, Gilbert Murray, Gilbert, Pinero, Chesterton, Conrad, James, Granville-Barker, Forbes-Robertson and Bennett gave, either in person or on paper, their opinion. One revelation, hitherto unannounced, was the existence of an advisory board, composed of theater managers, lawyers, a literary don and the lord chamberlain's comptroller, designed to improve the public image of the censor. Among the witnesses from the theatrical profession most managers and actors backed the current system; the managers because they preferred not to have the responsibility of self censorship and the actors because they preferred a central body to the caprices of provincial authorities. The censors opined that any

"healthy-minded author with a wholesome plot would have no difficulty in writing a good drama, if he is capable of writing a good drama at all."

In its 500,000-word report the committee decided that the lord chamberlain should stay in authority, but that it should be optional to submit plays to him for licensing. It would be legal to stage an unlicensed play but one must accept the risk of prosecution by the director of public prosecutions (acting against indecency), or the attorney-general (acting against graver offenses). If a court found against a play it could be banned for 10 years, then reassessed. The censor ought to pass any play unless it was judged: (1) indecent; (2) to contain offensive personalities; (3) to represent on the stage in an invidious manner a living person or a person recently dead; (4) to do violence to the sentiment of religious reverence; (5) to be calculated to conduce to crime or vice; (6) to be calculated to impair friendly relations with any foreign power; (7) to be calculated to cause a breach of the peace. The EXAMINER OF PLAYS was to be demoted and the lord chamberlain given sole responsibility for granting licenses. Presubmission of scripts was to be made two weeks before first night, and London theaters were to be licensed by the London County Council; music halls [vaudeville] and theaters were to have the same license.

The committee, the last major inquiry into censorship before its abolition in 1968, was condemned by Shaw as, "a capital illustration of … the art of contriving methods of reform that will leave matters exactly as they are." In trying to retain censorship while simultaneously abolishing it, the committee compiled what one critic called "one of the most chaotic and puzzling volumes that has ever been offered to the public." The committee's efforts generated much debate but no action. The government refused to act, and merely let the furor die away, while the censors took advantage of this apathy to make cuts in an unusually large number of works. SEE ALSO Theatres Act (1968, U.K.).

Joint Select Committee on Lotteries and Indecent Advertisements, 1908 (U.K.)   Among the deliberations of this wide-ranging committee was a review of Britain's OBSCENE PUBLICATIONS ACT (1857). It was noted that while prosecutions might easily be brought under the act, it was not always possible to prove in a court of law that the material in question was liable to "deprave and corrupt" as required by the HICKLIN RULE. Given what the committee saw as "a serious and growing evil," it proposed to make it illegal to publish or possess with the intent to sell any obscene or indecent books, pictures and similar publications or representations. Exemption would be offered those books or pictures with genuine claims to artistic or literary merit. It was further proposed that there should be diplomatic initiatives to stop the sending of pornography through the international mails, that the advertising of contraceptives should be banned and that cases of OBSCENE LIBEL would no longer be tried by a jury, merely by summary jurisdiction. The committee's proposals were noted but never adopted.

Joyce, James SEE *Ulysses.*

Joynson-Hicks, William Known generally to friends and foes as "Jix," Joynson-Hicks (1865-1939) was educated at Merchant Taylor's School and admitted as a solicitor in 1887. He was variously Conservative MP for North-West Manchester, Brentford and Twickenham and home secretary from 1924 to 1929. A staunch conservative, and president of the National Church League, Jix began his years as home secretary with a campaign to deport a variety of aliens whose presence, he felt, did not improve life in Britain. He then turned to a new target: sex, a phenomenon he considered to have been spawned in the aftermath of the First World War— and to be threatening to overwhelm the country. He was backed without question by the police force.

He prosecuted D.H. LAWRENCE for his paintings, RADCLYFFE HALL for her book, THE WELL OF LONELINESS, and, to general amusement, the drawings of William Blake. His policemen raided a number of bookshops with varying results. He also persuaded the LORD CHAMBERLAIN to exercise a stricter approach to his censorship of the theater. When the then lord chamberlain, Lord Cromer, suggested that theatrical censorship was too complex a topic for the responsibility of a single individual and that it should be taken over by the Home Office, Jix rejected the plan. He was by no means popular, and was satirized in 1929 in the book *The Policeman of the Lord* by P.R. Stephenson. In reply, he published the pamphlet, "Do we need a censor?" which question he answered in the affirmative. His own role he summed up thus: "The Home Secretary never moved against other than admittedly pornographic productions of his own volition."

Judicial Proceedings (Regulations of Reports) Act (1926) Under this act, passed in Britain in 1926, it is a crime to publish in relation to any judicial proceedings any indecent matter or indecent medical, surgical, or physiological details that would be calculated to injure public morals. It is also an offense to publish in relation to proceedings for a divorce or the annullment of a marriage any details other than: the names, addresses and occupations of those involved; the charges, legal argument and the judge's summing up and verdict. This latter constraint removed from the press the right to publish the once long-awaited lubricious details of the more scandalous divorce cases of the era.

Juliette, ou les Prosperites de vice SEE *Justine, or the Misfortunes of Virtue.*

Justine, or the Misfortunes of Virtue This novel, the most celebrated of the works of the Marquis de SADE, appeared in 1791. Entitled in the original French, *Les Infortunes de la*

Vertu, it had been scheduled for inclusion in de Sade's anonymous collection *Contes et fabliaux du XVIIIieme siecle par un troubadour provencal* (*Tales and Legends of the 18th Century by a Provincial Troubador*) but the *Contes*... never materialized, although the anthology was finally published in its unfinished state in 1930. De Sade decided to issue the novel, expanded into a book of its own and retitled *Justine, ou les Malheurs du vertu*, as a separate work. Written originally between June and July 1787 while in his cell in the Bastille, the 138-page manuscript was padded out with extra sex and extra philosophy for its publication as a novel in 1791. Although de Sade claimed in a letter to have written the book strictly for money, its dedication to his constant companion for his final 20 years, Marie-Constance Quesnet, belies such hackwork.

Within a decade of its publication, there appeared six reprints, each published in Paris but claiming on their title pages such disparate locations as London and Holland. Capitalizing on this success, de Sade wrote *La Nouvelle Justine*, which appeared in 1797, along with *Juliette, ou les Prosperites du Vice*, the story of Justine's sister, who had chosen to benefit from vice instead of suffering through virtue. This third book differs widely from its predecessors, notably in the increased cruelties worked out on the heroine. The two sisters were allegedly based on de Sade's wife Renee de Montreuil whom he left a year after their marriage, and on her younger sister Louise, with whom he eloped.

Justine was condemned as soon as it appeared. The public's fantasies as to its conception rivaled those included in its pages. Some had de Sade solitary in a cave, printing out every page; others claimed that Napoleon had executed any soldier caught with a copy; others believed that Robespierre read it to remind himself that his Terror paled in the face of the marquis' book. It remained an underground publication for many years. Twentieth-century editions of *Justine* have included that of Maurice Heine in 1930, which takes as its text the original manuscript of 1787; that included in the *Complete Works*, edited by Jean-Jacques Pauvert; and the Grove Press translation of 1965.

The heroine of de Sade's "philosophical tale" makes her hapless way through a world of wickedness, where evil rules unassailably. As written by de Sade, whose own attitudes had gradually hardened, the Justine of the 1791 and 1797 editions has changed. In the first she is the narrator, recounting her own martyrdom; in the second she has become an object, the endlessly vulnerable repository of the sexual violence of others. Unwilling or unable to benefit from her frequent humiliations, Justine appears to those who torture her as aberrant and absurd. She defies the logic and sense of the world through which she travels. As detailed in *La Nouvelle Justine*, she dies at last, destroyed by a bolt of lightning that enters her mouth and departs through her vagina. Her corpse is enjoyed by four libertines while her debauched sister Juliette watches and masturbates. For de Sade, the argument is complete: God, let alone more earthly powers, is on the side of evil.

As the critic Geoffrey Gorer pointed out *Justine* was created as an ironic appendix to Voltaire's *Candide*, offering the moral, "God helps those who help themselves." Her fate bears out de Sade's intention, not of titillation, but of using unassailable logic to destroy proclaimed moral certainties. As Gorer puts it, "… almost immediately de Sade saw that this subject necessitated more serious treatment … from being the Candide of Christianity, Justine became the Don Quixote. The parallel is very close. Both protagonists believe in a state of affairs and a humanity which in fact do not exist; both prefer to stick to their illusions rather than to learn from experience."

K

Kahane, Jack Kahane was born in Manchester, England, and fought in a British regiment in the First World War. He was gassed at Ypres. He returned only briefly to England, then moved permanently, with his French wife, to Paris. In 1931 he founded the Obelisk Press, with the direct intention of publishing a variety of books guaranteed to scandalize British opinion, and infiltrate them into his home country. His list included both reprints of novels banned in England—THE WELL OF LONELINESS by RADCLYFFE HALL, *My Life and Loves* by FRANK HARRIS, and the autobiography of a prostitute, Sheila Cousins' *To Beg I Am Ashamed*—and new works such as HENRY MILLER's TROPIC OF CANCER, Cyril Connolly's *The Rock Pool*, *The Black Book* by Lawrence Durrell and his own *Memoirs of a Booklegger*. Kahane died in 1939, leaving his son, MAURICE GIRODIAS, to carry on his literary subversion.

Kama Sutra, The SEE Australia 3. obscenity laws; Roth, Samuel; South Africa; *United States* v. *Thirty-Seven Photographs* (1971); Burton, Sir Richard.

Kansas

1. Criminal Syndication Act SEE *Fiske* v. *State of Kansas* (1937).

2. film censorship Kansas was one of the first states to institute its own film censorship, passing in 1913 a law entitled, "A act regulating the exhibiting or using of motion picture films or reels; providing and regulating the examination and approval of moving picture films and reels, and fixing penalties for the violation of this act, and making an appropriation for clerical help to carry this act into effect." The act stated that on or after April 1, 1913, "It shall be unlawful to exhibit or use any moving picture film or reel unless the same shall have been examined and approved by the Superintendant of Public Instruction. Films used in institutions of learning are exempt from the provisions of the act. It is made the duty of such officer to examine the films or reels intended for exhibition and approve such as he shall find to be moral and instructive and to withhold his approval from such as tend to debase or corrupt the morals." The censor was empowered to view any film exhibited in Kansas and "shall approve such as shall be moral and proper and disapprove such as are sacriligious, obscene, indecent or immoral, or such as tend to corrupt the morals." The Kansas censor operated until 1955, when such local censorship was declared unconstitutional by the U.S. Supreme Court in the case of *Holmby Productions* v. *Vaughan*, concerning an attempt to ban Otto Preminger's film THE MOON IS BLUE.

Kant, Immanuel Kant (1724-1804) was educated at the University of Konigsberg in Prussia and worked as a tutor. His first work, *A General Natural History of the Heavens*, appeared in 1755. In 1756 he began a 15-year appointment as an unpaid lecturer at Konigsberg, becoming in 1770 the university's professor of logic. In 1781 he published his most important work, *The Critique of Pure Reason*. Further books included *Prolegomena to Any Future Metaphysics* (1783), *Metaphysical Rudiments of Natural Philosophy* (1786), a second edition of the *Critique* (1787) and *Religion within the Boundaries of Pure Reason* (1793). The theories that Kant offered in this last volume were sufficient to bring him into conflict with the government, and the Prussian state encouraged by a strongly Lutheran church, suppressed the second part of the book. The order banning the book read in part: "Our sacred person you have with your so-called philosophy attempted to bring into contempt ... and you have at the same time assailed the truth of the Scriptures and the foundations of Creed belief ... We order that henceforth you shall employ your talents to better purpose and that you shall keep silence on matters whch are outside of your proper functions." When both parts appeared in Konigsberg in 1793, Frederick William II immediately barred Kant from continuing his lectures and from writing on religion. This prohibition stemmed less from any religious scruples than from the belicf that Kant was a supporter of the contemporary French Revolution. In 1827 the Catholic Church joined Kant's opponents when it added the Italian edition of *The Critique of Pure Reason* to the Roman Index (see Roman Index). The book remained there until the 20th century. Believing that Kant's philosophies undermined their own political doctrines, both the Soviet Union (in 1928) and Franco's Spain (in 1939) purged Kant's work from their libraries.

***Katzev* v. *County of Los Angeles* (1959)** Under ordinance number 6633 of the county of Los Angeles, it was forbidden on pain of six months in jail, a $500 fine, or both, to circulate or sell comic books to children under the age of 10 if those comics portrayed crime. Crime was defined as "an act of arson, burglary, kidnapping, mayhem, murder, rape, robbery, theft, trainwrecking, or voluntary manslaughter; or the commission of an act of assault with caustic chemicals or assault with a deadly weapon." Crime in comics was not restricted to actions by humans but also by "animals or any non-human, part-human or imaginary beings." This ordinance was declared unconstitutional in 1959 when Katzev, who had sold such a comic book, appealed his conviction to the California courts. The judge pointed out that the ordinance failed because there was "no showing ... of a clear and present danger of a substantive evil justifying suppression of the constitutional guarantee" (under the FIRST AMENDMENT); because the ordinance was too broad in its outlawing of all comic books that contain fictitious, nonreligious accounts of crime; because it established "arbitrary and unreasonable exemptions" (e.g., newspaper strips were exempt from the law, even though they were often identical to comic books). It was also noted that were such an ordinance to stand, then Bugs Bunny would be prohibited from stealing carrots from Elmer Fudd and Popeye from bashing Bluto.

Kauffmann, Stanley   SEE *The Philanderer*.

Keating, Charles H.   SEE Citizens for Decent Literature; President's Commission on Obscenity and Pornography (1970).

Kentucky's obscenity statute   Section 436.101 of Kentucky Revised Statutes (1973) states in part,

> Obscene matter, distribution, penalties, distribution. (1) As used in this section: (a) "Distribute" means to transfer possession of, whether with or without consideration. (b) "Matter" means any book, magazine, newspaper or other printed or written material or any picture, drawing, photograph, motion picture or other pictorial representation of any statue or other figure, or any recording, transcription or mechanical, chemical or electrical reproduction, or any other articles, equipment, machines or materials. (c) "Obscene" means that to the average person, applying contemporary standards, the predominant appeal of the matter, taken as a whole, is to prurient interest, a shameful or morbid interest in nudity, sex or excretion which goes substantially beyond customary limits of candor in description or representation of such matters.

Kenya   Kenya, which gained independence in 1963, has been a one-party state, ruled by the Kenya African National Union (KANU) and its President Daniel arap Moi, since 1982. Although section 79 of the 1963 constitution guarantees freedom of opinion and expression, such rights have become purely nominal; since the Preservation of Public Security Act (1967) the president has been empowered to suspend any such rights and regularly does so. He may also impose wide-ranging censorship. Although relatively few Kenyans can read English, all three main daily papers (two of which date from colonial days) appear in English, although two produce smaller, locally oriented Kiswahili editions. Two are owned by European multinationals.

There are no specific censorship laws, but the Office of the President maintains control either directly (issuing instructions for the running or abandoning of certain stories) or indirectly (through actual or threatened withdrawal of government advertising). Journalists may also be arrested and detained. Given the fear that such measures engender, even senior officials are unwilling to comment "on the record."

Broadcasting, administered by the Voice of Kenya broadcasting authority, is similarly controlled. Both radio and television are strictly vetted and feature substantial coverage of government news broadcasts and presidential speeches. Music programs are popular, although all subversive lyrics are censored.

Under section 57 of the Penal Code it is forbidden to utter any words with a seditious intention, although there is no legal definition of sedition. Seditious literature is also banned and even possessing it may lead to seven years in jail. Books and maazines do not have to be declared seditious as such: The government may withdraw any publication without further discussion. It is also forbidden to import anti-government material or to possess such material.

Film and theater are both censored, the former by a Film Censorship Board, the latter on a more ad hoc basis, with certain plays being permitted a performance at one time, and then banned at another. This censorship is primarily on political grounds.

King, George   SEE book burning in England 7. United Kingdom (1688-1775).

Kingsley International Pictures* v. *Board of Regents   SEE *Lady Chatterley's Lover* 3. film.

Knowlton, Charles   SEE *The Fruits of Philosophy*.

Kuwait   Prior to 1986 Kuwait's media were distinctly free, as opposed to those operating in many neighboring Arab states. In July 1986, following a series of disputes between the government, made up of the country's ruling families, and the elected deputies of the National Assembly, the amir dissolved the assembly and took over legislative authority. He suspended parts of the Constitution of 1962, which guarantees freedom of expression, albeit limited by "the relevant laws," and, as part of an attempt to undermine political opposition, established prior censorship.

Press control already existed, prescribed by the Printing and Publishing Law (1961), which allowed the government to fine or imprison those who created and distributed prohibited material. Such material included attacks on the government and reports that would undermine faith in the economy. The authorities had to authorize any publication and foreign material could be banned on the grounds of "public order or morals." A number of amendments followed in July 1986. Any newspaper that "served the interest of a foreign state or organization, whose policy conflicts with the national interest, or which receives help, support or benefit ... from any other state or source without permission from the Ministry of Information" was prohibited. Everything other than periodicals and commercial publications was to be submitted for prior censorship. Newspapers could be banned for up to three months and any employee who published "non-commercial advertisements" or the political statements of the opposition, faced three years in prison. Self-censorship, already accepted by Kuwaiti journalists even under a liberal regime, became more prevalent. On a harsher level, a number of non-Kuwaiti Arab journalists, catering to the country's high proportion of expatriates, were expelled. Stories criticizing the amir, pointing out sectarian conflicts and dealing with internal dissent will cause problems for the writer.

The Ministry of Information is responsible for controlling the state-owned television and radio stations, and for the censorship of books, films and plays. Radio and TV news never varies from the official line. The ministry checks the text of all books and many are banned, either for political, religious or moral reasons. Videotapes are scrutinized, mainly for their sexual content. Theater, once relatively free, is now subject, like the other media, to the current hard-line controls.

L

La Belle et la Bete In early 1810 the French artist Antoine du Bost was hired by Thomas Hope, a London gentleman, to paint a portrait of his wife. After it had been completed Hope quarreled with Du Bost over the picture. In June 1810 a picture appeared in a Hyde Park gallery: Entitled *La Belle et la Bete*, it caricatured both Hope (a notably plain man) and his wife (a notably attractive woman). In this new painting Mrs. Hope was seen wearing the same dress as in the original and there was inscribed on its label: "All this I will give thee,/Beauty, to marry me."

London society flocked to the gallery, keen to enjoy "a scandalous libel upon a gentleman of fashion and his lady." When Mrs. Hope's brother, the Reverend William Beresford, saw the picture on June 20, he refused to countenance the scandal and simply cut the picture to pieces where it hung. Du Bost then took Beresford to court, claiming damages for the destruction of the picture. In his judgment, Lord Ellenborough, the lord chief justice, declared that the plaintiff was both civilly and criminally liable for exhibiting the portrait in the first place. He refused to categorize it as a work of art worth £500, awarding damages of a mere £5, the value of the canvas, the paint and the stretcher. Subsequent to this case, it was accepted that while celebrities must suffer a certain degree of public abuse, less visible individuals can claim protection from such attacks and may, if they so desire, take the law into their own hands in destroying such offensive materials.

La Fontaine, Jean de La Fontaine (1621-1695) was the author of the *Fables* (*Contes et Nouvelles en Vers*), 12 books comprising some 240 poems, which appeared between 1668 and 1694. He drew on a wide variety of sources, recasting many old tales in a way best appreciated by his contemporaries. Despite the apparent innocence of his work, the fables were suppressed in 1675 for their alleged political satire and in 1703 placed on the Roman Index (see Roman Indexes), where the books remained until the 20th century.

Ladies' Directory, The In 1959 the Street Offenses Act removed prostitutes from London's streets. Given that customers could no longer ask girls in person just what specialities they might offer, there developed a place for a middleman to help both parties in the transaction. In 1960 one Frederick Charles Shaw, a publisher of Greek Street in Soho, was charged with "conspiring to corrupt public morals" in that he issued *The Ladies' Directory*, a simple 28-page contact magazine in which the "ladies" could advertise their favors, with such phone numbers and kindred details as they chose. In fact this charge was a novelty. The usual "living off

immoral earnings," used to prosecute pimps, did not appear fit. Since the police and the director of public prosecutions were determined to stamp out the *Directory* and any possible imitators, and had no desire, after the LADY CHATTERLEY'S LOVER trial to risk a "public good" defense, the authorities created the new offense of "conspiracy to corrupt public morals."

Shaw was tried at the Old Bailey in December 1960 and found guilty of the conspiracy, of living on the earnings of prostitution and of publishing an obscene article. He was sentenced to nine months imprisonment. Appeals both to the Court of Criminal Appeal and to the House of Lords were dismissed, and neither court was impressed by the argument that anyone who bought the *Directory*, knowing perfectly well what it was for, would more than likely be corrupt already. Five years later the contact magazines were back, initiated by the appearance in 1965 of *Way Out* and its many imitators. These were not prosecuted, and more respectable magazines began to run lonely hearts columns that might have been indictable in earlier years. Not until the prosecution of *IT* and its personal columns in 1970 was the conspiracy charge used again in this context.

Lady Chatterley's Lover

1. history Between October 1926 and January 1928 D.H. LAWRENCE wrote three versions of a novel in which he described the affair of the fictional Lady Constance Chatterley, wife of Sir Clifford Chatterley—an intellectual, writer and Midlands landowner who has been confined to a wheelchair by war wounds—with the estate gamekeeper, one Oliver Mellors, the son of a miner. While the book itself, which ends with the lovers each awaiting divorce and looking forward to their new life together, does not stray conspicuously from Lawrence's general moral and philosophical attitudes, his use of taboo language far exceeded anything acceptable in contemporary fiction. In his attempt to convey the animal passions of sexual intercourse, he included the sort of Anglo-Saxon vocabulary that scandalized most of society. Only James Joyce, whose use of such words in ULYSSES had ensured its outlaw status, had introduced such unabashed "obscenity" into supposed literature. Although the third version, which had the most lurid language, was unpublishable in England, Lawrence offered it to the publishers Jonathan Cape, Secker & Warburg and Chatto and Windus and mocked their instant rejections as hypocrisy. He then turned to Guiseppe Orioli, who ran an internationally famous bookstore in Florence, near which city the author was living. Lawrence knew that foreign editions of banned books were potentially highly profitable and he intended that *Lady Chat-*

terley should reap such benefits. A "dirty book" from a major novelist meant guaranteed sales.

Lawrence was not unduly perturbed by the ban. He considered his book "far too good for the ... gross public," suggesting rather that subscriptions should be solicited from "the right sort of people in the Universities." The first, Florentine edition of 1,000 copies duly sold out in 1928, even at the high price of two guineas (£2.10). As writer Colin MacInnes pointed out at the book's British trial in 1960, despite any ban, those who wanted the book and who were clever enough to appreciate it, would always find a way of obtaining it. Not all the copies survived Customs searches and as the demand for the book grew, so did the pirated editions. In 1929 Lawrence produced a cheaper edition through the Parisian publisher Edward Titus, including a preface in which he described his struggles with the censors, apostrophized as "My Skirmish with Jolly Roger." This edition sold well and Lawrence earned nearly 90,000 francs from it before his death in 1930.

For the next 30 years, until its trials (qqv) in Britain and America, *Lady Chatterley* remained either outlawed or so severely bowdlerized as to bear little resemblance to its author's work. For students of literature the book took on a ghostly quality; it was vital to have read it, and nearly all did, as was made clear by the procession of experts at the trials, but in theory such dissemination of an obscene work should have been impossible. Attempts were made to publish legitimate editions, notably in 1944 when the American publisher Dial Press brought out *The First Lady Chatterley*, an edition of Lawrence's first, 1926 draft, somewhat milder than the 1928 version. Urged on by anti-vice campaigner JOHN S. SUMNER, the Staten Island Court found the book "clearly obscene," basing this opinion on Lawrence's advocacy of adultery. On appeal the Court of Special Sessions reversed this opinion, but the book never appeared, due in part to fears of further prosecution and in part to problems with the Lawrence estate. In 1932 Knopf in America and Secker in Britain brought out an abridged (i.e., bowdlerized) version of the third draft, approved by Lawrence's widow, Frieda. In 1946 the New American Library took the U.S. paperback rights and sold 1.5 million copies of what was called a "mutilated and emasculated drugstore paperback" in the next 10 years. The book was promoted as "authorized," but the cuts were conveniently passed over without detailed explanation. No paperback appeared in the U.K.

In 1959, in order to test what seemed to be the wider opportunities for the publication of what had previously been condemned as obscene material, the Grove Press deliberately issued an unexpurgated edition, this, too, authorized by Frieda Lawrence Ravagli, of the 1928 version of *Lady Chatterley*. This edition, distributed through a book club called Readers Subscription, was seized by Post Office authorities. In a hearing before the U.S. Post Office the book was found obscene, but when Grove Press brought a countersuit to restrain the Post Office ban, Judge van Pelt Bryan of the U.S. District Court found in favor of the book. He found redeeming social merit in it and praised Lawrence's "descriptive passages of rare beauty." The decensorship of *Lady Chatterley* in America had an immediate effect in Britain. In 1960, emboldened by the OBSCENE PUBLICATIONS ACT OF 1959, Penguin Books announced their forthcoming complete edition. This led inevitably to a trial, and, after a procession of expert witnesses, to the freeing of the book in Britain. By the end of the 1970s the book had sold six million-plus paperbacks, even if the more cautious stores, in the aftermath of the acquittal, still kept copies beneath the counter, prepackaged in anonymous paper bags.

2. trials In 1959, after 30 years of smuggled, expurgated or pirated editions, the American publisher Grove Press decided to test the apparently liberal ruling on obscene publications embodied in the Roth decision of 1957 (see *Roth* v. *United States*)—in which a defense of "redeeming social importance" was permitted for the first time—by issuing an unexpurgated edition of the third version of D.H. Lawrence's *Lady Chatterley's Lover*. This edition, in which the Lawrence estate refused to take a royalty, believing themselves committed to the expurgated editions published by Knopf (hardback) and New American Library (paperback) in 1932 and 1946, was distributed through a small-circulation book club, Readers Subscription, patronized mainly by academics and scholars. The book cost the high price of $6. To confer suitable literary authority upon the edition, it had a preface by Archibald MacLeish, a former librarian of Congress, and an introduction by Mark Schorer, a leading Lawrence scholar and professor of literature at the University of California.

Inevitably, copies of the Grove edition were seized by the Post Office under the COMSTOCK ACT. The postmaster general declared the book obscene, despite the expert testimony of literary critics Alfred Kazin and Malcolm Cowley, and thus impermissible in the U.S. mails. He also banned any advertising of the work. Grove countered with their own suit, demanding a declaration not only that the book was not obscene, but also that the Comstock Act was unconstitutional, violating the FIRST and Fifth AMENDMENTs.

In the U.S. District Court, Southern District of New York, Judge Frederick Van Pelt Bryan found in favor of *Lady Chatterley*. In a day-long trial Judge Bryan completely vindicated the work. He accepted MacLeish and Schorer's assessment of the literary qualities of the book, adding to them his own praise of Lawrence's writing; he denied to the postmaster general the right to declare works obscene; he confirmed Roth in seeing the socially redeeming facets of the work. The U.S. government attempted to have Bryan's decision reversed, but on March 26, 1960, the U.S. Court of Appeals upheld the lower court, saying that "This is a major and distinguished novel, and Lawrence [is] one of the great writers of the age." The immediate aftermath of the Bryan decision was an explosion in sales of the book. Since Grove Press had no formal contract with the Lawrence estate, it could not establish copyright and the book remained in the public domain. A Pocket Books edition, appearing within eight days of the verdict, sold a million copies at 35 cents each in six days. A newspaper format edition was hawked by the Tabloid Publishing Company of New England at 25 cents. Even the expurgated NAL edition sold a quick 650,000 copies. When Grove Press attempted to stop this, the court decided in favor of NAL, who then brought out their own unexpurgated edition, making even more money.

The news of Grove Press' success made it clear that a similar attempt should be made in Britain. Both esthetic and commercial considerations, backed by the belief that the OBSCENE PUBLICATIONS ACT OF 1959 had offered wider latitude to "obscene publishing," made an uncut edition of *Lady Chatterley* alluring. On January 9, 1960, Penguin Books announced that, along with seven other Lawrence titles, a complete edition would be published to mark the 30th anniversary of the author's birth and the 25th of the imprints. In July, when Penguin sent his office sample copies of the 200,000 they had waiting in their warehouse, the Director of Public Prosecutions was unable to resist the challenge. A trial under the 1959 act was scheduled for October. Penguin froze its stock in anticipation. There was undoubtedly an increasingly liberal atmosphere in the U.K. Nabokov's *Lolita* had been published unscathed, but it lacked four-letter words and its sensuality was less overt. The real reason for the prosecution, it was opined, was that Penguin was offering the book at 3/6 (17 p.) a copy, a price that put a book once restricted to the connoisseur's locked bookcase on public sale to virtually anyone.

Unlike the U.S. trial, which was short and to the point, the five-day proceedings that opened at the Old Bailey on October 21, 1960, were a veritable circus. The defense lawyers had mustered 70 expert witnesses, of whom 35 were called. They included academics, the great and good of literature and the arts, a film critic, some teachers, clergymen and politicians. Their expertise was less important than what Charles Rembar, who had defended the book in America, called their role as "lobbyists ... [who] were not so much offering evidence as putting prestige into the claim that the book was innocent." The defense was substantially helped by the prosecution counsel, Mervyn Griffiths-Jones, who suggested to a jury, five of whose members stumbled over their oath, that it was not a book fit for "your wife or your servants." He also produced a grotesque word list, citing the "30 'fucks or fuckings,' fourteen 'cunts,' thirteen 'balls,' six each of 'shit' and 'arse,' four 'cocks' and three 'piss'" that had brought the book to court. The essentially patronizing tone of such statements certainly helped alienate the jury, although to what extent they were impressed by the procession of the liberal intellectual establishment is debatable. The most successful of the experts was Richard Hoggart, a former working-class scholarship boy who taught at a provincial university.

On November 2, after a trial adjourned to allow them to read the book, the jury retired for three hours before finding Penguin Books innocent. Their verdict reflected the era: The

Sixties, as a cultural phenomenon, dated from what Philip Larkin would call "the end of the Chatterley ban, and the Beatles' first LP." Penguin dedicated the next edition of the novel to the jury. It sold two million copies in a year, though many buyers were less than thrilled. In the long run, on both sides of the Atlantic, the result of the trials was to initiate a style of paperback, replete with a hitherto impossible interlarding of sex and violence, that could never previously have been contemplated. Not only were many strong but in no way pornographic hardbacks—Baldwin's *Giovanni's Room*, Donleavy's *The Ginger Man*—made available to the mass public, but also much acknowledged trash was equally available, to anyone who had the money.

3. film   The film of D.H. Lawrence's notorious novel was made in France in 1957 under the literally translated title of *L'Amant de Lady Chatterley*. It passed through U.S. Customs but was banned in New York under a provision of the New York Education Law, which stated that no license might be given to a picture if its subject "is adultery presented as being right and desirable for certain people under certain circumstances." The film's distributors chose to fight the ban, and the case, *Kingsley International Pictures Corporation* v. *Regents of the University of New York*, reached the U.S. Supreme Court in 1959.

The court, whose opinion was written by Justice Potter Stewart, rejected the Regents' case, declaring that since *Lady Chatterley* had been banned on the grounds of not an act but of an idea, the New York law was unconstitutional. The FIRST AMENDMENT specifically provided for the dissemination of any ideas, however abhorrent they might appear, unless, as in the case of outright obscenity, they fell outside its protection. This ban was not on the grounds of obscenity, merely on those of presenting adultery as an acceptable practice in certain circumstances. As such it could not be upheld. Justice Black, in a concurring opinion, added that any form of prior censorship, for whatever reason, violated the Constitution. He also stressed that "if this Nation is about to embark upon the dangerous road of censorship, my belief is that this Court is about the most inappropriate Supreme Board of censors that could be found. So far as I know, judges possess no special expertise providing exceptional competency to set standards and to supervise the private morals of the Nation."

Lamont v. *Postmaster General* (1965)   SEE United States 17. postal regulations (communist political propaganda).

L'Anti-Justine, ou les Delices de l'amour (1798)   This unfinished erotic novel was written by NICOLAS-EDME RESTIF DE LA BRETONNE (1734-1806), a prolific French novelist whose vast output is based on his experiences as a peasant in Paris and is culled from the diaries he kept, from the age of 15, as well as from his substantial correspondence with all sorts of women. Some authorities have claimed that Restif also wrote "Dom Bougre," an obscene pamphlet published in 1789, but this theory is generally dismissed. Although

Restif's 200-plus works consistently celebrate sex, *L'Anti-Justine* was more probably his sole contribution to hard-core erotica. It has also been surmised that its publication was the desperate stroke of a man who, failing to make money from relatively mild works, turned unashamedly to pornography. The author originally used the pseudonym "Jean-Pierre Linguet," an enemy of his who had been guillotined during the Terror. The novel was intended as a massive counterblast to the works of the MARQUIS DE SADE, an individual whom Restif particularly execrated and against whom he carried out a continuing vendetta. The book was originally to run to some seven parts, which would have totaled around 1,400 pages, but Restif finished only two and the book ends very abruptly.

The bibliographer LOUIS PERCEAU claimed that police attention to those parts that did appear put paid to any hopes Restif might have had of finishing his work: What there was of the book was banned in 1803. Such copies that had been circulated were regularly seized from brothels and bookshops, and it soon became one of the rarest of erotic works. Napoleon's order that henceforth two copies of all such seized pornography should be held in a special section of the Bibliotheque Nationale in Paris created the ENFER special collection. Four copies, including the author's original, are still held in the Enfer and a fifth has been traced through the collections of a number of variously distinguished bibliophiles, including ASHBEE's dissolute friend, FREDERICK HANKEY, and the millionaire, J.P. Morgan. Reprints of the novel began to appear in 1863, usually of poor quality. It first appeared in English as *The Double Life of Cuthbert Cockerton, Esq., Attorney-at-Law of the City of London*, published by CARRINGTON in 1895, although this version, which sets the action in Sheffield and may possibly have been the work of LEONARD SMITHERS, is hardly a faithful translation. A better English version was published by MAURICE GIRODIAS in 1955.

Although Restif announced in his preface that "no one has been more incensed than I by the foul performances of the infamous Marquis de Sade," *L'Anti-Justine* ranks among the world's more pornographic works. The book also offers its share of blatant cynicism and blasphemy a la Sade, although it would appear that Restif is less wholeheartedly committed to his philosophies than is de Sade and in the end prefers to celebrate the pleasure and not the pain of sex.

Last Exit to Brooklyn *Last Exit to Brooklyn* was written by American writer Hubert Selby Jr. and began appearing in America in its separate parts as early as 1957. The full book, a collection of six linked episodes, appeared in 1966 on both sides of the Atlantic. Set among the underclass of 1950s Brooklyn, *Last Exit* is an uncompromisingly brutal book, and the squalor of its action and its environment is leavened only by the excellence of Selby's writing. It describes the daily round of a group of Brooklyn youths: some straight, some gay, some undecided; most on drugs, all vicious, all seemingly devoid of the slightest vestige of human feeling, let alone conventional morality. The central episode of the book, and that which provoked its prosecution, is a section entitled "Tralala," the tale of an eponymous street whore, who suffers an appalling and horribly detailed gang-rape before being left for dead.

Last Exit, published by Grove Press in America and CALDER and Boyars in England, received what one critic has called "bruised respect." Selby's characters and their world were repellent, even terrifying, but the power of his writing was undeniable. By September 1966 the U.K. hardback had sold some 11,247 copies. At this point the Conservative MP Sir Charles Taylor was sent a copy by a member of the Oxford bookselling Blackwell family. Taylor was duly disgusted and told the attorney general about the book, although he refused to name it. The attorney general told Taylor not to worry, pointing out that the book was barely selling any more and that in any case he was too late to make an effective complaint. The director of public prosecutions, he explained, was "far from sure" that a prosecution would succeed. Tom Driberg and a number of other Labour MPs then proposed a motion of congratulation to the DPP for his sense.

This gesture outraged the hard-right Tory, Sir Cyril Black, a property dealer, lay preacher and member since the early 1950s of the PUBLIC MORALITY COUNCIL. Black brought a private prosecution against *Last Exit*, calling upon the publishers to prove why the book should not be forfeited and destroyed; the trial was heard at the Marlborough Street Magistrates Court in November 1966. Among the prosecution witnesses was H. Montgomery Hyde, who had recently defended the genteel classicism of FANNY HILL, but found himself unable to stomach the harsher contemporaneity of *Last Exit*. The magistrate, Leo Gradwell, was far from stereotypically conservative, but he too rejected Selby's book, finding it guilty as charged under section 3 of the OBSCENE PUBLICATIONS ACT (1959). Three copies of the book were burnt, although Gradwell's verdict only applied to his own area; elsewhere the book could continue to sell. The literary world was as disgusted by the conviction as Gradwell had been by the book. Britain, in the words of critic Martin Seymour Smith, "had made herself the laughing stock of the civilized world."

Calder and Boyars refused to accept the status quo and announced to the DPP their intention to continue publication. On February 6, 1967, the DPP announced a fresh prosecution, under section 2 of the act, which prohibited "possessing an obscene article for gain." The second trial lasted from November 13 to 22, 1967. The judge, Graham Rogers, directed that the jury should be all male, so as to spare ladies any embarrassment. The prosecution called ex-test cricketer and bishop of Liverpool-to-be, David Shepherd, who declared that he had indeed been left "not unscathed" by his reading of the book. The publishers countered with an impressive list of academics, critics, clergymen, media figures and the like. The jury were not swayed, and after retiring for five-and-a-half hours, found Selby's book guilty. The judge accepted that the book had been published in good faith by a respectable firm, so fined Calder and Boyars only £100, plus costs totalling some £500. The defense of the case had cost in all nearly £15,000. The need to find this substantial sum led to the founding of the DEFENSE OF LITERATURE AND THE ARTS SOCIETY, a body designed to coordinate future struggles against the censorious. More immediately, the defendants appealed. The Appeal Court accepted that the judge had not instructed the jury sufficiently as regarded the 1959 act and had thrown them "in at the deep end and [left] them to sink or swim in its dark waters." The court therefore overturned the conviction, and although this did not completely clear the book, it was apparent that a retrial would be highly unlikely in the contemporary political climate.

Last Judgment, The Michelangelo's fresco above the altar of the Sistine Chapel caused controversy from the moment of its unveiling on October 31, 1541. The Papal master of ceremonies, Biagio de Cesena, had already warned his master, Pope Paul III, after viewing the part-finished work in 1540, that its huge, nude figures were "better suited to a bathroom or roadside wineshop than to a chapel of the Pope." In 1558 the artist Daniele de Volterra was ordered to paint suitable coverings over the offending limbs. After masking them in a wardrobe of veils, draperies, breeches and skirts, Volterra earned himself the nickname "Il Braghettone" (the breeches-maker). In 1564 the work constituted the basis of Andrea Gilio da Fabriano's *Dialogo degli errori dei pittori* (*Dialogue on the Errors of Painters*), in which the theologian outlawed the nude from any form of church art.

Following suggestions by El Greco in 1566 that the whole fresco should be removed and a substitute prepared, Pope Pius V resisted complete destruction but ordered further disguise by drapery. This veiling continued under Popes Clement VII, who resisted destruction only after being petitioned by the Academy of San Luca, and Clement XIII (ca. 1760). Even now, when the ceiling is undergoing substantial cleaning, it has been decided that certain naked figures are to be left covered by the centuries-old grime. In 1931 U.S. Customs at New York banned a series of postcards of the original, undraped frescos. Two years later Customs was forced to drop its case against a set of pictures of the frescos, declared obscene in a New York court and detained for four days. The pictures—10 pamphlets of 30 reproductions in each—had been ordered from Italy by the city's Weyhe Gallery. Painted as copies of Michelangelo's work by Marcello Venusti before Volterra's "breeches" had appeared, they were released from custody only after the involvement of a senior customs official.

Lawrence, D.H. D.H. Lawrence (1885-1930), better known for his novels, including LADY CHATTERLEY'S LOVER, and his tempestuous private life, became seriously interested in painting in 1926. On June 14, 1929, there opened an exhibition of 25 of his paintings at the Dorothy Warren Gallery in London. Over the next six weeks some 12,000 people viewed the pictures, which aroused substantial comment, both favorable and adverse. The authorities noted those criticisms based more on moral than esthetic grounds and on July 5 an inspector and sergeant of police visited the show. They returned later to confiscate as indecent 13 paintings, plus four copies of a book of Lawrence reproductions published by the Mandrake Press, and removed a book of drawings by GEORGE GROSZ. In Lawrence's own opinion it was the fragments of pubic hair visible in the seized pictures that brought them to court. What might be acceptable in a full-time artist was not so in a novelist and poet known for his erotic work. His book of poems, *Pansies*, had already been seized by the postal authorities in 1928 and was substantially altered prior to its republication in 1929. Such luminaries as Rebecca West and Aldous Huxley condemned the police raid.

The octogenarian magistrate Frederick Mead who heard the case at Marlborough Police Court on August 8, apostrophized the works as "gross, coarse, hideous, unlovely and obscene." He refused to hear such expert witnesses as Augustus John and Arnold Bennett, declaring that it was "utterly immaterial whether they are works of art or not. The most splendidly painted picture in the universe might be obscene …" and should be "put an end to, like any wild animal which is dangerous." Despite his desire to take the case further, Lawrence was advised by his counsel to pay the five guineas costs levied against him and retire from the contest. The paintings were then returned to the gallery owners, Mr. and Mrs. Philip Trotter, on the proviso that they would never be shown publicly again. The four volumes of reproductions were destroyed. In 1951, the U.S. Customs refused to permit the import of the privately printed *Paintings of D.H. Lawrence*, ordered by one of his biographers, on the ground that it was obscene.

SEE ALSO *The Rainbow*.

Le Diable au corps (1785) SEE Andrea de Nerciat, Andre-Robert.

Legion of Decency Roman Catholic attempts to control the content of American films developed almost as soon as the medium was invented. The church banned A.M. Kennedy's *Power of the Cross* in 1916 and threatened Kennedy with excommunication if he released it. In 1922 the International Federation of Catholic Alumnae began publishing lists of recommended films, and a variety of similar bodies, some local, some national, all vied in setting their own standards of acceptability. The involvement of Martin Quigley and Daniel Lord, both prominent Catholics, in the drafting of the MOTION PICTURE PRODUCTION CODE in 1930 gave the church a far more important say. This developed even further after it became apparent that the code alone was still insufficient to control the industry. In 1933, spurred on by an influential group of American Catholics, the visiting apostolic delegate announced that "Catholics are called by God, the Pope, the bishops and the priests to a unified and vigorous campaign for the purification of the cinema, which has become a deadly menace to morals." Fired by this speech, Catholic reformers created the Legion of Decency in April 1934.

The initial object of the legion was the amassing of a petition from some 10,000,000 American Catholics who pledged, as members of the organization, "to rid the country of its greatest menace—the salacious motion picture." Members signed a pledge that read, "I wish to join the Legion of Decency, which condemns vile and unwholesome moving pictures. I unite with all who protest agianst them as a grave menace to youth, to home life, to country, and to religion ... Considering these evils, I hereby promise to remain away from all motion pictures except those which do not offend decency and Christian morality. I promise further to secure as many members as possible for the Legion of Decency. I make this protest in a spirit of self-respect, and with the conviction that the American public does not demand filthy pictures, but clean entertainment and educational features."

In February 1936 the legion developed a ratings system for the films it considered: Class A-I, morally unobjectionable for general patronage; Class A-II, morally unobjectionable for adults and adolescents; Class B, morally objectionable in part for all; Class C, condemned, "positively bad." The legion, with its triple threat of economic boycott, organized protest and lobbying of the official censors, terrified the industry's own HAYS OFFICE. Hays deputed Quigley to deal with the church, giving him full powers of negotiation. The MOTION PICTURE PRODUCERS AND DISTRIBUTORS ASSOCIATION (MPPDA) capitulated unreservedly. Its Studio Relations Department was renamed the Production Code Administration and placed under the control of former Philadelphia journalist, Joseph I. Breen, a Catholic layman who had been active in film reform since 1925. Breen was empowered to fine any MPPDA member who released a film without the legion's PCA certificate and seal of approval—$25,000.

The legion was further encouraged by Pope Pius XI who had made clear his admiration for the legion's activities, and in 1936 published the encyclical "VIGILANTI CURA" ("With Vigilant Care"). Hays, delighted by such support, embraced the encyclical as he had the legion; when he visited Rome himself, he received a private audience with Pius, and was rewarded with the Pope's congratulations as well as a personal encomium of the way in which "you sit at the valve in the conduit through which flows the principal amusement of the great majority of people in the world. Your impress is upon the quality of this entertainment and you are very important to us."

The cozy relationship between the MPPDA and the legion persisted throughout the 1930s, World War II and the 1950s. Even the landmark "MIRACLE" decision, which prompted the National Council of Catholic Men to warn that the Legion was now "the effective bulwark against pictures which are

immoral, short of being obscene," only ruffled the surface. The advent of America's first Catholic president, John F. Kennedy, changed the church's position in the country. With a newfound self-confidence, and inspired by urgings of Pope John XXIII for Catholics to move into the modern world, the legion found itself relaxing slightly.

In 1958 two new code categories were introduced: Class A-III, morally objectionable for adults; and a "separate category," morally unobjectionable for adults, with reservations, as regarded films that "required caution and some analysis and explanation as a protection to the uninformed against wrong interpretations and false conclusions." This latter was renamed Class A-IV in 1963. This liberalization was insufficient to preserve the legion's power, as was its being renamed in 1965 the NATIONAL CATHOLIC OFFICE FOR MOTION PICTURES. American mores were changing quickly and formerly acceptable moral standards were being abandoned. The NCOMP has continued to make its opinions known ever since, and its ratings system is still applied to films and publicized in the Catholic press and in diocesan newsletters, although its influence has waned.

Leighton, Alexander Leighton was a 17th-century British Presbyterian clergyman who made his dislike of the Anglican bishops clear. In his *Plea against the Prelacy* (1628) he condemned the episcopacy as "caterpillars, moths and cankerworms." The established church was even less temperate. Star Chamber fined Leighton £10,000, deprived him of his ministry, and sentenced him to be whipped, pilloried, to lose his ears, to have his nose slit, to be branded on both cheeks with the letters "S.S." (for "Sower of Sedition") and to be imprisoned for life. Sentence was carried out in November 1630. Leighton served 10 yeras in jail, prior to his release by the Long Parliament in 1640. In later life "rather insane of mind for the hardships he had suffered," he became keeper of Lambeth Palace and, ironically for one who had scourged bishops, fathered a future archbishop.
SEE ALSO Prynne, John.

Lennon, John The owner of the London Art Gallery was tried on April 1, 1970, for the alleged indecency of the display of a portfolio of 14 lithographs depicting John Lennon (1941-1982) and his wife, Yoko Ono. Three-hundred copies of each picture had been printed, for sale at £40 apiece. The defendant described the pictures illustrating the couple as "pornographic but not obscene." Lennon's erotic art was successfully exhibited later that year at the Upstairs Gallery in Long Beach, California, despite the London raid, with the full approval of the local Police Department.

Leon to Annabella SEE *Don Leon.*

L'Escholle des Filles, ou La Philosophie des Dames This 17th-century pornographic novel, attributed to Michel Melilot (Millot), was first published in Paris in 1655 and went into several later editions, appearing in translations throughout Europe, and in England as *The School of Venus* in 1680. *L'Ecole des filles, ou la Philosophie des dames leur indiquant le secret pour se faire aimer des hommes, quand meme elles ne seraient pas belles, et le plus sur moyen d'avoir du plaisir tout le temps de leur vie* ... is written in the form of a dialogue between an experienced older woman and a virgin and, unlike much pornography, it does not debase sex. While its plot is of no exceptional interest, its English translation replaced ARETINO's *Postures* as the country's favorite pornography. In the history of pornography it links the Renaissance (Aretino) to the 18th century (Cleland). It is renowned as "the most bawdy, lewd book I ever saw," according to Samuel Pepys. It is also mentioned in William Wycherley's play *The Country Wife* (1675), Learned's *The Rambling Justice* (1678) and Ravenscroft's *The London Cuckolds* (1681).

In 1730 JOHN CLELAND cited the overt grossness of its language as the stimulus for the writing of his own MEMOIRS OF A WOMAN OF PLEASURE, in which no single obscene word is found. The book, which was seized in Paris on its first publication, also featured in several contemporary and subsequent prosecutions of merchants selling "obscene and lascivious" books. Among these were Crayle and Streater, who had already been prosecuted in 1689 for their edition of ROCHESTER's SODOM. Further prosecutions followed in 1745 and 1788. The book has survived into the 20th century, its latest translation, *Lessons in Seduction*, appearing from Brandon House in California in 1967.

Lewis, Matthew Gregory   SEE *The Monk*.

Lewis, Sinclair   Lewis (1885-1951) failed to make a mark as a writer with his early work but with two novels, *Main Street* (1920) and *Babbitt* (1922), he found his real voice. Lewis revealed himself as the foremost satirist of America's Midwest, mocking its pretentions, its hypocrisies and the smug self-satisfaction of its small-town boosterism. Lewis later gave the same ironic treatment to the worlds of medicine, in *Arrowsmith* (1925), and evangelical preaching, in *Elmer Gantry* (1927). In 1930 Lewis became the first American to receive the Nobel Prize for Literature. *Elmer Gantry*, in which religion was held up to satirical analysis, was prosecuted and banned in Boston in 1927. Public libraries in America and in Britain refused to stock the book, and in 1931 Ireland banned the novel, following this in 1953 with the prohibition of *Ann Vickers* and *Cass Timberlane*. Germany banned all Lewis's books in 1954. Lewis' *Kingsblood Royal* was one of 6,000 books "relating to sex" which were purged from Illinois state libraries in 1953.

Liberty Leading the People   This picture, by Delacroix, was exhibited briefly in the Paris Salon in 1831. The picture had been commissioned by the French government for hanging in the Throne Room at the Tuileries, but prevailing bourgeois standards were so outraged at what was seen as a "glorification of the revolutionary spirit" that the government paid the artist, removed the picture from the Salon, and ensured that it was never subsequently exhibited.

Libya   Prior to the coup of September 1969, which brought Libya's present ruler, Muammar al-Qadhafi, to power, the country's media was comparatively diverse and relatively unrestrained. Sixteen newspapers—both national and provincial—were published by the private sector, giving journalists the chance to develop their talents and comment as they wished on national life. A television station had been established since 1966; four drama groups (two private, two state-backed) represented the theater; there were a number of women's magazines, an institute for the teaching of music and various similar establishments.

Qadhafi's new regime acted speedily to impose itself on the media. The entire newspaper press was shut down for a week; publication resumed under the control of in-house censors. All copy continues to suffer mandatory prepublication censorship. In 1972 the press was shut down again, and all printing presses declared government property. A blanket charge of "contributing to the former political corruption of the state" was leveled at all former editors and leading journalists. Since then a variety of titles have appeared, ostensibly different, but all dictated by the same ideology. A year later came Qadhafi's version of a "cultural revolution." People's committees took over the local administration of the state and many of the old laws were revoked. Whole libraries were burnt and 700 intellectuals arrested. The books destroyed were mainly Islamic texts and any material considered to represent left-wing ideology. The libraries became government departments, staffed exclusively by civil servants.

Subsequent to 1973 the government has an absolute monopoly of media control. In 1975 the president set up his own radio station, al-Watan al-Arabi. It is believed that his engineers have the technology to break into any transmission of the main stations in Tripoli and Benghazi. All news broadcasts begin with extracts from Qadhafi's Green Book (the collection of his thoughts and opinions, its cover colored Islamic green) and contain only material supplied by the country's newsagency, JANA. There are three television channels: a general channel, a foreign channel and the revolutionary channel, specializing in narrating and interpreting the Green Book.

Licensing Act (1662)   On the Restoration of Charles II in 1660 the censorship apparatus established under Oliver Cromwell (see Puritan censorship: The Commonwealth) was immediately abolished and Parliament was requested to create a new law for the prepublication censorship of the press. The initial attempt to implement this law in 1661 collapsed when the House of Lords demanded exemption from its provisions and the Commons preferred to reject the whole package rather than offer such a privilege. The Licensing Act regulating the whole nation was passed in 1662. Essentially it revived the "Decreee of Starre-Chamber Concerning Printing" of 1637 (SEE United Kingdom—Stuart Censorship), which had extended the number of official licensers and thus set up a bureaucracy for the precensorship of all publications. The act does not specify obscene literature, being concerned rather with "heretical, seditious, schismatical or offensive books or pamphlets," but does state that nothing may appear "contrary to good life or good manners." Roger L'Estrange was appointed surveyor of printing presses and lists of licensed books were published in the Term Catalogues that appeared until 1711. All unlicensed printing was forbidden, officials had powers of search and seizure and the number of master printers was limited to 20.

The act ran until 1679. It was due to be renewed but Parliament was dissolved in February of that year and the act did not appear before Parliament prior to the king's death in 1685. In the interim the common law provided adequate punishments for seditious, obscene, blasphemous and defamatory publications. There was also an increase in cases of "scandalum magnatum," an offense created under Edward I (1272-1307) whereby great men ("magnates") might claim legal protection against libelous attacks by their social inferiors. When Parliament met again in 1685 the Licensing Act was renewed until 1693, and then again until 1695.

In 1695 a parliamentary committee recommended that the act should be again renewed, but in February the Commons rejected this advice. The Lords sided with the committee and the two Houses met. The Commons put forward a list of 18 reasons for ending licensing, composed by the philosopher John Locke (1632-1704). Their main complaint was that the licensing system, as administered by the STATIONERS COMPANY, had become irredeemably corrupt. In addition to this, the logistics of the licensing system meant that it had never worked properly, corrupt or not. The choice of volumes to be censored was inconsistent. Prosecuted authors became martyrs, and their work merely vanished underground. Above all, the book trade had outgrown attempts to control it. Locke deliberately omitted any advocacy of freedom of the press. His arguments carried the day and licensing was thus abandoned, not from a desire to safeguard intellectual freedom, but through the pragmatic belief that it simply failed to work as required.

Literature at Nurse   George Moore (1852-1933) published his second novel, *A Modern Lover*, in 1883. Despite laudatory reviews, which compared it favorably with Zola, this story of contemporary Bohemian society proved too risque for Mudie's Library, which banned it, thus censoring Moore's work and denying him the substantial sales guaranteed by selection in this most influential of circulating libraries. W.H. Smith, which had initially accepted some copies, then rescinded any further orders, justifying the decision by citing a single complaint "from two ladies in the country." When in 1885 Moore's next book, *A Mummer's Wife*, was similarly

treated, the author produced *Literature at Nurse, or Circulating Morals*, a scathing attack on the hegemony of taste exercized by circulating libraries. He denounced the pusillanimity of the average circulating librarian, for whom "the artistic individualities of his employees count for as little as that of the makers of pill boxes ..." Such authorities had reduced English fiction either to "a sentimental misunderstanding which is happily cleared up in the end, or ... singular escapes over the edges of precipices, and miraculous recoveries of one or more of the senses of which the hero was deprived ..." He deplored the absence from modern publishing, dominated as it was by the libraries, of the novel of analysis and of observation, and wrote, "Let us renounce the effort to reconcile these two irreconcilable things—art and young girls." Neither Smiths nor Mudies were impressed and Moore's greatest novel, *Esther Waters* (1894), which dealt with the life of an unmarried mother and pictures scenes in a maternity ward, was excluded from their catalog. Moore's reputation among the discerning did not suffer, and he continued his fight against censorship throughout his career. Although it was subsequently judged to be a modern classic by the U.S Treasury Department, Moore's novel *A Story Teller's Holiday* was seized by the U.S. Customs in 1929 and declared obscene in 1932.

Little Black Sambo   On October 19, 1964, this children's storybook by Hazel Bannerman, hitherto untouched by scandal or controversy, was removed from the open shelves of the Lincoln, Nebraska, school system on the orders of School Superintendent Steven N. Watkins. Watkins had been alerted to what was cited as the inherent racism of the book, as alleged in a letter from the local Human Relations Council, in which a small black child is pursued by a ravening tiger. The superintendent then reallocated the book on the "Reserved" shelves, with a note explaining that while it was not "a part of the instructional program, it will be available to those who want to read it as optional material."

Little Red Schoolbook   The *Little Red Schoolbook* was first published in Denmark in 1970; this manual of "kids' rights" was inspired by the then still-popular bible of the Chinese Cultural Revolution, the "Little Red Book" of the thoughts of Chairman Mao Tse-Tung. It was translated and distributed in England in 1971 by Stage One, a publisher owned by Richard Handyside, whose list specialized in left-wing and alternative titles. The *Schoolbook* ran to 208 pages, of which fewer than a quarter dealt with drugs and sex; it cost 30p. An edition of 20,000 copies sold well, and another of 50,000 was scheduled. It appeared without adverse comment, receiving respectful, if not adulatory, notices in various intellectual journals.

Britain's censorship lobby, spearheaded by MARY WHITEHOUSE and Ross McWhirter, deplored the book. McWhirter, citing its suggestion that ideas might be gained from reading pornography, condemned the book as "not only obscene, but seditious." Inspired by such complaints, and urged on by the sensationalism of the popular press, the police raided Stage One, removing a large quantity of material, of which copies of the *Schoolbook* made up only a small part.

On April 14, 1971, Handyside was charged with possessing 1,201 copies of an obscene article for publication for gain. A group of 20 publishers immediately announced their support, promising to reprint the book under their own imprints. This solidarity, although encouraging, was short-lived, with an increasing flow of defections as the trial neared. With the threat of financial collapse, were the director of public prosecutions to become involved and invoke his powers to freeze stocks of the *Schoolbook*, Handyside waived his chance of a jury trial, opting for the quick and relatively simple justice of the Clerkenwell Magistrate's Court. Here he was defended by John Mortimer, QC, who was commuting between Clerkenwell and another obscenity trial, that of OZ at the Old Bailey. Although Handyside had prepared his case well, the subtleties of teenage relationships and the testimony of the expert witnesses for the defense did not impress the Bench. Handyside was found guilty and fined £50, with £115.50 costs.

The *Little Red Schoolbook* was banned, although duplicated copies of the original were circulated in many schools. Handyside brought out a revised edition of 100,000 copies, with the offending passages obscured by stickers. He also took his case to the Court of Appeal and to the European Court of Human Rights, both of which rejected it.

Locke, John   Locke (1632-1704) was educated at Westminster School and Oxford, and after holding various academic posts in Oxford became physician to the earl of Shaftesbury in 1667. After becoming embroiled in Shaftesbury's plotting against the king in 1683 Locke fled to Holland, where he took the pseudonym of Dr. Van der Linden and joined the court of William of Orange, soon to be William III of England. Locke returned to England after the Glorious Revolution of 1668 and became commissioner of appeals and a member of the council of trade.

Locke's initial clash with the authorities came when he published his "Letter from a Person of Quality to his Friend in the Country." This pamphlet discussed the parliamentary debates that took place in April and May 1675 concerning the passing of an act "to prevent the dangers which may arise from persons disaffected to the Government." Locke saw this act, which proposed a form of loyalty oath to the monarchy, as a new example of clerical mischief-making. His attack was condemned by the Privy Council and duly burned. More important was his major work, *An Essay Concerning Human Understanding* (1690, plus substantially revised editions in 1694, 1700 and 1706). This examination of the human mind and of its powers of understanding antagonized the Catholic Church. The French translation was placed on the Roman Index (see Roman Indexes) in 1700, where it remained until the 20th century. Oxford, from which he had been barred ever

since Charles II, in punishment for his alleged plotting, deprived him of his studentship at Christ Church and also chose to censor the *Essay*. A Latin version was permitted only on the proviso that "no tutors were to read with their students this essential investigation into the basis of knowledge."

Longford Report, The   Lord Longford, otherwise known as a publisher (Sidgwick and Jackson), and the father of the writer Lady Antonia Fraser, set up his committee to inquire into pornography in England in April 1971, after a debate on the subject in the House of Lords. Taking as his premise the view that "pornography had increased, was increasing and ought to be diminished," he collected some 52 supposed representatives of the public at large and 16 months later issued *Pornography: The Longford Report*.

The committee was composed of a variety of clergymen, schoolteachers, businessmen, academics, police and correction officers, conservative writers and journalists, and two members of the pop industry, supposedly representing "youth." The massing of information gave the public endless amusement, although the committee, which was heavily influenced by the NATIONAL VIEWERS AND LISTENERS ASSOCIATION, represented itself as a counterattack against moral laxity, an expression of widespread public discontent.

The committee's report appeared in September 1972. At only 60p it sold well. It provided few surprises and was, as the *Economist* pointed out, "broadly what one might expect of such an exercise: a report confirming and reinforcing the convictions and prejudices of the author and those of a like mind." The report criticizes contemporary society and its mores; the overall feeling is that "things have gone too far."

Unlike the American PRESIDENT'S COMMISSION ON OBSCENITY AND PORNOGRAPHY, whose methodology it echoed but whose liberal recommendations it found utterly alien, the Longford Committee urged substantial controls. It advocated a new definition of obscenity: "anything which outraged contemporary standards of decency or humanity, which were accepted by the public at large." But critics noted that this was open to debate as the traditional "deprave and corrupt." In the event the laws on obscenity remained unchanged. The crusade against pornography continued through the 1970s and beyond, but Lord Longford himself has gradually moved into other areas of concern.
SEE ALSO Festival of Light.

lord chamberlain   Descended from the medieval *Camerarus Hospitii*, Britain's lord chamberlain is a senior court functionary among whose various responsibilities, until abolished in 1968, was the censorship of the English stage. Like many aspects of stage censorship, the lord chamberlain's powers gradually accrued over the 200 years that followed the institution of such supervision under Henry VIII. As head of the Royal Household the lord chamberlain was the direct superior of the MASTER OF THE REVELS, who provided entertainment for the monarch. As the office of master fell gradually into disrepute, exploited by a succession of self-interested, venal holders, the lord chamberlain became increasingly responsible for the state of the stage.

The office of master of the revels vanished with the Stuarts, and by 1692 it was acknowledged (by Dryden) that the lord chamberlain's powers embraced "all that belongs to the decency and Good Manners of the Stage" and that he could "restrain the licentious insolence of Poets and their Actors, in all things that shock the Publick Quiet, or the Reputation of Private Persons, under the notion of 'Humour.'" In the STAGE LICENSING ACT OF 1737 and THEATRE REGULATION ACT OF 1843 this collection of powers was codified and given statutory authority. The lord chamberlain was an absolute censor. He was resonsible neither to Parliament nor to the courts of law. Every script had to be submitted to him and there was no appeal against his rulings, other than to the sovereign. By the same token, once he had passed a play, no other authority might seek to ban it. His office dealt only with theater managers, not with dramatists. The only way of avoiding censorship was by presenting one's work at a "theater club," a development of the 20th century, which, with its ostensibly restricted membership, made for a private performance. The lord chamberlain could invade such privacy, but on the whole he did not.

The lord chamberlain, a peer and often a former military man, held many demanding roles. For the purposes of censorship he was aided, and to a great extent practically replaced, by his assistant, the EXAMINER OF PLAYS, a job that had developed like his own, without any real definition, though with much de facto power. While lord chamberlains rarely stayed in office for long (the average was five years), the examiner might serve for 10 or 20 years and stamp his own, rather than his master's authority on the current stage. Relations between the two officials were usually close. The examiner tended to indulge the chamberlain's own foibles when reading the submitted scripts, and the lord chamberlain was satisfied to delegate the day-to-day decisionmaking to his subordinate. Early examiners did see themselves as independent figures, but after the 1843 act, they accepted a secondary, if still powerful role.

Lord chamberlains and their examiners were rarely malicious; their supporters, among whom were managers who felt that someone had to state what was acceptable on stage, and actors who had no desire to suffer the caprices of a provincial magistrate, accepted them as a necessary nuisance. Their views, it might be argued, represented those of the great British public. But for those, notably the writers, for whom any censorship was otiose, the lord chamberlain represented philistine, irrelevant interference. While individual playwrights, whose works had been savaged or even banned, had always railed intermittently against the censor, a more general movement against stage censorship started with the emergence of such modern writers as Shaw and Ibsen, both of whom had suffered the blue pencil. Ibsen was especially unpopular: In 1892 the examiner of plays stated that "all the

characters … appear to be morally deranged. All the heroines are dissatisfied spinsters … or dissatisfied married women in a chronic state of rebellion … and as for the men, they are all rascals or imbeciles."

The 20th century saw increasing agitation against the lord chamberlain. The 1909 JOINT SELECT COMMITTEE ON CENSORSHIP, inspired by the complaints of the literary establishment, pondered the problem, only to reinforce the status quo. Authors wrote letters, enlightened politicians proposed bills; very little changed. And in the late 1950s, after John Osborne's *Look Back in Anger* began a revolution in English drama, censor or no censor, many critics felt that the lord chamberlain might as well, for all his anachronistic powers, be tolerated. He might ostensibly maintain his control, but few producers, playwrites or actors, let alone intelligent audiences, seemed to care.

After the OBSCENE PUBLICATIONS ACT OF 1959, this tolerance collapsed, and the consensus was that state control of artistic expression had to go. In 1962 a bill to abolish the lord chamberlain's powers was defeated in Parliament by 137 votes to 77. The battle continued. In 1965 the text of *Saved*, a play by Edward Bond in which, in a horrific central scene, a baby is stoned to death in its pram, was submitted for reading. To avoid the inevitable cuts, the play was staged at a theater club, the Royal Court Theatre's "English Stage Society." For a change, the lord chamberlain refused to turn his blind eye to such a performance. The police joined the audience and in January 1966 the directors of the Royal Court were charged under the 1843 act with presenting an unlicensed play. They were found guilty and fined 50 guineas. Increased public protest reached Parliament. A private member's bill to end the censorship gained all-party support. The lord chamberlain, Lord Cobbold, responded with greater intransigence, even cutting a college production of Chaucer's *Miller's Tale*. In late 1967 Edward Bond submitted *Early Morning*, a viciously scurrilous treatment of Queen Victoria. Club performances were mounted in April 1968. The police appeared and charges were laid. There was no trial. In September 1968 the Theatres Bill became law. The lord chamberlain's office, after 400 years, was abolished.

SEE ALSO Theatres Act (1968, U.K.).

Los Angeles—possession of obscene matter   Under the Municipal Code of the City of Los Angeles, section 41.01.1:

It shall be unlawful for any person to have in his possession any obscene or indecent writing, book, pamphlet, picture, photograph, drawing, figure, motion picture film, phonograph recording, wire recording or transcription of any kind in any of the following palces: (1) in any school, schoolgrounds, public park or playground or in any public place, grounds, street or way within 300 yards of any school, park or playground; (2) in any place of business where ice cream, soft drinks, candy, food, school supplies, books, magazines, pamphlets, papers, pictures or postcards are sold or kept for sale; (3) in any toilet or restroom kept open to the public; (4) in any poolroom or billiard parlor, or any place where alcoholic liquor is sold or offered for sale to the public; (5) in any place where phonograph records, photographs, motion pictures or transcriptions of any kind are made, used, maintained, sold or exhibited.

SEE ALSO *Smith* v. *California* (1959).

Louis XIV's Anti-Protestant Decrees (1685)   In September 1685, one month before the revocation of the Edict of Nantes, which had allowed Protestants to follow their religion without official harassment, Louis XIV ordered the suppression and destruction of all Protestant writings. To effect this, Harlay, the archbishop of Paris, prepared at the request of the Parliament of Paris a list of the books in question. This list, which has little in common with the Indexes of the ROMAN or SPANISH INQUISITIONS, was occasioned when the Catholic authorities asked the king to forbid the Protestants to abuse or libel, in sermons or writings, the Roman Catholic Church. In August 1685 Louis therefore published an edict forbidding Protestants to preach or write against Catholicism; he also suppressed their right to print anything other than a statement of their own creed, the text of their prayers and the rules of Protestant discipline. Those who refused to obey this edict were to be banished and to lose their property. The printing or selling of prohibited books would be punished with a fine of 1,600 livres and the cancellation of the license to print. The list of codemned books was published in September 1685 under the title of *Catalogue des livres condamnes et deffendus par le Mandement de M. l'Archevesque de Paris*. The list was arranged in alphabetical order, followed by a supplementary list of 45 extra titles. All the books listed are printed in Latin or French, although a number of them were printed originally outside France. All versions of the Scriptures printed by Protestant ministers are condemned as "scandalous."

SEE ALSO Roman Indexes; index of Indexes.

Louys, Pierre   Frenchman Pierre Louys (aka Pierre Louis, 1870-1925) won fame in his lifetime as a poet and novelist, the creator of such works as *Aphrodite, moeurs antiques* (1896) and *La Femme et le pantin* (1898). All his erotic works were published after his death in 1925. Toward the end of his life Louys had eschewed fame and become a recluse, writing reams of erotic poetry and taking hundreds of photographs of naked prepubescent girls. After his death his widow and his former secretary, who subsequently married Madame Louys, sold off his papers as a job lot to the bookseller Edmund Bernard, who had already dabbled in erotic publishing. Bernard in turn sold off smaller lots of the papers, and from some of these were compiled a variety of erotic publications. The first of these was the *Manuel de civilite*, printed in an edition of only 600 copies in 1926. The *Manual* was a guide to erotic etiquette aimed at young girls who were taught how best to behave in a variety of social situations—in church, at home, at school, at the brothel etc.—and advised on a number of

sexual techniques. Louys' best known such work was *Trois filles de leur mere* (1926), concerning the adventures of a student who takes lodgings in a room next to a family of prostitutes—a mother and her two daughters. Four more works appeared in 1927: *Historie du roi Gonzalve et les douze princesses, Pybrac, Poesies erotiques* and *Douze douzains de dialogues ou Petites scenes amoureuses*. In 1927 a new edition of *Aphrodite, moeurs antiques* was published, including a chapter hitherto excluded and a scholarly introduction by the clandestine publisher Pascal Pia (1901-80). A number of works followed, the most important of which is *Les Chansons secretes de Bilitis*, limited on its publication in 1933 to 106 copies. These poems were based on his own hoax collection of 1894, *Les Chansons de Bilitis*, which were supposedly the work of a contemporary of Sappho. Louys enjoyed such hoaxes, and may well have been the true author of *Le verger des Amours*, attributed to APOLLINAIRE; he certainly faked one poem thought otherwise to have come from Baudelaire.

Louys's work was censored. In 1929 *Aphrodite, The Songs of Bilitis* and the *Twilight of the Nymphs* were all banned as "lascivious, corrupting and obscene" by the U.S. Customs. In 1930 a New York book dealer, E.B. Marks, was fined $250 for possessing a copy of *Aphrodite* in contravention of the state laws on obscene publications. In 1935 an attempt was made to import an edition de luxe of *Aphrodite* into America. This was banned, although the authorities overlooked a 49-cent edition, openly advertised in the *New York Times Book Review* and apparently, despite the postal regulations, available through the mail. *Aphrodite* was still being banned in the mid-1950s, and remains on the black list of the NATIONAL ORGANIZATION FOR DECENT LITERATURE.

Love Without Fear   *Love Without Fear* was a sex manual written by the distinguished psychiatrist and gynecologist Dr. Eustace Chesser. Chesser, who had practiced in the slums of Manchester, England, during the worst years of the Depression, was determined to produce a commonsense explanation of sexual behavior, along with a no-nonsense discussion of many quite widespread sexual habits that his patients enjoyed but which, mainly through ignorance and superstition, they found somewhat guilt-inducing and productive of shame and even neurosis. The book appeared in 1942 and sold some 5,000 copies before the director of public prosecutions ordered Chesser's arrest and the seizure of his book. His intention was to purge the nation of what he categorized as a pernicious work and to brand Chesser, his publishers and his manual as criminal and obscene.

Chesser chose to fight the case. The prosecuting counsel, Mr. Justice Byrne, was later to be the judge in the trial of LADY CHATTERLEY'S LOVER. Backed by three expert witnesses, who like him had been practicing in the slums, Chesser defended himself ably: "One cannot be in practise for long without realising that the physical ailments of most people are nothing as compared with mental troubles and difficulties. A large proportion, if not the greatest proportion, of these mental difficulties are the direct result of sexual difficulties … I felt that these sexual difficulties would, in a great many cases, never have arisen if there had been anything like a proper amount of sex teaching or sex books …" He added that he had described a range of what some might see as "perversions" specifically because they were not so abnormal; and for those who could not rest happy with their own proclivities, the knowledge that there were others similarly inclined might make it easier for them to seek professional help. He had refrained from the usual practice of using Latin words for the genitals and so on since, "if I use Latin words, then you do not even know what part of your anatomy it refers to."

The jury acquitted Chesser and his book in less than an hour and their decision proved a landmark in the history of sex education and obscenity laws. Chesser went on to sell literally millions of this and other manuals. In 1972 he appeared, the first-ever expert witness in an obscenity trial, in the case of *R. v. Gold*, and his claim that pornography was a liberating rather than a corrupting force, helped acquit a number of somewhat undistinguished soft-core men's magazines.

Lovelace, Linda (Linda Marchiano) SEE *Deep Throat*; *Inside Linda Lovelace*.

Luros v. *United States* (1968) Milton Luros was one of the tycoons of American sex publishing in the 1960s. Based in Los Angeles, he mailed his magazines and books throughout the country. In 1965, when a package of such material—mixing nudist magazines and books featuring lesbian pornography—was sent to Sioux City, Iowa, Luros was charged under the Federal Postal Regulations with sending obscene materials through the mails. The trial, in Sioux City, took three months and since it coincided with the harvest, few men were available to serve on the jury. The largely female jury, who obviously found the material embarrassing, found him guilty. His lawyer, the leading anti-censorship campaigner, Stanley Fleishman, who had argued in favor of HENRY MILLER and DEEP THROAT, appealed.

Reversing Luros' conviction Judge Lay accepted that Luros' nudist magazines had little to offer beyond their potential for making money and that even their own editors described them as "crap plus one." However he could see no "provocative or suggestive pose that smacks of a prurient appeal." As far as the "so-called lesbian books" went, they were undoubtedly "trash" and had "little if any literary value or social importance." They were written simply to sell. "They produce high profits for the appellants and can be described as distasteful, cheap and tawdry. Yet these facts do not alone constitute a crime." What did matter, Lay pointed out, was the extent to which, as the Postal Regulations attempted to carry out, government censorship might be permitted under the Constitution. "It is far better there be a tight

rein on authoritarian suppression, notwithstanding a conflict with some individuals' tastes or customary limits of candor, than that we live in a stifled community of self-censorship where men may feel apprehensive over the expression of an unpopular idea or theme. Still within our human possession is the free will to make an independent choice of values and to teach our children to do the same. Paternalistic censorship by government must continue to limit that choice only in the most extreme of circumstances."
SEE ALSO *United States* v. *Thirty-Seven Photographs* (1971); United States 17. postal regulations.

Lustful Turk, The This staple of Victorian and, thanks to reprints, subsequent pornography was first published in 1828 by J.B. Brookes. The book essentially combines the contemporary fascination with virginity, and more importantly its loss, and a sub-Byronic style of Mediterranean romance. It takes the form of a series of letters between two girls—Emily Barlow and Silvia Carey—the first of which details the misadventures of the former after she is captured by Moorish pirates while travelling to India and is given by their captian, an English renegade, as a gift to the dey of Algiers. The parallel fate of Emily's maid, who is similarly delivered to the dey of Tunis, is also revealed. The centerpiece of both tales is the girls' defloration. A further exchange of letters between two apparent clergymen—Father Angelo and Pedro—concerns a girl who, after being forced into an Ursuline convent and managing briefly to escape, loses her virginity, similarly under protest. The monks, it transpires, are actually white slavers working for the dey. The two strands of the book connect up in the final letter in which Emily, now pregnant by the dey, catches him in flagrante with Silvia, who herself has been abducted by the "monks." The two girls settle down with the dey, until he is unfortunately castrated by a rebellious Greek girl who refuses to be sodomized. The story ends with the dey's genitals pickled in wine and the girls returning to freedom.

Luther, Martin A German monk of the Augustinian order born to impoverished parents in Eisleben, Luther (1483-1546) was the founder of the Protestant Reformation in Europe. A visit to Rome convinced him of the essential corruption of the Roman Church and he worked consistently thereafter to undermine its influence. The climax of his campaign came in 1520, when he denounced the sale of indulgences (written absolutions from sin, varying in price as to the gravity of the offense) in his 95 Theses, nailed publicly to the doors of Wittenburg Church.

In 1516, at the Lateran Council, the church adopted a Papal Constitution that cited the increases in heresy and ordered that no book should henceforth be printed without examination and, if approved, a license. The duties of censorship were to be shared by the MAGISTER SACRI PALATII and the vicar-general in Rome, and the bishops in the provinces. On the whole the bishops were lax in this duty, whereas the Roman officials were increasingly assiduous, thus creating the basis for the ROMAN INQUISITION, with its wide-ranging powers.

On August 9, 1518, the bishop of Ascoli, charged by the Pope with dealing with the case of Luther, summoned the monk to Rome. If Luther proved recalcitrant when examined, he was to be arrested. In case he evaded arrest, he and his followers were to be excommunicated and any place that gave them refuge was to be placed under the Interdict (an edict that prohibited any religious practices to be carried out in a given area). In July 1520 Pope Leo X issued a bull, "Exurge Domine," ordering a search for and burning of all Lutheran books and pamphlets. This was followed in January 1521 by the bull "Decet Romanum Pontificem," confirming the excommunication of Luther and his supporters, and the burning of Lutheran works. In March 1521 the Pope wrote personally to England's Cardinal Wolsey to acknowledge his assiduous efforts in enforcing these orders. In 1521 the Papal Ban was pronounced on Luther at the Diet of Worms, and Luther's own books, and those of his followers were comprehensively and consistently banned and burned throughout Europe. In May 1521 he was denounced as a heretic at St. Paul's Cross in London and his books ordered to be burned. The continued dissemination of Lutheran books led in 1538 to Henry VIII's establishment of a royal licensing system, and initiation of 60-plus years of Tudor censorship.

SEE ALSO book burning in England 1. Tudor period; France 1. book censorship (1521-1551); Germany 1. book censorship (1521-1555); Netherlands 1. book censorship (1521-1550).

M

M The original *M* was made in Germany by Fritz Lang in 1931, starring Peter Lorre as the psychopathic killer of small children, and was loosely based on the actual case of the contemporary infanticide, Peter Kurten. Joseph Losey directed a remake of *M* in 1952; it starred David Wayne in the Lorre role. The state of Ohio, which in 1913 had been the first in America to establish its own board of film censors, banned the remake from exhibition on the grounds that: (1) its effect on "unstable persons of any age level could lead to a serious increase in immorality and crime"; (2) "[the] presentation of actions and emotions of a child killer emphasizing complete perversion without serving any valid educational purpose. [The] treatment of perversion creates sympathy rather than a constructive plan for dealing with perversion; (3) "Two brutal murders were depicted; the underworld boss who tracks down the killer is seen as infinitely more able than the chief of police."

The film's distributor, Superior Films, chose to fight the ban. The Ohio Supreme Court upheld the decision, claiming that, on the basis of THE MIRACLE decision in 1952, since *M* was of neither a "moral, educational or amusing or harmless character" the state censor had the right to ban it. In 1954 the U.S. Supreme Court reversed this decision, citing *The Miracle* once again, and stating that under that decision films fall "within the free speech and free press guaranty of the First and Fourteenth Amendments." Any interference with the film violated the Fourteenth Amendment, which extended the provisions of the First Amendment to individual states.

SEE ALSO *Reigen.*

Machiavelli, Niccolo Machiavelli, who has personified cynical political legerdemain for the past five centuries, was a Florentine statesman and political theorist (1469-1527). His popularity at the Florentine court fluctuated throughout his career, but he drew upon his experiences there under the Medici, and in a variety of diplomatic missions abroad, to write a number of works. These include the *Arte della guerra* (1517-20, *The Art of War*); *Storie Fiorentine* (1520-25, *History of Florence*); *Mandragola* (1518), a satire; and his best-known book, *Il Principe* (1513, *The Prince*), a treatise on political power. Calling for an idealized Italian savior to appear and rid the country of its endless procession of foreign rulers, Machiavelli takes a cold look at the necessities of statecraft, suggesting that the lessons of the past (notably of Roman history) should be used in the present and that to gain power and then to use it effectively may require an individual to transcend acceptable ethics.

The Prince, and his earlier work *Discorsi* (1503), were both placed on the Roman INDEX OF PAUL IV in 1559, and Machiavelli was included among those authors who were banned absolutely. He was equally unpopular among Protestants. In 1576 a selection of maxims from *The Prince* was published in France and attacked by the Huguenot, Gentillet. In 1602, when an English translation by Paterick appeared in Britain, Gentillet's views were taken as the basis for refuting Machiavelli's theories. The book's real effect was on literature, and the Machiavellian villain (and even the author's name) can be found in the works of Shakespeare, Webster, Marlowe and a number of other Jacobean and Elizabethan dramatists.

Mademoiselle de Maupin This novel was first published in Paris in 1835 by the French writer Theophile Gautier (1811-72). On November 17, 1917, JOHN S. SUMNER, secretary of the New York SOCIETY FOR THE SUPPRESSION OF VICE, purchased a copy from a bookseller called Halsey in New York City. Sumner read the book and cited certain passages as obscene under section 1141 of the New York penal law (1884), which dealt with literary obscenity in the state. The examining magistrate ruled that Sumner had no grounds for such a charge. Halsey then filed a countersuit, claiming damages for malicious prosecution, and in *Halsey* v. *New York Society for the Suppression of Vice* (1922), Sumner's defeat was compounded when the court ruled that the society was indeed liable for these damages. The majority opinion confirmed that Gautier's status as a major writer elevated him above such harassment, although a dissenting judge condemned the author as a degenerate and claimed that only his "polished style, with exquisite sayings and perfumed words," saved the book from the condemnation it would deservedly have received had its sentiments been delivered in the language of the streets.

Magic Mirror The films *Magic Mirror* and *It All Comes Out in the End* were exhibited in the Paris Adult Theater in Fulton County, Georgia, in 1971. The local board of censors banned both films under the state's Obscenity Statute of 1972. The cinema challenged the ban and took Slaton, Fulton Couty's district attorney, to court. After viewing the films the Superior Court of Fulton County overturned the ban and declared that the films were not obscene. Slaton appealed to the Georgia Supreme Court, and the ban was reinstated when the court assessed the two films as hard-core pornography and as such definitely obscene. The U.S. Supreme Court, in the case of *Paris Adult Theater* v. *Slaton District Attorney* (1973), affirmed the ban.

This case, which was decided on the same day as that of MILLER V. CALIFORNIA, set new standards for the status of obscenity in America, reflecting the newly conservative attitudes of Chief Justice Burger's Supreme Court. Reversing the decision in *Stanley* v. *Georgia* (1969), the court ruled that consenting adults would no longer be allowed to read the books and view the films of their choice, other than in the privacy of their own homes; this decision was left to the state. That the theater had advertised itself as "adult" and ensured that no minors were permitted entry was seen as irrelevant. In his majority opinion, Chief Justice Burger wrote, "one of the earmarks of a decent society ... resides in the prerogative of government to prevent consenting adults from engaging in degrading conduct." The weak, the uninformed, the unsuspecting and the gullible, in his view, had to be protected from the consequence of their own inadequacy. A state was quite at liberty to abandon all controls, but by the same token it had the power to set up those that it wished. The films were not judged to contain "wrong" or "sinful" conduct, but the public exhibition of and commerce in such material was likely to "jeopardize ... the State's rights to maintain a decent society." If a state felt that this sort of material was linked directly to a decline in community standards, then it might legislate accordingly, even if the matter could not be proved either way.

Justice Douglas dissented, pointing out inter alia that "in a life that has not been short, I have yet to be trapped into seeing or reading something that would offend me." Justice Brennan, also dissenting, accepted that his own ROTH STANDARD, established in 1957, was no longer a sufficient test for obscenity. But in a lengthy opinion he suggested that such tests were of secondary importance; what mattered was whether there even existed "a definable class of sexually orientated expression that may be totally suppressed by the federal and state government." Even if such a thing did exist, "the concept of 'obscenity' cannot be defined with sufficient specificity and clarity to provide fair notice to persons who create and distribute sexually-orientated materials, to protect substantial erosion of protected speech as a by-product of the attempt to suppress unprotected speech, and to avoid the very costly institutional harm." He added that the only legitimate and useful areas in which government should interfere in this area were in the possible involvement of children and in situations where such material was forced on unwilling recipients. Brennan's arguments, however, failed to persuade the majority of his fellow justices.

Magister Sacri Palatii   The "master of the sacred palace" was originally a Papal chaplain and, since the first magister was St. Dominic, traditionally a Dominican. His basic task was to advise the Pope on theological matters—initially, the interpretation of the Bible and, as such measures developed, the wider body of Catholic doctrine. It was also assumed that he would control the way in which theology was taught and preached to the faithful. While the Vatican never devleoped a theological faculty similar to that of the universities at Paris or Oxford, the magister's task was seen as similar to that of the head of such a faculty. This role evolved into that of the chief administrator of the censorship system of the ROMAN INQUISITION, in partnership with the members of the CONGREGATION OF THE INDEX of which he was given the ex officio title "perpetual assistant," which post was made official by Pope Leo X. From the start of the 17th century the magister was empowered to prohibit the reading and printing of certain books within the city of Rome.

Malaya   Malaya's federation of Malays, Chinese and Indians is governed by the Rukunegara, or "national ideology." This is based on five beliefs: a united nation and a democratic, just, liberal and progressive society; and five principles: belief in God, loyalty to king and country, upholding of the constitution, rule of law, good behavior and morality. Under this ideology the government sees the press as one more instrument of national development and unity. Journalists are meant to promote a positive image of the country and of its government's activities, and to eschew "the mindless aping of bourgeois values and styles of the West." During the 1970s there was to be no reporting on radio of bad news before lunchtime, so as not to upset those on the way to work. As of December 1987 the minister of information has the right to monitor all programs and ensure that they echo government policy. Any station that rejects such policy may be shut down.

In that same month the Printing Presses and Publications Act (1948) was amended. "Malicious" publishing was declared an offense—"malicious" being defined as "not taking reasonable measures to verify the truth." Journalists who wished to prove their innocence would have to reveal their sources in court if the state so demanded. Those convicted would be fined heavily or jailed for up to three years. The home affairs minister was empowered to ban any publication that he considered prejudicial to international relations, public order or morality, state security, national interests or that might alarm public opinion. Under the amended act there would no longer be any appeal against ministerial refusal or revocation of a publishing license. Not only could whole publications be banned, but any extract or precis was also liable to prosecution. A "publication" may be either Malayan or foreign and include "anything ... capable of suggesting words or ideas."

All news aimed at foreign consumption is channeled through the country's Bernama News Agency. A conscious proponent of the News International Information and Communication Order, the agency aims to correct what it sees as biased Western reporting of the Third World by putting out deliberately positive material. Material coming in from abroad is regulated by the Control of Imported Publications Act and the Official Secrets Act. The minister of information can ban anything he sees as unfit, whether for obscenity or simply for reporting that reflects poorly on his country. Support for the PLO means that anything classified as Zionist is rejected.

A further instrument of repression is the Internal Security Act, a measure promulgated by the British colonial administration and kept on the statute books. This act gives the government unlimited powers to act in the cause of "state security" and is used extensively to suppress opposition. The Malayan Special Branch uses the ISA to tap telephones, survey ideological opponents and monitor alleged subversives. The Official Secrets Act has been found especially useful against foreign correspondents whose stories may show up Malaysia in a poor light.

SEE ALSO New International Information Order.

malice Malice, as legally defined in both the U.K. and U.S. for the purpose of libel or slander cases, involves an evil intent or motive arising from spite or ill will; personal hatred or ill will; or recklessness or a wilful and wanton disregard of the rights and interests of the person defamed. In the area of libel, it consists in the intentional publication, without justifiable cause, of any written or printed matter that is injurious to the character of another. Malice is further defined as acting in bad faith and with knowledge of the falsity of the statements involved. In the context of a libel suit brought by a public figure or a public official malice is defined as publishing the false information knowing it to be false or with a reckless disregard of whether it is true or false.

Man with the Golden Arm, The *The Man with the Golden Arm* was filmed by Otto Preminger in 1956. Adapted from Nelson Algren's 1949 novel of the tragic life and wretched death of Frankie Machine, the hotshot poker dealer and hopeless junkie, it was given a totally spurious happy ending and starred Frank Sinatra and Kim Novak. Given that the portrayal of any form of narcotics use was outlawed by the MOTION PICTURE PRODUCTION CODE, the film did not receive the seal of approval from the MOTION PICTURE ASSOCIATION OF AMERICA. Preminger, like an increasing number of directors, chose to ignore the MPAA and released his film anyway. The film was screened without problem except in Maryland, where state censors demanded the removal of a scene in which the card dealer was "tying off" his arm preparatory to receiving an injection of heroin from his own dealer.

Faced with this demand, United Artists, the film's distributor, appealed to the Baltimore City Court, which sustained the censor's decision. The Maryland Court of Appeals overturned the ban, however, stating that the film failed to satisfy the law's condition as regarded the advocacy of narcotics abuse. It was indeed illegal to "debase or corrupt morals or incite to crime," but *The Man with the Golden Arm* merely illustrated drug use. It did not advocate it. If anything, even with Hollywood's happy ending, the film could be seen as a tract against the horrors of heroin addiction.

SEE ALSO advocacy.

Manet, Edouard SEE *Olympia.*

Manwaring, Roger Manwaring was a chaplain of England's Charles I and as such an enthusiastic proponent of royal prerogative in the face of an increasing demand for parliamentary rights. In 1627, when the king was pressing Parliament for a compulsory loan, Manwaring preached two sermons before his monarch, both advocating the king's right to impose any loan or tax without the consent of Parliament and adding that such absolute powers—known as the Divine Right of Kings—extended over any rights the subject might attempt to claim. These sermons were published as *Religion and Allegiance.* The increasingly Puritan Parliament was displeased, and the radical Pym delivered a lengthy condemnation of the sermons. The Commons then persuaded the Lords to pronounce judgment on Manwaring. He was to be imprisoned at the House's pleasure, fined £1,000, make a written submission at the bars of both Houses, be suspended for three years from holding any ecclesiastical or secular post, and prohibited for life from preaching at Court. The king was called upon to have the book recalled and burned.

Charles, still attempting to placate Parliament, duly issued a proclamation confirming the Lords' decision. On June 23 Manwaring made an abject submission to both Houses. On his knees, with tears in his eyes, he admitted that his sermons had been "full of dangerous passages, inferences and scandalous aspersions in most parts." The king had the sermons burnt but since anyone who annoyed Parliament was likely to please the Court, Charles soon had the bulk of the sentence remitted, gave Manwaring a royal pardon and a succession of ecclesiastical preferments, culminating in the Bishopric of St. David's.

Marlowe, Christopher SEE book burning in England 1. Tudor period.

Married Love Marie Stopes (1880-1958) was among the most important of Britain's sex educators. Her campaign to disseminate knowledge on what for many women was still something of a forbidden and slightly embarrassing mystery, was spearheaded by her book *Married Love.* Qualified as a paleobotanist, Stopes abandoned her studies in fossils for those concerning sex after she was forced to consult volumes in the British Museum before realizing that her marriage to fellow academic Reginald Gates, already several months old, had yet to be consummated. After extricating herself from this marriage, which required the pressing of a nullity suit and the parading in public of the hapless Gates' impotence, Stopes wrote *Married Love,* described as a "strange amalgam of purple prose, suffragist philosophy and sage advice on lovemaking." It was this latter that made the book both a vital sex guide and a source of notoriety for its author.

In 1917 Stopes married again, more happily, to Humphrey Roe, a 40-year-old ex-World War I pilot. With his money Stopes, already in demand as a purveyor of marital advice, and the author of a second book, *Wise Parenthood,* founded in 1921 Britain's first birth control clinic. Contentious and flamboyant, Stopes became an international figure. She fought the Catholic Church's antipathy to contraception, befriended George Bernard Shaw, became an outspoken proponent of eugenics, and fought what she called the perversion of homosexuality with the same fervor as she advocated contraception. She died of cancer in 1958.

Wise Parenthood was made a test case on its publication in England but was acquitted by the court. *Married Love* had been available in England for nearly 30 years and had already sold over 700,000 copies when copies were seized in 1931 as obscene by the U.S. Customs, which was empowered to make such seizures under the Tariff Act (1930). The act provided for the Customs to submit such material to a federal court of adjudication on its alleged obscenity, and *Married Love* was assessed by Judge Woolsey, who was responsible in 1934 for the ULYSSES STANDARD. The judge rejected claims that Stopes' book was obscene, stating in his judgment:

> Dr. Stopes' book … emphasizes the woman's side of sex questions. It makes also some apparently justified criticisms of the inopportune exercise by the man in the marriage relation in … his conjugal or marital rights, and it pleads … for a better understanding by husbands of the physical and emotional side of the sex life of their wives. I do not find anything exceptionable anywhere in the book and I cannot imagine a normal mind to whom this book would seem to be obscene or immoral within the proper definition of these words or whose sex impulses would be stirred by reading it. Whether or not the book is scientific in some of its theses is unimportant. It is informative and instructive, and I think that any married folk who read it cannot fail to be benefited by its counsels of perfection and its frank discussion of the frequent difficulties which necessarily arise in the more intimate aspects of married life … The book before me has as its whole thesis the strengthening of the centripetal forces in marriage, and instead of being inhospitably received, it should, I think, be welcomed within our borders.

By 1939 the book had sold a further one million copies in America. It remained prohibited only in Ireland where, influenced by the church, all advocacy of contraception was banned.

SEE ALSO *Birth Control*; *Love without Fear*; *The Sexual Impulse*; United States 21. Tariff Act (1930).

Martin Marprelate The "Martin Marprelate Tracts" were a number of anonymous pamphlets and short books issued secretly in England between 1588 and 1589 to attack the Anglican bishops, who were seen as increasingly corrupt, and to defend the Presbyterian system of discipline. The authors, who were eventually identified as a Welshman named Penry and a clergyman named Udall, were finally arrested. Penry was executed and Udall died in prison. A third man, Job Throckmorton, denied any invovement and was acquitted. The tracts, which were written in a populist style, were stimulated by Archbishop Whitgift's campaign to impose uniformity on liturgical practice, to promote royal supremacy and the authority of the Thirty-Nine Articles, first published in 1563 to define the Anglican Church's position on various important areas of religion.

The tracts, cited as some of the best prose satire of the period, included "The Epistle," "The Epitome," "Minerall and Metaphysical Schoolpoints" and "Hay any worke for Cooper" (alluding to a contemporary street cry and the current bishop of Westminster, Thomas Cooper). A typical example, "A Dialogue wherein is plainly laide open the tyrannical dealing of Lord Bishops against God's Church, with certain points of doctrine, wherin they approve themselves (according to D. Bridges his judgement) to be truely Bishops of the Divell," featured arguments among a Puritan, a Papist, a "jack of both sides," and an Idol (i.e., church) minister and concentrated on the alleged venality of the episcopacy. The work was burned in 1589. The tracts excited wide controversy, drawing such major figures as Lyly, Nashe, Gabriel and Richard Hervey and others into the debate. It ended only when Richard Hooker (1554?-1600) published his defense of the established church, *Of the Laws of Ecclesiastical Politie* (1593-97), in which he demolished the Marprelate contentions in a reasoned philosophical and theological discussion.

Martin, Herbert Henry Martin (1882-1954) was chosen in 1925 from 132 candidates as the secretary of Britain's Lord's Day Observance Society. He based his career on the credo, "neglect of God's Day is nearly always the first step in a downward career. Everyday experience proves this." "Misery Martin," as he was christened in the press, almost singlehandedly revived the fortunes of the society, much battered by the decline of sabbatarianism during and after World War I. He persuaded the solicitor general, Sir Thomas Inskip, to become president of the society and obtained W.S. Morrison (a future speaker in the House of Commons) as counsel. His efforts multiplied the society's income 10 times. In the election of 1929 Martin secured the promises of 259 MPs that they would resist the passing of a Sunday Theatres Act. Some 550,000 postcards were sent to politicians in a massive mail-out, and a mile-long petition was delivered, holding some 1,457,683 signatures. Despite all this the Sunday Entertainments Act was passed in 1932, authorizing Sunday cinema performances in London and certain provincial areas. Martin's efforts continued undaunted, and he had sports, games, dances and carnivals, radio debates and art exhibitions curtailed on Sundays. When the Second World War broke out the society added to its usual list the BBC radio Forces Program, suggesting that those likely to die in battle should better spend their Sundays in prayer. Martin's greatest victory came in 1941 when a government bill to open theaters and music halls on Sunday was defeated in the House. His final act (in 1951) was to ensure that the Festival of Britain pleasure gardens remained locked to the public on Sundays. He retired in 1951 and died three years later. His place as secretary was taken by Harold Legerton.

Marx, Karl Despite the enormous censorship apparatus that has been erected in the name of preserving and propagating his philosophy, Karl Marx (1818-1883) claimed to have no time for the restraint of free expression. In his words:

> The censored press has a demoralizing effect … The government only hears its own voice, knows that it only hears its own voice, yet acts under the illusion that it hears the voice of the people, and demands from the people that they should accept this illusion too. So the people for their part sink partly into political superstition, partly into political disbelief or withdraw completely from civic life and become a rabble … Since the people must regard free writings as illegal, they become accustomed to regarding what is illegal as free, freedom as illegal, and what is legal as unfree. Thus the censorship kills civic spirit.

Marx's works have themselves been subject to massive and continuing censorship. It is impossible to itemize every country in which Marxist works are prohibited, nor do such countries remain consistent in their bans, but it may be generally assumed that those governments pursuing right-wing totalitarian or dictatorial policies are keen to ban the founder of communism.

Maryland

1. film censorship Under Maryland's state law of 1955, chapter 201, article 66A, section 6 (itself an elaboration of the creation of the state's film censorship board in 1916), it is provided that:

> (a) The Board shall examine or supervise the examination of all films or views to be exhibited or used in the State of Maryland and shall approve and license such films or views which are moral and proper and shall disapprove such as are obscene, or such as tend, in the judgment of the Board, to debase or corrupt morals or incite to crimes. All films exclusively portraying current events or pictorial news of the day, commonly called newsreels, may be exhibited without examination … (b) … a motion picture film or view shall be considered to be obscene if, when considered as a whole, its calculated purpose or dominating effect is substantially to arouse sexual desires, and if the probability of this effect is so great as to outweigh whatever other merits the film may possess. (c) … a motion picture film or view shall be considered to … debase or corrupt morals if it portrays acts of sexual immorality, lust or lewdness, or if it expressedly or implicdly presents such acts as desirable, acceptable or proper patterns of behavior. (d) … a motion picture film or view shall be considered … to incite crime if the theme or the manner of its presentation presents the commission of criminal acts or contempt for the law as constituting profitable, desirable, acceptable, respectable, or commonly accepted behavior, or if it advocates or teaches the use of, or the methods of use of, narcotics or habit-forming drugs.

SEE ALSO *The Man with the Golden Arm.*

2. sale of objectionable material to minors As provided in article 27, section 421 of the Maryland Code (amended 1959):

> (a) It shall be unlawful and an offense for any person operating any newsstand, book store, drug store, market or any other mercantile establishment to wilfully sell or distribute to any child below the age of eighteen years, or permit the perusal of by any such child, or have in his possession with intent to sell, distribute or otherwise offer for sale or distribution to any such child, any book, pamphlet, magazine or other printed paper principally composed of pictures and specifically including but not limited to comic books, devoted to the publication and exploitation of actual or fictional deeds of violent bloodshed, lust or immorality, or which, for a child below the age of eighteen years, are obscene, lewd, lascivious, filthy, indecent or disgusting and so presented as reasonably to tend to incide a child below the age of eighteen years to violence or depraved or immoral acts against the person. (b) It shall be unlawful … to exhibit upon any public street or highway or in any other place within view of children below the age of eighteen years passing upon any such street or highway any book, pamphlet, magazine or other printed paper prohibited and made unlawful by sub-section (a) …

In the case of *Police Commissioner* v. *Siegel Enterprises Inc.* (1960) this statute was ruled unconstitutional by the U.S. Supreme Court (confirming the prior decision of the Maryland Court of Appeals) on the grounds of its being too vague, especially in subsection (b), which was considered to infringe upon the rights of adults to view these books.

Massachusetts's obscenity statute As provided in the Massachusetts General Laws, chapter 272, section 28A: "Whoever imports, prints, publishes, sells or distributes a pamphlet, ballad, printed paper, pornographic record, or other thing which is obscene, indecent or impure, or an obscene, indecent or impure print, picture, figure, image or description, or buys, procures, receives or has in his possession any such … [article] … for the purpose of sale, exhibition, loan or circulation, shall be punished."

Masses, The *The Masses*, a monthly socialist magazine based in New York City, was one of many similar left-wing publications barred from the mails in 1917 by the U.S. postmaster general, using as justification the ESPIONAGE ACT OF 1917 AND THE SEDITION ACT OF 1918, using the former's anti-sedition amendment. When the publisher offered to censor such portions as the Post Office required, this compromise was rejected. In official eyes "the whole purport" of the magazine was unlawful since, by its political stance, epitomized in four anti-war cartoons, a poem and in pieces supporting draft-resisters Emma Goldman and Alexander Berkman, it encouraged the enemies of the United States and hampered the war effort. Postmaster A.R. Burleson then withdrew from *The Masses* the second-class mailing privileges that were vital to its financial survival. Only magazines in regular production were granted these, he ruled, and since one issue had been missed (the August issue that had been seized), *The Masses* had failed to fulfil this criterion. This decision was reversed on appeal, but the appeal was subsequently quashed by the Circuit Court, which declared "the Postmaster's decision must stand unless clearly wrong." *The Masses* was forced to fold. At the same time, in September 1917, seven members of the staff went on trial under the Espionage Act for "obstructing the war effort." Particular governmental attention was directed at a cartoon—"Having Their Fling" by Art Young—which depicted an editor, a capitalist, a politician and a clergyman dancing in a shower of gold against a backdrop of armaments, death and destruction. Two juries failed to reach a verdict; the third acquitted the five editors and two artists involved.

master of the revels   The office of "Magister Jocorum, Revelorum et Mascorum omnium et singulorum nostrum, vulgariter nuncupatorum Revelles et Maskes" was established in England by Henry VIII in 1545. Initially the role of the master of the revels was to run the Revels Office, which supervized theatrical performances before the Court. He was responsible for the companies who performed there, and for the themes and content of their plays. His own superior was the LORD CHAMBERLAIN. He was not a censor as such; the regulation of Tudor drama, which concentrated on protecting state and church against political and religious dissension, appeared in a variety of acts, the details of which differed as to the religious persuasion of the current monarch.

In 1574 the master's powers were extended beyond the Court: when the queen permitted the earl of Leicester's players to perform in London and tour the country, the master was placed in overall charge. In 1579 a patent was issued to the current master, Edmund Tilney, confirming his absolute powers over the stage, although no powers of censorship were specified. The master of the revels became a true censor after the controversy over the MARTIN MARPRELATE tracts of 1588-89. The Privy Council, worried by the undisguised partiality of the stage for the established church in its struggle with the Puritan City of London, whose opinions the council tended to support, demanded the institution of a proper censor. Attempting to placate both parties, it was suggested that appointees both of the church and the city should "advise" the master on the licensing of plays. The advisors soon dropped out of sight, but the master's power was confirmed.

The role of censor carried with it an increasing potential for financial gain. Tilney was paid £3 a month, plus £100 a year by the queen. A fee of five shillings was charged for considering a play, whether or not it was approved. The master levied extra funds through licensing playhouses, giving dispensations to act during otherwise forbidden periods such as Lent, and other perquisites. The position reached its zenith under Sir Henry Herbert, who bought the office for £150 in 1623, held it until the advent of Cromwell in 1649 and then resumed it from 1660 to his death in 1673.

Like other masters, Herbert was less interested in censorship than profit. He maximized every source of income, extending to their extreme the limits of the stage and boasted an income of £4,000 per annum. Herbert's open venality did much to undermine the master's authority. His successor, Charles Killigrew, compounded this by continuing to pursue his own career as a dramatist while acting as censor. The creation in 1662-63 by Charles II of two patent theaters, the Theatres Royal of Drury Lane and Covent Garden—which were excluded from the master's fief—weakened the Revels Office still further.

The Revels Office had been very much the creature of the Stuarts. With their demise in 1688, the power of the master of the revels, though still technically intact, became defunct. Squabbles between Herbert and the managers of the patent theaters had meant that the lord chamberlain had been taking more actual responsibility for controlling the drama since the Restoration. By the 1690s he was the effective censor. In 1711 Queen Anne called for "a reformation of the stage"; the STAGE LICENSING ACT (1737) carried it out.

McCarthy, Joseph   Joseph "Tailgunner" McCarthy (1908-1957), the junior senator from Wisconsin, remains the embodiment of the anticommunist witch-hunting paranoia that ran through America in the late 1940s and early 1950s. While he was by no means the only energizer of the trend, he came to typify its worst excesses and to embody an era and its style, summed up by the eponymous "McCarthyism."

McCarthy specialized in brandishing lists of alleged communist sympathisers in the State Department, a technique first exhibited on February 9, 1950, when he informed a Republican women's club in Wheeling, West Virginia, "I have here in my hand a list of 205 that were known … as being members of the Communist Party and are still making and shaping the policy of the State Department." He was a master demagogue who had refined the traditional techniques of the HOUSE UN-AMERICAN ACTIVITIES COMMITTEE (HUAC) to a new perfection. His reign as supreme witch-hunter, from 1951 to 1954, has been termed "the great fear," and under his tutelage American anticommunist paranoia reached an intensity never paralleled.

At his peak, McCarthy was seemingly indestructible. When Senator Millard Tydings investigated his charges against the State Department (the famous list by then reduced to 10 people), he condemned McCarthy's allegations as "groundless," compared his technique to that of Hitler's "big lie," savaged his methods and ended by condemning "a fraud and a hoax perpetrated on … the American people." It made no difference; Tydings soon lost his senatorial seat to a McCarthy supporter. McCarthy's permanent Senate Subcommittee on Investigations spread fear among its targets. Professor Owen Lattimore, a respected orientalist, was charged with losing China in the wake of the Maoist Revolution. President Truman was attacked for withholding access to the loyalty oath files; then, when they proved relatively innocent upon release, McCarthy alleged that the files were incomplete. Whatever challenges were made against him, McCarthy counterattacked with subpoenas and smears. When the press turned against him, he simply branded it all as communist.

In January 1953 McCarthy hired Roy Cohn, a young lawyer, to manage his committee. Together they targeted the State Department's broadcasting and foreign library facilities. Cohn and an unofficial consultant, G. David Schine, toured Europe to check all U.S. offices; all "subversive literature" was seized and burned. In late 1953 McCarthy turned on the U.S. Army. Attempts to discover a spy ring in the Signal Corps failed, but McCarthy's treatment of military witnesses of all ranks was so savage that Army Secretary Robert Stevens demanded that some ground rules must be established before the hearings might continue. McCarthy was furious; Richard Nixon, a committee member, duly worked out a compromise. However, attacking the Army was McCarthy's mistake. In March 1954 broadcaster Edward R. Murrow used his television show, "See It Now," for an attack on McCarthy in which the senator was allowed to condemn himself out of own mouth. Simultaneously Senator Ralph Flanders criticized him in the Senate. The Army finally started fighting back, talking of McCarthyite blackmail. The investigating committee itself decided to hold hearings on the imbroglio, and McCarthy was forced to step down as chairman for the duration. He dominated proceedings as a witness but exposed his own chicanery. The committee was split between pardoning McCarthy outright and condemning him. Each member produced an individual report. On December 2, 1954, he was censured on a vote of 67-22 by his fellow senators. Ironically the charges did not relate to his witch-hunting, but to the abusing of fellow senators and his refusal to explain a business transaction. McCarthy lost power, support and credibility. He drank increasingly heavily, and died in May 1957.

SEE ALSO Dies, Martin; House Special Committee on Un-American Activities; Thomas, J. Parnell.

McGehee v. Casey (1983) Ralph W. McGehee agreed to sign the CIA Secrecy and Publishing Agreements (see CIA) on joining the agency in 1952. Under these agreements he was prohibited from divulging any information that he gained while working for the CIA unless authorized in writing. Accordingly, McGehee submitted to the agency's censors on March 20, 1981, an article he had written after leaving the agency, dealing with the CIA's role in the Central American state of El Salvador. In it he alleged that the CIA had gone out of its way to create an illusory picture of El Salvador, whereby "the revolt of poor natives against a ruthless U.S.-backed oligarchy" was portrayed for world comsumption as "a Soviet, Cuban, Bulgarian, Vietnamese, PLO, Ethiopian, Nicaraguan, International Terrorism challenge to the United States." To back up his allegations, McGehee cited a number of CIA disinformation programs that had already been carried

out in Iran, Vietnam, Chile and Indonesia. The agency censors informed the author that portions were "secret" and they would be cutting it accordingly. McGehee accepted these cuts, and on April 11, 1981, the amended article was published in *The Nation.*

With the article in print, McGehee then abandoned his acquiescence and sued the CIA, claiming that the censorship system in general, and in particular the cutting of his allegations as secret, was unconstitutional. The federal district court reject his suit, as did the appeal court. Appeals Court Judge Wald stated that:

(1) CIA censorship of "secret" information contained in a former agent's writings and obtained by a former agent during the course of CIA employment, did not violate the First Amendment, inasmuch as the government has a substantial interest in assuring secrecy in the conduct of foreign intelligence operations and criteria for what constitutes "secret" information are neither overbroad nor excessively vague. (2) The CIA properly classified as "secret" the censored portions of the ... article.

Despite this affirmation of CIA regulations, Judge Wald was constrained to add a lengthy rider to her judgment, in which she reminded readers of the "recent revelations about past indiscretions in the name of national security" and while accepting that judges had no special expertise in balancing the public's right to know with the need for protecting national security, she suggested that some "governmental institution, if not the classification system itself" ought to lay down suitable guidelines for such a balance. "By not weighing the value to the public of knowing about particularly relevant episodes in the intelligence agencies' history, we may undermine the public's ability to assess the government's performance of its duty," she wrote.

SEE ALSO *Haig* v. *Philip Agee* (1981); *Snepp* v. *United States* (1980).

Meese Commission, The (1986) SEE Attorney General's Commission on Pornography (1986).

Memoirs of Hecate County Edmund Wilson (1895-1972), one of the foremost American critics of the 20th century, saw his primary task as the writing of "a history of man's ideas and imaginings in the setting of the conditions which have shaped them." Such works as *Axel's Castle* (1931) and *To the Finland Station* (1940) have assured him of literary immortality. As readers of Wilson's autobiographies (covering the Twenties, Thirties, Forties and Fifties) were to discover, Wilson combined what many might otherwise have assumed to be an ascetic devotion to literature with an extremely active love life, all carefully detailed in his memoirs. In 1946, long before these reminiscences began to appear, Wilson published a collection of stories under the title *Memoirs of Hecate County.* The book consists of six interconnected stories of the lives of a variety of well-to-do residents of a fictional suburb of New York. One story in particular, "The Princess with Golden Hair," which depicted sexual relations with the sort of candor that was still rare for its era, caused some agitation, both among Wilson's peers, who feared that their doyen would both demean himself and overexcite the conservatives by this display, and among those same conservatives, who professed to find *Memoirs ...* shocking.

The New York SOCIETY FOR THE SUPPRESSION OF VICE, which was then operating as the New York Society for the Improvement of Morals, brought a suit against Wilson's publisher, Doubleday. In *People* v. *Doubleday* (1947) the book was duly convicted of violating New York's Obscenity Statute, as embodied in section 1141 of the statc's penal code. Although 50,000 copies were already in circulation the publisher was fined $1,000. The New York court presented no written opinion, stating merely that the book was obscene and that its conviction did not violate the FIRST AMENDMENT. In 1948 Doubleday's appeal, *Doubleday & Co.* v. *New York*, reached the U.S. Supreme Court. The court refused to overturn the lower court's decision and similarly avoided a written opinion, simply declaring in a 4-4 per curiam decision that the book was obscene. The book remained banned in New York State, although cases in San Francisco and Los Angeles resulted in acquittal.

SEE ALSO New York 5. Obscenity Statute.

Memoirs of a Woman of Pleasure, The

1. history   *The Memoirs of a Woman of Pleasure*, written by JOHN CLELAND, was published in two volumes in Britain by "G. Fenton" (actually Fenton Griffiths and his brother Ralph Griffiths) in November 1748 and February 1749. In 1750, faced by a government ban on the original version, Cleland created the expurgated, single-volume *Memoirs of Fanny Hill*, by which title the book, possibly the most famous work of erotic literature ever written, has since been generally known. Many clandestine editions of the original edition followed, although many of these omitted a homosexual scene witnessed by the heroine. Only that edition produced by MAURICE GIRODIAS in 1950 has restored this two-paragraph scene in the original version. The single-volume edition was rarely reprinted, an exception being that published by "H. Smith" (i.e., WILLIAM DUGDALE) in 1841. In 1963 and 1965 unexpurgated paperback editions, edited respectively by historians Peter Quennell and J.H. Plumb, faced trials in New York and London. While the American edition was acquitted, rendering it freely available there, a combination of circumstances resulted in the banning of the British paperback. Not until 1970, with little fanfare, did such an edition reappear. On its appearance the book was briefly and erroneously accredited to a well-known writer of erotica, Sir Charles Hanbury Williams.

According to its real author, the book was originated in the early 1730s while Cleland was in India. The plot was given to him by Charles Carmichael, a friend who died, aged 20, in Bombay in 1732. Cleland claimed that his intent was to prove that one could "write so freely about a woman of the town without resorting to ... coarseness." Indeed, there are no obscenities in the book, although Cleland's use of synonyms for the body's parts and metaphors for its acts seems limitless. Cleland wrote the first draft in India, finishing it off during his imprisonment for debt in 1748-49. As a piece of erotic fiction *The Memoirs of a Woman of Pleasure* differs, just as Cleland intended from such hard-core predecessors as MILLOT's L'ESCHOLLE DES FILLES (1655). Rather than pornography, Cleland's work is reminiscent of 17th-century erotic verse.

Although the story of Fanny Hill is the classic tale of the young country girl ensnared by corruption, Cleland's heroine differs from her traditional predecessors, even from DEFOE's *Moll Flanders*, to whom she has been compared. The usual moral ending is absent: Fanny marries for love and takes with her a dowry of £800, earned at her trade. More importantly, unlike Moll, Fanny enjoys the sex, a fact noted by some feminist critics. As an erotic, rather than a pornographic heroine, Fanny has her own moral standards. She enjoys, indeed, craves, heterosexual encounters, but quite definitely eschews homosexuality (especially between men), sodomy, masturbation and any form of fetishism. She also exists in a realistic world, a reasonable picture of contemporary London, populated by flesh-and-blood human beings, rather than against the featureless backdrop of wholehearted pornography, peopled only by endlessly copulating cutouts.

2. trials   John Cleland's erotic novel has the dubious distinction of being the most prosecuted literary work in history. It was banned, as an obscene book, on its first appearance in England in 1749—as was the expurgated edition of 1750. In America, where it was published in 1821, it was the first book to be banned, by the Massachusetts courts. In 1963 two unexpurgated paperback editions of the novel were issued, one by Putnam in New York, the other by Mayflower in London. Inevitably they went to trial. To the delight of Cleland's supporters in America his novel was acquitted. At its trial in July 1963—*Larkin* v. *G.P. Putnam's Sons*—Justice Arthur Klein stated, "While the saga of Fanny Hill will undoubtedly never replace 'Little Red Riding-Hood' as a popular bedtime story, it is quite possible that were Fanny to be transposed from her mid-18th century surroundings to our present day society, she might conceivably encounter many things which would cause her to blush." Nonetheless the book remained in the obscene category, a decision that was confirmed by the Massachusetts Supreme Court. Not until the case reached the U.S. Supreme Court as *Memoirs* v. *Massachusetts* (1966) was the local censorship statute that justified this prosecution finally overturned.

In 1963 the Massachusetts Supreme Court had declared in the case of *Larkin* v. *G.P. Putnam's Sons* that an edition of John Cleland's *Memoirs of a Woman of Pleasure*, popularly known as *Fanny Hill*, was obscene, as defined by the state's own board of censors, and as such could neither be published nor distributed in the state. Taking into consideration the

ROTH STANDARD of testing for obscenity the Massachusetts Court felt that *Memoirs* was both pruriently appealing and patently offensive, which characteristics outweighed any redeeming social importance the book might have had. The publishers appealed and in 1966 *Memoirs* v. *Massachusetts* reached the U.S. Supreme Court, where the state judgment was overturned.

The justices were not unanimous, but the overall opinion was that the book was not "utterly" without redeeming social importance and thus failed to satisfy Roth. Justice Douglas was particularly scathing of the attempt to censor Cleland's book, declaring that "judges cannot gear the literary diet of an entire nation to whatever tepid stuff is incapable of triggering the most demented mind. The FIRST AMENDMENT demands more than a horrible example or two of the perpetrator of a crime of sexual violence, in whose pocket is found a pornographic book, before it allows the nation to be saddled with a regime of censorship." Although Justice Clark recoiled from a book he found quite disgusting, totally devoid of redeeming social worth and "nothing more than a series of minutely and vividly described sexual episodes" and "designed solely to appeal to prurient interests," the Massachusetts ruling was overturned.

The long-term effect of the case was to redefine the Roth Standard into what was termed the Memoirs Standard. For obscenity to be proved, the following test must be applied:

> Three elements must coalesce: it must be established that (a) the dominant theme of the material taken as a whole appeals to prurient interest in sex; (b) the material is patently offensive because it affronts contemporary community standards relating to the description or representation of sexual matters; and (c) the material is utterly without redeeming social value.

Each of these criteria is to be applied separately; one aspect cannot be weighed against or cancel out one or two of the others.

Emboldened by these verdicts, and encouraged by the acquittal of LADY CHATTERLEY'S LOVER in 1960, Mayflower Books issued their 3/6 (17p) paperback edition in November 1963. Three days before publication there appeared in the window of G. Gold & Son's Magic Shop of Tottenham Court Road, London, a sign: "JUST OUT: FANNY HILL. BANNED IN AMERICA." The police were alerted, a warrant was obtained from the Bow Street Magistrate and in the subsequent raid 171 copies were seized. On December 18 the Golds, who would later capitalize on the men's magazine boom of the 1970s, were charged under section 3 of the OBSCENE PUBLICATIONS ACT OF 1959, whereby the retailer, not the publisher, was eligible for trial. Mayflower had distributed 82,000 copies by December; they froze further distribution until the trial, despite good reviews from such as V.S. Pritchett ("elaborate literary language") and Brigid Brophy ("literary charm"). Mayflower also paid for the Golds' defense.

The trial was a repeat of that of *Lady Chatterley* at a lower level. The defense offered two arguments: In the first place the book was an invaluable literary and historical source; in the second it was in no way obscene, but a bawdy romp, filled with straightforward sex. The prosecution, as in *Lady Chatterley* led by Mervyn Griffiths-Jones, QC, refuted this, concentrating its attacks on a flagellation episode. A parade of expert witnesses supported the book but circumstances were unfavorable to an acquittal. A combination of factors, notably the public's preoccupation with morality in the wake of the Profumo affair (the involvement of a married Tory minister with "model" Christian Keeler, an affair that nearly brought down the government), the undeniable association of the Golds with the Soho smut market and the book's low cover price, all worked to the advantage of the prosecution. After two minutes reflection, the magistrate, Sir Robert Blundell, found *Fanny Hill* guilty, and ordered the forfeiture of the seized copies.

The verdict enraged liberal opinion. An all-party motion deploring the condemnation was adopted in Parliament; the literary world and the media expostulated. The Obscene Publications Act was altered, giving publishers the right to demand trial by jury, whether or not they were directly involved in the initial charges. Mayflower decided not to appeal, but issued a bowdlerized edition of the book. In 1970, at the height of anti-censorship clamor, the original Mayflower edition returned to the shops. Although officially a banned book, there was no outcry. In 1985 the Oxford University Press brought out a critically annotated edition, priced at 1.95, as part of their World's Classics series. In 1965, when a second-rate film of *Fanny Hill* was presented to the British censors, they rejected it outright, but in 1968 released it with an X certificate.

SEE ALSO *Miller* v. *California*; Miller Standard.

Memoirs Standard, The   SEE *Memoirs of a Woman of Pleasure*.

Merry Muses of Caledonia, The   *The Merry Muses of Caledonia* is "a Collection of Favourite Scots Songs, ancient and modern, selected for use of the Crochallan Fencibles." It appeared around 1800 as the private songbook of an Edinburgh club. The collection was amassed by Robert Burns (1759-96), who had them printed, and who, it is now generally accepted, actually wrote as well as compiled the book. How the manuscript was first distributed remains a mystery; one theory is that it was stolen from his house after his death. That he was a collector of such songs is well attested in his own correspondence. The original edition contained 85 poems and songs; the second edition (1827) and subsequent ones have a further 42. Most of them deal with sex, and the use of taboo words is plentiful. Until the liberation of such material by the OBSCENE PUBLICATIONS ACT (1959), the *Merry Muses ...* was never published for mass consumption. In 1959, following the act, an edition was produced for distribution to members of a modern Edinburgh club, the Auk Society. In 1965, the full, unexpurgated edition became available in paperback form.

messenger of the press   Under the LICENSING ACT (1662) British government agents, called messengers of the press, were made responsible for tracing any form of unauthorized or undesirable printing and reporting its existence, as a prelude to subsequent legal censorship, to a secretary of state. Although the act lapsed officially in 1679, the messengers continued to be used by secretaries of state who required a convenient means of checking on publishers and printers they suspected of sedition. As well as acting as official informers, the messengers could prevent the publication or circulation of a book by employing a variety of devices to persuade a publisher to withhold a given volume. The government could also issue destruction oders (more usually associated with the OBSCENE PUBLICATIONS ACT [1857]), empowering them to seize materials from a printer or even, as a last resort, break up the set type. The messengers, many of whom had themselves been printers, were hated, few more so than Robert Stephens who prosecuted, inter alia, the works of the EARL OF ROCHESTER.

Mexico   Freedom of information and expression are guaranteed under articles 6 and 7 of the Mexican Constitution, which respectively state that "the expression of ideas will not be the subject of any judicial or administrative inquisition ..." and that "the freedom to write and publish on any matter cannot be violated. No law or authority can establish prior censorship." These guarantees are only limited by the Printing Laws and certain statutes regarding the protection of privacy and morals, notably the Organic Law of Public Education (1951), which deals with decency in the press. Thus there are no actual censorship laws—other than in the regulation of the cinema—but the letter of the law is generally undermined by the spirit in which it is enforced.

The government controls every aspect of the media through its Ministry of the Interior. This ministry, working on a brief to ensure that "information meets the established norms," has wide-ranging powers. It has a monopoly on the production and distribution of newsprint; it lays out and implements state media policies; it oversees the media through the Comision Calificadora de Publicaciones y Revistas Ilustradas; it issues printing certificates; it issues permits for and monitors national and local television and radio; it has absolute control over the production and content of film.

Further, the media is heavily influenced by the monopolistic nature of its ownership. Of Mexico's 118 TV stations, more than 100 are owned by a single conglomerate. Such concentrated power means that, although the government promises to guarantee the right of information, the stations simply refuse to implement such freedom of access. The media is further controlled by the ebb and flow of commercial and political (government) advertising. Errant newspapers face a concentrated boycott, rendering them uneconomic, although a limited critical press is tolerated, if not encouraged. Quiescent papers, on the other hand, receive many favors from the authorities, including public funds and tax exemptions.

The control of newsprint has, since 1935, been organized by PIPSA (Productora e Importadora de Papel SA). This company was designed to maintain a regular source of newsprint for all Mexico's papers, but soon came to be manipulated as a means of passive censorship. The government news agency, Notimex, is a further means of controlling information. This especially affects the provincial press, whose stories on government activity are dictated by the Notimex line. The government's control over the granting of permits for purchasing new technology also affects profitability, as does its restricting of access to the country's Morelos satellite.

As in a number of other Central American states, Mexican journalists are susceptible to bribery. Their pay is minimal, trades union organization is weak and both politicians and businessmen are happy to supplement reporters' wages in return for favorable coverage. It has been estimated that 90 percent of Mexico's journalists accept payoffs. For those who resist these temptations the punishments, if they investigate or criticize too assiduously, can be severe. Between 1984 and 1986 152 journalists were attacked physically, 12 of them murdered—a record exceeded only in COLOMBIA. Forty-two have been killed since 1971.

Michigan—protection of minors   The Michigan Penal Code, section 343, provides that "Any person who shall import, print, publish, sell, possess with intent to sell ... any book, magazine, newspaper, print, picture, drawing, photography, publication or other thing ... or obsene, immoral, lewd or lascivious prints, figures or descriptions, tending to incite minors to violent or depraved or immoral acts, manifestly tending to the corruption of the morals of youth, or shall introduce into any family, school or place of education ... any such book ... shall be guilty of a misdemeanor." In the case of *Butler* v. *Michigan* (1957), the U.S. Supreme Court rejected the constitutionality of this statute. Butler had sold John Griffin's novel *The Devil Rides Outside* to an undercover police officer and had been charged under section 343. He was duly convicted but his appeal to the Supreme Court was successful. Surely, stated the court, "this is to burn the house to roast the pig ... We have before us legislation not reasonably restricted to evil with which it is said to deal. The incidence of this enactment is to reduce the adult population of Michigan to reading what is only fit for children."

Miller Standard, The   In the case of MILLER V. CALIFORNIA (1973), the U.S. Supreme Court, led by its Nixon-nominated conservative Chief Justice Warren E. Burger, redefined the current test for obscenity in America. What has become known as the Miller Standard is a further definition of those standards that emerged from ROTH V. UNITED STATES (1957) and *Memoirs* v. *Massachusetts* (1966). As in the ROTH STANDARD and the MEMOIRS STANDARD, obscene material remained excluded from constitutional protection. What altered was the test for obscenity.

After Miller, the standard demanded that: "The basic guidelines must be: (a) whether the average person, applying contemporary community standards, would find that work, taken as a whole, appeals to prurient interest; (b) whether the work depicts or describes, in a patently offensive way, sexual conduct specifically defined by the applicable state law; and (c) whether the work, taken as a whole, lacks serious literary, artistic, political or scientific value." The important changes under Miller were that section (b) rejected the old concept of national consensus on obscenity, replacing it by standards set by each community; and that section (c) replaced the idea of being "utterly without redeeming social value" by a more tightly defined phrase. The alteration in (b) delighted those states that had deplored the gradual erosion of their right to maintain local censorship boards during the 1960s, as well as conservative organizations such as the MORAL MAJORITY and the CITIZENS FOR DECENCY THROUGH LAW.

Miller v. *California* (1973)   Marvin Miller was born in Chicago in 1920. He dropped out of the University of Chicago in his freshman year and devoted himself to a series of jobs, all of which were intended to make more money than a traditional education could provide. After serving a prison sentence for falsifying records and embezzlement he was released from jail in 1961. Based in Los Angeles he developed a reputation as a pornographer, concentrating his efforts on publishing hard-core but allegedly literary works, such as MY SECRET LIFE, bought for $50,000 by the Grove Press but serialized by Miller over 10 consecutive issues of a $1.25 magazine.

In 1971 Miller distributed an advertising brochure to thousands of randomly chosen clients. Among the items touted therein was a $3.25 paperback, *I, a Homosexual*, and two $10 picture books—*The Name Is Bonnie* (with 24 pictures of a naked blonde female) and *Africa's Black Sexual Power*. There was also available a $15 *Illustrated History of Pornography*, made up of reproductions of 150 classic erotic paintings, and an 8mm movie, *Marital Intercourse*, that cost $50. To gain lists of potential clients Miller paid $100 per 1,000 names to a specialist firm in Los Angeles, then solicited nearly 300,000 individuals, all of whom had regularly requested "adult" material. Despite this safeguard, some of the brochures did reach "innocent" hands, and complaints were made to California police departments. Charged with obscenity, Miller was found guilty in the California courts.

When in 1973 *Miller* v. *California* reached the U.S. Supreme Court, conservative Justice Warren Burger, backed by fellow conservatives on the bench, chose to use it as an example of the way in which their rulings would in future act against the liberal consensus of the previous decade. Com-

munity standards, rather than national ones, would judge whether material was or was not obscene. Conservatives such as the CITIZENS FOR DECENT LITERATURE professed their delight and promised "a holy war against the merchants of obscenity."

SEE ALSO Miller Standard, The.

Miller, Henry   Miller (1891-1980) was born in New York and destined for bourgeois respectability, but chose instead to reject college and spend the next 20 years enjoying a wide variety of adventures in America and, from 1930, in Paris. His first novel, TROPIC OF CANCER, was published in 1934 by the OBELISK PRESS, whose list mixed avant-garde literature with pornography; the book dealt frankly with his "wanderjahre," sparing the reader few details of his sexual escapades. Further adventures, detailing his own voyage of discovery, included TROPIC OF CAPRICORN (1939) and *The Rosy Crucifixion* (composed of *Sexus* [1949], *Plexus* [1953] and *Nexus* [1960]). Miller's frankness met inevitable censorship and the literary qualities of his books went generally unrecognized. In 1944 Miller returned to America, settling in California. As the moral climate changed, so did Miller's reputation and his books were reassessed favorably, although feminists found him an antagonistic male chauvinist and even the most charitable found it hard to term his work as literature. Miller's writing has contributed greatly to the expansion of naturalistic self-expression.

The most recent attempt to censor Miller came in England in 1988, when Care Campaign, an evangelical pressure group with particular interest in publishing, asked the director of public prosecutions (DPP) to look at Miller's *Opus Pistorum* (also known as *Under the Roofs of Paris*), which was published without any problem in London by W.H. Allen in 1985. The DPP refused to bring a prosecution at this stage, although he has left open the possibility of future proceedings; Care Campaign have the option of bringing a private prosecution. In either case the publishers have no intention of withdrawing Miller's work, and would fight a case.

Millot, Michel   SEE *L'Escholle des Filles* ...

Milton, John   SEE book burning in England 6. The Restoration.

Mirabeau, Comte de   Honore-Gabriel Riquetti (1749-91), Comte de Mirabeau, was formerly as celebrated for his libertine writings as for his role in the French Revolution, in the early stages of which he was president of the Constituent Assembly. His most famous book, *Le Libertin de qualite* (1783), the story of a young gigolo, was written while he was in jail for the abduction of a married woman. After its first edition, it subsequently appeared as *Ma Conversion*, of which he wrote to his mistress, "the idea is mad, but the details are rather jolly ..." His other erotic novels included *Le Rideau leve, ou l'Education de Laure* (1786), based on the supposed incest between the heroine and her father, and, of more dubious attribution, *Hic et hec, ou l'Eleve des RR. PP. jesuites d'Avignon* (the first edition of which is dated seven years after Mirabeau's death), which concerns the adventures of a Jesuit student as a tutor. Mirabeau also attempted a non-fiction work on sexuality, the *Erotikon Biblion* (1783), which attempted to fulfill his aim of researching throughout literature from the Bible onward the topics of "onanism, tribadism, etc., etc., in fact on the most indelicate subjects ..." and rendering such researches acceptable "to the most straight-laced class of person." Mirabeau achieved the research, but not the respectability. The book is hardly erotic or pornographic, and contemporary charges of blasphemy leveled against it are hard to prove, but the authorities detested it. Only 14 copies of the first edition are supposed to have survived, and it appeared on the INDEX LIBRORUM PROHIBITORUM after its second edition, subtitled "Amatoria Bibliorum," appeared in 1792. The book was prosecuted and destroyed in France on several further occasions throughout the 19th century.

Miracle, The *The Miracle* was a film made by Roberto Rossellini, taken from a story by Federico Fellini and starring Anna Magnani as a simple peasant woman who is seduced and impregnated by a stranger whom she believes to be St. Joseph. The child of this union, she believes, is Christ. The film appeared in Italy in 1948, where it was castigated by Catholic Church authorities but still allowed a general release. The film was imported into America in 1949, passed through Customs unopposed and received a license from the New York censor. Just 40 minutes long, it was shown with two other films (irrelevant to the case) as a trilogy called *Ways of Love*. Its distributor was Joseph Burstyn, born in 1901, a Polish-Jewish immigrant who had started life in America as a diamond polisher in 1921 and moved into the film business via the Yiddish theater in New York. In partnership with Arthur Mayer, publicity director for Paramount Pictures, he began distributing a mix of cheap exploitation movies and European "art" films, the profits from the former compensating for the low grosses of the latter. *The Miracle* fell into the second category.

While the official censors passed the film without comment, the Catholic Church, backed by the LEGION OF DECENCY, moved against the film. Cardinal Spellman denounced "this vile and harmful picture" as "a despicable affront to every Christian." He called on "all right-thinking citizens" to boycott the picture. Catholics duly avoided the picture and picketed the theaters in which it appeared. There were even bomb threats, and the Fire Department attempted to shut the theater and subpoena its manager. In February 1951 the Board of Regents of New York State met to consider the film: Acknowledging the religious pressure they declared it sacriligious. *The Miracle* lost its license and Burstyn, backed by the era's leading anticensorship lawyer, Ephraim London, went to court. The New York Appeals Court, in a 5-2 majority, backed the Regents.

When the case of *Joseph Burstyn Inc.* v. *Wilson* reached the U.S. Supreme Court in April 1952 London fought on simple principles: Local censorship of films was unconstitutional under the FIRST AMENDMENT and the influence of the church in the case violated the concept of separation of church and state. The court rejected the state's ban, declaring in a landmark decision that "motion pictures are a significant medium for the communication of ideas." Overturning the decision that had stood since MUTUAL FILM CORPORATION V. OHIO INDUSTRIAL COMMISSION (1915), the court accepted for the first time that film was entitled to constitutional guarantees of freedom of speech and expression. The court was careful not to outlaw local censors completely, but stated that as far as this case was concerned "a state may not ban a film on the basis of a censor's conclusion that it is 'sacriligous'" and added that, "It is not the business of government ... to suppress real or imagined attacks upon a religious doctrine, whether they appear in publications, speeches or motion pictures."

Burstyn had undoubtedly won a major victory, but mainstream Hollywood productions had little interest in what happened to art films like *The Miracle*. Burstyn, who had fought virtually without support from the industry, barely survived the case in which he had invested much time and money. He died of a heart attack in 1953.

Mishkin v. *New York* **(1966)** Edward Mishkin was a pornographer operating in New York City. In 1966 he was sentenced to three years' imprisonment for violating New York's obscenity statute, section 1141 of the state Penal Code, by writing, printing and possessing and selling some 50 hard-core books. Mishkin's product included some typical heterosexual titles, but on the whole concentrated on fetishism, sadomasochism and "bondage and discipline." Titles included *The Whipping Chorus Girls*, *Return Visit to Fetterland* and *Stud Broad*. One of Mishkin's authors testified that Mishkin ordered up rough, tough sex scenes, with blunt descriptions, detailing "abnormal and irregular sex." There was little doubt that Mishkin's books were intended simply as a form of moneymaking; they had no apparent or even hidden "redeeming social value." His lawyers made no attempt to hide this fact, basing their defense not on the virtues of Mishkin's product, but on its vices. So vile was the material, they claimed, that far from exciting any prurient desires, its only effect would be to disgust the average reader, on whose opinions the current MEMOIRS STANDARD was based. The U.S. Supreme Court was unimpressed by this sophistry and rejected Mishkin's appeal; the normally liberal Justice Brennan delivered the court's opinion. Only Justice Black, who rejected all form of speech or press censorship as unequivocally unconstitutional, delivered a dissenting opinion.

SEE ALSO New York 5. Obscenity Statute.

Mocket, Richard   SEE book burning in England 2. James I (1603-25).

Molinos, Miguel   Molinos was a Spanish theologian (1628-97) who lived in Rome and acted as a confessor to members of the church. In 1675 he published *The Spiritual Manual* (*Guia Espiritual*), which was translated from Italian into Latin and was reprinted with his earlier treatise on Holy Communion under the title of *A Spiritual Manual, releasing the soul and leading it along the interior way to the acquiring the perfection of contemplation and the rich treasure of internal peace*. The object of the work was to show that the pious mind must possess inner calm to attain any spiritual progress. Molinos' espousal of this form of religious mysticism, in which the will was to be extinguished, the senses ignored and one's efforts concentrated on spiritual devotion, inspired the Quietist movement. The work was approved by the mass of Catholic theologians and Pope Innocent XI. Pressure from Molinos' Jesuit rivals persuaded the ROMAN INQUISITION to examine the book; the inquisitorial assessors passed it as acceptable. Nevertheless Molinos was challenged by a number of enemies who charged him, variously, with Judaism, Mohammedanism and assorted allied heresies. Finally these enemies managed to persuade the king of Naples of Molinos' heresies, and in 1685 his book was reexamined by Cardinal Estraeus. This time his heresy was proved and in 1687 he was forced to make a public denunciation of some 68 articles that the Inquisition now condemned. He died in prison in 1697. A number of successors maintained the Quietist faith, notably Madame Guyon (1648-1717) and Francois Fenelon (1651-1716), whose own *Maximes des Saints* was similarly condemned by the church.

Molyneux, William   SEE book burning in England 7. United Kingdom (1688-1775).

Monk, The   Matthew Gregory Lewis (1775-1818) published his novel *The Monk* in England in March 1796. This story of a monk who is corrupted by a demon in female flesh, commits murder and suffers the tortures of the Inquisition and the fires of Hell, was in the tradition of the Gothic novels that began in 1764 with Horace Walpole's *Castle of Otranto*. Unlike the mainstream Gothic writers, Lewis' work had a macabre sensuality, with heavily sadistic overtones, and appeared to be trying deliberately, as Coleridge put it, "to inflame the fleshly appetites." In August 1797 the *Monthly Review* called for the book to be withdrawn from general circulation. As in many contemporary cases, worries about obscenity ran second to those concerning blasphemy. The innocent, 15-year-old Antonia is permitted to read the Bible in a version especially expurgated by her mother. There is, observes Lewis, "no reading more improper" than the uncensored work; "the annals of a brothel would scarcely furnish a greater choice of indecent expressions." Such lines were directly contrary to the Blasphemy Act of 1698, and it was

demanded that Lewis should be prosecuted for blasphemous libel and obscene libel. A case was prepared at the court of King's Bench but Lewis backed down before proceedings began. He entirely rewrote his novel, and in February 1798 there appeared the bowdlerized version—*Ambrosio, or, The Monk*—devoid completely of objectionable material. The case, as Lewis hoped, was promptly dropped.

Monkey Trial, The   SEE *Scopes* v. *State* (1927).

Montagu, Richard   The Rev. Richard Montagu was one of the more vociferous of those clergymen who, in the early 17th century, had chosen to back the king and the established church against Parliament and puritanism. For his pains Montagu suffered a number of attacks, accusing him of popery and Arminianism. He responded to these with his book, *Appello Caesarem*, written in his own defense and with the direct encouragement of James I. By 1628, after some years of debating Montagu's position, Parliament called upon the new king, Charles I, to punish Montagu and to suppress and burn his books. Charles obliged, issuing on January 17, 1628, a proclamation that cited Montagu's work as "the first cause of these disputes that have since much troubled the quiet of the Church" and threatened that if anyone else attempted to write on similar topics, "we shall take such order with them and those books that they shall wish they had never thought upon these needless controversies." Despite this apparent condemnation, Montagu was still made bishop of Chichester, and continued rising in ecclesiastical preferments until the Civil War.

Moon Is Blue, The   *The Moon Is Blue*, based on F. Hugh Herbert's play, was filmed by Otto Preminger in 1953. Ostensibly a light romantic comedy, and generally accepted as one of the director's lesser efforts, it fell foul of censorship boards in Milwaukee, Jersey City, Ohio, Maryland and Kansas. Censors disliked what they saw as a sex theme running through the plot, an excess of "sexy words" and "too frank bedroom dialogue." The Kansas censor banned the film, stating that he had found it to be "obscene, indecent and immoral, or such as to tend to debase or corrupt morals." This case, *Holmby Productions* v. *Vaughan*, reached the U.S. Supreme Court in 1955. Here the justices reversed the board's decision, stating that the words "obscene, indecent and immoral, or such as to tend to debase or corrupt morals" were too vague to support a licensing and censorship statute and "so broad as to be unconstitutional." In making this ruling, the court cited the cases of LA RONDE, M and THE MIRACLE.

Moore, George   SEE *Literature at Nurse*.

Moral Majority   The Moral Majority is probably the best-known of several groups based in America's fundamentalist Protestant community. The movement claims a membership of some 72,000 ministers and four million lay persons, all dedicated to promoting conservative values. Founded in 1979 by the Reverend Jerry Falwell, the Moral Majority describes itself as a "political movement dedicated to convincing morally conservative Americans that it is their duty to register and vote for candidates who agree with their moral principles." Falwell, whose use of TV and radio broadcasting has enormously widened his constituency, claims that the Moral Majority emerged spontaneously among right-minded Americans in response to the permissive liberality of 1960s and 1970s; he sees the movement as at the forefront of campaigns against such issues as abortion, homosexuality, women's rights and pornography. The Moral Majority is aggressively anti-communist and pro-nuclear defense.

SEE ALSO Christian Crusade, The; Citizens for Decency Through Law; Citizens for Decent Literature; Clean Up TV Campaign (CUTV/US); Coalition for Better Television; Committee on Public Information; Crusade for Decency; Eagle Forum; Morality In Media; National Federation for Decency; National Organization for Decent Literature; Parents' Alliance to Protect Our Children; People for the American Way.

Morality in Media   Founded in 1962 and originally called Operation Yorkville, the organization claims some 50,000 members and campaigns against the availability of pornography to minors. It aims to "educate and alert parents and community leaders to the problem of, the scale of and the danger in the distribution of obscene material; to encourage communities to express themselves in a unified, organized way to legitimate media requesting responsibility and to law enforcement officials urging vigorous enforcement of obscenity laws; to work for media based on the principles of love, truth and taste." Morality in Media operates the National Obscenity Law Center, which acts as a clearinghouse of legal information on obscenity cases, offering material for prosecutors, lawyers and other interested parties. The organization publishes its *Morality in Media Newsletter* every month and the *Obscenity Law Bulletin* every two months.

SEE ALSO Christian Crusade, The; Citizens for Decency Through Law; Citizens for Decent Literature; Clean Up TV Campaign (CUTV/US); Coalition for Better Television; Committee on Public Information; Crusade for Decency; Eagle Forum; Moral Majority; National Federation for Decency; National Organization for Decent Literature; Parents' Alliance to Protect Our Children; People for the American Way.

Morocco   Freedom of opinion and of expression are guaranteed to Moroccans under the Constitution of 1972. Various provisions modify these freedoms, notably with reference to the king, whose person is sacred and whose actions and words cannot therefore be criticized and whose messages to parliament may not be subjected to debate. Attacks on the monarchical system and on the state religion—Islam—are also seen as attacks on the king himself.

The Moroccan press is governed by the Press Code of 1958. All publications must be licensed. Under article 70 any publication that "is of a nature to disturb public order" may be banned, as can any that offends religion, the monarchy or the government. There is no provision for prior censorship in the law on Public Freedoms (1958), but the government has used it to control the media, especially after the coup d'etat of 1972, although the practice was abolished during the election campaign of 1976. Reintroduced after a riot in Casablanca in June 1981, prior censorship was extended throughout the country when more riots exploded in January 1984.

Mortimer, John   SEE *Inside Linda Lovelace*; *Little Red Schoolbook*; *My Secret Life*; *OZ* trial.

Motion Picture Alliance for the Preservation of American Ideals (MPAPAI)   SEE House Committee on Un-American Activities.

Motion Picture Association of America   In September 1945 WILL H. HAYS suddenly resigned from his position as head of the MOTION PICTURE PRODUCERS AND DISTRIBUTORS ASSOCIATION (MPPDA). He was replaced by Eric Johnston, the president of the U.S. Chamber of Commerce, which had been among the foremost supporters of the anti-communist purges that were stealing headlines in the postwar period. Johnston's administration was dominated by the investigations of the movie industry carried out by the HOUSE COMMITTEE ON UN-AMERICAN ACTIVITIES. In an attempt to improve the overall image of the movies he renamed the old MPPDA as the Motion Picture Association of America (MPAA).

Despite the influence of McCarthyism (see Joseph McCarthy), the mood of the country was gradually turning against censorship, and the MPAA and the Production Code that sustained it were appearing increasingly out of step. Otto Preminger's THE MOON IS BLUE had already defeated JOSEPH BREEN in 1953; but when the director made THE MAN WITH THE GOLDEN ARM for United Artists in 1955, a film starring Frank Sinatra and based on Nelson Algren's novel, the MPAA had to deny it a seal of approval—since no mention of any drug might appear on the screen. To the surprise of association members, Preminger needed only to delete a 30-second scene of Sinatra cooking up heroin in a spoon to placate the LEGION OF DECENCY, which gave his film a B rating, the first time the Legion had not automatically condemned a film rejected by the MPAA. Many MPAA members were appalled, but United Artists knew that box office potential superseded their complaints. United Artists then quit the MPAA. Johnston responded to this move by announcing that in 1956, for the first time, there would be an examination of the Production Code. The result of this was to remove the absolute ban on the portrayal of drug use, prostitution, abortion and kidnapping; these could now be shown if treated carefully. Miscegenation was no longer banned, but racial slurs were emphatically outlawed. Conversely, the code's attitude toward law was strengthened: The prohibition now read "Law—divine, natural or human—shall not be ridiculed, nor shall sympathy be created for its violation." There was also a new ban on blasphemy, which included the ridiculing of clergymen.

The clash between the Legion and the MPAA was repeated when Elia Kazan put Tennessee Williams' play BABY DOLL onto film in 1956. This time the Legion found the film unpalatable, while the MPAA gave it the necessary seal. Cardinal Spellman condemned the film from the pulpit of St. Patrick's Cathedral in New York, although he had never seen it himself. *Baby Doll* played in only 4,000 out of a potential 20,000 theaters, although it did good business where it appeared.

The considerable influence on Hollywood of the MPAA, the Legion of Decency, and the Production Code was eroded by a variety of factors throughout the 1950s. These included the startling rise of television, which decimated movie theater audiences, the gradual relaxation of American mores, the growing importance and sophistication of European films, and the pronouncement by the U.S. Supreme Court of a number of landmark decisions as regarded obscenity, notably those of ROTH V. UNITED STATES, and SMITH V. CALIFORNIA and the acquittal of the Grove Press edition of D.H. Lawrence's novel, LADY CHATTERLEY'S LOVER, and the Italian film adapted from it in 1959. At the same time the Supreme Court began regularly to reject the earlier decision of MUTUAL FILM CORPORATION V. INDUSTRIAL COMMISSION OF OHIO (1915), accepting at last that films were indeed eligible for FIRST AMENDMENT protection, and thus declaring that a number of local and state censorship laws were in fact unconstitutional. Despite this, the court refused to outlaw local censorship altogether.

As the series of Supreme Court decisions—JACOBELLIS V. OHIO, *Grove Press* v. *Gerstein* (see *Tropic of Cancer*), *Attorney General* v. *Naked Lunch* (see *Naked Lunch*), *Memoirs of a Woman of Pleasure* v. *Attorney-General* (see *Memoirs of ...*), among others—continued to refine America's definition of obscenity throughout the 1960s, the MPAA was forced to reassess its position. In May 1966 Jack Valenti, former special assistant to President Lyndon Johnson, was chosen to replace Eric Johnston, who had died in 1963, as president of the association. Valenti's first concern was to modify the Production Code, which he managed initially by creating a category of film known as SMA—Suggested for Mature Audiences—a label first attached to the film version of Edward Albee's *Who's Afraid of Virginia Woolf?*. The criterion that made a film SMA was that its subject matter be "blatant." When MGM refused to cut nude scenes from Antonioni's *Blow-Up*, preferring to relase it without an MPAA seal, the association was forced to compromise even further. It was obvious that the code was finally dead, but somethng had to be designed to replace it.

New regulations were developed in a scheme to classify films by stating which age-groups might be allowed to see them. The basis for this scheme was in two Supreme Court decisions, one regarding the film *Viva Maria* and the other in the case of GINSBERG V. NEW YORK, the result of which was the institution of different tests for obscenity as regarded minors and adults. Valenti polled the industry and created the Code and Rating Administration, under which the new system of classification by age was established.

The classifications, still in force, are: G, suggested for general audiences, including children of all ages. PG-13, parental guidance suggested, as some material may not be suitable for pre-teenagers. R, restricted, no admission to those under 17 unless accompanied by a parent or adult guardian; X, persons under 17 not admitted.

The standards that determine these ratings, which refer not to a film's quality but only to its relevance to the child viewer, include upholding the dignity of human life, exercising restraint in portraying juvenile crime, not demeaning religion, prohibiting extremes of violence as well as obscene language, gestures or movements; and limiting sexual content and nudity. No X-rated film may receive an MPAA seal. An appeal board, the Code and Ratings Appeals Board, composed of representatives of all areas of the industry, is empowered to alter the ratings of films.

Motion Picture Producers and Distributors Association

The MPPDA was established in March 1922 after the industry had failed to exercise self-censorship under the NATIONAL ASSOCIATION OF THE MOTION PICTURE INDUSTRY (NAMPI). Under MPPDA president, former U.S. Postmaster General WILL H. HAYS, the industry progressed from being seen by some as the most immoral of the American media in 1922, to standing foursquare for American values on Hays's retirement 23 years later. Hays was the ideal figure to calm conservative fears; he was a small-town Presbyterian elder whose own morality was immutable and who promoted the industry as a whole by subjecting it to the cultural and moral limitations of mainstream values.

Hays saw no point in federal or even state censorship, but was determined to purge the industry of its excesses. Making it clear to his membership that they either regulate themselves or face federal regulation, he advocated the involvement of the general public in the regulation of the industry. He gathered representatives of more than 60 civic, fraternal, religious, professional and educational bodies in the Committee of Public Relations (CPR). The CPR had a simple job: It was to oppose any film of which its members disapproved, and to promote those it liked. The end product was to force Hollywood in the direction of righteousness. Although the CPR gave a powerful voice to many of the industry's most vociferous opponents, who made sure that they were included in its numbers, it failed to solve the problem. When Hays attempted in 1924 to rehabilitate the hapless Roscoe "Fatty" Arbuckle, whose career had been destroyed by a sex scandal in 1921, many committee members resigned; the move undermined much of the CPR's credibility, although Hays, under general attack, remained in office. Many of the deserters allied in the Federal Motion Picture Council, a body that campaigned without success for federal censorship. The CPR itself was abandoned.

In 1926 Hays persuaded the producers to accept a Studio Relations Department. This was headed by Col. Jason Joy, former head of the CPR, who was charged with cooperating with state and local censorship officials throughout America. He also viewed films prior to release, and producers began to accept that by taking his advice as to compromise and moderation, they had far less trouble when the films faced local censorship. In October 1927 the SDR published its 11 "Don'ts and Be Carefuls." These excluded the following topics from the films: pointed profanity; licentious or suggestive nudity; illegal drug trafficking; any inference of sex perversion; white slavery; miscegenation; sex hygiene and venereal disease; actual childbirth; children's sex organs; ridicule of the clergy; willful offense to any nation, race or creed. On top of these were 26 further topics, all seen as potentially vulgar or suggestive. These included the use of the flag; a variety of larcenous crimes; murder; sympathy for criminals; sedition; rape; prostitution; men and women in bed together; wedding night scenes; surgical operations; seduction; the institution of marriage as a whole; anything to do with law enforcement and its officers et cetera.

The list, despite its exhaustiveness, was not compulsory. The Hays Office, as the MPPDA was generally known, set out to give its censorship more teeth and began remedying the situation in 1929 by the development of the MOTION PICTURE PRODUCTION CODE, which was finally adopted in 1931. For the next 40 years the code ensured that, with a few noteworthy exceptions, the industry's product was geared strictly to uncontroversial family entertainment. The code had been originated to a great extent by a Catholic theologian, Daniel A. Lord; and now Catholics, spearheaded by the national Council of Catholic Women, developed their own highly influential pressure group, the LEGION OF DECENCY, to force the code's near-universal acceptance.

The Legion terrified the Hays Office, claiming that 10,000,000 coreligionists had signed a pledge promising to "rid the country of its greatest menace—the salacious motion picture." In June 1934 the Studio Relations Department was renamed the Production Code Administration (PCA). The church's efforts were further boosted by the papal encyclical "VIGILANTI CURA" ("With Vigilant Care") of 1936, a document that was largely inspired by the code's own originator, Martin Quigley Sr., and which attacked the "lamentable state" of the movie industry and urged the faithful to keep up their fight against sin and corruption on the screen. Hays, who embraced the Legion and the code enthusiastically, was given a private audience by the Pope in Rome.

Hays resigned from the MPPDA in Septmber 1945, although he remained as an adviser until 1950. He was replaced by the moderate president of the U.S. Chamber of Commerce, Eric Johnston, under whom the association changed its name to that of the MOTION PICTURE ASSOCIATION OF AMERICA.

Motion Picture Production Code

1. history   The Motion Picture Code was developed in 1929 and put into practice in 1931. It originated as an attempt by the HAYS Office to provide some form of philosophical backdrop to its lists of acceptable and non-acceptable filmmaking standards and to create a system that would respond to the new circumstances occasioned by sound. (A silent film might be cut and still hang together; a "talkie" could not.) What was required was a whole new method of creating films that would require no further censorship.

The task of evolving this philosophy was given to Martin Quigley, a prominent Catholic layman and for the past 14 years publisher of the industry's leading journal, *The Exhibitors' Herald*. As his editorials in the *Herald* made clear, Quigley supported the sort of film that would be called family entertainment. If there had to be adult material, then such films should be restricted to a few specific theaters. With the assistance of another leading Catholic, Daniel A. Lord of St. Louis University, Quigley set about imposing on the industry a system whereby "clean" pictures would be the producers' staple product. Basing their scheme on an elaboration of the MOTION PICTURE PRODUCERS AND DISTRIBUTORS ASSOCIATION's (MPPDA) "Don'ts and Be Carefuls," they created the Motion Picture Production Code.

The code fell into two parts: the first, Quigley's responsibility, was a list of what might or might not be shown; the second, Lord's part, was titled "Reasons Underlying Particular Applications." When the code was published in 1930, the second half was left out, but the entire document did appear in 1934. The influence of Quigley and Lord on the regulation of the nation's film business was carefully excluded from code publicity; the Hays Office preferred to stress the participation of "church leaders ... women's clubs, educators, psychologists, dramatists and other students of our moral, social and family problems."

The code cited three basic principles: "(1) No picture shall be produced which will lower the moral standards of those who see it. Hence the sympathy of the audience shall never be thrown to the side of crime, wrong-doing, evil or sin. (2) Correct standards of life, subject only to the requirements of drama and entertainment, shall be presented. (3) Law, natural or human, shall not be ridiculed, nor shall sympathy be created for its violation." Lord's "Particular Applications" covered crime: murder, methods of crime, drug trafficking and (since Prohibition was still in force) drinking; sex: adultery, illicit sex, scenes of passion, rape, white slavery, miscegenation, scenes of childbirth, sex hygiene information, children's genitals; vulgarity; obscenity; profanity; costume (or rather its lack), as in nudity, undressing, dancing costumes and indecent or undue exposure; location; national feelings; religion; and repellent subjects, which included actual executions, torture, brutality, the sale of women and surgical operations. Sin might be portrayed, but only if compensatory retribution were meted out.

The code was put into practice in January 1931, setting in motion a censorship of American (and thus to a great extent worldwide) viewing that lasted until the 1970s. Under its provisions every script had to be submitted to the Association of Motion Picture Producers, a body that was legally separate but practically a part of the MPPDA. The AMPP readers would then return the script to the Hays Office with their recommendations. The system worked, but Hays still found, as he had done before the code, that maverick producers could and would ignore his strictures. Only when the LEGION OF DECENCY began threatening its own boycott of the industry, throwing the alleged outrage of 10,000,000 Catholics onto the side of censorship, did the producers capitulate to the code, a system that, as Edward de Grazia and Roger K. Newman have noted in *Banned Films* (1982), "imposed upon film-making a set of rigid requirements and taboos which would have destroyed Shakespeare, Ibsen and Shaw and which the lesser talents of Hollywood could not overcome …" Under the director of the Production Code Administration, JOSEPH I. BREEN, the code, at least as far as its critics were concerned, effectively destroyed any genuine artistic progress in American film for 20 years.

Although the code remained a power in the industry until the late 1960s, at least some of the mounting pressure to modify it was appeased in 1954 when, after the brief interregnum of Steven Jackson, 60-year-old Geoffrey Shurlock, a British-born intellectual and relative moderate, was appointed as the director of the Production Code Administration. Shurlock appreciated just how American mores were changing, and chose to administer the code on the basis of those changes. Despite the complaints of such conservatives as the Legion of Decency, the code's rigidity was gradually reduced.

In 1956 this moderation was incorporated in the first revision of the code (see below) in 25 years. While its basic morality and philosophy remained unchanged, detailed provisions were altered. The absolute taboos on drug use and drug trafficking, abortion, prostitution and kidnapping were abandoned: henceforth they could appear if handled carefully. The topic of miscegenation was no longer forbidden, and racial slurs were more actively prohibited. As a sop to the church, a ban was placed on blasphemy, but, after THE MIRACLE decision, it was noted that while films might be banned for attacking or ridiculing ministers of religion, the provision might not extend to challenges to religious beliefs themselves. A further revision, inspired by Jack Valenti of the MOTION PICTURE ASSOCIATION OF AMERICA (MPAA), was published in 1966 (see 3. amended text of 1966). By the 1970s it was clear the most useful aspect of a code seal was to keep major films out of the courts. Shurlock was succeeded in 1969 by Eugene "Doc" Dougherty, who was followed in 1971 by Dr. Aaron Stern, a practicing psychiatrist.

SEE ALSO Hays, Will H.; Motion Picture Association of America.

2. amended text of 1956 Although the Motion Picture Production Code has only a token role to play in contemporary Hollywood filmmaking, it still exists. The current version was compiled under the authority of the British-born Geoffrey Shurlock (b. 1894) who was director of the Production Code Administration from 1954 to 1969. The revised code runs to 12 sections; an appendix lists "Reasons Supporting the Code," "Reasons Underlying the General Principles" and "Reasons Underlying the Particular Applications," which later goes through all 12 sections, explaining what its administrators see as the need for such censorship. As accepted by Hollywood the code runs as follows:

General Principles:
1. No picture shall be produced which will lower the moral standards of those who see it. Hence the sympathy of the audience shall never be thrown to the side of crime, wrongdoing, evil or sin.
2. Correct standards of life, subject only to the requirements of drama and entertainment, shall be presented.
3. Law—divine, natural or human—shall not be ridiculed, nor shall sympathy be created for its violation.

Particular Applications:
1. Crime. (1) Crime shall never be presented in such a way as to throw sympathy with the crime as against law and justice, or to inspire others with a desire for imitation. (2) Methods of crime shall not be explicitly presented or detailed in a manner calculated to glamorize crime or inspire imitation. (3) Action showing the taking of human life is to be held to the minimum … (4) Suicide, as a solution of problems occurring in the development of screen drama, is to be discouraged unless absolutely necessary for the development of the plot, and shall never be justified, or glorified, or used specifically to defeat the ends of justice. (5) Excessive flaunting of weapons by criminals shall not be permitted. (6) There shall be no scenes of law-enforcement officers dying at the hands of criminals, unless such scenes are absolutely necessary to the plot. (7) Pictures dealing with criminal activities in which minors participate or to which minors are related shall not be approved … (8) Murder (a) The technique of murder must not be presented in a way that will inspire imitation; (b) Brutal killings are not to be presented in detail; (c) Revenge in modern times shall never be justified; (d) Mercy killing shall never be made to seem right … (9) Drug addiction or the illicit trade in addiction-producing drugs shall not be shown if the portrayal: (a) tends in any manner to encourage, stimulate or justify the use of such drugs; or (b) stresses … their temporarily attractive effects; or (c) suggests that the drug habit may be quickly or easily broken; or (d) show details of drug procurement or the taking of drugs … or (e) emphasizes the profits of the drug traffic; or (f) involves children … (10) Stories on the kidnapping or illegal abduction of children are acceptable … only (a) when the subject is handled with restraint and discretion and avoids details … (b) the child is returned unharmed.
2. Brutality: Excessive and inhuman acts of cruelty and

brutality shall not be presented. This includes all detailed and protracted presentation of physical violence, torture and abuse.

3. Sex: The sanctity of the institution of marriage and the home shall be upheld. No film shall infer that casual or promiscuous sex relationships are the accepted or common thing. (1) Adultery and illicit sex, sometimes necessary plot material, shall not be explicitly treated, nor shall they be justified nor made to seem right and permissible. (2) Scenes of Passion: (a) These should not be introduced except where they are definitely essential to the plot; (b) lustful and open-mouthed kissing, lustful embraces, suggestive posture and gestures are not to be shown; (c) ... passion should be treated in such a manner as not to stimulate the baser emotions. (3) Seduction or rape: (a) these should never be more than suggested ... they should never be shown explicitly; (b) they are never acceptable subject matter for comedy; (c) they should never be made to seem right and permissible. (4) The subject of abortion shall be discouraged, shall never be more than suggested, and when referred to shall be condemned ... The word "abortion" shall not be used. (5) The methods and techniques of prostitution and white slavery shall never be presented in detail, nor shall the subjects be presented unless shown in contrast to right standards of behavior ... (6) Sex perversion ... is forbidden [amended 1961 to permit "sex aberration" if treated with "care, discretion and restraint"]. (7) Sex hygiene and venereal diseases are not acceptable matter for theatrical motion pictures. (8) Children's sex organs are never to be exposed ...

4. Vulgarity: Vulgar expressions and double meanings having the same effect are forbidden. This shall include but not be limited to such words and expressions as chippie, fairy, goose, nuts, pansy, SOB, son-of-a. The treatment of low, disgusting, unpleasant though not necessarily evil subjects should be guided always by the dictates of good taste and a proper regard for the sensibilities of the audience.

5. Obscenity: (1) Dances suggesting or representing sexual actions or emphasizing indecent movements are to be regarded as obscene. (2) Obscenity in word, gesture, reference, song, joke, or by suggestion, even if it is likely to be understood by only part of the audience, is forbidden.

6. Blasphemy and Profanity: (1) Blasphemy is forbidden. Reference to the Deity, God, Lord, Jesus, Christ shall not be irreverent. (2) Profanity is forbidden. The [use of] the words "hell" and "damn" ... shall be governed by the discretion and prudent advice of the Code Administration.

7. Costumes: (1) Complete nudity, in fact or silhouette, is never permitted ... (2) Indecent or undue exposure is forbidden (this does not extend to documentaries of "actual scenes photographed in a foreign land of the natives ...").

8. Religion: (1) No film or episode shall throw ridicule on any religious faith. (2) Ministers of religion, or persons posing as such, shall not be portrayed as comic characters or as villains so as to cause disrespect on religion ...

9. Special Subjects: The following subjects must be treated with discretion and restraint and within the careful limits of good taste: (1) Bedroom scenes. (2) Hangings and electrocution. (3) Liquor and drinking. (4) Surgical operations and childbirth. (5) Third-degree methods.

10. National Feelings: (1) The use of the flag shall be consistently respectful. (2) The history, institutions, prominent people and citizenry of all nations shall be represented fairly. (3) No picture shall be produced that tends to incide bigotry or hatred among people of differing races, religions or national origins. The use of such offensive words as Chink, Dago, Frog, Greaser, Hunkie, Kike, Nigger, Spic, Wop, Yid should be avoided.

11. Titles: The following titles should not be used: (1) Titles which are salacious, indecent, profane or vulgar. (2) Titles which violate any other clause of this code.

12. Cruelty to Animals: outlawed.

SEE ALSO British Board of Film Censors 2. mandatory cuts (pre-1949).

3. amended text of 1966 In 1966 the Motion Picture Production Code was subjected to its second major revision since its inception in 1930. This revision was essentially the creation of Jack Valenti, a former adviser of President Johnson, who in 1966 was appointed head of the MOTION PICTURE ASSOCIATION OF AMERICA (MPAA). The intention and the function of the revised code were summed up in the "Declaration of Principles of the Code of Self-Regulation of the Motion Picture Association." This comprised a declaration of principles, a list of standards for production and a list of Production Code regulations. Compared with the all-encompassing provisions of the codes of 1930 and 1956, this was a liberal document. By the same token, the new code was also a sensible response to the fact that many Hollywood directors simply did not bother with a code seal if it stood in the way of their creative freedom.

The new code carefully mixed artistic freedom with traditional restraint:

> The revised code is designed to keep in close harmony with the mores, the culture, the moral sense and the expectations of our society ... Its objectives ... are: (1) to encourage artistic expression by expanding creative freedom; and (2) to assure that the freedom which encourages the artist remains responsible and sensitive to the standards of the larger society. Censorship is an odious enterprise. We oppose censorship and classification-by-law ... because they are alien to the American tradition of freedom. Much of this nation's strength and purpose is drawn from the premise that the humblest of citizens has the freedom of his own choice ... Censorship destroys this freedom of choice.

The next paragraphs affirm the ultimate role of parents as "arbiters of family conduct" and set the family at the heart of American society. To satisfy parental wishes, the MPAA is determined to maintain some degree of self-regulation since: "We believe self-restraint, self-regulation, to be in the tradition of the American purpose. It is the American society meeting its responsibility to the general welfare. The results of self-discipline are always imperfect because that is the nature of all things mortal. But this code and its administration, will make clear that freedom of expression does not mean toleration of license." While the authors admit that some films will ignore their code, parents can be assured that "the Seal of the Motion Picture Association on a film means that this picture has met the test of self-regulation."

The "Standards for Production" read as follows:

(1) The basic dignity and value of human life shall be respected and upheld. Restraint shall be exercized in portraying the taking of life. (2) Evil, sin, crime and wrong-doing shall not be justified. (3) Special restraint shall be exercized in portraying criminal or anti-social activities in which minors participate or are involved. (4) Detailed and protracted acts of brutality, cruelty, physical violence, torture or abuse, shall not be presented. (5) Indecent or undue exposure of the human body shall not be presented. (6) Illicit sex relationships shall not be justified. Intimate sex scenes violating common standards of decency shall not be portrayed. (7) Restraint and care shall be exercized in presentations dealing with sex aberrations. (8) Obscene speech, gestures or movements shall not be presented. Undue profanity shall not be permitted. (8) Words or symbols contemptuous of racial, religious or national groups, shall not be used to incite bigotry or hatred. (10) Excessive cruelty to animals shall not be portrayed, and animals shall be treated humanely.

Although the revised code aimed to adapt itself to the Sixties and beyond, its rules did not stray that far from the 1956 revision. It is briefer, more to the point, but essentially the same strictures obtain. Nonetheless, there is no doubt that Hollywood's production values have broadened, although to what extent this is in response to the code and what to the imperatives of the market place, remains debatable.

Mouth and Oral Sex, The   The *Mouth and Oral Sex* by Paul Ableman was published in America (as *The Sensuous Mouth*) in 1970, as a sex manual specializing in varieties of oral sex. Its author had graduated through MAURICE GIRODIAS' stable of literary-cum-porno authors and had not only won prizes for his writings but also had them banned.

British rights to *The Mouth* were purchased by the Running Man Press, owned by Christopher Kypreos, which dealt mainly in sexual and radical themes. It was decided to market *The Mouth* as a magazine, and four advertising brochures were mailed out to 100,000 potential customers. Kypreos received 2,000 subscriptions for the three guinea (£3.15) book, plus 17 complaints against his titillating advertising. The complaints proved sufficient for Kypreos to be charged with possessing an obscene article for publication for gain and sending an obscene article through the mails. He appeared at the Old Bailey in March 1971. Medical and literary experts testified for the book. The jury, after six and a half hours, found Kypreos not guilty of publishing an obscene article. The brochures were found indecent under the 1953 Postal Act. For these the publisher was fined £250 plus £100 costs; his legal costs totaled a further £6,500. In 1972 Sphere Books brought out a successful mass-market edition of the book.

Muggleton, Lodowicke   With his cousin John Reeve (1608-58), Muggleton (1609-98), an English tailor, believed himself to be one of the "two witnesses" to the prophets, as cited in Revelations 2:3-6, and who therefore had the power to sentence men either to eternal damnation or eternal blessedness. Muggleton denied the doctrine of the Trinity and claimed that matter was eternal and reason had been created by the Devil. Muggleton and Reeve founded their sect, the Muggletonians, around 1651. He was especially incensed by the Quakers and wrote a pamphlet titled "A Looking Glass for George Fox, the Quaker, and other Quakers, wherein they may See Themselves to be Right Devils" sometime in the 1650s. This work came to the notice of the authorities in 1676 and after a trial at the Old Bailey, Muggleton was condemned to stand for three days in the pillory at three of the most public places in the City of London, and to have his books burnt in three lots over his head. He was then jailed until such time as he could pay a fine of £500.

SEE ALSO Puritan Censorship: The Commonwealth.

Musset, Alfred de   SEE *Gamiani, ou une nuit d'exces.*

Mutual Film Corporation v. Industrial Commission of Ohio (1915)   This U.S. Supreme Court decision was taken as a result of the state of Ohio's establishment of the first state-level film censorship board in 1913. When the Mutual Film Corporation challenged the constitutionality of this board, the court delivered a ruling that effectively set the style of film censorship for the next four decades. Faced with the concept of regulating freedom as found in the first real mass medium, the court chose caution. The court compared films as "mediums of thought" to the circus, the theater and similar exhibitions, and concluded that: "It cannot be put out of view that the exhibition of moving pictures is a business, pure and simple, originated and conducted for profit, like other spectacles, not to be regarded ... as part of the press of the country or as organs of public opinion. They are mere representations of events, of ideas and sentiments published and known, vivid, useful and entertaining no doubt, but ... capable of evil, having power for it, the greater because of their attractiveness and manner of exhibition." Thus films were exempt from the FIRST AMENDMENT and the Ohio state censor was accepted as not only constitutional, but also necessary. The case of *Mutual Film Corporation v. Kansas* (1915) was decided at the same hearing. As in the argument over the Ohio censorship, the court upheld its constitutionality, citing the same grounds for its decision and adding that "Both statutes are valid exercises of the police power of the States and are not amenable to the objections urged against them—that is, [they] do not interfere with interstate commerce nor abridge the liberty of opinion; nor are they delegations of legislative power to administrative officers." Not until the case of *Joseph Burstyn v. Wilson* (1952), centered on the attempt to ban the film THE MIRACLE, did the court begin to alter its attitude toward the role of film.

***Mutual Film Corporation* v. *Kansas* (1915)** SEE *Mutual Film Corporation* v. *Industrial Commission of Ohio* (1915).

My Life and Loves Frank Harris (aka James Thomas, 1856-1931) was a major if ephemeral figure in the journalistic and literary world of London from the 1880s until his death. He edited the *Evening News* (1882-86), the *Fortnightly Review* (1886-94) and the *Saturday Review* (1894-98). In this last periodical he published Shaw, Wells and Max Beerbohm. Harris was an arrogant, extroverted acerbic figure who both impressed and infuriated. He promoted himself as the greatest Shakespearcan scholar of his age with his *The Man Shakespeare and His Tragic Life Story* (1909), although more academic figures disagreed. His shocking reputation was enhanced by the publication between 1922 and 1927 of *My Life and Loves*, a braggart collection of memoirs in which Harris mixed lurid sexual reminiscences with a catalog of name-dropping self-adulation.

My Life and Loves was compiled in Harris's relatively impoverished later years. The first volume was written in America and printed in Germany; the next three were written and printed in France, where he had been living since the end of World War I. The erotic chapters, a nonstop and inevitably repetitive list of conquests, were paginated separately from the more general experiences, but the total work shocked and alienated many former friends and admirers. Shaw, whose biography Harris wrote in 1931, burned his own copy rather than let his servants see it, although his own criticism was that, for all its vaunted self-revelation, it said nothing about its author. Harris' memoirs became almost instantly a staple of the prohibited book lists of Europe and America. The English Customs immediately outlawed any attempts at import. In 1926 the French attempted to confiscate Harris' own stock of the second volume and were stopped from prosecuting him for corruption of public morals by the pressure of his literary peers. In America the seizure and subsequent prosecution of 1,000 copies of the second volume made for one of the last successes of the SOCIETY FOR THE SUPPRESSION OF VICE. To compound his problems, the book was pirated extensively and Harris' hopes for substantial profits were destroyed.

My Life and Loves took Harris to 1900, when he was aged 45, and thus draws upon the years of his greatest success. His subsequent career saw a gradual decline in which his egocentricity overwhelmed his achievements. Among Harris' final acts was the selling of the rights to his memoirs to JACK KAHANE's THE OBELISK PRESS. In 1958 MAURICE GIRODIAS, Kahane's son, issued a pastiche called *The Fifth Volume*, which he claimed was in part derived from Harris' unpublished papers, but was actually written in its entirety by the Scottish poet ALEXANDER TROCCHI. *The Fifth Volume* naturally began life on the same banned lists as its progenitor, but when the complete memoirs were issued openly in the 1960s, the spurious addendum was included without com-ment and accepted, as far as any of Harris' "revelations" can be accepted, as the real thing.

My Secret Life (1890?)

1. history An 11-volume, 4,200-octavo-page autobiographical novel detailing an anonymous Victorian man's sexual career spanning some 40 years. The work was written by an aging roue and published privately at his request by a publisher who specialized in pornography. The title page attributes the book to "Amsterdam" but some experts believe it was published by AUGUST BRANCART, a prolific publisher of pornography in Brussels. This anonymity has survived until today, although the most feasible suggestion, albeit unproven, is that of Mr. Gershon Legman, that the ostensibly monogamous Victorian bibliographer of erotica, HENRY SPENSER ASHBEE, was responsible. Other critics have suggested that Ashbee might have written the introduction and, characteristically, the substantial index, but probably not the text itself.

Only six copies are estimated to have been printed, and even the British Library did not obtain its statutory copy until bequeathed one in 1964, but the authenticated existence of the book in a number of libraries, including those of Aleister Crowley, Harold Lloyd and Joseph von Sternberg, implies that the printer ran off a number of extras. The original appeared over several years and the full edition was not reprinted for 70 years. A French version of parts of volumes one and two—*Ma Vie Secrete*—appeared in 1923; in 1930 this selection reappeared in three volumes with illustrations. The SOCIETY FOR THE SUPPRESSION OF VICE banned a proposed English edition in New York in the early 1930s, but one volume—volume five—survived to appear as *Marital Frolics* in 1934. In 1967 the U.S. sexologists Drs. Phyllis & Eberhard Kronhausen produced a heavily edited selection published as *Walter: My Secret Life*. Only the Grove Press edition (1966) provides the full, unexpurgated 11 volumes. It was the original attempt to retail this edition in the U.K. that led to the book's trial in 1969.

It has been generally accepted that this stupendous catalog of copulation—with at least 1,200 women, the majority of them servants or prostitutes—is actually true and, with its picture of an otherwise unmentioned and unmentionable side of Victorian life, provides a view of the era at which such conventional chroniclers as Dickens could barely even hint. Whether, as Steven Marcus has suggested in *The Other Victorians* (1966), the author is a textbook exemplar of Freudian infantilism and emblematic of the entire Victorian age as regards its attitude to sex, or, in the Kronhausens' interpretation, *Walter* was a pioneer sexologist of awesome dedication, is open to the reader's interpretation. Possibly, to quote Marcus, *My Secret Life* "is the most important document of its kind about Victorian England"; certainly, it remains unique, a sociological document that, for all its repetitive and detailed couplings, offers a genuinely revelatory insight into actual life—a far cry from the simple cliches of THE LUSTFUL TURK and similar examples of unalloyed fantasy produced by the Victorian pornography industry.

2. trial A contemporary edition of *My Secret Life* was published in the United States in 1966 by the Grove Press. The 11 volumes were available for $20.00. In 1967 Arthur Dobson, a bookseller and publisher of Bradford, secured the rights to distribute the Grove Press edition in England. He managed to sell some 250 copies, at the then high price of £11.15.0 (£11.75) each. In February 1965 Bradford police had raided Dobson's shop, seizing a number of works, including an undistinguished contemporary "dirty book" entitled *Bawdy Setup*. Dobson was imprisoned for two years and fined £500, although *Bawdy Setup* itself was adjudged innocent of obscenity and returned. In July 1966 he was freed from jail on appeal. In August 1967 a further raid removed another set of books, once again including *Bawdy Setup*. The Bradford police, by then aware of his trade in *My Secret Life*, informed Dobson that this too was worth a prosecution and that a third raid would be forthcoming. When Grove Press appreciated the situation they withdrew from the distribution agreement with Dobson. Dobson responded by producing a one-volume paperback edition of the first two volumes of *My Secret Life*, but before this could be distributed, he was charged under the OBSCENE PUBLICATIONS ACT (1959) with selling a number of obscene books.

At Dobson's trial defense council John Mortimer managed to have *My Secret Life* considered separately from the modern books, and a parade of experts, including such top-ranking historians as J.H. Plumb and E.P. Thompson, attempted to prove that *Walter* was a vital guide to Victorian England. However, their intellectual arguments, which managed to avoid the tortuous paths confronting their peers at the OZ and LADY CHATTERLEY'S LOVER trials, did not impress the Yorkshire jury. Dobson was found guilty, imprisoned for two years (later reduced) and fined £1,000. His legal expenses ran

to £17,500. The main legal relevance of the trial was that the defense of "historical importance" could not be used in cases dealing with simple pornography; the upshot was that the practical position of *My Secret Life* was and remains unresolved. Ostensibly obscene, it remains generally available in England only as an imported Grove Press title.

Myron Gore Vidal's novel, *Myron*, a sequel to the best-selling *Myra Breckinridge* (1968), appeared in 1974, shortly following the U.S. Supreme Court's establishment in the case of MILLER V. CALIFORNIA of the MILLER STANDARD whereby it was left up to each community to decide what ranked as pornography. As the novelist put it in his foreword to the book, "although no link has yet been found between the consumption of pornography and anti-social behavior, any community may assume that such a connection exists if it wants to—in other words an outraged community may burn a witch even though, properly speaking, witches do not exist."

In response to this move Vidal, a lifelong campaigner for freedom of speech, no matter how offensive that speech may be nor which interested party may be offended, offered his own solution. In a jeu d'esprit that delighted his readers, he simply eliminated the potentially "dirty" words in *Myron* and offered what he saw as suitable substitutes:

> Since books are nothing but words a book is pornographic if it contains "bad" or "dirty" words. Eliminate those "bad" or "dirty" words and you have made the work "clean." In this novel I have replaced the missing bad words with some very good words indeed: the names of the justices who concurred in the Court's majority decision. Burger, Rehnquist, Powell, Whizzer White and Blackmun, fill, as it were, the breach; their names replaced the "bad" or "dirty" words. I have also appropriated the names of Father Morton Hill, S.J., and Mr. (CHARLES) EDWARD KEATING, two well-known warriors in the battle against smut.

N

Naked Amazon *Naked Amazon* was a pseudo-documentary travelogue made in 1957 by Zygmunt Sulistrowski who led a team of five fellow explorers into the Matto Grosso area of Brazil's Amazon River. Here they encoutered, among a variety of flora and fauna, the Camayura Indians, a tribe who do not wear clothes. Although the film was recognized throughout most of America for its anthropological qualities, the censorship board of Maryland demanded that all shots showing the Camayura below the waist were to be excised from the print before allowing the film its license. The chairman of the board was sure not only that many people would find such material shocking but also that it would tend to excite sexual desires in "irresponsible numbers of people." Any artistic or scientific merit that might be claimed for the film was deemed irrelevant. The distributors, the Times Film Corporation, took the censors to court. Both the Baltimore city court and the Maryland Court of Appeals, who heard the board's case in *Maryland State Board of Motion Pictures Censors* v. *Times Film Corporation* (1957), rejected the chairman's contention. The superior court pointed out that to censor the film on the basis of its effect on "irresponsible people" was the equivalent of assuming that one had to judge literature on the basis of its effect not on the average person but only on "the young and immature, the ignorant and those who are sensually inclined." The court also pointed out that, in any case, the version of the film submitted for its viewing had no below-the-waist close-ups. The case of *Naked Amazon* was similar to that of *Latuko*, another anthropological study, which had been produced in 1950 by the American Museum of Natural History and which portrayed the lifestyle and customs of the Latuko tribe in the Sudan. This film perturbed the censors in New Jersey, but when the distributors appealed against the state's ban, the judge rejected the censorship, saying flatly that "only a narrow or unhealthy mind could find any depravity in the film."

Naked Lunch, The *The Naked Lunch* was written by William Burroughs (1914-   ) and, after the initial appearance of certain sections in the magazines *Chicago Review* and *Big Table* in 1958 and 1959, was first published in full by the OLYMPIA PRESS in Paris in 1959. Its first American publication, by the Grove Press, came in 1962 and it appeared in England, published by JOHN CALDER, in 1964. While the latter edition caused some controversy, the novel found its greatest opposition in America where, before it was finally exonerated of all indecency in 1966, it was prosecuted or otherwise censored, either in magazine or book form, by academic institutions, the U.S. Post Office, the U.S. Customs and state and local government.

The first appearance in any form of Burroughs' novel came in the Fall 1958 issue of the *Chicago Review*, a "little magazine" produced by students at the University of Chicago and edited by Irving Rosenthal. The first piece in the magazine, chapter two of *The Naked Lunch*, was cited by *Chicago Daily News* columnist Jack Mabley as "one of the foulest collections of printed filth I've seen publicly circulated"; he likened such material to lavatorial graffiti. Mabley later apologized for this outburst, in which he attacked the "Beats" as "young, intellectual (and in need of) a bath," but the university authorities had noted his attack. Despite divisions in the faculty, the next (winter) issue of the *Review*, which was to have featured material by Burroughs, Jack Kerouac and Gregory Corso, was suppressed. Rosenthal, who had resigned over this extralegal censorship, took his copy to Paul Carroll, a former *Chicago Review* poetry editor, now running *Big Table* magazine. Carroll published the entire suppressed issue as *Big Table No. 1*, appearing in late 1959.

The banning of the *Review* added interest to *Big Table*, and among those requesting a review copy was August Derleth, a regional fiction and pulp horror writer and also the literary editor of the *Capitol Times* of Madison, Wisconsin. He loathed the material and volunteered himself to the postmaster of Chicago, whose department was already considering prosecuting *Big Table* for contravening the COMSTOCK ACT, as a witness in any possible case against the magazine. While Derleth made no formal complaint, his interest was seen to tip the scales against *Big Table*. The magazine was tried in June 1959. The prosecution claimed that all the material was worthless as literature; The Kerouac was filth-laden gibberish, the Burroughs utterly obscene and the Corso pacifist, anti-police and anti-Establishment. The language throughout failed to conform to community standards. Despite representations by such luminaries as Jacques Barzun, Lionel Trilling, Norman Mailer and LeRoi Jones, Judge William A. Duvall declared that *Big Table* was "obscene," "filthy" and its writing "not meritorious." A succession of appeals failed until Federal District Judge Julius Hoffman (to earn notoriety in 1970 in the Chicago Eight trial) overturned all previous verdicts and freed *Big Table* for distribution.

Once the Olympia Press, which had originally rejected *The Naked Lunch* in 1957, had brought out an edition in France, the Grove Press, which often followed Olympia's lead, determined to issue the whole book in America. Several copies of the typescript were dispatched, but only one arrived. Ten months after the disappearance it became obvious that they had been seized under provisions of the Tariff Act (1930), which provided for the seizure of allegedly obscene materials that were being imported into the U.S. Despite the acquittal of the *Big Table* excerpts in June 1960, the Customs continued to outlaw *The Naked Lunch* until ordered not to do so in January 1963 by the attorney general, whose office informed the commissioner of customs that it would be neither "appropriate nor desirable" to continue classifying the book as contraband.

The Grove Press edition appeared in November 1962 with maximum publicity. Almost immediately police acting under Massachusetts censorship laws seized copies on sale in a Boston bookshop owned by Theodore Mavrikos, a well-known seller of pornography. While Mavrikos was charged for selling the book, it was first necessary for the state to prove a charge of obscenity against the book *in rem*, as itself. The case against *The Naked Lunch* was heard in Boston in January 1965. Defense witnesses included leading writers, academics and psychiatrists, but they failed to sway Judge Eugene Hudson, who on January 13th found the book to be "obscene, indecent and impure … and taken as a whole … predominantly prurient, hardcore pornography and utterly without redeeming social importance." He rejected utterly the defense claim that the book was of social and scientific value, condemning it as trash by a "mentally sick" author. The basis of his decision was the case of JACOBELLIS V. OHIO, in which Justice Stewart had said of hard-core pornography: "I know it when I see it." Once the book was found guilty, the secondary charge against Mavrikos was dropped. The Massachusetts Supreme Court heard the appeal against conviction on July 7, 1966. In a majority decision they reversed the ban, declaring that the novel was "not utterly without redeeming social value" and thus not obscene. They added that it must not be advertised in Massachusetts under threat of reinstituting proceedings. For the first time *The Naked Lunch* was free of restraints. It was the last literary work to be thus prosecuted in America.

Namibia Namibia, as Southwest Africa a German protectorate until 1915 and under various degrees of South African rule since 1920, has existed in the shadow of South Africa since its creation in 1971. The United Nations has officially barred South African interference since 1971, and still-unresolved negotiations for the country's full independence have been under way since 1975. A mutually acceptable plan was agreed upon in 1988 and elections were scheduled for November 1989, intended to elect the post-independence government. But this process suffered when SWAPO guerillas, preferring to preempt the proposed orderly transfer of power, invaded and fought (for them) disastrous pitched battles with the South African army. However, whatever the future independent government may intend, it still remains subject to South African influence, including the imposition of censorship. Despite statements to the contrary, there remains a substantial South African military presence in Namibia, fighting the People's Liberation Army of Namibia (PLAN), the military wing of the South West Africa People's

Organization (SWAPO). It is to this end that much news control is aimed.

All the statutes, laws and regulations (q.q.v.) that make censorship work in South Africa are extended to Namibia. Under the Defense Act (1983), which outlaws the spreading of "alarm and despondency," no reports of PLAN successes are ever published, and any stories on the fighting, itself never officially announced, must be thoroughly vetted. What information does emerge is always heavily biased in favor of South Africa. Such material that does evade the Defense Act is further controlled by the Protection of Information Act, which prohibits the mentioning of a wide selection of official secrets, many of them of a military nature. Some journalists are flown into the area, but their credentials are checked and they are chosen carefully. Reporters who have refused to toe the line have lost their accreditation and, if persistent in their efforts, have been threatened and even attacked by South African paramilitaries. Reporters are further hampered by the Prisons Act, which bans the reporting of any stories on anything the authorities classify as terrorism, which includes anyone arrested by the security forces.

Nasty Tales *Nasty Tales* was founded in 1972 as England's first homegrown underground press comic magazine, aimed at a hippie readership and drawing on both American and English material. It was produced by the editorial staff of IT (see *IT*'s trial) and distributed through the major underground wholesalers. Its first number, which included U.S. underground cartoonist Robert Crumb's *The Grand Opening of the International Fuck-In and Orgy Riot*, was seized by the police. Its three editors, Mick Farren, his ex-wife Joy Farren and cartoonist Edward Barker, were charged under the 1959 OBSCENE PUBLICATIONS ACT and tried in January 1973. The jury returned verdicts of Not Guilty for all concerned.

The comic lasted barely another year, among the last, insubstantial flourishings of the "underground" banner.

National Association of the Motion Picture Industry The first attempt to institute federally controlled censorship in the United States came in 1915 when Congressman Dudley M. Hughes of Georgia proposed legislation under which a Federal Motion Picture Commission, a subdivision of the Bureau of Education in the Department of the Interior, would have been established. Hughes' own inspiration came from William Sheafe Chase, a Brooklyn clergyman who had testified to the House Education Committee, of which Hughes was chairman, that since at least a million children attended the films every day, any film that harmed a single one of them should be condemned as immoral and duly suppressed. Hughes' proposals were debated at length, but eventually defeated. A number of similar plans, appearing between 1915 and 1921, were also ousted by Congress. At the same time America's religious organizations began trying to regulate films, seeking, as yet without success, to ban all improper scenes.

The film business, desperate to avoid any form of centralized censorship, responded in July 1916 by forming the National Association of the Motion Picture Industry (NAMPI). NAMPI declared a twofold self-censorship program: One aspect was to gain for films the same protected status that print media were afforded under the FIRST AMENDMENT. However, this made no progress; the decision in MUTUAL FILM CORPORATION V. INDUSTRIAL COMMISSION OF OHIO (1915) ruled against such protection. The second aim was to back the 1920 review of the penal code in which films, like other communications media, were henceforth banned from transport by common carrier in interstate commerce if "lewd, obscene, lascivious, filthy, or of indecent character." The legislative result of this program was of secondary importance to the image it projected: Despite the 1915 decision, films were not linked in law and thus in the public eye with print, which was also subject to restraints as regarded interstate commerce.

In February 1921 NAMPI produced its own censorship standards, known as the Thirteen Points or Thirteen Standards. These were spurred on by a series of articles on the state of movie morals by Benjamin Hampton, who warned that "unless producers and exhibitors cleaned their own house and cleaned it thoroughly there might not be much house left." The "Points" listed a variety of taboo themes: "exploiting interest in sex in an improper or suggestive manner"; white slavery; illicit love that "tends to make virtue odious and vice attractive"; nakedness; "prolonged passionate love"; crime, gambling, drunkenness and "other unnatural practices dangerous to social morality"; instructing the "morally feeble" in crime; ridiculing or deprecating public or police officials or the military, and scenes that "tend to weaken the authority of the law"; offending any religion or religious figures; "vulgar" scenes, "improper gestures" and "salacious" titles. Any member of NAMPI who violated the code would be ejected from the association.

This effort was sabotaged by a number of factors. A leading member of the International Reform Bureau, a non-industry pressure group, lauded the Thirteen Points as no more than an industry-backed version of federal censorship. In 1921, against NAMPI's pleas for more time, the New York legislature passed a bill establishing a state censorship board, and 36 more states followed suit by the end of the year. The increasing domination of the business by Jewish immigrants fanned the nation's endemic anti-Semitism. Influential clergymen talked of "Patriotic Gentile Americans" whose censorship measures would "rescue the motion pictures from the hands of the Devil and 500 un-Christian Jews." The final straw was the 1921 sex and murder scandal involving then top-rated comedian Roscoe "Fatty" Arbuckle, who allegedly raped and murdered actress Virginia Rappe. The harm that this long-drawn-out, unsavory case did to the movies was underlined by a plethora of scandals, only marginally less lurid, that followed in short order. In December 1921, the industry decided to abandon self-regulation and turn to an external authority to regulate the business both on and off the screen. U.S. Postmaster General WILL H. HAYS was hired for $100,000 per year to run the newly formed MOTION PICTURE PRODUCERS AND DISTRIBUTORS ASSOCIATION. The MPPDA was organized in March, 1922. Its impotent predecessor, NAMPI, was dissolved that same month.

National Board of Review of Motion Pictures   On December 23, 1908, New York City Mayor George McLellan shut down all 600 of the city's movie theaters, claiming to be concerned by safety hazards but in fact driven by the current fear that the movies were subverting the impoverished masses who watched them in ever-increasing numbers. He also threatened to revoke the licenses of all exhibitors who showed films "which tend to degrade or injure the morals of the community." The exhibitors managed to obtain an injunction allowing them to reopen on December 26th, but on the following day city aldermen banned all under-16s from attending films unless accompanied by an adult. This hit at 25 percent of the regular audience, and theater owners were forced to hire adults to act as surrogate parents.

Faced by increased pressure from the politicians, the exhibitors decided to opt for self-regulation, rather than see the establishment of state censors as in Illinois. The New York State Association of Motion Picture Exhibitors asked the People's Institute (an organization dedicated to workers' education) to create a citizen's committee for this purpose. In June 1909 the National Board for the Censorship of Motion Pictures was established, drawn from the People's Institute, the City Vigilance League, the Children's Aid Society and similar groups. Films were initially examined by a five-man board but by 1914 this had expanded to 100 members. By 1915 there were 250 national affiliates, and they reviewed virtually all American movie product. The board claimed to offer "selection not censorship," and in 1915 it changed its name from the National Board for the Censorship of Motion Pictures to the National Board of Review of Motion Pictures. The board was self-financing, charging producers a fee for its examinations.

No producer was compelled to submit a film, but the board sent out a weekly bulletin to 450 "collaborators" in more than 300 cities, explaining what it had passed, passed with changes or condemned. These judgments were based on eight standards:

1. The Board prohibits obscenity in all forms.
2. The Board prohibits vulgarity when it offends, or when it verges towards indecency, unless an adequate moral purpose is served.
3. The Board prohibits the representation of crime in such a detailed way as may teach the methods of committing crime except as a warning to the whole public.
4. The Board prohibits morbid scenes of crime, where the only value … is in its morbidity or criminal appeal …

5. The Board prohibits the unnecessary elaboration or prolongation of scenes of suffering, brutality, vulgarity, violence or crime.

6. The Board prohibits blasphemy ...

7. The Board prohibits anything obviously or wantonly libelous ... anything calculated to cause injury to persons or interests from an obviously malicious or libelous motive, and films dealing with questions of fact which relate to criminal cases pending in the courts ...

8. In addition to the above specifications, the Board feels in general that it is right in forbidding scenes ... which ... have a deteriorating tendency on the basic moralities or necessary social standards.

Before the growth of state censorship boards reduced its affiliates, the board virtually fulfilled the role of a U.S. national censor, governing the viewing of its New York constituency, which counted for 5 percent of the nation's audiences, as well as the rest of the country. Many local boards only bothered to view films that the NBRMP had not passed, but as moviegoing increased, a number of major cities preferred to establish their own criteria.

National Catholic Office for Motion Pictures   The NCOMP was founded in 1966 as the newly retitled successor to the original organization designed to exert Catholic censorship of American films, the LEGION OF DECENCY. Like the legion, the office rates films as to their suitability both for adults and for children, and it uses the legion's classification system: Class A-I, morally unobjectionable for general patronages; Class A-II, morally unobjectionable for adults; and Class A-IV, morally unobjectionable for adults, with reservations; Class B, morally objectionable in part for all; Class C, condemned, "positively bad." The office continues to judge film on the basis of "basic Judaeo-Christian standards," the Ten Commandments and the belief that "there can be no compromise with evil, wherever it is." Like the legion, the office depends essentially on the threat of a potential boycott by America's 50 million Catholics of an expensive Hollywood project, although the faithful are far less easily persuaded today than they were in the legion's heyday.

The office is responsible to the Episcopal Committee for Motion Pictures, Radio and Television (composed of five bishops); the actual reviewing and allotment of ratings is performed by the International Federation of Catholic Alumnae (the original reviewing group for the legion), the office's New York Board of Consultors, and the board of consultors to the educational division of the office's National Center for Film Study in Chicago. Members of the alumnae, on whom the bulk of the work falls, must have had training in Catholic ethics and philosophy and undergo a six-month training period, during which they attend weekly screenings and lectures by senior reviewers. The training emphasizes, in the words of an administrator, "traditional standards of morality upon which the sanctification of the individual, the sacredness of the home and ethical foundations of civilization

necessarily depend ..." The New York Board of Consultors is drawn from a cross section of men, women, laity and clergy, involving educators and film critics as well as various professionals. The film center is mainly dedicated to film education workers in high schools and colleges.

National Coalition Against Censorship   The National Coalition Against Censorship is a loose federation of some 40 organizations dedicated to challenging the forces of censorship and to preserving the rights of freedom of thought, inquiry and expression in America. Among its member groups are the American Library Association, the National Association of College Bookstores, the Association of American Publishers, the American Society of Journalists and Authors, the Authors League of America and the American Association of University Professors. The coalition describes its credo as holding "that freedom of expression is the indispensable condition of a healthy democracy and that censorship constitutes an unacceptable dictatorship over our minds, and a dangerous opening to religious, political, artistic, and intellectual repression." The coalition helps all its participatory organizations to educate their own members about the dangers of censorship and the best ways in which it can be challenged. The coalition operates a legal information center, the National Information Clearing-house on Book-banning Litigation in Public Schools, which provides information to lawyers, the media and other interested parties. It circulates lists of banned books, sends their authors on speaking tours, backs lawsuits against censorship and makes anticensorship films for such TV stations as will broadcast them. The coalition files amicus curiae briefs in censorship cases and maintains an extensive library on FIRST AMENDMENT topics.

SEE ALSO Committee to Defend the First Amendment; First Amendment Congress; Freedom to Read Foundation; Reporters Committee for Freedom of the Press; Scholars and Citizens for Freedom of Information.

National Committee for Sexual Civil Liberties   The National Committee for Sexual Civil Liberties was founded in 1970 as a pressure group concentrating on challenging American laws on sexual conduct. It describes itself as being composed of "lawyers and scholars in government, sociology, religion, anthropology and history with experience in civil liberties." The NCSL works toward the dismantling of the entire structure of criminality and discrimination surrounding private sexual conduct between consenting adults. This includes the repeal of all laws convering adultery, fornication and sodomy to the extent that they punish such conduct. They also wish to see all offenses governing an individual's sexual orientation repealed. The organization further seeks the repeal of laws aimed at controlling the distribution, importation or sale of supposedly pornographic material to adults.

National Federation for Decency   The National Federation for Decency was founded in 1977 and is based in Tupelo, Mississippi. Its declared aims are to promote "the biblical ethic of decency in American society with a primary emphasis on television." It urges disgruntled viewers to write letters both to sponsors and to TV networks, protesting shows that they see as promoting violence, immorality, profanity and vulgarity and to encourage the airing of programs that are "clean, wholesome and family oriented." NFD monitors compile statistics on the use of liquor and profanity and the frequency of sex on TV shows.

SEE ALSO Christian Crusade; Citizens for Decency Through Law; Citizens for Decent Literature; Clean Up TV Campaign (CUTV-US); Coalition for Better Television; Committee on Public Information; Crusade for Decency; Foundation to Improve Television; Moral Majority; Morality In Media; National Organization for Decent Literature; People for the American Way.

National Organization for Decent Literature   The National Organization for Decent Literature was formed in America in 1938 by the Catholic hierarchy. Designed as a parallel organization to the film-related LEGION OF DECENCY, its intention was "to devise a plan for organizing a systematic campaign in all dioceses of the United States against the publication and sale of lewd magazines and brochure literature." The highly organized NODL has continued to impress its opinions on the arts in the U.S. through the large Catholic constituency there.

Its main methods of operation are: (1) the arousing of public opinion against material that its officers find offensive; (2) urging more rigorous enforcement of national and state laws controlling obscene literature; (3) promoting new and stricter legal controls over the media; (4) preparing a monthly list of disapproved publications; (5) visiting newsstands and stores to persuade the owners in person of the inadvisability of stocking certain material.

Literature is objectionable to the NODL if it falls into one of these categories: (a) it glorifies crime and the criminal; (b) its contents are largely concerned with sex; (c) its illustrations and pictures may be defined as "indecent"; (d) it carries articles on "illicit love"; (e) all journals and periodicals that carry "disreputable" advertising. Within a year of its founding magazine publishers began asking for interviews, hoping to make such modifications in their publications that would save them from the economically injurious threat of the NODL blacklist.

Over the years a large variety of authors fell afoul of the NODL. They include Mickey Spillane, James M. Cain, ERSKINE CALDWELL, James T. Farrell, PIERRE LOUYS, Somerset Maugham, John O'Hara, EMILE ZOLA, Nelson Algren, ERNEST HEMINGWAY, D.H. LAWRENCE, C.S Forester, James Michener, Irwin Shaw and many others.

The NODL is no longer in existence. Its nearest contemporary equivalent is CITIZENS FOR DECENCY THROUGH LAW, although many similar organizations are flourishing.

SEE ALSO Christian Crusade; Citizens for Decent Literature; Clean Up TV Campaign (CUTV-U.S.); Coalition for Better Television; Committee on Public Information; Crusade for Decency; Foundation to Improve Television; Moral Majority; Morality in Media; National Federation for Decency; People for the American Way.

National Viewers and Listeners Association   The National Viewers and Listeners Association (NVALA) was inaugurated in London in March 1965. It replaced the CLEAN UP TV CAMPAIGN (CUTV), which had been growing increasingly unpopular, even among its keen supporters, who had begun to condemn its constant "negativism." The new pressure group was designed to act not only to protest the objectionable but also to represent and lobby for the views of Britain's silent majority. Its president was John Barnett, chief constable of Lincolnshire; chairman was Major James Dance, MP (Con.). Vice Chairman Dr. E.E. Claxton was an active member of Moral Rearmament who believed, as stated in an article, "Venereal Disease and Young People," that VD was better cured by a "spiritual stimulus" than by antibiotics and felt that medical staff ought not to "waste their time" caring for the self-indulgent. Mrs. MARY WHITEHOUSE, cofounder of CUTV, was hon. general secretary and gave up her teaching career to devote herself to NVALA full-time. The London branch was headed by the Dowager Lady Birdwood.

NVALA initially promoted a six-point program: (1) to promote the moral and religious welfare of the community by seeking to maintain Christian standards in broadcasting; (2) to press for the creation of a Viewers' and Listeners' Council to influence all aspects of broadcasting; (3) to ascertain and collate public opinion on radio and television items and bring positive and constructive criticisms, complaints and suggestions to the notice of the proposed council and to Parliament; (4) to set up local branches of NVALA; (5) to ensure that the BBC maintains the high standards set out in its original charter; (6) to ensure that the ITA (now IBA) is encouraged to keep up the standards laid down in the Television Act (1964) and to honor its obligations to the nation.

Liberal opinion at first dismissed NVALA as a collection of cranks and BBC Director General Hugh Greene refused ever to meet them, but throughout 1965 it began to impinge on its target and claimed several successes in removing objectionable programs from the screen. Briefly opposed to NVALA was the Television and Radio Committee (TRACK), a group initiated by Avril Fox and seven other women from Harlow New Town who wrote to the *New Statesman* demanding to know why no one was standing up to NVALA. After holding an inaugural meeting at a public house in Cosmo Square, Holborn, it became the Cosmo Group. The group operated from the same address as the British Humanist Association but admitted to no formal links with that organization. The group barely outlasted the initial impetus of its formation.

NVALA became increasingly prominent through the late 1960s and involved itself with all the major obscenity prosecutions and allied causes celebres of the 1970s and beyond. In 1970, with the advent of a Conservative government, it proposed new reforms: (1) to amend the current obscenity laws; (2) to create a Broadcasting Council equivalent to the Press Council; (3) to create an independent Council of Viewers and Listeners; (4) to place all educational programs under the control of the Ministry of Education. The rejection of this scheme did not blunt its enthusiasm. It attacked the BBC's schools-oriented sex education programs; the comedy, *Till Death Us Do Part*; a proposed Danish film, *The Many Faces of Jesus Christ* (which dealt with the Messiah's supposed sex life); and kept up a continuous barrage of letters and pronouncements on each new, allegedly indecent broadcast, film, book or play. The association was involved, through the personal efforts of Mrs. Whitehouse, in the prosecution of GAY NEWS and the play, THE ROMANS IN BRITAIN. It backed the LONGFORD REPORT and deplored that of the WILLIAMS COMMITTEE.

Critics claimed that its 31,000 members are no more than a convenient platform for Mrs. Whitehouse's views. But whatever the reality, the NVALA continues to make itself heard. The Association can put 1.25 million signatures to a "Petition for Decency" and NVALA members remain a thorn in the side of liberal opinion.

National Vigilance Association The association, essentially a revival of the defunct British SOCIETY FOR THE SUPPRESSION OF VICE, which had collapsed in the 1870s, was launched at the monster demonstration in Hyde Park on August 22, 1885, that marked the culmination of journalist W.T. Stead's purity campaign against white slavery. Stead's attack on the trade, *The Maiden Tribute*, was a best-seller that year. Stead appointed as the society's secretary WILLIAM COOTE, an obscure compositor on the *Standard* newspaper and marshal at the rally. NVA chapters emerged throughout England, boosted by a triumphant tour by Stead and Coote in 1886. Coote grew from obscurity; George Bernard Shaw called him "a person of real importance ... [but] in artistic matters a most intensely stupid man and on sexual questions something of a monomaniac." Coote spent 34 years with the NVA and never differed from a single belief: The commercial exploitation of sex was a crime and should be punished as such.

The NVA was not initially particularly efficient, especially in the provinces. Local branches exaggerated evidence in order to parade their successes; there was rarely sufficient money, although local worthies often footed the bills, and both the judiciary and the public were less than supportive. Despite this the organization prospered, promoting its beliefs whever possible and gradually proving itself an invaluable, if often over-enthusiastic ally of the authorities. The association forwarded a stream of evidence to the relevant magistrates and police forces.

The NVA was by no means restricted to the prosecution of literary obscenity. It backed the recent laws of statutory rape, promoted the Criminal Law Amendment Act of 1885, attacked prostitution and white slavery (against which vice Coote himself departed on a successful European tour in 1898) and pushed for an incest bill. The Association's pamphlet, "Vicious Literature," made clear it was impossible that "such a society as the NVA, which soon after its formation incorporated the existing Society for the Suppression of Vice, should not repeatedly have attacked this form of literature."

The pornography trade had revived with the demise of the society, and the NVA returned to the attack. Acting in concert with Scotland Yard the association decimated the London trade, although supplies from France and Belgium, where many pornographers had fled, continued to arrive in bulk. Unlike the Vice Society, the NVA saw little reason to worry about the supposed classics. Using as its main weapon the OBSCENE PUBLICATIONS ACT (1857), it instituted prosecutions of a variety of allegedly immoral literature, including the DECAMERON, the works of RABELAIS, Henri de Balzac and a number of French authors and illustrators. The association was also responsible for the prosecution of HENRY VIZETELLY for the publication of ZOLA's *La Terre* in 1888. Its report for 1896 praises Lady Isabel Burton, who, with the association's help, had burned some 1,500 worth of the books of her late husband, the explorer Sir Richard. Coote helped her weed out the supposed obscene material and was made Burton's literary executor.

The NVA cast a wide net. In 1889 it procured the passage of the Indecent Advertisements Act, a measure that was written by its own legal subcommittee. In prohibiting the posting or distribution of advertisements relating to any sex-related problems or their possible alleviation, the law provided the sole legislation on indecency between the Obscene Publications Acts of 1857 and 1959. In 1890 Coote took personal charge of the campaign to suppress the highly popular poster of Zaoe, a female circus performer who was advertised with bare arms and legs protruding from her leotard. The poster sold 250,000 copies before Coote persuaded the London County Council to have it banned. The long-term result of this action was the establishment by the poster distributors of a secret committee of self-censorship, which agreed to secure prior NVA approval of all their product. This arrangement lasted until the late 1940s. The printers and distributors of postcards, which were enormously popular at the time, undertook similar self-censorship in the face of NVA campaigning. In 1896 the association joined the campaign against the new entertainment craze—living statuary, the *tableaux vivants* that predated striptease. For a change Coote was defeated and the tableaux survived, but he remained at the head of the NVA, a fanatical devotee of purity in all its forms, until his retirement in 1919.

The influence of the NVA waned with the outbreak of World War I, although it was not officially wound up until 1953. The PUBLIC MORALITY COUNCIL maintained a higher profile between the wars, especially as regarded questions of obscenity, although the association remained as resolutely opposed to corruption as ever and backed many of the efforts of Sir WILLIAM JOYNSON-HICKS, the home secretary. Coote was replaced by Frederick Sempkins, a former member of the Indian police, who in turn retired in 1940. Until its demise, the association shared the services of the PMC's secretary. It was reorganized after 1953 as the British Vigilance Association, which during its 20-year life was dedicated mainly to campaigning for the stricter regulation of employment agencies, although it did help unearth one white-slave operation, a London agency trafficking in Irish prostitutes.

Native Son   This film, made by Pierre Chenal in 1951 and starring Richard Wright as Bigger Thomas, was adapted from Wright's classic book, which draws its grim plot from the plight of the black man in white American society. Wright's book pointed up not merely the racial but also the social inequalities of his country, and was as unsparing of self-satisfied white liberals as of racist conservatives. Only Thomas' left-wing lawyer appears sympathetic, reflecting Wright's own political standpoint at the time. Released in 1951 the film was banned by the Ohio state censorship board in 1953 on the grounds that it contributed to "immorality and crime," even though the film shows that Thomas, who kills a white girl by mistake and a black one through fear, and who is presented as a victim rather than an aggressor, cannot escape death in the electric chair.

Classic Films, the distributor, appealed their case to the U.S. Supreme Court and *Native Son* was decided at the same time as another film, M. The court overturned the prohibitions on both films, rejecting the constitutionality of the state board's bans. The court cited THE MIRACLE decision as the basis for its ruling that films, like other forms of communication, were protected by constitutional guarantees of free speech and expression.

Nazi Germany   SEE book burning in Nazi Germany; Germany 4. Nazi press controls (1933-45); Germany 3. Nazi art censorship.

***Near* v. *Minnesota ex. rel. Olson* (1931)**   Under chapter 285 of the Session Laws for Minnesota for 1925 (1927) it was declared illegal for anyone to engage "in the business of regularly and customarily publishing a malicious, scandalous and defamatory newspaper, magazine, or any other periodical." Those who did this would be committing a nuisance and their publication could be suppressed.

Near was the publisher of the *Saturday Press*, an undisguisedly anti-Semitic tract, whose writing made his own attitudes more than clear. When a Jewish gangster had been charged with controlling Minnesota's gambling organization, Near weighed in with a number of hysterically anti-Semitic articles. Near compounded his offense by alleging that the state's law enforcement authorities were in cahoots with "anything with a hook nose that eats herring." The Minnesota courts believed that this writing fell under chapter 285 and that Near's pieces were malicious, scandalous and defamatory. He was ordered to cease publication and cited for comtempt of court when he refused to do so.

Despite the content of Near's pieces, the U.S. Supreme Court found itself unable to support the Minnesota statute, declaring it an unconstitutional prior restraint on the FIRST AMENDMENT right of a free press. For any authority to attempt such prior censorship was in contravention of the amendment. Near therefore had the right to publish what he wished, but if he, or anyone else, published material that was "improper, mischievous or illegal, he must take the consequence of his own temerity." The court cited the Minnesota libel laws as the right way of dealing with such material.

SEE ALSO *Smith* v. *Collin* (1978); *Terminiello* v. *Chicago* (1949).

Netherlands

1. book censorship (1521-50)   After the Emperor Charles V issued the Edict of Worms against the writings of MARTIN LUTHER in 1521 there followed a number of ordinances designed to control the spread of heretical literature in Europe. The initial extension of this censorship to the Netherlands was established by Charles V, who in 1522 gave a special permit to Franz van der Hulst to read the books of Luther and his followers in order to assess them for their heretical content. Van der Hulst was then appointed by Charles, and confirmed by Pope Adrian VI, as inquisitor of the Netherlands, aided, since he was a layman, by two ecclesiastics. Subsequent inquisitors were always clergymen, but appointment by the secular and confirmation by the spiritual authorities remained the accepted system of selection.

Contemporary reports speak of frequent bonfires of books and great masses of confiscated material. The Inquisition passed in 1524 an ordinance ordering the delivery of all heretical books for destruction, on pain of the confiscation of goods and of corporal punishment; banishment was added in 1526 and capital punishment in 1529. In 1526 it was ordered that no book should be printed or imported without a permit from the imperial commissioner. Miscreants would face banishment and the loss of one-third of their property. In 1529 all books dealing with religion, as well as receiving a permit from the state, had also to gain the approval of a bishop. Those who printed heretical material would be exposed on a scaffold and branded with the mark of a cross; failing this they were to lose either an eye or a hand. After 1546 the record of all permits issued was to be printed in each copy of the relevant book, and the printed text must be compared, prior to distribution, with the censored manuscript. From 1550 it was further ordered that if a book had been printed without a permit, and then found to be free of heresy, the printer would simply be fined and then banished for life. Possessing heretical material rendered the reader a heretic and, as such, prosecutable. The first offense of heresy could be purged by recantation. A further offense brought beheading for men and burial alive for women. A heretic who recanted but then lapsed again would be burned.

Among those authors forbidden in this period were LUTHER, WYCLIF, Huss, Marsilius, Oecolampadius, Zwingli, Melanchthon, Lambert, Pomeranus, Brunfels, Jonas and a number of other "libertarians," Aristotle, certain versions of the Bible that had already been condemned, and a number of histories of Germany.

2. film censorship Subsequent to 1977 there has been no censorship of films aimed at adults, but films intended for exhibition to those under 16 must first be submitted to a committee composed of educators and psychologists. Such films may be restricted to those over 14 or over 12, may have cuts required, or be made available to any age. The main criterion in restricting or cutting films is the concentration of sadistic, brutal or similarly harmful scenes. Censorship of videocassettes remains under discussion, although it is possible that this may be introduced specifically to protect children.

3. freedom of information Freedom of speech and information in the Netherlands is based on article 7 of the Dutch Constitution, promulgated in 1815 and revised in 1848, which states that no one requires prior permisison to publicize thoughts or opinions in the press, but that everyone must accept responsibility under the law for their own statements. The Netherlands also subscribes to the Treaty of Rome (1950) in which article 10 states: "Everyone has the right to freedom of expression. This right shall include freedom to hold opinions and to receive and impart information and ideas without interference by public authority and regardless of frontiers." There is no official censorship, and the government is empowered to impose restrictions on these freedoms only if the material concerned is seen to pose a threat to state security, public order or morals. The exclusion of such material is one of the criteria, under the Broadcasting Act (1967), which must be fulfilled by any organization wishing to begin broadcasting. Even in conspicuously liberal Holland, just what poses such a threat is, inevitably, subject to wide interpretation. In the absence of official censorship laws, the government is restricted to action through the courts and must uphold their judgments.

There is no specific legislation governing the right of individuals to reply to what they see as unfair or inaccurate treatment in the mass media, but in section 38 of the Broadcasting Act (1967) broadcasters are obliged to air a retraction and correction of inaccurate or incomplete information. The individual who has been directly affected by the program submits an application for rectification; the advisability of this is adjudicated by the president of the Amsterdam Court of Justice, who in turn may consult the government commissioner for broadcasting, who has overall responsibility for the conduct of the Dutch broadcasting media. In those cases where the program is involved in legal action, the broadcasting of a retraction does not free the company from its legal responsibilities.

Those who consider themselves wrongly reported by the Dutch press have two options: They may submit a complaint to the Council for Journalistic Conduct, a body appointed by the journalists' union (NVJ), the newspaper and magazine publishers and the state and private broadcasting organizations; alternatively, they may institute civil proceedings against the publication and the journalist concerned. The council has the responsiblity to "judge whether what was published was contrary to journalistic responsibility to society, including that responsibility for the citizen's right to information." It imposes no penalties, nor administers justice, but simply publishes its findings.

4. obscenity laws Subsequent to a government review in 1973, it was suggested that Dutch obscenity law be restricted to provisions protecting children and preventing obscene materials from being foisted on those who have no desire to encounter them. Although the law has not actually been changed, there appears to be a tacit acceptance of the pornography trade, certainly in Amsterdam. Sex shows, for instance, when restricted to private clubs, are tolerated by the police, who have developed municipal regulations to control them. Article 240 of the Penal Code makes it an offense to produce, distribute, import, export, transport or display publicly any writing, picture or object that offends decency. The test for obscenity—"offending decency"—is always interpreted in the light of current public attitudes as regards decency and how far one need go to offend it. There is no specified defense of artistic or literary merit, but such opinions are observed in practice.

New World Information Order The advocacy by UNESCO (United Nations Education, Scientific and Cultural Organization) of a revolution in world press communications, particularly as regards the Third World, was initiated in 1975 with the establishment of the MacBride Commission to investigate world journalism. This commission, under the chairmanship of former Irish Foreign Minister Sean MacBride, a Lenin and Nobel Prize winner, was rooted in the growing objection by such countries to what they felt was the inevitable Western bias that determined the reporting of their affairs. It was encouraged by the then director general of UNESCO, Amadou Mahtar M'bow of Senegal, a long-term opponent of the Western press (who in turn had little time for M'bow's methods and administration). The MacBride Commission's report, *Many Voices, One World*, was published in 1980.

The concept of the "new order" met strenuous Western opposition, with many delegates suggesting that UNESCO's program merely sanctioned the curbs on freedom of speech and similar press restraints that are found in many Third World nations. But what critics call the suppression of democratic freedoms, is what these governments see as the valid right to maintain their often unstable positions and thus the survival of their country, by advancing the positive aspects of their rule rather than fostering negative, destabilizing criticisms.

The Soviet bloc initially dismissed the new order as "meaningless and irrelevant," but soon appreciated its usefulness in the continuing struggle for influence in the Third World. Backing the implementation of the new order, the Soviets announced that it was due "to the joint action of the socialist and developing countries that international organizations have been able to adopt a number of important documents, dealing a blow at colonialism in the field of information." M'Bow, who has been awarded an honorary degree in a Soviet university, gained a partial victory at UNESCO's General Conference in Belgrade in November 1980. Here the West acceded to a resolution, which, while making sparse reference to freedom from censorship, the free dissemination of information etc., did set out a table of principles upon which the organization might debate the proposed "New World Information Order." It was also decided to establish the international program for the development of communications, designed to channel funds to needy governments. This was to have a governing body of 35 member states, under a director appointed by M'Bow.

This victory was marred in February 1981 when UNESCO staged a meeting on "the protection of journalists." This meeting was initially closed to the press (a decision overturned after angry remonstrations) and at the same time claimed to deal only with working journalists. This gave preeminence to virtually unknown Third World bodies, while outlawing as "publishers' associations" such major groups as the International Press Institute (IPI) and the Inter-American Press Association (IAPA). The meeting debated a paper prepared by a French marxist academic, which, inter alia, proposed the creation of an international press commission designed to protect journalists, subject to the "legitimate concern of states to preserve their sovereignty in the process of ensuring the regulation of journalists." Both IPI and IAPA, plus two other excluded bodies, rejected the paper.

In May 1981 some 20 Western countries issued the Talloires Declaration, prepared at the French village of that name, stating that journalists required no special protection or status but that they proclaimed a common standard: "a joint dedication to the freest, most accurate and impartial information that is within our professional capacity to produce." The concept of a double standard of press freedom in rich and poor countries was rejected absolutely, and the signatories added that they were "deeply concerned by a growing tendency in many countries to put the government's interests above those of the individual, particularly in regard to information."

In 1982 the 35 members of the IDPC conferred at Acapulco. Although the hopes of Third World countries, whose requests for communications-connected funds totalling some $80 million, were to a large extent dashed, a number of programs were initiated and some $910,000 was distributed. When the director general complained at the apparent reluctance of the rich nations to provide for the poor, the IDPC chairman stated that many such nations had refused to offer cash until the organization had proved itself as efficient and had guaranteed that none of the cash subscribed would in fact be used to suppress freedom of communication. The statement by a Cuban delegate that "the free flow of information and the new order are ... enemies" did nothing to reassure potential donors. To what extent the IDPC and the new order are genuinely committed to freedom of the press and to what extent they are merely funneling cash to the ideologically pure has yet to be resolved. On either count, the situation sufficiently displeased the U.S. and U.K. that both countries, as well as Singapore, quit UNESCO in protest at what they saw as its biased policies.

In 1988 the situation changed: After intense lobbying from his opponents, and a lengthy and sometimes acrimonious rearguard action by Director-General M'Bow, he finally lost his job. The new director-general, Federico Mayor, a former member of the Spanish government, has announced himself as determined to repair UNESCO's battered image. To this end he has removed implementation of the NWIO from the current agenda. It is presumably hoped that the U.K. and U.S., both major contributors to UNESCO's budget, will thus be tempted to return.

New York

1. civil service law   The law states in section 105:

> Subversive activities; disqualification. 1. Ineligibility of persons advocating the overthrow of the government by force or unlawful means. No persons shall be appointed to any office or position in the service of the state or of any civil division thereof, nor shall any person employed in any such office or position be continued in such employment, nor shall any person be employed in the public service as superintendent, principal or teacher in a public school or academy or in a state college or any other state educational establishment who (a) by word of mouth or writing wilfully and deliberately advocates, advises, or teaches the doctrine that the government of the United States or of any state or of any political subdivision thereof should be overthrown or overturned by force, violence or any unlawful means; or (b) prints, publishes, edits, issues or sells any book, paper, document, or written or printed matter in any form containing or advocating the doctrines; or (c) organizes or helps to organize or becomes a member of any society or group of persons which teaches or advocates [the doctrine]. For the purposes of this section membership in the Communist Party ... shall constitute prima facie evidence of disqualification for appointment to or retention in any office or position in the service of the state or any city or division thereof ... 3. Removal for treasonable or seditious acts or utterances. A person in the civil service of the state or of any civil division thereof shall be removable therefrom for the utterance of any treasonable or seditious word or words or the doing of any treasonable or seditious act or acts while

holding such points … A seditious act shall mean "criminal anarchy" as defined in the penal law.

(Penal Law: "'Criminal anarchy' is the doctrine that organized government should be overthrown by force or violence, or by the assassination of the head or any of the executive officials of government, or by any unlawful means. The ADVOCACY of such doctrine either by word of mouth or writing is a felony.")

The law was upheld in 1952, in case of *Adler* v. *Board of Edcation* when Adler lost his job for his political affiliations, but in *Keyishian* v. *Board of Regents* (1967) the Supreme Court reflected substantial differences in American society when it ruled that the law was vague, guilty of OVERBREADTH, and as such an unconstitutional restraint on FIRST AMENDMENT rights.

2. exposing minors to harmful materials   As provided by the New York Penal Law, section 484-h, "Exposing Minors to Harmful Materials":

1. Definitions. As used in this section: (a) "Minor" means any person under the age of 17 years. (b) "Nudity" means the showing of the human male or female genitals, pubic area or buttocks with less than a full opaque covering, or the showing of the female breast with less than a fully opaque covering of any portion thereof below the top of the nipple, or the depiction of the covered male genitals in a discernible turgid state. (c) "Sexual conduct" means acts of masturbation, homosexuality, sexual intercourse, or physical contact with a person's clothed or unclothed genitals, pubic area, buttocks, or, if such person be a female, breast. (d) "Sexual excitement" means the condition of the human male or female genitals when in a state of sexual stimulation or arousal. (e) "Sado-masochistic abuse" means flagellation or torture by or upon a person clad in undergarments, a mask, or bizarre costume, or the condition of being fettered, bound or otherwise physically restrained on the part of one so clothed. (f) "Harmful to minors" means that quality of any description or representation, in whatever form of nudity, sexual conduct, sexual excitement, or sado-masochistic abuse, when it: (i) predominantly appeals to the prurient, shameful or morbid interest of minors, and (ii) is patently offensive to prevailing standards in the adult community as a whole with respect to what is suitable material for minors, and (iii) is utterly without redeeming social importance for minors. (g) "Knowingly" means having general knowledge of, or reason to know, or a belief or ground for belief which warrants further inspection or inquiry or both: (i) the character and content of any material described herein which is reasonably susceptible of examination by the defendant, and (ii) the age of the minor, provided however, that an honest mistake shall constitute an excuse from liability hereunder if the defendant made a reasonable bona fide attempt to ascertain the true age of such minor.

2. It shall be unlawful for any person knowingly to sell or loan for monetary consideration to a minor: (a) any picture, photograph, drawing, sculpture, motion picture film or similar visual representation or image of a person or portion of the human body which depicts nudity, sexual conduct or sado-masochistic abuse and which is harmful to minors, or

(b) any book, picture, magazine, printed matter however reproduced, or sound recording which contains any matter enumerated in paragraph (a) of sub-division two hereof, or explicit and detailed verbal descripitons or narrative accounts of sexual excitement, sexual conduct or sado-masochistic abuse and which, taken as a whole, is harmful to minors.

3. It shall be unlawful for any person knowingly to exhibit for a monetary consideration to a minor or knowingly sell to a minor an admission ticket or pass or knowingly to admit a minor for a monetary consideration to premises whereon there is exhibited a motion picture or other presentation which, in whole or in part, depicts nudity, sexual conduct or sado-masochistic abuse and which is harmful to minors.

4. A violation of any provision hereof shall constitute a misdemeanor.

SEE ALSO *Ginsberg.* v. *New York* (1968).

3. minors and sexual performances   Under article 263 of the New York Penal Code the use of a child in a sexual performance is classified as a Class C felony. The article provides that: "A person is guilty of the use of a child in a sexual performance if knowing the character and content thereof he employs, authorizes or induces a child less than 16 years of age to engage in a sexual performance or being a parent, legal guardian or custodian of such a child, he consents to the participation by such a child in a sexual performance." For the purposes of the statute "sexual performance" is defined as "any performances or part thereof which includes sexual conduct by a child of less than 16 years of age"; "sexual conduct" means "actual or simulated sexual intercourse, deviate sexual intercourse, sexual bestiality, masturbation, sado-masochisic abuse, or lewd exhibition of the genitals"; a "performance" is "any play, motion picture, photograph or dance or any other visual presentation exhibited before an audience."

4. motion picture censorship   Under the New York Education Law it is unlawful "to exhibit or to sell, lease or lend for exhibition at any place of amusement for pay or in connection with any business in the State of New York, any motion picture film or reel … unless there is at the time in full force and effect valid license or permit therefor of the education department." Licenses will be issued unless a film or part of a film is "obscene, indecent, immoral, inhuman, sacriligious, or is of such a character that its exhibition would tend to corrupt morals or incite to crime." The term "moral" and the phrase "of such a character that its exhibition would tend to corrupt morals" are defined as referring to a film or part of a film, "the dominant purpose or effect of which is erotic or pornographic; or which portrays acts of sexual immorality, perversion or lewdness, or which expressly or impliedly presents such acts as desirable, acceptable or proper patterns of behavior."

SEE ALSO *The Miracle*; *Lady Chatterley's Lover* 3. film.

5. obscenity statute   Under section 1141 of the New York Penal Law (1884):

A person who ... has in his possession with intent to sell, lend, distribute ... any obscene, lewd, lascivious, filthy, indecent, sadistic, masochistic or disgusting book ... or who prints, utters, publishes, or in any manner manufactures or prepares any such book or ... in any manner, hires, employs, uses, or permits any person to do or assist in doing any act or thing mentioned in this section, or any of them, is guilty of a misdemeanor ... the possession by any person of six or more identical or similar articles coming within the provisions of sub-division one of this section is presumptive evidence of a violation of this section. The publication for sale of any book, magazine or pamphlet designed, composed or illustrated as a whole to appeal to and commercially exploit prurient interest by combining covers, pictures, drawings, illustrations, caricatures, cartoons, words, stories and advertisements or any combination or combinations thereof devoted to the description, portrayal or deliberate suggestion of illicit sex, including adultery, prostitution, fornication, sexual crime and sexual perversion or to the exploitation of sex and nudity by the presentation of nude or partially nude female figures, posed, photographed or otherwise presented in a manner calculated to provoke or incite prurient interest, or any combination or combinations thereof, shall be a violation of this section.

The statute was refined in 1974 to reflect current standards for testing for obscenity; under section 235.05 of the Penal Law any material or performance was to be judged obscene if:

(a) considered as a whole, its predominant appeal is to prurient, shameful or morbid interest in nudity, sex, excretion, sadism or masochism, and (b) if it goes substantially beyond customary limits of candor in describing or representing such matters, and (c) it is utterly without redeeming social value. Predominant appeal shall be judged with reference to ordinary adults unless it appears from the character of the material or the circumstances of its dissemination to be designed for children or other specifically susceptible audience.

***New York Times Company* v. *Sullivan* (1964)**   By the end of the 1950s the civil rights movement was conducting a well-publicized and increasingly successful campaign to alert the nation to the discrepancies between the lot of black and white Americans. In the era before the ghetto riots in Northern cities, its efforts were focused on the cities of the South, where the unequal status quo was often maintained by unregenerate racist administrations. On March 20, 1960, a group of black clergymen from Alabama, members of the National Association for the Advancement of Colored People (NAACP), published a full-page paid advertisement in the *New York Times* in which they attacked the behavior of the city officials of Montgomery, Alabama, as regarded civil rights. Included in the advertisement were a number of statements from students, alleging that the Montgomery police had performed a variety of illegal acts against them. Some of these allegations were subsequently proved to be untrue.

L.B. Sullivan, one of the three elected city commissioners in Montgomery, and responsible for the city's police, fire,

scales and cemetery departments, sued the *Times* and the subscribing clergymen for libel in an Alabama court, claiming that the attacks on the police were in effect attacks on him. The court awarded him $500,000 in damages. The Supreme Court of Alabama confirmed this ruling, but when the defendants took their case to the U.S. Supreme Court, the lower courts' decisions were overturned.

The court's ruling created what came to be known as the New York Times Rule, which stated that under the constitutional guarantees of a free press it was necessary for a public official who was suing for defamation to prove malice on behalf of the defendants. In this context malice was defined as "the publishing of material knowing it to be false, or with a reckless disregard of whether it is true or false." Presenting the court's opinion, Justice Brennan rejected Sullivan's allegation that normal constitutional guarantees were invalidated in the case since the material was published as a paid advertisement. An advertisement of this type, the court ruled, was not inserted for the purpose of selling a product, but was aimed to communicate information, express opinion, recite grievances, protest claimed abuses and seek financial support, for the NAACP. The carrying of editorial advertisements of this type was "an important outlet for the promulgation of information and ideas by persons who do not themselves have access to publishing facilities—who wish to exercise their freedom of speech even though they are not members of the press." If the court were to outlaw such advertisements, "the effect would be to shackle the First Amendment in its attempt to secure 'the widest possible dissemination of information from diverse and antagonistic sources.'" The opinion concluded that although some of the claims made in the advertisement had subsequently been proved false, Justice Brennan did not accept that they were made with actual malice as defined under the law.

New York Times Rule   SEE *New York Times Company* v. *Sullivan* (1964).

***New York* v. *Ferber* (1982)**   Ferber was the proprietor of a Manhattan bookstore who in 1982 was convicted under section 263.05 of the New York Penal Law for "promoting a sexual performance of a child under sixteen." The performance in question featured two 16-year-old boys masturbating. The State Supreme Court and its Appellate Division both convicted Ferber, but on appeal to the New York Court of Appeals Ferber's conviction was overturned because, in failing to define the difference between obscene and non-obscene sexual conduct performed by minors (and preferring to outlaw all such conduct), the statute suffered from "OVERBREADTH"—an insufficiently specific definition of its powers.

When the state appealed to the U.S. Supreme Court, the conviction was reaffirmed. The court stated that the statute did not violate the FIRST AMENDMENT. The justices differed slightly in their opinions, but the general ruling was that any state could outlaw the exploitation of children in sexual performances whether or not those performances were technically obscene as defined under the current tests. It was necessary to broaden the regulation of such sexual exhibitions as regards children because: (1) the First Amendment was no bar to the fact that such performances would do harm to the psychological, emotional and mental stability of the child; (2) the current MILLER STANDARD for judging obscenity was insufficient to deal with "kiddie porn"; (3) the exploitation of such material for gain, whether technically obscene or not, was in any case illegal in America; (4) there is only "modest at best" value to be derived from permitting either live performances or photographic reproductions of child sex; (5) excluding child pornography from the protection of the First Amendment did not clash with any previous Supreme Court decisions.

New Zealand

1. book censorship   Book censorship in New Zealand is operated by the Indecent Publications Tribunal. The body has the power to classify certain material as indecent and as such unsuitable for sale to persons under 18. Material thus classified is still available for display and sale, but its sale to a minor is a criminal offense. Publishers, police and customs officers may all request a ruling and all parties are offered an open hearing at which expert evidence, the opinions of readers and affidavits from authors may all be assessed. For the tribunal's purposes, indecency is defined as "describing, depicting, expressing or otherwise dealing with matters of sex, horror, crime, cruelty, or violence in a manner that is injurious to the public good."

The tribunal, which deals with sound recordings as well as books, must consider: (a) the dominant effect of the book or sound recording as a whole; (b) the literary or artistic merit, or the medical, legal, political, social, or scientific character or importance of the book or sound recording; (c) the persons, classes of persons, or age groups to or amongst whom the book or sound recording is or is intended or is likely to be published, heard, distributed, sold, exhibited, played, given, sent, or delivered; (d) the price at which the book or sound recording sells or is tended to be sold; (e) whether any person is likely to be corrupted by reading the book or hearing the sound recording and whether other persons are likely to benefit therefrom; (f) whether the book or the sound recording displays an honest purpose and an honest thread of thought or whether its content is merely camouflage designed to render acceptable any indecent parts of the book or sound recording. Finally the tribunal accepts that "where the publication of any book or the distribution of any sound recording would be in the interest of art, literature, science or learning and would be for the public good the Tribunal shall not classify it as indecent."

This system is generally seen as protecting real literature, although its one anomaly is in the banning of certain relatively soft-core men's magazines; the basis for this ban is that "entertainment value" cannot be taken into consideration when applying the tests for indecency. The makeup of the tribunal varies as to the current government, which chooses its appointees.

2. film censorship   Under the Cinematograph Films Act (1976) all films intended for exhibition must be submitted to the chief censor, the prime condition for whose approval is that they are not "injurious to the public good." When assessing a film, the censor must consider the dominant effect of the film as a whole and its likely audience; its artistic merit or social, cultural or similar importance; the extent and degree to which the film deals with violence, sex, indecent or offensive language or behavior and any form of antisocial behavior; the existence within the film of racism, sexism or antireligious sentiments; any other relevant circumstances relating to its exhibition.

Apart from those films that are banned absolutely, the censor classifies all films as follows: G, general exhibition; GY, general exhibition, more suitable to those of 13 and over; GA, general exhibition, more suitable for adults; G*, general exhibition, subject to any specific recommendations; R13, R16, R18, R20, restricted to audiences of the minimum age specified in the category; R FS, restricted to film societies; R FF, restricted to film festivals; R*, restricted to a specific audience or a specific place and time. Advertising material is also subject to censorship. An appeal against classification may be lodged with the Films Censorship Board of Review, whose seven members are appointed by the government. The minister of internal affairs may override the censor's decision.

3. obscenity laws   Since 1963 all considerations of obscene material have been referred to the Indecent Publications Tribunal. This five-member panel (always chaired by a lawyer and having two experts in either education or literature) must determine whether an article is broadly indecent or not indecent or must be subjected to certain restrictions regarding the age of its readers or the purposes of their reading. Any case involving allegedly obscene material, unless the defendant pleads guilty and admits the obscenity, is passed on to the tribunal by the comptroller of customs or the secretary of justice for a decision as to its status. The tribunal uses a test of "indecency": the "describing, depicting, expressing or otherwise dealing with matters of sex, horror, crime, cruelty, or violence in a manner that is injurious to the public good." When making their assessment the tribunal must consider the dominant effect of the work as a whole, its literary or artistic merit and its scientific, legal, medical, social or political character and importance, its target audience, its price, whether anyone is likely to be actively corrupted by it or benefit from it, whether it displays an honest purpose and a genuine plot, or whether it merely exists to parade the indecent passages. The author, publisher and other interested parties may appear before the tribunal to justify their work; appeals may be made against the Tribunal's decision to the Supreme Court and the panel may be asked after three years to reconsider any previously restricted or prohibited article. It is an offense to traffic in any way in material that is judged indecent.

Nicaea, Second Council of (787) Twenty-two disciplinary canons were laid down by Pope Hadrian I to cover all forms of religious art that might be created throughout Christendom. Ratified by both the Greek and Roman churches, these lasted for nearly 500 years and effectively ended the Iconoclastic Controversy that had begun in 730 over the role of images in the Byzantine Empire. In essence, the council declared that while the art itself belonged to its creator, the substance of what was created remained strictly in the hands of the church. Detailed, inflexible rules were established, covering every aspect of religious painting, up to and including the least item of clothing worn by those who might safely be depicted, without any heresy, by an artist.

Nicaragua As of the current Nicaraguan Constitution (article 30, January 1987), Nicaraguans "have the right to express freely their beliefs in public or private, individually or collectively, in oral, written or other form." However, under the state of emergency that has existed since March 1982, this constitution, like its predecessors, was automatically suspended. Censorship relaxed during 1984, immediately prior to the national elections, but the state of emergency was reimposed in October 1985, and with it the usual controls.

The Nicaraguan press is small and, by Western standards, unprofessional. Daily newspapers are *La Prensa*, the largest paper, and that which voices the main opposition to the new status quo; *El Nuevo Diario*, formed by ex-*La Prensa* journalists who promised "critical support" for the revolution; and *Barricada*, initially a strident pro-revolutionary propaganda sheet, but subsequently a useful, informative journal. The Sandinista government, which took over power in 1979, has always aimed to ensure that the press, often a destabilizing factor in a new situation, should support the revolution, which in part it had helped bring about. Thus *La Prensa* has suffered sporadic suspensions for going too far in its criticisms, and such extreme publications as the Maoist *El Pueblo*, which exhorted its 2,000 readers to sabotage the state economy, have been shut down. Notably, with the continuing vilification of the revolution by the U.S. and American backing for the Contra rebels, *La Prensa*, for all that it has received funds from the U.S., has chosen to mute its criticism and rally to the Sandinistas. This turnaround did not preclude its featuring on the cover of the June 25, 1986, of a photo of President Reagan giving a victory salute after Congress had voted $100 million to the contras. For this the paper was banned indefinitely, the government claiming that Nicaragua was at war with the U.S. and thus *La Prensa* was to be seen as "helping the enemy." Nicaraguan press laws remain vague. In August 1979 the junta issued a law that called upon the media to operate "within the bounds of social responsibility" and outlawed the publication of stories "harming the people's

interests and destroying the gains achieved by the people." It was further emphasized that the concept of press freedom was conditional on the press identifying with the aims of the revolution. Facts must accord with the aims of the government, although there is no restriction on leaders and editorial material, which may attack that government. The most obvious area of censorship is that which deals with counter-revolutionary activities, the reporting of which is generally banned.

Television stations are all state-run, but of the country's 30 radio stations only one is directly government-controlled. There is no prior censorship, but radio producers face sanctions if they overstep the bounds of acceptable criticism. In effect this means that all media must show reasonably active support of the revolution.

The position of Nicaraguan censorship altered in August 1987 when Nicaragua and four other Central American countries signed the Esquipulas II peace plan, which, among other measures for peace in the area, promised "complete freedom of press, television and radio ... for all ideological groups." The plan also promised the ending of all national states of emergency. In the event, Nicaragua did not end the emergency, citing as a reason America's continuing support for the Contra rebels, but it allowed *La Prensa* to recommence publication and the radio station Radio Catolica (banned in 1986) to broadcast once more.

Nichols, H. Sidney Nichols, a marginal but persistent figure in Victorian erotic publishing, was first an associate of LEONARD SMITHERS in Sheffield and London and then, forced to leave England by police pressure, a publisher in his own right in Paris and New York. Among his collaborative efforts may well have been the English version of RESTIF DE BRETONNE's L'ANTI-JUSTINE, which appeared in 1895 as a loosely based "translation" by Nichols and Leonard Smithers, published as *The Double Life of Cuthbert Cockerton*. In 1894 he was responsible for printing a translation of CASANOVA's *Memoirs* by the Welsh auhor, Arthur Machen (1863-1947).

While Smithers had undoubted pretentions to literary sophisticaton and produced many non-erotic works, Nichols was the driving force in the partnership's production of pornography. Under the imprint of the EROTIKA BIBLION SOCIETY a number of such works appeared. They included *Priapeia* (1888), a collection of "sportive epigrams" taken from risque Latin authors by Sir Richard Burton; *Les Tableaux Vivants* (1888), a collection of short erotic pieces written in France by Paul Terret and first published in 1870; *Opus Sadicum* (1889), an English version of JUSTINE first published in Paris by Isidore Liseux; and *Crissie, a Music Hall Sketch of Today*, which advertised itself as "A Narrative of Music Hall Depravity" and which was, in 1899, the last original erotic novel to appear in England in the 19th century. The two publishers fell out sometime during the 1890s and Nichols went on the run, first to Paris and then to America where he attempted to tout a number of badly forged

BEARDSLEY drawings. He died, supposedly in the 1930s, an inmate of Bellevue mental hospital.

Niclas, Hendrick SEE book burning in England 1. Tudor Period.

Nigeria

1. National Party Under the National Party of Nigeria (NPN) the position of the mass media in Nigeria was very much conditional on the unique structure of the country's administration. After the end of military rule in 1979, the country was composed of 19 state governments and a single federal government. Five major parties, each a loose confederation of ethnic or other interest groups, contested for power and each controlled at least two of the states. A total of 15 daily papers, at least 12 weeklies, 25 radio and 20 TV stations made up the mass media.

Under the 1979 constitution the media had an obligation to uphold the fundamental objectives of the constitution: notably, the establishment and maintenance of democracy, social progress, justice, liberty and national unity. They were also bound to "uphold the responsibility and accountability of the government to the poeple." All Nigerians were guaranteed freedom of expression and "the freedom to hold opinions and to receive and impart ideas and information without interference." They also had the right to "own, establish and operate any medium for the dissemination of ideas and information." The single restriction on the media was that only the federal or state government might operate radio or TV stations without permission from the president. There were no formal guarantees of press freedom; journalists had the same rights as other people and thus, it was assumed, the press was free.

There was little overt censorship, but the close relations between the various media outlets and the political parties, who liked to wage their political struggles through the media, tended to ensure that a given medium would offer a predictable party line. Radio and TV were controlled respectively by the Federal Radio Commission (FRCN, which replaced the Nigerian Broadcasting Company in 1978) and Nigerian Television (NTV), both ostensibly impartial bodies intended to give a single voice to Nigerian broadcasting in the international sphere. State governments, which already owned radio and TV stations and were keen to expand such facilities, complained of some bias from these agencies in favor of the ruling National Party but balanced this in the direction of the media they did control. There were few attempts to muzzle opposition to the NPN (although it was noted that the Presidential Press Corps, mustered for visits abroad, excluded opposition correspondents). The real restrictions on Nigerian media came not through fear of the authorities but through inadequate journalistic expertise and the practice of self-censorship. The media, by virtue of its political allegiances, tended to criticism and polemic, in place of investigation and fact. A lack of trained reporters, of sufficient funds and the investigative ethic meant that many good stories were simply ignored or missed and that the press thrived on opinion and rumor.

2. military rule In the fourth successful coup since Independence, the government of Nigeria was taken over on January 1, 1984, by the army under General Buhari, thus ending the civilian rule of President Shehu Shagari and the National Party of Nigeria. Although the media went out of its way to support the new regime and condemn the failings of the NPN, the army chose to impose a hitherto unknown censorship on what had been generally accepted as the freest press in Black Africa. Although the press remains vocal and varied, with at least 15 dailies and 30 weeklies, its freedoms, which critics felt it had abused with rumor-mongering and overt politicking under the NPN, have been curtailed.

On April 17, 1984, the Federal Military Government (FMG) published the Public Officers (Protection Against False Accusation) Decree of 1984 (Decree 4, under the law of February 1984), whereby the FMG could make laws immune to any challenge in the courts. Decree 4 enabled the authorities to reject a major criticism of the original Public Officers Decree: that it contradicted the 1979 Nigerian constitution, which guarantees the rights of the media to gather and disseminate news. The president has in any case promised to amend that particular article. The decree made it an offense for any person to report or publish information that is in any particular false and that in any way brings the government or its officials into ridicule. A special tribunal chaired by a High Court judge, with three military officers as members, presides over the trials of such offenses. Individuals may be fined or imprisoned; newspapers or the broadcasting media may be closed down for up to one year and journalists imprisoned. There is no appeal against the tribunal. The FMG also employs economic censorship, notably the restriction of the supply of newsprint by controlling its import licenses. Most of the country's press have had to cut down the size of their papers. Opposition papers cannot publish without paper and will thus vanish, even without the problems inherent in a legal prosecution under Decree 4.

Despite the hopes of many Nigerians, plans for a new constitution, to be promulgated in 1992, will not include guarantees of freedom of speech or the press. Despite the president's image as a supporter of human rights, many journalists see Nigeria's press as growing increasingly muzzled.

nodis No distribution; a classification level affixed to sensitive documents; such material is meant only for the individual to whom it is sent on a strict eyes-only basis.
SEE ALSO noforn.

noforn A notation on classified documents that prohibits anyone but a U.S. citizen from reading them.
SEE ALSO nodis.

North Briton, The   John Wilkes (1727-97) was elected MP for Aylesbury in 1757. An articulate opponent of the government, he founded in 1762 his weekly political periodical, *The North Briton*, a direct response to Smollett's *The Briton* and a general critic of the administration of Lord Bute. The running joke of the weekly was to pose as an English magazine edited by a Scotsman who delighted in his countryman Bute's success in usurping power from the English in London. Its first allegiance was to "The liberty of the press [which] is the birthright of a Briton and is justly esteemed the firmest bulwark of the liberties of this country."

On April 23, 1763, in issue no. 45, Wilkes and his coeditor, the satirist Charles Churchill (1732-64), went beyond Bute and attacked the king's Speech from the Throne, which dealt with the recent Peace of Paris under which the war with France and Spain had been ended. He attacked Bute for "ministerial affrontery" and, more dangerously, King George III for having, as regards his support of Bute, "sunk even to prostitution." Five years of legal maneuvering passed before Wilkes was arrested and charged with libel. While in spring 1763 the MP managed successfully to claim that parliamentary privilege gave him immunity from arrest, and even gain an award of £1,000 damages against the secretary of state for the manner of the searching of his house, in the fall the House of Commons declared issue no. 45 to be an OBSCENE LIBEL. The sheet was to be burned by the common hangman.

Crying their slogan, "Wilkes and Liberty!" the London mob rioted in his favor and made it impossible for the burning to take place. Wilkes was summoned before the House in December but departed to Paris. In January 1764 he was expelled from Parliament. In February he was found guilty in absentia of publishing the obscenely libellous article. When he refused to appear before the court he was declared an outlaw. In 1760 Wilkes returned to London. In March he was elected as MP for Middlesex. His outlawry was canceled but he was arrested to face two charges: the publication in the *North Briton* of a SEDITIOUS LIBEL; and the blasphemous and obscene libels contained in his scurrilous poem, "THE ESSAY ON WOMAN."

Guilty on both counts, Wilkes was fined £500 for each publication and sentenced to 10 months in jail for no. 45 and a year for the "Essay." The *North Briton* was suppressed. The mob rioted again and letters embarrassing to the government were published by Wilkes. This was construed as a further libel and his election as MP for Middlesex was declared invalid. Wilkes won back his seat three times while in jail, even though the government overturned the majority on each occasion. Before he left prison he was elected an alderman of London. Out of jail, Wilkes grew increasingly conservative. In 1774 he was elected lord mayor and in 1775 returned to Parliament, this time without contention. By the time of the Gordon Riots of 1780 Wilkes, once the darling of the mob, was fighting determinedly on the side of the Establishment. The issue that his career had raised whether Parliament truly had the right to control the press, remained central to the development of political censorship in Britain well into the 19th century.

North Korea   The North Korea constitution (1972) guarantees freedom of speech, the press, assembly, association and demonstration, as well as of scientific, literary and artistic pursuits. The country has also signed (in 1981) the International Covenant on Civil and Political Rights. Despite this, the policy of *juche* (self-reliance), created by Korea's President Kim Il Sung, leader since 1949, subordinates all such freedoms to the primacy of the Korean Workers' Party (KWP) and his own presidency. Freedoms of expression are counterbalanced by further articles of the constitution, demanding the "politico- ideological unity" of the nation and urging citizens to "heighten their revolutionary vigilance against … all hostile elements" opposing socialism.

The KWP controls all the country's media. Dominated by what it sees as a need for secrecy in the face of the threats posed by South Korea and the U.S., the party sets a tightly limited agenda of what topics may be discussed and the way in which they may be treated. Not only do all media employees work to quotas, but they also have their output strictly monitored. Newspaper stories are dominated by the Korean Central News Agency.

All published writers must belong to the Union of Writers and Artists. There are some 350 members, responsible among them for some 20 novels and 450 to 500 short stories each year. Censorship is extensive, commencing in discussion groups held at the writer's workplace and proceeding upward through various strata, including the Kim Il Sung University or Academy of Science for research works and the union itself for literary material. The Education Commission and the Ministry of Culture and Art add their comments; the highest level of analysis is that of the General Publications Bureau.

Radio broadcasts are strictly controlled. Most households have state-installed speakers, fixed permanently to the national and local networks. If an individual does own a radio, its dial is altered to receive nothing but these broadcasts. All radios are checked annually. The bulk of all broadcasting is pro-government material; approximately 50 percent of television programs are films focusing on the leader.

Northern Ireland   The law controlling allegedly indecent material in Northern Ireland remains the same as that governing England prior to the OBSCENE PUBLICATIONS ACT OF 1959. The OBSCENE PUBLICATIONS ACT OF 1857 and the crime of uttering an OBSCENE LIBEL remain in force. The THEATRES ACT (1968) does not apply to Ulster, where indecent theatrical exhibitions are still governed by section 4 of the VAGRANCY ACT (1824), dealing with making obscene exhibitions in a public street or place. English Customs and postal regulations, as well as those embodied in the Indecent Advertisement Act (1889) all extend to Northern Ireland.

Norway

1. broadcast censorship Radio and television broadcasting in Norway is controlled by the Act on Broadcasting of 1980, which replaced that of 1933. All broadcasting is controlled by the Norwegian Broadcasting Corporation (NRK: Norsk riksringkasting) as authorized by the king. There shall be no prior censorship of any program and no one, other than those concerned in making it or who have the responsibility for it, shall see a program prior to transmission. The NRK is duty-bound to broadcast any messages issued by government authorities.

The NRK is controlled by a board of directors. This board comprises seven members, each with his personal deputy. Its chairman, deputy chairman and three other members are appointed by the king for a four-year period; the other two members are elected by their fellow NRK employees in a secret ballot and serve for two years. Responsible for the day-to-day running of the NRK is a director-general, appointed by the king for a maximum of eight years. Beneath him are two managing directors, also appointed for eight years, with responsibility respectively for radio and television. The NRK is financed by television owners' license fees; there is no advertising.

National and regional advisory councils advise the NRK on its programming policies at national and regional levels. The National Council is made up of 25 members—14 appointed by Parliament, the remainder (including the chairman and deputy chairman) by the king—for four years in office. It adjudicates both on those programs submitted by the director-general and on those it has decided to review of its own accord. The board of directors, or the director-general, may ask the council's opinion on administrative and economic matters. The regional councils fulfill the same duties on a local level; they consist of five members appointed by the local legislative assembly for four years.

If an individual brings a formal complaint to the NRK within two months of the program being transmitted, this complaint will be assessed by the Complaints Tribunal. This tribunal has three members, appointed by the king for four years. It holds the right to decide whether a program has exposed the plaintiff to unwarranted prejudice or invaded his privacy; it can also decide whether the NRK, when asked to rectify alleged misinformation, has in fact done so adequately. Once the tribunal has reached a conclusion it must state its reasons and admit to any dissenting votes; the plaintiff is not legally bound by its decision.

2. press controls The first newspaper appeared in Norway in 1767, but the modern press stems from the late 19th and early 20th centuries. The press that emerged then was politically rather than profit-motivated. The various warring publications all set out to promote their own interests, usually that of a political party. The authorities did not interfere, preferring to stand by the Constitution of 1814, which declared "There shall be freedom of the press." This disinterest was helped by the fact that all of these idealistically based publications represented a relatively tiny and thus ineffectual constituency. As the major parties—the conservatives and liberals—grew stronger, so did the press that had attached itself to them. This situation has persisted, surmounting both the Nazi occupation during World War II and the coming of television (on which no advertising is permitted) in 1964.

As can be seen in the Norwegian Freedom of Information Act (see below), the country is committed to freedom of communication and there is no official press law. Pressure groups have campaigned for such legislation, but the press has united to rebuff these efforts. The laws that do govern the press are those that apply to every Norwegian citizen and are set down in the General Civil Penal Code (1902). These deal particularly with libel and slander. Conversely there exist a number of laws, notably as regards copyright, designed to further press interests. Like every other medium, the press benefits from the Freedom of Information legislation of 1970.

The press has accepted a degree of self-censorship since the founding in 1928 by the Norwegian Press Association of a press council designed to enforce journalistic ethics. This council promotes a "Be Cautious Code," which incorporates both the "Code for Editors" and the "Guidelines for Treatment of Court Cases in the Press," a document worked out with the country's leading lawyers. Until 1972 the press council drew exclusively on professionals working within the press; since 1972, when the council was reorganized, two members are elected from the general public. This alteration, plus certain procedural changes, is said to have imporved the performance of the council's main task, dealing with complaints from readers. There exists a second, parallel press council, formed by members of the specialist—trade, technical and professional—press, who are not members of the Norwegian Press Association.

3. Freedom of the Press Act (1971) The Norwegian Freedom of the Press Act was passed in 1971 on the model of the Swedish Act (q.v.) but, compared with that of its neighbor, has a wide variety of exemptions from disclosure, resembling in many ways the U.S. Freedom of Information Act. Most notably the government is able to take advantage of a substantial loophole whereby it may simply exempt documents from access by decree. Agencies may also refuse access if the documents under review would provide "an obviously misleading picture of the case." Documents are also refused to "the mentally ill, inebriates, small children, rowdies and slanderers." The act, like its American peer, replaced the Administrative Procedure Act (1967), which was based on the inquirer establishing a legitimate need to know prior to receiving the information. The authorities are not duty-bound to point the public toward any document, thus making it hard for the inquirer, who must specify the document that is required, to discover just what was available. This problem has been remedied in part by the provision of an index of documents, which can be demanded prior to further researches. In 1978 Norway passed a data protection act, the Privacy Act, and the Personal Registers Act to control computer-based personal information data banks and manually compiled files. Both individuals and companies may demand access to the files in which they appear and certain categories of information, e.g., private lists of political radicals, are forbidden. The only exceptions to access concern disclosures that would threaten the subject's mental or physical health and statistical information that cannot be easily retrieved on an individual basis. This law is regularly monitored by the independent Data Surveillance Service.

SEE ALSO United States 11. Freedom of Information Act.

Notes ... on Curious and Uncommon Books SEE *Index Librorum Prohibitorum.*

November *November* was written by the French author Gustave Flaubert (1821-80), better known for such works as *Madame Bovary* (1857) and *Bouvard and Pecuchet* (1881). The book was Flaubert's first novel, written around 1840 but suppressed as too revealing until 1914 when it was published in Paris. The English translation appeared in 1932. In 1935 JOHN S. SUMNER, secretary of the New York SOCIETY FOR THE SUPPRESSION OF VICE, brought suit against *November* in the New York courts, claiming that it violated the New York statute on obscenity, section 1141 of the state's penal code. The court rejected Sumner's suit, stating that while under the standards of his predecessor and founder of the society, ANTHONY COMSTOCK, *November* might possibly have been condemned, the law itself, even though it dated back to 1884 and Comstock's heyday, had to be interpreted in the light of contemporary attitudes. Thus *November* could not, in 1935, be considered as obscene: "To change standards of morals is the task of school and church; the task of the judge is to record the tides of public opinion, not to emulate King Canute in an effort to turn back the tide."

NOWA Prior to the liberalization that followed the elections of summer 1989, NOWA—the Independent Publishing House—was the largest and oldest unofficial publisher in POLAND. Like its peers, it acted to fill the gaps in Polish culture that were left after the excisions of the official censors. It was founded in autumn 1977 as the drive toward freedom, which culminated in the Solidarity movement, began to gain momentum. It began printing clandestinely, in basements and cellars, using duplicating machines to print and then distribute the work of those whose writing would never be authorized by the state. A slight relaxation in the power of the party meant that while such publishing would not be condoned, those who carried it on would not automatically be jailed. The founders of NOWA envisaged the development of an absolutely free publishing house, with a regular output of large-circulation publications—books, journals and magazines. But the sheer logistics, notably the strictly regulated paper supply and the need to purchase and then service the duplicating machines, made such hopes illusory. All such necessities—paper, ink, spare parts—had to be bought without attracting undue attention. Private individuals were suspect if they bought such things regularly and in bulk. Many items came from the black market.

NOWA was successful through massive popularity and support. A tradition of underground publishing starting during the Nazi occupation had inured people to obtaining literature in that way. Word of mouth and hand to hand circulation helped spread the titles. Every aspect of publishing and distribution, otherwise quite normal, was very complex. Stocks were kept in clandestine caches, constantly changed for safety. Distribution was by private car, in small quantities. The private lives of NOWA workers and organizers were intermeshed with publishing requirements. The skills of a variety of individuals were used: technicians, mechanics, printers, editors, translators and many more.

O

Obelisk Press, The   SEE Kahane, Jack.

obscene libel   Initiated in Britain in the mid-18th century, the offense of obscene libel formed the statutory basis for the majority of prosecutions for obscenity until the OBSCENE PUBLICATIONS ACT OF 1959. The word libel comes from the Latin *libellus*, meaning little book, and thus an obscene libel involves not speech but "a dirty little book." The concept of what constituted an obscene libel developed through a number of cases in the 18th century. During this time the main direction of censorship veered from the control of sedition, blasphemy and occasionally heresy (itself a concept more familiar to the original censors, the ecclesiastical courts) to control of published obscenity. The shift of responsibility for controlling obscene literature from ecclesiastical to secular jurisdiction took a little time. At the start of the century, in the prosecution of James Read and Angell Carter in 1707 for publishing THE FIFTEEN PLAGUES OF A MAIDENHEAD, the defendants were able to escape judgment by pleading successfully that the court, the Queen's Bench, had no right to try cases of obscene libel. The book, said Mr. Justice Powell, is "bawdy stuff ... [but] there is no law to punish it." In the prosecution of EDMUND CURLL in 1725, in which the defendant was clearly guilty, the judges in the court of King's Bench were unable to agree for three years of wrangling as to whether they were actually qualified to try the case. By mid-century, the offense had been fully recognized and sufficient precedent established to pursue offenders, if not always successfully.

The indictment for obscene libel, prior to revisions under the Indictment Act (1915), ran as follows:

> ... that [Name] being a person of wicked and depraved mind and disposition, and unlawfully and wickedly devising, contriving and intending, to vitiate and corrupt the morals of the liege subjects of our said Lord the King, to debauch and poison the minds of divers of the liege subjects of our said Lord the King, and to raise and create in them lustful desires, and to bring the said liege subjects of ... in the year of our Lord, etc., and within the jurisdiction of the said court, unlawfully, wickedly, maliciously, scandalously, and wilfully did publish, etc., a certain lewd, wicked, bawdy, scandalous and obscene libel, in the form of a book entitled [Name] in which said book are contained among other things divers wicked lewd impure scandalous and obscene libels ... To the manifest corruption of the morals and minds of the liege subjects of our said Lord the King, and his laws, in violation of common decency, morality, and good order, and against the peace of our said Lord the King, his Crown and Dignity.

Subsequent to the 1915 act, the charge became simply one of "publishing an obscene libel."
SEE ALSO Rochester, Earl of; Sedley, Sir Charles; *North Briton, The*.

Obscene Publications Act (1857)   When in May 1857 a bill intended to restrict the sale of poisons came before the House of Lords, Lord Campbell, the lord chief justice, referred in his speech to a particularly lurid pornography trial in which he was sitting and told their lordships of "a sale of poison more deadly than prussic acid, strychnine or arsenic": the pornography trade of London's HOLYWELL STREET. There were in fact two cases: the first was that of William Strange, a shopkeeper sentenced to three months in jail for selling two indecent magazines, *Paul Pry* and *Women of London*; the second was of WILLIAM DUGDALE, London's most notorious pornographer, who had been trapped for the ninth time by an agent provocateur of the SOCIETY FOR THE SUPPRESSION OF VICE and turned over to the police for prosecution. Dugdale, who was sufficiently incensed to brandish a penknife from the dock, was jailed for a year.

London's "dirty book trade" obsessed Lord Campbell, who then proposed in the Lords a new bill to regulate it. The bill created no new offense, and made no attempt to alter the current definition of what was obscene under common law, but concentrated on attacking the sale of obscene books by empowering the authorities to raid suspected stocks of such books and destroy them. Armed with the relevant search warrant, issued on sworn information (often procured through agents provocateurs) that the premises actually held obscene matter, the police could enter such premises and seize the allegedly obscene material. It was then the responsibility of the owner of that material to prove why it should not be destroyed.

The bill met vehement opposition in both houses of Parliament. The prevailing fear was that such a law would lead inevitably to the arbitrary destruction of whatever could be found to offend a conservative magistrate, irrespective of the true worth of such a book or picture. Lord Campbell promised that his bill would "apply exclusively to works written for the single purpose of corrupting the morals of youth and of a nature calculated to shock the common feelings of decency in any well-regulated mind ..." Thus assured, Parliament passed the bill as the Obscene Publications Act of 1857. As feared, the main effect of the act was the creation of a mass of arbitrary censors—the various societies dedicated to the prosecution of vice and the untutored but opinionated local magistrates. Since the magistrate who heard the case was usually the same one who had issued the initial summons, destruction orders were virtually impossible to resist. While supporters of the bill claimed that the Holywell Street pornography trade had been smashed, they were unable to produce material proof of this. Instead, the authorities were able to capitalize on an increasingly prudish public opinion to attack what had hitherto been recognized as classic works.

Obscene Publications Act (1959)   The need to reform the British laws on obscene publications, which dated back to the OBSCENE PUBLICATIONS ACT OF 1857 and Lord Cockburn's test established in *Hicklin* in 1868 (see Hicklin Rule), grew throughout the 1950s. Above all it was necessary to draw a line between serious literature and the product of the pulp pornography factories. While the 1857 act sought to control pornography, its successor was intended to protect art. A committee drawn from the Society of Authors, and chaired by Sir Alan Herbert (himself an MP), submitted its opinions to the home secretary in 1954. Its formation followed directly on the prosecutions of THE PHILANDERER, SEPTEMBER IN QUINZE and three other titles earlier that year. The findings of this committee formed the basis of the first attempt to change the law, a private member's bill, the Obscene Publications Bill, introduced in 1955 by Labour MP Roy Jenkins. This unsuccessful attempt was followed by the Obscene Publications Bill (1957), introduced by Lord Lambton. This did obtain a second reading and was referred to a select committee of the whole House. Due to the chronology of the parliamentary session, there was no time for anything more than a formal report in the 1956-57 session, but when Parliament reopened for 1957-58 the committee was asked "to reconsider whether it was desirable to amend and consolidate the law relating to Obscene Publications."

The committee duly heard much evidence, from all sectors of society, especially those involved in writing, publishing and prosecuting books. It noted a substantial trade in pornography: 167,000 books seized and destroyed in 1954, 22,000 postcards in 1957. When the committee reported to Parliament in October 1958, it was assumed that some reform would be undertaken. Again, nothing developed. Basing his proposals on the report, Roy Jenkins espoused a second private member's bill, the Obscene Publications Bill (1959). When this too was ignored, overall parliamentary pressure was aimed at the government. Sir Alan Herbert threatened to resign and seek reelection as an Independent. Eventually, the government set aside time to debate Jenkins' bill. After a variety of amendments, compromises and delays, the Obscene Publications Act (1959), "an Act to amend the law relating to the publication of obscene matter; to provide for the protection of literature; and to strengthen the law concerning pornography," became law on August 29, 1959.

The act, which has remained in effect in Britain, contains the following provisions and definitions. The old offense of publishing an OBSCENE LIBEL is abolished and the new one of publishing, for gain or otherwise, an obscene article is substituted. The offense may be tried before either a

magistrate (summary prosecution) or a judge (prosecution on indictment) and can be punished by a fine or imprisonment. Summary prosecution must be brought within 12 months, prosecution on indictment in two years. An "article" includes anything that can be read, as well as sound records and films. It originally made no provision on videotapes—since the technology did not yet exist. (This was remedied in 1980.) A person who "publishes" an article is one who distributes, circulates, sells, hires out, gives or lends it, or who offers it for sale or for hire. Publishing covers playing records, exhibiting films and showing artworks that are meant to be viewed by the public.

The act included a new test for obscenity, replacing Hicklin: "An article shall be deemed obscene if its effect or (where the article comprises two or more distinct items) the effect of any one of its items is, if taken as a whole, such as to tend to deprave and corrupt persons who are likely, having regard to all relevant circumstances, to read, see, or hear the matter contained or embodied in it." The word "article" was defined as "any description or article containing or embodying matter to be read or looked at or both, any sound record, any film or other record of a picture or pictures," but there were no exact definitions of the words "deprave" or "corrupt." A year later, during the trial of LADY CHATTERLEY'S LOVER, it was necessary for Mr. Justice Byrne to offer his own remedy for this deficiency, explaining that "to deprave means to make morally bad, to pervert, to debase, or corrupt morally. The words 'to corrupt' mean to render morally unsound, to destroy the moral purity or chastity of, to pervert or ruin a good quality, to debase, to defile ..."

Under a magistrate's warrant, and as specified under section three of the act, the police were allowed to raid and search premises suspected of harboring obscene articles and such articles could be seized. Section four accepted that a defense against conviction would be upheld if "it is proved that the publication of the article in question is justified as being for the public good on the ground that it is in the interests of science, literature, art or learning, or of other objects of general concern." It would be permitted to call expert witnesses into court to help make that defense.

The act was welcomed by those who had advocated reform, but it was clear to lawyers that much of its novelty had already been developed as practical law by enlightened judges and that the act merely gave it a statutory basis. The concept of assessing the whole, rather than a part of the work, the defense of "public good" and the use of expert witnesses had all emerged over the past decade. Certain important topics, notably the role of printers, the Customs and the Post Office, are not mentioned in the law. As the rash of trials that climaxed in the early 1970s proved, the success or failure of the act depended both on the current attitude of the country toward obscenity and whether one accepted that attitude. The power of a judge to impose his own opinion on the evidence seemed undiminished, although juries, often equally unimpressed by the protestations of the experts, seemed more willing than their predecessors to make up their own minds about what really did "tend to deprave or corrupt."

Certain modifications have been made to the 1959 act since its passage. The "public good" defense, which had once been used to persuade juries that obscene literature was actually of psychological benefit to certain individuals, was eroded in 1976 when the House of Lords ruled against this concept, and discarded completely in 1978 when the Court of Appeals stated conclusively that the educational effect of sexually explicit material was no longer admissible as a proof of public good. This judgment also ended the procession of expert witnesses who had featured so largely in the major obscenity cases of the early 1970s. The court ruled that it would no longer be acceptable to use such expertise in the assessment of whether or not an article was in fact obscene. A number of attempts have been made to revise the bill, particularly by the inclusion of television and radio broadcasting as objects of possible control. Mr. Winston Churchill's Obscene Publications Act (Protection of Children) Amendment of 1986 achieved a second reading in the House of Commons, but was abandoned at the committee stage. A private member's bill, sponsored by Mr. Gerald Howarth, passed its second reading in the House of Commons, although a major fight was promised for the third, decisive reading, and in May 1987 it was duly talked into oblivion by a concerted Labour Party effort. Further attempts at wholesale revision may well occur, but in the short run, while the 1959 act may continue to be used as Britain's central obscenity law, the Conservative government has promised, in the white paper on broadcasting of November 1988, to extend it to television in the very near future.

SEE ALSO Obscene Publications Act (1964); Criminal Law Act (1977); *Cain's Book*; *Fanny Hill*; *Inside Linda Lovelace*; *Lady Chatterley's Lover* 2. trials; *Last Exit to Brooklyn*; *Little Red Schoolbook*; *Longford Report*; *Mouth and Oral Sex, The*; *My Secret Life*; *Nasty Tales*; *OZ* trial; Williams Committee.

Obscene Publications Act (1964)   Britain's OBSCENE PUBLICATIONS ACT OF 1959 was found to hold certain loopholes. In addition, the abolition of currency controls, coupled with the fact that the United States had never signed the INTERNATIONAL CONVENTION FOR THE SUPPRESSION OF THE CIRCULATION AND TRAFFIC IN OBSCENE PUBLICATIONS (1923), meant that an ever-increasing amount of American and European pornography was flooding into Britain and seizures were running at millions of articles every year. After a number of cases had been decided by the courts, three new matters were added to the original statute. The first was the creation of the offense of "having an obscene article for publication for gain." This eliminated the problem that had arisen when the courts had determined that, under the 1959 act, the simple exposure of priced articles in a shop was not legally an offer for sale, which was an offense—and thus a number of defendants were able to escape conviction. From now on it was not necessary to prove that the allegedly obscene article had been

sold, merely that its owner was, by possessing it, intending at some stage to sell it. The second was the extension of the definition of the word "article" to include photographic negatives, under a blanket definition that now included anything intended for use in the reproduction of other articles. Finally, the courts were given powers within the act to order the forfeiture of obscene articles, thus eliminating the need for extra forfeiture proceedings.

obscene publications law: U.S. Mail   The first law covering the sending of obscene materials through the U.S. Mail was passed in 1865. Spurred by a variety of complaints about the type of reading material sent to soldiers fighting the U.S. Civil War, the law banned all such material from the mails and threatened offenders with fines of up to $500, 12 months imprisonment or both.

obscenity law   For details on the following international, national and local laws as regard the regulation of obscenity, both contemporary and historical, readers should consult the following entries:
Australia 3. obscenity laws
Belgium 2. obscenity laws
California 2. obscenity statute
Canada 2. censorship
Delaware's obscenity statute
Denmark 4. obscenity laws
Federal Anti-Obscenity Act (1873)
France 7. obscenity laws
Georgia 1. obscenity statute
Georgia 2. possession of obscene material
Germany—Federal Republic 3. obscenity laws
Illinois's obscenity statute
Italy's obscenity laws
Kentucky's obscenity statute
Los Angeles—possession of obscene matter
Massachusetts's obscenity statute
Netherlands 4. obscenity laws
New York 5. obscenity statute
New Zealand 3. obscenity laws
Northern Ireland
Obscene Publications Act (1857)
Obscene Publications Act (1959)
Obscene Publications Act (1964)
Obscene Publications Law: U.S. Mail
Ohio 1. obscene material
Scotland's obscenity laws
Tennessee
United States 15. obscenity laws
United States 17. postal regulations
United States 24. transporting obscene material

Official Secrets Acts (1889, 1911, 1920, 1929)
1. history   Successive British governments have established for themselves on the basis of these three acts, and in par-

ticular the second, a selection of wide-ranging powers, all of which tend to restrict the free flow of communications under the blanket justification of preserving the national security. Among them they have established some 2,324 separate offenses, under any of which the freedoms of unsuspecting citizens can be restrained.

A number of administrations had attemped to suppress a variety of official information throughout the 19th century. In 1837 the Foreign Office failed to halt the publication of a number of Lord Wellesley's 1809 dispatches; in 1847 the *Times* successfully fended off attempts to restrain its publication of Castlereagh's correspondence during the 1815 Congress of Vienna, pleading "the rights of the public." The inception of the 1889 act came through an escalation of leaks, all fed to the press. These involved a number of topics, many of which referred to information that was due anyway to be released in public, and notably to two cases, those of William Hudson Guernsey and Charles Marvin. Guernsey, who held a grudge against the colonial Office, where he had failed to obtain a job, had obtained and published some details of negotiations with Greece; Marvin, a free-lance journalist and Foreign Office clerk, revealed details of a secret Anglo-Russian agreement and received £42 from the *Globe* newspaper. Both were acquitted: There was no law governing the theft of information.

The flood of leaks proved too embarrassing to the government, and work was begun on the "Breach of Official Trust Bill," a title that demonstrated that while the content of the information might be slight, the breach of trust was considered much greater. With the addition of a clause dealing with foreign spies, and a revised title, the Official Secrets Act became law in 1889. The main drawback of this act was that it still failed to deal adequately with the problem of spies. Attempts to amend the act, in particular to include the receiver of the information in its provisions were made but abandoned in 1896 and 1908. The growing spy fever of 1910 and the trial of a German agent in 1911 helped the government pass the 1911 version of the act. It is this act, with its modifications in 1920 and 1939, that survives today.

As was always made clear, "An Act to re-enact the Official Secrets Act 1889 with Amendments" had been created against the background of the growing militarism and war propaganda of the era, and its essential purpose was to facilitate the entrapment of spies. As the Attorney-General Sir Gordon Hewart put it in 1920, "It is aimed at spying, the acts of spies and their accomplices and assistants." The most important changes were in placing the onus of proof on the defendant, who had to prove his innocence, and in section 2, the "catch-all" clause intended to staunch once and for all every type of civil service leak. The acts are uniformly wide-ranging. Under section 1 of the 1911 version it was a criminal offense to be in a prohibited place for a purpose prejudicial to the interests of the state security. For those prosecuted under this section, the onus is on proving one's innocence; the prosecution has no responsibility to prove

one's guilt. In addition, the prosecution can bring forward one's past character and activities as evidence in the current case. The accused may be denied the chance to argue that he or she was acting in the interests of the state or to show that the government is in error as to what those interests really are.

In 1920 the Coalition Government, fearing civil war in Ireland and facing a mounting campaign of IRA terrorism, determined to strengthen the 1911 law by passing the Official Secrets Act (1920). Its most notable provision was the introduction of a new offense: It was now a felony to do any act preparatory to the commission of a felony under the Official Secrets Act.

The acts apply to a diverse selection of individuals; among the ranks of those for whom it is a criminal offense either to pass on restricted information or, if such information has been obtained illegally, to keep records of it for oneself, are: (a) persons given information in confidence by holders of offices under the Crown, i.e., ministers, civil servants, judges, policemen; (b) persons who themselves hold office under the Crown; (c) persons who on contravention of the act have obtained any information; (d) persons who have contracts with the Crown (including those who supply stationery to government departments); (e) persons employed by those who hold office under the Crown; (f) persons employed by those who have contracts with government departments.

Section 2(2) makes it an offense to receive any information if one knows or should have known that communicating it is a violation of official secrecy. The sole defense is that the information was communicated "contrary to his desire." Material with no relevance to national security could nonetheless be suppressed under 2(2). To restrict the circulation of government papers even further, and ensure that the embarrassing as well as the genuinely secret were kept out of the public domain, section 1(2) of the 1920 act makes it illegal for someone given an official document not to hand it back to authorities.

In the eyes of critics the acts have been far from satisfactory ever since that of 1911 was pushed through Parliament in less than 24 hours from its introduction to its becoming law, with no debate whatsoever on the consistently controversial section 2. The acts, especially the notorious section 2(2), have become increasingly unpopular. A series of attempts at reform, notably the Franks Report of 1972, which found it "a mess" and proposed its replacement by an "Official Information Act," have failed to move successive governments. Juries have become increasingly intolerant of prosecutions brought under the acts; the acquittal, in 1985, of civil servant CLIVE PONTING (who leaked secret information prejudicial to the government's record in the Falklands War), underlined this new independence.

In January 1988 Richard Shepherd, a Conservative member of Parliament, attempted to promote his own reform of the acts as a private member's bill. The government did not wish to allow the alteration of so important a law to be left to a private member and ensured that Shepherd's bill was voted down—the first occasion on which the mandatory "three-line whip" had ever been used by a government against a measure proposed by one of its own back-benchers. Instead, in June, Home Secretary Douglas Hurd introduced his own reforms in the white paper, "Reform of Section 2 of the Official Secrets Act 1911." Although the government promoted the reforms as sorting out the complex and unsatisfactory act, criticis united in condemning what they saw as an even less liberal secrets law.

The heart of Hurd's proposal, which was scheduled to pass into law during 1989, is to "narrow the scope" of section 2 by limiting and clearly defining the circumstances in which the unauthorized disclosure of information is actually criminal. As well as expanding the ranks of those forbidden to disclose any information about their work—notably, in the wake of the Spycatcher case (see Peter Wright), all present and past members of the secret services—the white paper no longer accepts a defense of public interest regarding those who leak government or similarly actionable documents, nor will the fact that the information has already been published inside or outside the U.K. be permitted. Juries will need decide no more than whether a disclosure was made; if so, the defendent is guilty and reasons such as morality (as protested by SARAH TISDALL) will not be accepted. Proposed penalties under the revised law would be two years imprisonment or a fine or both if the case is tried by a judge; a maximum of six months imprisonment or a £2,000 fine or both if tried by a magistrate. SEE ALSO ABC Trial; *Crossman Diaries*; D Notices; IBA: broadcasting censorship; United Kingdom 3. Law of Confidence.

2. provisions

Penalties for spying: Section 1   This section is generally used against foreign spies. It is an offense:

> If any person for any purpose prejudicial to the safety or interests of the State
> (a) approaches, inspects, passes over or is in the neighbourhood of, or enters any prohibited place within the meaning of this Act; or
> (b) makes any sketch, plan, model or note which is calculated to be or is intended to be directly or indirectly useful to an enemy; or
> (c) obtains, collects, records or publishes, or communicates to any other person any secret official code word, or password, or any sketch, plan, model, article, or note, or other document or information which is calculated to be or might be or is intended to be directly or indirectly useful to the enemy.

Communicating official information: Section 2(1)   This section is aimed at suppressing leaks from within government offices. It is an offense if any person

> having in his possession or control any secret official code word, or password, or any sketch, plan, model, article, note, document or information which relates to or is used in a prohibited place or anything in such a place, or which has

been made or obtained in contravention of the Act, or which has been entrusted in confidence to him by any person holding office under His Majesty or which he has obtained or to which he had access owing to his position as a person who holds office under His Majesty, or as a person who holds or has held a contract on behalf of His Majesty, or as a person who is or has been employed under a person who holds or has held such an office or contract
(a) communicates the code word, password, sketch, plan, model, article, note, document or information to a person other than a person to whom he is authorised to communicate it or a person to whom it is in the interests of the state his duty to communicate it.

Receipt of official information: Section 2(2)   This section is aimed at journalists and is the basis for such trials as the ABC TRIAL of 1976. It is an offense for anyone who "receives any secret official code word, or password, or sketch, plan, mode, article, note, document or information, knowing or having reasonable ground to believe at the time when he receives it, that the codeword, password, sketch, plan, model, article, note, document or information is communicated to him in contravention of his Act … unless he proves that the communication … was contrary to his desire."

SEE ALSO Ponting, Clive; Tisdall, Sarah.

Ohio

1. obscene material   Under section 2905.34 of the Ohio Revised Code (1963), which deals with "Selling, Exhibiting, and Possessing Obscene Literature or Drugs, for Criminal Purposes," it was provided that

> No person shall knowingly sell, lend, give away, exhibit, or offer to sell, lend, give away, or exhibit, or publish or offer to publish or have in his possession or under his control an obscene, lewd, or lascivious book, magazine, pamphlet, paper, writing, advertisement, circular, print, picture, photography, motion picture film, or book, pamphlet, paper, magazine not wholly obscene but containing lewd or lascivious articles, advertisements, photographs or drawing, representation, figure, image, cast, instrument, or article of an indecent or immoral nature, or drug, medicine, article or thing intended for the prevention of conception or for causing an abortion, or advertise any of them for sale, or write, print, or cause to be written or printed a card, book, pamphlet, advertisement or notice giving information when, where, how, or of whom, or by what means any of such articles or things can be purchased or obtained, or manufacture, draw, print, or make such articles or things, or sell, give away, or show to a minor, a book, pamphlet, magazine, newspaper, story paper, or other paper devoted to the publication or principally made up, of criminal news, police reports, or accounts of criminal deeds, lust, or crime, or exhibit upon a street or highway or in a place which may be within the view of a minor, any of such books, papers, magazines or pictures. Whoever violates this section shall be fined not less than two hundred and not more than two thousand dollars, or imprisoned not less than one nor more than seven years, or both.

SEE ALSO *Jacobellis* v. *Ohio* (1964); *Les Amants*.

2. motion picture censorship   The state of Ohio was the first local authority to establish film censorship in America. On April 16, 1913, the Ohio General Assembly passed a law to establish the prior censorship of all films intended for exhibition in the state. The act created a Board of Censors, which was to examine all such films and either license them for exhibition or ban them from the state's theaters. Under section four of the act certain guidelines were laid down: "only such films as are in the judgment and discretion of the board of censors of moral, educational or amusing and harmless character shall be passed and approved ..." Section five allowed the Ohio board to work in conjunction with similar bodies that might be set up in other states and to form a "censor congress." The constitutionality of the board was tested and found satisfactory in the case of MUTUAL FILM CORPORATION V. INDUSTRIAL COMMISSION OF OHIO (1915).

Okeford, James   SEE book burning in England 4. Puritans.

Olympia   Edouard Manet's painting of *Olympia*, a reclining nude, was accepted by the Salon des Refuses in Paris in May 1865. Faced by a substantial critical and public onslaught, the gallery was forced to hire two policemen whose duty was to protect the painting at all times from visitors who wished to destroy it, brandishing knives, canes or other weapons. Halfway through the exhibition, the painting, which had hitherto occupied the position of honor, was rehung far above a high doorway, in an utterly undistinguished location but one that was at least safe from assault. Among the barrage of criticisms, *Olympia* was condemned as "a stripped fowl," "a yellow-bellied odalisque," "a parcel of filth" and "a tinted tart." The writer Edmond About called for the gallery to be fumigated, to dispel the rank corruption that was Manet's work.

Olympia Press, The   The Olympia Press was founded in Paris in 1953 by MAURICE GIRODIAS as a replacement for the OBELISK PRESS, created by his father, JACK KAHANE. Under a system of what he called "individualistic anarchy" Girodias offered two levels of publishing. On the one hand he continued his father's tradition of backing the new and the experimental, however such work might shock the authorities. Thus Girodias published Vladimir Nabokov's *Lolita*, J.P. Donleavy's *The Ginger Man*, William Burroughs' THE NAKED LUNCH, "Pauline Reage's" *Story of O*, AUBREY BEARDSLEY's *Under the Hill* and many other titles. Alongside these came what he called unashamedly the "DBs"—dirty books, written quickly for a 5,000-copy print run and equally quickly purchased. They included *White Thighs*, *With Open Mouth*, and *Whips Incorporated*; many were written by otherwise reputable, if young, authors, under a variety of pseudonyms.

Among those employed were the British poet Christopher Logue ("Count Palmiro Vicarion") and the author Alex Trocchi ("Frances Lengel"), whose autobiography, *Young Adam*, was issued in 1955 and who created the near-perfect pastiche, "The Fifth Volume" of MY LIFE AND LOVES by FRANK HARRIS (first published by the Obelisk Press). PAUL ABLEMAN also wrote DBs as did Terry Southern, as "Maxwell Kenton." Among Southern's efforts was *Candy*, written with Mason Hoffenberg. Unlike most DBs, this was considered too bookish and insufficiently dirty. It attracted a cult following but despite subsequent notoriety, was not at first an Olympia success.

The Olympia Press, with its green-jacketed "Travellers' Library" editions, thrived in postwar Paris, but when General de Gaulle became president in 1958 it proved a severe blow to the liberal consensus that had sustained Girodias. By 1960 his publications had been subjected to heavy conservative attack. In 1965 he closed down the office and moved to New York. He also attempted to set up in London in 1971, but neither venture was really successful. The climate that had encouraged the growth of the Olympia Press, had sustained it and given it its particular character, had vanished.

One for the Road   This poster by British artist Lynes was created in 1953 as part of a series designed to encourage safer driving by the Royal Society for the Prevention of Accidents (RoSPA). It featured a driver whose face was part normal flesh and part leering skull—a deliberate shock tactic aimed at countering the continual drift toward higher accident statistics. This proved too gruesome to many British local government authorities, and they refused to exhibit it. This poster, along with others similarly disturbing to the public, ranks among the most frequently censored images of the 1940s and 1950s.

One Hundred and Twenty Days of Sodom   The original manuscript of *Les Cent Vingt Journees de Sodome* was written by the Marquis de SADE between 1785 and 1789, during his incarceration in the Bastille. Penned in microscopic writing on a scroll of packing paper 12 centimeters wide and 12 meters long, the manuscript vanished, with much more of his writing, when the Bastille was stormed in July 1789. This book, a declaration of war on the society that saw it necessary to imprison him, had been intended to "outrage the laws of both nature and religion." De Sade wept "tears of blood" at its loss, and all his subsequent writing can be seen as an attempt to compensate for its disappearance. Although its author would never find out, the scroll had not been lost and was discovered in his old cell by one Arnoux de Saint-Maximin. From him it passed to the Villeneuve-Trans family, and thence, around 1900, to a German collector. The full text was published in Germany in 1904. It was laden with an excess of learned notes by the German psychiatrist Iwan Bloch, who wrote under the pseudonym "Eugene Duhren." Bloch justified his publication for its scientific importance and the fact that Sade found "amazing analogies" between the activities of his voluptuaries and the subjects of the later researches by such as Krafft-Ebing. The Sadeian scholar Maurice Heine published an authoritative edition in Berlin between 1931 and 1935. Since 1945 the book has been included in Jean-Jacques Pauvert's "Collected Edition." The first translation into English was published in 1966 in America by the Grove Press. A British reprint of this edition, with its introduction by the late Simone de Beauvoir, finally appeared in England in fall 1989.

The 120 Days of Sodom remains as its author intended, one of "the most impure tale(s) that has ever been told since the world began." It is a systematic catalog of sexual perversity, parodying the format of Boccaccio's DECAMERON, the scrupulous filing and delineation of which would have impressed de Sade's contemporaries, the Encyclopedists. It offers neither eroticism nor titillation to the average sexual palate but in its breadth of fantasy amazes rather than excites. Some 600 varieties of sexual experience are described, all of which, de Sade emphasized, were drawn strictly from the life and which are designed to illustrate his aphorism "Pleasure is proportional to the irregularity it occasions." They are divided into four parts, written as diary entries, which separate the excesses into simple, double (or complex), criminal and murderous. It is possible, however, that the original manuscript was not wholly preserved. As the endless copulations proceed, it is notable that the lavish detail of the earlier chapters becomes increasingly abbreviated with the later perversions more like shorthand descriptions of potential pleasures, listing in note form simply the participants required and the activities they should indulge, rather than giving full-blooded literary descriptions.

One Hundred Years Rule As in the THIRTY YEARS RULE, which controls the releasing of some public records, certain specified categories of information emerging from the conduct of British government are prohibited from public inspection for 100 years. The categories involved are: material that might cause distress to living individuals, their families or descendants (e.g., criminal or prison records); material that contains information received under a pledge of confidence (e.g., the census); certain papers relating to Irish affairs; any papers that can be seen as affecting national security; any material, the ownership of which is shared with "old" Commonwealth countries (Australia, Canada and New Zealand) and which cannot be released until all the governments involved have agreed.

Onze Milles Verges, Les SEE Apollinaire, Guillaume.

Oratory of Divine Love, The Developing between 1545 and 1563 under the auspices of the Council of Trent, the oratory represented a group of concerned members of the Catholic Church, shocked by the comparative worldliness of Pope Leo X and working toward the purification of the church from within. Their most conspicuous works were the creation of the INDEX LIBRORUM PROHIBITORUM, and the ROMAN and SPANISH INQUISITIONS.

Outlaw, The *The Outlaw*, an unexceptional film based on the adventures of Billy the Kid, was initially directed in 1940 by Howard Hawks. It starred Jack Buetel as Billy, Walter Huston as Doc Holliday and Jane Russell as Rio, Holliday's girl and, after a rape scene tempered only by the Kid's concern for her dress, Billy's girl too. Gregg Toland shot the film, and Jules Furthman wrote the script. The film was produced by Howard Hughes, who both tinkered with the script and determined on projecting Miss Russell's charms, notably her ample breasts, across the nation's screens; he finally fired Hawks and took over direction personally. The essence of Hughes' work was the unashamed exploitation of Russell's body. He concocted a cantilevered brassiere that maximized her cleavage but cut down on natural bodily movement; Toland's camera roved constantly over the actress' curves; a team of 20 still photographers were constantly compiling lurid publicity shots.

In December 1940 JOSEPH BREEN, administrator of the Production Code and thus Hollywood's censor, wrote to Hughes requesting a script. After reading it he suggested 23 cuts or changes. Hughes ignored Breen's suggestions. Both men appealed to Breen's superior, WILL HAYS. Hays arranged a compromise: Certain lines were altered, one cut, and Russell's breasts were covered in a bedroom scene. *The Outlaw* was given an MPPDA seal on May 23, 1941. The film opened in a single theater in San Francisco on February 5, 1943. To accompany the picture Hughes had designed an advertising campaign that more than made up for any earlier compromises. Huge posters of Russell adorned local billboards, asking "What are the two great reasons for Jane Russell's rise to stardom." Infuriated, the MPPDA revoked its seal, an unprecedented move, because Hughes had failed to have his publicity campaign approved.

Hughes counterattacked with an antitrust suit, claiming that the association had acted in restraint of trade. He stated quite simply that for all its voluntary basis, Hollywood's censorship was illegal. Hughes' motion was denied in June 1946 when Judge D.J. Bright stated that "the industry can suffer as much from indecent advertising as from indecent pictures." Hughes remained defiant, despite a near-fatal airplane crash in July 1946. He continued to show *The Outlaw*, now stripped of the seal that many theaters demanded before they would exhibit a film. These showings were increasingly curtailed not by individual theater managers, but by state and local boards of censors, who one after another banned the film. As a Baltimore judge stated, Russell's breasts "hung over the picture like a thunderstorm spread out over a landscape." But the dialogue between Doc and Billy proved equally contentious. Maryland, New York, Ohio and New Jersey all banned the film, as did many other major cities. It was equally vilified in Canada and Britain, although where it was shown, as in Los Angeles, theaters were packed out and the usual second feature was abandoned.

The controversy ended in 1949, when Hughes acceded to every demand. All the cuts and changes were made and the MPAA restored its seal. The LEGION OF DECENCY revised its "Condemned" rating to one of "B: morally objectionable in part for all." The censorship system remained intact, although some critics believe that Hughes and his film were substantially responsible for taking the first real steps to undermine its power.

SEE ALSO Motion Picture Production Code.

outrage aux bonnes moeurs   SEE France 4. freedom of the press; France 7. obscenity laws.

overbreadth   The concept of "overbreadth" has been developed by the U.S. Supreme Court to describe statutes or ordinances that may encompass in their general prohibitions certain actions or words that are in fact protected by the Constitution. As stated in *Thornhill* v. *Alabama* (1940), a law becomes void if "it does not aim specifically at evils within the allowable area of [government] control but ... sweeps within its ambit other activities that constitute an exercise of protected expressive or associational rights." Overbreadth is only applicable as regards those freedoms guaranteed in the Bill of Rights, and thus covers such areas as abusive language, annoying conduct, breach of the peace, distribution of literature, licensing, loyalty oaths, military laws, obscenity, picketing, prison regulations and public employment.

Ovid   Publius Ovidius Naso (43 B.C.-A.D. 18) was the author of both *Amores* (*Elegies*) and *Ars Amatoria* (*The Art of Love*) as well as a number of other historical, chronological and nostalgic works. As such he was one of Rome's most popular poets, his reputation surviving his exile by the Emperor Augustus in A.D. 8, the result of some unknown act of folly, coupled possibly with the risque content of the *Ars Amatoria*. Once the Emperor Constantine had converted to Christianity in 324, Ovid fell out of favor with the earnest new religion. His works vanished for 600 years, and even then would emerge only to be condemned. Ovid's verses were among the many books burned in 1497 by SAVONAROLA; they were proscribed in the TRIDENTINE INDEX of 1564, and in England in 1599 a translation by the poet Christopher Marlowe was burned at Stationer's Hall on the orders of the archbishop of Canterbury, on account of its immorality. In America the *Ars Amatoria* was still banned by the U.S. Customs as recently as 1928, and while home-produced copies were usually available, the city of San Francisco banned the book unilaterally in 1929, although the ban faded in a more permissive era.

OZ trial (*R.* v. *Anderson*)   *OZ* magazine, the title punning on the slang name for Australia, where it originated as a student publication in 1963, and on L. Frank Baum's fantasy land, so beloved of the hippie community, was first published in England in early 1967. Although the first issue featured established left-wing writers Paul Johnson, Colin MacInnes and a pastiche of the satirical magazine *Private Eye*, it soon graduated into the further reaches of psychedelia, advancing its editor Ricahrd Neville's credo that "the weapons of revolution are obscenity, blasphemy and drugs." Pornography was touted as a viable political weapon and if the more traditionally political members of the counter-culture decried its hedonism, *OZ* rivaled IT as Britain's most creative, exciting and popular alternative publication.

By 1970 *OZ* was devoting successive issues (these appeared sporadically, with undated covers) to various hip topics: the women's movement, gay power, LSD and flying saucers. *OZ* 28 was devoted to school children, whose participation in editing their own issue had been invited in an advertisement in *OZ* 26. Some two dozen applicants put together the issue, writing articles and creating the illustrations themselves. The cover, which featured a "camp-porn lesbian orgy" all tinted in blue, and such regular columns as the Personal Advertisements, were the responsibility of the adult staff. These classifieds often featured soft-core material and as such were far more explicit than the gay contact ads for which *OZ*'s fellow underground paper *IT* had been successfully prosecuted. Following two police raids in which vast quantities of material were seized from the *OZ* offices, the director of public prosecutions charged the *OZ* directors—Richard Neville, Jim Anderson and Felix Dennis—with publishing and possessing for gain an obscene publication as proscribed under the OBSCENE PUBLICATIONS ACT (1959) and with sending an indecent article through the mails, under the Post Office Act (1953). *OZ*'s publishing company was similarly indicted.

England's longest obscenity trial lasted nearly six weeks and cost some £100,000. The director of public prosecutions was represented by Brian Leary, QC: Anderson, Dennis and the company by John Mortimer, Britain's leading obscene publications defender. Neville defended himself. The defense argued that the issues at stake were not simply dirty magazines but liberty and freedom of speech. Mortimer linked the defendants' denunciations of the Establishment to the sermons of John Wesley. Neville reiterated, with commendable articulacy, the classic alternative position of revolutionary hedonism as stated in his book *Play Power* (1970). *OZ* was backed by what Mrs. WHITEHOUSE denounced as "Mortimer's Circus," a substantial array of expert witnesses who, as in the *Lady Chatterley's Lover* trial of 1960, were forced into somewhat tortuous convolutions in their attempt to justify the literary or artistic excellence of some of the schoolchildren's more exuberantly lavatorial contributions, especially as regarded certain illustrations. The content of the classifieds also helped the prosecution. The *OZ* trial created the "aversion theory": the defense that certain material, which was indeed "grossly lewd and unpleasant," would, far from encouraging its consumers toward perversion, actively repel them from it. This defense was subsequently used in a number of other obscenity trials.

All three defendants were found guilty, as was the company. During a weekend spent in prison awaiting sentence, their lengthy hippie locks were cropped to the regulation length, delighting the tabloid press but engendering a good deal of sympathy amongst the public. Neville was sentenced to 15 months in jail (followed by deportation), Anderson to one year and Dennis to nine months. The judge, Michael Argyll, was burned in effigy outside the Old Bailey, as the police fought 400 demonstrators. The pro- and anti-censorship lobbies took their traditional stances. Bail, pending appeal, was granted five days later, and the presiding judges made it clear that they too saw the sentences as excessively harsh, although the defendants were prohibited from any contact with their magazine.

When the appeal was heard, in November 1971, Mortimer convinced the court that Judge Argyll had misdirected the jury. The sentences of obscenity were all quashed, and that under the Post Office Act suspended. Judge Widgery, in summing up, stressed that obscenity, rather than titillating, might have an aversive, or "emetic," effect; he also suggested that the traditional ranks of expert witnesses were of little real use. For a brief period *OZ* flourished. Back copies of any issue were grabbed; previously unsold *OZ* 28s fetched £10 each in Soho sex shops, whose proprietors sent round vans to pick up the bundles for cash. In June 1973 *OZ* finally closed down. Neville had long since retired to television in Australia, Anderson to California. Dennis became a millionaire through his new company, which published martial arts and computer magazines.

SEE ALSO *Lady Chatterley's Lover* 2. trials.

P

P. and C. Letters   SEE D Notices.

Paine, Thomas   Paine (1737-1809), the son of a Quaker staymaker of Thetford in Suffolk, was working as a customs officer, the latest of various jobs, when in 1774 he was dismissed for demanding a pay increase. Taking the advice of his friend Benjamin Franklin, he moved that year to America, where he wrote his pamphlets "Common Sense" (1776) and "The Crisis" (a series, 1776-83), all of which backed the American struggle for independence. Further writing promoted the emancipation of women and the liberation of slaves. In 1787 Paine returned to England, via France, and published in 1791-92 the two parts of THE RIGHTS OF MAN, a radical answer to Edmund Burke's *Reflections on the Revolution in France* and *Appeal from the New to the Old Whigs*. Alerted by the artist William Blake against his imminent arrest for sedition, Paine fled back to France where he was well received and elected a member of the Convention. Here he narrowly escaped the guillotine (for his opposition to the execution of Louis XVI) and was jailed for a year. In 1793 he wrote *The Age of Reason*, which attacked Christianity and the Bible from the Deist standpoint, accepting a God on the grounds of reason rather than as proposed by religious credo. This rendered him even more unpopular to the English authorities and both his own effigy and copies of his works were regularly burned, paralleling more intellectual attacks, notably those of Richard Watson, bishop of Llandaff (1737-1816), in his *Apology for the Bible* (1796). Paine returned to America in 1802, but his opposition to the late President George Washington and his own views on religion undermined his former popularity. He died at his farm in New Rochelle, New York, in 1809, after several years of declining health. William Cobbett, a former opponent but likewise a radical, brought his bones back to England. Plans for a memorial were abandoned when the remains were lost, but Paine's status as an intellectual role model for generations of 19th-century radicals proved a more pertinent legacy.

Pakistan

1. general censorship   Under the military government of Pakistan, established in 1977, the control of freedom of expression operated in a variety of ways, all dedicated to creating a nation obedient to the theocratically fundamentalist "Nizam-i-Mustafa" (the system of Muhammad). Between the army itself, which is responsible for maintaining law and order and suppressing any possible uprising, and the hard-right theologians of the Jamaat-i-Islami, who have established stringent controls on all forms of culture, the country is strictly regulated. Although there is a large measure of underground publishing, clandestine distribution of video and musical cassettes and a variety of other attempts to defeat or bypass the censorship, the controls are remarkably successful.

The chief methods of control are as follows: (1) martial law: The provisions of martial law cover all aspects of national life and may be amended and increased as the authorities desire. Under them it is illegal to spread hatred between provinces or classes, excite dissaffection toward the army, spread despondency, express any opinions prejudicial to the state or its ideology, indulge in oppositional political activities and much more. All such transgressions are punishable by imprisonment, whipping or both. Suspects are presumed guilty until they can prove themselves otherwise; defense lawyers are not permitted, and there is no appeal to any higher court. (2) Islamic courts: These courts operate under the Sharia laws of Islam, based on interpretations of the Quran. These laws regulate every aspect of cultural and social life. Many leading opposition figures were successfully silenced and/or driven into exile. The blanket accusation of "undermining the ideology of Pakistan" is leveled at many, who may be severely punished for such activities. The main targets of the attack are nationalists, intellectuals, trade unionists and spokesmen for Pakistan's national minorities: All are condemned as foreign agents and subversives. (3) On the basis of "vulgarity" any publication critical of the government may be banned, and films, television programs and theatrical productions halted. Such censorship even extends to sport—and cricket and hockey have been condemned as anti-Islamic.

2. press censorship   The censorship of the press in Pakistan has remained governed by similar laws throughout the state's existence. The regulations enforced under the late President Zia-ul-Haq were inherited from and are much the same as those used by his predecessors. The press is controlled in four ways: the ownership of the newspapers, economic pressures, legal restraints used against printers and publishers and the arrest of the journalists themselves. Those journalists who protest the situation may face harsh penalties, notably under Martial Law Regulation 33, which prevents political activity and threatens up to seven years imprisonment and/or 20 lashes.

Most of the country's major newspapers are state-owned. One organization, the National Press Trust, is government-controlled and in turn owns and operates a number of national and regional papers, including two of the three English-language newspapers. A second organization, the People's Foundation Trust, was formerly owned by the family of the previous prime minister, Mr. Bhutto. This trust, which owns, among other papers, the largest circulation Urdu-language paper in Pakistan, was taken over by the state when martial rule began in July 1977. Economic pressure is exercized by the control of newsprint supplies and by the direction of advertising to papers favorable to the authorities.

Newsprint supplies are strictly regulated. Many major advertisers such as the banks and national airline are state-owned, and their accounts can be withdrawn when the state desires.

The main legal restraint on the press is the Press and Publication Ordinance, published by President Ayub Khan in 1963. This replaced a similar law of 1960, and in its turn was revised by the late Prime Minister Bhutto in 1975 and 1976. The real differences in such restraints today are the targets against which they are aimed—each regime simply reverses the ordinances of its predecessor. Under the ordinance all newspapers and journals are licensed. To obtain such a licence, printers and publishers must make a declaration promising that they will not publish any material contrary to the state's interest or critical of its policies. Unless they sign this document, they may not print or publish. All these documents must be counter-signed by a magistrate, and thus, simply by refusing this signature, the authorities can control any printer who, although otherwise obeying the law, is still considered a threat to the state. Everyone owning a press must deposit a financial security of up to 30,000 rupees ($2,500) with the government, and risks losing the press and the security if he defaults on the rules.

Under section 24 of the Ordinance, some 14 categories of offense under which this may happen are specified. These include causing public alarm and despondency, publishing stories on sex or violence or publishing anything that can be construed as seditious. On occasion these offenses may be made retroactive, and a paper may be prosecuted for its back issues. In certain cases the government can demand repeated securities. The imposition of excessive securities is a useful way of suppressing publications that it would be impolitic to ban outright. The ordinance is immune to challenge or question under the law. There are no definitions of what constitutes "objectionable material." A further law, section 99A of the Criminal Procedure Code (1898) (as amended) empowers the provincial government to shut down publications that are seen as promoting national discontent or setting one ethnic or social group against another. This law can be challenged in the courts.

In October 1979 after a transitional period since 1977 a variety of additional press curbs appeared, as part of the imposition of martial law and embodied in Martial Law Regulation 49. In effect these granted the president absolute control of the media. There was no appeal against the rulings of the military. An amendment of section 499 of the Penal Code has made libel an offense that may be tried in the criminal courts. Sedition is similarly cognizable. The Official Secrets Act is available as a backup measure. The Islamization of the country has also created a variety of rules, based in religious orthodoxy. A strict code of ethics governs radio and TV, with nudity, obscenity and vulgarity, rarely a major ingredient anyway, now strictly banned. Dancing and advertisements showing women smoking or riding motorbikes were removed, as were vulgar songs and folk music. Women announcers must appear with a dupate, a scarf covering their hair. Religious material has been introduced to the programming.

3. censorship of education The suspension of the rights of freedom of expression in Pakistan, most directly affecting the national media, similarly altered the role of education in the country under the military rule that existed from July 1977 until 1989. The basic tenet of the late General Zia's rule was the Islamicization of Pakistani life, including radical changes throughout the country's 20 universities and 600 colleges. Backed by official and unofficial organizations and laws, the government systematically set about destroying intellectual freedom in its institutions of higher learning. The major task of the Education Department was the wholesale revision of the syllabi of higher education and of the textbooks employed within it. By 1985 the department reported revision of some 550 textbooks, including subjects ranging from Robert Browning and D.H. LAWRENCE to Charles Darwin and similarly "atheistic" versions of history.

The military government set out to gain control of the formerly autonomous universities and colleges, purging both faculty and student body of socialists and secularists. Any administrators seen as supporters of the Pakistan People's Party (PPP), supporters of the late Mr. Bhutto and of his daughter Benazir (now in power), were removed from office. The government has wide powers of hiring and of dismissal within higher education, and all governing bodies are dominated by government supporters. A further check on subversion is the government's control of the transfer of teachers: Despite protests by teaching organizations, the authorities may move any teacher from one institution to another, thus breaking up any attempts to create an opposition cell. Such transfers are invariably demotions. Teachers must also face the annual confidential reports, gradings of their academic performance and ideological standing, which may be assessed by the government and used to promote or demote them. Teachers are also disciplined, often by actual physical violence or intimidation, by the fundamentalist Jamiat-i-Tulaba (IJT), the highly organized and armed student wing of the Jamaat-i-Islami religious party. The IJT is responsible for the compilation of lists of alleged undesirables, which form the basis of governmental dismissals, transfers and other punishments. It also offers suggestions on new appointments.

Palmer, A. Mitchell SEE House Special Committee on Un-American Activities.

pandering The concept of pandering is not included in any of the current legal standards—ROTH, MEMOIRS and MILLER—used to test for obscenity in American courts, but if proved it may be sufficient to tip the legal scales toward conviction when a case cannot be decided easily by the normal methods. In obscenity cases pandering is defined as "purveying textual or graphic matter ... to appeal to the erotic interest of ... customers." Some justices have accepted the role of pandering in such cases, but others feel that by condemning what is in effect the tone of advertising material, the prosecution is in fact threatening FIRST AMENDMENT guarantees.

SEE ALSO *Ginsburg* v. *United States* (1966).

Paraeus, David   SEE book burning in England 2. James I (1603-25).

Paraguay   The press in Paraguay, which was ruled from 1954 to 1989 by right-wing military dictator General Alfredo Stroessner, is ostensibly free, as guaranteed by article 73 of the state constitution of 1967. However each guarantee of freedom is balanced by a number of provisos, all of which ensure that the government maintains near-absolute control. Given that the country has remained almost permanently in a "state of siege," giving the government further wide-ranging powers, nothing subversive is permitted publication. No author may attack the regime and its principles, although minor criticism of government policies does pass unpunished. Prosecutions for criminal libel, which may be brought by government officials, acting as private citizens under article 126 of the Code of Criminal Procedure, and serve as blanket protection against journalistic comments, are also used to control the press. Some officials may never be criticized by name.

Radio and television are similarly restricted. Both TV channels are government-owned and permit no airing of opposition views, even during elections. Investigative journalism is minimal: Its exemplar, the magazine *ABC Color*, was banned indefinitely in 1984. The independent radio station, Radio Nanduti, after suffering years of attacks, was finally closed down in April 1986.

The relatively low profile maintained by Paraguay as a source of international news stories stems from the government's control of even the foreign news agencies working in its territory. All such agencies must be headed and staffed by native Paraguayans. Either such staff are directly paid by the government or they choose to exercise a high degree of self-censorship. Visiting foreign reporters suffer strict direct censorship, notably in the suppression of unfavorable stories by the state telecommunications center, Antelco, whose censors simply refuse to transmit them. Thus even stories that appear widely in the Paraguayan press need never appear outside the country.

Two major laws implement government policy. Law 294 (1950) restricts freedom of belief, opinion and expression, as well as outlawing the Communist Party. Supporting communist ideology is a criminal offense. Any school, college or university that employs party members may be shut down;

colleagues, under pain of imprisonment, are obliged to inform against such subversives. Law 209 (1970) is central to state power. Anyone who "publicly preaches hatred among Paraguayans, or the destruction of social classes" faces up to six years in prison. The law results in extensive journalistic self-censorship.

In April 1987, when the government chose not to extend the state of siege, a number of new media laws were proposed. Ostensibly liberal, critics believe that they are unlikely to improve matters. The Right to Reply law includes not merely "the weak" but also public figures amongst those who can challenge press coverage. Given the power of the government, this will mean a further check on media criticism. Even mentioning a government department could bring down an avalanche of mail, all of which would have to be given space. A new Penal Code has been prepared, amongst the provisions of which is a ban on using the press to disseminate politically "slanderous imputations" to attack the authorities, especially the police and the military. Such critics face up to eight years jail.

Parents' Alliance to Protect Our Children   The alliance was founded in 1979 and characterizes itself as a pro-life, pro-family organization. The aim of the alliance is to protect children from "manipulation in education and politics which leads to SECULAR HUMANISM which recognizes no higher authority than man himself." It provides information and opinions on children's welfare and protection and on parents' rights. This is carried out through the distribution of newsletters and educational material, the sponsoring of seminars and the conducting of research into children, parents and the secular and religious life of the traditional family. The alliance concentrates its interests on sex education, abortion, population control, child abuse, the curricula of both public and private schools, religious education, secular humanism and all legislation that affects the family.

SEE ALSO Christian Crusade; Citizens for Decency Through Law; Citizens for Decent Literature; Clean Up TV Campaign (CUTV-U.S.); Coalition for Better Television; Committee on Public Information; Crusade for Decency; Eagle Forum; Foundation to Improve Television; Moral Majority; Morality in Media; National Federation for Decency; National Organization for Decent Literature; People for the American Way.

Paris Adult Theater v. *Slaton District Attorney* (1973)
SEE *Magic Mirror*.

Parsons, Robert   Aided by the Jesuit Cardinal Allen and Sir Francis Englefield, Parsons (1546-1610) wrote in 1594 the book *A Conference about the next Succession to the Crowne of Ingland*. The aim of this book was to persuade the English to accept the infanta of Spain as a potential successor to Queen Elizabeth I, rather than the assigned successor, James VI of Scotland. Parliament was no more impressed than the population: The printer was hung, drawn and quartered and the book itself burned, with the proviso that "whoever should be found to have it in their house should be guilty of high treason." It was further burned in Oxford, where the university authorities particularly objected to the proposition that "birthright and proximity of blood do give no title to rule or government."

Pascal, Blaise Pascal (1623-62) was a French mathematician, physicist and moralist who combined theological and philosophical work with research into geometry, hydrodynamics and atmospheric pressure. As one of the leading proponents of JANSENISM he entered the convent at Port-Royal in 1655. Here he composed his most important nonscientific works: *Les Lettres Provinciales* (1656-57) and *Pensees* (1670). Despite Pascal's unswerving devotion to Rome both these works were condemned by the Catholic Church and gained the particular hostility of the Jesuits, who had been equated with the Massilian heretics in Jansen's original five propositions. Under pressure from the Jesuits Pope Innocent X was the first authority to condemn Pascal's work, in 1644. *Les Lettres Provinciales* was first burned in France for its alleged anti-religiosity in 1657. Louis XIV, who sided with the Jesuits and had Port-Royal closed down in 1710, ordered in 1660 that *Les Provinciales* "be torn up and burned ... at the hands of the High Executioner, fulfillment of which is to be certified to His Majesty within the week; and that meanwhile all printers, booksellers, vendors and others, of whatever rank and station, are explicitly prohibited from printing, selling, and distributing, and even from having in their possession the said book ... under pain of public, exemplary punishment." Only by carefully avoiding the scrutiny of the censors could his work be circulated. First placed on the Roman Index (SEE Roman Indexes) in 1664, Pascal's works remained there into the 20th century.

patent offensiveness The concept of "patent offensiveness" has been one of the tests for obscenity in America ever since the MILLER STANDARD was established in 1973. For the purposes of obscenity cases, material that is patently offensive usually means hard-core pornography. In the judgment in MILLER V. CALIFORNIA (1973), the court stated that while it had no right to propose regulatory schemes for adoption by the individual states,

> it is possible ... to give a few plain examples of what a state statute could define for regulation ... (a) patently offensive representations or descriptions of ultimate sexual acts, normal or perverted, actual or simulated; (b) patently offensive representations or descriptions of masturbation, excretory functions and lewd exhibition of the genitals. At a minimum, prurient, patently offensive depiction or description of sexual conduct must have serious literary, artistic, political, or scientific value to merit FIRST AMENDMENT protection.

Pennsylvania

1. Motion Picture Control Act Pennsylvania was among the first to create its own apparatus for censoring films. An act of 1915 created a board of censors that was given the right to examine and give or withhold a permit to every film intended for exhibition in the state. Acceptable films were "moral and proper," while the unacceptable were "sacriligious, indecent, immoral, or tend[ing] to debase or corrupt morals." The act was amended a number of times, most notably in 1959. Under the Motion Picture Control Act (1959) any exhibitor was required to register his film with the Board of Censors within 48 hours of its proposed first showing. The board was entitled to review all films and the exhibitor had to pay for the examination. If a majority of the board declared the film to be obscene it would be banned outright or marked as "unsuitable for children." A child was defined as anyone under the age of seventeen; the film was obscene if "to the average person applying contemporary community standards its dominant theme, taken as a whole, appeals to prurient interest." Films were unsuitable for children if they were simply obscene or incited the viewer to crime. Inciting to crime was defined as "that which represents or portrays as acceptable conduct or as conduct worthy of emulation the commission of any crime, or the manifesting of contempt for law." Those who violated the act were liable to fines of not less than $400 and not more than $1,000, a prison sentence of a maximum of six months, or both. Films that were to be shown for "purely educational, charitable, fraternal, family or religious purpose by any religious association, fraternal society, family, library, museum, public school or private school, or industrial, business, institutional, advertising or training films concerned exclusively with the advancement of law, medicine and the other professions" were exempted from censorship, provided that they were not exhibited in a cinema or similar "public place of entertainment."

2. Sedition Act Under the Pennsylvania Penal Code, section 207:

> The word "sedition" ... shall mean: Any writing, publication, printing, cut, cartoon, utterance, or conduct, either individually or in combination with any other person, the intent of which is: (a) to make or cause to make any outbreak or demonstration of violence against this State or against the United States, (b) to encourage any person to take any measures or to engage in any conduct with a view of overthrowing or destroying or attempting to overthrow or destroy, by any force or show of threat of force, the Government of this State or of the United States. (c) to incite or encourage any person to commit any overt act with a view [of placing] the Government of this State or of the United States into hatred and contempt. (d) to incite any person or persons to do or attempt to do personal injury or harm to any officer of this State or of the United States, or to damage or to destroy any public property or the property of any public official because of his official position ...

Sedition was classed as a felony and those who were convicted under the act faced a fine of up to $10,000, imprisonment for a maximum of 20 years, or both.

This act was abandoned, as were a number of other state sedition acts, after a Supreme Court decision. However, unlike many of those acts that were declared unconstitutional, the Pennsylvania statute was simply set aside as unenforceable in favor of the SMITH ACT (1940). In the case of *Pennsylvania* v. *Nelson* in 1956, in which an avowed member of the Communist Party was sentenced to 20 years in jail, fined $10,000 and required to pay $13,000 court costs, the Supreme Court of Pennslvania reversed the conviction. The court pointed out that while the state's act demanded that sedition against Pennsylvania as well as against the United States must be proved, "out of all the voluminous testimony, we have not found, nor has anyone pointed to, a single word containing a seditious act or even utterance directed against the Government of Pennsylvania." The U.S. Supreme Court, which heard the state government's appeal against this decision, confirmed the state Supreme Court's ruling.

Pentagon Papers, The   In mid-1967 Robert S. McNamara, then U.S. secretary of defense, commissioned a top secret history of the U.S. involvement in Indochina, specifically as regarded the war in Vietnam, an involvement that had by then been going on, either directly or by proxy, for the better part of 20 years. This history, which was officially titled *History of United States Decision-Making Process on Viet Nam Policy*, but came to be known as the Pentagon Papers, took 18 months to complete and ran to 3,000 pages of narrative history, plus 4,000 pages of illustrative documentation, all amassed in 47 volumes totaling 2.5 million words. It covered the period from 1945 to May 1968, the month the peace talks had begun in Paris following President Johnson's announcement that troop escalation in Vietnam would cease and that he would not be seeking a further term in office. Although the Papers did not represent a complete history, they offered a substantial archive of historical material, often written in the words of those who actually took the decisions it reported.

The material remained top secret until, on March 3, 1971, Daniel Ellsberg, a former deputy secretary of defense, sent a copy of the Papers to the *New York Times*, which began publishing selected, damning excerpts on June 13. The Papers made it clear that the realities of American foreign policy in this area were vastly contradictory to the public pronouncements of the administrations of four successive presidents and, although the Papers stopped short of Richard Nixon, by implication of a fifth. Although the Papers were not revealed to the public, nothing in them was in fact classified as secret. Nonetheless, as the government's response to their publication showed, they were seen as too sensitive for general dissemination.

The administration's response was twofold. The clandestine version was to set up the White House "plumbers," a group of undercover agents whose task was to repair the "leaks" in government. Among the plumbers' missions was the burglary of the office of Ellsberg's psychiatrist, in an attempt to smear the whistleblower. The ultimate result of these farcical junketings was the Watergate Affair and Richard Nixon's subsequent resignation. The administration's open response was through the courts. On the evening of June 14, Attorney General John Mitchell sent a telegram to the *Times*, demanding that since the publication was in breach of the ESPIONAGE ACT, it should stop at once. The *Times* sent its own telegram, respectfully turning down Mitchell's demand. After the first three daily installments of the Papers had appeared in the *New York Times*, the Justice Department obtained a temporary restraining order on further publication. The authorities claimed that if the material continued to appear "the national defense interests of the United States and the nation's security will suffer immediate and irreparable harm." For the next 15 days the issue was thrashed out in the courts, with the *Times*, the *Washington Post* and a number of other papers who had joined in publishing the material arguing that the restraining order was unconstitutional.

On June 30, 1971, the U.S. Supreme Court ruled on the cases of *New York Times* v. *United States* and *United States* v. *Washington Post*. By a majority of six justices to three the court found that the government had failed to justify its attempts to restrain publication of the material. In addition to the relatively brief three-paragraph per curiam opinion, several justices filed concurring opinions. Justice Black, supported by Justice Douglas, stated,

> I believe that every moment's continuance of the injunctions against these newspapers amounts to a flagrant, indefensible, and continuing violation of the FIRST AMENDMENT ... Our government was launched in 1789 with the adoption of the Constitution. The Bill of Rights, including the First Amendment, followed in 1791. Now ... the federal courts are asked to hold that the First Amendment does not mean what it says, but rather means that the government can halt the publication of current news of vital importance to the people of this country.

Justice Black went on to detail the history and intention of the First Amendment, noting that

> the Founding Fathers gave the free press the protection it must have to fulfill its essential role in our democracy. The press was to serve the governed, not the governors. The government's power to censor the press was abolished so that it could bare the secrets of government and inform the people. Only a free and unrestrained press can effectively expose deception in government. And paramount among the responsibilities of a free press is the duty to prevent any part of the government from deceiving the people and sending them off to distant lands to die of foreign fever and foreign shot and shell. In my view, far from deserving condemnation for their courageous reporting, the ... newspapers should be com-

mended for serving the purpose that the Founding Fathers saw so clearly.

People for the American Way

People for the American Way is a U.S. organization devoted to opposing all forms of censorship. It was founded in 1970 by television producer Norman Lear, and it has come to represent the most conspicuous opposition to such organizations as the MORAL MAJORITY and the EAGLE FORUM. PAW involves a variety of religious, business, media and labor figures who are "committed to reaffirming the traditional American values of pluralism, diversity, and freedom of expression and religion." The organization does not engage in political activity or the lobbying of politicians. Its main intention is to attack groups who advocate political repression and censorship. PAW seeks to "help Americans maintain their belief in self; and to reaffirm that in this society the individual still matters." The organization is devoted to sustaining a mass media campaign that underlines the importance of a positive climate of tolerance in which every individual is permitted to express his or her own sympathies and beliefs. Like all such pressure groups, PAW maintains a speakers' bureau, conducts research programs and disseminates educational material to interested parties.

SEE ALSO Committee to Defend the First Amendment; First Amendment Congress; Freedom to Read Foundaton; National Coalition against Censorship; Reporters Committee for Freedom of the Press; Scholars and Citizens for Freedom of Information.

People of the State of New York v. *August Muller*

In March 1882 August Muller, a 22-year-old clerk employed in the New York City book and picture store of Edmund F. Bonaventure, was found guilty of selling indecent and obscene photographs that represented "nude females in lewd, obscene, scandalous and lascivious attitudes and postures." The case had been brought by ANTHONY COMSTOCK, the country's leading anti-vice crusader, and was based on nine photographs of the offending material, which had been seized by Comstock who had personally raided the store. The paintings in question included *La Asphyxie* by Cherubino Pata, *After the Bath* by Joseph Wencker, *La Baigneuse* by Leon Perrault and *La Repose* by Chambord. Eight of the nine had already been exhibited without interference in Paris and the ninth in Philadelphia.

When, in October 1884, Muller's appeal against his conviction was heard by the New York Supreme Court he was unable to reverse the decision of the lower court. Six expert witnesses, all of whom were ready to swear that the pictures were indeed art and not obscenity, were not allowed to testify. The prosecution conceded that the pictures had been exhibited but stressed that "the object of the law was to protect public morals, especially as to that class of the community whose character is not so completely formed as to be proof against the lewd effects of pictures, photographs and publications prohibited ..." Muller drew from the court a new and lasting definition of obscenity, one that distinctly favored Comstockery over culture: "It would be a proper test of obscenity in a painting or statue whether it is naturally calculated to excite in a spectator impure imaginations." Expert witnesses were outlawed, their opinions taking second place in court to the gut feelings of the "ordinary juryman."

People on Complaint of Arcuri v. *Finkelstein* (1952)

Finkelstein was the owner of a neighborhood luncheonette and candystore in Brooklyn, NEW YORK. On his shelves were certain picture sets, featuring a variety of nude and semi-nude females. These packets of pictures were accompanied by material stating that they had been prepared purely as aides in the teaching of photography and carefully stressing their intrinsic artistic worth. The pictures were proved to have been purchased by a high school student, and Finkelstein was charged under section 1141 of the New York Penal Law, the state's statute against obscenity. City Magistrate Malbin, in sending the defendant for trial in the Special Sessions Court, railed against a situation in which minors could "come in, observe these pictures, purchase them and seek dark corners and privacy to snicker over [the] contents and pass the pictures around among their friends." It was not possible to cure the "abomination" of teenage prurience, but "when the opportunity arises to alleviate it, it should not be allowed to pass." Stating that the inclusion of the "artistic" disclaimer was irrelevant, Malbin ruled that "pictures are obscene which tend to stir sexual impulses or lead to sexually impure thoughts" and went back to the Victorian HICKLIN RULE to affirm that "an important ... test to be applied in determining whether a book offends the [New York] law against obscene publications is, does the matter charged as obscene tend to deprave or corrupt those whose minds are open to immoral influences and who might come into contact with it, ever bearing in mind ... that the statute looks to the protection not of the mature and the intelligent, with minds strengthened to withstand the influence of the prohibited data, but of the young and immature, the ignorant and sensually inclined." SEE ALSO New York 5. obscenity statute.

People v. *Birch* (1963)

This case was brought by the state of New York, citing its obscenity statute, section 1141 of the Penal Law, in an attempt to have certain books declared obscene and to prosecute their authors. The books in question were relatively anodyne soft-core fantasies: *Sex Kitten* (Greg Caldwell), *Clipjoint Cutie* (Monte Steele), *The Wild Ones* (Nell Holland), *The Hottest Party in Town* (Sam Hudson), *Passion Pit* (David Spencer), *Bedroom at the Top* (Bruce Rald), *Butch* and *College for Sinners* (Andrew Shaw). Judge Shapiro was unimpressed by the state's case and refused to declare the books obscene. He gave a number of reasons for his decision, dealing with what he saw as the state's inadequate case and giving a broad overview of contemporary legal attitudes to the way in which such cases ought to be treated, at least in the lower courts:

(1) While the State had claimed that the books would have a deleterious effect on any child who might read them, this in itself was insufficient ground to test for whether or not they were obscene. (2) The fact that the books were tawdry, lurid and ill-written did not qualify them for citation as hard-core pornography and thus for exclusion from the guarantees of the FIRST AMENDMENT. (3) If a book is to be banned as obscene, that judgment can be made only after constitutional and legal considerations, and not, the law being what it is, simply on the question of black and white fact. (4) Literary value or lack of it has no bearing on the obscenity of a book or the criminality of an author. (5) The most important factor in judging the obscenity or otherwise of a book was to what extent it breached the current community standards as to what was acceptable; even if a law had been promulgated when one set of such standards were in force, it could not be interpreted in the light of those same standards if public opinion had changed in the intervening period. The courts must take the new attitudes into consideration. (6) As cited in the decision in LADY CHATTERLEY'S LOVER, adultery might be portrayed as an acceptable relationship in certain circumstances and thus such portrayal was not automatically grounds for conviction. (7) The fact that the books' authors were not generally recognized as among the country's literary giants did not automatically render them susceptible to an obscenity prosecution. (8) The fact that certain "four-letter words," included in the books but not generally used in "polite society," are involved in a piece of writing does not automatically make it actionable. (9) It is vital that the courts guard against undue legal restraint of literary material, however good or bad, in order that a system of censorship may not be established and personal liberties, the foundation of a free society, be thus eroded.

SEE ALSO New York 5. obscenity statute.

Perceau, Louis   Louis Perceau (1883-1942), one of France's leading publishers of erotic literature during the 1920s and 1930s, combined a career in clandestine publishing with a continuing allegiance to activist left-wing politics. Both enthusiasms began in his youth. His arrest in 1906 for joining the signatories of an allegedly seditious poster was followed in 1909 by his first clandestine publication, *Le tresor des equivoques*, a collection of erotic spoonerisms, known as *contrepeteries* or "cross-fartings," for which he used the pseudonym of "Jacques Oncial." This was followed in 1913 by *Histoire d'hommes et des dames*, a further collection of erotic riddles, jokes and wordplays. In the tradition of many French pornographers, Perceau produced many reprints of the classics of erotic literature, scholarly editions of 17th- and 18th-century anthologies of libertine verse, and new editions of the major erotica of the 18th and 19th centuries, all of which appeared in de luxe, limited editions. He embellished them with his own learned introductions, signed pseudonymously "Helpey, Bibliographe poitevin" (bibliog-

rapher from Poitiers). The fact that some publications claimed such antiquity did not restrain the authorities, and they were often seized and destroyed in anti-pornography raids. He also issued a number of collections of his own verse, using the pseudonym "Alexandre de Verineau" for *Priapes* (1920) and "Au bord du lit" (1927, *At the Bedside*).

Perceau compiled what has been cited as the best bibliography of its genre, the BIBLIOGRAPHIE DU ROMAN EROTIQUE AU XIXE SIECLE, which appeared in 1930. This was preceded by his first bibliography, that of the L'ENFER, in Paris. This catalog, coauthored by the poet GUILLAUME APOLLINAIRE (1880-1918) and Perceau's fellow publisher of erotica, Fernand Fleuret (1883-1945), appeared in 1913. *Les Livres de l'Enfer*, which appeared in two volumes in 1978, was an updated version of this bibliography, expanded by another publisher, Pascal Pia (1901-1980), whose own lengthy invovement with erotica added substantially to the initial work. It was rumoured that Perceau had prepared similar works dealing with the erotic literature of the 17th and 18th centuries and the erotic poetry of the 17th to 19th centuries. His *Le Cabinet secret de Parnasse* (appearing in four volumes from 1928 to 1935) deals with French erotic poetry up to the 18th century.

SEE ALSO Gay, Jules; *Bibliographie des ouvrages relatifs de l'amour ...*

Perfumed Garden, The   SEE Fortune Press; Australia 3. obscenity laws; Roth, Samuel; South Africa 2. banned books; Burton, Sir Richard.

Peru   Prior to 1980, since when the country has been governed by two democratic governments, Peru was controlled by a repressive military regime that employed extensive control of all media. As a reaction to such controls the 1979 constitution (article 2) guaranteed Peruvians complete freedom of expression, extending this to information, opinion, expression and dissemination of thought by word, image or print without previous authorization, censorship or any other control, other than laws on defamation and the like. Under the constitution it is a criminal offense to suppress the media and neither the state nor any other institution can own a monopoly of press, radio or TV. Even under a state of emergency, during which four important rights may be suspended, freedom of expression remains unaffected. Only during a state of siege, which has governed several provinces since 1982 during the civil war against the Sendero Luminoso (Shining Light) Maoist guerillas, can censorship be used. This is justified by the creation of a "politico-military command" with extensive powers, although such censorship, while accepted, is not strictly constitutional. Journalists have sufferd at the hands of both sides, each of which are keen to have their policies publicized.

Φ (Greek letter phi)   The pressmark used in the catalog of the Bodleian Library, Oxford, to denote obscene, pornographic or otherwise prohibited books. The Greek letter is a pun on the adjuration "Fie!" addressed to readers of such volumes.

Philanderer, The   This novel, by American author Stanley Kauffman, had been published in the U.S. in 1952 as *The Tightrope* without any problems. It was published in England to some critical acclaim and sold 6,000 copies within 15 months. When the book first appeared in the U.K. in 1954 it was also subjected to two prosecutions. The first, under a local statute on the Isle of Man, the Obscene Publications and Indecent Advertisements Act (1907), culminated in the fining of Boots's Library for lending out the book. However, the high bailiff stressed that he acted only with reluctance and held the fine to £1. The second, on the mainland, was initiated by the director of public prosecutions who subpoenaed the publisher, Secker & Warburg, who decided to fight the case. The author was not in court, and the publisher Frederic Warburg, the defendant, was invited by the judge, Mr. Justice Stable, to leave the dock and sit with his solicitor. The jury were sent off to read the book "as a book. Don't pick out the highlights. Read it through as a whole." Mervyn Griffith-Jones prosecuted, as he would LADY CHATTERLEY'S LOVER in 1960.

In his summing-up the judge, who obviously sympathized with the defendants even if he had little time for the book, emphasized the need to view obscenity, and its test as defined in HICKLIN, in the context of the whole book, and not simply as regarded random passages within it. He stressed that while the law was unchanged, society was radically different and the jury must assess the book in that light. He trusted that as decent, average people they would find the middle way between the puritans and the pornographers:

> The charge is that the tendency of the book is to corrupt and deprave. Then you say "Well, corrupt and deprave whom?" to which the answer is: those whose minds are open to such immoral influences and into whose hands a publication of this sort may fall. What, exactly, does that mean? Are we to take our literary standards as being the level of something that is suitable for the decently brought up young female aged fourteen? Or do we go even further back than that and are we reduced to the sort of books that one reads as a child in the nursery? The answer to that is: of course not.

The Philanderer was duly aquitted, and the judge's summing-up hailed as a major breakthrough, the most important since Hicklin. That it was only one judge's opinion, however enlightened, and made no new law was demonstrated clearly three months later when SEPTEMBER IN QUINZE, by another American author, Vivian Connell (1903-   ), and published in the U.K. by Hutchinson, was tried and convicted at the Old Bailey in September 1954. While Mr. Justice Stable had been voicing an opinion that can now be seen as a precursor of the more substantial reforms of the OBSCENE PUBLICATIONS ACT OF 1959, Sir Gerald Dodson, the judge in the latter case,

revealed himself as a direct descendant of a less sophisticated age. Summing up in a way that left the jury in no doubt as to his own feelings Sir Gerald fined Hutchinson and its director, Mrs. Katherine Webb, £500, and delivered himself of a variety of determinedly "moral" opinions.

Philipon, Charles   Journalist and caricaturist Philipon published two satirical papers—LA CARICATURE and LE CHARIVARI—in mid-19th-century Paris. The chief target of Philipon's satires was King Louis Philippe, whom he characterized as "La Poire" ("the pear"), an image taken both from the French slang for "fathead" and from the shape of the monarch's head. So successful was this creation, with its overwhelming implications of smug, bourgeois stupidity, that it became a symbol of the opposition to Louis Philippe's government, which had been established after the Revolution of July 1830. On November 14, 1831, Philipon went on trial for "crimes against the person of the King." On November 19 Philipon was found guilty; the court rejected his plea that he had drawn only what he saw, despite his drawing for the judges a succession of four portraits of "La Poire," with accompanying text, showing the supposed metamorphosis of the royal head into a foolish fruit. "Can I help it," asked Philipon, "if His Majesty's face is like a pear?" He was fined 2,000 francs and jailed for six months. The "metamorphosis" was published, as an analysis of caricature, in *La Caricature* on November 24 and as a special woodcut supplement to *Le Charivari* on January 17, 1834.

In January 1833 Philipon returned to court, with his editor Gabriel Aubert, both charged with "an offense against the King" in their publication of a lithograph and an article entitled "Project for a Monument." The defendants were acquitted, but the offending material was destroyed. By 1834 Philipon had amassed some 13 months of imprisonment and 6,000 francs worth of fines, stemming from six adverse judgments against material published in his two papers. To pay his fines, and make up his losses, he produced *L'Association Mensuelle*, a lithograph supplement to *Le Caricature*. This supplement published such pointed satires as Daumier's *La Rue Transonian, le 14 Avril 1834*, which depicted the massacre of 12 working people, shot dead in an apartment by troops taking revenge for the death of an officer during the uprising of the Lyons silkworkers. Like many similar publications that offered prints, *L'Association* was effectively destroyed by the government's law that all prints must carry an official stamp, placed inevitably square in the middle of the image.

Philippines

1. censorship under Marcos   President Ferdinand Marcos maintained strict control of the press and allied media from his assumption of dictatorial powers in 1972 to his overthrow in 1986. The policy was directed throughout by a desire both to outlaw subversion and to entrench the authoritarian regime. His first act was to issue Letter of Instruction No. 1, providing for the taking over of all media by the authorities as part of the imposition of martial law. Except for the media he personally controlled—several radio stations and one newspaper—all others were shut down to prevent their succumbing to "communist subversion." The Department of Public Information (DPI) then issued Departmental Order No. 1 on September 25, 1972, setting out the guidelines for acceptable news reporting, stressing the need for "news reports of a positive national value." No criticism of martial law was permitted and no medium might make editorial comments.

The order stated that the media should print and broadcast "accurate, objective, straight news reports of positive national value, consistent with the efforts of the government to meet the dangers and threats that occasioned the proclamation of martial law, and the efforts to achieve a 'new society.'" In section four the order expressly prohibited material that might "inflame" people against the government, undermine popular faith in the government or disseminate sedition, popularize rumors or generate fear, panic and confusion. The law and its upholders were to be backed unreservedly. Material that undermined morals or promoted lawlessness, disorder and violence was banned. All news was to be cleared by DPI censors, including cables from corrrespondents to their non-Philippine newspapers or radio and TV stations. Printers had to submit anything on which they worked—from leaflets to newspapers. Photographers were permitted only to picture "normal city life" and "interviews with authorized officials and officers." Media censorship was coordinated by the establishment in October 1972 of the Committee on Mass Media, a body administered by army officers.

The Marcos attack on the media had no parallel in the whole of Asia, according to international monitors. Eight thousand people lost their jobs; of 18 newspapers, only two survived. Further controls were instituted by the Media Advisory Council, established on May 11, 1973, to ensure that the media continued to conform to the succession of edicts and regulations passed by the regime. All putative publishers were forced to sign "an instrument of allegiance" under which they promised their "whole-hearted support" to the MAC's rules, which were embodied in a 45-page directive. The committee further imposed a special levy on advertising revenues. All media outlets, includng public relations and advertising agencies, had to apply every six months for renewal of a license to operate.

News manipulation involved the aggrandizing of the government line, the suppression of meaningful criticism, and the presentation in all cases of a positive line regarding the state of the nation, under what were called the "Sunshine News Guidelines." All imported printed matter was subject to stringent checks. Attempts to censor the activities of the foreign press corps were opposed, but persistently difficult correspondents were refused entry visas. The MAC was abolished in November 1974. Ostensibly this was Marcos' response to foreign criticism of media repression; practically it was a move designed to eradicate the widespread corruption among MAC officers—particularly their use of government funds—and the dissension this was causing.

The MAC was replaced by two agencies: the Print Media Council and the Broadcast Media Council, but both of these were ultimately run by the DPI, reorganized with a substantially increased budget to facilitate the exercise of such powers. They coordinated the working of several government agencies designed to create and disseminate propaganda extolling Marcos' New Society, regulated internal and imported news, and licensed media organizations. They were also linked to the Board of Censors for Motion Pictures. The DPI issued regular policy directives to owners and editors, even to the extent of dictating the exact working to be used in describing certain key government activities.

2. censorship under Aquino The bloodless coup that in 1986 replaced the authoritarian power of President Ferdinand Marcos with the democratic government of Mrs. Cory Aquino had inevitable effects on Philippine media. In Proclamation No. 3, issued on March 25, 1986, Mrs. Aquino spelled out what has become known as the "Freedom Constitution," guaranteeing, inter alia, freedom of expression and of speech, as well as the reorganization of culture, the arts and the media and the creation of task forces to study film, information gathering, and all areas of police and military activity other than those that affect national security. Task forces have also been established to remodel the nation's broadcast media in the image of the British Broadcasting Corporation. Films are to be classified rather than censored, with a Film Classification Board replacing the Movie and TV Review and Classification Board.

Under the new regime the status of the press has been reversed: A number of previously high-circulation newspapers, once favored by Marcos, are now unpopular, facing inquiries into their ownership and finance, and losing readers; formerly banned opposition papers are now encouraged and increasingly successful. While Mrs. Aquino plans to dismantle much of the Marcos-era censorship, enough remains for it to be used against the vestigial pro-Marcos press, in ways, its owners and editors claim, that are as arbitrary and self-serving as anything Mrs. Aquino may have decried in her predecessor. Under the Commission of Good Government various measures were taken at once as regards the press: A new minister of information was appointed; editorial guidelines were presented to the press; the state news agency was reorganized, either with a view toward privatizing it or abolishing it altogether; all press attaches were recalled from Philippine embassies and the finances of two media conglomerates, formerly belonging to Marcos, were sequestered, and a further four newspapers, members of what was known as the "crony press," were placed under an audit. The sequestration of funds does not prohibit the newspapers from appearing, and the government has no interest in taking them over, but the move, along with the audits, is part of the general overhaul of the financial administration of the Marcos era.

The right-wing press defends itself by proclaiming its own commitment to democratic freedom and accusing the commission of double standards. Esthetic, rather than political critics, have claimed that the new freedoms have encouraged excessive license in the media, though defenders see it as a natural outpouring after 14 years of repression. The only press laws that exist govern libel; in the face of what has been called the freest but most licentious press in Asia, there are moves, as yet only suggested, to add new legislation to deal with "irresponsibility."

Philosophie dans le Boudoir, La *The Philosopher in the Bedroom*, written by the Marquis de SADE, was published in 1795 and, in a futile attempt to distract the authorities, subtitled "a posthumous work by the author of JUSTINE." It is one of de Sade's shorter books, but in its combination of philosophy, political pamphleteering and what ASHBEE called "cruel and crapulous" scenes of sexual violence, it epitomizes the Sadeian style as found in his lengthier works. Together with *Dialogue Between a Priest and a Dying Man* (1782), this is one of de Sade's two nontheatrical works written as a dialogue and as such resembles the style of a number of the major erotic works of the period.

In an introduction addressed "Aux Libertins" de Sade suggests that "voluptuaries of every age and of every sex ... lubricious women ... young girls ... and ... amiable debauchees" should join together in "sacrificing everything to the pleasure of the senses." Such excesses are worked out through the story of the sexual and philosophical education of a young girl, in which are featured many scenes of savage cruelty, including those in which the heroine takes as her victim her own mother, a model of probity. Sade's ironic epigraph suggests that "Mothers will make this volume mandatory reading for their daughters."

The work shows the extent to which de Sade yearns for his ideal world—one in which an individual's sexual preferences, however bizarre, would not mean his continual endurance of the degree of social ostracism that marked the author's own existence.

SEE ALSO *Juliette, ou les Prosperities de vice*; *Justine, or The Misfortunes of Virtue*; *One Hundred and Twenty Days of Sodom*.

Pierce v. United States **(1920)** Pierce and a number of fellow socialists had issed a pamphlet entitled "The Price We Pay" from the national office of the American Socialist Party in Chicago. They were charged under the ESPIONAGE ACT (1917) with attempting to cause insubordination and disloyalty and refusal of duty in the military and naval forces," and issuing a publication that contained "false statements with intent to interfere with the operation and success of these forces in the war with Germany."

This document, suitably fiery but hardly likely to influence many citizens, attacked the nation's involvement in World War I in terms that the U.S. Supreme Court found sensational. Its articles included such lines as "Your sons of military age ... will be taught not to think, only to obey without questioning. Then they will be shipped through the submarine zone by the hundreds of thousands to the bloody quagmire of Europe. Into that seething, heaving swamp of torn flesh and floating entrails they will be plunged ... screaming as they go. Agonies of torture will rend their flesh from their sinews, will crack their bones and dissolve their lungs; every pang will be multiplied in its passage to you."

The court confirmed Pierce's conviction, claiming not that his pamphlet had actually injured the war effort, but that it had been aimed to do so, that it set out to "interfere with the conscription and recruitment services; to cause men eligible for the service to evade the draft; to bring home to them, and especially to their parents, sisters, wives and sweethearts, a sense of impending personal loss, calculated to discourage the young men from entering the service." Justices Brandeis and Holmes dissented from this opinion, suggesting that "The Price We Pay" threatened no "clear and present danger" and that the leaflet "far from counseling disobedience to law, points to the hopelessness of protest ..."

SEE ALSO *Abrams* v. *United States* (1919); *Adler* v. *Board of Education* (1952); *Frohwerk* v. *United States* (1919); *Gitlow* v. *New York* (1925); *Lamont* v. *Postmaster General* (1965); *Schaeffer* v. *United States* (1920); *Schenck* v. *United States* (1919); *Sweezy* v. *New Hampshire* (1957); *Whitney* v. *California* (1927); *Yates* v. *United States* (1957).

Pinky *Pinky* was adapted from the novel of the same title, written by Cid Ricketts Sumner, and directed by Elia Kazan in 1949. It concerns the misadventures of a light-skinned black girl, Pinky, who works as a nurse in Boston, Massachusetts, where she has lived for the past dozen years and has become engaged to a white doctor. Pinky returns to visit her grandmother in the South, and after she nurses "Miss Em," the owner of the plantation on which her grandmother lives, during her last illness, Pinky is willed the plantation for her own. After suffering a variety of racist attacks, Pinky determines to abandon her "white" life in Boston and commit herself to working for the black community in the South.

In 1952 the film was banned in Marshall, Texas, under a local statute that empowered the authorities to deny a licence for the exhibition of any film that was "of such a character as to be prejudicial to the best interests of the people of said City." When the exhibitor, one Gelling, showed the film in defiance of the ban, he was convicted of violating the local statute, and the conviction was affirmed by the Texas Court of Criminal Appeals. This affirmation was given some five months prior to the U.S. Supreme Court's landmark decision regarding the film THE MIRACLE, a decision that granted film the same FIRST AMENDMENT guarantees as had the print media. Although Gelling's attorney had argued that film was not simply amusement, as accepted in the courts since the MUTUAL FILM CORPORATION V. INDUSTRIAL COMMISSION OF OHIO (1915), and was in fact a valid form of communication, the Texas courts had rejected this defense. Judge Beauchamp cited the immutability of "a constitution as solid as the rocks" and stressed that "the desire of a great industry to reap greater fruits from its operations should not be indulged at the expense of Christian character, upon which America must rely for its future existence." He further noted the importance of maintaining local and state rights against any federal interference.

When the case, listed as *Gelling* v. *Texas* (1952), came before the U.S. Supreme Court the *Miracle* decision was duly invoked. The court rejected the Texas law, citing it both as "too uncertain and indefinite" and "prior restraint ... in flagrant form." Judge Douglas added, "If a board of censors can tell the American people what is in their best interests to see or to read or to hear, then thought is regimented, authority is substituted for liberty, and the great purpose of the First Amendment to keep uncontrolled the freedom of expression defeated."

SEE ALSO *Near* v. *Minnesota* (1931).

Plumptre, Rev. James Plumptre (1771- ?) came from a distinguished English family, numbering MPs, clergymen and dons among his relations. He himself taught for 19 years at Cambridge University before taking up the living of Great Gransden, Huntingdonshire. From the age of 22 he had seen himself as the singlehanded savior of English literature. Finding it gross, irreligious and even obscene, he determined to filter for these impurities. Plumptre's works comprised 18 major books plus many lesser publications. He wrote eight plays of his own and expurgated 17 by other authors. In the pursuit of his abiding goal, the expurgation of the entire body of English literature, he composed studies of SHAKESPEARE (his expurgated collection of Shakespearian songs published in 1805 predated the BOWDLER's efforts), a BIBLE commentary designed to improve working-class-morals, an expurgated version of DEFOE's *Robinson Crusoe* (which kept selling for 60 years in America and England), two anthologies of expurgated poetry, a comic opera and a guide to becoming a successful smalltown butcher.

His major book is *The English Drama Purified* (1812). Dedicated to educating an audience in the ways of goodness, it promulgated the ground rules for "purified" drama. Everything potentially corrupting was to be cut. Comedy was accepted under sufferance—while nowhere does it state in the Bible that Christ laughs, neither does it say that he does not. Plays in which the status quo is attacked are firmly rejected. Plumptre's problem was that no one wished to publish his magnum opus. An appeal for subscriptions netted only 161 takers, who ordered 183 copies. The duke of Gloucester was persuaded to accept a dedication, and such notables as prime minister Spencer Perceval and the bluestocking, Harriet Bowdler, joined the list, but few others. The first three volumes appeared in May 1812. He asked Perceval to send extra copies to the royal family, but the prime minister was assassinated before he could act. Plumptre sent copies to every theater manager, to many actors and to the literati. Few replied, and none chose to popularize his work or produce his expurgated dramas. As a final gesture Plumptre attempted to send copies to the monarchs of France, Russia, Prussia and Austria. This too failed, even though he attempted to enlist British foreign ministers Castlereagh and later Canning as middlemen. In 1823 he abandoned his efforts at reform and deposited a single copy of *The English Drama Purified* in the Fitzwilliam Museum in Cambridge.

Pocklington, John The Rev. John Pocklington, D.D., had been one of the foremost campaigners against puritanism and upholders of the established church in the years leading up to the English Civil War. Once the king had been overthrown and the Long Parliament established, he found himself among the first of many writers whose works, once orthodox, were now heresy. In 1641 the House of Lords condemned two works—*Sunday No Sabbath* and *Altare Christianum*—to be burned by the common hangman in London, Oxford and Cambridge. The first of these had originally been delivered as two sermons in 1635. In these Pocklington had savaged the Puritan view of Sunday, condemning "these Church Schismatics" a "the most gross, nay, the most transparent hypocrites and the most void of conscience of all others. They will take the benefit of the Church, but abjure the doctrine and discipline of the Church." The second book, published in 1637, was designed as an answer to the work of WILLIAM PRYNNE and Henry Burton and aimed to prove that altars and churches had existed from the very earliest days of Christianity.

The punishment meted out to Pocklington was particularly vindictive: He was declared to have been "very superstitious and full of idolatry" and to have used many gestures and ceremonies "not established by the laws of this realm." He was similarly involved in proposing doctrines quite unacceptable to Puritan theology. Pocklington was deprived of all his livings and dignities and preferments, and forbidden ever to hold them again.

SEE ALSO Puritan Censorship: the Commonwealth.

Podsnappery Podsnappery, the excessive care as to the welfare of the supposedly impressionable young, derived from the character of Mr. Podsnap, in *Our Mutual Friend* (1864-65) by Charles Dickens. Podsnap, "a person embodying insular complacency and self-satisfaction and refusal to face up to unpleasant facts" (OED Supp. 1982), was introduced as a satire on the prevailing prurience and prudery that characterized much of contemporary Victorian literary criticism. At the heart of his concern, wrote Dickens, was "a certain institution called the 'young person' ... an inconvenient and exacting institution ... The question about everything was, would it bring a blush into the cheek of the young person."

Poems on Several Occasions *Poems on Several Occasions*, the collected erotic verse of John Wilmot, 2nd earl of ROCHESTER, was published posthumously in 1680, supposedly in Antwerp. Given Rochester's deathbed return to the church, it was assumed that these explicit celebrations of sex might have troubled his conscience, but once dead, he had no influence on their appearance. The verses included a number of poems that have subsequently been proved as the work of other authors, but of those which are definitely Rochester's work, may are as lubricious as the play SODOM, of which he is generally cited as the author.

The poems, though attacked for their immorality and the possibility that they might lure the innocent into sin, centered on the ironies of passion and the problems involved in sex rather than on any lustful celebrations. The first prosecution against the poems came in 1688, when Francis Leach, a contemporary pornographic bookseller, was arrested for their publication. In 1693 one Elizabeth Latham was fined five marks and imprisoned for issuing a similar publication, her arrest being for promoting the lasiviousness and vicious qualities of Rochester's work. The first prosecution for the crime of OBSCENE LIBEL in the higher courts, that of the King's Bench, was directed in 1698 at the poems. It has been suggested that these charges had all been brought by those who wished to whitewash the reputation of the late earl in the face of his deathbed conversion. The poems remained censored, even in those editions that were published for mass consumption, for several centuries.

poison shelf In British public libraries, the shelf or shelves on which are placed those books removed from open circulation after a reader has made a complaint about them.

SEE ALSO United Kingdom—contemporary censorship 7. public library censorship.

Poland

1. general Censorship in Poland under successive communist governments began in 1946 with an executive decree setting up the Central Office for the Control of Publications and Entertainment. This decree has undergone a number of revisions, but its essential feature remains: the institutionalized control of the Polish media. Its aim was first to consolidate and then to maintain political power. It is conducted on lines laid down by a 70-page document entitled "Memoranda and Recommendations from the Central Office for the Control of the Press, Publications and Performances." This document, known as "The Book of Rules," is backed up by a number of manuals, issued sporadically as "Censorship Information," by the bulletin *Information on Questionable Topics*, a fortnightly abstract of censored material with suitably illustrative quotations, and by a number of updates on the regulations as they change. A special bulletin, bound in yellow, covers material censored from the Catholic press.

All these documents deal with a number of subjects tabulated under six headings: "Taboo" topics, which must never be mentioned under any circumstances, notably any failures by the state in its promises, or by the U.S.S.R., and alternatively any positive references to the West; "Sacred" topics, to which reference is permitted only under strict rules; "Ideological" topics, which involve official doctrine; "Politically important" topics, which deal with the fluctuations of the party line; "Sensitive" topics, covering anything that must be treated with extreme caution; and "Allusive" topics, which may provoke undesirable reactions in the population.

The system also precensors the content of newspapers, books and other publications, and enforces a high degree of self-censorship on anyone who seeks to be published. Those authors and editors who resist the censor's "suggestions" are held responsible for whatever results on the publication of their untrimmed copy. Anyone may become a censor, although most recruits are humanities graduates, and often journalists or writers manque. Many are drawn by a good starting salary, although this increases only slowly and the job has a high turnover, with at least 75 percent of the personnel lasting no more than two years. Some small percentage are ideologically motivated, but most see censorship as an intellectual game. The censorship department is divided into various sections dealing with press, books, performances and analysis and training. All printed material, from books and newspapers to letterheads, business cards and death notices must be checked, as must films, theater and other performances. Press censors are considered the aristocrats of the profession, with a subsection, nicknamed the "Saints," who cover religious publications. The training and analysis department publishes an information bulletin advising on the best methods of censorship, illustrated profusely with cut or banned material.

There are branch offices of the censorship department in every local capital, but the main work devolves upon censors in the major cities.

The overall effect of such censorship is to promote the most optimistic, positive image of Poland, strictly on lines laid down by the prevailing orthodoxy. No constructive debate on the social or economic life of the country is officially permitted, although much takes place. Despite all such slavish attempts to promulgate the ideological line, many Poles are highly and vocally critical of their government. Both the Catholic Church, which itself is the subject of much censorship, and the Solidarity movement, outlawed until mid-1989, have helped maintain such opposition.

2. Act on Censorship (1981) Among Solidarity's major, if short-lived, achievements was the new Act on Censorship of July 1981. A reduction in censorship had been one of Solidarity's main demands and although the act survived only three months in its original form, before the imposition of the State of War in December 1981 cut it off short of a proper assessment, it introduced several revolutionary clauses. The concept of censorship was not abandoned; instead of concentrating on the extent of the censor's powers, it emphasized ways of restricting them. Authors or publications had the right to appeal against the censor's ruling; censors were to state next to each excision or alteration exactly which law the material transgressed; authors and publishers could then argue their case in court, or simply publish the censor's marks to leave the public in no doubt about what had happened to the text. Censors were also to abandon their practices of blacklisting certain names from publication and issuing guidelines as to the factual description of events.

3. Jaruzelski censorship   The period of liberalization and open dissent inspired by KOR (the association of Polish trade unions) and the Solidarity movement was abruptly cut off on December 13, 1981, when a military government under General Wojciech Jaruzelski was imposed on Poland under Soviet order. For the arts and media the immediate result was the suspension of their developing freedoms and the establishment of new controls. The Union of Polish Journalists was suspended at once and was dissolved altogether on March 19, 1982, a move that preceded a purge of at least 25 percent of its former members, with approximately 100 being detained, 1,000 losing their jobs and many more suffering a variety of punishments, including demotion and early retirement. Many papers, by no means only those supporting Solidarity, were shut down, effectively silencing the most articulate and experienced Polish journalists. Those who survived have been channeled into the provision of state propaganda. Book publishing was similarly purged, with its employees forced to undergo the "verification" of their ideological purity. Many have been purged, although such sackings were officially termed "reorganization." All books had to be resubmitted for censorship and a further level of censorship, dealing with the granting of permission to distribute material, was introduced. After the fall of Solidarity, all broadcasting media were proclaimed military institutions and their buildings immediately occupied by the army. Military broadcasters and technicians temporarily took the place of the regular staffs, who were suspended. Gradually these personnel were permitted to return to work but informed that they would still have to be verified. Many filmmakers, musicians and actors rejected these demands and boycotted radio and teleivion. The film business was forced to resubmit films that had been passed as satisfactory under the Solidarity censorship laws for further censorship. Members of the banned Association of Polish Film-Makers were also subject to verification. Artists boycott state galleries but continue with some underground production.

The Law on Censorship that had been worked out between Solidarity and the Polish authorities and passed on October 1, 1981, lasted only until the imposition of the rule of General Jaruzelski on December 13. Martial law, lasting until July 22, 1983, suspended many civil laws, among them large parts of the censorship act. The government specifically failed to state which parts were still binding and thus gave itself carte blanche. This power was further augmented by a variety of laws, all dealing with freedom of expression, passed during 1982-83. The most important of these was the Law on State and Official Secrets (December 14, 1982), which made it an offense to publish any information liable to damage national security or any military matters. The law also restricted the publishing of details of police organization, scientific research and economic statistics. An official secret is defined as any information that, if published, might threaten the public interest or legitimate interest of any organization, including the party.

When martial law was suspended, several new laws appeared, substantially modifying the censorship act of October 1981, in effect restoring the status quo prior to Solidarity. Any material deemed to be "a threat to State security or defense" or whose contents "obviously constitute a crime" will be banned automatically. Reprints of publications already passed by the censor must themselves be rechecked. The flow of information to and from other countries was severely restrained and made available only to a small group of academics and professionals, all chosen by the authorities. PAP (the Polish news agency) was placed under state control, and plans for a new press law, intended primarily to purge the press of "the sworn opponents of socialism," were developed.

As far as the role of the press is concerned, Jaruzelski stated in 1983, "You are operating in the first line of the class front ... In the interests of the nation and the socialist state it will not ... be possible to voice views that contradict the constitutional principles of the Polish People's Republic." This position was emphasized in the Press Law of January 28, 1984, which deprived journalists of autonomy, placing them at the direction of editors-in-chief. The law delineates the function of the journalist as being "to serve society and the state ... a journalist has the duty to implement the general programmatic policy of his editors and publishers." Any activities that contravene this concept render the journalist in violation of his duties as an employee.

The response of many artists and writers was to boycott the official media and devote their energies to a variety of underground ventures, including publishing, educational courses and clandestine cassette recordings. A new code of standards and ethics was developed, centering on this boycott, and published clandestinely. In addition to this, many members of the public refused to watch, listen to or read such programs and publications as were permitted, choosing for instance to walk out of their homes en masse rather than have it believed that they might be watching the 7:30 television news. Major artists and performers turned to internal emigration—refusing to lend their services to officially sponsored drama, concerts and other performances. So successful was this campaign that some television and radio stations temporarily suspended broadcasting or were reduced to running repeats. Those artists and writers who bowed to the regime became extremely unpopular, were ostracized, and had their cars and homes vandalized. Attempts to create new unions to replace the many creative organizations banned under martial law have not been highly successful.

4. Solidarity in power The union was permitted to contest in the elections of May 1989. Following Solidarity's overwhelming success in every seat, President Jaruzelski had no alternative but to accept Tadeusz Mazowiecki, a 62-year-old former lawyer and editor of a leading Catholic journal, and most recently the editor of *Solidarity Weekly*, as prime minister in August 1989. While Mazowiecki, Solidarity's first elected official, has stated that his immediate priority (at the time of writing) is to prepare a report on Poland's beleaguered economy for the International Monetary Fund, it may be assumed that an administration with Solidarity members, longtime victims of censorship, will work to reduce restrictions on freedom of speech and of information. In the necessary horsetrading that underlies the formation of this administration, it appears that Mazowiecki has offered the Communist Party both the defense and internal ministries, in return for Solidarity's retaining absolute control of the media. If this situation persists, it may be assumed that the former "underground" press will emerge into the open, that the "independent" (largely Catholic) press will be able to end its self-censorship, and that even the party press will, with the backing of glasnost (see U.S.S.R. 5) and the encouragement of the U.S.S.R. for the new regime, be able to write more freely in future.

Ponting, Clive Ponting (1946-) was seen as a high-flier as soon as he joined the British civil service in 1970. By 1974 he was an assistant principal in the Ministry of Defence and rising fast. In 1979, as a principal, he was deputed among other youthful stars to help Sir Derek Rayner, seconded from the retail trade, in his campaign to cut down civil service expenses. Ponting's success in pointing out overspending and suggesting cutbacks brought him to the attention of Prime Minister Margaret Thatcher, who had him moved up again, as assistant to Defence Secretary Francis Pym. Ponting's job was to help implement the economies he had suggested, but it soon became clear that Rayner's plans were evaporating in the face of Whitehall vested interests.

In March 1984 Ponting was appointed head of section DS5 at the Ministry of Defence, dealing with naval affairs, including fishery protection, the Gulf War and the Falklands task force. He found himself pitched into the center of a growing controversy over the May 2, 1982, sinking, by the British submarine HMS *Conqueror*, of the Argentine warship *General Belgrano*, with the loss of 368 lives. The question remains: Was the *Belgrano* a legitimate target or was she not only outside the British exclusion zone of 200 miles but actually, under Argentine naval orders, sailing away from the Falklands. The government case, which fluctuated as to detail but remained adamant as to British innocence, was represented by Michael Heseltine, the secretary of state for defense, and John Stanley, the minister for the armed services. Their leading opponent was Tam Dalyell, MP. The essence of his charges, which were highly detailed, was this: Had the sinking of the *Belgrano*, as the government claimed, been a military act, carried out by the *Conqueror* in pursuit of a legitimate target; or was it, as Dalyell claimed, a political one, carried out with cynical disregard for the "threat"; or actually lack of it, posed by the warship and in deliberate furtherance of Mrs. Thatcher's personal glory?

Ponting was initially given by Stanley the task of preparing two alternatives to set against the allegations made by the shadow spokesman for defense, Denzil Davies. One of these was to admit the truth—that the *Belgrano* had been sighted on May 1—and the other was to lie and claim that she had not been seen until May 2, and immediately sunk. For both parties, this time factor was vital: simultaneous sighting and sinking backed the government side; the 30-hour shadowing of the ship by the submarine, which Dalyell claimed, supported the MP's theory. This task was further refined when Ponting was asked by Heseltine's office to prepare an indepth review of the entire engagement, a detailed summary of signals, naval actions and allied information, all of which became known (adopting CIA parlance) as the "Crown Jewels" and was designed to be used as a basis for rebutting Dalyell. What Ponting discovered, and what was revealed at his trial, was that despite government assertions of a supposed Argentine pincer movement, of which the *Belgrano* represented one jaw, the ship in fact presented no threat to the British forces, and was indeed fleeing the 200-mile exclusion zone as stated.

The result of Ponting's labors was that on April 4 the prime minister replied to an opposition question on the sinking with the statement that the *Belgrano* had been sighted on May 1, but that the pincer formation, of which she formed a part, was a serious threat to the British Task Force; thus she had to be sunk. Ponting's own reaction was fury. On April 24 he sent an anonymous letter to Dalyell, stating that he had access to the truth, and suggesting certain questions that the MP ought to pursue. He also applied, without success, for a transfer to another ministry. He had already, on April 14, sent Heseltine a letter suggesting that the minister should answer Dalyell's questions honestly, as he (supposedly) would any less contentious parliamentary question—although he suggested that three answers should be refused.

The controversy continued, although Ponting was working on other tasks. He was reinvolved in July when, in answer to a request from the Commons Foreign Affairs Committee as to the alterations in the military rules of engagement during the Falklands War, another civil servant, Michael Legge, wrote a minute explaining that such disclosures "would provide more information than Ministers have been prepared to reveal ... I therefore recommend that we avoid these difficulties by providing the Committee with a more general narrative." Ponting's response was to send copies of the minute, plus page one of his own memo to Heseltine, dealing with the questions Heseltine should answer, rather than those he should reject, to Dalyell. Dalyell, in turn, made a copy, then passed the material to the chairman of the Foreign Affairs Committee who passed them on to Heseltine. Ponting was soon tracked down by ministry of defense police and on confessing told them, "I did this because I believe ministers within this department were not prepared to answer legitimate questions from an MP about a matter of public concern, simply in order to protect their position."

Charged under section two of the OFFICIAL SECRETS ACT, Ponting was tried in February 1985. The jury was stringently vetted and parts of the trial, notably those dealing with the "Crown Jewels," were held in camera. The essence of the prosecution's case, citing a phrase in the act, was that "the interests of the state" are the same as the current government policy. Although the judge, Mr. Justice McCowan, summed up very much in favor of the Crown, Ponting was acquitted. The ministry could not dismiss an innocent man, but they immediately stripped him of any security clearances, thus rendering it impossible for him to work, not merely at the Ministry of Defence, but also anywhere in Whitehall. He resigned, with some pension rights, and published his memoirs of the affair, *The Right to Know*.

SEE ALSO ABC Trial; Tisdall, Sarah.

Porteous, Bishop Beilby   SEE The Bible; Porteusian Index.

Porteusian Index   The first Bible to be published with a Porteusian Index appeared in 1796. This index was the creation of Bishop Beilby Porteous, the bishop of London and a leading member of the Society for the Reformation of Manners (see Societies for …) and was essentially a device to ensure that one could read the Bible and avoid all offensive material. Under Porteous' system, the Bible was annotated by four levels of marking, which were placed at the head of each chapter. They were, respectively: 1*, 1, 2 and unmarked.

Porteous included a key that explained them. "1*" meant the words of Christ plus all references to His coming found in the Old Testament. These markings were mainly in the New Testament, with some excerpts from Isaiah and the Psalms. "1" meant passages "of a more spiritual and practical nature" (than those marked "2" or left blank). These included those remaining parts of the Gospels that had not already been rated "1*," Job, Ecclesiastes, and various other passages, all of which were suitable for meditation on the grounds of their goodness and wisdom. "2" meant leading historical chapters—Samuel, Kings etc. These were not particularly improving but were still acceptable. Unmarked chapters included everything else, notably the Song of Solomon, the story of Lot etc. In his explanation of the key Porteous carefully resisted proscribing the unmarked chapters. Instead he pointed out how very dull most of it is, comprising as it does Jewish laws, lengthy genealogies and similar material. He neglects to mention the more sensational material. The Porteusian Index was reasonably successful; there was for a while a Porteusian Bible Society, based in Frith Street, Soho,

which distributed the indexed version. In the end the Bible failed: It offered safe passage through the scriptures, but did not, as the true expurgators required, create a genuinely purified bible.

Potocki de Montalk, Count Geoffrey Wladislas Vaile   Montalk was an eccentric living in England in the 1930s. Born in New Zealand, the son of an architect and grandson of a Polish professor, he had been educated for the law but preferred to live as a poet "by divine right" and in pursuit of what he claimed was his rightful throne as king of Poland. In January 1932, together with a companion, Douglas Glass, he attempted to find, in the area of the Old Bailey, a printer who would be willing to set of book of poems, *Here Lies John Penis*, incorporating Montalk's free translations of Rabelais and Verlaine plus 18 lines of his own, which included a number of taboo words. He eventually found the manager of a firm of linotype operators, a Mr. de Lozey, who offered to do the job for 25/- (£1.25). They left the manuscript with Mr. de Lozey, saying they would keep looking but if no cheaper offer could be found, he should proceed with the work. Before they could find another printer they were both arrested and held in Brixton prison.

At the preliminary hearing, at Clerkenwell police court, Glass was discharged and Montalk bailed. On February 8, 1932, the count, who chose to take his oath by Apollo, appeared at the Old Bailey before the recorder of London, Sir Ernest Wild. The recorder, who had recently published his own slim volume of verse, *The Lamp of Destiny*, made his position clear: "Are you going to allow a man, because he calls himself a poet, to deflower our English language by popularising these words?" He emphasized that "the highbrow school" had to abide by the same rules as lesser mortals. He referred to the offending words by their initials only and stated that "a man may not say he is a poet and be filthy." He then suggested that the jury need not leave the box, but could give their verdict without consultation. The jury did wish to retire, but returned to declare Montalk guilty. Montalk, who made his indignation clear, was sentenced to six months in jail.

The sole comfort for libertarians was the recorder's acknowledgment, although he denied its validiy for the count, of a defense in such cases of "public good (and) advancement of literature." An appeal fund was launched, backed by Aldous Huxley, J.B. Priestley, Walter de la Mare, Laurence Housman, T.S. Eliot and others. On March 7 Montalk, who had been imprisoned in the interim, appeared before the Court of Criminal Appeal. He failed to impress the court and his appeal was dismissed. After leaving Wormwood Scrubs prison he wrote up his experiences in a pamphlet entitled "Snobbery with Violence."

Poulet-Malassis, Auguste   Poulet-Malassis (1825-1878), the grandson of Jean-Zacharie Malassis, the publisher inter alia of MIRABEAU, was, with JULES GAY, one of the leading publishers of erotica in 19th-century France. He also published a number of legitimate works, although the most famous of these, *Les Fleurs du Mal* (1857) by Charles Baudelaire (1821-67), was itself prosecuted and both author and publisher fined. Poulet-Malassis' erotic publications featured excellent printing, fine illustrations and scholarly introductions, for the maintaining of which high standards he nearly bankrupted himself. His catalog included editions of such authors as Andrea de Nerciat, DE SADE and Pierre-Jean de Beranger (1780-1857) as well as collections of satirical verse. He also published *Le theatre erotique de la rue de la Sante* (1864), a collection of erotic plays written by French authors such as Henri de Monnier and performed not by humans but by puppets, secretly and before select audiences.

As did many of his peers in erotic publishing, Poulet-Malassis compiled some volumes of bibliography. He issued what were essentially his own sales catalogs under the title *Bulletin trimestriel des publications defendus en France imprimees a l'etranger* between August 1867 and December 1869. These give a useful overview of the trade in erotica, much of which he published himself, during the era.

SEE ALSO Perceau, Louis.

preferred position   Although the rights and freedoms guaranteed by the FIRST AMENDMENT to the U.S. Constitution are not absolute in each and every instance (a concept of limitation summed up in the dictum: "The most stringent protection of free speech would not protect a man in falsely shouting 'Fire!' in a crowded theater."), these guarantees are always seen as being of paramount importance. Any attempt to restrict or alter them is viewed as guilty until it can be proved innocent. This status is defined in U.S. law as a preferred position. The position was defined further in the case of *Schneider* v. *State* (1939) where the court stated:

> In every case ... where legislative abridgement of the rights is asserted the courts should be astute to examine the effect of the challenged legislation. Mere legislative preferences or beliefs respecting matters of public convenience may well support regulation directed at other personal activities, but be insufficient to justify such as diminishes the exercise of rights so vital to the maintenance of democratic institutions. And so, as cases arise, the delicate and difficult task falls upon the courts to weigh the circumstances and to appraise the substantiality of the reasons advanced in support of the regulation of the free enjoyment of the rights.

Presentation, The   The satirical cartoonist James Gillray (1757-1815) was arrested in London on January 23, 1796, for the publication two weeks previously of a print—*The Presentation–or–The Wise Men's Offering*—that depicted in an unflattering manner the presentation of the infant Princess Anne, born to the prince of Wales (later George IV) and his wife, Princess Charlotte. In the print the prince sways drunkenly into the room to meet an unidentified crone who is holding out the infant. Politician Charles James Fox and playwright Richard Brinsley Sheridan are pictured in groveling attendance. The picture's publication created a furor. One magazine condemned the scene as "vile ... most obscene" and claimed that decency had been shocked by its subject. Gillray was arrested on charges of selling the print, then released on bail. However, either through the intervention of politician George Canning, or simply through lack of interest, the case was soon afterward dropped.

President's Commission on Obscenity and Pornography, The   On October 23, 1967, President Lyndon B. Johnson signed Public Law 90-100 (HR 10347), creating the U.S. Commission on Obscenity and Pornography. The 18-member commission, composed of businessmen, academics, scientists, clergymen and lawyers, was charged with exploring four areas of responsibility: (1) analysis of the current U.S. legislation regarding the control and prosecution of alleged obscenity; (2) assessment of the distribution of and traffic in pornographic materials; (3) a study of the effects of pornography on the public, especially on minors, and the relationship, if it existed, between pornography and crime; (4) recommendation of any action for the future regulation of pornographic material.

In two years' work, nearly $20 million was spent on the commission as it labored to assess the "accepted standards of decency" in the U.S. As well as the commission's own staff, some 40 research countracts were distributed, bringing in academia, hard-core porno stores, colleges, prisons, hospitals and many other institutions and individuals. More than 200 allied bills, all attempting to limit pornography, were introduced in Congress. Well before the commission had finished its researches, in March 1970, the House of Representatives, acting on Richard Nixon's May 1969 message to Congress in which the new president had requested new laws to restrict the passage of offensive material through the mails, proposed a bill (HR 15693) drafted by the U.S. Civil Service Commission, that made it a federal crime to use the mails to deliver obscene materials to anyone under the age of 18. In response to a claimed 275,000 complaints against such deliveries, adults were able to give a written statement to their own post office declaring that they did not wish to receive any such material in their mail.

As drafts of the finished document began to appear in summer 1970, it became obvious that Nixon's hoped-for condemnation of pornography, linking it to crime, the corruption of minors and the general draining of America's moral reserves, would not be forthcoming. Conservative forces mustered to decry the report, claiming that it had been rigged, that its methods were unscientific and that its staff, with the exception of Charles H. Keating Jr. (the sole Nixon appointee and known in his hometown of Cincinnati as "Mr. Clean"), were incompetent at best. On September 30, 1970, the 874-page document was finally released. It proposed the repeal of all 114 existing state and federal laws that "prohibited importation, sale and display of pornography to adults ... Such laws ... are ineffective, are not supported by public opinion, and conflict with 'the right of each individual to determine for himself what books he wishes to read and what pictures or films he wishes to see.'" Also proposed were a number of state laws that would restrict distribution of all erotic material without parental consent, and the prohibition of any displays of visual erotica (although not books) that might be seen by children. The commission also called for a wide-ranging program of sex education and the encouragement of a public debate, based on factual information rather than emotional wrangling, on the topic of obscenity and pornography.

Dissenters, lead by Keating, who claimed he had been banned from writing a full counteropinion, claimed that the report was "biased in favor of protecting the business of obscenity" and that the whole enterprise had been a waste of taxpayers' money. All in all, said Keating, it was a "shoddy piece of scholarship that will be quoted ad nauseam by cultural polluters and their attorneys." On October 13 the U.S. Senate, which had initially pushed for the commission in 1967, repudiated it and its report and by a vote of 60-5 rejected its findings and its call for the blanket repeal of anti-obscenity laws. On October 24 President Nixon issued a 400-word statement in which he condemned the report as morally bankrupt and urged every state authority to fight even harder against pornography. "American morality is not to be trifled with," he added. The commission's efforts were quickly buried and its recommendations simply faded away.

In April 1971 a company that had published a deluxe version of the Report, interleaved with illustrations culled from hard-core Scandinavian pornography, and retailing at $12.50 (as opposed to the government's edition at $5.50), was charged in Dallas and San Diego with "interstate shipment of obscene matter and with conspiring to send obscene matter through the mails."

SEE ALSO Attorney General's Commission on Pornography; Citizens for Decent Literature; *The Illustrated Report*.

prior restraint (U.K.)   The British rejection of prior restraint censorship (the censorship of material prior to its publication, broadcasting or screening) and the concomitant acceptance of laws designed to punish unacceptable material once it has appeared, is based in William Blackstone's *Commentaries* (1765). Here the nation's most respected writer on the law stated, "The liberty of the press is indeed essential to the nature of a free state; but this consists in laying no previous restraints on publication, and not in freedom from censure for criminal matter when published. Every free man has an undoubted right to lay what sentiments he pleases before the public; to forbid this is to destroy the freedom of the press; but if he publishes what is improper, mischievous or illegal, he must take the consequences of his own temerity." Despite these unimpeachable sentiments, Britain's lack of a written constitution in whch they might be enshrined permanently (as they are in the U.S. FIRST AMENDMENT), has meant that prior restraint, while officially outlawed, has achieved certain inroads on the media's freedom.

Prior restraint injunctions are currently subject to three basic provisos: (1) an individual will not be permitted to silence an alleged libel if the publishers of that alleged libel have stated that they intend to call witnesses in court to prove the statement's truth; thus an aggrieved plaintiff cannot use the law of libel merely to gag an unpleasant revelation; (2) an injunction will not be granted on the grounds of breach of confidence, copyright or contract—even if such rules have obviously been abused—if the material in question reveals in the public interest matters of crime, fraud, misconduct or gross hypocrisy; (3) no injunction will be granted against material that allegedly contravenes the criminal law if the publisher concerned wishes to undergo a trial by jury to determine whether or not this is so.

prior restraint (U.S.)   Under United States law prior restraint governs any situation whereby an authority attempts to restrain the exercise of free speech or the free press prior to any judicial determination—with all the guarantees of due process of law—that the speech or press in question is not protected by the freedoms guaranteed by the FIRST AMENDMENT of the U.S. Constitution. Once speech or material has been adjudged unprotected, it can be subject to prior restraint without problem. Prior restraint is permitted far greater latitude within the Armed Forces, where, in common with a number of other laws, it can be set aside in the face of the allegedly greater importance of the "morale, loyalty and fighting discipline" of the troops. A similar limit to prior restraint exists regarding what may or may not be written or said in public by members of the nation's intellience services, who must sign an agreement whereby they promise not to divulge any professional secrets without submitting the material to the agency first.

SEE ALSO CIA 1. publishing agreements, 2. secrecy agreements; *Greer* v. *Spock* (1976); *McGehee* v. *Casey* (1983); *Near* v. *Minnesota* (1931); Pentagon Papers; *Snepp* v. *United States* (1980).

Private Case, The   The Private Case of the British Library, held in the British Museum in Bloomsbury, London, is a group of several thousand erotic and sexological works that comprises the greatest collection of indecent, obscene and pornographic books in the world. Including material published over more than three centuries, covering English, French, Spanish, Portuguese, Italian, German, Dutch and Latin texts, the Private Case surpasses similar "special" collections in France's Bibliotheque Nationale, the Vatican Library, Washington's Library of Congress and the Bodleian Library, Oxford. Private Case titles can be found in the General Catalog under the pressmark "P.C."

The Private Case was established circa 1856. Certainly there exist no Private Case pressmarks in the general catalog prior to 1857. The rationale behind the setting up of this special collection and the decision to omit all erotica from the main catalog is hard to pin down. Peter Fryer, whose study *Private Case—Public Scandal* (1967) broke the taboo on the hidden erotica, believes that it was most likely the personal decision of the Keeper of Printed Books John Winter Jones (1805-81), who assumed office in 1856. British Library authorities believe instead that Jones' superior and predecessor as keeper, Sir Anthony Panizzi (1797-1879), must have been behind the creation of the Private Case. The essence of the Private Case was that it dealt only with new acquisitions. Material that had been in the general catalog prior to 1856 stayed there. This led to anomalies: Certain items still accessible to the public were far more obscene than many confirmed to the museum's basement shelves.

The gradually expanding case of the 19th century reproduced in macrocosm the locked, secret shelves in the libraries of many collectors and connoisseurs of the period, men such as Richard Monckton Milnes (1809-95) or FREDERICK HANKEY (ca. 1832-82) who were as devoted to erotica as they were to more respectable literature. The collection was made available to such amateurs and they in turn might bequeath all or part of their own "facetiae" to the museum. Among the best-known of these collectors was HENRY ASHBEE, who as "Pisanus Fraxi" compiled the three-volume bibliography of erotica, NOTES ON CURIOUS AND UNCOMMON BOOKS (1877-85). Ashbee, whose own collection of erotica was among the 15,229 books willed to the library on his death in 1900, deplored the secrecy and inaccessibility of the case, writing of a collection that "to the shame of the British Museum authorities, is consigned to a dark room in the basement, difficult of access, and where the interesting specimens it comprises can only be inspected under the greatest disadvantages."

The modern Private Case, as Peter Fryer apostrophized it, represents "books weighed in the balance and found wanton." Its shelves engulfed books subversive of the monarchy and of religion, blasphemous books, obscene or erotic books and books that betrayed the secrets of freemasonry. Access to the case represented a freemasonry in itself, with the museum staff sedulously attempting to hide first the existence of the collection and then, if a reader proved adamant, the precise whereabouts of individual books. The actual catalog of the case was until very recently restricted to staff circulation. As recently as 1962 the official museum guide assured readers that all books held by the Museum could be traced through the General Catalog. This was simply untrue.

In 1963, under increasing pressure from legitimate researchers, it was announced that the Private Case, with its press marks, would be transferred, albeit gradually, into the General Catalog. By 1965 this had been done, although readers of books pressmarked "P.C." and "Cup." (for the "Cupboard" that contains restricted books) are still forced to sit at a special table in the North Library.

The current Private Case still concentrates on erotica. Its contents cover works of sexology, dictionaries of sexual slang or colloquialism; encyclopedias and histories of erotica and bibliographies of erotic works; a good deal of 17th- and 18th-century pornography; erotic classics and autobiographies that center on sex; hard-core pornography, including some of the contemporary products of Soho and 42nd Street; homosexual erotica; sado-masochistic and allied fetishist material. In 1981, following Fryer's pioneering work of 1967, *The Private Case* by P.J. Kearney was published. It lists, with all necessary details and a scholarly introduction, the titles, pressmarks and much allied and informative material as regards the once hidden collection.

SEE ALSO British Library: suppressed books.

Proclamation Society, The   In 1787 the social reformer and evangelical philanthropist William Wilberforce (1759-1833) determined to add to his campaign against the slave trade a campaign against what he felt was a parallel form of bondage: casual hedonism. The SOCIETIES FOR THE REFORMATION OF MANNERS, which had attempted a similarly uplifting task earlier in the century, had largely disintegrated. Wilberforce, one of the leading adherents of John Wesley's new sect, Methodism, sought to revive their aims, stating plainly that "God has set before me as my object the reformation of manners." In 1787 he persuaded the archbishop of Canterbury that a new campaign for such reforms could best be launched with royal backing.

On June 1, 1787, his efforts were rewarded. Under the signature of George III was announced "A Proclamation for the Encouragement of Piety and Virtue, and for preventing and punishing of Vice, Profaneness, and Immorality." The usual condemnations of drunkenness, sabbath-breaking and allied excesses were duly listed, but unlike earlier such pronouncements, there was included a specific reference to the need to suppress "all loose and licentious Prints, Books and Publications, dispersing Poison to the Minds of the Young and Unwary, and to punish the Publishers and Vendors thereof."

The country's bishops were then sent to their dioceses to promulgate the provisions of the proclamation. Wilberforce followed them one by one, offering encouragement and soliciting support for his new reform group, the Proclamation Society. By the end of his tour he had amassed the archbishops of Canterbury and York, 17 lesser bishops, six dukes and 11 other peers, as well as many lesser backers, such as Thomas BOWDLER, who toured the nation lecturing on prison reform, and the obsessively censorious Hannah More, who devoted her best efforts to the rooting out of corruption in the "hotbed of a circulating library." Wilberforce modeled the society on the ancient ROMAN CENSORS, who were the guardians of both the morals and the religion of their people. The society was headed first by Lord Montagu, then by Lord Bathhurst and then by Beilby Porteus, bishop of Chester, a veteran campaigner against "licentious Novels, licentious Histories and licentious systems of Philosophy"—the "grand corrupters" of innocent youth. His PORTEUSIAN INDEX provided readers with a safe means of discerning the acceptable and the dangerous passages of the Bible.

The society instituted a wave of prosecutions for obscene libel, netting a variety of works, mainly such pornographic classics as MEMOIRS OF A WOMAN OF PLEASURE and *The School of Venus* (L'ESCHOLLE DES FILLES), along with specimens of the new, "soft-core" sex-and-scandal periodicals such as *The Rambler's Magazine* and its various imitators. It is likely that the prosecution of HARRIS' LIST OF COVENT GARDEN LADIES in 1795 was initiated by the society. The Proclamation Society believed it was vital that the newly literate masses, susceptible without prior training to any kind of book, both good and evil, must be guided. If they would not be guided, then they must be led and the evil must be removed. Given the general tolerance and skepticism of the era, the censorial duty of a guarding religion, the second function of their Roman predecessors, was less easily exercised by the society. The Blasphemy Act of 1698 gave them a suitable weapon, but prosecutions were hard to maintain and the courts seemed less concerned than the society's activists with extirpating every vestige of possible corruption. One successful case was brought against an impoverished bookseller, Thomas Williams, prosecuted in 1797 for issuing THOMAS PAINE'S AGE OF REASON. When Williams' poverty became apparent to Lord Erskine, who was prosecuting the case, he suggested that the society might exercise a little charity. The society chose to resist Erskine's appeal, and the hapless Williams was duly condemned.

The Proclamation Society was a spent force by 1800. Its successes had been relatively few and the flow of objectionable literature and the movement toward religious tolerance had continued unabated. The masses grew more literate and the shelves of the circulating library offered superior entertainment to the tracts of the society. In 1801 it was proposed that a new reform group, the SOCIETY FOR THE SUPPRESSION OF VICE and the Encouragement of Religion and Virtue, should be established. It began work in 1802 and the Proclamation Society, overshadowed by the more vibrant newcomer, was absorbed quietly into its ranks.

Production Code Administration   SEE Legion of Decency; Motion Picture Producers and Directors Asociation (MPPDA).

Professor Mamlock   *Professor Mamlock* was made in Russia in 1938. It is an unashamedly propagandist film, dealing with the rise of the Nazi Party in Germany, the Nazi persecution of the Jews and other "enemies of the Reich," and the struggles of anti-Nazis, predominantly communists, against Hitler's brutality. The film had been adapted from a play of the same title by author Frederick Wolf, which had been produced without problem by a New York theater group. While the U.S. Customs saw no reason to hold up its import into America in 1939, the film did face a variety of censorship

problems: it was banned in England, in China, and in Chicago, Ohio and Massachusetts (on Sundays) in the U.S.

In 1939 the "amusement inspector" of Providence, Rhode Island, banned the film from his city, claiming that it was "communistic propaganda" and would "incite race hatred and class strife ... especially in view of the present condition of the public mind with respect to the underlying theme of the picture and also because of the nature of the scenes of brutality and bloodshed ..." The inspector added that his ban was further justified by the fact that the city would not exhibit any film that had not been previously approved by the NATIONAL BOARD OF REVIEW OF MOTION PICTURES, which body had not yet approved this film and which, when they did view it, refused to license it.

When the counsel for the distributors, the Amkino Corporation, filed for the reversal of these two denials, both the inspector and the National Board refused to alter their decision. The state supreme court backed the ban, refusing to accept the defendant's claim that there had been any error in law or that the board lacked the competence to judge the film.
SEE ALSO *Victory in the West.*

Protection of Children Act (1978, U.K.)   This British law was created to outlaw what was seen as a growing trade in child pornography. Children under the age of 14 were already protected by the Children Act (1960), but the new act dealt with those of 14 and 15, still below the age of consent (16 years of age). The test for prosecutions under the law is that of "indecency," a far wider concept than that of a "tendency to deprave and corrupt," which identifies obscenity in the OBSCENE PUBLICATIONS ACT OF 1959; it is thus possible to exert far more stringent controls over these films and magazines. Nonetheless, the courts have been unable to provide a meaningful definition of indecency; the best efforts include "offending against recognised standards of propriety" and "shocking, disgusting and revolting ordinary people."

It is an offense under the act, punishable by a fine of £1,000 or up to six months' imprisonment, to take indecent photographs (including films) of persons under 16 years, or permit them to be taken; to distribute (defined as parting with possession of or offering or exposing for acquisition by another person) or show indecent photographs of persons under 16; to posess such photographs with a view to distributing or showing them; and to publish or cause to be published advertisements that appear to offer indecent photographs of children.

Those charged with distributing or showing indecent photographs or posessing them with an intent of distributing or showing are permitted the defense of claiming a legitimate reason for so doing, or that he or she was ignorant of the content of the photographs. There is no such defense for those who have taken the pictures. The act does not define such "legitimate reasons." All prosecutions must be brought by the director of public prosecutions. The main problem found in the act is how to make an absolute identification of a pictured individual as being below the age of consent. In the end it is up to individual courts to decide this, when there exists no evidence other than the picture itself. As far as films are concerned, the indecency of the parts outweigh the effect of the whole, i.e., a single indictable frame may render an entire film illegal. Conversely a film that features indecent or obscene scenes portrayed by adult performers only, but in which all scenes involving children are perfectly innocent, does not fall under the act. The portrayal of a child, acting innocently in an indecent scene, does fall under the act.

The act was the culmination of Mrs. MARY WHITEHOUSE's campaign against what she and the tabloid press described as "kiddie porn," a campaign that was launched in the wake of her victory in the GAY NEWS BLASPHEMY case. Whitehouse captured as one of her first recruits the new leader of the Conservative Party, Margaret Thatcher, thus establishing for Mrs. Whitehouse, who had hitherto been ignored by major politicians, a rapport with the future prime minister that has persisted ever since. The incumbent Labour home secretary, Merlyn Rees, was less tolerant of Mrs. Whitehouse's grandstanding, preferring to wait for the Williams Report (see Williams Committee), which was still in its research phase.

The furor continued, and Mrs. Whitehouse, the FESTIVAL OF LIGHT and the tabloid press combined to demand legislation. Bowing to the pressure, the Labour government was forced to find room for MP Cyril Townshend's bill, which was passed into law on April 20, 1978. While reformers were delighted, author John Sutherland summed up most critics' views in his book *Offensive Literature* (1982), when he suggested that the act was not "useful or practical ... [it] merely mark[ed] the extraordinary lengths to which sanctimonious emotion and panic can occasionally drive the British public and its legislature."

prurient interest   This is defined in U.S. law as "having a tendency to excite lustful thoughts." It is embodied as a vital part of the tests for obscenity found in the ROTH, MEMOIRS and MILLER STANDARDS.

"Prurient Prude, The"   Charles Reade (1814-84), variously a lawyer, doctor, theatrical manager and dramatist, journalist and writer, and author of a number of novels promoting social reforms, published *Griffith Gaunt, or Jealousy* in 1866. His discussion of sexuality, especially as regards the enforced celibacy of religious life (which he had experienced personally as a don at Oxford and which he condemned as "an invention wholly devilish") proved too frank for the standards of the 1860s. American critics started the attacks, calling the book indecent and immoral; they were soon followed by their London peers who added that "the modesty and purity of women could not survive its perusal." When Reade was further accused of plagiarism, he began legal action. An appeal to Dickens, whose literary heir Reade was generally held to be, elicited no response. Dickens himself preferred on the whole to kow-tow to contemporary

restraint, claiming in 1867 in a letter to Wilkie Collins (from whose original idea the plot had been derived) that while the book was excellent, the uncultured mind might "pervert" certain passages. Collins and Matthew Arnold still offered themselves as "expert witnesses." Reade won his case, although receiving only derisory damages. He gained a better revenge on his critics with the publication of "The Prurient Prude," an open letter assailing his opponents. It begins "Dear Sir, There is a kind of hypocrite that has never been effectually exposed, for want of an expressive name. I beg to supply that defect from our language and introduce to mankind the PRURIENT PRUDE."

Prynne, William   Prynne (1600-69) was a barrister who combined his legal career with a growing preoccupation with the advancement of Puritan reform. His first pamphlets, against Arminianism (a religious doctrine that rejected many of Calvin's orthodox Puritan views, especially as regarded God's responsibility for evil), appeared in 1627. Government attempts to suppress these and subsequent works failed. In 1632, after seven years of work, he completed and had published *Histrio-mastix; or, the Player's Scourge*, an 1,100-page attack on such "immoralities" as the stage, hunting, dancing and other public pleasures, all of which he saw as "intolerable mischiefs to churches, to republics, to the manners, minds and souls of men." It was alleged that the book also attacked the queen, and Prynne was tried in February 1633 by Star Chamber. He was sentenced to be jailed in the Tower of London for life, to lose his ears and be whipped in the pillory, to be disbarred and to be fined £5,000. Not all of this sentence was carried out—he retained most of his ears—but his book was remorselessly seized and destroyed. Prynne, undaunted, continued to assail the government from his cell.

In 1637, in company with Dr. JOHN BASTWICK (1593-1654) and Henry Burton (1578-1648), both unregenerate anti-Catholic pamphleteers, he was tried for a second time, after the publication of a new book, *News from Ipswich*, written during his first term in jail. With his fellow defendants he was fined £5,000, ordered to have his ears cropped flush with his head and be branded on both cheeks with the letters "S.L.," standing in fact for "seditious or schismatical libeller" but reinterpreted by Prynne, whose sufferings had made him into something of a public hero, as "stigmata Laudis," referring to Archbishop Laud, who had ordered the sentence. He was to be confined for life in Carnarvon Castle. The execution of this sentence, on June 30, 1637, made it clear on whose side the mass of people were. The defendants' journey to the pillory and thence to their respective prisons was more a triumphant procession than a disgrace.

In November 1640 Prynne was released by the Long Parliament and his sentences declared invalid. His campaign aainst the stage duly influenced the Puritan prohibition of the theater, but his own dissident nature prevailed against the new government. He attacked Cromwell, his government and his army, being arrested for his pains. In 1660 he asserted the rights of Charles II and welcomed the Restoration. He was made keeper of the records in the Tower of London and published in 1662 his most important work, *Brevia Parliamentaria Rediviva*, a study of parliamentary practice.

public figure   As defined in cases of DEFAMATION in the American courts, a public figure, as opposed to a PUBLIC OFFICIAL, is anyone who, according to the U.S. Supreme Court decision in the case of NEW YORK TIMES COMPANY V. SULLIVAN (1964) has "some special prominence in the affairs of society, or the resolution of public questions, either by having achieved such pervasive fame or notoriety that he becomes a public figure for all purposes and in all contexts, or by voluntarily injecting himself or being drawn into a particular public controversy and thereby becoming a public figure for a limited range of issues."

public forum   SEE public place.

Public Morality Council, The   The Public Morality Council, dedicated to the suppression of all vice, especially that of the working classes, was founded in 1890 by Bishop Creighton and quickly established itself as the figurehead of the social purity movement that remained a power in England until World War II. Although it almost foundered in 1890, when Creighton became ill, it was triumphantly resuscitated in 1901 when the bishop of London, A.F. Winnington-Ingram, became chairman. The PMC, rooted in nonconformism, soon became an ecumenical movement, drawing on every denomination, including Jews. By 1930 it boasted representatives of 60 organizations on its General Council, and in 1935 a memorandum to the prime minister on "The Tendency of Present-Day Films, Plays and Publications" incorporated the views of 260 groups.

The PMC was Winnington-Ingram's personal fief for the next 38 years, until his retirement. He made no secret of his conservatism and dedicated the council to holding back a number of modern trends, especially contraceptives, of which he said he "would like to make a bonfire ... and dance round it." The PMC campaigned on all the abiding obsessions of the pre-1914 purity lobby: white slavery, incest, street prostitution, the advertising of birth control, the distribution of sex education manuals, and a variety of working class amusements, notably music halls, "tableaux vivants" (and later, striptease and all forms of stage nudity), obscene picture postcards and photographs, and the new Mutoscope (*What the Butler Saw*) machines.

The social purity campaign lost the bulk of its public support during World War I, but its activists, notably the PMC and its ally, the NATIONAL VIGILANCE ASSOCIATION, joined forces to form an effective pressure group. The two organizations considered actual amalgamation but compromised by giving responsibility for all questions of obscenity to the council. Its three committees—stage, film and literary—monitored all the contemporary media. The groundwork of

earlier years paid off: Both the LORD CHAMBERLAIN and in particular the newly formed BRITISH BOARD OF FILM CENSORS voluntarily cooperated with the PMC, and although book publishers were less amenable, Home Secretary Sir WILLIAM JOYNSON-HICKS proved a valuable ally. The PMC was involved in the prosecutions of THE WELL OF LONELINESS, THE SLEEVELESS ERRAND, *To Beg I Am Ashamed* and *Bessie Cotter*. A less obvious recruit was the American film censor WILL HAYS, for whom the council began analyzing the reactions of British audiences to American films.

The PMC deluged successive governments with complaints, one hundred or more per year, many of which were acted on. Nonetheless the authorities did resist backing some prosecutions, leading Winington-Ingram to wonder in 1937 whether Hitler or Mussolini might not be more useful to the cause. The PMC sent regular submissions to the authorities, specifying plays, books, even dancing styles that they felt should be censored. In 1934, for instance, they sent 22 books and two deputations on what they felt were obscene publications to the home secretary. Two years later the performance of the can-can featured among the 26 complaints against stage performances they itemized for action.

Winnington-Ingram retired in 1939 and was replaced by Bishop Wand. Under Wand the PMC waged new campaigns in the 1950s: against American "girlie" magazines and horror comics, contraceptive machines and a brand of Danish chewing gum containing pinups. The council was a major influence on Home Secretary Sir David Maxwell-Fyfe when in 1954 he prosecuted five works of serious literature. Among the council's new recruits was Sir Cyril Black, a leading Baptist, who in 1967 initiated the prosecution of LAST EXIT TO BROOKLYN. In 1956, it complained to London Transport about the advertising of ladies' underwear on the underground. Over the ensuing years, however, the PMC gradually faded away.

public official   A public official, as opposed to a PUBLIC FIGURE, has been defined by the U.S. Supreme Court in the case of NEW YORK TIMES COMPANY V. SULLIVAN (1964) as "one in the hierarchy of government having, or appearing to have, substantial responsibility for or control over the conduct of government affairs such that his position invites public scrutiny." Not all governmental employees are automatically public officials, but public officials may be assumed to be government employees.

public place   For the purposes of exercising one's FIRST AMENDMENT rights as guaranteed under the U.S. Constitution, a public place or public forum covers any place open to the public. However, a number of places are both open to the public and governed by a variety of intrinsic restrictions, e.g., courthouses, jails, public transport vehicles and military bases; so, such places may also exercise certain restrictions on the exercise of First Amendment rights. On the other hand, such areas as public parks, streets, sidewalks, libraries, stores, theaters and the area around public buildings are defined as public places or forums, and here one's rights may be exercised without fear of restriction. The doorbells of private homes are also defined as public places if the purpose of ringing them is to engage in political, charitable or religious solicitation; this right does not extend to purely commercial solicitation.

SEE ALSO *Greer* v. *Spock* (1976).

Puritan censorship (the Commonwealth) The Long Parliament, convened in 1640 during the English Civil War, set out to destroy the machinery of Stuart government. In 1641 it abolished the Star Chamber and its attendant ecclesiastical courts, the main instruments of Stuart censorship, and severely limited, but did not destroy the powers of the STATIONERS' COMPANY, the controller of the press. A reform group drawn from the less wealthy members sought a complete overhaul of the company, but their efforts were fended off by the vested interests. The company also proved to be the sole agency of stability within the printing trade that could be called upon by the new government. For about 18 months, in the first flush of revolution, there were no statutory restrictions on the press, which responded by issuing a flood of books, pamphlets and tracts. Tolerance soon abated, and in March 1642 Parliament commanded that "the abuse of printing be reformed" and began to prosecute an increasing number of printers and writers.

So massive and undisciplined was the flow of these publications that in March and June 1643 a series of general ordinances appeared, which first regulated the book trade and then reestablished full-scale censorship with the full compliance of the Stationers' if not of the more radical printers. Like the Tudors and Stuarts before them, the Puritans enforced the licensing of any publication, appointing an official searcher, himself a member of the company, to oversee the press and control what was printed.

The resumption of censorship drew from Milton in 1644 his famous "Areopagitica: a speech of Mr. John Milton for the library of the unlicenc'd printing, to the Parliament of England." The original *areopagitica* was the highest legal tribunal in Athens; Milton's pamphlet, which was neither registered nor licensed, and was written partially as a response to Parliament's suppression of his writings on divorce and partially as a condemnation of the Stationers' Company, attacked the ordinances of 1643. Pointing out that history's main advocates of censorship had been precisely those figures—kings and popes—most loathed by Puritans, and that any suppression of reading leads in turn to a suppression of knowledge and virtue, Milton urged Parliament to abandon its decrees. He also stresed pragmatically that censorship, however assiduously pursued, is like "the exploit of the gallant man who thought to pound up the crows by shutting the park gate." Truth was paramount, unpalatable or not, and new opinions ought to be infinitely preferable to a "gross conforming stupidity."

Parliament was not to be swayed. Indeed, the pamphlet that has come to epitomize perhaps the best arguments for freedom of speech was virtually ignored; it appeared in only one edition and was not republished in full until 1738. Milton himself acted in 1651 as the official licenser of newsbooks (prototype newspapers), a less ironic appointment than it might initially appear, since his plea centered on serious, rather than allegedly sensational publications. Only the chaos of the continuing Civil War and divisions in their own ranks between, among others, the Presbyterians and the Independents made Puritan censorship less than wholly efficient. The products of royalist opposition and Puritan factions continued to appear. Attempts by the army to destroy the royalist and Presbyterian press after Charles I had been executed were halfhearted. The Printing Act of 1649 and 1653 attempted to intensify censorship, drawing heavily on Tudor and Stuart models, but neither succeeded, even though 18 printers were arrested in 1653 and in 1654, under a general search warrant, the sergeant-at-arms smashed a number of unlicensed London presses. Special ad hoc committees were available for considering any particularly offensive publication. Newsbooks such as *Mercurius Britannicus* and *The Scottish Dove* were strictly controlled and occasionally prosecuted. Most successful was Oliver Cromwell himself, whose Order for the Control of the Press of August 28, 1658, went furthest to establishing effective, repressive censorship. His death left his system intact, and in April 1660 WILLIAM PRYNNE was entrusted by Parliament with drawing up an act to control the press. The Restoration of Charles II later that year curtailed those efforts, and those of the Puritan censorship.

SEE ALSO book burning in England 4. Puritans; United Kingdom: Stuart censorship.

Puttana Errante, La *La Puttana Errante* (*The Wandering Whore*), the product of an anonymous author or authors, appeared in 1650 and soon became one of the staples of 17th- and then 18th-century pornography, suffering the attentions of censors in various countries. Its dialogue form was patterned on ARETINO's *Ragionamenti* (1534-36) and thus gave rise to the false attribution of the book to that earlier writer. The book illustrates the sexual views of an older, experienced woman as passed on to her young companion. Once again it echoes Aretino, with the inclusion of 35 plates to illustrate positions of sexual intercourse. *La Puttana Errante* is the first known imaginative prose work that concentrates directly and exclusively on the pleasures of sex. A periodical, *The Wandering Whore*, was published in London by John Garfield later in 1660, but this capitalized on the book's reputation, rather than offering a direct translation. The earliest actual translation appeared in 1827 as *The Accomplished Whore*, published by the pornographer George Cannon.

Pynchon, William Pynchon's book, *The Meritorious Price of Our Redemption*, was the first one to be publicly burned in the United States, where it was destroyed by the Massachusetts Colony authorities in 1650. Although Pynchon (1590-1662) was one of the founders of the colony, and a signatory to its charter, his book proved so contentious in its criticism of the puritan orthodoxy that dominated the theological attitudes of the colony, that after it had been read by the General Council it was condemned to be burned by the common executioner in the Market Place. Pynchon himself was publicly censured and escaped further punishment only by sailing back to England.

Q

Quesnel, Pasquier Quesnel (1634-1719) was born in Paris and educated in the Congregation of the Oratory, of which he was appointed director. His first book, *Pensees Chretiennes sur les quatres Evangiles*, set the pattern for all his subsequent, more celebrated work. His major work appeared in 1671: *Le Nouveau Testament en Francais, avec des reflexions morales sur chaque verset*, which became known as *Les Reflexions Morales*. Further editions appeared in 1693 and 1694 in which he added new material, dealing not only with the Gospels, but with the Acts and Epistles as well. The book caused a sensation, influencing and dividing the whole church. Described by critics as "pernicious in practice and offensive to pious ears" and "scandalous, impious and temerarious," it became central to the ongoing controversy between the Jesuits and the Jansenists. A supporter of JAN-SENISM, Quesnel fled in 1684 to Brussels when he found himself unable to sign a document laid down by the Oratory in which the order accepted certain principles of DESCARTES, whose work was condemned by Arnauld and other leading Jansenists. In 1700 Quesnel was arrested on the orders of King Philip V of Spain, who was influenced by the Jesuits. In 1703 he escaped and returned to Amsterdam, where he died in 1719. Although its author was left in peace, the book was officially condemned by Pope Clement XI in 1708, and in 1712 a committee of five cardinals and 11 theologians sat in judgment on it. The result of their labors was the bull "UNIGENITUS", pronounced against Quesnel's work.

Quigley, Martin   SEE Motion Picture Production Code.

R

Rabbit's Wedding, The *The Rabbit's Wedding*, a children's book by Garth Williams, was published by Harper in 1958. By May 1959 it had without incident sold about 40,000 copies in the U.S. That month, as compulsory integration increased racial tensions in the Southern states, the book came under attack. Looking closely at an illustration of "The Wedding Dance" partway through the book, it was clear that of the lapine couple, the buck was black while the doe was white. Such miscegenation, stated an editor in Orlando, Florida, was "brainwashing ... as soon as you pick up the book and open its pages you realize these rabbits are integrated." The *Home News* of Montgomery, Alabama, added that the book was integrationist propaganda obviously aimed at children in their formative years. The public librarian in Montgomery removed the book from the "open" to the "reserved" shelves.

Rabelais, Francois Rabelais was a French physician, humanist and satirist (ca. 1494-ca. 1553) best known for his massive satires *Pantagruel* (1533), *Gargantua* (1535), the *Third Book* (1546), the *Fourth Book* (1548-52) and the *Fifth Book* (1562-64). The son of a lawyer, he became first a Franciscan monk and then the secretary of the bishop of Maillezais. He became a bachelor of medicine and published a number of works on medicine and archaeology, and acquired a reputation for his learning and medical expertise before beginning his cycle of satires. Despite enjoying the longtime patronage of Cardinal Jean du Bellay and the protection of Francois I of France, the nature of Rabelais' satires, often bawdy to the point of obscenity, and wasting no time on the observation of the social niceties, brought him into frequent conflict with the authorities.

The first two parts of *Pantagruel*, published in 1533 without the knowledge of their author, were listed immediately on the Index produced by the University of Paris and placed on the official literary blacklist of the Parliament of Paris. The fourth book was similarly proscribed in 1552. Despite the Papacy's absolution of Rabelais from attack in 1535, when a bull was enacted in his defense, the TRIDENTINE INDEX listed him as an author of the first class, and thus banned all his works completely. The United States banned his works until the Tariff Act (1930) ended the censorship of such acknowledged literary works, although certain editions, with what were termed obscene illustrations, remained forbidden. In 1938 Rabelais was banned comprehensively in South Africa.
SEE ALSO United States 21. Tariff Act.

Radeau de la Medusa, Le (The Raft of the Medusa) This painting by Gericault was put on show at the Paris Salon in 1819. The picture, of a heap of the dead and dying, in which pitiful survivors of a shipwreck raise themselves feebly, beseeching some final deliverance, commemorated the expedition to Senegal in July 1816 of the French frigate *Medusa*. The crew had mutinied and the survivors of that mutiny had spent 13 days and nights adrift on a raft in the open sea. The painting was generally vilified both by the critics, who immediately divided into two rival factions—classicists and romantics—and, more importantly, by the government, which claimed that Gericault's art was a deliberate, thinly veiled attack, imputing the disaster to the government's own incompetence. Further political inferences were read into the picture, claiming that it illustrated "the struggle of humanity for freedom," which could be construed as impermissible sedition. The government therefore refused to purchase the painting, and it was removed from the Salon for fear of any political repercussions.

Rainbow, The D.H. LAWRENCE began writing *The Rainbow* in 1912; it was published in 1915. Reviews were generally unfavorable, with certain writers condemning it as immoral or, as the *London Daily News* put it, "a monotonous wilderness of phallicism." Following these criticisms the police seized 1,000 copies of the book from the publisher's warehouse. In November 1915 the publishers, Methuen, were summoned to Bow Street Magistrate's Court to show cause why these thousand copies should not be destroyed. Appearing for the police, H. Muskett claimed that the book was "a mass of obscenity of thought, idea and action throughout" and made sneering reference to "language which he supposed would be regarded in some quarters as artistic and intellectual." Methuen neither informed Lawrence of the proceedings nor made any defense of the book, except for claiming that they had twice asked the author to make alterations and that he had refused to change it further. The magistrate, Sir John Dickson, regretted that a reputable firm such as Methuen should have lent their name to *The Rainbow* and wondered why, after the press had been so negative, they had not withdrawn it at once. In the House of Commons Philip Morrell, Liberal MP and husband of Lawrence's patroness, Lady Ottoline Morrell, questioned the activities of the police, but the government chose to permit the books' destruction. Lawrence spent the next three years repaying Methuen their advance. In addition, he lost his copyright in the book; he was stigmatized as an obscene author and became so notorious that few publishers or periodicals would give him work and such that he did undertake was often published under a pseudonym.
SEE ALSO *Lady Chatterley's Lover*.

Ramsay, Allan   The Scottish poet (1686-1758), one of the leading figures in contemporary Edinburgh literary society and the inspiration behind the 18th-century revival of Scottish vernacular poetry, was one of the earliest exponents of literary expurgation. In 1724, following various collections of his own work, he published *The Ever Green*, an anthology of Scottish poetry written before 1600. The notable feature of this collection was that Ramsay had chosen to expurgate a number of the poems. This surprised readers since Ramsay himself wrote reasonably bawdy verse and had opened one of the first lending libraries, which, unlike its 19th-century successors, made no attempt to censor the works it provided, making available even the "villainous, obscene and profane" books issued by EDMUND CURLL. Given Ramsay's sense of humor, it appeared that the excisions were both tongue-in-cheek and intended to maximize the sales of the anthology: The difficult words could be cut or replaced to satisfy the oversensitive, but the flavor of the poems could be retained. A penchant for teasing footnotes made it clear that Ramsay's intentions were less than devotedly censorious.

Ratchford, President, University of Missouri **v.** *Gay Lib* **(1978)**   Under the Missouri state law of 1939 homosexual acts, or "felonious acts of sodomy," are illegal: "Every person who shall be convicted for the detestable and abominable crime against nature, committed with mankind or with beast, with the sexual organs or with the mouth, shall be punished by imprisonment ... for not less than two years ..." Thus, when members of Gay Lib asked for official recognition for their movement from the authorities of the University of Missouri in 1978, this recognition was denied. Gay Liberation activists claimed that their movement would help set up a forum for the general discussion of homosexuality, but the university claimed that permitting a Gay Lib organization on campus would inevitably result in the promotion of homosexual acts.

The federal district court backed the university, but the Appeal Court overturned the ban, ruling that

> none of the purposes or aims of Gay Lib evidences AD-VOCACY of present violations of state law or university rules and regulations ... It is of no moment in FIRST AMENDMENT jurisprudence, that ideas advocated by an association may to some or most of us be abhorrent, even sickening. The stifling of advocacy is even more abhorrent, even more sickening. It rings the death knell of a free society. Once used to stifle "the thoughts we hate," in [Justice] Holmes' phrase, it can stifle the ideas we love. It signals a lack of faith in people, in its supposition that they are unable to choose in the marketplace of ideas ...

The judge added that being homosexual could not be assumed to render one automatically evil and, indeed, the Gay Lib movement was not composed uniquely of gays.

In a dissenting opinion Judge Regan sided with the university, claiming that it had the right "to protect latent or potential homosexuals from becoming overt homosexual students." He accepted that actions of this sort were prejudicial to homosexual students but that "the university was entitled to protect itself, in this small way, against abnormality, illness and compulsive conduct of [this] kind." The university took its case to the U.S. Supreme Court, but the court denied it a hearing.

Read, James   SEE obscene libel.

Reade, Rolf S.   SEE Rose, Alfred.

Red Channels   SEE blacklisting.

Redrup **v.** *New York* **(1967)**   In 1966 Robert Redrup, a newsdealer in Times Square, New York City, sold two supposedly pornographic paperbacks—*Lust Pool* and *Shame Agent*, at 75 cents each—to a plainclothes policeman masquerading as a customer. That day Redrup was only filling in on the stand as a personal favor for an ill friend. He had never heard of the paperbacks nor had he traded in such material until specifically requested to obtain some by this "customer." When Redrup had taken the money for the books, the policeman revealed his badge and charged the newsdealer under Section 1141 of the New York State Penal Law: selling an obscene, lewd and indecent book.

Redrup's bail and his legal defense were paid by the publisher of the paperbacks, WILLIAM HAMLING, a veteran of both state and national obscenity prosecutions. In a series of trials costing $100,000, Hamling fought the case through to the U.S. Supreme Court, where in May 1967 seven justices ruled that the books were not legally obscene. While the decision was per curiam—and thus did not carry a written opinion—Hamling and his peers concluded that if titillatory pulp of this nature was not legally obscene, then it would be extremely hard to cite material that was. As long as publishers kept their advertising scrupulously legal, thus avoiding the PANDERING charge used against Ralph Ginzburg (SEE *Ginzburg* v. *United States*), and kept such books away from minors, there seemed to be no limits, even those of including pro forma "socially redeeming qualiities," that they need observe. The immediate result of Redrup was the abandoning by the court of nearly 30 obscenity cases, all of which were rendered void by their ruling. A year later the publication of Philip Roth's *Portnoy's Complaint* by Random House was certainly rendered free of legal, if not critical controversy by the decision. In the longer term, the conservative backlash against Redrup can be seen as the inspiriation for the PRESIDENT'S COMMISSION ON OBSCENITY AND PORNOGRAPHY in 1968 and the subsequent erosion of the liberal position on such material.

Decided simultaneously in the U.S. Supreme Court were the cases of *Austin* v. *Kentucky* and *Gent* v. *Arkansas*. In the former case a woman resident of Paducah, Kentucky, approached a salesgirl in Austin's bookstore in Paducah and asked by name for two magazines—*High Heels* and *Spree*. As a result of this purchase, Austin was condemned in the Kentucky courts for violating the state's obscenity statute. In the latter case an Arkansas prosecuting attorney brought a suit under an Arkansas state law against obscenity, citing a number of soft-core men's magazines—*Gent*, *Swank*, *Bachelor*, *Modern Man*, *Cavalcade*, *Gentleman*, *Ace* and *Sir*. The local court ordered their distribution to be halted and for the magazines in question to be surrendered and destroyed. As in the case of Redrup, the court reversed the lower court convictions in both cases, affirming that all the magazines in question were protected by the FIRST AMENDMENT.

Regina* v. *Cameron   On May 21, 1966, Dorothy Cameron opened an adults-only exhibition—Eros '65—at her art gallery at 840 Yonge Street, Ontario, Canada. Sixty drawings, representing the work of 22 artists, were displayed. All the artists involved were reputable professionals, and the Cameron Gallery was one of the city's leading purveyors and exhibitors of art. Despite this, the police raided the gallery, confiscating seven pictures. As described in court "four of them ... portrayed two or more nude female figures, and of those, three portrayed acts of Lesbianism, one portrayed a single nude female 'in an act of sexual invitation,' and two purported to show a male and female figure engaged in sexual acts or positions." With only one dissenting opinion Cameron was found guilty on seven counts of exposing obscene pictures to the public view and fined $50 on each count.

***Regina* v. *Hicklin* (1868)**   In 1867 justices of the peace in Wolverhampton, England, had seized under the OBSCENE PUBLICATIONS ACT (1857) some 252 copies of a pamphlet entitled "The Confessional Unmasked: shewing the depravity of the Roman Priesthood, the iniquity of the Confessional and the questions put to females in confession." This pamphlet was the contemporary version of a Protestant tract that had originated in the early 19th century and had appeared in a variety of forms. It was specifically designed to discredit Roman Catholicism by quoting from the standard works on moral theology, as used by Catholic confessors, a variety of lurid passages, notably those referring to priests who had been overcome with lust while listening to particularly lubricious confessions. Such passages were usually in Latin, but had been issued with a translation (in parallel columns) for general distribution.

The copies in question had been obtained by Henry Scott, a local metal broker and organizer of the Protestant Electoral Union, who sold them at cost: one shilling a copy. When the pamphlets had been examined, the Wolverhampton authorities ordered that they be burned. Scott appealed to the Quarter Sessions, where the recorder, Benjamin Hicklin, found in his favor. The pamphlet was, he agreed, obscene, and its indiscriminate sale and circulation would indeed prejudice good morals. However, Scott's involvement was

purely innocent, intended only to promote the Protestant Electoral Union and expose the corruption of Rome.

The Catholic hierarchy refused to accept this, appealing beyond the recorder to the Queen's Bench sub nom *R.* v. *Hicklin*. Lord Chief Justice Sir Alexander Cockburn, in giving his decision, wrote: "The test of obscenity is this, whether the tendency of the matter charged as obscenity is to deprave and corrupt those whose minds are open to such immoral influences and into whose hands a publication of this sort may fall." The onus of this definition was that henceforth a book would be judged not upon its effect on the likely readership, the literate bourgeoisie, but by its effect on more susceptible individuals: women, children, the mentally incompetent and the lower classes. While this definition was not binding as law, being only judicial obiter dicta (an incidental remark), it was swiftly incorporated into textbooks and stood as the accepted test of obscenity until modified in the OBSCENE PUBLICATIONS ACT (1959).

Register Librorum Eroticorum   SEE Rose, Alfred.

Reigen   SEE Schnitzler, Arthur.

Remarque, Erich Maria   The German-born Remarque (1898-1970) is best known for his great antiwar novel, *All Quiet on the Western Front* (1929). Despite its being a Book-of-the-Month Club choice, it was banned on the grounds of obscenity by the Boston authorities in 1929, even though the club had already expurgated its edition. The book was similarly banned in Chicago. In Austria and Czechoslovakia soldiers were forbidden to read it, and in Germany and Italy its antiwar sentiments were deemed unacceptable for any reader. In 1953 the Irish banned three more of Remarque's novels: *The Road Back* (1931, a sequel to *All Quiet ...*), *Three Comrades* (1937) and *Flotsam* (1941).

Reporters Committee for Freedom of the Press   This organization, founded in the United States in 1970, claims just under 7,000 members. It defines itself as being "devoted to protecting the freedom of information rights of the working press of all media, and upholding the FIRST AMENDMENT." The committee conducts researches on how to subpoena on a reporter or on his or her notes and sources may jeopardize his or her ability to continue working with confidential sources. It also monitors all cases conducted wholly or in part in camera. Since 1972 the committee has filed amicus curiae briefs in most of the major lawsuits seen to affect the First Amendment rights of working journalists. Free legal advice is provided to any journalist who faces a case concerning his or her First Amendment rights.

SEE ALSO Committee on International Freedom to Publish; Committee to Defend the First Amendment; First Amendment Congress; Freedom to Read Foundation; National Coalition Against Censorship.

Restif de la Bretonne, Nicolas-Edme Restif de la Bretonne was born Nicolas-Anne Edme Retif (1734-1806), the son of a peasant who became a notary, in 1734. He produced many novels, each one based on his autobiographical adventures, especially those involving women, in contemporary Paris. Discarding his father's social advancement, Restif deliberately lived in squalor, ate little, drank only in company, lit a fire only when visitors appeared and worked from bed. He dressed roughly and paraded his body in macho display. Despite constant bouts of venereal disease, he seduced hundreds of women, including his own daughters, and claimed to have fathered the first of his 20-plus illegitimate children at the age of 10. His greatest pleasure was to surprise a pretty girl while she was still asleep. Above all he openly indulged his foot and shoe fetishism.

Restif worked first as the apprentice to a printer in Auxerre and then, from 1755 to 1759, as a journeyman printer in Paris. In 1759, after years of bachelor pleasures, he married an English girl named Harriet who soon left him, but bore him twins back in London. Restif returned to his old ways, adding voyeurism to his pleasures. In 1764, after he had become master of a printing house, he began writing more than just his own diaries and letters. His first book, *La Famille Vertueuse*, was a translation of a number of letters originally published in English. A career that produced some 200 works followed, every one celebrating the writer's enjoyment of cheerful, amoral promiscuity. Titles included *Pornographie* (1769), in which he advocated a system of state-run brothels in which responsible old bawds would take proper care of the youthful prostitutes, and *Le Pied de Fauchette* (1769), his hymn to feet and shoes. In 1775 appeared the first book to bring him national fame, *Paysan Perverti*, the story of a simple countryman corrupted by Parisian sophistication. Many others followed, some massive, such as the 24-volume *Contemporaines* and the 23-volume *Francaises, Parisiennes, Palais-Royal*, the two works comprising an enormous catalog of every variety of Frenchwoman.

Two works above all characterize Restif's output. One was L'ANTI-JUSTINE (1798), his answer to de SADE, a man included on his list of the three great human monsters (the others were his wife and his son-in-law). *L'Anti-Justine* remains a classic of 18th-century pornography and one that, despite its rejection of the Marquis' overt excesses and lengthy essays at philosophy, was as hard-core a work by its own lights as much of de Sade's efforts. Restif's other characteristic work was his intimate memoir *Monsieur Nicolas*, in its English translation subtitled "The Human Heart Unveiled." This book, which he called "the final adventure of a forty-five year-old" (Restif considered that after that age every man is betrayed by a woman), was begun in 1783 and appeared in 16 volumes between 1796 and 1797. As well as his usual foot fetishism, the theme of incest runs throughout this supposed autobiography, as indeed it does throughout *L'Anti-Justine*. The first 12 volumes of the book are narrative, the remaining four, subtitled "Mon Calendrier," are a list of his mistresses, arranged like a religious calendar of saints, with one (and often more) per day. Each mistress is given a brief biography and the year of her seduction.

Restif's works remained an essentially French taste, although European connoisseurs gradually began acquiring certain volumes. With the exception of *Pictures of Life* (1790) (which did not appear under his name) and *Cuthbert Cockerton*, the extensively bastardized version of *L'Anti-Justine* that appeared in 1895, nothing was translated into English until *Monsieur Nicolas* appeared in 1930. His reputation remains, as much as anything, for his role as an exemplar of shoe-fetishism.

retroactive classification The concept popular among many authorities that previously unclassified material, especially articles that have already been published and circulated publicly, were in fact secret—because of their topic—and should henceforth be withdrawn from all files and collections and never republished.

Return from the Meeting Gustave Courbet painted this picture of two drunken priests returning from a feast in 1863. Courbet, a devoted anticlericalist, chose his subject deliberately to pillory the church as an active supporter of the imperial regime. The police immediately removed the painting from where it was being exhibited, after its outright rejection by the jury of the Paris Salon. The painting was then bought by a devout Catholic who destroyed it.

Revenge at Daybreak *Revenge at Daybreak* was the English title given to a French film made in 1954 as *Desperate Decision* and released in America in 1964 by the Times Film Corporation. It was directed by Yves Allegret and starred Danielle Delorme and Henri Vidal. Set in Dublin in 1916 the film is the story of the revenge taken by a young convent girl on the Irish Republican Army leader who, in the guerilla fighting against the British and their supporters, had her boyfriend executed as an informer. While the film did not appear to contain anything that might be judged obscene or corrupting of morals, a man named Freedman, who was exhibiting it in Baltimore, Maryland, decided to use it as a means of defying the state censorship law, whereby every film had to be licensed for exhibition. He simply bypassed the licensing board and began showing the film. Charged under the state's laws, Freedman claimed violation of his freedom of speech, while the authorities claimed that the Board of Censors would have passed the film uncut had it been submitted as ordered. The exhibitor was duly convicted by the lower court and by the Maryland Court of Appeals. He was fined $25.

The U.S. Supreme Court, in *Freedman* v. *Maryland* (1965), reversed these verdicts unanimously, ruling that, while Maryland had the right to operate its own censorship, the procedure in this instance operated as an illegal PRIOR RESTRAINT. For the board to have acted correctly it should have adhered to three vital principles: (1) the burden of proving that a film was unprotected expression under the FIRST AMENDMENT rested with the censor; an exhibitor could not invite arrest as Freedman had done; (2) a censor might impose prior restraint, but this could not be taken as a final statement that the film was irretrievably unprotected by the Constitution; the censor must either license the film or go to court to suppress it, the restraint could not be imposed without a chance of adversary proceedings; (3) once the case has gone to court, a prompt adjudication on its obscenity or otherwise must follow; the censor cannot use long, drawn-out legal processes to keep a film from the screen. Considering this particular case, Freedman's conviction had to be nullified, since Maryland had adhered to none of the three conditions. In their concurring opinions Justices Douglas and Black accepted the court's ruling, but stressed that as far as they were concerned, it was simply unconstitutional for any of the individual states to operate a board of censors, no matter what procedures it accepted.

The immediate result of the Freedman decision was the restructuring of many local boards. Those in New York, Kansas and Virginia and in Memphis, Tennessee, abandoned the practice of prior censorship. Those of Dallas, Chicago and the state of Maryland reconstituted themselves as the new circumstances required.

Rights of Man, The   This political treatise by the English radical THOMAS PAINE was written in two parts, appearing in 1791 and 1792 and answering the conservative Edmund Burke's *Reflections on the Revolution in France* and *Appeal from the New to the Old Whigs*. Part one firmly embraced the principles of the Revolution and attacked Burke for substituting dramatic effects for meaningful arguments, and for "rancour, prejudice and ignorance." He traced the development of the French Revolution as far as the Declaration of the Rights of Man and condemned Burke for inaccuracy and sentimentality. He advocated any revolution, declaring that one generation has no right to impose its governmental style on its successor and stressed that a constitution represents the will of the people who at a given moment govern a country. He demanded the basic right of universal suffrage. In part two he analyzed the new constitutions of France and of America, comparing both very favorably to the British system. In this volume he also put forward a variety of proposals, many of which have been adopted in part by modern governments, calling for family allowances, maternity grants and other aspects of the Welfare State.

Although the British government deplored the book, on its initial appearance in 1791 it was not yet considered worthwhile prosecuting Paine himself. When part two appeared in 1792 England was at war with France, and a prosecution was instituted, but, warned by William Blake, Paine fled the country. He was tried in his absence, and *The Rights of Man* was declared seditious. It was regularly seized and burned in succeeding years, and like his later treatise, *The Age of Reason*, became a textbook for British radicalism.

Rivera, Diego   Rivera was perhaps Mexico's greatest 20th-century painter and in his time the world's leading painter of frescos. An unashamed socialist, who coauthored a revolutionary manifesto in Mexico City in 1922 but refused to accept ideological lines and was expelled from the Communist Party in 1929, he saw his work constantly come up against official disapproval. American critics attacked him, variously, for communism, sacrilege (when he painted a mural of a vaccination as a Nativity scene) or simply as "too Mexican."

In 1933 he was commissioned by Nelson Rockefeller to create for $21,000 a mural for the great hall of Rockefeller Center's RCA Building in New York City. Its subject was to be "human intelligence in control of the forces of nature." On May 22, 1933, Rivera was called down from his scaffold where he was still working on the unfinished mural. He was handed a check for $14,000, the balance of his fee, and informed that he had been dismissed. Within 30 minutes the mural had been covered by tarpaper and a wooden screen. Cause for complaint was that in the center of the 63 feet by 17 feet mural, in which Rivera had chosen to celebrate May Day, was a head of Lenin. In the original sketches for the mural a space had been left into which the head of a "great leader" was to be inserted. Rockefeller had assumed this would be an American, perhaps President Lincoln, but Rivera, whose socialist sympathies had never been disguised, chose the hero of the Russian Revolution. Seeking a compromise, Rockefeller suggested that Rivera should replace Lenin with some unknown face; the artist offered to add Lincoln but refused to expunge Lenin. Charged with wilful progandizing, he declared only that "All art is propaganda." Since he had accepted payment, Rivera was unable to force the Rockefellers to exhibit or even keep his work. The mural was chipped from the wall and subsequently replaced by one painted by Spanish artist Jose Marie Sert.

On November 21, 1936, Rivera, with "twenty other shouting Communists" and armed with five pistols, entered the Hotel Reforma in Mexico City to protest the "surreptitious" alteration of four of his panels depicting various scenes of recent Mexican history. Unlike the Rockefeller commission he had not been paid, but the management refused to hear his pleas and destroyed all the offensive panels. In 1949, hoping to rejoin the Communist Party, Rivera censored himself, refusing to submit photographs of three of the 21 panels of his "Portrait of America" to a retrospective of his own work: He feared that they might offend the party line. Throughout the 1950s Rivera's work continued to inspire controversy. In 1952 panels at the Detroit Institute of Arts, considered some of his finest work, were attacked as communist, decadent and blasphemous. Later that year murals that cast Mao Tse-tung and Stalin as near saints and others vilifying Western leaders were cut from a Mexican government exhibition. In April

1956 he accepted self-censorship again, painting over the words "God Does Not Exist" on a mural in Mexico City's Del Prado Hotel, thus permitting for the first time in eight years the public to view this work.

Rochester, John Wilmot, 2nd Earl of   John Wilmot (1647-80), second earl of Rochester, was a member of the circle of fast-living wits and courtiers, including his fellow earls of Dorset and Buckingham and SIR CHARLES SEDLEY, centered at the court of Charles II. Son of a Cavalier hero and a staunchly Puritan mother, he was educated as a typical contemporary aristocrat. Wadham College, Oxford, which he entered at the age of 12, preceded the Grand Tour of Europe, which in turn was followed by introduction at Court. Aged 18, after 18 months of fighting sea battles against the Dutch, he abducted and married his wife, the heiress Elizabeth Malet. He divided his life between his family in the country and a number of mistresses and fashionable menfriends in London. During one of his almost annual banishments from court, caused by extending the king's patience too far, he allegedly set up on Tower Hill as "Alexander Bendo," a German astrologer, whose predictions and cures delighted his erstwhile companions.

Rochester's wit and erudition were paraded in his poetry, which has been cited by critics as setting him among the last of the Metaphysical poets and the first of the Augustans. He died young, and thus his output, in which he could savage his own failings as acutely as those of others, was small, but it was varied and highly influential. Dryden, whose patron he briefly was, Swift and Pope were all influenced by him. For many people his subsequent reputation rests particularly on his lampoons, satires and erotic writings. In his POEMS ON SEVERAL OCCASIONS (1688) and the play he supposedly authored, SODOM: OR, THE QUINTESSENCE OF DEBAUCHERY, "he wrote more frankly about sex than anyone in English before the 20th century," according to Margaret Drabble. Unsurprisingly both these works were frequently prosecuted, almost from their first appearance.

In the words of Dr. Johnson, Rochester "blazed out his youth and health in lavish voluptuousness" and Edmund Gosse called him "a beautiful child which has wantonly rolled itself in the mud." By 1680 he was seriously ill and spent his last months debating with a number of theologians, particularly with Gilbert Burnet (1643-1715), a royal chaplain. Burnet, aided by the deist Charles Blount, convinced Rochester of the truth of deism, and he made, to the surprise of many, a deathbed conversion that was subsequently written up by Burnet. Rochester demanded that all his "profane and lewd writings" be destroyed; they were duly burned, but manuscript copies, some of which it is believed were doctored to make them dirtier than they had been written, remained in circulation. His subsequent reputation for scurrility and filth was guaranteed by the determined smear campaign waged by his enemies at court, notably John Sheffield, later duke of Buckingham. Apart from a number of more scholarly works

on the earl, the Victorian pornographer WILLIAM DUGDALE published in 1860 a spurious autobiography of Rochester, lavishly illustrated with pornographic lithographs and featuring his "Singular Life, Amatory Adventures, and Extraordinary Intrigues."

***Roman Index* (1559)**   SEE *Index of Paul IV*.

Roman Indexes (1670-1800)
1670   Under the instructions of Pope Clement X, an Index was printed containing the lists of Alexander VII (SEE *Index of Alexander VII*) and Clement VIII (SEE *Index of Clement VIII*). This was reprinted in 1675, with a supplement containing the new prohibitions of the previous five years.
1681   Jacobus Riccius, secretary of the CONGREGATION OF THE INDEX from 1749 to 1759, published an Index for Pope Clement XI; this contained the lists of 1670 and 1675 and brought them up to date. This Index was also notable for its compiler's attempt to correct the many typographical and bibliographical errors in its predecessors. A number of subsequent editions of this Index, each supplementing the last, appeared between 1682 and 1754.
1758   THE INDEX OF BENEDICT XIV. This laid down the foundations of all subsequent Roman Indexes. A number of supplements appeared in 1763, 1770 and 1779. A new Index appeared in 1786, with five appendices.
1785-98   A number of decrees of prohibition appeared during this period; they were published in the weekly *Giornale Ecclesiastico* and listed the decrees of the church against a number of specific titles, including works by Pascal and Voltaire.
19th-century   Indexes were published in 1806, although these were essentially a supplement to that of 1786. The first new index was published in 1819; this was followed by those of Gregory XIV in 1835 and 1841. Pius IX published two Indexes, in 1865 and 1877; Leo XIII added one in 1881 and one in 1900. All these Indexes were based on the standards established by Benedict XIV in 1758.

Roman Inquisition, The   Starting with the ecumenical councils of NICAEA Roman Catholicism was rigorously established as the mandatory religion of first the Roman Empire and later the individual European states that replaced that empire. Since a central purpose of the state religion was to uphold the secular status quo, any challenges to that religion in the form of heresy or blasphemy were seen as subversive of the state, as was sedition, and were prosecuted as stringently. The laws covering such crimes were, naturally, promulgated by the ecclesiastical authorities—the Pope in Rome and his bishops in the provinces.

The concept of an inquisition stems from the ecclesiastical legislature of the early Middle Ages. Spiritual courts offered three forms of action: the *accusatio*, a case brought formally by an individual accuser; the *denunciatio*, in which the accusation was made by a public officer, such as a deacon; and the *inquisitio* in which the ordinary (the church official in charge of a spiritual court) arrests a suspect and imprisons him or her if necessary. The indictment in this last, the *capitula inquisitionis*, was communicated to the suspect, who was then open to be interrogated on that indictment, although not on anything that fell outside, it. The final verdict was delivered by the ordinary.

The first inquisitors were basically officials who traveled through Europe searching out blasphemy and heresy and trying it in the spiritual courts. In 1184 Pope Lucius III ordered an "inquisition" into heresy; in 1215 his successor, Innocent III, proclaimed as a Christian duty the extermination of heretics. Hundreds of thousands were butchered to satisfy his exhortation. When Gregory IX established a formal "Tribunal of Inquisition" in Rome in 1231 he thus founded the centralized Papal Inquisition. The work involved was turned over to the newly formed orders of Dominican and Franciscan friars, who began pursuing heretics and their works with a new enthusiasm. In 1252 Innocent IV, in the bull "Ad Extirpanda," directed at the monarchs of the major European nations, authorized the establishment of a system designed specifically to root out heresy, including permitting the use of torture in the obtaining of confessions. The Inquisition, as the frontline defender of the faith, was established as above national laws, and monarchs who attempted to control its activities were considered as tampering with God's work and, in common with any subject who impeded the Holy Office, might be excommunicated. The office of inquisitor general was established in 1262 but lapsed in Rome after the 13th century. The continued appointment of this single, ultra-authoritarian figure under the SPANISH INQUISITION was undoubtedly a major cause of the greater efficiency and ruthlessness of the Spanish over the Roman system.

The Roman Inquisition was established in the form in which it championed the Counter-Reformation by the bull "Licet ab initio," issued by Pope Paul II on July 4, 1542. The tribunal was reconstituted under six inquisitors general, one of whom, Caraffa, became the actively anti-heretical Pope Paul IV in 1555. The inquisitors general were empowered to take action—with or without the aid of local bishops—for the detection and punishment of heretics, the examination of suspects, the destruction of pernicious literature and any other measures necessary for the extirpation of heresy. From 1550 onward these officials were to be cardinals.

The Papacy and Roman Inquisition issued a number of edicts duing the 16th century designed to reinforce and extend theological censorship. In 1543 the bookdealers of Italy were forbidden to trade in any heretical material and to make all their stocks available for examination. Similar instructions were issued to the printers. In 1563 Pope Pius IV gave permission for the Inquisition to prosecute clergymen as well as laymen. The CONGREGATION OF THE INDEX, designed to adminsiter the censorship system, was established in 1571. In 1595 the Inquisition was authorized to search for heretical material in the cargoes of all ships docking at Italian ports.

Unlike the Spanish Inquisition, the Roman organization was less effective in its persecution of heresy and in its suppression of heretical materials. The division of Italy into a variety of individual states made the enforcement of Papal decrees less simple, and such powerful entities as Venice chose, almost with impunity, to ignore many orders. The Roman Inquisition continued to compile and promulgate indices and issue regulations to control printing, publishing, bookselling and reading, but as Protestantism took hold and the Counter-Reformation wavered, the Holy Office began a lingering decline that drifted through the 18th and 19th centuries and may be said finally to have reached its end when the Index was abolished in 1966.

Romans in Britain, The   Playwright Howard Brenton's *The Romans in Britain* was staged by the National Theatre in October 1980. Its crude progagandist approach to the problems of Northern Ireland impressed few critics, but a scene in which a Roman soldier attempts to sodomize a captured Druid did scandalize both the theatrical and political establishments. While critical attacks were merely verbal, there were questions in the House of Commons, and the Greater London Council (GLC) first threatened and then actually did withhold the usual annual raise in the grant upon which the survival of the National largely depended. Mrs. MARY WHITEHOUSE led the legal battle against it. Unlike her private prosecution of GAY NEWS, in 1977, Mrs. Whitehouse was unable to gain permission from the attorney-general to initiate a case against Brenton's play under the OBSCENE PUBLICATIONS ACT (1959). Undaunted, she turned to the Sexual Offenses Act of 1956, which, coupled with a loophole in the THEATRES ACT OF 1968, made it possible for her to bring a private prosecution against the play's director, Michael Bogdanov, on the charge of "procuring an act of gross indecency between two actors in December 1980." The basis of this charge was section 13 of the Sexual Offenses Act, covering males who masturbate themselves or others in public parks or toilets. Legal experts noted that this part of the law was the narrowest of pretexts for an "obscenity" prosecution, and pointed out that if the soldier and druid had been women, section 13 would not have been relevant.

The case was heard at the Old Bailey in March 1982, after the defense had attempted unsuccessfully eight months earlier to have the prosecution thrown out in the magistrate's court. The press touted it as the biggest obscenity case since LADY CHATTERLEY'S LOVER in 1960, and the various forces—Mrs. Whitehouse's pro-censorship allies on one side, such theatrical heavyweights as Lord Olivier, Trevor Nunn and Harold Hobson on the other—were prepared for the struggle. The prosecution called a single witness, Mrs. Whitehouse's solicitor, Mr. Graham Ross-Cornes, who had been deputed to see the play for the NATIONAL VIEWERS AND LISTENERS ASSOCIATION. At the end of the testimony, Lord Hutchinson (who had argued for *Lady Chatterley's Lover* in 1960), submitted that there was no case to answer. Among other things, Ross-Cornes, who had been seated some 70 yards from the stage, accepted that what he initially claimed was a penis might in fact have been the actor's thumb. The judge, Mr. Justice Staughton, rejected the defense submission, but on the following day the prosecution announced that they were dropping their case, although Mrs. Whitehouse, who had not attended the proceedings, stressed to the press that this was not her decision. The attorney-general was forced to end this stalemate by a plea of nolle prosequi and a private statement that he was infuriated by NVALA's use of the courts for a publicity exercise.

Both sides claimed a victory, although Brenton and Bogdanov declared themselves frustrated by such inconclusiveness. Mrs. Whitehouse claimed absolute satisfaction: She had "made her point." While the immediate feeling in liberal circles was that she had been defeated, a longer term view appreciated that the Theatres Act of 1968, which had supposedly ended theatrical censorship, still left the stage open to private censorship attempts.

Ronde, La SEE Schnitzler, Arthur.

Rose, Alfred Rose (1876-1934) was born in Warwickshire, England, the son of a small gentleman farmer. He was largely self-educated and spent some time in America, where he worked in Mobile, Alabama. On returning to London after World War I he set up the Addressing Company, a small mail addressing company that specialized in the distribution of publicity material to the medical profession. He died of pneumonia in 1934. Writing under the anagrammatic pseudonym "Rolf S. Reade," Rose compiled his *Register Librorum Eroticorum*, which was published posthumously in 1936. This massive two-volume bibliography, itself consigned to the PRIVATE CASE in the British Museum but available in a number of large public libraries in the U.S. and U.K., lists some 5,000 prohibited books, in English, French, Italian and German. The register is essentially an update of HENRY S. ASHBEE's 19th-century researches, now including the BIBLIOTHECA ARCANA (1884) and the PERCEAU and APOLLINAIRE catalog of the Paris L'ENFER and Rose's own research, including the listing of the titles and press marks of the Private Case (then a herculean task). It drew on a wide variety of previously published bibliographies of erotica, including those of the Vatican and the Guildhall Library in London (subsequently merged into the Private Case). Rose's bibliography contains some errors, and the author died before he could eliminate them, but it remains the best guide to the whereabouts and availability for research of much modern erotic writing, even if critics warn the user against over-reliance on Rose's opinions. After his death his bibliography, on file cards, was turned over to W.J. Stanislas, an otherwise unknown London bookseller, who duly published it, prefaced by a brief essay on the otherwise anonymous "T.O.I."

Rosen v. *United States* **(1896)** In 1896 New York publisher Lew Rosen was found guilty of obscenity by the U.S. Supreme Court under the Post Office regulations covering the mailing of obscene material (SEE United States 17. postal regulations) for an issue of his magazine *Broadway*. In this, the first federal, rather than New York State, prosecution brought by vice crusader ANTHONY COMSTOCK, it was alleged that on one of its 12 pages there were pictures of women "in different attitudes of indecency." It was particularly stressed that the lampblack which had been used to cover up the women's "offending parts" was easily removable by rubbing with a piece of bread. In his defense Rosen pleaded that *Broadway* had only been sent through the mails (which made it liable to a COMSTOCK ACT prosecution) at the request of a government agent provocateur and that he was personally unaware of the ease with which the lampblack could be removed. He also testified that he had not known that the pictures were in fact obscene. The Supreme Court remained unimpressed and sentenced Rosen to 13 months hard labor.

Rosset, Barney Rosset was born in 1923, the son of a wealthy Chicago banker and businessman. In 1953, he acquired the Grove Press and devoted himself to publishing the work of various important avant-garde writers, notably JEAN GENET, Samuel Beckett, Eugene Ionesco, Alain Robbe-Grillet and Simone de Beauvoir. Rosset spent much time in Paris, where he attempted to recreate the era of American expatriate pleasures epitomized in Hemingway's *A Moveable Feast*. By the 1960s the Grove Press began to slant its list away from the specialist avant-garde to titles with greater sales potential, albeit more challenging to established literary standards.

In the wake of the Roth ruling of 1957 (SEE *Roth* v. *United States*), which made "redeeming social importance" a defense against obscenity, Rosset decided to issue the hitherto bowdlerized LADY CHATTERLEY'S LOVER in an unexpurgated edition. Despite its prosecution in 1959, the U.S. courts permitted this edition to appear. Rosset then printed the first U.S. edition, in 1962, of William Burroughs' NAKED LUNCH. This sold 14,000 copies, found itself banned in Boston and in due course taken to court. After a much-publicized trial Grove Press was acquitted and the book was generally available in the U.S. in 1965. In 1964 Grove also offered LAST EXIT TO BROOKLYN by Hubert Selby. The book shocked many readers, but in the U.S. did not go to trial.

In 1961 Rosset bought from a German collector for $50,000 what he assumed were the exclusive rights to publish the anonymous Victorian "memoir," MY SECRET LIFE. Rosset's intention was to publish this erotic classic in a deluxe two-volume ediiton. This scheme, while ultimately profitable, was briefly held up when Marvin Miller, a no-frills pornographer who boasted no literary pretensions, serialized the whole "Life" in 10 issues of a magazine, retailing at a mere $1.25 each. Only by making Miller a substantial out-of-court payment could Rosset continue with his plans. When *My Secret Life* proved a major success, Rosset continued the series by issuing the Marquis de SADE's *Juliette* and 120 DAYS OF SODOM. By the standards of previous editions of these works, Grove Press was putting on the market very hard-core material at relatively giveaway prices. Rosset concentrated on bringing mass-market techniques to the "art porn" market, and his techniques, fortified by the increasing liberality both of the courts and of the potential consumers, certainly worked.

Roth Standard, The   SEE *Roth* v. *United States* (1957); Ulysses Standard.

Roth v. United States (1957)   SAMUEL ROTH was one of America's leading pornographers in the 1950s. His career extended back to the 1920s, and he had been in constant battle with the authorities for years. In 1956 he was convicted in a New York federal district court of sending obscene materials through the mails. This decision was affirmed on appeal, although a concurring opinion by Judge Jerome Frank listed a detailed critique of the current obscenity laws, which brought the whole concept of such prosecutions into question.

When the case reached the U.S. Supreme Court, Justice Brennan delivered the majority opinion. Brennan, 51, was a recent appointee to the court and proved to be one of its more liberal members, a consistent champion of freedom of speech. Roth's lawyer argued not only that postal censorship was unconstitutional but also that the current definition of obscenity, based on the British HICKLIN RULE of 1868, was too vague to permit due process of law. Brennan rejected Roth's appeal but delivered a ruling that changed the status of obscenity in American law.

The problem, as perceived by Brennan, was to determine whether, as perceived by the framers of the Constitution and of its FIRST and Fourteenth AMENDMENTs, which guarantee freedom of speech and expression, obscenity could be proved to have any redeeming social importance. The amendments stressed that however repugnant certain ideas might be, if they could be seen to have such importance, then they were duly and properly protected. As far as Roth's case was concerned, Justice Brennan could see no justification for declaring his undoubtedly obscene books and pamphlets socially important, but in considering the larger sphere of obscenity, Brennan established a new test, which came to be known as the ROTH STANDARD. It was necessary to determine "whether to the average person, applying contemporary community standards, the dominant theme of the material taken as a whole appeals to prurient interest." Obscenity per se remained beyond the protection of the Constitution, but if material passed this new test, then such protection might be justifiably claimed.

Justices Douglas and Black filed a dissenting opinion, noting that the Roth Standard made "the legality of a publication turn on the purity of thought which a book or tract instills in the mind of the reader ... punishment is inflicted for thoughts provoked, not for overt acts or anti-social con-

duct." They worried that Roth did not "require any nexus between the literature which is prohibited and action which the legislature can regulate or prohibit." Prosecuting the arousing of sexual thoughts, rather than the concrete commital of an illegal action seemed to them to be a contravention of the spirit of the amendments in question. Brennan's decision stood nonetheless, and, with certain modifications, is still central to U.S. obscenity law.

SEE ALSO *Miller* v. *California*; Ulysses Standard.

Roth, Samuel   Roth, born in 1895 to Orthodox Jewish parents in an Austrian mountain village, immigrated to the United States in 1904. By 1925, after a precocious career at high school and a faculty scholarship at Columbia University, he set up a literary magazine—*Two Worlds Monthly*—and a mail order service, specializing in the notorious, though scarcely lurid works of ZOLA, Maupassant, Balzac and FLAUBERT. Roth's coup was to offer in early editions of the magazine a serialized version of James Joyce's ULYSSES. Joyce himself had not given permission, even when offered double serialization rates of $50 an episode, but Roth claimed that Ezra Pound, who in turn claimed to be Joyce's agent, had done so. *Two Worlds* also censored Joyce's more explicit language slightly. This impressed neither the readers who found the great novel too complex, nor the authorities, who ordered him to stop the serialization. This he did, and eschewed *Ulysses* until 1930 when, for distributing entire unexpurgated editions of the complete book, some three years before the courts accepted that it was not obscenity but art, he served 60 days in jail.

Having gained his avant-garde spurs with *Ulysses*, Roth turned to more profitable, and more generally lurid, publications. He produced editions of two Indian love manuals, the *Kama Sutra* and *The Perfumed Garden*. By now Roth had gained sufficient notoriety to be pursued by agents of the New York SOCIETY FOR THE SUPPRESSION OF VICE, and at its instigation he was prosecuted and sentenced to 90 days' hard labor. On his return from jail, now garlanded with a certain cachet among pornographers and avant-garde writers, Roth continued unabashed. A distinctly unauthorized biography of President Hoover was ignored by the press but sold 200,000 copies. Roth also distributed several illegal editions of LADY CHATTERLEY'S LOVER and his own biography of the self-styled libertine, FRANK HARRIS.

By 1936 Roth was a marked man. His office on East 46th Street was surveyed through a telescope on an adjacent building, his mail was opened and his customers plagued by federal inspectors. Roth finally wrote a letter of complaint to the postmaster general. His answer was an indictment charging him with sending obscenity—notably *The Perfumed Garden* and *Lady Chatterley's Lover*—through the mails. He was convicted at the subsequent trial and served three years. In 1939 he returned to New York and to his former occupation, declaring himself at war with the authorities. Diversifying his companies, multiplying his imprints, even leaving packages of books at special drops for selected customers—Roth's business was as much concerned with evasion as distribution. Through the 1950s he stood as the nation's leading "smut king" (and was so denounced by Walter Winchell) and found himself facing almost continual prosecution for books ranging from *Waggish Tales of the Czechs* to *Self Defense for Women*. After his unbowed self-defense in 1954 before Senator Estes Kefauver's inquiry into pornography, he was charged with 26 indictments of obscenity. Twenty-two of the counts—against AUBREY BEARDSLEY's *Venus and Tannhauser*—were proven, and on February 7, 1956, Roth, aged 62, was given five years in jail and a $5,000 fine.

In April 1957, after having had his guilt confirmed by a succession of appeal courts, ROTH V. UNITED STATES OF AMERICA was heard by the Supreme Court. The justices decided 6-3 to uphold Roth's sentence, but William J. Brennan, in writing the majority opinion, created a test for obscenity that was significantly different from what had existed since Hicklin (see Hicklin Rule) in 1868. Obscenity depended on "whether to the average person, applying contemporary community standards, the dominant theme of the material taken as a whole appeals to prurient interest." That the dominant theme must be obscene, rather than letting one single paragraph condemn an entire work, opened the way to new, liberal standards in U.S. publishing. The stranglehold that the COMSTOCK ACT had held over the arts in America since 1871 had been broken. Ironically, as the Roth ruling cancelled out a mass of obscenity convictions and freed many works from the threat of prosecution, the man whose trial had inspired it remained in jail where, it was noted, he could now receive through the mails many of those volumes that had brought him there.

Rousseau, Jean-Jacques   Rousseau (1712-78) was born to a Protestant artisan family in Geneva, and was educated by an aunt and uncle after his mother died and his father left for France. After leaving his job as an apprentice engraver in 1727 he began a lifetime of traveling around the Continent, relying on the help of a number of friends and patrons and on a succession of clerical, secretarial and tutorial posts. His first important publication, which won him a prize from the Academy of Dijon, was *Discours sur les sciences et les arts* (1750). He followed this in 1755 with *Discours sur l'origine de l'inegalite*, both books proposing his theories of the superiority of natural man to his more civilized and sophisticated cousins. To Rousseau the primitive enjoyed innocence and contentment in his state of nature, requiring nothing other than that which would sustain life; social man embellished his life with superfluities and was condemned by modern society to a form of legally sanctified, perpetual servitude known as work.

Further books included *Emile* (1762), in which he proposed a system of education suitable for encouraging the development of a natural man, and included his plans for his own form of Christianity, a type of deism that rejected the institutionalized religion of the contemporary world. This outraged the church; the parliament of Paris, backed by the archbishop, who issued a pastoral against its author, condemned Rousseau's book to be torn and burned. Rousseau exiled himself to Geneva to escape any personal harm. In 1763 the council of Geneva also condemned him, whereupon Rousseau renounced his citizenship and published the *Lettres de la Montagne*, attacking the council, prior to moving on to Neuchatel, where he enjoyed the protection of Frederick the Great.

Rousseau's greatest popular success, *Julie, ou la Nouvelle Heloise*, appeared in 1761. His best-known work, *Du Contrat Social*, was published in 1762. The latter was the summation of his political theories in which he advocated universal justice through equality before the law, and a fairer distribution of wealth. He defined government as essentially a social contract under which power was exercized along lines dictated by the general will and for the common good. Both books were included on the ROMAN INDEX, as were *Emile*, the *Lettres de la Montagne*, the posthumous *Confessions* (1781-88) and the rest of Rousseau's oeuvre. He remained prohibited to Catholic readers until the 20th century. The *Confessions* was banned in America in 1929, as being injurious to public morals, and from 1935 to 1936 his works were proscribed in the U.S.S.R.

Rowan v. *United States Post Office Department* (1970)
Rowan operated a small mail order business and attempted in 1970 to use the courts to have enjoined the U.S. postal regulations governing unwanted mail, whereby an individual could inform the postal service he no longer wished to receive unsolicited mail of an erotically arousing or sexually provocative nature. Rowan claimed in the U.S. Supreme Court that the statute violated his constitutional right to communicate, stating that "the freedom to communicate orally and by the written word and, indeed, in every manner whatsoever is imperative to a free and sane society." The court accepted this theory, but placed above it the concept of individual privacy, whereby a "zone of privacy" extended to and included an individual's mailbox.

> The court has traditionally respected the right of a householder to bar, by order or notice, solicitors, hawkers, and peddlers from his property ... Nothing in this Constitution compels to listen to or view any unwanted communication, whatever its merit; we see no basis for according the printed word or pictures a different or more preferred status because they are sent by mail. The ancient concept that "a man's home is his castle" into which "not even the king may enter" has lost none of its vitality, and none of the recognized exceptions includes any right to communicate offensively with another ... In effect, Congress has erected a wall—or more accurately permits a citizen to erect a wall—that no advertiser can penetrate without his acquiescence ... The asserted right of a mailer, we repeat, stops at the outer boundary of every person's domain.

SEE ALSO United States 17. postal regulations.

Rowlands, Samuel   SEE book burning in England 1. Tudor period.

Rubbish and Smut Bill, The   Germany's Weimar government passed the Schund und Schmutz law (the Rubbish and Smut Bill) on May 17, 1927, as a belated response to a growing conservative outcry against what was seen as a flood of permissive "moral dirt," in the form of plays, literature, art and performances (especially in nightclubs) potentially corrupting for German youth. The bill was opposed by the artistic community, but the concentration by its framers on the protection of the young, rather than on proposing full-scale controls, ensured that the bill became law, with the exception of a discarded section that had sought to establish national and state boards of censorship. Under the new law people under 18 were automatically banned from exhibitions "not certified as pure by the board of police censors" and were not permitted to join life classes, with their nude models, at the art schools. The police were given wide powers of enforcement, including unrestricted entry into private homes and the supervision of dancing in private homes, and delegates from the churches were to have seats on the art commission established by the Berlin police.

Rumania

1. press censorship   The Rumanian press under President Ceausescu is strictly controlled, and no editor, even of a minor publication, is permitted to leave the country without personal permission from the president. The Law of the Press, enacted on March 28, 1974, as "the first uniform regulation meant to fix the legislative framework for the operation of the press in Rumania," governs journalism in the country. The law is divided into eight chapters, prefaced by a general statement of the spirit in which the law has been made.

Chapter one, article one explains the role of the press both as an instrument of propaganda and simultaneously as a platform for public expression which secondary role can also function in the propaganda sphere by spreading "valuable ideas to encourage initiative" in the masses. Article two places the entire press under the control of the Rumanian Communist Party (RCP). Article three defines freedom of the press as "a fundamental right enshrined in the Constitution. This right is guaranteed to all citizens, and the necessary conditions have been created for them to be able to express, through the press, their opinion on matters of general interest and of a public character, to be informed on all domestic and international events." Chapter two explains the political and social duties of the press, essentially to make suitable contributions to maintaining the status quo as represented by the RCP. Chapter three deals with regulations that govern the organization and the operation of newspapers and magazines. The right to publish is granted to political, state, mass and public organizations and other legal entites. All such publi-

cations must be registered with the Press and Printing Committee. The responsibility for the content of each publication rests with its publisher. Such publishers include a variety of political, administrative and cultural bodies. Each publisher appoints an executive council to "guide and coordinate the entire work of publication, to supervise its orientation to accord with the RCP programme." In addition to the self-censorship exercized by editors and individual journalists, the publisher and the executive councils represent the primary level of censorship. Chapter four deals with the rights and obligations of a journalist, notably demonstrable ideological purity and sufficient professional requirements.

Chapter five, section three, article 67, "Defending the Interests of Citizens and Society Against Abuse of the Freedom of the Press," specifies the limitations set on freedom of the press. They include a ban on the publication of anything declared illegal by the Rumanian Constitution; attacks on socialism and on RCP internal or foreign policy; attacks on party or state officials; information that disturbs public order or that endangers state security; instigations to break or disrespect state laws; the spreading of fascist, obscurantist, anti-humanistic, racist or nationalist propaganda; offenses against good manners or ethics; information on pending lawsuits or attempts to anticipate decisions by the courts; libelous statements that may damage the reputation or legitimate interests of a citizen.

Chapter five also defines the relationship between journalists and state officials. Other than party officials, state, mass and public organizations must communicate to the press such of their affairs as are in the public interest. Journalists have the right of professional secrecy as regards their sources, and the coercion of journalists to reveal such sources is forbidden. No one is permitted to impede the right of the press to criticize, within the terms of press freedom. Members of the public also have the right to bring their criticisms of the status quo to press, and the press is obliged to act on these criticisms, either by publishing them or sending them to the institution under attack, which must respond positively to that criticism within 30 days. Articles 68 and 73 of section three emphasize that the editor-in-chief and the journalists employed on a given publication are responsible for maintaining all censorship regulations as embodied in article 67.

The Press and Printing Committee supervises all publications to ensure that no subversive material appears. Journalists who transgress the censorship may jeopardize their careers. Chapters six and seven deal respectively with the rights and duties of foreign correspondents and the penalties accruing to those disseminating illegal publications, recordings or films.

2. new censorship (1977)   Speaking at the National Writers' Conference in Bucharest in 1977, President Ceausescu hinted vaguely at the abolition of state censorship, promised to end direct interference in literary production, and stated that the literary committees of the Writers' Union would become self-managing entities. In June 1977 similar freedoms were promised to visual artists. The promised freedoms, which seemed to herald a cultural thaw, came to little. Most of the old censors were simply absorbed into the new managing councils set up throughout the media. The government substituted for direct censorship the more subtle system of "diluted responsibility," i.e., self-censorship.

Publishers, editors, authors and journalists were to be responsible both as individuals and in their collective committees for what appeared. The onus was transferred, as the government put it, "from the bureaucrat to the creative artist" and as such made the artist's responsibilities even harder. As Ceausescu stated, "I am firmly convinced that everyone who is aware that no other person will correct him, and that everything depends on him, will think things over long and hard before reaching a decision." The inference was plain. The committees, to which all writers belong, are a further guarantee of rectitude: All are headed by senior members of the Writers' Union, of the party or of the Council on Socialist Culture and Education.

To underpin the supposed revolution, the old state Press and Printing Committee, the organ of censorship, was abolished in December 1977 and its responsibilities were taken over by the Council on Socialist Culture and Education. The organization, part of the central government apparatus, has even greater powers than its predecessor and exists to "guide the publishing houses and exert control over their output." It is further responsible for the political and ideological censorship of all imported films, books and records as well as for all performances within Rumania. The council is also a proscribing agency, issuing to editors of the print and audiovisual media lists of unacceptable news and feature topics. It ensures that writers and journalists conform to a variety of laws, all designed to support the state and its policies. The vital supply of newsprint is controlled by the council. Article 67 of the former Press Law (1974) has been revised, by the council's Decree 471 (December 1977), to provide for the suspension of any publication that breaks any part of the law.

Current media regulations are contained in the Amended Press Law of 1978, which declares that freedom of the press is a fundamental right of all citizens. The press is to pursue an educational end, developing the social awareness of the people, and fostering "love for the Romanian Communist Party and the socialist fatherland [and] respect for the glorious traditions of the workers' class struggle ..." The duty of a journalist is to "devotedly serve the cause of socialism, and to struggle for implementing the party and state domestic and international policy." Journalists who reject this role will lose their credentials and face "transfer to another activity."

To help sustain the law, every press organ (including radio and television) has a "leading council" and an editorial board drawn from this council. As well as journalists, the board is made up of party and trade union members. It is responsible for ensuring that the press organ sticks firmly to the party line,

guiding and controlling its activity and dictating the ideological content and quality of materials published or broadcast.

Under a decree of 1983, which has not been revised, the government has the right to make records of any ownership of typewriters, copiers and similar equipment, including ink and typewriter ribbons. Only socialist units may have copiers and all such machinery must be registered with the local police. To buy a typewriter one must apply to the local militia. People with police records or those considered a threat to state security may not own a typewriter. All typewriters must be checked annually and specimens of their typeface held by the militia. These specimens must also be handed in if the machine is repaired. Inherited machines, or those given as gifts, must still be registered, and if the owner moves, the militia operating near his or her new home must be informed of the typewriter within five days. No one may lend or rent out a machine.

Russia

1. press censorship pre-1801 Printing arrived late in Russia. The first native press was not established until 1564 and, with its relatively few successors, was absolutely dedicated to serving the Russian Orthodox Church. Not until the reign of Peter I (1682-1725) was the press employed for secular purposes. The czar himself established and edited the nation's first printed newspaper, *Vedomsti* (*The Bulletin*), published in Moscow beginning in 1702. The paper lasted until the Revolution of 1917, operating generally as an official mouthpiece, with news on Russian successes at home and abroad, and the publication of all imperial ukases. Peter also set up a state printing plant in 1719, to be supervised by the Senate. The production of secular books brought with it censorship, and a law of October 1720 restricted the printing of such material without the prior censorship of the church. This censorship was based in the laws covering lese majesty and treason, established in the Code of Czar Alexis in 1649. The lack of independent printing curtailed the need for special censorship laws. Peter's special police agency, the Preobrazhensky Commission, could arrest anyone breaking the code and subject him to a variety of punishments, including torture.

Under Peter II (1727-30), prepublication ecclesiastical censorship was continued. The czar transferred the Holy Synod press and all other religious printing to Moscow; secular printing was split between the Senate press (for official ukases, or decrees) and the Academy of Sciences (for other, secular books). Until 1750, when under the Empress Elizabeth (1741-61) the academy gained control of its own publications, the Senate had the power of approving academy-produced books. Private printing began in 1759 with the publication through the academy of A.P. Sumarokov's journal, *Trudoliubivaia Pchela* (*The Industrious Bee*). This project was abandoned, as was a further unofficial journal, *Prazdnoe vremia v polzu upotrenblennoe* (*Leisure Time Usefully Employed*), which was printed through the press of the Cadet Corps, also in 1759. Both official bodies proved rigorous censors and permitted little opportunity for either journal to promote its own opinions without interference.

The Empress Catherine (1762-96), seeing herself as an agent of enlightenment, set up a commission in 1767 to draft a new code of laws, including provision for the control of publishing. She urged its members to err toward liberalism rather than repression when considering published libels and ostensible treason. Although the state and church maintained their monopoly on printing, with the empress as self-appointed chief censor, the mood did accentuate relative liberalism, with Catherine herself anonymously founding and then editing a satirical journal, *Vsiakaia Vsiachina* (*The Miscellany*). By 1767 moves toward establishing private printing were underway. Both the Academy of Sciences and the police offered themselves as censors. When in 1771 Catherine's ukase approved the first private press, it and its successors were duly subjected to the authority of the academy, which operated around the basic premise that nothing would appear that opposed "Christianity, the government or common decency."

In 1783, responding to demand, Catherine granted general permission for private presses in a statute. The academy in St. Petersburg and the university in Moscow would censor their own publications, but the bulk of private printing would be subject to the police, who were empowered to excise any material contravening "the laws of God and the state," or considered to be of a "clearly seditious" nature. Publishing flourished but the precise definition of sedition varied with Catherine's tastes. In 1784 attacks on the Jesuits, a sect she favored, by an author who supported the Freemasons, a sect she deplored, were punished with confiscation of the publication concerned. In 1787 she banned the printing of religious material by private, secular publishers and forbade its sale in secular bookshops. The French Revolution promoted government fears of sedition, and the empress clamped down on critics of her own authority, notably Alexander Radishchev, whose *Journey from St. Petersburg to Moscow* (1790) had failed to find a printer although it satisfied the police censor. Radishchev published his book, an attack on alleged Court sycophants, himself. The empress was furious and the author was exiled to Siberia for 10 years. A further official attack on N.I. Novikov, founder in 1784 of the Moscow Typographical Company and author of the banned attacks on the Jesuits, who was sentenced in 1792 to 15 years' imprisonment, thoroughly scared the press and ensured that the censors worked scrupulously.

In September 1796 Catherine confirmed her powers by abolishing the free press she had authorized in 1771 and giving the state absolute control over all but a very few government-approved private presses. Censorship offices, under the supervision of the Senate, were opened in Moscow and St. Petersburg and, to check imported material, in Riga and Odessa. Each board of censors took one member from the academy or university, one from the church and one from the Senate. Anything might be banned that was "against God's law, government orders or common decency." Imports that violated these strictures were to be burnt. The Holy Synod continued to censor spiritual works by itself.

Catherine died in 1796 and was succeeded by Czar Paul I who ruled until deposed by his son Alexander in 1801. His first act was to pardon both Novikov and Radishchev, but at the same time to strengthen the censorship. The whole apparatus was centralized in an office in St. Petersburg that reviewed all publications and books. Foreign books that attacked "faith, civil law [and] morality" were automatically outlawed. He banned all references to the Enlightenment and to the French Reovlution, declaring that the one had led inexorably to the other. He created a special censorship committee to which all questionable publications were to be referred and took personal charge of its deliberations. Censors were ordered to board ships with the customs inspectors and check all printed matter before it arrived in port. Sending prohibited material through the mails was banned.

2. censorship under Alexander I (1801-25)   Alexander I, who approved of the coup that overthrew his father Paul I in 1801 and brought him to the Russian throne, at first treated the press with a liberalism that in no way had been presaged by his earlier life. He had no interest in books, his main knowledge of them having been gained as a member of his father's censorship committee. His first act, as regards the press, in 1801, was to abolish Paul's restrictions on foreign works and return to the system preferred in 1796 by Catherine the Great. A year later he went further, abolishing the 1796 system and returning to that of January 1783, thus permitting once again a relatively free private press. Under his regulations censorship was no longer the responsibility of the police but fell to the directors of the public schools, thus conferring an educational, rather than repressive aspect on the censorship. In September 1802, Alexander began moves to alter the whole structure of cultural control. The new Ministry of Public Education was given responsibility for developing a single, centralized system for secular publications. In 1803 a committee, the Chief Administration of Schools, was created to advise the minister and to oversee the reform of the system. The administration was headed by two of the czar's intimates, A.A. Czartoryski and N.N. Novosiltsev, both senior academics, entrusted with advising the monarch on the optimum means of censorship.

The statute on censorship became law on July 9, 1804. It consisted of 47 short, general articles, all reflecting the administration's liberalism and the czar's belief that reasonable people did not need elaborate guidelines. It was assumed that at some stage journalistic criticism of the authorities might go too far and would then be dealt with, but it was hoped that a rational approach to such problems, as opposed to blind repression, would advance knowledge and improve civic liberty. The Ministry of Public Education was given absolute responsibility for secular works, although their precise definition blurred somewhat into that of religious publications. The nation's three existing universities, in Moscow, Vilna and Dorpat, and the new ones at Kazan and Kharkov, were to provide the censors; St. Petersburg, which lacked a university, was to have its own special censorship committee. The dean of each university was to find his committee from among the faculty. Elsewhere civil governors were to draw on the staffs of local schools.

As was usual in Russian censorship all contraventions of God's law, state law and morality were to be excized, with the addition of attacks on an individual's honor. Censors were to act quickly in assessing publications, and when demanding cuts or complete withdrawal were to give their reasons. The benefit of the doubt was to lie with the author. Only the name of the printer, the place and date of publication had to be printed in a book. Second and subsequent impressions, if identical to the first, did not require resubmission to the censor. The keynote of the statute was toleration, as epitomized in article 22, which states, "A careful and reasonable investigation of any truth which relates to the faith, humanity, civil order, legislation, administration or any other area of government not only is to be subjected to modest censorship strictures but is also to be permitted complete press freedom, which advances the cause of education."

The war with France, lasting off and on from 1805 to 1815, inevitably tightened censorship. Committees were set up in 1805 and in 1807 to combat internal subversion by French fifth columnists and to ferret out dangerous books. These committees had the power to instruct all government departments on censorship problems. In December 1811 the new Ministry of Police was given powers of decentralizing all security functions, including censorship. The police now had to approve new printing plants, theater productions and posters. The police censorship proved inefficient and was abandoned in 1819, its powers reverting to the Minister of the Interior. Prewar permissiveness returned.

For the remainder of Alexander's reign censorship developed as a focus of conflict between two vital areas of interest: the Orthodox Church and the pietists and mystics whose Western ideas were seen as tainting Russian ecclesiastical purity. The czar initially backed the pietists. He placed Prince Golitsyn, founder of the Bible Society, an organization devoted to the dissemination of Bibles in modern rather than Old Church translations, at the head of the Ministry of Spiritual Affairs and Public Education, thus giving him authority over both the ecclesiastical and the censorship apparatus. The church, alleging that Golitsyn's power undermined its own authority and thus promoted dissent, demanded that spiritual censorship should be its own responsibility. Fighting back, Golitsyn's censorship became increasingly repressive and moralistic, eroding the spirit of 1804. In 1824 the church, whose influence was too important a prop for the monarchy, won its way. Alexander abolished the Ministry of Spiritual Affairs and Public Education and dismissed Golitsyn. Spiritual censorship returned to the Holy Synod. The old Ministry of Public Education was revived under Admiral

Shishkov, an opponent of mysticism. The czar died in November 1825 and was succeeded by his brother, Nicholas I.

3. censorship under Nicholas I (1825-55)   After the relative liberalism of censorship under Czar Alexander I, the system initially created by his brother and successor Nicholas I was typified by its conservatism. In early 1826 Admiral Shishkov, minister of public education and chief censor, proposed a new censorship law of some 230 articles (that of 1804 held a mere 47). The czar, still preoccupied by the abortive Decembrist insurrection that had greeted his accession on December 14, 1825, passed the new statute without changes in May 1826. The essence of Shishkov's reforms was to eradicate literary, academic censorship and replace it with professional, bureaucratic censorship. University-based censors were dismissed, and four censorship committees were established in St. Petersburg (the main censorship committee), Moscow, Dorpat and Vilna. The minister of public education was replaced as chief censor by a Supreme Committee consisting of a number of senior ministers. With the director of the chancellory, the administrative arm of the system, the Supreme Committee formed the Chief Administration of Censorship.

Shishkov's intent was to ensure that publications "have a useful or at least not-dangerous orientation for the welfare of the fatherland" and to "direct public opinion into agreeing with the present political circumstances and views of the government." To implement this, all "metaphysical discussion of natural, civic or judicial rights" was banned and no works that defended or described either secular or religious dissent were permitted. The benefit of the doubt lay always with the censor, who was to remove any ambiguous material. General discussion of religion was allowed, but the final arbiter of its orthodoxy was the church. The church applauded the new law but there was widespread opposition to the "cast-iron statute," and the czar soon regretted his condoning of Shishkov's measures. Using a committee he had established for the drafting of rules on foreign publications (which were not controlled by Shishkov) he began to have the censorship reformed again. On April 23, 1828, a ukase established the new censorship statute law. Shishkov immediately resigned and was replaced by the moderate Prince Lieven.

Under the new law anything that endangered the church, the monarchy or the morals and personal honor of Russian citizens was to be outlawed. The benefit of the doubt returned to the author of a text, and a censor could make no changes without consultation. Ministers forfeited their right to control any references to their administrative activities, and authors were no longer legally liable for material that, despite its approval by the censor, was later deemed unacceptable. The administration of censorship returned to the universities; Shishkov's Supreme Committee was disbanded and the ministerial members of the Chief Administration of the Censorship were replaced by senior cultural figures. A Foreign Censorship Committee, responsible to the Chief Administration, was to deal with imports, and a special Post Office

Department, later nicknamed the "Black Office," censored foreign periodicals sent through the post. The Foreign Committee issued monthly lists of proscribed titles, running at some 150 titles every month, until 1848—when it rose by 400 percent. The czar also approved, separately from the statute, Russia's first copyright law.

The liberal basis of the new statute was balanced by the czar's belief that it failed to cover all contingencies. Thus he created under a secret directive of April 25, 1828, a parallel censorship, the responsibility of the secret police of the third section of the Chancellory. Although its only stated responsibility was the censorship of the stage, the third section was empowered to oversee all censorship affairs in the czar's interest and to intervene in them when it saw fit. It was to watch particularly for material "inclined to the spread of atheism or ... violations of the obligations of loyal subjects." Any author seen as liable to such criticisms could be interrogated by the secret police and possibly charged with a crime, although in practice the third section used such powers only in situations of general political instability. The third section also managed to persuade the czar to authorize a further secret directive, of March 28, 1831, whereby writers were once again held resonsible for published material, even when previously passed by the censor, thus rendering them targets for harassment and post-publication censorship. Individual ministerial complaints against the press were also favored by the czar, who granted ministers certain censorship powers over matters pertaining to their own ministries. Liberalism was further tempered by the passing on April 22, 1828, of a law restoring ecclesiastical censorship and giving to the church the control of any material that could be in any way interpreted as being religious.

By the early 1830s the reforms of 1828 had been largely wiped out; liberal censorship was hamstrung by many restrictive modifications, and writers, caught between the liberal letter of the law and its repressive implementation, often opted for self-censorship. The czar's lack of concern for culture meant that he continually bungled attempts to protect it, believing in any case that he had the right to dictate his people's reading matter, and interfering increasingly in its creation by recruiting private authors to pen pro-government copy. The growing demands of the public for cheap, accessible magazines, newspapers and similar popular publications were rejected. Nicholas's intense nationalism meant that progressive Western ideas were excluded from Russia and that internal and external criticism of the state and church was rigorously put down. The third section worked both at home and, more clandestinely, abroad to mute such attacks and encourage favorable propaganda.

The revolutions of 1848 only proved the czar's fears, and he launched a terror against the press, desperate to crush the least example of alleged subversion. On April 2, 1848, Nicholas created the Committee for Supreme Supervision over the Spirit and Orientation of Private Publications, headed by D.P. Burturlin, director of the Imperial Public Library. This committee was kept secret, but acted ruthlessly to intensify censorship, encouraging informers and spies, urging the censors to greater vigilance, overruling those who seemed too liberal and creating an overall atmosphere of panic in the literary and journalistic worlds. Writers dealing with the two most important topics of the era—the status of the various Slavic nations and the position of the serfs—suffered in particular. Despite the repression, the unofficial, radical press, catering to the increasingly sophisticated intellectual bourgeoisie, continued to develop. When the terror slowed and the czar died, this press, despite the attacks, was flourishing.

4. censorship under Alexander II (1855-1881) On his accession in 1855 the primary concern of the new czar, Alexander II, was the emancipation of the serfs, a topic that had been growing in importance throughout the century. Unlike his predecessor, Nicholas I, whose censors had banned most references to emancipation, Alexander appreciated the necessity of permitting public debate on the topic, in the hope of persuading the population of the government's pro-emancipation line. To foster such debate it was necessary to alter the style of press censorship and in January 1858 new rules, gradually liberalizing printed discussion of the question, were announced. Efforts toward a general redefinition of the censorship system remained muddled: One minister described press control as "a plaything of the fates." The social, economic and political complexities of the emancipation debate were reflected in the czar's inability to settle on a new direction for censorship; debate must be encouraged, but bias and special pleading kept at bay.

The appointment of A.V. Golovnin as minister of public education in 1861 was an attempt to impress some form of direction on the chaos, in this case a liberal one. Golovnin sought suggestions from journalists as to how censorship should proceed: They advocated post- rather than prepublication censorship, and intimated that the better disposed the government was toward the press, the more the favor might be returned. Golovnin duly encouraged the press, permitting many new journals to be launched and allowing them for the first time to carry advertisements. In 1862, hoping to implement a policy of firm but fair censorship, he established the Commission for the Revising, Altering and Supplementing of the Regulations on Press Affairs (the Obolensky Commission), requesting that it should work out ways of ending prepublication control and devise new restraints in its place. These attempts to liberalize censorship were sabotaged by political circumstance.

The increasingly unstable situation led to demands both by the czar and by the minister of the interior, Count Valuev, for a strengthening of censorship. New regulations, giving increased powers to the conservative Valuev, were duly enforced: The ministers of education and the interior could together suspend any periodical having "a dangerous orientation" for up to eight months; criticism of the government was strictly controlled and neither could officials be named nor alleged malpractices cited; no official could write for the press and any anonymous author had to be identified if the authorities so demanded. Valuev also created new, temporary regulations for the supervision of the press, notably the licensing of printshops and the regular recording of all publications and censorship rulings. Any manufacture, sale or purchase of printing equipment was to be recorded and licensed. The minister's police were empowered to inspect all printers and publishers; their owners and staff, if charged, were liable to criminal prosecution.

In November 1862 the Obolensky Commission began revealing its proposals for censorship reform. Although it concurred in almost every way with Golovnin's generally liberal attitudes, accepting that a free press should be allowed to develop in Russia as it was doing in Europe, it stated that in order to provide the unity and independence that the system lacked, the whole apparatus should be transferred to the Ministry of the Interior. Golovnin opposed this transfer, but the czar, faced with growing political problems, was adamant; the change was effected in March 1863. With his power secured, Valuev now charged Obolensky with reforming the censorship system under the Ministry of the Interior. After lengthy debates, a ukase of April 6, 1865, created a statute embodying the new system.

Broadly, the new law diminished prepublication censorship and for the first time involved the courts as co-censors. The overall feeling of the statute was Western, giving the press a variety of new legal rights and an unprecedented ability to stave off, under the legal system, government interference. Its regulations fell into five sections: (1) all censorship matters (other than those supervised by the church) were to be controlled by the Chief Administration of Press Affairs in the Ministry of the Interior; this section also defined the personnel and hierarchy of the censorship system; (2) periodical publications and the procedures under which they would be allowed to appear were defined; all periodicals were to submit copies to the censorship officials and the penalties for noncompliance were described; (3) rules were formulated for printing plants and bookshops; (4) procedures were instituted for the initiating of cases against unacceptable published works; it was also made an offense to print, or to speak on stage certain words; (5) rules and regulations were established for theatrical censorship. Various injurious words as defined in the statute became articles in the criminal code. These words included: (1) those undermining public confidence (the equivalent of the U.K. SEDITIOUS LIBEL); (2) defamation, covering printed attacks on the honor, reputation or good name of an individual or an institution and against which truth was not a defense; (3) abuse, which was similar to defamation but dealt in name-calling rather than in the imputation of facts; and (4) libel.

In December 1866 a number of supplementary rules, requested by Valuev and the minister of justice, Count Panin, were added to the statute. These defined the exact position of the courts as regarded various aspects of censorship: The

court could confiscate an allegedly illegal work pending the case against it; the censorship administration could initiaite a case, directing the procurator to act against a book and providing the relevant evidence; most press misdemeanors were to be assigned to the circuit courts; more important charges, as specified by Valuev and Panin, to be assigned to the Court of Appeals; the procuracy alone could institute cases in defense of attacks against the government, its institutions and officials; private individuals who were biased in the press had to act alone. The new rules were defined as temporary, with the proviso that they formed only a part of the continuing expansion of press freedom in Russia, although that freedom must continually be tempered by responsibility. This responsibility, in its widest sense, was imposed on the press by prosecutions for the "injurious words" cited above. Prosecutions under these articles, 1035, 1039, 1040 and 1055 in the criminal code, were frequent, especially those under 1035, dealing with alleged threats to the security of the state. The system survived through this czar's reign.

5. censorship under Alexander III (1881-94) and Nicholas II (1894-1917)   As the 19th century drew to a close, Russian radical movements grew increasingly pervasive. The government responded with a variety of new regulations to tighten the censorship. The assassination of Alexander II in 1881 and the accession of Alexander III, a long-time proponent of harsher censorship, led to the creation of various so-called temporary measures, approved on August 27, 1882. A Supreme Commission on Press Affairs was set up with sweeping powers to close papers and ban many topics from press discussion. Any papers that had been closed would be permitted to appear in the future only if they accepted regular preliminary censorship, submitting copies to the authorities every night before printing. A more subtle form of control was the opening of a "reptile fund," providing government cash for the bribing of newspapers. The press continued to flourish, however, both at the serious and popular ends of the market. Radical publications did suffer, but between 1864 and 1890 the overall Russian press multiplied by seven times, from 181 publications to 1,299.

Alexander III died in 1894 and was succeeded by Nicholas II, the last of the czars. By 1905 the press was virtually unfettered. The government gave up attempts to discipline even the radical press in the face of a large and confident publishing establishment. Throughout the period of the 1905 Revolution the press was instrumental both in making news of the uprising generally available and in lobbying for an end to its own regulation. As the Revolution reached its height in the "days of freedom" of late 1905, the censorship system simply collapsed: Neither the Printers Union nor the journalists with whom they worked obeyed the censorship any longer. The czar made one final attempt to regain control in the statute of November 24, 1905. This supposed charter of press freedom, which dismantled all vestiges of preliminary censorship (other than in the provinces), simultaneously called for responsible editors who would submit to their local press affairs committee each issue of their publication as it started to circulate. If a publication held criminal content all unsold copies could be seized as long as the Appeals Court had agreed to initiate a case; ecclesiastical censorship in the cities was ended and the courts given sole jurisdiction over the press; a new law prohibited the incitement of disorder in print. For all its supposed freedoms the statute was immediately employed to launch a campaign of prosecutions, but with the end of preliminary and church censorship, the Russian press was, until the Revolution of 1917, technically free of administrative control. This freedom was absolutely confirmed by the rules issued in March 1906 by the Council of Ministers and designed to eliminate certain loopholes in the 1905 law.

(For censorship after the Russian Revolution, see entries at U.S.S.R.)

Rutherford, Samuel SEE book burning in England 6. the Restoration.

S

Sacheverell, Dr. Henry Dr. Sacheverell (d. 1724), a High Church and high Tory cleric and friend of Joseph Addison, preached two sermons in 1709 that resulted in his impeachment before the House of Lords on charges of SEDITIOUS LIBEL. At Derby, in August, he took as his text "The Communication of Sin" and lambasted the Nonconformists and their allies for "Wild, Latitudinarian, Extravagant Opinions and Bewitching False Doctrines, the Impudent Clamours, the Lying Misrepresentations, the Scandalous and False Libels, upon both the King and the Church." Three months later, preaching in St. Paul's on "The perils of False Brethren in Church and State," he extended his attack beyond the Noncomformists to holders of high office who would "renounce their creed and read the Decalogue backwards … fall down and worship the very Devil himself for the riches and honors of this world." Among his targets were named Dr. Gilbert Burnet, bishop of Salisbury (1643-1715), and Benjamin Hoadley (1676-1761), bishop of Bangor. A number of thinly veiled allusions made it clear that Sacheverell deplored the Glorious Revolution of 1688, a topic on which any criticism was absolutely forbidden.

The second sermon caused a furor. Forty-thousand copies were purchased by the doctor's supporters, while Parliament voted it a seditious libel and impeached him before the House of Lords. Both the London mob, who sacked a number of the Dissenters' meetinghouses, and a wide range of influential figures backed Sacheverell. His speech to the Lords was described as "studied, artful and pathetic," and he claimed to have recanted all his controversial views. This effort reduced a number of female spectators to tears but failed to impress the peers. He was convicted, but the margin—69-52 total, 7-6 among the bishops—was so narrow as almost to confer a victory. Given the uproar that he had caused, Sacheverell's sentence was lenient: The sermon was condemned to be burnt and the doctor suspended from preaching for three years. Sacheverell remained a hero until his death in 1724. During the trial one fervent supporter, the rector of Whitechapel, commissioned an altarpiece in which the figure of Judas Iscariot was represented by that of Kennett, dean of Peterborough, who was one of the doctor's most virulent critics. Twenty-three years after his death, Sacheverell's lead coffin temporarily vanished from his grave at St. Andrew's Holborn; the sexton was arrested for the theft.

Sacra Conversazione, The This picture, created in 1518 by Giovanni Battista Rosso, is cited as the first painting to create a scandal among critics and connoisseurs. The picture, ostensibly showing the Virgin and Child enthroned with Four Saints, was commissioned by the church of Santa Maria Novella, in Florence. The church administrator, Monsignor Buonafede, refused to accept the finished work. Rosso had allegedly abandoned the acceptable serenity of classicism and in creating what the monsignor called "all the diabolical saints," had crafted a work quite unsuitable for display in a church. Claiming that Rosso had cheated him, Bonafede supposedly thrust back the picture and rushed at once from his house.

Sade, Donatien Alphonse Francois, Marquis de The Marquis de Sade (1740-1814), not the first but certainly the most notorious holder of this aristocratic name, was born in Paris, the son of a French nobleman and diplomat and a lady-in-waiting to the Princess de Conde. The family came from Avignon, deriving its name from the nearby village of Saze, and de Sade could claim direct descent from Petrarch's Laura, who had married an ancestor, Hugues de Sade. After education at a Jesuit school, de Sade was commissioned into a cavalry regiment, with which he fought against Prussia. It is also alleged that his development of the sexual tastes that now bear his name occurred during army service, and he certainly devoted much time to the pursuit of women. In 1763, under protest but complying with his father's wishes, he married Renee-Pelagie de Montreuil, even though he preferred her 13-year-old sister, Louise. A year after the marriage he eloped with Louise. Renee entered a convent, where she died in 1790.

De Sade appears to have developed his sexual tastes in the army, but his actual libertinage seems to have fallen well below the excesses and inventiveness of his fictional heroes. In 1763 he spent a month in the Vincennes fortress for excesses committed in a brothel, and a year later the owner of a Parisian establishment was warned against him by the police. In April 1768, on Easter Sunday, he picked up one Rose Keller, a 36-year-old pastrycook's widow, who had been reduced to begging. De Sade took her to a rented cottage, forced her to strip at knifepoint, flogged and allegedly lacerated her, although there were no apparent wounds. When Keller brought suit against the marquis, he managed to pay her off with 2,400 livres. In November the marquis was released and the charges dropped. His detention had satisfied public opinion, which was becoming increasingly intolerant of aristocratic excess.

In July 1772 de Sade, accompanied by his servant, one Armand, arranged an orgy with four girls in Marseilles. After the orgy, in which de Sade was birched some 800 times, a fifth girl, Marguerite Coste, who had been procured later, was dosed with the supposed aphrodisiac Spanish Fly (cantharides); she became ill. The matter was reported to the royal prosecutor. Despite his efforts to escape prosecution, de Sade and his servant were found guilty of poisoning and sodomy. They were condemned to death in absentia and duly hanged in effigy. The marquis fled to Italy but was arrested in Rome. In December 1772 de Sade began the first of a number of prison sentences, which would eventually total 27 years. A further scandal, involving a number of 15-year-old girls, taking place after the marquis had been released from jail, is barely documented.

In 1778, after claims from servants that he had tried to bribe them for sexual favors, and from a father whose daughter Justine had been allegedly abducted by the marquis, de Sade was imprisoned in the Vincennes jail. He remained there, in severe discomfort and deprived of writing materials, until 1784, when he was transferred to the Bastille. He was released in 1790, and he held for a while an official post in the Revolutionary government. For the next decade he lived as an intellectual anarchist, publishing many books, both philosophical and sexual, all characterized by his savage attacks on accepted beliefs of every sort. In 1801 he was sent to the mental asylum at Charenton on trumped up charges of insanity, after he published a pamphlet—"Zoloe et ses deux Acolytes," which he may not actually have written—attacking Napoleon and his wife, Josephine. He lived there until his death, dedicating himself to theatrical productions, gourmandise and refining his sexual fantasies.

In prison, and later in the asylum, de Sade wrote all his major works, including JUSTINE, OR THE MISFORTUNES OF VIRTUE (1781). THE 120 DAYS OF SODOM (1785), the autobiographical novel *Aline and Valcour* (1788), LA PHILOSOPHIE DANS LE BOUDOIR (1795), *Juliette, or the Prosperities of Vice* (1796), and *The Crimes of Love* (1800). Less than a quarter of his entire output has survived; many of his papers were destroyed at the storming of the Bastille in 1789 and many more, including obscene tapestry illustrations for *Justine*, were seized in 1800.

De Sade died in 1814; phrenologists judged from his skull that he had "motherly tenderness and great love for children." His own opinion, taken from his last will, was less kindly: "Imperious, choleric, irascible, extreme in everything, with a dissolute imagination the like of which has never been seen, atheistic to the point of fanaticism, there you have me in a nutshell, and kill me again, or take me as I am, for I shall not change." He commanded that acorns be scattered on his grave "in order that the spot may become green again, and the copse grow back thick over it, the traces of my grave may disappear from the face of the earth, as I trust the memory of me shall fade out of the minds of men." The marquis dreamed of an ideal world, in which those with bizarre sexual tastes were neither condemned nor preached at "because their bizarre tastes no more depend upon themselves that it depends on you whether you are witty or stupid, well-made or hump-backed." In such a society, said Simone de Beauvoir in her essay "Must We Burn Sade?" (1955), he would have been included for his

genuine abilities, rather than excluded for his aberrant fantasies.

His works, as the critic Geoffrey Grigson has stressed, may be "deplorable morally and as literature, [but] are of considerable historical and philosophical interest." As Aldous Huxley noted, there is a great deal more philosophy than pornography, and turgid slabs of pure opinion outweigh the flagellation and the incest. His attitudes to property presage those of Proudhon and Max Stirner and his dealings with sex show a knowledge of sexual psychology unique in his era. His works were proscribed throughout the world almost from their first publication, but have always maintained their fascination in pirated, underground, clandestine editions. The first recognized English translation—of *Justine*, appearing as *The Inutility of Virtue*—appeared in 1889, but the pornographer George Cannon had been tried for selling de Sade's works in 1830 and Swinburne and JOHN CAMDEN HOTTEN, writing their *Romance of Chastisement* (ca. 1860), may well have borrowed from *Justine* and *La Nouvelle Justine*.

The French poet Apollinaire, who claimed that de Sade was "the freest spirit that ever lived," drew on researches in the ENFER of the Bibliotheque Nationale in Paris to compile a selection of de Sade's works in 1909. Publication then passed to two major Sadeian scholars. Maurice Heine (1884-1940) published various of the canon in the 1930s before ceding his authority to Gilbert Lely on his death. Starting in 1947 Jean-Jacques Pauvert began publishing his edition of the Complete Works, encountering some trouble in 1954 when *La Philosphie dans le Boudoir*, *Justine*, *Juliette* and *The 120 Days of Sodom* were issued and promptly charged with being an "outrage aux bonnes moeurs." Andre Breton and Jean Cocteau appeared for the defense, but the case was lost. The full *Oeuvres Completes* did not appear until 1973. The first mass-market editions were produced by the Grove Press in New York between 1964 and 1968. An attempt by Corgi Books to reproduce Grove's success in England began with the publication of *Justine* in 1965. The association of de Sade with the horrors of the "Moors Murders" trial in 1966, in which the defendants used his philosophies to justify brutal child murders, put an end to any further such marketing in England; there were no further attempts to publish any of the heavier novels there until the appearance in 1989 of *The 120 Days of Sodom*.

Saint Paul   In character with his strictures on sex, St. Paul may be cited as one of the earliest of censors. The Ephesians, urged on by the Apostle, destroyed their "bad books" as recounted in Acts 19:19: "And many that believed came and confessed and showed their deeds. Many of them also which used curious arts brought their books together and burned them before all men: and they counted the price of them and found it 50,000 pieces of silver." Paul's initiation of clerical censorship inspired and indeed justified the Roman Catholic Indexes of the 16th and later centuries; in fact, some of the more lavishly produced of these featured as a frontispiece an

illustration of the Pauline converts destroying their books, beneath which print was the verse quoted above.
SEE ALSO Index Librorum Prohibitorum.

samizdat The word *samizdat* describes those literary works, political writings, newsletters, petitions, open letters, trial transcripts and allied materials (including illustrations and photographs) that are disseminated outside the officially sanctioned channels in the Soviet Union and its allies, by a variety of private individuals and organizations. The colloquialism that describes such works is a literal translation of the Russian for "self-publishing house." The name parodies such state or cooperative publishing agencies as Gospolitizdat or Akademizdat. In essence, samizdat provide an official substitute for services more usually provided by such organizations.

Samizdat publishing began around 1966, although earlier instances have been recorded, and at first concentrated on essays and belles lettres. The distribution network thus created soon developed as a useful channel for the dissemination of overtly political material. Authors are generally, although not exclusively, dissidents or representatives of national and religious minorities or other groups who have no officially sanctioned voice. All samizdat publications, whatever their origin, act to circumvent state guidelines and evade government censorship. In many eyes the best Russian writing of the last 20 years has appeared exclusively in samizdat.

Samizdat can be produced by professional printing, in typewritten manuscripts, mineographed sheets or on audio tapes. They can be distributed by mail or by hand. They need not be published in the sense that an edition (as of an official publication) exists; some are simply circulated around a small group of trusted friends. Alternatively, material that has in fact been officially published enters this category when earlier editions have sold out and are not being reprinted or, in the case of such works as Alexander Solzhenitsyn's *One Day in the Life of Ivan Denisovich*, they were no longer permitted by the state book trade and had been withdrawn from the open shelves of libraries. Samizdat that appear outside the Soviet Union become *tamizdat*, "published out there"; foreign broadcasts, illegally recorded and distributed on tapes, are *radizdat*, "radio publication."

It is not actually illegal to produce samizdat, and an author, according to the Fundamental Principles of Civil Legislation of the U.S.S.R. and Union Republics, is simply exercising his "right to publish, reproduce and circulate his work by any method allowed by the law." Where he falls foul of the law is in the content of the material, which may be deemed as failing to combine the interests of individual citizens with those of society at large. If the authorities consider that an author has failed in this duty, he and his work may be liable to a variety of penalties. All forms of opposition publishing were suppressed three days after the Revolution of October 1917 by a "temporary" edict that has yet to be repealed.

Although the Soviet Constitution guarantees freedom of the press, the precise limits of this freedom vary greatly according to the prevailing political consensus. Publications are tolerated only as far as they conform with "the interests of the working people" and "strengthen the socialist system."

Errant self-publishers can thus find themselves arraigned for crimes against the rights of citizens (e.g., distributing a samizdat edition of an out-of-print work); against the socioeconomic order (i.e., distributing material for profit); and against public order of the state (i.e., publishing material considered subversive). Making, publishing or disseminating any statements considered to be politically harmful carries criminal responsibility, and the content of many samizdat publications—religious, nationalist etc.—falls under such a prosecution. Zionists, Baptists, members of Baltic and other national minorities, as well as such dissidents as SINYAVSKY and DANIEL have been tried on such charges.

Mikhail Gorbachev's policy of glasnost (see U.S.S.R. 5.) is undoubtedly liberalizing areas of the Soviet media, but it is notable that members of the dissident community, from whose ranks samizdat emerge, are vocal in their warnings to the West not to be over-convinced by these supposed freedoms. Given this caution, and the fact that "openness" still has many powerful enemies, it may be assumed that the flow of samizdat will continue for the foreseeable future.

Sanger, Margaret (1883-1966) SEE *Birth Control*.

Satanic Verses, The The *Satanic Verses*, by Indian-born English writer Salman Rushdie, was published in England on September 26, 1988, by Viking/Penguin. It was Rushdie's fourth novel. His first was unnoticed but the second, *Midnight's Children*, won the prestigious Booker Prize in 1981 and placed Rushdie among the younger generation of Britain's best-respected writers. *The Satanic Verses* deals in Rushdie's usual magic realism style with the foundation of Islam, Britain in the era of Thatcherism, the Asian immigrant community and a variety of allied concerns. It appeared to mixed reviews: as many critics admitted to finding the book impenetrable as praised it as Rushdie's best yet. There were no mentions of any possible offense to the British or the international Muslim community.

The first attacks on the book predated its U.K. publication. Two Indian magazines published interviews with the author early in September. The content of these pieces led to an Indian opposition MP, Syed Shahabuddin, launching a campaign to have the book banned in India. By the end of 1988 India, Pakistan, Saudi Arabia, Egypt, Somalia, Sudan, Malaysia, Qatar, Indonesia and South Africa had all forbidden publication.

The campaign to ban the book in England began slowly. A fortnight after publication the Islamic Foundation in the Midland town of Leicester (a center of Asian immigration) circulated allegedly offensive passages through the Muslim community. It was claimed that these passages directly blasphemed Islam and its holy book, the Koran. After calls for a prosecution of the book under U.K. BLASPHEMY laws were rejected by the prime minister, Muslim leaders began planning an all-out campaign. On January 14, 1989, the book was publicly burnt in Bradford, Yorkshire, launching a series of protests and further demands for prosecution and for the withdrawal of the book. The British government refused to prosecute, stating that, fairly or not, blasphemy in Britain refers only to the Christian Church, and the book remained available at most bookshops.

The international outcry escalated in Pakistan on February 12 when five people died and 100 were injured in riots against the book. Another man died a day later in Kashmir. On February 14 Ayatollah Khomeini issued a *fatwa* or religious edict, stating "I inform the proud Muslim people of the world that the author of *The Satanic Verses*, which is against Islam, the prophet and the Koran, and all those involved in its publication who were aware of its content, have been sentenced to death." Iran-watchers suggested that Khomeini's edict was aimed more at rallying his own wavering supporters, disillusioned after Iran failed to win the Iran-Iraq war, than at Rushdie's "blasphemy." This made no difference. Rushdie vanished into hiding, guarded by the Special Branch, Britain's political police. The world's Muslims rose to echo Khomeini's death sentence, marching, burning the book and vowing to kill its author. In Iran it was announced that were the killer a foreigner he or she would receive $1 million. An Iranian assassin would get 200 million rials (approximately $750,000) plus automatic martyrdom. Four days later, on February 18, Rushdie issued an apology. He acknowledged that some Muslims might have been offended, and duly regretted this. The apology was not accepted in Iran and the death sentence remained.

Since Khomeini's *fatwa* the position has remained unresolved. Some publishers—in Italy and France—at first decided to withdraw their translations, and then issued them. Profits, presumably, outweighed the fear of an Iranian hit-squad. Rushdie stands to make £1 million in America alone. Few Muslims have read the book but there have been demonstrations against British embassies and cultural centers in Muslim countries, and in England the community remains determined to have the book withdrawn. The European Community has withdrawn its diplomats from Iran; France has promised to prosecute anyone who calls for Rushdie's death.

The English government has been less forceful. The prime minister, who appears in the book as "Mrs. Torture," has been keen to state her sympathy for Muslim sensibilities; Foreign Secretary Sir Geoffrey Howe has declared that the book is not actually very good. Although all concerned claim to stand by the principles of freedom of speech, its practice has seemed to be harder to stomach. As well as forcing Rushdie into hiding, the death threat has persuaded a number of hitherto liberal spokesmen and women to restrain their comments and a number of libraries, notably the British Museum, to remove the book from open shelves. Penguin's proposed paperback edition may well not appear.

Satyra Sotadica SEE *L'Academie des Dames.*

Saudi Arabia Censorship in Saudi Arabia is part of a general state program to control freedom of expression. While King Saud (1953-64) distrusted all writers and their publications, his attacks on the media were never fully institutionalized. Since his fall in 1964 the process of censorship has been formalized and delegated to a variety of government bodies. The main agent of such activity is the Ministry of Information, which has responsibility for all the Saudi media and other channels of information. Its main activity is the "purification" of culture prior to its being permitted circulation to the public. A special unit, the Management of Publications Department, analyzes all publications and issues directives to newspapers and magazines stating the way in which a given topic must be treated. Such directives are ostensibly unofficial; there is no precensorship of publications but if any material goes against a directive, or more generally qualifies as "impure," the department will check it and notify the minister of information, who decides in what way and to what extent the publication and its employees are to be punished.

The main effect of this system has been to impose on journalists rigorous self-censorship. Certain emotive words—struggle, revolution, civil rights—are taboo, as are the larger concepts connected with them. Two further departments augment the ministry's controls. The Higher Council for Information was established in 1980 after the fundamentalist-inspired disturbances at Mecca. Under the control of the ministers of information and the interior, backed by eight other members recruited from a variety of government departments, the task of the council is to provide a religious context within which governmental policies may be seen. The Committee for Intellectual Security, a department of the Ministry of the Interior, is composed of a number of specialists drawn from various fields. It exists to analyze all publications produced within Saudi Arabia and to classify their writers by ideological and political groupings. From this analysis lists of sympathetic or seditious writers may be drawn up and those considered a threat to national security proscribed or even expelled. The listing of "enemies" is helped by the compilation of constantly updated files, held in the Ministry of the Interior, on all journalists.

Two religious organizations, their members appointed by the king, exist separately from the government but support its censorship system. The General Command for Departments of Research and Missionary Works is headed by the country's general mufti (the chief religious authority), who holds absolute power in the arena of theological pronouncements. The command is powerful enough to make itself felt throughout Saudi life, offering "interpretations" on a wide variety of topics, which statements are automatically incorporated in

Saudi law. These opinions are written in answer to any unsuitable points of view that have been published in the Arab press. Once stated, the interpretation is passed on to the Saudi media, which are duty-bound to broadcast or publish it as an official document. A second religious body—the Authority for Ordering Good and Stopping Evil—under the hereditary control of the al-Sheikh family (staunch supporters of the al-Saud monarchy), sets down the nation's ethical standards. Members of the authority have absolute control of all Saudi cultural activities and may order imprisonment or other punishments for what they see as unethical behavior.

Savonarola, Fra Girolamo A Dominican monk and religious reformer, Savonarola (1452-1498) campaigned against what he saw as the artistic and social excesses of Renaissance Florence. As leader of the democratic party after the expulsion of the Medicis, notable patrons of the arts, Savonarola preached vehemently against every aspect of luxury. In 1495, to add action to his words he began substituting for "the profane mummeries of the carnival" regular "Bonfires of Vanities." Artists and collectors were requested to consign voluntarily a variety of precious objects to the flames. Backsliders were corrected by teams of *piagnoni* (weepers) who proceeded from house to house, sparing no owner, however powerful, in their quest for prohibited objects. They carried away anything they considered objectionable, piling onto the bonfires a vast catalog of irreplaceable manuscripts, ancient sculptures, antique and modern paintings, priceless tapestries and many other valuable works of art, as well as mirrors, musical instruments, books of divination, astrology and magic. Among the leading painters who reluctantly queued at the flames were Botticelli and Lorenzo di Credi. Works by OVID, Propertius, DANTE and BOCCACCIO were earnestly destroyed.

For the next three years, despite the nominal authority of the Medicis, Savonarola was the real ruler of Florence. He wrote a number of books, and these treatises against excess provided an excuse for Savonarola's enemy, Pope Alexander VI (a Borgia), to act against him. The Dominican's espousal of the cause of Charles VIII of France had angered the Pope. Now he moved. Savonarola was arrested, tortured and tried on the grounds of his having attempted to demand church reforms and allege corruption in the Papacy. He was ceremonially degraded, hung upon a cross and burned, with all his works, as a heretic. His ashes were thrown into the River Arno.

scandalum magnatum SEE seditious libel.

Schad v. Borough of Mount Ephraim (1981) Schad operated an adult bookstore in the commercial section of Mount Ephraim, New Jersey. Included in the bookstore was a peepshow: Customers could enter a booth, insert money in a slot, and a covered window would open, behind which a nude girl could be watched dancing for a few minutes. Schad was charged with violating Mount Ephraim's zoning ordinance against entertainment in that area. The ordinance approved the operation of certain businesses only; adult bookstores with peepshows were not included. The New Jersey courts, while accepting that nude dancing in itself was protected by the FIRST AMENDMENT, convicted Schad on the principle that the zoning ordinance excluded his business from the amendment's protection. A majority of the U.S. Supreme Court reversed this decision, Justices Burger and Rehnquist dissenting, stating that other businesses in the area offered live entertainment without suffering from the zoning ordinance and that the ordinance, which had been drawn up specifically to combat Schad's bookstore, was in itself insufficient to overturn the basic rights guaranteed by the First Amendment.

Schaeffer v. United States (1920) Five German-Americans—Peter Schaeffer, Paul Vogel, Louis Werner, Martin Darkow and Herman Lemke—were convicted by the Philadelphia courts under the ESPIONAGE ACT OF 1917 for publishing between June and September 1917 17 articles in a German-language newspaper. When the case reached the U.S. Supreme Court in 1920 Schaeffer and Vogel were acquitted—the court could find no evidence to link them to the publication—but the convictions of the other three for "wilfully making and conveying false reports and statements ... with intent to promote the success of Germany and to obstruct the recruiting and enlistment service of the United States to the injury of the United States" were upheld. The newspaper's publishers had been taking news dispatches from other papers and reprinting them with omissions, revisions and a generally anti-American slant. The court stated that this rewriting was undertaken in a deliberate manner to create a false impression and thus undermine the U.S. war effort; such abuse of press freedoms was not protected by the FIRST AMENDMENT. Dissenting opinions cited the anti-German hysteria of the period and suggested not only that such convictions would never have been upheld in a calmer national state of mind, but also that any restriction on free speech, even during wartime, was likely to undermine the essential freedom to criticize government polocy.

SEE ALSO *Abrams* v. *United States* (1919); *Adler* v. *Board of Education* (1952); *Frohwerk* v. *United States* (1919); *Gitlow* v. *New York* (1925); *Lamont* v. *Postmaster General* (1965); *Pierce* v. *United States* (1920); *Schenck* v. *United States* (1919); *Sweezy* v. *New Hampshire* (1957); *Whitney* v. *California* (1927); *Yates* v. *United States* (1957).

Schenck v. United States (1919) Schenck was one of a group of defendants convicted under the ESPIONAGE ACT OF 1917 for mailing printed circulars intended to obstruct the recruiting and enlistment effort of the United States government. The circular attacked the draft, stating that conscripts were little better than convicts and that the whole idea of conscription typified the worst aspects of despotism, as organized to further the interests of a "chosen few" capitalists. The document also called upon its readers to "Assert Your Rights" and fight conscription, claiming that such opposition was a right guaranteed to all citizens and that any pro-conscription arguments were the specious outpourings of a capitalist press and dubious policitians.

The U.S. Supreme Court upheld the convictions and in its judgment created the doctrine of CLEAR AND PRESENT DANGER. Under this doctrine, speech that would usually be protected by the FIRST AMENDMENT would forfeit that protection if it could be proved to have been of such a type and used in such circumstances as to create a "clear and present danger" of bringing about the sort of evils that Congress is empowered to prevent. The court admitted that other than in wartime such a circular would not have been prosecuted, but since it was obviously designed to undermine the war effort, and "the character of every act depends upon the circumstances in which it is done," the convictions should stand. Said the court:

> The question in every case is whether the words used are used in such circumstances, and are of such a nature as to create a clear and present danger that they will bring about the substantive evils that Congress has a right to prevent. It is a questions of proximity and degree. When a nation is at war many things that might be said in time of peace are such a hindrance to its effort that their utterance will not be endured so long as men fight and that no Court could regard them as being protected by any constitutional right.

SEE ALSO *Abrams* v. *United States* (1919); *Adler* v. *Board of Education* (1952); *Frohwerk* v. *United States* (1919); *Gitlow* v. *New York* (1925); *Lamont* v. *Postmaster General* (1965); *Schaeffer* v. *United States* (1920); *Sweezy* v. *New Hampshrie* (1957); *Whitney* v. *California* (1927); *Yates* v. *United States* (1957).

Schlafly, Phyllis   SEE Eagle Forum.

Schnitzler, Arthur   Schnitzler (1862-1931) was the outstanding chronicler of the culture and the mores of the Austrian, and particularly of the Viennese, bourgeoisie during the 20 years that preceded World War I. The most celebrated of his works, many of which had enormous impact in their time, is *Reigen* (1903), of which the literal translation is *The Ring*, in French *La Ronde*, but which has also been published in New York as *Hands Around* (1930) and in London as *Merry-go-round* (1953). The book offers in a series of 10 short, cyclical episodes an overview of Viennese sexual habits as practiced by individuals from all levels of the city's society. The first couple are a prostitute and a soldier, then the soldier and a parlor maid, the maid and a young man, the young man and someone else's wife, the wife and her husband, the husband and a young girl, the young girl and a poet, the poet and an actress, the actress and a count, the count and the original prostitute.

The American translation was seen as sufficiently corrupt for the state of New York to bring the case of *People* v. *Pesky* (1930). *Hands Around* was charged with violating New York's obscenity statute, section 1141 of the New York Penal Law. The judge made it clear that in his opinion Schnitzler's book was filth incarnate, had "nothing to recommend it ... and is properly held to be disgusting, indecent and obscene."

In 1950 the story was filmed by the French director Max Ophuls (1902-57) as *La Ronde*. Europe's sophisticated audiences enjoyed the film, and in America 17 states allowed its exhibition without comment, but the New York Board of Regents, using the state's motion picture censorship law, the New York Education Act (1953) (see New York 4. motion picture censorship), banned it, claiming that it would "tend to corrupt the morals" of viewers. The New York Appellate Division confirmed the ban, claiming that the regents were right to "take such reasonable and appropriate measures as may be deemed necessary to preserve the institution of marriage and the home ..." The court warned against "the vice of indiscriminate sexual immorality" and claimed that the film, which "panders to base human emotions [and is] a breeding ground for sensuality, depravity, licentiousness and sexual immorality" constituted a CLEAR AND PRESENT DANGER to New York's citizens. The distributors, Commercial Pictures, appealed to the Supreme Court, which reversed the Appellate Division's decision in a judgment given in *Commercial Pictures* v. *Board of Regents* (1954). The crux of its ruling was that immorality alone was not sufficient grounds for censorship.

Another of Schnitzler's works, *Casanova's Homecoming* (1918), was indicted for obscenity by a U.S. court in 1924. The case was never brought, after the publisher chose to withhold publication. America's large German-speaking population remained at liberty to read the book in the original. When the SOCIETY FOR THE SUPPRESSION OF VICE attempted to have the same book banned in 1930 the case was dismissed, although in Italy, in 1939, Mussolini did ban it.

SEE ALSO New York 5. obscenity statute.

Scholars and Citizens for Freedom of Information   This organization was formed to support the freedom of access to government information that is enshrined in the Freedom of Information Act. The members are determined to "support the Freedom of Information Act [FOIA] in maintaining and protecting the nation's records and in guaranteeing public access to them; to promote a greater understanding of the FOIA as a research tool and as a protective instrument for the vital interests of a democratic society." The group monitors legislative and executive efforts to bypass, reduce or revoke the act and organizes opposition to any such attempts. It also raises funds and fosters channels of communication between professional organizations and between scholars and the public.

SEE ALSO United States 11. Freedom of Information Act.

Schultze-Naumberg, Prof. Paul   In 1928 Schultze-Naumberg, a noted German architect and town planner, published his book *Art and Race*, which explained the phenomenon of "hereditary determinism" in art, which held that "the artist cannot help but produce his own racial type in his creations." Immediately espoused by Adolf Hitler, such theories became the basis of the Nazi concept of "degenerate art" and the rationale for the censorship of art, literature and other cultural products. In Alfred Rosenberg's *Der Mythus des 20. Jahrhunderts* (*The Myth of the 20th Century*), which provided Nazism with some of its intellectual underpinnings, the concepts embodied in art and race were elevated to the status of absolute doctrine. In 1930 Schultze-Naumberg was appointed director of the Weimar Art School, where he banned the use of live models and offered in his lectures such apercus as "anyone who finds esthetic pleasure in Expressionism is not a German."

SEE ALSO Germany 3. Nazi art censorship.

Scopes v. *State* (1927)   Under the Tennessee Anti-Evolution Act (1925)—"An act prohibiting the teaching of evolutionary theory in all the Universities, normals and all other public schools in Tennessee, which are supported in whole or in part by the public school funds of the state, and to provide penalties for the violations thereof"—it was unlawful for any teacher "to teach any theory that denies the story of the divine creation of man as taught in the Bible, and to teach instead that man has descended from a lower order of animals." In 1925 one John Thomas Scopes, an otherwise mild-mannered young biology teacher in the town of Dayton, Tennessee, was convicted by a jury of contravening this act; he was fined $100. Scopes had volunteered himself as a test case in order that evolutionists might challenge Tennessee's recently promulgated statute. Clarence Darrow, America's most celebrated legal defender, took the case with no fee. As a carnival atmosphere took over the usually peaceful small town, the forces of God and the Devil, as the creationists saw it, entered on their cataclysmic struggle. One hundred journalists descended on Dayton, extra teletypes were installed and the *Chicago Tribune* set up equipment to broadcast the trial to those who, failing to find a seat in court, waited eagerly outside.

The trial opened on Friday July 10, 1925. Darrow set the tone for the 11-day hearing when he objected to Judge John T. Raulston's pretrial prayers and had a sign proclaiming "Read Your Bible" removed from the courtroom. The selected jury included one admitted illiterate; Scopes was charged on the evidence of three of his pupils, who testified that he had indeed taught them Darwinian theory. Darrow amassed a legion of expert witnesses, and the prosecuting counsel, District Attorney A.T. Stewart, proved himself as melodramatic as Darrow when, challenging the admission of such expert opinion as evidence, he raised his hands to heaven and asked "Would they have me believe I was once a worm and writhed in the dust? I want to go beyond this world to where there is eternal happiness for me and others." Judge Raulstone refused to admit the evidence of the scientific experts.

By the second weekend the trial appeared to have lost its momentum and the crowds of sensation-seekers were leaving town. The situation changed radically with the appearance as an unfriendly defense witness of William Jennings Bryan, three times a candidate for president, a devotedly fundamentalist Protestant, generally known as "the Great Commoner." Prosecutor Stewart objected to what he knew would be one of Darrow's virtuoso performances, but Raulston overruled him and Bryan ascended the stand to promise that he would defend the true faith and reject the false witness of agnostics and infidels. Darrow, savaged by Bryan as "the greatest atheist and agnostic in the United States," systematically eviscerated the Great Commoner's fundamentalist certainties. In a two-hour cross-examination he reduced the courtroom to laughter as he goaded Bryan into exhibitions of greater and greater absurdity. Bryan himself was reduced in the end to answering every paradox and inconsistency with the statement, "The Bible states it, it must be so."

Darrow made his point, and that of the evolutionists, but since at no time had he denied Scopes' teaching of evolution in contravention of the act, he failed to win an acquittal. Scopes then appealed to the Tennessee Supreme Court. Chief Justice Green declared that there was little merit in the contention that the act in itself violated the state's constitution. He accepted that that constitution stated, "It shall be the duty of the general Assembly ... to cherish literature and science" but refused to accept that the state's refusal to accept evolutionary theory, even though a preponderance of contemporary scientists did accept it, was in contravention of that statute. "If the Legislature thinks that, by reasons of popular prejudice, the cause of education and the study of science generally will be promoted by forbidding the teaching of evolution in the schools of the state, we can conceive of no ground to justify the court's interference." He rejected the criticisms of the act based on another part of the state constitution, which held "that no preference shall ever be given, by law, to any religious establishment or mode of worship." He said, "We are not able to see how the prohibition of teaching the theory that man has descended from a lower order of animals gives preference to any religious establishment or mode of worship. So far as we know, there is no religious establishment or organized body that has in its creed or confession of faith any article denying or confirming such a theory ... the denial or affirmation of such a theory does not enter into any recognized mode of worship." He concluded: "Those in charge of the educational affairs of the state are men and women of discernment and culture" and confirmed that what was good enough for them was adequate for the court. Thus the act stood.

The court, however, still reversed Scopes' conviction and nullified the fine, on a purely legal technicality: It had been the duty of the jury to assess his fine, and not that of Judge

Raulston, who had in fact taken this task upon himself. Thus Scopes was declared not guilty. He was no longer working as a teacher, and Judge Green ended proceedings by declaring "we see nothing to be gained by prolonging the life of this bizarre case."

SEE ALSO *Epperson* v. *Arkansas* (1968).

Scot, Reginald   Scot (1538?-99) was educated at Oxford and stood as MP for New Romney between 1588 and 1589. He read widely and in 1584 published his own work, *The Discovery of Witchcraft*. This was designed specifically "on behalf of the poor, the aged and the simple" and aimed to rid them of a variety of long-standing superstitions as regarded witchcraft and sorcery. Scot's book both deflated the impostures of the so-called sorcerers, and pointed out to the credulous how foolish they were to believe such nonsense. Attacking those who claimed that such beliefs must be valid since so many generations had accepted them, he replied "Truth must not be measured by time, for every old opinion is not sound." By the same token he attacked the law for its cruel treatment of those condemned as witches.

Scot's pioneering, rational work found an important enemy. King James I (of England) devoted his own *Demonologie* to attacking *The Discoverie*. A firm believer in the literal interpretation of the spirits, up to and including the angels in heaven, even though a careful reading of Scot would have found the line, "I deny not that there are witches or images; but I detest the idolatrous opinions conceived of them." One of the first acts of James' reign was to have every accessible copy of Scot's book burned. Scot himself, who had died in 1599, before James became king of England, escaped punishment.

SEE ALSO United Kingdom: Stuart censorship.

Scotland's obscenity laws   Scotland, governed by its own judicial system, is not subject to the English OBSCENE PUBLICATIONS ACT (1959). The sale of such material can be dealt with at Scottish common law or under various specific statutes.

Common Law: It is an offense at common law to publish an obscene work intended to corrupt public morals. The last reported prosecution for this offense was in 1843, although there have been a number of unreported prosecutions since. Criminal proceedings may be taken either summarily or on indictment. Articles seized in such a prosecution may only be forfeited and destroyed after a conviction.

Statutory Law: Section 380(3) of the Burgh Police (Scotland) Act (1892) makes an offense the publishing, printing or offering for sale or distribution, or selling, distributing or exhibiting to view, or causing to be published, printed or exhibited to view, or distributed, any indecent or obscene book, paper, print, photograph, drawing, painting, representation, model or figure, or publicly exhibiting any disgusting or indecent object, or writing or drawing any indecent or obscene word, figure or representation in or on any place

where it can be seen by the public, or singing or reciting in public any obscene song or ballad. The maximum penalty is a fine of £10 or no more than 60 days imprisonment. Section 380(5) makes it a further offense to exhibit obscene posters or similar material or to send such material through the posts. Section four of the VAGRANCY ACT (1824), as used in England, makes it an offense for any person wilfully to expose to view in any street, road, highway or public place any obscene print, picture or other indecent exhibition. A variety of local laws underline the general ones. The THEATRES ACT (1968) extends to Scotland, as do England's customs and postal regulations.

SEE ALSO United Kingdom—contemporary censorship 1. customs and post office legislation.

Screw   Launched in New York City in November 1968, *Screw* was the first tabloid newspaper devoted exclusively to sex. The idea of such a publication came from two men, one a writer and photographer, the other a typesetter and editor, who had met at the *New York Free Press*, one of New York City's emergent underground newspapers. Al (Alvin) Goldstein had been born in 1937 in one of Brooklyn's tougher neighborhoods, the son of a photographer for the Hearst organization. Between the end of his obligatory Army service in 1958 and the launch of *Screw* a decade later, Goldstein wroked variously as an insurance agent, a taxi driver, a salesman of both rugs and encyclopedias, a carnival pitchman, an industrial spy and the writer of bizarre tales for the *National Mirror*, a sensational tabloid weekly. Jim Buckley was born in Lowell, Massachusetts, in 1944. His youth was spent shuttling between first orphanages and then schools as his parents fought over his custody. After a hitch in the U.S. Navy he ran through a number of jobs—teletype operator, underground press street-seller, fudge maker—before joining the *Free Press* as a sub-editor.

In summer 1968 both men were looking for a change. Goldstein's free-lance writing career was failing, sub-editing held no appeal for Buckley. Investing $175 each they put together the first edition of *Screw* in November 1968. Loosely modelled on the defunct *Fuck You: A Magazine of the Arts*, *Screw* ran to 12 pages, its cover featuring a pretty brunette fondling a large, kosher salami, with a blurb (by Goldstein) extolling "the most exciting new publication in the history of the West." Four thousand copies of the 7,000-print run were sold at 35 cents each. By issue number 10 there were 24 pages and the circulation approached 100,000. The offices moved from Union Square to 11 West 17th Street, a building once occupied by wealthy realtor Edward West "Daddy" Browning (1874-1934), whose quinquagenarian antics with his 16-year-old child bride "Peaches" had scandalized 1920s society.

Although *Screw* concentrated on sex, running pictures, editorial and personal ads hitherto unavailable on the city's newsstands, it took an indisguised political stance that paralleled the preoccupations of the wider, contemporary underground press. With a little photographic sleight-of-hand a pair of military commanders were shown enjoying the act of sodomy against a background of Vietnam war atrocities; politicians and judges appeared practicing the very perversions they condemned. Radical populism combined with sexual liberation to savage what the magazine saw as the double standards that dominated Establishment mores, particularly in its analysis of the world of commercial sex. *Screw* also backed the customer in the sexual marketplace. Its famous "peter meter" established standards for porno movies; its reviewers checked out massage parlors, book stores, brothels, marital aids, the special requirements of a variety of fetishists and much more, with all the assiduity of less notorious consumer advocates. Praise from *Screw* boosted one's profits; condemnation might destroy one's business.

On May 30, 1969, the police raided *Screw*, Mayor John Lindsay having taken exception to a collage in which he sported a massive penis, with accompanying copy that implied his performance in office was much inferior to his efforts in bed. The editors were charged with obscenity but the paper kept appearing and the case was defeated. After a year's publication, sales topped 150,000. Imitators followed, such as *Pleasure* and the *New York Review of Sex*. A further trial for obscenity, in 1973, was less successful. In *Buckley* v. *New York* (1973) the magazine was found to be obscene, and the U.S. Supreme Court refused to hear the appeal. The conviction failed to stop publication; *Screw* continues to appear.

secular humanism   Secular humanism is the term developed by American religious fundamentalists to categorize any educational philosophy that denies the primacy of absolute values and refuses to base its central tenets on a literal reading of the Bible. On the basis of this charge a variety of conservative pressure groups have sought to ban both courses and textbooks that attempt to deal with various topics in ways with which they disagree.

Among such unacceptable topics are the theory of evolution; critical appraisals of the Vietnam war, government scandals and the arms race; liberal analyses of such social problems as poverty, teenage pregnancy, unemployment, drug use, and the shifting status of the American family. The discussion of sex, especially homosexuality, is taboo in the classroom. These groups oppose such products of secular humanism as the open classroom, the new math and creative writing programs, asserting that such relatively unstructured academic approaches break down standards of right and wrong, encourage "socialistic" non-competitiveness and thus promote rebellion, sexual promiscuity and crime.

What schools should do, they state, is to return to many of the teaching practices and textbooks of 30 years ago, as well as the Christian values and principles upon which, they argue, the country was founded. History texts should emphasize the positive side of America's past, economics courses stress the strengths of capitalism, and literature should avoid divorce, suicide, drug addiction and similar "negative" topics. Above

all they want a curriculum and an approach to teaching that clearly and unquestioningly delineates between right and wrong.

In 1986 a *New York Times* report cited the censorship, on the grounds of their secular humanism, of some 239 titles, among them: *Brave New World* (Huxley), *Catcher in the Rye* (Salinger), *Run Shelley, Run*, *The Kinsman* (Ben Bova), *Howl* (Allen Ginsberg), *Getting Down to Get Over* (June Gordon), *Our Bodies, Ourselves* (Boston Women's Health Collective), *Sports Illustrated*, *Ms*, *Death of a Salesman* (Arthur Miller), *Slaughterhouse Five* (Kurt Vonnegut Jr.), *The Fixer* (Bernard Malamud), *Down These Mean Streets* (Piri Thomas), *The American Heritage Dictionary*, *Of Mice and Men* (Steinbeck), *Lord of the Flies* (William Golding), *A Doll's House* (Ibsen), *The Diary of Anne Frank*, and major works by Langston Hughes, James Baldwin, Poe, Hawthorne, Stevenson and Hemingway.

Sedition Act (U.S., 1798)   The Sedition Act, passed by the Fifth American Congress on Bastille Day, July 14, 1798, was a remarkably punitive law, especially in its disregard for the freedoms of speech and communication guaranteed in the FIRST AMENDMENT (itself only seven years old) and in the substantial fines it levied on transgressors; it lasted only three years. The act was inspired by the rivalry between the current president, John Adams, a Federalist, and the republican followers of Thomas Jefferson. The latter had been assailing the government with a number of contentious broadsides, and the Sedition Act was intended to silence their attacks. There already existed, on the English model, a law against SEDITIOUS LIBEL, but it was felt that it did not extend to this type of material. Twenty-five people were prosecuted under the act, often pro-Jefferson newspaper editors and usually for relatively minor attacks. Even drunks who were overheard condemning Adams were duly charged and fined.

Section one of "An Act in addition to the act, entitled 'An Act for the punishment of certain crimes against the United States'" stated:

> That, if any persons shall unlawfully combine or conspire together, with intent to oppose any measure or measures of the government of the United States, which are or shall be directed by proper authority, or to impede the operation of any law of the United States, or to intimidate or prevent any person holding a place or office in or under the government of the United States, from undertaking, performing or executing his trust or duty; and if any person or persons, with intent as aforesaid, shall counsel, advise, or attempt to procure any insurrection, riot, unlawful assembly, or combination, whether such conspiracy, threatening, counsel, advice or attempt shall have the proposed effect or not, he or they shall be deemed guilty of a high misdemeanour, and on conviction ... shall be punished by a fine not exceeding five thousand dollars and by imprisonment during a term of not less than six months nor exceeding five years, and further, at the discretion of the court may be beholden to find sureties

for his good behavior in such sum, and for such time, as the court shall direct.

Section two:

That if any person shall write, print, utter and publish, or shall cause or procure to be written, printed, uttered or published, or shall knowingly and willingly assist or aid in writing, printing, uttering or publishing any false, scandalous and malicious writing or writings against the government of the United States, of either house of the Congress of the United Stats, or the President of the United States, with intent to defame the said government, or either house of the said Congress, or the said President, or to bring them, or either of them, into contempt or disrepute; or to excite against them, or either or any of them, the hatred of the good people of the United States, or to stir up sedition within the United States, or to excite any unlawful combinations therein, for opposing or resisting any law of the United States, or any act of the President of the United States, done in pursuance of any such law, or the powers in him vested by the constitution of the United States, or to resist, oppose, or defeat any such law or act, or to aid, encourage or abet any hostile designs of any foreign nation against the United States, their people or government, then such person, being thereof convicted … shall be punished by a fine not exceeding two thousand dollars, and by imprisonment not exceeding two years.

When Adams was succeeded by Jefferson himself in 1801, the act was promptly repealed and all those convicted under its provisions were pardoned. Jefferson, whose efforts the acts had sought to silence, typified the law as "to be a nullity as absolute and as palpable as if Congress had ordered us all to fall down and worship a golden image."

seditious libel The concept of seditious libel was developed in Britain as an attempt to control the growing power of public opinion, which by the 17th century was no longer susceptible to the old law of treason. The new laws took their basis in the medieval statutes of *Scandalum Magnatum*, a series of measures enacted in 1275 to suppress rumors affecting the king and nobles, which might otherwise inflame the masses to rebellion. A century later the statute was amended, broadening the range of those who could be thus offended. By the 16th century it had evolved into seditious libel. The law remained somewhat self-defeating: The falsity of a rumor had to be proved by the prosecution and while spreading rumors was in itself illegal, making them up, which was far harder to prove, was a much worse crime. Truth remained an adequate defense until 1606, in the case *De Libellis Famosis*, when Star Chamber overturned this restriction. As the jurist Sir Edward Coke reported, libel against a private individual could be punished since it might provoke revenge and thus a possible breach of the peace; libel against the authorities was an even greater offense "for it concerns not only the breach of the peace, but also the scandal

of government." The case created the legal aphorism "The greater the truth the greater the libel"; what mattered was not the libel, but the potential it might have for public disorder. Prosecutions for seditious libel by Star Chamber remained at the center of Stuart Censorship (see United Kingdom: Stuart censorship) and their unpopularity hastened the destruction of that court.

The restoration of the Stuarts in 1660 initiated a resurgence of seditious libel prosecutions as printers and publishers were harassed by official searchers such as Roger L'Estrange, whose responsibility it was to seek out and destroy seditious printing. The Puritans had abolished Star Chamber, but they left intact this law, a convenient catchall for any government whose position was insufficiently secure for it to permit unfettered criticism. Seditious libel prosecutions formed the main area of conflict between the government and the press in the 18th century, during which period the power of the law was gradually eroded. In 1704, in *R. v. Tuchin*, Chief Justice Holt opined that "a reflection on the government" must be punished since "if people should not be called to account for possessing the people with an ill opinion of the government, no government can subsist. For it is very necessary for all governments that the people should have a good opinion of them."

The first part of the century merely carried on the practices of the later Stuarts, with prosecutions such as that of Richard Franklin (or Francklin) for publishing in 1731 a political paper, *The Craftsman*, in which the government was criticized. The increasingly prevalent idea of freedom of the press, inspired by the ZENGER trial in America and by Milton's AREOPAGITICA, dominated the mid-century. Such a freedom was defined in Blackstone's *Commentaries on the Laws of England* (1765-69) as "indeed essential to the nature of a free state, but this consists in laying no previous restraints upon publications, and not in freedom from censure for criminal matter when published." However, Blackstone's approval of postpublicaiton culpability and the "fair and impartial trial" that this should receive ignored two basic elements of such a trial: Defendants were not allowed to prove the truth of the alleged libel, and a judge, rather than a jury, decided the verdict.

In 1752 the first jury rejected a judge's instructions to convict and instead acquitted one William Owen, charged with attacking the government in a pamphlet. So antagonistic toward the law did juries become that soon acquittals were the norm, and the authorities found it increasingly hard to secure a conviction. The furor and farce that typified the prosecution of JOHN WILKES for the NORTH BRITON accentuated the diminishing power of the law. The prosecution of the widely published Junius Letter No. 35 in 1770, in which, in the absence of the anonymous author, five printers and a bookseller were tried, led to a public uproar and demands for a review of the law. The review that followed, radically altering the judicial procedure in such cases, did not repeal the law but altered its import. Above all, it was no longer dangerous merely to criticize the government. In 1792 the Libel Act, pioneered by Charles James Fox and the leading contemporary advocate, Erskine, established for good that it was up to the jury, and not the judge, to determine whether or not a libel was seditious.

As originally defined in English law an opinion constitutes a seditious libel when it is made "with an intention to bring into hatred or contempt, or to excite disaffection against the King or the government and constitution of the United Kingdom as by law established, or either House of Parliament, or the administration of justices, or to excite British subjects to attempt otherwise than by lawful means the alteration of any matter in Church or State by law established, or to promote feelings of ill will and hostility between different classes." This interpretation was modified in 1886 when the judge who was trying a number of socialists for their speeches at a meeting in Hyde Park cited this definition and then added,

An intention to show that her Majesty has been misled or mistaken in her measures, or to point out errors and defects in the government or the constitution as by law established, with a view to their reformation, or to excite Her Majesty's subjects to attempt by lawful means the alteration of any matter in Church or State by law established, or to point out, in order to their removal [sic] matters which are producing or have a tendency to produce feelings of hatred and ill-will between classes of Her Majesty's subjects, is not a seditious intention.

Later interpretations narrowed down this definition, which, if taken at face value, would outlaw much serious political debate. In 1947, in the trial of one Gaunt, who had commented adversely on the reaction toward British Jews when their compatriots in Palestine were attacking British troops, Mr. Justice Birkett pointed out that: "Sedition has always had implicit in the word, public disorder, tumult, insurrection or matters of that kind." Merely pointing out the inadequacies of national institutions or promoting class warfare did not qualify.

SEE ALSO *The Age of Reason*; *The Rights of Man*.

Sedley, Sir Charles Sedley, sometimes known as Sidley, was a dramatist and poet (1639?-1701), a friend of Dryden and Lord ROCHESTER as well as of King Charles II. He was equally well known, as were most of his circle, for his drunken excesses. In June 1663, he indulged in an escapade that, despite its having no literary connotations, brought him within authority of the law against OBSCENE LIBEL, the forerunner of modern obscenity laws. Sedley and some friends appeared, "inflam'd with strong liquors," on the balcony of the Cock public house in Bow Street, Covent Garden. From here they proceded to lower their breeches and "excrementiz'd in the street," following this display with a shower of bottles, which they had, during their drinking bout, filled with urine. They also berated the crowd that gathered below with a variety of blasphemous speeches. The upshot of this prank was the appearance of Sir Charles and his companions at Westminster Hall, where Sir Robert Hyde, the lord chief justice, claiming the right of *custos morum* (the right to punish or prohibit any act seen as contrary to the public interest) fined him 2,000 marks (or £500), committed him to prison without bail for one week and bound him over to keep the peace for a year. The plaintiff "made answer that he thought that he was the first man that paid for shitting." His crime, however, was his assault on the people below, and his blasphemous remarks, which constituted an obscene libel. This verdict created the precedent for all subsequent obscenity laws and for the offense of CONSPIRACY TO CORRUPT PUBLIC MORALS.

SEE ALSO *Fifteen Plagues of a Maidenhead*.

Sellon, Edward Sellon (1818-1866) was born the son of a "gentleman of modest fortune whom I lost when I was quite a child" and went at the age of 16 to serve in the East India Company. Here he gained a captaincy by the precocious age of 21 and divided his time bewteen Indian antiquities and "the salacious, succulent houris of the East." He fought one duel. In 1844 he returned to London to marry Augusta, a girl selected by his mother. Fortunately she was attractive, though not as rich as he had supposed. His marriage was always stormy. Unable to resist other women, including the housemaid, he was continually leaving home, then reconciling himself with his wife. For two years he drove the London to Cambridge coach, using an assumed name, then for a while ran a fencing school in London and later taught in a girl's school where his wife, yet again, found him seducing the pupils. He also wrote several books on India, notably *Annotations of the Sacred Writings of the Hindus*, *The Monolithic Temples of India*, and a translation of the *Ghita-Radhica-Khrishna*, a Sanskrit poem. After Sellon's mother died, leaving him relatively penniless, he and Augusta retired to the country, enjoying three years of connubial bliss, curtailed only by the arrival of a child. Sellon left his family, for the last time, and in 1860 began working in London as a writer for WILLIAM DUGDALE, the pornographer.

By 1866 Sellon had written a number of works for Dugdale, including *The New Epicurean; or, The Delights of Sex, Facetiously and Philosophically Considered, in Graphic Letters Addressed to Young Ladies of Quality* (1865) and its sequel, *Phoebe Kissagen; or, the Remarkable Adventures, Schemes, Wiles, and Devilries of Une Maquerelle* (1866). He also illustrated *The Adventures of a Schoolboy* (1866), a homosexual novel by JAMES CAMPBELL) and *The New Lady's Tickler; or, the Adventure of Lady Lovesport and the Audacious Harry* (a novel of flagellation, and still extant during World War I). In 1866 he sold to Dugdale the manuscript of his allegedly autobiographical work, *The Ups and Downs of Life*. In it, "The nearest thing to a classic Victorian erotology has" (R. Pearsall op. cit.), he detailed the career of what ASHBEE called a "thoughtless, pleasure-seeking scamp." It remains one of the rarest works of erotica and only one copy of the first edition is known to exist. A reprint, titled *The Amorous Prowess of a Jolly Fellow* (1892), is just as rare. *The Ups and Downs* ... , published in 1867, was Sellon's last testimony. In April 1866 this adventurer, a man "by no means devoid of talent, and undoubtedly capable of better things" (Ashbee), shot himself through the head in a room in Webb's Hotel, Piccadilly. He left a note for his latest mistress, a poem entitled "No More," and a final tag, "Vivat Lingam/Non Resurgam" ("Long live cock. I shall not return").

Senegal   Independent Senegal passed its own press law (Law No. 79-44) in 1979 to replace a number of earlier laws passed by both the colonial French and earlier Senegalese governments. The intention of the law is to control the country's press, by observing the constitutional guarantees of freedom but at the same time curtailing "excesses, abuses and anarchy" that such freedom allows. The law is supposed to protect the persons, goods, honor and dignity of the citizens.

The law falls under three headings: (1) the definition of a press organ as any journalistic publication, barring the professional, special or technical and those that appear less than four times a year. It specifies the legal position regarding ownership, management and allied aspects of the business, plus circulation and distribution; (2) the qualifications and obligations required of a journalist, notably the professional identification card; (3) the administrative and legal sanctions that may be exercised over anyone who breaks Law 79-44. The law is extended to cover all forms of printed material—books, photographs, journals etc.

Every individual involved in the newspaper business, from owners to vendors, is made strictly answerable under the law. All publications, both foreign and Senegalese, must be submitted for predistribution censorship. All publications must carry the printer's name and address and the names of all those "directing" the organ, either in law or in fact. Every publication must have a director, usually the majority shareholder or, if the paper is owned by a political party, a senior member of that party. The real names of any pseudonymous writers must be known by the editor who must divulge them if required. Distributors and vendors must be registered with their local police. Street vendors have legal responsiblity for what they sell. Two commissions exist under the law: the National Press Commission and the Commission for Control of Press Organs (CCPO). The NPC, who members are drawn from the newspaper owners, journalists and the Ministry of Information, ensures that everything published is subject to the law. It also controls the distribution of journalists' ID cards. The CCPO, made up of senior judges, a representative of the Ministry of Information and the director of the largest-selling newspaper (invariably government-sponsored), oversees the business side of publishing: auditing the accounts, checking circulation figures etc.

September in Quinze   *September in Quinze*, by American author Vivian Connell (1903-   ) and published by Hutchin-

son, was tried and convicted at the Old Bailey in September 1954. Connell's earlier novel, *The Chinese Room* (1942), had already been attacked in the United States, but despite the objections of a citizens committee in Middlesex County, New Jersey, was exonerated. This book punned on Quinze/Cannes and dealt with the Mediterranean amours of a Middle Eastern monarch who had recently been dethroned and was dedicating himself to hedonistic self-indulgence.

Following the recent case of *Julia* by Margot Bland, published by T. Werner Laurie, which had been dispatched speedily by a magistrate at the cost of a £30 fine and £10 costs, both the police and the publishers wanted the case disposed of in the lower court, but the Marlborough Street magistrate sent it on to the Old Bailey.

SEE ALSO *The Philanderer*.

September Laws, The   These laws were passed in France on September 9, 1835, as an attempt to curb the rash of parodies, satires, caricatures and similar political attacks on the government of Louis Philippe, established after the Revolution of July 1830. Freedom of the press had been proclaimed by the new king, but when this seemed only to legitimize a spate of attacks on the Throne, he turned increasingly to prosecutions for lese majesty and allied offenses. The September Laws declared that any attacks on the king equalled threats to public security and must as such be outlawed. All prints, lithographs, engravings and similar illustrations would fall henceforth under the jurisdiction of the minister of the interior in Paris or the departmental prefects in the provinces. Penalties for transgression ran from one to 12 months imprisonment, fines of 100 to 1,000 francs and the automatic confiscation of all offending material. The laws survived until the overthrow of Louis Philippe in the Revolution of February 1848.

SEE ALSO *Caricature, La; Charivari, Le*.

September Morn   This painting by Paul Chabas of a young French girl bathing nude on the shores of Lake Annecy in the Upper Savoy was first exhibited, to general approval, at the 1912 Salon in Paris. A reproduction was published for American readers in *Town and Country* magazine. In 1913, when a full-sized reproduction was exhibited in the window of Jackson and Semmelmeyer's Photographic Store on Wabash Avenue in Chicago, the authorities ordered it removed. Led by Alderman "Bath House John" Coughlin, Chicago's political boss, they prohibited the painting from being displayed publicly anywhere in the city. The picture found many defenders, and a jury was empanelled to hear all the rival opinions. Despite the pronouncements of such as the Chicago Vice Committee, who declared that since the girl was bathing in a public place, which was "definitely against the law," the picture should be prohibited, the jury refused to support the ban.

September Morn was then bought by Harry Reichenbach, the contemporary maestro of grossly inflated publicity campaigns. He took the picture to New York, where he exhibited it in the window of Braun & Company of West 46th Street. Here, hired for $45, a "small gallery of urchins" leered, grimaced, pointed and made suggestive comments. An anonymous phonecall ensured that ANTHONY COMSTOCK appeared on the scene to declare, "There's too little morning and too much maid." He did not, however, consider the picture worthy of prosecution. Reichenbach maximized the spurious dramatics of Comstock's visit, firing up a bogus controversy over art, morals, nudity and obscenity, all centered on *September Morn*. Postcards of the painting were forbidden in various American towns, a New Orleans art dealer was arrested for displaying a reproduction. Reichenbach steadfastly maintained the hype until his picture became the best-known image in America. More than 7,000,000 reproductions were sold—appearing on dolls, statues, umbrella handles, tattoos and many other places—in a merchandising orgy rarely surpassed until today's calculated exploitations of films, rock stars and royal weddings. Chabas died in 1937, both famous and enriched from the royalties he had received on his picture. He never revealed the name of the model, saying merely that she was married with three children. The original picture was not publically exhibited again until 1957, when it appeared at the Metropolitan Museum of Art in New York City.

Servetus, Michael   Servetus (aka Miguel Serveto, 1511-53) was a Spanish physician and theologian, a graduate of medicine in Paris and a lecturer there in geometry and astrology. As a doctor, practicing in various parts of France, he published in 1531 *De Trinitatibus Erroribus*, an attack on the doctrine of the Trinity, and in 1533 *Christianismi Restitutio*, a collection of theological treatises. After the latter were published in secret at Vienne in France, and the printer, Balthazar Arnouillet, deliberately excluded his own name and that of the author (other than his initials, "M.S.V."), a letter from CALVIN in Geneva denounced Servetus as the author and as a heretic. Calvin even offered a sample of Servetus' handwriting as proof of his guilt. Servetus was tried at Vienne under the auspices of the inquisitor general of Lyons (Mathieu Ory, who appears in RABELAIS as "Doribus"). He was found guilty and imprisoned, but managed to escape thanks to his friendship with Piere Paulmier, the archbishop of Vienne. His enemies had to make do with burning only his books and his effigy. He then moved to Geneva where, while waiting for a boat, he was recognized and arrested again. After a notably unfair trial, Servetus was found guilty, and, largely thanks to the vindictiveness of Calvin, burned at the stake with his condemned works. Green wood was used for the pyre, straw and leaves sprinkled with sulfur were placed on his head and his book was tied to his arm. In 1554 Calvin issued a book in which he attempted to justify his persecution of Servetus, claiming that the author had attacked the authority of the Bible and of Moses in an edition of Ptolemy's *Geography*.

"Sex Side of Life"   Under United States regulations regarding the mailing of obscene matter (see United States 17. postal regulations) it is forbidden to send material dealing with sexual education through the mails. In 1930 one Mrs. Dennett, the mother of two boys aged 11 and 14, decided that she wished her sons to learn the facts of life. To help her in explaining these facts she consulted some 60 publications of varying merit, none of which she found satisfactory. Instead, she decided to write and publish her own pamphlet, which she called "The Sex Side of Life." When it was discovered by the authorities that she had mailed a copy of this pamphlet to another housewife, Mrs. Miles of Grottoes, Virginia, she was charged and convicted by a federal district court of contravening the postal regulations. Her counsel pointed out that her pamphlet was intended only to help other parents in the sex education of their children, and that circulation had been strictly limited to interested parents and to social agencies; the judge was unimpressed. He told the jury that their task was to determine whether, under the law, the pamphlet was "obscene, lewd, or lascivious" and explained the HICKLIN RULE to them as a means of making their judgment. He added that "even if the matter sought to be shown in the pamphlet ... were true, that fact would be immaterial, if the statement of such facts were calculated to deprave the morals of the readers by inciting sexual desires and libidinous thoughts." Dennett was fined $300.

In *United States* v. *Dennett* (1930) the federal appeal court overturned the verdict. It described the pamphlet in admiring tones and went on to suggest that sex education, within certain limits, was to be recommended. It also rejected the Hicklin Rule as an outmoded means of assessing alleged obscenity. The court added that:

> It may be assumed that any article dealing with the sex side of life and explaining the functions of the sex organs is capable in some circumstances of arousing lust. The sex impulses are present in every one, and without doubt cause much of the weal and woe of human kind. But it can hardly be said that, because of the risk of arousing sex impulses, there should be no instruction of the young in sex matters, and that the risk of imparting instruction outweighs the disadvantages of leaving them to grope about in mystery and morbid curiosity and of requiring them to secure such information as they may be able to obtain from ill-informed and foul-mouthed companions, rather than from intelligent and high-minded sources ... The statute we have to construe was never thought to bar from the mails everything which might stimulate sex impulses. If so, much chaste poetry and fiction, as well as many useful medical works, would be under the ban.

SEE ALSO *Birth Control*; *Birth of a Baby, The*; *Love Without Fear*; *Married Love*; *Sexual Impulse, The*; *Sexual Inversion*.

Sexual Impulse, The   This sex instruction manual written by Edward Charles was published in Britain in 1935 by the left-wing firm of Boriswood Ltd., which already, the previous year, suffered the banning of James Hanley's *Boy*. Although it was generally assumed that legitimate sex manuals were outside the obscenity laws, Boriswood, aware of the firm's reputation, had been especially careful in preparing this volume. A variety of eminent medical men, including Lord Horder and Professor Julian Huxley, had given it their imprimatur. The publication had been advertised throughout the medical press; the major subscription was from a leading medical bookseller. The bulk of the book propounded biochemical technicalities and abstruse philosophical tenets, but an important section dealt with techniques of sexual intercourse as made comprehensible for the average reader. Freed from jargon, the author indulged his more lyrical side when discussing what he obviously saw as pleasurable experiences.

The Sexual Impulse and its publishers appeared before the magistrate of the Westminster Police Court in October 1935, charged with publishing an obscene book. A variety of experts testified to the educational and scientific value of the book. The magistrate, Mr. A. Ronald Powell, was unimpressed, asking whether it was "fit and decent for people of the working class to read." He also made clear his dislike of suggestions advocating sex in the open air and during menstruation. Boriswood Ltd. was convicted of obscene publication. The book was ordered to be destroyed. An appeal to the London Sessions was unsuccessful. It has never been republished.

SEE ALSO *Birth Control*; *Birth of a Baby, The*; *Love Without Fear*; *Married Love*; "Sex Side of Life"; *Sexual Inversion*.

Sexual Inversion   Henry Havelock Ellis (1859-1939) was a pioneer of literary taste and scientific knowledge whose advocacy of free thought and free love led in 1896 to the publication of *Sexual Inversion*, volume one of his *Studies in the Psychology of Sex*. Ellis was a leading member of the late-Victorian avant-garde; he had discovered Ibsen and Whitman, edited with HENRY VIZETELLY the unexpurgated Mermaid Series of Elizabethan dramatists, produced a work on criminology (albeit based on the somewhat unscientific theories of Lambroso) and edited the journal *Contemporary Science*. He was a founder member of the Fellowship of New Life, a protoptye of the Fabian Society.

In 1892 it was suggested to him by the writer John Addington Symonds that he should produce for the Science Series a study of homosexuality: *Sexual Inversion*. Symonds, himself a homosexual, wished to see a book exalting his own form of sexuality. Ellis, whose own sexuality was swamped into near-impotence by all-consuming shyness, and who in 1891 had married the lesbian Edith Lees (1861-1916), planned an objective scientific work. He also planned for it to be used as propaganda against the Criminal Amendment Act (1885), into which the muckraking journalist and MP Henry Labouchere had inserted a clause outlawing all homosexual intercourse, even between consenting adults in private.

Symonds died in 1893, unable, as he had planned, to collaborate on the book. Its first edition appeared in 1896, published in Leipzig, Germany, as *Das Kontrare Geschlechtsgefuhl*. Finding a London imprint proved harder. The trial of Oscar Wilde in 1895 had spread homophobia throughout England and Ellis' book frightened legitimate publishers. He turned eventually to a private press, the University Press in Watford, run ostensibly by one George Astor Singer, a permanent absentee who proved indeed to be pure fiction, and one Dr. Roland De Villiers, a gaudy adventurer who would turn out, to Ellis' surprise, to be in fact George Ferdinand Springmuhl von Weissenfeld, the son of an eminent German judge, whose love of luxury was financed by his career as a swindler and a large-scale wholesaler of pornography.

As well as Ellis' work, the University Press issued the *University Magazine and Free Review*, devoted to a variety of progressive causes, and *The Adult*, the journal of the Legitimation League, an organization devoted to securing rights for illegitimate children. The publication of *Sexual Inversion* went generally unremarked until the volume was cited at a league meeting by its secretary George Bedborough (formerly George Higgs) as an admirable work. It was noted that copies of the book were available from Bedborough whose home in John Street doubled as a league bookshop. This recommendation was noted by Detective Inspector John Sweeney, an undercover policeman who attended league meetings.

When Scotland Yard received a complaint from a youth who had been sent a copy of *Sexual Inversion* in error and whose parents demanded its suppression, Sweeney was able to act. Bedborough was arrested and charged, erroneously, with publishing Ellis' work. He was then loaded with 10 further charges regarding *The Adult*. A raid in 1899 on De Villiers' house netted two tons of pornography. De Villiers was found hiding on the roof. He died of apoplexy at the police station, although legend had it that he committed suicide, aided by a poison ring. While Bedborough's supporters felt that he should capitalize on this opportunity for martyrdom, the bookseller was less sanguine. Ellis himself, in his pamphlet "A Note on the Bedborough Case," made it clear that he had no stomach for such legal battles and Bedborough had no desire to take his place. Charged with "uttering an OBSCENE LIBEL," he confounded his supporters, who had arranged petitions, legal aid funds and a number of expert witnesses by accepting Sweeney's offer: Plead guilty to the Ellis charges and the rest would be dropped. Bedborough was duly bound over, and the recorder of London, Sir Charles Hall, admonished him, "You have acted wisely for it would have been impossible for you to have contended with any possibility whatever ... that this book, this lecture and this magazine were not filthy and obscene works ..." Ellis was bitter, but accepted in his autobiography *My Life* (1939) that the long-term, worldwide success of his work far outweighed his courtroom tribulations. Further volumes were consigned to F.A. Davis of Philadelphia, Krafft-Ebing's publisher. The Legitimation League collapsed.

Shakespeare, William In the last 400 years the works of Shakespeare (1564-1616) have been more often expurgated than those of any other English-language author except Chaucer. From the first excisions of the Restoration to the present day, when expurgated school editions are still studied, the bowdlerized editions of the Bard have persisted. The first example of such censorship was that of Elizabeth I, who found the passage in *Richard II* in which the king is deposed so infuriating that she had it cut from all performances and it was only restored after her death. The next recorded expurgation of Shakespeare was carried out by Sir William D'Avenant, who held a monopoly of licensed plays in London, in 1660. In what was basically a sop to Puritan interests, he trimmed seven of the plays with the general intention "that they may be reformed of prophanes and ribaldry." It was a patchy effort: Some scenes or words were changed, some cut, and some left intact. Once the Restoration was firmly established, such acknowledgments to the Cromwell years disappeared. For the next 100 years Shakespeare was made if anything more ribald, as in Dryden's version of *The Tempest* in which Miranda is given a sexier twin sister, Dorinda. Such editing as existed was esthetic, for instance George Steevens' removal of the gravediggers from *Hamlet* on the premise that such low comedy disgraced so great a play.

The first substantial expurgation appeared in 1774, prepared by Francis Gentleman for the publishers Bell. His intention was to give Shakespeare classical form and a sense of dignity, i.e., nowhere should kings be ridiculed or seen as anything but divine. His decision to put mildly indecent passages in italics—so that readers could skip them (he cut without comment those he considered beyond the pale)—only drew attention to Shakespeare's alleged tastelessness. In 1795 William Henry Ireland (1777-1835), best known as a forger, produced an expurgated *King Lear*. This appeared not on moral or artistic grounds but to reinforce the prevalent theory that true Shakespeare lacked any ribaldry, which excess stemmed from later additions. Thus, to forge an original manuscript Ireland avoided all indecency. His ruse was discovered, but not before his forgeries had deceived many experts and Boswell had even kissed the phony parchment. *King Lear* was disliked by George III and it was prohibited from the English stage during his reign, supposedly out of respect for the royal insanity.

In 1818 the FAMILY SHAKESPEARE, edited by Thomas BOWDLER appeared. Its success spawned a number of imitators, most notably the Rev. J.R. Pitman's *The School-Shakspeare* (1822). Pitman aimed to undercut Bowdler, offering just the "celebrated passages" from 26 plays, linked with the minimum necessary plot for 18/- (90p); Bowdler's 36 plays cost three guineas (£3.15). He also produced a more stringent expurgation. His book lasted 40 years and five editions. Also in 1822 appeared Elizabeth Macauley's *Tales of the Drama*, dealing with a number of playwrights and influenced more by Mary Lamb's *Tales from Shakespeare* (1807) than by the *Family Shakespeare*, but still expurgated severely when dealing with Shakespeare. Expurgation paused briefly until the late 1840s; henceforth a rash of "select," "family" or "school" editions appeared, rendering any uncut version of Shakespeare almost invisible.

In 1849 the first successful American bowdlerization appeared, *The Shaksperian Reader*, edited by Professor (of elocution) John W.S. Hows of Columbia University. Bowdler had already been issued in America but had proved so unpopular that in its second edition its cuts had had to be restored. Hows' expurgations far exceeded those of Bowdler. *Othello* stops at act three, Falstaff completely vanishes from *Henry IV, Part 1* and so on. Linguistic cuts were equally extensive, excluding much that Bowdler had tolerated. *The Shaksperian Reader* appeared in new editions until 1881, and even had a sequel, *The Historical Shaksperian Reader*.

In England there were more and more expurgations. Titles included *Selections from the Plays of Shakespeare Especially Adapted for Schools, Private Families and Young People* (1859), edited by Charles Kean; Charles Kemble's *Shakspere Readings* (1883); *Shakespeare's Plays for Schools* (1883-85), edited by Charlotte M. Yonge; *The Boudoir Shakespeare* (1876-77), edited by Henry Cundell; and many more. Even Lewis Carroll started work (although he only finished *The Tempest*) on *The Girl's Own Shakespeare*, aimed at readers from 10 to 17. These and others reflected the contemporary opinion of Rev. Thomas Best, regretting in a sermon in November 1864 the "almost idolatrous honor [paid] to the memory of a man who wrote so much that would not be tolerated in any decent or domestic circle and whose works … are, I doubt not, an abomination in the sight of God."

The Household Edition of the Dramatic Works of William Shakespeare (1861) by William Chambers & Robert Carruthers represents the first scholarly attempt at expurgation. The editors wished above all to avoid the practice of previous expurgators who had offered no indication of what was the original and what had been changed; thus, while they still cut without comment, all changes are placed within quotation marks. Some of the most highly "delicate" expurgations appeared in the 1860s. They included Rosa Baughan's *Shakespeare's Plays* (1863), most notable for its excision of all humor, and a great deal else, from all the plays; it was praised in *The Critic* as a "thorough weeding." In 1864 came the equally restrained *Cassell's Illustrated Shakespeare* by Charles and Mary Cowden Clarke. In 1865 Thomas Bulfinch edited *Shakespeare Adapted for Reading Classes and the Family Circle*, especially popular in America.

By the 1870s every major U.S. publishing hosue had its own expurgator, and in 1872 Ginn (of Boston) produced a three-volume edition of 21 plays "selected and prepared for use in Schools, Clubs, Classes, and Families." This eventually expanded to 38 volumes, one per play, including even the doubtful ones. This American equivalent of *The Family Shakespeare* sold five million copies bewteen 1880 and 1890 and a further 750,000 after that; some plays in the series still remain in print. Its editor, Henry Norman Hudson, was a respected Shakespearian scholar who also put out two unexpurgated editions, one before and one after the Ginn canon. His authority as a scholar made his cuts more influential, and, although they remained expurgations, his revisions were "models of care and wisdom" (Perrin op. cit.). *The Hudson Shakespeare* was replaced after his death by *The New Hudson Shakespeare* (1909). Unlike the original edition this admitted to no cuts or alterations (Hudson had scrupulously indicated his by brackets) but claimed only to note "every variation from First Folio." Early expurgators at least admitted to their efforts. The code words "family," "selected" or "school" made it clear that cuts had been made, but often the young people to whom such books were given had no idea how little what they read resembled Shakespeare's original work. By 1910 such editions as those of Rolfe (1884) and Meiklejohn (1880) dominated Shakespearian study, certainly up to undergraduate level. Dense and often valuable scholarly notes bedecked every volume, but no admission of the accompanying censorship was permitted.

The First World War saw the end of these bowdlerized editions. In 1916, writing in the *English Review*, Richard Whiteing debunked Bowdler for the first time. By 1925 the *Family Shakespeare* was a spent force. Hudson was similarly treated in America in 1929, and George Lyman Kittredge launched his unexpurgated school edition in 1939. Nonetheless, cut editions are still read in schools, including the Oxford University Press' "New Clarendon Shakespeare" and Cambridge University Press' "Pitt Press Shakespeare."

Shaw, George Bernard SEE Comstock, Anthony; Douglas, James; examiner of plays; Harris, Frank; Joint Select Committee on Censorship (1909); lord chamberlain; United States 13. library censorship (1876-1939); *The Well of Loneliness.*

She Should'a Said No! SEE *Wild Weed.*

Sierra Leone Under the Newspapers Amendment Act (1980, amended 1983) the government of Sierra Leone moved toward a comprehensive control of free expression in the national press. The essence of the law makes it compulsory for a proprietor to register his publication with the minister of information and broadcasting. The registration fee is nearly $4,000 in the first year and almost $2,000 for each subsequent year. The simple effect of this was to drive out of existence many small, low-budget opposition newspapers. The government claimed that such a diminution of the press would improve the quality of such papers that survived. In addition the ministry may refuse, cancel or withdraw the registration of any publication.

Censorship in Sierra Leone has been in force since the State of Emergency was proclaimed in 1973. There are no explicit rules and journalists must be cautious. Those who criticize the government face punishments against which there is no appeal. Those reporters who are seen as security risks are dismissed. The censors, operating mainly from the Ministry of Information and Broadcasting, but sometimes drawn from the newspaper's editorial staff, have destroyed manuscripts.

significant proportion Under British law the test for obscenity, as established in the OBSCENE PUBLICATIONS ACT (1959), is that the material in question is likely to deprave and corrupt those encountering it; for this test to be proved, not one or two but a significant proportion of the likely readers or viewers must be affected. This concept was established by the Court of Appeal in the trial of LAST EXIT TO BROOKLYN in 1967. It pointed out that the material clearly could not be assumed to affect all persons, nor could it mean just one individual, "for there are individuals who may be corrupted by almost anything." Instead, the court opted for the concept of a "significant proportion of persons likely to read [the material]," although it stressed that "what is a significant proportion is a matter entirely for the jury to decide." This was slightly narrowed in 1972 when, in the case of *DPP* v. *Whyte*, Lord Cross stated that "a significant proportion ... means a part which is not numerically negligible but which may be much less than half."

All subsequent British obscenity trials have hinged to some extent on this hypothetical number, varying as to the opinion of the juries responsible. It may work for either the defense (who do not have to worry about the effect on a single impressionable youngster who chances on the material) or for the prosecution (who do not have to prove that the majority, or even many people might be corrupted).

Sinclair, Upton Sinclair (1878-1968) was born in Baltimore and worked his way through college by writing novels, a career he pursued for the rest of his life. His best known work is *The Jungle* (1906), an expose of conditions at the Chicago meat-packing yards. The book aroused such public indignation that the federal government was forced to mount its own investigation. Like the hero of his novel, what he found in Chicago turned Sinclair into a socialist, and his work unashamedly promoted left-wing values. His novel *Oil!*, which dealt with the Teapot Dome scandal and its effects on the notably corrupt administration of President Warren Gamaliel Harding (1921-23), was banned in Boston in 1927—although Harding had died in 1923 and his cronies were long dispersed. Sinclair defended the case himself, at a cost of $2,000, and addressed a crowd of some 2,000 people on Boston Common, explaining at length the character and the intent of his book. The court suppressed nine pages of the book, including a substantial portion of the Biblical "Song of Solomon." The bookseller from whose store the book had been seized was fined $100 and the offending pages were blacked out. Sinclair, whose campaign to become the Democratic governor of California in 1933 was met with a fierce counter-campaign (from both Republicans and a majority of Democrats), was equally vilified abroad. His work was banned in Yugoslavia in 1929, burned in Nazi Germany in 1933, banned in South Africa in 1938 and in Ireland in 1953.

Singapore   Under the Newspaper and Printing Presses Act of August 28, 1974, controls were established over the Singapore press that are designed to eliminate media opposition to the government. Throughout 1971 Prime Minister Lee Kuan Yew had attempted to purge the press by strongarming its various factions into submission. The resulting well-publicized struggles between Lee and the press did undermine the opposition press but simultaneously weakened Lee's own reputation as a supposedly democratic figrue. The 1974 act, which institutionalized censorship, was the product. Under this act (most recently amended in 1986) newspapers must obtain (as they had to under the repealed Printing Presses Act of 1920, revised 1970) an annual license to own a printing press and to issue publications. The main innovation was the division of newspaper stock into two classes: management and ordinary. Management shares, which have greater voting rights, may be owned only by individuals approved by the Ministry of Culture. Once that approval has been obtained, the newspaper cannot refuse management shares to the individual in question. Non-Singapore citizens may not hold management shares without direct permission from the minister. If any newspaper fails to meet governmental requirements as regards the issuing of management shares to approved individuals, the ministry has the power to place its own nominees on the board of directors.

All newspaper directors must be Singapore citizens; no foreign investments, all of which must be declared, may be accepted without the approval of the Ministry of Culture. If the minister vetoes such investment it must either be returned to the donor or placed in a charity of the minister's choice. The government has the right to search any premises, without a warrant, and to seize outlawed publications. No Malaysian publication may circulate in Singapore without ministerial permission. A press council was introduced, with responsibility for laying down guidelines for acceptable journalistic behavior and for monitoring the ideological acceptability of key newspaper personnel. Those violating the act face fines and/or imprisonment. The result of the act was to force newspapers to become public corporations, thus breaking up old family monopolies. Given the government power over management shares, papers can be censored and indeed closed down by the withdrawal of those shares, which will automatically render the running of such a paper illegal.

Further to the 1974 act the government uses various other censorship measures. The Undesirable Publications Act (1967) covers the censorship by the Ministry of Culture of all imported publications and audio recordings. The Cinematograph Act created a Board of Censors to assess the acceptability of all films for viewing or sale. In 1972 all films depicting any form of brutality were banned. The Essential Regulations Ordinances deal with sedition and the protection of national security. The libel laws are used to ensure that the opposition cannot point out the abuses of various government officials and to stifle the opposition press. Bookshops are advised to be cautious and carry out their own censorship of the books they stock. Above all the media are expected to prop up the regime. As the prime minister stresses: "we want the mass media to reinforce, not undermine the cultural values and social attitudes being inculcated in our schools ..." The Internal Security Act (created for Malaysia by the British colonial administration and adopted by Singapore on its independence in 1965) is a further instrument of control. Under section 20 the minister of home affairs may ban any publication seen as "prejudicial to the national interest, public order or security" of the country. The act has been used extensively to punish opponents of the government.

Sinyavsky and Daniel Trial (1966)   Russians Andrey Donatovish Sinyavsky and Yuli Markovich Daniel, the latter a Jew and son of the Yiddish short story writer Mark Daniel-Meerovich, were both born in 1925. Both served in World War II and turned to writing afterward. Like many of their intellectual peers, each was deeply affected by the de-Stalinization measures encouraged by Premier Khrushchev's speech at the 20th Party Congress in 1956. Sinyavsky, the more prominent of the two, was a disciple of Boris Pasternak (both men were pallbearers at the writer's funeral in 1960), and his first major work was a preface to a collection of Pasternak's poetry in 1956. Like Pasternak he believed fully in the 1917 Revolution, but found the rigid Marxist ideology that dominated Russia quite unsatisfactory. Writing as a critic in the influential journal *Novy Mir* Sinyavsky continually outraged the literary establishment. Taking the pseudonym "Abram Tertz" he began publishing books outside the Soviet Union, notably *On Socialist Realism* (1959), *The Trial Begins* (1960), *Lyubimov* (*The Makepeace Experiment*) (1964), all of which featured in his trial.

In comparison Daniel had a very minor reputation in the U.S.S.R., based only on his verse translations. A single attempt to have an original work published legally was forbidden. Like Sinyavsky he began publishing abroad, writing as "Nikolai Arzhak." His work included *This Is Moscow Speaking* (1963), *The Man from MINAP* (1963), *Hands* (1966) and *Atonement* (1964). More sombre than Sinyavsky's work, Daniel's offered even sharper political satire. All four books were cited at his trial.

The two writers were arrested in September 1965. Western observers heard the news at the start of October, but Soviet citizens were not informed until *Izvestia* published an attack headlined "The Turncoats" in mid-January 1966; it was typical of the campaign that would continue through their trial.

Neither publishing abroad nor adopting a pseudonym was actually illegal, but the pair were condemned as "double-faced agents of Western anti-Soviet propaganda, moral delinquents and near-pornographers," whose reputations, if they had any, had been earned through fraud and deception.

The two writers were charged under section 70 of the Soviet Criminal Code with "Agitation or progaganda carried out with the purpose of subverting or weakening the Soviet regime or in order to commit particularly dangerous crimes against the State, the dissemination for the said purposes of slanderous inventions defamatory to the Soviet political and social system, as well as the dissemination or production or harboring for the said purposes of literature of similar content are punishable by imprisonment ..." Sinyavsky's and Daniel's work was thus supposedly seditious and potentially destructive of the state, even though it was totally unavailable to Soviet readers and distributed only abroad.

What mattered was their intent, and Dmitri Eremin, in *Izvestia*, claimed they had slandered, among others, Chekhov, Lenin and the Soviet Army. The trial took place February 10-14, 1966. It was the first time that Soviet writers were on trial for what they had written; many others had been condemned, but they had not been tried in open court, with their books as the main prosecution evidence. It was also the first time that the accused in a show trial refused to plead guilty. The accused were allowed a defense but the court was openly biased, as was all the reporting. The press condemned them before the trial even began and their side was never put to the public.

Sinyavsky was given seven years in a labor camp, Daniel five. The foreign response was predictably outraged, typified by the lifelong French Communist Louis Aragon, who condemned the trial in a major piece in *L'Humanite*. More important was the reaction of the majority of the Russian intellectual community, many of whom openly attacked the verdict, with as little success as their Western peers. The only major Soviet writer to come out against the defendants was Mikhail Sholokov (author of *And Quiet Flows the Don*) who savaged the "two renegades" and their allies at the 23rd Party Congress in April 1966. Both men served their sentences, but their conduct in court, notably their refusal to accede to the normal formalities of a show trial, probably did more than all their writing to decry censorship.

SEE ALSO socialist realism.

Sinyavsky, Andrei (aka Abram Tertz) SEE Sinyavsky & Daniel Trial (1966).

Sleeveless Errand, The This novel by Norah James appeared in Britain in 1929. Written as a two-day-long conversation in which the characters reveal their most intimate thoughts, the book had been heavily influenced by James Joyce and suffered a fate similar to that of ULYSSES. The director of public prosecutions applied for a destruction order, claiming that the book tolerated and even advocated adultery.

The words "God" and "Christ" were said to appear overly often; as an example of the book's "shocking depravity" he cited the sentence "For Christ's sake give me a drink." The defense claimed that such unpleasantness as occurred in the book merely reflected life as it was and that the author's intent had been "to portray and condemn the mode of life and language of a certain section of the community." The magistrate was unimpressed and, in granting the destruction order, stated that *The Sleeveless Errand* would certainly suggest "thoughts of the most impure character" to readers of all ages. The home secretary, Sir WILLIAM JOYNSON-HICKS, was questioned in the House as to his own responsibility for the prosecution. He replied that he "thought it was a proper case to be sent to the D.P.P.," which he had done, after which he disclaimed all responsibility in the proceedings. The main result of the case was the inception of a period in which defenses claimed repeatedly, and usually without success, that if a book that allegedly portrayed obscenity also condemned that obscenity, it ought to be immune from prosecution.

Smith Act (U.S.: 1940, 1948) The Smith Act was originally passed in 1940, revised in 1948 and slightly refined in 1957. It remains the United States' federal sedition act and may be employed to prosecute anyone who attempts to overthrow the elected government of the United States. The act was tested in the case of *Dennis* v. *United States* (1951), when Dennis, a leading member of the American Communist Party, was convicted under the act for advocating the overthrow of the U.S. government. Accepting that his plans provided a CLEAR AND PRESENT DANGER to the national security, the U.S. Supreme Court delivered a majority opinion in favor of upholding the conviction, although Justices Black and Douglas both dissented, claiming that the conviction owed a great deal more to the contemporary intensity of the public's anti-communism than to the constitutionality of the act. The court refined the act in 1957 by its ruling on the case of YATES V. UNITED STATES. Mere ADVOCACY, as proved in *Dennis* v. *United States*, was henceforth insufficient grounds for a Smith Act conviction; the urging of direct, immediate action was necessary for a clear and present danger to be established.

The important part of the act states,

> Whoever knowingly or wilfully advocates, abets, advises, or teaches the duty, necessity, desirability or propriety of overthrowing or destroying the government of the United States or the government of any State, Territory, District or Possession thereof, or the government of any political subdivision therein, by force or violence, or by the assassination of any officer of any such government; or Whoever, with intent to cause the overthrow or destruction of any such government, prints, publishes, edits, issues, circulates, sells, distributes or publicly displays any written or printed matter advocating, advising, or teaching the duty, necessity, desirability or propriety of overthrowing or destroying the government of the United States by force or violence, or attempts to do so;

or Whoever organizes or helps or attempts to organize any society, group, or assembly of persons who teach, advocate or encourage the overthrow or destruction of any such government by force or violence; or becomes or is a member of, or affiliates with, any such society, group, or assembly of persons, knowing the purposes thereof—Shall be fined not more than $10,000 or imprisoned not more than ten years or both, and shall be ineligible for employment by the United States or any department or agency thereof for the five years next following his conviction.

SEE ALSO Espionage Act (U.S., 1917) and Sedition Act (U.S., 1918).

Smith v. California (1959) Eleazer Smith, a bookstore owner in Los Angeles, California, was convicted under the local regulations governing obscene material (LOS ANGELES—POSSESSION OF OBSCENE MATTER) for having in his store, with intent to sell, a book that had been adjudged obscene in the courts. Smith claimed that while the book, *Sweeter Than Life*, might be obscene, he never read the stock he sold and was thus immune from prosecution. Smith was defended by the veteran anti-obscenity lawyer, Stanley Fleischman, who had begun his career by defending members of the film industry who had been branded as subversives by the HOUSE UN-AMERICAN ACTIVITIES COMMITTEE. Fleischman managed to persuade the U.S. Supreme Court that Smith was innocent of disseminating obscene matter, even though the book in question would have been condemned as such under the prevailing ROTH STANDARD. In its opinion the court stated,

By dispensing [in cases of obscenity] with any requirement of knowledge of the contents of the book on the part of the seller, the ordinance tends to impose a severe limitation on the public's access to constitutionally protected matter. For if a bookseller is criminally liable without knowledge of the contents, and the ordinance fulfills its purpose, he will tend to restrict the books he sells to those he has inspected; and thus the State will have imposed a restriction upon the distribution of constitutionally protected as well as obscene literature. It has been well observed of a statute construed as dispensing with any requirement of scienter [proof that the act complained of was done knowingly] that: "Every bookseller would be placed under an obligation to make himself aware of the contents of every book in his shop." It would be altogether unreasonable to demand so near an approach to omniscience.

The court added that the self-censorship to which booksellers would have to submit themselves would rebound onto the public, who would then gain access only to those books that the seller felt were safe.

Smith v. Collin (1978) The majority of the 70,000 population of the town of Skokie, Illinois, were in 1977 Jewish, many of them refugees from the Nazi extermination camps of World War II. As a calculated insult the National Socialist Party of America, which described itself as a Nazi organization, chose Skokie as the site of a full-dress assembly, scheduled to be held outside Skokie Village Hall in the summer of 1977. Collin, the party's "führer," announced these plans in March 1977. On May 2 Skokie's authorities passed three ordinances designed to place restrictions on parades in general and the proposed Nazi demonstration in particular.

These forced any potential paraders to take out substantial public liability and property insurance; forbade the dissemination of racial and religious hatred; and banned the wearing of military-style uniforms at political demonstrations. On June 22 Collin applied for a permit as prescribed under Ordinance 994. He stated that the meeting was to take place on July 4, would be made up of persons demonstrating outside the village hall, would last about 30 minutes and would not disrupt traffic. Those parading would wear their usual uniforms, bedecked with swastikas and other Nazi insignia, and would carry placards demanding free speech; they would not distribute any form of literature. The permit was denied.

Collin took the party's case to a federal district court, where he argued that the Skokie ordinances were unconstitutional. The court was faced with the paradox: On the one hand, FIRST AMENDMENT rights were being claimed by a political organization among whose first acts, in the unlikely event of their ever coming to power in America, would be to suppress those rights; on the other hand, those rights were now being curtailed by a group who, on emotional grounds alone, appeared to most democratic Americans to be "the good guys." The court chose, as did the appeals court above it, to opt for the long view, and duly dismissed the Skokie ordinances as unconstitutional. Simply creating an ad hoc set of regulations to restrict the Nazis was unacceptable, and Collin's demand for an injunction against the ban was granted. The National Socialists were permitted to hold their meeting in Skokie on June 25, 1978, but in the event, having won their point, chose to transfer their activities to Chicago where they paraded on June 24 and July 9. The village attempted to take its own case, *Smith v. Collin*, to the U.S. Supreme Court, but the court, in an opinion written by Justice Blackmun, denied them a hearing. Blackmun itemized the lengthy chronology of the affair, and pointed out that the Constitution demanded that freedom of speech be upheld, whether or not the courts involved liked what they were forced to do.

SEE ALSO *Near* v. *Minnesota ex. rel. Olson* (1931); *Terminiello* v. *Chicago* (1949).

Smithers, Leonard Charles "The most learned erotomaniac in Europe," in the words of his son Jack, Smithers (1861-1907) was born in Sheffield and began his career as a lawyer. In 1891, with a friend, H.S. NICHOLS, he moved to London, where he used a legacy to set up a publishing firm in Soho Square and subsequently, as the Walpole Press, at 39

Charing Cross Road. Nichols knew the business, and had been involved with Smithers in the production of Sir Richard Burton's *Arabian Nights*; Smithers himself collaborated with Burton on *Priapeia* (1889), an anthology of "sportive epigrams" culled from the more lurid Latin authors, and an edition of Catullus' *Carmina*. The Walpole Press concentrated on similarly risque material and was raided, the first of many raids on Smithers' businesses, by the police, who removed two tons of set type. Nichols, on bail, fled to Paris in 1890, where he began publishing obscene pamphlets. When this activity alerted the authorities he moved on to New York City.

Smithers sacrificed his type in the raid but stayed on in London to continue publishing, in which occupation he flourished. Pornography bought him a house in London, apartments in Paris and Brussels and, temporarily, a large country house. He amassed a coterie of genuinely talented writers and artists, many of whom doubled as both pornographers and respectable authors or illustrators. Star of this group was AUBREY BEARDSLEY, whose illustrations for the *Yellow Book* brought him to Smithers' notice. Smithers, described by the antiquarian bookseller Bernard Quaritch as "the cleverest publisher in London," flourished for 10 years as the capital's leading distributor of pornography. His speciality was masking such material as the highest of literary art. He founded *The Savoy* as a showcase for Beardsley's talents, where the artist could indulge his perverse imagination in illustrations to Pope's "Rape of the Lock" and his own "Under the Hill."

Other Smithers titles included the homosexual novel *Teleny, or the Reverse of the Medal* (1893), featuring its hero's experiences as a transvestite masochist and attributed to a London barrister, Stanislas de Rhodes; and *White Stains* (1898) by the self-proclaimed magician, Aleister Crowley (1875-1947), whose other clandestine works include *Snowdrops from a Curate's Garden* (ca. 1904), which features a number of Sadeian perversions. Smithers also indulged his own passions. As Wilde, whose work he published, said, "He loves first editions, especially of women; little girls are his passion." Smithers' reign lasted a scant decade. He went bankrupt in 1900, bedeviled by police raids and the instabilities of his alcoholic wife. He died in Islington in 1907, a pauper, forgotten by those whose tastes he had once delighted.

SEE ALSO Carrington, Charles.

Snepp v. United States (1980) Frank Snepp worked as an operative of the American Central Intelligence Agency from 1968, when he was recruited as an expert on nuclear strategy and NATO, until 1976, when he resigned in the wake of the Vietnam War. His agency career began in the sphere of European strategic affairs, but Snepp moved to Vietnam in 1969, serving two tours of duty at the U.S. Embassy in Saigon, as the agency's principal analyst of North Vietnamese political affairs. He was also responsible for preparing strategic estimates and briefings and handling interrogations and informant networks. His second tour ended with the fall of Saigon in April 1975 and America's ignominious departure from Southeast Asia. Back in America Snepp attempted to interest his superiors in an official "after-action" report on the last days of American involvement in Vietnam, but there was no response. He resigned from the agency in 1976 and began writing his own report, culled from many interviews and from his personal experiences, which had been set down in a detailed briefing notebook and the personal diaries that he kept between 1973 and 1975. As he pointed out in his introduction, he had deliberately avoided quoting any colleagues, in or out of the CIA, and he had been at pains to preserve the identities of those who "still belong to the shadowy world of espionage," mentioning them only by an alias, unless their cover had already been blown by the press.

Snepp realized that submitting his manuscript to the agency for its own precensorship, as agreed in the official publishing agreement he had signed on joining the CIA, would prove destructive of his work and of his intention to publicize just what had gone on in Vietnam. He decided, therefore, to bypass what the agency termed prepublication review. Thus, when his book appeared in 1977, titled *Decent Interval*, Snepp was charged by the agency with violating the publishing agreement.

At no time did the government allege that Snepp's book had revealed any secrets, but concentrated on the fact that it had appeared without the authorization, which in 1968 he had agreed to accept. By doing this they charged, irrespective of whether it contained secrets or not, the book had "irreparably harmed" America's national security by raising doubts both at home and abroad concerning the CIA's ability to control its own agents and thus the flow of information to which they were party.

The government therefore demanded that while the book could no longer be suppressed, all its profits should be forfeited and that Snepp should never again be permitted to publish any book based on his involvement with the CIA. The district and the appeals courts of the state of Virginia both accepted the government's position. In 1980 the U.S. Supreme Court accepted that under the strict interpretation of the First Amendment, the agency's publishing agreement was illegal PRIOR RESTRAINT but accepted that the demands of national security overrode freedoms that would be mandatory were their subject not working for the CIA. This decision had cost Snepp at least $200,000 by 1985. This case, reminiscent of constraints under Britain's OFFICIAL SECRETS ACT, was the first to make it illegal for an American intelligence official to publish any information, secret or otherwise, that had been gleaned from official sources.

SEE ALSO CIA 1. publishing agreements; *Haig* v. *Agee* (1981); *McGhee* v. *Casey* (1983); *United States* v. *Marchetti* (1972).

social purity SEE National Vigilance Association; Public Morality Council.

socialist realism   "Socialist realism" is the pervasive standard against which the ideological excellence, and thus acceptability, of any product of any Soviet artist must be judged. The concept was originated by Maxim Gorky, the founder of the Writers' Union, and the politicians N. Bukharin and Andrei Zhdanov, the party spokesman on literature, at the 1st Writers Congress in 1934. The basis of socialist realism is a positive attitude to every aspect of Soviet life, and it may include the rewriting of texts both published and unpublished to conform with the party line. Realism in this context means the reflection of reality as defined by its revolutionary development. Above all it promotes all-encompassing optimism, in which all actions must be achievments and all individuals exemplary ("the positive hero"). In the eyes of many critics socialist realism has hamstrung the progress of the Soviet arts, especially in painting, where acceptability has appeared to run hand-in-hand with late-19th century bourgeois realism. The policy reached its zenith as ZHDANOVISM between 1945 and 1948, but it remains the basis of Soviet art today. As N.S. Khrushchev said in 1957, summing up the party's attitude before and after his leadership: "What our people need is works of literature, art and music properly rendering the pathos of labor, and understandable to the people." The method of socialist realism provides unlimited possibilities for supplying such works.

Societies for the Reformation of Manners, The   T h e s e societies were the direct development of the Religious Societies, associations of puritanical young Anglicans, that had emerged in England in the 1670s and were actively promoted from 1691 onward by Queen Mary. This religious revivalism, with its distaste both for the studied excesses of the Stuart court and the gin-soaked debaucheries of the masses, provided the new monarchy with an ideal means of making up for the absence of a statutory body opposed to immorality. The societies, like so many of their successors, drew on the respectable lower-middle classes, the small tradesmen and craftsmen in whose economic and social interest it was to promote a work-orientated morality. Notable among their recruits was Edward Stephens, a Gloucestershire squire who took holy orders and devoted himself to anti-Catholic pamphleteering. Stephens proposed a variety of measures, including national fasting, mass public confession and a bill to confer the death penalty on adultery, transportation for brothel-keeping, and massive fines for the drinking of toasts.

The first society was founded in 1690, when the parish officers and leading citizens of Tower Hamlets responded to King William's proclamation against robbers and highwaymen by forming a society to suppress local brothels. In 1691 a second society appeared, formed by Edward Stephens. Both societies were noticed by the queen, and in July 1691 she issued a letter to the Middlesex bench of justices, urging them to clamp down on vice. Not only the Middlesex bench, but many other authorities responded by forming a local

"Society for the Reformation of Manners." Directed by a central panel of lawyers, members of Parliament and similar figures who dictated general policy and helped out with expenses, the societies reached their peak around 1700. There were at least 20 societies in London, 13 in Edinburgh and 42 elsewhere in Britain. Those in the provinces were promoted from its founding in 1698 by the Society for Promoting Christian Knowledge (SPCK), before it turned to education and abandoned reform. They spread beyond Britain to Protestant Northern Europe, America and the West Indies.

The aim of the societies was not to initiate new laws, but to ensure the enforcement of old ones. Thus, while they used such existing tools as the Blasphemy Act (1698) to attack profanity on stage, they rarely pursued literature, since there existed as yet few laws for its control. It was also true that the masses, whose manners were due for reform, flocked to the theater but rarely picked up a book. In 1694 the society's administrators published *Some Proposals for the National Reformation of Manners* and a black list of those whom they had already prosecuted. The crimes they deplored included prostitution, Sabbath-breaking and drunkenness, but not obscenity.

The first "reformation" was duly aimed at "the Play Houses—those Nurseries of Vice and Prophaneness," as apostrophized in Jeremy Collier's pamphlet of 1698, "A Short View of the Immorality and Profaneness of the English Stage." A group of actors were successfully fined for using the word "God" as an expletive. By 1738 the society and its many branches claimed that they had prosecuted 101,683 individuals, in the London area alone, for such "publick Enormities" as sabbath-breaking, swearing, drunkenness, lewdness, brothel-keeping and sodomy. Their methods were based on informing to the magistrates against alleged sinners. Not all magistrates approved of such activity, but enough did for the societies to prosper. Informers were generally unpopular, but a member, Nottingham vicar John Disney, offered an excuse to his fellows in his Second Essay of 1710: "There is nothing we need to blush at in turning Informers against Vice; 'tis an honorable undertaking, and cause of God, and whosoever is ashamed of it deserved neither the Work nor the Reward." There followed a catalog of directions, instructing the informers against whom they should act and how their own lives should be conducted.

Aside from pursuing the blasphemer and the sodomite, whose brothels they purged as rigorously as they did heterosexual establishments, the societies specialized in the prosecution of sabbath-breaking, often entering inns or coffeehouses, therein to assail the customers with words and even blows. They also managed to suppress several Sunday markets. By 1760 they societies appear to have vanished, their last recorded statement being a denial that their members were attempting to gain prosecutions against people cooking their Sunday lunch. For all their lists, the societies achieved relatively little in the form of cultural censorship. Their legacy was more important than their lifetime: Simply through publicity a climate of moral opinion had been developed in which the public, and the government, would be increasingly sympathetic toward any campaign to outlaw what might be considered improper.

SEE ALSO Proclamation Society, The; Society for the Suppression of Vice (U.K.) and (U.S.).

Society for the Suppression of Vice (U.K.) In 1801 the British pro-censorship lobby, which viewed with alarm the decline of the PROCLAMATION SOCIETY, published "A Proposal for Establishing a Society for the Suppression of Vice and the Encouragement of Religion and Virtue." The Society originally planned to take in the areas of false weights and measures, the prevention of cruelty to animals, the punishment of those who lured women and children into prostitution and the prosecution of fortune-tellers. It began with three subcommittees: one devoted to obscene and blasphemous publications, a second to the sabbath and a third to a wide range of working-class amusements, all seen as worthy of repression. In the event, the promise to suppress publication of "Licentious and Obscene Books and Prints" took absolute precedence and ancillary topics were discarded in the fight against pornography and blasphemy.

Like all the vice societies, its main aim was to purify the lives of the masses, newly literate and thus for the first time exposed to the potential corruption of print. As Sydney Smith satirized it, it was "a society for suppressing the vices of persons whose incomes do not exceed £500 p.a." The society's first efforts were directed against questionable literature. It attacked both the classically pornographic and, taking upon itself a task that the law chose to neglect, the prosecution of such material as might "bring a blush to the cheek of modesty." Even the society's own officials were considered vulnerable, and seized materials were entombed in a box with three keys, each held by a separate administration. Despite its noble purposes the society was no more popular among some sections of the privileged than it was among the masses. Members of both parties condemned its interference with mass culture, with one Tory even pointing out in defense of such pleasures that it had been "proved incontestably that bear-baiting was the great support of the constitution in church and state."

The society's vital support came from the rising bourgeoisie, and to their satisfaction a number of prosecutions were launched. James Aitken, already condemned in 1795 for selling HARRIS' LIST OF COVENT GARDEN LADIES, was now jailed for *The Amours of Peter Aretin* (ARETINO). His wife, Ann, was also jailed for a print, *The Convent Well Supplied*. Alexander Hogg was charged with OBSCENE LIBEL for selling "A New and Compleat Collection of the Most Remarkable Trials for Adultery," part of the growing genre of quasi-pornography, tales of sex and scandal in high places culled from the more lurid court reports. The burgeoning field of periodicals—*The New Rambler* and its peers—also suffered in court. By 1817, in which year the society brought nearly 40

successful prosecutions, the pornographers had been driven virtually underground. Their product, once in the margins of more respectable publishing, had been enclosed in a cultural ghetto; as a byproduct, a variety of topics that might once have been dealt with by a legitimate author, were declared off-limits by an increasingly smut-conscious public.

The campaign against pornography was followed by that against blasphemy. The prevailing attitude outside the society was that such religious disputation that might, by law, be prosecuted for blasphemy had sufficient intellectual status to be deserving of debate, but the Vice Society, as it had come to be known, rejected such moderation. It concentrated its attacks on two books and a single publisher. In 1819 Richard Carlile, publisher of the periodical *The Deist, or, Moral Philosopher*, issued both THE AGE OF REASON (1793) by THOMAS PAINE and *Principles of Nature* (1801) by Elihu Palmer. The former condemned the Bible as both fallacious and disgusting; the latter, in denying the Trinity, committed a BLASPHEMOUS LIBEL. The society's attempts to suppress Carlile's publications extended over seven years and encompassed his entire family. First Carlile himself, then his wife, his sister, and a number of friends and relations put themselves forward for trial, imprisonment and fines, of increasingly severe magnitude, in defense of Paine and Palmer. As quickly as the society brought prosecutions, 14 in all by 1825, so did the "blasphemers" accept their legal martyrdom and produce a new individual ready to carry on issuing the books. Not until 1827, with Carlile out of jail and running his business once more, did the society accept its defeat.

For the next 40 years the Society concentrated once again on pornography. As the main instrument of censoring literature prior to the OBSCENE PUBLICATIONS ACT OF 1857, the society worked ceaselessly, seeking to destroy the flourishing Victorian pornography trade. A new brand of pornographer, highly professional, resilient in the face of repeated prosecutions, had emerged. The society fought assiduously to undermine such individuals as WILLIAM DUGDALE, George Cannon, John and Edward Duncombe and John Benjamin Brookes, who centered their activities on London's HOLYWELL STREET, as well as many lesser traders in obscene literature. The 1857 act, while proposed by Lord Chief Justice Campbell, was indirectly the result of the society's efforts. The case, which so enraged Campbell and impelled him to promote the new measure, was that of Dugdale, who had been trapped for the ninth time by a society agent provocateur. As had Lord Campbell in 1857, the society claimed it bore no animus toward literary classics, but serious writers feared its investigators as much as did pornographers. As a correspondent of the *Atheneum* remarked in 1875, "So timid are Englishmen where there is a question of being charged with encouraging vice that I fancy the effect upon an average bookseller of a visit [from the Society] is like that which would once have been produced by the call of a functionary of the Inquisition upon a Spanish Jew."

In 1824 it secured the passage of the VAGRANCY ACT, catchall legislation to amalgamate the various long-standing laws governing "rogues and vagabonds," and including the prohibition of the public sale or display of indecent or obscene material. This act coincidentally destroyed the once flourishing trade in bawdy street ballads, although their singers merely removed themselves to the concert taverns, the precursors of the music halls, themselves to become a target for the society's censors.

In 1868 the society produced a report itemizing its successes. Since 1845 there had been 159 prosecutions, 154 of them successful. Some 37 shops had been closed down, netting 129,681 obscene prints; 16,220 books and pamphlets; five tons of letterpress sheets; 16,005 sheets of obscene songs, catalogs and handbills; 5,503 cards, snuffboxes etc.; 844 engraved steel and copper plates; 428 lithographic stones; 95 woodblocks; 11 printing presses; and 28 hundredweight (3,136 pounds) of type. Paradoxically, the society was already near to collapse. In 1870 it admitted that it had lacked the funds to pay for its last 28 prosecutions. Despite the conservatism of the era, no further support appeared. It maintained a presence until 1880 when it finally ceased work. Its function was revived in 1886 with the founding of the NATIONAL VIGILANCE ASSOCIATION.

SEE ALSO Societies for the Reformation of Manners.

Society for the Suppression of Vice (U.S.) This crusading society was established in New York City on May 16, 1873. Among its many supporters were William E. Dodge Jr., Morris K. Jessup, J. Pierpont Morgan and Robert B. McBurney. Its New York secretary was the country's leading crusader against vice, ANTHONY COMSTOCK. The national society was the direct descendant of Comstock's Committee for the Suppression of Vice, which had set up originally under the auspices of the YMCA. Under a special act passed by the New York State legislature the society was given "a monopoly of vice, and its agents the rights of search, seizure and arrest." It was also granted 50 percent of all fines levied on those successfully prosecuted by the society or its agents. The society persisted in its efforts throughout Comstock's career and after his death in 1915, when JOHN S. SUMNER replaced him as secretary. In 1924 Sumner announced that in its career the society had "confiscated an average of 65,000 obscene pictures per annum." In the 1930s members of the society spearheaded the attempt to prosecute SAMUEL ROTH. Gradually, as the climate of public opinion eroded Comstock's grasp on American culture, the society began to collapse. By the Second World War it was obsolete.

Sodom: or, The Quintessence of Debauchery This play in five acts, a prologue and two epilogues, was written by the Earl of ROCHESTER and published in Antwerp in 1684 as a play "by the E. of R." Rochester disclaimed responsibility for his "scatalogical romp" (Donald Thomas), and for a while it was attributed to John Fishbourne, a barrister. Neither his contemporaries nor generations of scholars have been willing to accept Rochester's disclaimer and the *Dictionary of National Biography* includes *Sodom*, a work of "intolerable foulness," in Rochester's bibliography. More recently a number of scholars have supported the earl, claiming on both stylistic and chronological grounds that Rochester was innocent of the play's authorship. Either Fishbourne did indeed write it or it was the joint production of various authors, one of whom admittedly might have been Rochester.

The play itself, the first example of English libertine writing, satirizes the literary and moral pretensions of works written in the popular heroic couplet form, the form in which it appears itself. It has also been suggested that it pokes fun at Rochester's Oxford college, Wadham. The entire play is devoted to debauchery, and a cast of characters named Bolloxinion, king of Sodom, Cuntigratia, his queen, General Buggeranthos, Princess Swivia, the maids of honor Cunticula and Clitoris, and the like copulate ceaselessly. The supreme pleasure, as underlined in the title, is sodomy, although such pleasures as incest are not overlooked. The play ends with the apocalyptic destruction of the kingdom. *Sodom* entered no professional repertory, but it was supposedly performed once, before King Charles' court. None of the early printed editions have survived, although there were allegedly two printings by 1707. One of these may have survived until at least 1865. The earliest extant printed edition of the play appeared in 1904, published in Paris by H. Welter.

Sodom was frequently condemned in court, the first prosecution coming in 1689. Joseph Streater and Benjamin Crayle, who had already been prosecuted for the publication of *The School of Venus* (L'ESCHOLLE DES FILLES) in 1688, were charged at the Guildhall Quarter Sessions with the selling of "librum flagitosum et impudicum" (obscene and lascivious books). Crayle, for unspecified reasons, signed the indictment against his fellow bookseller, but in court he suffered more. He was fined £20, imprisoned (although this was subsequently commuted) and had an inventory taken of his goods. In 1707 another dealer, John Marshall, was prosecuted successfully for selling the play, as were many others thereafter.

SEE ALSO *Poems on Several Occasions.*

Sod's Opera, The The *Sod's Opera* is an almost unknown operetta by William S. Gilbert (1836-1911) and Sir Arthur Sullivan (1842-1900), which deals with the proclivities of the homosexually inclined. Its cast, reminiscent of that created for the Earl of ROCHESTER's SODOM, included such characters as Count Tostoff, the Bollox brothers, "a pair of hangers on," and Scrotum, "a wrinkled old retainer." This obscene work by the late-19th-century exemplars of satirical comic operas, has never been performed, but for many years a copy could be found in the guardroom of St. James' Palace.

South Africa

1. literary censorship   A variety of laws combine to censor publications in South Africa on political and moral grounds. As well as 106 laws aimed specifically at restricting freedom of the press, there is also the Suppression of Communism Act, under which it is an offense to publish or disseminate "any speech, utterance, writing or statement or any extract from or recording or reproduction of any speech, uttering, writing or statement" of any person listed as a member of the Communist Party or any other banned organization, or any person prohibited from attending gatherings. This provision affects hundreds of individuals, including almost all the leaders of the African liberation movement and the majority of African writers. Opponents of apartheid both at home and abroad, including many exiled activists and writers, are thus restrained from making their views felt. The Customs and Excise Act prohibits the importation of "indecent, obscene or objectionable goods" (including soft-core men's magazines), while the Publications and Entertainments Act prohibits the manufacture or publication of such material within the country. This act, passed in 1963 and supplemented by the Publications (Amendment) Act of 1986, controls all publications, films, entertainments, art and sculpture. All such productions may be undesirable if they fulfill one of five categories, if they: (a) are indecent, obscene, offensive or harmful to public morals; (b) are blasphemous or offensive to any religion in the republic; (c) bring any section of (white) South Africa into ridicule or contempt; (d) harm relations between sections of the population; (e) are prejudicial to public safety or the security of the state. Originally it required no more than an announcement in the *Government Gazette* for a ban to take force.

Since the early 1970s the government has attempted to modify the structure of its censorship system. All three acts are administered by the director of publications, who works through two offices: the Publications Control Board and the Publications Appeal Board. The director's office can thus place its wide-ranging ban on a vast spectrum of material deemed not only obscene but also, more importantly, subversive: anti-racialist, anit-colonialist, anti-apartheid and Marxist publications head this list. Material describing Marxist and socialist states is automatically banned. The committee, which also gives or withholds its imprimatur to films, posters, shows and entertainments, does not always ban unreservedly. The Appeals Board exists to assess any material that may be considered contentious. Writers and publishers are invited to submit manuscripts for prepublication review, and booksellers are urged to check with the board any material that they may feel is potentially unsuitable for sale. Literature, as defined by the board, is that material passed as neither pornographic nor injurious in any way to some vestige of "State security." In 1987 the names of board members were published for the first time.

2. banned books   Other than IRELAND, where books were banned on religious grounds, no modern country prohibits writing on so large a scale as does South Africa, where an estimated 18,000 titles are currently proscribed. A wide selection of laws exist simply to ensure that no such material is permitted distribution. These include the Suppression of Communism Act, the Customs and Excise Act and the Internal Security Act (see South Africa 4.); there are more than 20 acts in all that focus on or include censorship in their provisions. The current state of national emergency has created an almost absolute news blackout in addition to the normal strictures. The forbidden titles range from those otherwise acknowledged as classics of literature, to more generally popular titles, political writing by both blacks and whites, South Africans and others, allegedly communist tracts and so on. Anything that deals with struggles against colonialism or speaks in favor of racial equality is barred. In the mid-1970s the United Nations Unit on Apartheid compiled a selected list of prohibited publications:

Peter Abrahams, *A Night of Their Own*

Thomas R. Adam, *Government and Politics South of the Sahara*

African National Congress (ANC), *Brute Force—the Treatment of Prisoners in South Africa's Jails*

Alan Aldridge, *The Beatles' Illustrated Lyrics*

American Committee on Africa, *Would You Give South Africa Nuclear Power? … The U.S. Did*

Herbert Apthekar (ed.), *And Why Not Every Man?*

James Baldwin, *Another Country*, *Blues for Mister Charlie*, *The Fire Next Time*

W.A. Ballinger, *Call It Rhodesia Congo*

John Barth, *The End of the Road*

AUBREY BEARDSLEY, *Under the Hill*

Brendan Behan, *Confessions of an Irish Rebel*

Sally Belfrage, *Freedom Summer*

Mary Benson, *The African Patriots*, *At the Still Point*, *The Badge of Slavery* (pamphlet on the pass laws), *South Africa: Struggle for a Birthright*

H. von Dach Bern, *Total Resistance*

Alvah Bessie, *The Symbol*

Robert M. Bleiweiss (ed.), *Marching to Freedom: the Life of Martin Luther King*

E.R. Braithwaite, *To Sir With Love*

Michael Braun, *Love Me Do—The Beatles' Progress*

Bertolt Brecht, all works

George Breitman (ed.), *Malcolm X Speaks*

Douglas Brown, *Against the World—a Study of White South African Attitudes*

Brian Bunting, *The Rise of the South African Reich*

Wilfred Burchett, *Come East Young Man*

Martin Burger, *Dr. Verwoerd of South Africa—Architect of Doom*

Robert Burns, THE MERRY MUSES OF CALEDONIA

William Burroughs, *Dead Fingers Talk*, *Junkie*, *The Naked Lunch*

Horacio Caio, *Angola—Os Dias Do Desespero*

ERSKINE CALDWELL, *The Bastard and the Poor Fool, In Search of Bisco, The Last Night of Summer*

James Cameron, *The African Revolution*

Guy & Candie Carawan (eds.), *We Shall Overcome—Songs of the Southern Freedom Movement*

Stokeley Carmichael and Charles V. Hamilton, *Black Power*

Nick Carter, *Rhodesia*

Christian Action (London), various pamphlets on Apartheid, Nelson Mandela etc.

Edward Clayton, *Martin Luther King: the Peaceful Warrior*

Eldridge Cleaver, *Soul on Ice*

Daniel Cohn-Bendit, *Obsolete Communism—the Left Wing Alternative*

Ernest Cole, *House of Bondage*

James Collier, *Somebody Up There Hates Me*

Canon L. John Collins, *Faith Under Fire*

Mercer Cook and Stephen E. Henderson, *The Militant Black Writer in Africa and the United States*

Jack Crone, *The Dawn Comes Twice*

Suzanne Cronje, *Witness in the Dark*

Basil Davidson, *Which Way Africa*

John A. Davis and James K. Baker (eds.), *South Africa in Transition*

Regis Debray, *Strategy for Revolution*

Angelo del Boca, *Apartheid*

Margrit de Sablonniere, *Apartheid*

Jacob Drachler, *African Heritage—Intimate Views of the Black Africans from Life, Love and Literature*

Patrick Duncan, *South Africa's Rule of Violence*

Lawrence Durrell (ed.), *The Best of Henry Miller*

Allen Edwardes, *Death Rides a Camel*

Paul Edwards, *Through African Eyes*

Cyprian Ekwensi, *Jagua Nana*

Episcopal Churchmen for South Africa, various pamphlets

Bernard Fall (ed.), *Ho Chi Minh on Revolution*

Frantz Fanon, *The Wretched of the Earth, Toward the African Revolution*

Jules Feiffer, *Harry the Rat with Women*

Edward Feit, *South Africa: the Dynamics of the African National Congress*

Ruth First, *One Hundred and Seventeen Days*

Ian Fleming, *The Spy Who Loved Me*

Lionel Forman, *Chapters in the History of the March to Freedom*

A.C. Forrest, *Not Tomorrow—Now (The Middle East and Africa Today*

Margaret Forster, *Georgy Girl*

Marion Friedmann (ed.), *I Will Still Be Moved—Report from South Africa*

William R. Frye, *In Whitest Africa—the Dynamics of Apartheid*

Roger Garaudy, *Marxism in the 20th Century*

Jane Gool, *The Crimes of Bantu Education in South Africa*

Nadine Gordimer, *The Late Bourgeois World*

Nadine Gordimer and Lionel Abrahams (eds.), *South African Writing Today*

Lieut. Col. T.N. Green, *The Guerilla—and How to Fight Him*

Che Guevara, *Bolivian Diary, Reminiscences of the Cuban Revolutionary War*

Jack Halpern, *South Africa's Hostages*

John Hatch, *A History of Post-War Africa*

Joseph Heller, *Catch-22*

Alex Hepple, *South Africa: a Political and Economic History, Verwoerd*

Sidney Hook, *From Hegel to Marx*

Tom Hopkinson (ed.), *Life World Library: South Africa*

Langston Hughes, *The First Book of Africa*

Aldous Huxley, *Island*

Christopher Isherwood, *Down There on a Visit*

A. Jacob, *White Man, Think Again*

Hewlett Johnson, *Soviet Strength*

Le Roi Jones, *Dutchman & The Slave, The System of Dante's Hell*

Helen Joseph, *Tomorrow's Sun: A Smuggled Journal from South Africa*

Kenneth Kaunda, *Zambia Shall Be Free*

Elia Kazan, *America America, The Arrangement*

Nikos Kazantzakis, *The Last Temptation of Christ*

Jack Kerouac, *Big Sur*

Martin Luther King, *Why We Can't Wait*

Hans Kohn and Wallace Sokolsky, *African Nationalism in the 20th Century*

Leo Kuper, *An African Bourgeoisie—Race, Class and Politics in South Africa*

Alex La Guma, *A Walk in the Night, And a Threefold Card*

Colin and Margaret Legum (eds.), *African Handbook: Eight South Africans' Resistance to Tyranny*

Doris Lessing, *Going Home*

Deirdre Levinson, *Five Years, An Experience of South Africa*

Joseph Lewis, *The Bible Unmasked*

Oscar Lewis, *The Children of Sanchez*

Allard Lowenstein, *Brutal Mandate: a Journey to South-West Africa*

Albert Luthuli, *The Road to Oslo and Beyond*

Norman Mailer, *An American Dream*

Malcolm X, *The Autobiography of Malcolm X*

William Manchester, *The City of Anger*

Nelson Mandela, *I Am Prepared to Die, Apartheid*

Irving L. Markovitz (ed.), *African Politics and Society*

Ralph G. Martin, *Black and White*

Richard Mason, *The World of Suzie Wong*

Andre Maurois, *September Roses*

Govan Mbeki, *South Africa: the Peasant's Revolt*

Tom Mboya, *Freedom and After*

Mary McCarthy, *The Group*

Vernon McKay, *Africa in World Politics*

Dr. T.P. Melody, *The White Man's Future in South Africa*

Grace Metalious, *Peyton Place* (Dutch translation)

Henry Miller, *Tropic of Cancer, Nexus, Plexus*

Bloke Modisane, *Blame Me on History*, *De Wet is Blank*
A.M. Mohammed and M.A. Foum, *Forge Ahead to Emancipation*
Eduardo Mondlane, *The Struggle for Mozambique*
Ezekiel Mphahlele, *African Writing Today*
S.B. Mukherji, *Indian Minority in South Africa*
Vladimir Nabokov, *Lolita*
Lewis Nkosi, *Home and Exile*, *The Rhythm of Violence*
Kwame Nkrumah, *Africa Must Unite*
Martin Oppenheimer, *Urban Guerilla*
Ferdinand Oyona, *Houseboy*
S.E.M. Pheko, *Christianity Through African Eyes*
Willard Price, *Incredible Africa*
Philip W. Quigg (ed.), *Africa—A Foreign Affairs Reader*
Martin Redmann, *Potsdam: Agreement and 20 Years Later*
Rt. Rev. Ambrose Reeves, *South Africa—Let the Facts Speak*
Richard Rive, *African Songs*
Philip Roth, *Portnoy's Complaint*
Leslie and Neville Rubin, *This Is Apartheid*
Lord Russell of Liverpool, *South Africa Today and Tomorrow*
Albie Sachs, *The Jail Diary of Albie Sachs*
E.S. Sachs, *The Anatomy of Apartheid*
Francois Sagan, *Bonjour Tristesse*
Robert Scheer (ed.), *Eldridge Cleaver—Post-Prison Writings and Speeches*
Stuart R. Schram, *The Political Thought of Mao Tse-Tung*
Ronald Segal, *Into Exile*
Ronald Segal and Ruth First (eds.), *South-West Africa: Travesty of Trust*
Leopold Sedar Senghor, *Nation et Voie Africaine du Socialisme*
Herbert L. Shore (ed), *Come Back Africa: 14 Short Stories*
Alan Sillitoe, *Key to the Door*
Ndabaningi Sithole, *African Nationalism*
Louis L. Snyder, *The Idea of Racialism—Its Meaning and History*
Terry Southern and Mason Hoffenburg, *Candy*
Herbert J. Spiro, *Politics in Africa*
John Russell Taylor (ed.), *New English Dramatists: 8* (Charles Wood, James Broom Lynne, Joe Orton)
Massimo Teodori (ed.), *The New Left*
Sekou Toure, *La Guinee et l'Emancipation Africaine*
Pierre van den Burghe, *Race and Racism*
Vatsyayana, *The Kama Sutra*
Mary Ann Wall, *The Dominee and the Dom-Pass*
Walter T. Waubank, *Documents on Modern Africa*
Charles Webb, *The Graduate*
Jack Woddis, *Africa: the Way Ahead*
World Council of Churches, *Christians and Race Relations in Southern Africa*

3. media censorship laws   Aside from any special restrictions, particularly as levied on both the internal and foreign press during periods of Emergency Rule, the South African state has evolved a number of laws to regulate broadcasting, publishing and the exhibition of material. The authorities claim that there is no censorship, merely control, since against true censorship there would be no appeal. As Deputy Minister of Information Louis Nels explained when defining the Emergency Regulations of 1986: "To us censorship means that every report must be approved before it can be published. We do not have censorship—what we have is a limitation on what newspapers can report." Against the most draconian of these regulations, which give the authorities broad powers, there is indeed no appeal. In addition to the specific legislation cited below, there are a number of acts restricting freedom of movement, especially for black journalists.

Bantu Administration Act (1927), section 29(i): "Any person who utters any words or does any act or thing whatever with intent to promote feelings of hostility between natives and Europeans shall be guilty of an offense."

Riotous Assemblies Act (1914): The state president has the power to prohibit the publication of any "documentary information" that he feels promotes "feelings of hostility between the European inhabitants of the Union on the one hand and any other section of the inhabitants of the Union on the other hand." Unlike the Bantu Administration Act there need be no proof of intent and the act does not deal with relations between blacks and blacks, or blacks and coloreds. Under the Riotous Assemblies Act (1956) it is forbidden to make public in any way news of an assembly that has been banned.

Entertainment (Censorship) Act (1963): This act created a Board of Censors whose initial task was the control of films and advertising. This was soon expanded to advising the minister of justice on the banning, when seen fit, of imported books and other publications. Material falling under the ban includes representations of political controversy, of adverse relations between capital and labor, and of the intermingling of the black and white races.

Suppression of Communism Act (1950): The state president is empowered to ban any individual or any publication that he considers to be abetting "any of the objects of communism." There is no appeal. Additional clauses make it possible to suppress the statements of any banned person, whether alive or dead, within South Africa. It is also possible to restrict banned individuals from writing for publication outside South Africa, and certain newspapers, suspected of communistic leanings, must produce a large cash indemnity against the publication of such "subversive" material.

Criminal Law Amendment Act (1953): It is an offense either to speak or act to protest a law in such a way that any other person may be encouraged to break a law. Letters and publications sent through the post may be seized if suspected of encouraging such activity. The penalty for such incitement is up to five years jail and/or up to 10 strokes of the whip.

Public Safety Act (1953): This act provides for the institution of a State of Emergency under which any newspaper may be banned.

Customs Act (1964): All publications may be banned from importation as indecent or obscene; they may also be banned if they are considered "on any ground whatsoever objectionable."

Official Secrets Act (1956): It is illegal to publish any material relating to the military, the police and the Bureau of State Security (BOSS).

Extension of the University Education Act (1959): Under this act, which created separate tribal colleges for black students, it was made illegal to circulate any form of student publication without precensorship by the rector. No student may speak to the media without similar checks.

Prisons Act (1959): It is illegal to publish any material, unless sanctioned by the commissioner of prisons, regarding individual prisoners, the administration of prisons.

Defense Amendment Act (1967): It is illegal, unless sanctioned by the Ministry of Defense, to publish any material—factual, rumor or comment—referring to the composition, movement or dispositions of the South African armed forces.

Publications and Entertainments Act (1963): Within this act are 98 specific definitions of what is considered undesirable in terms of what may be censored from any publication or entertainment.

General Law Amendment Act (1969): The minister of justice may declare any place or area to be officially protected; once an area has been thus classified, the media may not identify it either in text or by an illustration.

The General Law Amendment Act, "The BOSS Act" (1969): Any communication as regards the personnel of the Bureau of State Security or those it has detained is illegal. The government may bar from court any evidence that implicates BOSS in a trial, even if that evidence is germane to a defendant's case.

Publications Act (1974): This act replaced the Publications and Entertainments Act (1963) and strengthens the censorship of non-newspaper publications, records and tapes, films and stage shows, artwork and amateur photography. Censors may ban not only current but also future editions of undesirable periodicals and fine or imprison those who possess undesirable material, which term embraces anything the authorities consider offensive to public morals or religious feelings, or that "brings any section of the inhabitants of the Republic into ridicule or contempt," undermines peaceful relations between sections of the population or is prejudicial to state security.

Newspaper and Imprint Registration Act (1971): All newspapers must declare their "intended nature and contents," register personal and social details of their editors and staff and must deposit an indemnity against the possibility of their breaking the Suppression of Communism Act (above).

Proclamation R123 (August 1987): This proclamation, which reinforced and extended the state of emergency proclaimed on June 12, 1986, was aimed at "newspapers which fostered and promoted a climate of violent overthrow of the state." A new and anonymous panel of censors was set up to make a "scientific evaluation" of potentially illicit material. The government claimed that previous censorship measures were still insufficient to deal with the new situation. Under the new rules the government will first warn offenders. If the warning has no effect then official censors will start imposing prepublication curbs. Finally, the publication can be banned for 90 days at a time.

Emergency Regulations (1986, 1987): On December 11, 1986, the government announced new press controls, based on the Public Safety Act (1953, see above) and designed to control the media further under the current State of Emergency. Journalists were no longer permitted "to be on the scene, or at a place within sight, of any unrest, restricted gathering or security action"; no information may be published regarding the deployment of security forces, "subversive" speeches or restricted gatherings; no information on detained individuals may be published, even after their release; newspapers may not leave blank spaces to indicate censorship; any report that might be considered "subversive" must be submitted to the authorities before broadcasting or publication; the government can seize any film or videotape; no opposition politicians may be quoted, if their statements are ruled as subversive, other than when speaking in Parliament.

On December 29, 1986, further regulations were added, mainly aimed at suppressing the boycott of schools by black schoolchildren; and on January 8, 1987, a further group targeted the ANC, prohibiting any material—published, broadcast or in advertisement—that might "improve or promote the public image" of a banned organization. The newspaper proprietors successfully challenged these regulations in the courts on January 29, but their victory was reversed by the government within hours. The authorities now have the power to ban the publication—on radio or television, in newspapers or advertisements—of "any matter." The definition of subversive was extended to include any statement supporting an "unlawful" organization.

4. The Internal Security Act (1982) This act, which succeeded the Suppression of Communism Act (1950), serves to consolidate the bulk of the wide-ranging security apparatus existing under South African law. It is under the ISA that individuals and organizations may be banned. Censorship is dealt with under section 5(1): Publications may be banned if the minister is satisfied that any periodical or publication: (a) "serves inter alia as a means for expressing views or conveying information the publication of which is calculated to endanger the security of the state or the maintenance of law and order"; (b) "professes, by its name or otherwise, to be a publication for propagating the principles or promoting the spread of communism"; (c) "serves inter alia as a means of expressing views or conveying information the publication of which is calculated to further the achievement of any of the objects of communism"; (d) "is published by, or under the direction or guidance of, an organization which has been declared unlawful"; (e) expresses views propagated by any organizations included under paragraph (d); (f) "serves inter alia as a means for expressing views or conveying information the publication of which is calculated to cause, encourage or foment feelings of hostility between different population groups or parts of population groups"; (g) is a banned publication appearing under a new name or in further issues under its original name.

South Korea   Prior to 1987, when the civilian government of Roh Tae-Woo took over from the military rule of General Chun Doo-Hwan, South Korea had sufferd extensive censorship under Chun and his predecessor, Park Chung-Hee, who between them had controlled the country since 1961. Park effectively eliminated political opposition by taking over the media; when Chun replaced Park in 1980 he too purged the press. Some 172 publications and 617 publishing companies were closed, and 683 reporters lost their jobs. Only one newspaper in each province was allowed to operate; a single news agency dealt with all news, and ony two television stations were permitted. In December 1983, faced by increasing opposition, Chun attempted to calm the situation by relaxing the censorship. A number of dissident publications were permitted and some critical reporting began to appear in the press. This freedom increased during the election campaign of 1985. When in May 1985 Chun attempted to clamp down again, the populace refused to be cowed. The confict between government and governed intensified until in June 1987 Roh Tae-Woo, of the ruling democratic Justice Party, announced direct elections for the presidency and once again relaxed censorship, as well as restoring civil rights to 2,300 political prisoners, including opposition leader Kim Dae-Jung. A new constitution, replacing that of 1980, was approved in October 1987 and instituted in February 1988. It included a ban on licensing or censorship of speech. At the election, in December 1987, Roh became president after the opposition were unable to put up a single candidate.

The main instrument of state control, the National Security Law, which dated back to the Chun era, has not been repealed under Roh. Aimed at anyone seen as "aiding the cause of anti-state elements," it has been widely used against political and media opposition. Seven-hundred political prisoners were still detained under the law in late 1987 and the police regularly seize "communist" materials (including Bertrand Russell's *History of Western Philosophy*) from Seoul bookshops.

Prior to 1987 the press was controlled by the Basic Press Act (1980) under which all publishers had to obtain an official license. Once in business, they had to submit all material to the Department of Public Information Control; these restrictions covered broadcast material too. Songs, books, films and theater were submitted to the Ethics Committee for Public Performance. Officials monitored the press, down to specifying the placement of stories and the pictures that might be printed with them; advertisements were similarly subjected to an advertising council, which allotted ads according to the loyalty of a given publication.

In November 1987 the Basic Press Law was repealed and replaced by two new laws, dealing with periodicals and with broadcasting. Under the Registration of Publications Law, the minister of culture and information forfeited the power to revoke the registration of newspapers and magazines. Only the courts may do this, although papers must still hold a license. More controls are exercised by demanding that Korean-language newspapers must have a press capable of printing 20,000 copies of a four-page tabloid in an hour. Foreign-language dailies and Korean monthlies have similar regulations as to equipment. In all, this means that only the relatively wealthy papers will be permitted. The smaller opposition sheets must collapse. The Broadcasting Act states that TV and radio may serve the public interest with government interference, but it also bans private enterprises from running broadcasting companies, a move aimed at the Christian Broadcasting System, the country's only non-government service.

Day-to-day control by the Ministry of Culture is augmented by the extensive "Information Guidelines"—instructions to the press that are sent each day to each newspaper publisher by the Department of Public Information Control. Stories are broadly categorized as "possible," "impossible" and "absolutely impossible" to print, and editors will respond as required, cutting the latter categories completely, and drastically amending the first. Every detail is considered: the form and content of a story, its headline, crossheads and the page and position on the page in which it should, if permitted, appear. The guidelines state whether or not certain events or individuals may even receive coverage. They dictate the size and "angle" of an illustration.

Spain

1. censorship (1502-1810)   Printing arrived in Spain in 1470, the year following the creation of a united Spain by the marriage of Ferdinand of Aragon and Isabella of Castile. Initially they welcomed books, ordering in 1480 that imported publications should be exempted from tax, but in 1502, reflecting the efforts of the SPANISH INQUISITION as regarded religious censorship, the dual monarchs began dealing with secular material. Their Pragmatic Sanction of July 8, 1502, stated that: No book was to be published nor imported without a royal license; such licenses were to be granted by the presidents of the *audiencias* (royal courts), archbishops and certain bishops. Each of these officials would be aided by salaried examiners who were to check all work for possible faults. Any book that was published or imported without a license was to be seized and destroyed, as was any manuscript that had been altered between licensing and publication. The printer or bookseller who dealt in such works was to be removed from his profession and fined double the money he had made from copies already sold.

As the centralization of governmental power increased in Spain, so did censorship. In 1554 Emperor Charles V, acting with his son Prince Philip, empowered the Royal Council of

Castile with the censorship and regulation of the press. In future no licenses were to be issued by any authority other than the president or members of the council. Copies of all manuscripts or imported books were to be deposited with the council so that a check might be made on any attempts to alter them after the license had been granted. Heresy, an abiding concern, remained the prerogative of the Inquisition. Philip acceded to the throne as Philip II in 1556 and issued a further Pragmatic Sanction in September 1558. This forbade the import of foreign books and reaffirmed the licensing powers of the council. Anyone, including booksellers, who owned works condemned by the Inquisition were ordered, on pain of death, to deliver the offending material to the authorities for burning. Anyone circulating a banned book or manuscript on a religious subject also faced the death penalty if they did not hand over such material to the council either for burning or for possible licensing.

In 1568, noting the spread of Protestantism in France, Philip added special measures, providing for even more severe censorship along Spain's northern borders. By 1600 the *relaciones*, prototype newspapers and essentially factual reports of important events, which had gradually become politicized and anti-government, were also subjected to censorship. Editors became subject to government interference, ordered either to improve the good news for public consumption or to suppress the bad. The details of the censorship have remained vague, but a royal order of June 13, 1627, forbade the publication of court reports or allied legal information without government permission, authorized the Royal Council to delegate one of its members to be the official licenser and granted the universities permission to print classroom exercises and scholarly papers. The king himself occasionally checked the proofs of important *relaciones*. In 1682 Charles II issued his own order, simply reaffirming those of his predecessors.

In 1762 Charles III attempted to increase the use of print as an adjunct to spreading popular education. A Royal Order of November 14, 1762, suppressed "the regulation, the requirement of soliciting permission to print, the privileges for books, the correctors, the laws of censorship, the publication of approvals, and all the other turns of the labyrinthine gears which chain the cultural intelligence transmitted by the vehicles of public communication." This freedom did not extend to the press, which was still censored, and to the need to obtain licenses. Despite this, the press did expand, and in 1781 there was launched *El Censor*, a newspaper published by the Royal Council lawyer Luis Canuelo, an advocate of the philosophies of VOLTAIRE, ROUSSEAU and Montesquieu, a Francophile and a Mason—all beliefs guaranteed to alienate the Spanish authorities. His newspaper railed constantly against the Spanish establishment, and after a number of warnings and the retraction by Canuelo of several pieces, was shut down by a royal order of November 29, 1798. This order was too late to suppress a number of imitators, and on October

2, 1788, Charles III issued a new "Reglamento de Imprentas." These rules stated that:

> Censors as much as authors and translators will take care that the papers and writings [entrusted to them] shall include neither lewd nor slippery expressions and no satires of any type, not even in political matters; nor things which discredit persons, the theater and national instruction: much less those things which may blacken the honor and esteem of communities and persons of all classes or stations, dignitaries and employees. [They shall] abstain from all words which might be interpreted as having or have direct allusion against the Government or its Magistrates, for which offense the penalties established by the laws will be imposed or demanded.

As of mid-1789 any manuscript scheduled for inclusion in a periodical was to be submitted to the authorities "written in a clear hand and enough ahead of time to allow it to be perused without haste."

The worries that the French Revolution caused the Spanish authorities were accentuated when in June 1790 a Frenchman attempted to assassinate the Conde de Floridablanca, Charles IV's chief minister and a keen monarchist. Floridablanca then imposed strict censorship on all printed material coming from France. In February 1791 the king himself promulgated a new decree suppressing all of Spain's leading newspapers other than the official *Gazeta de Madrid* and the *Diario de Madrid*, although this latter was specifically barred from printing "verses or other political ideas of any kind." On June 25, 1792, the border with France was closed to printed matter and anything that was seized by customs was to be inspected by the Ministry of State. No new publications were permitted in Madrid for the rest of the year. All copy was to be submitted for censorship six days prior to publication or "however long the President of the Council may order."

On April 11, 1805, with Spain involved in the European wars between France and England, Charles IV produced more printing regulations, which established, among other things, the first court devoted exclusively to controlling the print media. In 1808, as Charles abdicated in favor of his son Ferdinand VII, the French invaded Spain, their nominal ally, and established Marshal Murat as lieutenant-general. The French took immediate control of the press, suborning it to propagandist purposes and assuring Spanish loyalists that "the authors, distributors or sellers of seditious printed matter ... will be considered agents of England, and shot." This situation persisted until 1810, when the French left Spain.

2. censorship (1810-1937) After the expulsion of the French from southern Spain in 1810, the Cortes passed the new Constitution of Cadiz. Incorporated as article 371 was a new press law, the "Ley de Libertad de Imprenta" (law of freedom of the press), passed on October 19, 1810, which made freedom of publishing absolute; any Spanish citizen could freely "publish their political thoughts and ideas, not only as a brake on the arbitrariness of those who govern, but also a means of enlightening the nation in general and as the only means of arriving at knowledge of true public opinion." Article I specified that "all groups or particular persons, regardless of their condition or state, [shall] have the freedom to write, print and publish their political ideas without the need for licensing, or any approval prior to publication." The law left religious affairs to the church and established a Supreme Censorial Commission to "ensure freedom of printing and keep abuses in check." The result was the launch of many newspapers, often outspokenly opposed to the authorities and especially to the church.

In May 1813 the French were ejected from Madrid and King Ferdinand VII returned to take power. In May 1814 he annulled the Constitution of Cadiz and all its decrees stating, "His Majesty has resolved that no poster may be put up, no announcement distributed, no daily [newspaper] nor anything written may be printed without its prior presentation to the person who is in charge of the government, who will deny or grant permission for printing or publication [after] having heard the opinion of the learned person or learned persons who are impartial and who neither served the invaders nor manifested seditious opinions." Liberal papers were shut down at once, but their conservative rivals also came to infuriate the king and on May 2, 1815, Ferdinand issued a new decree that emphasized his displeasure at "the diminishing of the prudent use which ought to be made of the press" and its use for "impudence and personal exchanges which not only offend the persons against whom they are directed, but also offend the dignity and decorum of a prudent nation ..." He then shut down all papers other than two official publications.

For the next 60 years, until the major new press law of 1868, the status of press freedom in Spain fluctuated along lines dictated by the reversals of national politics. In March 1820 Ferdinand was forced by liberal pressure to reverse his position and accept the Constitution of Cadiz. The press duly benefited, and many new titles appeared, notably those launched by the patriotic societies and by the secret Communeros, a revolutionary group who attacked the monarchy, the church and the liberals with equal vigor. On October 22, in a timid attempt to restrict such writing, the Cortes passed a new press law, similar to that of 1810. It reaffirmed the complete freedom of publication, other than on religious topics. A Committee for Protection of Freedom of the Press was established. Five offenses might be leveled against the press: (1) Subversion; (2) Inciting to rebellion; (3) Inciting to disobedience to the law or authorities; (4) Moral offenses; (5) Injuries to a particular person (libel). The law was ineffectual; it excluded any graphic material and failed to offer an exact definition of the crimes. This omission was remedied in February 1822.

By August 1823 the liberal era had collapsed and, after a further brief occupation by the French, Frederick annulled all previous liberal measures, including those regarding freedom of the press, in a proclamation of October 1, 1823. The next new press law was passed on January 4, 1834, promulgated by Francisco Cea Bermudez, the centrist prime minister who ran the government for Ferdinand's successor, the Queen-Regent Maria Cristina. This law, the "Reglamento que ha de observarse para la censura de los periodicos" (laws that must be observed for the censorship of publications), stated that "the absolute and unlimited freedom of the press, the publication and circulation of books and papers cannot exist without offense to our Catholic religion and detriment to the public welfare." It reinstituted royal licensing for newspapers, put the provincial press under the control of the provincial governors and demanded a deposit from each paper against possible fines. All articles were to be censored before publication, and if anything had been cut there must be no blank spaces—new copy must be inserted. There were to be no attacks on the government, head of state or national religion nor on foreign leaders or governments. Censors themselves were not permitted to form associations in case they "pervert their judgments." Any censor who failed in his job would suffer the same penalties as those who published unacceptable material. To encourage their probity they were to have substantial salaries, far larger than those of journalists.

This law was supplemented in March 1837, when either the editor (in the case of unsigned articles) or the writer was made personally responsible for their own words and the deposit was doubled. This law, part of the new Constitution of 1837, set out the concept of the responsible editor, who must himself contribute to the paper and would face prosecution with his writers. A copy of all publications must be submitted to the authorities before distribution; those claiming to be offended in print were allowed a right of reply, which had to be printed. The next constitution, that of May 23, 1845, reaffirmed the right to publish without precensorship but set up tribunals to deal with the five press crimes. Press laws continued to fluctuate during a period of constant governmental change. In 1852 the 1837 law was upheld again, with increased fines and increased jail terms for those criticizing the monarch or the state religion "or that which is moral" and substantially larger deposits against the fines. These were increased further in 1856.

In 1866 a conservative government reestablished prior censorship, giving the authorities the right to ban anything containing "ideas, doctrines, accounts of events, or news offensive to the Catholic Religion, the Monarch, the Constitution, members of the Royal family, the Senate, the Chamber of Deputies, Foreign Sovereigns and to the Authorities; also anything that tends to relax the discipline of the army, alter the public order, or which may be contrary to that which is moral and decent." Any paper that offended three times would be shut down. Only "decorous and non-calumnious" criticism of the government would be permitted. Only with the establishment of the federal government in 1868 did the fluctuations halt. Its official manifesto of October 1868 affirmed the freedom of the press, "the lasting voice of intelligence." The new Constitution of February 1869 stated: "No Spaniard can be deprived of the right to utter freely his ideas and opinions, both in speech and in writing ..." With a few minor adjustments, this freedom was maintained until 1923, although governments were still averse to letting themselves be attacked, and they censored where necessary. In 1883 a new print law, the "Ley de imprunta de 26 de junio de 1883" formed that basis of law for the next 75 years. Graphics were now liable to control; a company's directors must be registered and a detailed breakdown of the publication's intentions set out; no one deprived of civil or political rights would be allowed to publish; the responsible editor or director was responsible for all content. In 1923 the military government of General Miguel Primo de Rivera established strict press censorship, prohibiting the publication of any political material unless authorized by the government. After further turmoil a Republic was declared in April 1931. As part of the "Ley de defensa de la republica" all "acts of aggression against the republic" by the press were prohibited. Transgressors could be punished by fines, jail or even exile. This law helped suppress a wide variety of opposition and was essentially picked up by Franco after 1938. A new Constitution of December 1931 affirmed freedom of the press but in article 25 added: "The rights and guarantees stated in the corresponding articles can be totally or partially suspended ... when it is imperative to the security of the state ..." This was frequently done.

3. censorship under Franco   Among the immediate results of the nationalist victory in the Civil War was the reorganization of the Spanish press. Stating that "One of the old concepts which the new Spain has most urgently to revise is that of the press," the goverment ratified the "Ley de Prensa de 22 de abril de 1938," a measure designed to "awaken in the press the idea of service to the State and to return to the men who live from the press the dignity which is merited by anyone who dedicates himself to such a profession." Control of the press was vested in the Ministry of the Interior and the government was given the right of: (1) regulating the number and size of periodicals; (2) participating in the designation of directive personnel; (3) ordering the journalistic profession; (4) supervising press activity; (5) censoring all publications. In addition Franco resurrected the concept of the responsible editor, making the director of a newspaper legally responsible for any alleged transgressions. The company owning the paper was in turn responsible for the sins, either by "commission or omission," of the director. The ministry could punish all writings that "directly or indirectly may tend to reduce the prestige of the Nation or Regime, to obstruct the work of the government of the new State, or sow pernicious ideas among the intellectually weak." Any acts already illegal under the criminal code might also be punished, as were those that deviated in any way, including passive resistance, from the standards laid down for the operation of the press. Punishment consisted of a fine, the dismissal of the director from his post or from the profession of journalism or, in extreme cases, the confiscation of the publication.

The major left-wing papers—*El Sol* and *El Heraldo* (both of Madrid)—had not survived the Civil War. The new press was led by the pro-Franco organs: *ABC*, *Ya* and *Informaciones*. There followed a large-scale purge of journalists: Many were arrested and 40 were executed. The law gave the government "sole authority to organize, watch over and control the press as a national institution." The 1938 law further developed an official theory of news reporting. The basis of this was the belief, written into the law, that "the existence of a Fourth Estate cannot be tolerated. It is inadmissable that the press can exist outside the State. The evils that spring from 'freedom of the democratic kind' must be avoided ... The press should always serve the national interests; it should be a national institution, a public enterprise in the service of the State." This attitude persisted throughout the Franco era and was written into textbooks of journalism into the 1960s.

Under this theory political news was heavily censored and generally repressed. Culture, religion and sport filled the papers, while politics, local and national news was given minimal coverage. Until 1962 all material, other than that written for the official Falangist press, was precensored by officials of the Ministry of Information and Tourism in Madrid or by specific censors appointed to check the provincial press. Paradoxically, the word censor itself was rarely used officially, either within the government or in statutes. The only specific rules designated as "censorship" dealt with immorality and attacks on Franco himself. The day-to-day regulation of the press was supervised by the head of the National Press Service, in turn responsible to the Director General of the Press. Censors gained their jobs through a competitive examination, as did any other bureaucrat. They needed no special qualifications. Material used by the national news agency, EFE, and coming from foreign sources was similarly scrutinized, although it was rarely censored. The press was further controlled by government's allocation of newsprint and by an oath of allegiance that journalists swore to the state prior to gaining official press credentials. This read: "I swear before God, for Spain and its Leader, to serve the Unity, the Greatness and the freedom of the Fatherland with complete and total faithfulness to the principles of the Spanish State, without ever permitting falsehood, craft or ambition to distort my pen in its daily labor." Just what constituted "distortion" was up to the carefully self-censoring newsman, who might find that merely reporting events or even statistics less than favorable to the regime brought him into error.

In 1941 Gabriel Arias Salgado took over as the press overlord, first as vice secretary of national education and then as minister of information, or of "Non-Information" as he was nicknamed. Working from the premise that "Freedom of information has installed the freedom of error ..." and blaming "libertinism of information" for modern problems, he proved himself an absolute hardliner on the press.

The first attempts to modify the 1938 law came in 1950 when the primate of Spain, Enrique Cardinal Pla y Deniel, stated: "It is highly deplorable that it is not recognized that between the liberties of damnation—the unrestrained license of the press for cheating and corrupting the public, always condemned by the Church—and the absolute state control of the press, exists the happy medium of a responsible freedom of the press, proper to a Christian and civilized society ..." The governmental response was to acknowledge the comment but to take little action. Individual editors were granted slightly greater autonomy, but the basic taboos were maintained. A number of similar efforts followed: In 1952 the National Council of the Catholic Press submitted a list of proposed reforms, notably those that would reorganize censorship, in a way that would do less harm to editorial content, and establish a special tribunal to deal with press offenses. In 1953 the National Congress of the Spanish Press attacked censorship abuses, demanding the elimination of controls and the elaboration of a new law. In 1954 another leading clergyman, Father Jesus Iribarren, editor of the official Catholic paper *Ecclesia*, attacked the controls and was dismissed for his pains.

In December 1954 the government did begin debating the problem, although such information was kept well away from the public. Arias Salgado presented a bill that only strengthened government controls, allowing the authorities an absolute veto on all senior appointments. This bill did not become law, but in April 1955 the government issued a new code of journalistic ethics, the essence of which was to conform journalistic loyalty to the interests of the state. In 1959 the government set up a special commission to study the press law, explaining that it was "somewhat out of date, considering the dynamism and needs of modern journalism." By 1960 a draft law had been worked out; for prepublication censorship it substituted a lengthy list of "Crimes of the Press," which effectively maintained control at the same level. In July 1962 Arias Salgado retired and was succeeded by the relatively liberal Manuel Fraga Iribarne. Fraga promised speedy liberalization, but his enthusiasm was checked by the realities of government conservatism, and in 1965 he was still calling for patience and equanimity in the progress of reform. He did make some quick changes, permitting the launch of a flood of new publications and loosening the controls on book publishing and importing. In the light of his claim that "we want to encourage all free discussion which is in the national interest" some criticism of the government was permitted to appear. The lack of strict guidelines created confusion, and writers, still not sure of how far they could go, found themselves pulled up apprently arbitrarily. Nonetheless Spanish readers were somewhat better informed, even if the information was often dictated to the press by government agencies.

In 1964 there was drafted a new press law, the "Ley de Prensa e Imprenta." This affirmed "liberty of expression in the print media" but amplified this to mean that "freedom of expression shall have no limits other than those imposed by the considerations of morality and truth, respect for existing public and constitutional order; the demands of national defense, of the security of the State and of internal and external public peace; the reserve owing to the action of the government, of the Cortes and of the administration; the independence of the tribunals in the application of the law and the safeguarding of private affairs and honor." Prepublication censorship was abandoned, and publications were to be permitted to choose their own directors. However, the government still maintained the right to prosecute errant publications, punishing them with fines and/or suspension of publication for up to six months. The law was debated in the Cortes in early 1965, and 52 of the 72 original articles were altered, though none substantially. Franco signed the new law on April 9, 1966, and it remained in force until his death.

4. censorship post-Franco The Constitution of 1978 guarantees "the right to communicate freely or receive any accurate information by any means of dissemination whatsoever ... the exercise of these rights cannot be restricted by any form of prior censorship." Despite these promises, freedom of expression is restricted by "the right to honor, privacy, personal reputation and the protection of youth and children." Rights are further curtailed by Organic Law 8/1984 (dealing with terrorism) and Organic Law 1/82 (also dealing with honor and personal reputation). All freedoms may be suppressed during a state of emergency. The concept of "accurate information" means that individuals who feel information published about them is not accurate have the right to demand a correction.

The press in post-Franco Spain faces two forms of control: under the Penal Code, itself largely a creation of the Franco era, and under a number of laws that ostensibly exist to combat terrorists, notably the Basque separatist organization, ETA. On the death of Franco and the accession of King Juan Carlos there developed a consensus among the Spanish establishment that while democracy should be implemented, there should be no major and disturbing changes—a policy of gradualism embodied in the phrase "reforma sin ruptura" (reform without rupture). The result of this policy has been compromise with the right-wing leadership, which still holds many important and influential positions, notably in the military, judicial, industrial and business sectors. For those democratic journalists, allied to members of the other media, who see the new government as an opportunity thoroughly to investigate the Franco years, this policy remains a hindrance.

Legal controls over the press stem first from the Penal Code, under which a variety of blanket charges restrain journalists from public scandal, injury, calumny and disrespect. Several hundred cases have been brought against journalists, invariably on democratic and never on Francoist papers (which still urge a return to fascism), who have been accused of attacks on the army, the civil guard, the judiciary, the church, the royal family and public morality. By such charges it is made almost impossible for writers to conduct proper investigations into allegations of corruption, torture, bad prison conditions, the fascist background of certain individuals etc. Some cases are brought by private citizens, but the bulk are taken up by an official of the Ministro Fiscal (the equivalent of the attorney general) who applies for a writ and briefs a judge to take up the prosecution. The judge summons the journalist in question, who must make a statement and is then bailed pending a trial. This trial may not come to court for many months, even years, and the accused, aware that bail will be revoked if he or she is accused of any further crimes, is forced to suffer lengthy self-censorship. Once found guilty, the accused faces a variety of punishments, including short periods of house arrest, jail terms, fines, temporary suspension from his or her job, banishment from the city where the paper is produced and prohibition from working as a journalist for lengthy periods. Sentences are often suspended, but may be reimposed in the event of additional offenses.

Since 1977, when the Audiencia Nacional was instituted to replace Franco's Public Order Tribunal (TOP) and to suppress terrorism in Spain, two laws have provided for further control of journalism. Under the "Ley de Defensa de la Constitucion" and the "Ley de Defensa de la Cuidadania" (laws in defense of the constitution and of the citizen), the crime of making an apology for terrorism has been introduced. These laws have produced a parallel legal system specifically designed to deal with terrorism and a number of loosely allied crimes, including pornography, prostitution, gunrunning and drug sales, all of which have "a grave effect on the nation." This system, which presumes an individual to be guilty until proven innocent (in contravention of Spain's national constitution), allows the government, represented by individual *fiscales*, to overrule judicial rulings, subordinates the judiciary to police, denies the privacy of lawyer-client consultations and permits people to be held without trial for up to 15 years. Journalists may be charged with the crime of professional negligence and the plant and machinery used to produce an offending publication may be impounded, as well as the article itself. The main result is to inhibit the press, since it is very hard to determine at what stage the mere recounting of facts blurs into apologizing for terrorism.

Given the continuing presence of pro-Franco figures in influential positions of power, these controls are frequently and effectively implemented. Pressure groups use physical threats as well as attempts at bribery (through the "fundo de reptiles" or reptile fund) to suppress embarrassing material. Right-wing business interests, using both legitimate and illegal means, have made attempts to buy up shares, and thus gain control of opposition papers. In 1987, after the Constitutional Tribunal had in December 1986 reversed a decision of the Madrid Supreme Court and cleared a Basque newspaper of condoning terrorism, the government dropped six articles of the antiterrorism laws. The most important article to be repealed was #21, under which the courts could shut down any newspaper or broadcasting station thus condemned "as an exceptional precautionary measure."

Spanish Inquisition

1. general censorship　The censorship imposed by the Inquisition in Spain was established as a counterattack on the new and heretical ideas that developed during the 16th-century Protestant Reformation. By the time the Inquisition was formally suppressed in 1834, that censorship had been in operation, in varying degrees, for over three centuries. It interfered in religious and secular life, attempting to silence as best it could Protestant and other heresies as well as the liberal views of humanism and the Enlightenment and the revolutionary ideas developing in France. It confirmed the independence of Spanish Catholicism from that of the Pope in Rome and of the church in Spain from the crown. It attacked literature and scholarship, driving many authors into fearful self-censorship, although critics remain divided over the extent to which the undeniable decline in Spanish creativity can be attributed to the Inquisition. It hamstrung Spanish trade through its incessant searching for smuggled literature, and by denying progress, helped imprison scientific progress in a blind alley of neglect.

Prior to the Reformation there was little censorship in Spain, where a liberal state and an urbane, secure church tolerated a variety of opinions, including those of the large Jewish and Moorish populations, and where the humanist ERASMUS was more popular than anywhere else in Europe. Some Jewish and Moorish manuscripts and the writings of some mystical sects had been burned by zealous inquisitors, but these actions had had no legal authority.

The first serious censorship law in Spain, laying down regulations on the printing and issuing of books, was authorized not by the Inquisition, of which the law made no mention, but by the monarchs Ferdinand and Isabella. Their law of 1502, which formed the basis of all subsequent legislation, created stringent regulations: No books were to be printed, imported, distributed or sold without submitting to preliminary censorship and, if satisfactory, obtaining a license. Only the presidents of the high courts of Valladolid and Granada, and the prelates of Toledo, Seville, Granada, Burgos and Salamanca could issue such licenses, working through teams of salaried inspectors. Once licensed and printed, the sheets had to be checked against the manuscript to ensure that there had been no changes. Any book found to be evading the censorship was to be confiscated and burned; the printer or vendor was fined twice the amount he received for selling the book and was prohibited henceforth from engaging in his trade.

MARTIN LUTHER was unknown in Spain in 1520, and although the threat of Protestantism developed only gradually, it was sufficient to involve the Inquisition in censorship for the first time. On April 7, 1521, the inquisitor general, Cardinal Adrian of Utrecht, issued a decree in response to a call from the Holy See for Spain to help in the suppression of Protestant texts. The Inquisition was not cited as such, but its authority in making effective the ban and its various regulations, and the penalties their nonobservance carried, was assumed. No Protestant texts might be imported; anyone selling or owning such material would be severely punished unless they produced them for public burning; anyone who knew of someone owning heretical works had to denounce them—failure to do so would render him liable to the same penalties as the owner. The operation of this ban meant that the Inquisition gradually accrued to itself increasing powers of de facto censorship. In the absence of an official Index (see *Index Librorum Prohibitorum*), regular lists (*Cartas acordadas*) were circulated to the Inquisition's tribunals, updating the catalog of forbidden material. A clause was added to the Edict of Faith obliging individuals to inform against the owners of heretical works. By 1535 the Inquisition, still without official recognition, had extended its powers to include the condemnation, searching out, seizure and destruction of books and the punishment of their owners or sellers. An attempt to take over the royal prerogative of licensing was abandoned when the Inquisition realized that fluctuating standards of orthdoxy might mean that today's acceptable text was tomorrow's heresy. The Crown was thus allowed all such licensing authority and the Inquisition maintained its infallibility.

The growth of Protestantism alarmed among others the Emperor Charles V, in retirement in Spain. His letter of May 25, 1558, to the Infanta Juana, regent of Spain during Philip IV's absence abroad, instigated the major vehicle of Inquisitorial censorship—the *Index of 1559* (see *Index of Valladolid*). The emperor demanded that Philip should imitate his own tough policy toward heresy in Flanders and offer a "quick remedy and exemplary punishment" to "so great an evil." On his return the king acted. In a series of autos-da-fe he began burning the Protestant believers and, following the decree issued by the regent on September 7, 1558, instituted a rigorous system of censorship. The decree ordered that no foreign books translated into Spanish might be imported, and that all printers must be licensed; it also laid down the rules of the censorship. Contravention of any of these points would result in death and the confiscation of one's property. The Index (still the 1551 edition) was to be circulated to all bookshops, in which it was to be displayed for public access. All books must include a copy of the licence, the price, the names of the printer, author and city of publication. Every page of the manuscript must be signed after its censorship by the secretary of the royal chamber and all printed sheets rechecked against the manuscript. Handwritten manuscripts were subject to the same penalties and they too were to be licensed. The Inquisition was made immune to any such orders and given absolute power to impose the regulations. The decree lasted until the 19th century.

In 1559 Fernando de Valdes, the obsessively orthodox inquisitor general of Seville, who had spearheaded the attacks on Protestantism and humanism, issued the *Index of 1559* to back up the Inquisition's new role. The first Spanish Index had appeared in 1551, commissioned from the University of Louvain (see *Index of Louvain*), and intended to provide a single catalog of prohibited works that would supplant the various *cartas acordadas*. Its main aim was to ban all vernacular trnaslations of the Bible, as well as books of ritual and commentaries on the scriptures. The *Index of 1559* followed suit, on a more elaborate level. Anything that fell into one of these categories was banned: books by heresiarchs; all religious works written by those condemned by the Inquisition; all books on Jews and Moors biased against Catholicism; all vernacular translations of the Bible, even by Catholics; all devotional works in the vernacular; all works of controversy between Catholics and heretics; all books on magic; all verses using the scriptures "profanely"; any book printed since 1515 without the name of its author and publisher; all anti-Catholic works; all irreligious illustrations.

Indexes prepared for and used by the Spanish Inquisition continued to appear throughout its effective life. Using its listings the Holy Office was able to filter European culture along lines acceptable to Spanish Catholic orthodoxy. Where the Spanish Indexes differed from those of Rome (see Roman Indexes), with which they often concurred, was in the admission of a category of expurgations, passages that could be cut, rather than, in the Roman style, the assumption that a single passage rendered the whole book unfit for reading. The first Expurgatory Index appeared in 1554, specifying a number of passages that had to be blotted out (*borrado*), and several more followed. The implementation of the censorship extended to the searching out of heresy in public and private libraries, religious foundations, bookshops and universities. Even the dead were not immune: No bequest of books might be permitted without an Inquisitorial check. Books thus confiscated were sent to a local tribunal for assessment and then, if condemned, destroyed. The overall effect was to create a network of informers and blackmailers, on whose evidence the Inquisition pursued its policies. In fact, it was the malice of such informers, rather than that of the Inquisitors themselves (though such functionaries doubtless existed), that created the greatest opposition toward and resentment of the Holy Office. Whether, as some critics maintain, Spain suffered an intensive war against learning, or, as others claim, the majority of writers and virtually all of the general populace were untouched by its operations, the desire of the Inquisition to eradicate heresy and the machinery to effect this desire remained substantial.

As well as rooting out heresy within Spain, the Inquisition also attempted to stop its entry into the country, either through otherwise legal importing or through smuggling. Such Protestant enclaves as had developed had been centered on the ports, especially Seville, and under the "Visitas de Navio" the Inquisition was empowered, along with a variety of other authorities, to board incoming vessls and check their cargoes for heretical contraband before they were permitted to off-load. Merchants were particularly irritated by the fact that the Inquisitors charged the ships for such searches; foreign ambassadors regularly complained, but were met with counter-complaints against heresy. The continuing flow of clandestine texts into Spain proved that these efforts were not wholly successful. The Inquisition also worked in its own self-interest, using the censorship to ensure both its independence from the church in Rome and from the Crown in Spain. Church and state maintained a precarious alliance that solidified only in the face of the growing revolutionary threats of the late 18th century, although there is no doubt that without state cooperation (exemplified in the legislation of 1558-59) the Inquisition would not have been able to act so assertively.

2. *Index Librorum Prohibitorum* The Indexes of banned literature used by the Inquisition in Spain were quite independent, though often coinciding in their prohibitions, from the TRIDENTINE INDEXES used in Rome. They developed from the *Cartas acordadas*, regular letters of instruction sent from the 1520s to the 1540s to the Inquisition's regional tribunals, instructing them on the latest titles to be banned. Outside Spain both the Emperor Charles V and King Henry VIII of England had issued such lists of heretical works in the 1520s, but the first example of a unified list in Spain can be traced to a letter written from the Inquisition's Supreme Council (the *Suprema*) to the Inquisitor of Barcelona, urging him to take action against imported books and enclosing a list of forbidden titles. In 1546 the University of Louvain (see *Index of Louvain*) was ordered to compile a comprehensive list, which would replace these accumulated letters. This list was submitted to the Suprema in 1547, enlarged by the scholars in 1550 and reprinted for mass circulation in 1551, at which point it became the first autonomous Spanish Index.

In 1559, following the censorship legislation enacted by the Infanta Juana, the inquisitor general of Seville, Fernando de Valdes, an obsessive prosecutor of every variety of heresy, produced the Index of 1559 (or *Index of Valladolid*). This far-reaching example of ecclesiastical censorship confirmed the primacy of the Inquisition in such affairs and acted as the focal point of a campaign, initiated in 1521 by a decree of Inquisitor General Cardinal Adrian of Utrecht, to control the orthodoxy of Spanish culture. This INDEX OF VALLADOLID was also the first product of the Spanish Inquisition to be based on the autonomous efforts of Iberian authorities, rather than simply recasting previous European Indexes. Its comprehensiveness showed the extent to which, compared with Rome, Spain had taken over as the leader in the suppression of heresy.

Unlike the Roman Index, the Spanish variety did not consider it necessary to ban wholesale every volume in which some heretical comment appeared. Under the INDEX EXPURGATORIUS, the first edition of which appeared in 1554, devoted solely to the Scriptures, those passages that had to be *borrado* (blotted out) were specified, and once this task had been performed, the mutilated book could be returned to its owner or library. The 1559 Index soon fell behind the Inquisition's needs, and in 1572 the University of Salamanca was commissioned to prepare a full-scale revision. Despite regular urging, this was not completed until 1583, when it appeared in two volumes, one a list of banned books and one an expurgatory index (a list of those volumes scheduled for expurgation, published in 1584). This Index, named for the current inquisitor general, Gaspar de Quiroga (see *Index of Quiroga*), expanded on its predecessors, specifying the names of 600 new heretics (none of whose works might be published), mainly incorporating those cited in the TRIDENTINE INDEXES of 1564 and 1571, and proscribing a further 682 volumes. Under the 1583 Index the Inquisition extended its interest over the entire range of contemporary European culture, banning or expurgating Dante, BOCCACCIO, PETER ABELARD, RABELAIS, William of Ockham, MACHIAVELLI, Thomas More and many others, including classical authors and fathers of the church. The Index represented the efforts of Spanish advocates of the counter-Reformation to impose their own intellectual preferences through censorship.

Indexes continued to appear throughout the Inquisition's existence, each named for the current inquisitor general. The 1612 INDEX OF SANDOVAL y Rojas put both outright bans and partial expurgations into one outsize volume. Unlike earlier Indexes, which had divided the material into Latin and the vernacular, this compilation divided its subjects into three classes: authors who were absolutely banned; books that were banned, regardless of author; books not bearing the name of an author. The INDEX OF ZAPATA (1632) and the INDEX OF SOTOMAYOR (1640) were even larger and went even further than had Quiroga in isolating Spain from current European thought. No further revision appeared until that of 1707, authorized by Vidal Marin and incorporating 67 years of new material discovered in a special search of libraries and bookshops carried out in 1706. The *Index of Prado y Cuesta*, in 1747, was prepared by the Jesuits, whose undisguised biases led to its swift discredit; despite this it was not replaced until 1790, by the INDEX ULTIMO, a rationalized version of all the earlier versions, with much duplication cut out and the titles arranged in alphabetical order. However, the lack of expurgatory directions meant that censors still had to check with their old editions. The suppression of the Inquisition in 1834 led to the lapse of the Spanish Indexes. Catholics who required direction in their reading turned to the ROMAN INDEXES, which survived until 1966.

SEE ALSO the separate entry, *Index Librorum Prohibitorum*.

3. art censorship The Inquisition evolved gradually throughout the Middle Ages as the established church struggled to suppress heresy. Basing its actions on the literal meaning of heresy as "selection," the Special Office or "Holy Office" fought against anyone who attempted to choose their own beliefs, rather than accept the doctrines of the church. Among the earliest acts of the Inquisition was the promulgation of the "Interian de Ayala," a strict code governing in detail the exact limits of the style permitted to Spanish painters. Any deviation from these rules—crosses must be scaled at 15 feet by 8 feet, the timber must be cut flat, not rounded etc.—was heresy. Once a work was approved, it was sacrilege to tamper with it. Pietro Torrigiano, who destroyed his *Madonna* in 1522 when he felt the price offered by its commissioner, the Duke d'Arco, was too low, was condemned to death by the Inquisition. He starved himself to death in his cell.

In 1558 a decree of Philip II of Spain granted to the Holy Office full authority over artistic and literary censorship. No foreign books might be imported, all printing must be licensed, any deviation from the censorship laws meant automatic confiscation and death. The Index of prohibited books (see *Index Librorum Prohibitorum*), originally drawn up in 1547 (published 1551), was revised and consolidated, with different regional editions appearing throughout the country. Among the blanket condemnations was one covering "all pictures and figures disrespectful to religion." Thus, when in 1573 Veronese put a dwarf, jesters, a parrot and a dog into his *Last Supper*, he was ordered to make suitable alterations. He resisted most of these, but changed the title to *Feast in the House of Levi*, thus avoiding New Testament implications. His plea that "painters claim the license that poets and madmen claim" failed to impress.

A century later the Inquisition had extended itself beyond doctrine into morality, inspecting illustrated snuffboxes for signs of pornography and forcing hairdressers either to remove from their shop-windows or to render decent the wax busts on which they advertised their skills. The busts, it was felt, might inflame the suggestible young. Art remained under the sway of the Inquisition. Francesco Pacheco, grand inquisitor and father-in-law to the painter Velazquez, issued in 1649 his *Arte de la Pintura* (*The Art of Painting*) in which he set down regulations for religious depictions, any diversion from which would be prosecuted. When Bartolomeo Murillo suggested on canvas that the Madonna might have toes, he was duly rebuked. The creation of a nude—as picture or sculpture—in a secular context brought excommunication, a fine and a year's exile.

Spirit of '76, The This film, produced in 1917 by Robert Goldstein, was a glorification of the American Revolution of 1776, featuring all the classic events: Paul Revere's ride, Patrick Henry's speech, the Declaration of Independence, Washington at Valley Forge and so on. It also portrayed a variety of bloodthirsty activities on the part of the British troops. It was banned in Los Angeles, and Goldstein was charged under the ESPIONAGE ACT (1917) with "knowingly, wilfully, and unlawfully attempting to cause insubordination, disloyalty, mutiny and reprisal of duty in the military and naval forces of the United States during war." The film was ostensibly patriotic, but its portrait of America's allies, the British, was seen as destructive of the war effort and "calculated to arouse antagonismsm and to raise hatreds." Goldstein was jailed. Despite the fact the most defendants under the Espionage Act claimed ther constitutional rights under the FIRST AMENDMENT, Goldstein merely claimed that his film was not advocating mutiny. He lost the appeal and served his term.

Stage Licensing Act (1737) Sir Robert Walpole (1676-1745) became prime minister of Great Britain in 1721. His was not a popular ministry, and dramatists joined writers, journalists and pamphleteers in decrying his authority. By 1728 the attacks were irritating enough for him to have *Polly* by John Gay (1685-1732), a sequel to Gay's *The Beggar's Opera*, banned. A more virulent opponent was Henry Fielding (1707-54). Starting in 1730 Fielding wrote a string of plays, beginning with *The Author's Farce*, *Rape Upon Rape* and *Tom Thumb*, that proceeded more and more mercilessly to lambaste Walpole's government. Despite increasingly severe warnings from the LORD CHAMBERLAIN and the banning in 1732, with threats of prosecution for treasonable libel, of *The Fall of Mortimer*, Fielding produced in 1736 *The Historical Register for the Year 1736*. This savage exposition of corruption within British politics proved insupportable.

Walpole announced to Parliament that he had received from Henry Giffard, manager of the theater in Goodman's Fields, the text of *The Golden Rump*, a play allegedly obscene and written by Fielding. Walpole did not display the manuscript, nor did he reveal that Giffard's assistance had been procured with a bribe of £1,000. Parliament was sufficiently impressed to permit Walpole to push through the Stage Licensing Act, condemned by critics as a hasty and ill-conceived piece of legislation, but one that dominated the English stage, with only minor alterations in the THEATRE REGULATION ACT (1843), until 1968. Under the guise of preserving public morals, rather than his own parliamentary status, Walpole stamped the government's authority on the stage. There was opposition, notably that of Lord Chesterfield, but it failed to halt the legislative stampede.

All plays and players were to be sanctioned by the lord chamberlain. Any actor working independently would be classed as a rogue and vagabond and punished accordingly. The two patent theaters, established by Charles II, would have a monopoly of all British stage performances. There could be no new plays, operas or stage entertainments of any kind without the lord chamberlain's approval. The lord chamberlain was given unlimited powers of censorship. Under the terms of the act he could demand at least 14 days before the first night a "true copy" of every play to be acted "for hire, gain, or reward," and "It shall be lawful to and for the said lord chamberlain, for the time being, from time to time, and when, and as often as he shall think fit, to prohibit the acting, performing or representing any interlude, tragedy, comedy, opera, play, farce or any other entertainment of the stage, or any act, scene, or part thereof, or any prologue, or epilogue." The law did not usually act retroactively, but it could if required, and did so in cutting Thomas Otway's *Venice Preserv'd* (1682) and certain Shakespearian passages.

The immediate result of the act was the shutting of various unlicensed theaters. Its passage was also responsible for the term "legitimate theater," a phrase coined to cover the work performed at the permitted theaters. Fielding forsook the stage for prose, thus ending the career of one whom Bernard

Shaw called "the greatest practising dramatist, with the exception of Shakespeare, produced … between the Middle Ages and the 19th century." The act also created for the first time a specific and permanent theatrical censor: the "Licenser of the Stage," a salaried member of the lord chamberlain's staff who, with his own assistant, worked full time to regulate the theater.

Stamp Acts, The (1712 et seq.)   The first Stamp Act was passed in 1710 as a response by the British government to growing pressure from printers and publishers for the creation of a substitute for the LICENSING ACT of 1662, which had lapsed, after years of inefficient operation, in 1694. Neither the government, which disliked an uncontrolled press, nor the publishers, who feared for their profits were they to suffer prosecution, felt secure without some specific controlling measure. Queen Anne responded to requests from both sides and issued a series of proclamations, the first in 1704, but they proved impotent in the face of so many "licentious, schismatical and scandalous" publications. The eventual expedient was to extend the Revenue Act of 1710, which already provided for the taxation of almanacs and calendars, to cover periodicals, notably weekly newspapers and pamphlets. The revenue thus generated would be a bonus; the real target was the suppression of the cheap, sensational and critical press.

At first the act worked: Many newspapers were forced off the streets. But the success was short-lived: As many survived as went under, and within a year the publishers had worked out schemes to avoid the stamp duty and make the revenue uncollectable. Exploiting every loophole, notably the discrepancy between papers printed on a single sheet and those of larger dimensions (which paid less tax for larger editions), the press regrouped. By 1714 the government admitted defeat. Probably the most important result of the 1712 act was its making possible the development of the provincial press, because country subscribers refused to pay new, higher London prices.

A new Stamp Act (11 George cap. 8), intended to fill the loopholes, was passed in 1724, urged on by Chancellor Sir Robert Walpole. It aimed to remove the possibilities of evasion and for the first time made a distinction between newspapers and pamphlets, concentrating its attack on errant newspapers only. The act was as futile as its predecessor, and although some marginal publications did vanish, no established one suffered and within a few years evasion was general. Stamp Acts followed throughout the century, including that of 1765, which so angered the American colonists. Few newspapers collapsed, although their profits were impaired, but the acts did establish real control over periodicals. The need for cash by all concerned also opened up a further, more subtle means of control—the acceptance by the press of government subsidies and more or less open, politically motivated bribes.

Stanley v. Georgia (1969)   While Georgia police raided Stanley's home, suspecting him of illegal bookmaking activities, they discovered a number of films in his bedroom. These films were seized and, on being screened, were judged obscene. Stanley was tried under Georgia's statute on the possession of obscene material and duly found guilty. His conviction was upheld by the state Supreme Court. The U.S. Supreme Court reversed this decision, stating that while one may not produce, sell, distribute, transport, or give away obscene material, one may still possess it within one's own home, which the court defined as a zone of privacy. The court ruled that the government, whether federal or state, has no right to determine what materials, literary or pictorial, one may enjoy within that zone. If such a right is ignored, then the authorities may censor private libraries and control every individual's emotional and intellectual choices. "If the First Amendment means anything," wrote Justice Brennan, "it means that a state has no business telling a man, sitting alone in his own house, what books he may read or what films he must watch." The fact that in this case the material might have been legally obscene was seen as irrelevant.

SEE ALSO Georgia 1. obscenity statute.

Star v. Preller (1974)   Star was the owner of a number of adult bookstores in Baltimore, Maryland, in which he had also installed coin-operated viewing machines by which customers were enabled to watch erotic films. These films were seized by the city's vice squad, which justified its raid by citing the state's regulations on film censorship, whereby the exhibitor of any film required a prior license from the state board of censors. Star retaliated by seeking an injunction on the seizure, claiming that the establishment and operation of such a board was unconstitutional. Unlike a number of cases that had indeed overturned a variety of state censorship boards, this one failed to impress the U.S. Supreme Court, which denied Star a hearing. In an earlier case, *Freedman* v. *Maryland* (see *Revenge at Daybreak*) the defendant had managed to defeat the state laws, but since then they had been amended on lines that no longer contravened the constitution.

State of New Jersey v. Hudson County News Company (1962)   The Hudson County News Company was the distributor of a wide range of men's magazines, including *Action for Men*, *Expose for Men*, *Male*, *Untamed* and *Glamorgirl Photography*. The company was charged in 1962 under a New Jersey law that prohibited the sale and distribution of obscene and indecent publications. In the Essex County court the presiding judge, Judge Matthews, made it clear that he despised the material in question, which he had "no hesitation in classifying as absolute trash … The obvious intent of these is to appeal to man's taste for bawdy things and to pander to the cult of pseudosophisticates represented by certain members of our male population who conceive the ultimate in values to be the perfect dry martini and a generously endowed, over-sexed female. To my mind they exist as forlorn evidence of the irresponsible efforts of the publishers concerned to contribute to the mediocrity of society."

Despite this disdain, the judge was unable, under the law, to find the magazines and their distributor guilty as charged. However distasteful their contents might be, Matthews put FIRST AMENDMENT freedoms before personal moral standards:

> In a pluralistic society the courts ... cannot and should not become involved in the attempts to improve individual morals, nor should they become involved as arbiters in the war between the literati and the philistines over the standards to which our literature is to adhere. The function of the courts and our law is clear: to provide, insofar as it is humanly possible, a climate free of unnecessary restraints in which our citizens will be able to express themselves without fear. It is, or should be, apparent to all that everything we have been, are, or will be as a nation has or will come as the result of the unfettered expression of individual ideas. Responsible citizens should realize that our freedoms are inextricably bound together so as to constitute a vital whole, which is much more than a mere sum of its parts; and that whenever we deal with any area of freedom we are necessarily dealing with the living whole. If we cannot with reasonable certainty know every possible effect that will flow from the regulation of any specific area of social freedom when we consider the whole, self-restraint must be exercised ... It must be agreed that if we are to continue to have the freedom of expression as it has been guaranteed, and which we have cherished since the Revolution, the existence of the type of trash involved here must be tolerated as part of the price which we must pay.

Stationers' Company   The term "stationer" developed in the early 16th century as a description for the publishers and sellers of books, as opposed to their printers. It derived from the Latin *stationarius*, one who kept a shop, usually assumed to be a bookshop, in one place, rather than trading as an itinerant vendor. A society of the writers of court hand (a style of handwriting used in British courts until the 18th century) and text letters (specially written capital letters) had been established in London in 1357, and was incorporated with binders, sellers and illuminators of books as a guild in 1404. Printers were admitted by 1500. The stationers applied in 1542 for their separate incorporation as a specific craft organization but were not given a charter until 1557. While it may be assumed that in common with many crafts, the stationers sought both civic honor and the recognition and regulation of their practices, the Crown used their charter, the preamble of which stated that their purpose was to control "scandalous, malicious, schismatic and heretical" printing, for its own political ends. The stationers received wide-ranging powers to control printing.

English printing was limited to members of the London Company or others that could secure a special royal license. No provision was made for provincial printing. Officers of the company held the right to enter and search any premises for evidence of unlawful printing and to fine and imprison anyone thus convicted. Elizabeth I confirmed her sister's charter, and the stationers became a liveried company in 1560. Central to the charter was the right to establish a monopoly on printing and thus, concomitantly, to maintain the Crown's desire to restrict the number and allegiance of printers. The structure of the company upheld these twin aims, combining the self-interest of the stationers with that of the authorities. The company cooperated fully with all measures to control the press, such as the Injunctions of 1559, the Council Order of 1566 and the Star Chamber Decree of 1586, which, respectively, required monetary recognizances from printers, set up detailed regulations regarding the right to print, and established strict ecclesiastical censorship, including the right of the ecclesiastical Court of High Commission to name master printers. Members were further bound to obtain a new license from the company prior to printing any work. Modern copyright owes its development to the rights of patentees granted to members of the company.

All Elizabethan legislation regarding printing supported the rights of search and seizure enjoyed by the company. These extended throughout the country, although the officers restricted themselves to London, leaving local authorities to act as proxies elsewhere. From 1566 they were further empowered to deal with imported material, checking rigorously for smuggled books and pamphlets. From 1576 on the company ordered that all printers were to be searched weekly and that reports were to be made on the number of presses, on who was employed at the printshop and on what they were working. Printers found to be working illegally had their presses and type smashed and the printed material destroyed. As long as the Crown held unassailed power, so did the stationers. The gradual erosion of royal prerogative undermined the absolutism of the company, and its power under the Tudors did not extend into Stuart rule.

The company gained its greatest influence shortly before the fall of Charles I when in 1637 it gained the control of all printing. The Star Chamber Decree of that year, which attempted to remove the abuses and evasions that had developed in the operation of its previous decree of 1586, made the company an official censor as well as licenser of all new printing. The company was restored to power along with the Stuarts in 1660 but its preeminence had passed. A number of factors were present: growing discontent within the trade, the glaring discrepancy between the rich, monopolistic master printers and their lesser craft brethren, the residuum of Puritan sentiment among printers who resented the Stuart return, increasing resentment against printing patents and the reluctance of members to reject the burgeoning market in popular literature, which the government was trying to break up. When in 1669 the company was invited to help the surveyor of the press develop new ways of enforcing press regulations this disenchantment was noticeable. As the century passed, the stationers' resentment and their increasing desire for profits, notwithstanding government restrictions, became increasingly apparent and influential.

Steinbeck, John   Although some 360,000 copies of Steinbeck's (1902-68) most famous novel, *The Grapes of Wrath*, were in print within a year of its publication in 1939, a number of groups attempted to ban the book. Public libraries in St. Louis confined it to the adults only shelves, a number of towns in Kansas and Oklahoma banned it outright, and the Associated Farms of Kern County, California, campaigned against its use in California's schools, since it showed the state in a poor light. In 1953 Steinbeck's Pulitzer Prize-winning novel *The Wayward Bus* (1947) was censored in many U.S. cities. Steinbeck's complete works were banned in Ireland.

Stopes, Marie   SEE *Married Love.*

Strange Fruit   This 250-page novel by Lillian Smith, published in 1945, concerned the topic of miscegenation, as practiced between a lackluster white youth and his girlfriend, an educated black girl. It contained a number of scenes of sexual intercourse, a murder and a subsequent lynching, masturbation, an indecent assault on a young girl, as well as numerous instances of physical description, which might be seen as deliberately titillatory and which appeared with a frequency that, it was felt, "had a strong tendency to maintain a salacious interest in the reader's mind and to whet his appetite for the next major episode." The book's distributor, a Mr. Isenstadt, was charged in 1945 under the Massachusetts laws governing obscene material (see Massachusetts's obscenity statute), in that he had distributed a publication that was "obscene, indecent, impure, or manifestly tends to corrupt the morals of youth." The court found Isenstadt guilty and fined him $200, later reduced to $25.

The court ruled that although the book was undoubtedly written with a serious purpose, that it possessed great literary merit, that the reviewers admired it, and that it put forward a legitimate theme, it remained obscene and indecent as specified by the law. The theme of "a love which because of social conditions and conventions cannot be sanctioned by marriage and which leads to illicit relations" had, after all, been handled "without obscenity" in George Eliot's classic *Adam Bede*. The fact that *Strange Fruit* might promote "lascivious thoughts and ... arouse lustful desire" outweighed any artistic merit that it might undoubtedly possess. The fact that it had already sold 200,000 copies was similarly unimportant, and a number of bookstores—notably in Detroit, Boston and New York—accepted a gentlemen's agreement whereby the book was quietly taken off their shelves.

Stranger Knocks, A   This film was made in Denmark in 1963, winning three "Bodils," the Danish equivalent of an Oscar. It concerned the story of a woman, living in an isolated, seaside cottage, who one stormy night lets a stranger in. She is lonely, he is amorous, they make love keenly. In bed she discovers that he is not only a former Nazi, on the run from Danish justice, but also the same man who tortured and killed her late husband during the war. The film was released in America in 1963 by the Trans-Lux Film Corporation. At least 250,000 people in 23 states saw the film before the state censors of New York banned it in 1964; those of Maryland followed suit a year later.

In New York, after the Board of Regents had refused to license the film on the grounds that its portrayal of the couple's love-making was obscene under the state's film censorship law, the Appellate Division of the New York Supreme Court reversed the ban, freeing the film for exhibition. The New York Court of Appeals then reinstated the ban and the case, *Trans-Lux Distributing Corporation* v. *Board of Regents* (1964) went to the U.S. Supreme Court. The court saw no need to write an opinion, but simply cited its recent decision in the case of FREEDMAN V. MARYLAND (1965) in which the Maryland system of state film censorship was declared unconstitutional in its attempt to ban the film REVENGE AT DAYBREAK; the court extended this ruling to the New York system and allowed *A Stranger Knocks* to be shown.

The Maryland authorities had altered their censorship system to conform with the Supreme Court's earlier ruling in *Freedman*, but their attempt to ban *A Stranger Knocks* had been initiated at an earlier date. The board had objected to the entire film, rather than to specific scenes. This decision was reversed by the Maryland Court of Appeal in *Trans-Lux Distributing Corporation* v. *Maryland State Board of Censors* (1965). The court stated that not only had the board not offered to the lower court any evidence of the film's obscenity as defined in the tests established by the U.S. Supreme Court, but also that in their view the film was a serious work of art and should as such be permitted exhibition. They cited the ruling in LES AMANTS (JACOBELLIS V. OHIO [1964]) as justification for this decision.

Stubbs, Sir John   Stubbs (ca. 1541-90) was educated at Trinity College, Cambridge, and became a barrister of Lincoln's Inn. In 1579, when it was strongly rumored that Elizabeth I was intending to marry Francois, duke d'Alencon, the brother of the French King Henri III, Stubbs wrote "The Discoverie of a Gaping Gulf whereinto England is like to be swallowed by another French marriage, if the Lord forbid not the banes by letting her Majestie see the sin and punishment thereof," suggesting that such a marriage to a Catholic prince would drag England back to the days of Queen Mary and her Spanish husband, Philip. The pamphlet, which apostrophized France as "a den of idolatry, a kingdom of darkness, confessing Belial and serving Baal," and hoped that Elizabeth would marry someone "as had not provoked the vengeance of the Lord," infuriated the queen. She issued a proclamation on September 27, 1579, in which Stubbs' work was condemned as "a lewd, seditious book ... bolstered up with manifest lies, &c." It was to be destroyed in public and such copies as were found were duly burned in the kitchen stove of Stationers' Hall. Stubbs was arrested, imprisoned and had his right hand cut off after a cleaver was driven through his wrist by a mallet, "whereupon he put off his hat with his left hand and said with a loud voice 'God save the Queen.'" Despite this mutilation he continued to write, with his left hand, and after his imprisonment was rehabilitated at Court.

Stzygowski, Josef Stzygowski (d. 1940) was an Austrian art critic who supported the Nazi party and hated all forms of modern art. A self-proclaimed believer in Nazi race theories, his work concentrated on providing an intellectual basis for racist theories of art. According to Bernard Berenson, writing in *Aesthetics & History in the Visual Arts* (1948), a typical Stzygowski statement declared that "Nothing good could come from the Aegean and from the South. Only in the North was there art, and that art was Aryan and Germanic, owing nothing to races tainted with Negroid blood as were the Greeks and the Semites." He set himself up as the prophet of anti-iconic art, typified by its absolute horror of the nude. Ironically, Stzygowski's greatest influence was in America, the U.K. and in France, rather than in Axis countries.

Suarez SEE book burning in England 2. James I (1603-25).

Sumner, John On the death of ANTHONY COMSTOCK in 1915, his place as secretary of the New York SOCIETY FOR THE SUPPRESSION OF VICE was taken by John S. Sumner. While the heyday of the society had undoubtedly passed, and Sumner lacked Comstock's vindictiveness, he attempted to keep up his predecessor's standards in an increasingly hostile world. In 1917, shortly after taking office, he suffered a reversal that might have seemed prophetic of changing attitudes. His attack on a bookseller who stocked Gautier's MADEMOISELLE DE MAUPIN was rejected by the courts, and substantial demages were awarded for malicious prosecution. Later attacks on other great French authors were similarly foiled. But he did not always fail.

In April 1921 Sumner had Louis Brink, a New York art dealer, arraigned on charges of displaying in his window obscene and lewd pictures and prints, either nude or partly nude. While the magistrate was unwilling to prosecute Brink himself, he ordered that those pictures found most objectionable should be destroyed. In May 1922 Sumner's laying of information before the New York courts was instrumental in Lorenzo Dow Covington, an archaeologist of international distinction, a leading Egyptologist and fellow of the Royal Geographical Society in London, being given a sentence from six months to three years in jail for the possession of obscene pictures and literature in his own home. Sumner had acted after two men who had already been convicted of possessing obscene pictures claimed that they had obtained them from the explorer and lecturer. Covington, who underwent 240 days' observation in New York's Bellevue mental hospital, told the court that he had bought the pictures and literature in Spain and felt that they "would help me in my studies of human nature."

Subsequent attempts in the 1930s by Sumner to seize and have prosecuted various materials proved a failure, as his conservative constituency began to weaken. ERSKINE CALDWELL's *God's Little Acre* and Radclyffe Hall's THE WELL OF LONELINESS withstood his denunciations. The society, however, was a prime mover in the continuing attacks on pornographer SAMUEL ROTH. In 1938, shortly before the society went into its final decline, Sumner issued a statement in which he defended his own efforts in fighting "commercialized vice," which supplied "an illegitimate thrill to old fools and young boys and girls."

SEE ALSO Flaubert, Gustave; *If I Die*; *Lady Chatterley's Lover* 1. history; *November*.

Sunshine and Health Before the advent of *Playboy* and the many lookalikes that followed on its success, the most common precursor of the men's magazine was the nudist magazine, where men, women and often children, were seen disporting themselves in a variety of activities that often seemed more humorous than titillating. *Sunshine and Health* was the official publication of the American Sunbathing Association, Inc., a group of American nudists. It suffered, along with various similar nudist magazines, a number of prosecutions, notably in Ohio in 1948, and in New York in 1952. In *State of Ohio* v. *Lerner* (1948), Lerner, a Cincinnati bookshop owner, was charged under the state's obscenity statute (see Ohio) with offering for sale a magazine that, while not actually obscene, still contained "lewd and lascivious photographs and drawings." Lerner was acquitted, the judge pointing out that "an obscene book must be held to be one wholly obscene and that necessarily in testing a literary work for obscenity it must be viewed in its entirety and only when and if the obscene contents constitute the dominant feature or effect does it fall within the forbidden class." He added that "these ... views are of God's own children as he made them in His own image. There cannot be any obscenity in God's own handiwork."

In 1952 Edward T. McCaffrey, New York City's commissioner of licenses, who had authority over the distribution of publications, circularized the city's newspaper distributors, informing them that their licenses to distribute would be suspended if they continued to display or offer for sale a number of nudist magazines, i.e., *Sunshine and Health, Sunbathing for Health Magazine, Modern Sunbathing and Hygiene, Hollywood Girls of the Month* and *Hollywood Models of the Month*. The publisher of *Sunshine and Health* chose to sue McCaffrey, seeking an injunction against his threat. In *Sunshine Book Co.* v. *McCaffrey* (1952) the Supreme Court of New York County duly confirmed the commissioner's rights in this area, stating that his action was "a reasonable regulation to aid [him] in performing the duties assigend to him by statute, and did not constitute prior restraint." Judge Corcoran found that while both sexes, young and old, attractive and plain, were featured inside the magazines, only "shapely and attractive young women in alluring poses" were used for the covers. He felt that this proved that the publishers were aiming to "promote lust ... The dominant purpose of the photographs in these magazines is to attract the attention of the public by an appeal to their sexual impulses ... They will have a libidinous effect upon most normal, healthy individuals. Their effect upon the abnormal individual may be more disastrous. Their sale and distribution are bound to add to the already burdensome problem of juvenile deliquency and sex crimes."

Sunshine and Health came before the courts again in 1957. In *Sunshine Book Company* v. *Summerfield* (1957), the magazine was charged under the U.S. postal regulations that govern the mailing of obscene matter. Both a district and an appeals court ruled that the magazine was indeed obscene and confirmed its conviction as charged. The appeals court cited the 1952 New York case as justification. In 1958 the U.S. Supreme Court reversed the conviction, freeing the magazine and ruling that it could not be found obscene under the test of the ROTH STANDARD.

SEE ALSO United States 17. postal regulations.

Sweden

1. broadcast media Swedish radio and television developed too late to be included in the provisions of the Freedom of the Press Act (1766) (see Sweden 3.). Instead they are governed by the Radio Act (1967) and the Broadcasting Liability Act (1967), both acts most recently amended in 1978. Under the Radio Act the government has the right to allot franchises to broadcasting companies and to ensure that those who are granted such rights shall exercise them factually and impartially and in full accordance with Swedish laws governing freedom of expression. The act states that the companies shall "promote the basic principles of democratic government, the principles of the equality of Man, and the liberty and dignity of the individual." The act further provides for the establishment of a Radio Council that will examine programs after they have been broadcast to ensure that they satisfy the requirements of the act and any allied agreements relevant to broadcasting. There is no prior censorship, but the council has the right to investigate complaints brought by the public. The eight-member council is absolutely independent and may also examine, on its own initiative, any program that it feels may have gone beyond the acceptable standards. Any company that is subject to council investigations must publicize its findings fully.

The Broadcasting Liability Act is modeled on the concept, used in the print media, of a responsible publisher. Every company is bound to appoint a program supervisor to ensure against any infractions against the broadcasting laws and to stand responsible for any material that may place the company in court. As guaranteed to print publications, all journalistic sources may remain anonymous and their names may not be used or cited in court. Neither of these acts is part of Swedish constitutional law, but in 1984 new legislation, embodying their provisions, was being prepared for inclusion

in the constitution. The intent is to extend the Freedom of the Press Act to all mass media—including radio, TV, film, audio and video tapes and gramophone records, the theater and exhibitions. In common with other European countries Sweden is gearing up for cable and satellite television, and a law will be passed to cover this new technology. While it is still at a research stage, it is assumed that it will on the one hand maintain the rights of freedom of expression, and on the other prohibit portrayals of sexual violence, grievous violence against people or animals and pornography. Neither advertising nor sponsorship will be permitted.

2. film censorship Sweden established a National Board of Film Censors in 1911, and its two advisory bodies, the 10-member National Council for Film Inspection and the National Board for Film Inspection for Children, in 1954 and 1972 respectively. Repeated attempts over the years to have film censorship completely abandoned have always been defeated. All films must be submitted to the National Board before exhibition. If the film is aimed at an over-15 audience, then only one censor need view it; two censors, as well possibly as the Children's Board, must see films aimed at the juvenile market. The board is obliged to consult the National Council for Film Inspection before banning a film entirely or cutting considerable parts; before cutting a film that has gained recognition as being of substantial artistic value or that is very likely to gain such recognition; and before making any censorship decision of fundamental importance to the overall discharge of the board's duties. The board bases its potential decision to ban a film on four factors: it may have a coarsening or highly exciting effect, or incites to crime; it is harmful either to Sweden's international relations or to defense or international security; it obviously contravenes a law; it may cause psychological harm to children. An analysis of those films that are banned or severely cut shows that Swedish censorship worries more about violence than about sex. Those films that may be exhibited are categorized as those restricted to adults (those over 15); films restricted to those over 11; and those passed for general exhibition.

3. Freedom of the Press Act Sweden has been consistently the most liberal of all European states in its attitudes to press control. Under its Constitution of 1766 and a statute of 1812 (with its subsequent amendments) publications are free of precensorship. They can only be confiscated by officers of the courts, and not the police, and then only pending trials for specific crimes. These include libel, the undermining of the political and social status quo, abuse of religion, attacks on the honor of individuals and obscenity. Punishment is by fine, levied on daily newspapers at twice the rate of those on periodicals. Editors who wished to check the acceptability of given material can consult the Liberty of the Press Committee.

The Freedom of the Press Act is part of the 1766 Constitution and has been in operation, with the exception of a brief period of royal absolutism ending in 1809, ever since. It was affirmed in the most recent constitution, of 1949, that laid down the libertarian principles endemic to current Swedish life. It cannot be abrogated or amended unless the decision to do so is carried out by two successive parliaments, with a general election between the first and second readings. Central to the act is the concept of the responsible publisher, an individual who must be appointed by the owner of any periodical that appears more than four times a year, and who is made responsible for any violations of the act. The responsible publisher may appoint a substitute, who will take his or her place when he is absent or indisposed; but only in the unlikely event of both individuals being unable to answer charges would anyone else appear in court. The act provides a chain of responsibility; the owner, then the printer and then the distributor, to cover such an event. A Code of Ethics, devised by Sweden's Press Council (founded 1916), was established in 1978 and is administered by the press ombudsman (an office established in 1969).

Reporters themselves are inviolate from prosecution. Their sources are protected, and they may shelter behind their legal representative, the responsible publisher. State and municipal employees who wish to blow the whistle on their employer are also protected and their names may not be admitted as evidence in court. Of course, this anonymity is limited, mainly by the exigencies of state security. Publications may offend against the act as specified by a variety of offenses laid down in the state penal code, e.g., by "crimes against the State" (treason, instigation of war, incitement to riot, conspiracy and sedition), libel threats to or contempt of minority groups on racial or ethnic grounds etc. Libel actions are the most common, although the press is rarely involved in any actions. No prosecution can be brought without the approval of the chancellor of justice, thus precluding any arbitrary decisions by a local authority. If a newspaper does reach court, it is tried by a jury—an exception to normal Swedish procedure—on the premise that laymen will be more favorable to the press than would a judge. Conviction requires a 6-3 majority of the nine-person jury and while a judge can overrule the jury, reversing a guilty verdict, he or she cannot reverse an acquittal.

The Freedom of the Press Act also covers freedom of information. Under its provisions all government information is to be made available to the public unless it falls into one of the seven categories of exemption, such as that affecting matters of national security and including one that protects species of animals and plants, that are specified by law. If a civil servant has no legal grounds on which to refuse access to information he or she may be reprimanded. Other than for certain kinds of ministerial documents, the final decision as to whether secrecy is legally justified rests with the ombundsman or the Supreme Administrative Court.

Although many commentators point to the act as the exemplar of open government in Sweden, its incorporation of the Secrecy Act (1981) (see Sweden 4.) means that freedom of information is still substantially controlled when the government wishes to do so. The act was revised in 1981 and,

as well as including the Secrecy Act, it created three types of official information: information to which the public has access (the bulk of that produced by government); documents that are not open to public access but may be talked about freely by civil servants whose role as anonymous sources is still protected under the law; documents that are neither to be made public nor to be leaked. Outside the government sphere, the law regulating commercial and financial interests remains unresolved, although a Data Protection Act deals with computer-generated information held on individuals, licensing any collection of such materials and making all data banks of this type open to inspection by the Data Inspection Board. If an official document is made available by the Press Act, it must be provided within a maximum specified period. This Swedish system has latterly been imitated, in a more restrained way, in Finland, Denmark and Norway.

4. The Secrecy Act (1981)   This act was passed in an attempt by the Swedish government to reduce the ease whereby journalists could take advantage of information leaked by civil servants (and to which the authorities, despite the acceptance of such freedoms in the constitution, take exception). Unlike the Freedom of the Press Act, the Secrecy Act is not part of the constitutional law and is thus open to far easier alteration and amendment. Under Swedish law there are only two categories of information: records that are open for public access and material that is protected by statutes of the criminal law. Within these categories there exists sufficient latitude for leaks from government sources, and under the constitution journalists are protected from having to reveal their sources when publishing such leaked material. This attitude is reflected in the Freedom of the Press Act (see Sweden 3.), under which only one person is legally responsible for what is published, usually the editor of a publication or the author of a book. If legal actions are taken under the act, a special type of jury, elected by proportional representation, must be empaneled.

The Secrecy Act was developed when these leaks became too embarrassing, particularly that referring to the illicit actions of one of Sweden's security services, the Information Bureau (IB), in 1973. Hitherto, even the existence of the IB was unknown to the citizens it purportedly served, let alone the details of its operations, especially its cooperation with foreign security agencies. Given the relatively liberal provisions of the Freedom of the Press Act as regarded legal proceedings, the journalists concerned were tried (in camera) and convicted under the espionage section of the Penal Code. The outcry that followed their convictions led to the establishment of a royal commission to consider alterations to the Press Act. At the same time the constitution was being amended, and the added freedom of speech it accorded civil servants made the government keen to curtail the more enthusiastic whistleblowers. The result was the Secrecy Act, now incorporated into the Press Act.

The main provision of this act is that anonymity of journalistic sources is now subject to three conditions. Sources must be named if: (1) the material affects national security, notably spy cases; (2) the charge includes the intentional handing over of classified secret material; or (3) the source is in violation of a duty not to reveal information, when that duty is set down in another piece of legislation.

***Sweezy* v. *New Hampshire* (1957)** Under the New Hampshire Subversive Activities Act (1951) the state reflected the contemporary concern with communism and "sedition" by enacting a wide-ranging law to deal with such a perceived threat to the fabric and stability of its authority. Subversive organizations were outlawed and ordered to be dissolved, and subversive persons were not permitted employment by the state government or in educational institutions. A loyalty program was created to check for such subversives, and a loyalty oath became mandatory on all government and educational employees. As defined in the act,

> a "subversive person" is any person who commits, attempts to commit, or aids in the commission, or advocates, abets, advises or teaches, by any means, any person to commit, attempt to commit, or aid in the commission of any act intended to overthrow, destroy or alter, or to assist in the overthrow, destruction or alteration of the constitutional form of the government of the United States or of the state of New Hampshire, or any political subdivision of either of them, by force or violence, or who is a member of a subversive organization.

In 1954 Sweezy was a teacher at the University of New Hampshire, lecturing in humanities. He was questioned on March 22, 1954, regarding a lecture he gave as part of his course to some 100 students. Under the subversion law the state attorney general was empowered to question any teacher as to the content of his or her teaching as a means of determining whether he or she were loyal or subversive. Sweezy refused to answer any questions that focused on the allegation that he had been teaching communist propaganda, and was convicted of contempt of court, a decision confirmed in the state Supreme Court.

The U.S. Supreme Court overturned Sweezy's conviction and stated that the interrogation violated his rights of academic freedom and political expression:

> areas in which government should be extremely reticent to tread. The essentiality of freedom in the community of American universities is almost self-evident. No one should underestimate the vital role in a democracy that is played by those who guide and train our youth. To impose any straitjacket upon the intellectual leaders in our colleges and universities would imperil the future of our Nation ... Equally manifest as a fundamental principle of a democratic society is political freedom of the individual. Our form of government is built on the premise that every citizen shall have the right to engage in political expression and association.

SEE ALSO *Abrams* v. *United States* (1919); *Adler* v. *Board of Education* (1952); *Frohwerk* v. *United States* (1919); *Gitlow* v. *New York* (1925); *Lamont* v. *Postmaster General* (1965); *Schaeffer* v. *United States* (1920); *Schenck* v. *United States* (1919); *Whitney* v. *California* (1927); *Yates* v. *United States* (1957).

symbolic speech Under American law the principle of symbolic speech is defined as conduct that is performed in order to communicate an idea. The conduct and the communication must be inextricably linked, otherwise the definition does not hold. Examples of symbolic speech, as allowed by the U.S. Supreme Court, include the wearing of black armbands as an anti-war protest, the wearing of a jacket bearing the slogan "Fuck the Draft," the wearing of a military uniform by an actor who is attacking U.S. foreign policy, and a number of cases in which the U.S. flag was allegedly misused.

SEE ALSO *Cohen* v. *California* (1971).

Syria Modern censorship in Syria began in 1947, following the coup d'etat by Housni al-Zaim. Subsequent coups led to a gradual tightening of controls, until, after the takeover in 1970 by Hafiz al-Assad, Syria's current president, the developing apparatus was formalized into a full-scale system of state censorship, covering all internal and foreign publications, films, videocassettes and records. The censorship is pervasive and all-powerful, although, in the absence of official guidelines, what is or is not acceptable at a given moment appears to vary.

All publications, whether national or local, are state-owned. Underground publishing does not exist, neither does independent journalism. Strictly monitored education—personal files on each pupil begin in elementary school and many teachers at every level work as well for the intelligence services— ensures that today's newspaper writers work strictly along official guidelines. The university courses in journalism promote a state-designed curriculum, administered by state-appointed staff. All editors must be members of the ruling Ba'ath party. Many journalists were executed in the aftermath of Assad's coup, and many more fled into exile. Such rebels as exist today, i.e., anyone who deviates from the party line, is barred from writing and reduced to a minor role in the Ministry of Information.

Since 1974 virtually all foreign publications are banned, whether in Arabic or otherwise. Such publications may apply for distribution by submitting an application to the office of the censor in the Ministry of Information. Even if distribution is permitted, every issue must be submitted for pre-distribution assessment, and offending articles are deleted. Printed material sent to individuals through the mail is checked before being delivered. Foreign books are similarly restricted. Books and periodicals brought in by travelers are usually confiscated by the Customs. A list of material, stamped by the ministry, is compiled and the owner must hand this list over on leaving, at which point the publications will be returned.

Private publishers do operate in Syria, but they too face censorship. All manuscripts must be read by the censor, who will stamp the pages he approves. Like anything else that is published, the finished work must be resubmitted, to check that the censored manuscript and the printed text are identical. The final arbiter of all censorship disputes is the Cultural Office of the Ba'ath Party. The Ministry of the Interior publishes regular lists of censored publications, and officials make spot-checks on bookshops to ensure that nothing thus proscribed is available.

Members of the Ba'ath Party control every major post in radio and television, but their controls are further backed by the relevant censorship committee. No film may be made until the film committee has passed its script and distribution is forbidden until the final cut has been approved; foreign films suffer similar restrictions as do foreign publications and books. Even the sermons preached in the mosques are censored, written down and checked by the Ministry for Religious Affairs.

T

tableaux vivants These prototype strip-shows gained initial popularity in New York City in the 1840s. Audiences were able to look through a thin gauze curtain at a succession of "tableaux," staged by women clothed in sheer tights. One "Dr. Collyer" had taken the growing interest in the fine arts and developed this new form of exhibition—"esthetics sweetened by sex," as a commentator put it. Launching his ladies at Palmo's Opera House, the Doctor promised "Living men and women in almost the same state in which Gabriel saw them in the Garden of Eden on the first morning of creation." At 50 cents a customer, Collyer and his various imitators found such "art" most profitable. By the end of the decade the tableaux were virtually extinct, victims of criminal prosecutions and the mass interventions of indignantly moral crowds.

Taiwan Taiwan's constitution guarantees freedom of speech, teaching, writing and publication, and in addition to these guarantees there exist certain clauses that permit the government to control all such freedoms, to impose martial law and censorship. During the long period of military rule, from 1949 to 1987, successive Taiwanese governments chose to control freedom of speech. Those who stirred up sedition or otherwise spread rumors that "harmed the social order or created disturbance in people's minds" were jailed by tough military courts. Although the end of military rule led to some relaxation in such controls, the National Security Law (1987) still bans all advocacy of communism; it does, however, abolish the military trials of civilians.

Taiwanese print media are controlled by the Publications Law. All publications must be licensed and the Government Information Office is empowered to fine publishers and ban publications that commit offenses "against the public order." Between 1951 and 1987 no new papers were permitted, ostensibly due to the cost of newsprint; this restriction was lifted in January 1988, although no paper may exceed 24 pages. There is no overt censorship of the copy; most editors and reporters belong to the ruling Nationalist (Kuomintang) Party. The Department of Cultural Affairs regularly calls editors to suggest the best way of handling a given topic; only if self-censorship fails does actual suppression take over. There do exist a number of declared opposition journals, but these are heavily censored and dare not overstep government limits without facing a ban, the reasons for which do not have to be given. Alternatively, their license is removed, although this punishment can be circumvented by reissuing the journal under another name. (Opposition publishers often have a number of what they call "spare tires," other licensed titles ready for use.) Finally they can be confiscated. In 1986 some 62 percent of the issues of opposition journals were banned, 145 issues faced some degree of confiscation and 1.1 million copies were seized.

Talmud, The SEE Christian Church 3. censorship of Hebrew texts (150-814).

Tennessee Sections 39-3003 and 39-3007 of the Tennessee Code state: "It shall be a misdemeanor for any person to knowingly sell, distribute, display, or exhibit; or to publish, produce, or otherwise create with the intent to sell, distribute, display or exhibit any obscene material ... Every person who is convicted of violating this section shall be punished by imprisonment ... for not more than eleven (11) months and twenty-nine (29) days and a fine of not more than $5000 in the discretion of the jury ..." Obscene material is defined as:

> any material, matter, object or thing, including but not limited to, any written or printed matter, film, picture, drawing, or any object or thing is obscene if, considered as a whole, its predominant appeal is to prurient interest, that is, a shameful or morbid interest in nudity, sex or excretion, and if in addition, (a) it is patently offensive to the public or if it goes substantially beyond customary limits of candor in describing or representing such matters, and (b) it is devoid of any literary, scientific or artistic value and is utterly without social importance. The phrase "predominant appeal" shall be considered with reference to ordinary persons.

Tennessee's Anti-Evolution Act (1925) SEE *Scopes* v. *State* (1927).

***Terminiello* v. *Chicago* (1949)** As stated in the Municipal Code of Chicago (1939), "All persons who shall make, aid, countenance, or assist in making any improper noise, riot, disturbance, breach of the peace or diversion tending to a breach of the peace within the limits of the city ... shall be deemed guilty of disorderly conduct." In 1949 a defrocked Catholic priest, Father Arthur Terminiello, was charged under this statute after he had addressed an 800-strong meeting in a Chicago auditorium under the auspices of the Chicago Veterans Association. The burden of Terminiello's speech was an unrestrained attack upon "the scum ... the atheistic communistic Jews" whom he urged "to go back where they came from." The former priest's speech had been well advertised, and a crowd of 1,000 people surrounded the auditorium, protesting his presence and fighting with the police, who sought to protect the speaker. The result of these tussles was that Terminiello was found guilty of disorderly conduct by the district court, the Illinois Appeals Court and the Illinois Supreme Court.

The U.S. Supreme Court overturned the conviction, ruling that a state cannot convict someone simply because his speech "invites dispute" or "stirs people to anger." The essence of the FIRST AMENDMENT and the freedoms it guarantees is that just such speech may be protected from prosecution. Justice Douglas pointed out,

> The vitality of civil and political institutions in our society depends on free discussion ... it is only through free debate and free exchange of ideas that government remains responsive to the will of the people and peaceful change is effected. The right to speak freely and to promote diversity of ideas and programs is therefore one of the chief distinctions that sets us apart from totalitarian regimes. Accordingly a function of free speech under our system of government is to invite dispute. It may indeed best serve its high purpose when it induces a condition of unrest, creates dissatisfaction with conditions as they are or even stirs people to anger. Unless such speech, however contentious, causes a clear and present danger, it must be allowed free rein.

Justice Jackson, dissenting, suggested that this case pointed up the difference between the theories of free speech, "with which, in the abstract, no one will disagree," and the harsher, more immediate practicalities of a situation where the exercise of that freedom causes a riot. Jackson suggested that, far from limiting Terminiello's rights, it was only through the "suffrance and protection" of the Chicago authorities that he was allowed to speak in the first place. The speech he chose to make was a provocation to an immediate breach of the peace and it was for that, not his actual ideas, that he was being punished. "Riot is a substantive evil, that I take it no one will deny the State and the City have the right and duty to prevent and punish ..." he wrote.

SEE ALSO *Near* v. *Minnesota ex rel. Olson* (1931); *Smith* v. *Collin* (1978).

Texas State Textbook Committee   Texas is one of 18 states to operate a centralized system for the authorization of the textbooks to be used in its public schools. Given the size of the state, the concomitant spending power of its educational authority, and the enthusiastic lobbying of the committee by fundamentalist censors such as MEL AND NORMA GABLER of Educational Research Analysts, the activities and decisions of this committee have become far better known than those of any of its peers. The committee consists of 27 elected members, one drawn from each of the state's congressional districts; it approves an annual textbook budget of over $65 million, a sum that makes Texas the fourth largest market for such publications in the country. Between 1974 and 1984 the committee, at the urging of the Gablers and their colleagues, adopted a set of guidelines for judging the suitability of textbooks for Texas school systems. These guidelines reflect activists' criticisms of SECULAR HUMANISM and challenge the

hegemony of evolutionary theory, stressing that it is as much a theory as is Bible-based creationism.

The guidelines read: (1) "Textbooks that treat the theory of evolution shall identify it as only one of several explanations of the origins of humankind and avoid limiting young people in their search for meanings of their human existence"; (2) "Each textbook must carry a statement on an introductory page that any material on evolution included in the book is clearly presented as theory rather than fact." With an eye to the economic clout of the Texas educational system, publishers have overhauled their textbooks to satisfy the system. In some cases, publishers sold the same altered textbooks to a number of school districts in other states that had not demanded any alterations.

The guildelines were repealed in April 1984, when the committee substituted for them the provision that "theories should be clearly distinguished from fact and presented in an objective educational manner." Although campaigning liberals claimed that this revision was brought about by a threatened lawsuit from the anti-censorship pressure group, PEOPLE FOR THE AMERICAN WAY, it appears that the committee changed its edict when the Texas attorney general stated that the original guidelines were an unconstitutional intrusion into religion and that he would not defend the committee if any lawsuits arose. The Gablers claimed that the committee had been blackmailed by the PAW suit, and decried "rule by intimidation and threat."

SEE ALSO *Scopes* v. *State* (1927).

Theatre Regulation Act (1843, U.K.)   In 1823 a House of Commons Select Committee under Edward Bulwer-Lytton was established to examine British laws on theatrical licensing, dramatic copyright, censorship, and to repair the many deficiencies in the STAGE LICENSING ACT (1737). Lytton, a writer himself, disliked censors, stating, "A censor upon plays seems to me as idle and unnecessary as a censor upon books," and citing censorship as an "almost unconstitutional power." He would have substituted the power of public taste, backed by the "vigilant admonition" of the press. He also deplored the monopoly held by the two patent theaters. After hearing 12 days of expert witnesses Lytton's committee recommended the abolition of censorship and of the theatrical monopoly. Parliament was unimpressed. In 1833 the committee's findings were rejected.

The Theatre Regulation Act of 1843 accomplished what Parliament had intended Lytton to do: The 1737 act was patched up, the LORD CHAMBERLAIN established even more firmly in his place, and various anomalies that had accrued during the past century were adapted to contemporary demands. The lord chamberlain's absolute power over the nation's drama was affirmed again. A stage play was comprehensively defined as "every Tragedy, Comedy, Farce, Opera, Burletta, Interlude, Melodrama, Pantomime or other Entertainment of the Stage or any Part thereof." All plays had to be submitted to his office seven days before the proposed first night. He could ban any performance "whenever he shall be of opinion that it is fitting for the Preservation of Good Manners, Decorum or of the Public Peace." Those who refused to accept the ban faced a fine of £50; the theatre might even lose its license. His responsibilities were extended to censoring any theater in England, although his licensing powers were restricted to Westminster; justices of the peace dealt with other theaters.

The work of the EXAMINER OF PLAYS, which had existed de facto for 100 years, was given statutory legitimacy. The examiner was given a salary, rising over the years from £400 annually in 1843. A set licensing tariff was established—£2 for a full play, £1 for a two-act play and five shillings (25p) for a song, epilogue or prologue. The 1843 act, itself only a refinement of that of 1737, confirmed the pattern of British theatrical censorship until its abolition in 1968. Although the character of the lords chamberlain and their examiners might change, the act and its provisions did not. In 1737 the theater had been made safe for the politicians; in 1843 it was dedicated to the taste of the emergent Victorian bourgeoisie and thus it remained for a century and a quarter more.

Theatres Act (1968, U.K.)   "An Act to abolish Censorship of the Theatre and to amend the law in respect of Theatres and Theatrical Performances" was passed on September 26, 1968, ending more than 400 years of state censorship of the British stage. Based on the deliberations of the Joint Committee on Theatre Censorship, established in 1966 in response to increasing anti-censorship agitation, it repealed the THEATRE REGULATION ACT OF 1843 and abolished the LORD CHAMBERLAIN's role as censor. Following from the OBSCENE PUBLICATIONS ACT (1959), the act accepted a test of obscenity that held that "a performance of a play shall be deemed to be obscene if, taken as a whole, its effect was such as to tend to deprave and corrupt persons who were likely, having regard to all relevant circumstances, to attend it."

Despite this, as specified in the act, there remain a number of areas in which the law may still control theatrical performance. Plays no longer require a license, but theaters do, for the purposes of health and safety regulations. Parts of a script may be charged with being obscene; if so, the same defense of public good as exists in the Obscene Publications Act (1959) may be offered. Expert witnesses may be called to prove that a performance is in the interest of "drama, opera, ballet, or any other art, or of literature or learning." Performances are also excluded from prosecution as "obscene, indecent, offensive, disgusting or injurious to morality"; from the VAGRANCY ACT (1924), which bans indecent exhibitions; and the Burgh Police (Scotland) Act (1892), which deals with obscene performances in Scotland. The same test of indictable obscenity exists as in the 1959 act, and anyone who presents or directs, for gain or not, an obscene performance of a play given either in public or in private (other than as a domestic event in a private dwelling) may be prosecuted. The play's author, however, is not liable; although he or she technically "publishes" the play by offering it to a producer, the play does not become an "obscene article" unless it can be proved to corrupt those who have read it (the cast) rather than those who merely attend the theater (the audience). Only if the script is blatantly obscene or in some other way likely to deprave or corrupt, can an author be prosecuted directly.

Rehearsals and performances given for the purposes of being filmed, recorded or broadcast are exempted. DEFAMATION on stage comes under the libel laws rather than, as formerly, under the less serious crime of slander; the incitement of racial hatred is a criminal offense, as is a performance that uses threatening, abusive or insulting words or behavior if these are intended to cause a breach of the peace. Any proceedings against a play must be initiated by the attorney general in person or by someone authorized to do so by him. This ensures that management cannot be prosecuted at the whim of a private individual. Prosecutions of plays on charges of SEDITIOUS LIBEL, criminal libel and BLASPHEMY are still feasible. Censorship of plays does remain, but only indirectly in that local authorities, by refusing licenses to theaters or grants to certain companies, can and do impose a degree of restriction, although under the main provisions of the act such authorities may no longer impose conditions regarding the content of a play or the way in which it is performed.

SEE ALSO *Romans in Britain, The.*

Thirty Year Rule   This is a regulation governing British public records, as set down in the Public Records Acts of 1958 and 1967, whereby no records of the cabinet or of central government departments are made available for public inspection until 30 years have elapsed from the January that follows the year in which these records were originally complied. The documents in question are placed in the Public Records Office, where they are duly released after 30 years. Certain particularly sensitive material, notably that regarding Britain's secret services, the police, putative rebellions and any areas in which government activity might be seen to have been less than admirable, are subject to a 100-YEAR-RULE. However, as many historians and researchers have found, the idea that every government record is preserved is misleading. Current records are continually destroyed, to limit the mass of paperwork, and much important material is never filed. Critics contend that in addition there is the deliberate excision of difficult material, and the active sanitizing of possibly contentious records.

SEE Official Secrets Acts.

Thomas, J. Parnell   SEE House Committee on Un-American Activities.

Thomas, William   Thomas (d. 1554) was considered one of the ablest men of his era, holder of a church living and at one time clerk to the council of Edward VI. He wrote prolifically, among his most notable works being a defense of Henry VII entitled *Peregryne*. His *Historie of Italie*, published in 1549, included a number of attacks on Pope Paul III, and on the Vatican in general. Among Thomas' revelations was his statement that "by report, Rome is not without 40,000 harlots, maintained for the most part by the clergy and their followers ... Oh! what a world it is to see the pride and abomination that the churchmen there maintain." Although Edward VI ostensibly supported his father's Protestant doctrine, such an attack was considered unacceptable, and the *Historie* was burned, supposedly by the common hangman, a fate that was not repeated until PRYNNE's *Histriomastix* was similarly treated in 1633. Thomas was executed under Queen Mary in 1554 after Wyatt, the leader of a failed rebellion against the queen, claimed that the writer had been the instigator of the revolt. Thomas was hanged and quartered in May 1554, and his head was exposed on London Bridge. The *Historie* was republished in 1561, under Elizabeth I.

time-place-manner   Under the U.S. legal system, the concept of "time-place-manner" refers to the imposition of valid restrictions on the exercise of otherwise absolute freedoms as guaranteed by the FIRST AMENDMENT of the Constitution. Time-place-manner considerations have thus made it possible to prohibit freedom of political speechmaking and the distribution of campaigning material on military bases, the limiting by zoning requirements of areas where adult films may be exhibited, the restricting of certain material that includes filthy words to periods when minors will not be listening, regulations that control traffic, keep the streets clean, control noise and so on.

***Times Film* v. *Chicago* (1961)**   SEE *Don Juan*.

Tindal, Matthew   SEE book burning in England 7. United Kingdom (1688-1775).

Tisdall, Sarah   In 1983 Tisdall (1960-   ) had been a civil servant for three years, earning an exemplary record in the private office of Sir Geoffrey Howe, then foreign secretary of the Conservative government. On October 21, 1983, she was told to photocopy two documents; both had been written by Defense Secretary Michael Heseltine and were addressed to the prime minister, Mrs. Thatcher. Copies were distributed to the six senior members of the government. The papers referred to the imminent arrival in England of some 160 ground-launched "cruise" missiles—the Tomahawk BGM-109, or "glockum" in the jargon. Francis Pym, then defense secretary, had agreed in 1980 that the U.K. would accept the American missiles; 96 would be sited at the RAF base at Greenham Common and 64 at RAF Molesworth.

The first memo dealt with the arrival of the missiles, scheduled for November 1. Heseltine put forward his suggestions as to how best the government might maximize favorable media coverage and negate any opposition attacks. The second memo, potentially more damaging, dealt with

plans for increased security at Greenham, where a peace camp of women, regularly augmented by mass demonstrations, was creating both negative publicity and considerable disruption. The memo stated that were the protesters to penetrate too deeply into the camp, the security forces would be authorized to open fire on them; British troops, rather than the Americans also stationed at Greenham, would be responsible for the first shots. Tisdall read the documents, was appalled at their content and took an extra copy, which she delivered labeled "The Political Edition," to Britain's leading liberal daily newspaper, *The Guardian*.

After checking out the veracity of the documents through covert Ministry of Defence sources, the paper's defense correspondent wrote an 800-word lead story headlined "Whitehall sets November 1 cruise arrival." It appeared on October 22 and drew heavily on both memos although it made no specific references to either until, after a massive uproar from both the government and the anti-nuclear lobby, the paper published the text of the first document on October 31. There was no publcation of the second memo, which the paper saw as too sensitive for complete exposure, although a further lead story, on November 1, excited the controversy even further by referring directly to the official rules of engagement at Greenham that provided, in the last resort, for the use of weapons against demonstrators.

On November 11 the treasury solicitor, the government's lawyer, demanded the return of the published document, stating simply that it was government property. Rather than quickly destroy the memo the *Guardian*'s editor, Peter Preston, asked his lawyers whether such a move would be illegal. They told him yes. He then, in many eyes, compounded a tactical mistake by a strategic one: He informed the government that he did have the document but since it had markings that "might disclose or assist in the identification of the source" he wished to destroy them. He backed what might appear a naive belief in the inadequacy of police technology with the invocation of section 10 of the Contempt of Court Act (1981): "No court may require a person to disclose, nor is any person guilty of contempt of court for refusing to disclose, the source of information contained in a publication for which he is responsible, unless it be established to the satisfaction of the court that disclosure is necessary in the interests of justice or national security or for the prevention of disorder or crime."

The High Court rejected the *Guardian*'s plea on December 15th, and the Court of Appeals confirmed that judgment on the next day. National security was considered more important than the anonymity of a source, and the paper was to hand over the document at once, even though it had been given leave to appeal to the highest tribunal, the House of Lords. (The Lords, which did not adjudicate on the case until October 1984, only narrowly upheld the appeals court, by three votes to two). The *Guardian* then appeared to panic, and not only handed over the one document but, allegedly believing that the government knew all about the second memo anyway, admitted to its existence. This, the *Guardian* explained, was not capitulation but the sensible manipulation of a useful bargaining chip, intended to save the paper from a prosecution under the OFFICIAL SECRETS ACT. The paper was indeed saved, and its staff brought into line with threats of crippling contempt of court fines and thus the loss of their jobs. Tisdall was less fortunate: once the documents had been turned over, it was simple for government investigators to trace the material back to her. She confessed her action on January 9, 1984, and was charged under section two of the Official Secrets Act.

Her trial on March 23 lasted only 90 minutes. Guilty as charged, she was sentenced by Mr. Justice Cantley to six months in jail; she served four. Ironically the second memo was almost ignored in court. According to one's loyalties Tisdall was either a martyr or thoroughly deserving of her fate. A Freedom of Information campaign was launched, but its impetus barely survived Tisdall's incarceration.

Titicut Follies   Director Frederick Wiseman made this film in 1967. It was a documentary on the life of inmates at the state prison for the criminally insane at Bridgewater, Massachusetts. Wiseman had received permission from the Massachusetts attorney general in March 1966 and started shooting at the prison in April. Some 80,000 feet of film were exposed, and the finished documentary, in which nothing was faked, included scenes of the forced feeding of an inmate on hunger strike and of that inmate's subsequent death and burial; of one inmate's emotional outburst against the officers who had repeatedly taunted him with his failure to keep his cell clean; of body searches; of the interrogation by a staff psychiatrist of a sex attacker; of the condemnation by a schizophrenic inmate of the treatment he received from the staff, and of several similarly emotional situations. Wiseman undertook to accept four conditions when filming: (1) the rights of all inmates and patients would be fully protected; (2) only those inmates competent to sign the relevant releases would be included in the film; (3) each of those who appear on the film would have first to provide such a written release; (4) the completed film would require the approval of the prison's commissioner and superintendent before it could be exhibited in public.

When the commissioner viewed the final cut on June 1, 1967, his first objection was to the "excessive nudity" portrayed. When U.S. Attorney General Elliot Richardson saw it he felt that it constituted an invasion of privacy of those seen on the screen in a variety of humiliating and highly intimate situations. He suggested that if Wiseman really had obtained the required releases, they were not valid. On September 22, 1967, the commissioner told Wiseman that the film, as seen by him, could not be exhibited. Faithful to his contract with Grove Press for the distribution of the film, Wiseman ignored the ban and exhibited *Titicut Follies* in public. The state of Massachusetts immediately sued him and demanded that all potential income from exhibiting the film

be placed under a "constructive trust," whereby the filmmaker would be unable to touch any money accruing to his work.

The judge suggested that Wiseman had made his film under false pretenses, since the material he had shot was far more extensive than that which he had specified to the state attorney general when obtaining permission to film in the prison. He had also promised that the film would be non-sensational and non-commercial; in fact it was "crass commercialism, a most flagrant abuse of the privilege" given to the director. The entire film was a gross invasion of privacy. He then ruled that: (1) any releases that may have been obtained from the inmates were "a nullity"; (2) the film "is an unwarranted intrusion into the rights of privacy of each inmate pictured, degrading these persons in a manner clearly not warranted by any legitimate public concern"; (3) the public's right to know did not entail the humiliation of those whom it was attempting to find out about; (4) the state had a responsibility to protect the rights of inmates from exploitation; (5) the state must protect the rights of privacy of those in its custody. He then upheld the injunction against exhibiting the film, although the constructive trust applied only to future profits, not to those Wiseman had already made.

In an attempt to extend the provisions of the trust the state appealed to the Massachusetts Supreme Judicial Court, which refused to overturn the lower court decision and modified the original injunction to permit the film's being shown to "legislators, judges, lawyers, sociologists, social workers, doctors, psychiatrists, students in those or related fields and organizations dealing with the social problems of custodial care and mental infirmity." In their case, the public interest superseded the privacy of the inmates. Wiseman then attempted to appeal this decision to the U.S. Supreme Court, which refused to hear the case. In a dissenting opinion Justice Harlan, who with Justices Brennan and Douglas had wanted to hear Wiseman's appeal, pointed out that the film was "at once a scathing indictment of the inhumane conditions that prevailed at the time of the film and an undeniable infringement of the privacy of the inmates filmed ..." *Titicut Follies* was a perfect example of the clash between the Constitution's "committment to the principle that debate on public issues should be uninhibited, robust and wideopen ... and the individual's interest in privacy and dignity ..." The film remained limited to the categories of professional viewer listed above.

A related suit brought in New York by the officers of the prison, who claimed that the film had defamed them and invaded their privacy, was rejected. The federal district court ruled that the content of the film was protected by the free speech guarantees of the FIRST AMENDMENT. Since the plaintiffs could not prove that it was either obscene or "a false report made with knowledge of its falsity or in reckless disregard of the truth" it remained under that protection.

Tobacco Road   SEE *God's Little Acre*.

Toland, John Born in Ireland, Toland (1670-1722) rejected the "grossest superstition," i.e., Roman Catholicism, in his teens and turned to freethinking and pantheism, a term that he coined. Among other ideas was the formation of a society called "Socratia." Its hymns were to be the odes of Horace and its prayers blasphemous attacks on Rome. Alexander Pope was unimpressed, but Swift called him "the great Oracle of the Anti-Christians." In 1696 Toland wrote his major work, *Christianity not Mysterious*, which proposed the natural religion of Deism, in which a Supreme Being was the source of finite existence, rather than the received religion of Christianity, with its supernatural doctrines and revelations. The book was burned in Dublin in 1696 on the orders of the Committee of Religion of the Irish House of Commons, and some members even demanded that Toland should be burned with it. His position was not helped by his own arrogant intransigence, and William Molyneux, a campaigner for Irish independence, pointed out in a letter to the philosopher John Locke in May 1697: "He has raised against him the clamour of all parties; and this is not so much by his difference in opinion as by his unseasonable way of discoursing, propagating and maintaining." Toland traveled in Europe and continued to write until his death; his works included a *Life of Milton* (1698) and the *Pantheisticon* (1720), although no book ever rivaled the notoriety of his first.

Tomorrow's Children The subject of this film, made in 1934, is sterilization. Its plot concerns an unfortunate family in which both parents are alcoholics, a son is in jail and a daughter physically handicapped. Only a second, adopted daughter is untainted. The Welfare Board persuades the parents to have themselves and all three children sterilized, and the plot revolves around the last-minute escape of the "normal" daughter from the knife. The film's moral is that sterilization decisions must be taken with proper care and not on the basis of arbitrary bias. It included a court scene that cast an unfavorable light on the honesty of the legal process in such decisions.

With such a topic, the film was duly banned by the New York censor on every occasion on which it was presented for review between 1934 and 1937. It was cited as immoral and tending to corrupt the morals of those who saw it. In 1937 the owners, Foy Productions, took the censor to court, but three successive levels of New York courts affirmed the ban. Foy argued that the banning of the film was unconstitutional. The courts were unimpressed, defining *Tomorrow's Children* as "a studied creation inherently tending to distort the minds of the unwary and of children, to teach the corruption of courts, and to portray devices for circumventing the Penal Law." The court added that "many things may be necessary in surgery that are not proper subjects for the movies." As well as being immoral and distasteful, the court also ruled that the film was "a clear violation" of the statutory prohibition on any material disseminating information on contraception or sex education. In their dissenting opinion, two judges in the New York Court of Appeals attacked this verdict, claiming that the film was not prurient, did not advocate sterilization as an alternative form of contraception and was "a forceful and dramatic argument against the enactment of statutes" that are "a disputatious matter of public concern." They added that to ban the discussion of sterilization or any kindred topics "presents the issue of whether our people may govern themselves or be governed; whether arguments for and against proposed and impending legislation may be presented directly in the public prints, on the stage and by films, or whether a Commission or Commissioner is to determine the limit and character of information to be given to the public. Ministers of propaganda are favored in certain jurisdictions, but agencies of that kind have never been approved here."

Trevelyan, John John Trevelyan (1903-86), "the film censor with the diplomatic touch" (London *Times* obituary), was born in Beckenham, Kent, the son of a parson and educated at public school and Cambridge University. He worked briefly for a bank and then as teacher in West Africa. After being invalided home he started 20 years of work as an educational administrator in the U.K. While working in occupied Germany, establishing schools for the children of Allied servicemen, he wrote a letter attacking the BRITISH BOARD OF FILM CENSORS (BBFC) for its failure to take into account the effect of films on the young. In 1951, back in England, he was asked to apply for a vacancy as an examiner for the BBFC. In 1959 he became the board's secretary and as such the official censor of films shown in Britain.

Trevelyan's administration of British film censorship coincided with the permissive Sixties, an era when traditional restraints were being discarded in many areas of society, especially in the mass media. Unusual in being what he called "a censor who did not believe in censorship as a principle," Trevelyan had a massive effect on the development of film in the U.K. Compared to many of his predecessors, he stood out as a superliberal, and as such was vilified by more conservative pressure groups, but his concern for the young was never relaxed, however much he was determined to ensure that film sensibilities kept abreast of contemporary changes. He made it possible for many of the talents that were emerging at the time to flourish, relatively unrestricted by his cuts. His most celebrated act was his personal attempt to halt the police seizure of the Andy Warhold film FLESH while it was being screened at the Open Space theater club in London. The raid was not stopped, although the prosecution failed, but Trevelyan was confirmed as a champion of artistic freedom. He resigned from the BBFC in 1971, publishing his memoirs, *What the Censor Saw*, in 1973. Before his death he briefly worked to coordinate Britain's flourishing print pornography industry, appointed by a committee of men's magazine owners to represent their interests to the authorities.

Tribun du Peuple, Le SEE Babeuf, Francois.

Tridentine Index

1. history This Index was the first one to be backed by the authority of a papal general council. It dated from the council's fourth session in April 1546, when a papal decree, "De editione et usu librorum sacrorum," laid out the principles for the reading and interpretation of the Bible and called upon the council to establish regulations for the control of printing. Although some members felt that the ROMAN INDEX OF 1559 had preempted for the time being any further such edict, the Tridentine Index, or Index of Pius IV, duly appeared in 1564, at the 18th session of the council. It represented both the most efficient codification to date of the Catholic system of censorship and the realization by the church that, even though it was impossible to stamp out the ever-strengthening Protestant revolt, it was still advisable to set down regulations governing members of the true faith, and to justify those regulations by a wide-ranging reform of the church. The Tridentine Index embodied the censorship system of the Counter-Reformation.

The most important creation of the new Index was its Ten Rules (see below). Although they were occasionally modified and even temporarily suspended in subsequent Indexes, the rules formed the basis of all such edicts, both in Rome and in Spain, until the 20th century. As such the Index was distributed far more widely than any previous such compilation and extended church censorship further, and more successfully, than any previous effort. A number of regional Indexes followed, based to a large extent on the Tridentine. They included those of Antwerp (1569, 1570, 1571), Parma (1580), Lisbon (1581) and Madrid (INDEX OF QUIROGA, 1583). These naturally differed in detail from the Tridentine, but may be seen as extensions of the major Roman index.

Its effect was to modify, albeit slightly, some of the more sweepingly condemnatory regulations of the 1559 Index, giving a greater voice to the church's moderates, notably the delegates from Germany. Where Paul had issued blanket prohibitions, Pius attempted to be more discriminating, expurgating rather than banning wholesale. However, this moderation was in itself somewhat watered-down, since no guidelines were included as to which such cuts and emendations should be made. The Index turned the task of expurgation over to "Catholic divines" but few dioceses actually held men of sufficient theological expertise. The CONGREGATION OF THE INDEX, established in 1571, was created to fill this gap, but few expurgated texts appeared prior to the 1590s. The Index was further complicated by the contradictions implicit in its relatively vague rulings, tending to the moderate in the lists of those authors prohibited. If in doubt the local official would err to the conservative, excluding for safety's sake the permitted works of those authors whose other books were definitely proscribed. The one detailed rule, rule 10, which dealt with the printing, distribution and selling of books, was unmistakably repressive, ensuring that all such functions remained strictly under ecclesiastical control.

SEE ALSO Index of Indexes.

2. the ten rules Under the Tridentine Index the following material was prohibited and the following rules promulgated as regards reading, printing and distributing printed works:

1. All books condemned by the supreme pontiffs, or general councils, before the year 1515, and not comprised in the present Index are, nevertheless, to be considered as condemned.
2. The books of heresiarchs, whether of those who broached or disseminated their heresies prior to [1515] or of those who have been, or are, the heads or leaders of heretics ... are altogether forbidden, whatever may be their titles or subjects. And the books of other heretics, that treat professedly upon religion, are totally condemned; but those that do not treat upon religion are allowed to be read, after having been examined and approved by Catholic divines ... Those Catholic books are also permitted to be read that have been composed by authors who have afterwards fallen into heresy, or who, after their fall, have returned to the bosom of the Church, provided these have been approved ...
3. Translations of ecclesiastical writers, which have been hitherto published by the condemned authors, are permitted to be read, if they contain nothing contrary to sound doctrine. Translations of the Old Testament may also be allowed, but only to pious and learned men, at the discretion of the bishop; provided they use them merely as elucidations of the Vulgate ... But translations of the New Testament, made by [heresiarchs] are allowed to no one, since little advantage, but much danger, generally arises from reading them ...
4. ... bishops or inquisitors ... may ... permit the reading of the Bible, translated into the vulgar tongue by Catholic authors, to those persons whose faith and piety, they apprehend, will be augmented and not injured by it; and this permission they must have in writing. But if anyone shall have the presumption to read or possess it without permission, he shall not receive absolution until he have first delivered up such Bible to the ordinary. Booksellers ... who sell or otherwise dispose of Bibles in the vulgar tongue ... not having such permission, shall forfeit the value of the books ...
5. Books of which heretics are the editors, but that contain little or nothing of their own, being mere compilations from others ... may be allowed ... after there have been made ... such corrections and emendations as may be deemed requisite.
6. Books of controversy between the Catholics and heretics of the present time, written in the vulgar tongue, are not to be indiscriminately allowed, but are to be subject to the same regulations as Bibles in the vulgar tongue.
7. Books professedly treating of lascivious or obscene subjects, or narrating or teaching these, are utterly prohibited, since not only faith but morals, which are readily corrupted by the perusal of them, are to be considered; and those who possess them shall be severely punished by the bishop. But the works of antiquity, written by the heathen, are permitted to be read, because of the elegance and propriety of the language; though on no account shall they be suffered to be read by young readers.
8. Books, the principle subject of which is good, but in which some things are occasionally introduced tending to heresy and impiety, divination or superstition, may be allowed, after they

have been corrected ... The same judgment is also given concerning prefaces, summaries, or notes, taken from condemned authors and inserted in the works of authors not condemned ...

9. All books and writings of geomancy, hydromancy, aeromancy, pyromancy, cheiromancy and necromancy; or that treat of sorceries, poisons, auguries, auspices or magical incantations are utterly rejected. The bishops shall also diligently guard against any persons reading or keeping any books, treaties or indexes that treat of judicial astrology or contain presumptuous predictions of the events of future contingencies ... or of those actions that depend upon the will of man. But such opinions and observations of natural things as are written in aid of navigation, agriculture and medicine are permitted.

10. ... if any book is to be printed in the city of Rome, it shall first be examined by the vicar of the pope or the MAGISTER SACRI PALATII or by any other person chosen by our most holy Father ... In places other than Rome, the examination ... shall be referred to the bishop with whom shall be associated the inquisitor of heretical depravity of the city or diocese in which the printing is done, and those officials shall ... affix their approbation to the work in their own handwriting, such approval being subject, however, to the pains and censures contained in the said decree ... an authentic copy of the book to be printed, signed by the author himself, shall remain in the hands of the examiner ...

The houses or places in which the work of printing is carried on, and also the shops of booksellers, shall be frequently visited by persons deputed for that purpose ... so that nothing that is prohibited may be printed, kept or sold. Booksellers ... shall keep in their libraries a catalogue ... of the books that they have on sale, nor shall they keep, or sell, nor in any way dispose of, any other books without permission ... under pain of forfeiting the books, and of liability to other penalties ... If persons import foreign books ... they shall be obliged to announce them to the deputies ... and no one shall presume to read or lend or sell any book that he or any other person has brought into the city until he has shown it to the deputies and obtained their permission ... Heirs and testamentary executors shall make no use of the books of the deceased, nor in any way transfer them to others, until they have presented a catalogue of them to the deputies and have obtained their license ...

Finally it is enjoined on all the faithful that no one presume to keep or read any books contrary to these Rules or prohibited by this Index. But if anyone read or keep any books composed by heretics, or the writings of any author suspected of excommunication, and those who read or keep works interdicted on another account, in addition to the burden of mortal sin, shall ... be severely punished.

Trimmer, Sarah Kirby   SEE The Bible.

Trocchi, Alexander   SEE *Cain's Book*; *My Life and Loves*.

Tropic of Cancer   Of Henry Miller's many books, "the Tropics," respectively of *Cancer* (1934) and of *Capricorn* (1939), are the best-known and have been the most frequently

censored. For those who subscribed regularly to JACK KAHANE's Paris-based OBELISK PRESS Miller's first novel, a memoir of amatory and other escapades in contemporary Paris, might have seemed at home in the mix of youthful experimentation by such authors as Lawrence Durrell and Cyril Connolly and the companion volumes of pseudonymous pornographers. The U.S. Customs was less liberal. It seized *Tropic of Cancer* in 1934, using the provisions of the Tariff Act to submit Miller's book to a district court, which classified it as obscene, confiscated and destroyed the seized copy and proscribed any further attempts to import the title. Its successor, *Tropic of Capricorn*, was treated similarly in 1939, and neither of the two books was freely available in America until 1961 in the Grove Press used the provisions of the ROTH STANDARD to publish new editions. In the meantime successive courts decried the novels as likely to "incite to disgusting practices and to hideous crimes" and as standing "at the nadir of scatology." As for Miller, he "descends into the filthy gutter" and his writing is "filthy, disgusting and offensive to good taste."

Once the Grove Press edition appeared, a number of cases were instituted against *Tropic of Cancer*. It was acquitted of obscenity in California (*Zeitlin* v. *Arneburgh* [1963]) and in Wisconsin (*McCauley* v. *Tropic of Cancer* [1963]), but condemned in the lower courts of Massachusetts (*Attorney General* v. *The Book Named Tropic of Cancer* [1962]), New York (*People* v. *Fritch* [1963]) and Florida (*Grove Press* v. *Gerstein* [1963]). The appellate courts of both Massachusetts and New York reversed the convictions of Miller's book, the former accepting that it was a genuine literary work, and the latter that to ban it would be to take on "the role of the censor, a role that is incompatible with the fundamentals of a free society." Only in Florida, where the court held that the book was one "into which filth was packed," did the state's obduracy drive the defendants into the U.S. Supreme Court. In 5-4 per curiam decision (a decision that represents the overall views of the justices and is not considered to require any expanded explanation) the court simply declared that *Tropic of Cancer* was not obscene and freed it for all future American readers.

SEE ALSO Miller, Henry; United States 21. Tariff Act (1930).

Tropic of Capricorn   SEE *Tropic of Cancer*; Miller, Henry.

Tsin Chi Wang-Ti   In 213 B.C., this emperor of China, whose public works included the construction of the Great Wall (between 214 and 204 B.C.), launched a crusade agaisnt books. He attempted, according to Edmund Gosse, "the extinction of all literature, root and branch, with the exception of those books dealing specifically with medicine, agriculture and science. Not only were the books burned, but five hundred of the literati who had offended him most were executed and banished."

Turkey Article two of the Constitution of 1982 guarantees human rights "within the concepts of public peace, national security and justice," but article 13 restricts those rights "by law … with the aim of safeguarding the state … [its] national security, public order, general tranquility … public morals and public health …" Censorship of the Turkish media exists under three laws: the state constitution, the Penal Code and the "New Police Law" of June 1985, itself a series of amendments of the Police Duties and Powers Act of 1934.

Anyone who "writes or prints any news or articles that threaten the internal or external security of the State … or that tend to incite offense, riot or insurrection" is breaking the law and faces punishment. Article 140 of the Penal Code provides for the imprisonment of those who make allegations or statements detrimental to Turkey's reputation abroad. This article has been used to ban newspapers and imprison critical reporters. Article 163 of the code forbids the advocacy of religious sects. Police powers are greatly increased under the 1985 act; officers may now close down plays, films or videotape performances that may be construed as "harmful to the individisible integrity of the State." They may arrest without warrant anyone seen as continuing "to disturb the peace and tranquility of the public." While the relaxation in the overall control of Turkish society (with the end of martial law) has obviously included the less aggressive implementation of censorship, the machinery remains in place, although less actively implemented. No prior censorship exists but a number of books are still banned and writers and publishers face suspension from their job or even imprisonment if they overstep what the state decrees as acceptable limits.

There is no prior censorship of the press, which is all in private hands. Following the end of military rule in 1985 there has been an upsurge in the freedom to criticize the government and to cover major issues—such as torture—that were hitherto untouchable. Conversely a number of journalists who were imprisoned under martial law remain in jail, and it was reported in February 1987 that the writers, translators and publishers of 240 publications had been charged under the Press Act since 1984. A major source of such prosecutions is the crime of "insulting" the government.

The banning of books continues. After a comprehensive list of banned titles—all branded "means of separatist propaganda"—was circulated by the Ministry of Justice to the country's educational institutions in October 1986 some 39 tons of material were sent for pulping. Titles included a number of Western atlases and the *Encyclopedia Britannica*. The publishing of the Law to Protect Minors in 1986 has helped control magazines, authors and publishers. Ostensibly aiming at pornography, its supervisory committee (that meets eight or nine times each month to examine current publications), has used the law to attack a variety of material, including the film *Gandhi* and the philosopher David Hume's *On Religion*. A number of allegedly obscene magazines have been banned. The Committee also threatens to ban any material that contains slang. Criticizing the law can also lead to suppression of the magazine in which the attack appears.

Further press controls are exercized by the Press Council, a self-regulating body established in July 1986. The Council claims to be a defender of the free press and the public right to know; it also wishes to safeguard the dignity and integrity of the press. Its members, mainly television officials and print media proprietors, subject themselves to a voluntary moral code and can penalize journalists who report "false" information.

Radio and television are both state-owned and duly censored of contentious material. Since 1985, however, this censorship has been gradually relaxed and stories on opposition politicians, once invisible, are now common. The civilian government has moved the censorship of film from the Ministry of the Interior to that of Tourism and Culture. This raised hopes of a greater liberalization, but this has yet to materialize. The Ministry of the Interior, and the military, still have a large say in the control of Turkish cinema.

Tyndale, William Tyndale (1495?-1536) was one of the foremost scholars of the Reformation who in 1522 commenced his major work: the translation of portions of the Bible into the vernacular. When the pursuit of this project in England proved difficult, and the work was described as "pernicious merchandise," he moved to Germany, visiting LUTHER at Wittenberg and printing the first sections of his translation of the New Testament at Cologne in 1525. The Pentateuch followed in 1530 and the Book of Jonah in 1531. The whole translation was completed at Worms, then smuggled back into Tyndale's native England. Here it was denounced by the bishops, who objected to what they interpreted as his seditious notes on the scriptures, and burned publicly at St. Paul's Cathedral. Of 6,000 copies, all but one were destroyed. As well as destroying every copy discovered in England, the authorities attempted to hunt down those circulating abroad. Pursued by Cardinal Wolsey, who ordered him arrested, Tyndale immigrated to Antwerp, where he embraced the doctrines of the Swiss protestant reformer, Ulrich Zwingli (1485-1531), and continued his scholarly work, engaging in a major dispute with Sir Thomas More. In 1530 his book, *The Practise of Prelates*, a treatise attacking the Catholic clergy and condemning the divorce of Henry VIII, was banned in Germany. Tyndale was betrayed to the imperial authorities in 1535 and arrested on charges of heresy. He was strangled and burned at the stake in Vilvorde in 1535, accompanied by copies of his works (of which 50,000 copies were already in circulation) and despite a plea for clemency from Thomas Cromwell. His last words were, "Lord, open the King of England's eyes!" In 1546 the archibshop of Canterbury ordered Tyndale's works to be burned, specifically because in them he had described the church authorities as "horse-leeches, maggots and caterpillars." His work was banned again by Queen Mary in 1555 as part of her general drive against Protestant heresies.

U

Uganda Following the repressive government of Idi Amin (1971-79), with all its commensurate censorship and arbitrary attacks on freedom of expression the Ugandan press enjoyed a period as the freest and most prolific in Africa. Thirty-plus papers appeared regularly, reflecting a rainbow of ideologies. This situation was short-lived. After the election of Milton Obote's Uganda People's Conference in 1980 press freedoms faced new restrictions and by 1984 few journals offered anything but the official line. As well as censorship, the UPC began detaining writers whose work was seen as designed to "spoil the name of the government." Obote's regime was overthrown in 1986 and replaced by the National Resistance Movement, which is the current government, and the media began once more to experience less stringent controls.

There are no actual censorship laws in Uganda, but a limited supply of newsprint, due to high costs, limits all publications. All topics are open to discussion, although the authorities have warned editors against "exaggerated and false" reporting. President Musveni is particularly keen to quell any reports of alleged human rights violations during the war with rebel forces in the north. Journalists have received a number of directives urging the importance of positive writing, rather than "blowing up negative issues."

Ulysses

1. book James Joyce's novel *Ulysses* was first published in 1921 by Shakespeare & Co. in Paris. The first edition was of 1,000 copies, printed in Dijon and distributed to subscribers throughout the world. A second edition of 2,000 copies, for the Egoist Press, was printed, also at Dijon, in October 1922. These were distributed, without hindrance, to individual purchasers, bookshops and their agents. In January 1923 there was a third printing, of 500 copies, also for the Egoist Press. Of these, only one copy reached its London destination, the remaining 499 were seized by English customs at Folkestone. Under the 1867 Customs Act, the confiscated volumes were burned before their publisher, Harriet Weaver, could save them. Sylvia Beach, of Shakespeare & Co., continued to print *Ulysses* in order to meet a growing demand for the book. British customs continued to search for copies in the luggage of tourists returning from France. Those copies discovered were confiscated and destroyed. Alfred Noyes, a poet and writer with an obsessive hatred for Joyce and kindred Modernist writers, campaigned against the book and managed to have a broadcast referring to it canceled and to have a copy withdrawn from a sale in 1930 of the library of the late Lord Birkenhead. Sotheby's, the auctioneers, did not dare to put the corrected proofs into one of its sales.

The book received similar treatment in America, starting with the prosecution of Margaret Anderson, who began serializing episodes from the yet-unpublished novel in her magazine, *The Little Review*, in 1919. In February 1921 she was fined for this publication and would have gone to prison rather than pay, but another woman, who disliked the book, paid off her fine rather than let her become an imprisoned martyr. When the complete book was published many copies eluded the Customs ban on its importation. Some 30,000 bowdlerized and pirated editions appeared to supply the massive American demand. In 1928 SAMUEL ROTH serialized the book, with some cuts, in his *Two Worlds Monthly* and later served 60 days in jail for distributing an unexpurgated edition in 1930.

In 1933 Random House, which was preparing an uncut edition for publication, decided to challenge the Customs ruling. It carefully primed the authorities, then attempted to "smuggle" in an unexpurgated edition. The Customs failed to respond, but the charade was enacted again, and the vital copy was duly seized under the Tariff Act (1930). Random House was charged under the act. In a ruling by Federal Judge John M. Woolsey, subsequently upheld in the Supreme Court by Justice Augustus Hand, *Ulysses* gained official recognition as art and was confirmed as not being obscene under the Tariff Act or any other regulation.

Woolsey made four explanatory points to set his landmark decision in context: If a book was deliberately written as titillatory pornography, then there was no valid defense against its prosecution; if obscene means "tending to stir the sex impulses or lead to sexually impure and lustful thoughts," then the person likely to have those impulses or thoughts must be "l'homme moyen sensuel," the average person, the equivalent to the "reasonable man" in the law of torts; works of physiology, medicine, science and sex instruction were to be immune from prosecution; "the proper test of whether a given book is obscene is its dominant effect." The opinions of experts were of paramount importance, since "works of art are not likely to sustain a high position with no better warrant for their existence than an obscene content."

Woolsey then made an order for the book to be allowed in America and declared:

It may be that *Ulysses* will not last as a substantial contribution to literature, and it is certainly easy to believe that in spite of Joyce's laudators, the immortals will still reign, but the same thing may be said of current works of art and music and of many other serious efforts of the mind. Art certainly cannot advance under compulsion to traditional forms, and nothing in such a field is more stifling to progress than limitation of the right to experiment with a new technique … We think *Ulysses* is a book of originality and sincerity of treatment and that it has not the effect of promoting lust …

After 1933, when the decision in the U.S. courts freed the book from any future censorship, *Ulysses* gained general currency, particularly in the unexpurgated edition that appeared in England and America in 1937. In England the prosecutions simply faded away. Some quiet censorship did remain: In the Caedmon Records Literary series recording of the Molly Bloom soliloquy that ends the book, certain passages were excised, although no mention was made of this on the record's cover.

SEE ALSO Ulysses Standard; United States 21. Tariff Act (1930).

2. film Joyce's novel faced its last prosecutions before World War II. Afterwards it was generally acknowledged as a literary masterpiece, but this essentially limited tolerance did not extend to the wider world of film. In 1965 director Joseph Strick began making a film of the book; it was completed for release in 1967. This version antagonized the BRITISH BOARD OF FILM CENSORS, which demanded substantial cuts. The proposed changes were generally on the same lines as those once demanded by earlier opponents of the book: Buck Mulligan's cod Mass that opens the book, scenes from the "Night-town" sequence, a variety of references to sex. The Molly Bloom soliloquy that ends the novel was particularly savaged, with 18 separate cuts—some of them quite lengthy—required. The submission of *Ulysses* to the BBFC happened to coincide with the prosecution of Hubert Selby's *Last Exit to Brooklyn* in the British courts. Given this background, the board felt that if it was to fulfill its "responsibility to protect film companies from court actions" (Trevelyan, op. cit.) Strick's film must be substantially altered.

Strick was unimpressed by this ostensible solicitude. He claimed that the board was the only censor in the world to demand alterations (true enough, since it was the only one to have seen the film), and he fought back by making the cuts, but in a novel way. Either the soundtrack was excised and the visual left, or the visuals cut and the soundtrack untouched. Where the track had been cut, there were now notable "bleeps." The board duly awarded an X certificate, although neither party was satisfied. Strick then took his film to the Greater London Council, which chose to pass it uncut. The board eventually followed, allowing Strick to restore the cuts in 1970.

Ulysses Standard Making his ruling in the case of *United States* v. *One Book Entitled Ulysses* (1934), which had been brought to determine whether or not the book was obscene under the provisions of the Tariff Act (1930), Judge John M. Woolsey laid down a test for obscenity that replaced the archaic HICKLIN RULE, which had been taken from Victorian England and used since 1868. This revised test had set the ground rules for all subsequent standards adopted in America. Woolsey stated: "We think the same immunity should apply to literature as to science, where the presentation, when viewed objectively, is sincere, and the erotic matter is not introduced to promote lust and does not furnish the dominant note of the publication. The question in each case is whether the publication taken as a whole has a libidinous effect."

"Unigenitus" The Papal bull "Unigenitus" was issued in September 1713 by Pope Clement XI, who had been urged by Louis XIV of France to condemn the allegedly heretical doctrines of JANSENISM, which were especially popular in his country. The bull is specifically aimed at the *Commentary on the New Testament*, a book first published in 1671 by PASQUIER QUESNEL (1634-1719), and it condemns 101 propositions found in the *Commentary*, many of them already given the authority of the scriptures. The bull was accepted by the parliament of Paris but after Louis' death in September 1715, the theological faculties of the French universities, backed by 30 bishops, demanded modificatons and clarifications in its text. Two groups emerged: the Apellants, who were calling for changes in the bull, notably for the precise definition of why certain propositions had been condemned; and the Acceptants, who abided by the bull as promulgated.

This controversy soon moved into a debate over papal infallibility: Could the Pope lay down dogma without challenge? The papal response was to reject the Apellants and confirm the Pope's position in a second bull, issued in 1719. This confirmed the condemnations and demanded absolute and unquestioning obedience from the church. The Apellants then split further, into those who now accepted the papal will and those, called Re-Apellants, who continued to question it. The controversy continued through the first half of the 18th century, gradually fading away after Pope Benedict XIV modified the papal position on infallibility, although not the condemnation itself, saying that the bull was not a final and immutable conclusion, but a papal utterance that deserved respect. He continued to ban works relating to Quesnel and Jansenism in his general decrees.

United Kingdom—contemporary censorship

1. customs and post office legislation Under the Customs Consolidation Act (1876), the importation into Britain of any indecent or obscene works (including films) is forbidden and Customs is empowered to seize such materials. This ban, which was listed between regulations dealing with coffee and snuff, was retained when the act was modernized in 1952. As stated in section 42, these materials include "indecent or obscene prints, paintings, photographs, books, cards, lithographic or other engravings, or any other indecent or obscene articles." Many of the items that are confiscated and destroyed, the numbers of which run into hundreds of thousands every year, would have been acquitted in court, but are subject at Britain's points of entry to the personal judgment of individual Customs officers. Officers are, however, instructed to ignore the odd "dirty book" or magazine (other than any item featuring child pornography), obviously imported for personal rather than commercial use and such material as may be needed for academic research etc.

Since 1978 Customs has extended its responsibilities to dealing with indecent or obscene matter passing through the overseas post. The Commissioners of Customs and Excise compile a constantly updated black list of such material, based largely on the titles of books that have already been prosecuted. This list is not regarded as comprehensive, but provides the running basis on which officers can conduct searches. The list is classified for Customs use only and is not published. Under the Customs and Excise Management Act (1979) anyone whose books are seized has a month in which to make an objection to the commissioners; after that period, if no complaint has been registered, the books are automatically forfeited without opportunity for proceedings, although Customs is under no obligation to inform the public of this right, nor will it do so. If the individual does object in time, the matter can go to court, although Customs need not return the material in question for use in the preparation of the defendant's case. Even if the books are acquitted in a lower court, Customs may appeal its case all the way to the House of Lords.

An attempt to make the destruction of the material subject to a court order, whether or not an individual has actually complained against the seizure, was rejected by Customs, which alleged that it would be expensive and time-consuming. When material seized by Customs does come to court, the defendant has no recourse to the defense of "literary merit"; expert witnesses are not permitted and the material may be condemned if only parts, rather than the whole work, are found to be obscene.

Under the Post Office Act (1953) (see below) it is forbidden to send a postal packet that contains indecent or obscene material. The Post Office authorities are authorized to detain and destroy such matter. No evidence as to whether or not the material is obscene is allowed, and the fact that the sender may have had some laudable purpose in posting the material is no defense. The provisions of the OBSCENE PUBLICATIONS ACT (1959) are irrelevant to cases brought under the Post Office act. Material found acceptable under one, may still be obscene under the other. When the OZ TRIAL defendants appealed against their convictions in 1972, the sentence under the Obscene Publications Act was duly reversed; that stemming from the Post Office Act was upheld. The majority of seizures, which run at around 800 per year, are from overseas. Under the Unsolicited Goods and Services Act (1971), the mailing of unsolicited material of a sexual nature is illegal. The Post Office has the power under both pieces of legislation to open sealed packets that it suspects of containing prohibited matter. Under section 66 of the act it is similarly prohibited to "send any message by telephone that is grossly offensive or of an indecent, obscene or menacing character."

2. Indecent Advertisements Act (1889)   This act provides an extra means of enforcing the banning of indecent and obscene material from public eyes, and as such is allied to the VAGRANCY ACT (1824) and its concomitant bylaws and local variations. It was the brainchild of the NATIONAL VIGILANCE ASSOCIATION, the figurehead organization of the late-19th-century social purity movement in England, and was drafted by the association's legal department. The act, which has remained in force ever since, states:

3. Whoever affixes or inscribes on any house, building, wall, hoarding, gate, fence, pillar, post, board, tree, or any other thing whatsoever so as to be visible to a person being in or passing along any street, public highway, or footpath, and whoever affixes to or inscribes on any public urinal, or delivers or attempts to deliver or exhibits, to any inhabitant or to any person being in or passing along any street, public highway, or footpath, or throws down the area of any house, or exhibits to public view in the window of any house or shop, any picture or printed or written matter that is of an indecent or obscene nature, shall ... be liable to a penalty not exceeding forty shillings, or ... to imprisonment for any term not exceeding one month ...
4. Whoever gives or delivers to any other person such pictures, or printed or written matter mentioned in section three of this Act, with the intent that the same, or some one or more thereof, should be affixed, inscribed, delivered, or exhibited as therein mentioned, shall ... be liable to a penalty not exceeding five pounds, or ... imprisonment for any term not exceeding three months ...
5. Any advertisement relating to syphilis, gonorrhoea, nervous debility, or other complaint or infirmity arising from or relating to sexual intercourse, shall be deemed to be printed or written matter of an indecent nature within the meaning of section three of this act, if such an advertisement is affixed to or inscribed on any house, building, wall, hoarding, gate, fence, pillar, post, board, tree, or any other thing whatsoever so as to be visible to a person being in or passing along any street, public highway, or footpath, or is affixed to or inscribed on any public urinal, or is delivered or attempted to be delivered to any person being in or passing along any street, public highway, or footpath.

Public indecency is further regulated by two more laws. The Indecent Displays (Control) Act (1981) makes it an offense to display indecent matter in, or so as to be visible from, any public place. The law is aimed particularly at the window displays of Britain's adult bookstores, which shops, with their windows filled with potentially shocking material, had burgeoned during the 1970s. Since the passage of the act, all such premises have emptied their windows, displaying instead a notice that states, "WARNING. Persons passing beyond this notice will find material on display which they may consider indecent. No admittances to persons under eighteen yeras of age." The Local Government (Miscellaneous Provisions) Act (1982) enables local councils to state the conditions for the regulation of the display and advertising of licensed sex shops and sex cinemas, and to withdraw those licenses—and thus close down the premises—if those conditions, which invariably prohibit the display of indecent matter, are breached.

3. Law of Confidence The Law of Confidence, which is not a statutory law but one made in court by a judge, developed in the mid-19th century. The plaintiff in an action to stop a publication on the grounds of confidentiality is claiming a right to protect privacy, or at least private property. This claim then puts in opposition the public interest of the plaintiff and the public interest of publishing the information under dispute. When the plaintiff is attempting by his or her claim to cover up fraud, crime or iniquitous behavior, then the court can easily rule for disclosure. But such cases are often more finely balanced, and courts must decide between what is in the end sensationalism, and what actually makes a useful contribution to public debate. In these cases the law does allow for a public interest defence, but at the same time offers the public no cut-and-dried right to know. Plaintiffs can often persuade a judge to grant an interim injunction, which does not preclude a trial, but puts it off for what may be several years, thus permitting what might be a highly contentious issue, if tried immediately, to recede from the public interest.

Legal confidentiality was invented for the specific purpose of stopping one Strange from exploiting the royal family by publishing a catalog of some privately printed etchings made by Queen Victoria and Prince Albert. From there it was extended to cover commercial secrets. In 1967 the law was extended further, to encompass private rights, when it was used to grant an injunction against publication to the Duchess of Argyll, who wished to stop a Sunday newspaper from publishing her husband the duke's memoirs of their less than peaceful marriage. More notoriously the law was used, without success, in the cases of the CROSSMAN DIARIES and in the thalidomide case, both of which involved the London *Sunday Times* and in the prosecution of Peter Wright's *Spycatcher*.

Breach of confidence is a civil remedy that protects a plaintiff against the disclosure or use of information, which is not publicly known and which has only been handed over on the basis that it will not be further disseminated until the person from whom it originally came gives permission to do so. Thus when a journalist obtains secret information, his or her editor must decide whether it is confidential, in legal terms; whether, even if it is confidential, it should be published on the grounds of public interest; and if it is published, does there remain the danger of an injunction? That the information may be marked "Confidential" or that it has been obtained in an underhand way—tapping a telephone or making a clandestine film—does not matter; there must be an existing and enforceable legal relationship of confidentiality.

The law is unique to Britain; when the European Court of Human Rights was asked to assess it regarding the suppression of information on the thalidomide affair it was unable to find anything in the Declaration of Human Rights that dealt with breaches of confidence and could not thus adjudicate in favor of the *Sunday Times*.

4. Northern Ireland: censorship laws Although Northern Ireland is a part of the British Isles, sectarian warfare there between Catholics and Protestants, and the presence since 1969 of British troops, has ensured the existence of certain special provisions concerning the reporting of events in the Six Counties. Two statutes deal with "the troubles," and each one deals at least in part with the censorship of information.

Under section 22 of the Emergency Provisions (Northern Ireland) Act (1978) it is forbidden to collect, record, publish or attempt to elicit any information (including the taking of photographs) concerning the army, police, judges, court officials or prison officers, which might be used by terrorists. It is similarly an offense to collect or record any information that might be used by terrorists to further an act of violence, or to possess any record or other document that contains information of this sort. While the act is primarily aimed at espionage, this section can easily be extended to journalistic research. A defendant charged under the act can offer a plea of reasonable excuse or lawful authority, but the onus of proof is placed on the defendant rather than, as is usual under British law, on the prosecution. These offenses apply only to Northern Ireland, and no prosecution can be undertaken without the express approval of the director of public prosecutions.

Under section 11 of the Prevention of Terrorism (Temporary Provisions) Act (1976), which applies in mainland Britain as well as in Northern Ireland, all subjects have a positive duty to inform the police of any facts that might assist either in preventing an act of terrorism or lead to the arrest, prosecution and conviction of someone suspected of terrorist activities. This section can be extended to those journalists who interview members of the Provisional IRA, the INLA or similar proscribed organizations. The police and army are empowered to question anyone about any terrorist activity, e.g., bombings, and journalists who have obtained their own interviews are bound to answer such questions.

Television coverage of Northern Ireland is regularly censored. Scenes that might present the IRA or their allies in a favorable light are excised from British news or current affairs programs. On occasion such programs are scheduled for the least accessible viewing slots, usually very late at night. Interviews that give the IRA a chance to air its views, even if the program makes it clear that such views are absolutely unacceptable, are taboo. The BBC, on the whole has shown itself more resistant to government pressures in this area than has the IBA.

5. Northern Ireland: media bans Whether or not Northern Ireland is Britain's Vietnam, as some like to claim, remains debatable, but the "troubles" are certainly still the most sensitive domestic issue facing successive governments. On these grounds there exist specific and stringent media controls as regard the province (see above). The British media are by no means as free to report on the situation there as are the many international news teams whose reporters and camera crews put out a view of Anglo-Irish relations very different from that sanitized for domestic consumption.

Until 1969, when British troops began their as yet unfinished role in the area, government policy on the media in Northern Ireland was simple: Nothing that undermined the supposed authority of the central govrnment might be permitted. In 1959 the actress Siobhan McKenna, appearing on Ed Murrow's American television program *See It Now*, suggested that some members at least of the IRA might be "young idealists." The BBC refused to run a second program, also featuring McKenna. A year later the BBC governors chose to drop from BBC-TV's highly popular *Tonight* program a piece in which a reporter looked at the border tensions between Northern Ireland and Eire.

Once the situation had escalated toward its current violent stalemate, the bans were more frequent. In 1971 the Granada TV program, *World In Action*, well-known for its investigative reports, was prohibited by the IBA from transmitting its program, *South of the Border*, a look at the effect tensions in the North had on the rest of Ireland. The program was carefully balanced, but appearances by IRA leaders meant that it survived beyond the editing suite. In 1973 the idiosyncratic actor-director Kenneth Griffiths made *Hang Out Your Brightest Colours*, a profile of Michael Collins, a Republican leader whose decision to make peace with the British in 1922 led to his own assassination. This was banned by the company that commissioned it, ATV. A number of documentaries made by the program *This Week* were similarly banned by the IBA, although one, dealing with police brutality, was cheekily excerpted by the BBC and broadcast as "The program the ITV bosses wan't let you see." The BBC was not always so liberal: In 1978 a program on Derry, offering Republican as well as "loyalist" views, as duly banned.

Since 1979 the government, with its determinedly hard line vis-a-vis terrorism and helped by what some critics denounce as an increasingly subservient BBC, has attempted to ensure that the government viewpoint remains the media's only authorized viewpoint. In July 1985 the program "Real Lives," which dealt with IRA leader Martin McGuiness, was dropped after pressure from the government. On October 19, 1988, the government produced its most far-reaching ban to date. An official notice from Home Secretary Douglas Hurd, backed up a week later by a letter of clarification from the home office, banned interviews by any British television company with any member of a listed Northern Ireland organization, e.g., Sinn Fein (the legal political wing of the IRA) and the Protestant UDA.

The notice states that no speech or statement made by a member of one of these organizations can be broadcast live, although the same statements can be repeated, word for word, by an actor or newsreader. In addition there are the following prohibitions on broadcasting: actuality (live broadcasting) of a speech by a foreign leader or politician in support of a listed organization; actuality of words of support for these organizations spoken by a politician in the European parliament or by a defendant in court; shouts of support for a listed organization by members of crowd, including crowds at sporting occasions; actuality of acceptance speeches by members of listed organizations successful in an election (although their electioneering speeches may be carried); certain historical documentary footage of members of listed organizations. Print journalism is not subject to the notice.

6. Post Office Act (1953)   Under section 11:

> (1) A person shall not send or attempt to send or procure to be sent a postal packet that … (b) encloses any indecent or obscene print, painting, photograph, lithograph, engraving, cinematographic film, book, card or written communication, or any indecent or obscene article whether similar to the above or not; or (c) has on the packet, or on the cover thereof, any words, marks or designs that are grossly offensive or of an indecent or obscene character.

SEE ALSO United Kingdom 1. customs and postal regulations.

7. public library censorship   In the same way as once did their predecessors, the employees of Mudies' and W.H. SMITH's circulating libraries, individual librarians and library committees have removed various books from library shelves. It would be impossible to itemize every single instance of library censorship. Instead, this list sketches the wide variety of material purged at one time or another by British librarians of the 20th century.

Books

Baldwin, James, *Another Country*

Barnes, E.W., Bishop of Birmingham, *The Rise of Christianity*

BLYTON, Enid, various works, including "Noddy" series

Boccaccio, THE DECAMERON

Chaucer, Geoffrey, *Canterbury Tales*

Chesterton, G.K., *The New Unhappy Lords*

Cleland, John, MEMOIRS OF A WOMAN OF PLEASURE

Connell, Vivian, SEPTEMBER IN QUINZE

Cory, D.W., *The Homosexual Outlook*

Crompton, Richmal, "William" series

Dali, Salvador, *The Secret Life of Salvador Dali*

Dudley, Ernest, *Picaroon*

Edington, May, *The Captain's House*

Evans, May, *The Girl with X-Ray Eyes*

Fielding, Henry, *Tom Jones*

Flowerdew, H., *The Celibate's Wife*

Forester, C.S., *The Ship*

Furness, Lady, *Double Exposure*

Genet, Jean, various works

Gibbon, Lewis Grassie, *Sunset Song*; *Cloud Howe*, *Grey Granite*

HALL, Radclyffe, THE WELL OF LONELINESS

Hardy, Thomas, various works

HARRIS, Frank, MY LIFE AND LOVES

Haye, Alec, *In Love*

Hitler, Adolf, *Mein Kampf*

HUGO, Victor, *La Terre*
Huxley, Aldous, *The Art of Seeing*
Johns, Captin W.E., "Biggles" series
Jones, James, *From Here to Eternity*
Joyce, James, ULYSSES
Kama Sutra
Kauffmann, Stanley, *The Philanderer*
Kinsey, Alfred, *Sexual Behavior in the Human Female*, *Sexual Behavior in the Human Male*
Kravchenko, V., *I Chose Freedom*
LAWRENCE, D.H., *The Prussian Officer*, LADY CHATTERLEY'S LOVER
Linklater, Eric, *Magnus Merriman*
Mailer, Norman, *The Naked and the Dead*, *Barbary Shore*
Marshall, Bruce, *The Fair Bride*
Meersch, M. van der, *Bodies and Souls*
Merle, Robert, *Weekend at Zuydcoote*
MILLER, Henry, TROPIC OF CANCER, TROPIC OF CAPRICORN
Mitchell, Don, *Thumb Tripping*
Morrill, George, *Dark Seas Running*
Nabokov, Vladimir, *Lolita*
Nichols, Beverly, *Crazy Pavements*
PERFUMED GARDEN, THE
RABELAIS, Francois, *Gargantua and Pantagruel*
Richards, Frank, "Billy Bunter" series
Robbins, Harold, *The Carpetbaggers*
Sartre, Jean-Paul, *The Age of Reason*
Selby, Hubert, LAST EXIT TO BROOKLYN
Sharp, Alan, *A Green Tree in Geddye*
Shaw, George Bernard, various works
Trocchi, Alexander, CAIN'S BOOK
VOLTAIRE, *Candide*
Wells, H.G., *Ann Veronica*
Whitney, L.F., *The Natural Method of Dog Training*
Wildeblood, Peter, *Against the Law*
Wilson, Edmund, MEMOIRS OF HECATE COUNTY
Winsor, Kathleen, FOREVER AMBER
WODEHOUSE, P.G., various works

Magazines, Newspapers and Journals

Action
An Alternative Vision
Baptist Times
Christian Science Monitor
DAILY MIRROR
Daily Sketch
DAILY WORKER
Evergreen Review
Freedom
GAY NEWS
Labor
Liberal News
Peace News
Picture Post
Soviet Weekly
Sun, The

Tribune
Welsh Nation

8. film censorship The exhibition of films in Britain is controlled by the voluntary self-censorship of the trade itself as well as by the powers of local government. Film censorship in Britain works on four levels. The most important is that operated by the BRITISH BOARD OF FILM CENSORS (BBFC), a body initially set up by the British film industry in 1921, which assesses films, makes cuts and alterations, and issues ratings governing the age-groups for which each film is suitable. Local councils also have the statutory right to give or withhold permission for the screening of films, but they are generally guided by the decision and ratings of the BBFC. They may, on occasion, either prohibit a film or, even when the board has chosen to ban a film outright, award it a local certificate, which overrides the national rating. Under the OBSCENE PUBLICATIONS ACT (1959), as amended in 1977 and 1979, the director of public prosecutions (DPP) may bring charges against a film or a videocassette if it is considered likely to deprave and corrupt its audiences. The Customs authorities are empowered to prohibit the import of any film that they consider to be "indecent," a category far broader than "obscenity."

Any prosecution of a film by the DPP must be initiated by the DPP applying for a warrant under which it can be seized. The aim of this proviso is to cut down on the likelihood of frivolous or vexatious prosecutions and to give the county's public cinemas, film clubs and societies a measure of statutory protection from arbitrary police raids—although once armed with a warrant, the police have extensive powers of search and seizure. Defendants may offer a "public good defense," although this is narrower than that allowed to books, and covers only the interests of "drama, opera, ballet, or any other art, or of literature or learning." Science, included in the public good of books, is omitted. The archival function of film is assumed to be a part of "learning."

United Kingdom—Stuart censorship

1. James I (1603-25) and Charles I (1625-49) Under the first two Stuarts, facing increasingly militant Puritan agitation, the ecclesiastical courts became more and more active as censors, but, as in the Tudor era, they took little notice of literature. The enthusiasm with which the various decrees were enforced tended to vary according to the policies of the current archbishop of Canterbury. Bancroft (1604-10) was generally illiberal; his successor, George Abbot, was so moderate as to find himself deprived of his see in 1627, after the accession of Charles I. The ultraconservative Archbishop Laud took his place and operated the censorship with increasing severity. Sentences upon those convicted of flouting its laws grew more harsh. In 1630 ALEXANDER LEIGHTON was sentenced by Star Chamber for his book *Syon's Plea Against Prelacy* in which he had attacked members of the Court and the church. He was removed from his office, sentenced to life imprisonment in the Fleet Prison, to be pilloried and whipped, to have his ears cut off, his nose split and his cheeks branded. He escaped briefly from custody but was recaptured and the sentence carried out. He was awarded compensation by the Puritan Parliament in 1641.

Other individuals, such as Richard Blagrave, arrested for stocking forbidden books, and the king's printers, Barker and Lucas, arraigned for printing a "wicked bible" in which a misprint commanded readers "Thou shalt committ adultery," as well as those condemned for dispersing popish books and publishing fanatical pamphlets, were prosecuted by Star Chamber. The most notable case was that of WILLIAM PRYNNE, condemned in 1633 for *Histrio-mastix*, an 1,100-page attack on drama, which it was alleged had coincidentally attacked the queen. Prynne was fined, imprisoned, branded and had his ears cut off. Despite this he continued his campaigns from his cell in the Tower of London. While the king and the Church defended their status, Parliament was notably jealous of its privileges. Dr. Cowell of Cambridge was prosecuted for his dictionary of political and legal terms, *The Interpreter*, in 1610; Floyd, an aging Catholic barrister, for openly delighting in a Protestant military defeat in 1621 and thus commenting, in a way forbidden to Parliament itself, on religious affairs abroad; two future bishops, who made their support for the monarch clear, despite growing parliamentary animosity, were attacked.

Star Chamber made its final, punitive attempt to suppress Puritan publications in July 1637. The powers allotted to the STATIONERS' COMPANY under Mary and Elizabeth I were reinforced and there was instituted a system of licensing more complex and far-reaching than any previous one. Every loophole in the previous censorship laws was carefully closed. Still, the system did not work. Censorship was merely one part of the problem facing Charles I and his advisers; more pressing difficulties undermined its efficiency and the pamphleteering continued unabated until the Long Parliament abolished Star Chamber, the ecclesiastical courts and the Court of High Commission in 1641.

SEE ALSO book burning in England 2. James I; book burning in England 3. Charles I; and below.

2. The Restoration (Charles II: 1660-85)

In dismantling the structure of Puritan government the restored Stuarts had no wish to destroy at the same time the machinery of censorship that earlier Stuarts had used and that had been maintained, albeit in different forms, by Cromwell. Sedition remained a potent threat to stability and in 1662 the LICENSING ACT ensured that a stringent censorship was established. The act returned to the punitive efforts to regulate printing initiated by Star Chamber in 1637, with an extended range of interests to encompass the vast expansion in the press and its products that had developed during the Commonwealth. Unlicensed printing was forbidden, a variety of officials, each of whom maintained control over a specific part of the press—divinity, philosophy, medicine etc.—had extensive powers of search and seizure, and the number of master printers was limited to 20. The mix of politics and theology that still informed contemporary censorship—as opposed to questions of obscenity—was implicit in the act's first section, which stressed the primacy of the religious doctrines established by the Church of England and the state government and condemned any deviations as "heretical, seditious, schismatic [and] offensive." Every book had to print its license as a preface to all other text and the printer's name must always be included. Import regulations included the prohibition of the opening of any package unless an official observer were present. The office of surveyor of the press was established to control the press under the terms of the act; the first holder, Sir Roger L'Estrange (1616-1704), was appointed in August 1663.

While sedition was ostensibly controlled by the Licensing Act, more innocent pleasures, similary restrained by puritanism, were readmitted to decent society. The playhouses, banned as of 1642, were restored. Two companies held the monopoly of performances, one under Thomas Killigrew (The King's) and the other under William D'Avenant (The Duke of York's), which became respectively the Theatre Royal, Drury Lane, and the Theatre Royal, Covent Garden. These two companies controlled the "legitimate" theater until the THEATRE REGULATION ACT of 1843. When the Licensing Act lapsed in 1679 it was not immediately renewed, but James II's first Parliament remedied this omission. It was temporarily renewed once again by William and Mary but lapsed for good in 1695. The long process of censorship by a combination of the church and the state lapsed with it and a new style of purely secular censorship, with an emphasis on obscenity rather than sedition took its place.

SEE ALSO Stationers' Company.

United Kingdom—Tudor censorship (1485-1603)

The basic premise of Tudor censorship of the press was that the safety and peace of the realm could be preserved only if all dissenting opinion was firmly suppressed. The instrument of that suppression was the Crown itself. The new spirit of learning and inquiry, growing throughout Europe, tended to undermine the status quo. As such it was to be strictly controlled. Although the Reformation, the break with Rome and the creation of the Church of England all developed during the reign of Henry VIII, heresy of any sort was judged to be as politically seditious as it was threatening to the established church. The development of the press and the concomitant spread of literacy was seen as a potential problem for the status quo were it not controlled and, for all that Henry had rejected Catholic divorce laws, he had no desire to welcome Protestant reformers. To proclaim a religious faith other than that of the monarch was de facto seditious, and Tudor censorship, no matter what religion the monarch preferred, concentrated on making this clear. The system emphsized the linkage of politics and theology, seeking to reinforce the established versions of each; obscenity was barely considered yet, and literature, if devoid of politics and religion, was allowed a relatively free rein.

Almost from its inception under Caxton in 1476, the control of printing had been assumed by the Crown as a royal prerogative. The first Stationer to the king (Peter Actors) was appointed in 1485 and the first official printer (William Faques) in 1504. Theological developments soon justified the licensing of the press, controlling not merely who should print, but also what should be printed. The clergy had been empowered to suppress heresy from the time of WYCLIF (1382) but their efforts proved decreasingly successful. Attempts to suppress Lutheranism (see Martin Luther) commenced in 1520, when the archbishop of Canterbury asked Cardinal Wolsey to compile a list of Lutheran writers and to add their works to the list of prohibited material held at Oxford University. In 1529 a number of proclamations against heretical and seditious books were issued, listing the offending titles and thus predating the Catholic INDEX LIBRORUM PROHIBITORUM. Under these proclamations the clergy and the judiciary were empowered to prosecute the printers and owners of heretical works in the ecclesiastical courts. A further proclamation (and list) of 1530 established the outline of a secular licensing system, dealing only with theological works, and appointed the church as the licensing authority.

In 1538, alienated from Rome and now master of the English clergy, Henry instituted a system of royal licensing. Under royal control the press was to be employed both to suppress opposition and to disseminate information favorable to the Crown. No English books, whether theological or otherwise, were to be printed without authorization from the king, his privy council or a bishop. Similar restrictions were placed on the importing of books. A new concept of seditious opinions, against which the proclamation was specifically aimed, was introduced. Transgressors were to be fined and/or imprisoned. The proclamation was occasionally modified throughout Henry's reign, with special orders appearing in response to unforeseen political developments. It does not appear, however, that the decree was very often observed. A further constraint on printers was embodied in the Act of Six Articles, whereby the doctrines of transubstantiation (the belief that the communion bread and wine were transformed into the actual body and blood of Christ) and auricular confession (the hearing of confessions by a priest), among other doctrines, were strictly upheld; anyone attacking them in writing or in print would on the first offense be imprisoned at the royal pleasure and forfeit his goods and the profits of his lands for life. A second offense assumed guilt of felony without benefit of clergy (the clergyman's privilege of being exempted from trial in secular courts), leading automatically to execution.

Under Edward VI, in 1547 and 1549, there appeared orders forbidding the publication or use of popish books of prayer or instruction. A new prayer book was introduced and orders were given to destroy its predecessors. All printing was to be licensed first by three secretaries and, after the fall of the Protector Somerset, the privy council. The increasing religious factionalism led to nine proclamations, all in restraint of any publications tending to favor the opponents of the Crown.

Under Mary, who had temporarily reconciled England with Rome, a proclamation of 1553 forbade any printing without her special license and attempted to ban from England the importation of any Protestant materials. She also banned Edward's new prayer book. In 1556 Mary created for the first time an effective means of royal censorship by her incorporation of the STATIONERS' COMPANY, a step that influenced the censorship of British print for a century and a half. The company, effectively the printers' trade union, was given a royal charter, the monopoly on printing and various other perquisites. In return, the printers promised to search out and destroy all unlicensed, illegal and subversive books. They were given the necessary powers of seizure and destruction to back up these actions. In 1559 Elizabeth I, who had reestablished Protestantism, confirmed this charter in a number of "Injunctions" that stated that no book, pamphlet, play or ballad should be printed unless licensed by the monarch, six members of the privy council, the chancellor of Oxford or Cambridge University or certain ecclesiastical dignitaries. No political or religious work was to be reprinted without recensorship. No work might be published without the inclusion of the name of its licensers. This system lasted in essence until 1695.

No scheme could or ever did prove watertight. The frequent reissuing of Elizabeth's "Injunctions," as in the Council Order of June 27, 1566, and the Star Chamber Decree of June 23, 1586, makes it clear that not everyone was willing to be constrained. Her officials pursued first papists, such as Father Persons, the Jesuit Robert Southwell and printer Hames Duckett, and later Puritans, whose position was epitomized in the MARTIN MARPRELATE Tracts of 1588-89, attacking Archbishop Whitgift's attempts to impose a uniform liturgy on the English church. Whitgift responded by appointing a panel of 12 individuals, specifically commanded to suppress Puritan pamphleteering. In 1599 certain satirical works, notably those of Gabriel Harvey and Thomas Nashe, were burned, and a ban was pronounced on the further publication of satires and epigrams, as well as on unauthorized plays and histories.

In their turn the emergent Puritans, presaging their greater successes in the 17th century, began making efforts to extend the censorship to literature, attacking bawdy ballads and the like, but with no real impact. In 1580 the lawyer and magistrate William Lambard proposed an "Act of Parliament for the Establishment of the Governors of English Print," aimed directly at controlling literature. This prototype Obscene Publications Bill concentrated less on lewdness but more on maintaining the profits and interests of licensed publishers in competition with the unlicensed printers. It proposed censorship by lawyers rather than clergymen or politicians, and aimed to embrace popular as well as serious literature. It was never even presented to Parliament.

SEE ALSO book burning in England 1. Tudor period; United Kingdom—Stuart censorship.

United States v. *Gray* **(1970)**   In 1970 Claude Gray, a U.S. Marine, was charged with contravening article 134 of the Uniform Code of Military Justice, which states, "all disorders and neglects to the prejudice of good order and discipline in the armed forces, all conduct to bring discredit upon the armed forces … shall be punished at the discretion of [a] court." Gray had written and spoken as follows:

> We have not served in Vietnam but we have not been deaf or blind to the testimony of our brothers who have gone and were lucky enough to return. In the brig, one meets Vietnam veterans and conscientious objectors, and from them one gets a different view of the war. In the barracks we talk to each other; at demonstrations we have read leaflets and pamphlets. We have heard and encountered both sides of the war. We have heard death tolls calmly announced over TV and radio. We have read of whole villages wiped out by our forces accidentally, and we have reason to believe our war there is a huge mistake made possible in part by inhumane and dictatorial practices within the military. We can no longer cooperate with these practices or with the war in Vietnam. We are not deserting; we are simply taking a stand to help others like us. Positively, we favor an immediate end to the war and the establishment of a voluntary military service to defend the nation, together with the needed reforms within the military to attract volunteers. Article 134 [of the UMC] should be struck from the code, free speech guaranteed and individual conscience respected; a conscientious objector's status should be easier to obtain for those with moral doubts about a war. In general soldiers should have a greater say about the rules they live under, and certainly about a matter of life and death, and the destruction of another country.

Gray was cashiered from the Marines for his violation of article 134 and what were termed his "disloyal statements." The court-martial ruled as irrelevant the fact his writing was confined to a personal "rough log" and that he had previously been of good conduct. If anything his previous reputation as a good Marine would make it more, rather than less, likely that his statements would be taken seriously by his fellows.

United States v. *Kennerley* **(1913)**   Mitchell Kennerley was convicted in 1913 under the U.S. postal regulations governing the sending of obscene material through the mails. He had sent by post the novel *Hagar Revelly*, which concerns the misadventures of Hagar, a young New York girl, and contains what contemporary critics termed "scenes of frankness and detail." These were sufficient to bring Kennerley to court. When the case reached the U.S. Supreme Court, Justice Learned Hand, who would later support Judge Woolsey's ruling on ULYSSES in 1934, showed in his opinion that even this early in the century he appreciated the limitations of the traditional test for obscenity, the HICKLIN RULE. He accepted that the rule was generally used in the lower courts and "it would no longer be proper for me to disregard it" but offered his own, contradictory opinion:

> I hope it is not improper to say that the rule as laid down, however consonant it may be with mid-Victorian morals, does not seem to me to answer to the understanding and morality of the present time, as conveyed by the words "obscene, lewd, or lascivious." I question whether in the end men will regard that as obscene that is honestly relevant to the expression of innocent ideas, and whether they will not believe that truth and beauty are too precious to society at large to be mutilated in the interests of those most likely to pervert them to base uses. Indeed, it seems hardly likely that we are even today so lukewarm in our interest in letters or serious discussion as to be content to reduce our treatment of sex to the standard of a child's library in the interests of a salacious few, or that shame will long prevent us from adequate portrayal of some of the most serious and beautiful sides of human nature …
>
> Should not the word "obscene" be allowed to indicate the present critical point in the compromise between candor and shame at which the community may have arrived here and now? If letters must, like other kinds of conduct, be subject to the social sense of what is right, it would seem that a jury should in each case establish the standard much as they do in cases of negligence. To put thought in leash to the average conscience of the time is perhaps tolerable but to fetter it by the necessities of the lowest and least capable seems a fatal policy. Nor is it an objection, I think, that such an interpretation gives to the words of the statute a varying meaning from time to time. Such words as these do not embalm the precise morals of an age or place; while they presuppose that some things will always be shocking to public taste, the vague subject-matter is left to the gradual development of general notions about what is decent.

SEE ALSO United States 17. postal regulations.

United States v. *Levine* **(1936)**   Levine was convicted by a federal district court under the U.S. Postal Regulations concerning the sending of obscene material through the mails. The material in question comprised three publications: the *Secret Museum of Anthropology*, a collection of photographs of naked women from native tribes around the world; *Crossways of Sex*, a supposedly scientific treatise on sexual pathology; and *Black Lust*, a novel that describes the adventures of an English girl who is captured by Dervishes at the fall of Khartoum and kept in a harem until the battle of Omdurman, when she is killed. As far as the court was concerned, all three, fact or fiction, were equally obscene. The judge stressed that the regulations were designed to protect "the young and immature and ignorant and those who were sensually inclined" and told the jury to relate the books' content to them, rather than to more sophisticated readers. He also advised the jury that, on the basis of the HICKLIN RULE, only a part of the work need be obscene for the whole to be condemned.

Levine was convicted but the conviction was reversed in the appeals court, which applied the more recent ULYSSES STANDARD, which demanded that a whole work, rather than individual passages, must be proven obscene. The court's opinion stated that the Hicklin Rule:

> naturally presupposed that the evil against which the statute is directed so much outweighs all interests of art, letters or science, that they must yield to the mere possibility that some prurient person may get a sensual gratification from reading or seeing what to most people is innocent and may be delightful or enlightening. No civilized community not fanatically puritanical would tolerate such an imposition, and we do not believe that the courts that have declared it would ever have applied it consistently. As so often happens, the problem is to find a passable compromise between opposing interests, whose relative importance, like that of all social or personal values, is incommensurable.

SEE ALSO United States 17. postal regulations.

***United States v. Marchetti* (1972)**   Victor Marchetti was a former executive assistant to the deputy director of the CIA, who, after his resignation from the agency, decided to capitalize on his experiences as an intelligence agent by writing *The Rope Dancer* (1972), a novel set in the loosely fictional "National Intelligence Agency," as well as a number of free-lance non-fiction articles. One of these had appeared in *The Nation* magazine in April 1972, entitled "CIA: The President's Loyal Tool." He had also offered a number of magazines, most notably *Esquire*, an outline of a piece based on his own memoirs. Since, like all CIA agents, Marchetti had signed the agency's secrecy and publishing agreements (see CIA), and on his resignation signed a further secrecy oath, his former employers claimed that his journalistic pieces were in breach of this agreement and that they "contained classified information concerning intelligence sources, methods and operations." The agency then took Marchetti to court to press its right, under the agreements, to precensorship of all such writing. The federal district court ordered Marchetti to submit all material to the agency at least 30 days prior to publication.

The appeals court confirmed this injunction, stating that by accepting employment with the CIA, and by signing the relevant agreements, Marchetti had submitted himself to certain constraints on his FIRST AMENDMENT rights that would have been unconstitutional if applied to a private citizen, but that were justified for intelligence, the Armed Forces and similar areas of activity. The court stated that Marchetti might speak and write about the agency but could not disclose any classified information unless it had already entered the public domain. The CIA had the right to check his writing to judge what was and was not classified. In Marchetti's favor, the agency must finish this review promptly, within 30 days, and

the writer was entitled to obtain a judicial review of any revisions and cuts the agency might wish to make.

The U.S. Supreme Court's refusal to hear Marchetti's appeal confirmed this judgment. Marchetti continued to write, and in 1975 came up against the courts and the agency once again. In collaboration with a former State Department employee, John Marks, who had also signed a secrecy agreement as part of the terms of his employment, Marchetti began writing a book, entitled *The CIA and the Cult of Intelligence*, for the publisher Alfred A. Knopf, Inc. When this book was submitted for censorship the agency found some 339 classified items in the manuscript. After some argument, this list was pared down to 168 items, each represented by a blank space in the published book. Knopf, with the two authors, took the agency to court, seeking an order to overturn this censorship. This case—*Alfred A. Knopf, Inc.* v. *Colby* (1975)—came before the same appeals court judge, Judge Haynsworth, and had the same outcome as its predecessor: The CIA's rights were upheld. Marchetti and Marks had made "a solemn agreement ... at the commencement of [their] employment" and by so doing had "effectively relinquished [their] first amendment rights." The U.S. Supreme Court, as in 1972, refused to hear a further appeal. When researchers using the Freedom of Information Act (see United States 11.) obtained details of the cuts, it appeared that most stemmed from embarrassment, rather than the needs of security. In 1982, when a revised edition of the book appeared, some 25 percent of the cuts had been reinstated.

SEE ALSO *Haig* v. *Agee* (1981); *McGehee* v. *Casey* (1983); *Snepp* v. *United States* (1980).

***United States v. Morison* (1985)**   Samuel Morison, an employee of the Naval Intelligence Center in Maryland, was, with the knowledge and approval of his employers, the U.S. editor of the British publication, *Jane's Fighting Ships*, the internationally accepted catalog of the world's naval vessels. For this he was paid $5,000 per year. In 1985, in what he claimed was no more than an error of judgment, he sent three photographs of a Soviet aircraft carrier under construction to the weekly magazine, *Jane's Fighting Weekly*; the pictures had been taken by a U.S. satellite and were classifed as secret. When this was discovered Morison was prosecuted under the ESPIONAGE ACT and for the theft of government property. He was accused of having sent off the pictures in the hope of gaining a full-time job with Jane's, and of revealing, given the detail of the pictures, the sophistication of U.S. satellite technology. Morison faced up to 400 years imprisonment and a fine of up to $40,000. He was found guilty, but the sentence was two years in prison.

***United States v. One Book Entitled Ulysses* (1934)**   SEE *Ulysses*.

***United States v. Reidel* (1971)**   Reidel was the distributor of a pamphlet entitled "The True Facts About Imported

Pornography." He advertised his wares in certain newspapers, stating that no one under 21 was permitted to answer his advertisement. In 1971 he mailed to a recipient who turned out to be a postal inspector a copy of the pamphlet and found himself charged under the U.S. Postal Regulations (see United States 17.) dealing with the sending of obscene matter through the mails. The district court accepted that by warning off those under 21 Reidel had not been attempting to solicit minors or an unwilling or captive audience. They dismissed the federal case. On appeal to the U.S. Supreme Court, the acquittal was reversed. Referring to the case of STANLEY V. GEORGIA, which determined the rights of individual privacy as regarded the consumption of possibly obscene materials, the court stated that while one was permitted to enjoy whatever one liked at home, this did not confer on another person the right to sell or deliver such material Furthermore, Reidel's warning gave insufficient guarantees that minors would genuinely be protected from receiving his pamphlet.

The court's liberals, Justices Black and Douglas, dissented from this opinion, complaining,

> For the forseeable future this Court must sit as a Board of Supreme Censors, sifting through books and magazines and watching movies because some official fears they deal too explicitly with sex. I can imagine no more distasteful, useless, and time-consuming task for the members of the Court than perusing the material to determine whether it has "redeeming social value." This absurd spectacle could be avoided if we would adhere to the literal command of the First Amendment that "Congress shall make no law ... abridging the freedom of speech, or of the press."

United States* v. *Thirty-Seven Photographs (1971) Milton Luros was one of America's major distributors of sex-related publications in the 1960s and 1970s. In 1971, returning from a holiday in Europe, his luggage was searched by U.S. Customs and there were discovered some 37 photographs, which the Customs officers considered to be obscene and seized as such, pending federal adjudication under the terms of the Tariff Act (1930) (see United States 21.). Luros claimed that seizure of the pictures, which were to be used as illustrations for a forthcoming deluxe illustrated edition of the classic Indian sex manual, the *Kama Sutra of Vatsyayana* (already widely distributed without legal hindrance), was unconstitutional. The U.S. Supreme Court refused to overturn the district court's ruling. In the majority decision it stated that even if obscene material were to be enjoyed only in the privacy of one's own home, as laid down in STANLEY V. GEORGIA (1969), that conferred no rights on anyone to import it into the U.S. The Tariff Act was confirmed as constitutional. Justices Black and Douglas, dissenting, claimed that Luros's FIRST AMENDMENT rights had been violated, and that the "zone of privacy," which is accepted as extending to the limits of one's home, should also cover the suitcases with which one travels, and any material held in them.

SEE ALSO *Luros* v. *United States* (1968).

***United States* v. *Three Cases of Toys* (1842)** In 1842 the U.S. government's Tariff Law made the importation of an indecent and obscene painting cause of forfeiture of all the goods included on the same invoice. In September 1842 U.S. Customs seized a consignment of three boxes of toys, imported from Germany. In amongst the innocent toys were nine snuffboxes, on each of which was a false bottom, hiding a variety of obscene pictures, painted onto the box. The jury did not even leave the courtroom but found in the government's favor, confiscating the entire shipment, worth approximately $700. That the importer of record was completely ignorant of the snuffboxes, which had been ordered through another firm, was no defense.

***United States* v. *Two Tin Boxes* (1935)** SEE *Ecstasy*.

United States
1. banned films The following is a list of the most important of those films that have been banned in America since 1908. Many of these attempts at censorship were subsequently overturned by higher courts, and many failed to get a hearing from any court, but a variety of local, state and national authorities, and certain anti-obscenity pressure groups have all targeted these films for censorship. In the main they have been cited for obscenity, but the list includes a number considered to have been seditious. Not all of these films appear elsewhere in this volume, but the most important are included under their own heading and are printed in small capital letters.

Alibi (1929)
Alimony Lovers (1968)
AMANTS, LES (THE LOVERS) (1958)
Amok (1947)
Anatomy of a Murder (1959)
And God Created Woman (1958)
Angelique in Black Leather (1969)
Art of Marriage, The (1971)
BABY DOLL (1956)
Bachelor Tom Peeping (1964)
Bedford Incident, The (1965)
BEHIND THE GREEN DOOR (1973)
BIRTH CONTROL (1917)
Birth of a Nation (1915)
BIRTH OF A BABY (1939)
BLUE MOVIE/FUCK (1969)
Body of a Female (1967)
Brand, The (1919)
Bunny Lake Is Missing (1965)
CALIGULA (1981)
Candy (1969)
Carmen, Baby (1968)
CARNAL KNOWLEDGE (1972)

CHANT D'AMOUR, UN (1966)
Cindy and Donna (1971)
Class of '74 (1974)
Collection, The (1970)
Computer Game (1971)
CONNECTION, THE (1962)
Cry Uncle (1972)
CURLY (1949)
DEEP THROAT (1972)
Desire Under the Elms (1959)
DEVIL IN MISS JONES, THE (1975)
Dirty Girls, The (1965)
DON JUAN (1959)
Easiest Way, The (1918)
Ecstasy (1935)
Emmanuelle (1981)
Exorcist, The (1973)
Female, The (1968)
Fit to Win (1919)
Four Nine One (1964)
Fox, The (1968)
Fur Piece (1971)
Game of Love, The (Le Ble en herbe) (1956)
Garden of Eden, The (1956)
Gun Runners (1975)
Hand That Rocks The Cradle, The (1917)
Have Figure Will Travel (1964)
I AM CURIOUS—YELLOW (1968)
I Am Sandra (1975)
I, A Woman (1967)
It All Comes Out in the End (1971)
It Happened in Hollywood (1975)
JAMES BOYS IN MISSOURI (1908)
Killing of Sister George, The (1971)
LADY CHATTERLEY'S LOVER (1957)
Language of Love, The (1969)
Last Tango in Paris (1973)
Last Picture Show, The (1973)
Latuko (1952)
Libertine, The (1970)
Little Sisters (1975)
Lorna (1964)
Lysistrata (1971)
M (1952)
MAGIC MIRROR (1971)
MAN WITH THE GOLDEN ARM, THE (1956)
Married Bachelors (1971)
MIRACLE, THE (1951)
Miss Julie (1952)
Mom and Dad (1958)
Mondo Freudo (1967)
MOON IS BLUE, THE (1953)
NAKED AMAZON (1957)
NAKED CAME THE STRANGER (1975)
Naked Truth, The (1926)

Native Son (1953)
Never on Sunday (1961)
Newcomers, The (1973)
Night Riders (1908)
Odd Triangle (1969)
Ordeal, The (1915)
OUTLAW, THE (1946)
Pattern of Evil (1969)
Picture Is Censored, The (1966)
PINKY (1949)
Pornography in Denmark (1971)
PROFESSOR MAMLOCK (1939)
Remous (Whirlpool) (1939)
Rent-a-Girl (1967)
REVENGE AT DAYBREAK (1964)
Road to Ruin, The (1929)
RONDE, LA (1951)
School Girl (1974)
Secret Sex Lives of Romeo and Juliet, The (1970)
Sex Lure, The (1917)
Sexual Freedom in Denmark (1971)
SHE SHOULD'A SAID NO! (1956)
Sinderella (1972)
Spain in Flames (1937)
SPIRIT OF '76, THE (1917)
Spy, The (1917)
Starlet (1970)
Stewardesses (1974)
STRANGER KNOCKS, A (1965)
Therese and Isabelle (1968)
TITICUT FOLLIES (1968)
TOMORROW'S CHILDREN (1937)
Twilight Girls, The (1964)
Unsatisfied, The (1965)
VICTORY IN THE WEST (SIEG IM WESTEN) (1941)
Virgin Spring, The (1962)
VIVA MARIA (1966)
Vixen, The (1970)
Where Eagles Dare (1970)
Wicked Die Slow, The (1968)
WILD WEED (1956)
WILLARD-JOHNSON BOXING MATCH (1915)
Without a Stitch (1970)
Woman's Urge, A (1966)
Women of the World (1963)
Woodstock (1970)
Yellow Bird (1969)
Youth of Maxim, The (1935)

2. book banning The following is a list of those titles most frequently banned from public educational institutions between 1966 and 1975. The number in parentheses is the number of attempts (of which 51-58% have been successful) at censorship that have been made on each title.

(41) *Catcher in the Rye*, J.D. Slinger (1951)
(20) *Soul on Ice*, Eldridge Cleaver (1968)
(15) *Manchild in the Promised Land*, Claude Brown (1965)
(14) *Go Ask Alice*, Anonymous (1971)
(10) *Catch-22*, Joseph Heller (1961)
(10) a variety of photographic and art books featuring the nude.
(9) *The Grapes of Wrath*, John Steinbeck (1939)
(7) *Of Mice and Men*, John Steinbeck (1937)
(7) *Slaughterhouse Five*, Kurt Vonnegut, Jr. (1969)
(7) *To Kill a Mockingbird*, Harper Lee (1960)

3. censorship of newsreels The production of regular film newsreels in the United States, to be shown in cinemas along with the main feature, began in 1914, reached its heyday in the 1930s and 1940s and only declined with the advent of the superior immediacy of television. Among the main companies producing such material were Movietone News, RKO Pathe News, Universal News and MGM News. In 1921 New York state enacted a law that required the "publishers" of such material to submit all their newsreels to the state film censor for his approval, just as they would a feature film. In the case of *Pathe Exchange Inc.* v. *Cobb* (1922) Pathe sought to have this law overturned, alleging that since newsreels were documentary records of current events, they should have the same status regarding freedom of speech as did the print media. The New York courts rejected this, claiming that the nature of film made it a "spectacle or show," and that the audiences for film, often including the "child and illiterate adult," were more susceptible to influence than newspaper readers. This judgment was upheld by the appellate court and by the New York Supreme Court, both of which denied that "the biweekly motion picture newsreel ... is a part of the press of the country," citing as precedent the U.S. Supreme Court decision in MUTUAL FILM CORPORATION V. INDUSTRIAL COMMISSION OF OHIO (1915). A variety of other states followed New York in censoring the newsreels.

This censorship ended in 1952 after the case of *State* v. *Smith* (1952) in which the exhibitor of a Warner-Pathe newsreel refused to submit his film, which covered such topics as the U.S. presidential elections and the Olympic Games, to the Ohio state censor. Fortified by the recent decision in THE MIRACLE case, which had overturned the exclusion of feature films from FIRST AMENDMENT protection, the court accepted that newsreels too had a right to constitutional protection.

4. child pornography Under federal law, it is illegal to disseminate any obscene material involving minors. In addition to this every state has passed some form of legislation covering the creation and distribution of pornography involving minors, colloquially known as "kiddie porn." Twenty states have banned the distribution of material depicting children engaged in sexual conduct, regardless of whether that material could actually be judged as obscene under the current tests for obscenity as set down in U.S. law. These

states are: Arizona, Colorado, Delaware, Florida, Hawaii, Kentucky, Louisiana, Massachusetts, Michigan, Mississippi, Montana, New Jersey, New York, Oklahoma, Pennsylvania, Rhode Island, Texas, Utah, West Virginia and Wisconsin. Fourteen states restrict their prohibition of such material to that which can be proved obscene in court: Alabama, Arkansas, California, Indiana, Maine, Minnesota, Nebraska, New Hampshire, North Dakota, Ohio, Oregon, South Dakota, Tennessee and Washington. Connecticut and Virginia prohibit distribution only if the material is obscene. Twelve states prohibit only the use of minors in the making of such material: Alaska, Georgia, Idaho, Iowa, Kansas, Maryland, Missouri, Nevada, New Mexico, North Carolina, South Carolina and Wyoming.

5. The Civil Service Reform Act (1978) SEE United States 25. The "Whistleblowers" Act (1978).

6. classified information Although American courts are generally opposed to censorship that depends on PRIOR RESTRAINT by their government, stating consistently that such measures violate constitutional guarantees of freedom of speech, this stance is almost always modified when the restraints cover the sensitive areas of national security and intelligence gathering. Even those documents obtained under the Freedom of Information Act (see United States 11.) are heavily censored, where they impinge on security matters, by the relevant intelligence organizations and are issued only in sanitized versions. But the demands of national security are constantly challenged by those who see it as a convenient blanket that hides both incompetence and illegality. On the whole, despite these reservations, the government generally has its way on security. Several important regulations cover classified information.

First is 18 USC section 797:

On and after thirty days from the date upon which the President defines any vital military or naval installation or equipment as being [classified], whoever reproduces, publishes, sells, or gives away any photograph, sketch, picture, drawing, map or geographical representation of the vital military or naval installations so defined, without first obtaining permission of the commanding officer of the military or naval post, camp, or station concerned, or higher authority, unless such photograph, sketch, picture, drawing, map or geographical representation has clearly indicated thereon that it has been censored by the proper military authority, shall be fined not more than $1000 or imprisoned not more than one year, or both.

Second, 18 USC section 798: "Whoever knowingly and wilfully communicates, furnishes, transmits, or otherwise makes available to an unauthorized person, or publishes, or uses in any manner prejudicial to the safety or interest of the United States or for the benefit of any foreign government to the detriment of the United States any classified information ... shall be fined not more than $10,000 or imprisoned for not more than ten years, or both." Classified information is defined as material concerning: (1) "the nature, preparation or use of any code, cipher or cryptographic system of the United States or any foreign government"; (2) "the design, construction, use, maintenance, or repair of any device, apparatus, or appliance used or prepared or planned for use by the United States or any foreign government for cryptographic or communication intelligence purposes"; (3) "the communication of intelligence activities of the United States or any foreign government"; (4) "information obtained by the process of communications of any foreign government, knowing the same to have been obtained by such processes."

Under 18 USC section 793 (e), a fine of $10,000 or up to 10 years in prison or both is leveled against anyone who obtains unauthorized possession, whether deliberately or accidentally, of classified material and fails to turn such material over to the authorities or deliberately passes it on to a foreign power.

Under the Carter administration, there was an attempt to redefine what might and might not be classified. Under Executive Order 12,065 (1979) classifiable material included:

(a) military plans, weapons, or operations; (b) foreign government information; (c) intelligence activities, sources or methods; (d) foreign relations or foreign activities of the U.S.; (e) scientific, technological, or economic matters relating to the national security; (f) U.S. government programs for safeguarding nuclear materials or facilities; (g) other categories of information which are related to national security ... designated by the President, by a person designated by the President ... or by an [intelligence] agency head.

The Reagan administration took this list further and classified an increasing amount of government information. Under Reagan's Executive Order 12,356 (1983) the Carter list was reaffirmed, and expanded to include "cryptology; a confidential source; and the vulnerabilities or capabilities of systems, installations, projects, or plans relating to the national security." In 1983 President Reagan also proposed a system of prior restraint censorship that would have required any federal employee with any access to classified material to obtain prepublication approval for any writing they might wish to do throughout their life. This plan was postponed for further discussion.
SEE ALSO United States 16. Pentagon censorship.

7. United States Constitution SEE First Amendment.

8. desecration of the flag Under section 700(a) of 18 United States Code, "Whoever knowingly casts contempt upon any flag of the United States by publicly mutilating, defacing, defiling, burning, or trampling upon it shall be fined not more than $1000 or imprisoned for not more than one year, or both." The individual states have their own anti-desecration statutes, largely modeled on this one. Most of the cases arising under this law deal with the commercial exploitation of the flag, as in its use in a beer advertisement in the case of *Halter* v. *Nebraska* (1907). But in the Vietnam War era, there arose a number of instances where individuals,

as part of their protest against the war, chose in some way to attack the nation's symbol. Given the freedom of speech guarantees embodied in the FIRST AMENDMENT, the Supreme Court has ruled on a number of occasions that while it is constitutionally unacceptable to burn the flag, there is nothing to prohibit those who wish to speak defiant or contemptuous words about it.

In the case of *Street* v. *New York* (1969) the Supreme Court reversed the conviction of one Street who had burned a flag and stated "We don't need no goddam flag" as part of a protest against the murder of civil rights leader James Meredith. Street was convicted under a New York state anti-desecration statute, under which it is illegal "publicly to mutilate or publicly to defy or cast contempt upon any American flag either by words or act." The court ruled that the restraint of his comments, reprehensible though many Americans might find them, was unconstitutional; the defendant's freedom of expression had to be preserved. The court ruled similarly in *Smith* v. *Goguen* (1974), when Goguen was convicted under Massachusetts law for treating the flag contemptuously, after he sewed a small facsimile of the flag to the seat of his trousers. Again, in *Spence* v. *Washington* (1974), the defendant, who in this case had been convicted under Washington state law for hanging a flag upside down from his window, after attaching a peace symbol to it, was acquitted on the grounds of his constitutional rights to freedom of expression. His action was seen by the court as SYMBOLIC SPEECH.

9. The Federal Advisory Committee Act (1972) This act represented the first attempt by Congress to open up the meetings of federal bodies. It concentrated on dismantling the closed consultative system that existed between regulatory bodies and the industries with which they dealt. Although the act provided for the listing of such meetings in the *Federal Register* and the keeping of records and minutes of the proceedings of such committees, the exemptions to the act were so many and so widely interpreted that such cases as did come to court invariably upheld a committee's rights to privacy. The act was amended in 1976 to conform with the Sunshine Act (see United States 19.), which was passed in the same year.

10. film censorship Thomas Edison demonstrated his kinetoscope for the first time on April 14, 1894. The first recorded protest against a film came 14 days later, directed at *Dolorita in the Passion Dance*, a peep-show running in Atlantic City. Others followed: A film featuring a bride preparing for her wedding was denounced as "an outrage upon public decency"; another, of *The Great Thaw Trial* (a real-life sex-and-murder scandal), was attacked because children were allowed to watch it; in 1895 the mayor of New York tried in vain to close down the nickelodeons as places of immorality. At first the authorities charged high prices for cinema licenses, but escalating profits more than compensated. In 1907 Chicago introduced pre-exhibition censorship, making the police chief responsible for assessing the city's films. In 1909 came the first censorship case, *Block* v.

Chicago, dealing with two films: THE JAMES BOYS IN MISSOURI and Night Riders. The Illinois Supreme Court backed the city censors. New York's National Board of Censorship (later National Board of Review) fulfilled the same function.

The first instance of official film censorship on a state level came on April 16, 1913, when the state of Ohio passed a statute to establish a board of censors to precensor all films proposed for exhibition in the state. The basis of its judgment was a clause stating that "only such films as are in the judgment and discretion of the board of censors of a moral, educational or amusing and harmless character shall be passed and approved ..." This law was tested in 1915 and upheld by the Supreme Court in the case of MUTUAL FILM CORPORATION V. INDUSTRIAL COMMISSION OF OHIO. Film, as far as the court was concerned, was simply one more American business; the concept of free speech did not enter into the topic. Not until the 1950s did this federal approval of local censorship begin to lapse; in 1952 the court overruled its earlier decision, and the power of local censorship was weakened.

In the interim the range of such censorship was substantial. Depending on local sensibilities films lost even the most restrained references to sex, violence, race relations, venereal disease, communism, divorce, abortion and a number of other topics deemed too sensitive for mass consumption. The attitude of local censors was summed up by the Chicago police sergeant who stated baldly, "Children should be allowed to see any movie that plays in Chicago. If a picture is objectionable for a child, it is objectionable period."

Only when the courts, like the producers who controlled the industry, began to consider film as a medium of communication rather than simply as a commercial enterprise, did local censorship begin to wither. The increasingly liberal attitudes of the 1960s made it possible to produce and screen films on topics that would have been unthinkable in Hollywood's "golden age." There was no attempt to abandon local licensing, but a series of court decisions depleted the grounds upon which permits might henceforth be refused. Based on the premise that all such censorship would be in violation of FIRST AMENDMENT freedoms, it was no longer possible for local authorities to ban films on the grounds that they were sacriligious, prejudicial to the best interests of the people of the city, tending to corrupt morals, harmful rather than educational, or undermining confidence that justice can be carried out. The tenor of such judgments, taken as a whole, was to emphasize that films might be made about real life, rather than being the optimistic, sentimental fare that seemed safer to many local censors. It is for the return of those "positive, wholesome values" that conservative groups such as the MORAL MAJORITY are campaigning.

Unlike most countries, the United States has never operated a system of national censorship. Imported films may be checked by Customs, under the Tariff Act (1930) (see United States 21.), but internally produced material is regulated not by the federal government but by the industry itself.

The American film industry was the first to institute self-regulating censorship, directed from within its own ranks and voluntarily accepted by all the members of that industry. From 1922 to 1968 the MOTION PICTURE ASSOCIATION OF AMERICA (first known as the MOTION PICTURE PRODUCERS AND DISTRIBUTORS ASSOCIATION), colloquially known as the Hays Office from its first director, WILL H. HAYS, had controlled film censorship, issuing general (and often stifling) guidance through its Production Code Administration. Other than the code, which was rigorously enforced and which set the standard for the moral simplicities of much mainstream Hollywood production, there was and is no formal, national film censorship. The MPAA issued its guidelines, the major companies followed them as requested, and, since these same companies owned the cinema chains where most Americans watched their products, these standards determined what might be shown at the nation's theaters.

Two factors altered this cozy situation. One was the Supreme Court decision on THE MIRACLE in 1952, which robbed the studios of their absolute control of the cinemas; the other, less concrete but perhaps more relevant to the popular mood, was the growing desire of filmmakers to present films that reflected contemporary life more realistically than permitted by the Hays Office. The MPAA, fearful of losing its authority, joined with the National Association of Theater Owners (NATO) and the International Film Importers and Distributors of America (IFIDA) to create, as of November 1, 1968, the Classification (originally Code) and Rating Administration (CARA). Thus censorship remains the industry's own affair.

Under the supervision of a Policy Review Committee made of members of MPAA, NATO and IFIDA, which sets guidelines and ensures that they are carried out as required, CARA operates through a seven-member Ratings Board, based in Hollywood. This full-time board, for which there is no formal qualification other than industry membership, is responsible for its own decisions, although its ultimate direction comes from the Policy Review Committee. Each film submitted for rating is seen by each member of the board. They discuss it and decide on the appropriate classification. Their basic test is to decide how the parents of an American child of under 17 would classify the material under discussion. Each film is rated on a variety of themes, including sex, violence, language, nudity, and overall theme and then given an overall rating based on these aspects. There is no compulsion to submit films, but virtually all producers, other than pornographers who themselves give their product an X rating, do so; some 500 films are rated a year.

American films fall into four categories: G, general audiences, all ages admitted and offering nothing offensive either to parents or children; PG-13, parental guidance suggested, some parts may not be suitable for children although there will be no extreme violence, grotesque horror or explicit sex; R, restricted, under-17 year-olds must be accompanied by a parent or guardian, an adult film with horror, violence, or coarse language etc., but no explicit sex; X, no admission to those under 17, a genuinely adults-only film with few restrictions as to sex, violence or coarse language. Film trailers are similarly censored by the Advertising Code Administration, a subcommittee of the MPAA; these are rated either G, for exhibition with any feature film, or R, restricted to exhibition with R- or X-rated features. Filmmakers may appeal against a given rating; the Ratings Appeal Board, similarly drawn from the industry's governing bodies, assesses arguments from CARA and from the complainant. A two-thirds majority, ballotted in a closed session, is necessary to change the original rating.

SEE ALSO Chicago: film censorship; Kansas 2. film censorship; Maryland 1. film censorship; New York 3. motion picture censorship; Ohio 2. motion picture censorship; Pennsylvania 1. Motion Picture Control Act.

11. Freedom of Information Act   This act, similar to the Swedish Freedom of the Press Act (see Sweden 3.), was passed in 1966, after a lengthy campaign by Rep. Carl Moss of California, and went into effect in 1967. Its purpose is to make as wide as possible a volume of government information, including that held by law enforcement agencies, available to the general public. As opposed to the 1946 Administrative Procedure Act, those seeking information no longer had an onus upon them to prove a demonstrable need to know. It put into law the dictum of President James Madison: "A people who mean to be their own governors must arm themselves with the power that knowledge gives. A popular government without popular information or the means of acquiring it is but a prologue to farce or a tragedy or both." In 1974, in the wake of the revelations of the FBI's COINTELPRO surveillance operations and despite a veto by President Ford, the act was amended to eliminate many of the loopholes whereby federal agencies had attempted to circumvent the law.

The act is designed to uphold the public's right of access, and the responsibility is on the government and its agencies to justify restrictions upon that right. Three types of disclosure are provided for: rules followed by agencies must be published in the *Federal Register*; other records must be disclosed on request; made available in reading rooms and suitably indexed. When an agency refuses to honor a request, the judicial rather than the executive branch of government determines the rights in the case. Agencies subject to the act are all those involved in the executive branch of the federal government (including the semi-autonomous regulatory commissions); the judiciary, Congress and state governments are exempt, although most states have their own version of the act.

Nine exemptions from disclosure exist: (1) information that must be kept secret in the interest of foreign relations or national defense, although all such information must already have been classified as secret; (2) the internal rules and practices governing the personnel and the operation of a given agency, although once these stray beyond the mundane such

as sick leave and parking permits and enter what the courts judge to be public interest, the exemption lapses; (3) information that has been exempted from disclosure by a statute other than the act, e.g., individual tax records are not generally available for scrutiny because of provisions in the tax laws; (4) trade secrets and privileged and confidential commercial and financial information; such information has created many lawsuits between trade rivals under the act, with such rivals appearing as defense and as plaintiff; (5) "inter-agency or intra-agency memoranda that are not available at law," i.e., the disclosure of any information that would thus impair the efficiency of an agency's operations—not statistics or similar factual material, but the confidential discussions that take place before a decision is reached; (6) any personal information the release of which would be an invasion of privacy; individuals may request their own files (although these are often precensored on the grounds of security) but may not see, inter alia, reports of ethics hearings as regards agency personnel; (7) investigatory records compiled for the purpose of law enforcement, assuming disclosure would cause one of six types of harm: interference with investigations, depriving a person of a fair trial, invasion of privacy, prejudicing confidential sources and information, revealing investigative methods, endangering law enforcement personnel; (8) information on the supervision of banks and financial institutions; and (9) information regarding petroleum, a rarely used exemption inserted as a price of his signature by President Johnson, loyal to his oil-rich state of Texas.

The act has been used continually for a variety of researches, by historians, journalists, companies, pressure groups and many individals, including foreign nationals who are thus able to obtain information on their own government and industry that remains secret at home. Only that information that is specified in the nine general provisions of the act may be kept from public access. Some 150,000 inquiries under the act are made annually. No administraiton has made it easy for the act to operate.

12. Intelligence Identities Protection Act (1982)   Under this act, passed on June 29, 1982, it is a crime for anyone to publish material that names a specific individual as a covert agent either of the CIA or the FBI. This prohibition is sustained even if such material has already been published, either cited in publicly accessible records or derived from public sources. The text of the law reads:

> Whoever, in the course of a pattern of activities intended to identify and expose covert agents, and with reason to believe that such activities would impair or impede the foreign intelligence activities of the United States, discloses any information that identifies an individual as a covert agent to any individual not authorized to receive classified information, knowing that the information disclosed so identifies such individual and that the United States is taking affirmative measures to conceal such individual's intelligence relationship to the United States, shall be fined not more than $15,000 or imprisoned not more than three years, or both.

13. library censorship (1876-1939) Although a number of circulating and social or subscription libraries had been established earlier, the burgeoning of U.S. public libraries came in the mid-19th century. These libraries were dedicated simultaneously to bringing knowledge to the masses and to ensuring that such knowledge as was available was strictly certified and "useful." Such intentions, with their strong leavening of religious and moral strictures, assumed a code of censorship. This worked on two levels, moral and social. Such "degenerate" European classics as BOCCACCIO, RABELAIS, Balzac, Sterne, Richardson and Fielding were proscribed on moral grounds alone. More immediately important to many librarians were popular modern works. As self-appointed guardians of the newly literate workforce, they felt that the popular, sensational novel was not sufficiently educative. They also worried that too much novel-reading would undermine the work ethic. More positively, it was hoped that, were trash excluded from the library, a wider range of genuinely stimulating material could be offered.

Based on such criteria, there operated a tacit, informal censorship based on taste rather than morals. As long as all books had to be requested from closed shelves, librarians could try to direct the reading tastes of their patrons. Certain books could be borrowed or consulted only with written permission; others were restricted to a certain age group or to those holding scholarly status.

The librarian's role as censor was defined in a number of local controversies, in Boston, Los Angeles and elsewhere, during the 1880s. While librarians were by no means obsessive censors, certain individuals attempted, like the contemporary anti-vice societies, to impose their own opinions on the public. In 1881 James M. Hubbard, a minister and cataloger, attacked the Boston Public Library for its "vapid and sensational" acquisitions, demanding that the young should be protected by a board of censors, a separate catalog and children's borrowing card and the labeling of harmless books. By 1885 Hubbard had defeated the library trustees and much of Boston's press who dismissed his worries. His suggestions were adopted. Hubbard attempted to extend his influence to control the nation's libraries, calling for the exclusion of anything touching on crime and sex, especially adultery, and decrying the works of female novelists. While Hubbard was not wholly successful, contemporary morals ensured that libraries grew more censorious. At the same time the developing professionalism of librarians encouraged them to dictate the public's reading.

This elitist role was challenged in the 1890s as the readers sought increasing access. Shelves were opened to patrons, and they were allowed to borrow two books, not one (although only one might be fiction). The new realism of authors such as ZOLA and the growing volume of socially critical investigative writing provided the censor with another problem. Established as the guardians of public consciousness, many librarians eschewed the "morbid and unsavory pessimism" of social realism, preferring to circulate the once excluded trashy popular novels. In 1893 the president of the American Library Association (ALA) compiled a list of 5,000 titles suitable for the small library. G.A. Henty, Hall Caine and Conan Doyle were included, as were selected volumes by FLAUBERT and GAUTIER (preferably not in translation), but Wilde and GEORGE MOORE were not. The duty, as they saw it, of librarians to avoid pessimism, was seen in the absolute exclusion of any such works.

Between 1900 and 1918 the librarian worked against a background of political liberalism and moral conservatism. The missionary educative spirit was faced by accelerating advances in human knowledge. The desire to disseminate information was balanced by worries as to what information was "correct." Library trustees and the communities who both appointed them and used their collections were essentially conservative. Librarians who embraced the new attitudes were unpopular; several lost their jobs. Local censorship crusades flared up continually, ostensibly guarding the young and seeking to purge libraries. The further a library from a metropolis, the more anodyne its shelves. The authorized ALA catalog of 1904 banned OVID, Rabelais, Boccaccio, Smollett, Richardson, Henry James, George Moore, Wilde, Stephen Crane, Flaubert, Dostoyevski ("sordid") and Gorky. Only certain works of Bennett, SHAW, VOLTAIRE, Tolstoy, and H.G. Wells appeared. In nonfiction, radicalism, atheism, socialism and disreputable (i.e., extreme) social criticism were all excluded.

The tide of progressive writing and the gradual liberalization of society inevitably affected the libraries. Old concepts of value consensus were collapsing. As writing became more radical and outspoken and writers challenged prevailing standards of obscenity in court, there developed growing attacks on librarian censors. Many felt their informal censorship was much more dangerous than legal censorship, and too elusive for an outright challenge. The librarians grew defensive, alleging that people could read what they wanted if they bought it, but that libraries had the duty to buy "good" books. This attitude, they claimed, was sanctioned by "sound preference in the community." The 1904-11 ALA catalog supplement underlined this stance. There was no socialism and no muckraking, but a plethora of popular best-sellers. The bellicosity of 1914-18 promoted a general jingoism that sought to purge libraries of suspect socialist, pacifist and similar volumes. Librarians helped compile the Army Index of 100 books forbidden to soldiers, although this was abandoned in late 1917. The nationalist fervor encouraged by the ESPIONAGE ACT (1917) AND SEDITION ACT (1918) further depleted library shelves. Only those librarians who saw themselves as custodians of an international body of knowledge, unaffected by partisan politics, fought the excisions. Postwar political conservatism affected the libraries. A survey by *Library Journal* in 1922 revealed that libraries still had restricted sections, closed stacks, locked cases, and special sections reserved for study or for a variety of interested professionals. Branches often lacked certain books held only by the central library.

As moral standards became more liberal, the 1920s and 1930s saw librarians abandoning their role as censor. The average librarian now opposed rather than promoted censorship as a professional belief. The 1926 ALA catalog, the first completely new one since 1904, reflected the new ideology: Moore, Wilde and Flaubert were now included, and many novelists, such as James, who had formerly been represented only by uncontroversial works, were now accepted in entirety. But JOYCE and Scott Fitzgerald were still barred, as were Zola, Gide and Proust. The 1931 supplement persisted in excluding Fitzgerald, along with Faulkner, HEMINGWAY and Huxley. Radical nonfiction was similarly proscribed.

While the debate on censorship had been essentially internal in the 1920s, the Depression at home and totalitarianism abroad forced libraries into a greater political awareness; librarians now saw their mandate as making all information available and letting readers form their own opinions, even if extremism, usually of the left, was still censored. In 1939 the ALA adopted the Library Bill of Rights, originated by the Des Moines library in 1938. It made three points: (1) books should be chosen for their value and this choice should not be influenced by the politics, race, religion or nationality of the writer; (2) all sides of a question should be represented by the books selected; (3) the library premises should be available for public discussions to all interested parties, irrespective of their beliefs or affiliations.

14. military regulations

Air Force It is provided under Air Force regulation 35-15 (3) (a) (1970) that:

(1) No member of the Air Force will distribute or post any printed material other than publications of an official governmental agency or base regulated activity within any Air Force installation without permission of the commander or his designee. A copy of the material with a proposed plan or method of distribution or posting will be submitted when permission is requested ... (2) When prior approval for distribution or posting is required, the commander will determine if a clear danger to the loyalty, discipline or morale of members of the Armed Forces, or material interference with the accomplishment of a military mission, would result. If such a determination is made, distribution or posting will be prohibited ... (3) Mere possession of materials unauthorized for distribution or posting may not be prohibited unless otherwise unlawful. However, such material may be impounded if a member of the Armed Forces distributes, or posts, or attempts to distribute or post such material within the installation ... (4) Distribution or posting may not be prohibited solely on the ground that the material is critical of Government policies or officials.

Post commanders are encouraged to promote the availability of material on as wide a range as possible of public interest topics. Obviously, by civilian standards, any such prohibitions are directly opposed to FIRST AMENDMENT rights, but as upheld in the case of *Brown, Secretary of Defense* v. *Glines* (1980), individual freedom takes second place to the military need for the maintenance of loyalty, discipline and morale.

Army Political campaigning is completely outlawed, as are "demonstrations, picketing, sit-ins, protest marches, political speeches and similar activities." The distribution or posting of any publication must be approved by a post commander, although since soldiers may vote in national elections, campaign literature must be allowed to circulate. The basis for the prohibition of any material is that it "presents a clear danger to the loyalty, discipline, or morale of troops ..." If a commander does prohibit a given publication, he must inform his immediate superior as well as the Department of the Army and receive approval to carry out the prohibition. Pending the receipt of that approval, the commander may delay the distribution of the material in question. Soldiers may not be polled as to their personal political preferences, nor may they be solicited for contributions to a campaign, and no officer or NCA may attempt to influence any soldier to vote for any given candidate.

SEE ALSO *Greer* v. *Spock* (1976).

Navy and Marine Corps As underlined by the U.S. Supreme Court decision in *Secretary of the Navy* v. *Huff* (1980), Naval and Marine commanders have the right to suppress FIRST AMENDMENT rights when these rights can be proved to interfere with the maintenance of loyalty, discipline and morale. Varying only as to specific geographical command, the Navy and Marine regulations state: "No ... personnel will originate, sign, distribute or promulgate petitions, publications, including pamphlets, newspapers, magazines, handbills, flyers, or other printed or written material, on board any ship, craft or aircraft, or in any vehicle ... or any military installation on duty or in uniform, or anywhere within a foreign country irrespective of uniform or duty status, unless prior command approval is obtained." Commanders are directed "to control or prohibit" the circulation of materials that they feel would

(1) materially interfere with the safety, operation, command, or control of his unit or the assigned duties of particular members of the command; or (2) present a clear danger to the loyalty, discipline, morale or safety to personnel of his command; or (3) involve distribution of material or the rendering of advice or counsel that causes, attempts to cause or advocates insubordination, disloyalty, mutiny, refusal of duty, solicits desertion, discloses classified information, or contains obscene or pornographic matter; or (4) involve the planning or perpetration of an unlawful act or acts.

Uniform Code of Military Justice Under the Uniform Code of Military Justice members of the Armed Forces are excepted from certain freedoms enjoyed by civilians under the U.S. Constitution. These include article 88: "Any commissioned officer who uses contemptuous words against the

President ... shall be punished as a court-martial may direct";
article 133: "Any commissioned officer, cadet or midshipman
who is convicted of conduct unbecoming an officer and a
gentleman shall be punished as a court-martial may direct";
article 134: "... all disorders and neglects to the prejudice of
good order and discipline in the armed forces, all conduct of
a nature to bring discredit upon the armed forces ... shall be
punished at the discretion of [a] court."

Among the various cases that have emerged under the
UCMJ was that of *Parker* v. *Levy* (1974). Levy was an army
physician working in a hospital. After he made statements to
black soldiers urging them to refuse orders to go to Vietnam
and had attacked the Special Forces as "liars and
thieves ... killers of peasants ... and murderers of women
and children," Levy was court-martialed, dismissed from the
Army, ordered to forfeit all pay and serve three years of hard
labor in the stockade. Levy appealed his sentence to the U.S.
Supreme Court but was unable to have it quashed.

15. obscenity laws   The Constitution, under the FIRST
AMENDMENT, states that "Congress shall make no
law ... abridging the freedom of speech or of the press" and
thus outlaws a national system of censorship. The federal
system of government means that obscenity laws may vary
widely, and the prominence and power of various pressure
groups can mean that in the short term local prohibitions may
have greater force than do the pronouncements of the federal
authorities. The current test for obscenity, as set down by the
U.S. Supreme Court, derives from the case of MILLER V.
CALIFORNIA (1973) and requires that all these conditions be
satisfied: the AVERAGE PERSON, taking contemporary community standards, would find that a work, taken as a whole,
appeals to the prurient interest; the work depicts or describes
sexual conduct in a patently offensive manner; the work,
taken as a whole, lacks serious literary, artistic, political or
scientific value. The Supreme Court further defined patently
offensive sexual conduct as either patently offensive representations or descriptions of intimate sexual acts, normal or
perverted, actual or simulated, or patently offensive representations or depictions of masturbation, excretory functions
or lewd exhibition of the genitals. The general effect of such
definitions is for all cases dealing with obscene publications
to be restricted to allegedly hard-core pornography. A number
of other federal laws deal with the sending by mail and
importation of obscene articles, the interstate transportation
of such articles, the making of obscene broadcasts and the
prohibition of child pornography (in which a child is defined
as anyone under 16). The Anti-Pandering Act (1968) bars the
unsolicited mailing of advertisements promoting potentially
offensive material. State laws generally ban all trafficking in
obscene materials, but the compulsion under *Miller* to define
such materials by a specific test has forced some states to
reenact old laws or create new ones for their own use.

SEE ALSO California 2. obscenity statute, 3. offensive language; Delaware's obscenity statute; Georgia 1. obscenity
statute, 2. possession of obscene material; Illinois's obscenity
statute; Kentucky's obscenity statute; Los Angeles—possession of obscene matter; Maryland 2. sale of objectionable
material to minors; Massachusetts's obscenity statute; New
York 5. obscenity statute; obscene publications law: U.S.
Mail; Ohio 1. obscene material; Tennessee; United States 24.
transporting obscene material; United States 17. postal
regulations; United States 21. Tariff Act (1930); United
States 22. telephone regulations (federal and state).

16. Pentagon censorship   The concept of national security
is invoked as the justification for limiting the availability of
information in many countries, including the U.S., where the
Department of Defense is empowered to classify as secret an
enormous volume of material. With the lapsing of wartime
censorship in 1945, the Pentagon attempted to institute an
all-embracing censorship system. In 1947 the Security Advisory Board of the joint State Department/Army/Navy/Air
Force Coordinating Committee suggested an automatic ban
on any information likely to cause "serious administrative
embarrassment." The vagueness of this definition ensured
that it was not taken up, any more than was Defense Secretary
James Forrestal's broadbased scheme, in 1948, to ban all
information "detrimental to our national security."

The situation remained undefined until the Korean War,
when President Truman laid down four security classifications, ordering the Pentagon to sort its secrets into "Top
Secret," "Secret," "Confidential" and "Restricted." This too
was seen as overly vague and the media in particular campaigned against so wide and unspecific a system. In 1953
President Eisenhower responded by cutting out the Restricted
category and limiting the number of agencies that were actually permitted to classify material. This system lasted until
1972, when President Nixon's Executive Order 11,652 further reduced the agencies allowed to classify material and
attempted to promote faster declassification of no longer
sensitive material. The Freedom of Information Act (1966)
had further weakend the domination of the classifiers, but
loopholes in the law ensured that little information became
free if a relevant agency did not wish it.

The result of all this secrecy is a massive amount of
classified material. The Department of Defense has amassed
more secret files than can be counted. The Pentagon had in
1979 some 1,020,000 cubic feet of classified files, the
equivalent of 2,297 stacks, each the height and volume of the
555-foot-high Washington Monument. Even government officials admit that this is somewhat excessive, and one veteran
of the civil service, William G. Florence (with 43 years of
government work behind him), stated that "less than one half
of one per cent of the ... documents ... actually contain information qualifying for even the lowest defense category."

SEE ALSO United States 6. classified information.

17. postal regulations

communist political propaganda   Under section 305(a) of
the Postal Service and Federal Employee Salary Act (1962):

mail matter, except sealed letters, which originates or which is printed or otherwise prepared in a foreign country and which is determined by the Secretary of the Treasury pursuant to rules and regulations to be promulgated by him to be "communist political propaganda," shall be detained by the Postmaster General upon its arrival for delivery in the United States, or upon its subsequent deposit in the United States domestic mails, and the addressee shall be notified that such matter has been received and will be delivered only on the addressee's request, except that such dentention shall not be required in the case of any matter which is furnished pursuant to subscription or which is otherwise ascertained by the Postmaster General to be desired by the addressee.

"Communist political propaganda" is defined in the Foreign Agents Registration Act (1938) as including:

> any oral, visual, graphic, written, pictorial, or other communication or expression by any person (1) which is reasonably adapted to, or which the person disseminating the same believes will, or which he intends to, prevail upon, indoctrinate, convert, indice, or in any other way influence a recipient or any section of the public within the United States with reference to the political or public interests, policies, or relations of a government of a foreign country or foreign political party or with reference to the foreign policies of the United States or to promote within the United States racial, religious, or social dissensions, or (2) which advocates, advises, instigates, or promotes any racial, social, political or religious disorder, civil riot, or any other conflict involving the use of force or violence in any other American republic or the overthrow of any government or political sub-division of any other American republic by means involving the use of force or violence.

The practical enforcement of this regulation was operated through 11 postal checkpoints, which screened all incoming unsealed mail from a list of designated foreign countries for possible communist propaganda. Only material that was addressed to government or educational institutions or was already guaranteed exemption under a reciprocal international cultural agreement was exempted. If the mail in question was deemed to be communist political propaganda the recipients were sent a notice informing them of this fact and requesting that, if they wanted their mail, they return an attached reply card within 20 days. Otherwise the mail would be destroyed. In the case of *Lamont* v. *Postmaster General* (1965), when the mail in question was a copy of the *Peking Review*, the Supreme Court found that these regulations were unconstitutional. In particular, the obligation to return the reply card was cited as "unconstitutional because it requires an official act as a limitation on the unfettered exercise of the addressee's FIRST AMENDMENT rights." Such a regulation was in direct opposition to "the uninhibited, robust, and wide-open debate" that was supposedly intrinsic to the amendment.

mailing obscene material   Under this statute, passed in 1865 and cited at Title 18 USC, section 1461, it is illegal to send "any obscene, lewd, lascivious, filthy book, pamphlet, pic-

ture, print or other publication of a vulgar or indecent character" or "any letter upon the envelope of which, or postal card upon which scurrilous epithets may have been written or printed, or disloyal devices printed or engraved" through the U.S. mails. As such the statute has been responsible for the bulk of federal prosecutions in this area ever since. It runs as follows:

> Every obscene, lewd, lascivious, indecent, filthy or vile article, matter, thing, device or substance; and Every article or thing designed, adapted, or intended for producing abortion, or for any indecent or immoral use [this originally included a prohibition on articles for "preventing conception"] and Every article, instrument, substance, drug, medicine, or thing which is advertised or described in a manner calculated to lead another to use or apply it for producing abortion, or for any indecent or immoral purpose; and Every written or printed card, letter, circular, book, pamphlet, advertisement, or notice of any kind giving information, directly or indirectly, where, or how, or from whom, or by what means any of such mentioned matters, articles, or things may be obtained or made, or where or by whom any act or operation of any kind for the procuring or producing of abortion will be done or performed, or how or by what means abortion may be produced, whether sealed or unsealed ... is declared to be nonmailable matter and shall not be conveyed in the mails or delivered from any post office or by any letter carrier ...

Those who contravene this regulation might be fined a maximum of $5,000 or face up to five years jail, or both for the first offense; subsequent offenses doubled all penalties. SEE ALSO Comstock Act (1873); President's Commission on Obscenity and Pornography; *United States* v. *Three Cases of Toys* (1842); *Birth Control*; *Ginsburg* v. *United States*; *Grimm* v. *United States* (1895); *Hamling* v. *United States*; *Lady Chatterley's Lover*; *Lamont* v. *Postmaster General* (1925); *Luros* v. *United States* (1968); *The Masses*; *Rosen* v. *United States* (1896); *Roth* v. *United States* (1957); *Rowan* v. *United States Post Office Department* (1970); *Sex Side of Life*; *Sunshine and Health*; *United States* v. *Kennerley* (1913); *United States* v. *Levine* (1936); *United States* v. *Reidel* (1971); *Voltaire*.

unwanted mail   Under section 4009 of the Postal Service and Federal Employee Salary Act (1965), entitled "Prohibition of Pandering Advertisements," every individual is allowed to take action against what he "in his sole discretion believes to be erotically arousing or sexually provocative." The statute declares that

> (a) Whoever for himself, or by his agents or assigns, mails or causes to be mailed any pandering advertisement which offers for sale matter which the addressee in his sole discretion believes to be erotically arousing or sexually provocative shall be subject to an order from the Postal Service to refrain from further mailings of such materials to designated addresses thereof ... (c) The order of the Postal Service shall expressly prohibit the sender and his agents or assigns from making any further mailings to the designated addres-

ses ... (e) Failure to observe such an order may be punishable by the court as contempt thereof ... (g) Upon request of the addressee, the order of the Postal Service shall include the names of any of his minor children who have not attained their nineteenth birthday, and who reside with the addressee.

18. The Privacy Act (1974)

The Privacy Act was passed when Congress was amending the Freedom of Information Act (see United States 11.) in 1974, and although it works essentially as a data protection measure, it overlaps and acts in concert with the Freedom of Information Act. The act is designed to protect information on individuals and applies only to the federal government and does not infringe upon commercial data banks, although these are subject to other statutes. It covers both manual and computer-generated records. Under the act any American citizen (foreigners excluded, as opposed to the Freedom of Information Act, which extends its benefits to any enquirer) has the right to inspect, and equally importantly to have corrected, any file that may exist on him or herself. The act also prohibits agencies from circulating the information they may have gathered on a person to other agencies. An individual may consent to such interchange of information, except that no information movement may occur without written records. And when an agency requests information from an individual, it must explain why the government needs that information and what may happen if the individual refuses to provide it.

The act holds two general exemptions, covering the nation's main collectors of personal information, the CIA and the FBI, but also extending to lesser law enforcement bodies. The act is enforced through the federal courts and anyone can sue to enforce any part of its provisions. Agencies may be fined for failure to comply with the act and an individual may sue for damages, which he claims have been caused by an agency's actions. Given that most suits come under the Freedom of Information Act, there have been few cases based on the Privacy Act; the latter's provisions have not been fine-tuned by legal decisions.

SEE ALSO Austria: Federal Ministries Act (1973); Denmark 3. Law on Publicity in Administration (1970); Norway 3. Freedom of the Press Act (1971); Sweden 3. Freedom of the Press Act.

19. The Sunshine Act (1976)

This act, designed to make more accessible the closed meetings of a variety of federal agencies, was passed in 1976 and went into effect a year later. It covers what are called "collegial" agencies, which are headed by a body comprising two or more members, appointed by the President but designed to operate in relative independence from his authority. Such agencies include the Federal Trade Commission, the Securities and Exchange Commission and around 50 others, all dealing in regulatory, licensing and quasi-judicial functions.

The act states that the meetings of these bodies must be open to the public if they result in the disposition of official agency matters. Ten statutory reasons exist to keep the meeting closed, the majority of which are the same as those used as exemptions from the Freedom of Information Act (see United States 11.) and members may vote for such a private meeting, citing one of those reasons. Whether open or closed, under the act there must be kept official records of the discussions, usually in the form of tape-recordings or transcripts rather than minutes. Once such records are compiled they become available to public scrutiny under the Freedom of Information Act.

20. court cases and legislation index

(1) obscene publications, books, magazines etc.
Board of Education v. *Pico* (1982)
Ginsberg v. *New York* (1968)
Ginzburg v. *United States*
Grimm v. *United States* (1895)
Hamling v. *United States*
In Re Worthington (1894)
Maryland 2. sale of objectionable material to minors
Memoirs of a Woman of Pleasure 2. trials
Memoirs of Hecate County
Memoirs v. *Massachusetts* (1966)
Miller Standard, The
Miller v. *California* (1973)
Mishkin v. *New York* (1966)
Myron
Naked Lunch, The
People of the State of New York v. *August Muller*
Redrup v. *New York* (1967)
Rosen v. *United States* (1896)
Roth v. *United States* (1957)
Schad v. *Borough of Mount Ephraim* (1981)
Screw
Smith v. *California* (1959)
Star v. *Preller* (1974)
Sunshine and Health
Tropic of Cancer
Ulysses
United States v. *Kennerley* (1913)
United States v. *Reidal* (1971)
United States v. *Thirty-Seven Photographs* (1971)
United States 15. obscenity laws
Winters v. *New York* (1948)

(2) films
A Stranger Knocks
Amants, Les (*The Lovers*)
Birth of a Nation, The
Blue Movie/Fuck
Caligula
Carnal Knowledge
Chant d'Amour, Un
Don Juan
I Am Curious—Yellow
James Gang in Missouri
Lady Chatterley's Lover 3. film
M

Magic Mirror
Miracle, The
Moon Is Blue, The
Native Son
New York v. *Ferber* (1982)
Pinky
Revenge at Daybreak
Titicut Follies
Viva Maria
Wild Weed
Willard-Johnson Boxing Match

(3) miscellaneous
Chaplinsky v. *New Hampshire*
Cincinnati v. *Karlan* (1973)
Commonwealth vs. *Sharpless*
Ratchford, President, University of Missouri v. *Gay Lib* (1978)
Rowan v. *United States Post Office Department* (1970)
Epperson v. *Arkansas* (1968)
Scopes v. *State* (1927)

(4) espionage, sedition etc.
Abrams v. *United States* (1919)
Aliens Registration Act, 1940 (U.S.)
Frohwerk v. *United States* (1919)
Gitlow v. *New York* (1925)
Haig v. *Philip Agee* (1981)
Pierce v. *United States* (1920)
Schaeffer v. *United States* (1920)
Schenck v. *United States* (1919)
Smith Act (1940, 1948)
Snepp v. *United States* (1980)
Sweezy v. *New Hampshire* (1957)
United States v. *Marchetti* (1972)

(5) radio, television, broadcasting etc.
Federal Communications Act (1934) 1. equal time
"Filthy Words"
Hair

(6) freedom of speech, libel, slander etc.
Cohen v. *California* (1971)
Goldwater v. *Ginzburg*
Greer v. *Spock* (1976)
Hatch Act
Near v. *Minnesota ex. rel. Olson* (1931)
New York Times Company v. *Sullivan* (1964)
New York Times Rule
Pentagon Papers, The
People v. *Bruce* (1964)
Smith v. *Collin* (1978)
Stanley v. *Georgia* (1969)
Terminiello v. *Chicago* (1949)
United States 14. military regulations
United States 17. postal regulations
Whitney v. *California* (1927)

Yates v. *United States* (1957)

21. Tariff Act (1930) Under the Tariff Act U.S. Customs is empowered to seize any material that is being imported into the country and that it feels might be obscene; it must then submit that material to a federal court in order for its obscenity, or otherwise, to be judicially determined. If anything, Customs tends to be more liberal than America's internal censors, accepting more potentially obscene films than many local authorities. Conversely, customs represents the only example of national censorship in America, and if material seized by them is upheld by the courts as obscene, then it is effectively deprived, at a stroke, of the entire U.S. market.

The act states:

All persons are prohibited from importing into the United States from any foreign country ... any obscene book, pamphlet, paper, writing, advertisement, circular, print, picture, drawing, or other representation, figure, or image on or of paper or other material, or any cast, instrument, or other article which is obscene or immoral, or any drug or medicine or any article whatever for the prevention of conception, or for causing unlawful abortion ... No such articles whether imported separately or contained in packages with other goods entitled to entry, shall be admitted to entry; and all such articles and, unless it appears to the satisfaction of the collector that the obscene or other prohibited articles contained in the package were enclosed therein without the knowledge or consent of the importer, owner, agent, or consignee, the entire contents of the package in which such articles are contained, shall be subject to seizure and forfeiture as hereinafter provided ...

Provided, further, that the Secretary of the Treasury may, in his discretion, admit the so-called classics or books of recognized and established literary or scientific merit, but may, in his discretion, admit such classics or books only when imported for non-commercial purposes. Upon the appearance of any such book or matter at any customs office, the same shall be seized and held by the collector to await the judgment of the district court as hereinafter provided; and no protest shall be taken to the United States Customs Court from the decision of the collector. Upon the seizure of such book or matter the collector shall transmit information thereof to the district attorney of the district in which is situated the office at which such seizure has taken place, who shall institute proceedings in the district court for the forfeiture, confiscation and destruction of the book or matter seized. Upon the adjudication that such book or matter is of the character the entry of which is by this section prohibited, it shall be ordered destroyed and shall be destroyed. Upon adjudication that such book or matter thus seized is not of the character the entry of which is by this section prohibited, it shall not be excluded from entry under the provisions of this section. In any such proceeding any party in interest may upon demand have the facts at issue determined by a jury and any party may have an appeal or the right of review as in the case of ordinary actions or suits.

SEE ALSO *The Decameron*; *Ecstasy*; United States 10. film censorship; Grosz, George; *Hellenic Sun*; *I Am Curious—Yellow*; *Married Love*; *The Naked Lunch*; Rabelais, Francois; *Tropic of Cancer*; *Ulysses*.

22. telephone regulations—federal and state   Under title 47 USC, section 223:

> Whoever—(1) in the District of Columbia or in interstate or foreign communications by means of telephone—(A) makes any comment, request, suggestion or proposal which is obscene, lewd, lascivious, filthy, or indecent; (B) makes a telephone call, whether or not conversation ensues, without disclosing his identity, and with intent to annoy, abuse, threaten or harass any person at the called number; (c) makes or causes the telephone of another repeatedly or continuously to ring, with intent to harass any person at the called number; or (D) makes repeated telephone calls, during which conversation ensues, solely to harass any person at the called number; or (2) knowingly permits any telephone under his control to be used for any purpose prohibited by this section, shall be fined not more than $500 or imprisoned not more than six months, or both.

This legislation, which deals mainly with the use of the telephone by one individual to harass another, was supplemented in 1983 by a federal law aimed at controlling, and in fact driving out of business, the rash of "telephone sex" services, christened by their opponents as "Dial-a-Porn."

The Federal Communications Commission (FCC) may impose fines upon and the U.S. attorney general may seek to prosecute anyone or any firm who operates a telephone service that is determined as being obscene or indecent and that is available to anyone under the age of 18. Most states have their own local telephone regulations, which are similar to the federal ones and which all declare it illegal to make a telephone call in which there is an "intent to annoy or to abuse."

23. text book censorship   The 1980s have seen a number of attempts by individuals and local authorities to censor publications held by a variety of American public institutions, notably schools and libraries. Parents' committees and school boards have been active since the late 1970s in mounting such attacks, and several hundred cases of local censorship per year are reported to the Office for Intellectual Freedom of the American Library Association. It is presumed that this figure is but a fraction of the whole. Such censorship has become recognized as a major tool in the crusade for the preservation of "American values" and against SECULAR HUMANISM.

A variety of individuals and groups spearhead the campaign, which extends throughout the U.S. and which in its most extreme form has indulged in the burning of books. Most campaigns are initiated by parents, often backed by clergymen, who lobby school boards to gain the exclusion of certain textbooks, notably those dealing with such issues as feminism, minority rights, poverty and sexual freedom.

Facing such pressure, a number of textbook publishers have begun to excise such material form their works.

Notable among private censor organizations is Educational Research Analysts Inc., founded in 1973 by MEL AND NORMA GABLER of Longview, Texas. The Gablers monitor every textbook used in Texas, and have successfully had a number of dictionaries barred from school use on account of their "vulgar language and unreasonable definitions," and they exercise a continuing influence on the reading lists of Texas schools.

SEE ALSO Christian Crusade; Citizens for Decency Through Law; Citizens for Decent Literature; Clean Up TV Campaign (CUTV-US); Coalition for Better Television; Committee on Public Information; Crusade for Decency; Foundation to Improve Television; Moral Majority; Morality in Media; National Federation for Decency; National Organization for Decent Literature; People for the American Way.

24. transporting obscene material   Under title 18 USC, section 1465, "Whoever knowingly transports in interstate or foreign commerce for the purpose of sale or distribution any obscene, lewd, lascivious, or filthy book, pamphlet, picture, film, paper, letter, writing, print, silhouette, drawing, figure, image, cast, phonograph recording, electrical transcription or other article capable of producing sound or any other matter of indecent or immoral character, shall be fined not more than $5,000 or imprisoned not more than five years, or both."

25. The "Whistleblowers" Act (1978)   This act, more formally listed as the Civil Service Reform Act, was designed to protect civil servants who choose to reveal government malfeasance or allied wrongdoing. It was passed following a number of incidents in which civil servants had chosen to leak sensitive information and were subsequently punished for their allegiance to what they saw as a duty to the public. Information covered under the act is defined as that which the employee reasonably believes to illustrate or cover up "a violation of any law, rule or regulation" or "mismanagement, a gross waste of funds, an abuse of authority, or a substantial and specific danger to public health or safety." Employees are not protected if the information in question is itself protected by statute or required by an executive order to be kept secret in the interest of foreign relations or national security.

The act is enforced by the Office of Special Counsel, from which an ombudsman is appointed by the President, subject to senatorial approval, to serve for five years. This ombudsman has substantial powers and can stop the actions of an agency that is attempting to punish a civil servant, require that agency to answer allegations referring to the case and discipline those officials who abuse their power in trying to attack the whistleblower. The office ensures that employees are protected when disclosing information both to the public or to Congress and to the office itself or to inspectors general of government agencies.

26. World War II press censorship   The U.S. government set up its censorship of the homefront wartime media within a week of Japan's attack on Pearl Harbor in December 1941.

President Roosevelt appointed Byron Price to head the office of censorship, which had developed out of the old Committee on Public Information of World War I. Price was empowered to coordinate the voluntary self-censorship of the U.S. home media and to control any material that was written for consumption outside the U.S. He had no responsibility for propaganda as such. To explain the censorship system to the press, Price issued the "Code of Wartime Practices for the U.S. Press." This slim, 12-page document was revised several times, but remained essentially the same. The basis of all controls was that nothing might be published that might help the enemy war effort. The code specified those areas about which the press might not write without the "appropriate authority": the location of troops, planes and ships, production contracts and capacities, casualty reports and ship sinkings.

The code was by no means popular, but the media, like most Americans, supported the war effort and, albeit grudgingly, joined in. Their acquiescence was undoubtedly helped by Price's enumeration of the principles behind his system: Voluntary censorship must be restricted completely to those matters that really did affect national security. The press must not be asked to censor itself on the grounds of any request that did not genuinely further that security. The threat to security must be real, and the press must be given a solid, reasonable explanation. There must be no interference with editorial opinion. Requests for censorship must not be influenced by nonsecurity, politically orientated considerations or interests. The press must not be put in the position of policing or withholding from publication the statements and opinions of responsible public officials. No material already circulating abroad could be censored from the U.S. press. Finally, the code must be explained to the public and they must understand exactly why the censorship was necessary. The code was enforced until August 1945, when it was abandoned with the end of the war.

Universal Declaration of Human Rights   The declaration was proclaimed in 1948 and while never set down as a legal treaty, it is seen in many countries as de facto customary international law. Article 19 states: "Everyone has the right to freedom of opinion and expression; this right includes freedom to hold opinions without interference, and to seek, receive and impart information and ideas through any media regardless of frontiers."

SEE ALSO American Convention on Human Rights; European Convention on Human Rights; International Covenant on Civil and Political Rights.

unofficial classification   A method of countering journalistic inquiries whereby a government official claims that the requested piece of information has been classified as secret when in fact it has not been.

unprotected speech   Unprotected speech, as defined under U.S. law, covers such varieties of speech that are not protected by the FIRST AMENDMENT. As Justice Brennan of the U.S. Supreme Court explained during the case of ROTH V. UNITED STATES (1957): "The guarantees of freedom of expression [under the Constitution] gave no absolute protection for every utterance." The aim of the amendment was not to protect libel, obscenity and the like but "to assure unfettered interchange of ideas for the bringing about of political and social changes desired by the people." Thus "all ideas having even the slightest redeeming social importance—unorthodox ideas, controversial ideas, even ideas hateful to the prevailing climate of opinion—have ... full protection." Unprotected speech includes obscenity, child pornography, FIGHTING WORDS, situations where a CLEAR AND PRESENT DANGER can be proved, libel, slander and DEFAMATION, and commercial speech that can be proved to be false or fraudulent.

U.S.S.R.

1. art censorship   In the immediate aftermath of the 1917 Revolution the Soviet government was at pains to encourage a wide spectrum of artistic talent, both conventional and experimental. Exhibitions were mounted of Constructivists, Suprematists and similar progressive movements, but with the accession to power of Joseph Stalin in 1929 this freedom was utterly curtailed. In 1930 the state of the arts in the Soviet Union was systematized under a variety of provisions established at the "Kharkov Conference for mass organization of Art and Literature." Working under the slogan "Art must be a class weapon," as defined that year by the Soviets' International Bureau of Revolutionary Artists, the Congress declared "Artists are to abandon 'individualism' and the fear of strict 'discipline' as petty-bourgeois attitudes ... Artistic creation is to be systematised, 'collectivized,' and carried out according to the plans of a central staff like any other soldierly work ... Every proletarian artist must be a dialectic materialist. The method of creative art is the method of dialectic materialism." To underline this policy, the Artists' International produced a series of slogans, including "Art renounces individualism. Art is to be disciplined. Art is to be created under the 'careful yet firm guidance' of a political party ..." By 1931 artistic standards had been further refined, with the demand that ideologically acceptable creativity embody three fundamental aspects: *partynost* (party character), *ideinost* (Socialist content) and *narodnost* (national roots).

On April 23, 1932, against the new slogan "All art must be propaganda," the Association of Soviet Artists was established. This submitted to centralized control all painting and sculpture in Russia. In its resolution "On Reconstruction of Literary-Artistic Organizations" the Central Committee of the CPSU ordered the liquidation of all independent or unofficial artists' organizations or movements, replacing them with strict party control and an ideologically acceptable unionized structure promulgating the official artistic line. Henceforth no artists who wished to work in the U.S.S.R.

could avoid joining the union or subordinating his or her creativity to its directions. In 1934, declaring that "the masses are the final arbiters of taste," the U.S.S.R. adopted a new name for state-sanctified art: SOCIALIST REALISM.

In 1939, setting down the role of the artist in Soviet society, Stalin coined the definition "the engineer of men's souls" to define his or her task. The engineers' jobs were admittedly limited, with all acceptable art restricted to pictures of the "new Soviet man" perfecting the "new Soviet society." Soviet artists were to use *kritika i samokritika* (criticism and self-criticism) to ensure the purity of their own efforts. The struggles of the Great Patriotic War (World War II) superseded artistic problems, but the official controls never weakened. In 1947 modern art was condemned as "decadent, anti-humanist and pathological" and any backsliding artists were expelled from the Artists Union. Any form of artistic revisionism was cited as "subjective anarchy."

2. broadcasting censorship Soviet broadcasting, serving probably the largest viewing and listening network in the world, under the aegis of the State Committee for Television and Broadcasting, is guided, as are all Soviet media, by the principles and ideological needs of the Communist Party and the government. All media are thus controlled and staffed by party members or at least its definite supporters. Delegates who represent the broadcasters in the various unions are invariably members. The most senior personnel are drawn from party functionaries of suitable standing. As one of these put it in 1970: "For each of us there is nothing more dear than to extol our Communist party, our Socialist Fatherland, our fraternal international people. There is nothing more noble … than to spread propaganda for the experience of building Communism in our country."

The censorship of broadcasting, like that of books, is controlled by GLAVLIT (Central Board for Literature and Press Affairs). In the context of broadcasting the most obvious result of such censorship is a virtual prohibition on live programs, the content of which cannot be easily regulated. Supposed studio discussions are not spontaneous, but depend on prepared and precensored texts delivered by the participants. In addition to the wide spectrum of generally taboo topics that might present Soviet government and society in a negative light, broadcasting is further restricted by its own rules: There are no religious programs, and when religion is mentioned it is only as a butt of ridicule; accurate documentaries are almost impossible to make, so risky would be the discussion of the Soviet economy or crime rate. The censors also deal with the adaptation of Western films for TV, mutilating them substantially.

It is also forbidden to record and disseminate the output of the various foreign stations broadcasting information and/or propaganda to Soviet citizens. Such activities come under the description of "distribution of hostile information." Radio Free Europe, Radio Liberty, Voice of America, Deutsche Welle and the BBC broadcast some 683 combined hours of programs per week to the Soviet Union and a further 783 to

eastern Europe. It has never been a crime to listen to these programs, even under the harshest years of Stalinism, but Soviet bloc authorities have tried in a variety of ways, from simple jamming, to political pressure on Western governments, to infiltrating the staff of the stations with pro-Soviet employees and publishing attacks on the probity of such stations in the press—all intended to undermine the effect these broadcasts have on their populations. Rumania and Hungary, then the most liberal of socialist states, abandoned jamming in 1964 and 1963 respectively; the result of glasnost has been the wholesale shutdown of all Soviet jamming efforts.

Soviet jamming was widespread and costly, with some 3,000 transmitters, a 5,000-member staff engaged in 24-hour-a-day interference with foreign broadcasts. The cost of such efforts ran into several hundred million dollars and was last assesed (in 1971) at six times that of the U.S.S.R.'s own external broadcasts, which run to 2,000-plus hours per week. Despite all this effort, jamming was by no means universally effective and listeners in the countryside, as opposed to the towns where jamming was concentrated, could always obtain relatively good reception.

3. censorship of publications (Glavlit) Post-Revolutionary censorship was initiated in the U.S.S.R. by Lenin, who signed a decree in 1918 to authorize temporary press censorship for the duration of the Civil War; it was to be abandoned once that war was over. In 1920 this position was reversed when Lenin flatly refused to annul the decree, claiming that unrestricted freedom would merely help "monarchists and anarchists" and thus undermine the still fragile Bolshevik power base.

Contemporary literary censorship operates under Glavlit—*Glavnoye upravlenie po delam literatury i pechati*, the Central Board for Literature and Press Affairs—which was initially set up in the 1920s. The official title of Glavlit is "The Central Board for Safeguarding of State Secrets in the Press under the Committee for Press Affairs of the U.S.S.R. Council of Ministers," although in practice censorship is quite independent of the authority of the committee, a vaguely defined department that was created in 1964 by the then-powerful A.I. Adzhubey, former Premier Khrushchev's son-in-law. Glavlit takes responsibility for all U.S.S.R. censorship from its headquarters in Moscow. It is responsible to the Department for Agitation and Propaganda of the CPSU Central Committee, which in turn takes orders from the CPSU Central Committee for Ideological Questions. Its operations can also be controlled directly by the CPSU Central Committee Secretary. Censorship on the regional and district level is exercised by individual Glavlit boards; cities have their own local "Oblit" officials. In all, the department employs some 70,000 people, invariably party or Komsomol members. The censorship system employs many KGB officers, arts graduates and former journalists.

All major regional or city newspapers, publishing houses and major printers have their own permanent or visiting censors. Specialist censors operate to "read" or "service" (i.e., censor) the copy in various specialist magazines and periodicals. The decision of any local official can be overruled by his superiors at U.S.S.R. Glavlit in Moscow. The censorship of specific material is further controlled by a number of organs. The largest of these is the military censorship of the General Staff of the U.S.S.R. Armed Forces. Material dealing with nuclear and atomic power is controlled by the State Atomic Energy Commission. This office must license any mention of nuclear energy, both pacific and military, and even checks science fiction; it is notorious for its slow deliberations. All material dealing with space flight and exploration is similarly controlled by the Commission for Research and Exploration of Cosmic Space, under the U.S.S.R. Academy of Sciences. This was established in 1957, contemporaneous with the launch of Sputnik I. Further departments exist to censor texts dealing with radio, electronics and chemistry. Finally, "KGB censorship" controls all matters deemed relevant to state security.

Glavlit censors are sent two copies of every article in proof; these proofs must include the page layout so that no tricks may be played with adjacent headlines or illustrations. The censor notes such areas that are unsound and informs the relevant editor. This editor can debate the proposed cut; the actual writer cannot defend his or her work in person. Such alterations as are made are, as far as official correspondance is concerned, those suggested by the editor. No mention is ever made of Glavlit or censorship to an author. The official euphemism when instructing the printer is "author's corrections." The censor is guided primarily by THE INDEX OF INFORMATION NOT TO BE PUBLISHED IN THE OPEN PRESS. The full "Talmud" (as it is known) runs to 300-plus pages dealing with general and specific topics and is aimed specifically at maintaining as pure as possible an image of the Soviet government and the ideology it promotes. It also deals with material that might threaten national security or reveal any weaknesses in the socialist system, such as agricultural failures or crime statistics. In the wake of glasnost (see U.S.S.R. 5) the list has been cut by around one third—in the main, material that is not considered as detrimental to Soviet defense or economic interests and material that, ostensibly secret, is known to be accessible to sophisticated foreign spy technology. Work on shrinking the "Talmud" yet further is in progress.

Once material has been passed for printing it receives the official Glavlit stamp (on every printer's sheet or every newspaper double page) and one copy of the proof is returned for production, while the other is held in Glavlit files. For printing any material without the stamp an editor, printer or other person responsible faces up to eight years in prison. The printed copy is then compared with the Glavlit proof and, if identical, is given a further stamp authorizing publication. There exists in addition a higher level of censor who can reread the proofs and force further changes. In theory, Glavlit has no right to demand textual changes unless the material deals with military or state secrets and an editor can refuse to comply. Few editors risk taking this course.

In June 1986, at the Union of Soviet Writers' Congress, it appeared that the hegemony of Glavlit might at last be modifed. With the deposition of First Secretary Georgy Markov, aged 75, for 15 years a hardline advocate of extreme control, and his replacement by the younger Vladimir Karpov, 64, a former victim of the Stalinist era, the opportunity to diminish censorship may have emerged. Whether the entire apparatus will be dismantled is unlikely, but some relaxation of the censorship bureaucracy, in harmony with similar changes throughout the Soviet system advocated by President Gorbachev's policy of glasnost seems feasible. Glavlit's chief censor, Dr. Vladimir Baldyrev, has stressed that the department now exists as a vehicle for the destruction of the "cult of secrecy" and the transformation of the Soviet press into "an information culture," but in the same interview he affirmed that prepublication censorship will remain a staple of the Soviet press.

4. censorship of science   The censorship of science in the Soviet Union, which was instituted with the founding of the state, falls into four basic areas, all justified by the ostensible desire to safeguard the secrets of Soviet science from its enemies: (1) the control of fields of knowledge in which it is permitted to do research; (2) the setting down of those sources of primary scientific information one may use; (3) censorship of the contents of scientific papers, journals and books; (4) the strict monitoring of contacts between Soviet scientists and their Western colleagues.

In the 1930s Einstein's relativity theory was prohibited, as was the study of paramagnetic resonance. Biologists might not deal in "formal genetics"—those theories based on the work of G.J. Mendel. Eugenics was absolutely forbidden as was paediatrics. The study of sociology was forbidden until the 1960s. The limits on genetics continued in the 1940s and were joined by those on linguistics. In the 1950s no physiological research that contradicted Pavlov might be undertaken; cybernetics was condemned as a reactionary science.

The state monitors clsoely all laboratories and the experiments conducted inside them, as well as any data, sociological and economic, that is gathered. It is almost impossible, due to the policy of the KGB, which actively discourages such trips, for a scientist to undertake research outside the country. Those scientists who are permitted to do so are often of the second rank, and all such trips are under heavy KGB surveillance. Within the U.S.S.R. the collection of data by questionnaires or mass surveys is very hard. The KGB, plus several other agencies, must give permission. Even when research is encouraged, such as into an epidemic or disease, the scientists involved receive little information from the authorities. Access to statistical data is virtually impossible: 50-year-old material remains restricted and thus economists are severely hampered in their research.

Libraries and archives suffer extreme censorship. The Principal Archive Bureau actively discourages research into the material it holds, denying much primary source material to scholars. The Soviet Union's main library, the Lenin Library, restricts access to 25 percent of its stock. The favored few who are allowed to read controlled material, in Room 13, must sign a declaration promising not to make use of anything they have read. The state's scientific libraries are equally secretive, especially as regards foreign publications. There is no open shelving and permission must be given to read each book. Banned volumes include the work of any Soviet scientist who has died in jail or left the country. Nothing formerly or currently proscribed by state policy as politically harmful may be read, and no sex research. Foreign journals must be read and censored, either in part or as a whole issue, prior to releasing them to readers.

The publication of one's research, for internal or external consumption, follows rigid lines. First one must read the paper to one's colleagues, who must approve its publication; it is then submitted to a foreign affairs expert commission, one of which, staffed by bureaucrats and a KGB member, exists in every scientific research establishment specifically to monitor all published work. They give their expert opinion, formulated in a document that states: The work has no new elements, makes no discoveries or inventions, and all problems and questions raised in it have already been discussed in various other papers and articles. It is then sent to the ministry in Moscow where it is rechecked; such checks can take up to two years and unsatisfactory papers may simply vanish into the bureaucracy. Articles for internal consumption will be further checked by the GLAVLIT hierarchy. Many reasons exist for rejecting a paper but overall is the desire of the censor to keep Soviet science a secret.

Personal contacts between Soviet scientists and their Western peers are strictly monitored. The stated aim of the U.S.S.R. is to extract the maximum of information from the West and give as little as possible in return. To this end all incoming letters to scientists are opened and may possibly never be delivered. Scientists may not send their Western colleagues copies of any manuscript or of Soviet archive material. The exchange of natural specimens is almost impossible. Only the most official links are permitted, with minimal personal fraternization condoned. Returning Soviet scientists must write reports for the KGB and the military. Those who refuse will not be allowed abroad again. Even the complaisant are unable to take up the many invitations they receive to conferences and seminars. Western scientists who visit the U.S.S.R. are banned from many institutions and their laboratories, sometimes from whole towns.

5. glasnost   There can be little doubt that Mikhail Gorbachev's policy of glasnost or "openness" has set in motion the greatest revolution in Soviet life since the last war and possibly since the Revolution itself. Successive governments have paid lip-service to employing the media to publicize the shortcomings of the system, but Gorbachev's determination to reform Russia as never before has unleashed a tide of complaint, analysis and self-criticism hitherto unknown to the Soviet people. Starting as a way of using the media, in the traditional manner, to help push forward economic and social reforms, glasnost initially meant the unprecedented discussion of official corruption and economic waste, alcoholism, drug abuse, dissatisfaction among the young and a variety of other topics previously censored out of the nation's media. This spread to the highlighting of disasters, notably that of the explosion at the Chernobyl power station, when incompetent officials were openly pilloried for their failings. As Gorbachev's reforms have pushed forward, so has the scope of glasnost broadened. Stories akin to Western investigative journalism have begun to appear, dealing with blundering police, corrupt KGB men and similar individuals whose activities had previously remained sacrosanct. The condition of Russia's labor camps has even come under discussion and the past, notably the excesses of Joseph Stalin, has come more and more to be disinterred from the official histories and placed under a new and searching light. A number of "non-persons" have been rehabilitated, and even Trotsky, the Antichrist of the Revolution, seems scheduled for forgiveness.

The extent to which glasnost will persist remains debatable. While it has undoubtedly modified some of the excesses of Soviet censorship—newspapers seem freer, the arts are noticeably liberalized—there is still no hard-and-fast law enshrining the new mood. It could all be reversed very easily. Clandestine SAMIZDAT publishing still exists, with around 400 titles in print, and it is still a basic truth of all Soviet publishing that nothing, however ostensibly "liberal," appears without permission. A new press law was promised for 1986, but remained in embryo. The intention is that it should provide a firm basis for the new forms, casting journalists as watchdogs, offering far better access to information and simultaneously defining limits to "openness" in the hope of calming Gorbachev's more conservative critics. Those involved with drafting the law have stated that it still has no precise definition of freedom of the press. Nonetheless the law is supposed to redefine the structure and role of censorship in the Soviet Union. Even if Glavlit and similar organizations are not abandoned, it is to be assumed that they will be brought up to date in the light of the new reforms.

6. music censorship   The control of music in Russia dates back to well before the 1917 revolution, with controls being imposed for religious, nationalist and political reasons. But while Czarist censorship was often ignored, the revolutionary government at once established far tighter controls, giving almost unlimited powers of censorship to the authorities. Orchestral and operatic works were scanned for ideological impurities and those that failed to reflect a sufficiently militant spirit were either banned or "not recommended" for performance. "Decadent bourgeois" music, especially "class hostile" church music, was condemned, and a new "proletarian" music proclaimed.

During the New Economic Policy (NEP) period, initiated by Lenin in 1921, these restrictions were largely relaxed and Russians were able to enjoy the worldwide interest in tangos, foxtrots and other modern dancing. Private music publishing reappeared. This openness was short-lived. The government established ORKIMD (the Association of Revolutionary Composers and Musicians) to direct music along party lines and established Glavrepertkom (the Chief Directorate of the Repertoire Committee) as an official censorship office. The office's main responsibility was for sheet music, all of which was to be checked, especially when the music incorporated literary works, since if an author had been banned for his or her writing, there should be no chance of those same works appearing as song lyrics. The work of emigre composers was banned and their names systematically blackened. The formation of the Russian Association of Proletarian Musicians (RAPM) accentuated attacks on "decadent" music, condemning modernism, and setting out to replace such compositions with robust, militarist songs aimed at the masses.

A further relaxation of music censorship began in April 1930 when the RAPM was dissolved and replaced by the Union of Soviet Composers (USC), a body that encouraged music development, favored modernism and presided over a revival of Soviet music. By 1936, as Stalin's purges gathered momentum, censorship returned, spearheaded by officials of USC. The resurgence of private music publishing was eradicated. Every composition was submitted to the union, checked for political rectitude and "reflection of reality." It was then either permitted, as an exemplar of SOCIALIST REALISM or subjected to one of two levels of censorship, an outright ban or limited publication with a proviso that actual performance would not be encouraged.

This system has remained the basis for the control of music. Dissident composers appear but are forced into silence or, if fortunate, gain permission to emigrate. Emigre composers are vilified by the authorities. The absolute control of music publishing by the USC means that many composers are forced to curb their creativity along political lines. Those who refuse are expelled from the union, thus losing any opportunity to pursue their career. The volume of banned works is substantial, although occasionally the changed status of an individual composer may reintroduce once forbidden material into the repertoire. A large proportion of the censorship is based on attacks on "nationalist tendencies," a euphemism for the suppression of the traditional music of various Soviet minorities, notably the Crimean Tatars. The work of Jewish composers, both modern and traditional, is generally banned as "Zionist propaganda." Permitted works will be widely performed by a variety of orchestras, encouraged by the media and generally promoted. Composers thus tolerated are in line for good salaries, prizes and similar inducements. Such underground music that does escape censorship appears in the form of ballads, often performed and recorded in secret and circulated, at the risk of imprisonment merely for their possession, on clandestine tapes.

7. press control As stated in the Constitution of 1977, Soviet citizens "are guaranteed freedom of speech, of the press, and of assembly, meetings, street processions and demonstrations." The strict proviso that such freedoms be "in accordance with the interest of the people and in order to strengthen and develop the socialist system ... in accordance with the aims of building communism" provides the basis for all-embracing controls, inter alia, of the Soviet press, a body apostrophized by Lenin in his pamphlet "What Is to Be Done?" (1902) as "not only a collective propagandist and collective agitator, but also a collective organizer." The Soviet journalist, according to Pravda "is an active fighter for the cause of the Party. It is not enough for him to have good intentions, he must also have clear views, a knowledge of life and the ability to present his thoughts convincingly and brilliantly from Leninist positions."

Apart from the overt censorship, the press both of Russia and its satellites is controlled in a variety of ways, the most important of which are noted here:

News agencies: TASS, the main Soviet news agency, and its peer *Novosti* (APN) represent the world's largest transnational news agencies. For the authorities of the Soviet bloc these agencies, paralleled by their equivalents in each satellite country, act as a filter for all printed and broadcast information. TASS is the supreme example, but it is accepted that no one bloc country will attempt to cover the news of another other than in the way in which the national news agency has set it out. All bloc newspapers, radio and TV depend on these agencies as primary sources of party-generated news and opinion. Material is written to an agency tape to the length and with the headline that will be required in the newspaper or bulletin. The party can also use the agencies to transmit a variety of "messages," both for internal and Western consumption. Material that is not filtered through the agencies does not, in effect, exist. TASS reports are color-coded, indicating the exclusivity of the information contained: "green" and "blue" TASS are relatively innocuous, containing no material that overtly contradicts the party line; "white" TASS is more complete and refers to problems in bloc countries; "red" TASS goes only to the elite and offers an almost uncensored view of world and Soviet affairs; there is also a "colorless" top-secret version read only by a tiny elite.

Pravda, the party newspaper: *Pravda* (*Truth*) is the model for all party papers throughout the bloc, although the imitations are less slavish, especially in design, than they were in the 1940s and 1950s. The newspaper remains the primary source of authentic party-orientated news, and readers have learned to read between the editorial lines for inferences regarding leadership power struggles and similar information. Until 1960 nothing could be written or broadcast by TASS, Radio Moscow and other media before it had been printed in *Pravda*. Its senior editors are linked firmly to the party apparatus.

Objectivism: In Marxist jargon, objectivism or "bourgeois objectivism" is a rightist disease, and thus a pejorative, implying the desire to see problems even when the party has denied their existence. This version of Western "impartiality" is rigorously expunged from the Soviet-bloc press.

Non-Party Press: Ostensibly non-party organizations, this press includes the provincial media and the various papers that represent youth organizations, trade unions, the Labor Front and others. In fact, their senior personnel are invariably party members and, backed by the censorship apparatus, maintain the usual controls.

Instructional conferences: Soviet media are guided by a mix of large-scale public conferences, debating the overall direction of the press, and unpublicized but continual monitoring and direction. The major briefing, held twice a month, is conducted by the chief of the agit-prop department and attended by only the most senior media figures. The current party line is expounded as regards current news topics and major priorities are detailed. Instructional conferences, with less high-ranking officials, are repeated at lower levels of the media, with concomitantly less detail provided. While such briefings seem to echo the off the record and deep background sources used by the West, the difference is that here the news is dictated rather than revealed.

8. special bulletins There has evolved throughout the Soviet bloc countries a system of special bulletins, the contents of which are far more detailed than are those of more public information sources, and which are distributed only to a small group of the ruling party. The U.S.S.R.'s main news agency, TASS, appears in a variety of color-coded editions, indicating the exclusivity of the information contained: green and blue TASS are relatively innocuous, containing no material that overtly contradicts the party line; white TASS is more complete and refers to problems in bloc countries; red TASS goes only to the elite and offers an almost uncensored view of world and Soviet affairs; there is also a colorless top secret version read only by a tiny elite. No more than 1,000 to 5,000 copies each of the more confidential editions are produced.

Other countries and agencies have their own systems. In Rumania there are three levels: the highly confidential yellow, the more accessible red and the widely circulated green (mainly economic topics) bulletins. The Hungarian news agency MTI produces a special bulletin with a red stripe and a more general collection of material bound in green. Bulgaria's BTA has a special summary, and Poland's PAP produces a white edition for the elite, both circulated among only a few hundred readers. All the most sensitive bulletins concentrate on foreign reports and internal politicking in the national leadership, and often include emigre literature and journalism.

9. theater censorship Censorship of the theater in the Soviet Union has always been designed to work on two levels: to read, assess, permit or prohibit the plays that it oversees, and to intervene at every stage in the production of those plays. Thus the censor may not simply expedite a variety of given rules but may, in the words of a former senior official,

"penetrate to the very core of the creative process in the theater." Control of the theater appeared gradually. Initially there was no overt political censorship, only the repertory section of the Commissariat for Education, headed by the poet Alexander Blok. This merely read plays and assessed them in the light of the contemporary requirements of both the theater and its audiences. The party inevitably took over. The apparatus of assessment, Glavpolitprosvet, was declared in 1921 "a direct instrument of the Party within the system of organs of the State" and in 1923 was replaced by Glavrepertkom, a direct instrument of the party, although the Commissariat of Education remained the nominal authority.

Glavrepertkom censored new plays, compiled and circulated lists of recommended and banned plays, and interfered ad lib in the plans for each production. The text of each play and the season's repertoire had to be sanctioned, the proportion of classical to modern plays and of Russian work to translations adjusted as required. Everything was judged by the current ideological line. By the end of the Stalin era it had become a mechanical process. Once a play was accepted by Glavrepertkom it would be copied and circulated by a special distribution section to all theaters. Once a production began, up to the final rehearsals, it might be checked by the Glavrepertkom representative who decided on the spot whether it could go on or must be altered or even banned. In 1934 Glavrepertkom was reorganized as GURK (Main Directorate of Control over Repertoire and Places of Entertainment) and combined the functions of censorship and artistic direction. The formation in 1936 of the Committee for Arts Affairs took it formally from the administration of Commissariat for Education, giving direct control to the party, bypassing all ministries.

Some opposition to the censorship was possible under Lenin, but it failed to survive the advent of Stalin in 1929. As the standards of SOCIALIST REALISM took effect, truly creative theater vanished beneath the stricter guidelines. All remotely sensitive topics were prohibited, especially mention of the purges and the Gulag, the decimation of minorities and particularly that of the Jews. A number of leading playwrights, notably Meyerhold, were purged. A playwright might be praised in public, but theaters would be warned off actually producing his work. A variation on this latter theme was "supra-censorship," a system whereby the censor did not actually ban the play but simply made so many demands that the theater was forced to withdraw it from the repertoire.

For a brief period, following Stalin's death in 1953, and the replacement of GURK by bureaucrats working for the Ministry of Culture, the theater enjoyed a brief period of freedom. Forced by the post-1956 de-Stalinization to amend their image even while maintaining their powers, the new censors extended supra-censorship. Plays were passed, but theater directors were informed in person that an actual production would not be approved. This situation has continued, although a degree of thaw can be seen and the new policy of glasnost should improve things further. The fact remains, despite some breakthroughs, that the more socially or politically pertinent a play is, the less favorable reception it will receive from the state.

10. underground press   In parallel and in opposition to the state's censored media, there exist in the Soviet Union many publications, usually appearing in SAMIZDAT, that serve as unofficial but important mouthpieces for a wide variety of dissident movements. *Current Events* attempts to incorporate coverage of the entire dissident movement, and religious, national and political groups all publish their own underground journals, produced with difficulty and in the face of persecution, suppression and, for the editors, arrest.

These publications are distributed from person to person, and the information they record is amassed by word of mouth, each piece of "copy" moving steadily backward along the distribution chain until it reaches the actual editors. These chains operate under the strictest security, using codes, specially prepared envelopes if the normal mails are employed, and generally secret methods. Above all the journalists involved maintain utmost caution. The publications tend to appear sporadically, and their staff and its editorial policy may change from issue to issue. The most popular of these journals come from the national and religious minorities—Lithuanians, Ukrainians, Estonians, Crimean Tartars, Volga Germans, Catholics, Jews and others. Less widespread are those issued by the politically ideological, not merely dissident Marxists of both left and right, but monarchists and even fascists. The liberal-democratic dissidents, perhaps best known in the West, also produce their own samizdat.

11. Union of Soviet Writers   As well as a variety of laws governing censorship, the Soviet system relies to a great extent on the self-censorship of its writers. Such discipline is primarily maintained by the Union of Soviet Writers. This all-embracing trade union of Soviet writers was formed in 1932 under the chairmanship of Maxim Gorki (1868-1936). This initially appeared as a liberal move, since it replaced the ultra-left RAPP (Russian Association of Proletarian Writers), the dominating force in Soviet literature since 1929, which was dedicated to suborning all writing to ideology. In fact by consolidating all writers in one organization, and thus placing them under one censorship, the production of Soviet literature was incorporated effectively into the machinery of the Soviet state.

The Writers' Union is the vital center of Soviet literary life, the heart of the vast bureaucratic apparatus that supervises and surveys the entire range of literary creativity. The stated intention of the USW is to bind together through its statutes all those who wish "to participate through their creative work in the class struggle of the proletariat and in socialist construction"; the aim is "the creation of artistic works worthy of the great epoch of socialism." It was also intended that the union should provide a forum of intellectual exchange and a means whereby writers could benefit from each other's experience and knowledge, as well as a channel through which the party could work out more fully the meaning of SOCIALIST REALISM and the task of Soviet literature. The union also provides the ideal means by which the party can guide writers along the paths of ideological purity and ensure they do not blunder into producing anti-socialist works.

As power concentrated at the top of the union's pyramidal structure, as its basic democratic processes atrophied and the original bylaws were openly ignored, this ideological supervision became the union's most potent function. The party organization of the USW maintains its ideological vigilance through daily surveillance exercised over its members through a network of lower party groups that permeate every national and local level. Through its first secretary, who delegates real authority only to one or two other individuals, the USW controls all literary matters from the broad aspects of Soviet literary policy to the minutiae of local administration. The union dominates the influential literary journals and the whole apparatus of publishing. The journals, in which all official literary criticism appears, ostensibly exist as creative workshops, but fulfill a more fundamental role as instruments of screening and censorship. The editors of such magazines often revise manuscripts along ideological lines and Soviet authors have to accept such corrections as the price of publication.

Criticism does not constitute a discussion of the work, merely its checking for the correct political stance, a position that is based on "an objective truth which can be known"—Marxism-Leninism. A senior rank in the literary bureaucracy is often the reward for those writers who have dutifully followed the vicissitudes of the party line throughout their career, and such bureaucrats form the front line of conservative resistance to liberal changes.

The Writers' Union also offers valuable material rewards to conforming writers, not the least of which is authorized publication. Alternatively waverers can be expelled from the union and will lose such perquisites. The most important financial aid comes from the union's literary fund (*litfond*), which administers extensive and diverse operations on a national and regional level, providing sanitoriums, medical clinics, writers' clubs, retreats for creative work, special apartments for writers, summer cottages, nurseries and summer camps. It makes loans to writers and to their families, provides research funds, money for stays at health centers, and much more.

The basics of publishing also exert controls. Literary prizes can set a writer up for life. A complex royalty system designed deliberately to encourage conformity awards a greater percentage of sales to those writers who have the widest distribution: the better the writer serves the state, the better will be the scale of royalties fixed by the state. Ideological purposefulness and timeliness and importance are ranked far higher than literary ability—all of which tends to the bureaucratization of literature, in which the powerful elite prefer to administer rather than to write. Artistically there is little experiment, innovation or originality in the mainstream of Soviet literature, dominated as it is by the *khalturshchiki* (party hacks) who actively support the status quo. In 1923 Viktor Shklovsky claimed that, "The greatest misfortune of Russian art is that it is not allowed to move organically, as the heart beats in the breast of man, but is regulated like the movement of trains."

V

Vagrancy Act (1824) This act is the oldest extant statute covering the regulation of public exhibitions under the common law of England. The law, a revised version of one passed in 1822, was intended to reform and consolidate the many laws passed over the centuries to punish "idle and disorderly Persons and Rogues and Vagabonds." Among such miscreants included in the original act were "all persons openly exposing or exhibiting in any street, road, public place or highway any indecent exhibition." In 1824 this was slightly amended to "every person wilfully exposing to view … any obscene print, picture or other indecent exhibition." Supplemented by various later statutes in 1838, 1847 and 1889, this law has survived as the basis of all those statutes governing indecent public displays. It overlaps with a variety of local acts, notably the Town Police Clauses Act (1847), which deals with "Every person who publicly offers for sale or distribution, or exhibits to public view, any profane, indecent, or obscene book, paper, print, drawing, painting or representation, or who sings any profane or obscene song or ballad, or uses any profane or obscene language to the annoyance of residents or passengers." Recent prosecutions brought under the Vagrancy Act include the DPP's conviction of works by the artist JIM DINE in 1969 and Mrs. WHITEHOUSE's unsuccessful attempt to censor the film *Blow-Up* in 1967. The acts and bylaws have also been used to harrass street-sellers of racial magazines and censor T-shirts that feature designs "in poor taste."

Venus dans le cloitre, ou, la religieuse en chemise This piece of 17th-century pornography was allegedly written by Jean Barrin, a senior French clergyman, or by Francois Chavigny de la Bretonniere, an unfrocked Benedictine monk whose other writings included *La Galante hermaphrodite* (1683). It was first published in Paris in 1683 and takes the form of three dialogues, supposedly between two nuns: 19-year-old Sister Angelique and 16-year-old Sister Agnes. The tenor of their conversation is that religious devotion and sexual pleasure may be combined, so long as one obeys certain rules. Religious orders themselves are merely political establishments, and their rules differ widely from Christ's actual teachings and thus these rules have no moral force. Although the sisters indulge in mild lesbian and some heterosexual activity, the sexual passages are generally glossed over and there is no deliberately obscene writing. Subsequent editions from 1719 included a further dialogue between two new characters—Virginie and Seraphique—and the reprint of a religious pamphlet, "L'Adamiste, ou le Jesuite insensible." The book gained its greatest notoriety when its English translation, *Venus in the Cloyster, or, the Nun in her Smock* (originally issued by Henry Rhodes in 1683), was published by the Grub Street pornographer and hack of all trades EDMUND CURLL in 1724 and again in 1725. Curll's trial at the Court of King's Bench led to the establishment of OBSCENE LIBEL as a crime under common, rather than ecclesiastical, law.

Venus de Milo This statue, most popularly known for her missing arms, has distressed the authorities on a variety of occasions. In 1853, in Mannheim, Germany, the statue was tried in court for her nudity and was convicted and condemned. A decade later, in America, reproductions of the statue were popular, but only after she had been freed from her classico-erotic associations and renamed "The Goddess of Liberty." The "Goddess" became a widely purchased postcard, but she was still *Venus* at heart. In March 1911, in what critics ridiculed as "an elephantiasis of modesty," the *Venus* was one of several classical statues, long since accepted in their undraped form, which Alderman John Sullivan of Buffalo, New York, backed by the local Catholic clergy, sought to have either covered up or removed from general public view. In the event, Sullivan and his allies were not taken seriously. Eighteen years later the statue was censored again in the U.S. and Europe. A reproduction of the *Venus* in a Palmolive Soap advertisement carried a white patch to cover the breasts, while in Hungary the police banned the exhibition of a photograph of the *Venus* mounted in a shop window.

As recently as the 1950s the statue has had its opponents. In December 1952 the Cyprus Tourist Office used the figure on posters sent to Kuwait, hoping to attract Arab tourists. Sheik Abdullah al Salimal Sebah banned them. The problem was not the nudity, which offended no one, but the lack of arms. Under Islamic law persistent thieves have their hands cut off, and the Kuwaitis, seeing the mutilated statue, might assume all Cypriot girls were hardened criminals. Back in America, in July 1955, firemen in Winona Lake, Indiana, were called to the local park. A full-scale reproduction of the *Venus* had been covered in poison ivy, which had been planted by a local woman to disguise *Venus'* nudity.

Victory in the West (Sieg im Westen) *Victory in the West* was the English title given to a supposed current events documentary made in Germany as *Sieg im Westen*. The film deals with the devastating successes of the German armies in the campaigns of 1940, when they swept through Belgium and France and destroyed the British Expeditionary Force. Alongside this factual material, presented with the same gloating exultation, is a good deal of purely political propaganda, attempting to justify the rise of the Nazis, their policies and their warmongering.

The film was released in New York in May 1941. As a documentary film it was exempt from censorship, but a private citizen, Richard R. Rollins, filed a civil action (*Rollins v. Graves* [1941]) to compel the New York State Department of Education, the body responsible for the censorship of feature films, to view the film, subject it to licensing and to deny it a license on the grounds that it would incite public disorder. While the department did view the film as requested, it refused to classify it as anything but a documentary and thus left it free from any legal constraints. The court refused to reverse this ruling and suggested that if the film really did cause riots, "there are public officers charged with the duty of preserving the public peace."

SEE ALSO *Professor Mamlock.*

Vietnam

1. Law on Counter-Revolutionary Crimes   This law, a major plank in the implementation of the *thanh loc* (see below) or cultural purification program of the Vietnamese government since 1975, was promulgated in North Vietnam in 1967 and extended to the whole country after the war. Among its 22 articles, article 15 deals with publications: Those who, for the purposes of counterrevolutionary propaganda commit the following crimes will be punished by imprisonment for two to 12 years.

> (1) Carrying out propaganda and agitating against the people's democratic administration and distorting socialism; (2) propagating enemy psychological warfare themes, distorting the war of resistance against the U.S. aggressors for national salvation, independence, democracy, and national reunification, and spreading baseless rumors to cause confusion among the people; (3) propagandizing the enslavement policy and depraved culture of imperialism; (4) writing, printing, circulating or concealing books, periodicals, pictures, photographs or any other documents with counterrevolutionary contents and purposes.

2. thanh loc (purification of culture)   Subsequent to the takeover of South Vietnam by revolutionary forces on April 30, 1975, all cultural affairs, notably cinemas, theaters, newspapers, publishers, printing plants, bookshops and tearooms were shut down and told to await orders as to their future activities. The policy of *thanh loc* (cultural purification) was established and all media were to be reevaluated on ideological lines under the direction of the new government's propaganda branch. The old culture, it was declared by General Tran Bach Dang (head of propaganda and, under aliases, a poet and journalist), was "a slave culture promoted by the American imperialists in order to destroy the Revolution." As such it was to be checked and decadent and reactionary culture was to be extirpated.

The purging of literature commenced almost at once and took approximately four months. After all the relevant infor-

mation was collected, lists of banned authors were posted in the Ministry of Information and Culture and in many public places. A copy of all banned works has been preserved in the National Library, but this has a registered membership of only 800 individuals. A list of criteria for such an evaluation was established. It was divided into four negative categories (A-D) and two positive ones (E-F):

Category A: works that in any way opposed communism. These fell into sub-groups: the ideological opponents like Solzhenitsyn, Pearl Buck, Andre Gide, Koestler and a number of Vietnamese writers, including Nguyen Manh Con, Doan Quoc Sy and Vu Khac Khoan; writers (all Vietnamese) who had been "poisoned" by years of pro-American reading or who were ex-members of the ARVN (South Vietnamese army) and hence unlikely to regard the North Vietnamese with favor; and women fiction writers, whose romantic tales preferred love to party duties.

Category B: works considered as decadent by the authorities. Vietnamese authors, often women such as Tuy Hong and Trung Duong, whose works featured reasonably explicit sex or dealt with otherwise taboo sexual topics and were as such judged indecent and immoral. Various Westerners, including HENRY MILLER, Elia Kazan, Francoise Sagan, D.H. LAWRENCE Sartre, Camus and Simone de Beauvoir. Any celebration of sensual pleasures fell under the ban.

Category C: romantic works. Any authors, both Western and Vietnamese who preferred the individualistic pleasures of the bourgeois life to the harsher demands of duty to the party. Enjoyment of nature was similarly proscribed.

Category D: works on philosophy and religion, both Western and Vietnamese, Christian and Zen.

Category E: works considered by the cultural authorities to be healthy, constructive and progressive. These were books in which the evils of Western society were pointed out and condemned, such as those by ZOLA and Balzac. Any attacks on class, structural and allied ideological impurities were also praised, as were Vietnamese rulers Diem or Thieu. Works devoted to rural life, elevating the lot of the peasant rather than celebrating the beauties of nature, were included here.

Category F: works based on Marxist thought and written by true revolutionaries, even though when originally published their ideological orientation may have been disguised in order to fool the previous, repressive regime. Maxim Gorky's *The Mother* was seen as the exemplar, and all the most praiseworthy Vietnamese authors, who had attacked either the French, the Americans or the "puppet" regimes, were included in this, the highest category.

As well as purging the libraries, the new government purged individuals, and a number of writers and artists were detained in labor camps. A number of these had been working in the South Vietnamese Psychological Warfare Department, writing propaganda material whose threat to the new republic was seen as "more dangerous than nuclear radiation." Their reeducation was considered vital. Journalism was similarly attacked, and the number and freedom of Vietnamese newspapers was drastically curtailed. The majority of papers are state-controlled and the remainder are semi-official. Political commissars also interfere strongly in the theater and the opera, both institutions vital to a country with only limited literacy. As in Cultural Revolution-era China, the entertainments produced are deliberately utilitarian and the public is less than impressed.

"Vigilanti Cura"   Pope Pius XI's 1936 encyclical "Vigilanti Cura" ("With Vigilant Care") was heavily influenced by the LEGION OF DECENCY's Martin Quigley, who had been lobbying hard for the church to extend its traditional censorship of literature, through the Index, to the new popular medium of film. The Pope pointed out that "the cinema speaks not to individuals but to multitudes and does so in circumstances, time, place and surroundings which are the most apt to arouse unusual enthusiasm for good as well as bad and to conduct that collective exultation which, as experience teaches us, may assume the most morbid form." He noted the rule of films as "instruments of seduction" and warned the industry that "when one thinks of the havoc wrought in the souls of youth and childhood, of the loss of innocence so often suffered in motion picture theaters, there comes to mind the terrible condemnation pronounced by Our Lord upon the corrupters of the little ones: Whosoever shall scandalize one of these little ones who believe in Me, it were better that a millstone be hanged around his neck and he be drowned in the depths of the sea." In conclusion he praised the American Catholics for their efforts and abjured them to continue the good work so that the industry might recognize and accept its "responsibility before society."

SEE ALSO *Index Librorum Prohibitorum.*

Viva Maria   *Viva Maria* was an all-star French movie, directed by Louis Malle in 1965 and starring Brigitte Bardot, Jeanne Moreau and George Hamilton. The plot concerned the adventures of Bardot and Moreau, both called Maria, who mixed revolution with their love lives in a romp through a fictitious banana republic. The film was a worldwide success and while esthetically limited, provided good popular entertainment. Although Bardot came complete with her "sex kitten" reputation, it could hardly be judged obscene or even indecent. Nonetheless when the film was submitted to the Motion Picture Classification Board of Dallas, Texas, the local censor classified it as "not suitable for young persons" and barred it to anyone under 16. The basis for this ban was that the board considered the film to portray: "(1) brutality, criminal violence, or depravity in such a manner as to incite young persons to crime or deliquency; or, (2) sexual promiscuity, or extra-marital or abnormal sexual relations in such a manner as ... likely to incite or encourage delinquency or sexual promiscuity on the part of young persons or appeal to their prurient interests."

The distributor, United Artists, challenged this ruling before the Texas Court of Appeals. The state court confirmed the censor's classification, but the U.S. Supreme Court, in *United Artists Corp.* v. *City of Dallas* (1968) and *Interstate Circuit Inc.* v. *City of Dallas* (1968), reversed the ruling as unconstitutional. The court ruled that the statute as constituted was too imprecise, particularly as regards its definition of the division between what adults might see but minors might not. Said the court: "Such vague standards, unless narrowed by interpretation, encourage erratic administration, whether the censor be administrative or judicial ... individual impressions become the yardstick of action and result in regulation in accordance with the beliefs of the censor rather than regulation by law."

Vizetelly, Henry   Publisher, journalist, engraver and editor, Vizetelly (1820-94) bears a great deal of responsibility for defying the strictures of late-Victorian taste, as prescribed by the circulating libraries and the demands of the three-decker novel, and introducing into England the works of more cosmopolitan and sophisticated authors. In 1885 he began producing cheap, single-volume editions of literary works, starting with *A Mummer's Wife* by GEORGE MOORE. In 1886 he began, in association with HENRY HAVELOCK ELLIS (1859-1939), the Mermaid series of unexpurgated reprints of "The Best Plays of the Old Dramatists." He also published translations of FLAUBERT, Gogol, Tolstoy, the Brothers Goncourt and early detective fiction from Gaboriau and du Boisgobey. By 1888 he had published, with some deletions, 17 novels by EMILE ZOLA, an author whose fame in his native France was balanced only by his lurid reputation in England where such an authority as Tennyson condemned his books as "the drainage of your sewer."

The authorities had not hitherto bothered with Vizetelly, but his publication of Zola's *La Terre* in 1888 excited the interest of the NATIONAL VIGILANCE ASSOCIATION, a contemporary anti-vice society particularly exercised by the French novel, and simultaneously provided the Establishment, increasingly agitated by French "naturalist" writing, an excuse to attack this bugbear. Samuel Smith, MP, the NVA's spokesman on obscenity, dismissed the books as "only fit for swine." The government initially refused to prosecute, but NVA pressure told and Vizetelly was charged with "uttering and publishing certain obscene libels," notably the Zola and books by de Maupassant, Daudet, Flaubert and GAUTIER.

After a trial in which one juryman objected to passages from the novel being read out in court, Vizetelly was fined and the *Times* condemned the book as "... mere and sheer obscenity, naked, shameless and unutterably vile" and stated "We cannot but rejoice, therefore, that Mr. Vizetelly has acknowledged his offense and been punished for it." One MP stated that "nothing more diabolical has ever been written by the pen of man."

In 1889 Vizetelly repeated the offense, publishing works by Zola, de Maupassant and Paul Bourget. Despite a petition for his release, signed by many eminent figures, and his obvious ill health he was sentenced to three months in prison.

His company was bankrupted and he died in 1894, bereft of everything but his many friends in the artistic and literary worlds. Two years after Vizetelly's death Zola came to London; he was feted and praised without a hint of prosecution.

Voltaire   Pseudonym of Francois-Marie Arouet (1694-1778), a French satirist, novelist, historian, poet, dramatist, polemicist, moralist and critic. As the presiding genius of the Enlightenment and a noted freethinker, his career oscillated between praise and persecution. He was imprisoned in the Bastille between 1717 and 1718 for his political satires and exiled to England for similar writings from 1726 to 1729. For the rest of his life he alternated short spells in the great cities of France and Germany with prudent self-exile in the provinces, enjoying the protection of noble patrons. A wide variety of his works earned the condemnation of both the secular and the ecclesiastical authorities, both in his native France and elsewhere.

In 1716 he was exiled from Paris for composing lampoons against the regent, the Duc d'Orleans, and his spell in the Bastille was for two further satires, *Puero Regnante* and *J'ai Vue*, libels on Louis XIV. In 1734 the *Lettres Philosophiques sur les Anglais*, which had appeared in 1733 as reflections culled from his years in England, was burned by the high executioner on the grounds that it was "scandaleux et contraire a la Religion." A further satire, the *Temple du Gout* (*Temple of Taste*), which mocked the state of contemporary French literature, was also seized and burned and a warrant was issued against Voltaire, who sensibly decided to make one of his excursions out of Paris. In 1752 a diatribe against Emperor Frederick II of Prussia—*Diatribe du Docteur Akakia*—was banned there. Voltaire was briefly arrested and the book burned. The *Lettres Philosophiques* was placed on the ROMAN INDEX in 1752, followed by the *Histoires des Croisades* in 1754 and the *Cantiques des Cantiques* in 1759. Voltaire remained absolutely proscribed by the Index until the 20th century. In 1764 his *Dictionnaire Philosophique* was banned in Geneva, where he had chosen to live out his final years.

Voltaire's best-known work, the comprehensively satirical *Candide* (1759), achieved the dubious success of being banned both by the U.S. Customs, in 1929, and by the Soviet authorities, in 1935. *Candide* remained anathema to American authorities as late as 1944 when Concord Books, issuing a sale catalog that included the book, was informed by the Post Office that such a listing violated U.S. postal regulations on sending obscene matter through the mails. The catalog was only permitted after the offending title had been expunged from its pages.

SEE ALSO United States 17. postal regulations.

Vorst, Conrad   SEE book burning in England 2. James I (1603-25).

W

W. H. Smith & Son, Ltd. The first newsagent established by a Smith was opened in little Grosvenor Street, London, in 1792 by Henry Walton Smith. When he died shortly afterward he left the shop to his wife Anna. On her death in 1816 the shop passed to her younger son, William Henry Smith (1792-1865). When his son, also William Henry (1825-91), became a partner in 1846, the current title was established.

Smith took full advantage of the need for railway bookstalls, opening its first at Euston Station in 1848. Their strict Methodist consciences ensured that no dubious works were stocked on their stalls, a revolutionary reversal of the traditional railway bookstall, on which could be found a wide selection of rubbish, including pornography. But even Smith was unable to satisfy the more prudish and those who spotted the works of Byron or Dumas fils among the piles of improving literature were swift to complain.

When Smith set up its circulating library, which lasted until 1961, it formed, with Mudie's, a major force within English publishing. With their potential for bulk-buying, coupled with their strict rejection of anything regarded as even remotely salacious they became a major influence on mainstream British writing. Publishers would not publish, and many writers preferred not to attempt, subjects that would not gain Smith's approval. As Smith grew more powerful and more profitable, it appeared that public opinion shared their views. W.H. Smith II was known as "The Schoolmaster," and his principles of selective education were much admired. Not all writers appreciated the Smith hegemony. GEORGE MOORE (1852-1933), whose work was banned on several occasions, excoriated both Smith's and Mudie's libraries in his LITERATURE AT NURSE in 1885.

The paradoxical effect of Smith and Mudie censorship was the gradual decline of the three-volume novel upon which the mainstram depended. Not content to write for the middle class, many preferred to find alternative methods of publication. The rise of cheaper single-volume editions may be attributed largely to the prohibitions of Victorian tastes.

Watson, John SEE The Bible.

Webster, Noah SEE The Bible.

Well of Loneliness, The *The Well of Loneliness* by RADCLYFFE HALL (1883-1943) appeared in Britain in July 1928, published by Jonathan Cape. It became notorious for its treatment of female homosexuality, and was a fictional version of the world of Nathalie Barney and her literary and artistic set in Paris. Serious critics applauded the work, lauding Hall's somewhat over-earnest sincerity, but it was loathed by the popular press, personified by JAMES DOUGLAS of the *Sunday Express* who claimed that he would rather give a child a bottle of prussic acid than permit him or her to read the book, charting as it did the "insolently provocative bravado ... [of] the decadent apostles of the most hideous and loathsome vices." The *Sunday Chronicle*, which specialized in vice exposes, followed suit, as did a number of low-circulation papers.

Faced by such hysteria, and fearing prosecution, Cape offered to withdraw the book. The home secretarty, Sir WILLIAM JOYNSON-HICKS, urged them to do so. The literary community, and Ms. Hall herself, complained bitterly. In September 1928 it was revealed that a new, unexpurgated edition was being prepared in Paris by the Pegasus Press; subscribers could obtain copies for 25/- (1.25) plus postage. When the first consignment of the book arrived in Dover in October, it was seized by British Customs, and both Cape and Pegasus were charged under the OBSCENE PUBLICATIONS ACT (1857). The home secretary made it clear that the prosecution was central to his personal anti-vice campaign. The authorities applied, under the act, for a destruction order.

At the trial, held at Bow Street magistrates court on November 9, 1928, the magistrate, Sir Chartres Biron, rejected out of hand a massive collection of expert witnesses, prepared to testify on behalf of the book. Ms. Hall, present only as a spectator, made one effort to interrupt and was threatened with expulsion were she to make another. The court found against the book, which "glorified unnatural tendencies," and ordered it to be destroyed. The magistrate was especially upset by a portrayal of lesbianism "as giving these women extraordinary rest, contentment and pleasure." So too was the judge at the Quarter Sessions, where an appeal against destruction was heard. A letter of protest to the *Manchester Guardian* was signed by a variety of distinguished writers—Bernard Shaw, Rose Macaulay, John Buchan, Arnold Bennett and others—but failed to alter the verdict. The seized copies were burned. Not until 1949 was the book republished in England, since when it has suffered no further harassment. In 1974 it was read, without comment, on BBC Radio's "A Book at Bedtime."

Hall's book was also prosecuted in New York, after it had been published there in 1929. In the case of *People* v. *Friede* (1929) the defendants were charged under New York's obscenity statute (see New York 5.). The magistrate recounted this story of a "female invert" and the "unnatural and depraved relationships" that the book portrayed and "idealized and extolled." In convicting the defendant as charged he stated: "The book can have no moral value since it seeks to justify the right of a pervert to prey upon normal members of a community ... The theme of the novel is not only antisocial and offensive to public morals and decency, but the method in which it is developed, in its highly emotional way attracting and focusing attention upon perverted ideas and unnatural vices, and seeking to justify and idealize them, is strongly calculated to corrupt and debase those members of the community who would be susceptible to its immoral influence." He used the HICKLIN RULE to prove that since certain passages might be seen as obscene, the entire work was therefore obscene, and upheld New York's prosecution.

Wentworth, Peter   SEE book burning in England 1. Tudor Period.

Wesley, John   The founder of Methodism, which in the 19th century lay behind much of the censorship of classical and contemporary literature. Wesley (1703-91) produced one of the first serious expurgations of English literature. While Wesley's love of literature was undeniable and his reading wide, his love of decency transcended it. In 1744, as a fellow of Lincoln College, Oxford, he declared that little literature could be read except "at Hazard of Innocence or Virtue." Prompted by the countess of Huntingdon's wish to see an anthology of "clean" poetry he produced in 1744 the three-volume *Collection of Moral and Sacred Poems, From the Most Celebrated English Authors*. The collection contained 250 poems (of which 25 were written by Wesley himself or his brother Charles).

One hundred and fifty of the poems remain as written, or appear as uncut extracts of original work. The remaining 100 are all expurgated, although Wesley makes no mention of this. Lines have been cut and words changed. Many of the missing lines were considered by Wesley simply too boring or too metaphysical for 18th-century taste, but large amounts of Pope, Dryden, Cowley and Prior were expurgated for morality's sake. Wesley's efforts attracted little interest at the time; few readers bothered to differentiate between stylistic changes and expurgation. After this Wesley resisted further expurgations, resisting "moral" alterations in his edition of Milton's *Paradise Lost* and removing only such parts as were otherwise incomprehensible to the working-class Methodists for whom it was intended. Subsequent to the *Collection* he tended to disregard literature completely, believing that its distractions diminished the wholehearted concentration on religious matters that was required by the devoted evangelical.

White, Harry Dexter   SEE House Committee on Un-American Activities.

Whitehouse* v. *Lemon   SEE *Gay News*.

Whitehouse, Mary   Mary Whitehouse (1910-), the figure who for more than 20 years has more than any other been associated with the advocacy of censorship in Britain, was born Mary Hutcheson on June 13, 1910. She enjoyed a traditional middle-class upbringing, and after training she began working as a teacher in Wolverhampton in 1932. In 1935 she joined the evangelistic Oxford Group, otherwise known as Moral Re-Armament, and met her husband, Ernest Whitehouse, at a group meeting. They have three sons and one foster-child.

MRA was founded in June 1908 by an American Lutheran minister, Frank Buchman, who, on a visit to a church in Keswick, England, received "a poignant vision of the crucified Christ" and a "dazed sense of a great shaking up." On this basis Buchman, whose followers are also known as "buchmanites," created a major evangelistic movement, which in its most extreme form proposes the establishment of a theocratic state in which religion would dominate every aspect of life. The movement also embraced an obsessive anticommunism in the 1950s and declared itself opposed in every way to the permissive society of the 1960s. While Mrs. Whitehouse is by no means a tool of MRA, its four absolute standards—absolute honesty, absolute purity, absolute unselfishness and absolute love—have dominated her own life and her campaigns ever since.

Mrs. Whitehouse abandoned teaching in 1940 but returned to it in the 1950s after a lengthy illness. After some years as a part-time teacher she became in 1960 the senior mistress with special responsibility for art and, later, for sex education at Madeley Secondary Modern School in Wolverhampton. In January 1964 with Norah Buckland, a clergyman's wife and MRA member, she launched the CLEAN-UP TV CAMPAIGN (U.K.) as an attempt to challenge the moral laxity that they felt stemmed directly from the increasingly liberal standards of television in general and the BBC in particular. After a manifesto had exhorted the "Women of Britain" to "revive the militant Christian spirit" of the nation, and a packed public meeting in Birmingham Town Hall proved that traditional views still had a large constituency, CUTV could claim 235,000 signatures on the manifesto by August 1964. In March 1965 CUTV became the NATIONAL VIEWERS AND LISTENERS ASSOCIATION (NVALA), under which title it continues to operate. Since then Mrs. Whitehouse has been at the heart of every controversy that touches on morals and the media in Britain.

Among the major trials and campaigns in which she has been involved are those of THE LITTLE RED SCHOOLBOOK (1971), Schoolkids' OZ (1971), the Nationwide Petition for Public Decency (1972), the FESTIVAL OF LIGHT (1972), THE ROMANS IN BRITAIN (1982), GAY NEWS (1976), DEEP THROAT (1973), *Growing Up,* a BBC documentary on artist Andy Warhol (1973) and the PROTECTION OF CHILDREN ACT (1978). She is a continual campaigner to toughen up the OBSCENE PUBLICATIONS ACT (1959), especially as to bringing the broadcasting media within its control. The BBC has been a long-term bete noir, and NVALA maintains a barrage of complaints about the Corporation's output.

SEE ALSO BBC 2. broadcasting censorship; blasphemy; *The Longford Report.*

Whitney v. California (1927)   Under California's Criminal Syndicalism Act "criminal syndicalism" is defined as "any doctrine or precept advocating, teaching or aiding and abetting the commission of crime, sabotage (which word is hereby defined as meaning wilful and malicious physical damage or injury to physical property), or unlawful acts of force and violence or unlawful methods of terrorism as a means of accomplishing a change in industrial ownership or control, or effecting any political change." Whitney, who had been one of the founding members of the American Communist Labor Party, was charged under the act with advocating criminal syndicalism as here defined. Although her involvement had been limited to words and not actions, the U.S. Supreme Court upheld the constitutionality of the California law. The court stressed that in such cases the interest of the authorities must be given every benefit of the doubt, given that they have responsibility for the security of their citizens. It was further ruled that advocating forbidden doctrines was just as culpable as actually carrying them out: "The ADVOCACY of criminal and unlawful methods partakes of the nature of a criminal conspiracy. Such united and joint action involves even greater danger to the public peace and security than isolated utterances and acts of individuals." This equation of words and deeds as far as criminal syndicalism was concerned remained an article of legal faith until the position was reversed in the case of *Brandenburg* v. *Ohio* (1969), at which time the court stated that a "CLEAR AND PRESENT DANGER" must be found in the advocacy; words alone would no longer justify a prosecution. SEE ALSO *Abrams* v. *United States* (1919); *Adler* v. *Board of Education* (1952); *Debs, Eugene; Frohwerk* v. *United States* (1919); *Gitlow* v. *New York* (1925); *Lamont* v. *Postmaster General* (1965); *Pierce* v. *United States* (1920); *Schaeffer* v. *United States* (1920); *Schenck* v. *United States* (1919); *Sweezy* v. *New Hampshire* (1957); *Yates* v. *United States* (1957).

Wilberforce, William (1759-1833)   SEE the Proclamation Society.

Wild Weed   The film *Wild Weed* was made in 1949; it was typical of a number of drug-scare movies, the classic of which was the earlier *Reefer Madness*. It traced the story of a young chorus girl (who has only taken so sordid a job in order to put her brother through college) who first falls prey to marijuana and then turns stool pigeon, helping narcotics agents to break up a ring of drug traffickers. When the film was exhibited in Pennsylvania in 1950 it was refused a permit by the Pennsylvania state censor. The board rejected the film under a new title, *Devil's Weed*, in 1951. When the film's owners, Hallmark Productions, tried with a third title—*She Should'a Said No!*—they were equally unsuccessful and the board offered a list of 20 reasons for its refusal to license the film,

all summed up in its contention that it was "indecent and immoral and … tended to debase and corrupt morals." Scenes that the board found particularly objectionable were those that implied or depicted a relationship between drug use and sexual desire.

The Pennsylvania Supreme Court finally heard the owners' appeal—*Hallmark Productions* v. *Carroll*—in 1956. In its ruling the court stated that Pennsylvania's censorship was unconstitutional. It ruled that the terms under which the film was censored were too vague to form the basis of due legal process, and that precensorship regulations by their very nature contravened the FIRST AMENDMENT. He cited the U.S. Supreme Court's judgemnt in the case of the film THE MIRACLE as a basis for this opinion.

Wilkes, John   SEE *The North Briton; "Essay on Woman."*

Willard-Johnson boxing match   In 1908 boxer Jack Johnson defeated Tommy Burns in Australia to become the world's first black heavyweight champion. The fact that Johnson was a superb stylist and towered above most of the contemporary contenders failed to abate the horror with which many of America's white boxing fans viewed the new champion. A succession of "Great White Hopes" were put up against Johnson, and he demolished them all. In 1912 a federal law was enacted to ban the importation of any films depicting a "prize fight or encounter of pugilists" intended for public exhibition. This came in direct response to Johnson's defeat in 1910 of the former white champion, James Jeffries. Congress claimed that the sight of a black man beating a white would trigger race riots and must thus be suppressed. In 1915 Johnson lost a fight (deliberately, he later claimed) to the current white hope, Jess Willard, who took the title after a grueling match staged in Cuba. When its maker attempted to import the film of the fight into America, U.S. Customs, followed by the federal and then the U.S. Supreme Court unanimously banned it from the country (even though Johnson had *lost* the fight). The law was not repealed until 1940.

Williams Committee, The   British Labour Party Home Secretary Roy Jenkins announced the creation of a committee to investigate "obscenity, indecency and violence in publications, entertainments and displays" in June 1977. It was to be headed by Professor Bernard Williams, a man decried by the pro-censorship FESTIVAL OF LIGHT as "a leading humanist," and a witness for the defense in the LAST EXIT TO BROOKLYN trial in 1966. A number of Tory MPs attempted to block this appointment, claiming that Williams' admitted atheism prohibited him from considering obscenity, but Jenkins ignored their pleas.

The committee was composed of 12 distinguished individuals who worked from September 1977 until they presented their conclusions in October 1979. It accepted the premise that "for many years the obscenity laws have been in retreat" but, unlike the censorship lobby, went on to suggest that this fact should be embodied in law. "The printed word should be neither restricted nor prohibited since its nature makes it neither immediately offensive nor capable of involving the harms we identify," it concluded. Williams believed that it was not ncessary for the authorities to impose moral standards. Individual choice was paramount and everyone should be permitted to exercise their own reason in the pursuit of morality. Pornography was not a threat because for most people it was simply rubbish. Whether in fact the majority of people were able to justify Williams' faith in their rationality was not a question the committee chose to consider. With its assumptions regarding the intelligence and perception of the average person, Williams opted for rationality and tolerance. Perhaps its most important suggestion was the abandoning of traditional terminology: Such loaded words as "obscene," "indecent," "deprave and corrupt" should be scrapped. In their place there should be the discussion of "harms," in which context one asks not whether pornography is evil or depraved but simply whether it causes harm and whether its abolition would merely increase that harm.

To replace the existing laws Williams suggested that material involving minors (under 16) and material depicting violence should be banned. Those trafficking in such material might be jailed for up to three yeras. While written material was absolutely unrestricted, pictorial pornography should be sold only in specific sex shops, and only to those over 18. Such shops would display a warning notice outside and would not be permitted to display their wares in the window. Pictorial material thus restricted was to be defined as that "whose unrestricted availability is offensive to reasonable people by reason of the manner in which it portrays, deals with or relates to violence, cruelty or horror, or sexual, faecal, or urinary functions or genital organs." Unsolicited mailing of pornography, the selling of material to those under 18 and the contravention of the regulations on window displays and advertising would be tried by a magistrate and punishable by up to six months in jail and fines of up to £1,000.

Unsurprisingly the Festival of Light, the NATIONAL VIEWERS AND LISTENERS ASSOCIATION (NVALA) and similar bodies condemned Williams as "a pornographer's charter," and demanded that the government reject the report. More influential opinion-makers disliked the report as well, contending that Williams had not taken the problem seriously enough. The Conservative government, as opposed to the Labour administration that had commissioned Williams, promised that "no early action" would be taken on its suggestions. In the event the report was quietly forgotten, although certain of its suggestions, notably those dealing with sex shop displays, were embodied in the Indecent Displays (Control) Act (1981) and the Local Government (Miscellaneous Provisions) Act (1982).

Williams, Roger   Williams (ca. 1603-1683) was one of the founders of the Massachusetts Bay Colony, but his outspoken attitudes, notably his refusal to accept that the state had authority over individual conscience and his general intransigence in civil matters, led to his being "enlarged" out of the colony. In 1635 he moved to Rhode Island and founded the city of Providence. In 1644 Williams wrote *The Bloudy Tenent of Persecution*, a book that was essentially an attack on one of his Massachusetts rivals, John Cotton. It set out an argument for religious toleration, democratic liberty and the necessity for intellectual freedom under both secular and ecclesiastical governments. In England the Puritan House of Commons ordered that the book should be burned in public. Cotton offered his refutation in 1647, "The Bloudy Tenent Washed and Made White in the Bloud of our Lamb," and in 1652 Williams offered his counterblast, *The Bloudy Tenent yet More Bloudy; by Mr. Cotton's Endeavour to Wash it White in the Bloud of the Lamb*. In 1936, 300 years after Williams had been banished from the state, the Massachusetts legislature formally rescinded the order of expulsion.

Wilson, Edmund (1895-1972)   SEE *Memoirs of Hecate County*.

Winnington-Ingram Bishop   SEE Public Morality Council.

Winters v. New York (1948)   Under the New York Penal Law covering the writing and dissemination of crime stories it was illegal to sell or distribute any publication "principally made up of criminal news, police reports, or accounts of criminal deeds, or pictures, or stories of deeds of bloodshed, lust, or crime." This law, which had its peers in many states, was presumably derived from an era when the salacious (for its time) *Police Gazette*, with its pictures of "actresses" and other ladies of the night, was the nearest thing to a modern men's magazine that those in search of cheap thrills could find. In 1948 the defendant Winters was charged with violating this law and putting on sale "a certain obscene, lewd, lascivious, filthy, indecent and disgusting magazine, entitled *Headquarters Detective, True Cases from the Police Blotter, 1940*. Given that the content of *Headquarters Detective* was unsurprisingly focused on "criminal news, police reports, or accounts of criminal deeds, or pictures, or stories of deeds of bloodshed, lust, or crime," Winters was convicted in both the lower court and the New York appeal court.

The U.S. Supreme Court reversed the conviction, ruling that the definition of culpability within the act was too vague and the whole act was in contravention of the freedoms guaranteed by the FIRST AMENDMENT. The court did not particularly admire the magazine but "though we can see nothing of any possible value to society in these magazines, they are as much entitled to the protection of free speech as the best of literature." Justice Frankfurter dissented, pointing out that such magazines were not only passively not good, but also actively bad, and definitely contributed to the criminality of those who read them.

Wither, George SEE book burning in England 4. Puritans.

Wodehouse, P.G. In 1940 P.G. Wodehouse (1881-1975), albeit often living either in America or France, was Britain's leading humorist. He had written more than 70 books, helped revolutionize the Broadway musical, created a number of immortal characters—notably Jeeves and Bertie Wooster—and had, for more than a decade, been earning at least £100,000 per year. In 1940, as the Germans advanced through France, he and his wife were living at their French home in Le Touquet. The Wodehouses attempted to escape to England, but the war cut them off. Because Wodehouse was 59, and the Germans were interning every male under 60, he was arrested, and between February 1940 and June 1941 held in a variety of internment camps in Germany. He was released in June 1941 and lodged in the Hotel Adlon in Berlin. The sole restrictions on his freedom were that he did not attempt to leave Germany. He continued working on his books and in late June and July made five broadcasts to America over the German radio. The broadcasts were humorous, utterly non-political and dealt with the privations of camp life. They were lightweight, self-deprecatory, and Wodehouse's involvement proved totally naive.

The reaction in England, where Wodehouse had been something of a national institution, was almost wholly negative. Wodehouse's supporters, such as Ian Hay, attempted to defend the writer's essential innocence, pointing out how, like the characters of whom he wrote, he was insulated from "real life" and had been thus incapable of seeing how the Germans had exploited his propaganda value. The literary journals generally accepted this view. His detractors, who included E.C. Bentley, demanded the fiercest of punishments. The affair escalated when, after questions had been asked in the House of Commons, William Connor, who wrote an acerbic "voice of the people" column in the *Daily Mirror* under the byline "Cassandra," was allowed to broadcast on the BBC regarding Wodehouse. The BBC deplored the program, described as "ten minutes of irrelevant smearing, pseudo-dramatically delivered," but it was backed by the minister of information, Duff Cooper.

The immediate result of the Cassandra broadcast was the banning of Wodehouse's books by a number of public libraries. Portadown and Larne in Northern Ireland, Sheffield, Southport, Blackpool and a number of other libraries in the north of England removed his books from their shelves. Despite a spate of letters from Wodehouse's backers, the library committees had their way. Wodehouse's books were at best placed in storage and at worst pulped. Most of these bans lapsed after 1945, although that in Sheffield lasted until 1954. Wodehouse himself was investigated and exonerated in 1945, although he chose voluntary exile from Britain, living until his death in America. He was awarded a belated knighthood in 1975, just six weeks before he died, working on a new novel.

Women Against Pornography This feminist organization was founded in 1979 by a group of women who included Susan Brownmiller, author of *Against Our Will*, a major study of rape and its effects. It has around 5,000 members. The group seeks to change public attitudes to pornography, especially the libertarian beliefs that the consumption of such titillatory images is socially acceptable and sexually liberating. WAP campaigns in every area of American society to drive home its belief that "the essence of pornography is ... the degradation, objectification, and brutalization of women." It offers adult and high school slide shows, a speaker's bureau, and tours of New York's Times Square area, generally accepted as "the porn capital of the country." Critics of WAP and similar feminist campaigns against pornography claim that such attacks create a bizarre alliance between left-wing women and the hard-right, fundamentalist crusaders of the MORAL MAJORITY and other essentially religious organizations, the fruit of which is a mutal desire to curtail what some would claim as basic civil liberties.

SEE ALSO Dworkin-McKinnon bills; Women Against Violence Against Women; Women Against Violence in Pornography and Media.

Women Against Violence Against Women This organization was founded in 1976 and has about 3,000 members. Its objective, in common with other feminist groups, is "to stop [the] gratuitous use of images of physical and sexual violence against women in mass media and end the 'real world' violence it promotes." WAVAW sponsors public education in this area, consciousness-raising and mass consumer action. The organization in particular seeks to persuade the film industry to modify its use of "sexist-violent" images of women, especially in the advertising of films.

SEE ALSO Dworkin-McKinnon bills; Women Against Pornography; Women Agaisnt Violence in Pornography and Media.

Women Against Violence in Pornography and Media This movement was founded in 1976 and claims just under 5,000 members. It describes itself as "A feminist organization opposed to the association of violence with sexuality and to media portrayals encouraging the abuse of women. It confronts pornography store and theater owners, newspaper publishers who advertise pornographic material, and producers of record jackets portraying images of violence." The organization monitors current trends in pornography and offers public education schemes, slide shows and tours of major pornography centers; it coordinates a number of allied pressure groups, advising on the writing of protest letters, maintaining a speaker's bureau, an anti-pornography exhibit and preparing various "media protest packets" to aid its members' efforts.

SEE ALSO Dworkin-McKinnon Bill; Women Against Pornography; Women Against Violence Against Women.

Wood, Robert   In 1940 Wood was the state secretary of the Communist Party in Oklahoma and ran a left-wing bookstore in Oklahoma City. The store was raided by a group of vigilantes who seized much of his stock, including Lenin's *The State and Revolution*, a number of works of fiction and economics, the Declaration of Independence and the U.S. Constitution. All these were burned as "Communist literature" at the City Stadium. Wood and his wife, as well as customers in the shop and a carpenter who had been hired to repair some shelves, some 18 people in all, were arrested on charges of criminal syndicalism and held incommunicado. Twelve were freed, but the Woods and four others were held. Robert Wood was charged with distributing literature that advocated violence, and Mrs. Wood and two others were charged with belonging to an illegal organization, to wit, the Communist Party. All six defendants were tried, found guilty and sentenced to 10 years imprisonment and a fine of $5,000. The prosecution made no attempt to prove that any of the defendants had actually engaged in a conspiracy, attempted to overthrow the goverment, or did anything but run the bookshop or purchase items from there. In 1943 the State Court of Appeals overturned the verdicts.

Worthington, In Re **(1894)**   In 1894 ANTHONY COMSTOCK, the anti-pornography crusader and spearhead of the SOCIETY FOR THE SUPPRESSION OF VICE, brought this case against the receiver of the assets of the Worthington Company. The receiver had obtained as part of the company's assets a number of fine editions of various books, e.g., Payne's *Arabian Nights*, Henry Fielding's *Tom Jones*, the works of RABELAIS, OVID's *Ars Amatoria*, Boccaccio's DECAMERON, the *Heptameron* of Queen Margaret of Navarre, ROUSSEAU's *Confessions, Tales from the Arabic* and *Aladdin*. In a decision that pointed toward the ULYSSES STANDARD of 1934, and made it clear that the days of the HICKLIN RULE were numbered, Judge O'Brien of the New York Supreme Court unreservedly threw out Comstock's suit. His ruling stated "It is very difficult to see upon what theory these world-renowned classics can be regarded as specimens of ... pornographic literature ... The works under consideration ... have so long held a supreme rank in literature that it would be absurd to call them now foul and unclean. A seeker after the sensual and degrading parts of a narrative may find in all these works, as in those of other great authors, something to satisfy his pruriency. But to condemn a standard literary work because of a few of its episodes, would compel the exclusion from circulation of a very large proportion of the works of fiction of the most famous writers of the English language." He added that the works in question would not be bought or "appreciated by the class of people from whom unclean publications ought to be withheld" and that the young would not be corrupted since the books "are not likely to reach them."

Wright, Peter   After public school and the School of Rural Studies at Oxford Wright (1916-   ) joined in 1940 the Admiralty Research Station at Teddington, the main Royal Navy scientific laboratory. His main efforts were concentrated on the defusing of magnetic mines. In 1950 Wright's superior, Frederick Brundrett, a veteran of Admiralty research since 1919, was asked to appoint a committee to advise Britain's intelligence services, MI5 and MI6, on scientific affairs. Among others Brundrett chose Wright. Wright joined MI5 full-time in 1955 as a scientific advisory officer.

He was involved in the breakup of the Portland Ring (Harry Houghton and Ethel Gee, both Admiralty clerks who had been passing information to "Gordon Lonsdale," actually the KGB man Conon Modoly) and in the case of American fugitives Morris and Lorna Cohen. More vitally, he became a believer in the views of the Soviet defector Anatoly Golitsin, who "walked in" to a CIA overseas station in 1961 and who convinced the West that its intelligence services were riddled with KGB moles. Wright's faith in Golitsin was reinforced by his own interrogation in 1964 of Sir Anthony Blunt—the Fourth Man—who was given immunity from prosecution despite his proven KGB involvement. Wright further claimed that the current head of MI5, Sir Roger Hollis, was himself a mole.

Although Wright was by no means alone in his beliefs, and an investigation was made into Hollis' position, he was unable to prove his point. Instead he was vilified by many colleagues and he left MI5 in 1976, immigrating to Tasmania, where he set up a stud farm. In 1979 Blunt's spying activities were revealed to the public and the prime minister made a statement to the Commons in which she justified the immunity deal, claiming that in 1964 there had been insufficient evidence to prosecute. Wright was infuriated and began compiling a dossier to refute Thatcher's claim. This developed first into a Granada TV program, broadcast in 1984, and then in 1986 into his memoirs, *Spycatcher*, in which he not only reiterated his views on Hollis and on Blunt, but also added that he had evidence of a group of 30 MI5 officers who in 1974 had been attempting to undermine, through a variety of dirty tricks, the administration of the Labor Prime Minister Harold Wilson.

When the British government heard news of this book, for which the Australian office of British publishers Heinemann had paid Wright an advance of £17,000, they immediately demanded an injunction on its future publication. In the case, heard before Mr. Justice Powell of the Equity Division of the Supreme Court of New South Wales, Wright was represented by the flamboyant Australian barrister Malcolm Turnbull, and the British government sent Sir Robert Armstrong, head of the Civil Service. The trial proved a disaster for Armstrong, whose mandarin style did not equip him for the rigors of sophisticated cross-examination. His unfortunate euphemism for bureaucratic lying, "economy with the truth," has entered the language. Despite the efforts of the British press, fueled by government leaks, to picture the judge as both anti-British and stupid, and Turnbull as a showboating fraud, the court failed to sustain the government's plea for censorship.

Powell's judgment ran to 85,000 words, some 279 pages. It hinged in the end upon the fact that another book, British journalist Chapman Pincher's *Their Trade Is Treachery* (1983), with substantially similar details, had been permitted by the government. A number of other books had also been published without problems, and even more senior intelligence figures had been able to write about their years in power without interference. The government policy had been inconsistent; Wright's material would not jeopardize U.K. security and thus the court would not uphold the censorship. A ban in England, of course, could not be overturned and in May 1987 the government attempted vainly to persuade the U.S. government to follow suit. By 1988 Wright's book had been printed in over a dozen languages, topping the bestseller lists in Europe and the U.S. Wright himself has become a millionaire. Even England had not remained immune: Apart from thousands of copies imported by returning travellers from abroad, many bookshops obtained copies of the Australian paperback and for a while sold them openly. Only one such shop was prosecuted, and the case is outstanding.

The career of *Spycatcher* in the British courts has been cited by many critics as the extreme example of the Thatcher government's alleged drive against freedom of speech. The first injunction against the book came in June 1986, when the *Observer* and the *Guardian* newspapers (and later the *Sunday Times*) were banned from reporting on the contents of what was still an unpublished manuscript. In April 1987 the *Independent* carried reports on Wright's revelations, claiming that it was not affected by the previous injunctions. The government responded by obtaining from the House of Lords a blanket injunction on any further references to *Spycatcher*; ignoring it would place the newspaper in contempt of court. The BBC received a further injunction, forbidding it to name Wright, although the title could be mentioned. This was subsequently modified, leaving all the media powerless to discuss the book's contents until legal proceedings against the original whistleblowers—the *Observer* and the *Guardian*—were concluded. The government further attempted to have the book banned in Hong Kong (successfully) and New Zealand (without success).

In December 1987 the injunction against the *Guardian* and the *Observer* was set aside; Mr. Justice Scott in his judgment emphasized the necessity of a free press in a democratic society and rebutted government claims that national security was more important. He also refused to accept that the duty of confidentiality (see U.K. 3. law of confidence) bound secret service employees such as Wright until they died. Such confidentiality could not be imposed when dealing with useless information or information already in the public domain. The government appealed his decision, but in October 1988 the Law Lords affirmed the earlier decision. Injunctions on all the media were lifted and *Spycatcher* became freely available. Lord Keith, announcing the judgment, stressed however

that "I do not base this upon any balancing of the public interest nor on any considerations of freedom of the press, nor on any possible defenses of prior publication or just cause of excuse, but simply on the view that all possible damage to the interest of the Crown has already been done by the publication of *Spycatcher* abroad and the ready availability of copies in this country." The concept of confidentiality was in no way undermined. The whole case was further devalued when Wright himself, appearing on BBC-TV in the wake of the judgment, admitted that the most contentious part of the book, the alleged MI5 plot against former Prime Minister Wilson, was "unrealiable." Rather than the 30 conspirators he cites in his memoirs, there was only one really serious plotter, himself, although some commentators suggested that this "revelation" might be yet more MI5 disinformation.

In November 1988 the government announced the Security Services Bill, designed specifically to silence any future Peter Wrights. Under this bill members of the security and intelligence services will be bound by law to keep silent about their professional lives. There will be no external scrutiny or accountability for these services, and disaffected members will be unable to appeal to anyone outside their own service.

Wunderlich, Paul Wunderlich, a German graphic artist and teacher at the Hamburg Academy of Fine Arts, mounted an exhibition in Hamburg in 1960. His work, which has been described as erotic, sensual, macabre and intellectual, was found to be obscene by the local police, who closed the exhibition on these grounds. The most offensive items were lithographs of couples in love-making postures, entitled "Qui s'explique."

Wyclif, John John Wyclif (or Wycliffe, ca. 1330-84) was born in North Yorkshire, educated at Merton College, Oxford, and gained the patronage of John of Gaunt. At the urging of his patron he began attacking the established church in the person of William of Wickham, John of Gaunt's rival for power in Britain. As a scholastic philosopher he wrote extensively on logic and began to develop his own radical opposition to the contemporary ecclesiastical establishment. With his followers, the Lollards, Wyclif suffered increasing persecution, starting at least as early as 1378. In 1380 his writings were officially condemned and in 1381 he was forced to retire to his parish at Lutterworth. In 1382 the Synod of Oxford again denounced his views as heretical. A statute was passed in March 1400 to suppress his heresy and although he had died in 1384, the campaign against his followers saw many of them executed in the early 15th century.

As a further prescription against heresy, at the Oxford Synod of 1407 Archbishop Arundel drew up a series of provincial constitutions to control the publication and distribution of heretical books. Among other rules, these constitutions, the most important of which were subsequently included in an act of Parliament, provided for the censorship of all books read in universities and schools, the prohibition of any translation of the Scriptures and an absolute ban on the reading of any Lollard literature. In 1410 an additional statute appeared, punishing anyone who wrote books against Catholicism.

Y

Yates v. *United States* (**1957**)   In 1951 Yates and 13 other defendants were leaders of the Communist Party in California. They were indicted under the SMITH ACT, America's federal anti-sedition law, for conspiring to advocate and teach the overthrow of the U.S. government by force, and to organize, in the form of the Communist Party of the United States (CPUSA), a group of people dedicated to promoting such advocacy and teaching. Both the district and the appeal court found all 14 guilty as charged. When in 1957 the case reached the U.S. Supreme Court it reversed the convictions. Its ruling was a reversal of the last major case involving this matter, *Dennis* v. *United States* (1951), in which a majority of the court had confirmed that ADVOCACY, as in CRIMINAL SYNDICALISM cases, was as culpable as was the actual committal of the revolutionary acts that it proposed. Now the court redefined the status of advocacy within the Smith Act, ruling that advocacy of abstract doctrine was no longer sufficient cause for prosecution or conviction. On these grounds the court reversed five convictions absolutely, but ruled that the remaining nine defendants be tried again.

In his dissenting opinion Justice Black, joined by Justice Douglas, called for the absolute acquittal of all 14 defendants and stated that in his opinion "the statutory provisions on which these prosecutions are based abridge freedom of speech, press and assembly in violation of the FIRST AMENDMENT." He pointed out that while the invariably lengthy Smith Act trials apparently turned on vast accumulations of evidence and on the fine points of contrasting left-wing ideologies, the crucial issue was really "the propriety of obnoxious or unorthodox views about government" and in such cases "prejudice makes conviction inevitable, except in the rarest circumstances ..." Black pointed out that by suppressing what they saw as plots to overthrow democracy and establish a totalitarian government in its place, the U.S. authorities were acting exactly as such a totalitarian power would itself do: "Governmental suppression of causes and beliefs seems to me to be the very antithesis of what our constitution stands for."

SEE ALSO *Abrams* v. *United States* (1919); *Adler* v. *Board of Education* (1952); Debs, Eugene; *Frohwerk* v. *United States* (1919); *Gitlow* v. *New York* (1925); *Lamont* v. *Postmaster General* (1965); *Pierce* v. *United States* (1920); *Schaeffer* v. *United States* (1920); *Schenck* v. *United States* (1919); *Sweezy* v. *New Hampshire* (1957); *Whitney* v. *California* (1927).

Yugoslavia   Yugoslavia's constitution (1974) guarantees (article 166) "freedom of the press and of other information media, of public expression, of gatherings and of public assembly." This is balanced by article 203, which prohibits the use of such freedoms to attack or undermine the state, to jeopardize the constitution, endanger Yugoslavia's foreign relations, stir up "national, racial or religious hatred or intolerance, or to instigate the commission of penal offenses." No freedom may be used "in a manner offensive to public morals."

As in Hungary (q.v.) there is little overt censorship in Yugoslavia; the control of the media is considered best achieved by the appointment of politically responsible editors and the replacement of any who have fallen into a variety of ideologically unacceptable deviations. The press is further limited by certain controls on the setting up of a newspaper. Ten citizens must initiate the launch of a new paper, and none of them can ever have been charged with any ideologically based offenses. All publishers must submit an outline of their paper's style and content to the Socialist Alliance, the country's official ideologues, who will judge it on the basis of its social justificaion. Similar tests must be undergone in all of Yugoslavia's six federal republics and two autonomous provinces, each of which have powerful local regulations. All editorial staff must show "ideological-political commitment" and "moral and practical eligibility." This amounts, in effect, to the capacity for judicious self-censorship.

Only in the field of foreign news reporting that relates to the Soviet Union and fellow Warsaw Pact states is control consistently exercised from above. Under the 1974 constitution the "endangering of friendly relations" with other states has been made a crime. This clause gives a wide opportunity for the state to interfere when it feels the media are claiming too great an independence from the party line. On several occasions newspapers have been confiscated or banned because of the style of their reporting of events within the Soviet bloc. As regards visiting foreign journalists, Yugoslavia is relatively liberal and appears to have tried hard to implement the suggestions of the HELSINKI FINAL ACT, but makes no pretense about affording greater privileges and access to those whom the regime feels are most sympathetic.

Book and magazine publishing has increased dramatically in the last few years. A wide range of periodicals appear, including explicit sex magazines. These latter are rarely prosecuted, although anti-pornography laws do exist; the censor prefers to check political errors. Censors can use a number of laws to control literary content, including the law on the Fundamentals of the System of Public Information and the Law on the Prevention of Abuse of Freedom of Press and the Media. These cover a wide range of prohibited topics, from military secrets to over-enthusiastic criticism of the government and socialism. Printers and publishers must submit the first two issues of any printed material—prior to binding—to the Office of the Public Prosecutor. These laws, administered by the public prosecutor, are also extended to radio and television, film and video.

Yugoslavia also has a number of "verbal crimes" under which free speech can be controlled. All are based on "the crime of thought," a term borrowed from the French *delit d'opinion*. Such crimes come under the definition of hostile propaganda, which is defined under article 118 of the Yugoslav Criminal code, section 1:

> Whoever, by means of writing, speech or in any other way, advocates or incites the violent or unconstitutional change of the social system or State organization, the overthrow of the representative agencies or their executive offices, the break up of the brotherhood and the unity of the peoples of Yugoslavia, or resistance to the decisions of representative agencies or their executive offices significant for the protection and development of socialist relationships, the security of the defense of the country; or whoever maliciously and untruthfully represents the social situation in the country shall be punished by imprisonment for not more than 12 years.

Section 2: "Whoever infiltrates himself into the territory of Yugoslavia for the purpose of carrying out hostile propaganda, or whoever commits the offense specified in (1) of this article, assisted or infuenced from abroad, shall be punished by strict imprisonment." There are no distinctions between violent or non-violent advocacy. Local governments have similar laws, forbidding "untruthful news." Cases against hostile propaganda number between 400 and 700 each year.

Z

Zaire Zaire is a one-party state, governed by the Popular Revolutionary Movement (MPR), dedicated to the doctrine of Mobutism, the creation of its president Mobutu Sese Seko. The Constitution of 1978 guarantees freedom of expression, but the Manifeste de la N'Sele, which expounds the fundamentals of Mobutism, stresses that the enjoyment of human rights is not possible other than in a "politically structured state" and that "the freedom of the individual cannot be allowed to lead to anarchy of the state." In effect the presidential word is incontrovertible law and all efforts to dilute Mobutism are rigorously suppressed. The concept of *bonnes moeurs* (moral and social standards) establishes a framework in which the law may be used to govern freedom of expression, and by extension quell opposition.

The press is controlled by the Press Law of 1981, itself part of Zaire's penal code. As in the more general constitution, while the press is under article 1 guaranteed the "freedom to print, publish and disseminate written material subject to the press laws and relevant regulations," article 19 states that all journalists are bound by the *bonnes moeurs* concept. Any information that deals with Mobutism faces prior censorship. A paper may be banned if it contravenes *bonnes moeurs*. Although there are no state-owned newspapers, the MPR must license any publication and its proprietor and editor will face detailed scrutiny before being appointed. Those chosen are usually MPR activists. All journalists must belong to the National Union of Journalists, and cards are issued by the authorities.

Radio and television are wholly state-controlled. Equally important are music, and songs in particular. There has been a Censorship Commission of Music since 1967, regulating lyrics to the *bonnes moeurs* standards of other media. Only songs that have been authorized and registered with the authorities may be performed.

Zambia Zambia's ruling United National Independence Party (UNIP) banned opposition parties in 1972. Under the national constitution a Bill of Rights guarantees (article 21) freedom of conscience and belief, and (article 22) the right to hold opinions, and receive and communicate ideas without interference and the right to freedom of expression. Regulating such rights are laws of libel and slander, the prohibition of any defamation—written or spoken—of the president, and the laws on sedition (dating from the colonial era). Under article 53 of the Penal Code the president may ban any publication seen as contrary to the public interest. Such restrictions apply to foreign as well as local publications, although anyone may apply to import foreign material.

Zambia's Censorship Board deals with all the media, including songs and films. The premise of such censorship is that the material be "inimical to the nation." In 1980 the government published the Press Council Bill (renewed in 1984). This bill has yet to become law, but with its provisions for party control of the press (including the banning of publications and the dismissal of errant journalists), it is seen as a continual and potential threat to press freedom. Both radio and television are fully state-controlled.

Zenger, John Peter Zenger (ca. 1680-1746) was the publisher of the *New York Weekly Journal: containing the freshest Advices, Foreign and Domestic*. An emigrant from the German Palatinate, Zenger was by no means fluent in English, but the use of the *Journal* by prominent opposition spokesmen ensured that it achieved a wide reputation. Its first number appeared on November 5, 1733, in direct opposition to the government paper, the New York *Weekly Gazette*. In its second number an article was published on the liberty of the press and this article was reprinted in a variety of subsequent editions. In October 1734 a committee was appointed to investigate Zenger's newspaper and look into charges of seditious libel that had been alleged against it. The committee found numbers 7, 47, 48 and 49, which contained the reprinted article, to be libelous as charged and ordered them to be burned. Zenger was arrested and jailed.

At his trial he was defended by Andrew Hamilton, a distinguished Philadelphia lawyer nearly 80 years old, and by James Alexander, a founder of the American Philosophical Society, a legal reformer, a member of the governments of both New York and New Jersey and the editor of the *Journal*, as well as attorney general of New Jersey. Alexander hired Hamilton, but continued to mastermind the defense tactics.

The essence of his argument, which provided the basis of all subsequent libertarian arguments regarding libel, was simple: "Truth ought to govern the whole Affair of Libels"; it rejected the Star Chamber ruling on SEDITIOUS LIBEL whereby the greater the truth the greater the libel, since the plaintiff would be even more inclined to take revenge and cause a breach of the peace. In Alexander's eyes, truth should render any defendant immune from punishment. The court rejected his position and he offered another: Juries, not judges, should determine the law as well as the facts in such cases. Hamilton's peroration appealed not merely to the jury's sense of justice, but to the growing anti-British feeling of the colony and to "every Freeman that lives under a British Government on the Main of America." The jury was persuaded, returning a verdict of not guilty, but the common law did not change until sometime after the Revolution.

Zenger's defense set a precedent for use in many later trials concerning freedom of speech and of the press and many subsequent defendants consulted Alexander's *A brief Narrative of the Case and Tryal of John Peter Zenger*, published in 1736. Other than the trial of a New Yorker in 1745 for "singing in praise of the Pretender" and a similar prosecution in South Carolina, Zenger's was the last case of this sort to be held prior to the Revolution. The organization that spearheaded Zenger's defense was called "The Sons of Liberty." The Sons were leading opponents of the Stamp Act and thus proponents of the American Revolution. They developed in the 19th century into the Tammany Society, which for many years represented the machine that dominated New York politics.

SEE ALSO Cato; Father of Candor.

Zhdanovism

Andrei Zhdanov (1896-1948) was one of the founders of SOCIALIST REALISM in 1934. By 1936, the era of the Stalinist purges, Zhdanov had gained control over much of Soviet culture, and saw a number of leading writers and artists executed or imprisoned, but the period of his absolute ascendancy, the *Zhdanovshchina* (Zhdanov's time), came between 1945 and his death in 1948.

The era of Zhdanovism was one of calculated repression after the relative freedoms of the war years. On August 14, 1946, the Central Committee issued a decree on literature, "Resolutions on the Journals *Zvezda* and *Leningrad*." This decree, plus its elaboration in two speeches by Zhdanov, established post-war Soviet literary policy. Two further decrees dealt with theater and cinema. It concentrated on emphasizing the educative value of literature, the duties of the writer to people, party and state, and above all the necessary political orientation of art. As the decree stated, "the task of Soviet literature is to aid the state to educate the youth correctly and to meet their demands, to rear a new generation strong and vigorous, believing in their cause, fearing no obstacles and ready to overcome all obstacles. Consequently any preaching of ideological neutrality, of political neutrality, of 'art for art's sake' is alien to Soviet literature and harmful to the interests of the Soviet people and the Soviet state." Zhdanov, expanding this further, referred to Lenin's article "Party Organization and Party Literature" as justification for the new policy. Obsessively anti-capitalist, he demanded that Soviet literature should "boldy lash and attack bourgeois culture" and take its part in the cold war.

The application of Zhdanovism meant the persecution of many writers, notably Akhmatova and Pasternak, an attack on the current (1946) leadership of the Writers' Union and its replacement by sounder men, and above all the drive toward obsessive patriotism coupled with the condemnation of those whose work failed to reach the required socialist realist standards. Much work was rewritten to incorporate the new status quo and many novels, previously acceptable and even praised, suffered major attacks. The party justified its interference by alleging that once a work had been revised according to Zhdanov doctrines, only then was it successful—which success was held to prove that the revision had thus been necessary.

In 1948 a full-scale campaign was launched against the growing ranks of "antipatriotic cosmopolitans"—those who resented the growing displacement of art by ideology. The cosmopolitans replied that such resentment was far from unpatriotic, but born of a desire to preserve the once-high standards of Soviet literature; the party replied that if literature was in decline, then the writers were to blame for failing to adhere slavishly to the current doctrine. Anti-Semitism was also central to the campaign against the cosmopolitans, with specific charges that there was an international plot, basically Jewish, to link cosmopolitan literature to international counter-Revolution. By 1950, when it was considered that the antipatriotic group and the "rootless cosmopolitans" (Jews) had been routed, even hardliners began to realize that Zhdanovism had not entirely benefited Soviet literature and tried to reverse it. The basic tenets of socialist realism were not changed, however, and the original decree on literature was published as a pamphlet. More party stalwarts began to complain about the stale, tedious nature of the arts and when Stalin died in 1953 a certain liberalization was permitted.

Zhdanov died in 1948 but his master plan essentially outlived him. The various thaws, frosts, liberalization and repression that followed in sequence until today still maintain the basic Zhdanov doctrine and persist in severely limiting Soviet writing. Only in SAMIZDAT does experimental creative work persist.

Zola, Emile

Zola (1840-1902) was the leading member of the French school of naturalistic fiction and the author of many novels, including *Therese Raquin* (1867), *Germinal* (1885), *La Terre* (1887), *Nana* (1880), and the 19-volume saga of the Rougon and Macquart families, which appeared between 1871 and 1893. Zola's detailed depiction of French life, often accentuating the miseries, corruption and the baser human appetites over the comfortable annals of the genteel bourgeoisie central to the work of less determinedly worldly writers, typified for the Victorians what came to be known as the French novel. The English publisher HENRY VIZETELLY was jailed in 1888 for publishing *La Terre*, albeit in an expurgated edition. Zola perhaps remains best known for his impassioned statement on the Dreyfus Affair of the 1890s, *J'Accuse*, published in *L'Aurore* in 1898. Zola had studiously avoided involvement in this affair, which pitted the Army establishment against a single Jewish officer, victimized unfairly for the treachery of a fellow soldier, an aristocratic gentile. In 1898 he acted, writing a trenchant attack on the entire case. The Army retaliated with a libel suit and Zola decamped to England, spending 11 months there before returning to Paris. Zola's work continued to offer a frisson to those so disposed: The ROMAN INDEX banned his complete works in 1894; Yugoslavia followed suit in 1929 and Ireland in 1953. *Nana*, which makes a heroine of a prostitute, held a prime place on the blacklist of the NATIONAL ORGANIZATION FOR DECENT LITERATURE.

BIBLIOGRAPHY

Amnesty International, *Voices for Freedom*. London: AI Publications, 1986.

Article 19, *Information, Freedom and Censorship: World Report 1988*. London: Longman, 1988.

Ashbee, Henry S. and Peter Fryer, *Forbidden Books of the Victorians*. London: Odyssey Press, 1970.

Atkins, John, *Sex in Literature*, 4 vols. London: John Calder, 1982.

Barker, Martin (ed.), *The Video Nasties*. London: Pluto Press, 1984.

Barnes, Clive (ed.), *Report of the President's Commission on Obscenity and Pornography*. New York: Bantam Books, 1970.

Barrier, N.G., *Banned: Controversial Literature and Political Control in British India, 1907-1947*. Columbia: University of Missouri Press, 1974.

Barrow, Andrew, *The Flesh Is Weak*. London: Hamish Hamilton, 1980.

Barton, Frank, *The Press of Africa: Persecution and Perseverance*. London: Macmillan, 1979.

Bertrand, Ina, *Film Censorship in Australia*. St. Lucia: University of Queensland Press, 1978.

Bloch, S. and P. Reddaway, *Russia's Political Hospitals: The Abuse of Psychiatry in the USSR*. London: Gollancz, 1977.

Boyer, Paul S., *Purity in Print*. New York: Scribners, 1968.

Bristow, Edward J., *Vice and Vigilance*. Dublin: Gill and Macmillan, 1977.

Broun, Heywood and Margaret Leech, *Anthony Comstock: Roundsman of the Lord*. New York: Boni, 1927.

Bullock, Alan and Oliver Stallybrass (eds.), *The Fontana Dictionary of Modern Thought*. London: Fontana, 1977.

Buranelli, Vincent, *The Trial of Peter Zenger*. New York: New York University Press, 1957.

Burchfield, Robert (ed.), *Supplements to the Oxford English Dictionary*. Oxford: Clarendon Press, 1972, 1976, 1982, 1986.

Calder-Marshall, Arthur, *Lewd, Blasphemous & Obscene*. London: Hutchinson, 1972.

Campbell, Duncan and Steve Connor, *On the Record: Surveillance, Computers & Privacy*. London: Michael Joseph, 1986.

Caute, David, *The Espionage of the Saints: Two Essays on Silence and the State*. London: Hamish Hamilton, 1986.

Censorship Today. London: 1968-69.

Chandos, John, *To Deprave and Corrupt* ... London: Souvenir Press, 1962.

Clapp, J., *Art Censorship*. Metuchen, N.J.: Scarecrow, 1972.

Cleland, John, *Memoirs of a Woman of Pleasure*. Oxford: Oxford University Press, 1985; first published 1749.

Cockerell, M., P. Hennessy and D. Walker, *Sources Close to the Prime Minister*. London: Macmillan, 1984.

Collins, Irene, *The Government & the Newspaper Press in France, 1814-1881*. Oxford: Oxford University Press, 1959.

Coulton, G.C., *Inquisition & Liberty*. Gloucester, Mass.: Peter Smith, 1959.

Cox, Barry, John Shirley and Martin Short, *The Fall of Scotland Yard*. Harmondsworth: Penguin Books, 1977.

Craig, Alec, *The Banned Books of England and Other Countries*. London: George Allen & Unwin, 1962.

Darnton, Robert and Daniel Roche (eds.), *Revolution in Print: The Press in France, 1775-1800*. Berkeley: University of California Press, 1989.

De Grazia, Edward, *Censorship Landmarks*. New York: R.R. Bowker, 1969.

De Grazia, Edward and Robert K. Newman, *Banned Films: Movies, Censors and the First Amendment*. New York: R.R. Bowker, 1982.

De Sade, Donatien-Alphonse-Francois, Marquis de, *Justine, or the Misfortunes of Virtue*. New York: Grove Press, 1964; first published in Paris, 1791.

————, *Juliette, ou les prosperites de vice*. New York: Grove Press, 1968; first published in Paris, 1797.

————, *The 120 Days of Sodom*. New York: Grove Press, 1966; first published in Paris, 1785.

————, *La Philosophie dans le Boudoir*. New York: Grove Press, 1965; first published in Paris, 1791.

Deakin, Terence J., *Catalogi Librorum Eroticorum*. London: Cecil & Amelia Woolf, 1964.

Dewhirst, Martin and Robert Farrel, *The Soviet Censorship*. Metuchen, N.J.: Scarecrow Press, 1973.

Ditchfield, P.H., *Books Fatal to Their Authors*. London: Elliot Stock, 1903.

Drabble, Margaret (ed.), *The Oxford Companion to English Literature*, 5th ed. Oxford: Oxford University Press, 1985.

Ernst, Morris L., *Censorship*. New York: Macmillan, 1964.

Ernst, Morris L. and W. Seagle, *To the Pure*. Milwood, N.J.: Kraus, 1973; first published 1928.

Evans, Harold, *Good Times, Bad Times*. London: Weidenfeld & Nicolson, 1983.

Farrer, J.A., *Books Condemned to Be Burnt*. London: Elliot, Stock, 1892.

Faust, Beatrice, *Women, Sex and Pornography*. Melbourne: Melbourne House, 1980.

Findlater, Richard, *Banned: A Review of Theatrical Censorship in Britain*. London: McGibbin & Kee, 1967.

Foxon, David, *Libertine Literature in England, 1660-1745*. New Hyde Park, N.Y.: University Books, 1965.

Fryer, Peter, *Private Case—Public Scandal*. London: Secker & Warburg, 1966.

————, *Mrs. Grundy*. London: House & Maxwell, 1963.

Gay, Peter, *The Bourgeois Experience*, vol. 1. Harmondsworth: Penguin Books, 1984.

Geller, Evelyn, *Forbidden Books in American Public Libraries (1876-1939)*. Westport, Conn.: Greenwood Press, 1984.

Gerber, Albert B., *Sex, Pornography & Justice*. New York: Lyle Stuart, 1965.

Gillett, Charles R., *Burned Books*, 2 vols. Westport, Conn.: Greenwood Press, 1975; first published 1932.

Goodman, Michael B., *Contemporary Literary Censorship: The Case History of Burroughs'* Naked Lunch. Metuchen, N.J.: Scarecrow, 1981.

Goodman, Walter, *The Committee*. New York: Farrar, Straus & Giroux, 1969.

Graves, Robert and Alan Hodge, *The Long Weekend*. London: Faber and Faber, 1940.

Green, Jonathon, *Newspeak: A Dictionary of Jargon*. London: Routledge & Kegan Paul, 1984.

Grendler, Paul F., *The Roman Inquisition and the Venetian Press, 1540-1605*. Princeton: Princeton University Press, 1977.

Haight, Anee L., *Banned Books*, 2nd edn. New York: R.R. Bowker, 1955.

Hale, Orton J., *The Captive Press in the Third Reich*. Princeton: Princeton University Press, 1964.

Hall, Richard V., *A Spy's Revenge*. Harmondsworth: Penguin, 1987.

Haney, Robert W., *Comstockery in America*. New York: Da Capo, 1974; first published 1960.

Heise, J.A., *Minimum Disclosure*. New York: Norton, 1979.

Hohenberg, John, *Free Press/Free People*. New York: The Free Press/Collier-Macmillan, 1973.

Home Office Report of the Committee on Obscenity and Film Censorship (The Williams Committee Report). London: H.M. Stationery Office, 1979.

Hooper, David, *Official Secrets*. London: Coronet Books, 1988.

Humana, Charles, *World Human Rights Guide*. London: Pan Books, 1987.

Hurwitz, Leon, *Historical Dictionary of Censorship in the United States*. Westport, Conn.: Greenwood Press, 1985.

Hyde, Montgomery, *History of Pornography*. London: Four Square Books, 1965.

Johnson, Priscilla, *Khrushchev & Art: Politics of Soviet Culture*. Cambridge, Mass.: MIT Press, 1965.

Kamen, Henry A.F., *The Spanish Inquisition*. London: Weidenfeld & Nicolson, 1982.

Kearney, Patrick J., *A History of Erotic Literature*. London: Macmillan, 1982.

————, *The Private Case*. London: Jay Landesman, 1981.

Kertesz, G.A., *Documents in the Political History of the European Continent, 1815-1939*. Oxford: Oxford University Press, 1968.

Kuh, Richard H., *Foolish Fig Leaves*. New York: Macmillan, 1965.

Labedz, Leopold and Max Hayward (eds.), *On Trial: The Case of Sinyavsky and Daniel*. London: Collins and Harvill Press, 1967.

Lea, Henry C., *A History of the Inquisition in Spain*. London: Macmillan, 1907.

Legman, G., *Love and Death: A Study in Censorship*. New York: Hacker, 1963; first published 1949.

Lendval, Paul, *The Bureaucracy of Truth*. London: Burnett Books, 1981.

Levy, Leonard W., *Legacy of Suppression: Freedom of Speech and Press in Early American History*. Cambridge, Mass.: Belknap Press, 1960.

Liston, Robert A., *The Right to Know: Censorship in America*. New York: F. Watts, 1973.

Longford, Lord, *Pornography: The Longford Report*. London: Coronet, 1970.

Loth, David G., *The Erotic in Literature*. London: Secker & Warburg, 1961.

Marcus, Steven, *The Other Victorians*. London: Corgi Books, 1964.

Markun, Leo, *Mrs. Grundy*. Westport, Conn.: Greenwood, 1969; first published 1930.

Michael, James, *The Politics of Secrecy*. Harmondsworth: Penguin Books, 1982.

Michael, R. (ed.), *The ABZ of Pornography*. London: Panther, 1972.

Moore, George, *Literature at Nurse, or, Circulating Morals*. Hassocks, Sussex: Harvester Press, 1976; first published 1885.

Munro, C.P., *Television, Censorship and the Law*. London: Saxon House, 1979.

Murphy, Terence G., *Censorship: Government & Obscenity*. Baltimore: Helicon Press, 1963.

Murray, James A.H., Henry Bradley, W.A. Craigie and C.T. Onions (eds.), *Oxford English Dictionary*. Oxford: Clarendon Press, 1933.

Navasky, Victor S., *Naming Names*. New York: Penguin Books, 1980.

New York Public Library, *Censorship: 500 Years of Conflict*. New York: Oxford University Press, 1984.

O'Higgins, Paul, *Censorship in England*. London: Nelson, 1972.

Palmer, Tony, *The Trials of* OZ. London: Blond and Briggs, 1971.

Pearsall, Ronald, *The Worm in the Bud: The World of Victorian Sexuality*. London: Weidenfeld & Nicolson, 1969.

Peckham, Morris, *Art and Pornography*. New York: Harper and Row, 1969.

Perrin, Noel, *Dr. Bowdler's Legacy: A History of Expugated Books in England and America*. London: Macmillan, 1970.

Phelps, Guy, *Film Censorship*. London: Gollancz, 1975.

Pisanus Fraxi (aka Ashbee, H.S.), *Librorum Prohibitorum*. London: privately printed, 1877.

————, *Centuria librorum absconditorum*. London: privately printed, 1879.

————, *Catena librorum tacendorum*. London: privately printed, 1885.

Putnam, George H., *The Censorship of the Church of Rome*, 2 vols. New York: G.P. Putnam's Sons, 1906.

Randall, Richard S., *Censorship of the Movies: The Social and Political Control of a Mass Medium*. Madison: University of Wisconsin Press, 1970.

Reade, Rolf S. (aka Rose, Alfred), *Register Librorum Eroticorum*, 2 vols. London: privately printed, 1936.

Rembar, Charles, *The End of Obscenity: The Trials of* Lady Chatterley, Tropic of Cancer *and* Fanny Hill. London: Andre Deutsch, 1969.

Richards, J., *The Age of the Dream Palace*. Boston: Routledge and Kegan Paul, 1984.

Rickards, Maurice, *Banned Posters*. London: Evelyn Adams & MacKay, 1969.

————, *Posters of Protest and Revolution*. Newton Abbott, Devon: David & Charles, 1969.

Roberts, Edwin A., *The Smut Rakers*. Silver Spring, Maryland: National Observer, 1966.

Robertson, Geoffrey, *Obscenity: An Account of the Censorship Laws and Their Enforcement in England and Wales*. London: Weidenfeld & Nicolson, 1979.

Robertson, Geoffrey and Andrew G.L. Nichol, *Media Law*. London: Sage Publications, 1984.

Robertson, James C., *The British Board of Film Censors, 1896-1950*. London: Croom Helm, 1985.

Rogers, W.G., *Mightier Than the Sword*. New York: Harcourt Brace Jovanovich, 1969.

Rolph, C.H., *Books in the Dock*. London: Andre Deutsch, 1969.

Roth, Cecil, *The Spanish Inquisition*. New York: Norton, 1964.

Ruud, Charles A., *Fighting Words: Imperial Censorship and the Russian Press, 1804-1906*. Toronto: University of Toronto Press, 1982.

Schlesinger, Philip, *Putting "Reality" Together: BBC News*. Beverly Hills, Calif.: Sage, 1979.

Schulte, Henry F., *The Spanish Press, 1470-1966*. Urbana: University of Illinois Press, 1968.

Schumach, Murray, *The Face on the Cutting Room Floor*. New York: William Morrow, 1975.

Scribner, Robert W., *For the Sake of Simple Folk*. Cambridge: Cambridge University Press, 1981.

Seymour-Ure, Colin, *The Press, Politics and the Public*. London: Methuen, 1968.

Shanor, Donald R., *Behind the Lines: The Private War against Soviet Censorship*. New York: St. Martin's Press, 1985.

Sheehan, Neil et al., *The Pentagon Papers*. New York: Bantam Books, 1971.

Siebert, Frederick S., *Freedom of the Press in England, 1476-1776*. Urbana: University of Illinois Press, 1952.

Speculator Morum (aka Sir William Laird Clowes), *Bibliotheca Arcana*. London: George Redway, 1885.

St. John Stevas, Norman, *Obscenity and the Law*. London: Secker & Warburg, 1956.

Stephens, J.R., *The Censorship of English Drama, 1824-1901*. Cambridge: Cambridge University Press, 1980.

Street, Harry Freedom, *The Individual and the Law*, 5th edn. Harmondsworth: Penguin Books, 1982.

Sutherland, John, *Offensive Literature: Decensorship in Britain, 1960-82*. London: Junction Books, 1985.

Svirsky, Grigori, *A History of Post-War Soviet Writing*. Ann Arbor, Mich.: Ardis, 1981.

Swayze, Harold, *Political Control of Literature in the U.S.S.R., 1946-59*. Cambridge: Harvard University Press, 1962.

Thomas, A.H., *Censorship in Public Libraries*. Epping, Essex: Bowker, 1975.

Thomas, Donald, *A Long Time Burning: A History of Literary Censorship in Britain*. London: Routledge & Kegan Paul, 1969.

Tomkinson, Martin, *The Pornbrokers*. London: Virgin Books, 1982.

Tracy, Michael and David Morrison, *Whitehouse*. London: Macmillan Press, 1979.

Trevelyan, John, *What the Censor Saw*. London: Michael Joseph, 1973.

Tribe, David, *Questions of Censorship*. New York: St. Martin, 1973.

Wagner, Peter, *Eros Revived*. London: Secker & Warburg, 1988.

Webb, Peter, *The Erotic Arts*, rev. edn. London: Secker & Warburg, 1983.

Werth, Alexander, *Russia: Hopes and Fears*. Harmondsworth: Penguin Books, 1969.

Whitehouse, Mary, *Who Does She Think She Is?* London: NEL, 1971.

Woodward, Bob and Scott Armstrong, *The Brethren: Inside the Supreme Court*. New York: Simon & Schuster, 1980.

Writers and Scholars International, *Index on Censorship*. New York: Random House; 1969-80, published several times annually.

Young, Wayland, *Eros Denied*. London: Weidenfeld & Nicolson, 1964.

Bold face type indicated main essays.